THE ROUTLEDGE HISTORY OF TERRORISM

Though the history of terrorism stretches back to the ancient world, today it is often understood as a recent development. Comprehensive enough to serve as a survey for students or newcomers to the field, yet with enough depth to engage the specialist, *The Routledge History of Terrorism* is the first single-volume authoritative reference text to place terrorism firmly into its historical context.

Terrorism is a transnational phenomenon with a convoluted history that defies easy periodization and narrative treatment. Over the course of 32 chapters, experts in the field analyze its historical significance and explore how and why terrorism emerged as a set of distinct strategies, tactics, and mindsets across time and space. Chapters address not only familiar topics such as the Northern Irish Troubles, the Palestine Liberation Organization, international terrorism, and the rise of al-Qaeda, but also lesser-explored issues such as:

- American racial terrorism;
- state terror and terrorism in the Middle Ages;
- tyrannicide from Ancient Greece and Rome to the seventeenth century;
- the roots of Islamist violence;
- the urban guerrilla, terrorism, and state terror in Latin America;
- literary treatments of terrorism.

With an introduction by the editor explaining the book's rationale and organization, as well as a guide to the definition of terrorism, a historiographical chapter analyzing the historical approach to terrorism studies, and an eight-chapter part that explores critical themes in the history of terrorism, this book is essential reading for all those interested in the past, present, and future of terrorism.

Randall D. Law is Associate Professor of History at Birmingham-Southern College in Birmingham, Alabama, where he teaches courses on Russia, Modern Europe, and terrorism. He is the author of *Terrorism: A History* (2009) and is frequently interviewed by national and international reporters on matters related to terrorism and Russian politics. His current research is on terrorism, violence, and criminality in the city of Odessa in the Russian Empire in the early twentieth century.

THE ROUTLEDGE HISTORIES

The Routledge Histories is a series of landmark books surveying some of the most important topics and themes in history today. Edited and written by an international team of world-renowned experts, they are the works against which all future books on their subjects will be judged.

THE ROUTLEDGE HISTORY OF WOMEN IN EUROPE SINCE 1700
Edited by Deborah Simonton

THE ROUTLEDGE HISTORY OF SLAVERY
Edited by Gad Heuman and Trevor Burnard

THE ROUTLEDGE HISTORY OF THE HOLOCAUST
Edited by Jonathan C. Friedman

THE ROUTLEDGE HISTORY OF CHILDHOOD IN THE WESTERN WORLD
Edited by Paula S. Fass

THE ROUTLEDGE HISTORY OF SEX AND THE BODY
Edited by Kate Fisher and Sarah Toulalan

THE ROUTLEDGE HISTORY OF WESTERN EMPIRES
Edited by Robert Aldrich and Kirsten McKenzie

THE ROUTLEDGE HISTORY OF FOOD
Edited by Carol Helstosky

Forthcoming:

THE ROUTLEDGE HISTORY OF GENOCIDE
Edited by Cathie Carmichael and Richard Maguire

THE ROUTLEDGE HISTORY OF EAST CENTRAL EUROPE
Edited by Irina Livezeanu and Arpad von Klimo

THE ROUTLEDGE HISTORY OF MEDIEVAL CHRISTIANITY
Edited by Robert Swanson

THE ROUTLEDGE
HISTORY OF TERRORISM

Edited by Randall D. Law

LONDON AND NEW YORK

First published 2015
by Routledge

2 Park Square, Milton Park, Abingdon, Oxfordshire OX14 4RN
52 Vanderbilt Avenue, New York, NY 10017

Routledge is an imprint of the Taylor & Francis Group, an informa business

First issued in paperback 2019

Copyright © 2015 Randall D. Law for selection and editorial matter; individual extracts © the contributors

The right of the editor to be identified as the author of the editorial material, and of the authors for their individual chapters, has been asserted in accordance with sections 77 and 78 of the Copyright, Designs and Patents Act 1988.

All rights reserved. No part of this book may be reprinted or reproduced or utilized in any form or by any electronic, mechanical, or other means, now known or hereafter invented, including photocopying and recording, or in any information storage or retrieval system, without permission in writing from the publishers.

Notice:
Product or corporate names may be trademarks or registered trademarks, and are used only for identification and explanation without intent to infringe.

British Library Cataloguing-in-Publication Data
A catalogue record for this book is available from the British Library

Library of Congress Cataloging-in-Publication Data
The Routledge history of terrorism / edited by Randall D. Law.
    pages cm.—(The routledge histories)
  Includes bibliographical references and index.
  1. Terrorism—History.   I. Law, Randall David.
  HV6431.R686 2015
  363.32509—dc23   2014039877

ISBN: 978-0-415-53577-9 (hbk)
ISBN: 978-0-367-86705-8 (pbk)

Typeset in Baskerville
by Keystroke, Station Road, Codsall, Wolverhampton

CONTENTS

Notes on contributors ix
Acknowledgments xiii

1 Introduction 1
RANDALL D. LAW

PART I
State terror, tyrannicide, and terrorism in the pre-modern world 13

2 Tyrannicide from Ancient Greece and Rome to the crisis of the seventeenth century 15
JOHANNES DILLINGER

3 Pre-modern terrorism: the cases of the Sicarii and the Assassins 28
DONATHAN TAYLOR AND YANNICK GAUTRON

4 Terrorism in the Middle Ages: the seeds of later developments 46
STEVEN ISAAC

PART II
The emergence of modern terrorism 61

5 The French Revolution and early European revolutionary terrorism 63
MIKE RAPPORT

6 Terrorism in America from the colonial period to John Brown 77
MATTHEW JENNINGS

CONTENTS

7 **Entangled terrorisms in late Imperial Russia**   92
MARTIN A. MILLER

8 **Anarchist terrorism and counter-terrorism in Europe and the world, 1878–1934**   111
RICHARD BACH JENSEN

9 **Anarchist terrorism in the United States**   130
THAI JONES

10 **American racial terrorism from Brown to Booth to Birmingham**   143
R. BLAKESLEE GILPIN

PART III
Terrorism in the twentieth century   157

11 **State terrorism in early twentieth-century Europe**   159
PAUL M. HAGENLOH

12 **Britain's small wars: the challenge to Empire, 1881–1951**   177
BENJAMIN GROB-FITZGIBBON

13 **Britain's small wars: the Empire strikes back, 1952–68**   190
BENJAMIN GROB-FITZGIBBON

14 **The Northern Irish Troubles**   204
CILLIAN McGRATTAN

15 **Violence in the Algerian War of Independence: terror, counter-terror, and compliance**   218
MARTIN C. THOMAS

16 **Israel and the Palestine Liberation Organization**   239
BOAZ GANOR

17 **The roots of Islamism and Islamist violence**   258
JOHN CALVERT

18 **Islamist terrorism from the Muslim Brotherhood to Hamas**   270
DAVID COOK

CONTENTS

19 The urban guerrilla, terrorism, and state terror in Latin America — 284
JENNIFER S. HOLMES

20 Militant organizations in Western Europe in the 1970s and 1980s — 297
HANNO BALZ

PART IV
Recent decades — 315

21 Contemporary domestic terrorism in the United States — 317
CAROLYN GALLAHER

22 The genesis, rise, and uncertain future of al-Qaeda — 333
DAVEED GARTENSTEIN-ROSS

23 Politics, religion, and the making of terrorism in Pakistan and India — 351
EAMON MURPHY

PART V
Critical themes in the history of terrorism — 367

24 Modernity and terrorism — 369
ROGER GRIFFIN

25 Terrorism and insurgency — 383
GERAINT HUGHES

26 Suicide terrorism — 397
SUSANNE MARTIN

27 Counter-terrorism and conspiracy: historicizing the struggle against terrorism — 411
BEATRICE DE GRAAF

28 Media and terrorism — 428
ROBERT A. SAUNDERS

29 Terrorism and technology — 442
ANN LARABEE

CONTENTS

30 International terrorism   **456**
GERAINT HUGHES

31 The age of terrorism in the age of literature   **470**
LYNN PATYK

PART VI
The historiography of terrorism   **485**

32 The literary turn in terrorism studies   **487**
RICHARD JACKSON

Index   501

CONTRIBUTORS

Randall D. Law is Associate Professor of History at Birmingham-Southern College in Birmingham, Alabama, where he teaches courses on Russia, Modern Europe, and terrorism. He is the author of *Terrorism: A History* (2009), soon to be published in a second edition, and is frequently interviewed by national and international reporters on matters related to terrorism and Russian politics. His current research is on terrorism, violence, and criminality in Odessa in the Russian Empire in the early twentieth century.

Hanno Balz is Visiting Assistant Professor in German and European History at Johns Hopkins University in Baltimore, Maryland. His fields of research are the history of social movements, media, and discourse history; Cold War studies; the history of anti-communism; and the Shoah and Nazi rule. He has published extensively on media and terrorism in West Germany.

John Calvert is Professor of History at Creighton University in Omaha, Nebraska. His research deals variously with the Muslim Brotherhood, radical Islamist ideologies, and British policy in the Arab world in the early 1900s. His most recent book is *Sayyid Qutb and the Origins of Radical Islamism* (2010).

David Cook is Associate Professor of Religion at Rice University in Houston, Texas. His areas of specialization include early Islamic history and development, Muslim apocalyptic literature and movements (classical and contemporary), radical Islam, historical astronomy, and Judeo-Arabic literature. His books include *Understanding Jihad* (2005), *Martyrdom in Islam* (2007), and *Understanding and Addressing Suicide Attacks* (with Olivia Allison, 2007). He received his PhD from the University of Chicago.

Beatrice de Graaf is Professor for the History of International Relations and Global Governance at Utrecht University in the Netherlands. She is the author of many articles and books on the history of national security in the West, counter-terrorism and political violence, and securitization and international relations, including *Evaluating Counterterrorism Performance: A Comparative Study* (2013).

Johannes Dillinger is Professor in Early Modern History at Oxford Brookes University in Oxford, England, and Honorary Professor in Modern History and Regional History at the Johannes Gutenberg University in Mainz, Germany. He has also been guest lecturer at Georgetown University, Stanford University, the German Historical Institute in Washington, and Nehru University in New Delhi. His main research interests include political crime, representative government, magic, and folk religion.

CONTRIBUTORS

Carolyn Gallaher is Associate Professor in the School of International Service at American University in Washington, DC. She is an expert on political violence by non-state actors, including militias, paramilitaries, and drug cartels. Her first book, *On the Fault Line: Race, Class, and the American Patriot Movement* (2002) followed the rise and eventual fall of the Kentucky State Militia. Her second book, *After the Peace: Loyalist Paramilitaries in Post-accord Northern Ireland* (2007) examines why Loyalist paramilitaries took nearly a decade after the 1998 peace agreement to decommission their weapons and stand down their armed units.

Boaz Ganor is the Founder and Executive Director of the International Institute for Counter-Terrorism, the Ronald Lauder Chair for Counter-Terrorism, and the Dean of the Lauder School of Government, Diplomacy, and Strategy at the Interdisciplinary Center, Herzliya, Israel. He is also the founder and President of the International Academic Counter-Terrorism Community. He is the author or editor of many books and articles on counter-terrorism, including *The Counter-Terrorism Puzzle: A Guide for Decision Makers* (2005).

Daveed Gartenstein-Ross is a Senior Fellow at the Foundation for Defense of Democracies and an Adjunct Assistant Professor in Georgetown University's Security Studies Program in Washington, DC. He is the author or volume editor of 14 books and monographs and holds a PhD from the Catholic University of America.

Yannick Gautron is a doctoral candidate at the University of Poitiers in France, working on Arab-Muslim mountain communities in medieval Syria. He has published several articles and book chapters about the Druze community and Western and Muslim historiographical traditions concerning the Assassins.

R. Blakeslee Gilpin is an Assistant Professor of History at Tulane University in New Orleans, Louisiana. His research interests revolve around slavery and its legacies in history, literature, and art. He is the author of *John Brown Still Lives!* (2011) and the editor of *The Selected Letters of William Styron* (2012).

Roger Griffin is Professor in Modern History at Oxford Brookes University in Oxford, England. His many publications on a wide range of phenomena relating to generic fascism and related forms of extremism include *The Nature of Fascism* (1991), *Modernism and Fascism* (2007), and *Terrorist's Creed: Fanatical Violence and the Human Need for Meaning* (2012).

Benjamin Grob-Fitzgibbon is Associate Professor of History at the University of Arkansas. He has published widely on political violence and terrorism, including the books *Imperial Endgame: Britain's Dirty Wars and the End of Empire* (2011) and *Turning Points of the Irish Revolution: The British Government, Intelligence, and the Cost of Indifference, 1912–1921* (2007).

Paul M. Hagenloh is an Associate Professor of History in the Maxwell School of Citizenship and Public Affairs and Chair of the Maxwell Program in Citizenship and Civic Engagement at Syracuse University in Syracuse, New York.

Jennifer S. Holmes is Professor and Head of Political Science and Public Policy and Political Economy at the University of Texas at Dallas. She received her AB from the University of Chicago and her PhD from the University of Minnesota. Her major area of research is political violence, terrorism, and political development, and she is a co-author of *Guns, Drugs, and Development in Colombia* (2008).

Geraint Hughes is a Senior Lecturer at the Defence Studies Department, King's College London. He has taught at the Joint Services Command and Staff College, Shrivenham, UK, since 2005, and is the author of *Harold Wilson's Cold War: The Labour Government and East–West Politics, 1964–1970* (2009), *The Military's Role in Counterterrorism: Examples and Implications for Liberal Democracies* (2011), and *My Enemy's Enemy: Proxy Warfare in International Politics* (2012).

Steven Isaac teaches at Longwood University in Farmville, Virginia. He has published on medieval military history in books, encyclopedias, *The Journal of Medieval Military History*, and *Les Cahiers de Civilisation Médiévale*. His current projects are threefold: the role of mercenaries, the impact of being besieged on urban populations, and the War of 1173–4.

Richard Jackson is Professor of Peace Studies at the National Centre for Peace and Conflict Studies, University of Otago, New Zealand. He is editor-in-chief of the journal *Critical Studies on Terrorism* and the author or editor of eight books on terrorism and conflict resolution. His latest book is a novel entitled *Confessions of a Terrorist* (2014).

Matthew Jennings is Associate Professor of History at Middle Georgia State College in Macon, Georgia, where he teaches Native American history, among other subjects. His first book, *New Worlds of Violence: Cultures and Conquests in the Early American Southeast* came out in 2011, and he continues to study violence in early American history.

Richard Bach Jensen is Professor of History at Louisiana Scholars' College, Northwestern State University, in Natchitoches, Louisiana. He is the author of *The Battle against Anarchist Terrorism: An International History, 1878–1934* (2014) and *Liberty and Order: The Theory and Practice of Italian Public Security Policy, 1848 to the Crisis of the 1890s* (1991).

Thai Jones is the Herbert H. Lehman Curator for US History at the Rare Book & Manuscript Library of Columbia University in New York City. He is the author of two books: *More Powerful than Dynamite: Radicals, Plutocrats, Progressives, and New York's Year of Anarchy* (2014 [2012]) and *A Radical Line: From the Labor Movement to the Weather Underground, One Family's Century of Conscience* (2004). Jones is working on a new book on the labor movement and the environment in a Nevada boomtown tentatively entitled *Goldfield: Dreams, Greed, Destruction, and the Fall of the Old West*.

Ann Larabee is Professor of English and American Studies at Michigan State University in East Lansing, Michigan. She is the author of *The Dynamite Fiend: The Chilling Tale of a Confederate Spy, Con Artist and Mass Murderer* (2005) and *The Wrong Hands: Popular Weapons Manuals and Their Challenges to Democracy* (2015).

Susanne Martin is Assistant Professor of Political Science at the University of Nevada, Reno. She earned her PhD in Government from the University of Texas at Austin and has published articles on political violence and terrorism; political parties; and war and insurgency. She recently co-edited a special issue of *Terrorism and Political Violence* with Leonard Weinberg and Mary Beth Altier.

Cillian McGrattan lectures in Politics at the University of Ulster in the UK. He is the author/editor of four books and numerous articles on Northern Irish history and politics.

CONTRIBUTORS

He is currently completing a monograph on the politics of trauma and an edited collection on the Sunningdale agreement.

Martin A. Miller is Professor in the Department of History and the Department of Slavic and Eurasian Studies at Duke University in Durham, North Carolina. He is the author of *Kropotkin* (1976), *The Russian Revolutionary Emigres* (1986), *Freud and the Bolsheviks* (1997) and *The Foundations of Modern Terrorism* (2013) in addition to numerous scholarly articles.

Eamon Murphy is Adjunct Professor in the Department of Social Sciences and International Affairs of Curtin University in Perth, Australia. His recent major publications include *The Making of Terrorism in Pakistan: Historical and Social Roots of Extremism* (2013), and *Contemporary State Terrorism: Theory and Practice* (2009) edited with Richard Jackson and Scott Poynting.

Lynn Patyk is Assistant Professor of Russian at Dartmouth College in Hanover, New Hampshire. Her research interests are nineteenth and twentieth century Russian literature, the revolutionary tradition, and the history of terrorism. She has published several articles and book chapters on the intersection between Russian revolutionary terrorism and literary culture.

Mike Rapport is a Reader in European History at the University of Glasgow, Scotland. He specializes in the French Revolution, including its international impact, and is author of *The Napoleonic Wars: A Very Short Introduction* (2013), *1848: Year of Revolution* (2009), *Nineteenth Century Europe* (2005), and *Nationality and Citizenship in Revolutionary France* (2000).

Robert A. Saunders is a Professor of History and Political Science at Farmingdale State College–SUNY, where he teaches courses on comparative religions, international politics, and world history. He holds a PhD in Global Affairs from Rutgers University.

Donathan Taylor is the R. N. Richardson Professor of History at Parker College, Hardin-Simmons University in Abilene, Texas. His primary area of specialization and research is ancient Mediterranean history with emphasis on Roman warfare. In addition, he is a freelance historical illustrator.

Martin C. Thomas is Professor of Imperial History and Director of the Centre for the Study of War, State and Society at the University of Exeter in England. His most recent publications are *Violence and Colonial Order: Police, Workers and Protest in the European Colonial Empires, 1918–1940* (2012) and *Fight or Flight: Britain, France, and their Roads from Empire* (2014).

ACKNOWLEDGMENTS

The editor of any book as large as this one incurs many debts if the book is to actually see the light of day. It is with great pleasure that I take stock of those debts.

This volume would obviously not have been possible without the hard work and extraordinary cooperation of a large team of talented contributors. I have thanked each of them personally many times, and I thank them publicly here. More than once I have told my friends and the contributors themselves that working on this book was like herding cats – or for the Dutch, as one of my contributors told me, like trying to keep all the frogs in the basket – but the project has been enormously satisfying. Editing a volume of essays is quite a different beast from writing a book; the latter turns you inward, while the former always turns you outward, creating a community. While this book is now done, I look forward to enjoying the results of our collaborations in future projects, at conferences, and in the enjoyment of each other's scholarship.

I would also like to thank the faculty, staff, and students at my home institution, Birmingham-Southern College (BSC). In particular, I want to acknowledge my extraordinary colleagues in the History Department: Will Hustwit, Mark Lester, Matt Levey, and Victoria Ott. They have offered ceaseless encouragement, advice (most of it solicited), and camaraderie. Most importantly, they have provided a friendly and stimulating environment that has helped me to become a better teacher and scholar. For that and much more, I thank them. Many others at BSC have aided me in one way or another, including Gen. Charles Krulak (USMC, retired), Guy Hubbs, Mark McClish, Mark Schantz, Steve Cole, Shane Pitts, David Resha, Janice Poplau, and Pam Sawallis.

There were many others beyond BSC who have provided invaluable advice and/or encouragement throughout this project. They include Col. Ed Rowe (US Army, retired), Special Agent Jack Owens (FBI, retired), Mary Habeck, Beverly Gage, Christopher Waldrep, David Andress, David Goldfrank, Michael Fellman, Arie Perliger, Ami Pedahzur, and Sergio Catignani. I also want to thank the many wonderful people at Routledge and Keystroke with whom I have had the pleasure of working: Eve Setch, Amy Welmers, Laura Pilsworth, Paul Brotherston, Jo Aston, Liz Dawn, Jane Canvin, and Maggie Lindsey-Jones.

Lastly, I want to thank my wife, Hannah Wolfson, and my son, Alexander. They have given me love, support, and encouragement beyond compare, and I love both of them dearly. My daughter, Vera, is still too young to appreciate the import of the gifts she has given me, but I will remind her when she gets a little older. This book is dedicated to my wife, the best life partner anyone could hope to have.

1

INTRODUCTION

Randall D. Law

The history of terrorism is old – as this volume demonstrates – but the study of it and its defining features is relatively young. In this volume, we will look at actors and events stretching back more than 2,000 years and across five continents. We will explore examples of terrorism used in pursuit of secular and religious aims, by states and conspiratorial groups, against humans and property, and against specific targets and randomly chosen ones. Indeed, there are many ways of defining the phenomenon, most of them shaped by our present circumstances. I ask that as you begin to read you set aside your current understanding so that you might gain a deeper, more nuanced understanding of terrorism, as it exists now and through history.

One of the great questions is when "modern terrorism" – that is, terrorism as we know it – began. Russia in the 1860s and 1870s is often cited as its birthplace. One of the most articulate commentators on Russian revolutionary terrorism during this era was Sergei Kravchinsky who had himself been a participant in the campaign of targeted assassination against the tsar and his henchmen. In 1878, Kravchinsky stabbed to death General Nikolai Mezentsev, the head of Tsar Alexander II's political police; soon after, he fled to London, where he continued to promote Russian revolutionary terrorism under the nom de plume Stepniak. He admitted that "terrorists cannot overthrow the government" but was adamant that they could "render its position untenable" by forcing the authorities to act out of fear. Moreover, terrorism could produce martyrs and heroes – "proud as Satan rebelling against God" – who could rouse the people against the state, "to render them the arbiters of their own destinies."[1]

Around this time in the United States, terrorism was also being practiced by conspiratorial groups but on a far grander scale, with mass, indiscriminate violence. This was the era of the Ku Klux Klan after the American Civil War, and it constituted a sustained campaign against black emancipation and empowerment in the South. Angry, disenfranchised former Confederates and other white supremacists burned, maimed, and killed African Americans, often under cover of night but sometimes in front of crowds. As an Alabama newspaper reported about one attack (a castration), such violence "has had a salutary influence over [other blacks]. They now feel their inferiority, in every particular, to the white men."[2]

States can and should be understood to be users of terrorism as well. Certainly Stepniak-Kravchinsky and Reconstruction-era Klansmen would have been quick to agree that it was the state that was illegitimate, brutally violent, and ultimately terroristic. Indeed, the term "terrorist" was first used in English to describe state terror when in 1795 Edmund Burke denounced the French revolutionaries of 1793–4 as "those hell-hounds called Terrorists."[3]

He got the term "terror" from the Jacobins themselves who used it – positively at the time – to describe the violence used not only against actual enemies who schemed against the revolution but also against those who, given their backgrounds and worldviews, might merely contemplate it. Shortly after the Jacobins were driven from power, one of the organizers of their fall, Jean-Lambert Tallien, gave a speech in which he adroitly identified the key feature of state terrorism. Unlike a legitimate government that "may limit itself to keeping watch over improper *actions*, threatening and punishing them with appropriate penalties, . . . if the government of terror pursues a few citizens for their presumed intentions, it will frighten all citizens."[4]

The French revolutionaries' vision was secular, but, as we all know today, acts of terrorism can also be motivated by religious extremism. One of the clearest examples of this came in 2006 during the United States' occupation of Iraq when Samara's al-Askari Shrine, one of the holiest sites for Shi'a Muslims, was bombed. The perpetrators were almost certainly Sunni insurgents working through or in alliance with al-Qaeda in Iraq. The terrorists attacked early in the morning, causing no human casualties but almost completely destroying the shrine's golden dome. Over the next few days, Shi'ite militias retaliated, killing well over a thousand Sunnis and destroying scores of their mosques. Thus although the strike itself caused no fatalities, it spurred communal violence, strengthened the hands of militia leaders, and pushed Iraq closer to civil war.[5]

What do these examples tell us? They certainly make clear the difficulties associated with defining terrorism, but they also have one thing in common: the celebration of violent spectacle. These disparate acts of violence were meant to induce change by swaying the behavior of many by targeting the relatively few. Herein is the key to understanding terrorism, since we cannot grasp its significance by looking at only one dimension. Instead, the nature of spectacle – and thus terrorism – demands that we consider three dimensions: the perpetrator, the act against the few, and the reaction of the many. There, at the intersection of those three elements, lies terrorism.

This was long understood by many perpetrators, but overlooked by scholars. Both Tallien and Kravchinsky grasped it, as did the Russian anarchist Peter Kropotkin. Although the latter never fully embraced terrorism and actually came to denounce it late in life, he nonetheless provided one of the clearest articulations of its utility.[6] In 1880, he wrote:

> When a revolutionary situation arises in a country, before the spirit of revolt is sufficiently awakened in the masses to express itself in violent demonstrations in the streets or by rebellions and uprisings, it is through *action* that minorities succeed in awakening that feeling of independence and that spirit of audacity without which no revolution can come to a head.[7]

Kropotkin shied away from identifying what he meant by "action," but elsewhere he implied that he was talking about work stoppages, posters, graffiti, minor acts of sabotage – perhaps closer to what we today might call civil disobedience. But some of his contemporaries understood that violence – arson, bombings, killings – would fit the bill quite nicely. Such violence became known as "propaganda of the deed," and while historians debate who is to be reviled or credited with first coining the term, Kropotkin certainly captured the intent. An act could function primarily as a *message*, one intended to provoke responses from those who witnessed or heard about it, not necessarily – or even – those against whom it was specifically directed. This was the idea behind the "direct actions" or *attentats* ("attempts") of late nineteenth- and early twentieth-century anarchist terrorists.[8] These anarchists chose violent methods of carrying out their attacks – bombings of public venues, the targeting of vilified figures, the use of poisonous chemicals and various "infernal machines" – that promoted the appreciation of their acts as spectacle and insured that they were widely covered in newspapers, illustrated journals, and tabloids.

In the twentieth century, many terrorists explicitly articulated the power of the spectacle and the relationship between perpetrator, act, and response. Ramdane Abane, one of the principal architects of the National Liberation Front's (FLN) campaign of terrorism against France in pursuit of Algerian independence in 1954–62, once asked rhetorically, "Is it preferable for our cause to kill ten enemies in a dry river bed [far from the cities] when no one will talk of it or a single man in Algiers which will be noted the next day by the American press?" As if that needed clarifying, he was fond of saying that "one corpse in a [civilian's] jacket is always worth more than twenty in a uniform."[9] In other words, French military deaths in the hinterland made little difference for the FLN in its pursuit of military victory, but dead French civilians in urban areas could help achieve dramatic gains for the FLN in both the domestic and international courts of opinion.

Some officials charged with countering terrorism have proven adept at analyzing the phenomenon as well, but this was rare before the mid-twentieth century. As Richard Bach Jensen, Thai Jones, and Beatrice de Graaf observe in this volume (Chapters 8, 9, and 27, respectively), during the heyday of anarchist terrorism, state officials rarely showed an interest in describing the essential nature of terrorism. On the contrary, they were interested in describing terrorism as nothing more than a set of destabilizing tactics such as assassination, public violence, or incitement to riot; the pure expression of a single ideology, anarchism; or simply the natural condition of deranged, dirty immigrants or margin-dwellers. Surprisingly little effort seems to have been expended at the international conferences called to combat terrorism around the turn of the century to move beyond these limited – albeit politically useful – descriptions of terrorism. What terrorism fundamentally *was* still seemed a question of little importance to counter-terrorists of this era.

Likewise for academics. To the pioneering Italian criminologist Cesare Lombroso (d. 1909), terrorism was the product of innate personal defects – he championed the pseudo-science of phrenology, after all – and the weakening hold of the conservative elite on the masses. Most academics and casual observers tended not to see the difference between revolutionary motivations and terroristic practices. And in time, even that sort of interest waned. For instance, an article on terrorism in the 1933 *Encyclopedia of the Social Sciences* claimed that it had become "outmoded as a revolutionary method," something "irrelevant and unnecessary."[10]

This was not so with authors, playwrights, and poets of the fin de siècle, who displayed a knack for understanding the nature of the terrorist spectacle – small surprise, given that communicating meaning to an audience via the use of provocative symbols is the bailiwick of literature every bit as much as for the terrorist. (For confirmation of this and an analysis of some of the literature of terrorism, see Chapter 31 by Lynn Patyk in this volume.) But, like academics, in time creative writers grew more interested in the size and consequences of great wars, great states, and great disasters.

After World War II, the recognition of terrorism's import began to emerge among jurists and legal scholars but not among academics broadly. Those at the Nuremberg Trials appreciated its existence, as exercised by the Nazis both before and after their rise to power in Germany in 1933. But in keeping with the circumstances, the use of the term by Allied judges to describe Nazi violence reflected more of an interest in denouncing Nazi criminality than in devising an analytically useful category. At some points during the indictment and the guilty verdicts, judges described the Brownshirts' street violence as part of an effort "to undermine and overthrow the German Government by 'legal' forms supported by terrorism." Elsewhere in the proceedings, however, the word "terrorism" was used vaguely to describe the use of concentration camps or various brutal actions against civilians. The Soviet judge issued the broadest denunciation when he stated that Hitler's entire regime was "terroristic."[11] Alas, such generic uses of the word "terrorism" did not reveal an interest in exploring the various ways in which violent spectacle might be used by sub-state and state groups alike; rather, "terrorism" was simply a convenient way to condemn an enemy that everyone already agreed was beastly.

World War II and its aftermath helped lead to the emergence of de-colonization and the spread of ethno-nationalist movements waged by those who typically had passion but few resources – fertile ground for the adoption of terrorist tactics. Perpetrators of terroristic violence such as Menachem Begin and George Grivas, supporters of it such as Frantz Fanon and Ghassan Kanafani, and counter-insurgents/counter-terrorists such as Harold Briggs and Roger Trinquier all grasped that "terrorism" described a set of tactics to be used in pursuit of a range of ideological goals. While it overlapped with criminality or warfare, it constituted something different, something that hinged on spectacle and that could, alternately, intimidate or empower various audiences – and perhaps several simultaneously. Meanwhile, the few scholars who explored terrorism conceptually, such as Eugene Walter or the host of academics who studied the Soviet Union or Nazi Germany, remained concerned with what is generally regarded as "state terror," the use of terrorizing violence by a state against its own civilians.[12] Valuable, yes, but they failed to recognize the similarity with what is today widely recognized as terrorism.

By the 1970s, international bodies finally began to explore the nature of terrorism as a category of violence and not just as an epithet with which to impugn one's enemies. In response to the advent of international terrorism, particularly the hijacking of airplanes and then the Munich Massacre, the United Nations (UN) began efforts to define terrorism so that its perpetrators and supporters could be stigmatized, isolated, and sanctioned. The core of the definition – the use of any means to "unlawfully and wilfully . . . cause death, injury or serious bodily injury to a civilian, or to any other person not taking an active part in the hostilities in a situation of armed conflict, when the purpose of such act, by its nature or context, is to intimidate a population, or to compel a government or an international organization to do or abstain from doing any act" – has been effectively agreed upon since at least the 1990s and was used in a UN convention to combat the financing of terrorism.[13] And while it is overly broad and still fails to explicitly capture the notion of seeking results by engaging in violence before an audience, it has proven to be a step forward in international law. A "comprehensive convention" on international terrorism, however, remains to be passed. The definition itself has never been the problem; the stumbling block has been the inability of negotiators to agree on whether such a definition should be applied to sub-state movements pursuing self-determination or, in fact, states themselves. Among members of the international community, the definition of terrorism has still been held hostage to the relativism embedded in the well-worn cliché that one person's terrorist is another's freedom fighter.

Also in the 1970s, academics began to turn their attention to analyzing the core features of terrorism with more productive results. Western experts such as David Rapoport, Brian

Jenkins, Martha Crenshaw, Walter Laqueur, and Richard Clutterbuck identified key elements of the terrorists' toolbox, including assassination, the mass casualty event, the role of the media, and the importance of provocation. In 1975, lawyer and historian David Fromkin sketched out one of the first brief histories of terrorism and asserted that terrorism is "a form of mass communication," the intent and significance of which hinges more on its representation in the media before an "audience" than on its impact on particular victims. In fact, he wrote, "the uniqueness of the strategy [of terrorism] lies in this: that it achieves its goals not through its acts but through the response to its acts."[14]

By the 1990s, a small subset of terrorism experts, led by important figures such as Alex Schmid and Richard Leeman, were exploring terrorism as a communicative act that while violent, primarily served to function as a message to one or more audiences.[15] As such, terrorism as a message hinged on the symbolic value of the act as perceived by distant targets.

This form of analysis, however, opened the door to perceptive critiques of terrorism studies itself. Some of these critiques amounted to little more than counter-claims concerning the biases inherent in the use of the term "terrorism," but they highlighted the sometimes close relationship between terrorism experts and the state. The implication, made explicit in the 1980s in the works of Edward Herman, Gerry O'Sullivan, and Noam Chomsky, was that most experts restricted their application of the term "terrorism" to sub-state actors, thus providing the government with the means to denounce leftist revolutionaries while turning a blind eye to the reactionary violence of the state.[16]

Such accusations suggested that terrorism still existed as an objective reality and could be productively studied – that is, the space between fact and propaganda could be accurately gauged and bridged – if only a more expansive and balanced definition of terrorism could be deployed. The anthropologists Joseba Zulaika and William Douglass undermined this proposition in their book *Terror and Taboo* when they applied Foucaultian post-structural analysis to the subject of terrorism – what they tellingly called "terrorism discourse" – and proclaimed that the emperor had no clothes: terrorism was a cultural and linguistic construct with no underlying reality that could be identified as fundamentally "terrorism." An act became "terrorism" when it was called such by an observer, usually a government and usually in accordance with some sort of political agenda. Moreover, Zulaika and Douglass revealed much about how "terrorists" (or those who promote our fear of them) exercise power over the public by creating narratives that individuals can inhabit, thus distorting their ability to assess the true danger of such forms of political violence.

Meanwhile, much of the scholarly – and what might be called sub-scholarly – investigation into the nature of terrorism fell into two traps. The first was the pursuit of definitions that relied on proposing more and more criteria that focused not on the relationship between the perpetrator, the act, and its reception – the triangle described above and in countless terrorist memoirs and manifestos – but rather on various elements in isolation: state or sub-state, the context of war or peace, the pursuit of political or religious change, human or material target, a single action or extended campaign, etc.[17] The second trap was to closely associate terrorism with a particular ideology or worldview, that is, to investigate terrorism with the foregone – and mistaken – conclusion that it could only be employed by a *certain type* of agent working toward a *certain type* of aim. This was what had happened during the era of anarchist terror around the turn of the previous century. The epitome of this approach in the late twentieth century was Claire Sterling's 1981 book, *The Terror Network*, which alleged that virtually all acts of international terrorism in the 1970s were funded and orchestrated by the Soviet Union as a means of covertly destabilizing the United States and its Cold War allies.[18]

The seminal moment in the emergence of terrorism studies was, of course, September 11, 2001, and the subsequent "War on Terror." Before then, terrorism experts, including those described above, had existed in relatively small numbers, inhabiting the fringes of academia and public consciousness, more frequently identified as consultants or policy experts than true academics. This was the case even in West Germany, Italy, France, and the United Kingdom, countries that had suffered from serious and sustained terrorist campaigns at home or abroad in their empires. But after 9/11, the demand for terrorism expertise quickly grew, and it was met by a rapid expansion in the number of such experts – many of whom were self-styled pundits – who churned out scholarly and popular works, blogs, journals, and opinion pieces. The West's sudden awareness of the threat of terrorism produced horror and puzzlement about this "new" phenomenon, even in countries that had experienced it since the 1960s. Most Americans, for instance, seem to have genuinely forgotten that President Ronald Reagan waged a "war on terrorism" in the 1980s, much less that anarchist terrorists carried out a campaign of violence in the US in the 1910s, culminating in the explosion of a massive bomb on Wall Street in 1920 that killed dozens. Indeed, the present-day obsession with the "new" phenomenon of terrorism has revived the old assumption from the 1890s and the 1980s that terrorism is essentially an ideology. Now, of course, it is expressed in the oddly well-meant refrain that while not all Muslims are terrorists, certainly all terrorists are Muslims. Not many scholarly works maintain this stance, but it is unfortunately widespread among popular commentators.

This leads us to two core assertions of this volume. First, to be appropriately and productively analyzed, terrorism needs to be understood as a means to an end. It is often described as a tactic, but, in fact, terrorism is best understood as a strategy that undergirds other actions. After all, killing, kidnapping, and arson are not "terrorism" per se. They are crimes that might be committed while engaging in terrorism as part of a broad strategy, one that might involve other forms of violent struggle. In other words – and this is the volume's second core assertion – a particular campaign of violence can only be understood as terrorism and its significance appreciated within and because of a particular context.

In terrorism studies, there exists an oft-noted divide between those who work within the social sciences and the humanities. This is often described as a contrast between quantitative and qualitative methodologies, but that captures only some of the difference. Of all the ways that we might characterize it, perhaps the most helpful is to observe that most scholars in the humanities explore the creation over time of a phenomenon that could be called terrorism but are generally obliged to do so while looking at only a particular time and place, while those in the social sciences are adept at analyzing it comparatively across time and place but only through the lens of a particular moment's – i.e., the present's – definition of it. In other words, if historians/humanists are primarily concerned with the development of the definition and thus the pattern, social scientists are focused on analyzing the present-day result of a process of historical change and projecting it back in time. To be even more blunt, historians, at their best, problematize the definition, while social scientists, when carrying out their best work, apply the definition.

Let us be clear: no scholarly discipline has a monopoly on the truth. Rather, each has advantages and disadvantages. As a historian, I am obviously trained and committed to pursue a certain sort of truth-telling. But if there are any doubts as to my conviction that social scientists have much to contribute to our understanding of terrorism, just simply look at the "notes on contributors." There you will see that of 31 contributors to this volume, five primarily identify themselves as social scientists, and another six describe themselves as humanists from other disciplines besides history. I am confident that readers will agree that the social scientists who have contributed to this book have added immeasurably to its quality, complementing the strengths and mitigating some of the weaknesses of the historical approach.

But the framework of this volume is unmistakably historical, both in its chronological organization and its methodological treatment. As such, another word on the particular strengths and weaknesses of the historical investigation of terrorism is warranted. As I suggested above, the historical study of terrorism suffers from a "forest for the trees" problem. Historians have the skills necessary to make sense of the significance of individual terrorist actors, incidents, and eras since they are highly trained in the art and science of deep investigation and rich contextualization. For that very reason they tend not to venture far outside of their temporal and geographic fields, due also to their use of sometimes difficult-to-reach archival sources that may require specialized language abilities. Thus although there is an increasingly large and sophisticated number of studies that examine the use of and the response to terrorism, unfortunately these studies tend to exist in isolation from one another.

Therefore, one of the main goals of the book you hold in your hands is to strive to indeed see the forest as well as the trees and thus produce a comprehensive history of terrorism that not only captures the particularities of this or that agent or event but also puts them in an expansive context that encourages us to find continuities and distinguish real changes. To do this, we have brought together between two covers some of the world's foremost historians of terrorism and ensured that their contributions speak to each other.

To provide a common starting – if not ending – point for these exchanges, I asked contributors to consider Schmid's "revised academic consensus definition," which appeared in 2011. While I doubt that any "consensus" definition of terrorism can live up to that billing, Schmid's definition comes as close as I believe is possible, at least as it concerns mid to late twentieth-century incarnations of terrorism. Schmid describes terrorism, in part, as a

> doctrine about the presumed effectiveness of a special form or tactic of fear-generating, coercive political violence and . . . a conspiratorial practice of calculated, demonstrative, direct violent action without legal or moral restraints, targeting mainly civilians and non-combatants, performed for its propagandistic and psychological effects on various audiences and conflict parties.

As noted above, the definition of terrorism risks becoming a string of criteria and caveats designed to counter various protestations based on the peculiar traits of this or that terrorist in this or that particular time and place – and Schmid's definition does include 12 points and is based on responses to two questionnaires distributed to academics regarding the viability of his 1984 and 1988 "academic consensus definitions." But in general, he captures the essential nature of terrorism as it has evolved in the modern era. Namely, he emphasizes that "the *direct victims* [of a terrorist act] *are not the ultimate target* . . . but serve as message generators, more or less unwittingly helped by the news values of the mass media, to reach various audiences and conflict parties that identify either with the victims' plight or the terrorists' professed cause."[19] In this, Schmid endorses several decades of academic work by scholars in terrorism studies that have emphasized that what makes terrorism unique is the centrality of symbolic violence, the performative act, or the communicative act.

Within individual chapters or groups of chapters in this volume, the definition of terrorism can appear fairly stable. Accordingly, a given contributor's primary task might be to describe and analyze the manifestations of terrorism in a specific time and place, which may or may not neatly fit a given definition. But over great sweeps of geography and eras, no single definition can fully capture the meaning and significance of terrorism. Nor should it. In fact, that creeping awareness should come second only to the recognition that *terrorism is old* as a clear point of significance for this volume.

Within and across the contributions to this volume, readers can explore how terrorism emerged from and was in some ways prefigured by pre-modern varieties of violence, including tyrannicide, private violence, and state terror. For the late modern era – that is, since the eighteenth century – readers can compare and contrast sub-state terrorism, state-sponsored terrorism, and state terror(ism). In Chapter 32, Richard Jackson directly challenges historians to broaden our frameworks for understanding state and sub-state violence, despite the ontological challenges. And several authors – de Graaf, Martin A. Miller, Roger Griffin, and, in particular, Paul M. Hagenloh (Chapters 27, 7, 24, and 11, respectively) – have tackled the issue quite directly and productively. Many others, including Jensen, Jones, Jennifer S. Holmes, and Steven Isaac (Chapters 8, 9, 19, and 4, respectively), have approached it more tangentially.

Most of the scholars included here imagine terrorism as objective, historical, generalizable, and stable, at least for short periods of historical time, while a few treat it largely or entirely as linguistically and culturally constructed (here I am thinking of de Graaf and Jackson as well as Patyk [Chapters 27, 32, and 31, respectively]). Generally speaking, the longer the period covered in a chapter, the more the author must recognize the essentially contested and constructed meaning of the term, as well as the ways the meaning of the term evolves from the standpoint of the state, the public, and the perpetrators of violence.

Let us be clear on this point, however: some scholars' belief that terrorism is culturally constructed is not meant to imply that somehow there is no *real* violence present. On the contrary, such an approach accepts that real blood is spilled and that real lives are destroyed. The issue is how we describe such violence and thus how societies react to it. How, such scholars might ask, is our reaction altered when we perceive that "terrorists" are at fault? What then do we demand of our governments and ourselves? Conversely, how do we react when it is our governments, militaries, or police forces spilling the blood? Do we accept the possibility, cultural constructivists might ask, that our governments might be terrorists?

The subject of religiously inspired violence also deserves a word of explanation. At first I was uncomfortable including a chapter focusing on Islamist thought, in addition to one detailing the activities of Islamist-inspired terrorists. In an ideal world, a volume on the history of terrorism would not have to survey the doctrines of a large subset of one of the world's largest and most significant religions just to draw, in part, the conclusion that John Calvert (Chapter 17) does, that Islam's – as well as Islamism's and *salafism*'s – connections to violence are limited, often gravely misunderstood, and primarily driven by specific contexts. In other words, that link is subject to the same caveats and asterisks that are routinely applied to other world religions. I suspect that I have already tipped my hand as to my reason for including Calvert's chapter in suggesting earlier that Islam and terrorism have become linked in the public imagination of much of the West for many reasons that are regrettable or simply wrong. I hope this chapter will set the record straight for some readers. This concern is also expressed in Chapters 8 and 9 by Jensen and Jones, respectively, on anarchism and terrorism; there is a long and storied history of broad movements becoming known to outsiders through the activities of their violent fringe. If readers

INTRODUCTION

need to be reminded that adherents of other religions have found inspiration for violence in their faiths, they can turn to Donathan Taylor's portion of Chapter 3 on pre-modern terrorism that addresses the Sicarii; Isaac's (Chapter 4) on terror in medieval Christian Europe, including the Crusades; Matthew Jennings's (Chapter 6) on the subjugation and terrorization of the New World by European Christians; Eamon Murphy's (Chapter 23) discussion of Hindu extremism; and Susanne Martin's (Chapter 26) discussion of the participation of Christians and Buddhists in suicide attacks in recent decades.

While a historical approach to terrorism provides many advantages, the search for its origins raises its own questions, in particular, how to address the history of terrorism in those eras before the term entered widespread use (which did not happen until the latter part of the nineteenth century). A different concern is how to analyze "terrorism" before the rise of modern conceptions of the state and the individual. This makes the group of chapters that address pre-modern "terrorism" fraught with dangers and conceptually challenging but also tremendously fruitful. As Johannes Dillinger, Taylor and Yannick Gautron, Isaac, and Jennings demonstrate in Chapters 2, 3, 4 and 6, respectively, most of the elements that constitute modern terrorism existed before "terrorism" was "invented." Or should that be "discovered"? And Mike Rapport, Jennings, and Griffin (in Chapters 5, 6, and 24, respectively) explore those moments of invention/discovery.

As de Graaf proposes in Chapter 27 on counter-terrorism, one way to avoid the possibility of overly imposing the present on the past and thus risking anachronisms is to historicize the debate, striving to restrict ourselves or at least hyper-consciously trace (à la *Begriffsgeschichte*, the German term for the history of concepts) the use of terms in historically accurate ways. Isaac is particularly careful to do this in Chapter 4, in part because he takes on directly the challenge of historicizing violence in an era that lacked our clear modern distinctions between public and private killing.

The questions – as well as some of the possible answers – that I have outlined concerning the nature of terrorism in this introduction make clear the importance of gaining a clearer-eyed understanding of the phenomenon. And while the contributors to this volume might differ in their application of definitions of terrorism – and in their willingness to accept the possibility that the phenomenon we call "terrorism" can even be defined – there would certainly be broad agreement among them that it is incumbent upon all of us to learn from the historical record.

Speaking for myself, I believe that terrorism has often been employed in the past as a strategy that can be comprehended, analyzed, and countered, and that terrorism constitutes a real – if not existential – threat to the national security of the world's states and peoples. As such, I hope that this volume is read, absorbed, and addressed by those in the military, intelligence community, and national security apparatus of the United States and other countries. We should address the real danger posed by modern terrorist movements, but the contributions to this volume are valuable in reminding readers that those who use terrorism are more likely to cause casualties and destabilize states and societies than to achieve the full extent of their goals. And let us add to that the warnings from fiction writers of a century ago and of some academics of more recent decades: that our governments might do grave damage to themselves and to their populations in the name of fighting terrorism. Popular ignorance invites states to act hastily to reassure their peoples and opens the door to abuses of authority, human rights, and civil liberties.

Our concern about terrorism as a national security issue should also be tempered by the awareness that terrorism is indeed a strategy and can be used by those to whom we might be more favorable. If terrorism is to be a useful analytical category, we should also question the means and ends of terroristic violence when used by those whose aims we endorse.

In the end, the study of terrorism's history probably raises more questions than it provides answers. But if, as suggested throughout this introduction, terrorism is a slippery beast that terrifies most when its very nature is questioned the least, perhaps the asking of better, more informed questions is the first step toward enlightenment.

Notes

1 Sergei Stepniak-Kravchinskii, *Underground Russia: Revolutionary Profiles and Sketches from Life* (New York: Charles Scribner's Sons, 1883), 41, 42, 257. For more on Kravchinsky and Russian revolutionary terrorism, see Chapter 7 by Martin A. Miller and Chapter 31 by Lynn Patyk in this volume.
2 Quoted in Lisa Cardyn, "Sexual Terror in the Reconstruction South," in *Battle Scars: Gender and Sexuality in the American Civil War*, ed. Catherine Clinton and Nina Silber (Oxford: Oxford University Press, 2006), 148. For more on Reconstruction-era white supremacist terrorism, see Chapter 10 by R. Blakeslee Gilpin in this volume.
3 Edmund Burke, "Fourth Letter […] to the Earl Fitzwilliam," in *The Works of the Right Honourable Edmund Burke* (London: John C. Nimmo, 1887), 6:70.
4 "J.-L. Tallien on the Terror," in *The French Revolution: A Document Collection*, ed. Laura Mason and Tracey Rizzo (Boston: Houghton Mifflin, 1999), 264, 266. Emphasis in original. For more on terrorism during and immediately after the French Revolution, see Chapter 5 by Mike Rapport in this volume.
5 See Juan Cole, "Iraq's Worst Week – and Bush's," March 1, 2006, www.salon.com/2006/03/01/worst_3/ (accessed September 13, 2014).
6 After many decades of encouraging revolutionary activity, Kropotkin admitted in the 1890s that "a structure based on centuries of history cannot be destroyed with a few kilos of explosives." Quoted in Martin A. Miller, *Kropotkin* (Chicago: University of Chicago Press, 1976), 174.
7 Peter Kropotkin, "The Spirit of Revolt," in *Kropotkin's Revolutionary Pamphlets*, ed. Roger N. Baldwin (New York: Dover, 1970), 39. Italics in original.
8 For more on the phenomenon, see Chapters 8 and 9 in this volume by Richard Bach Jensen and Thai Jones, respectively.
9 Quoted in Bruce Hoffman, *Inside Terrorism*, rev. and expanded ed. (New York: Columbia University Press, 2006), 61; and Alistair Horne, *A Savage War of Peace: Algeria 1954–1962* (New York: Viking Press, 1978), 132. For more on terrorism in the Algerian War of Independence, see Chapter 15 by Martin C. Thomas in this volume.
10 Quoted in Joseba Zulaika and William Douglass, *Terror and Taboo: The Follies, Fables, and Faces of Terrorism* (London: Routledge, 1996), 17.
11 *Trial of the Major War Criminals before the International Military Tribunal at Nuremberg* [The so-called "Blue Series"] (Nuremberg, 1947), 1:31–3, 46, 290, 298, 301, 329, 350.
12 See, for example, E. V. Walter, *Terror and Resistance: A Study of Political Violence* (London: Oxford University Press, 1969); Robert Conquest, *The Great Terror: Stalin's Purge of the Thirties* (London: Macmillan, 1968); and William Shirer, *The Rise and Fall of the Third Reich* (New York: Simon & Schuster, 1960).
13 "The International Convention for the Suppression of the Financing of Terrorism," United Nations, 1999, Article 2.1, https://treaties.un.org/doc/db/Terrorism/english-18-11.pdf (accessed September 20, 2014). The treaty entered into force in 2002, and 185 countries have ratified it.
14 David Fromkin, "The Strategy of Terrorism," *Foreign Affairs* 53, no. 4 (1975): 692.
15 See, for instance, Alex P. Schmid and Janny de Graf, *Violence as Communication: Insurgent Terrorism and the Western News Media* (London: Sage Publications, 1982); Anthony Kubiak, *Stages of Terror: Terrorism, Ideology and Coercion as Theatre History* (Bloomington, IN: Indiana University Press, 1991); and Richard Leeman, *The Rhetoric of Terrorism and Counterterrorism* (New York: Greenwood Press, 1991).

INTRODUCTION

16 Edward S. Herman, *The Real Terror Network: Terrorism in Fact and Propaganda* (Boston: South End Press, 1982); Edward S. Herman and Gerry O'Sullivan, *The "Terrorism" Industry: The Experts and Institutions that Shape Our View of Terror* (New York: Pantheon Books, 1989); and Noam Chomsky, *Pirates and Emperors: International Terrorism in the Real World* (New York: Claremont Research and Publications, 1986). For a valuable analysis of the discipline of "terrorism studies," see Lisa Stampnitzky, *Disciplining Terror: How Experts Invented "Terrorism"* (Cambridge: Cambridge University Press, 2013).

17 The opening chapter of a standard work in the field – Jonathan R. White, *Terrorism: An Introduction*, 4th ed. (Belmont, CA: Wadsworth/Thomson, 2002) – surveys much of this literature, including many mind-boggling definitions of terrorism that concentrate, in turn, on the motives of the perpetrator, his/her means, target, and, only occasionally, the broader reaction to the violence. Conversely, in *The Lessons of Terror* (New York: Random House, 2002), Caleb Carr reveals why resorting to a single-factor definition of terrorism – "warfare deliberately waged against civilians with the purpose of destroying their will to support either leaders or policies that the agents of such violence find objectionable" (p. 6) – doesn't work in the first place.

18 Claire Sterling, *The Terror Network: The Secret War of International Terrorism* (New York: Henry Holt, 1981). For more information on Sterling, her allegations, and the US government's embrace of her thesis, see Chapter 27 by de Graaf on counter-terrorism and Chapter 30 by Geraint Hughes on international terrorism, both in this volume.

19 Alex P. Schmid, "The Definition of Terrorism," in *The Routledge Handbook of Terrorism Research*, ed. Alex P. Schmid (Abingdon: Routledge, 2011), 86–7. Italics in original.

Further reading

Crenshaw, Martha. *Terrorism in Context*. University Park, PA: Pennsylvania State University Press, 2001. First published 1995.

Fromkin, David. "The Strategy of Terrorism." *Foreign Affairs* 53, no. 4 (1975): 683–98.

Hoffman, Bruce. *Inside Terrorism*. Rev. and expanded ed. New York: Columbia University Press, 2006.

Laqueur, Walter. *A History of Terrorism*. New York: Little, Brown, 1977.

—, ed. *Voices of Terror: Manifestos, Writings and Manuals of al Qaeda, Hamas, and Other Terrorists from around the World and throughout the Ages*. New York: Reed, 2004.

Law, Randall D. *Terrorism: A History*. Cambridge: Polity, 2009.

Rapoport, David C. "The Four Waves of Modern Terrorism." In *Attacking Terrorism: Elements of a Grand Strategy*, edited by Audrey Kurth Cronin and James M. Ludes, 46–73. Washington, DC: Georgetown University Press, 2004.

Reich, Walter, ed. *Origins of Terrorism: Psychologies, Ideologies, Theologies, States of Mind*. Washington, DC: Woodrow Wilson Center Press, 1990.

Schmid, Alex P., ed. *The Routledge Handbook of Terrorism Research*. Abingdon: Routledge, 2011.

Stampnitzky, Lisa. *Disciplining Terror: How Experts Invented "Terrorism."* Cambridge: Cambridge University Press, 2013.

Zulaika, Joseba, and William Douglass. *Terror and Taboo: The Follies, Fables, and Faces of Terrorism*. London: Routledge, 1996.

Part I

STATE TERROR, TYRANNICIDE, AND TERRORISM IN THE PRE-MODERN WORLD

2

TYRANNICIDE FROM ANCIENT GREECE AND ROME TO THE CRISIS OF THE SEVENTEENTH CENTURY

Johannes Dillinger

This chapter surveys the development of the doctrine of tyrannicide from its earliest beginnings in the ancient world until the early seventeenth century. It will discuss the interrelation between theoretical debates and concrete political violence. Since the loaded terms "tyrant" and "tyrannicide" are not objectifiable and are unsuitable as categories of historical analysis, I will use them only in order to investigate the origins and changes in the concept that an unjust ruler (a "tyrant") could or should be killed legitimately ("tyrannicide"). I will not address the objectivist or moral questions concerning whether some concrete person should be seen as a "tyrant" or if killing any such person could be excusable. The idea of tyrannicide is relevant for a discussion of the history of terrorism, which I define as asymmetrical conflict including the partisan use of media in which an actor without official government mandate employs violence or the threat of violence against some state in order to further political change. At least in the initial stage of their fight, terrorists – in contrast to the organizers of a coup d'état, insurrectionists, or guerrilla fighters – do not yet aim at exercising military control over a certain region.[1] Terrorist tactics include assassinations of rulers, which the terrorists sometimes present as legitimate tyrannicides. This definition implies that terrorism is not necessarily a modern phenomenon. Such a recognition might help us to acquire a deeper understanding of terrorism if we allow that the roots of the phenomenon reach into the remote past.[2] The fact that we tend to see persons who fought pre-modern monarchs in a positive light does not contradict that suggestion: the old and unsolvable problem that one person's terrorist is another person's freedom fighter is, after all, an integral part of the discussion of terrorism.

Ancient Greece

According to tradition, the first Greek statues paid for out of public funds not depicting a god were those of tyrannicides: in 514 BC, Harmodios and Aristogeiton stabbed to death Hipparchus, a tyrannical ruler of Athens.[3] However, the Greek historians who dealt with the event hesitated to praise the killers. They already voiced some of the criticism that would help to shape the discussion of tyrannicide until the present. According to Herodotus, the killing achieved nothing for it did not end the tyrannical rule of Hipparchus' two surviving brothers.[4] When Thucydides discussed Hipparchus' assassination, he addressed major points of the discussion of tyrannicide that was to come: the motives of the killers, the guilt of the tyrant, the risks taken, and the eventual outcome. He arrived at the sobering conclusion that a rather lenient tyrant had been killed by persons who had acted not out of love of liberty but out of injured pride and fear for their personal safety. With their ill-planned assassination, they had merely provoked the tyrant's successors to punish the Athenians harshly.[5]

Nevertheless, the democratic faction of Athens not only celebrated the tyrannicides but tried to give the resistance against tyranny a legal basis. Aristotle mentioned that according to an ancient law anyone aspiring to tyrannical rule would be outlawed, as would all his supporters. He might have been alluding to a law by Dracon. Laws enacted under Solon, Cleisthenes, Pericles, and Eucrates – roughly between 600 and 400 BC – obliged the Athenians to fight all attempts to overthrow democracy. In 410 BC, a decree of Demophantos legalized the killing of anybody who overthrew Athens' "constitution" and of anyone who accepted a public office after such an overthrow. Indeed, all Athenian citizens were required to swear an oath to fight tyrants with all possible means. The *polis* promised to honor the memory of anyone – even foreigners – who killed an Athenian tyrant.[6] These laws might serve as good examples of symbolic legislation; rather than playing any practical role in law enforcement, they served as an expression and confirmation of the democratic awareness of Athens.

When Plato studied the state and dealt with tyranny and tyrannicide, he had little time for historical arguments. In *The Republic*, Plato sketched a portrait of the tyrant as a personality type. The tyrannical man comes from democratic stock, but the relative luxury his background allows him corrupts him so that he loses all sense of propriety. The tyrannical man was not necessarily a ruler. However, tyrannical rule was first and foremost the rule of a person of the tyrannical type, and the tyrannical ruler was the worst kind of tyrannical person.[7]

Plato explained that tyranny arose from the lack of structure the democratic society suffered from. The commoners were unable to reconcile liberty with stability and longed for a strong leader who protected them from people of the upper classes. This leader could easily turn into a tyrant. Indeed, any leader who had tasted power over the docile *demos* and had killed in political conflict inevitably became a tyrant. The only way out of this development was to kill that leader before he rose to full tyrannical power. Plato's views here corresponded to the gist of the Athenian laws against tyranny: tyrannicide was pre-emptive in character. It was the last defense of the political system one had to resort to before a would-be tyrant fully solidified his power. According to Plato, after the tyrant had gained full power, he would still feel far from safe. The tyrant lived in fear – that was part of the tyrannical personality – but he was also positively driven by the concrete fear of assassination: all the benefits he ostentatiously bestowed on the population were meant to appease his would-be rebellious subjects. The enemies of the tyrant were clearly the upper classes who would plot his assassination. The tyrant would eventually ask the *demos* for troops for his personal protection. As the tyrant had to fear all people with any moral standards, he had to rely on mercenaries whose loyalty was questionable at best. The tyrant caught himself in vicious circles of distrust that made both his political and physical survival ever more unlikely.[8] Thus, for Plato the fear of tyrannicide was one of the motors that drove tyranny.

Plato's doctrine of tyranny implied a version of terrorism rather different from how the term is usually used today, one understood in the broadest sense of the political use of terror. Terror was a central element of tyranny not because the tyrant used terror as a weapon against would-be rebels but because the tyrant's constant fear of assassins was the structuring principle of his reign. The problem that would play a major role in later centuries – whether the killing of a tyrant was right or lawful – was of hardly any interest for Plato. He simply did not discuss it as a legal problem or a moral dilemma.[9]

Aristotle wrote at length about tyranny. For him, the yardstick of all political systems was the common good. Not only did tyranny not serve the common good, it negated it. Tyranny was not really a form of government. Rather, it was per se a violation of the "constitutional" order: the tyrant was a demagogue, a king, a magistrate, or a member of the oligarchy who created for himself a unique position of power beyond anything allowed by the rule of law or tradition. This construction of tyranny as a kind of pseudo-government that was always in itself unlawful begged the question what exactly lawful government was. For practical purposes, Aristotle seemed prepared to admit that the support of the people made the difference between a king and a tyrant. He might have echoed a suggestion by Socrates here. In this context, Aristotle even envisioned a way in which the tyrant could consolidate – if not legitimate – his rule: if the tyrant played the role of the pious and dignified monarch, he could minimize the risk of attacks on him. Ideally, he gave both the commoners and the upper class the impression that he was all for them and would defend them against the other group. At the same time, as Aristotle remarked ironically, it was best for the tyrant to foster discord and distrust among his subjects, to do everything to keep them from uniting against him, to deprive them of potential leaders, and to surveil them with unceasing vigilance. It was most important for the tyrannical ruler to keep a close watch over everyone who might feel wronged by his regime. Aristotle's sober view of the tyrant corresponded to his detached treatment of tyrannicide. He did not see the assassin as an idealist. As the case of Harmodios and Aristogeiton had shown, tyrannicides had usually some ulterior motive for their attack on the ruler: fear, greed, vengeance, or ambition. The last two might even lead the tyrannicide to attack even though he had hardly any chance to escape after the killing. In this way, Aristotle envisaged the suicide assassin: no enemy of the tyrant was more dangerous than the one who felt he had suffered so much under his rule that he was prepared to die if he could take the tyrant with him. In any case, Aristotle acknowledged that a blatant abuse of power could justify tyrannicide. He, like Plato, expected members of the elites to fight tyrants successfully.[10]

Ancient Rome

The Roman republic had laws against tyranny roughly corresponding to those of Athens. Given the republic's natural hostility to all things monarchical, the laws were not explicitly directed against tyrants but against people who attempted to re-establish the *regnum*. It was legal to put anyone to death who tried to create a new office without the consent of the people and outside of the ceremonial and political framework, i.e., anyone who wanted to overthrow the republican order. These laws were apparently enacted in the late sixth and fifth centuries BC, and they belonged to the very bedrock of the republican constitution. According to Livius, in 486 BC a consul who appeared to be about to gain permanent rule by bribing the *plebs* with new land grants was executed. Spurius Maelius, a rich plebeian, was killed by the *magister equitum* Ahala when he attempted a similar coup in 439 BC. Ahala went into exile.[11]

On the basis of these traditions and urged on by Caesar's rise to power, Cicero became one of the most outspoken advocates of tyrannicide ever. For Cicero, tyranny spelled the end of law and freedom. Anyone who thought that such a government could be honorable was not just stupid or corrupt but was also clearly mad. The tyrant himself was not even a human being. His life was a burden to him because it was necessarily full not only of intrigue but also of fear. Echoing Plato, Cicero presented the threat of tyrannicide as an integral part of the tyrant's reign. Killing him was not only just; it was a noble deed and as necessary as the amputation of a diseased limb. Whereas killing a friend was a most heinous crime, killing a former friend who had become a tyrant – that is, abusing the trust of a tyrant in order to kill him – was "the most beautiful of all great deeds."[12]

Cicero demanded the killing of tyrants in power as well as the killing of everybody aspiring to tyrannical rule. He praised tyrannicides emphatically as liberators worthy of ritual worship and claimed that given the opportunity he would kill a tyrant even if it cost his own life.[13] According to Cicero, tyrannicide was justifiable homicide par excellence, for it was really killing in self-defense. As such, it was in accordance with natural law, which was the yardstick of positive law. As such, it would be utterly absurd to question the rightfulness of tyrannicide.[14]

It should be obvious that Cicero's fierce advocacy of tyrannicide reflected the changes in the political structure in Rome he lived through. When he spoke about tyranny, he did not discuss theoretical matters but mounted polemical attacks on his political adversaries who were about to overthrow Roman republicanism. Cicero and Brutus, who famously led the conspiracy to kill Caesar, had been in close contact. Even though Cicero was not part of that conspiracy, the connection between the fact that Brutus owed much of his career to Caesar and Cicero's suggestion that not even personal obligation should keep a conscious citizen from attacking a tyrant seems obvious. However, the Senate failed to celebrate Brutus as a tyrannicide. It merely pardoned him as a murderer. Given the political power of Caesar's faction, Brutus had to flee the city a few days later.[15]

Given the preoccupation of antiquity with the tyrant as a person who wanted to overthrow the "constitutional" order, one might argue that the tyrant rather than the tyrannicide was a precursor of modern-day terrorists. In the modern era, many define terrorism as asymmetrical conflict in which an actor with no official mandate from any government fights a government in order to further political change. If we accept that, we need to see pre-modern tyrants who wanted to overthrow the existing political structures as akin to modern terrorists, not the tyrannicides who aimed at defending that political structure.

The Middle Ages: John of Salisbury and Thomas Aquinas

Concerning active resistance and tyrannicide, Biblical traditions were equivocal. Even if we exclude those passages of the Bible in which God demands the killing of some person and focus narrowly on questions of legitimate disobedience against authority, we find a variety of opinions. While the history of the Maccabees, Daniel 7:27, and Acts 5:29 seemed to justify (violent) resistance, Exodus 22:27–28, Proverbs 8:15, Romans 13, and 1 Peter 2:13–18 advocated obedience towards the authorities even if they were pagan. In contrast to Greek and Roman authors, the Bible focused on resistance or non-resistance against actual rulers, not against persons about to overthrow the political order. Some early Christian authors praised tyrannicide. For example, Sozomen enthusiastically reported the (wrong) story that Julian the Apostate had been killed by a Christian as a tyrant because he had fought the Church. There were even legends about a saint who came down from Heaven in order to kill the tyrant Julian.[16] Augustine did acknowledge that if the commonwealth had fallen prey to criminals and persons indulging their personal ambition, it was just to fight them and give the government back to those who would use it rightly. However, his main argument was that Christians should respect the lords of the *civitas terrena* (the City of Man).[17] Augustine more or less set the tone for the Christian discussion of tyrannicide until the High Middle Ages.[18]

John of Salisbury, a protégé of Thomas Becket, was the only theologian of the High Middle Ages who tried to defend tyrannicide vociferously. John, who drew upon Cicero, thought that his time suffered under a number of tyrants, among others the German Emperor Frederick Barbarossa. For John, the decisive difference between a king and a tyrant was that the king respected the law whereas the tyrant did not. The king was the image of God's majesty that founded and guaranteed all law, while the tyrant was the image of the devil. While John conceded that unjust government was a form of divine punishment, this did not mean that Christians had no right to fight unjust rulers. The abuse and destruction of the law was not to be tolerated and could not go unpunished. Therefore, John allowed tyrannicide as the *ultima ratio* in the conflict with unjust princes, including princes of the Church. He went so far as to suggest that in most cases of unjust government, tyrannicide was rightful because tyranny would not allow the intervention of legitimate authorities. However, John did respect norms of feudal society, for it was illegitimate for a tyrannicide to violate the bonds of honor and mutual trust implied in feudal obligations. In the end, John seemed to be unhappy with his own daring, explaining that prayer was the most effective weapon against tyrants.[19]

In the thirteenth century, Thomas Aquinas set out to describe the origins and nature of monarchy, integrating historical experience, Greek philosophy, and Christian tradition. Tyranny, Aquinas explained, might also arise out of the rule of the majority with its factionalism as well as out of monarchy. The latter case was less damaging as it avoided party strife. The main characteristic of tyrannical rule was that it served the interests of those in power and not the common good. If tyranny triumphed over the precautions recommended by Aquinas – such as a limitation of monarchical power – the *doctor angelicus* suggested that it would be best to tolerate it for a while if it was at all tolerable. The dangers arising out of an open fight against a moderate tyrant might be worse than his tyranny itself. If the tyrant prevailed, he might resort to harsh countermeasures against the rebels. If the tyrant lost, a permanent destabilization of the political system could still ensue. A more aggressive tyrant might arise out of the ruin of his predecessor. In case of an intolerable tyranny, Aquinas had as a young theologian defended tyrannicide following Cicero. Later on, Aquinas declared soberly that the deposition of a ruler was a "constitutional" question: elective monarchies might give the subjects a chance to resist. In accordance with Aristotle, but also reflecting the political realities of his time, Aquinas thought that first and foremost powerful elites had the right and the duty to fight tyrants. In other political systems, the subjects could only pray for relief from tyranny. Thus, Aquinas advocated a right to resist that should take its concrete form according to the specific customs of each country. This did not necessarily exclude tyrannicide as the *ultima ratio*, but the direct and adventurous course of tyrannicide should never be the first option. Given the fact that Aquinas was a nephew of emperor Frederick Barbarossa and given his Aristotelian orientation, it is probably not surprising that the theologian was reluctant to praise tyrannicide. Nevertheless, Aquinas' new respect for "constitutional" conditions and his level-headed acknowledgment of the realities of power that saw resistance primarily not so much as the privilege but as the responsibility of rich and influential persons made Aquinas a remarkable theoretician of tyrannicide.[20]

The Middle Ages: Petit and Gerson

In 1407, John the Fearless, Duke of Bourgogne, had killed his cousin, Louis, Duke of Orléans, who had ruled France de facto as the vicegerent of his feeble-minded brother, King Charles V. The death of Louis sparked a major debate on tyrannicide. John the Fearless asked one of the protégés of his family, Jean Petit, a priest with a doctorate in theology and a sound knowledge of law and politics, to defend him. John himself assembled a committee of nobles to hear his case. This official hearing was part and parcel of a propaganda campaign launched by John; writings praising his killing of the king's brother were already circulating in Paris. Petit defended John by declaring Louis a tyrant and a traitor whom the duke of Bourgogne had rightly killed. After Petit's speech, John admitted openly that he had killed Louis. The assembly of nobles acquitted him immediately. Two patents issued in the name of the king exculpated him. Thus, John did not only avoid any punishment, he achieved a major propagandistic victory.[21]

Petit revised his speech two times between 1408 and his death in 1411, but he never changed his basic arguments. Petit's defense of his client and sponsor was a piece of propagandistic aggrandizement rather than a legal plea. Petit might have decided to present John's deed as tyrannicide since it allowed him to shower the greatest possible praise on him, drawing on Cicero and John of Salisbury.[22] In Petit's speech, John was a tyrannicide in the classical sense of a man of high standing who intervened in order to stop an ill-suited person's illegitimate rise to power. His pre-emptive strike against Louis had saved the king whom the duke of Orléans had conspired to replace. All of the kingdom had lived in fear of Louis, whom Petit described as a typical tyrant, an unprincipled despot who lived to indulge himself. When John ordered his men to kill Louis, he was like the archangel Michael who threw Lucifer into hell. Divine law, natural law, moral law, and positive law all demanded tyrannicide. Therefore, nobody needed an official mandate or an instruction from some superior person in order to kill a tyrant legally. Petit stated that any subject of the king could legitimately kill a tyrant. The supreme obligation to kill the tyrant outweighed all personal or feudal obligations. Thus, Petit removed the last safeguard implied in the chivalrous ideal of feudalism that even John of Salisbury had respected. The assassination was even more honorable when the power of the tyrant was already strong enough to make it impossible for the courts to bring him to justice. Petit explained that if tyrannicide was legitimate, meritorious, and even a positive duty for any subject of the king of France, it was even more so for Duke John because he was an aristocrat of the highest rank.[23]

Jean Gerson, arguably one of the most respected theologians of that time, attacked Petit's very construction of the just tyrannicide. Gerson had Petit's theses condemned by a "Concile de la Foie" (Council of Faith) in Paris in 1414. This small assembly was already under the influence of Emperor Sigismund, an adversary of Duke John.[24] Sigismund was the *spiritus rector* of the Council of Constance; Gerson was one of the Council's leading theologians. It comes as no surprise that in 1415, the Council of Constance anathematized the notion that "any tyrant may and ought to be killed, licitly and meritoriously, by any of his vassals or subjects, even using plots, subtle blandishments or flattery, notwithstanding any oath taken or treaty made with him, and without waiting for a sentence or a mandate given by any judge."[25] The Council's text targeted mainly Petit but also the Dominican monk Johannes Falkenberg who supported the Teutonic Order of Knights against the king of Poland and had called for the king's liquidation.[26] The Council's decision was not the last word of the Catholic Church concerning tyrannicide since the clause about sentences and mandates left some room for debate. In addition to that, the Council's legitimacy was questionable. Gerson later returned to the subject of tyrannicide. He stressed that persons of legitimate authority, not just any disgruntled subject, had to deal with the tyrant. He demanded that the tyrannical ruler should be given the chance to repent for his sins and thus save his soul, i.e., he should not die suddenly in an assassination.[27]

There was a shift of emphasis from antiquity to the Middle Ages concerning tyrannicide. Even though both epochs knew both concepts of tyranny, the tyrant as a person aspiring to unlawful rule was apparently more prominent in the debates of antiquity when tyrannicide was primarily understood as a pre-emptive strike. After Augustine, authors tended to see the tyrant as a person who had already established his rule. Thus, tyrannicide became a way to liberate the people who already suffered from suppression. The influence of the Bible helped to foreground this understanding of tyrannicide. To be sure, there were exceptions from that trend. The killing of Louis, Duke of Orléans, seems to be the most prominent one. Nevertheless, the Council of Constance's decision and the further debate about violence against rulers rather neglected the old concept of the pre-emptive tyrannicide. This relative shift reflected another large-scale development. With the decline of the Roman Empire, government had lost much of its structure. It is a truism that the Middle Ages did not know states in a modern (or Roman) sense of the word. Laws like those of Athens and Rome that positively protected an abstract "constitution" against the tyrant as its enemy would have made little sense. Laws against treason were probably the best equivalent of the old laws against the rise of a tyrant. Treason laws like Edward III's act of 1352 or the German Golden Bull of 1356 punished attacks on the royal dynasty or on the princes who elected the king. Ancient Greece and Rome as well as Europe in the Middle Ages had mostly stressed that tyrannicide – if it was admissible at all – was the duty or rather the privilege of political elites. Given the relatively weak legal structure of medieval monarchies, this aspect became even more crucial. It corresponded to the all-encompassing estates system and the concept of *ordo:* the structure of society, including the privileges of the clergy and the aristocracy, were supposed to be part of the God-given hierarchical order mankind had to live in. It was consistent with this kind of thinking to assume that a political action of the magnitude of tyrannicide must be among the prerogatives of the ruling elites. Thus, all pre-modern authors condemned tyranny and many advocated tyrannicide while they maintained that the actual attack on a tyrant was a privilege reserved for a very small elite. This might alienate the modern democratic mind, but it was totally in keeping with pre-modern ideas of an ordered and structured world. Not even the Reformation would change that basic concept.

The Reformation and the monarchomachs

The Reformation challenged all traditional structures of power. In Germany, France, and England, denominational controversies led to armed resistance against the king. The legitimacy of a whole cosmos of power, that of the Church of Rome, was called into question. Nevertheless, the reformers' view of tyrannicide was not significantly more positive than that of the medieval Church. Martin Luther explained that Christians should pray for tyrants and not resist them actively. God would punish them eventually. Such an attitude was necessary, given that Luther's rejection of papal rule had obliged him to emphasize the authority of the temporal powers. Even if they neglected their God-given power to order and protect the Christian community, violent resistance – like the German Peasants' War – let alone tyrannicide was out of the question. Luther explained that neither the traditions of the Bible nor those of antiquity could ever justify killing a tyrant. That the Swiss had freed themselves from feudal rule or that the Danish had dethroned King Christian II was for the Wittenberg theologian plainly unjust. Luther only changed his mind to a certain degree, when in 1530, under pressure from Protestant princes, he declared it right for them to defend themselves with military force against the emperor. Nine years later, he confirmed this view and explained that armed resistance against the pope and those princes fighting Protestants at the beck and call of Rome was essentially self-defense. In rhetorical hyperbole, Luther declared the pope an outlaw who – according to German law – could be killed legally by anyone as if he were a wild beast.[28] The irony of this concept of "papacide" was, of course, that Luther himself had been an outlaw since 1521. It comes as no surprise that the Augsburg Confession embraced the concept of legitimate resistance against ungodly rulers.

In contrast to Luther, John Calvin directly commented on the nature of tyranny. The tyrant was a ruler who used fear not as an instrument of coercion (as it might be done in a well-ordered state) but as an instrument of suppression: fear helped to spread senseless confusion among the subjects. Even though Calvin maintained that the subjects owed obedience to their lords, he too was deeply troubled by the persecution of his own adherents by Catholic authorities. Rulers who did not respect God's will – i.e., who fought Protestantism – did not deserve loyalty. In 1562, early in the French civil wars, Calvin demanded that kings and princes who did not serve God should be arrested. However, he made it very clear that this was not a license to rebel, let alone a call to tyrannicide: persons of authority had to lead the resistance.[29] Calvin did not just echo medieval doctrines about tyrannicide here: it would have been difficult for him to say anything else in the concrete context of civil war.

The so-called monarchomachs of the sixteenth century, some of them Huguenots, essentially shared Calvin's view. The term "monarchomachs" (monarch slayers) is misleading: these authors – most prominently Hotman, Bèze, and Buchanan – stressed the right of rebellion and the estates' prerogative to check the monarch's power. The monarchomachs wanted the old elites of the estates to unite against the monarch that had grown too powerful. Thus they advocated armed resistance and open revolt against a tyrannical system rather than tyrannicide.[30]

In the late sixteenth century, Jean Bodin, one of the fathers of the concept of absolutism, took the opposite view. Bodin claimed that nobody, not even a person from the political elite, had the right even to think about killing his sovereign monarch. Only the intervention of a foreign power to bring down the tyrannical government in another country could be legitimate.[31]

The Jesuit debate and the assassinations of rulers around 1600

For a number of later authors, Juan de Mariana, a sixteenth-century Spanish historian and Jesuit priest, was the apostle of tyrannicide.[32] Indeed, his 1599 treatise was more aggressive than the Council of Constance's decision seemed to permit, and it did suggest a slightly new perspective. Anyone was allowed to kill a tyrant if the tyrant had been condemned by "*publica vox populi*" (the public voice of the people). One was to assume that such a condemnation took place automatically and silently if the tyrant prevented all meetings of persons of high standing that could have summoned the power to condemn him officially. In a way, a ruler who permanently kept the elite from uniting against him dethroned himself by that very act. This argument might have been derived from canon law: a pope who had evidently lost his Catholic faith automatically lost papal authority. More importantly, Mariana had in mind a concrete tyrant and concrete elites who were potentially dangerous to him. Henry III of France had killed the duke and the cardinal of Guise, both leading figures of the opposition against him. According to Mariana, this crime against the estates system, the political privileges of the elites, made him a tyrant. Henry's willingness to cooperate with the Protestant Henry of Navarre seemed to be less important for Mariana. Henry III was a tyrant because he violated the basic principles of the French monarchy (and any well-ordered state) that would at least guarantee the prerogatives of the high aristocracy. According to Mariana, the assassination of Henry by the radical Dominican Jacques Clément in 1589 had been justifiable tyrannicide, not murder. Mariana was no champion of popular sovereignty; usually he is not even counted under the monarchomachs. His treatise was an educational book written for the young Philip III of Spain. It was neither a radical political pamphlet nor a theological treatise but an instructive and practical manual for good government. Mariana warned the prince in no uncertain terms and pointed out the limits of his power: between him and potential assassins stood only the magnates of his kingdom among whom the bishops figured prominently.[33]

The most prolific critic of Mariana was probably Francisco Suárez, a fellow Jesuit who discussed tyrannicide in the context of a polemic against Anglicanism.[34] Suárez' tyrants were clearly the Protestant monarchs of England, especially Henry VIII and James I. Suárez reminded his readers of a fundamental distinction between two kinds of tyrants: those who had no legitimate claim to authority and those whose rule was essentially legitimate even if their governmental practices had become questionable, e.g., Nero. A tyrant of the latter kind might be especially dangerous if he supported heresy. Tyrants with no legal claim to rule had no authority, thus no law and no biblical call to obedience could protect them. However, as private persons were not allowed to kill murderers sentenced to death, private persons were not supposed to liquidate unjust rulers, even those whose rule was fundamentally illegitimate. Suárez repeated the basic thought that the fight against a tyrant should be left to persons of authority. This was even more important if the tyrant to be fought had some legitimate claim to authority. However, every ruler who turned his back to Catholicism lost any such claim. According to Suárez, the pope could officially depose heretical rulers because Rome's main responsibility (and prerogative) was the preservation of the Church all over the world. Thus, no resistance, let alone a physical attack on the person of a prince, could be legitimate without the foregoing approval of the pope. As to the concrete and practical role of private persons in a conflict with the tyrant, Suárez stressed explicitly that they should not take any action, no matter if the tyrant had any legitimate claim to power or not. Self-defense was the only exception from this rule as it was a God-given right. Nevertheless, even in self-defense the would-be assassin should ask himself if his own death or that of the tyrant would cause more hardship for the community.

Suárez took the old idea that tyrannicide was a kind of political privilege to extreme heights. This was more than a reflection of the estates system he lived in or a vestige of the medieval concept of *ordo*. Suárez vainly tried to dispel the anti-Catholic and anti-Jesuit odium the debate about Mariana had caused.[35] In addition to that, two attacks on monarchs loomed large over Catholic political theory. The first was the Gunpowder Plot. Eight years before Suárez wrote his treatise on the English monarchy, a small group of radical English Catholics led by Robin Gatsby – and allegedly Jesuit priests – had tried in vain to assassinate James I. The state trials that followed maintained that Jesuit teachings were ultimately responsible for the attempt on the king's life. We know precious little about the plotters, but they might have seen themselves as tyrannicides. A Jesuit apparently tried to dissuade them from their plans.[36] Suárez probably hoped to discourage further attempts on the monarch's life, which might have made the situation of the Catholic minority in England completely untenable even as he upheld papal authority and the condemnation of the English king as a heretic. The second attack had succeeded: François Ravaillac had stabbed Henry IV – Henry of Navarre, who had succeed Henry III as king of France – to death in 1610. The assassin had been no Jesuit but a radical Catholic disenchanted with Henry who had himself converted to Catholicism but failed to make the other Huguenots fall in line. In addition to that, Ravaillac had feared that Henry would attack the pope. The assassination itself and rumors about Jesuit involvement did not help to improve the situation of the Church and the Jesuit order.[37]

Both Mariana and his Jesuit counterpart Suárez developed their doctrines against the background of concrete attacks against kings. However, they dealt with them in very different ways: whereas Mariana tried to defend the assassination of Henry III as rightful tyrannicide, Suárez cautioned against the very concept of legitimate tyrannicide. Suárez not only feared reprisals against his co-religionists. He apparently saw the justification of tyrannicide as another source of irritation that threatened to destabilize the already explosive political situation even further.

We might call the plotters and assassins of the sixteenth and seventeenth centuries terrorists: they were non-state actors who attacked (members of) governments in order to further political change. Their actions were widely publicized and became parts of propaganda wars, much like those of their modern counterparts. Writers in antiquity had stressed that the tyrant was a person who wanted to overthrow the political order. Therefore, he, not the tyrannicide, could be regarded as the equivalent of a modern terrorist. The same analogy does not hold true for the Middle Ages and the early modern period, when writers tended to see the tyrant primarily as an unjust but well-established ruler. Accordingly, it was more difficult to justify a fight against him. The assassin turned from a heroic defender of the political order to its criminal enemy, resembling the modern conception of the terrorist. At any rate, the concepts of tyrannicide we discussed here were hardly revolutionary. Rather, they appeared to be integral parts of cultures that mostly respected the privileges and the political vocation of small elites. The link between the old doctrines of tyrannicide and ideas of popular sovereignty is tenuous: from Greek antiquity onwards, most authors stressed time and again that not just anybody but rather influential people should fight tyrants, be it because it was their privilege to do so or because of practical reasons. The real assassins and plotters of the period around 1600 hardly fitted the image of very high-ranking persons entitled to kill a tyrant; not even the Gunpowder Plotters were high aristocracy. With the exception of the ambiguous text by Mariana, the theorists of tyrannicide were reluctant to praise these terrorist-style regicides.

Later in the seventeenth century, the Thirty Years' War and the English Civil War would challenge monarchical power as it had never been challenged before. The execution of Charles I established a new concept of revolutionary violence against rulers, which the old concepts of tyrannicide were not even fit to describe.[38]

Notes

1 Johannes Dillinger, *Terrorismus* (Freiburg: Herder, 2008), 10–18.
2 Dillinger, *Terrorismus*, 21–5.
3 Heinrich Schlange-Schöningen, "Harmodios und Aristogeiton, die Tyrannenmörder von 514 v. Chr," in *Das Attentat in der Geschichte*, ed. Alexander Demandt, 15–38 (Erftstadt: Area, 2003); Mario

Turchetti, *Tyrannie et tyrannicide* (Paris: PUF, 2001), 46–69, 100–2; and Conal Condren, "The Office of Rule and the Rhetorics of Tyrannicide in Medieval and Early-Modern Europe," in *Murder and Monarchy: Regicide in European History, 1300–1800*, ed. Robert von Friedeburg, 48–72 (Basingstoke: Palgrave, 2004). Note that the term "tyrannicide" can not only refer to the act but to the person who carries it out.

4 Herodotus, *Hist.* 5, 55–62, www.paxlibrorum.com/books/histories/ (accessed February 27, 2013).
5 Thucydides, *Hist.* 6, 54–59, www.perseus.tufts.edu/hopper/text?doc=Perseus:text:1999.01.0247 (accessed February 27, 2013). See also Pedro Barceló, "Thukydides und die Tyrannis," *Historia. Zeitschrift für Alte Geschichte* 39, no. 4 (1990): 401–25.
6 Turchetti, *Tyrannie*, 97–107.
7 Plato, *Republic*, 9, www.perseus.tufts.edu/hopper/text?doc=Perseus%3Atext%3A1999.04.0094% 3Abook%3D9%3Asection%3D571A (accessed February 27, 2013). See also Roger Boesche, *Theories of Tyranny* (University Park: Pennsylvania State University Press, 1996), 27–39. For Plato's interpretation of the assassination of Hipparchos, see Plato, *Symposium*, 182, www.perseus.tufts. edu/hopper/text?doc=Perseus%3Atext%3A1999.01.0174%3Atext%3DSym.%3Asection%3D1 82c (accessed February 27, 2013).
8 Plato, *Republic*, 8, 555–557, www.perseus.tufts.edu/hopper/text?doc=Perseus%3Atext%3A1999. 04.0094%3Abook%3D8%3Asection%3D555B (accessed February 27, 2013); Plato, *Laws*, 4, 711–713, www.perseus.tufts.edu/hopper/text?doc=Plat.+Laws+4.711&fromdoc=Perseus%3Ate xt%3A1999.01.0166 (accessed February 27, 2013); and Boesche, *Theories*, 39–48.
9 Franklin Ford, *Political Murder* (Cambridge, MA: Harvard University Press, 1985), 34–7, 41–7; and Hans Georg Schmidt-Lilienberg, *Die Lehre vom Tyrannenmord* (Tübingen: Mohr 1901, reprint Aalen: Scientia 1964), 11.
10 Aristotle, *Politics*, 5, 1310–1315, www.perseus.tufts.edu/hopper/text?doc=Perseus%3Atext%3A1 999.01.0058%3Abook%3D5%3Asection%3D1310a (accessed February 27, 2013); Boesche, *Theories*, 49–84; Turchetti, *Tyrannie*, 83–99; and Ford, *Political*, 44–6.
11 Livius, 2, 8, 2; 3, 55, 5; 10, 9, 3–6, www.thelatinlibrary.com/livy/liv.3.shtml (accessed February 27, 2013); and Turchetti, *Tyrannie*, 129–36.
12 Cicero, *De Rep.* 2, 26, 48, www.thelatinlibrary.com/cicero/repub.shtml (accessed February 27, 2013); Cicero, *De off.* 3, 4, 19; 3, 7, 32; 3, 21, 82–4, www.thelatinlibrary.com/cicero/off.shtml (accessed February 27, 2013); and Ingo Gildenhard, "Reckoning with Tyranny: Greek Thoughts on Caesar in Cicero's Letter to Atticus," in *Ancient Tyranny*, ed. Sian Lewis, 197–212 (Edinburgh: Edinburg University Press, 2006).
13 Cicero, *Phil.* 2, 46, 117–119, www.thelatinlibrary.com/cicero/phil2.shtml (accessed February 27, 2013).
14 Cicero, *Pro Milo*, 4, 9–11, 29, 80, www.thelatinlibrary.com/cicero/milo.shtml (accessed February 27, 2013).
15 Ulrich Gotter, *Der Diktator ist tot!* (Stuttgart: Steiner, 1996); Robert Miola, "Julius Caesar and the Tyrannicide Debate," *Renaissance Quarterly* 38, no. 2 (1985), 271–89.
16 Brian Johnstone, "Political Assassination and Tyrannicide: Traditions and Contemporary Conflicts," *Studia Moralia* 41, no. 1 (2003): 24–46, 32–3; www.heiligenlexikon.de/BiographienM/ Mercurius.html (accessed July 31, 2014).
17 Augustinus, *De libero arbitrio*, 1, 6, 14, www.augustinus.it/latino/libero_arbitrio/index2.htm (accessed February 27, 2013).
18 Stefan Heid, "Der Umgang der frühen Kirche mit Tyrannenmord," *Die neue Ordnung* 56, no. 2 (2002): 125–36; and Johnstone, "Political," 33.
19 John of Salisbury, *Policraticus*, ed. Cary Joseph Nederman (Cambridge: Cambridge University Press, 2000), 25–30, 190–225; and Cary Joseph Nederman and Catherine Campbell, "Priests, Kings and Tyrants," *Speculum* 66, no. 3 (1991): 572–90.
20 Thomas Aquinas, *De regimine principum (De regno)*, 1, 2. 4–7. 11–12, www.corpusthomisticum.org/ orp.html (accessed February 27, 2013); Schmidt-Lilienberg, *Lehre*, 29–36; Johnstone, "Political," 34–7; and Turchetti, *Tyrannie*, 267–74.
21 Bertrand Schnerb, *Jean sans Peur* (Paris: Payot, 2005); Bernard Guenée, *Un meurte, une société: L'assassinat du duc d'Orléans* (Paris: Gallimard, 1992); Turchetti, *Tyrannie*, 320–1; Ford, *Murder*, 129–32; and Jürgen Miethke, "Der Tyrannenmord im späteren Mittelalter," in *Friedensethik im Spätmittelalter*, ed. Gerhard Beestermöller, 24–48 (Stuttgart: Kohlhammer, 1999).

22 When Turchetti suggested that Petit made "une erreur de tactique" when he presented John as a tyrannicide he did not take the propagandistic possibilities of tyrannicide into account. Turchetti, *Tyrannie*, 327.
23 Petit even suggested that the king would have overstepped the limits of his power had he tried to prevent the killing of his brother. Jean Petit, Second justification, entire text in Otto Cartellieri, *Beiträge zur Geschichte der Herzöge von Burgund* (Heidelberg: Winters, 1914), 21.
24 Jean Gerson, *Oeuvres complètes* (Paris: Desclée, 1960–1973), 10:180; Cartellieri, *Beiträge*, 13–14; and Turchetti, *Tyrannie*, 322.
25 Quoted in Harro Höpfl, *Jesuit Political Thought* (Cambridge: Cambridge University Press, 2004), 317.
26 Hartmut Boockmann, *Johannes Falkenberg, der Deutsche Orden und die polnische Politik* (Göttingen: Vandenhoeck & Ruprecht, 1975); and Jürgen Miethke, "Heiliger Heidenkrieg?" in *Heilige Kriege*, ed. Klaus Schreiner, 109–25 (Munich: Oldenbourg, 2008).
27 Gerson, *Oeuvres*, 10:164–286;Turchetti, *Tyrannie*, 325–31; and Ford, *Political*, 132,155.
28 Martin Luther, *D. Martin Luthers Werke: kritische Gesammtausgabe* (Weimar: Böhlau 1883–2009), 39.2:41–2; Cynthia Grant Shoenberger, "Luther and the Justifiability of Resistance to Legitimate Authority," *Journal of the History of Ideas* 40, no. 1 (1979): 3–20, 18–19; Turchetti, *Tyrannie*, 379–80; Wolfgang Schild, "Missetäter und Wolf," in *Wirkungen europäischer Rechtskultur*, ed. Gerhard Köbler, 999–1031 (Munich: Beck, 1997); and Esther Hildebrandt, "The Magdeburg Bekenntnis as a Possible Link between German and English Resistance Theories in the Sixteenth Century," *Archiv für Reformationsgeschichte* 71 (1980): 227–53.
29 Max Engammare, "Calvin monarchomaque?" *Archiv für Reformationsgeschichte* 89 (1998): 206–25; and Harro Höpfl, *The Christian Polity of Jean Calvin* (Cambridge: Cambridge University Press, 1982), 170–1, 210–16.
30 Roger Mason, "People Power? George Buchanan on Resistance and the Common Man," in *Widerstandsrecht in der frühen Neuzeit*, ed. Robert von Friedeburg, 163–84 (Berlin: Dunker & Humblodt, 2001); and Turchetti, *Tyrannie*, 418–42.
31 Jean Bodin, *Les six livres de la république* (Paris: DuPuy, 1576; Paris: Fayard, 1986), 1:2, 4–5, 5, 6; 2:63–4; 5:176–8.
32 See for example Schmidt-Lilienfeld, *Lehre*, 40–50.
33 Juan de Mariana, *De rege et regis institutione libri tres* (Toledo: Rodríguez, 1599, reprint Aalen: Scientia, 1969); Pierre Chevallier, *Les Régicides: Clément, Ravaillac, Damiens* (Paris: Fayard, 1989), 114–19; Harald Braun, *Juan de Mariana and Early Modern Spanish Political Thought* (Aldershot: Ashgate, 2007), 82–6; Höpfl, *Jesuit*, 317–19; Nicole Reinhardt: "Juan de Mariana: Bibelexegese und Tyrannenmord," in *Die Bibel als politisches Argument*, ed. Andreas PeĐar and Kai Trampedach, 273–94 (Munich: Oldenbourg, 2007); and Nicolas Le Roux, *Un regicide au nom de Dieu* (Paris: Gallimard, 2006).
34 Francisco Suárez, "Defensio fidei Catholicae adversus Anglicanae sectae errors," in *Francisci Suárez opera omnia*, ed. Michel André and Charles Berton, 24:675–83 (Coimbra: Gomez de Loureyro, 1613, Paris: Vivès, 1856–1878); the comments in Braun, *Juan*, 83, 87, are not totally convincing.
35 Braun, *Juan*, 6–9.
36 Antonia Fraser, *The Gunpowder Plot* (London: Phoenix, 2002); and Mark Nicholls, *Investigating Gunpowder Plot* (Manchester: Manchester University Press, 1991).
37 Roland Mousnier, *L'assassinat d'Henri IV* (Paris: Gallimard, 1964; reprint Folio, 1992).
38 Glenn Burgess, "Regicide: The Execution of Charles I and English Political Thought," in *Murder and Monarchy: Regicide in European History, 1300–1800*, ed. Robert von Friedeburg, 212–36 (Basingstoke: Palgrave, 2004).

Further reading

Boesche, Roger. *Theories of Tyranny*. University Park: Pennsylvania State University Press, 1996.
Braun, Harald. *Juan de Mariana and Early Modern Spanish Political Thought*. Aldershot: Ashgate, 2007.
Demandt, Alexander, ed. *Das Attentat in der Geschichte*. Erftstadt: Area, 2003.

von Friedeburg, Robert, ed. *Murder and Monarchy: Regicide in European History, 1300–1800*. Basingstoke: Palgrave, 2004.

Guenée, Bernard. *Un meurte, une société. L'assassinat du duc d'Orléans*. Paris: Gallimard, 1992.

Johnstone, Brian. "Political Assassination and Tyrannicide: Traditions and Contemporary Conflicts," *Studia Moralia* 41, no. 1 (2003): 24–46.

Lewis, Sian, ed. *Ancient Tyranny*. Edinburgh: Edinburg University Press, 2006.

Turchetti, Mario. *Tyrannie et tyrannicide*. Paris: PUF, 2001.

3

PRE-MODERN TERRORISM
The cases of the Sicarii and the Assassins

Donathan Taylor and Yannick Gautron

Those searching for the pre-modern roots of modern-day terrorism must usually be content with finding the occasional tactical similarity, the rare parallel strategic consideration, or an intriguing rhetorical construction of violence. More often, the analysis of ancient or medieval violence illuminates the character of modern terror by highlighting the presence or absence of critically important elements, what Steven Isaac in Chapter 4 describes as the utility of a photographic negative of our own time. While the chapters directly preceding and following this one demonstrate the timelessness of killing, they reveal the difficulties associated with analyzing violence that induced terror or mimicked modern tactics – such as assassination – but took place in societies that did not possess modern conceptions of the state, the ideological availability of revolutionary political change, or now-common delineations between public and private acts. Two examples stand out in the pre-modern world, however, for their eerie familiarity to our modern modes of violence: the Sicarii of Judaea and the Assassins of Persia and Syria. This chapter analyzes these two movements, explains their uses of violence within the contexts of their times, and explores the appropriateness of describing them as terrorists within both their contexts and ours.[1]

Romans, Jews, and Sicarii in Judaea

In the Southern Levant, a unique set of circumstances arose by the mid-first century of the Common Era that created an environment conducive to a unique expression of violence among the Jewish population which modern society has subsequently identified as terrorism. In the Roman province of Judaea, decades of foreign rule, together with the collaborative acquiescence of the largely Hellenized Jewish social and religious elite, finally compelled certain radical groups within the local community to oppose both in an expression of self-determination. Among these was a band of violent dissidents called the Sicarii whose identity has generated endless debate among modern scholars of Jewish history.

The circumstances which gave rise to the Sicarii found their origin in the social and political events which unfolded within Judea[2] during the preceding century. In 63 BCE, the Roman general Pompey (106–48 BCE) undertook to resolve a dispute between rival Hasmonean claimants to the high priesthood of the country as part of his efforts to further secure Rome's control over former Seleukid territories in the Levant. This task ultimately necessitated a three-month siege of Jerusalem, followed by the inexorable application of Roman authority. After a fresh round of internal disorder several years later, an additional reorganization of Judea occurred during the tenure of Aulus Gabinius, proconsul to Syria (57–55 BCE). Among other things, this involved a reduction in the political authority of the high priesthood and the rebuilding of several towns, the latter of which subsequently experienced an influx of colonists from various parts of the Mediterranean.[3]

These and other internal changes administered by Rome, though acceptable to the upper social and economic elite, generated growing agitation within the greater Jewish community. Governed by foreign rulers, subject to the authority of local Hellenized leaders, and surrounded in their ancestral lands by thousands of "Gentiles," many Jews found recourse in their religious teachings. Given the nature of Israelite cultural tradition, derived largely from the Bible, Jewish resistance to objectionable forms of rulership, whether foreign or domestic, inevitably assumed potent religious overtones.[4] And by the latter half of the first century CE, Jewish discontent with Roman rule generated a constant tension that provided a fertile environment from which the Sicarii pursued their goal of liberating the Jewish people from Roman authority.

In 6 CE, Rome formally joined the regions of Judea, Idumea, and Samaria into the Roman Province of Judaea and then moved to further consolidate its authority through the application of a tax census by the governor of Syria, P. Sulpicius Quirinius (6–12 CE). Under the subsequent constraining effects of these new changes, relations further deteriorated between the local Jewish population and their foreign overlords, and resistance to Roman authority hardened. For Rome, the matter was not made easier by the fact that a succession of later procurators, such as Ventidius Cumanus (48–52 CE), Lucceius Albinus (62–64 CE), and Gessius Florus (64–66 CE), who were appointed by the emperor to maintain supervision over the province of Judaea, callously mishandled domestic relations with little care shown for the welfare of the Jewish population. These periodic bouts of maladministration paired with the sometimes indiscriminant application of military force only added fuel to the growing civil unrest.[5]

Among the small minority of extremist groups that emerged at this time to oppose Roman authority in Judaea, the Sicarii stood apart. The ability of current scholarship to unravel the character of this elusive sect is complicated by the fact that almost all extant knowledge is derived from a single biased source – the works of the Jewish historian and former general during the opening stages of the First Roman–Jewish War (66–73 CE), Yosef ben Matityahu, later to be called, after his acquisition of Roman citizenship, Flavius Josephus.[6] Through two of his works, *The Jewish War* and *The Antiquities*, Josephus collectively portrays the Sicarii as an indigenous group of violent religious radicals that emerged in the mid-first century during the governorship of the Roman procurator Antonius Felix (52–60 CE).[7] Their appearance was the result of a confluence of factors that came together at the interface between Roman authority and Jewish culture.

From certain intertextual evidence in Josephus and lesser Talmudic sources, some modern historians have posited a link between the Sicarii and the Zealots (Kanna'im), the most widely identified opposition group to Roman rule in the events ending with the fall of Jerusalem in 70 CE. Since the nineteenth century, the potential existence of this relationship between the two sects has fueled passionate discussion among scholars, although no definitive connection can, in fact, be derived from any of the extant works.[8]

Sicarii violence and terror

In a careful analysis of Josephus, two characteristics can be ascertained that distinguish the sect from all other opposition groups in Judaea: their extreme doctrine of "No lord but God" and their utter commitment to carry out acts of violence against members of the Jewish community that dared reject this belief.[9] In essence, the targets of their violence were Jews, particularly prominent leaders in the community – such as priests – who cooperated with Roman authorities or otherwise acquiesced to the foreign influences permeating Jewish society.

The terror inspired by the Sicarii was magnified by the manner in which they intimidated their enemies. Josephus says that unlike the rural bandits common to Judaea, the Sicarii originated in Jerusalem and relied on anonymity as an instrument to instill fear. They

> committed murders in broad daylight in the heart of the city. The festivals were their special seasons, when they would mingle with the crowd, carrying short daggers under their clothing, with which they stabbed their enemies. Then, when [the victim] fell, the murderers joined in the cries of indignation and, through this plausible behavior, were never discovered.

Such tactics inevitably resulted in widespread psychological anxiety within the Jewish community.

> The panic created was more alarming than the calamity itself; every one, as on the battlefield, hourly expecting death. Men kept watch at a distance on their enemies and would not trust even their friends when they approached. Yet, even while their suspicions were aroused and they were on guard, they fell; so swift were the conspirators and so crafty in eluding detection.[10]

The first victim of this tactic was the High Priest Jonathan, doubtless selected because he was perceived to be a high profile collaborator with the Romans and his death would serve as a stark warning against such behavior to both the Jewish ruling elite and the common population.[11]

The instability generated in Jerusalem by this and other such sensational incidents quickly captured the attention of Roman authorities in Judaea who almost certainly assigned the name Sicarii, a Latin term derived from the fact that the assassins carried out their attacks with the use of a distinctive weapon whose design most resembled the curved Roman dagger called a *sica*. This term has no other currency in Greek or Jewish literature before Josephus.[12]

In addition to assassination, the Sicarii also resorted to the kidnapping of prominent Jews for purposes of political extortion. They began this practice during the procuratorship of Albinus when they seized Eleazar, secretary of the temple captain and son of the current high priest, Ananias (63 CE). They then offered his release in exchange for the freeing of their fellow Sicarii currently imprisoned by the Romans. Following Ananias' entreaties, Albinus eventually granted the request, but Josephus notes that "this was the beginning of greater troubles."[13] Emboldened by their success, the Sicarii continued to employ the abduction of prominent Jews as a means to secure the freedom of their incarcerated associates.

The activities of the Sicarii likewise extended into the countryside where they proved no less significant. In a less furtive manner, they sought to intimidate and punish the rural Jewish elite for willingly acquiescing to Roman authority. Josephus says that the Sicarii moved against those Jews "who consented to submit to Rome and in every way treated them as enemies."[14] To this end, they plundered and destroyed the estates of the wealthy in select acts of reprisal.

In each instance, the tactics of the Sicarii were specific, violent, and calculated to curtail popular collaboration with Imperial officials through the application of terror. By targeting the Jewish social and religious elite, the Sicarii were carefully selecting individuals who were of high symbolic political value in order to discourage pro-Roman grassroots cooperation from among the wider population. At the same time, an immediate tangible result was to disrupt the unchecked flow of information from Jewish leaders who provided the Romans the means to anticipate and thereby control the course of events in the province. Collectively, these actions served to further isolate Roman forces while simultaneously driving a wedge between the Jewish people and their traditional leadership, whom the Sicarii saw as generally corrupt. Perhaps most notable is the fact that Sicarii attacks of this nature targeted only Jews. Extant evidence indicates that Roman civilians and military personnel suffered few direct reprisals in the form of assassination, kidnapping, or property destruction. That the psychological purpose of these attacks was aimed primarily at the Jewish population is further confirmed by the fact that such incidents occurred at religiously significant times and places, such as pilgrimage festivals and the Temple of Jerusalem.[15]

Yet the Sicarii were in many ways as much a symptom of the unstable social and political conditions present in Judaea as they were a contributor to its further breakdown in the immediate years prior to the outbreak of the first-century revolt. Faced with a protracted inability to exercise self-determination because of the Roman occupation, a growing segment of the Jewish population became increasingly resolved to free their country by violent means.

The Roman–Jewish War and the end of the Sicarii

When the general uprising finally began in the summer of 66 CE, the Sicarii were only briefly involved in the events in Jerusalem before the tyrannical actions of their leader Menachem, which included the murder of the high priest Ananias, led to his own death by other Jewish rebels who opposed his brutal methods. Because of their perceived extremism, the remainder of the Sicarii in the city were likewise killed in the purge, although a few managed to escape to the isolated Herodian mountain fortress of Masada, roughly 30 miles south-southeast of Jerusalem, overlooking the Dead Sea.[16] There, in the remoteness of the eastern Judaean Desert, the Sicarii continued to stubbornly proclaim their doctrine of "No lord but God."

The occupation of Masada was the last significant chapter in the history of the Sicarii in Judaea, and the site of the final event of the First Roman–Jewish War (66–73 CE). In the seventh year of the conflict, the newly appointed Roman governor of Judaea, L. Flavius Silva (73–81 CE), besieged Masada with a single legion, the Legio X Fretensis, and supporting *auxilia*. His purpose was to overcome this last remaining pocket of resistance in the revolt. The leader of the Sicarii atop Masada was Eleazar ben Yair, an individual whom Josephus claims was a descendant of one Judas the Galilean of Gamala in Gaulanitis, who was instrumental in raising the standard of revolt at the time of Quirinius' census 67 years earlier.[17]

At Masada, the terroristic nature of the Sicarii once again fully manifested itself. During the early stages of the fortress' occupation, they raided neighboring communities for supplies, but in time the manner of their attacks grew more violent. Unlike previous incursions, the Sicarii carried out a vicious assault against the village of Engedi on the shores of the Dead Sea in order to collect needed supplies and foodstuffs. The attack, which occurred on

Passover, ended with the massacre of some 700 villagers, including women and children, and Josephus tells us, "they made similar raids on all the villages around the fortress, and laid waste the whole district."[18]

Josephus does not say why the Sicarii altered their methods from the time of Engedi. The attack may have been nothing more than simple banditry – the exercise of brute violence for personal profit. But given the depth of their ideological convictions which emanated from the doctrine of "No lord but God," it is reasonable to conclude that the Sicarii believed their actions at Engedi were as virtuous as those in Jerusalem that ended in assassination and kidnapping. Fully inculcated in their beliefs, no moral impediment was allowed to detract from their righteous cause, and certain acts of terror, regardless of how heinous, could be justified as helping to sustain their order's fanatical resistance to Roman occupation. If need be, anything and anyone could be sacrificed on behalf of their conviction.

When the 10,000-strong legionary force of Silva finally reached Masada, the Sicarii doubtless saw the inevitability of the situation, a certainty made all the more manifest in subsequent weeks as the Romans systematically enclosed the entire plateau in a wall of circumvallation and constructed a siege ramp on a spur of bedrock on the western side of the rock face. In a speech given by Yair to his fellow Sicarii, as related to Josephus by two survivors of the Masada siege, the dissident leader compelled those around him to freely choose suicide rather than submit to Roman slavery.[19]

Like terrorists centuries later, the fanaticism of their beliefs persuaded Eleazar ben Yair and his followers to perceive each circumstance of their lives in apocalyptic terms. The righteousness of their beliefs justified each violent act throughout their existence, including their own deaths. For the Sicarii, the mass suicide of 960 people that followed Yair's exhortations was seemingly stark validation of their mantra.

From Josephus, it is evident that the actions of the Sicarii were unique among the events of the First Roman–Jewish War. They were intended from their inception to incite panic and fear, through acts of internecine assassination and kidnapping, as instruments to destabilize Jewish–Roman relations and provoke broad popular resistance to foreign rule.

The exceptional nature of the Sicarii is further underscored by the fact that such a highly concentrated application of "terror" tactics, especially against one's own people, is found nowhere else in antiquity. During the first century, other serious Native revolts against Roman authority occurred, most notably in North Africa (17–24 and 45 CE), Britain (60 CE), and Germany (69–70 CE), but any expressions of opposition comparable to that of the Sicarii did not emerge in the midst of these uprisings.[20] Both the African and German struggles at some point included episodes of guerrilla warfare, yet neither uprising involved practices intended to drive a wedge between the indigenous population and Roman authorities through the premeditated use of terror by dissidents against their own people. Josephus' observation in Book 7 of *The Jewish War* emphasizes this overt and unique extremism of the Sicarii. Here he notes that the Sicarii "in every way . . . treated [their Jewish brethren who consented to submit to Rome] as [foreign] enemies."[21] Within the context of Jewish religious and cultural tradition, this statement is revealing. In essence, the Sicarii relegated their Jewish opponents to the status of "foreigners" or non-Jewish enemies of no greater intrinsic worth than Roman adversaries.[22]

In Judaea, the critical component that provided the conditions necessary for the emergence of such an exceptional form of resistance was religious. Josephus' accounts make it clear that by the mid-first century, an active perception existed within certain sectors of the Jewish community that Roman authority infringed upon the otherwise unfettered expression of

Mosaic tradition. The sensitive nature of this situation was further aggravated by the prevalence of apocalyptic and messianic–eschatological influences in Judaism, particularly among some of the emerging revolutionary sects in the immediate years prior to the destruction of the Second Temple. Likewise, the prominent acceptance within Israelite cultural tradition of resistance to foreign domination as a precursor to divine deliverance further energized the vociferous nature of Jewish opposition to Roman rule.[23] In the end, the commingling of distinct social, political, cultural, and religious factors in Judaea generated a volatile environment that inevitably moved the situation to open war, a result achieved, in part, by the violence perpetrated by the Sicarii on their fellow Jews.

That the conditions that brought about the First Roman–Jewish War – and in consequence local terrorism – were unique to the place and moment is perhaps further illuminated by the fact that in 73 CE some Sicarii fled from Judaea to Egypt where they again sought to incite the Jewish community in Alexandria to revolt against Roman authority. Using the same tactics, they initially murdered some of the moderate Jews of social rank in the city, but this time the actions of the Sicarii failed less to inflame the Egyptian Jews than alarm the community out of fear of Roman retribution. In response, hundreds of Sicarii were seized and turned over to the Romans, ending the threat of insurrection. A second incident in Cyrene likewise failed in its original purpose.[24]

Though they were an aberration in their own time, significant parallels can be identified between the character of the Sicarii and more contemporary terrorist movements in the twentieth and early twenty-first centuries. Like many of their modern counterparts, such as al-Qaeda and the Islamic State of Iraq and Syria (ISIS), the Sicarii sought both political and religious outcomes through their actions.[25] In order to achieve their ideological goals, the Sicarii deliberately worked to instill fear among the civilian leaders and non-combatant population of Judaea by the application of specific, lethal tactics for the purpose of undermining relations between the general public and their colonial overlords, thereby fomenting broad resistance to Roman rule.

In the end, the ideology of the Sicarii, along with the extreme violence it generated, not only isolated the group from the greater Jewish community but inhibited its exportation. As subsequent events demonstrated, the group's raison d'être was proven to be exclusively the result of the rarified social and political environment created in Judaea by events during the century leading up to 70 CE. Without those preconditions, the Sicarii eventually ceased to exist. But the First Roman–Jewish War was not the last time in the pre-modern era that religious and political circumstance combined to inspire the birth of a dissident group that modern anti-terrorism experts would label as terrorists.

The Assassins

As made clear above, the Assassins were hardly the first to use political assassination or the first to support such targeted violence with ideological or religious justifications. Nevertheless, they provide a very instructive case to all who want to understand the historical roots of terrorism. Organized in a tight community with precise objectives, they systematically resorted to assassinations that followed specific methods, as much for the strategic effectiveness as for the significant psychological impact. Many authors like Bernard Lewis regard the Assassins as probably the first terrorists in history.[26]

Regardless of the ways in which such an assertion might be qualified and as modern as the notion of terrorism is, the Assassins' deep impact remains incontestable: not only their name passed into common usage, but they left a lasting impression on the Western collective imagination, from medieval myths concerning the "Old Man of the Mountain" to fictional works such as the *Assassin's Creed* videogaming saga. But this often romantic vision hides much more complex historical, political, religious, and cultural realities.

Those whom the Western Christians referred to as "Assassins" since the twelfth century were in fact the Nizaris, adherents of a radical trend born in Persia from Isma'ili Shi'ism at the end of the tenth century. Although the Nizari movement officially originated in 1094, its identity, religious particularism, and its methods of struggle arose from a process of reflection initiated by the founder Hasan-i Sabbah several years earlier.

Cornerstones of the Nizari struggle

A Persian from the city of Qum, Hasan was a *da'i* ((pl. *du'at*) literally, in Arabic, "one who summons," that is, an evangelizing missionary), charged, as the authorized representative of the imam, with spreading Isma'ili doctrines. The headquarters of the *da'wa* ("invitation" or "summoning" to the doctrine/mission) was then based with the Fatimid Caliphate of Cairo, the chief political, religious, and military rival of the Abbasid Caliphate of Baghdad, the "orthodox" Sunni headquarters defended (in reality, ruled) by the Seljuk Turks. Dispatched by the Fatimid Caliphate, Hasan operated in Persia from 1081 onwards. His assignment was within the core of the Seljuk Empire where Sunnism was the official religion, especially in the towns. Due to their remoteness from the Fatimid Caliphate and its own internal difficulties, Isma'ili Persian communities could not rely on effective support from Cairo. The strength and talent of Hasan lay in analyzing and taking advantage of certain aspects of Seljuk rule, plus conceiving tactical schemes that could be adapted to the circumstances of the Seljuk empire. He succeeded in making Persian Isma'ilism, which used to be an underground religious current, into an open and rebellious movement that defied the Seljuks' overwhelming military strength with a deadly reputation.

Isma'ilism had already received a favorable response from the populace in Persia. Its adherents showed fervor and a kind of determination that originated from the very nature of Shi'ism. Deprived of the opportunity to lead the Muslim community by the Sunnis shortly after the death of the prophet Muhammad, the Shi'ite party has since developed a fervor that draws upon themes of martyrdom, suffering, and, above all, struggle against an iniquitous and usurping governing power. Arising from a schism that shook Shi'ism in the eighth century, Isma'ilism was much more radical. It represented both a religious and political opposition movement, coherent and centralized, and secretly spreading even as it was condemned and hounded by Sunni "orthodoxy."

While the Sunni follow the exoteric or apparent meaning (*zahir*) of the Qur'an, Isma'ilism relies on the idea that its texts have esoteric and secret meanings (*batin*) that contain divine truths (the equivalent of what is referred to in Christian tradition as gnostic wisdom). As such, Isma'ilism offered its adherents several degrees of initiation and interpretation, adapting to all levels of popular understanding as well as responding to intellectual questioning. These divine truths were delivered by the figure of the imam and his *du'at*; thus Isma'ilism was based on *ta'lim*, a concept of absolute authority that requires faithfulness and the unquestioned obedience of followers. Claiming to be the legitimate way of Islam, Isma'ilism proposed an alternative to the Sunni establishment, which the Isma'ilis considered liable for the Muslim world's splintering, and it seemed widespread and strong enough to overthrow the existing order.

As a cradle of older dissident traditions, Persia provided a context favorable to Isma'ili preaching. Many Persian dynasties had already opposed the caliphate of Bagdad and rekindled Persian cultural identity then under Arabic domination. The emergence of Turkish dynasties and especially the Seljuk triumph revived both local people's discontent and a Persian sense of identity. The Isma'ili *da'wa* had been well established in Persia since the tenth century, and from the year 1070, Persian Isma'ilis acknowledged only one *da'i* based in Isfahan. When Hasan, who probably shared this sense of Persian identity and enjoyed his autonomy from Cairo, became the main *da'i* in charge of preaching Isma'ilism in Seljuk territories, he could take advantage of the already vibrant Isma'ili momentum to launch an open revolt against the Seljuk empire.

Hasan gave up Isfahan as a base, ill-suited as it was for open activities against Seljuk power, and turned to the mountainous region of Daylam, to the south of the Caspian Sea. Strongly imbued with a sense of their political and religious identity and autonomy, the region's population was already open to Isma'ili preaching. Hasan was searching for his own *dar al-hijra*, a place of refuge according to the Muslim tradition, that he could use as headquarters for the Persian *da'wa*. The seizure of strongholds in mountainous districts to be used as refuges became one of the cornerstones of Hasan's strategy. He selected the famous citadel of Alamut, a veritable eagle's nest reputed to be impregnable. The *da'wa* revealed its effectiveness on this occasion: Hasan sent his *du'at* to Alamut and its hinterland in order to convert the garrison and local people. In the year 1090, when the newly converted Isma'ilis openly revealed themselves, the lord of the place, who held Alamut from the Seljuk sultan, had to give up the stronghold. The seizure of Alamut was the first direct blow against Seljuk authority and essentially marked the foundation of an Isma'ili (and later Nizari) state. The Isma'ilis subsequently captured many strongholds, sometimes by siege, most of the time by conversion of the local people. Some of these places were recaptured by the Seljuks, but the Nizari state was definitely established by the year 1118. Although scattered among the regions of Rudbar and Qumis in Daylam, as well as far to the southeast in Quhistan, near the frontiers of present-day Iran, Pakistan, and Afghanistan, the Isma'ili network of strongholds operated cohesively due to the central leadership of Alamut, seat of the major *da'i*.

Isma'ili preaching and seizure of strongholds proved that there were alternatives to a direct confrontation with the Seljuk empire. With Hasan now acting in broad daylight, the use of assassination soon became one of his tactics. The declaration of the Isma'ili community and the emergence of a state inevitably led to a reaction from the Seljuks. The vizier Nizam al-Mulk had paid attention to the activities of Hasan in the Daylam since 1088 and became the fiercest opponent of the Isma'ilis. It was likely on his advice that the Seljuk sultan Malik Shah engaged in a military campaign against Isma'ili strongholds. Nizam al-Mulk was therefore targeted by the Isma'ili community, and his death in the year 1092 was the first of the many assassinations that mark the history of the Assassins.

Juwayni, a Persian author of the thirteenth century, provided a detailed account of the assassination of Nizam al-Mulk, basing the story on lost Isma'ili sources. According to Juwayni:

> Hasan-i Sabbah spread the snare of artifices in order at the first opportunity to catch some splendid game, such as Nizam-al-Mulk, in the net of destruction and increase thereby his own reputation. With the juggling of deceit and the trickery of falsehood, with absurd preparations and spurious deceptions, he laid the basis of the *fida'is* ("those who sacrifice themselves"). A person called Bu-Tahir, Arrani by

name and by origin, was afflicted "with the loss both of this world and of the next," and in his misguided striving after bliss in the world to come on the night of Friday the 12th of Ramazan 485 [October 16, 1092] he went up to Nizam-al-Mulk's litter at a stage called Sahna in the region of Nihavand. Nizam-al-Mulk, having broken the fast, was being borne in the litter from the Sultan's audience-place to the tent of his harem. Bu-Tahir who was disguised as a Sufi, stabbed him with a dagger and by that blow Nizam-al-Mulk was martyred. He was the first person to be killed by the *fida'is*.[27]

A further step in the renewal of the Persian Isma'ili movement led to the very birth of the Nizari community. The Fatimid Caliphate experienced a succession crisis in the year 1094: contrary to the provisions laid down by the caliph al-Mansur designating his elder son Abu Mansur Nizar as successor to the caliphate and thus to the Isma'ili imamate, vizier Badr al-Jamali installed Nizar's young brother in power. Hasan upheld the legitimacy of Nizar, however, even as the latter and his supporters were eliminated in Egypt. By refusing to recognize Nizar's brother as the legitimate Isma'ili imam, Hasan consequently split the Fatimid *da'wa*. As undisputed leader of Persian Isma'ilis and, in reality, of all Isma'ilis living in the Seljuk empire, Hasan now spearheaded a new and totally independent Nizari *da'wa*. Since Nizar was executed, Hasan became – according to Isma'ili doctrines – the *hujja* ("proof") of the occulted imam, that is, his legitimate representative on Earth and dispenser of the divine knowledge. The authority of Hasan, buttressed by the notion of *ta'lim*, was naturally accepted and recognized by the whole Persian Isma'ili community. With the founding of Nizarism achieved, the talent of Hasan showed in how he cultivated and directed their fervor and devotion.

Muslim perceptions of the Nizaris

The Nizari phenomenon was unequivocally and fiercely condemned by the whole Muslim world: by Sunnis and the Fatimid Isma'ilis, as well as other Shi'ite movements. In 1091, the year before he became the Nizaris' first victim, Nizam al-Mulk had written *Siyar al-Muluk* ("Rule for Kings"), a treatise of governance intended for Sultan Malik Shah. Grounded in the history of both Persia and Islam, it vehemently condemned heresies:

> Seceders have existed in all ages, and from the time of Adam (upon him be peace) until now in every country in the world they have risen up in revolt against kings and prophets. Never has there been a more vile, more perverted or more irreligious crowd than these people, who behind walls are plotting harm to this country and seeking to destroy the religion. Their ears are alert for the sounds of sedition and their eyes are open for signs of the evil eye.[28]

Nizam al-Mulk devoted long sections to denouncing Isma'ilis, named Batinis (from *batin*), as he worried about their increasing importance and the danger that they represented: "their whole purpose is only to abolish Islam and to lead mankind astray."[29]

There was no better exemplar of the official view than the treatise of Nizam al-Mulk, and it doubtless guided Sunni religious and political orthodoxy towards the Nizaris. Subsequent Sunni and Shi'ite treatises aggressively denigrated the Nizaris as the *malahida* ("heresy") par excellence, undermining Islam from within. Sunnis already regarded Shi'ism as a religious error, since it dared to interpret the Qur'an via *batin*. But both Sunni and Shi'ites believed that Isma'ilism threatened religious law and Islam by extending even further the interpretation of the Qur'an and placing exclusive emphasis on *ta'lim*, thereby giving the imam too important a place. One key issue in these treatises was to determine if Nizaris could be regarded as true Muslims – or even Muslims of any sort.

In addition, some texts ascribed licentious habits to the Nizaris in violation of the religious prohibitions. One expression of contempt appeared first in 1123 and then again from time to time: during an ideological dispute, the Fatimid caliph al-Amir described the Nizaris as *hashishiyya* ("hashish users"), without any justification but undoubtedly in a very pejorative way.[30] This fairly rare term was repeated by the Shi'a Zaydis of Persia, in the thirteenth century, when they mention the Nizaris as *hashishis*. Hashish use was severely condemned by Islam, owing to its adverse effects on the integrity and morality of the faithful, to the point that hashish abusers were considered criminals by Muslim society.[31] Characterizing a community as *hashishiyya* was therefore particularly offensive and infamous, a virulent way of casting the Nizaris as outlaws from the Muslim community. However, it is quite doubtful that they used hashish; they practiced, to the contrary, asceticism and moral discipline. Although rare, the use of the term *hashishiyya* seems to have come to the knowledge of Crusaders: the first historical mentions of the Nizaris among Westerners took the form "Al-Hachichine," "Heyssessini," etc., which eventually became "Assassins" over time.

Never was a Muslim community more severely condemned, nor subject to such unanimous feelings of hostility. What most astounded the Muslim world was not so much the dangerous emergence of the Nizaris in the heart of the Seljuk Empire but their systematic use of assassinations. As stated above, the Assassins did not invent this. Physical elimination of an opponent is as old as humanity itself. Ideological, religious, or political justifications of such acts were not the preserve of the Nizaris either: several groups have used it since antiquity, starting with the Sicarii and, in the eighth century, several radical Muslim groups (like the Kharijites) had made it a religious duty, justifying their deeds by an antinomian sense of rectitude.[32] But recurring assassinations played an essential part in the Nizaris' methods of struggle. They used it often enough and in an identifiable manner that medieval sources attributed all similar acts to them.

The use of assassination

It is virtually impossible to analyze the thinking of Hasan regarding assassination, as most of the Nizaris' sources were destroyed during the fall of Alamut in the thirteenth century. Nevertheless, the use of assassination seems to have come about in a natural and logical way. On the one hand, Isma'ilis and Nizaris, as radical Shi'ite traditions, were nurtured by allied concepts of legitimate revolt and martyrdom. Bernard Lewis goes further, saying that the concept of tyrannicide, as a religious obligation to rid the world of an illegitimate ruler, could have justified these methods.[33] Rashid al-Din, a Persian chronicler of the thirteenth century who, like Juwayni, relied on Nizari sources, thus had Hasan say, about Nizam al-Mulk's assassination, "the murder of this demon is the beginning of bliss."[34] On the other hand, any consideration of the very nature of the Seljuk power must recognize that the unity of the empire was based on personal ties of loyalty. Since direct confrontation with Seljuk military might was virtually impossible, assassinating key characters seemed the best option for keeping opposing forces off-balance. The killing of Nizam al-Mulk, who was an outstanding administrator and a fierce opponent of the Isma'ilis, considerably undermined the empire. The death soon after of Sultan Malik Shah led to the withdrawal of the troops besieging Alamut and opened a period of civil war among his potential successors.

The ultimate purpose of the assassinations carried out by the Nizaris was therefore strategic, whether in a defensive or a repressive way. Their most symbolically meaningful victims besides Nizam al-Mulk were the Fatimid caliph al-Amir in 1130 and the Sunni Abbasid caliphs al-Mustarshid and al-Rashid, in, respectively, 1135 and 1138. Nizaris mostly targeted political and military dignitaries, such as viziers, emirs, or other officials, and religious figures such as *qadis* (Judges with religious, civil, and judicial functions) involved in ideological campaigns against the Nizaris. They aimed occasionally at civilian officials, such as prefects or jurists, but they never aimed randomly and blindly with terror itself as the sole justification.

While it was not, properly speaking, a religious duty, Lewis notes, "The killing by the Assassin of his victim . . . had a ritual, almost a sacramental quality."[35] Nizaris involved in such deeds were designated by the term *fida'i* (pl. *fida'iyin*), "he who devotes, sacrifices himself," as a signal of their commitment or even their sacrifice in the interests of the community. Kamal al-Din, a Syrian chronicler of the thirteenth century, recounted an anecdote that underlines this exaltation. In 1126, several *fida'iyin* stabbed to death Bursuqi, the *atabeg* (governor) of Mosul, in a mosque; although most of his attackers were slaughtered on the spot, one of these managed to escape. Kamal al-Din then tells us:

> This young man, who managed to escape, had a mother of an advanced old age; when she learned of the death of both Bursuqi and his murderers, and knowing her son was a part of them, she showed great satisfaction and made up her eyes with kohl as a token of gladness. When she saw him back safe and sound a few days later, she was distressed by this and, in her pain, she shaved her hair and blackened her face.[36]

Although it is difficult to assess the veracity of this story, Juwayni and Rashid al-Din do confirm the existence at Alamut of a roll of honor featuring the names of the *fida'iyin* and their victims. A poem written by Hasan Ibn Salah Birjandi, a Nizari historian of the thirteenth century, for the glory of three *fida'iyin* who eliminated Qizil Arslan, governor of Azerbaidjan in 1191, has also come to us: "Praise, glory, and thousands of benedictions be upon the three heroes, the brave swordsmen, capturers of kings!"[37]

Assassinations committed by the Nizaris had their own modus operandi, which, aside from reinforcing the ritual character of these deeds, had a significant psychological impact. Lewis emphasizes that "Assassins always used a dagger; never poison, never missiles."[38] They approached their victims, sometimes disguised as Sufis or beggars, and generally acted in full daylight, in a public place: at the court, in military camps, or, in a more striking way, in the heart of mosques, during the days of prayer or the month of Ramadan. It would be an overstatement to call these suicide missions, as chroniclers often mention *fida'iyin* trying to flee the scene and sometimes succeeding. Although they had little chance to live through their mission in such circumstances, the primary intention was more a display of boldness without any limit than a search for death; they aimed to impress the popular imagination and to discourage the potential adversaries of the community. Birjandi perfectly epitomized this in his poem: "Brothers, when the blessed time arrives, and the good luck of both worlds accompanies us, the king, who possesses more than a hundred thousand cavalry, would be frightened by a single warrior."[39]

Initial reactions to the acts carried out by the *fida'iyin* were the slaughter of Nizari communities in many towns through popular uprisings driven by uncontrollable fear or by orders from authorities. The Damascene al-Dahabi relates that in 1129, the lord of Damas "put to death six thousand people accused of following Nizari doctrines."[40] Mistrust was such that opponents of the Assassins adopted hyper-elaborate protections. The Fatimid vizier al-Afdal was "extremely distrustful and precautious, was always standing on guard and alert, especially against the sect of the Batinis, and surrounded himself against them with weapons of all types, a large number of servants, slaves, and black guards, plus various tools and sharpened sabres."[41] Bursuqi, killed in 1126 by the Nizaris, "kept his mind alert and stood on guard against an attempt on their part [the Batinis]; he surrounded himself with squires and bodyguards, with soldiers armed from head to toe. . . . He wore chain mail in addition which neither the point of the sabre nor the blade of the dagger could penetrate."[42]

Western perceptions of the Nizaris

The Western medieval reaction to the Nizaris and their assassinations was out of proportion with that of the Muslim world. At the beginning of the twelfth century, Nizari activity spread to Syria. The geographic context, unlike in Iraq, plus its political and religious fragmentation offered advantageous conditions. Isma'ili doctrines had been disseminated by the Fatimid Caliphate since the tenth century and communities with strong religious identities (Druzes, Nosayris) were potentially open to the Nizari *da'wa*. They lived in the mountain range that provided a natural boundary between, on the one hand, the Seljuk governors of Aleppo and Damascus and, on the other, the four Crusader states along the coastline. After settlement attempts in Aleppo and Damascus failed, Nizaris began seizing a network of strongholds in the Jabal Bahra (near the northwestern coast of present-day Syria) after 1130. The Syrian Nizaris originally depended on Alamut, and its leaders were appointed by the Persian headquarters, but they asserted their independence after 1169, under Rashid al-Din Sinan's reign, known through Western sources as the first "Old Man of the Mountain."

The first Western figure assassinated by the Nizaris was Count Raymond of Tripoli in 1152. But Western chroniclers did not mention the community until the last third of the twelfth century. Unaware of the terms "Nizaris," "Batinis," or "Mulahid," they identified the Assassins only with great difficulty as belonging to the Muslim world, sometimes recounting in vivid contrast licentious habits that went against Muslim laws.

Nizari religious practice or identity were not the focus of Western writers. Instead, it was their use of assassination and particularly the recruitment, training, and indoctrination of the *fida'iyin*. As Benjamin of Tudela pointed out in a simple summation: "they are feared everywhere because they kill kings with disregard for their own life."[43] Burchard of Strasbourg, who traveled through the Holy Land around 1175 on behalf of Emperor Frederick Barbarossa, reported that the Assassins were brought up from a very young age in palaces cut off from the world, where they learned several languages such as Latin, Greek, and Arabic; once they reached adulthood and were fully imbued with the idea that their salvation depended on their unquestioning obedience to their lord, they were ordered by the latter to kill princes with a golden dagger.[44] At the beginning of the thirteenth century, Arnold of Lübeck was the first to report that the Old Man of the Mountain administered a narcotic beverage to his followers; he afterwards promised them eternal possession of the delights they had seen in their drug-induced dreams, provided that they fulfilled his command.[45]

"The Old Man of the Mountain" quickly became the central figure of the Western stories about the Assassins. The first mentions of him coincided with the reign of Rashid al-Din Sinan, who played an important role on the Syrian political chessboard, alternating diplomacy and confrontation with neighboring powers, including the Crusaders. The title of "Old Man of the Mountain" had first been a local designation for him before it became a generic title adopted by the Western sources to refer to the successive leaders of the Syrian Nizari community. It seems to have been a purely Western creation, as it is absent from the Arab–Muslim sources. Lewis proposes that Nizaris naturally referred to their leader as *Shaykh* ("wise person" or "elder" with a connotation of intellectual and moral authority). Westerners seem to have only retained the meaning of "elder" and to have combined it with the entrenched mountainous location of the Assassins.[46]

In 1192, near the end of Rashid al-Din Sinan's leadership, Conrad of Montferrat, a claimant to the kingship of Jerusalem, was murdered by two Assassins who had infiltrated his entourage over several months. This event made a deep impression on Westerners and sparked a wave of political anguish built on wild rumors. The English king Richard the Lionheart was accused of having contracted with the Old Man of the Mountain to kill Conrad. French chroniclers even claimed that he sent Assassins into France in order to kill King Philip Augustus, who kept himself protected by sergeants-at-arms, both day and night, in fear for his life. The accusations got so out of hand that the English chancellery forged a letter from the Old Man of the Mountain proclaiming Richard's innocence.[47] And the rumors persisted so long that at the beginning of the thirteenth century, Guillaume Guiart claimed in a poem that Richard the Lionheart himself had raised and indoctrinated young men, aiming to send them to assassinate his opponents.[48]

The disproportionate reaction of Westerners is quite notable, especially in view of the small number of Christians who fell victim to the Assassins: while Nizaris claimed several dozen Muslim victims throughout their history, they only killed five Crusaders (not counting some of the unsuccessful attempts). Indeed, although the Muslim world knew well with whom it was dealing, Westerners were still assessing the Nizari community, along with its murderous reputation, striking behavior, and unheard-of methods, all of which represented a constant threat. Rumors spread throughout the thirteenth century, and Western authors involved the Old Man of the Mountain in many political cases in Europe. While some lords and sovereigns were alleged to have paid tribute to the Old Man so as to be spared by the Assassins' daggers, others were accused of infiltrating Assassins into their opponents' entourages. Whatever the truth, these stories had such an impact that in 1245, during the Council of Lyon, Pope Innocent IV provided provisions in the decree *De sentencia et re iudicata* ("Of Sentencing and Judicial Matters") that anyone who killed another on his own or by sending Assassins was to be sentenced to excommunication and the loss of any dignity, order, office, or benefice.[49]

But in the end, Western fascination outpaced Western fear. Legends built around the Old Man of the Mountain and his Assassins fed a fantasized vision of the Middle East and the Holy Land, far exceeding the mundane realities of the Nizari community. The unquestioned loyalty of the Assassins toward the Old Man of the Mountain attracted as much attention from authors as did their methodical use of assassination. One chronicler reported that in 1194, as Henri of Champagne visited him, the Old Man ordered some of his Assassins to throw themselves from the top of a tower to certain death on the rocks below in order to prove their obedience. They reportedly did so without the slightest hesitation.[50] The term "Assassin" thus seemed for a while synonymous with absolute faithfulness. Several Provençal troubadours used this theme as ornaments in their courtly poetry near the end of the thirteenth century, delivering some surprising verses, such as: "You have me more fully in your power than the Old Man his Assassins"; "Just as the Assassins serve their master unfailingly, so I have served Love with unswerving loyalty"; and "I am your Assassin, who hopes to win Paradise through doing your commands."[51]

The Western slant on the story of the Assassins allows us to fully assess the psychological impact of the assassinations carried out by the Nizaris, an impact strong enough to have occluded most other aspects of the sect. But assassination was not an exclusive weapon for the Nizaris; they were not above establishing alliances and diplomatic relations, according to the potential benefits for their cause or their territorial consolidation. They thus supported certain emirs against others in the heartlands of the Seljuk empire; they approached the governors of Aleppo and Damascus when they wanted to begin their mission in Syria; and they exchanged embassies and maintained relationships with certain Frankish lords and even with King Louis IX of France. Furthermore, political assassination was only truly effective if the edifice of power was susceptible to collapse with the death of the figure on whom it relied. Thus it is not surprising that the Orders of the Temple and of the Hospitallers in Syria were able to exact tribute from the Assassins. Jean de Joinville explained this when he told the story of the embassy sent by the Old Man of the Mountain to Saint Louis, in 1253: "[The Old Man of the Mountain] paid a tribute to the Temple and to the Hospitallers, because these orders dreaded nothing from the Assassins, because he would gain nothing if he had the master of the Temple or of the Hospitallers killed. He knew that, if he killed one, another one as good as the former would be brought back in place; and for this, he did not want to lose Assassins where there is nothing to be gained."[52]

Born as a rebel movement in the very heart of the Sunni establishment and perfectly suited to its environment, Nizari Isma'ilism launched a serious threat to the established order. Although considered both a religious and political danger by the powers of the day, the Nizaris failed to overthrow their rivals. They were reduced over time to one faction among many on the complex and unsettled, always moving, chessboard of Persia and Syria. Their influence and their methods of struggle proved ineffective against the two conquering powers that swamped the Middle East in the second half of the thirteenth century. The Nizaris were eliminated from Persia by the Mongols and then dispersed after the capture and destruction of Alamut in 1256. In Syria, the Mamluks forced them to submit once and for all in 1271. They were reduced to being used for a short while by Sultan Baybars for one-off assassinations. In any event, the Nizaris had lost their substance and their way.

Their terrifying reputation nevertheless outlasted them. While the account of Marco Polo at the very end of the thirteenth century proved to be the most accomplished mythification of the Old Man of the Mountain, of his gardens of Paradise, and of the mystical Assassins, Guillaume Adam warned King Philippe VI of France, in 1332, in his treatise on how to recapture the Holy Land:

> I name in sixth place the Assassins, cursed and to be avoided, who sell themselves, who lust after human blood, who kill an innocent for a certain price and do not take into account salvation of the soul. They transfigure themselves into angels of light, as the devil does, when they adopt the gestures, language, lifestyle and facts of various nations, people and specific individuals; thus covered with sheep skins, they

kill before being recognized. . . . And the only cure that I know for the guard and the protection of the king is that in his household, for whatever service, however fleeting or vile it may be, we do not receive anybody except those whose country, place, lineage, condition and person are completely known.[53]

Hasan-i Sabbah doubtless never imagined that the reputation of his *fida'iyin* would have such an impact: despite the disappearance or withdrawal of the Nizari communities, the myth of the Assassins not only remained very much alive in Europe, but it still represented a tangible threat, as we see from the treatise of Guillaume Adam. His recommendations let us measure the extent to which the strategy of political assassination and its psychological impact, developed by Hasan-i Sabbah 250 years earlier, was effective.

Conclusion

As described throughout this chapter, the Sicarii and the Assassins were each unique in their respective eras. No other groups of their times used the tactic of assassination so extensively nor promoted terror so actively. Historians today can endlessly debate whether these two groups warrant being called terrorists, but in an important way, the application of such terminology is beside the point. With the invention of the word "terrorism" and the recognition of it as a distinct category of violence still hundreds of years away, its invocation in the first and twelfth centuries cannot help but be anachronistic. After all, the application of a modern rhetorical device to pre-modern behaviors and actors unavoidably calls forth misleading connotations. Nonetheless, the identification of key similarities between the Sicarii, the Assassins, and many modern terrorists is illuminating. At the least, it demonstrates that groups could use terror tactics to great effect without modern media, weapons, or ideologies. But the rarity of such tactics in the pre-modern world also suggests that terrorism was still an idea whose time had not quite yet come. That no other groups – at least as far as we know – mimicked the Sicarii or the Assassins reveals the existence of a significant divide between the pre-modern and modern worlds, for, as we know, the sheer mutability and vast applicability of terrorist tactics is one of its more important contemporary hallmarks.

Notes

1. Yannick Gautron and Randall D. Law would like to thank Steven Isaac for his invaluable aid in translating the section on the Assassins into English.
2. Throughout this chapter, the region is referred to as "Judea" until it was incorporated into a new Roman province in 6 CE, at which time it becomes the Roman province of "Judaea."
3. Josephus, *Jewish War*, trans. H. St. J. Thackeray et al. (Cambridge, MA.: Harvard University Press/Loeb Classical Library, 1926–8), 1.127–57, 160–70; and Josephus, *Antiquities*, trans. H. St. J. Thackeray et al. (Cambridge, MA.: Harvard University Press/Loeb Classical Library, 1930–65), 14.28–79, 91.
4. Richard A. Horsley, *Jesus and Empire: The Kingdom of God and the New World Disorder* (Minneapolis, MN: Fortress Press, 2003), 37–8, 81.
5. Josephus, *Jewish War*, 2.223–57, 271–84, 301–9; and Josephus, *Antiquities*, 20.
6. Josephus, *Jewish War*, 1.3.
7. Josephus, *Jewish War*, 2.252–4.
8. Morton Smith, "Zealots and Sicarii, Their Origins and Relation," *Harvard Theological Review* 64, no. 1 (1971): 18; and Solomon Zeitlin, "The Sicarii and Masada," *Jewish Quarterly Review* 57, no. 4 (1967): 263–4. Reference is made to the Sicarii in a select number of Talmudic passages.

For examples, see *Avot de-Rabbi Nathan* and the *Ecclesiastes Rabbah*. In *Jewish War*, 7.253–74, Josephus makes a deliberate effort to differentiate between the Sicarii and Zealots by describing each separately. For further insight into the distinctions between "Zealots" and "Sicarii" see the chapter, "Fourth Philosophy, Sicarii, Zealots," in Richard A. Horsley and John S. Hanson, *Bandits, Prophets and Messiahs: Popular Movements in the Time of Jesus* (Harrisburg, PA: Trinity Press International, 1999); and David M. Rhoads' balanced assessment in "Zealots" in the *Anchor Bible Dictionary* (New York: Doubleday, 1992), 6:1043–54.
9 Mark A. Brighton, *The Sicarii in Josephus's Judean War: Rhetorical Analysis and Historical Observations* (Atlanta, GA: Society of Biblical Literature, 2009), 148–9.
10 Josephus, *Jewish War*, 2.254–7.
11 Ibid., 2.240, 256; and Josephus, *Antiquities*, 20.164–5.
12 Brighton, *Sicarii in Josephus*, 144; and Josephus, *Antiquities*, 20.186.
13 Josephus, *Antiquities*, 20.210.
14 Josephus, *Jewish War*, 7.254. The Latin term *sicarius* (Gr. σικάριοι) is commonly used in Roman sources to identify an assassin or murderer. A notable example of such use is the *Lex cornelia de sicariis et veneficis* [Cornelian Law of Assassins and Poisoners] (*Institutes* 4.18.5 and *Digesta* 48, Title 8). This law was enacted in 81 BCE by the dictator Lucius Cornelius Sulla.
15 Richard A. Horsley, "The Sicarii: Ancient Jewish 'Terrorists,'" *Journal of Religion* 59, no. 4 (1979): 439–41; and Horsley, *Jesus and Empire*, 44.
16 Josephus, *Jewish War*, 2.433–8.
17 Ibid., 2.118; and Josephus, *Antiquities*, 18.4.
18 Josephus, *Jewish War*, 4.398–405.
19 Ibid., 4.323–6.
20 Tacitus, *Annals*, trans. J. Jackson (Cambridge, MA: Harvard University Press/Loeb Classical Library, 1925–37), 2–4, 14.29–39; and Tacitus, *Histories*, trans. C. H. Moore (Cambridge, MA: Harvard University Press/Loeb Classical Library, 1925–37), 4–5.24.
21 Josephus, *Jewish War*, 7.254–5.
22 The Greek word Josephus selects to use in 7.255 is ἀλλόφυλοι, *allophyloi*, "foreigners" (literally, "of another tribe").
23 David C. Rapoport, "Fear and Trembling: Terrorism in Three Religious Traditions," *American Political Science Review* 78, no. 3 (1984): 669; and Horsley, *Jesus and Empire*, 37, 81–5. Aside from allusions in Josephus, evidence for the prevalence of apocalyptic and messianic–eschatological influences in Judaism before the First Roman–Jewish War can be found in the corpus of intertestamental literature from the period. For examples, see the books of Ethiopic Enoch and 2 Esdras.
24 Josephus, *Jewish War*, 7.409–17, 436–50.
25 ISIS is also sometimes identified by government, international aid, and media sources as the Islamic State (IS) or the Islamic State of Iraq and the Levant (ISIL). For more on ISIS, see Chapter 22 by Daveed Gartenstein-Ross on the history of al-Qaeda in this volume.
26 Bernard Lewis, *The Assassins: A Radical Sect in Islam* (Oxford: Oxford University Press, 1987), 129.
27 Juwayni, *The History of the World-Conqueror*, trans. John Andrew Boyle (Cambridge, MA: Harvard University Press, 1958), 2:676–7. For more on the term *fida'i*, see later in this chapter.
28 Nizam al-Mulk, *The Book of Government or Rules for Kings*, trans. Hubert Darke (London: Routledge and Kegan Paul, 1960), 193.
29 Ibid., 238.
30 Al-Amir, *Al-Hidaya al-Amiriyya*, trans. A. A. A. Fyzee (Calcutta: P. Knight, 1938).
31 Franz Rosenthal, *The Herb: Hashish versus Medieval Muslim Society* (Leyde: E. J. Brill, 1971).
32 For more on the Kharijites, see Chapter 17 by John Calvert on the origins of modern Islamism and salafi jihadism.
33 Lewis, *The Assassins*, 125–7.
34 Rachid al-Din, *Jami al-Tawarikh; qismat-i Isma'iliyyan*, ed. Muhammad Taqi Danichpazhuh and Muhammad Mudarrisi Zanjani (Teheran, 1960), 110. Translation by Yannick Gautron.
35 Lewis, *The Assassins*, 127.
36 Kamal al-Din, "Extraits de la chronique d'Alep par Kemal al-Din," in *Recueil des Historiens des Croisades. Historiens orientaux* (Paris: Imprimerie Nationale, 1884), 3:654. Translation by Yannick Gautron.

37 Wladimir Ivanov, "An Ismaili Poem in Praise of Fidawis," *Journal of the Bombay Branch of the Royal Asiatic Society* 14 (1938): 66.
38 Lewis, *The Assassins*, 127.
39 Ivanov, "An Ismaili Poem," 67.
40 Al-Dahabi, *Kitab duwl al-Islam*, ed. and trans. Arlette Nègre (Damascus: Institut français de Damas, 1979), 93. Translation by Yannick Gautron.
41 Ibn al-Qalanisi, *Damas de 1075 à 1154*, ed. and trans. Roger Le Tourneau (Damascus: Institut français de Damas, 1952), 153. Al-Afdal was assassinated in 1121 by order of the Fatimid caliph, but the Assassins were accused of it. Translation by Yannick Gautron.
42 Ibn al-Qalanisi, *Damas*, 167. Translation by Yannick Gautron.
43 Benjamin de Tudèle, *Les voyageurs juifs du XIIè siècle: Benjamin de Tudèle*, ed. and trans. Haïm Harboun (Aix-en-Provence: Massoreth, 1998), 209–10.
44 Burchard de Strasbourg, *Itinera Hierosolymitana crucesignatorum*, ed. Sabino Sandoli (Jerusalem: Franciscan Printing Press, 1980), 2:407.
45 Arnold de Lübeck, "Chronica Slavorum," in *Monumenta Germaniae Historica Scriptores* (Hanover, 1884), 21:178–9.
46 Lewis, *The Assassins*, 8.
47 Matthieu Paris, *Grande Chronique de Matthieu Paris*, trans. A. Huillard-Bréholles (Paris: Paulin, 1840), 2, 207–9.
48 Charles E. Nowell, "The Old Man of the Mountain," *Speculum* 22, no. 4 (1947): 510.
49 "Chronica Minor Auctore Minorita Erphodiensi," in *Monumenta Germaniae Scriptores* (Leipzig, 1925), 24:200.
50 "L'Estoire de Eracles Empereur," in *Recueil des Historiens des Croisades: Historiens occidentaux* (Paris, 1859), 2:210 and 230–1.
51 F. M. Chambers, "The Troubadours and the Assassins," *Modern Language Notes* 64 (1949): 245–51.
52 Jean de Joinville, *Vie de Saint Louis*, ed. and trans. Jacques Monfrin (Paris: Garnier, 1995), 222.
53 Guillaume Adam, "Directorium ad passagium faciendum," in *Recueil des Historiens des Croisades: Documents Arméniens* (Paris, 1906), 2:496–7.

Further reading

The Sicarii

Brighton, Mark A. *The Sicarii in Josephus's Judean War: Rhetorical Analysis and Historical Observations*. Atlanta, GA: Society of Biblical Literature, 2009.

Horsley, R. A. "The Sicarii: Ancient Jewish 'Terrorists.'" *Journal of Religion* 59, no. 4 (1979): 435–58.

—. *Jesus and Empire: The Kingdom of God and the New World Disorder*. Minneapolis, MN: Fortress Press, 2003.

Josephus. Translated by H. St. J. Thackeray et al. 10 vols. Cambridge, MA: Harvard University Press/Loeb Classical Library, 1926–65.

Rapoport, David C. "Fear and Trembling: Terrorism in Three Religious Traditions." *American Political Science Review* 78, no. 3 (1984): 658–77.

Smith, Morton. "Zealots and Sicarii, Their Origins and Relation." *Harvard Theological Review* 64, no. 1 (1971): 1–19.

Tacitus. Translated by C. H. Moore et al. 5 vols. Cambridge, MA: Harvard University Press/Loeb Classical Library, 1925–37.

Zeitlin, Solomon. "The Sicarii and Masada." *Jewish Quarterly Review* 57, no. 4 (1967): 251–70.

The Assassins

Daftary, Farhad. *The Isma'ilis: Their History and Doctrines*. Cambridge: Cambridge University Press, 1990.

—. *The Assassin Legends*. London: I. B. Taurus, 1994.

Hodgson, Marshall G. S. *The Order of Assassins: The Struggle of the Early Nizari Isma'ilis against the Islamic World*. The Hague: Mouton, 1955.

—. *The Venture of Islam*. Vol. 2, *The Expansion of Islam in the Middle Periods*. Chicago: University of Chicago Press, 1974.

Laoust, Henri. *Les schismes de l'Islam*. Paris: Payot, 1977.

Lewis, Bernard. *The Assassins: A Radical Sect in Islam*. Oxford: Oxford University Press, 1987.

Madelung, Wilferd. *Religious Schools and Sects in Medieval Islam*. London: Variorum Reprints, 1985.

4

TERRORISM IN THE MIDDLE AGES

The seeds of later developments

Steven Isaac

There is no shortage of problems in trying to speak consistently of terrorism per se in the Middle Ages. This historical period has the burden of covering three continents across a period of at least one thousand years of changes. To this historiographical headache, this chapter poses another disjunction: namely, how to find aspects of terrorism, as understood today, in these periods and places that generally lacked the organizing principle and legitimacy of the nation-state, that struggled to define the warrior against the innocent bystander, and whose ideological police (the Church) preached both pacifism and physically enforceable dogma.

Nonetheless, medieval people did know and experience instances of terror. Its ability to shock and gall, however, was less formidable in a time when dangers abounded, when neighbors and four-legged predators were as much a threat to survival as were any groups who might constitute a threat just because they were "Other." When we find medieval condemnations of violence, the rhetoric usually camouflages a simple resentment that the writer's camp was simply on the wrong (that is to say, receiving) side of the nastiness. If the reverse opportunity arose, it is not at all clear the behavior would have been different.

What then is the point in studying the medieval contexts of terrorism? Certainly not to make us feel better for having supposedly progressed away from a more barbarous epoch. Nor is it to craft a photographic negative of our own time, to highlight by inversion how terrorists today act, although that effect inevitably occurs. The Middle Ages allow us, however, to examine the boundaries of the Weberian dictum that a state is defined by its monopoly of the legitimate use of physical force. As the medieval period synthesized the legacies of Greece and Rome with the new arrivals, Germanic culture and Christianity's still-developing doctrines, it sought to define both who could legitimately inflict force on another and what limits (if any) there were on that very violence. Thus, the millennium and more after the fall of Rome dealt with the problems of illicit violence, of who could wage war and who ought (or not) to be on the receiving end of such acts, of those moments when war's cruelties became outright atrocities, and which authorities had the right to referee these debates. In addition, the period saw the creation of Holy War in both its Christian and Islamic forms.[1]

Doctrinal developments within Christendom

Christianity built upon many Roman cultural foundations, including the concept of "just war" (and its inverse: unjust or impermissible wars). The Roman Empire had a centuries-long tradition, sometimes hollow but still important for its symbolic value, of theoretically limiting its wars to just causes and appropriate means. From the beginning, Rome had its fetial priests who confirmed that a Roman grievance was just in the eyes of the gods, and who then informed Rome's foes that a militant response was coming unless Rome's complaint was satisfied. Cicero followed this tradition in his development of a theory of just war in *De Officiis*, further stipulating that there were limits on how severely a war could be prosecuted to redress an injury.[2]

Augustine of Hippo (d. 430) built upon Cicero's foundation, in effect "baptizing" his ideas so that they worked within a Christian worldview. Against the pacifism inherent in Jesus' preaching, Augustine noted the Old Testament examples of warfare conducted by David or Moses, plus Jesus' own advice to a soldier to be content with his pay. In this last case, Jesus did not counsel the soldier to change his career but rather, as Augustine spun it out, to avoid the worst pitfalls of warfare, such as unlicensed violence or plunder. In effect, argued Augustine, sin makes war inevitable, and Christians have to be ready to engage in it if the cause is worthy enough, such as the protection of the innocent. Following the Ciceronian model, wars should only correct wrongs; in doing this, but now in a Christian context, such correction had to be based on spiritual love for the transgressor. To safeguard this ideal, Augustine put the responsibility for war with a community's leader, thereby ruling out individual or private forms of warfare.[3] This enabled him to square the pacifism of Christianity with the military needs of the Late Empire, but once that empire had faded, it left open the question of where the frontier really was between private and communally sanctioned violence.

One obvious candidate for such communal leadership was the Church itself, as the new moral referee of the Mediterranean world. Augustine's own teacher, Ambrose of Milan, had put these ideas into direct action when he called Emperor Theodosius to account in 390 for the massacre he had authorized in Thessaloniki after citizens there killed several Roman officials. In a letter that explained both his position and Theodosius' need to submit to the bishop's moral authority, Ambrose denounced the massacre of perhaps up to 7,000 townspeople as an event without precedent.[4] After eight months of stalemate, Ambrose gained his point via the emperor's public repentance. A century later, Pope Gelasius I summed up this tug-of-war in his letter to Emperor Anastasius which outlined the doctrine of the Two Powers (or the Two Swords). In unambiguous terms, he claimed that secular power got its authority from the spiritual power and had to submit to that spiritual power when called to account.[5]

The new Christian message was hardly free of ambiguity, however. Ambrose enjoyed a close relationship with Theodosius – aside from the Thessaloniki incident – and commended his zeal for the faith in the same letter. That zeal included forceful expulsions of Arian heretics from the Empire and destruction of paganism's last vestiges. Augustine himself, as a result of his long contest with the Donatist heresy in North Africa, moved from a position against coercion (which he noted only produced outward confessions and no real internal change of heart) in 392 to an acceptance by 417 of its utility. Augustine tried to retain a moral high ground by insisting on a context of love and correction for regretfully necessary acts of violence. In the end, though, he conceded that some people were only brought around by force, and in particular he mentioned how instances of blinding (Paul) and whipping (Jesus) had produced moral exemplars for the faith. The essence of his argument has echoed ever since: that undesirable force was sometimes needed to forestall greater injury (such as the corruption of others by heresy). Augustine preferred an approach based on persuasion, but he left the door open to force. When the Donatists turned to murder and riots, the emperor applied stern laws to break the Donatists, and Augustine gave way to the state's solution.[6]

Christianity's summons to a higher moral code continued to coexist uneasily with the violence of the physical world. Gregory of Tours, whose sixth-century chronicle gives us so much information about early Frankish society, reveled at moments in the miraculous feats of violence exercised by Saint Martin of Tours against those who disrespected holy spaces. His prose shows a certain glee in seeing disbelievers and malefactors "get theirs" but also the belief that such manifestations of power were the best witness to Christianity's supernatural truth.[7] Moreover, medieval scriptural texts and sermons were replete with images of tortures being gruesomely visited upon the damned. By the High Middle Ages, a popular genre of literature showcased individuals at risk of being damned in visits to purgatory or hell in a dream; there, they saw the many sin-specific tortures which awaited the unrighteous. Not surprisingly, the dreamer awoke with a newfound impulse to live uprightly.[8] For the illiterate, the surfaces of churches had many of the same pictorial messages painted all around. Since those in hell were damned by the incontestably correct judgment of God, what was there to question in the terrors that awaited evildoers? The problem, of course, was that God by definition knew perfectly when and what violent tool best suited a situation; the theologians of the day, however, remained uncomfortable condoning human violence, even when it benefited the Church. As complicated as this was for violence within Christendom, it was hardly less so when the violence was directed outwards.

Dealing with external threats

Once Christianity had transformed Greco-Roman culture, Church leaders found their fortunes tied to the political ups and downs of Rome's heirs. Although problematic, the Church turned to force to combat internal rivals, as seen above. The arrival of Islam and other external foes strengthened this dynamic, seemingly legitimating the destruction or forceful assimilation of outside groups.

The early medieval Church had already made a hard choice in the sixth century by legitimizing Clovis' Merovingian dynasty; his baptism into orthodox doctrine and the relative peace that he enforced kept the Church rather mute on his habit of murdering family members who might threaten Christendom with feuds. By the time the Merovingians devolved into figureheads, Pope Zachary agreed with Pepin the Short that it was indeed aberrant for the one with the power (i.e., Pepin) not to have the crown. The last Merovingian was not so much a bad king or a tyrant as just a rather ineffectual ruler; and so he was dumped into monastic retirement in the papally sanctioned coup of 751.[9] Pepin's Carolingian dynasty had already proved itself under his father by blocking Muslim forces in 732 near Poitiers; under his son Charlemagne, it reached its greatest extent through both vigorous military action as well as spiritual coercion. As with all the accommodations with secular powers, the Church – in this case, the popes – had to square high ideals with often brutally pragmatic Carolingian tactics.

Charlemagne's biographer Einhard presented the monarch's Saxon wars as a necessary consequence of the raids and arson committed first of all by the Saxons. This *casus belli* helped offset the three decades of war that Einhard judged the most brutal and bloody ever undertaken.[10] Additionally, the Royal Frankish Annals, written yearly as their name indicates, recorded the horrors of the combat with an even closer perspective and without knowing how it was going to end. Violence on one side led to cruelty on the other, and the Annals reported both. Thus, we can feel the frustration in the Carolingian camp that the successful military campaigns were not creating permanent submission.[11] In order to win hearts and minds, Charlemagne decided to bring the Saxons willy-nilly into the Christian fold; they were converted en masse after his victories, but when he was far away, they reverted to their former beliefs and sacked the churches imposed on them, often killing the priests. In his most vicious reprisal, Charlemagne ordered the massacre of his Saxon prisoners of war, which resulted in 4,500 killed in a single day at Verden. In his 785 Capitulary (law code) for the Saxons, he decreed death not only for attacks on his agents and Church officials but also for any Saxons that simply refused to convert.[12] Charlemagne's mentor, Alcuin of York, tried to restrain this approach, but the softer attitude shown by Charlemagne in the revised Capitulary of 797 seems to have resulted more from the resignation of the Saxons to their new master than any sense on his part that he had stepped over a line.

In 777, meanwhile, Charlemagne was asked for help by a rebel against the Muslim caliph of Cordoba, and the opportunity proved too tempting. Historian Jean Favier has proposed that Charlemagne may have been influenced by the very religious arguments he was using to justify his Saxon campaigns.[13] Whatever his motivation(s), Charlemagne soon recognized the power of his new foe and skillfully negotiated a withdrawal that nonetheless gave him new territory in Barcelona's hinterland. As he crossed back over the Pyrenees, however, his rear guard was attacked by Basques at Roncevaux and wiped out. This incident was transformed in following centuries into an ambush by perfidious Muslims; in its new form, the tale of Roland's epic death and that of his men encapsulated and strengthened Christian hatred for their Islamic rivals.[14] The *Chanson de Roland* and its Rambo-like cousins (consider, for example, the 24 "sequels" that make up just the William of Orange cycle) made religious hatred of Muslims a normative thing, portrayed their gruesome deaths with almost pornographic titillation, and, for the most part, dehumanized them to the point of meriting the deaths that Christian heroes doled out to them. Germinating in the centuries after Charlemagne's death, these songs exploded into popularity right alongside Europe's crusading fervor.

While Islam's growth was a constant anxiety for Christian Europe, it was eclipsed by the terror caused by the advent of the Vikings. Not only did Western Christendom lose a sense of guaranteed security, it moved quickly into a state of overall siege. The nature of Viking raids put virtually everyone under the same threat. Their boats allowed them to appear without warning and to strike far inland as well, so that few regions felt genuinely safe. They came for plunder, and they went wherever it was found: coastal and riverine settlements but also, most especially, churches and monasteries. The latter were particularly tempting, situated as they often were in isolated locales, away from immediate military aid. A number of factors came together to augment how the Vikings terrorized much of Europe. Their ability to strike seemingly anywhere was paramount but so too was their choice of targets: their impiety in destroying holy places and killing men and women sworn to God's service, not to mention lurid tales of sexual violation, created shock waves of stories told over and over, reinforced by the refugees who arrived amid the panic.[15]

Some of this was surely deliberate; each tale of atrocity weakened the Vikings' victims' will to resist. "God save us from the savage race of Norsemen," were the words of church liturgies in some of the afflicted areas. The Annals of St. Vaast describe fatalities everywhere during the siege of Paris in the 880s, with an emphasis on the defenseless: women, children, and still-nursing infants.[16] One of the more controversial atrocities attributed to the Vikings was the ritual execution ceremony of the blood eagle.[17] As described in several sagas and

Skaldic poetry, it involved cracking open the victim's ribs from the spine, splaying them outward, and then pulling out and displaying the victim's lungs across his open back. The problem is that no source is clear (in historical terms) that this ritual truly took place. The Anglo-Saxon Chronicle is rather laconic in its entries, focusing more on the large numbers killed by the Vikings rather than the method. While the question may remain unsolvable, their reputed thirst for atrocity was not a reputation they bothered to deny. This paid off most clearly in the case of England, where the Anglo-Saxon kings began levying the Danegeld with which to pay the Vikings to go somewhere else. The historical jury is still out on just what conditions in Scandinavia drove the Viking phenomenon, but no one proposed then or now that the Vikings terrorized Christian Europe as part of an ideological program. Certainly, except in the case of obtaining easy tribute, they were not seeking to change the behavior of their victims or reduce a perceived threat. On the other hand, medieval Christians explained the Vikings as being unwitting agents of God, sent to punish Europe for its sins.

A "society organized for war" vs. the Peace and Truce of God

With the dissolution of the Carolingian Empire in the later ninth century, those who stood the best chance of survival in this militarized reality were the local powerbrokers that constructed the most defensible sites and built up the most effective protection networks. This was the birth of what was once termed feudalism, although that model has now been largely abandoned by scholars. Still, what comes into particular view for a chapter on terrorism is the distinction that did matter: the renewed question of who could exercise legitimate force. In other words, just as conditions led to the heyday of private warfare (necessarily accepted because it provided a means of resisting the very real threats on all sides), the Middle Ages sought both a conceptual framework and a practical tool for curbing that very phenomenon. Thanks to Church leaders and theologians, a framework grew out of the synthesis of ideas that Georges Duby famously analyzed in his study *The Three Orders*. Finding a means to check the violence of castle-based lords (castellans) and the rising group of horse-borne warriors without descending into the same cycle of raids and counterstrikes was, however, a more problematic headache, only partially answered by efforts like the Peace and Truce of God.

Duby focused on theologians like the tenth-century's Adalbero of Laon and Gerard of Cambrai for their expression of three social functions in Christendom: those who prayed (*oratores*), those who fought (*bellatores*), and those who toiled (*laboratores*). As a model championed by ecclesiastical thinkers, it unsurprisingly prioritized the work of the first group and set up the professionally religious as the social order best positioned to regulate the whole of medieval society. In trying to define these three orders, theologians struggled to find the traits that most accurately applied to each grouping and could be presented as being under the divine plan. For everyone not in the second order, i.e., the career warriors, the model focused on the fact that they spent most of their lives without weapons, and the idea began to grow that not only should they not carry weapons, but, by living thus, neither were they targets of permissible violence.[18]

These ideas came to a head in 989 at the Council of Charroux, followed quickly by other councils across Aquitaine and Burgundy, which sought to protect the unarmed populace from predatory warriors under decrees known collectively as the Peace of God (*Pax Dei*). The empowerment of castellans derived from the networks of armed protection they could draw upon and put into action. Against raiders like the Vikings, this decentralized approach had the advantage of rapidly fielding a force able to block such incursions. As the threat of external raids tapered off, these local aristocrats-on-the-make continued to grow their own networks at the expense of their neighbors. This led to a cycle of small-scale but nearly incessant and often vicious raids and counter-raids, usually targeted at the lands and persons of small farmsteads or unfree serfs, whose demise was seen by the combatants as a legitimate means of pressuring rival lords.[19] When bishops across France gathered to forbid these actions, labeling them, in fact, as "criminal actions," they were not only genuinely concerned about blocking such suffering but also sought to protect laborers who literally fed the Church.[20]

How, though, was the medieval Church to police violence exercised by the very group otherwise sanctioned to engage in it? Church leaders looked first to deterrence: in the Peace of God movement at Charroux, they brought along the bodies of saints in ritual processions so as to add spiritual punch to their decrees. For anyone who violated the statutes of the coalescing Peace of God movement, they excommunicated that person. These efforts were so popular that ensuing Peace of God councils had to be held outdoors due to the numbers who showed up. Ralph Glaber's account of one meeting has the commoners showing up in deafening numbers, shouting: "Peace, peace, peace."[21] Besides their own spiritual levers, Church leaders realized this popular verdict could work for them as well, and, riding the wave, they compelled many lesser knights to swear to respect the peace. In the words of one such oath from 1023, warriors promised not to invade churches, seize people for ransom, or attack pilgrims or merchants unless they had committed a crime. A further effort to limit violence came about at this time as councils across France moved to make certain seasons off-limits to warfare. At first, the season of Lent was the main focus, but by 1041, a council at Arles included major saints' days, Thursdays through Sundays (in honor of Jesus' death), and the Advent season. This effort to restrain all violence during short periods of time was the Truce of God.

Still, the problem of enforcement ran up against those willing to flout popular desires or to take their chances on going to hell. This led the archbishop of Bourges in 1038 to create a Peace League at the same time that the injunctions of the *Pax Dei* were implemented at a public meeting; virtually every male over 15 in the region had to swear to meet illegal violence with now-sanctioned violence. According to Adam of Fleury, the new peace enforcers, including churchmen who led the effort, met success on every front, benefiting from such "divinely inspired terror" that some violators abandoned their castles rather than face this militia. In the end, though, Count Odo of Déols was unwilling to submit to a force he deemed just a vigilante mob. Adam of Fleury explained the ensuing defeat of the League as a result of it having exceeded its spiritual mandate through unrestrained violence; he vividly described the defeat as the result of superior numbers and skill on the side of the "rebels" against the League.[22] Despite this drastic setback, and because spiritual causes were available to explain it, the Peace of God was far from finished and continued to endure as a social ideal.

Odo of Déols was actually typical of the age, a time which saw an unprecedented rise of private warfare. To varying degrees across Europe, new power blocs arose as local lords built networks of patronage and protection that gave them growing levels of control inasmuch as they also managed to provide promised safety to the inhabitants of their territories. While kings and emperors still insisted on their primacy, the facts on the ground often meant that various counts, dukes, and lesser magnates were the real arbiters of what kinds of violence could be practiced by the sheer fact of getting away with all kinds of mayhem. While many identified themselves according to linguistic or geographic affinities, the most important trait, as Marc Bloch showed in his still classic study, was that of being "the man of a man."[23] In other words: identity (and authority) came from one's lord. His personal goals were legitimate (and normative) by virtue of succeeding; and his permission, or mere acquiescence, sufficed to legitimate the same for his vassals.

This personal bond had already shaped violence in the medieval world for centuries through vendetta and self-help justice, and it continued to affect the use of force as both the tools of war and statecraft grew more sophisticated. It also meant, in counterpoise to the Church's arguments in the *Pax Dei*, that there were no neutrals in the power struggles of European lords, arguably even no non-combatants. Studies in the last few decades have shown that the former tendency to denigrate medieval warfare as a chaotic cycle of senseless violence missed the strategic maneuvers in the destruction of peasantry and church structures or the raids on towns.[24] Medieval leaders knew that finances were the foundation of any successful war: to have secure resources was to have the upper hand, and to be deprived of the same was the first step in being compelled to enter negotiations. Those without the luck to be born into privileged positions – titled, well-armed, with access to fortifications, and related advantages – had little more than the spiritual injunctions of the Church to protect them, protections which were only too flimsy unless buttressed by some other tool.

Medieval elites recognized this fact of politics and war. Let us consider the practice of not just taking but of giving hostages. The practice itself of giving over persons as guarantees long predated the Middle Ages. Charlemagne, unsurprisingly, demanded and got hostages from the Saxons in his effort to compel them to conform to his wishes. These were tools of statecraft, guarantees expected and given by one or both parties (at the risk of death, mutilation, or physical abuse to the hostages) to ensure that a particular agreement endured. Thus, they were not hostages in the modern sense, not bystander victims, whose peril was meant to change a public authority's policies. Their captive status was instead the foreseen result of negotiations. Still, the fact that hostage-taking was normative did not mean that the threat to their lives was not real and, on occasion, brutal. Nor did kinship necessarily work to mitigate the problem. Welsh rulers regularly did horrible things to the nephews, nieces, and cousins in their custody.[25] Henry I of England permitted his own granddaughters to be blinded by their custodian as a just retribution against his son-in-law's own mistreatment of another hostage.[26]

Besides blood relatives, political associates were just as valuable in this high-stakes game by the simple fact of having their political weight defined by their lord. At the upper end of medieval warfare, this resulted in the practice of regularly taking other knights captive so as to ransom them. Monastic observers like Orderic Vitalis (d. 1142) saw this development as a sign of more humane warfare due to less blood being spilled, but he was rather deliberately missing the point in the hope of portraying contemporary wars as adhering to Church teachings. Much of his writing shows wars in their full nastiness, especially for those not among the military elite. Orderic particularly blasted one contemporary, Robert of Bellême, for his depredations against ordinary folk. To cripple his rivals, Bellême regularly carted off peasants and townspeople to his own fortresses. He thereby put the entire local food chain at risk, besides torturing the captives for his own pleasure.[27] If Bellême's pathology was singular, however, the value of ordinary people as captives was recognized far and wide. So habitual was the practice, so unquestioned was the idea of being the "man of a man," that non-knights sought freedom from being taken captive for their putative lord's debts.[28] At the same time, the growing power of non-feudal forces compelled lords like the Germanic emperors to take literally hundreds of captives from towns that had rebelled; these hostages were drawn deliberately from all across a town's social and economic makeup, thus demonstrating the practice's aim of controlling as much of the recalcitrant population as possible.

A final twist on the phenomenon of hostages deserves mention: the role of women either as hostages or in the not necessarily different situation of being a politically compelled bride. As Adam Kosto pointed out in his study of medieval hostages, women were as liable to be given as hostages as men, but there were prohibitions against this on the part of Christian powers when it came to Islamic rivals, mostly from fears of sexual violation[29] (a recurring theme in the popular *chansons*). Part of the revolt against King John of England derived from rumors that women in his custody were similarly not safe. In cases where women were given over as brides, they could find themselves in stunning misery. Duby recounts the tale of Ghodelive, eventually sainted for her suffering at the hands of her husband and in-laws, a torment that ended with her strangulation by her husband's servants. A similar tale of fortitude comes in Guibert of Nogent's memoirs, where he praised his mother's courage and fidelity in the face of intense animus from her new husband's family.[30] Ghodelive's story is a hagiography and that of Guibert's mother was bucking to become one, so we should be careful treating such tales as fact. Still, their narrative, even their tropes, display norms and expectations that let us see the precariousness of any existence beyond the reach of family or similar networks of protection.

One of the key elements in Europe's development at the turn of the millennium was a transition from considering who *could* be protected to who *ought* to be protected. The Peace and Truce movements began the effort to codify the latter. Concurrently, however, the practice of giving hostages conceded the fact that the apparatuses did not yet exist to extend such security to everyone.

Religious violence: crusades, jihad, and the Inquisition

A revolutionary development of Christian thinking on war came with the formalization of crusading ideology from 1095 onwards. It was both a surprising twist on prior teaching as well as an almost inevitable conclusion of the trends in play. The 1054 Council of Narbonne had declared that Christian-on-Christian violence was tantamount to shedding Christ's own blood.[31] This was a natural legacy of the Peace and Truce movements. As the papacy became ever more active in contemporary events, it began endorsing some military affairs, notably events like the Norman Conquest or whoever supported the Gregorian reformists in their struggles against the Germanic emperors. Notably, though, even William the Conqueror and his soldiers had to do penance for the fellow Christians killed in the papally sanctioned invasion of England. For those outside the Christian fold, however, the implications were much direr. As warfare now understood to be commanded by God himself, crusading made the very act of killing opponents (and risking one's own death thereby) an act of penance.

The launch of the crusading movement, however, is quite the historiographical nightmare because the inaugural speech by Pope Urban II has been obscured and changed by the multiple versions of the event. What is firm, though, is that the pope did promise that the expedition to Jerusalem counted as a penance, so long as the Crusader went for the right motives (i.e., not for personal gain).[32] Within a decade of Jerusalem's capture, writers like Guibert of Nogent or Robert the Monk pushed forward the apocalyptic themes latent in the whole endeavor, stressing the role of Western Christians as God's chosen people who must combat the evil supposedly present in Islam. Their after-the-fact versions of Urban's speech wallowed in gruesome accounts of atrocities against Christians that were misreported as regular practices of Muslims and were mirrored in the gratuitous carnage of the *chansons de geste*.

The Church's legitimation of faith-based violence had immediate consequences as Crusaders in German lands launched pogroms against local Jewish populations. Once in the Middle East, the armies engaged in further brutalities. At Antioch and Jerusalem, days of butchery followed the initial capture; at Ma'arat al-Numan, Crusaders turned to cannibalism of their recently slain foes, all this being reported by Christian sources rather than as atrocities by outraged Muslim authors.[33] The success of the First Crusade vindicated the theological revolution – whatever Urban II actually proposed – as understood by the medieval "man on the street." Even when Jerusalem was lost in 1187 and later crusades failed to meet their goals, the failures were explained as the result of sin. Few contemporary voices criticized the Church's embrace of the formerly off-limits secular sword, and centuries passed before the institutionalized Church (as well as its later Protestant rivals) relinquished the option of physical force.

Within the Muslim world, it took a generation or more before theologians and generals were able to begin using the Christian invasion as grounds for ideological and political counter-attacks. As Carole Hillenbrand amply demonstrated in her rich study, jihad in its military format had grown rather moribund in Islamic practice. The Crusades changed that, then and since.[34] Within six years of Jerusalem's fall, the cleric al-Sulami argued for a return to spiritually motivated warfare; only by the 1130s, however, did the general Zengi begin to campaign under this aegis when it suited him. His son Nur al-Din took up the banner even more so after 1146, and Salah al-Din legitimized his political ascendancy with his prosecution of jihad against the Kingdom of Jerusalem.

Religious violence risks turning inward, and this was true for all the great monotheisms. In the case of Islam, the most famous example was the Assassins, a splinter group which turned to assassination as the tool best suited to their small numbers. For a century and a half, as demonstrated in this same volume, the choice seemed to pay off before they were almost wholly eradicated by the Mongols. Their dramatic killings caught the imagination of Muslim and Christian alike, leading to many mythologized stories about the sect. On the Christian side, the turn to internal violence came when Pope Innocent III authorized Crusade as a tool against domestic heretics as well as external foes. Across most of southern France, the Albigensian Crusade against the Cathars unleashed round after round of reciprocal atrocity. The tone was set at Béziers in 1209 when the Crusaders asked how to differentiate Cathars from Catholics. The papal legate threw the problem in God's lap: "Kill them all," he reportedly said; "God will know which ones are his."[35] Each winter, when Crusader numbers dwindled, the local inhabitants returned the favor. After a few years of campaigning, it was no longer enough just to kill many opponents; both sides turned to mutilation and dramatic executions to break the other's will. Captured opponents suffered blinding or the splitting of their noses; no one had immunity, as the female castellan of Lavaur learned. Once her castle fell, some 400 defenders were burned as heretics while she herself was flung screaming down the castle's well and then finished off when the attackers filled the well with boulders.[36] This cycle of vengeful retribution continued for roughly twenty years as southern resources and resistance were ground down.

The horrors of the Albigensian Crusade and the mass executions regularly perpetrated by the Crusaders highlight the problem that confronted the Church in the High Middle Ages:

the desire to bring about conversions through doctrinal persuasion ran up against the imperative to protect believers at all costs. In a related trend, the plodding argumentation of the Church could not always match the excitable passions of street-level faith. One result of this dilemma was the medieval Inquisition, an effort to find and correct heresy through careful investigation. The Inquisition's original goal was to locate heretics amid the faithful and, having identified them, convince them to return to approved doctrines. Real world dynamics, however, upset this approach. In particular, the Church's idealized effort ran up against the position of secular rulers that religious deviance was equivalent to political treason. Second, those under investigation often did their best to give unusable answers to the Inquisitors. Rulers like Peter of Aragon and Emperor Frederick II made clear statements to this effect, with the latter decreeing death by fire in 1224 for heretics.[37] At the fall of Montségur in 1244, 215 heretics were burned by the besiegers, without recourse to the Inquisition.[38] In comparison to these heavy-handed rulers, the Inquisition's techniques could almost look sane and merciful. Almost, that is. At first, the Church took care not to use force in extracting confessions, but eventually such lines blurred, then disappeared. In 1252, Pope Innocent IV opened the door completely with his Bull, *Ad Exstirpanda*, which permitted limited torture so as to get those under questioning to reveal their concealed beliefs. Succeeding popes continued to relax the prohibitions, so that a number of techniques came into use, like the rack, the *strappado*, and imprisonment amid harsh deprivations. In addition, convoluted rules evolved so as to prohibit certain testimony, especially if it helped defendants; most accusations were kept protectively anonymous.[39] Interestingly, while Christendom's great theologians, like Thomas Aquinas, seemed to agree to judicial execution of heretics (see the *Summa* II–II.11:4), day-to-day inquisitors like Bernard Gui actually decried torture's utility for gaining valid confessions. In the end, whatever the medieval Inquisition's high ideals, it set precedents that were amplified terribly by its Spanish descendant and by the secular state apparatuses that supplanted it in Early Modern Europe.

Chivalry and the laws of war

Randall D. Law argued in his study of terrorism that one key trait is the performative nature of such violence; its perpetrators expect to have an audience and know its significance is determined by that audience.[40] Medieval violence was almost always performative, a kind of political theater, and it became ever more so with the popularity of chivalric customs. The problem, though, is that in its earliest manifestations, the practices of chivalry demonstrated a penchant for violence, not a horror arising from such acts. Across several centuries, the norms that glorified specific forms of violence developed into codes that aimed to constrain the violence by defining unacceptable acts in wartime. These conventions were the seeds of the later "laws of war" that dominate any conversation concerning (il)licit violence.

Christendom may have eschewed the blood sports of the Roman arena, but it found replacements, not least of all in the preparatory war games – i.e., the tournament – that came to be a hallmark of chivalric culture. The risks inherent to these so-called games was such that the Church tried to suppress them by decreeing that anyone who died in a tournament could not be buried in consecrated ground, being effectively guilty of a form of suicide. In the twelfth century, the pre-eminent part of the tournament was the mêlée, the open-field combat which swirled across the countryside like real war. Teams practiced tactical maneuvers, ambushes, and took no thought of the peasant lands and habitations they wrecked along the way. Through these tactics, the tournament showcased how the secular elite's militant ethos was at odds with Church ideals. In the following centuries, the joust grew into its own, replete with, and confined by, the rules that governed such specialized combat. Heralds appeared as a profession, concerned with tallying the scores of the participants, both for gloriously vicious blows as well as those considered unsporting. The litany of dramatic wounds and famous deaths across the centuries, however, testifies that the introduction of equipment and technique was meant to keep the show vivid and explosive for the spectators. The growth of urban tournaments indicates the attraction for all of medieval society, not just the traditional knights. Nor were women immune to the spectacle; they were prominent in the stands, and the literature shows them cheering just as heartily for forceful blows and strikes violent enough to cause showers of sparks.[41]

Just why the Church relaxed its anathemas against tournaments is hardly answerable in this space, but several major factors deserve mention. One primary explanation rests on the fateful turn already taken when the Church legitimized religious warfare in the Crusades. Like the secular rulers who came to accept tournaments for their value in training cadres of professional warriors, the Church appears to have caved in similarly because of the need to have capable knights available for the Holy Land.[42] Another idea notes that chivalry offered a package of values and attractions sufficient to rival the message of the Church. Richard Kaeuper has noted how both the action and the literature of chivalry legitimized the private violence of the secular elite, effectively approving predation against churches, women, and the defenseless.[43] In this light, the Church made its bargain with chivalry's cult so as to domesticate it.

As for the secular elites, their motives are clearer than those of the Church. The pageantry of chivalry let the arms-bearing elite confirm its status as such. Just as critical, as Maurice Keen showed decades ago, the economics of war undergirded the whole scheme.[44] When combatants claimed the protection of laws of war during moments of surrender, they did so in the assurance that the other side knew these laws and honored them likewise. If not, the risks of engaging in war would have outweighed any potential profits. Such laws had to be operant from the very start of conflict in order for combatants to qualify for rules-based protection, and tournaments provided a socialization into violent norms that crossed international lines. Those who appeared to fight under other paradigms, as in the Celtic peripheries, Islamic territories, or worse, the freebooters internal to Europe, received no such protections.[45]

Conclusion(s)

Moving too quickly across a thousand years of history, this survey has attempted to showcase how the Middle Ages dealt regularly with some elements of what is today called terrorism, if not with the full combination of elements that make up its modern sense. Ideas about how and when to use lethal force evolved as those ideas migrated from ancient Rome to Early Modern Europe, with a tension constantly in play between secular agendas and religious models. Throughout the whole period, private violence flourished in ways distinctly at odds with modern ideas. With feud as a mostly accepted form of justice, sudden violence was an expected part of daily existence. For a long time, despite the Church's efforts, there was an assumption that everyone was "fair game" in war; modern ideas about non-combatants were germinating in the Peace and Truce movements but were not wholly accepted, as the darker side of chivalry shows. With the exception of the Crusades and the institutionalized persecution of the Inquisition, ideologically driven violence was rare. Terror, of the sort practiced by the likes of the Vikings or Robert of Bellême, was a tactic adopted and discarded for practical reasons. Even Charlemagne's forced conversion of the Saxons was arguably driven more by military pressure than by Christian fervor.

Because the traits of modern terrorism do not align with the facts of medieval history, it may seem that the Middle Ages cannot much increase our understanding of the phenomenon. The mismatch of categories, however, gives us profitably blurred lines that better nuance our questions of the past and the present. Was the Inquisition, for instance, a form of state terror or perhaps instead a counter-espionage program run amok? Or, to consider another angle: what of the role of publicity in validating an act of terror as such? Obviously, the Middle Ages had nothing like modern-day media coverage, but news still got around, and sometimes at a startling pace. When Charles the Good, Count of Flanders, was murdered in a Bruges church by would-be tyrannicides, word of the deed was rocketing through the wharves of London within forty-eight hours. While such speed was, in fact, physically possible, the point that our source makes in this instance was that the speed of dissemination matched the enormity of the deed.[46] Thus, jaw-dropping, performative instances of violence were possible to achieve for a medieval audience; it was not the act itself, however, that triggered the shock, but the social conventions flouted along the way. Count Charles was hardly the first or last feudal lord assassinated by vassals who resented his authority;[47] his murder at the moment of his prayers, however, did serve to make the deed all the more heinous. Similarly, clerical chroniclers expressed horror over violence committed against women (often with lurid overtones), children, and the defenseless. It is hard not to see the fear in such writers of becoming the next targets if such behavior continued. It may well be that their moral outrage was selfish, but they nonetheless built the foundations for later conventions regarding licit and illicit forms of violence. Born of both idealism and practical self-interest, medieval ideas about acceptable forms of violence planted the seeds for our ongoing debates.

Notes

1 This chapter only deals obliquely with Islam's traditions, since Chapter 3 by Donathan Taylor and Yannick Gautron on pre-modern terrorism covers the Middle East far more directly.
2 Cicero, *De officiis*, trans. Walter Miller (Cambridge, MA: Harvard University Press, 1913), 1.11.33–1.13.41.
3 Frederick H. Russell, *The Just War in the Middle Ages* (Cambridge: Cambridge University Press, 1977), 16–25.
4 Ambrose of Milan, "Ambrose to Theodosius I 390 [Letter 51]," at the *Internet Medieval Sourcebook*, www.fordham.edu/halsall/source/ambrose-let51.asp (accessed July 1, 2014).
5 Gelasius, "Gelasius I on Spiritual and Temporal Power, 494," at the *Internet Medieval Sourcebook*, www.fordham.edu/halsall/source/gelasius1.asp (accessed July 1, 2014).
6 Peter Brown, *Augustine of Hippo* (Berkeley: University of California Press, 1969), 240–3, 335–6.
7 Gregory of Tours, *Historia Francorum*, trans. Lewis Thorpe (New York: Penguin, 1974), 255–8, 340–1.
8 For one popular example: *The Vision of Tnugdal*, trans. Jean-Michel Picard (Dublin: Four Courts Press, 1989).
9 Royal Frankish Annals, in *Carolingian Chronicles*, trans. B. W. Sholz and Barbara Rogers (Ann Arbor: University of Michigan Press, 1970), s.a. 750.
10 Einhard, "The Life of Charlemagne," in *Two Lives of Charlemagne*, trans. Lewis Thorpe (New York: Penguin, 1969), 61.
11 Royal Frankish Annals, s.a. 775–85.
12 Alessandro Barbero, *Charlemagne: Father of a Continent*, trans. Allan Cameron (Berkeley: University of California Press, 2004), 44–8.

13 Jean Favier, *Charlemagne* (Paris: Fayard, 1999), 228.
14 *The Song of Roland*, trans. Glyn Burgess (London: Penguin, 1990).
15 Excellent summations of these issues are in Paddy Griffith, *The Viking Art of War* (Havertown, PA: Casemate, 1995), 28–37, 82–98, 203–11.
16 The Annals of St. Vaast, available in translation at: http://deremilitari.org/2013/07/viking-raids-in-france-and-the-siege-of-paris-882-886 (accessed July 14, 2014).
17 Roberta Frank, "Viking Atrocity and Skaldic Verse: The Rite of the Blood-Eagle," *English Historical Review* 99 (April 1984): 332–43.
18 Georges Duby, *The Three Orders*, trans. Arthur Goldhammer (Chicago: University of Chicago Press, 1980), 90, 98–100 passim.
19 For an analysis of these principles, see John Gillingham, "Richard I and the Science of War in the Middle Ages," in *War and Government in the Middle Ages*, ed. J. Gillingham and J. C. Holt, 78–91 (Woodbridge: Boydell, 1984).
20 Thomas Head, "The Development of the Peace of God in Aquitaine (970–1005)," *Speculum* 74, no. 3 (1999): 656–86.
21 Rodulphus Glaber, *Opera: Historiarum Libri Quinque*, ed. and trans. John France (Oxford: Oxford University Press, 1989), 194–5.
22 Andrew of Fleury, "Activities of the Peace League of Bourges in 1038," trans. Thomas Head, in *The Peace of God*, ed. Thomas Head and Richard Landes, 339–42 (Ithaca, NY: Cornell University Press, 1992).
23 Marc Bloch, *Feudal Society*, trans. L. A. Manyon (Chicago: University of Chicago Press, 1961), 1:145.
24 See note 19 above.
25 See *Brut y Tywysogion*, ed. John Williams ab Ithell (London: Rolls Series, 1860), s.a. 1126–9 for a particularly gruesome round of atrocities.
26 Orderic Vitalis, *The Ecclesiastical History of Orderic Vitalis*, trans. Marjorie Chibnall (Oxford: Clarendon Press, 1978), 6:210–12.
27 Orderic Vitalis, 4:232–4, 296; 5:242.
28 See, for example, the charter granted by Henry II in 1177 to the clerics of Grammont. *Recueil des Actes de Henri II*, ed. Léopold Delisle and Élie Berger (Paris: Imprimerie Nationale, 1916), document no. 507.
29 Adam Kosto, *Hostages in the Middle Ages* (Oxford: Oxford University Press, 2012), 85.
30 Georges Duby, *The Knight, the Lady, and the Priest: The Making of Modern Marriage in Medieval France*, trans. Barbara Bray (New York: Pantheon, 1983), 130–5, 146.
31 Mansi, *Sacrorum Conciliorum* (Venice: 1774), vol. 9, col. 817.
32 Thomas Madden, *The Concise History of the Crusades*, 3rd ed. (Lanham, MD: Rowman & Littlefield, 2014), 7–13.
33 John France, *Victory in the East* (Cambridge: Cambridge University Press, 1994), 265–8, 315, and especially 355–6, where France diminishes the enormity of the violence following the capture of Jerusalem.
34 Carole Hillenbrand, *The Crusades: Islamic Perspectives* (New York: Routledge, 2000), esp. Chapters 3 and 4.
35 Mark Pegg, *A Most Holy War* (Oxford: Oxford University Press, 2008), 77.
36 William of Tudela, *The Song of the Cathar Wars*, trans. Janet Shirley (Burlington, VT: Ashgate, 1996), 41.
37 *The Catholic Encyclopedia* (New York: Robert Appleton Company, 1910), s.v. "Inquisition" (by Joseph Blötzer), www.newadvent.org/cathen/08026a.htm (accessed July 17, 2014).
38 Bernard Hamilton, *The Medieval Inquisition* (New York: Holmes & Meier, 1981), 64.
39 C. H. Lea, *The Inquisition of the Middle Ages*, abridged ed. (New York: Macmillan, 1961), 204–20.
40 Randall D. Law, *Terrorism: A History* (Cambridge: Polity, 2009).
41 Among the key works on the subject: David Crouch, *Tournament* (London: Hambledon, 2005); and Maurice Keen, *Chivalry* (New Haven, CT: Yale University Press, 1984).
42 Juliet Vale, "Violence and the Tournament," in *Violence in Medieval Society*, ed. Richard Kaeuper (Woodbridge: Boydell, 2000), 154.
43 Richard Kaeuper, *Chivalry and Violence in Medieval Europe* (Oxford: Oxford University Press, 1999), 50, 58–9, 225–30.

44 Keen, 224–33.
45 See Matthew Strickland, *War and Chivalry* (Cambridge: Cambridge University Press, 1996), 304–13.
46 Galbert of Bruges, *The Murder, Betrayal, and Slaughter of the Glorious Charles, Count of Flanders*, trans. Jeff Rider (New Haven, CT: Yale University Press, 2013), 25–6.
47 For more on the ancient and medieval practice of tyrannicide, see Chapter 2 by Johannes Dillinger in this volume.

Further reading

France, John. *Victory in the East*. Cambridge: Cambridge University Press, 1994.
Head, Thomas, and Richard Landes, eds. *The Peace of God*. Ithaca, NY: Cornell University Press, 1992.
Hillenbrand, Carole. *The Crusades: Islamic Perspectives*. New York: Routledge, 2000.
Kaeuper, Richard. *Chivalry and Violence in Medieval Europe*. Oxford: Oxford University Press, 1999.
Pegg, Mark. *A Most Holy War*. Oxford: Oxford University Press, 2008.
Moore, R. I. *The Formation of a Persecuting Society*. 2nd ed. Malden, MA: Blackwell, 2007.
Russell, Frederick H. *The Just War in the Middle Ages*. Cambridge: Cambridge University Press, 1977.
Stalcup, Brenda, ed. *The Inquisition*. San Diego, CA: Greenhaven Press, 2001.
Strickland, Matthew. *War and Chivalry*. Cambridge: Cambridge University Press, 1996.
Tracy, Larissa. *Torture and Brutality in Medieval Literature: Negotiations of National Identity*. Woodbridge: Boydell & Brewer, 2012.

Part II

THE EMERGENCE OF MODERN TERRORISM

5

THE FRENCH REVOLUTION AND EARLY EUROPEAN REVOLUTIONARY TERRORISM

Mike Rapport

> Terror is nothing but prompt, severe, inflexible justice. . . . It is less a special principle than a consequence of the general principle of democracy applied to our country's most pressing needs.[1]

On February 5, 1794, Maximilien Robespierre chillingly defined what he meant by "terror." It was not a political program or an ideology but a means to an end: the triumph of republican democracy over its many enemies. The revolutionaries only used the precise terms "terrorist," "terrorism," or "the Terror" later, in a hostile, retrospective way as they distanced themselves from the system as it had functioned in France in 1793–4.[2] The word "terror" already had many uses, emotional, religious, military, and judicial,[3] but the idea that France had endured a "system of terror" was first expressed by the repentant Jacobin, Bertrand Barère, on July 29, 1794 – the day after his erstwhile colleague Robespierre had been guillotined.[4] The *Académie française* dictionary in 1798 defined *terrorisme* as a "system, or regime of terror" and *terroriste* as "an agent or partisan of the Terror that arose through the abuse of revolutionary measures."[5] "Terrorism," the surviving revolutionaries hoped, was an aberration, not a practice that might be employed in other times or places. Yet the dark memories of 1793–4 have imprinted themselves on revolutions ever since. This chapter falls into five sections. The first considers the Terror's antecedents; the second and third discuss the two main forms of French revolutionary terror: state-imposed coercion and popular violence. The fourth explores the revolutionaries' attempts to use terror for "regeneration," and the final section traces the impact of the French Revolution on the practices of terror up to 1848.

Antecedents

Medieval and early modern states used violence (and the threat of it) to overawe their subjects and opponents, but the relationship between these earlier practices and those of the French Revolution are ambiguous. There were two ways in which the early state might have used terror: coercive violence to impose policy and a demonstration of the sovereign's punitive might. The organized persecution of religious dissent, such as the Albigensian Crusade, the medieval and the Spanish Inquisitions, and the system imposed on Tudor England by Thomas Cromwell, Henry VIII's minister, when he enforced the Protestant

Reformation, all foreshadowed later forms of state-imposed terror, although the militantly secular French revolutionaries would have denied any inspiration from these confessional models.[6] Indeed, the revolutionaries used the memory of the Saint Bartholomew's Day massacre of 1572, when French Protestants were slaughtered on royal orders during the Wars of Religion, as a fearful example of what, in vain, they wanted to avoid. Equally, the revolutionaries knew about the work of Niccolò Machiavelli. The sixteenth-century Florentine outlined the political uses of fear in *The Prince*: a prince should not worry about being thought cruel if that kept his subjects united and obedient. Ideally a ruler would want to be both loved and feared, but since these two qualities did not easily coexist, it was better to be feared than to be loved. The French revolutionaries believed they were forging a new, transparent political order based on citizenship, so they explicitly shunned Machiavelli as a model, but he did make one pragmatic observation that would resonate, if unacknowledged, in revolutionary France: "he who quells disorder by a very few signal examples will in the end be more merciful than he who from too great leniency permits things to take their course and so to result in rapine and bloodshed."[7]

Machiavelli thus justified terror as demonstrative violence, which can be found in the torture and execution of state enemies, such as (to cite two French examples, of which the revolutionaries were well aware) Henri IV's assassin François Ravaillac in 1610 and François Damiens, who had lightly wounded King Louis XV with a dagger in 1757. Such publicly inflicted agonies went beyond the punishment of an individual and demonstrated the punitive might of the sovereign. Michel Foucault argued that such demonstrative, penal violence was eventually supplanted as a means of disciplining subjects. Punishment became less a public spectacle, chastising the victim's mind and disciplining the body through more routinized forms of penalty, such as the prison.[8]

The French Revolution was part of this transition in the uses of terror. On the one hand, it asserted sovereignty through punitive violence, a process whose ultimate expression lay in the execution of Louis XVI on January 21, 1793. Having inverted the old order's location of sovereignty (it was no longer in the body of the king, but vested in the "nation"), executing Louis aimed not only at vindicating the republic, but (as Robespierre argued) to "nourish in the spirit of tyrants, a salutary terror of the justice of the people."[9] Robespierre thereby turned the "logic" behind Damiens' agonies against the dethroned monarch on behalf of the new sovereign, the people itself. On the other hand, the Revolution "routinized" political oppression. Executions were just one part of a web of daily practices of coercion, surveillance, and mobilization. The "people" were no longer meant to be only awestruck spectators but active citizens cooperating with the machinery of terror.

The French revolutionaries found examples in their classical education, particularly the Roman *delatores* (who brought evidence in prosecutions) and *censores* (who watched over the morality of citizens).[10] They did not use such Latin terms, but the name of the most powerful of all the Terror's central organs, the Committee of Public Safety, deliberately recalled Cicero's dictum that *salus populi suprema lex est* – the supreme law is the security of the people.[11] Yet there was no historical blueprint for the Terror of 1793–4, which emerged erratically as the revolutionaries thrashed about in the complex interaction between, on the one hand, the intense circumstances of the moment and, on the other hand, the ideology and cultural inheritance through which they interpreted these circumstances and which shaped their responses. That terror was a practice rather than a principle is illustrated by the fact that it was used by political actors on both left and right. Just as there was a "Red" (Jacobin) Terror, so there were outbreaks of a countervailing "White" (Royalist) Terror in the later 1790s and in 1815.

Robespierre and his later detractors agreed that "terror" in the context of 1793–4 was "fear-generating, coercive political violence" rather than the "conspiratorial practice" of violence for the purposes of psychological shock and propaganda – two of the forms discussed by Alex Schmid.[12] Conspiratorial violence directed *against* the regime certainly existed but was more prevalent among nineteenth-century revolutionaries, some of whom regarded themselves as the legatees of the French Revolution.

The Terror was purportedly directed *against* counter-revolutionary conspiracy, which was held to be the very antithesis of the republican transparency to which the revolutionaries aspired. The practitioners of 1793–4 imposed what is now called "state terror" (Arno Mayer calls it "top-down" or "enforcement" terror)[13] against the country's own citizens. While this anticipated twentieth-century practices,[14] it was also rooted in the past, for other forms of terror coexisted and interacted with it. For one, there was tyrannicide, which had precedents going back to ancient Rome and Greece: Cicero argued that a tyrant was no different from an enemy soldier or criminal, so could be legitimately killed.[15] When the French revolutionaries put Louis XVI on trial, they alluded to such precedents. Deploying rhetoric foreshadowing the language of the Terror proper, some Jacobins argued that Louis was an enemy of the nation from the very fact that he was a king: "no man can reign innocently," declared Louis-Antoine Saint-Just. "Every king is a rebel and a usurper." If, he argued, the would-be tyrant Caesar could be slain in the midst of the Senate for challenging Roman liberty, then Louis, who posed no less a threat to the French Republic, could also be killed.[16]

Yet tyrannicide cut both ways. Louis-Michel Le Peletier de Saint-Fargeau, a Jacobin deputy, was knifed by an ex-noble in January 1793 for voting for the king's death. On June 13 that year, Charlotte Corday stabbed another Jacobin deputy, Jean-Paul Marat, and there were alleged attempts on Robespierre and Collot d'Herbois, his colleague on the Committee of Public Safety, in May 1794. Corday's assassination of Marat showed just how contested the meaning of tyrannicide was. For Corday, the revolution had been derailed when the Jacobins had purged their bitter opponents, the Girondins, from the Convention on June 2. Marat, bloodthirsty and demagogic, seemed to represent the worst Jacobin traits. Corday's act represented a throwback to older ideas that the killing of an individual tyrant could remedy the ills that afflicted the entire body politic. Yet, as Randall D. Law has argued, the French Revolution helped to forge modern conceptions of how "tyranny" should be overthrown: tyranny was embedded within an entire political system, which had to be revolutionized.[17] No one pretended that the decapitation of Louis XVI alone would secure the Republic. Even royalists saw assassination as merely the prelude to a wider (counter-revolutionary) transformation. In December 1800, an attempt was made to blow up Napoleon Bonaparte with a carriage laden with explosives. The elimination of the first consul would have been the first step in the restoration of the monarchy, but this still left wide open the question as to how far the clock would be turned back towards the old regime. In this vein, the Jacobins interpreted Marat's assassination as a blow aimed not just at one deputy but against their entire order, which in turn strengthened their impulses towards political coercion.

The French Revolution also linked the past with the future in another fundamental way: in the role played by the revolutionary crowd, which formed the second form of French revolutionary terror. The collective revolutionary violence began with the murderous retribution inflicted on authority figures in July 1789, through the horrifying bloodletting of the September Massacres in 1792, to such acts of violence as the decapitation of the deputy Jean-Bertrand Féraud during the Prairial uprising of May 1795. Mayer calls this violence "bottom-up," "spontaneous," or "primitive" terror,[18] meaning a throwback to earlier upheavals, in which crowd action sought vengeance, redress of grievances, the elimination of foes, or the defense of traditional ways of life. Such violence haunted contemporaries and the generations that followed.

"Top-down" or state terror

State terror consisted of a network of formal institutions that were developed in an ad hoc way as the hydra-like crisis of 1793 developed. Yet the French Revolution had opened with emancipating promise. The absolute monarchy of the Bourbons had collapsed under the weight of a fiscal, political, and economic crisis in the summer of 1789. The monarchy did not survive the subsequent struggle to establish a new constitutional order. The reluctance of Louis XVI to share power with an elected National Assembly (among other grievances) led to his attempt to flee in June 1791, stirring a republican movement which, although suppressed temporarily, gained momentum after the outbreak of war against Austria and Prussia in the spring of 1792. As invading armies converged on the capital, the Revolution was radicalized, the popular movement in Paris mobilized, and the provinces galvanized in defense of the new order. The monarchy was overthrown on August 10, 1792, and a republic was proclaimed on September 22. Power now lay with the newly elected assembly in France, the National Convention, based on a broad (though not quite universal) male suffrage. After a bruising political trial, the Convention found Louis guilty of treason and he was guillotined on January 21, 1793 – a sentence that bitterly split the republicans between hardline Jacobins and their Girondin opponents, who wanted clemency, a schism that aggravated revolutionary politics in their descent into terror.

The nascent Republic had turned the tide in the conflict, but the French invasion of the Low Countries, the Rhineland, as well as Nice and Savoy, combined with the diplomatic furor over the regicide, set France on a collision course with every major European power in Western Europe. By the spring of 1793, the Republic was at war against Austria, Prussia, the rest of Germany (the Holy Roman Empire), Britain, the Netherlands, Spain, Portugal, and the northern Italian state of Piedmont-Sardinia. Moreover, Russia was making ominous noises in support of this coalition. France was being invaded on every frontier, but there was also a crisis within, which took many faces, including a peasant counter-revolution in the west of the country (the Vendée, Brittany, and Normandy), sparked by the imposition of conscription but also against the Revolution's secularizing attack on the Catholic Church and led by royalist nobles. There was a desperate economic crisis that brought the threat of insurrection from the Parisian popular movement, the *sans-culottes*. These were the radicalized men and women of the capital's working population: artisans, craft-workers, retailers, journeymen, apprentices, and laborers who sought to defend their place in the Republic's emerging democratic politics, to defend their economic independence against the pressures of larger-scale business, and to seek radical, redistributive economic controls to weather the social crisis. It was with *sans-culotte* support that the Jacobins ousted the Girondins from the Convention and government on June 2, 1793, thereby provoking a civil war, called the "federalist revolt" because of its provincial base (it was mainly concentrated around the cities like Marseille, Toulon, Lyon, Bordeaux, and Caen). The disasters of 1793 are at the source of debate as to why the French Revolution fell into terror. Traditionally, historians such as Georges Lefebvre and Albert Soboul claimed that these circumstances forced extraordinary measures onto the Revolution. More recently, "revisionists" such as François Furet, Lynn Hunt, and Keith Baker have suggested that terror was an integral part of the Revolution from the very start, that it was "scripted" or inherent within revolutionary rhetoric and ideology from 1789.[19]

Jacobins like Robespierre certainly developed sophisticated theories of terror as they defended their policies, drawing on the ideological and cultural resources that had informed the Revolution since 1789: these rested not just on the rights of the individual (proclaimed in the Declaration of the Rights of Man and the Citizen in August 1789) but also on national sovereignty. The revisionist argument suggests that, in rhetorically transferring sovereignty from the king to the "nation" in 1789, the Revolution replaced one form of absolutism with another. If, as the revolutionaries claimed, political legitimacy rested only in the nation, then they could only ever claim to speak for it, rather than for specific social interests, which left no room for political pluralism or the concept of a loyal opposition. Robespierre, Saint-Just, and Barère, among others, argued that the Terror was "revolutionary," by which they meant that it was not so much illegal as extra-legal, not unconstitutional but applicable in circumstances where normal constitutional rule was dangerous to the very survival of the nascent Republic. When, on October 10, 1793, Saint-Just persuaded the Convention to declare the government "revolutionary until the peace," he explained that "in the light of the situation confronting the Republic, the constitution cannot be put into effect: it would be used to destroy itself."[20]

Terror was, in other words, temporary but open-ended, since no one could tell for sure when it would be safe to return to regular forms of law and government. The Jacobins were well aware that "revolution" is an extra-legal transformation in the political and social order. For as long as the new civic order was endangered, so the revolutionary process – the struggle of a free people to protect its liberties against its enemies – had to continue. Terror was the means of waging that struggle: there could be no middle ground in the combat between "liberty" and "despotism." "Social protection," argued Robespierre, "is due only to peaceful citizens," adding that "there are no citizens in the Republic but the republicans."[21] Such arguments were one of the French Revolution's dark gifts to later revolutionary terrorism, which denies the legitimacy of opposition and punishes it accordingly.

Yet ideology does not provide the only explanation for the Terror, which in 1793 seems primarily to have aimed at confronting the crisis, explaining why its apparatus developed piecemeal between March and September 1793. To create a strong, fast-reacting executive, the Convention elected two committees, of Public Safety (CPS) and of General Security (CGS). The former was to supervise the war effort, foreign policy, the armies, and the government ministries, while the latter was to control internal security and policing. These two committees would emerge as the central political authority of the Terror, albeit one answerable to the Convention. A Revolutionary Tribunal was established to try traitors without appeal. Rebels caught bearing arms were to be summarily executed. "Representatives on mission" – deputies from the Convention – fanned out across the provinces to mobilize society for the war effort and to suppress counter-revolution. The *levée en masse* introduced universal conscription and requisitioned France's resources. Committees of surveillance were established in every urban section and every rural commune. Reporting to the CGS, they were charged with watching foreigners, arresting "suspects," and with issuing the *certificats de civisme*, identity papers that attested to the holder's patriotism and without which no citizen could hold public office, travel around the country, and find work.[22] "Suspects" were expansively defined by the Law of Suspects on September 17, 1793, as "those who, by their conduct, relations, utterances or writings have shown themselves to be partisans of tyranny, of federalism, and enemies of liberty," as well as a variety of other groups, including former nobles and their families "who have not constantly demonstrated their attachment to the Revolution."[23] The economic crisis was attacked by the imposition of economic controls. The death penalty was imposed on food hoarders; a forced loan was imposed on the rich; public granaries were established; "revolutionary armies" of *sans-culottes* were created to requisition grain in the countryside; the Law of the Maximum fixed both prices and wages; and the whole system was capped off by the Subsistence Commission to oversee the controlled economy.[24]

"Bottom-up" or popular terror

The economic measures and the surveillance committees formed the juncture between the state terror and the "bottom-up" terror from the *sans-culottes*. Indeed, the two overlapped, even as the Jacobins in the Convention and the popular movement pressed their own, separate agendas. The former wanted to preserve the Republic and forge a civic order based on republican citizenship and virtue, while the latter sought a more direct form of democracy and to defend the economic interests of the capital's working population. Despite these differences, the revolutionary leadership harnessed popular violence for its own purposes – either by justifying it retrospectively or by directing it against their own opponents, as the purge of the Girondins had shown. David Andress has argued that, far from being an external force exerted on state terror, popular violence was a fundamental, constituent part of the process, serving the purposes of the revolutionary elites as much as it did the *sans-culottes*. There was therefore a symbiotic, if fraught, interrelationship between "state" and "popular" terrors, each finding in the other a political use, encouraging popular action and at the same time ratcheting up the scale of state violence.[25] While the more draconian economic measures, such as the death penalty for hoarders and even the Maximum, were driven primarily by insurrectionary pressure on the Convention, ultimately the controls helped the government to stabilize the economy, ease the social crisis, and keep the armies supplied. When the Jacobin Georges Danton proposed the creation of the Revolutionary Tribunal in the Convention on March 10, 1793, he argued that it would prevent a repeat of the mob violence in the September Massacres in the previous year, when a murderous crowd, directed by some of the more radical Parisian revolutionary leadership, slaughtered hundreds of imprisoned, counter-revolutionary suspects. "Let *us* be terrible," Danton roared, "to prevent the people from being terrible themselves."[26] The furies of the September Massacres justified the strengthening of the revolutionary state's coercive arm. The intermeshing of "state" with "popular" terror was formally structured in local institutions, especially the surveillance committees. In Paris, where they were called "revolutionary committees," they had in fact been spontaneously created by popular militants in August 1792, and they remained the hotbeds of *sans-culotte* activism, but after September 1793 they reported directly to the CGS and were salaried by the government, whereby they were effectively co-opted as an arm of "state terror."[27]

Moreover, private citizens also had a part to play, not least in offering denunciations and information on "suspects." The revolutionaries made a subtle distinction between "informing," which they saw as an old regime practice, and "denunciation" which was a civic act. For the revolutionaries, "informing" was done in secrecy and so could be driven by personal motives, but "denunciation" was the duty of all good citizens, an expression of their vigilance for the public good, and, since it was done in public, the very publicity guaranteed against abuses. Yet with the creation of the committees of surveillance, denunciations were now made to a small group of men behind closed doors, where "public opinion" was no protection against false accusations. This change, in fact, reinforced the role of the committees as an arm of state repression: since they also had powers of arrest, they became the first staging-post of a victim's tortuous journey to imprisonment, trial, and, for the unfortunate, the guillotine.[28]

A similar shift occurred in the Terror as it unfolded in the provinces. The Convention's representatives on mission were legally vested with the full authority of the nation and so became, in effect, local dictators, issuing edicts "by virtue of the unlimited powers invested in [them] by the National Convention."[29] While many of these representatives managed to mobilize their departments without resorting to bloodletting,[30] others committed horrifying atrocities, the worst in areas afflicted by civil war or counter-revolution, most infamously in Lyon (where captives were mown down by grapeshot), Nantes (where hog-tied prisoners were drowned en masse), and the Vendée.[31] Two points arise from this "anarchic" Terror, as it is commonly remembered by historians. One is that, in the strict legal sense, it was not "anarchic" at all: the powers that these representatives exploited were devolved to them by the Convention, and they used them in defense of the state, not against it.[32] This is especially true in the Vendée, where an estimated 200,000 people may have perished. The other point is that, just like the "popular terror," it served the purposes of the revolutionary state, even if, ultimately, the Jacobins reined it in. Like the violence of the "bottom-up" terror, the "anarchic terror" was legitimized by the rhetoric and orders of the Convention until the threat of civil war and counter-revolution was contained. By December, Robespierre and his closest associates had come to consider the "anarchic" Terror to be more of a liability than a help, and, by the law of 14 Frimaire (4 December), the government centralized control of the Terror and scaled back the powers of the representatives on mission, recalling the most extreme to Paris to account for their actions. Yet by then the "anarchic Terror" had done most of the work of ending the civil war and containing the counter-revolution.

The relationship between the politicians and the popular movement was fraught with friction, and slowly, erratically, and opportunistically, the Jacobin dictatorship asserted itself and steered the Terror unambiguously towards the needs of the state. In September 1793, the *Enragés* (literally, the "madmen"), who provided some of the most radical leadership of the Parisian popular movement, were arrested. In December 1793, the Convention put a stop to the *sans-culotte* assault on the Church – a full-blown campaign of "dechristianization" which closed down churches and destroyed religious images – citing the need for public tranquility as a motive.

Underlying these conflicts was a struggle over the direction of the Terror itself. The *sans-culottes*, seeing in it a means of defending their social interests, and their Hébertist spokesmen, a motley group of radicals around the journalist Jacques-René Hébert, wanted to intensify it. Other voices, particularly those of Georges Danton and Camille Desmoulins, alarmed that good patriots were now threatened by terror, had demanded clemency. After some wavering, the government struck down the middle: the Hébertists were guillotined on March 24, 1794, decapitating the popular movement (literally), but the Dantonists followed them twelve days later. The "revolutionary armies" were abolished and the seats of militant power, including the war ministry, the Paris Commune, and *sections* (the Parisian districts) were purged. That spring, local administrations that had shown too much initiative were closed down or replaced; a police bureau was established to scrutinize the conduct of public officials, answering to the CPS; all political prisoners held in the provinces were to be transported to Paris and tried by the Revolutionary Tribunal there; and all government ministries were subjected to CPS supervision.[33]

Terror as regeneration

From now on, the Terror certainly went beyond a defensive response to the crisis to an ideologically driven attempt to "regenerate" French society as a "Republic of Virtue." The program aimed to create citizens whose moral universe had expunged the habits of the old order and was devoted to the self-sacrificing, republican egalitarianism of the new. The process had begun earlier: a new revolutionary calendar, for example, was introduced to the Convention in September 1793. Yet now such a transformation meant changing the way people thought and how they behaved. It therefore demanded not just political conformity and obedience but active commitment to the Jacobin vision of the future. This involved a "cultural revolution" that anticipated Stalin's *Homo Sovieticus* (a new breed of human being immersed in communist values and culture).[34] Political and moral messages were transmitted to the public through symbols, festivals, the theater, the press, the arts, and the Jacobin clubs. There was a plan for a national system of education, inspired by the Spartan example. Place and personal names were changed: religious and royal terms were dropped or replaced by impeccably republican ones, such as "Marat" and "Libre" ("free"). The polite form of address – "vous" – was dropped in favor of the egalitarian "tu" – *tutoiement*: there was to be no deference among equal citizens.[35]

The Terror became a means of enforcing a more rigid form of political orthodoxy and of suppressing all dissent. Thus the last months of the Terror are the most controversial because they witnessed a quickening pace of the killing even as the Republic's external and domestic situation was improving. The Law of 22 Prairial (June 10, 1794) accelerated the work of the Revolutionary Tribunal: defendants were stripped of legal counsel, the definition of crimes against the Republic was expanded dramatically, the jury could convict on the grounds of "moral proof" if there was no hard evidence of guilt, and the only sentence available was death. Together, these measures routinized the Jacobins' hazardously narrow conception of "virtuous" citizenship. The tempo of executions sped up: in the fifteen months since March 1793, the Tribunal acquitted roughly half of the accused but passed 1,251 death sentences, with an average of three people a day being guillotined. After 10 June, in the six weeks remembered as the "Great Terror," 1,376 people were sentenced to death, averaging thirty daily beheadings. Antoine-Claire Thibaudeau, a member of the Convention who survived, recalled that the Terror "hovered over everyone's head, striking them down indiscriminately; it was as arbitrary and swift as Death's scythe."[36]

This was the whole point: since no one could feel secure, their safety lay in unquestioning loyalty to the government. It was not enough that this loyalty was publicly expressed: a virtuous citizen was meant to internalize the egalitarian, self-abnegating values of the new Republic.[37] Ultimately, the Terror aimed to root out those whose patriotism was insincere: Robespierre frequently spoke of "unmasking" such people. Yet, once it became an instrument of moral transformation, no one could see when and how it would end. Saint-Just wrote that "the revolution must stop when its laws have brought happiness and public liberty to perfection.... One speaks of the high point of the revolution. Who will determine it? It changes."[38]

The Jacobins themselves could see no safe way of ending the Terror. The transition back to constitutional law meant that the "terrorists" would be vulnerable to the vengeance of those whom they had hurt. The repentant "terrorist" Jean-Lambert Tallien later recognized this dilemma. How, he asked, could its practitioners "return to the crowd, after having made so many enemies? How could they not fear revenge after committing so many crimes?"[39] Moreover, how could the Jacobins repudiate the Terror without appearing to reject the Revolution itself? By the summer of 1794, they had passed the point at which they could simply declare that the crisis had abated: their own regenerative project was now too tightly interwoven with the Terror itself. Both practically and ideologically, the Jacobins had painted themselves into a corner with toxic paint. So it was that the Terror ended when the government's enemies – politicians who felt targeted themselves, the *sans-culottes* angry that the Maximum was also imposed on wages – marshaled their forces and overthrew and guillotined Robespierre and his associates, including Saint-Just, on 9–10 Thermidor (July 27–8, 1794).

The uses of terror in early nineteenth-century Europe

The Terror horrified the European imagination and cast its shadow over revolutionary movements in succeeding generations. In the period between the fall of Napoleon Bonaparte and the Revolutions of 1848, European revolutionaries included a spectrum from liberal, constitutional monarchists to the early revolutionary socialists, all opposed in different degrees to the authoritarian order that emerged in 1815. For most, the state terror of 1793–4 was a warning to be heeded. It was more than of symbolic importance that, when the Second Republic was proclaimed on the ruins of France's last monarchy in 1848, one of the first decrees of the provisional government was to declare the abolition of the death penalty for political crimes.

Yet for a small, hard kernel on the radical left, terror would be necessary to complete the revolutionary transformation. These hardliners were explicitly inspired by the experience of the Jacobin Terror and by the figure who in hindsight now appears to be the first "professional revolutionary," Gracchus Babeuf, who took his name from the Gracchi, the brothers in Ancient Rome who pursued reforms for the poor. Babeuf had been arrested in 1796 as he and his secret organization, the "Equals," planned to overthrow the Directory (the regime that ruled France between 1795 and 1799) and ultimately establish an egalitarian social order. Babeuf ominously argued that measures would be needed "to eliminate whatever obstacles stand in the way."[40]

Revolutionaries who explicitly embraced such tactics in the first half of the nineteenth century sat on the radical fringe. They included the French revolutionary socialists Louis-Auguste Blanqui and Armand Barbès, whose "Society of Seasons" sought to seize power and exercise a revolutionary dictatorship in the pursuit of an egalitarian society.[41] The Russian revolutionary Pavel Pestel, the "Russian Jacobin," represented the radical wing of the Decembrist movement.[42] Pestel's manifesto, *Russian Justice*, envisaged a Russian republic, peasant emancipation, and the public ownership of half the country's agricultural land, to be achieved by the coercive rule of a "Revolutionary Senate" modeled on the Committee of Public Safety.[43] Most European revolutionaries in this period wanted to avoid such measures. The Italian nationalist Giuseppe Mazzini emphasized national self-determination and popular sovereignty but stressed that the rights of the individual were paramount. In the *Duties of Man* (1841–60), he wrote: "there are certain things that are constitutive of your individuality and are essential elements of human life. Over these, not even the People have any right. No majority may establish a tyrannical regime."[44]

Yet of necessity European revolutionaries shared with the Blanquists a commitment to secrecy and conspiracy. Republicans, socialists, and even liberals who were otherwise horrified by the prospect of terror were nonetheless willing to adopt methods that were conspiratorial in preparing for an insurrection. Yet the intention was rarely to sow fear or to make a propagandist point through demonstrative violence, even if these were the effects.

Rather, the revolutionaries were motivated by two possible goals. First, they were working for a direct confrontation with the authorities, in the shape of an insurrection or a coup d'état. The Carbonari, for example, were Italian secret societies whose membership included liberal and Bonapartist army officers and officials alienated by the conservative order that had replaced Napoleonic rule. Such organizations were particularly prevalent in states where the freedom to organize openly was severely circumscribed. Liberals saw parliaments as the only legitimate sphere of formal political action and aspired to a society based on civil liberties. Where these existed, liberals tended to avoid conspiracy, as they did in Britain, the Low Countries, southern Germany, and France (where the Charbonnerie, an imitation of the Carbonari, mostly consisted of former Bonapartists and republicans). Yet in absolute monarchies where such rights were limited, the challenge was how to achieve the goals of a constitution, civil rights, and national freedom. Some liberals therefore chose conspiracy as the middle road between supine submission to absolutism and full-blown revolution "from below." This point reveals the essential elitism at the heart of early European liberalism, but it was an elitism conditioned by a real fear of the dangers of "bottom-up" terror.[45] After 1815, liberal revolutionaries pursued regime change while avoiding the unpredictable violence of a popular uprising. Thus the first European revolutions after 1815 were conspiracies unleashed by liberal army officers seeking an ordered transition imposed "from above." Such were the *pronunciamientos* in Spain and Portugal, which triggered the liberal revolutions of 1820; the Carbonari revolutions in Italy in 1820–1; the Decembrist uprising in 1825; and – initially – the Polish insurrection of 1830–1.

Yet the failures of these revolutions spurred a change of tactics, giving conspiracy its second main purpose. The ultimate goal was still an insurrection and the methods were still conspiratorial, but the ideal revolution would be driven by a genuinely popular uprising. The most important example of this change of direction was the creation of Mazzini's "Young Italy" in 1831. It expected its members to work towards subverting the political order and to sacrifice themselves in the cause of Italian unity and freedom. Yet it diverged from earlier underground organizations by having a published program, a broad membership which paid subscriptions, and a messaging service keeping its various branches in touch with each other. In short, though operating outside the law, it shared many features of an organized political party. This, in fact, suited its immediate purpose, which for Mazzini was education and propaganda to convince the public of the republican and nationalist cause. Yet Mazzini also believed that Italy's despotic regimes would only be ousted by an insurrection. The uprising would target only the regime, securing the support of the local people, respecting their property and the Church. The goal, in other words, was not terror but a revolution supported by a willing population.[46]

Other forms of "direct action," such as assassination, were not unknown, but they were rarely the weapons of choice. The most notorious assassinations after the French Revolution were committed by people acting on their own: in 1819, Karl Sand, a German student radical, murdered the conservative playwright August von Kotzebue; the next year the Duc de Berry, third in line to the French throne, was stabbed to death by another lone assassin, Louis-Pierre Louvel, a Bonapartist. It was only after the Revolution of 1830, which bitterly disappointed French republicans because it replaced one monarchy with another, that in France assassination was seriously considered as the beginning of the revolutionary process. The Decembrists may have planned to kill the tsar in 1825 and the Polish revolutionaries the Russian viceroy in 1830, also as the beginning of the transition. Even so, many revolutionaries still disapproved of the tactic. One of the grisliest assassination attempts of this period was committed by Joseph Fieschi on King Louis-Philippe of France in 1835, which only grazed its target but killed eighteen others and seriously wounded twenty-two.[47]

Fieschi was only indirectly connected with the republican underground, and few voices were raised in his support. Committed republicans, such as those in the closest French equivalent to Young Italy, the Société des Droits de l'Homme et du Citoyen (SDHC), regarded assassination as an "egotistical" act. They preferred open insurrection because it required a large, organized group dedicated to the same ideology, illustrating that the people as a whole were rising up. As one republican leaflet explained in 1837 (after another attempt by a lone would-be assassin), "it is not enough to kill the tyrant, one must also annihilate the tyranny," as the French Revolution itself had apparently shown with the death of Louis XVI. Such a broader, revolutionary transformation could only be achieved through a union of all republicans, not by "isolated attacks" on the monarchy.[48] It was for this reason that the barricade – not the terrorist's bomb or the assassin's knife – became the pre-eminent symbol of revolution between 1830 and 1848. In Paris alone, streets were barricaded in uprisings in 1832, 1834, 1839, and 1848.[49]

Yet revolutionaries often fell short of condemning the overall *goals* of the assassins – and in this ambiguity lay another feature of modern terrorism: it can flourish in an environment where a broader section of the public may disapprove of terrorism's *means* but broadly relate to its grievances. What shocked authorities in Germany after Sand's murder of Kotzebue was the reaction of some public figures. Friedrich Carové, one of Georg Hegel's colleagues at the University of Berlin, argued that while Sand's action was wrong, it showed that Germany's national spirit had not been entirely corrupted, and it was such corruption that the German people should guard against.[50] Carové's response reflects the tortured relationship between terrorism and the wider community from which it springs. A terrorist act may be condemned by the majority, but the condemnation might be tempered by a shared sense of malaise with the existing order. It is in such circumstances that terrorism as conspiratorial, demonstrative violence can flourish.

Conclusion

The French Revolution left a constructive gift to the world in its emancipating ideology of human rights and political freedom, but it also formulated the modern theories and rhetoric of terror – and the revolutionaries themselves were well aware of the contradiction. They seeded the essential problems of modern terrorism: can peace and justice ever emerge from the evils of violence, particularly violence directed by a state against its own citizens, or by one group of citizens against the existing order? To what extent should a democratic state abandon its own rules to defend itself? What, if any, forms of political violence are legitimate? The French revolutionaries were among the first to elevate political terror into a complete system, supported by a network of institutions reaching from the political center to the most localized level, and explained by a justificatory rhetoric and ideology. Central to such practices was the idea of terror as all-pervasive, deriving its power not just by the force of example but also by fostering the sense that it could strike at anyone and anytime, which is how modern terrorism sows fear.

Moreover, in seeking not only to defend the Republic but also to "regenerate" society itself, the Jacobin Terror anticipated later terrorism in its messianic sense of mission, one which allowed terrorists to qualify not only active opponents as enemies but also the indifferent or apathetic. Political violence could come to be regarded by terrorists as a salutary, regenerative process in itself, in which perhaps the most important blood to be sacrificed would be their own. Within Jacobinism, as in later revolutionary and terrorist ideologies, lay the nihilistic sense that the cause would flourish on sacrifice and martyrdom. As Robespierre exclaimed on February 5, 1794, "let us, in sealing our work with our blood, see at least the early dawn of universal bliss."[51] Yet while every human being wants the free pursuit of happiness, not all want to shed blood to achieve it.

Notes

1 Richard T. Bienvenu, ed., *The Ninth of Thermidor: The Fall of Robespierre* (New York: Oxford University Press, 1968), 38.
2 David Andress, "The Course of the Terror, 1793–94," in *A Companion to the French Revolution*, ed. Peter McPhee (Malden, MA: Wiley-Blackwell, 2013), 307.
3 Annie Jourdan, "Les discours de la terreur à l'époque révolutionnaire (1776–1798): Étude comparative sur une notion ambiguë," *French Historical Studies* 36, no. 1 (2013): 54–8.
4 Bronislaw Baczko, *Ending the Terror: The French Revolution after Robespierre* (Cambridge: Cambridge University Press, 1994), 49.
5 *Dictionnaire de l'Académie française* (Paris, 1798), 2: 775.
6 For more detail on medieval forms of terror and demonstrative violence, see Chapter 4 by Steven Isaac in this volume.
7 Niccolò Machiavelli, *The Prince* (New York: Cosimo, 2008), 43.
8 Michel Foucault, *Discipline and Punish: The Birth of the Prison* (New York: Vintage, 1994), 3–11. See also Chapter 24 by Roger Griffin on modernity and terrorism in this volume.
9 Keith Michael Baker, ed., *The Old Regime and the French Revolution* (Chicago: University of Chicago Press, 1987), 307–11.
10 Colin Lucas, "The Theory and Practice of Denunciation in the French Revolution," *Journal of Modern History* 68, no. 4 (1996): 772–3.
11 David Andress, *The Terror: Civil War in the French Revolution* (London: Little, Brown, 2005), 164.
12 Alex. P. Schmid, "The Definition of Terrorism," in *The Routledge Handbook of Terrorism Research*, ed. Alex Schmid (London: Routledge, 2011), 86.
13 Arno Mayer, *The Furies: Violence and Terror in the French and Russian Revolutions* (Princeton, NJ: Princeton University Press, 2000), 101–2.
14 On forms of state terror during the first half of the twentieth century, see Chapter 11 by Paul M. Hagenloh in this volume.
15 Chapter 2 by Johannes Dillinger in this volume, "Tyrannicide from Ancient Greece and Rome to the Crisis of the Seventeenth Century," explores these examples in greater detail.
16 Baker, *The Old Regime and the French Revolution*, 304–7.
17 Randall D. Law, *Terrorism: A History* (Cambridge: Polity, 2009), 58–9, 61–2.
18 Mayer, *The Furies*, 118.
19 This debate is neatly summarized by Hugh Gough in *The Terror in the French Revolution* (Basingstoke: Macmillan, 1998), 6–9. Subsequent pages (9–11) ably discuss developments in historical research on the subject.
20 Marc Allan Goldstein, ed., *Social and Political Thought of the French Revolution, 1788–1797: An Anthology of Original Texts* (New York: Peter Lang, 1997), 497.

21 Bienvenu, *The Ninth of Thermidor*, 38, 39.
22 Andress, *The Terror*, 163.
23 J. M. Thompson, *French Revolution Documents 1789–94* (Oxford: Blackwell, 1933), 258–60.
24 William Doyle, *The Oxford History of the French Revolution* (Oxford: Oxford University Press, 1989), 264–5.
25 David Andress, "La violence populaire durant la Révolution française: révolte, châtiment et escalade de la terreur d'État," in *Les politiques de la Terreur (1793–1794)*, ed. Michel Biard, 69–80 (Rennes: Presses Universitaires de Rennes, 2008).
26 Norman Hampson, *Danton* (Oxford: Blackwell, 1978), 102.
27 Albert Soboul, *Les sans-culottes parisiens en l'an II: movement populaire et gouvernement révolutionnaire (1793–1794)* (Paris: Seuil, 1968), 180–3.
28 Lucas, "The Theory and Practice of Denunciation," 779.
29 John Hardman, *French Revolution Documents* (Oxford: Blackwell, 1973), 2:152.
30 See, for example, Bernard Bodinier, "Un département sans terreur sanguinaire: l'Eure en l'An II," in *Les politiques de la Terreur*, 111–27.
31 Doyle, *The Oxford History of the French Revolution*, 254, 257.
32 Andress, "Course of the Terror," 299.
33 Ibid., 303; and Gough, *The Terror in the French Revolution*, 66–7.
34 Anne Applebaum, *Iron Curtain: The Crushing of Eastern Europe 1944–56* (London: Penguin, 2013), 163.
35 Emmet Kennedy, *A Cultural History of the French Revolution* (New Haven, CT: Yale University Press, 1989), 304, 347–50; and Andress, *Terror*, 306–7.
36 Bienvenu, *The Ninth of Thermidor*, 51. The term "Great Terror" was later revived and applied to the period 1937–8, the worst years of Stalinist political violence in the Soviet Union. For more on this, see Chapter 11 by Hagenloh in this volume.
37 William M. Reddy, *The Navigation of Feeling: A Framework for the History of Emotions* (Cambridge: Cambridge University Press, 2001), 173–210.
38 Goldstein, *Social and Political Thought of the French Revolution*, 556.
39 Baczko, *Ending the Terror*, 51.
40 John Anthony Scott, ed., *The Defense of Gracchus Babeuf before the High Court of Vendôme* (New York: Schocken, 1972), 48.
41 Jill Harsin, *Barricades: The War of the Streets in Revolutionary Paris, 1830–1848* (New York: Palgrave, 2002), 7.
42 The Decembrists are explored in greater detail in this volume, by Martin A. Miller in Chapter 7 on "Entangled Terrorisms in Late Imperial Russia."
43 Patrick O'Meara, *The Decembrist Pavel Pestel: Russia's First Republican* (Basingstoke: Palgrave, 2003), 81.
44 Stefano Recchia and Nadia Urbinati, *A Cosmopolitanism of Nations: Giuseppe Mazzini's Writings on Democracy, Nation Building, and International Relations* (Princeton, NJ: Princeton University Press, 2013), 8.
45 Michael Broers, *Europe after Napoleon: Revolution, Reaction and Romanticism, 1814–1848* (Manchester: Manchester University Press, 1996), 41–3.
46 Denis Mack Smith, *Mazzini* (London: Yale University Press, 1994), 5–7.
47 Harsin, *Barricades*, 147–8.
48 Ibid., 175, 183.
49 Martyn Lyons, *Post-Revolutionary Europe, 1815–1856* (Basingstoke: Palgrave, 2006), 66–8.
50 Matthew Levinger, *Enlightened Nationalism: The Transformation of Prussian Political Culture, 1806–1848* (Oxford: Oxford University Press, 2000), 142–4.
51 Bienvenu, *The Ninth of Thermidor*, 34.

Further reading

Andress, David. *The Terror: Civil War in the French Revolution*. London: Little, Brown, 2005.
Baczko, Bronislaw. *Ending the Terror: The French Revolution after Robespierre*. Cambridge: Cambridge University Press, 1994.

Biard, Michel, ed. *Les politiques de la Terreur (1793–1794)*. Rennes: Presses Universitaires de Rennes, 2008.

Doyle, William. *The Oxford History of the French Revolution*. Oxford: Oxford University Press, 1989.

Gough, Hugh. *The Terror in the French Revolution*. Basingstoke: Macmillan, 1998.

Linton, Marisa. *Choosing Terror: Virtue, Friendship, and Authenticity in the French Revolution*. Oxford: Oxford University Press, 2013.

Lucas, Colin. "The Theory and Practice of Denunciation in the French Revolution," *Journal of Modern History* 68, no. 4 (1996): 768–85.

Lyons, Martyn. *Post-Revolutionary Europe, 1815–1856*. Basingstoke: Palgrave, 2006.

Mayer, Arno. *The Furies: Violence and Terror in the French and Russian Revolutions*. Princeton, NJ: Princeton University Press, 2000.

Soboul, Albert. *The Parisian Sans-Culottes and the French Revolution: 1793–4*. Oxford: Clarendon Press, 1964.

6

TERRORISM IN AMERICA FROM THE COLONIAL PERIOD TO JOHN BROWN

Matthew Jennings

As far back as we can see into the North American past, terror-inducing tactics are present. They were one piece of a larger toolkit that featured violence of various kinds in Native America. The arrival of Europeans challenged Native ways of violence and brought new technologies and styles of terrorism to bear. There is no shortage of provocative and symbolic acts of violence associated with European colonization; an attempt to catalog all of these acts would run to an absurd length. On colonial plantations, Europeans relied upon terror to keep a large enslaved population in check and at work. When the seaboard colonies rebelled against British authority in the late eighteenth century, both sides relied upon acts of violence to terrorize their adversaries. As the newly independent United States established itself as a continental power, it relied on something akin to state terror to stake its claim to a wide swath of North America, and Native people and the Mexican republic responded in kind. Finally, as the fight over slavery and slavery's expansion became the consuming political passion, pro-slavery and anti-slavery partisans used terror tactics to advance their cause. The fact that "terrorism" as a term is of comparatively recent vintage presents some difficulties when it comes to applying the concept to the distant past, and many of the incidents below do not fall into neat categories.[1] For example, the European and later US genocide against Native peoples could be considered "state terror" from the perspective of the United States, since Native land claims were seen as invalid. Native nations perceived the conflict between themselves and colonizers as between sovereign entities, so the use of the phrase "state terror" would privilege the US perspective. Other terminological problems arise because few people in early America drew the same lines that contemporary commenters might between public and private violence, or state and non-state violence. Rather than dissect each violent act which follows to figure out which specific brand of terrorism it may constitute, this chapter focuses on events which provoked controversy in their own time or seem striking for some other reason, in an effort to show that violence intended to provoke terror has been present from the very beginning of American history.

Terrorism before the advent of Europeans

When discussing the use of terror-inducing tactics in early North America, scholars face an intriguing and frustrating historiographical dilemma. Most of the sources left behind from the early years of colonization were produced by the invaders, who viewed their violence and terrorism as legitimate tools to conquer and pacify a strange land. At the same time, from the very moment of the first European presence in the Americas, two powerful and remarkably long-lived images of Native American violence took hold. On the one hand,

Europeans could sometimes view Native people as peaceful, even admirable, albeit in a primitive way. On the other hand, Europeans believed that Native people engaged in extraordinary, shocking acts of violence, which fed the notion that Native people were somehow savage – the "noble savage" and, for lack of a better term, the "just plain savage."[2] This dichotomy of stereotypes began when Columbus questioned his guileless and virtuous Taíno hosts about their neighbors and learned of the presence of another group of islanders, the Caribs, who were grotesque and fierce and prone to extreme acts of violence. The juxtaposition persists in modern times as well. Witness the New Age romanticizing of a peaceful Native past before savage Europeans ruined an American Eden, as well as the wide array of United States military equipment named after Native people, nations, and weapons. It is necessary to set aside these stereotypes since Native American societies were no more "warlike" or violent than other societies around the world. Violence played an important role in Native America, but American Indian violence was not savage, and it was not the sole salient feature of indigenous communities.

North America had been home to large, complicated societies in the centuries prior to European colonization, and all of these societies likely employed terror-inducing violence. The archaeological record, oral history, and documents from the earliest European expeditions can help scholars reconstruct, at least in an imperfect way, the ways in which terrorism functioned in early America. The large polities of the Native Southwest, such as those that flourished at Chaco Canyon, New Mexico, from 900 to 1250 or so, may have relied on forced labor and provocative acts of violence to construct their great houses (*casas grandes*). There is some evidence that widespread, provocative violence marked the rise of the elites at Chaco Canyon and that this violence also included public episodes of terror-inducing violence that may have served to demonstrate the price of resistance or enforce subjugation to Chacoan authority.[3] During roughly the same time period, the rule of elites at Cahokia, a massive city that grew on the east side of the Mississippi River near modern St. Louis, appears to have rested at least in part on a state monopoly on violence. Archaeologists believe that highly provocative sacrifices of war captives or people given as tribute occurred on top of the platform mounds and served as a graphic reminder of the costs of opposing the regime. Archaeological evidence from Mound 72 supports such assertions: the two elite men buried there were joined by dozens of others who probably met a violent end.[4]

Though the Chaco and Cahokia civilizations dispersed, their descendants, as well as other societies throughout indigenous America, continued to use terrorizing tactics as part of a varied toolkit. The Crow Creek site in South Dakota speaks to mass violence. An attack, dated tentatively to 1325, totally annihilated nearly 500 townspeople. Many of the remains showed signs of scalping and other forms of mutilation. The large number of victims at Crow Creek is extraordinary, but evidence of terrorizing violence in Native America before the arrival of European is not.[5] Sources from the early Spanish exploration and invasion tend to bear this out. The accounts associated with Hernando de Soto's expedition, which encountered the descendants of Cahokia in the form of Mississippian-era towns as it tore through the indigenous Southeast from 1539 to 1543, show the world of Mississippian violence in some detail. In one notable incident, soldiers from the town of Alimamu confronted de Soto's army in April 1541 from atop a fortification they had constructed. The Alimamu men wore only breechclouts, but their bodies were painted black (to represent death) and red (to represent success in war), and some wore horns and feathers. Their appearance was carefully cultivated to terrorize their adversaries, as was their behavior. They taunted the Spaniards and pantomimed roasting one of the invaders over a fire. Once

Spanish reinforcements arrived and the force breached the barricade's outer wall, the Alimamu soldiers retreated to a strategic location, safe from Spanish assaults. All in all, nearly two dozen Spanish fighters died, while the Alimamu defenders lost just three.[6] While this incident would likely not qualify as "terrorism" in the modern sense of the term since it was enacted between opposing soldiers, in other ways it fits quite well. Not only does it include the symbolic violence of certain colors (even if only understood by the Alimamus) and the threatened roasting, but the violent pageantry was staged *outside of* battle.

The terror of colonization

The early Spanish expeditions in North America not only witnessed and experienced Native violence as it existed in the mid-1500s, they also unleashed a vast amount of violence, often using tactics designed to terrorize as they did so. As de Soto's army probed the interior Southeast, it seized hostages from both the top and bottom of Mississippian society. Kidnapping elites might ensure safe passage through their provinces, given ordinary Mississippians' reverence for their leaders. At Cofitachequi (in present-day South Carolina), the Spanish seized the female leader and held her hostage until she escaped with one of the African slaves accompanying the expedition. Taking hundreds of ordinary townsfolk hostage also guaranteed that plenty of people would be available to carry Spanish luggage and otherwise labor to assist the expedition.[7] When the Spanish met military resistance, they often responded with highly provocative acts of violence. For instance, de Soto's army brought along a number of dogs trained to attack human adversaries. It also employed group executions, as well as other terrifying acts such as the cropping of ears and noses, the amputation of hands and feet, and burnings at the stake. Even when Mississippian communities did not offer resistance, the presence of wealth could provoke the Spanish to use terror tactics. Upon learning that deceased elites at Cofitachequi underwent elaborate burials in which their body cavities were stuffed with freshwater pearls, one of the Spanish officers ordered the bodies cut open and the pearls removed. While perhaps not intentionally designed to terrorize, such desecrations almost certainly had that effect. The Spanish entry into the Southwest also featured the use of terrorizing violence. When the Pueblo of Arenal resisted Spanish incursions in the winter of 1540–1, Francisco Vázquez de Coronado's expedition made an example of it. Spanish officers put the town to the torch, captured the residents as they fled their burning homes, and burned them at the stake.[8] The Pueblos were familiar with some forms of violence, but this was novel.

Neither the de Soto nor the Coronado expedition managed to establish a permanent colony. But the Spanish returned in later years and once again employed terror tactics. The Spanish foundation of St. Augustine is described in detail below, but beyond that particular spasm of violence, Spanish armies were not at all timid about the use of terrorism. In fact, they believed they had divine sanction for doing so, based upon their understanding of the twentieth chapter of Deuteronomy, in which God lays out the rules of war against enemies of Israel: "Thou shalt save nothing alive that breatheth." Sometimes this type of conflict is referred to as a "war of fire and blood." If non-Christians resisted the introduction of Christianity into their homelands by invading armies, then any tactics, no matter how terroristic, were fair, and, by Spanish logic, the blame for the harsh tactics lay with the resisters themselves.[9]

Backers of English colonization recounted the terrorism of the Spanish presence in the Americas with great zeal, primarily because it helped justify their own presence in North America and stressed the difference between Protestant virtue and Spanish cruelty. Richard

Hakluyt, an early, vociferous advocate of English colonization, wrote in his *Discourse of Western Planting* that the Spanish had committed "moste outrageous and more then [sic] Turkishe cruelties" in their invasion of the Americas. They were "without manhodde, emptie of all pitie, behavinge themselves as savage beasts, the slaughterers and murderers of mankind."[10] English armies might use terrorizing tactics on occasion, but they paled in comparison to the atrocities attributable to the Spanish that later became known as the Black Legend. English readers snapped up translated copies of the writings of Bartolomé de Las Casas and others who criticized Spanish mistreatment of indigenous peoples.[11] In reality, English colonization also featured terrorism at the outset. In 1585 at Roanoke, Ralph Lane (a veteran of Elizabethan campaigns in Ireland), became convinced that a massive conspiracy was brewing among the local Algonquian communities. It may well have been, as the English had been ruthless in pressing their hosts for relatively scarce food stores. Lane determined to stop the plot, and so, after gathering many Native leaders together under the pretense of a peace talk, Lane's soldiers ambushed the party and beheaded one of the most powerful men in the region, Wingina (also known as Pemisipan). Relations deteriorated thereafter, and the English abandoned the colony.[12]

In the contest between English and Powhatans in early seventeenth-century Virginia, both sides used the tactics of terror to get their point across. Powhatan himself was no stranger to violence, having used open hostilities in combination with economic pressure and intimidation to rise to rule most of eastern Virginia.[13] The arrival of the English presented a grave threat to American Indians in Virginia, but it provided an opportunity as well. In late 1607, Powhatan's soldiers captured the English military chieftain John Smith, and, after a lengthy tour of Powhatan's dominion, Smith came face to face with the man himself. After consulting his religious advisors, Powhatan raised his war club over John Smith's head. That's when the leader's daughter, Pocahontas, intervened to save, or rather ritually adopt, Smith. The act was a terrifying prelude to Smith's (and by extension the English) adoption into Powhatan's world. The English failed to recognize what had happened and continued to expand, sometimes quite violently, beyond the pale at Jamestown. There are plenty of incidents one could highlight, but George Percy's attack on the town of Paspahegh stands out for the level and type of violence employed. As the English force approached Paspahegh, it fanned out in small groups. After an initial surprise attack routed the defenders, the English beheaded one of their captives, then proceeded to burn the town, including the adjacent cornfields. The English also started to carry the "Queen" and her children back to Jamestown, before they decided it was a mistake to let them live. They executed the children by "throweing them overboard and shoteinge owtt their Braynes in the water," before eventually putting their mother to the sword, according to Percy's account. While Native Virginians were certainly familiar with terror tactics as perpetrators and victims, this level of brutality seems to have been exceedingly rare before the English arrived. By 1622, any slim chance of peaceful coexistence had been exhausted, and Powhatan's successor, his brother Opechancanough, spearheaded an attack against the English who had broken the rules by moving beyond Jamestown. Hundreds of colonists perished, and the Native army employed a provocative form of violence in an effort to teach the English a lesson: some English victims were beheaded or otherwise mutilated after death. The English claimed such attacks were unwarranted and proof of Native savagery and used them to justify an all-out war of their own.[14]

Farther to the north, many elements of this drama were replayed near the first English colony in the land they called New England. From the Plymouth colonists' grave robbing and provocative militia exercises to the mass slaughter of the Pequot War, the religious zealots who founded New England made great use of terroristic violence, and their Native neighbors responded in kind. In 1637, in conflict over trade and land, the New English army and the Pequot army marched against one another – and missed. The English happened upon a large fortified town on the Mystic River. The fact that the main Pequot force was out after the English meant that a disproportionate number of the inhabitants of the town were women, children, and men above military age. In modern terminology, they were non-combatants. The New English set fire to the town, and Captain John Mason estimated that between 600 and 700 Pequots died. Most were burned alive, but the few that managed to escape the flames suffered a systematic genocide at the hands of the English soldiers. Mason wrote that "God was above them, who laughed his Enemies and the Enemies of his People to scorn, making them as a fiery Oven . . . filling the place with dead bodies." William Bradford of Plymouth described the scene thusly:

> It was a fearful sight to see them thus frying in the fire and the streams of blood quenching the same, and horrible was the stink and scent thereof, but the victory seemed a sweet sacrifice, and they gave praise thereof to God, who had wrought so wonderfully for them, thus to enclose their enemies in their hands and given them so speedily a victory over so proud and insulting an enemy.[15]

Native people in southern New England took away several key lessons from the Pequot War and deployed their own military forces to great effect in Metacom's War, also known as King Philip's War, which raged in the mid-1670s. Native soldiers put entire towns to the torch and also demonstrated an affinity for flintlock muskets, which most of the English deemed too expensive to be practical.[16] The violence of the early stages of Metacom's War mirrored that of the Pequot War as Native armies sought to terrorize the English. It seems clear that attacking Wampanoags and their allies sought to destroy the very things on which the English based their identity of themselves as "civilized." Entire families were murdered in their homes, and the attackers destroyed houses and cattle as well. Scores of English who survived the attacks were taken captive, which carried its own brand of terror.[17] Many Native groups took captives – European, Native, and African – in the course of conflict, and the experiences of these captives varied widely. Some found themselves adopted and integrated into Native communities to the extent that they preferred not to return to their homes. Others lived in a state of constant fear, while some were tortured.

Episodes of Europeans committing acts of terror-inducing violence against other Europeans were not unknown in early America, and one of these incidents occurred near the very outset of a permanent European presence in what would eventually become the United States. A small colony of French Protestants in northern Florida was too close to Spanish treasure shipping lanes for that empire's comfort, and the Spanish responded swiftly. After destroying Fort Caroline (near present-day Jacksonville) and over 100 of its inhabitants, Governor Pedro Menéndez de Avilés met two separate forces of French soldiers who had just survived shipwrecks. The first surrendered and tried to negotiate for safe passage back to Fort Caroline, only to have Menéndez announce that

> their fort had been taken and those who had been inside had their throats slit, because they were there without the permission of Your Majesty and because they

were sowing their evil Lutheran sect in these provinces of Your Majesty I made *war with fire and blood* as governor and captain-general of these provinces.[18]

Menéndez put most members of both of these unfortunate parties to death, employing a sort of state-endorsed terrorism that was going out of style in Europe itself, where non-combatants were increasingly understood to be illegitimate targets of warfare.[19] Terror and colonization went hand in hand in North America.

Terror in the fight for empire and the birth of the United States

As Europeans expanded from precarious coastal footholds further and further into the interior of North America, they employed state terrorism to dominate their weaker neighbors when it was possible to do so. At the same time, Native communities also employed tactics that would today be considered terrorist in their attempt to push back against the invaders. When the European superpowers of the day, Great Britain and France, struggled over North America in the Seven Years' War, both relied on Native proxies to strike terror into the hearts of the other side's colonists. It should come as no surprise that when thirteen of Great Britain's mainland colonies declared independence and went to war to win it, both sides used tactics designed to inspire terror. As the war spread into Indian Country, the Continental Army deliberately sought to undermine Native independence through attacks on food supplies and civilian populations.

The main exports of the European colonies are well known: furs, fish, timber and naval stores, grain, as well as more profitable crops such as sugar, indigo, tobacco, and rice. Less well known is the fact that Europeans also exported violence from their settlements into the interior of the North American continent. According to the hoary mythology of the Black Legend, the Spanish were the main perpetrators. A clear-eyed reading of the evidence indicates that all of the European powers were capable of committing acts of state terrorism. To note just a few examples, traders from Charles Town led joint Anglo-Creek expeditions in the first decade of the eighteenth century that captured thousands of Native slaves from the mission towns of Spanish Florida. In New France, the governor expressed fear of Native violence, describing it as "the cruelest war in the world. They are not content to burn the houses, they also burn the prisoners they take, and give them death only after torturing them continually in the most cruel manner possible."[20] Of course, the French also sowed terror on occasion. In the 1720s, France declared war on the Fox, or Mesquakie, Indians, described by colonial officials as "cunning and malignant" and "insolent." The campaign hit home in the 1730s, with the French governor Charles de la Boische de Beauharnois ordering his soldiers to "kill Them without thinking of making a single Prisoner, so as not to leave one of the race alive in the upper Country." In campaigns in what is now Wisconsin and Illinois, the French and their Native allies routinely killed Mesquakie soldiers and their families, enacting a terrifying, though ultimately failed, genocide.[21]

The subject of slavery poses an interesting conundrum for students of the history of terrorism. After all, the European practice of taking and exploiting slaves of color was, at root, an economic endeavor, although one rooted in deeply entrenched notions of racial and civilizational superiority. Slavery was not intended as a form of symbolic violence: victims and audience were one and the same. But in some ways, it makes sense to view the enslavement of thousands of Native Americans and exponentially more Africans and African Americans as a form of terrorism. From the perspective of those caught up in the abominable practice, it surely was terrifying. And within the context of the plantation, the forms of violence that were deployed to maintain slavery were clearly performative. Well-recognized rituals of violence against the few were used to intimidate the many and to reinforce racial hierarchies.

And yet, from the perspective of the people doing the enslaving, slavery entailed a form of violence so banal that it rarely elicited mention in plantation records, save in cases of extraordinary violence. Disrupting the efficient harvest of a valuable staple crop could certainly bring down the wrath of the planter class. Francis Le Jau, employed as an Anglican missionary in Carolina, wrote of one suspected arsonist that the "poor Slavewoman was burnt alive near my door without any positive proof of the Crime she was accused of."[22] Such public violence enacted upon the living bodies of enslaved people, to say nothing of the mutilation of the deceased bodies of slaves or their descendants who faced lynchers' ropes and desecration in future generations, carries such symbolic weight that it is difficult to consider them anything else than a state-sanctioned form of terrorism. Slaves who attempted to run away could face cruel punishments as well. Enslaved women and men who consistently absented themselves from their plantations for short periods of time faced an increasingly violent progression of punishments. They were whipped publicly at first, and subsequent offenses brought brandings, ear croppings, severed Achilles heels, castration for male slaves, and death (with the accompanying loss of property to be reimbursed by the colonial government).[23]

On one memorable occasion in 1739, enslaved Africans, newly arrived from Angola and forced to labor on a public works project near the Stono River in South Carolina, repaid the mundane terror employed by slave owners with a spectacular episode of terrorizing violence of their own. Scholars dispute whether the Stono Rebellion was a long-germinating conspiracy or an impromptu response to ill-treatment, but the violence employed by the slaves clearly had a terror-inducing component. After breaking into a store and seeking food and drink – or perhaps firearms – a group of slaves surprised two men in the store, killed, and then beheaded them, placing the severed heads on the steps of the store. The slave rebels, who eventually numbered between 60 and 100, managed to kill 23 white colonists before meeting a force of colonial militia. The militia dispersed the rebels and captured the leaders. In the aftermath of the Stono Rebellion, Carolina's colonists took trophy heads and, according to one account, set these heads on pikes, perhaps as a warning to future would-be rebels.[24]

In the imperial contest known in Europe as the Seven Years' War and in America as the French and Indian War, the British, the French, and Native Americans from diverse nations used terror tactics to inspire fear and send messages across cultural lines. Tanaghrisson, the so-called Half King, joined Colonel George Washington of Virginia on a mission to reconnoiter Fort Duquesne at the Forks of the Ohio in 1754 and stunned those present when he killed the leader of a French patrol, Joseph Coulon de Villiers de Jumonville. Though the precise motives for killing the officer remain fuzzy, it is possible that Tanaghrisson intended to spark a conflict between imperial powers that could restore some measure of Native autonomy.[25] He succeeded in the former but failed in the latter. The war that ensued between Great Britain and France, the superpowers of the day, quickly spun out of any individual's ability to control, and terrorist violence was present in nearly every chapter of the conflict. Civilian populations wedged between competing armies and associated guerrilla forces fared particularly poorly. The early phases of the war witnessed massive attacks on the western edges of the British colonies of Pennsylvania, Maryland, and Virginia by the French and their Native allies. While in today's conflicts some of this might be described as "collateral damage," there are enough instances, in which the British and their allies specifically sought to target and destroy Indian settlements, and Native people infuriated by squatters and ill-treatment sought to do likewise to English towns, that these should probably be understood as terrorism. Civilians also suffered in the aftermath of the surrender of the garrison that defended Fort William Henry, though not nearly as badly as viewers of the film *Last of the Mohicans* might be led to believe. As the siege of Quebec unfolded in 1759, the British general James Wolfe ordered his soldiers to pillage the farms and Native towns in the area, in part to force the French into battle, in part to terrorize the French and their allies.[26] This is another example of the trickiness of applying modern terminology to early conflicts: Wolfe used terror as a legitimate, to his mind, piece of his tactical toolkit. War erupted in the southern theater in the late 1750s when English colonists surprised Cherokee families, scalped them, and sold the scalps for bounty money. Cherokees protested, but when a delegation of headmen came to Charles Town to talk, they were detained and several were executed. A bitter partisan conflict between Cherokees and backcountry colonists occurred, and both sides committed atrocities.[27]

The racial situation deteriorated in the aftermath of the war as Great Britain struggled to administer vast new territories and, to a lesser extent, tamp down violence between Native people and colonists. Multiple Native nations attacked British forts in the West in a conflict the British laid at the feet of the Ottawa war leader Pontiac, calling it Pontiac's War (he was the nominal mastermind of a much wider-ranging conflict); bloody and terroristic violence ensued. In one of the more closely examined incidents of terrorism associated with this conflict, Jeffrey Amherst, a British general who had himself accused the French of dishonorable tactics, may have ordered the distribution of blankets from smallpox patients to Native Americans near Fort Pitt (on the site of the former Fort Duquesne). If he did not explicitly order it, he certainly would have approved it. Amherst's feelings about Native Americans in general, and those who opposed the British in particular, are well documented: they were "the Vilest Race of Beings that ever Infested the Earth & whose Riddance from it must be Esteemed a Meritorious Act for the Good of Mankind."[28] For their part, groups of Native people surrounding English forts like Pitt often shouted stories designed to terrify garrisons and speed their surrender.[29] In a chilling closing chapter to this already bloody era, a vigilante band in Pennsylvania, the Paxton Boys, carried out a genocidal assault on their Conestoga Indian neighbors in late 1763 and early 1764. The racialized terrorism of their campaign would have long-lasting effects in the mutual mistrust between English colonists and Native people, as well as the fairly violent form of white identity forged by colonists.[30]

As most schoolchildren in the United States know, the American patriots declared their independence in July of 1776. As fewer know, the contest began years before that pivotal date, and both the British and their colonial adversaries resorted to terror-inducing tactics. The Patriot movement in Boston drew strength from groups like the Sons of Liberty. There is little doubt that the British Empire looked upon the Sons of Liberty as a terrorist organization, even though the first uses of the term were still a couple of decades away, as the group endorsed the use of violence, sometimes symbolic and other times more concrete, to bring about their desired political ends. Violence between Patriots and Loyalists predated Lexington Green and continued alongside the official War for Independence. Tarrings and featherings, beatings, and even extra-legal killings were not infrequent occurrences. These acts, while they may have been directed at individuals, were designed to intimidate larger populations, helped to determine who was on which side, and, as they accumulated, undermined the chance for a peaceful rapprochement.[31] Nor was violence limited to persons: in the best known of many instances, Patriots in "Mohawk" disguise destroyed an enormous amount of tea belonging to the British East India Company. General Thomas Gage wrote in 1775 that the colonists were waging a campaign of "daily and indiscriminate invasions upon private property, and with a wantonness of cruelty . . . carry[ing] depredation and distress wherever they turn their steps."[32] The British responded with demonstrations of force designed to cow the colonial population into submitting to Parliament's authority. One result was the onset of open hostilities at the Massachusetts towns of Lexington and Concord in April 1775. Farther to the south, the royal governor of Virginia, Lord Dunmore, believed he had hit upon a tactic that would terrify that colony's insurgent planters into giving up their rebellious schemes. Dunmore offered freedom to any slave of a rebel master who served the British military. Eventually, hundreds of African Americans took up arms against their owners in Dunmore's Ethiopian Regiment. Though not terribly effective militarily (and weakened by disease), the sight of armed slaves fighting for their freedom in the service of the British could not have been more frightening to Virginia's Patriot planters. It also spurred rebellious sentiment. One Patriot noted that "men of all ranks resent the pointing [of] a dagger to their Throats, thru the hands of their slaves."[33]

As the War for Independence unfolded, regular and irregular forces on both sides sought to terrorize their enemies. To remain in the field required food and fuel, and both armies availed themselves of civilian resources at every turn. Both armies also deployed sexual violence, though incidences of rape were likely underreported.[34] In occupied cities and in the backcountry, civilians lived in constant fear of whichever army happened to be operating in the area. The conflict in the southern backcountry was a particularly nasty undertaking, as small groups of partisans, operating only loosely in conjunction with the larger militaries, ravaged their opponents' farms. More regular forces were only slightly better behaved: in the aftermath of the battle at King's Mountain, Major Patrick Ferguson's body was stripped and left where he died as Patriot forces rushed to seize souvenirs. At least one account suggests that enraged colonists took turns urinating on Ferguson's corpse. Banastre Tarleton noted that "mountaineers . . . used every insult and indignity toward the dead body of Major Ferguson." And Tarleton was intimately familiar with insult and indignity. Indeed, "Tarleton's Quarter" was a phrase used to describe the bayoneting of wounded or surrendering soldiers, as Tarleton's dragoons had used that tactic at the Waxhaws massacre in 1780.[35]

It should come as no surprise that some of the most savage instances of violence occurred when the Continental Army moved against its Indian enemies. The Declaration of Independence made reference to "merciless Indian savages whose known rule of warfare, is undistinguished destruction of all ages, sexes and conditions," and while Native people did commit atrocities, this more accurately describes the way the American armies behaved in Indian country. George Washington desired that John Sullivan's army invade Iroquois country in 1779 to "carry the war into the Heart of the Country of the six nations; to cut off their settlements, destroy their next Year's crops and do them every other mischief of which time and circumstances will permit." George Rogers Clark invaded Shawnee country believing that "to excel them in barbarity was and is the only way to make war upon Indians." Clark practiced what he preached when he ordered Indian prisoners bound and tomahawked at Vincennes.[36] American armies committed similar atrocities in repeated invasions of the Cherokee towns over the course of the war.[37] The United States was born in a struggle that involved terror tactics on all sides, and the young nation secured its independence through the use of such tactics against its Native American neighbors.

Terrorism in the early republic and antebellum America

From the era of the American Revolution to the crisis that resulted in the Civil War, terrorism shaped American communities in myriad ways. The United States continued to terrorize the denizens of Indian Country as it pressed western land claims. On the international scene, terror tactics accompanied the American army as it invaded British North America in the 1810s and again when it invaded Mexico in the 1840s. Americans inspired by nativist sentiment terrorized recently arrived immigrants. Enslaved African Americans and their free cousins in northern cities routinely faced terrorism of various kinds. As the sectional crisis heated to a boil in the middle of the nineteenth century, white Americans terrorized each other based on their beliefs regarding slavery, culminating in the spectacular raid on Harpers Ferry in 1859.

The threat of violence was at the very heart of the United States' expansion across North America. Long after the guns had fallen silent at Yorktown in 1781, the US continued to terrorize its Native neighbors. Violence at the edge of the country became mundane, and the pattern was broken only by spasms of large-scale conflict, such as the massive victory a confederacy of nations won over the American army led by Arthur St. Clair in 1791 on the Wabash, or the retaliatory blow struck by the Americans at Fallen Timbers in 1794.[38] By the early nineteenth century, white ideas about race were changing and hardening, and US policy took a harder edge as a result. Though it may not fit a narrow definition of terrorism, Indian removal should probably be seen as a series of episodes of state-sponsored terrorism.[39] While an evenhanded rendering of the violence of the early nineteenth century must admit that Native American fighters took a heavy toll, as at Fort Mims in August in 1813, the end result was clear and lopsided.[40] The United States carried out a military and administrative campaign that sought to ethnically cleanse the lands east of the Mississippi and very nearly succeeded. The architects of this campaign would have found the notion that there was any such thing as an Indian civilian or non-combatant laughable – not only were they the heirs of a long tradition of perceived European superiority, they were of the mind that Providence had set aside all of North America for their unique blend of Protestantism, capitalism, and democracy. Examples such as the Cherokee removal of 1838 and 1839, which cost that southeastern nation approximately one-quarter of its population, are certainly stark and well known, but it is sometimes difficult for citizens of the modern United States to fully comprehend the havoc wrought on Indian communities by the republic in its early years.[41] California's Native communities, for instance, suffered a perfect storm of racist violence when their lands came under the purview of the United States by the terms of the Treaty of Guadalupe Hidalgo in 1848. Regular forces and vigilantes alike committed atrocity after atrocity in their drive to exterminate California's Indians. The *Yreka Herald* put it succinctly in 1853: "Extermination is no longer a question of time – the time has arrived, the work has commenced, and let the first man that says treaty or peace be regarded as a traitor."[42] The US campaign of terror had the desired effect of securing the nation's claims to a wide swath of North America by the middle of the nineteenth century. Consolidation of American rule over the Great Plains would proceed apace in the years after the Civil War.

When the United States went to war against other imperial powers in the first half of the nineteenth century, it suffered opponents' terror tactics but certainly employed its own as well. American forces invaded British North America in 1813, and while General Henry Dearborn decried some of his soldiers' more outlandish actions in the campaign, his American army inflicted a great deal of damage on targets of questionable military worth, such as civilian homes and abandoned governmental buildings in the burning of York (present-day Toronto). The next year, a British force returned the favor by burning Washington.[43] Something approaching state terror – or perhaps what are identified by today's international law as war crimes – could play an even larger role when invading American armies believed themselves racially superior to their foes. Such was the case when the United States went to war against Mexico on dubious grounds in 1846. The regular army fought reasonably honorably against Mexican regulars, but the volunteers that fought alongside it did nothing of the sort, choosing to wage a war that featured sexual violence against Mexican women, confiscation of civilian property, and the too-frequent destruction of non-combatants.[44]

Mob violence regularly struck fear into marginalized populations in antebellum America, and groups as varied as Irish immigrants, Mormons, and free people of color found themselves targeted by mobs in the first half of the nineteenth century. Irish people had been migrating to the United States since before there had been a United States, but famine and British imperialism swelled their ranks in the 1840s, and they came to the States in ever larger numbers.[45] Native-born Protestant whites – who feared economic competition, mistrusted Irish culture, and hated Catholicism passionately – tried to terrorize the Irish into submission. In one striking incident at Kensington, outside of Philadelphia, a group of Protestants, believing the Protestant flavor of their public schools to be in danger, took to the streets in a series of "Bible Riots" in 1844. Angry crowds descended in force upon local Catholic institutions and people, reflecting the notion that the very foundation of the republic was at risk: "if the BIBLE should be suppressed and liberty of conscience destroyed . . . the walls of our glorious Republic would be thrown down, and the foot of Roman power be set upon our sons, and our daughters become subject to the control of the Papal priests." In all, the fighting left a handful dead and dozens more wounded.[46] Latter-day Saints faced persecution almost from the moment the sect came into being, and anti-Mormon sentiment, as well as terrorizing violence, drove Joseph Smith and his followers from upstate New York to Missouri and eventually to Nauvoo, Illinois, where they attempted to set up their own version of a godly community. Mob violence ensued, and in June 1844, Smith and his brother Hirum were lynched by anti-Mormons. Smith's successor, Brigham Young, led the Mormons to the shores of the Great Salt Lake.[47] American mobs seem to have reserved special fury for free communities of color. African American freedom in northern cities was fragile and imperfect, and free blacks tended to exist at the margins in poor-paying jobs with little security. These tenuous conditions worsened at various points in the nineteenth century, as mobs vented their racialized rage in countless incidents targeting black schools, churches, and other institutions.[48]

American slaves continued to face the constant terrorism of the master class prior to the coming of civil war. The fact that there were comparatively few large-scale slave revolts should not be taken to mean that slaves were complacent and content in their bondage. Rather, it speaks to the demographic realities that confronted the victims of slavery. There were plenty of ways to cope with enslavement and resist it apart from taking up arms.

Of course, few events inspired terror among southern whites more than the actual occurrence of rebellion, and one name was synonymous with the practice: Nat Turner. Nat was born in southern Virginia in 1800 and from a young age demonstrated extraordinary gifts. As a young man, he described events that preceded his birth and also claimed to have visions of black and white spirits fighting in the sky. By the 1830s, he had come to interpret these signs to mean that he had been specially chosen to lead an uprising against slavery: "by signs in the heavens . . . it would make known to me when I should commence the great work . . . . I should arise and prepare myself and slay my enemies with their own weapons." In the late summer of 1831, Nat and a dedicated band of followers struck terror into whites in Virginia (and beyond) as they moved from plantation to plantation, killing nearly sixty people. Nat was eventually apprehended and executed, but not before local whites, wielding their own brand of terrorism, captured alleged rebels, beheaded them, and placed their severed heads on pikes along the road, an action that hearkened back to prior episodes of corpse mutilation designed to terrify and send a message.[49]

The institution of slavery as practiced in the United States clearly carried within it the potential for terroristic violence in a variety of contexts, as described earlier. What may be a bit more surprising is the ferocity with which white people attacked each other over their views on the subject. Some of these white actors were intimately connected to the struggle to free African Americans or to the desire to keep them in bondage, while others fought for or against slavery in a more abstract sense. Indeed, one recent account has described the long-simmering conflict that flared wherever slavery and freedom abutted one another as a "border war." Each side of this border war employed tactics designed to terrorize its opponents.[50] Attempts to recapture fugitive slaves and browbeat those who harbored them often ended in violence. Such was the case at Christiana, Pennsylvania, in 1851. Anti-abolitionist mobs were especially prone to violence: witness the 1837 death of the abolitionist newspaper editor Elijah Lovejoy in Alton, Illinois. Finally, in the 1850s, a nasty guerrilla war took shape in Kansas, as pro- and anti-slavery territorial governments and their partisans skirmished throughout the middle of that decade. One of the anti-slavery heroes of that particular contest was John Brown, a man who fits most definitions of terrorism quite well. It also bears mentioning that the causes he adopted, the social equality of the races and the destruction of slavery, are ones that are more or less universally applauded today. Brown came to understand that slavery was violence, even terrorism, at its core, and he dedicated his life to its destruction. His tactics, borrowed from Toussaint L'Ouverture and other slave rebels, including Nat Turner, were explicitly aimed at striking terror into the supporters of slavery. At Potawattomie Creek in 1856, Brown directed the murder of pro-slavery settlers, ostensibly as repayment for the beating of Charles Sumner by Preston Brooks on the floor of the Senate earlier that year. After going into hiding and raising an army to "carry the war into Africa," as he put it, by invading the slaveholding South, Brown and a biracial strike force raided the federal arsenal at Harpers Ferry, Virginia, intending to distribute the captured arms to slaves, thus enabling them to liberate themselves in a sort of rolling revolution. Though Brown may have failed to spark the massive slave uprising he had envisioned, his actions and his performance at trial in 1859 certainly succeeded in terrorizing white southerners. Brown expressed no regret for his actions and reminded the jury, as well as the riveted, news-hungry American republic, that "had I so interfered in behalf of the rich, the powerful, the intelligent, the so-called great . . . every man in this court would have deemed it an act worthy of reward rather than punishment." (For more on John Brown and particularly his legacy, see Chapter 10 by R. Blakeslee Gilpin in this volume.) There is also no small irony that whereas in 1859, Brown was executed as a traitor to Virginia for attempting to liberate slaves, the federal government itself, spurred by secession and war, would encourage slave rebellion in the rebellious states and act as a liberating force by late 1862 and early 1863.[51]

Terrorism, though perhaps not known by that particular term, has deep roots in American history. Indigenous communities used terror tactics against each other before Europeans ever arrived. Once Europeans did arrive, they employed terror tactics against each other and their Native hosts. European colonies established their dominance using terror, and the struggles for empire and independence of the mid- to late-eighteenth century unleashed a bewildering array of violent possibilities. The newly established American republic lashed out at neighbors north, south, and west as it secured its dominion over much of North America. Using terror-inducing tactics, forces within the United States threatened to pull the country apart at the seams in the conflict that prefigured the Civil War.

Reflecting on the violence that shaped early American history can be a sobering experience, but it is necessary – not just as a corrective to jingoist versions of the past, but because it moves us toward a fuller, more accurate rendering of that past. And by placing terrorisms past in the proper historical context, we can begin to see our own violent times more clearly. From this perspective, terrorism is not an aberration or something that al-Qaeda imported on September 11, 2001, but rather a crucial aspect of American history from the very beginning.

Notes

1 For more on the problem of naming acts of terrorism before "terrorism" was named, see Chapter 4 by Steven Isaac in this volume.
2 Robert F. Berkhofer, Jr., *The White Man's Indian: Images of the American Indian from Columbus to the Present* (New York: Vintage Books, 1979).
3 Stephen A. LeBlanc, *Warfare in the Prehistoric Southwest* (Salt Lake City: University of Utah Press, 2007).
4 Timothy Pauketat, *Ancient Cahokia and the Mississippians* (Cambridge: Cambridge University Press, 2004); and Pauketat, *Cahokia: Ancient America's Great City on the Mississippi* (New York: Penguin Books, 2009).
5 Colin Calloway, *One Vast Winter Count: The Native American West before Lewis and Clark* (Lincoln: University of Nebraska Press, 2003).
6 Robbie Ethridge, *From Chicaza to Chickasaw: The European and the Transformation of the Mississippian World, 1540–1715* (Chapel Hill: University of North Carolina Press, 2010).
7 Matthew Jennings, *New Worlds of Violence: Cultures and Conquests in the Early American Southeast* (Knoxville: University of Tennessee Press, 2011); and Charles Hudson, *Knights of Spain, Warriors of the Sun: Hernando de Soto and the South's Ancient Chiefdoms* (Athens: University of Georgia Press, 1997).
8 David Weber, *The Spanish Frontier in North America* (New Haven, CT: Yale University Press, 1992).
9 Patricia Seed, *Ceremonies of Possession in Europe's Conquest of the New World: 1492–1640* (Cambridge: Cambridge University Press, 1995), 69–99. Seed discusses the *Requirimiento*, the legal document which justified violence and blamed it on Native people, in great detail.
10 Richard Hakluyt, *Discourse of Western Planting*, ed. David B. Quinn and Alison M. Quinn (London: Hakluyt Society, 1993), 59.
11 Las Casas's work was published in English as early as 1583 under the title *The Spanish Colonie*. See also William S. Maltby, *The Black Legend in England: The Development of Anti-Spanish Sentiment, 1580–1660* (Durham, NC: Duke University Press, 1971).
12 Michael Leroy Oberg, *The Head in Edward Nugent's Hand: Roanoke's Forgotten Indians* (Philadelphia: University of Pennsylvania Press, 2008).
13 "Powhatan" here refers to the specific leader who was in power in eastern Virginia at the time the English arrived. It can also be used, sometimes in plural, to describe the various peoples ruled by Powhatan.

14 Frederic Gleach, *Powhatan's World and Colonial Virginia: A Conflict of Cultures* (Lincoln: University of Nebraska Press, 1997). George Percy's account, *A Trewe Relacyon* . . ., appears in Edward Wright Haile, ed., *Jamestown Narratives: Eyewitness Accounts of the Virginia Colony* (Champlain, VA: Roundhouse, 1998). The excerpt quoted appears in James Horn, ed., *Captain John Smith: Writings with Other Narratives of Roanoke, Jamestown and the First English Settlement of America* (New York: Library of America, 2007), 1104.
15 Quotations appear in Alfred Cave, *The Pequot War* (Amherst: University of Massachusetts Press, 1996) 151, 152.
16 Patrick Malone, *The Skulking Way of War: Technology and Tactics among the New England Indians* (Lanham, MD: Madison Books, [1991] 2000).
17 Jill Lepore, *The Name of War: King Philip's War and the Origins of American Identity* (New York: Alfred A. Knopf, 1998).
18 Pedro Menéndez de Avilés, *Cartas Sobre la Florida, 1555–1574*, ed. Juan Carlos Mercado (Madrid: Iberoamericana, 2002), 143, quoted in Matthew Jennings, *New Worlds of Violence*, 74 (emphasis added); and John McGrath, *The French in Early Florida: In the Eye of the Hurricane* (Gainesville: University Press of Florida, 2000).
19 For more on medieval Europe's shifting understanding of the "rules of war," the role of non-combatants, and the protections that should be afforded them, see Chapter 4 by Steven Isaac in this volume.
20 Quoted in Alan Taylor, *American Colonies* (New York: Viking Penguin, 2001), 370.
21 Quoted in Calloway, *One Vast Winter Count*, 322, 324.
22 Francis Le Jau, *The Carolina Chronicle of Doctor Francis Le Jau, 1706–1717* (Berkeley and Los Angeles: University of California Press, 1956), 55. See also Jennings, *New Worlds of Violence*, 158–9.
23 A. Leon Higginbotham, Jr., *In the Matter of Color: Race and the Americans Legal Process, the Colonial Period* (Oxford: Oxford University Press, 1978), 167. See also Thomas Cooper and David J. McCord, eds., *Statutes at Large of Carolina* (Columbia, SC, 1840), 7:352.
24 Peter Charles Hoffer, *Cry Liberty: The Great Stono River Slave Rebellion of 1739* (New York: Oxford University Press, 2012), esp. 82, note 26; and James Taylor Carson, *Making an Atlantic World: Circles, Paths, and Stories from the Colonial South* (Knoxville: University of Tennessee Press, 2007), 113–14.
25 Fred Anderson, *Crucible of War: The Seven Years' War and the Fate of Empire in British North America, 1754–1766* (New York: A. A. Knopf, 2000), 56–8.
26 Daniel Marston, *The Seven Years' War* (New York: Osprey Publishing, 2001), 83.
27 John Oliphant, *Peace and War on the Anglo-Cherokee Frontier, 1756–63* (Baton Rouge: Louisiana State University Press, 2001).
28 Quoted in Colin Calloway, *The Scratch of a Pen: 1763 and the Transformation of North America* (New York: Oxford University Press, 2006), 73.
29 Gregory Evans Dowd, *War Under Heaven: Pontiac, the Indian Nations, and the British Empire* (Baltimore, MD: Johns Hopkins University Press, 2002), esp. 128–30.
30 Kevin Kenny, *Peaceable Kingdom Lost: The Paxton Boys and the Destruction of William Penn's Holy Experiment* (New York: Oxford University Press, 2009); and Peter Silver, *Our Savage Neighbors: How Indian War Transformed Early America* (New York: W. W. Norton, 2008), esp. 177–82.
31 Thanks to Randall D. Law for helping to clarify this point.
32 Quoted in T. H. Breen, *American Insurgents, American Patriots: The Revolution of the People* (New York: Hill and Wang, 2010), 13–14.
33 Quoted in Douglas R. Egerton, *Death or Liberty: African Americans and Revolutionary America* (New York: Oxford University Press, 2009), 73.
34 Carol Berkin, *Revolutionary Mothers: Women in the Struggle for America's Independence* (New York: Vintage, 2005), 38–42.
35 Walter Edgar, *Partisans and Redcoats: The Southern Conflict that Turned the Tide of the American Revolution* (New York: Harper Perennial, 2003), 55–6; quoted material from 119.
36 Colin Calloway, *The American Revolution in Indian Country: Crisis and Diversity in Native American Communities* (Cambridge: Cambridge University Press, 1995), quoted material from 48 and 51.
37 Tyler Boulware, *Deconstructing the Cherokee Nation: Town, Region and Nation among Eighteenth-Century Cherokees* (Gainesville: University Press of Florida, 2011), 152–77.

38 Frederick Hoxie, Ronald Hoffman, and Peter J. Albert, eds., *Native Americans and the Early Republic* (Charlottesville: University Press of Virginia, 1999).
39 Ronald N. Satz, *American Indian Policy in the Jacksonian Era* (Norman: University of Oklahoma Press, 1975).
40 Gregory A. Waselkov, *A Conquering Spirit: Fort Mims and the Redstick War of 1813–1814* (Tuscaloosa: University of Alabama Press, 2006); and Jeremy Black, *Fighting for America: The Struggle for Mastery in North America, 1519–1871* (Bloomington: Indiana University Press, 2011), 160–229.
41 Theda Perdue and Michael D. Green, *The Cherokee Nation and the Trail of Tears* (New York: Penguin Books, 2008).
42 Quoted in James J. Rawls, *Indians of California: The Changing Image* (Norman: University of Oklahoma Press, 1984), 180.
43 J. C. A. Stagg, *The War of 1812: Conflict for a Continent* (Cambridge: Cambridge University Press, 2012).
44 Paul Foos, *A Short, Offhand, Killing Affair: Soldiers and Social Conflict during the Mexican–American War* (Chapel Hill: University of North Carolina Press, 2002); and Timothy J. Henderson, *A Glorious Defeat: Mexico and its War with the United States* (New York: Hill and Wang, 2008).
45 Kerby A. Miller, *Immigrants and Exiles: Ireland and the Irish Exodus to North America* (New York: Oxford University Press, 1985).
46 Katie Oxx, *The Nativist Movement in America: Religious Conflict in the Nineteenth Century* (New York: Routledge, 2013). Quoted material appears on 133.
47 Kenneth Winn, *Exiles in a Land of Liberty: Mormons in America, 1830–1846* (Chapel Hill: University of North Carolina Press, 1989), 208–27.
48 James Oliver Horton and Lois Horton, *In Hope of Liberty: Culture, Community, and Protest among Northern Free Blacks, 1700–1860* (New York: Oxford University Press, 1997), esp. 163–4.
49 Kenneth Greenberg, ed., *The Confessions of Nat Turner and Related Documents* (Boston, MA: Bedford/St. Martin's, 1996), quotation from 48; see also Greenberg, ed., *Nat Turner: A Slave Rebellion in History and Memory* (New York: Oxford University Press, 2003), esp. 79–102.
50 Stanley Harrold, *Border War: Fighting Over Slavery before the Civil War* (Chapel Hill: University of North Carolina Press, 2010).
51 Robert McGlone, *John Brown's War Against Slavery* (Cambridge: Cambridge University Press, 2009); Brian McGinty, *John Brown's Trial* (Cambridge, MA: Harvard University Press, 2009); and Jonathan Earle, *John Brown's Raid on Harpers Ferry: A Brief History with Documents* (Boston, MA: Bedford/St. Martin's, 2008), trial transcript quoted on 86–7.

Further reading

Breen, T. H. *American Insurgents, American Patriots: The Revolution of the People:* New York: Hill and Wang, 2010.

Ethridge, Robbie. *From Chicaza to Chickasaw: The European Invasion and the Transformation of the Mississippian World, 1540–1715*. Chapel Hill: University of North Carolina Press, 2010.

Fellman, Michael. *In the Name of God and Country: Reconsidering Terrorism in American History*. New Haven, CT: Yale University Press, 2010.

Greenberg, Kenneth, ed. *Nat Turner: A Slave Rebellion in History and Memory*. New York: Oxford University Press, 2003.

Jennings, Matthew. *New Worlds of Violence: Cultures and Conquests in the Early American Southeast*. Knoxville: University of Tennessee Press, 2011.

McGlone, Robert E. *John Brown's War against Slavery*. Cambridge: Cambridge University Press, 2009.

Richter, Daniel K. *Before the Revolution: America's Ancient Pasts*. Cambridge, MA: Harvard University Press, 2011.

Silver, Peter. *Our Savage Neighbors: How Indian War Transformed Early America*. New York: W. W. Norton, 2008.

Slotkin, Richard. *Regeneration through Violence: The Mythology of the American Frontier, 1600–1860*. Middletown, CT: Wesleyan University Press, 1973.

7

ENTANGLED TERRORISMS IN LATE IMPERIAL RUSSIA

Martin A. Miller

The problem of terrorism in historical perspective

In 1908, at the same time that Russia was engulfed with terrorisms from above and below, the British writer G. K. Chesterton published his novel *The Man Who was Thursday*. The story concerns a police detective, Gabriel Syme, who poses as an anarchist in order to gain entrance to an underground group in London so as to gather intelligence. In the course of the narrative, he learns that five of the six members of the circle are all police agents spying unwittingly on one another instead of combating the bomb threats of the real anarchists.[1]

That same year, in Russia, Evno Azef was at the height of his influence as a double agent working for the government's national police force, the Okhrana, while also providing state information to his comrades in the Combat Organization of the Socialist Revolutionary Party. More than once he confronted a dilemma that many insurgents have faced in similar situations of being entangled simultaneously in both of the warring arenas of political violence. In 1904, to take one glaring episode, he was charged by the Combat Organization to head the group assigned to assassinate the current Okhrana chief, Vyacheslav von Plehve. Azef's stark choice was either to carry out the mission to murder his own boss in order to remain embedded in the underground or to blow his cover and face being revealed as a police informant by refusing.

I mention these two examples, one fictional and the other factual, because they vividly illustrate one of the most important characteristics of the phenomenon we call terrorism, namely its entanglement of defenders and antagonists of the state. This paradigm, however, has not been subject to serious inquiry in spite of the rich literature on the general subject. There have been essentially two approaches to the study of terrorism in Russian and Soviet history. Most frequently, terrorism is confined to the radical underground, from Dmitry Karakozov's attempt on Emperor Alexander II onward through the upheavals of 1905 and 1917.[2] In this perspective, the state is often understood as a responder to the violence from below when it orders harsh measures of repression, which are sometimes referred to as justifiable counter-terrorism. Those historians who have emphasized the tsarist regime's brutal use of force by the army, police, and security services represent the other model.[3] Rarely, however, do they use the term "terrorist" to designate the violence of the imperial era, in contrast to its accepted use in reference to the state violence of the Stalin years, where it has been conjoined with the concept of totalitarianism.[4]

I am proposing a more integrated approach to the problem of what I consider the entangled nature of Russian terrorism in the late imperial era. This involves recognizing that, in reality, both of these elements – the state and its revolutionary competitors –

constitute the phenomenon of terrorism.[5] As I shall demonstrate in this chapter, the police at both the national and provincial levels and the insurgent organizations operating throughout the country were locked in an ambivalent embrace that fueled the very violence that each proclaimed it was dedicated to abolishing. For the government, the problem was in finding forceful ways to end the violence from below that threatened its authority. For the radicals in the underground, the issue was how to generate sufficient force to bring an end to the violence of the state.

Both sides considered the other as illegitimate and immoral. Though entirely hostile to one another, both the police and the revolutionaries employed spies, often acting as double agents in the manner dramatized by Azef, whose tasks were not only to gather intelligence about planned acts of violence but also, if so ordered, to provoke the other side into initiating those very actions. On both sides of the barricades, civilian casualties were accepted as necessary and unavoidable collateral damage in the mutually antagonistic struggle for strategic success. As long as neither wished to recognize the other in order to open some level of dialogue, these violent acts would speak in lieu of negotiated words.

Further, they mirrored one another by creating a similar culture within their respective redoubts. Both learned to communicate in coded languages that ended up often in the hands of the other side thanks to the skills of the infiltrators. Both honed their expertise in deceit and subterfuge to the point where it seemed they could no longer exercise independent judgment apart from their rigid ideological commitments. Equally noteworthy is the astonishing resemblance their manuals, manifestos, and policy statements had with one another, with the application of violence uppermost in their calculations to gain ultimate victory.[6]

With respect to the many efforts scholars have made at defining terrorism, my own contribution to this varied discourse emerges from the features described above. First, there must be a constant reliance on the use of violence to achieve certain proclaimed political objectives. Second, these tactics of violence involve an invasive assault either against sectors of the civilian population when utilized by authoritarian governments or against representatives of the state when employed by clandestine, insurgent groups operating within the confines of the nation-state or across national borders. Third, the acts of violence must be repeated and, on occasion, expanded in their brutality in order to create a pervasive atmosphere of fear. The violence is justified, whether from above or below, by deeply held convictions that posit an unacceptable, unjust, and illegitimate present that must be replaced by a more benign future order. To reach this new order, large numbers of targeted people designated as threatening must be eliminated by violence.[7]

The origins of political violence in Russia

Long before there were menacing insurgent movements within Russia seeking to violently undermine the government, the state's security forces had already established a pattern of terrorizing their own subjects. Perhaps the earliest institutional example of this tendency was the Oprichnina established by Ivan IV in the mid-sixteenth century, whose victims ranged from clerics to clans, and from formerly trusted government advisors to entire towns suspected of treasonous activities.[8]

This tradition of instilling fear and utilizing violence against suspected opponents of the regime intensified in the early eighteenth century with Peter the Great's endorsement of his security force, the Preobrazhensky Prikaz, which functioned in tandem with the Secret

Chancellery (*Tainaia kantseliariia*) relied on earlier by his father, Tsar Aleksei.[9] From this point on, as the imperial Russian nation-state was coalescing, there was not a single ruler who felt sufficiently secure to rule without a security force commissioned to employ violence.

The emergence of a genuine political opposition – apart from either competing court factions or the Cossack–peasant alliances that fueled occasional mass violence mainly in the rural provinces – became undeniably visible during the era of the French Revolution, when the modern nation-state made its debut. The creation of a democratic republic in France in 1792 and its evolution into a state-declared government of terror devoted to extinguishing its royalist enemies stirred mortal fears within the courts of Europe and Russia. Divine right as the legitimate foundation of government had now been successfully challenged by the coming to power of a regime passionately committed to the concept of popular sovereignty.[10]

This Enlightenment-inspired notion brought into the political arena the reality that governments had responsibilities toward their citizens that kings did not. More importantly, citizens had rights of their own since they, not the ruler, were now sovereign. The consequence of this new polity was that, theoretically at least, any citizen had the right to propose his political agenda. The underlying and largely unforeseen problems, however, were whether words or deeds were to be used in realizing these proposals and to what ends. It soon became clear that tactics of violence were to be accepted from the start by both the state in the hands of Maximilien Robespierre and Louis-Antoine Saint-Just, and its competitors within the Republic, including Fillipo Buonarroti, Gracchus Babeuf, and Jacques-René Hébert.

In Russia during the first quarter of the nineteenth century, the fear of similar challenges to the legitimacy of the autocratic regime motivated the government to enhance its security forces. In spite of the fact that the Ministry of Police gathered hundreds of dossiers with potentially damaging information, none of its officials were able to anticipate the most threatening organizations that were operating secretly at the time, namely the Northern and Southern Societies, which eventually generated the first violent political rebellion that was neither a peasant uprising nor a court conspiracy. To be sure, there were reports on the plans of these two organizations that found their way into the hands of the security chiefs, including General Alexander Benckendorff, who was at this moment the chief of staff of the Corps of the Imperial Guards, yet another security agency. Spies even described these groups as possessing "revolutionary intentions," but it seems that what was being planned was too fantastic for the authorities to take seriously enough to act on in time.[11]

Information about possible political violence from below was conveyed directly to Alexander I from an English industrialist indicating that the Southern Society was intent not only on provoking an overthrow of the regime but also planned "to exterminate the entire royal family."[12] The warning was accurate. Pavel Pestel, leader of the Southern Society and admirer of Robespierre's radical politics, had made plans for a post-imperial regime that included an assassination squad he called his *garde perdue* whose mission was to murder the entire Romanov family. Moreover, he favored a permanent security force modeled loosely on Robespierre's protective unit for the Committee of Public Safety to enforce the new republic's legitimacy. Because of the failure of the Northern Society to take advantage of the power vacuum created by the death of Alexander I during the violent confrontation over the succession in the capital on December 14, 1825, none of this terror was to be realized – at least, not at this time. The intentionality was, nonetheless, a chilling harbinger of the future.[13] Knowledge about the two societies, buried by censorship during Nicholas I's reign, would surface decades later as the insurgent–inspirational movement known historically as the Decembrists.

Once safely ensconced on the throne, Nicholas I made clear his acknowledgment of the danger to the legitimacy of the imperial regime that the Decembrists represented. "The revolution is at the doors of Russia," he thundered in a proclamation soon after his accession, "but it shall not effect an entry, I swear, as long as I am Emperor by the Grace of God."[14] His wrath was realized in edicts permitting aggressive judicial punishments for the perpetrators of sedition – the execution of five of the leaders of the two societies, and the torture and exile of hundreds of supporters who were forced to walk to their prison camps in Siberia where they would spend the rest of their lives reflecting, Nicholas hoped, on their immoral acts.

To ensure that the government was properly protected against any further manifestations of political rebellion, Nicholas moved quickly to create a more extensive security bureaucracy. Benckendorff is credited with formulating the new plan centralizing the entire police force under government control, the goal of which was to instill sufficient fear in educated society to forestall any surviving radicalism. Nicholas accepted the plan, creating the Third Section of his Majesty's Imperial Chancellery with Benckendorff as chief. The Third Section, as it became known, was given wide latitude in conducting surveillance, gathering intelligence from local police offices through hired spies, making arrests, and, when so ordered, punishing detained political suspects.

Terrorism, whether carried out by the state or by its opponents, must have enemies to function. When they do not exist, they can be invented. The Third Section's inability to locate political conspiracies under the influence of the Decembrists compelled its agents to turn to other sectors of society. One of Benckendorff's directives in setting up his bureau recognized the importance of potential violence implied in the publication of dangerous words in addition to the surveillance and spying necessary to uncover threatening deeds. He made clear that among the police's important functions was the suppression of any publication advocating criticism of the regime. Toward this end, he set up the country's largest censorship division to date, responsible for the "perlustration" of suspicious correspondence in the mails as well as for the examination and categorization of all published material, whether issued in Russia or imported from abroad.

In response, thousands of people with no official connection to the police were falling over themselves to provide denunciations of alleged political machinations. Most were taken seriously but nonetheless proved scurrilous. This spontaneous activity was evidence, however, of something else, namely, the widespread acceptance in the society at large of one's patriotic duty to support the government's claims of public danger.[15]

The purpose of Benckendorff's protocols for the Third Section was to maintain public order and regime loyalty by establishing an atmosphere of fear within the "dangerous" sectors of educated society. To ensure this situation, the Third Section declared open warfare on editors and writers suspected of fomenting opinions that strayed outside the boundaries of "Orthodoxy, Autocracy and Nationality," the cornerstones of Nicholas I's Official Nationality policy. That said, not everyone in the division was in agreement. M. Ya. von Vock, who had once headed an earlier version of the security chancellery and was now working directly under Benckendorff, thought the plan to target the literary community might backfire and might even prove to be completely counter-productive if the public found the enhanced tactics of surveillance, censorship, and arrest unwarranted. He was concerned that the repressive censorship could provoke the very rebellion it was committed to preventing.[16]

As it happened, the truly serious political challenges to the regime's legitimacy during Nicholas I's reign occurred in occupied Poland in 1830–1. Benckendorff received permission to dispatch agents to Warsaw to monitor discontent in the aftermath of that revolt, though they were apparently taken largely by surprise when the next uprising broke out there in 1848. Closer to its St. Petersburg headquarters, a small group called the Kritsky circle distributed pamphlets and proclamations denouncing the Romanovs. They also announced their intentions to assassinate the ruling family, as Pestel had earlier intended. An agent provocateur working for the police who managed to gain access to the circle discovered their plans. Following their arrest and a search of the meeting site, the group was found to be stashing weapons in preparation for their violent attacks. One of the members of the circle also possessed in his pocket at the time of his arrest a broadside titled "Liberty and Death to Tyranny."[17] Their intentions were certainly clear, even if the chances of achieving their goals were quite remote.

The police devoted considerable attention throughout Nicholas' reign to harassing, restricting, and exiling writers, whom they saw as a direct threat by virtue of their ability to disseminate sedition via literature. Few were spared direct encounters with the Third Section's agents. The country's most prominent poet Alexander Pushkin as well as the writers Mikhail Lermontov, Ivan Turgenev, Nikolai Gogol, and Fyodor Dostoevsky all suffered the punishing terror of the police in varying degrees. In addition, the philosopher Peter Chaadaev was arrested and placed in an insane asylum for daring to publish an essay, blandly titled "A Philosophical Letter," in which he criticized Russia for having no independent history apart from the West and attacked the values and practices of the Orthodox Church. Nikolai Nadezhdin, the editor of *The Telescope*, where Chaadaev's article appeared, was sentenced to exile in Siberia and his paper permanently banned. Another paper, *The Moscow Telegraph*, was also shut down when its editor, Nikolai Polevoi, dared to publish a critique of a crudely patriotic play that happened to be the emperor's favorite drama. The future socialist writer and editor Alexander Herzen, then a student at Moscow University, was arrested and sentenced to confinement in Viatka near the Ural Mountains. The charges against him are more suggestive of the insecurity of the government than they were of identifying criminal acts. He and other students were blamed for publicizing songs critical of the emperor as well as being in the vicinity of suspicious fires that were raging on the university grounds in 1834. After being interrogated by Benckendorff himself, Herzen claimed in his memoir that, far from being intimidated into renouncing his critical ideas, he felt driven to further engage with political radicalism.[18]

The year 1848 in Russia was by no means the transformative force that it was in Europe, but the events were threatening enough for Nicholas I to further expand his security operations. Fearful of spillover from the rebellious overthrow of monarchies across the continent that occurred that year, Nicholas I focused his attention on investigative reports about a socialist-oriented circle in the capital that held meetings at the apartment of a low-level Foreign Ministry official, Mikhail Petrashevsky. They were primarily concerned with searching for ways to introduce judicial reform measures and serf emancipation, and some members possessed censored French socialist works. With the help of police undercover agents, the circle was exposed. Nicholas overreacted and had the entire circle arrested in April and kept in solitary confinement for almost eight months in the dungeons of the Peter and Paul Fortress prior to being sentenced to execution by firing squad. The sentence was altered to Siberian exile at the last minute, as famously recorded by one of the members, a young, aspiring writer named Fyodor Dostoevsky.[19]

The outbreak of political violence

The era of political violence began in earnest during the succeeding reign. Structurally, the scenario was even established before Alexander II came to the throne. As we have seen, the police had already set up the mechanisms of repression, and the underground was now aggressively coalescing as both sides moved closer toward a collision course, one that triggered the outbreak of a sustained period of terrorism.

The regime's insecurity under the new monarch, Alexander II, was visible soon after his coronation in 1856. After acknowledging defeat in the Crimean War, Alexander II began a multi-pronged reform policy for his administration. Simply put, he was committed to figuring out how to emancipate Russia's huge serf population while ensuring a peaceful process acceptable to both the landowning class, who stood to lose their customary labor, and the peasants themselves, whose impoverished lives would hardly be improved. He had to avoid, in other words, the potential violence of a gentry Fronde, on the one hand, and peasant upheavals, on the other. To accomplish this delicate political strategy, a crackdown on provocative criticism was necessary.

Toward this end, Alexander appointed Vasily Dolgorukov in 1856 to command the Third Section's bureaucracy. During the next few years, as the emperor began enacting his plans for emancipating the enormous serf population, Dolgorukov's field agents were reporting on peasant disturbances in many provincial areas, some of which had turned into violent events. The agents also uncovered and sent Dolgorukov copies of pamphlets and broadsides supporting peasant aspirations for land and emancipation.

Investigations provided evidence that these inflammatory and illegal publications originated in London at the radical Russian language press run by Herzen, now living in permanent exile there. Copies of Herzen's paper, *The Bell* (*Kolokol*), were discovered in police searches from Kiev to Moscow and St. Petersburg. Most issues contained information on censored news within Russia, particularly peasant rebellions and corruption in the court, much of it based on reliable information brought to him in London by travelers from Russia. Merely being in possession of an issue during a police raid resulted in a jail sentence.[20]

Police attention also focused on the influence among the emerging urban intelligentsia of a literary journal, *The Contemporary* (*Sovremennik*). The editors, Nikolai Chernyshevsky and Nikolai Dobroliubov, were (correctly as it happened) suspected of publishing thinly veiled anti-regime criticism. Dolgorukov was convinced that the journal was responsible for provoking what he considered a crisis of confidence in the government at the crucial moment when the emperor was planning to announce the emancipation legislation. The situation soon worsened. After the decree ending legal serfdom was made public, ominous dissatisfaction surfaced from elements in society who found the terms of the 1861 Emancipation Proclamation extremely unfair to the peasantry. Pamphlets predicting a wave of armed rebellion in the countryside with rivers of landowners' blood flowing on their estates were confiscated in the spring, soon after the decree was published.[21] Dolgorukov held Chernyshevsky responsible for the escalating volume of protest and launched an aggressive campaign against him and the journal, resulting in his arrest. Charged with seditious language capable of fomenting rebellion, he was sentenced to life imprisonment and the journal was banned from further activity.[22]

In spite of the numerous predictions of violence, the police were not prepared for Dmitry Karakozov's attempt to assassinate the emperor on April 4, 1866, in broad daylight during an imperial procession on the main boulevard in St. Petersburg. Alexander II survived the incident, but Dolgorukov accepted responsibility for not having prevented the attempt and resigned. Justice proceeded apace nevertheless. According to police reports, peasants in the crowd restrained Karakozov after he misfired his revolver until the authorities apprehended him. He was then swiftly brought to trial, convicted, and executed on October 3.[23]

An experienced intelligence operative, Peter Shuvalov, was appointed Dolgorukov's successor. He in turn placed the important security position of governor-general of the capital in the hands of General Fyodor Trepov. Between them, police surveillance was heightened to the point that the late 1860s has been called the era of "The White Terror." More journals were closed, including *The Russian Word* (*Russkoe Slovo*), and its leading writer, Dmitry Pisarev, placed under arrest. The assassination attempt on the emperor led to his ordering a comprehensive review of the Third Section. Hoping to intercept the planning of future *attentats*, the Third Section's budget was increased, more agents assigned to policing functions, greater surveillance was applied to the public mail service, and the entire imperial railway system from Poland to the Caucuses was placed under police monitoring.

Fear of this police terror was rampant but not ultimately successful in that the violence from below grew exponentially in the ensuing years. In 1869, just as the authorities were in a congratulatory mood for seemingly quelling the threats posed by anti-imperial publications, an unprecedented act of violence occurred at Moscow University that once again took the police by surprise. A student at the university, Sergei Nechaev, led a small radical group that was planning an attack on the tsar. Nechaev was inspired by Karakozov's attempted assassination and was determined to accomplish the mission. On the night of November 21, 1869, a member of his circle who wanted out was murdered either by Nechaev himself or by a comrade at his order. By morning, Nechaev had fled to Switzerland where he gained access to Mikhail Bakunin, the aging anarchist revolutionary.

Nechaev put his schemes into a small manifesto titled "The Catechism of a Revolutionist."[24] This document is significant because it is the inaugural manifesto of Russian insurgent terrorism. In it, Nechaev openly described life in the radical underground as a total commitment to the cause of violent revolt in which participants were to abandon all connections to family, friendships, and society. Most chilling, he detailed, in terms of categories, the sectors of the Russian government and its supporters in the larger society targeted for assassination. It is noteworthy that in the last clause he advocated the importance of including women sympathetic to the cause, and in roles equal to those of men. To Bakunin, he also claimed, falsely, to be in command of a brigade across Russia of more than eighty people drawn from his group, the People's Vengeance, who were waiting for the sign to unleash a violent revolt with the goal of overthrowing the tsarist state.

Meanwhile, Shuvalov ordered his gendarmes to conduct a massive search for suspects. Hundreds were detained, searched, and prepared for the first public trial of political criminals. Confusion over the legality of the evidence reduced the number of suspects who could be charged with subversive intent against the government, leaving the court no choice but to release all but thirty-four defendants. Shuvalov, determined to justify his department's arrest record, over the next two years secretly sentenced some 200 others whom the court had released.[25]

By this time, however, the administration had even greater challenges to deal with. A new generation of educated and politically conscious youth emerged at this time seeking new strategic approaches to address the continuing mood of dissatisfaction over the unchanging conditions of impoverishment of the post-Emancipation peasantry. At the same time, they were repelled by both the repressive tactics of the police and the violence associated with

Nechaev's manifesto while also deeply influenced by the critical attitudes expressed in the publications of Herzen abroad and Chernyshevsky at home. They further identified with what they now perceived as a line of continuity stretching back to the Decembrists, whose challenges to the imperial regime many of them first learned about from clandestine copies of Herzen's uncensored *Bell*.

The result was the opening of a new form of protest across a decade that began with nonviolence and climaxed with unparalleled insurgent terrorism. Frustrated with the lack of progress in improving the lives of the former serf population and inspired by the admonitions from Herzen, Chernyshevsky, and, more recently, Peter Lavrov, to "go to the people," several thousand students abandoned their privileged lives in the early 1870s to overcome the class divide by moving to peasant villages. Their purposes were varied. Some wanted primarily to improve literacy and health care, but others, driven by the exclamatory rhetoric of Bakunin's underground publications, sought to foment outright rebellion by denouncing local clerics, court corruption, and police brutality.

The police, caught once more without adequate intelligence ahead of time, moved in with force during the summer of 1874, arresting over 700 suspects. Though most memoirists of the "movement to the people" blamed their failure on police repression, the fact is that, in many instances, the peasants themselves were disturbed by the criticism of their respected religious and secular authorities and were relieved to have the outsiders removed.[26] Of that total, 193 were actually brought to trial in 1877. The number would surely have been higher had not over seventy of those detained not died or gone mad in confinement. There was also a separate Trial of the 50, which included mainly laborers and peasants who were sympathetic to, or implicated in, the actions of the student agitators.

The minister of justice, Konstantine Pahlen, and his Third Section chief, General Nikolai Mezentsov, had little time to feel relief; on the day after the verdicts were announced at the Trial of the 193, the first significant act of political violence since the Karakozov Affair occurred. On January 24, 1878, Vera Zasulich, one of the many radicalized activists disheartened by the trial, made an appointment to meet with Trepov, the St. Petersburg governor-general, and, in his office, pulled a revolver out of her muff and shot him.

She claimed at her trial that she was seeking revenge for the flogging of one of her jailed comrades and decided on violence only after her requests were repeatedly denied. Trepov survived and surprisingly Zasulich was exonerated at her trial two months later.[27] Shortly thereafter, she went to Europe where she became associated with a nascent Russian Marxist exile group in Switzerland and campaigned against the tactic of insurgent terror. Nonetheless, her shooting of Trepov stirred others in the underground to act in a similar manner, leading to very grave consequences.[28]

The wave of violence from below was inaugurated by what seemed to the police as individual acts, perhaps committed by criminals rather than revolutionaries. Just months after Zasulich's attack on Trepov, Sergei Kravchinsky, inspired by her deed, succeeded in assassinating Mezentsov, stabbing him to death with a knife after stalking him meticulously on the street a block from his Third Section office. Kravchinsky escaped abroad where he published his exculpatory accounts justifying his vengeful killing of Mezentsov as the official who oversaw and ordered the imprisonment, torture, and exile of his comrades.[29]

The police soon discovered that Kravchinsky was affiliated with an insurgent organization called Land and Freedom (*Zemlia i volia*) made up of survivors of the security dragnet following the 1874 "mad summer" mass arrests as well as new recruits to the anti-tsarist cause. The group functioned mainly in St. Petersburg and Moscow, but its branch in Kiev sent a letter to A. A. Lopukhin, procurator of the Petersburg criminal court, in which the Executive Committee asserted what they called their "modest and rational demands." These included the right to a fair trial for all who were detained by the state, freeing those for whom there was no reliable evidence, and treating detained prisoners humanely, without any form of torture. The group admitted responsibility for assassinating Mezentsov in addition to fatally wounding G. E. Geiking, a local Kievan police official, and promised to act again with violence if their demands were not accepted.[30]

Instead of reforming the law and using more rigorous oversight to enforce its practice by the police, however, the government chose to work around it, including ignoring some of the terms of the 1864 judicial reforms when the threat to the state made this necessary. The new chief of the Third Section, General Alexander Drenteln, further centralized the unwieldy security bureaucracy, requested (and received) additional funding, and vastly expanded the networks of infiltrators and spies on the state payroll.[31]

Simultaneously, the Land and Freedom Party expanded its ranks and its commitments to engage in more violent activities or, in their own vocabulary, to greater amounts of "agitation" instead of "propaganda," the weapon of the earlier "movement to the people." In spite of all the efforts by Drenteln's agents to monitor their activities, the members of the party managed to meet secretly to plan tactics and strategy in Voronezh without interference from the authorities. However, the internal disputes proved irreconcilable between those activists who favored a return to the tactics of peaceful propaganda in peasant villages and urban factories and those who advocated terror as the only possibility for successfully challenging the autocracy. The result was a schism that left the terrorist faction dominant within the country, renamed the People's Will (*Narodnaia Volia*), while the minority assumed a new identity as Black Repartition.

People's Will's campaign of insurgent terror moved quickly into high gear. In February 1879, Grigory Goldenberg shot to death Prince Dmitry Kropotkin, governor of Kharkov (and a relative of the anarchist Peter Kropotkin). A month later, Drenteln himself narrowly escaped an attempt on his life, as did the emperor on April 2 when Alexander Soloviev errantly fired his revolver at Alexander II outside the Winter Palace. In response, a virtual state of emergency was declared as the Third Section was permitted to arrest and censor without first gaining court permission.

Terrorisms ascendant

Both the police and the insurgents became obsessed with the habits and codes of their enemies to the point where the two sides became intimately entangled in each other's increasingly destructive violence. They continued to mirror one another's tactics and strategy as time went on, operating now in a shadowy zone outside the boundaries of civil society, establishing their own culture of intelligence gathering and violent acts. In many ways, this was the realization of Nechaev's portrait of the obsessed, totally committed activist functioning beyond all ties to law, family, and friendships to realize their goals by any means. They would soon be more familiar with one another than either was with the worlds they had left behind to accomplish their assignments.

One such example concerns the relationship established between Alexander Mikhailov, a prominent member of People's Will, and Nikolai Kletochnikov, whom he convinced in 1878 to join the security service of the Third Section in order to report back to the party. The plan worked well for several years as Kletochnikov ascended to higher positions with access to sensitive intelligence that he secreted to Mikhailov. Eventually, he was discovered as a spy early in 1881 and spent the rest of his life languishing in prison after a commuted death sentence.[32]

The information provided by Kletochnikov was useful as People's Will continued its relentless assault. On February 4, 1880, Stepan Khalturin bribed his way into the labor detail at the Winter Palace and blasted the imperial dining room with dynamite he smuggled inside. Eleven people were killed and over fifty injured in the explosion, but the tsar had not entered the room at the time and was unharmed. In the aftermath, Alexander II relieved Drenteln of his command, abolished the tarnished Third Section, and created a new body with the pretentious title of the Supreme Executive Committee for the Preservation of State Order and Public Tranquility, with General Mikhail Loris-Melikov as its chief with near-dictatorial powers.

These administrative changes were codified in Russia's first authentic emergency legislation. Such laws had been promulgated in Europe, particularly in France during the Terror of 1793–4 and again in the aftermath of the savage violence during the Paris Commune in 1871. However, no Russian ruler in the modern era had placed the country under an effective state of siege, which was the case at this point. Loris-Melikov was permitted "to give any regulations and take any measures" that would guarantee "the preservation of the state order and public peace."[33] The police were permitted and encouraged to carry out extensive searches, arrests, solitary confinement, and extraction of testimony by force (i.e., torture).

To be sure, People's Will had lost its best source of police intelligence when Kletochnikov was arrested, but he was quickly replaced by Goldenberg who, imprisoned after his assassination of Kharkov Governor-General Kropotkin, was persuaded to betray his former comrades. In addition, Nikolai Rysakov was also enticed into police service when it became clear that he possessed valuable intelligence as a former radical activist. When promised that his earlier participation in preparing bombs for People's Will would be forgiven, he was more than willing to betray his former comrades. As a consequence, Andrei Zhelyabov, a leading member of the Executive Committee of People's Will and one of the architects of the plans for the tsaricide, was arrested in February 1881. Other arrests followed, but the police were unable to prevent the March 1 bombing of Alexander II's carriage during a public procession in the capital, which finally killed him.[34]

Alexander III succeeded his father and instituted a revival of the "White Terror." The emergency decree of 1879 was now codified into law officially on August 14, 1881, transforming what were once considered security measures of extraordinary magnitude into the norm of quotidian conditions. Political dissent was now criminalized with responsibilities for enforcement of the harsh emergency conditions handed to Konstantine Pobedonostsev, former tutor to the new emperor and now head of the Holy Synod, and Count Dmitry Tolstoy, the recently appointed interior minister.

These two reactionary statesmen played key roles in the ensuing state terror. No restraint was placed on General Drenteln, now Governor-General in Kiev, when he permitted the vicious anti-Semitic pogroms that broke out in that city and surrounding villages under his jurisdiction.[35] A more enduring development was the establishing of a new state security force, called the Security Section, or Okhrana (from *Okhrannoe otdelenie*), in the wake of the failures of the Third Section to stem the tide of anti-regime bombings. One of its earliest functions was to approve a special subdivision, the Holy Brotherhood

(*Sviashchennaia druzhina*), which was essentially a government hit squad with permission to pursue and punish Russian revolutionaries who had fled abroad.

Plans for the Holy Brotherhood called for a budget of one million rubles and a force of around 1,000 recruits.[36] In many ways, it was a mirror image of its enemy. Two squads were dispatched to hunt down and assassinate the populist activist Lev Hartmann and the prominent anarchist Peter Kropotkin. Although they did not manage to accomplish these killings, the Brotherhood did set up a periodical in Geneva with the interesting title of *Pravda* (*Truth*), edited by a former member of the Third Section. The purpose was to imitate the kinds of anti-regime articles that the revolutionary press abroad printed, hoping to provoke a disturbance that would justify arrests of the Russian radicals who were operating outside the reach of the Russian authorities. However, the material turned out to be so inflammatory and extreme in advocating violence that it was soon closed due to its inability to gain influence among the Russian community abroad.[37]

The Holy Brotherhood did have some minor successes, including the bombing of a bookstore whose owners were known to be close to the populist exile Peter Lavrov, but Dmitry Tolstoy saw a better way to accomplish its purpose. He closed the Holy Brotherhood's operations in the spring of 1883, while envisioning a far more effective form of anti-revolutionary police activities in Europe. With the cooperation of several governments, particularly the French Republic, the Okhrana set up offices in a number of urban areas near the ever-growing Russian émigré neighborhoods and established a permanent working relationship with the local gendarmes of those countries.

These operations, together with the increasing ability to penetrate the subterranean networks established by the opponents of the regime both at home and abroad, led to a close – virtually intimate – relationship between the two sides. Just as groups like People's Will had learned how to gain access to their targets, regardless of how protected they seemed to be, so too the police became experts at imitating the culture of their enemies. Starting in the 1880s, the hunters and the hunted became almost indistinguishable since they began playing dual identity roles and employing similar tactics of violence.

One of the most dramatic examples of this linkage of police and insurgents was the Degaev Affair. Colonel G. P. Sudeikin was a former participant in the student movement who gained admission to the ranks of the Okhrana with the intention of helping to create a reformed monarchy with less central authority. His plan was to engage the radical underground in a joint association toward that end. The plan, ingenious despite being highly improbable, was put into place when he engaged the services of Sergei Degaev, detained as a member of People's Will, whose task was to provide intelligence to the police in return for his release.

As a double agent, his initial success was to locate and capture Vera Figner, one of the most prominent revolutionaries still at large, early in 1883. At the same time, Degaev also deceived Sudeikin by providing information back to his comrades in the underground. Sudeikin then arranged for Degaev to travel to Geneva to abduct another revolutionary, Lev Tikhomirov, and return him to Russia. Simultaneously, People's Will asked Degaev to use his proximity to Sudeikin to assassinate him, which he accomplished on December 16, 1883.[38] Other police agents played similar dual roles, such as P. S. Statkovsky.[39]

This cooperation and interchange between hostile elements responsible for security and sabotage also led the police directly into committing illegal and criminal actions. It was increasingly easy to cross the line since both sides were essentially operating with the same tactics, despite their antithetical strategic orientations. Both sides actively recruited agents from the enemy camp. Although we are accustomed to consider such careers as choices rooted in deep loyalties either to the state or its overthrow, the consequences of this entangled terrorism included a heightened sense of insecurity and uncertainty regarding commitments. Establishing trust within this clandestine culture became ever more difficult to establish and maintain. A police agent one day could (and did) become an insurgent the day after and vice versa. Some of these informers, as one study puts it, "managed to help both sides substantially and it is extremely difficult even today to calculate and compare their contribution to the police as against their contribution to the revolutionaries."[40]

For the last two decades of the nineteenth century, Peter Rachkovsky headed the special Foreign Branch of the Okhrana, with its central headquarters in the Paris Russian Consulate building. Rachkovsky's budget, considered lavish for the time, permitted him to hire not only additional Russian agents to combat the influence of the growing émigré communities abroad but also employ a number of French police officials to aid in their work. One of his most trusted Russian agents was Abram Hekkelman, who, using the nom de guerre of Landezen (and later, as A. M. Harting), managed to gain access to exile groups of People's Will survivors in Paris and Zurich involved in preparing bombs for assassinating Russian officials in Moscow and St. Petersburg. In 1888, Landezen, acting under Rachkovsky's instructions, proposed a plan to the Paris circle to assassinate Emperor Alexander III, paid for the explosives with funds directly from the Okhrana, and worked in the group's French bomb factory constructing the devices. Prior to implementing the action, Landezen alerted the French police who arrested the entire group. To be certain that the public understood the proper narrative of the roundup, Rachkovsky hired a reporter to plant stories in the French press that they had destroyed a vicious plot by anarchists – the current bête noire of the police throughout Europe – to murder a number of unnamed state officials.[41]

The final spasms of political violence in Imperial Russia

Although the struggle between the Russian police agents and the émigré revolutionaries continued throughout the period leading up to World War I, the home front, relatively quiescent during the 1890s after the complete collapse of People's Will, became the scene of extraordinary political violence as the new century dawned. Once more, just as security officialdom relaxed under the assumption that the terror from below had been largely repressed, a new wave of unprecedented insurgent violence emerged that, in turn, enjoined the police to interact.

Both sides perpetrated acts of extraordinary terror in the years prior to, during, and following the tumultuous 1905 revolution. New Okhrana directors replaced their predecessors who maintained the commitment to preserve the autocratic order, while new revolutionary organizations arose dedicated to continuing past insurgent efforts to overthrow that regime. With the country now moving rapidly into the industrial era, the possibilities for greater damage to the enemy increased with advancing technology. The state, as always, had the advantage of superior arms, resources, and personnel, but weapons considered part of the government's monopoly found their way into the hands of the underground. Both sides continued to compete for the sympathy of the larger population in the ongoing contestation over regime legitimacy. As the security establishment remained committed to the fantasy of a timeless autocratic polity, however outmoded its functions and significance had become, the political opposition retained its own dream world of a future egalitarian social structure attainable only through regime change, regardless of how improbable this outcome was.

Neither side had much respect for contemporary legalities, visibly evidenced by their willingness to use acts of extreme violence to achieve their ends, which were, simply put, to destroy the other. They were, nevertheless, quite willing to learn tactics and strategy from one another in the process.

The array of the nascent political parties were, with the exception of the far right, largely formed abroad since the autocracy was unwilling to recognize them within the Empire. The most significant of the emerging radical parties were the Marxist Social Democrats and the populist Socialist Revolutionary Party. Most of their early congresses and conferences were held in Western Europe, although Okhrana agents always managed to infiltrate them.

State and anti-state entanglements emerged in new social terrain as a consequence of the government-sponsored factory system expansion in the 1890s under the direction of Sergei Witte, the minister of finance. The increase in the number of factories, many larger than their European counterparts, provided the locus for the consequent rise of a serious labor movement. To head off the increase of strikes and work stoppages, Sergei Zubatov, a young and aspiring Okhrana official who had already proven himself skilled at penetrating and provoking the radical underground toward violence, received permission in 1901 to have the police run its own trade union. The theory was that by enrolling sufficient numbers of factory workers, the government could redirect their loyalties away from anti-regime sentiments and increase industrial productivity. Supported by both the governor-general of Moscow, Grand Duke Sergei Aleksandrovich, and the deeply reactionary chief of police, Dmitry Trepov (son of Fyodor Trepov), Zubatov succeeded in enlisting thousands of workers, including an unintended number of radical activists, before chaos overtook events.[42]

A renewed opposition movement emerged at the same time, generated in part by the restrictions imposed by the rector of St. Petersburg University on political meetings and peaceful demonstrations in February 1899. When the students called for a demonstration to protest the rules, the police were ordered to quell the speeches. Whether they were provoked is not clear, but there is no doubt that the police used excessive violence to break up the demonstration. Arrests and further restrictions followed, which drove one of the students, Peter Karpovich, to assassinate Nikolai Bogolepov, the minister of education. Further acts of repression and resistance followed quickly. Another student, Stepan Balmashov, assassinated Dmitry Sipiagin, the minister of the interior, on April 15, 1902. Balmashov claimed membership in a new violent group, the Combat Organization, a fragment of the Socialist Revolutionary Party led by Grigory Gershuni. The Combat Organization was poised not only to fight the efforts of the new minister of the interior and police, Vyacheslav von Plehve, but also to move with tactics of intense violence in a comprehensive attack on the state.

Yet another disturbing development in this period was the emergence of rightist, nationalist militias willing to engage in their own forms of terrorism to support the state in its war against the left. Disagreements remain among scholars as to the extent to which the police at the highest levels supported and encouraged this violence. What is clear, however, is the absence of the kind of large-scale prosecution and trials that the revolutionaries of the left had been subjected to at least since the 1870s.

Local neighborhood squads, loosely organized under the umbrella of the Black Hundreds, carried out much of this violence, often in the guise of aiding the police in repressing "threatening elements" working to undermine the monarchy. The numerous pogroms, attacks on civilian Jewish communities, represented some of the most vicious terrorism of these vigilantes. In many instances, the regional governors-general provided the link between the Black Hundred groups on the one side and the Ministry of Interior on the other.

Regardless, thousands of Jews were victims of the anti-Semitic violence in urban areas such as Kiev and Odessa as well as many smaller towns across the Pale of Settlement, a version of a national ghetto where most of the Empire's Jewish population was compelled to dwell.

At the same time, one of the most prominent of the few legal political parties accepted by the state was the monarchist Union of the Russian People, which also sponsored the Black Hundreds and their assaults against suspected revolutionaries and non-Russian ethnicities in addition to Jews. The leaders of the Union of the Russian People included Vladimir Purishkevich and A. I. Dobrovin, who enjoyed direct access to the Okhrana. In addition, their racist newspaper articles had wide circulation. Also, they delivered vitriolic speeches against minorities in the State Duma, an elected administrative assembly with highly restricted representation created as a concession to end the lengthy and violent nine-month revolution in 1905. These speeches were widely available on a daily basis in the published proceedings of the State Duma.[43]

Perhaps the most dramatic story of entangled terrorism during the 1905 era was the career of Evno Azef, who was mentioned at the outset of this chapter. He had already worked as a police spy in Rostov-on-Don and in Karlsruhe, Germany, where he studied engineering and informed on anti-regime exiles there, when Zubatov recruited him into the higher ranks of the Okhrana in St. Petersburg in 1899. Over the next several years, Azef was assigned to join the Moscow circle of the Socialist Revolutionary Party as a police informer. He became admired and trusted by party members. With police knowledge, Azef became a founding member of the party's Combat Organization, making him a central figure in their assassination plans. After Gershuni's arrest, Azef was delegated to head the terrorist faction. To obtain finances for the violence against the state, Azef organized bank robberies, known as "expropriations" in the radical lexicon, which often ended with civilian casualties.

Far more complicated was the party's plan to assassinate the minister of interior, Plehve, who was in fact Azef's boss and paymaster. The police were informed but could do little without blowing Azef's cover. As a result, on July 15, 1904, Igor Sazonov hurled a bomb into Plehve's carriage, killing him instantly. Even more dramatic was the assassination of Grand Duke Sergei Aleksandrovich, the governor-general of Moscow and the tsar's uncle, on February 4, 1905, by Ivan Kalyaev. The next target was Peter Stolypin, who was certainly the most powerful minister at the time. The Combat Organization, still headed by Azef, infiltrated the minister's villa outside the capital on August 12, 1906, and set off several bombs. More than a dozen people were wounded and killed, but Stolypin escaped without injury.

All through this period, Azef met regularly with the new head of the Okhrana, A. V. Gerasimov. Gerasimov's justifications for accepting the violence perpetrated against his own government were, first, that the situation would have been worse if he were not informed by Azef and, second, that without Azef in place as a police informer at the center of the Combat Organization's attack command, the arrests of the revolutionaries could not have taken place. Moreover, Gerasimov was not without his own plans for repressive violence.

These events were all part of the momentous upheaval that dominated Russia through all of 1905 and into the spring of the following year before order was restored. The revolutionary upsurge, which began in January with a strike in the main St. Petersburg artillery factory, was certainly the most threatening moment for the Romanov regime in its 300-year history, which, before it was over, flirted with the possibility of a complete collapse. The shutdown of the factory ended with a peaceful procession on January 22 to the Winter Palace to present a petition to the tsar. Troops responsible for protecting the palace opened fire on the demonstrators, with casualties in the hundreds. The event remains engraved historically as "Bloody Sunday," memorializing the snow speckled with crimson from the wounds on that day.

For the next nine months, Russia was overwhelmed with unprecedented transformation and violence. Border guards were replaced with activists who permitted exiles such as Lenin and Trotsky to return. Local councils (soviets), many elected in the provinces, sprang up to replace local administrations. Printing presses were taken over by radical publicists who issued volumes of previously censored materials. In addition, trams were overturned, upscale stores were sacked, and, most ominously, assassinations and reprisals became everyday occurrences.

The void in imperial power permitted a direct confrontation between the agencies of terrorism on both sides. The Combat Organization, along with separate actions by anarchists and rightists, utilized the weakening of national security to carry out the killing of "anyone in a uniform," as Boris Savinkov put it. At the same time, the police and the army, now returned from the disastrous war against Japan, dealt savagely with the revolutionaries and were responsible for thousands of casualties as well. Severely weakened, with the regime's very legitimacy at stake, Nicholas issued his October Manifesto promising parliamentary reforms, which contributed to the government's gradual restoration of authority.

One of the government's most notorious measures was to operationalize the field court martial system in 1906–7 under the aegis of the Military District judiciary. This permitted the regional police, aided when necessary by local military authorities, to make wholesale arrests based on information provided by their informers. Rather than following the legal code, which provided for a trial and lawyers, these suspects were taken immediately to a sentencing tribunal within twenty-four hours, the results of which were almost uniformly a death sentence by firing squad.

These executions numbered around 1,000 in the immediate aftermath of the 1905 Revolution and were carried out empire-wide from Warsaw and Riga to Kiev and Vladivostok, in addition to the areas in and around Moscow and St. Petersburg. The executions continued even after the revolutionary upheaval was quelled, killing some 5,000 people suspected of anti-regime activities by 1909.[44] Despite the huge losses suffered, the Combat Organization finally caught its primary target. Dmitry Bogrov, who was himself an agent of the Okhrana, carried out his mission successfully on September 1, 1911, at the Kiev Opera House by assassinating Stolypin. Nevertheless, the judgment remains valid that "in the early twentieth century, the imperial authorities came nearer to operating a political reign of terror than on any previous occasion."[45]

The Azef story wound down in an unexpected manner. He was denounced and "outed" as a spy for the police not by a Combat Organization comrade but by Vladimir Burtsev, an ex-activist whose files on informers, compiled in his London exile center, were widely respected by all sides in the conflict of terrorisms. Also astonishing was the validation of Burtsev's charges against Azef by a former Okhrana chief, A. A. Lopukhin, who traveled to London to deliver his testimony.[46] Slippery to the end, Azef, once realizing he could no longer function either as a revolutionary or in the Okhrana, fled abroad and reinvented himself again, this time as an ordinary and very unpolitical shop owner in Berlin.

The end of this long entanglement of the imperial police and its revolutionary antagonists came about quickly and, for many, unexpectedly. In retrospect, the signs appear clearer than they did to the protagonists at the time. Labor strikes had risen dramatically in the years before the outbreak of the Great War, often being repressed by the security forces violently.

The economy was in peril as the prioritized costs of war left the civilian population deprived of food and services, which were either scarce or too expensive. The credibility of the government had plummeted as Nicholas could not reverse the fortunes of battle even after his celebrated appearance at the front, nor could he repair the corrupt image and damage traceable to Rasputin's assertion of authority in his absence. Above all, the nationalist passion for victory could no longer be relied on among the troops in the trenches after so many losses. Instead, sectors of society normally loyal to the regime, including in the Duma, which had been dominated by rightist parties since its inception in 1906, turned increasingly against the house of Romanov. Voices, some at the highest level, had not only warned of the impending dangers but went so far as to predict a revolution unless attention was devoted to these issues; their calls of distress were left unheeded.[47]

Collapse finally came in February 1917, when demonstrations in Petrograd and Moscow overwhelmed the security forces. Nicholas was compelled to abdicate and was replaced by a group of officials from the Duma, self-selected and unelected, who assumed power as the Provisional Government. For the next few months, there were attempts to end the longstanding entangled and violent relationship between the security agencies and the revolutionary parties. For some, this meant avenging the "crimes" committed by the police against those who wished to replace the autocracy with a more just structure of governance.

Now that those formerly repressed were in positions of authority, space was opened up for acts of justified vengeance, such as the burning of police buildings and attacks on former security officials. For others, the task at hand was to comprehensively compile data on the Okhrana and its constituencies to reveal its criminal violence. Much work in this direction was accomplished until the next revolution interrupted its being concluded.[48]

The Bolshevik seizure of power in October also provided the opportunity for the re-establishment of a Russian state secret police force. This variant proved to be more sinister and terroristic than its predecessor – so much so that, whenever it lacked a sufficiently realistic threat to its questionable legitimacy, it invented one. This "enemies list" would include innovative poets and film makers as well as oppositional parties, "former people," wreckers within, bourgeois capitalist influences abroad, and ordinary citizens with critical political perspectives in need of denunciation. As a result, the legitimacy of the state remained in question, ensuring that the entanglement of the terrorisms would endure, in a futile search to realize the goal of justifying violence to create a state in which violence would be unnecessary.

Notes

1 See Chapter 31 by Lynn Patyk in this volume for more discussion of Chesterton's novel.
2 Claudia Verhoeven, *The Odd Man Karakozov: Imperial Russia, Modernity and the Birth of Terrorism* (Ithaca, NY: Cornell University Press, 2009); O. V. Budnitskii, *Terrorizm v Rossiiskom osvoboditel'nom dvizhenii* (Moscow: ROSSPEN, 2000); and Anna Geifman, *Thou Shalt Kill: Revolutionary Terrorism in Russia, 1894–1917* (Princeton, NJ: Princeton University Press, 1993).
3 Ronald Hingley, *The Russian Secret Police: Muscovite, Imperial Russian and Soviet Political Security Operations, 1565–1970* (London: Hutchinson, 1970); Jonathan W. Daly, *Autocracy Under Siege: Security and Opposition in Russia, 1866–1905* (Dekalb: Northern Illinois University Press, 1998); Charles A. Ruud and Sergei A. Stepanov, *Fontanka 16: The Tsars' Secret Police* (Montreal: McGill Queen's University Press, 1999); and Fredric S. Zuckerman, *The Tsarist Secret Police Abroad: Policing Europe in a Modernising World* (New York: Palgrave/Macmillan, 2003).
4 This has been the case at least since Trotsky's denunciations of Stalin during his years of exile in Mexico in the 1930s, and it has become embedded as an interpretive trope in the literature as a

result of the immense impact of Hannah Arendt's *Origins of Totalitarianism* (New York: Harcourt, Brace, 1951) and solidified by Robert Conquest in his book *The Great Terror* (New York: Macmillan, 1968), which continues to inform studies of political violence in the Stalin era. Historians in post-Soviet Russia have adopted a similar divisional analytic approach of the two separate terrorisms. For more on terrorism, state terror, and totalitarianism, see Chapter 11 by Paul M. Hagenloh in this volume.

5   For more on the subject of state terror, particularly in regard to its development alongside and not apart from sub-state terrorism, see Chapter 24 by Roger Griffin in this volume.
6   For a more extensive discussion of this interpretation, see Martin A. Miller, *The Foundations of Russian Terrorism: State, Society and the Dynamics of Political Violence* (Cambridge: Cambridge University Press, 2013), 240–58.
7   For more on the definition of terrorism, see Randall D. Law's introduction to this volume.
8   The English diplomat Jerome Horsey was astonished by the violence of the *oprichniki*. See his "Travels" in Giles Fletcher, *Russia at the Close of the Sixteenth Century* (London: Hakluyt Society, 1856).
9   B. I. Veretennikov, *Istoriia tainoi kantseliarii petrovskogo vremeni* (Moscow: Librokom, [1910] 2011).
10 For more on state terror/ism in the French Revolution, see Chapter 5 by Mike Rapport in this volume.
11 Sidney Monas, *The Third Section: Police and Society in Russia under Nicholas I* (Cambridge, MA: Harvard University Press, 1961), 56; and P. S. Squire, *The Third Department: Establishment and Practices of the Political Police in the Russia of Nicholas I* (Cambridge: Cambridge University Press, 1968), 35.
12 Edward A. B. Hodgetts, *The Court of Russia in the Nineteenth Century* (New York: Scribner's, 1908), 197. The message was from John Sherwood and told to Alexander personally at a meeting.
13 Pestel's "Green Book," the main document containing his political strategy and tactics, was discovered in the police search once the conspiracy was uncovered and the members of both societies were arrested. On the Decembrist rebellion, see especially Marc Raeff, *The Decembrist Movement* (Englewood Cliffs, NJ: Prentice Hall, 1966).
14 Hodgetts, *The Court of Russia*, 203.
15 Ruud and Stepanov, *Fontanka 16*, 21.
16 Ibid., 20. The letter from von Vock to Benckendorff was penned in July 1826, at the time of Nicholas I's coronation.
17 M. N. Gernet, *Istoriia tsarskoi tiur'my, 1825–1870* (Moscow: Gosizdatel'stvo iiuridicheskoi literatury, 1961), 2:418–23.
18 Herzen's account of the encounter is in his memoir, *My Past and Thoughts* (Berkeley: University of California Press, 1982), 202–7. On the police campaign against the writers, see Hingley, *The Russian Secret Police*, 37–44. For more on the broader context of Russian and European censorship regarding terrorism and sedition, see Chapter 28 by Robert A. Saunders in this volume.
19 For his thinly veiled autobiographical fictional account, see Dostoevsky's *House of the Dead*. On the circle, consult P. Ye. Shchogolev, *Petrashevtsy v vospominaniiakh sovremennikov* (Moscow, 1926); and John L. Evans, *The Petrashevskii Circle, 1845–1849* (The Hague: Mouton, 1974).
20 M. I. Mikhailov, *Zapiski* (Petrograd: Gosizdat, 1922), 20; and N. Ia. Eidel'man, *Tainy korrespondenty "Poliarnoi Zvezdy"* (Moscow: Gosizdat, 1966), 93–4. A network of professional smugglers were responsible for transporting Herzen's publications across occupied Poland and Western Russia to reach their subscribers, who took great risks distributing them in the Russian countryside.
21 Among the most inflammatory were "To the Younger Generation" by Mikhail Mikhailov and "Young Russia" attributed to P. G. Zaichnevskii, while another, "The Great Russian," argued for the necessity of further reform to alleviate the peasant hunger for land without the huge burdens attached in the Emancipation Proclamation.
22 Two reliable sources for these events are the published diaries of state censor A. V. Nikitenko and Interior Minister P. A. Valuev.
23 See Claudia Verhoeven's recent study, *The Odd Man Karakozov*.
24 For a full biographical account and the manifesto, see Philip Pomper, *Sergei Nechaev* (New Brunswick, NJ: Rutgers University Press, 1979).
25 Ruud and Stepanov, *Fontanka 16*, 36–7.
26 One good example is the account found in Gleb Uspensky's "Village Diary" in his *Pol'noe sobranie sochinenii* (Moscow: Gosizdat, 1949), 5:125–47.

27 See Chapter 31 by Patyk in this volume for her discussion of two literary responses to Zasulich's shooting of Trepov.
28 On Zasulich, consult Jay Bergman, *Vera Zasulich* (Stanford, CA: Stanford University Press, 1983); and Lynn Ellen Patyk, "'The Double-edged Sword of Word and Deed': Revolutionary Terrorism and Russian Literary Culture" (PhD diss., Stanford University, 2006).
29 Kravchinsky (his *nom de guerre* was Stepniak) eventually settled in London and renounced any involvement in violence, though in his many books and articles, he portrayed the Russian regime as the provocative agent of terror. His active career as a publicist was suddenly silenced in 1895, not by the Russian agents seeking to kill him, but by a train accident while he was walking near the tracks and absorbed in reading. See especially his *Career of a Nihilist* (New York: Hurst, 1889) and *Underground Russia* (Westport, CT: Hyperion Press [1883] 1973). For an interesting interpretation of his admiring memorialization of his comrades among the revolutionary terrorists, see Lynn Ellen Patyk, "Remembering 'The Terrorism': Sergei Stepniak-Kravchinskii's *Underground Russia*," *Slavic Review* 68, no. 4 (2009): 758–81.
30 "Pis'mo Kievskogo 'Ispolnitel'nogo komiteta Russkoi Sotsial'no-revolutionnoi Partii,'" in *Politicheskaia politsiia i politicheskii terrorizm v Rossii (vtoria polivena XIX–nachalo XX vv.)*, ed. N. I. Dedkov, 46–8 (Moscow: AIRO-XX, 2001).
31 On Drenteln at this time, see Christine Johanson, *Womens' Struggle for Higher Education in Russia* (Toronto: McGill-Queens University Press, 1987), 67–8.
32 P. Koshel, *Istoriia nakazanii v Rossii. Istoriia Rossiiskogo terrorizma* (Moscow: Golos, 1995), 260–2.
33 Alexander N. Domrin, *The Limits of Russian Democratisation: Emergency Powers and States of Emergency* (London: Routledge, 2006), 72. For the terms of the entire law, see N. I. Dedkov, ed., *Politicheskaia politsiia*, 64–6.
34 For more on the use of explosives by the People's Will – and particularly the role of the bomb maker Nikolai Kibalchich – see Chapter 29 by Ann Larabee on terrorism and technology in this volume.
35 P. A. Zaionchkovskii, *Kriziz samoderzhaviia no rubezhe 1870–1880-kh godov* (Moscow: Gosizdat, 1964), 379.
36 To gain a sense of the significance of this financial outlay, Peter Gatrell has calculated that 28 percent of the national budget in 1885 went to defense, most of which, in the absence of war, was channeled to the security forces. By contrast, 22 percent went to the administration (the court and ministries) and 3 percent to education. See his *The Tsarist Economy, 1850–1917* (New York: St. Martin's, 1986), 221. Thanks to Steven Marks for this reference.
37 See Hingley, *The Russian Secret Police*, 72–3.
38 Lev Tikhomirov, "Neizdannye zapiski," *Krasnyi arkhiv* 29 (1928): 170–1. The fullest account in English is Richard Pipes, *The Degaev Affair: Terror and Treason in Tsarist Russia* (New Haven, CT: Yale University Press, 2005).
39 Ruud and Stepanov, *Fontanka 16*, 65–7.
40 Ruud and Stepanov, *Fontanka 16*, 68.
41 Budnitskii, *Terrorizm v rossiiskom osvoboditel'nom dvzhenii*, 97; Zuckerman, *The Tsarist Secret Police Abroad*, 136–7.
42 Feliks Lur'e, *Tainy i istorii: Politseiskie i provokatory* (St. Petersburg: Chas-pik, 1992), 197–209.
43 See the discussion and evidence in Martin A. Miller, *The Foundations of Modern Terrorism*, 90–3. Ruud and Stepanov have archival evidence to substantiate the claim that the total number of Black Hundred recruits and volunteers in 1906 was more than 91,000 and rose to over 253,000 the next year. See *Fontanka 16*, 108.
44 Gernet, *Istoriia tsarskoi tiur'my*, 4:106–8 and 5:67–9. Jonathan Daly puts the total executed from 1906 to 1913 at 3,382. In addition, almost 9,000 people were sentenced to hard labor and exiled to Siberian camps and prisons in 1906 where many either died or endured conditions of living death. See his book, *The Watchful State: Security Police and Opposition in Russia, 1906–1917* (DeKalb: Northern Illinois University Press, 2004), 42–3.
45 Hingley, *The Russian Secret Police*, 102.
46 See A. A. Lopukhin, *Otryvki iz vospominanii*, introd. M. N. Pokrovskii (Moscow: Gosizdat, 1922); and Nurit Schliefman, *Undercover Agents in the Russian Revolutionary Movement: The SR Party, 1902–1914* (New York: St. Martin's Press, 1988), especially 190–5. Burtsev was, to his dismay, severely criticized by Socialist Revolutionary Party members for his exposures, which they felt were more

damaging than helpful to their own cause. Some continued to support Azef, refusing to see him as a spy.
47 One of the most insightful was the warning presented to Nicholas as early as February 1914 by Peter Durnovo, his minister of interior, former police official, and member of the State Council. See his "Memorandum to Nicholas II," in *Documents of Russian History, 1914–1917*, ed. Frank Golder, 3–23 (New York: Century, 1927).
48 See Pavel Eliseevich Shchegolev, *Padenie tsarskogo rezhima*, 6 vols. (Moscow: Gosizdat, 1924–7).

Further reading

Anemone, Anthony, ed. *Just Assassins: The Culture of Terrorism in Russia*. Evanston, IL: Northwestern University Press, 2010.

Engel, Barbara Alpern, and Clifford N. Rosenthal, eds. *Five Sisters: Women against the Tsar; The Memoirs of Five Young Anarchist Women of the 1870's*. New York: Knopf, 1975.

Geifman, Anna. *Thou Shalt Kill: Revolutionary Terrorism in Russia, 1894–1917*. Princeton, NJ: Princeton University Press, 1993.

Hingley, Ronald. *The Russian Secret Police: Muscovite, Imperial Russian and Soviet Political Security Operations, 1565–1970*. London: Hutchinson, 1970.

Miller, Martin A. *The Foundations of Russian Terrorism: State, Society and the Dynamics of Political Violence*. Cambridge: Cambridge University Press.

Pipes, Richard. *The Degaev Affair: Terror and Treason in Tsarist Russia*. New Haven, CT: Yale University Press, 2005.

Pomper, Philip. *Sergei Nechaev*. New Brunswick, NJ: Rutgers University Press, 1979.

Ruud, Charles A., and Sergei A. Stepanov. *Fontanka 16: The Tsars' Secret Police*. Montreal: McGill Queen's University Press, 1999.

Stepniak-Kravchinsky, Sergei. *Underground Russia*. Westport, CT: Hyperion Press, [1883] 1973.

Venturi, Franco. *Roots of Revolution: A History of the Populist and Socialist Movements in Nineteenth-Century Russia*. Translated by Francis Haskell. Chicago: University of Chicago Press, [1960] 1983.

Verhoeven, Claudia. *The Odd Man Karakozov: Imperial Russia, Modernity and the Birth of Terrorism*. Ithaca, NY: Cornell University Press, 2009.

8

ANARCHIST TERRORISM AND COUNTER-TERRORISM IN EUROPE AND THE WORLD, 1878–1934

Richard Bach Jensen

Soon after an anarchist shot United States President William McKinley in September 1901, the *St. Paul Pioneer Press* of Minnesota editorialized that: "It is not too much to say that the whole of Europe in the last two years has been in a condition of constant terror as to when and where the murderous brotherhood who style themselves anarchists would find their next victim."[1] While doubtless an exaggeration, the comment does convey a sense of the moral panic that seized much of the world at various times between the late 1870s and the mid-1930s. A significant number of anarchist bombings and assassinations occurred during this period, but the phenomenon of anarchist terrorism that exercised such a powerful impact on the mentality of the world was much greater than these violent deeds. Overwhelmingly it was a cultural construction. The present chapter will discuss the causes, progress, and decline of anarchist terrorism as a worldwide phenomenon (Chapter 9 will examine it in the United States). A second focus of this chapter will be on government and police reactions to anarchism.[2]

The origins of anarchist "propaganda of the deed"

Anarchist terrorism can only be understood as the product of multiple social, economic, and political causes, as well as of the personal motivations of the terrorists themselves. Government and media responses were integral to the creation of this violent phenomenon. The words "anarchist" and "anarchism" became synonyms for "terrorist" and "terrorism," and many who were nationalists, radicals, socialists, mentally unbalanced, or police agent provocateurs were labeled anarchists because of their violent deeds.

The relationship between anarchism as an ideology and terrorism is problematical. Although there were some pacifist anarchists, the majority favored a violent social revolution and the abolition of law and all governmental and authoritarian social and economic structures.[3] However, neither the Frenchman Pierre-Joseph Proudhon nor, except for a brief period, the Russian Mikhail Bakunin, the founders of the nineteenth-century anarchist movement, called for assassination attempts and terrorist bombings. Only in 1869–70 did Bakunin briefly come under the spell of the ruthless Sergei Nechaev and assisted him in writing *The Catechism of a Revolutionary*, which advocated robbery and assassination.[4] While Bakunin called for terrible and bloody revolts (and organizing workers and peasants to bring them about), he soon became disillusioned with Nechaev and rejected his *Catechism*.

Anarchist-led uprisings, however, failed badly in the 1870s, in part because of excellent police intelligence and spies who had penetrated Bakunin's organization.[5] Governments in France, Spain, Italy, and Germany overreacted to these events and suppressed the socialist, or First, International, the Social Democratic Party in Germany, and various labor organizations. This was despite the fact that the Marxists, at least outside of Russia, not to mention the non-Marxist labor organizations, increasingly emphasized peaceful involvement within the parameters of established institutions in order to build up the socialist and labor movements, rather than violence and instigating an immediate revolution.[6] Nonetheless, governments and many bourgeois feared, or at least claimed to fear, the International as an extremely dangerous instrument of social revolution.

The practice of "propaganda by the deed," a name initially applied to any illegal act of protest but that later came to be associated with anarchist terrorism, developed in the context of the failure of Bakunin's "collectivist" approach, increasing government repression, and the excitement produced by a series of non-anarchist assassinations and attempted assassinations. Between 1877 and 1881, the French anarchist Paul Brousse, the Italian Carlo Cafiero, and the Russian Peter Kropotkin all had a hand in devising and publicizing the concept of propaganda by the deed, although they seem to have had somewhat different ideas about what exactly it entailed.[7] All agreed, however, that it implied illegal acts by individuals as well as bands of conspirators.

A series of assassination attempts in 1878 initiated the era of anarchist terrorism. In January, the brutal governor of St. Petersburg was shot by the Russian revolutionary Vera Zasulich; in May and June, German Kaiser Wilhelm I was fired at and wounded; and in October and November, the kings of Spain and Italy were attacked. In these cases, only two of the assailants – Max Hoedel, in Germany, and Juan Oliva y Moncasi, in Spain – could definitely be considered anarchists (or Bakuninist members of the First International), but the newspapers, authorities, and some anarchists attributed all, except perhaps Zasulich's attack, to the "Black International," i.e., the anarchists. Another defining moment came in March 1881 when the People's Will, an offshoot of the Populist movement, used a dynamite bomb to murder Emperor Alexander II of Russia. The People's Will was not an anarchist organization, but its action thrilled the anarchists, who considered the Russian tsar to be the most despotic ruler in Europe. Under the influence of this assassination, in July 1881 an international congress of anarchists, including Kropotkin and Errico Malatesta, the foremost Italian anarchist, met in London. The congress officially adopted a policy of "propaganda by the deed" and called for the study of the technical sciences, such as chemistry, in order to make explosives.[8] There were several secret agents at the conference, and at least one, a French police informer, vehemently urged the use of bombs. From the very beginning, then, the police – acting on behalf of the authorities who wished to discredit the anarchists and others on the Far Left – played a shadowy role in instigating anarchist terrorism. Whatever the role of the police, the majority of the anarchists in attendance were enthusiastic for a policy of terrorism, given their bitterness against government repression and the success of the People's Will in killing the tsar.

The writings of the German anarchist firebrand Johann Most and others provided even more explicit incitement to terrorism. Between late 1880 and 1885 the columns of Most's newspaper, *Die Freiheit* (*Freedom*), urged workers to engage in propaganda by the deed and provided information on bomb making (some of which was inaccurate and led to premature explosions) and how to poison food and daggers. In 1885, this information was published in German in booklet form as *The Science of Revolutionary Warfare*.[9] The booklet sold tens of thousands of copies, was translated into many languages, and influenced radicals in Germany and America, although it is uncertain how influential it was among French, Italian, and Spanish anarchists.[10] But the anarchists amongst the "Latin races," as they were referred to at the time, had their own advocates of terrorism and published equally bloodcurdling calls for firearms, daggers, and explosives to be employed against the bourgeoisie.[11] What is surprising is that, for example in France, prior to 1892 a decade of ceaseless preaching of propaganda by the deed led to so few actual violent acts and no moral panics. (Part of this incendiary rhetoric was once again due to the police, who funded the first anarchist newspaper in France, a journal, according to Kropotkin, of "unheard-of-violence").[12] A comparable pause occurred in Argentina, where, during the 1890s, anarchist periodicals exalted violence and the glory of dynamite, but, until 1905, this led to no violent deeds.[13] Both cases again suggest the problematical link between anarchist words and terrorist deeds.

The invention of dynamite also shaped the development of anarchist terrorism. The Swedish chemist Alfred Nobel created this unprecedentedly powerful explosive in 1864. The Russian and Irish revolutionaries pioneered its use for terrorist bombings and assassinations since they saw it as a way to differentiate their violent acts from those of common criminals, although for assassinations, at least, the traditional dagger and pistol were more effective weapons. The anarchists followed in the footsteps of these two groups, either stealing dynamite or concocting it on their own according to often faulty recipes.[14] Some anarchists developed an overblown faith in dynamite as a miracle weapon that might level the playing field between the oppressed masses and the state and enable a successful revolution. None of the famous anarchist murders of major political leaders, however, were carried out with dynamite.

Other factors as well played a part in fomenting anarchist terrorism. These included the increasing influence after Bakunin's death in 1876 of Kropotkin's "communism," which, while not overtly championing terrorism, encouraged organizing in small groups and discouraged anarchist involvement in the labor movement. In Spain, small groupings of anarchists provided fertile soil for the growth of violent plots.[15] The last two decades of the nineteenth century witnessed a "Great Depression" that brought a decline in agricultural prices and a marked slowing of general economic growth. Especially hard hit were people living in the countryside and artisans, the latter a social group to which many anarchists belonged and the source of many terrorists. Economic hardship exacerbated the so-called Social Question, "the consciousness of a contradiction between economic development and the social ideal of liberty and equality" (a notion that the French Revolution had popularized).[16] The failure of late-nineteenth-century society to resolve glaring injustices and end severe economic suffering goaded some anarchists into taking extreme actions. Contributing to the outbreak of violence were also regional and national traditions of social warfare and justified regicide that had little to do with anarchist ideology. For example, in the early- and mid-decades of the nineteenth century, the Italian Risorgimento had glorified tyrannicide as a weapon for the achievement of national unification.[17] It should therefore have come as no surprise that in the 1890s Italian anarchists became infamous as the great assassins of Europe.

Since publicity provides the nourishment on which terrorism thrives, the emergence of the "New Journalism" in the 1880s also helped create the mystique of anarchist terrorism as a powerful force. Originating in the United States and Britain, the "New Journalism" was more interested than older forms of journalism in producing exciting news for popular consumption and entertainment. Newspapers in England and France cut their prices and reached circulations of a million or more by the turn of the century.[18]

Worldwide news coverage was only one aspect of the first great era of economic and social globalization (1890s–1914) in which international trade and migration reached unprecedented levels.[19] Anarchists, and in some cases anarchist terrorists, traveled throughout the world as part of this migration. It should be emphasized, however, that conditions in those countries to which the immigrants traveled had to be congenial for the outbreak of anarchist terrorism to occur and that migration alone was not sufficient. Despite the fact that London was a major destination for immigrating anarchists, England experienced only a few insignificant acts of anarchist violence. With the post-World War I clampdown on immigration into the United States and elsewhere, the most significant phase of anarchist terrorism came to an end. In other words, the epoch of anarchist terrorism coincided quite closely with and was to a certain extent the product of the first great period of globalization.

The first phase of anarchist terrorism: 1878–1880s

While the era of anarchist terrorism can plausibly be described as a great wave, within this wave were four more or less distinct phases: 1878 through the 1880s, 1892 through 1901, 1904–14, and 1917–34.[20] Most characteristic of the 1880s were violent acts involving labor disputes and acts of simple criminality. In 1882 authorities accused a mysterious "Black Band" of violent acts against mine operators and religious and political officials in the French town of Montceau-les-Mines. In 1883–4, a second series of dynamite explosions occurred, this time more clearly at the hands of anarchists, although at least one agent provocateur was involved.[21] About the same time in Andalusia, Spain, the even more obscure "Black Hand" was accused of various violent deeds, although it may have only existed in the imaginations of the police and the newspapers. Nonetheless, the anarchists were blamed and ultimately seven were garroted, i.e., iron collars were progressively tightened around their necks until they were strangled or their necks broke.[22] The most famous of all labor disputes associated with anarchist violence, and discussed in the next chapter, was the Haymarket bombing of May 1886 in Chicago. This led to the hanging of innocent anarchists, who became the first great anarchist martyrs and, in the years to come, inspired anarchists throughout the world. The blood of martyrs provided the seeds for many subsequent acts of anarchist terrorism.

During the 1880s, several violent deeds associated with anarchists were entirely or almost entirely criminal. In Austria between 1882 and 1884, alleged anarchists robbed and murdered a number of people, including a moneychanger and his young sons. Anarchists also carried out murders and robberies in Germany and France. Italian anarchists in Paris used part of their proceeds from robberies to finance an anarchist publication; some French intellectuals justified these deeds as revolutionary acts against private property.[23] "Illegalism," expropriation of "bourgeois" property in the name of the revolution, would also crop up later in both anarchist and Russian socialist history.

No anarchist assassinations of major political figures succeeded during the 1880s. In September 1883, however, an anarchist plot may have come close to blowing up the German kaiser, crown prince, and many top generals during the dedication of a monument symbolizing Germania. Otto von Bismarck used the horrified reaction to this incident to renew his anti-socialist law, although the socialists had nothing to do with the plot. This was but one example of many in which governments during this period attempted to exploit anarchist terrorism for ulterior ends. The September 1883 plot even had a link to the authorities since a German police agent lent money to one of the anarchist conspirators to enable him to travel to the site of the planned assassination.[24]

Most anarchist terrorism was carried out in hopes that it might spark a revolution or at least deal a justified blow against repressive employers and other authorities. The desire to take revenge against a perceived wrong is certainly one of the most primal of human impulses. Occasional acts of propaganda by the deed, however, were more *coups de theatre*. Such was the case of Charles Gallo's assault on the Paris Bourse in March 1886, when he tossed a bottle of hydrogen cyanide among and then fired three shots at the stockbrokers. No one was killed, although two people were nearly asphyxiated. Subsequently, Gallo turned his trial into a media circus as he loudly proclaimed his anarchist beliefs.[25] During the 1880s, acts of anarchist violence were, on the whole, isolated and had little impact. Except for the Haymarket bombing in the United States, the public was only momentarily disturbed by these deeds.

Anarchist terrorism and counter-terrorism during the 1890s

All this was to change in the 1890s when anarchist violence erupted across ten countries, primarily in Europe, but also in Cuba, the United States, and Australia. The increasingly wide geographical sweep of anarchist terrorism – ultimately it affected every inhabited continent – differentiated it from all previous forms of terrorism and has not been equaled until the present day. Moreover, during the 1890s, chain reactions of violence, repression, and revenge simultaneously unfolded across multiple countries and for a time seemed impervious to normal methods of police control. The pre-eminent era of anarchist terrorism began in March 1892 with a series of dynamite bombings in Paris carried out by François Claudius Ravachol and prompted initially by the harsh treatment and sentencing of some anarchists involved in a May Day demonstration. Later explosions damaged a mining company, an army barracks, three cafés and restaurants, the French parliament while in session, a church, and a police station. Émile Henry's unprecedented act in February 1894 of killing innocent café goers was particularly shocking. The culminating anarchist act occurred in June 1894 when the Italian Sante Caserio assassinated the French president at Lyon. While the office of president was largely symbolic, President Sadi Carnot had refused to commute the death sentence of Auguste Vaillant, the parliament bomber, despite the fact that that explosion had produced no deaths and little injury and had so been intended.[26]

In the years 1892 to 1894, almost coinciding with events in France, a series of anarchist bombings took place in Belgium, Spain, and then Italy. While the bombings in Belgium, principally in Liège, damaged some buildings, including a church, no one was killed.[27] Soon Spain surpassed France as the site of the world's most lethal anarchist terrorism. The execution in February 1892 of anarchists blamed for an insurrection in Jerez in southern Spain began a cycle of protest, repression, and revenge. Barcelona, the greatest anarchist center in Europe, subsequently witnessed several bombings responding to the Jerez executions and labor disputes. More famously, in September 1893, the idealistic anarchist Paulino Pallás threw bombs at the chief Spanish military commander in Catalonia, slightly wounding the general but killing two others. A November 1893 explosion in Barcelona's opera house, the center of social life for the city's wealthy, led eventually to the death of thirty people, more than those who died in France during the entire decade of the 1890s. Just as horrific was the June 1896 bombing of a religious procession proceeding along Cambios Nuevos (or Canvis Nous) street in Barcelona, which killed twelve people, including women and children. Anti-clericalism was a strong motivating factor behind terrorist attacks in Catholic countries since the Church was seen as a pillar of an oppressive society. Moreover, in the 1896 case, political and military, as well as religious, leaders headed up the procession.[28] Since the anarchists rarely targeted women and, even more rarely, children, the deaths of these innocents produced enormous public outrage. This in turn pushed the government to carry out extravagant measures of repression, which eventually discredited it. The government declared martial law in Barcelona for six months and arrested over 400 anarchists and others suspected of being sympathetic to the anarchists. These included radicals, Catalan republicans, and anti-clericals.[29] Since the jails of Barcelona were filled to overflowing, many of the arrested were imprisoned in the Montjuich fortress overlooking the city. There they were subjected to horrible tortures to extract confessions.[30] In a secret trial characterized by many illegalities, a military court condemned five anarchists to death, although it is almost certain that none of them was responsible for the bombing.[31] The misdeeds of the authorities were widely publicized and did much to blacken their reputation, so much so that the horror over a new "Spanish Inquisition" overshadowed the original horror over the Barcelona bombing. In August 1897, to revenge the cruel deeds carried out in the Montjuich fortress, an Italian anarchist assassin shot and killed Prime Minister Antonio Cánovas del Castillo.

One might ask whether the cruelty of the 1896 anarchist bombing was part of the anarchists' strategy, i.e., to lure their enemies into self-destructive behavior. Since the true author of the bombing was never discovered, it is hard to say. Certainly few if any anarchists overtly praised the bombing and on the whole it seems unlikely that such a Machiavellian goal was the anarchists' intention.

While outside Italy the Italian anarchists were consolidating their title as the foremost assassins of Europe, within the peninsula anarchists provided a similar if less deadly version of events in Spain and France. In March 1894 a bomb exploded outside the parliament building in Rome, killing two people, and in June an anarchist shot at and slightly wounded the prime minister. In May 1894 explosions went off near the Justice and War ministries, and in July an anarchist stabbed to death a Tuscan journalist who had been critical of anarchist tactics. In a fashion almost as extreme as that of Spain, the Italian Parliament passed draconian anti-anarchist laws that were used to round up 3,000 people, many of whom were not anarchists, and detain them on islands off the Italian coast. The government subsequently dissolved the Socialist Party and arrested its leaders, although the socialists had distanced themselves from the anarchists and played no part in their terrorist deeds. As in France, the anarchist terror culminated with the assassination of the head of state, King Umberto I. Killed in July 1900 by an Italian migrant who had been living in Paterson, New Jersey, the murder of Umberto demonstrated the global reach of anarchist violence.[32]

But if anarchist terrorism had a global reach, little evidence proved that it was the product of a grand conspiracy, despite the fears of governments and the press.[33] Before 1905, at least, individuals, perhaps assisted by one or more friends and relatives, carried out the bombings and assassinations. These individuals could often count upon a degree of assistance from informal national and international networks of anarchists, although their precise role, since largely clandestine, remains little known and quite speculative.[34]

The police and governments facilitated these individuals' lethal success because of their grossly deficient knowledge of anarchist actions and their inadequate measures to protect heads of state and government. Around 1900–1, several countries began expanding and professionalizing their executive protection services. Heads of state and government disliked all the restrictions imposed by bureaucratized systems of bodyguards and still held to traditional attitudes that it was unmanly or undemocratic to allow oneself to be surrounded by huge security details.[35] Nonetheless, it was now increasingly recognized that personal preferences must be subordinated to raison d'état in this new age of terrorism. Aided by luck, these systems successfully shielded American heads of state until 1963 and Italian leaders in office until the present day.[36]

While these efforts at prevention proved to be a success, the brutal methods of repression following assassinations and bombings during the 1880s and 1890s produced mixed results. The imprisonment of hundreds and thousands of suspected anarchists and terrorists in France, Italy, and Spain, often without due legal process, and their torture in Spain, may have chastened but also embittered the anarchists, some of whom sought violent revenge. In Spain and Italy, these excessive policies were the product of weakness, not strength. The police forces in both countries were backward, poorly trained and educated, divided into multiple forces, including militarized and civilian branches, and lacking such important tools of scientific policing as effective identification systems. They were also underfunded and undermanned, at least compared to the French and the Metropolitan Police of London. The Spanish authorities resorted to torture and the use of military tribunals to dispense flawed justice, not because they were the descendants of cruel sixteenth-century inquisitors, but because their intelligence services and police forces – at least until the reforms of 1907–12 – were woefully inadequate. Recent research has also emphasized that the Spanish, Italians, French, Germans, Russians, and even, to a moderate extent, the British all resorted to agents provocateurs not only to provoke violent attacks and therefore facilitate the apprehension of extremists but also to achieve other political goals (such as winning elections).[37]

Britain suffered much less from anarchist violence than the continental countries due to a number of causes. These included the greater popularity of its political leaders and stability of its political institutions and its continued adherence to Victorian liberal values. Foreign anarchists appreciated the asylum that England provided them and, despite the occasional crackdown, the freedom to publish what they liked. The British labor movement was highly developed and served to channel worker discontent into non-violent channels. Finally, the British police was perhaps the best in the world. It carefully monitored the anarchists without needlessly provoking them. On occasion it may even have found them jobs.[38]

Reacting to the threat of Fenian and nihilist, as well as anarchist, violence, a number of northern and central European countries passed laws against the criminal use of explosives (e.g., Britain, 1883; Germany, 1884; Austria, 1885; Belgium; 1886; Switzerland, 1894). During the 1890s and the first decade of the twentieth century, some thirteen countries enacted legislation specifically designed to curb propaganda by the deed. These laws ranged from penalizing the abusive use of explosives and prohibiting anarchist associations and publications, to restricting the publication of the proceedings of anarchist trials, trials that often provided the opportunity for inspiring anarchist speeches and the creation of anarchist hero-martyrs.[39] Once again, these laws had a limited and uneven impact since in some cases they exacerbated the situation by provoking anarchist acts of revenge.

In 1898, an Italian anarchist's assassination of Austro-Hungarian Empress Elisabeth while she was visiting Geneva, Switzerland, led to the calling of an international conference in Rome. This was the first anti-terrorist conference ever held and attended by every European state. The conference's first action during its month-long meeting in November–December 1898 was to define an anarchist act as one aiming at "the destruction of all social organization by violent means." This sweeping definition implied that the anarchists were out to destroy all political, religious, social, and even family structures. This frightening prospect differentiated anarchist terrorism from other varieties of contemporary terrorism, such as Socialist Revolutionary terrorism in Russia, which appeared more limited in its goals and put it into a category all its own.[40] While most of the conference's legislative, extradition, and expulsion proposals were never enacted, some of its measures, including measures concluded off the record, were of importance. The recommendations that all countries adopt *portrait parlé*, the French system of personal identification, and that attempts on the lives of heads of state always be liable to extradition (the so-called Belgian Clause) were very influential. Sir Howard Vincent, a British delegate and founder of the Criminal Investigation Department at Scotland Yard, initiated secret meetings of European police officials attending the conference at which arrangements were made for closer cooperation against and communication regarding the anarchists.[41] For fifteen months following the conference, no anarchist *attentats*, or violent deeds, took place. This may have been due to happenstance, but Vincent claimed that the cause had been the "international system . . . established" at Rome and increased police vigilance.[42]

Around 1900-1, following the assassinations of King Umberto and President McKinley, anarchist terrorism went into remission for a more or less extended period depending on the locale. Instead of ordering massive arrests and the curbing of civil liberties, the governments of Italy and the United States reacted relatively mildly, although both countries, but particularly the United States, experienced a popular backlash against the anarchists and sympathy for the assassinated victim. Such a strong popular backlash also occurred in France after the assassination of its president in 1894 and in Argentina after the anarchist bombings of 1909-10 and seems to have been a factor in the temporary halt to anarchist terrorism in those countries. Much of this backlash was due to nationalism, e.g., against the assassination of a French president by an Italian and against anarchist threats to sabotage the 1910 centenary celebrations of Argentine independence. By contrast, during the 1890s, Ravachol had become something of a folk hero since his targets were hated judges and prosecutors who had overlooked police brutality and condemned maltreated anarchists to harsh prison sentences. Vaillant's throwing of an ineffectual bomb into the French parliament in December 1893 had disturbed few ordinary people both because of the lack of injuries and because the parliamentarians were unpopular and considered corrupt.[43]

In the aftermath of the 1900-1 assassinations, both the Italian and American governments enacted significant reforms. As described earlier, both opted to improve protection for their heads of state. The United States passed laws to prohibit anarchist immigration (1903 and 1907), although by 1921 these laws had affected fewer than forty people.[44] Italy expanded and modernized its police force and created an unprecedented international network of policemen and informers in Europe, the Ottoman Empire, and the Americas to spy on the anarchists. In both Italy and the United States, the authorities also adopted more socially progressive policies toward organized labor and, in Italy, toward the socialists. It was the latter policies that exercised the greatest impact on anarchist terrorism by opening up a safety valve for the energies of anarchists and other proletarians, and draining away or redirecting some of their discontent.[45]

Internationally, the impact of the two assassinations was to catalyze efforts to bring about a fuller implementation of the 1898 Rome Accord and to include the United States in these efforts. President Theodore Roosevelt seemed interested in international anti-anarchist cooperation, as indicated by his fiery address to Congress in December 1901 in which he denounced the anarchists in the most extreme terms. But Secretary of State John Hay distrusted the Germans and the Russians, who were spearheading international efforts, and probably believed that the United States lacked the policing apparatus necessary for such cooperation. No national policing organization, such as the Federal Bureau of Investigation, existed before 1908, and the Secret Service could provide only fitful help to the European states.[46] Since for several years following McKinley's assassination anarchist *attentats* did not reoccur, the necessity of an anti-anarchist accord seemed less urgent and this helps explain why not only the United States but also Britain, France, and Italy ultimately declined to join the new initiative.

Nonetheless, in March 1904 lengthy negotiations finally led about two-thirds of the European states to sign a secret anti-anarchist protocol in St. Petersburg. Eventually twelve European countries (Germany, Austria-Hungary, Denmark, Romania, Russia, Serbia, Sweden-Norway [Norway continued in compliance even after separating from Sweden in 1905], Turkey, Bulgaria, Spain, and Portugal) formally adhered to the protocol. Switzerland became a de facto adherent although it never formally signed the accord, and Luxembourg signed a modified agreement with Russia and Germany alone. While never joining, Britain indicated that it had adopted the Swiss attitude "as our model" and "in practice" followed "most" of the protocol's provisions.[47] The agreement specified procedures for expulsion, called for the creation of central anti-anarchist offices in each country, and regularized international police communication regarding the anarchists.[48] While this agreement certainly improved international communication regarding the anarchists and facilitated their expulsion, it is difficult to find evidence that it actually prevented *attentats*.

The third phase of anarchist terrorism: 1904–14

The pause in anarchist terrorism ended around the time of the outbreak of the Russo-Japanese War in 1904 and the Russian 1905 Revolution. Even before then, beginning in 1901, the Russian Socialist Revolutionaries had launched a well-organized series of assassinations targeting tsarist officials.[49] The "Russian Method" of a centrally controlled terrorist campaign (as opposed to the anarchist preference for spontaneous individual action) made a great impression on the world's radicals and revolutionaries. While the Russian Method was not characteristic of the anarchist approach to terrorism, it was often confused with propaganda by the deed, especially outside of Europe in such places as British-ruled India, China, and Japan. Indeed, the anarchist Most may have been one of the first to use the term when he praised the Russian Method following the assassination of Tsar Alexander II.[50] With the outbreak of the chaotic 1905 Revolution, Russian anarchism, which had previously been unimportant inside Russia, experienced exponential growth. An extreme form of terrorism developed, characterized by random, "motiveless" acts of violence with seemingly no connection to ideology; nonetheless, they were attributed to the anarchists. Cases were reported of anarchist suicide bombers. According to one source (although this may well be an exaggeration given the lack of accurate records), "anarchists" were responsible for the majority of the 17,000 Russian casualties from terrorism between 1901 and 1916.[51] After the tsar's concessions brought an end to the revolution, his government resorted to ruthless methods in order to suppress terrorism.[52] Harsh government repression played a role in ending most terrorist acts by late 1907, although government reforms and the general exhaustion of the revolutionary movement played important roles as well, once it was clear that terrorism by itself was unlikely to topple the regime. A turncoat anarchist, who had become a police agent, assassinated Prime Minister Stolypin in 1912. This tragedy was due to the tsarist police's inept handling of its double agents and its excessive use of agents provocateurs.[53]

The draconian repression of terrorism in Russia forced many anarchists and other extremists to flee the country and bring their sometimes violent propensities to France, Switzerland (where two people were killed in 1906–7), the United States, Britain, and, perhaps most spectacularly, to Argentina. In 1907, the French police reported that nearly 1,500 Russian terrorists were living in Paris. While this was presumably an exaggeration, the French capital did became a refuge and networking center for revolutionaries and terrorists from Spain, the Balkans, India, China, and elsewhere, as well as Russia. Russians in Paris gave bomb-making lessons and manuals to Indians battling British rule of India.[54]

In part because of this help from Russian revolutionaries, between 1907 and 1915 a series of bombings and assassination attempts took place in India, leading to the death of at least five people and, in December 1912, the severe injury of the British viceroy. In July 1909 in London, an Indian student killed an aide to the secretary of state for India. While the Indian terrorists were nationalists and not anarchists, the mainstream British, and in some cases the American, press, linked these violent deeds directly to the anarchists and to the Russian Method, which was incorrectly identified as anarchistic.[55]

In 1908, a series of violent deeds, some apparently committed by Russian anarchist immigrants, led to a major anarchist scare in the United States. Given the importance that President Roosevelt gave to anarchist terrorism at this time, it is plausible to infer that one of the reasons for his creation in July 1908 of the embryonic, and initially nameless, Bureau of Investigation may have been his consciousness of the anarchist threat.[56]

In 1909–10, immigrant extremists from the Russian Empire, often identified as anarchists but mostly members of the Latvian Social Democratic Party, carried out several notorious robberies in England. These attacks at Tottenham in January 1909 and Houndsditch in December 1910 culminated in a ferocious shootout with the police on Sidney Street, in the east end of London, in early January 1911. Altogether some five policemen and five Latvians were killed and more than a dozen injured during the three incidents.

The second major source of the worldwide wave of anarchist terrorism after about 1903 was Spain. That country, like Russia, was one of the most backward states in Europe, with many unresolved social and political problems. Rafael Núñez Florencio emphasizes that the harsh repression of a strike in southern Spain in 1903 – together with reports of the police use of torture, leading to the deaths of two workers – exercised "a decisive influence on the perpetuation of new *attentats*."[57] Once again, as in the 1890s, a cycle took shape of protest or strike activity, brutal police crackdowns, and anarchist revenge. In April 1904, an anarchist attacked Prime Minister Antonio Maura. Between 1903 and 1909, over eighty bombs exploded in Barcelona bestowing on it the name "city of bombs." The explosions killed at least eleven people and injured over seventy. A moral panic seized the city, a number of rich people emigrated, and the tourists stopped visiting. Many blamed the anarchists for the Barcelona bombings, although at least some of them were carried out by an agent provocateur named Joan (or Juan) Rull and his family in order to coerce money out of the city authorities. The instigators of many of the other explosions remain unknown.[58]

In 1905–6, serious attempts on the life of King Alfonso XIII took place and led to many deaths. These may have been the product of rather widespread conspiracies and suggest that anarchist terrorists had begun to organize themselves more thoroughly than in the past. This would make sense given that in the twentieth century the anarchists increasingly embraced organized activity as part of their struggle against the established order. For example, they became more and more involved in the labor movement, adopting the syndicalist ideas propounded by the French anarchist Fernand Pelloutier. The new, more highly organized anarchist conspiracies may also have reflected the influence of the Russian Method. At the heart of the conspiracies against Alfonso may have been Francisco Ferrer y Guardia, the wealthy anarchist revolutionary and educational reformer. Ferrer's recent biographer makes a well-documented, if unproven, case for Ferrer's involvement.[59] The first conspiracy occurred when Alfonso visited Paris in May 1905. A bomb attack left the king unharmed but injured seventeen bystanders. Ferrer knew all the suspects in the Paris bombing. Bloodier was an assault in Madrid exactly a year later. A bomb thrown at the king and his new bride missed its target but killed about thirty bystanders and injured over one hundred. This was the deadliest anarchist *attentat* in history up until this point and one of the most widely publicized since it took place in the full glare of the international media and with 200,000 people lining the streets to see the newly married couple. The assassin, Mateo Morral, was Ferrer's librarian and publishing assistant at the Modern School in Barcelona. Morral's girlfriend was a Russian nihilist and perhaps a terrorist herself.[60]

At the time, Ferrer's involvement in either the 1905 or 1906 *attentats* could not be proven. Yet, the Spanish government's deep conviction of his complicity led it to blame him for a destructive uprising in 1909 that led to a week-long revolt in Barcelona and the burning of many churches. The government arrested Ferrer and tried him before a military tribunal that condemned him to execution by firing squad. This judicial murder instantly created a major anarchist martyr and provoked a whole series of acts of revenge. The chief among these was the murder of Prime Minister José Canalejas in November 1912 and yet one more unsuccessful attack on the Spanish king in April 1913.[61]

In 1909–10, the two major sources of anarchist, and world, terrorism came together in Argentina. Here Spanish anarchists and Russian terrorists ignited a brief but intense period of terrorism and moral panic. Beginning in 1905, two attempts on the life of the president of Argentina were followed by a series of bombings. In 1908, the press accused the Russians of introducing terrorism to Argentina, and the police claimed to have discovered a Russian bomb factory and plans to blow up the public water works and the main electrical power plant of Buenos Aires.[62] In October and November 1909, in protest against the Spanish execution of Ferrer, Catalonians carried out a bombing of the Spanish consulate in Rosario and Russians an attempted bombing of a church in Buenos Aires. The most sensational act of anarchist violence occurred on November 14, 1909, when an immigrant Russian Jewish anarchist named Simon Radowisky assassinated Ramon Falcon, the police chief of Buenos Aires and one of the most powerful men in the country. In May–June 1910, the Cathedral of Buenos Aires and the Colon opera house were bombed, leading to one death and more than a dozen wounded, some seriously. Clothing its actions in the language of "social defense" as propounded by European criminologists, the Argentine government acted as ruthlessly as in Spain or Russia. The authorities declared martial law for months and arrested thousands of suspected anarchists, torturing some and deporting others.[63]

During the 1905–14 period, real or alleged anarchist acts of violence also took place in Sweden, Denmark, Italy, Belgium, Germany, the Balkans, and the Ottoman Empire. While the assassin of King George I of Greece in March 1913 has often been written off as simply a madman, evidence from people who knew Aleko Schinas when he lived in the United States attests to his intelligence and firm anarchist convictions.[64] Following the assassination, the Greek government demonstrated how worried it was about the anarchists by requesting that nearby countries send it lists of their resident "militant anarchists" who might be of danger to "the security of prominent persons." It also created a special security service to protect its sovereign and other noted persons.[65]

China and Japan also experienced the impact of anarchist terrorism and the Russian Method. This was due in part to Chinese students studying in Paris who brought back anarchist ideas to China. For a time "assassinationism" was in vogue, drawing inspiration from both the anarchists and the Russian Socialist Revolutionaries, groups that the Chinese radicals often conflated. "Assassination squads" or "corps" were organized to murder Imperial Chinese officials and in January 1912 succeeded in killing a leading Manchu noble. This devastating blow was a major factor in the decision of the imperial court to abdicate on behalf of the child emperor.[66] Japanese anarchists arrested in 1910 were apparently plotting to carry out a "revolution of terror" and the assassination of the emperor.[67]

In the Balkans, many of the most extreme south Slav opponents of the Habsburg Empire were enamored of the Russian Method and looked to Socialist Revolutionary émigrés in Switzerland and France for advice on terrorism. A powerful tradition of tyrannicide also existed among the south Slavs. The Austrian authorities, however, frequently described Young Bosnia, one of the principal nationalist groups, as "anarchist," and, indeed, a few of its members were anarchists and many more were influenced by anarchist ideas. Presciently, in 1898 the Russian foreign minister had expressed to the Austrians his fears that should the anarchists spread into the Balkan peninsula where they could be monitored only with difficulty, they would cause embarrassment to both governments.[68] This premonition seemed to be coming true in June 1914 when Nedeljko Čabrinović, a confirmed anarchist – at least for a time – and formerly employed at an anarchist print shop in Belgrade, threw the first bomb at the Archduke Franz Ferdinand. Already, beginning in 1910, Slav nationalists had initiated a systematic campaign of political assassination against Austrian officials in Croatia and Bosnia that culminated in the murder of the heir to the Austro-Hungarian throne.[69] Franz Ferdinand was unprotected by the elaborate security system that since 1853 had effectively safeguarded the Emperor Franz Joseph.[70]

With the outbreak of World War I in 1914, anarchist terrorism came to an end in most countries. People's energies and, even more crucially, the mass media were focused on the war effort, and young men, the source of most terrorists, were drafted into the military. Moreover, European anarchists split over the issue of whether or not to support the western Allies, as Kropotkin did. In general, terrorism declines during wars between states[71] but peaks during periods of intense civil conflict and revolution. There were no anarchist assassinations or bombings in any of the belligerent states during World War I, except in the United States, where two incidents occurred in Milwaukee in 1917. On the other hand, during the Russian Revolution of 1905 and its aftermath, the Russian civil war of 1918–20, and the quasi civil war in Barcelona during the era of the *pistoleros* between 1919 and 1923, many hundreds, if not thousands, of violent anarchist acts took place.

Anarchist terrorism after the Russian Revolution

The Russian Revolution of 1917 opened the way for the final phase of anarchist terrorism because it excited and inspired the extreme Left and destabilized several countries. The economic recession and social turmoil that followed in the wake of World War I compounded the revolution's impact. Russian anarchists, after initially welcoming the Bolshevik triumph, came to see their government as the world's worst despotism. Anarchists began forming groups that instigated terrorist acts, especially in southern Russia. On September 25, 1919, a clandestine organization of anarchists together with some left-wing Socialist Revolutionaries blew up the Moscow headquarters of the Communist Party while a meeting was in progress. The explosion killed 12 people and wounded 55 others. The anarchists now called for a new "era of dynamite" to destroy Communist tyranny, but the Bolsheviks prevented this through wholesale arrests and executions.[72]

In Spain, postwar political and economic problems spawned an era of terrorism fully comparable to, if not indeed more severe than, the contemporary anarchist terrorism in Russia. Following a period of artificial wartime prosperity, an acute economic recession caused Spanish employers to demand drastic wage cuts for their workers. They also wished to humble, if not destroy, the CNT, the anarcho-syndicalist union, which had begun to expand during the war. By 1919, it had reached a membership of 500,000. Members of the CNT, and the anarchists generally, were thrilled by the outbreak of the Russian Revolution and believed that it might portend a similar revolution in Spain. They were in no mood to compromise with business owners, who were supported by the government and army. It was in this tense and volatile situation that Catalonia and particularly Barcelona descended into conditions of near civil war and rampant terrorism. Rival groups of gunmen, known as *pistoleros*, some backed by the government and the employer associations and others affiliated with the anarchists and the CNT, engaged in a series of revenge assassinations and bombings. Between January 1919 and December 1923, rival gangs killed over 700 people.[73] Right-wing *pistoleros* killed dozens of syndicalist leaders, including moderates. In revenge, anarchist "action groups" assassinated various employers; the editor of a newspaper; the former civil governor of Barcelona; Prime Minister Eduardo Dato (in March 1921); and the Cardinal Archbishop of Saragossa (in April 1923). (Dato was the last head of government or state anywhere in the world to be killed by the anarchists.) The Spanish government proved ineffectual in curbing the violence. Due in part to this, in September 1923 a Spanish general overthrew the constitutional regime and installed a dictatorship. He also destroyed the CNT and by December 1923 had ended terrorism in Barcelona.[74]

The postwar chaos, violence, and terrorism in Catalonia were also replicated in postwar Italy. Bombings, allegedly by anarchists, killed people in Milan in October 1920 and in Turin in May 1921. The worst bombing took placed on March 23, 1923, when an explosion at the Diana Theater in Milan led to the death of twenty-one and the injury of 172 people. This was the bloodiest terrorist incident in Italy until 1980. It was also largely an accident. The anarchist conspirators, including a woman, had intended to protest the imprisonment of Malatesta by striking at the chief of police, who was staying in a hotel next door to the theater.[75] Nonetheless, even the bombing of a hotel, which might very well have led to the death of innocent people uninvolved in policing or politics, represents a significant break from the past practice of Italian anarchists. The Italians, unlike the French and Spanish, had hitherto avoided such targets. Italian anarchists were also involved in attempts on Benito Mussolini's life, none of which even wounded the *Duce*, but all served as excellent excuses for consolidating his dictatorial rule.

Between 1919 and 1923, the anarchists carried out a number of violent acts in France. In February 1919, Prime Minister Georges Clemenceau was shot in the shoulder. Perhaps the most notable attempt, however, occurred in January 1923 when Germaine Berton became the first woman anarchist to succeed in an assassination after she killed the right-wing editor of the *Action Française* newspaper. A little over a year before, the anarchist May Picqueray claimed to have tried to assassinate the American ambassador by sending him a hand grenade inside a perfume box.[76]

This greater prominence of female anarchist terrorists probably reflects increased female participation in a whole range of traditionally male activities due to their mobilization during World War I. While before the war anarchist women had assisted their lovers in carrying out terrorist plots, none of them had actually perpetrated violent deeds themselves. For example, during the 1890s, Emma Goldman had helped provide money for Alexander Berkman's attack on Henry Clay Frick, and the police accused several French women of assisting anarchist men in propaganda by the deed.[77] Their merely secondary role stood in marked contrast with that of the female Russian populists of the 1870s and 1880s, who had played a prominent part in carrying out assassinations. Although in theory the anarchists believed in equality between the sexes, they also dismissed feminism as a bourgeois distraction and suspected women of being more conservative and traditional than men.[78]

Between 1917 and 1932, Latin America became a major site of anarchist terrorism leading to the signature in February 1920 of the last international anti-anarchist agreement, although doubtless it was also aimed at revolutionary Bolshevism.[79] Bombings and assassinations occurred in Argentina, Brazil, and Uruguay. Especially in Argentina, this was often due to Spanish and Italian anarchists fleeing the dictatorships recently established in their home countries. Apparently in protest against an "anarchist trial," the Palace of Justice in Buenos Aires was bombed in August 1920.[80] In February 1921, anarchist bombs damaged the stock exchange and foreign ministry buildings in Rio de Janeiro.[81] In January 1923, a German anarchist assassinated Colonel Hector Varela in revenge for his ruthless repression of strikers in Patagonia. Between 1926 and 1930, the immigrant Italian Severino di Giovanni and his gang carried out numerous bombings and a huge robbery. In May 1926, he bombed the US embassy in Buenos Aires, destroying the building's entire façade, in protest against the death sentence handed down to the American anarchists Sacco and Vanzetti. For the same reason, in December 1927 he bombed two American banks in Buenos Aires, killing two persons and wounding twenty-three. Di Giovanni's bloodiest terrorist deed occurred in May 1928, when he and others bombed the Italian consulate, killing nine and injuring thirty-four. In December 1929, another Italian anarchist came close to killing Argentine President Hipólito Yrigoyen.[82]

The second important anarchist gang leader of the time was Arcangel Roscigna. He was the leader of the "anarchist expropriators" and robbed several banks, once in collaboration with the famous Spanish anarchist Durruti. Fleeing to Uruguay after the death of a policeman, the expropriators were captured and tortured by the police chief of Montevideo. Revenge-seeking anarchists gunned him down in February 1932. After this event, anarchist terrorism in South America largely subsided for many years. In Argentina, the military dictatorship of General José Félix Uriburu in 1930–1 harshly repressed the anarchists. Spanish and Italian anarchists were expelled and native anarchists sent to Terra del Fuego, the Argentine Siberia.[83]

While in Spain anarchist violence and terrorism flared up in the 1930s after the downfall of the military dictatorship of Primo de Rivera and in the tumultuous years leading up to the Spanish Civil War, in the rest of the world they went into steep decline. The anarchists had long lost to the communists their publicity and their reputation as the pre-eminent threat to world civilization. Therefore idealists and notoriety seekers had less and less incentive to wrap themselves in the anarchist mystique before committing acts of violence leading to martyrdom. In Italy and Russia, powerful dictatorships supported by political parties that mobilized the masses and controlled the media had consolidated their power by the late 1920s or early 1930s. They crushed anarchist opposition and mostly eliminated the possibility of terrorism. The same occurred in Spain after General Francisco Franco's triumph in 1939. The collapse of international migration, due to restrictive laws in the 1920s in the US and elsewhere and later to the economic depression of the 1930s, constricted or halted the flow of anarchists, and in some cases anarchist terrorists, around the world. Rivalries and disputes among the anarchists themselves paralyzed action. Changes in legal thinking, which had previously equated anarchism with terrorism, symbolized the end of the era of anarchist terrorism. After a member of the right-wing Macedonian terrorist organization VMRO, with the assistance of Croatian nationalists, and with the direct or indirect support of Mussolini, assassinated Yugoslav King Alexander and the French foreign minister in Marseille in April 1934, it was no longer possible to view terrorist deeds as primarily the acts of anarchists. In 1937, the League of Nations drew up a convention for the prevention and punishment of terrorism that made no mention of anarchist or social crimes.[84]

Notes

1 *St. Paul Pioneer Press*, September 8, 1901.
2 For a more detailed discussion of anarchist terrorism and its repression, including many references omitted from the present text, see Jensen, *The Battle against Anarchist Terrorism, 1878–1934: An International History* (Cambridge: Cambridge University Press, 2014).
3 For a further discussion of anarchist ideology, see Chapter 9 by Thai Jones on "Anarchist Terrorism in the United States" in this volume and chapter 1, "The Origins of Anarchist Terrorism," in Jensen, *The Battle against Anarchist Terrorism*.
4 For further information on Nechaev and Russian terrorism in general, see Chapter 7 in this volume by Martin A. Miller, "Entangled Terrorisms in Late Imperial Russia."
5 Giampietro Berti, "La sovversione anarchica in Italia e la risposta giudiziaria dello State (1874–1900)," *Quaderni fiorentini per la storia del pensiero giuridico moderno* 38 (2009): 579–600, especially 579–83.
6 For a comparison between the anarchist and the socialist approaches to violence and direct action, see Chapter 9 in this volume by Jones, "Anarchist Terrorism in the United States." While the anarchists advocated direct action and violent revolution, this did not necessarily imply the adoption of a strategy of terrorism. As I have tried to indicate in this chapter, its genesis had a much more complicated origin. Moreover, some socialists, especially inside Russia, did engage in terrorist tactics.
7 Even earlier, in 1857, Carlo Pisacane had distinguished between "propaganda of the idea" and propaganda by conspiracies, plots, and other "deeds." The anarchists rediscovered Pisacane's writings in the 1870s. Pisacane, *Saggio sulla rivoluzione* (Milan: Universale Economica, 1956); Nunzio Pernicone, *Italian Anarchism, 1864–1892* (Princeton, NJ: Princeton University Press, 1993), 13; George Richard Esenwein, *Anarchist Ideology and the Working-Class Movement in Spain, 1868–1898* (Berkeley: University of California, 1989), 60–1; and Ze'ev Ivianski, "Individual Terror: Concept and Typology," *Journal of Contemporary History* 12, no. 1 (1977): 45; Cafiero, "L'Action," *Le Révolté*, December 25, 1880, quoted by Pernicone, *Italian Anarchism*, 186–7. Cafiero's famous article advocating propaganda by deed is often erroneously attributed to Kropotkin, e.g., Walter Laqueur, *The Age of Terrorism* (Boston, MA: Little, Brown, 1987), 48; and James Joll, *The Anarchists* (London: Eyre and Spottiswoode, 1964), 109. Caroline Cahm, *Kropotkin and the Rise of Revolutionary Anarchism, 1872–1886* (Cambridge: Cambridge University Press, 1989), 140, points out Kropotkin's reservations about Cafiero's approach.
8 Cahm, 152–77. The resolutions of the London Congress were published in *Le Révolté* (July 23, 1881), 1–2, and are reproduced, in English translation, in Cahm, 157–8, and Andrew Carlson, *Anarchism in Germany*, vol. 1, *The Early Movement* (Metuchen, NJ: Scarecrow Press, 1972), 62–3.
9 Johann Most, *Military Science for Revolutionaries* (Cornville, AZ: Desert Publications, 1978).
10 Paul Avrich, *The Haymarket Tragedy* (Princeton, NJ: Princeton University Press, 1984), 66; and Jensen, "The Evolution of Anarchist Terrorism in Europe and the United States from the

Nineteenth Century to World War I," in *Terror from Tyrannicide to Terrorism*, ed. Brett Bowden and Michael Davis (St. Lucia: University of Queensland Press, 2008), 138, 330.

11 The Italian chemist Ettore Molinari provided information for the explosives manual *La Salute è in Voi!* published by the anarchist Luigi Galleani. *L'indicateur anarchiste* provided similar information for the French. See Chapter 29 by Ann Larabee in this volume.

12 Jean Maitron, *Histoire du Mouvement Anarchiste en France (1880–1914)*, 2nd ed. (Paris: Société universitaire d'éditions et de librairie, 1955), 134, 198; and Kropotkin, *Memoirs of a Revolutionist*, ed. and introd. by Nicolas Walter (New York: Dover, 1988), 479–80.

13 Iaacov Oved, *El anarquismo y el movimiento obrero en argentina* (Mexico City: Siglo XXI, 1978), 64.

14 For the problems involved in and the high failure rate of amateur bomb making, see Chapter 29 by Larabee. On the Irish Fenians' dynamite campaign of the 1880s, see Chapter 12 by Benjamin Grob-Fitzgibbon in this volume.

15 Joaquín Romero Maura, "Terrorism in Barcelona and its Impact on Spanish Politics 1904–1909," *Past and Present* 41 (1968), 51–4.

16 Adolph Wagner cited by Ira W. Howerth, *American Journal of Sociology* 12, no. 2 (September 1906): 259.

17 For early nineteenth-century terrorism, see Chapter 5 in this volume by Mike Rapport, "The French Revolution and Early European Revolutionary Terrorism."

18 Robert A. Saunders, "Media and Terrorism," Chapter 28 in this volume; Anthony Smith, *The Newspaper: An International History* (London: Thames and Hudson, 1979); and Micheline Dupuy, *Le Petit Parisien* (Paris: Plon, 1989), 60, 71.

19 E. J. Hobsbawm, *The Age of Empire, 1875–1914* (New York: Random House, 1989), 53.

20 David C. Rapoport, "The Four Waves of Modern Terrorism," in *Attacking Terrorism: Elements of a Grand Strategy*, ed. Audrey Kurth Cronin and James M. Ludes, 46–73 (Washington, DC: Georgetown University Press, 2004).

21 Maitron, *Histoire du mouvement anarchiste*, 156–7.

22 Temma Kaplan, *Anarchists of Andalusia, 1868–1903* (Princeton, NJ: Princeton University Press, 1977), 126–34; and Esenwein, *Anarchist Ideology*, 88–92.

23 Carlson, *Anarchism in Germany*, 256–69; and Maitron, *Histoire du mouvement anarchiste*, 182–3.

24 Carlson, *Anarchism in Germany*, 288–9.

25 Maitron, *Histoire du mouvement anarchiste*, 201–2; and Ettore Sernicoli, *L'anarchia e gli anarchici: Studio storico e politico*, 2nd ed. (Milan: Treves, 1894), 1:270–2.

26 Henri Varennes [Henri Vonoven], *De Ravachol à Caserio* (Paris: Garnier Frères, 1895).

27 For a brief discussion of Belgium, as well as the Netherlands, see Beatrice de Graaf, "The Black International Conspiracy as Security Dispositive in the Netherlands, 1880–1900," *Historical Social Research/Historische Sozialforschung* 38, no. 1 (2013), 142–65.

28 Temma Kaplan, *Red City, Blue Period: Social Movements in Picasso's Barcelona* (Berkeley: University of California Press, 1992), 28–35; and Angel Herrerin, "España: La Propaganda por la Represión, 1892–1900," in *El nacimiento del terrorismo en occidente*, ed. Juan Avilés Farré and Angel Herrerin, 103–39 (Madrid: Siglo XXI de España, 2008).

29 Herrerin, "España: La Propaganda," in *El nacimiento del terrorismo*, 103–39; Esenwein, *Anarchist Ideology*, 193; and Rafael Núñez Florencio, *El terrorismo anarquista (1888–1909)* (Madrid: Sigloveintiuno, 1983), 58.

30 Esenwein, *Anarchist Ideology*, 195.

31 Romero Maura, "Terrorism in Barcelona," 131.

32 *La Tribuna* (Rome), March 9–10; May 31–June 1, 1894; Francis Nichols, "The Anarchists in America," *Outlook*, August 10, 1901, 859–63; Captain George McClusky of the New York City Detective Bureau, report, August 1900, copy included with letter of Ambassador Fava to Acting Secretary of State, A. A. Adee, September 19, 1900, RG 60, Department of Justice, National Archives (College Park, MD); and Arrigo Petacco, *L'Anarchico che venne dall'America* (Milan: Mondadori, 1974).

33 For more on the relationship between counter-terrorism and conspiracy, including during the turn-of-the-century wave of anarchist violence, see Chapter 27 by Beatrice de Graaf in this volume.

34 Vivien Bouhey, "Anarchist Terrorism in Fin-de-Siècle France and its Borderlands," *Oxford Handbooks Online* (February 2014), 10, Online at: www.oxfordhandbooks.com (accessed May 13, 2014).

Like Bouhey (although he does not discuss terrorism), Davide Turcato (*Making Sense of Anarchism: Errico Malatesta's Experiments with Revolution, 1889–1900* [New York: Palgrave Macmillan, 2012]) argues that anarchist actions were more planned and organized than has previously been thought.

35 Carola Dietze and Frithjof Benjamin Schenk, "Traditionelle Herrscher in moderner Gefahr: Soldatisch-aristokratische Tugendhaftigkeit und das Konzept der Sicherheit im späten 19. Jahrhundert," *Geschichte und Gesellschaft* 35, no. 3 (July–Sept 2009): 368–401.

36 The Italian partisans' murder of Mussolini in 1945 was more an act of war and civil war than terrorism. Even after 1900, mere heads of government continued to be provided with less protection than heads of state. Examples include Spanish prime ministers Canalejas (1912) and Dato (1921) and Austrian Minister President von Stürgkh (1916). The first two were assassinated by anarchists and Stürgkh by a socialist.

37 Alex Butterfield, *The World That Never Was* (New York: Pantheon, 2010); and Louis Andrieux, *Souvenirs d'un Prefect de Police* (Paris: Memoire Du Livre, [1885] 2002), 256–61.

38 Bernard Porter, *The Origins of the Vigilant State: The London Metropolitan Police Special Branch Before the First World War* (London: Weidenfeld and Nicolson, 1987); and [Guillermo J. de Osma y Scull] "Tanteo confidencial sobre concertar la repression internacional del anarquismo de accion, Entente cordiale," July 1906, Archivo Maura (Madrid), Arm.Inf.N.3/G.2.

39 Richard Bach Jensen, "The International Campaign against Anarchist Terrorism, 1880–1930s," *Terrorism and Political Violence* 21, no. 1 (2009): 91–2.

40 In 1903, for example, the Socialist Revolutionary Mikhail Gotz (or Gots) was denied extradition from Italy to Russia although accused of organizing the assassination or attempted assassination of two government ministers. An important part of the justification for this denial was that these violent deeds were protected by a clause in the Italo-Russian extradition treaty that excluded persons who had committed illegal acts for political reasons. Anarchist crimes were almost never afforded such protection or considered "political" by the courts ("Memoria sulla domanda di estradizione del cittadino russo Michele Gotz," *La scuola positiva* 12, no. 1–2 (January–February 1903): 4–25; and *Enciclopedia giuridica italiana*, s.v. "Estradizione" by Pietro Lanza, 549).

41 Chapter 5, in Richard Bach Jensen, *The Battle against Anarchist Terrorism*.

42 *Times* (London), June 5, 1906, 3.

43 *Enciclopedia giuridica italiana*, s.v. "*Estradizione*" by Pietro Lanza, 5:547 n.5; interview with Francesco Saverio Merlino, *La Stampa* (Turin), June 18, 1907, in *Gli anarchici: Cronaca inedita dell'Unità d'Italia*, ed. Aldo De Jaco, 699 (Rome: Editori Riuniti, 1971); Maitron, *Histoire du mouvement anarchiste*, 244–6; David Rock, *Argentina 1516–1982* (Berkeley and Los Angeles: University of California Press, 1985), 187; Juan Suriano, *Paradoxes of Utopia: Anarchist Culture and Politics in Buenos Aires, 1890–1910*, trans. Chuck Morse (Oakland, CA: AK Press, 2010), 224–6; and Varennes, *De Ravachol à Caserio*, 98, 208.

44 William Preston, *Aliens and Dissenters: Federal Suppression of Radicals, 1903–1933*, 2nd ed. (Urbana: University of Illinois Press, 1963), 33.

45 Mauro Canali, *Le spie del regime* (Bologna: Mulino, 2004); Jensen, *The Battle against Anarchist Terrorism*, especially chapters 6 and 8; and Richard Bach Jensen, "Police Reform and Social Reform: Italy from the Crisis of the 1890s to the Giolittian Era," *Criminal Justice History: An International Annual* 10 (1989): 179–200.

46 Richard Bach Jensen, "The United States, International Policing, and the War against Anarchist Terrorism, 1900–1914," *Terrorism and Political Violence* 13:1 (Spring 2001), 15–46.

47 W. E. Davidson, 8 June 1908, FO371/78; A. H. D[ixon], "Memorandum as to the Protocol of 1904 respecting Anarchist Crimes", 13 July 1906, HO144/757/118516, Public Record Office (now the National Archives), Kew, UK.

48 Jensen, "The International Campaign."

49 For details, see Chapter 7 by Miller in this volume.

50 Edward Krebs, *Shifu, Soul of Chinese Anarchism* (New York: Rowman and Littlefield, 1998), 4, 33–8. Steven Marks (*How Russia Shaped the Modern World* (Princeton, NJ: Princeton University Press, 2003), 17–37) discusses the "Russian Method" abroad. For Most's statement, see James H. Billington, *Fire in the Minds of Men* (New York: Basic Books, 1980), 414.

51 Anna Geifman, *Thou Shalt Kill: Revolutionary Terrorism in Russia, 1894–1917* (Princeton, NJ: Princeton University Press, 1995), 124–5.

52 Miller, Chapter 7 in this volume.
53 Geifman, *Thou Shalt Kill*, 231–2; 237–40.
54 Peter Heehs, *The Bomb in Bengal: The Rise of Revolutionary Terrorism in India, 1900–1910* (Delhi: Oxford University Press, 1993), 90–1.
55 *Times* (London), May 4, 1908; *Times*, February 16, 1909, 7; "Indian Anarchism," *Times*, February 12, 1909, 11; "Anarchism in India. The Influences of Western Propaganda," *Times*, February 15, 1909; "The Indian Anarchists," *Times*, February 16, 1909; "The Attempted Assassination of Lord Hardinge," *Times*, December 24, 1912, 5; and George McDermot, "Anarchism in India and its Consequences," *American Catholic Quarterly Review* (July 1909), 521. Also see Chapter 12 by Grob-Fitzgibbon in this volume.
56 Jones, "Anarchist Terrorism in the United States"; and Jensen, "The United States, International Policing," 31–4.
57 Núñez Florencio, *El terrorismo anarquista*, 103.
58 Eduardo Gonzàlez Calleja, *La razón de la fuerza: Orden público, subversión y violencia política en la España de la Restauración (1875–1917)* (Madrid: Consejo superior de investigaciones científicas, 1998), 398–400; Romero Maura, "Terrorism in Barcelona," 156–7; and Núñez Florencio, *El terrorismo anarquista*, 80–2, 164–8.
59 Juan Avilés Farré, *Francisco Ferrer y Guardia* (Madrid: Marcial Pons, 2006).
60 Ibid., 152, 168–9, 189–90.
61 Avilés Farré, ch.7. With Canalejas, it is a question of probability, rather than certainty, since the assassin committed suicide immediately after the murder. S. Sueiro Seoane, "El asesinato de Canalejas y los anarquistas españoles en Estados Unidos," in *El nacimiento del terrorismo*, 159–88; and E. Comin Colomer, *Un siglo de atentados politicos en España* (Madrid: [Editorial N.O.S.], 1951), 209–10.
62 Jose Moya, "The Positive Side of Stereotypes: Jewish Anarchists in Early-Twentieth-Century Buenos Aires," *Jewish History* 18, no. 1 (2004), 30.
63 Osvaldo Bayer, "Simón Radowitzky," in *The Argentina Reader: History, Culture, Politics*, ed. Gabriela Nouzeilles and Graciela Montaldo, 219–30 (Durham, NC: Duke University Press, 2002); Jose Moya, "The Positive Side of Stereotypes," 19–48; and Richard Bach Jensen, "Global Terrorism and Transnational Counterterrorism: Policing Anarchist Migration Across the Atlantic; Italy and Argentina, 1890s–1914," in *Oxford Handbooks Online* and *The Oxford Handbook of the History of Terrorism*, ed. Carola Dietze and Claudia Verhoeven (Oxford: Oxford University Press, 2014, and forthcoming).
64 *New York Times*, March 20, 1913, 3.
65 "King's Murderer is Educated Anarchist," and "The Assassin Lived Here," *New York Times*, March 20, 1913, 3. *Note-Verbale*, Greek Legation, to Italian Foreign Ministry, Rome, October 23, 1914, "Z" b. 49, Italian foreign ministry archive, Rome. The new security service was instituted by decree on January 3, 1914. Italian Foreign Ministry, April 27, 1914, Div. AA.GG.RR. Massime, b. 3/A3, Archivio Centrale dello Stato, Rome.
66 E. J. M. Rhoads, *Manchus and Han: Ethnic Relations and Political Power in Late Qing and Early Republican China, 1861–1928* (Seattle: University of Washington Press, 2000), 21, 23, 154–5, 222.
67 Ira Plotkin, *Anarchism in Japan: A Study of the Great Treason Affair 1910–1911* (Lewiston/Queenston/Lampeter: Edwin Mellen, 1990).
68 Austrian embassy, St. Petersburg, to foreign ministry, Vienna. September 28/16, 1898. Politisches Archiv. Interna XXVII/64. N. 94. A-B. Haus- Hof- und Staatsarchiv, Vienna.
69 V. Dedijer, *The Road to Sarajevo* (New York: Simon and Schuster, 1966), 181, 200, 226, 236, 244, 357, 435.
70 For Franz Joseph's security system, see Jensen, *Battle against Anarchist Terrorism*, 205–7.
71 Franklin L. Ford, *Political Murder: From Tyrannicide to Terrorism* (Cambridge: Cambridge University Press, 1985), 246.
72 Paul Avrich, *The Russian Anarchists* (New York: W. W. Norton, 1978), 185–90.
73 Florian Grafl, "A Blueprint for Successfully Fighting Anarchist Terror?: Counter-Terrorist Communities of Violence in Barcelona during the *Pistolerismo*," in *An International History of Terrorism: Western and non-Western Experience*," 51–64; and Gerald Brennan, *The Spanish Labyrinth* (Cambridge: Cambridge University Press, 1971), 74n2.
74 Robert Kern, *Red Years/Black Years: A Political History of Spanish Anarchism, 1911–1937* (Philadelphia, PA: Institute for the Study of Human Issues, 1978), 34–68.

75 Vincenzo Mantovani, *Mazurka blu: La strage del Diana* (Milan: Rusconi, 1979).
76 Richard Sonn, *Sex, Violence and the Avant-Garde: Anarchism in Interwar France* (University Park: Pennsylvania State University Press, 2010).
77 Paul Avrich and Karen Avrich, *Sasha and Emma* (Cambridge, MA: Harvard University Press, 2012); and Richard Sonn, "Gender and Political Violence in Nineteenth Century France and Russia," *Proceedings of the Western Society for French History: 2000 Annual Meeting*, ed. Barry Rothaus, 199–206 (Boulder, CO: University Press of Colorado, 2002).
78 Sonn, *Sex, Violence and the Avant-Garde*, 30–8.
79 *Control of Terrorism: International Documents*, ed. Yonah Alexander et al. (New York: Crane Russak, 1979), 11–16.
80 *New York Times*, August 15, 1920, 2:1.
81 Ibid., February 10, 1921.
82 *New York Times*, January 26, 1923, 19; Moshik Temkin, *The Sacco–Vanzetti Affair: America on Trial* (New Haven, CT: Yale University Press, 2009), 40; Osvaldo Bayer, *Los anarquistas expropriadores* (Buenos Aires: Planeta, 2003), 11–88; and Víctor Alba, *Politics and the Labor Movement in Latin America* (Redwood City, CA: Stanford University Press, 1968).
83 Osvaldo Bayer, "L'influenza dell'immigrazione italiana nel movimento anarchico argentino," in *Los anarquistas expropriadores*, 123–46.
84 Bogdan Zlataric, "History of International Terrorism and its Legal Control," in *International Terrorism and Political Crimes*, ed. M. Cherif Bassiouni, 474–84 (Springfield, IL: Charles Thomas, 1975).

Further reading

Carlson, Andrew. *Anarchism in Germany*. Vol. 1, *The Early Movement*. Metuchen, NJ: Scarecrow Press, 1972.

Dietze, Carola, and Frithjof Benjamin Schenk. "Traditionelle Herrscher in moderner Gefahr. Soldatisch-aristokratische Tugendhaftigkeit und das Konzept der Sicherheit im späten 19. Jahrhundert." *Geschichte und Gesellschaft* 35, no. 3 (July–Sept 2009): 368–401.

Esenwein, George Richard. *Anarchist Ideology and the Working-Class Movement in Spain, 1868–1898*. Berkeley: University of California, 1989.

Farré, Juan Avilés, and Angel Herrerin, eds. *El nacimiento del terrorismo en occidente*. Madrid: Siglo XXI de España, 2008.

Jensen, Richard Bach. *The Battle against Anarchist Terrorism, 1878–1934: An International History*. Cambridge: Cambridge University Press, 2014.

—. "The First Global Wave of Terrorism and International Counter-terrorism, 1905–1914." In *An International History of Terrorism: Western and non-Western Experience*, edited by Jussi Hanhimäki and Bernhard Blumenau, 16–33. London: Routledge, 2013.

Maitron, Jean. *Histoire du Mouvement Anarchiste en France (1880–1914)*. 2nd ed. Paris: Société universitaire d'éditions et de librairie, 1955.

Núñez Florencio, Rafael. *El terrorismo anarquista (1888–1909)*. Madrid: Siglo veintiuno, 1983.

Oved, Iaacov. *El anarquismo y el movimiento obrero en argentina*. Mexico City: Siglo XXI, 1978.

Pernicone, Nunzio. *Italian Anarchism, 1864–1892*. Princeton, NJ: Princeton University Press, 1993.

Rapoport, David C. "The Four Waves of Modern Terrorism." In *Attacking Terrorism: Elements of a Grand Strategy*, edited by Audrey Kurth Cronin and James M. Ludes, 46–73. Washington, DC: Georgetown University Press, 2004.

Romero Maura, Joaquín. "Terrorism in Barcelona and its Impact on Spanish Politics, 1904–1909." *Past and Present* 41 (1968): 130–83.

Varennes, Henri [Henri Vonoven]. *De Ravachol à Caserio*. Paris: Garnier Frères, 1895.

9

ANARCHIST TERRORISM IN THE UNITED STATES

Thai Jones

For Americans, anarchism and terror share an enduring bond. The grenade-wielding anarchist – impoverished, foreign, insane – remains an instantly recognizable cultural construct even today. A century ago it was a central social archetype. "Bombs and anarchists are inseparable in the minds of most of us," a New York journalist wrote during World War I. "Mysterious destroyers of life and of property, merciless men who have pledged their lives or their knives or their guns to some nefarious cause or another."[1]

Always small in numbers, anarchists in the United States were brash and active nonconformists and dissenters. Opposed to government and organized religion, their controversial beliefs ensured an outsized presence in national political debates. Though they advocated for the working class, they usually operated outside of the institutional boundaries of labor organizations and often earned hostility from the nation's most prominent unions.[2]

In the United States, a series of spectacular dynamitings and assassinations from 1886 to 1920 elevated these adherents of an egalitarian political philosophy to the level of a fearsome "Red Peril." Yet, though some of these acts of "propaganda by deed" targeted leading figures or led to significant loss of life, the aggregate death toll of the campaign was paltry when placed in context with the rampant violence of the industrial era. Furthermore, the turn to violence was usually disastrous for the workers' cause, ushering in severe reprisals and allowing authorities to discredit all local radicals. Instead of sheer numbers or political success, then, it was the continuous din of supposed conspiracies, "discovered" plots, and thwarted actions, drummed up by law enforcement officials and reported eagerly in the newspapers, that made the anarchist in the United States a bugbear par excellence.

Without assaying a formal definition of anarchism, it is nevertheless necessary to specify the field of discourse for this inquiry. While the label "anarchist" was embraced as a positive descriptor by those who identified themselves with the movement and political philosophy of anarchism, the word is also an epithet that has been employed widely and indiscriminately since at least the mid-nineteenth century. Journalists, police officials, and politicians rarely cared to differentiate precisely between radical factions, so that the term "anarchist" was habitually applied to union leaders, socialists, communists, and others. In the popular consciousness, of course, its meaning is even more broad: anarchy is merely a synonym for chaos.

As a result of this undifferentiated use of the term, American terrorists ranging from the libertarian Timothy McVeigh and the white supremacist Ku Klux Klan to the trade unionist Structural Iron Workers and the Leninist Weather Underground have all been described as proponents and practitioners of anarchism.

Adding further to the difficulty of definition is the fact that characterizations of anarchism proposed by the highest authorities make no mention of violence of any sort, let alone terrorist violence. Of these, without a doubt the most famous definition was offered by Peter Kropotkin, a Russian aristocrat who dedicated his life to the cause, in the 1910 edition of the *Encyclopedia Britannica*:

> Anarchism ... the name given to a principle or theory of life and conduct under which society is conceived without government – harmony in such a society being obtained, not by submission to law, or by obedience to any authority, but by free agreements concluded between the various groups, territorial and professional, freely constituted for the sake of production and consumption, as also for the satisfaction of the infinite variety of needs and aspirations of a civilized being.

It was only near the end of the 5,000-word-long entry that Kropotkin grudgingly acknowledged that well-publicized attacks by anarchists had "created in the general public the impression that violence is the substance of anarchism, a view repudiated by its supporters."[3]

But no amount of repudiation could counteract the view – dinned in to the popular mind by constant repetition – that anarchism and terror were inextricably linked. A small minority of violent extremists, and their spectacular actions, shaped the reputation of the entire movement. For those who chose to call themselves anarchists, this would be an insoluble publicity problem. For historians it remains a fascinating paradox: that the very political philosophy that advocates the most humane ideals of equality and self-government should simultaneously possess such a notorious legacy of terror and assassination.

One last problem must be considered before transitioning to an examination of specific events. More perhaps than any other radical movement in history, anarchism was international. Ideologically, anarchists rejected the legitimacy of national governments and often identified themselves as citizens of the world. Leading anarchist organizers found themselves hounded from state to state – Mikhail Bakunin literally circumnavigated the globe in search of asylum – while movement journals were much more likely to discuss foreign developments than to deign to mention local affairs. Though the United States boasted a domestic tradition of individualist anarchism stemming from the thought of Josiah Warren and Henry David Thoreau, the anarchists who would come to be identified with terrorist violence were often European or Russian immigrants. As a result, a discussion of American anarchist terror that restricts itself to the geographic boundaries of the United States inevitably constricts the subject matter in ways that run counter to its history. (Chapter 8 by Richard Bach Jensen examines anarchist terror in these years from a worldwide, particularly European perspective.)

With these caveats in mind, this inquiry will focus on the facts and controversies surrounding the employment of terrorism by anarchists in the United States during the period from the 1880s through the Red Scare of 1919–20. After discussing the most significant terrorist incidents in those years, I will examine the secondary instances – failed attacks, suspected plots, newspaper hysteria, political agitations, and police provocations – that did so much to magnify the sinister reputation of the anarchist movement. Finally, I will consider the legacy of American anarchism's reign of terror.

The appearance in the United States of anarchists prepared to use bombs and pistols to achieve their ends was neither the first nor the last time in American history when terrorist violence would be employed as a political tool. Writing at the end of the 1960s, Richard Hofstadter, the eminent historian, had rediscovered a latent aspect of the US tradition. "We are now quite ready to see that there is more violence in our national heritage than our proud, sometimes smug, national self-image admits of," he wrote. "Americans certainly have reason to inquire whether, when compared with other advanced industrial nations, they are not a people of exceptional violence."[4]

Though noting a tradition of urban riots stretching back to the colonial era, Hofstadter argued that the vast majority of American violence had been conservative in nature: employed by owners against workers, native-born against immigrants, and – most calamitously – by white supremacists against Indians and African Americans.[5]

In this sense, anarchists in the 1870s and 1880s did represent something new. Rarely had working-class spokespeople advocated so stridently for the forcible abolition of wage labor and even the national state. These anarchists possessed other troubling characteristics, as well. They were armed with a newly invented weapon – dynamite – as well as a mature political philosophy capable of devastating critiques of the system of capitalist production. And, unlike many previous advocates for social change, many of them were recent arrivals to the country agitating among fellow immigrants in suddenly teeming and uncontrollable industrial metropolises.

The origins of American anarchism

As early as 1791, Jeremy Bentham was defining the anarchist as anyone who "denies the validity of the law . . . and calls upon all mankind to rise up in a mass, and resist the execution of it."[6] By mid-century, Pierre-Joseph Proudhon had taken the next step and had identified himself as an anarchist.[7]

But revolutionary anarchism only emerged as an international mass movement in the aftermath of the Paris Commune of 1871. Taking a romanticized view of the events in Paris, anarchists in the United States soon canonized these few stunning weeks as a moment when the proletariat of the French capital conjured up and then defended a democratic free city against the forces of reaction. Though few communards considered themselves anarchists, their legacy was quickly claimed by Mikhail Bakunin in his long-running struggle with Karl Marx for the leadership of international working-class radicalism. As against Marx's vision of structured, gradual change, Bakunin advocated direct action and immediate insurrection. The Commune, though unsuccessful, was taken as evidence that such methods might succeed.[8]

In the following decades, radicals in Europe and America divided over questions of tactics and strategy. Most socialist parties took the Parisians' failure as a sign that their insurrection had been premature. Until World War I, socialists and trade unionists of Europe and America would commit themselves to gradual reforms achieved by electoral means and workplace organizing. Anarchists took a different lesson. Although some urged collective action and others proposed to take individual steps, all agreed that the time had come for deeds to further the struggle. The proletarian and peasant masses were ready to rise up, they believed, if only a few courageous anarchists would appear to inspire them to action. To this end, anarchists throughout Europe began engaging in abortive revolts, assassination attempts, and industrial sabotage. "One such act," Peter Kropotkin wrote in 1880, "may, in a few days, make more propaganda than thousands of pamphlets."[9]

Anarchist assassinations had begun to roil the capitals of Europe in 1878. The year 1880 saw the creation of the Social Revolutionary Club in New York City, the first anarchist organization in the United States. Though no acts of terrorism were associated with the group, its members committed themselves to self-defense and cheered the successful assassination of Tsar Alexander II in 1881.

In the United States, the foremost early advocate of "propaganda by deed" was Johann Most, a former member of the German Reichstag who arrived in New York City in 1882. Though he never personally engaged in an act of terror, the violence of his rhetoric in favor of revolutionary action earned him unparalleled notoriety. In speeches during a nationwide tour, he advocated targeted assassinations of leading politicians and capitalists that would inspire workers to resist the degradations of wage labor. Ominously following up these exhortations by working at an explosives factory, Most would publish a technical booklet on explosives. With a wild black beard grown to mask a disfigured jaw, Most's visage – more than that of any other individual – would become the inspiration for the archetypal figure of the anarchist bomber.[10]

In 1883, American anarchists held a national convention in Pittsburgh. Johann Most joined others there – including Albert Parsons and August Spies, both of Chicago – in drafting a statement for the movement. Opening with a quotation from the Declaration of Independence, the Pittsburgh Manifesto combined Marxist theory with American radical traditions. But it was most notable for its explicit insistence on the value of deeds. It was "self-evident," the framers claimed, that "the struggle of the proletariat with the bourgeoisie must have a violent revolutionary character." First among its stated principles was "destruction of the existing class rule, by all means, i.e., by energetic, relentless, revolutionary and international action."[11]

Whether such rhetoric alienated, inspired, or even reached the American audience (considering how few newspapers printed the anarchists' declaration) is impossible to tell, but it is clear in retrospect that these years were something of a heyday for anarchism in the United States. Adherents numbered in the tens of thousands, vibrant anarchist periodicals existed in several cities, and radicals across the country faced the decision of accepting gradualist socialist party strategies or embracing the call to action embodied by the new faction. Although opponents would perennially brand anarchism as a foreign contagion brought to American shores, it was actually the experience of repression and exploitation in the United States that turned most apolitical immigrants into homegrown radicals. And anarchism seemed to them an attractive doctrine.

This changed dramatically in Chicago in 1886, when mass strikes for an eight-hour workday climaxed in a series of violent confrontations between radicals and authorities. On the evening of May 4, a phalanx of police charged a peaceful demonstration near the city's Haymarket Square. During the skirmish, an explosive device flew into the midst of the officers' formation, killing seven policemen. Though authorities could not identify the bomb thrower, they quickly arrested eight leading local anarchists and charged them with conspiracy to murder. Following a six-week trial, the defendants were found guilty. Four were hanged; a fifth evaded the noose by committing suicide in his cell, and the three others were sentenced to long prison terms.[12]

Although working-class animosity against elites and their public servants had grown during the strike wave, this deliberate and deadly attack on individual officers in the Haymarket was itself enough to make many activists forswear anarchism. But the repressions that followed vastly magnified the disaster for radicals. Detectives abandoned all pretense of civil liberties, raiding apartments without warrants, holding suspects incommunicado, and freely employing "third degree" methods. A prominent social theorist who visited Chicago in the days following the explosion reported witnessing a "period of police terrorism" in the second city.[13] Newspapers around the nation fomented a Red Scare that discovered terrorist plots in every immigrant district. In this sense, working-class organizers realized, the bomb had been a windfall for those who opposed the labor movement.

With Haymarket a rough pattern had emerged: violent acts – either committed by or attributed to anarchists – would be followed by sharp Red Scares, when newspaper sensationalism would foment anti-radical feelings and law enforcement officials would take extraordinary new measures in the vain hopes of preventing future outrages.

Anarchist attacks and state responses

If a majority of Americans accepted mainstream depictions of anarchists as mad bombers, there were others who understood the Haymarket affair differently. In Rochester, New York, a young Emma Goldman – soon to be the most notorious American anarchist of all – was radicalized by the martyrdom of the executed Chicago leaders. Though he had come from a political family in Russia, Alexander Berkman also experienced Haymarket as a catalyst for revolution. In New York City, Berkman and Goldman were influenced by Johann Most to embrace the tactic of "propaganda by deed."

The 1890s witnessed a massive escalation of anarchist terrorism worldwide, from Europe to Australia, and the United States was not spared. In 1892, when Carnegie Steel locked out its workers in Homestead, Pennsylvania, Berkman and Goldman saw an opportunity to put theory into action. After failing to construct a workable dynamite bomb, they procured a revolver and dagger. Berkman traveled to Pittsburgh and gained entry – on July 23 – to the office of Henry Clay Frick, Carnegie's chief lieutenant. Berkman fired three times and then wrestled his target to the ground, stabbing him repeatedly, before he himself was subdued by some workmen.

Frick survived. Following a two-hour trial, Berkman would spend the next fourteen years in prison. For the *attentat* (the anarchist term for a bombing or an assassination attempt) he was unrepentant. But if he had thought to aid the cause of the workers at Homestead, he had seriously miscalculated. The strikers expressed only disgust for his actions, which had severely discredited their own movement. Within a few months, their union would be broken. Even Johann Most, the longtime apostle of propaganda by deed, decried Berkman's attempt as an impulsive mistake – a betrayal that would earn him a public horsewhipping at the hands of Emma Goldman.[14]

Throughout the 1890s, the campaign of anarchist violence throughout Europe ensured a continuous paranoia among politicians, elites, and law enforcement officials. In 1900, when Italian King Umberto I was assassinated by an anarchist who had lived for several years in Paterson, New Jersey, fear of domestic terror spiked further. This anxiety was then disastrously confirmed on September 6, 1901, when US President William McKinley was shot twice at close range by an assassin during a visit to Buffalo, New York. The killer, Leon Czolgosz, was sentenced to death by electrocution after an eight-hour trial.

The assassination of a president demanded a systemic response beyond merely punishing the individual attacker. Officials insisted that anarchist assassinations were not political acts inspired by economic and social conditions but rather the violent expressions of defective minds or the result of lax immigration policies that allowed entry to foreign radicals.

Within a year of the president's murder, individual states had passed statutes rendering the public expression of anarchist ideas illegal.[15]

Ignoring the awkward fact that Czolgosz had been born in the United States, nativist activists used his deed to further confirm their long-held vision of anarchism as a foreign contagion. In 1903, the US Congress passed sweeping immigration reform. Widely referred to as the Anarchist Exclusion Act, the new law provided:

> That no person who disbelieves in or who is opposed to all organized government, or who is a member of or affiliated with any organization entertaining or teaching such disbelief in or opposition to all organized government . . . shall be permitted to enter the United States.

Though enforced on only a handful of occasions (only thirty-eight anarchists were deported in all the years before the Red Scare of 1919–20), the Anarchist Exclusion Act nevertheless represented a landmark in US government policy: it was the first time that immigration restrictions had been set solely on the basis of ideas.[16]

Although the nation's industrial cities would remain the storm centers for anarchism, a kindred movement was growing in western coalfields, lumber camps, and mining districts. Unions in these extractive industries were rough, militant, and casual with violence. Most members had had lifelong experience with rifles and dynamite. Attacks on company property had been commonplace in labor conflicts for decades. Although they tended not to identify themselves as anarchists per se, they embraced key anarchist tactics and concepts, including syndicalism, direct action, and industrial sabotage.

In 1905, representatives of these unions gathered together in Chicago to create a new labor organization, the Industrial Workers of the World (IWW). "Big Bill" Haywood, the delegate from the Western Federation of Miners, called the meeting as "the Continental Congress of the Working Class." For the next decade and a half, the IWW members – or Wobblies, as they were called – would become the nation's most sensationalized and feared working-class organization. Though they would be on the receiving end of far more violence than they ever perpetrated, the Wobblies struck a militant tone from the first sentence of the preamble of their constitution, which stridently declared: "The working class and the employing class have nothing in common. There can be no peace so long as hunger and want are found among millions of working people and the few, who make up the employing class, have all the good things of life."[17]

On December 30, 1905, the new organization faced its first test when a bomb killed Frank Steunenberg, a former governor of Idaho with an anti-labor reputation. The bomber, Harry Orchard, was quickly detained and agreed to turn state's evidence. Haywood and other officials of the Western Federation of Miners were arrested and charged with the murder. The Haymarket scenario seemed to be playing out for a second time. Prominent union leaders were being prosecuted for a crime that they had not personally committed. In effect, they were on trial for their beliefs. Representing the defense, Clarence Darrow asserted as much in the courtroom, telling jurors that it was the labor movement itself that was being assailed. The stunning not-guilty verdict was understood to prove the great strides that workers' organizations had taken in the intervening two decades since Haymarket.[18]

Five years later – on October 1, 1910 – an enormous explosion demolished the offices of the *Los Angeles Times*, killing a score of workers and injuring dozens more. Although early suspicion fell on local anarchists, an international investigation eventually resulted in the capture of labor leaders connected with the International Association of Bridge and Structural Iron Workers.[19] Although neither the assassination of Steunenberg nor the attack on the virulently anti-labor *Los Angeles Times* had ended up being the work of avowed anarchists, the associations between working-class organizations and violent tactics no doubt further cemented the association of anarchists and terrorists in the public mind.

Back east, these years had brought several spectacular anarchist failures. March 1908 began with the Chicago police chief opening his front door to discover a ragged-looking assailant poised to attack. In the ensuing melee, the suspected anarchist was killed, the chief received a stab wound, and various bystanders were shot. Later during that same month, a second Haymarket horror was avoided by the narrowest of margins. After NYPD officers had violently dispersed a rally of socialists in New York City's Union Square, an anarchist attempted to toss a grenade into the midst of a formation of police. The device – a brass bed knob crammed with broken nails, nitroglycerine, and gunpowder – detonated a moment early, killing the attacker while leaving his intended victims dazed but unharmed.[20]

These assassination attempts raised calls for stricter enforcement of the Anarchist Exclusion Act and prompted President Theodore Roosevelt to attempt to block radical publications from the mails. "When compared with the suppression of anarchy, every other question sinks into insignificance," Roosevelt warned in a message to Congress. "The Anarchist is the enemy of humanity, the enemy of all mankind."[21]

Despite the president's warnings, radicals continued to perpetrate propaganda of the word and deed. A huge resurgence of anarchist activity occurred in New York City in 1914, fostered by police brutality and a crushing industrial depression. When news arrived in the metropolis that John D. Rockefeller's Colorado Fuel and Iron Company had been responsible for a military-style assault on striking coal miners in Ludlow, Colorado, radicals in the city demanded revenge. Two women and eleven children had been killed in the coalfields; loud calls for revenge could be heard from around the country. On Independence Day, 1914, a devastating explosion on Lexington Avenue, in East Harlem, panicked the holiday-seeking crowds. A large tenement house crumbled halfway to the street. In the wreckage, police discovered the bodies of three well-known anarchists. Their bomb had gone off accidentally; no one knew for sure what the target had been, but speculation immediately centered on the Rockefeller estate in nearby Westchester County.[22]

Responding quickly to this latest anarchist threat, New York City founded a secret policing unit known as the Anarchist Squad, which was dedicated to combating future acts of propaganda by deed. Special officers insinuated themselves into radical groups using elaborate disguises and subterfuges and the latest surveillance technologies. Despite these efforts, the city soon found itself in the midst of the most virulent bombing campaign in its history. On October 13, 1914, bombs targeted St. Patrick's Cathedral and St. Alphonsus' Church, site of a mass arrest of homeless activists. On November 11, the anniversary of the Haymarket executions, unknown bombers attacked the Bronx County Court House. A few days later, another bomb was disabled before it exploded underneath a seat in a courtroom in Lower Manhattan.[23]

Unable to prevent these attacks or convict any perpetrators, the Anarchist Squad turned to other means. Officers who infiltrated radical organizations usually made themselves the most vocal militants in the group. Their most extreme use of the methods of the agent provocateur occurred in 1915, when a detective convinced two youths – Carmine Carbone and Frank Abarno – to detonate a bomb in St. Patrick's Cathedral. The provocateur planned the attack, provided the explosives, and – according to the radicals – even lit the fuse, only to have other detectives race in and "prevent the attack." Despite the obviousness of the frame-up, a judge sentenced the two defendants to six to twelve years in Sing Sing Prison.[24]

The first Red Scare

This offensive was just one front in a national campaign of radical terrorism. In these years, anarchist followers of Luigi Galleani, an Italian immigrant who embraced the ideology of propaganda by deed, were likely responsible for bombs that exploded in Boston, Milwaukee, Washington, San Francisco, and Philadelphia. Like Johann Most before him, Galleani was an ardent proponent of propaganda by deed. His published works included hagiographies of anarchist martyrs and detailed instructions for the construction of dynamite bombs. Unlike Herr Most, Galleani also put these fiery words into practice. In the coming years, he and his circle of followers would be behind the most audacious acts of anarchist terrorism in the nation's history.[25]

As World War I progressed in Europe, the Anarchist Squad's mission widened to encompass investigations of German saboteurs and Russian Bolsheviks. When the United States joined the conflict in April 1917, the full force of the US government directed itself at subduing domestic dissent. New deportation laws, as well as the Espionage and Sedition Acts of 1917 and 1918, drastically increased the federal bureaucracy's repressive powers against free speech. Suddenly, it was illegal to use "disloyal, profane, scurrilous or abusive language about the form of government of the U.S. or the constitution of the U.S." Emma Goldman and Alexander Berkman were imprisoned for urging audiences to avoid the draft. Citizen vigilance committees instigated mob justice. Pacifists were attacked and jailed. Radical publications were banned from the mails. Wobbly agitators were tortured and lynched throughout the western states. And even respectable radicals, including Eugene V. Debs – a perennial Socialist Party candidate for the US presidency – found themselves behind bars.[26]

Nor did armistice bring peace to the home front. Instead, 1919 witnessed the apex of industrial conflict in US history, as the dislocations of war, mass unemployment, race riots, and radical militancy involved more than four million workers in strikes and brought the spectacle of class warfare to cities from Boston to Seattle. Combined with the frightening specter of the Bolshevik Revolution, these disturbances themselves nearly ensured a panicked anti-radical reaction.

Then a brazen campaign of bombings all but guaranteed it. Around May Day, a first attempt to send mail bombs to dozens of targets – ranging from prominent politicians and capitalists to minor officials who had somehow earned the anarchists' enmity – was averted by alert postal workers. A month later, powerful time bombs detonated in seven cities. Among the damaged targets was the Washington, DC, home of US Attorney General A. Mitchell Palmer. Communiqués found near each of the explosions were signed by "The Anarchist Fighters," a clue that they had been set by followers of Galleani. Historians have estimated that the well-coordinated, multi-city attack would have required the work of at least fifty determined conspirators.[27]

In short order, the most notorious anarchists in the United States were all deported. Luigi Galleani was returned to Italy just weeks after the bombings. Six months later, Emma Goldman, Alexander Berkman, and hundreds of others were transshipped from New York harbor to the Soviet Union. In December 1919 and January 1920, the attorney general and his protégé J. Edgar Hoover authorized a series of mass arrests on radical groups that netted roughly 10,000 arrests.

Anarchism roars into the 1920s

The Palmer Raids marked the high-water mark in the decades-long conflict between anarchist terrorism and government authorities in the United States. Yet, even as the Red Scare of 1919–20 was reaching its peak, the tide was set to recede. Official obsession was already transferring itself from anarchism to communism: the persistence of the Soviet regime ensured that the newly created Communist Party USA would soon replace the unaffiliated, decentralized anarchists as the red menace of the twentieth century. Relative prosperity in the 1920s would make industrial relations a less central social concern. And a reaction against the severity of Palmer's and Hoover's methods would encourage federal agencies to keep their anti-radical contingency plans safely away from public scrutiny.[28]

In these circumstances, the most devastating pre-9/11 terrorist attack in US history came like an aftershock rather than as a bolt from the blue. At 12:01 p.m., on September 16, 1920, dynamite in a horse-drawn cart detonated halfway between the Wall Street headquarters of the House of Morgan and the federal treasury. The timing was cataclysmic. It was lunch hour and the street was packed. Nearly forty people were killed, another 400 harmed. Historians suspect that the followers of Galleani had perpetrated this attack – as they had the previous year's campaign. But despite a massive manhunt, the actual identities of the perpetrators were never discovered. Perhaps this explains why despite a terrible death toll, the Wall Street bombing was soon forgotten, while another anarchist controversy from the same years has remained a touchstone in the history of the American Left.[29]

Boston had long been a center of anarchist terrorism. That's where Nicola Sacco and Bartolomeo Vanzetti settled when they both arrived in the United States in 1908. Their experiences in America had radicalized them into firm devotees of propaganda by deed. Among Boston anarchists they were well known. Those beliefs had undoubtedly drawn them into terrorist conspiracies, but that did not necessarily make them guilty of a fatal payroll robbery that occurred south of Boston on April 15, 1920. Nevertheless, the two anarchists were tried for murder, convicted, and sentenced to death. Evidence for their participation in the robbery was contradictory, and their trial had been poorly handled. Dragging on for most of the decade, their appeals would garner unprecedented worldwide attention. As with the Haymarket defendants forty years earlier, the anarchists were to die for their beliefs rather than for their supposed crime. The weeks leading up to their execution – on August 23, 1927 – were marked by bombings in cities in the United States and around the world.[30]

Although the global anarchist movement would arguably reach the pinnacle of its relevance during the 1930s with the Spanish Civil War, in the United States the execution of Sacco and Vanzetti marked the last notable episode in a long-running drama of terrorism, paranoia, repression, and fear.

Anarchist tendencies in the New Left

Violence continued as a central strain in American life throughout the twentieth century. The labor conflicts of the 1930s were as bloody as anything that had come before. Civil rights activists in the North and South during the 1950s and 1960s faced the threat of beatings and murder. But it was the Black Power and anti-war movements of the late 1960s and early 1970s that carried radical violence to the same pitch – and beyond – that had characterized the anarchist years. According to the Treasury Department, from the start of 1969 to mid-April 1970 there were 40,934 bombings, attempted bombings, and bomb threats, leading to forty-three deaths and almost $22 million in damage. Out of this total, 975 had been explosive, as opposed to incendiary, bombings.[31]

This was propaganda by deed on a scale rarely, if ever, attempted by US radicals before or since. And there were certainly those who believed they were seeing another resurgence of the black flag of anarchism. When the Weather Underground claimed credit for setting a bomb inside a women's lavatory in the Pentagon, the *New York Times* was quick to denounce ultra-radicals who hoped to use "acts of terror" to recruit followers into "their anarchist ranks." Others, too, equated this sort of violence with the direct action tactics of a previous era. Fred Hampton, leader of the Black Panthers in Chicago, was appalled by the plans by the Weatherman faction of Students for a Democratic Society to confront the city's police with the militant demonstrations that would come to be known as the Days of Rage. Fearful for the reprisals that would fall on his own constituency, Hampton denounced the protest as "anarchistic, opportunistic, individualistic, chauvinistic, and Custeristic."[32]

There were anarchist factions affiliated with the anti-war movement. In New York City's Lower East Side, a group known as the Motherfuckers embraced direct action with a series of provocative gestures. Most notable among these was the dumping of garbage into the fountain at Lincoln Center in the spirit of "cultural exchange." But their bent was artistic and counter-cultural rather than political and revolutionary, and their methods involved figurative as opposed to literal dynamite. Anarchist foremothers, particularly Emma Goldman, were lovingly resurrected as heroines by the feminist movement of the 1970s. But the Weather Underground and Black Panthers considered themselves to be engaged in a revolutionary nationalist struggle along an ideological axis that encompassed Marx, Lenin, Trotsky, and Mao but held no room for the ideas of Berkman or Kropotkin. A saying of the period encapsulated their stance on the matter: anarchist by choice, communist by necessity.[33]

Anarchism in the age of neo-liberalism

In a political milieu still largely defined by a Manichean divide between capitalism and communism, anarchism did not seem to provide most activists in the United States with a practical alternative. This changed dramatically after the collapse of the Soviet Union and the end of the Cold War. Beginning in the 1990s, anarchist-identified protest groups emerged once again as a visible radical faction. The 1999 showdown in Seattle between police and demonstrators protesting the globalization policies of the World Trade Organization marked the first time in decades that tactics of direct action had been directly linked to recognizably anarchist ideas. Embracing Internet technologies that could facilitate leaderless, or horizontal, organizing, the new activists reflected the influence of anarcho-feminism and tended to be far more sensitive than their classical forebears to questions of racism and patriarchy. Accompanying the rise of this new breed of anarchist came the inevitable response by authorities. For the first time in decades, Americans regularly began to read about anarchist plotters and the law enforcement officials who were working to thwart them.[34]

Beginning with Henry David Thoreau's experiments at Walden, an ecological critique had always been central to anarchist political philosophy. Kropotkin's *Fields, Factories, and Workshops*, published in 1912, argued for a revolutionary re-imagining of social spaces that would replace global commerce with self-sufficient regional communes. On the individual level, this new system would have also replaced the drudgery of factory labor with a diversity of employment for every citizen. Writing in the US postwar period, Murray Bookchin formally placed ecology at the center of anarchist thought, arguing that environmental crises and social conflicts were inseparably linked. But it was the Earth Liberation Front (ELF) and Animal Liberation Front (ALF) that translated these theoretical leanings into direct action. Since 1979, according to the Federal Bureau of Investigation, actions by these and other groups have been responsible for more than $100 million in damage to international corporations, lumber companies, animal testing facilities, and genetic research firms.[35]

The Occupy Wall Street movement of late 2011 and early 2012 represented by far the largest fluorescence of anarchist thought and action since 1919. From New York City to Oakland, California, and in thousands of cities and towns in between – and, indeed, around the globe – protesters against globalization, corporate ecological depredations, political corruption, and a constellation of other issues joined in a leaderless, decentralized movement that demonstrated all of the vital possibilities – and many of the limitations – inherent to anarchist politics. Although few of the tens of thousands of participants in the Occupy encampments, demonstrations, and related activities would have self-identified as anarchists, they were all nevertheless utilizing anarchist practices and ideas. The decision to occupy and liberate a literal space within a capitalist city harkened back to the days of the Paris Commune. Modes of governance – ranging from the nightly held general assemblies to the volunteer-run kitchens, libraries, and classrooms – were all practical reflections of the most deeply held tenets of anarchist thought. Refusing pressures to nominate leaders or an official platform gave the movement flexibility and a creative spirit, while also drawing frustrated critique from mainstream media.

One tactic of classical anarchism which the Occupy Movement eschewed was propaganda by deed. Although street demonstrations often became confrontational and frequently featured violence against property and police, at no time did participants decide to attempt a terrorist action. Law enforcement officials made several highly publicized arrests during the months-long movement, and news media frequently announced the foiling of anarchist bomb plots. But without a single exception, these supposed terrorist plots had been the work of agents provocateurs. Much like the case of Carbone and Abarno in 1914, undercover police had planned the attacks and supplied the materiel, only to have their colleagues swoop in at the last second to "foil" the plot.[36]

Conclusions

Looking back over the history of anarchist terrorism in the United States, the use by government of agents provocateurs forms one of the most notable themes. This is not to deny the agency of radical anarchists. From Alexander Berkman to the followers of Galleani, there have always been individual anarchists determined to translate the violent rhetoric of bomb talk into the literal employment of explosives. But, even taken together, their actions hardly account for the bloodcurdling reputation that anarchism in America has incurred. To understand anarchism's place in the nation's cultural memory, it is necessary also to include the vastly more numerous incidents that were either planned by government agents or invented out of whole cloth by politicians or journalists.

This phenomenon was well understood by anarchists themselves, who were constantly aware of the spies and eavesdroppers in their midst. Furthermore, it is manifested by the fact that the possibility of provocateur action inevitably accompanied an attack that couldn't be precisely ascribed to the hand of an anarchist. This category includes many of the most notorious acts of anarchist terror in US history: the Haymarket bomb, the Lexington Avenue explosion in 1914, the Preparedness Day bombing of 1916, and even the Wall Street bombing of 1920. The hand of Pinkertons and other provocateurs was suspected by radicals at the time of all these acts. These claims obviously were self-serving for those who might potentially stand accused of murder, but their existence nevertheless reflects a widespread reality of official provocation, and historians cannot conscientiously reject them out of hand.

The anarchist movement in the United States has always related to the contours of the American scene. Although detractors invariably have seen it as a foreign import – the handiwork of "outside agitators" – in fact, it was shaped to a large degree by domestic economic and political relations. For every Johann Most who came to the United States as a committed European radical, there were numerous Albert Parsons and Emma Goldmans who were radicalized by the iniquities and oppression that they witnessed here. Although the anarchists were deeply connected to international affairs and considered themselves to be citizens of the world participating in a global movement, their politics and activism were local in their goals and tactics.

The anarchist use of terrorism – or propaganda by deed – especially in the years 1886 to 1920, reflected this dichotomy. Political assassinations and the targeting of innocent civilians were prevalent throughout Europe in these years. Numerous attempts were made by radicals on the lives of tsars, kings, and prime ministers. When these same tactics appeared in the United States, it seemed self-evident to American politicians and journalists that the sins of the Old World were being visited on the New. This was not so. Bloodshed and terror were homegrown here, in fields, factories, and tenements. The anarchists were merely participating – spectacularly at times, it is true – in a period in US history that many scholars refer to as the Age of Industrial Violence.

Notes

1 Guidano Bruno, "Anarchists at Close Range," *Current Opinion* (September 1916): 212.
2 For a more detailed discussion of anarchist terrorism in the United States, with a special emphasis on anarchism and policing, see Thai Jones, *More Powerful than Dynamite: Radicals, Plutocrats, Progressives, and New York's Year of Anarchy* (New York: Walker, 2012).
3 Peter Kropotkin, "Anarchism," in *The Encyclopedia Britannica*, 11th ed. (1910–11).
4 Richard Hofstadter, *American Violence: A Documentary History* (New York: Alfred A. Knopf, 1970), 5, 6, 11.
5 For more on American violence – including against Indians and African Americans – during the colonial and antebellum eras, see Chapter 6 by Matthew Jennings in this volume. For white supremacist violence from the Civil War to the Civil Rights Movement, see Chapter 10 by R. Blakeslee Gilpin. For white supremacist violence in recent decades, see Chapter 21 by Carolyn Gallaher.
6 Jeremy Bentham, "A Critical Examination of the Declaration of Rights," in *The Works of Jeremy Bentham* (Edinburgh: William Tait, 1839), 8:498.
7 Daniel Guérin, *No Gods, No Masters: An Anthology of Anarchism* (Oakland, CA: AK Press, 2005), 37–126.
8 *Writings on the Paris Commune: Marx, Engels, Bakunin, Kropotkin, and Lenin* (St. Petersburg, FL: Red and Black Publishers, 2008), passim.
9 "The Spirit of Revolt," in Peter Kropotkin, *Kropotkin's Revolutionary Pamphlets* (New York: Dover Publications, 1970), 40.
10 Beverly Gage, *The Day Wall Street Exploded: A Story of America in its First Age of Terror* (New York: Oxford University Press, 2009), 41–50.
11 Timothy Messer-Kruse, *The Haymarket Conspiracy: Transatlantic Anarchist Networks* (Urbana: University of Illinois Press, 2012), 181.
12 James Green, *Death in the Haymarket: A Story of Chicago, the First Labor Movement and the Bombing that Divided Gilded Age America* (New York: Pantheon, 2006), passim.

13 Paul Avrich, *The Haymarket Tragedy* (Princeton, NJ: Princeton University Press, 1984), 222.
14 Emma Goldman, *Living My Life* (Mineola, NY: Dover, 1970), 1:105–6.
15 William Preston, *Aliens and Dissenters: Federal Suppression of Radicals, 1903–1933*, 2nd ed. (Urbana: University of Illinois Press, 1963), 30.
16 Ibid., 33.
17 Melvyn Dubofsky, *"Big Bill" Haywood* (Manchester, UK: Manchester University Press, 1987), 160.
18 For an exhaustive treatment of the Steunenberg case, see J. Anthony Lukas, *Big Trouble: A Murder in a Small Western Town Sets Off a Struggle for the Soul of America* (New York: Simon & Schuster, 1998).
19 Howard Blum, *American Lightning: Terror, Mystery, the Birth of Hollywood, and the Crime of the Century* (New York: Crown Publishers, 2008).
20 Jones, *More Powerful than Dynamite*, 128–30.
21 Richard Bach Jensen, "The United States, International Policing and the War against Anarchist Terrorism, 1900–1914," *Terrorism and Political Violence* 13, no. 1 (2001): 32.
22 Jones, *More Powerful than Dynamite*, 248.
23 Ibid., 280–2.
24 Ibid., 281.
25 Paul Avrich, *Sacco and Vanzetti: The Anarchist Background* (Princeton, NJ: Princeton University Press, 1991), 45–103.
26 Jones, *More Powerful than Dynamite*, 294.
27 Avrich, *Sacco and Vanzetti*, 149.
28 Stanley Coben, *A. Mitchell Palmer: Politician* (New York: Columbia University Press, 1963).
29 Gage, *The Day Wall Street Exploded*, passim.
30 Avrich, *Sacco and Vanzetti*, passim.
31 Thai Jones, *A Radical Line: From the Labor Movement to the Weather Underground, One Family's Century of Conscience* (New York: Free Press, 2004), 213. For more on recent American terrorism, see Chapter 21 by Gallaher in this volume.
32 Jones, *A Radical Line*, 204.
33 Ibid., 182.
34 Thai Jones, "Occupy Protests Show Radical Potential: Through Decades, Confrontation and Consensus Can Coexist," *Jewish Daily Forward*, December 2, 2011.
35 For more on ALF and ELF, see Chapter 21 by Gallaher.
36 Todd Gitlin, "The Wonderful American World of Informers and Agents Provocateurs," thenation. com, June 27, 2013: www.thenation.com/article/175005/wonderful-american-world-informers-and-agents-provocateurs (accessed August 6, 2014).

Further reading

Adamic, Louis. *Dynamite: The Story of Class Violence in America*. New York: Viking Press, 1934.

Avrich, Paul. *Sacco and Vanzetti: The Anarchist Background*. Princeton, NJ: Princeton University Press, 1991.

Gage, Beverly. *The Day Wall Street Exploded: A Story of America in its First Age of Terror*. New York: Oxford University Press, 2010.

Green, James. *Death in the Haymarket: A Story of Chicago, the First Labor Movement and the Bombing that Divided Gilded Age America*. New York: Anchor Books, 2007.

Hofstadter, Richard. *American Violence: A Documentary History*. New York: Alfred A. Knopf, 1970.

Kropotkin, Peter. *Kropotkin's Revolutionary Pamphlets*. New York: Dover Publications, 1970.

Preston, William. *Aliens and Dissenters: Federal Suppression of Radicals, 1903–1933*. New York: Harper & Row, 1963.

10

AMERICAN RACIAL TERRORISM FROM BROWN TO BOOTH TO BIRMINGHAM

R. Blakeslee Gilpin

Although terrorism of the late antebellum era is best characterized by violence in the cause of racial liberation, terrorism in the century that followed most often took the opposite tack: violence designed to preserve white supremacy. This chapter chronicles the character of those acts of suppression. American racial terrorism from John Wilkes Booth to the Birmingham 16th Street Church bombing in 1963 encompasses diverse acts but some common themes. So while that century saw terrorist acts in the service of many causes – from attempts by Puerto Rican nationalists to gain independence for their island to the dawn of the airplane hijacking age, the bombing of Wall Street to the assassination of Medgar Evers – racial violence in the United States established common patterns and responses.

Brown, Lincoln, and Booth

When John Brown led his ragtag interracial army into Harpers Ferry, Virginia, in October 1859, he was well aware of the symbolic importance of his actions. Brown hoped to eradicate slavery by initiating an abolitionist guerrilla war (which he plotted as the first step towards a new abolitionist state), but he also knew from his murderous time in Kansas that his deeds, successful or not, could inspire more than immediate earthly rewards. Brown would never have called himself a terrorist, but in his willingness to use violence to further the anti-slavery cause and his embrace of propaganda by deed, Brown would certainly fit any modern definition of the term.[1]

With a similar understanding of the propaganda of his deeds, Brown sits comfortably alongside the suicide bombers and airplane hijackers of recent decades. Brown's efforts did not immediately produce his desired results, as he himself perhaps expected. What made Brown a terrorist was not simply his use of violence as a tool of public relations, although he certainly saw such acts as a way of separating true abolitionists from milquetoast men like the journalist William Lloyd Garrison. Brown also understood that his actions could attract more zealous converts and set in motion a national reckoning with the evil of slavery. In his dramatic capture and trial, the abolitionist demonstrated that even an attempt to violently effect political change can produce devastating repercussions. Brown's trial ended with his conviction by the state of Virginia on charges of treason, murder, and attempting to incite a slave insurrection.

When Brown was convicted, knowing he was to hang, he delivered a speech in the courtroom that spoke to his intuitive understanding of terrorist violence. The Bible "teaches me," Brown explained:

to "remember them that are in bonds, as bound with them." I endeavored to act up to that instruction. . . . I believe that to have interfered as I have done as I have always freely admitted I have done in behalf of His despised poor, was not wrong, but right. Now, if it is deemed necessary that I should forfeit my life for the furtherance of the ends of justice, and mingle my blood further with the blood of my children and with the blood of millions in this slave country whose rights are disregarded by wicked, cruel, and unjust enactments, I submit; so let it be done![2]

As if working from a twenty-first-century handbook, Brown spent the month before his execution propagandizing from his jail cell. He entertained visitors and produced reams of commentary about his beliefs, American slavery, and the future course of the nation. His final words speak powerfully to his claim as the first American terrorist. On his way to the gallows, Brown passed a note to his jailer that read: "I John Brown am now quite certain that the crimes of this guilty land: will never be purged away; but with Blood. I had as I now think: vainly flattered myself that without very much bloodshed; it might be done."[3]

With those ideas in mind, Brown supporter E. C. Stedman printed and scattered a poem around Charlestown before Brown's execution: "each drop from Old Brown's life veins, like the red gore of the dragon, May spring up a vengeful Fury, hissing through your slave-worn lands!"[4] In such a context, it should not be surprising that contemporaries and modern writers alike have called Brown "the spark" that began America's bloodiest conflict, a righteous achievement for any terrorist.

Brown's execution took place in a heavily guarded field outside of Charlestown, West Virginia. Among those in attendance was a Maryland man who had purchased a counterfeit Virginia militia uniform in order to watch the old man hang. At the time still an actor in a famous family troupe, John Wilkes Booth lied when he claimed to have "aided in the capture and execution of John Brown." He "was proud of my little share in that transaction," Booth falsely recalled, "for I deemed it my duty [to help] our common country to perform an act of justice." Brown's life and death had a profound influence on Booth and the course of the nation. Booth's letters to his sister revealed both his "unlimited, undeniable contempt" for Brown as well as his grudging admiration for that "brave old man" and "rugged old hero." In short, Booth learned from Brown that a symbolic death could reach thousands of Americans. As Booth explained, "John Brown was a man inspired, the grandest character of this century!"[5]

However, Booth's sense of justice and his notion of a "common country" was deeply upset when shots were fired on Fort Sumter in 1861. Identifying (somewhat dubiously) as a native Southerner, Booth was outraged by President Abraham Lincoln's suspension of habeas corpus in his home state of Maryland and the steady drift by the Union towards an emancipationist war. In turn, the president would quickly replace John Brown "as the hated symbol of abolition."[6] For all of Booth's respect for Brown's bravery and willingness to die, he abhorred Brown's specific cause and thus considered Lincoln not only a coward but the perpetrator of ever more outrageous acts upon the South.[7] After the dizzying changes of fortunes that the war produced – from the Confederacy's victories at Bull Run to the Emancipation Proclamation to the Union victory at Gettysburg – Lincoln's re-election in 1864 and the fearful possibilities of Reconstruction turned Booth to more deadly thoughts and more direct mimicking of Brown's violent effort to change the course of history. While Lincoln might have been "walking in the footprints of old John Brown" in moving against slavery, the president, according to Booth, was not "fit to stand with that great hero."[8]

For Booth, one glaring example of Lincoln's offenses was the president's final public speech, delivered in Washington, DC, just two days after Robert E. Lee's surrender. What scared Southern sympathizers like Booth were the clues Lincoln gave about his plans for postwar Reconstruction. Explaining Louisiana's early decision to ratify the Thirteenth Amendment, Lincoln celebrated "the colored man [who] in seeing all united for him, is inspired with vigilance, and energy, and daring" for the cause of freedom. Unlike his earlier statements about Reconstruction, Lincoln expressed a clear desire for black enfranchisement. In the crowd, John Wilkes Booth remarked to a friend, "that is the last speech he will make."[9]

When Booth shot Lincoln in the back of the head with a .44 Derringer on April 14, 1865, he initiated a new age and character of American violence. Lincoln's assassination was "the last terrorist act of the Civil War," historian Michael Fellman argues, and

> the first act of terrorist resistance to Reconstruction [which] demonstrated the continuity of systematic political violence used to enforce white domination of African Americans during two hundred years of slavery in the past and a hundred years of segregation to come. White hegemony would once again demand terrorist means.[10]

In one capacity, like Brown, Booth did inspire other would-be assassins, those hungry for change or fame, to imitate him. On the other hand, Booth also inaugurated a broader kind of terror, a unique American terrorism that served a formal political party; underwrote the social, economic, and political hierarchies of the South; and virulently fought to forestall change. With his cry of "sic semper tyrannis," Booth fired the opening shot in a century-long campaign of terrorism. That violence had a simple goal: keep black Americans as a permanent social and economic underclass.

Terrorism during Reconstruction

A rare and brief notice appeared in *The New York Times* on November 5, 1872, reporting on political terrorism in the state of Kentucky. "For the purpose of intimidating Republican voters," a black, Republican, voter-registration leader named Samuel Hawkins, along with his wife and his daughter, were lynched in Fayette County. "The Kuklux," the paper reported, "hung all three to the same limb of a tree. Hawkins leaves a family of helpless children." As if by necessity, the paper also pointed out that "he was a quiet, inoffensive man, and his only crime was being a Republican."[11]

For most of the past 150 years, the violence that was invented, practiced, and perfected in the two decades following the end of the Civil War hardly warranted mention, particularly in mainstream American histories. Only in recent decades has sustained scholarly attention been paid to the systematic and systemic violence directed against emancipated slaves. By necessity, those studies have explored the terrorist clout of the Ku Klux Klan, the horrific extent of lynching, and the racial mythology that underpinned white supremacy. In this context, it is especially important to underscore that several states (most notably South Carolina) still ignore the period of Reconstruction in high school curricula altogether because it is considered too controversial to teach. Recounting incidents of violence, these bowdlerized accounts of American history skip neatly from Booth to the anarchist bombing of Chicago's Haymarket in May 1886.

Historian James Green has accordingly called Haymarket "the biggest news story since Lincoln's assassination."[12]

Of course, those headlines reveal the awful tendency of Americans to avert their eyes from the more terrible story: the savage acts that dominated the years between Lincoln's assassination and the Civil Rights Movement. The story of 1865–1963 is the story of racial terrorism by (mostly Southern) whites against (mostly Southern) blacks and the national complicity that allowed this violence to continue and eventually spread beyond the former Confederacy's borders. As Grace Hale explains, "southern whites constructed their racial identities on two interlocking planes: within a regional dynamic of ex-Confederates versus ex-slaves and within a national dynamic of the South, understood as white, versus the nation."[13]

In this sense, to understand racial terrorism is to explore the kind of loss that the South endured during the Civil War. In May 1861, the Confederate States of America (CSA) was one of the wealthiest nations on Earth. But the CSA made a "gamble of world historical proportions" on the "reactionary dream" of a society based on human chattel. "Their vision of the future" was tried and did not merely fail but brought unprecedented destruction. Southerners experienced defeat on such a devastating scale that it still remains singular in the country's experience. Two-thirds of the entire assessed wealth of Southern society was simply gone. Three hundred thousand men had been killed, and nearly as many wounded, a massive toll in human terms. Much of the Southern landscape, from forests to farms to cities, was in ruins. Nearly half the livestock in the South was killed, and two-thirds of all farm machinery destroyed. During this same time, the North was virtually untouched. Moreover, the wealth of the Union increased by more than half from 1861 to 1865. Industry and population would continue to grow at an unprecedented pace for the next decade.[14]

After Lincoln's assassination, former Confederates, despite being shaken at home by black emancipation, sensed that Northern will to protect black freedom was shaky at best. Thus began a process Americans soon dubbed "Redemption," which literally meant the return of states of the former Confederacy to Southern Democratic control. The term also came to encompass the return to something as socially, economically, and politically close to the antebellum slave South as possible. After the end of the "peculiar institution," the possibilities of black freedom (citizenship, suffrage, and equality) were too much for ex-Confederates to bear. As one Texan revealingly (and with exceptional self-awareness) explained to a Congressional committee in 1866: "I have some ethnological theories that may perhaps warp my judgment; but my judgment is that the highest condition the black race has ever reached or can reach, is one where he is provided for by a master race."[15] Such deeply held beliefs in black inferiority helped steer Southerners amidst the roiling seas of military and economic devastation along with the added humiliation of federal occupation and black political participation.

The South's answer, at once highly organized and deeply political as well as disturbingly widespread and organic, was the Ku Klux Klan. With its origins somewhere between a "social fraternity dedicated to playing pranks" and "a terrorist organization aiming at the preservation of white supremacy," the Klan began in Pulaski, Tennessee, immediately following the Civil War. Though the organization was new, it had deep roots in Southern soil. "The precedent of the ante-bellum slave patrol" informed every aspect of the Klan and its imitators, borrowing its methods meant to keep first slaves, then freed blacks in whatever whites defined as "order." "Thus duty and inclination combined," describes Allen Trelease, "to produce bands of postwar regulators and vigilantes throughout the South."[16]

The Klan subsequently enjoyed three distinct eras. The initial Klan spread like a disease across the former Confederacy (and beyond its borders) in the 1860s and 1870s before being threatened, mostly ineffectively, by the federal government in the 1870s and made obsolete by Southern Democratic Redemption in 1877. The second Klan re-emerged in the 1920s and petered out in the 1940s. The third (and current) incarnation reformed in response to the Civil Rights struggle and has soldiered on through the present day.

The Klan organized across many states and eventually similar groups were founded under many different names: the White Line, the Knights of the White Camellia, the White Caps, and others. What these groups shared, beyond a penchant for violence, was a common goal: the rollback of any postbellum black advancements and the restoration of some semblance of the antebellum racial order. The advance of Lincoln's party in the former Confederacy became the target and its characterization as illegitimate became the lever by which Southerners would reclaim their region. Outrages during election times got so terrible – murders, riots, and blatant political fraud – that the federal government was eventually forced, despite great reluctance, to get involved. In 1871, Republicans began a joint House–Senate committee to investigate the Klan. South Carolina's ongoing and brutal repression of black political activity in 1871 convinced President Ulysses S. Grant and Congress to respond with the Ku Klux Klan Act. The Act allowed Grant to suspend the writ of habeas corpus, which allowed federal troops to arrest Klansmen when local police were unwilling to do so. Of course, such a federal response was truly very rare, but Grant's actions were enough to drive the Klan underground or cause members to reorganize in other paramilitary terrorist groups.

The story of Georgian Scipio Eager is emblematic of the treatment of freedpeople in the South after 1865. One hundred hooded Klan members came to his house

> where he lived with his parents, brothers, and children. The Klansmen announced that they were going to kill everyone who hadn't voted the Democratic ticket. . . . One of Eager's brothers, moreover, was accused of being "too big a man" because he could read and write and talked of starting a Negro school. When this brother now tried to escape from them he was riddled with bullets and buckshot, and he died the next day.[17]

Eager himself was beaten and threatened. Klansmen returned to his house on several occasions. He recalled that on one occasion, his terrorizers "had dogs with them, 'what they call "nigger-hounds" such as they had in old slavery times.'" Even though Eager eventually could positively identify his assailants, what difference did it make? "I did not know what to do. I was just like the rabbit when the dogs are after him; I had to do anything that I could to try and save my life." Eager fled to Atlanta, "leaving behind a blind father, a helpless mother and house full of children with no means of support."[18]

Abram Colby was another victim of Klan violence. Colby was dragged from his bed and whipped "three hours or more and left . . . for dead." Colby explained that his torturers asked him just one question: "Do you think you will ever vote another damned radical ticket?" When Colby defied his captors, "they set in and whipped me a thousand licks more, with sticks and straps that had buckles on the ends of them." Colby's testimony to the House–Senate investigative committee revealed one of the most distressing aspects of the Ku Klux Klan and its intractability. Some of the men who broke Colby's door down were "first class men in our town. One is a lawyer, one a doctor, and some are farmers."[19]

Those first class men, the leaders of business and politics across the South, made any governmental remedies incredibly difficult. Thus, despite briefly defeating the Ku Klux Klan as an individual organization, its imitators fought on, and the beliefs that underpinned this terrorist violence became ever further entrenched. The White Line was particularly intent on "forbidding blacks to beat drums and cutting the drums up" at political rallies or election times. "This is a white man's country, and we don't allow that," black Republicans were informed before they were beaten with sticks and pistols. "On election day . . . White Liners dragged a [twenty-four-pound cannon] to the polling place and then began beating potential black voters." The votes told the story of racial terrorism in the South: in one district in Mississippi, Republican votes plummeted from 1,400 in 1873 to 90 in 1875.[20] The story was the same across the former Confederacy.

Frequently cited as a relatively clearheaded observer of the horrors of Redemption, Adelbert Ames, the carpetbagger governor of Mississippi, captured the flavor of these efforts quite well at the time. "Through the terror caused by murders and threats, the colored people are thoroughly intimidated," he explained. They "are disenfranchised [and] are to be returned to a condition of serfdom – an era of second slavery."[21] Ames was witnessing the Klan's successors, organizations like the White League as well as the White Line that wrote an even bloodier chapter in terms of violence against blacks and the attendant political rollback.

In his narrative of the horrific violence of early 1870s Mississippi, author Nicholas Lemann highlights that while the White League "drew emotional sustenance" from the same cluster of racist boilerplate and fears of miscegenation, they were, in fact, a far scarier and more open affront to the aftermath of the war than even the Klan had been. The White League was "less secret, better organized, and more explicitly political in its aims," he writes, and "its purpose was to use extralegal violence to remove the Republican Party from power, and then to disenfranchise black people . . . – all aims that were to be accomplished by any means necessary."[22] One Mississippi White Liner unapologetically explained, "It is no secret that there has not been a full vote and a fair count in Mississippi since 1875. We have been preserving the ascendancy of white people by revolutionary methods. In other words we have been stuffing ballot boxes, committing perjury, and here and there in the state carrying the elections by fraud and violence."[23] The role these white supremacist groups played was always more than merely political; this violence was also profoundly psychological, as Lemann notes. This resistance to the federal government and to local Republican political power helped rehabilitate whites still wounded from the experience of Civil War defeat. Restoring white supremacy through terrorist violence proved both cathartic and deeply advantageous for the economic and political futures of white Southerners.[24]

In Louisiana, where some of the most brutal terrorist violence in American history took place, one white planter defended the violent tactics of white citizens. For B. W. Marston, white Republicans, particularly carpetbaggers, were simply trying "to organize the freedmen element against the interests of the white people." With such "incendiary purposes" in mind, Marston explained to Congress that blacks and whites who supported the Republican Party would be dealt with "promptly." Marston was referring, however obliquely, to the Coushatta Massacre, where the local White League assassinated six white Republicans and as many as twenty blacks who witnessed the killings.[25]

The legacy of Reconstruction terrorism

Despite the audacity and extent of racial violence and political fraud, it is especially outrageous that popular understandings of Reconstruction still most closely resemble the heroic narrative popularized by turn-of-the-century North Carolinian novelist, Thomas Dixon. Dixon's bestselling trilogy celebrating the Klan represents the depraved and ahistorical interpretation of Reconstruction at its finest. Dixon depicted a period of Northern vengeance "where evil outside forces attempted to destroy southern white civilization and mongrelize the population." The books are nearly pure stereotype, complete with venal carpetbaggers and scalawags, beastly blacks and innocent white women. Southern whites fight to save not just themselves but civilization. While these exaggerated caricatures, factual manipulations, and racist interpretations may seem absurd to us now, they distilled the core beliefs and felt truth of many Americans.[26]

Dixon's work was immensely popular, especially in the South, and was adapted for the stage and eventually the screen. D. W. Griffith's 1915 film, *The Birth of a Nation*, took Dixon's Klan trilogy and embedded a white supremacist vision of the past, present, and future in America's consciousness. Indeed, the film remains a signature achievement in American film making as well as American racism. "Ku Klux Fever" gripped the South, where the film was treated as a "sacred epic," but beyond the region as well. The rest of the United States showed "overwhelming enthusiasm" for Griffith's film and one New Englander remarked that the film made him "want to go out and kill the first Negro I see."[27]

Griffith's film recounts the history of the Civil War and Reconstruction through the eyes and experiences of Southern whites. Thus, the film represented history retold by those who vehemently opposed any political and social progress by African Americans. Both book and film show Southern blacks lusting after white women and brutally exercising their newfound freedom. White Southerners are rescued by the heroic Klan. With *The Birth of a Nation*, Griffith created the first blockbuster – a film that grossed over $60 million, single-handedly established the American film industry, and made Hollywood, where the film was shot, the motion picture capital of the world. Of course, *The Birth of a Nation* would eventually trigger race riots and revive the Ku Klux Klan for the twentieth century.[28]

Because widespread black protests greeted the dramatic staging of Thomas Dixon's *The Clansman* nine years earlier (the National Association for the Advancement of Colored People [NAACP] would boycott the film as well), both Griffith and Dixon knew it would be important to drum up support among prominent Americans for their historical vision. Dixon called up his old friend, native Virginian and the twenty-eighth president of the United States, Woodrow Wilson, asking him to endorse the film. Dixon called the movie "the birth of a new art – the launching of the mightiest engine for molding public opinion in the history of the world." Dixon's gambit worked and *The Birth of a Nation* became the first movie ever screened in the White House. Wilson embraced both Dixon and Griffith when the film ended. "It is like writing history with lightning," the President famously remarked. "My only regret is that it is all so terribly true."[29]

After this dramatic imprimatur, Dixon sought an audience with the chief justice of the Supreme Court, Louisianan Edward White. White, 70 years old, thought the idea of moving pictures "absurd" and remarked that he did not have "the slightest curiosity to see one." But Dixon did not give up, telling White that *Birth* "told the true story of Reconstruction and the redemption of the South by the Ku Klux Klan." White softened. "I was a member of the Klan, sir," he replied. "Through many a dark night, I walked my sentinel's beat through the ugliest streets of New Orleans with a rifle on my shoulder." The chief justice, along with several senators and congressmen, gave the film a rousing standing ovation.[30]

World War I served only to "intensify the racist climate and sparked another deadly new wave of mob violence in America."[31] In 1919 alone, the country witnessed twenty-five "race riots" – events that usually involved rampaging white mobs killing individuals before burning down the black sections of cities North and South. In the midst of this terrible racial terrorism, the black intellectual W. E. B. Du Bois exposed the entrenched racism and ignorance that fed such violent acts. His masterful *Black Reconstruction*, first published in 1935, revisited the birthing ground of America's terrorist crimes. Far from the typical critiques of the folly of Reconstruction, Du Bois celebrated 1865–77 as an unprecedented experiment in progressive government while revealing the ways the government failed its people. More relevantly, Du Bois exposed how generation upon generation of American historians had, in the words of his biographer Daniel Levering Lewis, "congealed racist interpretations of Reconstruction in the popular mind as solidly as had D. W. Griffith's film."[32]

Du Bois himself lamented that Reconstruction was "a field devastated by passion and belief" and that "sheer necessity" required his work to serve as "an arraignment of American historians and an indictment of their ideals." Why had the historical profession systematically ignored the many black triumphs and countless white outrages and wholly misunderstood the American tragedies of the postbellum years? Du Bois explained:

> With a determination unparalleled in science, the mass of American writers have started out so to distort the facts of the greatest critical period of American history as to prove right wrong and wrong right. . . . It simply shows that with sufficient general agreement and determination among the dominant classes, the truth of history may be utterly distorted and contradicted and changed to any convenient fairy tale that the masters of men wish.[33]

Lynching

The earlier discussion of Scipio Eager sets Du Bois's concerns about the historiography of Reconstruction in great relief. Statistics – that is, the act of measuring the number of blacks lynched or the decline in Republican voting rolls – are woefully inadequate to described racial terror in the United States. In Eager's case, this blatantly political terrorism directly eliminated at least two Republican voters in Washington County, Georgia. But when lynching statistics simply add Eager's brother to the tally of April 1871, historians miss the forest for the trees. To be sure, death counts are certainly a useful historical measure, but historians deploy and debate them with special vigor. In the history of racial violence in the United States, this practice is especially important because early race reformers fought against white supremacist terrorism initially by publicizing statistics and incidents in black-owned newspapers and magazines.

At the dawn of the twentieth century, those statistics indicated that two blacks were being lynched every week in the South. Based on the pioneering reporting of anti-lynching activist Ida B. Wells-Barnett, even by the 1890s as many as 10,000 "black Americans [had been] put to death in the South." And Wells-Barnett's staggering estimate is likely conservative. Moreover, no one in 1900 could report even a fraction of the terrorist violence being committed in the name of white supremacy. This horrific catalog of whippings, shootings, hangings, robbery, and rape that preceded and pervaded the Civil War and saturated the century that followed is particularly problematic. We want to know the scope of such violence in order to understand it. However, even if underreported violence like lynching provides some hard statistics, it is futile to try and count the innumerable threats and small acts of violence – the matrix of daily terror – that helped maintain the political, social, and economic basis of white supremacy. Instead of numbers, Philip Dray's landmark study of American lynching relies on prose; racial terrorism was simply an American "holocaust."[34]

That holocaust was a direct result of the cultural identity as well as the very real social and political chaos of the 1860s South. Few Southerners, even the former plantation aristocracy, knew the shape their society was in or would take. In the absence of a functioning government and an almost complete judicial vacuum, the Klan was born. According to one historian, the Ku Klux Klan "wrapped itself in the Stars and Bars, recited the racist litanies which had been devised to justify Negro slavery, threatened death to unbelievers, and thereby rendered itself unassailable by orthodox Southerners."[35]

Upending the sexual and racial proclivities of the antebellum era – a time of relentless sexual violence by white males against black women – groups like the Ku Klux Klan reversed the script with the active encouragement and complicity of white political leaders. Stoking "white anxiety about the political, economic, and social meanings of emancipation," the ominous specter of the black rapist emerged. The turn-of-the-century race-baiting Southern activist Rebecca Felton tried to make the case that this fear was also historical and thus legitimate. In the antebellum years, all feared for "the rape of their wives and daughters," and this fear was "born in the blood and bred in the bone." Thus, the black rapist had "deep roots in both the slaveholding south and the white southern imagination." Conveniently, this logic encouraged increasingly harsher repression and psychological terrorizing. The postbellum script of whites defending the barricades of civilization took on new potency and encouraged violent reprisals when some vague crime against order had been committed, even if there was no pretext. During Reconstruction, in service of social and political repression, the portrayal of "black men as beastly and unable to control their sexual desire served to justify the practice of lynching, segregation laws, and disenfranchisement of black men."[36]

For the next century (and beyond), *The Birth of a Nation* provided the cultural tropes and schema for white supremacy. Lynchings and further terrorist violence were justified by the belief, however unconscious or cynical, that white women needed to be protected.[37] This process only worsened over time. As the Civil Rights Movement gained momentum, all blacks and whites sympathetic to the cause were potential victims.[38] Mob actions were neither aberrations nor the acts of rogue individuals but the backbone and lifeblood of an entire region. The public ritual murder, the midnight tortures, and the constant terrorizing of the black population consumed the societies where they took place. The ubiquity of this violence and the explosive possibility of it erupting at any time for any perceived offense became essential to the maintenance of white supremacy and – conveniently for the white males in power – patriarchy as well. One particularly corrosive aspect of this disturbing creation was the notion of anonymity. According to Philip Dray, "The coroner's inevitable verdict, 'Death at the hands of persons unknown,' affirmed the public's tacit complicity: no *persons* had committed a crime, because the lynching had been an expression of the community's will."[39] But of course, someone had committed these crimes.

The Scottsboro case, which began in March 1931 in northeastern Alabama, was so commonplace in the details of its injustice, it is surprising that historians know so much about it. Countless innocent black youths had been arrested, tried, and lynched or executed by kangaroo courts since 1865. In this case, an interracial fight on a train led to rape charges, an attempted lynching, and nine guilty convictions for nine innocent men. What made the Scottsboro case notable was that it was suddenly deemed outrageous enough to generate a public outcry.

Indeed, the most dramatic change in the interwar years was the emergence of lynching in particular as a national public issue. As activism to combat lynching moved from reformers like Wells-Barnett and Du Bois to mainstream left-wing circles, lynching became a cultural phenomenon, a symbol of the racism and brutality of the South to self-righteous if genuinely concerned Americans. A good example of that cultural shift can be found in "Strange Fruit," originally a poem published in *The New Masses* in 1937. New York schoolteacher Abel Meeropol, an amateur writer and composer, penned the words in response to the increasingly commonplace but no less horrific imagery of a Southern lynching, and his song eventually found its way to Billie Holiday. Holiday immortalized the words and captured growing outrage against extra-legal white supremacist Southern violence with the song's powerful metaphors. The opening stanza underscores both the shocking brutality of lynching as well as its long history in the American landscape.

> Southern trees bear a strange fruit,
> Blood on the leaves and blood at the root,
> Black bodies swinging in the southern breeze,
> Strange fruit hanging from the poplar trees.[40]

The cultural phenomenon of lynching and the cultural products that white Southerners in particular created has led to new understanding of the spectacle of lynching and the way these very public acts "rather than the violence itself . . . wrought psychological damage, that enforced black acquiescence to white domination."[41] For historians like Amy Louise Wood and Kristina DuRocher, "the cultural power of white supremacy itself" lies in its existence as "spectacle" and is found in the ritualistic aspect of lynching: "the crowds, the rituals and performances, and their sensational representations in narratives, photographs, and films."[42]

The African American Civil Rights Movement

With the character of racial terrorism so firmly established, the intensification of the campaign for black civil rights in the 1950s spurred whites to respond. The murder of Emmett Till, the assassination of Medgar Evers, and the bombing of the 16th Street Baptist Church in Birmingham all fit the pattern of violence and terror created during Reconstruction. There was one important difference: 100 years after the Civil War, the nation could no longer ignore what was happening. Television and newspaper coverage and public attention meant that the 1950s and 1960s were dominated by images of sit-ins and school integrations accompanied by the kind of vicious racism and brutal everyday violence that defined the white supremacist campaign in the South.

Like Samuel Hawkins in 1872, Medgar Evers committed the "crime" of advocating black political involvement, especially by organizing local chapters of the NAACP. When President John F. Kennedy gave a speech on national television in support of civil rights on June 12, 1963, Evers was targeted and killed, shot in the back with a high-powered rifle. Within weeks of Evers's murder, Bob Dylan had written a song. "The laws are with [his assassin]," Dylan described, "to protect his white skin, to keep up his hate, so he never thinks straight."

Dylan's song, "Only a Pawn in Their Game," used Evers's murderer to underscore that poor Southern whites were merely tools in the hands of a white supremacist culture.[43] However, where John Brown's terrorism – violence in the service of slave liberation – was briefly used by the US government before being prematurely discarded, white supremacist practice and ideology became deeply embedded in the culture, society, and politics of the American South. Such threads are deeply deserving of future scholarship.[44]

Notes

1. For a longer discussion of Brown as terrorist, see Chapter 6 by Matthew Jennings in this volume, which explains that Brown understood the institution of slavery itself as terrorism. Jennings also makes the compelling point that Brown's actions in 1859 seemingly opened the door for the federal government to endorse similar acts once the Civil War was underway. For further discussions of Brown as a terrorist, see Tony Horwitz, "The 9/11 of 1859," *The New York Times*, December 1, 2009. See also David W. Blight, "He Knew How To Die," History News Network, December 2009: http://hnn.us/article/120730 (accessed September 4, 2014). For more on the origins of the term "propaganda of the deed," see Chapter 8 by Richard Bach Jensen on European and world anarcho-terrorism in this volume.
2. Zoe Trodd and John Stauffer, eds., *Meteor of War: The John Brown Story* (Maplecrest, NY: Brandywine, 2004), 132.
3. Ibid., 159. Punctuation reproduced from the original.
4. E. C. Stedman, "Raid of John Brown," also known as "John Brown's Invasion," reprinted in *New York Tribune* and *The Liberator*, November 28, 1859.
5. Thomas Goodrich, *The Darkest Dawn: Lincoln, Booth, and the Great American Tragedy* (Bloomington: Indiana University Press, 2005), 60–1.
6. Edward Steers, Jr., *Blood on the Moon: The Assassination of Abraham Lincoln* (Lexington: University of Kentucky Press, 2001), 36.
7. The connections between Brown and Lincoln were hard to avoid. Lincoln himself denied any similarity repeatedly, most notably in his famous Cooper Union speech. Derogatory political cartoons from the era depict Lincoln removing his face to reveal either John Brown's face or the devil's.
8. Michael Fellman, *In the Name of God and Country: Reconsidering Terrorism in American History* (New Haven, CT: Yale University Press, 2010), 95. Fellman also connects the two men directly, explaining, "As Booth was himself aware, his desire to enact an anarchy of the deed in order to change the course of American history made [him] the direct descendant of John Brown."
9. "Lincoln's Last Speech," www.abrahamlincolnonline.org/lincoln/speeches/last.htm (accessed September 4, 2014).
10. Fellman, 96.
11. *The New York Times*, November 5, 1872.
12. Like Brown unleashing a Civil War or Booth unleashing a tide of conservative terrorism, the Haymarket bombing christened the age of anarchist violence in the United States. Caleb Crain, in reviewing a popular historical work on the Haymarket in *The New Yorker*, explained that "for the generation that came of age during the Civil War, ideas and violence were closely entangled." One of the most tantalizing aspects of these pioneers of anarchist terrorism is that the actual bomb maker might have melted down metal type to make the bomb itself – "the literal transformation of their words into deeds." It is also worth noting that all the accused mentioned John Brown, abolitionism, Abraham Lincoln, and Fort Sumter in their defense. See Caleb Crain, "The Terror Last Time: What Happened at Haymarket," *The New Yorker*, May 13, 2006. For more on the Haymarket bombing and anarchist violence in the US, see Chapter 9 by Thai Jones in this volume.
13. Grace Elizabeth Hale, *Making Whiteness: The Culture of Segregation in the South, 1890–1940* (New York: Vintage, 1999), 9.
14. Stephanie McCurry, *Confederate Reckoning: Power and Politics in the Civil War South* (Cambridge, MA: Harvard University Press, 2012), 1–2.

15 *The Report of the Committees of the House of Representatives Made during the First Session, Thirty-Ninth Congress, 1865–1866* (Washington, DC: Government Printing Office, 1866), 2:129–32.
16 Allen W. Trelease, *White Terror: The Ku Klux Klan Conspiracy and Southern Reconstruction* (Baton Rouge: Louisiana State University Press, 1995), xi, 11.
17 Trelease, 321–2.
18 Ibid.
19 *Testimony Taken by the Joint Select Committee to Inquire into the Condition of Affairs in the Late Insurrectionary States* (Washington, 1872), reprinted in *Trouble They Seen: The Story of Reconstruction in the Words of African Americans*, ed. Dorothy Sterling (New York: Da Capo Press, 1994), 374–5.
20 Fellman, 125.
21 Stephen Budiansky, *The Bloody Shirt: Terror after Appomattox* (New York: Viking, 2008), 207.
22 Nicholas Lemann, *Redemption: The Last Battle of the Civil War* (New York: Farrar, Straus and Giroux, 2006), 25.
23 Judge Chrisman, quoted in James G. Hollandsworth, *Portrait of a Scientific Racist: Alfred Holt Stone of Mississippi* (Baton Rouge: Louisiana State University Press, 2008), 57.
24 Fellman, 131.
25 *Testimony of B.W. Marston Re: The Coushatta Affair*. House Reports, 44th Congress, 1st Session, No. 816, 645–727.
26 John Boles, *The South through Time: A History of an American Region*, 3rd ed. (Upper Saddle River, NJ: Pearson, 2004), 2:469.
27 Wyn Craig Wade, *The Fiery Cross: The Ku Klux Klan in America* (New York: Oxford University Press, 1998), 138.
28 "The Birth of a Nation and Black Protest," Roy Rosenzweig Center for History and New Media, http://chnm.gmu.edu/episodes/the-birth-of-a-nation-and-black-protest/ (accessed September 4, 2014).
29 Jennifer D. Keene, "Wilson and Race Relations," in *A Companion to Woodrow Wilson*, ed. Ross A. Kennedy (London: John Wiley, 2013), 144.
30 Wade, 126–7. Over the next twenty years, *The Birth of a Nation* went on to become one of the most admired and profitable films ever produced by Hollywood, replaced finally in 1940 by another piece of Redemptive propaganda, *Gone with the Wind*, another film about the Civil War and Reconstruction era based on a novel by a Southerner that told the story of gallant Southern cavaliers and their ladies and the "Lost Cause" of the Confederate South.
31 Crystal Feimster, *Southern Horrors: Women and the Politics of Rape and Lynching* (Cambridge, MA: Harvard University Press, 2009), 220.
32 Daniel Levering Lewis, introduction to *Black Reconstruction in America, 1860–1880*, by W. E. B. Du Bois (New York: Free Press, 1992), vii.
33 Ibid., xvi. If the attentions and arguments of contemporary American historians are any indication, we are still distracted by the flash and bang of an anarchist bomb. Rather than cordon one kind of violence off from the other, we might be inclined to view the driving dynamics of American terrorism during this era as closely related phenomena. On the one hand, white Americans fought for a century after the abolition of slavery to preserve the economic and social hierarchy that had kept blacks subservient since the seventeenth century. On the other hand, anarchists (most of whom would be considered ethnically white within a half-century) fought to upend the tools of economic oppression that kept people like themselves marginalized. Racial violence during these hundred years only underscores the continuities and characteristics that have defined Americans' relationship with violence in the name of change.
34 Philip Dray, *At the Hands of Persons Unknown: The Lynching of Black America* (New York: Modern Library, 2002), vii, xi.
35 Trelease, xi.
36 Feimster, 7, 4–5.
37 Kristina DuRocher, *Raising Racists: The Socialization of White Children in the Jim Crow South* (Lexington: University Press of Kentucky, 2011), 5.
38 Ibid., 164.
39 Dray, ix.
40 Billie Holiday, "Strange Fruit," Commodore Records, 1939; lyrics by Abel Meeropol, published originally under the pseudonym Lewis Allan, "Bitter Fruit," *The New York Teacher* (January 1937).

Meeropol and Holiday were not alone in their interest. Like many of the left-leaning artists of 1930s, the regionalist painter John Steuart Curry was drawn to lynching. The murder of department store scion Brooke Hart in San Francisco and the lynching of his killers inspired Curry to paint images of mob justice. The Hart lynching came in the midst of a series of legal fiascoes like the Scottsboro case in Alabama and increasingly brazen lynchings across the South. Because Hart was a white victim, the lynching provided the NAACP with a pretext to reinvigorate their longstanding campaign for federal anti-lynching legislation.

41 Amy Louise Wood, *Lynching and Spectacle: Witnessing Racial Violence in America, 1890–1940* (Chapel Hill: University of North Carolina Press, 2009), 2.

42 Wood also manages to inscribe an inspirational story in her catalog of inhumanity, brutality, and injustice. By the mid-1930s, anti-lynching activists, through their relentless attention to making national the local phenomena of lynchings, transformed lynching imagery into "icons of oppression." However, Wood notes that such progress came at a cost, since it "unwittingly succeeded in detaching them from history itself." Wood, 3, 269.

43 Bob Dylan, "Only a Pawn in Their Game," from *The Times They Are a-Changin'*, Columbia Records, 1964.

44 Ashraf Rushdy, *American Lynching* (New Haven, CT: Yale University Press, 2012), xii. Rushdy explains that the memory of slavery as well as its legal apparatus "directly produce[d] the very cultural values that inspired and gave [racial terrorism] its impetus in America." This violence is thus "distinctively American" because of the "fundamental contradictions" of the founding moment. The founders "solved a set of intractable problems by . . . promot[ing] an act of collective violence, directed in certain ways at specific groups of people" that was "meant to exhibit a particular kind of social power and exercise a particular kind of social control."

Further reading

Budiansky, Stephen. *The Bloody Shirt: Terror after Appomattox*. New York: Viking, 2008.

DuRocher, Kristina. *Raising Racists: The Socialization of White Children in the Jim Crow South*. Lexington: University Press of Kentucky, 2011.

Feimster, Crystal. *Southern Horrors: Women and the Politics of Rape and Lynching*. Cambridge, MA: Harvard University Press, 2009.

Fellman, Michael. *In the Name of God and Country: Reconsidering Terrorism in American History*. New Haven, CT: Yale University Press, 2010.

Lemann, Nicholas. *Redemption: The Last Battle of the Civil War*. New York: Farrar, Straus and Giroux, 2006.

Trelease, Allen W. *White Terror: The Ku Klux Klan Conspiracy and Southern Reconstruction*. Baton Rouge: Louisiana State University Press, 1995.

Wood, Amy Louise. *Lynching and Spectacle: Witnessing Racial Violence in America, 1890–1940*. Chapel Hill: University of North Carolina Press, 2009.

Part III

TERRORISM IN THE TWENTIETH CENTURY

11

STATE TERRORISM IN EARLY TWENTIETH-CENTURY EUROPE

Paul M. Hagenloh

Assessing the nature of state terrorism in Europe in the first half of the twentieth century is difficult. The terms "terror" and "terrorism" were in wide use in this period but had varied meanings, not all of which correspond to the way we think about the term today. Even if we accept current definitions that focus on violence committed by (or supported by) governments and directed at non-combatants with clear political goals, often related to national security, we are still left with fundamental questions of definition and scope. Early twentieth-century states, especially dictatorships, mobilized a stunning variety of forms of violence against their populations – structural, paramilitary, legal, extra-legal, often genocidal. Which aspects of this violence qualify as "state terrorism"? Does terrorism occur by definition only in times of peace, or can it occur on the battlefield? Can one state practice "terrorism" vis-à-vis another or only vis-à-vis non-combatant populations (its own or another's)? Does spontaneous ethnic, religious, or class-based violence count as state terrorism if supported, initially or eventually, by a state? What, if anything, is gained by thinking in terms of "state terrorism" in regards to regimes that operate almost exclusively through violence, intimidation, and fear, or that take genocide as a primary policy goal? One might argue that all violence committed by a genocidal dictatorship should be construed as terroristic, but doing so provides little analytic help in understanding the nature and causes either of state terrorism or of modern state violence in general.

I argue in this chapter for a relatively narrow understanding of state terrorism, one that focuses on overt, immediate, public violence that is intended not only to instill fear and intimidate but also to reshape the basic social makeup of the society at which it is aimed. I argue as well that European state terrorism in the early twentieth century can only be understood in the context of the momentous changes in the nature of European states themselves in this period, especially the changing nature of state administration during war. The brutal wars of the early twentieth century – civil wars, World War I, anti-colonial struggles, World War II, and resistance in Eastern Europe after both world wars – brought many of the tactics that we today call "terrorism" into the mainstream of modern military practice, while at the same time war and revolution brought these terroristic military tactics into the mainstream of modern European statecraft. In short, war made terrorism one of the constituent tools of modern European dictatorships: it is simply impossible to imagine the Stalinist or Nazi dictatorships without the massive application of terroristic violence to civilian populations that took place in colonial struggles and global conflicts alike in the early twentieth century. In sum, war changed "terrorism" from a limited tactic, one that had the most resonance in revolutionary situations, to an almost ubiquitous aspect of modern European conflict and state violence, for states as well as sub-state actors. By the twentieth century, terrorism was politics by other means; and it was war that made it so.

As many recent works on European history have shown, the connections between modern European statecraft, violence, and war are evident in virtually every corner of the continent, in democracies as well as dictatorships. Yet it was in dictatorships that the potential for violence inherent in modern European statecraft was unleashed with most fury: dictatorships were least restricted by concerns of public responsibility and political culture, especially in peacetime, and interwar European dictatorships were particularly dedicated to using state violence, including state terrorism, to effect massive social and economic transformations in the territories that they controlled. This chapter, then, will focus on the German, Italian, and Soviet cases: these are among the strongest states in interwar Europe as well as the least democratic. In these three cases, we find widespread application of a particular kind of state violence that fits current definitions of state terrorism quite well: these regimes carried out widespread, sometimes random acts of violence against civilian, non-combatant populations, in both wartime and peacetime, for explicitly political ends. These examples show that state violence that emerged and was perfected in wartime in numerous contexts (military, anti-insurgent, colonial) could be transferred to peacetime state activity; and they show how far tactics that were developed during times of war could be taken, under the right conditions, against civilian populations in peacetime.[1]

State terror before the Great War

Without repeating what has been said in previous chapters, we begin by noting that state terror, including the kind we identify as the "modern" variant, certainly took place well before the twentieth century. The French Revolution is perhaps the paradigmatic case of modern state terrorism, one that fits our own contemporary definitions quite closely: revolutionary Jacobins, as described by Mike Rapport in Chapter 5 in this volume, made explicit use of the apparatus of the state to carry out widespread, unpredictable violence against not only internal political enemies, understood as "counter-revolutionary conspirators," but also against representatives of social classes thought to be inimical by nature to the interests of the new regime. Revolutionary terror was an ad hoc response to the existential threats posed by internal rebellion and by invading European powers, but it was also an extra-legal method of forcing a complete transformation of the existing social and political order, carried out by representatives of a greatly expanded French revolutionary state (and often assisted by popular violence, including that carried out by the infamous *sans-culottes*). The fact that Jacobins viewed "terror" as a constructive avenue of political and social change is often noted when linking them to later violent revolutionaries (fascists, Bolsheviks, National Socialists), but the mere positive connection between terroristic violence and political change is not particularly unusual for any era of human history. More important is the fact that Jacobins used terror as an instrument with which to operate directly on the French body politic: the revolutionary state used terroristic violence (including but not limited to the guillotine) to forge a new political consensus, to effect direct social transformation (e.g., reshaping demographic realities, forced change of cultural and political norms, vicious attacks on religious belief), and to create a new mode of modern civic participation and French republican citizenship.[2]

Yet the French Revolution was, perhaps surprisingly, something of an anomaly in the use of terrorism by states in Europe for most of the nineteenth century, at least domestically. Various revolutionary movements and figures on the far left, it is true, viewed the French experience with state terror as a model to be emulated, but few had any opportunity to put such plans into place – with the notable exception of the Paris Commune, which revived many of the traditions of the Jacobins. More ominously, numerous instances of military conflict, revolutionary uprisings, and insurgency in the nineteenth century also produced state actions that we might deem "terrorism," beginning with French atrocities against Spanish civilians during Napoleonic campaigns and continuing through independence movements on the Italian peninsula through the numerous nationalist uprisings in the crumbling Ottoman and Austro-Hungarian empires late in the century. Yet for most of the long nineteenth century, European states shied away from actions that bore too close a resemblance to the state terror of the French revolutionaries, not only domestically but also in times of war, as during the Franco-Prussian War of 1870–1, when Otto von Bismarck urged his military commanders to burn entire French villages to the ground in order to terrorize the population into submission – a suggestion rejected by the chief of the Prussian General Staff, Helmuth von Moltke.[3]

This situation began to change for numerous reasons in the late nineteenth and early twentieth centuries, including the emergence of a new mass politics that brought "the public" to the center of political action; the growing propensity of European states to embark on progressive, Enlightenment-inspired schemas for social change (and the growing technical expertise of such states to carry them out); and the increasingly tense political atmosphere created by struggles for national liberation, from the Balkans to Ireland. But none of these factors was more important in expanding the repertoire of modern states to include terroristic violence against their own populations than the colonial experience. Extreme violence was nearly universal in the European (and North American) colonial experience, with counter-insurgency campaigns in particular often entailing widespread, instrumental use of terror against non-combatant populations. This trend was strengthened by the emergence of a group of state functionaries schooled, quite literally, in the application of violence against non-combatants and by a growing sense of historical mission among European elites that made any tactics possible in the pursuit of the "civilizing mission" or "military necessity."[4]

Yet there is little sense in searching for the roots of future state terrorism, or lack thereof, in the more or less barbaric nature of colonial violence in one case or another. Nearly all European powers participated in state terrorism in the colonies in a way that could be seen as a precursor to more terrible events to come, and many of the most brutal examples of colonial repression were carried out by nations that had a democratic future – indiscriminate burning of Boer settlements by the British in the Transvaal and Orange Free State, for example, or the murderous campaigns of Indian removal carried out by the military and administrative representatives of the United States as it expanded across the North American continent (for the latter, see Chapter 6 by Matthew Jennings in this volume). The proper analytic question, rather, is: how did this colonial violence metastasize into state terrorism during and after World War I in each individual case, and how did these colonial experiences become permanent parts of domestic statecraft in dictatorial countries but not (or much less so) in democratic countries? The answer lies in the concrete experiences of each of these countries during the era of world war (and ongoing civil war) stretching from 1914 to at least the mid-1920s; and it is to these experiences that we now turn.

Nazi Germany

We begin with Germany, because the National Socialist regime has for decades been the paradigmatic case of a modern European dictatorship that ruled by terroristic violence. The Nazi system (along with the Union of Soviet Socialist Republics [USSR], discussed below) was key to Hannah Arendt's immensely influential concept of totalitarianism, which posits that totalitarian dictatorships ruled precisely through ruthless, unpredictable terror. In Arendt's model, these regimes terrorized their populations with a broad array of both public and private violence – show trials, mass executions, vast secret police networks, forced denunciations – in order to produce fear and create social atomization, reducing all people to ciphers that could be manipulated with ease as these revolutionary totalitarian states redefined completely the basic social, political, and economic structures of the nations they controlled.[5] Arendt's model was for decades so influential that it constrained academic research on interwar dictatorships, as most commenters simply assumed that "terror" was a, perhaps *the*, foundational element of both the Nazi and Stalinist regimes. Arendt's influence has hardly disappeared, but the last several decades of research on interwar Europe have greatly complicated our understanding of how authoritarian European regimes actually functioned, as well as raised the question of the extent to which all modern states employ various modes of violence and coercion in order to define, categorize, and dominate populations under their control.[6]

The widespread understanding of Nazi Germany as a "terror state" is understandable, particularly in light of the regime's self-presentation and the inarguable importance of street-level terrorism and paramilitary violence in the National Socialist rise to power. Key to this narrative are the infamous *Freikorps*, or volunteer paramilitary units of young men, often too young to have served directly in World War I, which were created in the wake of Imperial Germany's defeat in 1918.[7] The *Freikorps* served initially to protect Germany's interests in the East vis-à-vis Soviet Russia, in addition to preventing further left-wing revolution within Germany. Although any military rationale for this paramilitary force vanished quickly in the 1920s with the solidification of international borders and the creation of a stable, democratic Weimar system, their brand of paramilitary street-fighting, imbued with a hatred of "the East" (disorderly, Jewish, Bolshevik), became a foundational part of right-wing political culture during the fragile Weimar years. The infamous "Brownshirts" (Sturmabteilung, or SA) of the National Socialist Party took up the mantle of the *Freikorps* in the 1920s, and paramilitary violence became a widespread part of the Weimar political landscape – on the left as well as the right, as the SA clashed in brutal street battles with opponents from the center and left, most notably the paramilitary Red Front-Fighters Alliance (Roter Frontkämpfer-Bund, or RFB) associated with the German Communist Party (KPD).[8] As the Weimar system faltered under the weight of the Great Depression, street-level terrorism and paramilitary action carried out by the Brownshirts helped usher the Nazi regime into power. Ultimately, the centrality of right-wing popular violence in the overthrow of the Republic ensured that the *Freikorps'* ethos of existential struggle, leader worship, and transformative violence would be a major part of the new political system that emerged in Germany in the mid-1930s. In this analysis, state terror *was* popular terror in Nazi Germany, with the regime not merely co-opting the violent politics of the street but consciously institutionalizing it as a central part of an anti-liberal fascist state.

Yet National Socialist state terrorism was something far more radical, destructive, and transformational than mere Brownshirt thuggery. Most research now suggests that the kind of "popular terror" represented by the SA was limited internally by the structure of the National Socialist state and that it played far less a role in the daily life of German citizens within the Reich after 1933 than previously assumed.[9] As in the case of the French Revolution, the National Socialist state and popular violence initially coexisted in a symbiotic relationship, with the state relying on the SA for support but with the SA exerting a substantial influence on the nature of state violence carried out by the regime. But, unlike the French case, the National Socialist state rather quickly dispensed with popular violence as an instrument of rule, a process both symbolically and literally summed up in the purge of the SA leadership in 1934 and the subsequent subordination of the SA to the more professionalized SS (Schutzstaffel). "Popular terror," though important, was only one part of a more complex nexus of anti-democratic populism, scientific racism, eliminationist anti-Semitism, and militarized colonialism, all of which were embodied in and carried out by an exceedingly powerful, modern, National Socialist (i.e., German) state apparatus.

Most new research also suggests that state repression was far less widespread within German society than previously assumed and that the regime ruled on the basis of a substantial amount of popular support for its policies – along with, it must be stressed, a tremendous amount of terroristic violence directed at "externalized" populations both within Germany and especially outside its borders during war. The regime enjoyed popular, sometimes enthusiastic, support for its exclusionary policies, from the infamous pogroms in 1938 known as Kristallnacht (Night of the Broken Glass) through the chaotic and increasingly pointless resistance to the Allied assumption of control over central Europe in 1945. Ultimately, Nazi Germany was a majoritarian dictatorship: a political system in which a group of elites ruled by violence and terror but to the advantage of most of the population, most of whom accorded the regime passive, if not active, support.[10]

National Socialist violence was carried out primarily in the context of a strong German state, both military and civilian; and it is in this context that we can most profitably discuss the concept of "state terrorism" and differentiate between "state terror" and other forms of violence widely employed by the regime, both within and outside its own borders. As the National Socialist regime moved from internal consolidation in the mid-1930s to external conquest later in the decade, the ethos of violence and terrorism inherent in the Nazi political movement was subsumed into a broader political structure that unleashed these destructive terroristic impulses primarily on "externalized" populations in the context of total war. This was true even of Jews, who found themselves progressively excluded from the polity but even so did not face annihilation until they were transported outside the boundaries of the Reich and subsumed fully into the category of "other" in the East. Once war with Poland began in 1939, the occupied lands were freed of any sort of legal or conceptual restrictions on the exercise of state power. The strong German tradition of a Rechtsstaat, a "state of law" based on a written constitution that constrains even the most powerful institutions (e.g., the police, the military), remained in place inside Germany, no matter how battered or abused; but it vanished completely in Eastern Europe, where virtually every part of the military and administrative machinery of the German occupation viewed untrammeled terror as a means of conquest, a strategy for maintaining order, and a tool for the total refashioning of social and political structures in conquered areas. As has been well documented, even the highly conservative Wehrmacht leadership accepted (if in the case of some high-ranking officers only begrudgingly) that conquest in the East would entail mass terrorism and murder of civilian populations by all parts of the National Socialist state apparatus, its own soldiers included.

The sources of this ethos of violence are many. Readers should consult Chapter 24 by Roger Griffin on terrorism and modernity in this volume for a discussion of one crucially important set of such sources: the potent mix of political ideology, instrumental rationality, and modern bureaucracy summed up in the metaphor of the "gardening state." Yet this amorphous set of assumptions about the nature of modern governments was only one such influence, and the German colonial experience in prior decades had a more direct, and generally underestimated, effect on National Socialist administration in the East. Like most other European powers, German colonial officials made wide use of terroristic violence in the late nineteenth century to control colonial populations and especially to quell local insurgencies. Such violence was an accepted part of colonial practice, enshrined in military doctrine of the time and virtually codified in Charles Callwell's 1896 handbook, *Small Wars: Their Principles and Practice*.[11] German troops combated irregular forces with a wide array of terroristic methods that generally remained off-limits in conflicts between European powers: mass hostage taking, ruining natural and agricultural resources on which local populations depend, and punitive campaigns against particular villages as punishment for specific anti-colonial actions. German colonial violence in South West Africa, against the Herero and Maji-Maji revolts between 1904 and 1907, was shocking then as now: General Lothar von Trotha's troops veered far outside any accepted traditions of military conflict, shooting male Herero insurgents out of hand and driving women, children, and the infirm out of villages to die of starvation. When forced to moderate his tactics under pressure from Berlin, von Trotha turned to branding all Herero men who surrendered and conscripting them into forced labor. Such tactics, termed *schrecklichkeit* (frightfulness), were little different, according to one scholar of counter-insurgency, from the Nazi tactics of *abschreckung* ("terror tactics") of over three decades later.[12]

The German army employed very little of this kind of overt terrorism during World War I, in part because occupations in the East were carried out under the framework of German administrative law, even in an area that had already been culturally redefined as "external" to the Reich and full of populations understood as ethnically (and civilizationally) "other." War in the East after 1939, however, entailed no such restrictions. Without recounting the entire history of Nazi occupation and the Holocaust, we note that civilian and military officials (Wehrmacht, Waffen-SS, Einsatzgruppen) all engaged in what they saw as counter-insurgency efforts, in which a rhetoric of national security (protecting the Reich from opposition from "hostile" yet "weak" populations) merged with an ideologically conditioned drive to cleanse the East of populations seen as "subhuman" (Poles, Roma, and Jews, among others). Terror was chief among the strategies employed from the beginning of the occupation, made possible by the effective suspension of even military (not to speak of civil) law in zones behind the advancing front lines: Einsatzgruppen and Wehrmacht troops confiscated property, conducted summary arrests, deported both individuals and entire communities, and organized mass executions of populations deemed threatening (Polish elites, left-wing activists, and Jews first and foremost). The Security Police in most areas then attempted to resettle these "cleansed" spaces with "Germanic" populations, with the explicit goal of creating secure military spaces and promoting strong state administration, as well as creating the kind of homogenous social order characteristic of the National Socialist dream of modern "Aryan" society.

Civilian and military officials alike understood such actions as explicit (and proper) "terrorism" in that they were intended to repress representatives of "undesirable" populations (Polish intellectuals, for example) in order to terrorize the remainder into submission. Yet the relationship between "terrorism" and the broader National Socialist project (including mass violence of various sorts, genocide, forced resettlement, labor camps, etc.) is complicated and underscores some of the dangers of relying on accepted definitions of terrorism when discussing European state violence in the twentieth century. Many of the actions of the Nazi state in the East correspond closely to widely accepted definitions of terrorism that focus on a triangular relationship between perpetrator, victim, and intended audience: Nazi officials often intended to communicate a threat to target populations via the repression of "message generators," in Alex Schmid's terminology, in order to instill fear or break resistance.[13] Yet the "threat" being communicated was often the regime's intent to eliminate a particular group of people altogether, and the initial targeting of "message generators" often served as only the first step in a more comprehensive program of resettlement, internment, and annihilation. Hence the difference between "state terrorism" and "genocide" in the Nazi case is arguably one of scale and state capacity rather than intent or essence. The events of Kristallnacht, for example, were not (yet) intended to eliminate the Jewish population entirely in the target areas, whereas the actions of battalions of reserve soldiers charged with ransacking and murdering Jewish populations behind advancing front lines certainly were; the former was carried out by a still relatively weak state apparatus and involved a considerable amount of spontaneous popular participation, the latter by a highly structured, militarized bureaucracy that nonetheless relied on the consent of the perpetrators to this specific action, if not the overall project of genocide. And yet these actions themselves were so similar in nature that it seems analytically untenable to call the first "terrorism" and refuse to give the same label to the latter merely because its effect was so much greater.[14]

This is a difficult problem to address, and we will return to it below in our discussion of Stalin's USSR. For now we suggest that it is unhelpful to bracket off "totalitarian" violence from other modes of modern European state violence, as does Griffin, on the assumption that the ultimate goals of these states (i.e., total social and political transformation, with mass violence up to and including genocide as viable tools to effect that transformation) make their concrete methods of violence (including terrorism) somehow unique among techniques of violence carried out by modern states. Nor is it wise to rely on a definition of terrorism, including state terrorism, that rules out mass state actions, including genocide, only because the targets are really the targets and not "message generators." A robust definition of state terrorism in the twentieth century must take into account the reality that the European state (gardening, surveillance, bio-political, military, etc.) became powerful enough, for the first time, to bridge this gap, and to bring to fruition the dream of the French revolutionaries, which was to operate directly on the body politic with methods that included, but are not limited to, the application of massive amounts of violence, much terroristic, in the effort to create a homogenous, unambiguous, uniform social, political, and ethno/national space.[15] In doing so, modern states, including dictatorships, create their own "ideologies" of power: acts of state terrorism carried out against broad categories of people are inevitably a process of definition and dehumanization, as well as a "tactic" in support of a broader goal. A definition of terrorism that focuses on "doctrine" and "tactic" is, in short, insufficient in attempting to come to grips with the immense potential for violence inherent in the modern state.

Stalin's USSR

If the past two decades of research have complicated the idea that Nazi rule was based on terror, they have only strengthened this claim in the case of the other major "totalitarian" regime of the twentieth century, the Soviet Union. The USSR served for several decades after the beginning of the Cold War as the analytic twin of Nazi Germany: Stalin's dictatorship was, in this account, based entirely on the fear engendered by various overlapping forms of repression, including the Gulag system of labor camps, public show trials, surveillance carried out by the secret police (the infamous NKVD), and the ever-present threat of denunciation by a colleague, friend, or family member that marked the beginning of a hellish descent into any or all of the above. The analytic connection between Soviet communism and state terrorism was so strong, in fact, that the single best-known repressive event of Stalin's rule, the wave of arrests and executions that left nearly a million people dead in the space of eighteen short months in 1937 and 1938, became known in academic and popular texts alike as "The Great Terror," a phrase that both invoked comparisons to revolutionary France and designated "terror" as the central function of the Soviet state.

The first wave of research completed after the collapse of the USSR in 1991 did little to soften this characterization, and most accounts now argue that state terrorism was central to the Bolshevik project from the very beginning. One hardly needs to pore over the writings of the early Bolshevik leaders to find evidence that they viewed terrorism as a perfectly legitimate means of effecting revolutionary change. The fledgling Bolshevik regime swiftly carried out mass repressions of potential rivals from other socialist camps – first summary arrests and executions of anarchists in Moscow in early 1918, then arrests of mainstream opposition leaders, mostly Mensheviks and Socialist Revolutionaries, and then violent repression of working-class dissent in the summer, all leading to a much broader wave of repressions known as the "Red Terror" over the second half of 1918. The Red Terror, which likely claimed some 10,000 to 15,000 lives, was explicitly punitive, and it was intended to send a strong message to potential opponents as much as to repress individuals seen as active threats, but the tactics had more to do with contemporary political realities than with French-revolutionary precedent: hostage taking and subsequent executions from among the families of leading oppositionists or old-regime figures, arrests and executions among unruly peasant populations that were described as "prophylactic" measures, and the initial creation and population of the labor-camp system – the Gulag – that would come to virtually define the Soviet experience. A strong connection between military action, administration, and state terror was also established immediately – and irrevocably – in the post-revolutionary period. Not only did the new Red Army take part in massive campaigns against peasants resisting the Bolsheviks' grain procurement campaigns between 1918 and 1921, but the rapidly expanding secret police, the Cheka (later the NKVD), created its own military force, known as the Internal Troops for Defense of the Republic, that numbered by 1919 at least 200,000. These Troops carried out direct martial repressions of rebellions major and minor throughout the entire Soviet period, using all means at their disposal, including artillery and even poison gas, during the most dire moments of post-revolutionary conflict.[16]

The regime continued with overtly terroristic repression of entire social categories over the following years. Such actions included the well-known repressions of the unfortunate remnants of the Russian Empire's upper classes, culminating symbolically if not numerically in 1922 and 1923 with the forced expulsion of hundreds of the most talented Russian intellectuals and their families, many of whom would go on to make incalculable contributions to world and Russian culture from their exile abroad. Yet military and police administrations also targeted broad swaths of the population deemed threatening to the new regime, such as Orthodox priests, rebellious peasants on the unstable periphery, and entire socio-ethnic groups like the Don Cossacks. The latter were identified as inherently anti-Soviet based on their corporate (if not quite ethnic) identity and targeted with a process termed "de-Cossackization" – mass arrests, execution of political elites, destruction of homelands, and forced migration of populations to all reaches of the former Russian Empire. That the de-Cossackization campaign was abruptly halted after only several months, as the political situation shifted in the region, did not prevent more than 10,000 Cossacks from being executed by military representatives of the new Bolshevik state.[17]

As in the German case, many of these more explicitly terroristic strategies have their roots in colonial violence; in contrast to the Wehrmacht, however, the tsarist military made widespread use of exactly these kinds of tactics just before and during World War I. The tsarist military was already in the mid-nineteenth century engaged in massive ethnic cleansing in the Caucasus, expelling more than half a million Chechens and Circassians and resettling their villages with Cossacks; and Kazakh and Kirgiz uprisings in 1915 were met with deliberate acts of genocide by imperial troops and settlers that killed or displaced several hundred thousand people.[18] It was a small step, then, to a massive expansion of these tactics on the western borderlands during World War I, where nearly a million imperial subjects were categorized as "internal enemies" by the military authorities – Germans, Balts, Jews, and Turkish Muslims – and subjected to a wide range of repressions: deportations, property confiscations, internment in concentration camps, and pogroms against both Jews and Germans that often occurred with the only thinly veiled support of local military and civilian authorities alike.[19]

Such tactics continued almost uninterrupted across the revolutionary divide of 1917. A surprising number of tsarist military officials, deemed "bourgeois specialists" but highly valued by the new regime for their professional skills, successfully navigated from one side of that divide to the other, serving in the Red Army in the 1920s and 1930s and forming a direct link between tsarist and Soviet military terror.[20] To be sure, the massive amount of ethnic cleansing, state-supported pogroms, and explicitly punitive operations perpetrated by all sides – Red, White, Green – during the highly confused situation of the Russian Civil War (1918–ca. 1921) make it difficult to discern which instances of "terrorism" in this era deserve to accrue to the tally of the "state." To take just one example, the city of Kiev in the aftermath of the 1917 revolutions experienced at least a dozen major and minor military coups and changes of power – first the overthrow of the Ukrainian Central Rada by the pro-German Pavel Skoropadsky, then a coup carried out by the Ukrainian nationalist Semyon Petliura, then the Red Army, then White forces under General Denikin, then the Red Army again, the Polish military, and the Red Army a final time. Each change of power was accompanied by waves of arrests, retribution, public executions, resettlement, and pogroms, all of which left the city and the entire area devastated. In Ukraine, as across the wide swaths of lawless territory in which the new regime battled its foes both internal and external, these brutal occupation tactics, usually rooted in a very loose application of military law, became a standard part of both military occupations and civilian administration, for Red as well as White forces.[21]

Taken together, the entire history of Russian and early Soviet state violence ensured that state terrorism – explicit, targeted violence intended to punish, to instill fear, and to reshape the social structure of the country – was engrained in basic Soviet administrative practices by the mid-1920s and that terror would be among the most important strategies of control that the Stalinist state would turn to as it attempted to force the USSR into its version of "socialism" in the 1930s.[22] Parallel trends set the stage for Stalinist repression as well, including a creeping re-emergence of ethno-nationalism in Soviet political culture, along with the emergence of highly utopian and modernized visions of cultural progress among the new Soviet political elite that correspond closely to Zygmunt Bauman's concept of the "gardening state" in Western Europe.[23] Yet in the early Soviet case, it was most emphatically war – world war, military occupation, military tactics, civil war, and the complex responses of populations who were subject to all of the above – that cast the die for the massive upheavals that would follow under Stalin.[24]

After a brief period of retrenchment and relative calm in the mid-1920s, the Soviet regime reverted to overtly violent tactics in support of Stalin's first policy initiatives during the First Five-Year Plan (1928–32): collectivization of agriculture, forced industrialization, and the expulsion from the Soviet state of remnants of the "bourgeoisie" and their replacement by a new cadre of "proletarian" elites. The Stalinist regime made use of virtually every violent state technique available to it in pursuing these goals, including show trials of technical specialists and foreign industrialists in the late 1920s, state-sanctioned purges of places of employment and other local institutions, the rapid expansion of the labor camp system (the Gulag) and the surveillance activities of the secret police, state-exacerbated (perhaps induced) famine, and mass arrest, resettlement, and execution of large numbers of peasants who resisted or could be expected to resist collectivization of agriculture.

Yet not all of these myriad acts of state violence should be construed as state terrorism. Many are better understood as systemic or structural violence, enmeshed in the basic nature of the Stalinist state/society interface and pervading the entire social fabric of the country by the mid-1930s. For example, the successive waves of deadly purges of the Soviet Communist Party in the 1920s and 1930s, which resulted in the expulsions of thousands of party members and culminated in the infamous show trials of the late 1930s (e.g., Bukharin et al.), were the product of highly complex social and bureaucratic trends that included but extended far beyond the actions of the Soviet state: generational conflicts within Soviet officialdom, shop-floor politics that pitted the working classes against the social-climbing elites who became their new bosses, as well as the direct intervention of the secret police (the NKVD).[25] It makes little analytical sense to refer to such violence as "state terrorism," given our definition of the term above, unless we simply assume that all violence perpetuated by a "totalitarian" state should be construed as "terrorism" – a position that might be consistent with Arendt's analysis but provides little understanding either of state terrorism as a modern phenomenon or of the nature of the Stalinist system.

Some Stalinist state violence, however, was indeed terroristic. Much of the post-1991 research on the Stalin era, in fact, shows that the most repressive and destructive actions of the regime are entirely consistent with the definition of state terrorism outlined above, that is, actions carried out directly by an increasingly powerful Soviet state apparatus that used violent techniques, up to and including mass executions, to target specific populations, instill fear, and in some cases eliminate target categories of people entirely. Collectivization of agriculture in the late 1920s and early 1930s, for example, was accompanied by "dekulakization" – a coordinated attack on "counter-revolutionary" peasant populations, with local officials of the Communist Party and secret police in charge of devising lists of three categories of "kulaks" (moderately well-off peasants) in the countryside and subjecting them to incarceration in labor camps, deportation to distant regions of the Soviet Union, or dispossession and resettlement within their home regions, respectively.[26] Not surprisingly, such actions provoked violent resistance from peasant populations across the USSR, some reaching thousands of peasants in size; and the state responded in kind, with mass arrests, tens of thousands of summary executions, and unprecedented deportation operations – with arrested families shunted via overcrowded railway cars through a makeshift system of barracks, transit camps, and labor colonies to final destinations on the inhospitable eastern and northern peripheries of the empire – that totaled some 1.8 million people by the end of 1931, with as many as 300,000 perishing along the way.[27]

By the mid-1930s, the Stalinist regime was fully engaged in numerous such campaigns, which targeted specific categories of individuals deemed threatening or undesirable: petty criminals, vagrants, homeless children, and, with increasing intensity as the decade wore on, numerous ethno-national categories that were seen as a national security threat. The latter included Germans, Japanese, Poles, and others seen as potential "fifth columnists" in the event of an increasingly likely war in the West or East. Such campaigns were generally carried out by the state apparatus and entailed relatively little popular participation or support. Not only the notorious NKVD but the NKVD's Internal Troops, mentioned above, the federal Border Guard administrations, as well as Red Army divisions responsible for security in border regions all played a major role in such repressions, so much so that some accounts of the era now speak of a "militarized" dictatorship under Stalin.[28]

These trends culminated in a wave of mass repressions carried out by the Stalinist state in 1937–8, referred to internally as "mass operations of repression of kulak, criminal, and other anti-Soviet elements." These operations, in which over 700,000 individuals were shot and roughly a million more incarcerated, arose directly from the regime's national security concerns, as looming conflict with Germany and Japan goaded the regime into punitive actions against broad categories of potential fifth columnists. Germans, Latvians, Finns, Estonians, and shortly thereafter Japanese, Koreans, Poles, and a raft of other ethnicities seen as unreliable in time of war were targeted, alongside populations of dispossessed peasants, social marginals, and those with any connection to the remnants of the former elite classes. State officials were provided with quotas by region for arrests and executions, and they selected targets based on previous convictions, ethno-national status as ascribed in identification documents, or in many cases random sweeps of public areas that were designed to fill quotas as quickly as possible. Unlike Germany, the Stalinist regime made little distinction of place while targeting suspect populations: a Korean in Kiev was as likely a target as one in the Far East. These operations, which are best understood as a combination of ethnic cleansing and social prophylaxis, were highly organized, directed from Moscow, and carried out almost exclusively by the Stalinist state – as clear an example of state terrorism on a mass scale as we find in the early twentieth century.[29]

Although most of the people who lost their lives in 1937–8 fell victim precisely to these "mass operations," it bears repeating that they represent only one of the numerous types of violence, state and otherwise, that took place under the Stalinist regime in the 1930s. Arendt was correct in arguing that violence, intimidation, and fear pervaded Stalinist political culture, even if her analysis focused primary on highly visible, obviously irrational aspects of Stalinist violence, especially denunciations, show trials, and confessions – the "whirlwind" of terror that enveloped loyal party members like Nikolai Bukharin and that served as the basis for our understanding of the Stalinist system for decades after World War II.[30]

It should be no surprise that these tactics carried over into Soviet actions during World War II, usually without even a veneer of social prophylaxis. As Red Army and NKVD officials swept into Poland, then the Baltics, they unleashed explicit programs of terror – arrest, execution, deportation – against elites, suspect nationalities, and families of the repressed. The German advance into the USSR likewise resulted in fresh campaigns against suspect nationalities: Volga Germans, Crimean Tatars, Chechens, and a dozen others were deported to Central Asia. The surprisingly small amount of resistance was met with barbaric violence: in one case, in the Caucasus, an entire village population – some 700 people – was locked into a barn and burned alive.[31] Similar campaigns were carried out as the war came to an end, often in the same areas that suffered at its beginning: Ukrainians, Germans, Estonians, and numerous others fell victim to a system for which terror (arrest, deportation, execution) had become a completely unremarkable aspect of basic Soviet governance.

Ultimately, then, the account that has dominated the field since the collapse of the USSR is the one that we previously applied to the National Socialist case: terror was widespread within the Soviet body politic, and it was applied with abandon outside it, both supporting a dictatorial system based primarily on violence and fear. I have focused here on the less-known aspects of Soviet repression because much of the standard story – denunciations, the show trials, the Gulag – is known to most readers already, if only in outline. In the Stalinist case, the close connection between military operations and state terrorism is impossible to miss: Stalinism was a highly militarized system in which the Communist Party, the domestic security services, and the Red Army ruled much of the country via systemic (and systematic) terror. Perhaps paradoxically, although much of the state violence carried out by the Stalinist regime was indeed publicly demonstrative, this is emphatically not true of several of the most destructive actions of the era: the "mass operations" of 1937 and 1938, for example, were carried out secretly and had little value as a "threat-based communication process," in Schmid's terminology. Yet such actions were explicitly intended to reshape the basic demographic, ethno-national, and cultural structures of Soviet society, and they were certainly part of a broad campaign of political state violence that served to "destabilize, coerce, and compel" – key aspects of any consensus definition of terrorism. As in the National Socialist case, however, the most salient analytic criteria in understanding state terrorism under Stalin all related to the immense power of the Soviet state – from the power to collect and analyze demographic information, to the power to arrest, deport, resettle, and execute millions of people in time of peace as in war.

Fascist Italy

Finally, the case of Fascist Italy provides a highly useful counterpoint to the above discussion of totalitarian dictatorships. Despite the explicit importance of terror and violence to the self-conception of Mussolini's regime, the Fascist state mobilized far less overt violence against its own citizens than either Nazi Germany or the USSR – though, it must be stressed, Fascist Italy was anything but benign, as the dictatorship was shot through with violence at all levels. At the same time, the connection between military violence and terrorism is quite clear in the Italian case: colonialism and war shaped the nature of the Fascist state, and in turn Fascist state practices shaped exceptionally brutal colonial actions in the 1930s. Fascist Italy did employ state terrorism against its populations, and it was, at its core, a political system based on terror in the service of complete social transformation; hence it can be understood as a "totalitarian" system. Yet the regime was far less destructive than either Nazi Germany or Stalin's USSR, or indeed than Franco's nationalists during the Spanish Civil War; the Italian case thus underscores both the usefulness of the concept of "state terrorism" in modern Europe and the limits of any analysis that conflates terrorism, terror, and totalitarianism.

Italian fascism was, in some sense, the model for contemporary dictatorships in Greece, Spain, and Romania, as well as Nazi Germany. Mussolini's rise to power was made possible by explicitly terroristic street violence aimed at overthrowing the existing political system, and the new regime understood violence – purifying, anti-liberal, spiritual violence – as the bedrock of the new political order. As in the German case, however, the initial popular impetus towards spontaneous street violence that animated Mussolini's *squadristi* was quickly subsumed under a broader Fascist state; but unlike the Nazi case, the primary goals of Fascist state violence remained internal, and violent practices were generally not "externalized" onto populations that were deemed an existential threat and hence slated for annihilation. Fascist violence was a means of national regeneration, a spiritual imperative in the process of refashioning the Italian *uomo fascista* (fascist man), while externalized violence, while necessary, was merely legitimate, an unavoidable part of the Italian people's struggle for existence.[32] Nonetheless, both forms of violence, taken together, were integral to the Fascist project of creating a new, anti-liberal, supra-national political identity, and they were integral to the basic political structure of the regime.

Perhaps surprisingly, the first several decades of research on Mussolini's Italy in the mid-twentieth century de-emphasized the role of this kind of violence in the Fascist system of power, arguing that Italian fascism was relatively ineffectual, even benign, and that it became radicalized only under the influence of Nazi Germany.[33] Recent work has reversed this trend completely, arguing that Fascist Italy was indeed based on widespread application of terroristic violence, both structurally and in terms of concrete state action. Even though the Fascist state after 1926 curbed much of the spontaneous street violence associated with the *squadristi*, it began to build a state system based on much the same thing. Italian police, often with the assistance of Fascist party operatives or militiamen, routinely beat, harassed, and publicly humiliated Italian citizens, both for perceived political unreliability and for civil infractions as routine as public drunkenness or theft. At the same time, the increasingly powerful and stable Fascist state employed many of the same strategies to control its population and repress dissent that characterized other interwar dictatorships: surveillance, denunciation gathering, extra-legal arrests and imprisonment for both political opponents and non-political offenders.[34]

This combination of systemic terror, on the one hand, and the comparatively modest application of concrete acts of state terrorism to the population – "ordinary violence" in the words of one recent commentator – on the other, may have been less destructive than comparable state practices in Nazi Germany and the USSR, but it was intended nonetheless to effect a utopian social transformation within Italy, one that saw violence as the key to the moral and physical regeneration of the Italian nation.[35] Such an account therefore squarely places Fascist Italy among the nations that deserve to be called "totalitarian"; and yet Italian fascism did not entail anywhere near the same level of internal repression as did the Soviet or Nazi dictatorships. Best estimates suggest that several tens of thousands of Italians were arrested and deported to "confinement colonies" in the south. Fascist violence, though totalitarian, was far from "totalizing" in the more common sense of the word: the Fascist system left large parts of the existing Italian social structure in place, including the Catholic Church, traditional nationalist and local identities, and the family, in sharp contrast to the USSR.[36] Italian fascism also lacked an explicit drive to externalize its brand of political terror, and it did not take extermination of suspect populations as a specific goal. Mussolini embarked on a broad set of anti-Jewish policies in the mid-1930s, for example, that culminated between 1940 and 1943 in a campaign to intern Jews in camps, but it was only with the Nazi occupation between 1943 and 1945 that these Jews, many of foreign origin, were targeted for annihilation.[37] Ultimately, Mussolini's state apparatus explicitly claimed the right to mete out punishment to any and all citizens with impunity, subjecting the population to sporadic public exercises of punitive and often random violence as a method of instilling widespread fear of punishment; it therefore applied clearly terroristic practices in support of a totalitarian ideology but with drastically less capacity and effect, at least domestically, than its contemporary regimes in Germany and the USSR.

Yet Fascist practices in Italian colonies in the 1930s show just how entrenched state terrorism had become in the Italian political system and just how far the regime was prepared to take violent methods of rule in a context completely outside the boundaries of Italian political culture (again, as with the German case, battered but still present in Italy itself). Long-standing tensions in Italy's Libyan colonies prompted Mussolini to launch pacification campaigns as early as 1923, which spiraled by the end of the decade into genocidal military actions intended to stamp out local Sanusi bands for good. The Italians used not only overwhelming force but also spoiled resources, slaughtering cattle and poisoning water supplies, in order to cause misery and starvation; they also carried out public hangings of rebel leaders in order to demoralize the opposition. Italian actions in Ethiopia in 1935 and 1936 were even worse: Italian troops bombed hospitals, razed entire villages to the ground, and publically executed rebels and civilians alike before taking Addis Ababa in 1936.[38] In the Italian colonial context, fascistic notions of purifying violence came full circle: as one commentator notes, colonial conflict, rather than the domestic political sphere, was "fascism's first true mass mobilization," an "experimental field of violence" in which the regime terrorized non-combatant populations with all the instruments available to a modern state, from aerial bombings and chemical weapons, all filtered through the spirit of "masculine freedom and transgression" that animated the *squadristi* from the beginning.[39]

Comparatively little research exists to connect these experiences to the battlefields of World War II, but that which does suggests that Italian troops in occupied territories (e.g., Greece and Yugoslavia) often replicated the kind of street violence that emerged two decades before – arson, public beatings, and ritualized shamings involving the forced ingestion of castor oil – and combined them with the violent techniques of the modern military state, including internments, deportations, and executions.[40] The Italian colonies, by the mid-1930s, were a de-civilized space in which the terroristic governance strategies that were a constituent part of the Fascist system could be put into place by eager statesmen, trained in the atmosphere of the *squadri* but now operating with the full force of the Italian state at their disposal.

The Italian case shows, perhaps even more clearly than the Nazi or Soviet cases, that "state terrorism" is a useful analytical construct in understanding the violence in the modern era, as long as it is kept separate from the admittedly overlapping categories of systemic violence and totalitarianism. Fascist Italy was totalitarian in its ideology and goals, if not implementation; it employed numerous violent techniques in order to control the populations under its control, all situated in a state structure that used violence to instill fear and maintain control; and it carried out concrete acts of terroristic violence against both domestic and external populations, usually in a way that supported the overall structure of the regime. The most destructive examples of Fascist state terrorism, furthermore, were carried out in explicitly military contexts, often colonial, while a militarized, masculinized culture of action and power had a reciprocal and equally important effect on the Italian state itself. Fascist Italy may have been less destructive, in terms of sheer number of victims, than the USSR or

Nazi Germany, but the widespread application of terroristic violence was nonetheless a basic and fundamental part of the dictatorial system that kept the regime in place.

Conclusion

The European state system changed drastically in the first half of the twentieth century. Several concrete goals of European statesmen that were highly obvious as far back as the French Revolution came to fruition in these years: a drive to understand and control demographic trends, strict controls on migration and international borders, increasing government intervention into national and global economic systems, and a whole range of policies, based in the Enlightenment-era dream of social perfectibility and modern social homogeneity that made populations easy to "read" and act upon. At the same time, the capacities of the modern European state grew tremendously: European states gained the ability to count populations, to survey them with a vast array of legal and extra-legal institutions (from the census bureau to the secret police), and to act on them with an equally broad array of economic, medico-social, and judicial agencies. Given that much of this growth in institutions was fueled by war (colonial war, world war, civil war), it is hardly surprising that many of these powerful state institutions of the early twentieth century, especially those functioning in dictatorships, had at their disposal a broad array of techniques of violence that were as at home within the national boundaries of a given state as on the battlefield, from the secret and bureaucratic (perlustration of correspondence) to the public and highly personal (public beatings, summary arrests, public executions).

Not all of these instances of state violence deserve to be termed "state terrorism," but those that do share certain qualities. They are carried out by hypertrophied institutions, often military or militarized, and often with the explicit intention of protecting the polity from existential threats, real or imagined. They take as a primary goal the fundamental reshaping of the social structure of the nation – to be clear, a goal that was widespread in European statecraft in the early twentieth century, and not only in "violent" political systems. This goal took on fundamental importance in the dictatorships that we term "totalitarian," but this fact should not blind us to the reality that all modern states seek to transform the populations under their control. Finally, state terrorism entails the application of often deadly force to civilian populations in what is seen as an effective and legitimate means of achieving these ends.

It should be clear from the above discussion that the idea of "modern state terrorism" is meaningless without the existence of a powerful, interventionist, modern state: states have carried out more or less violent actions against non-combatants from the beginning of human history, but it is the particular combination of goals and means that emerged in the twentieth century that gives the category analytical purchase. As one analyst notes, barbarism in the twentieth century cannot be understood as an unfortunate (and temporary) reversion to an older sort of human cruelty; rather, the "finest creations of the century" – technological, intellectual, and institutional – were themselves "sown with the seeds of authoritarianism and cruelty" and were "employed to terrorise."[41]

Policy makers and analysts alike would do well, then, to look not merely to ideology, nor strictly to the effects of dictatorship, when searching for the root causes of state terrorism in the contemporary era. State violence is ubiquitous in the modern era, and it tends not to remain compartmentalized in one field of action or another. Terroristic policies that are justified – correctly or not – as legitimate in certain contexts rarely remain limited to those contexts, at least not without the vigorous public discussion and contestation that occurs in modern liberal democracies. The experience of the twentieth century shows that nearly all strong states have the capacity to engage in terroristic actions, and that those that resist are the states that maintain the strongest sense of civic political culture (not necessarily liberal–democratic) in *all* contexts: military, colonial, as well as domestic.

Notes

1. The definition proposed by the European Union in 2002 seems most useful here: terrorism is violence directed at non-combatants "with the aim of intimidating people and seriously altering or destroying the political, economic or social structures of a country (murder, bodily injuries, hostage taking, extortion, fabrication of weapons, committing attacks, threatening to commit any of the above, etc.)." See Brett Bowden, "Terror(s) throughout the Ages," in *Terror: From Tyrannicide to Terrorism*, ed. Brett Bowden and Michael T. Davis (Brisbane: University of Queensland Press, 2008), 4–5.
2. In addition to Chapter 5 by Rapport in this volume, see Hugh Gough, "The Terror in the French Revolution," in *Terror: From Tyrannicide to Terrorism*, 77–91.
3. Ian F. W. Beckett, *Modern Insurgencies and Counter-Insurgencies: Guerrillas and their Opponents since 1750* (London: Routledge, 2001) 24–31.
4. On the topic of counter-insurgency and terrorism, see Douglas Porch, *Counterinsurgency: Exposing the Myths of the New Way of War* (Cambridge: Cambridge University Press, 2013). The most important account to date of the connection between colonial violence and world war is found in Isabel V. Hull, *Absolute Destruction: Military Culture and the Practices of War in Imperial Germany* (Ithaca, NY: Cornell University Press, 2004).
5. Hannah Arendt, *The Origins of Totalitarianism* (New York: Harcourt, Brace, 1951). For a perceptive discussion of the Soviet and National Socialist cases, see Peter Holquist, "State Violence as Technique: The Logic of Violence in Soviet Totalitarianism," in *Landscaping the Human Garden: Twentieth-Century Population Politics in a Comparative Framework*, ed. Amir Weiner, 19–45 (Stanford, CA: Stanford University Press, 2003).
6. On the latter point, in addition to Foucault's immensely influential work, see especially Zygmunt Bauman, *Modernity and the Holocaust* (Ithaca, NY: Cornell University Press, 2000); and James Scott, *Seeing Like a State: How Certain Schemes to Improve the Human Condition Have Failed* (New Haven, CT: Yale University Press, 1999). For discussion of Bauman, see Chapter 24 by Roger Griffin in this volume, but note that none of these commentators, including Bauman, exclude liberal democratic societies from their analysis of the perils of modernity.
7. The classic study of the *Freikorps* in English remains Robert G. L. Waite, *Vanguard of Nazism: The Free Corps Movement in Post War Germany, 1918–1923* (Cambridge, MA: Harvard University Press, 1952).
8. For street violence on the left, see Eve Rosenhaft, *Beating the Fascists?: The German Communists and Political Violence, 1929–1933* (Cambridge: Cambridge University Press, 1983).
9. For a recent and comprehensive discussion of paramilitary violence in interwar Europe, see Robert Gerwarth and John Horne, "Vectors of Violence: Paramilitarism in Europe after the Great War, 1917–1923," *Journal of Modern History* 83, no. 3 (2011): 489–512. Gerwath and Horne conclude that paramilitarism, while having a substantial influence on the overall political culture of the era, had relatively little direct role in the politics of those continental states that featured strong civic institutions, including Germany and Austria.
10. The single most important commentator in English remains Robert Gellately. See his *The Gestapo and German Society: Enforcing Racial Policy 1933–1945* (Oxford: Clarendon Press, 1990); and *Backing Hitler: Consent and Coercion in Nazi Germany* (Oxford: Oxford University Press, 2001).
11. Beckett, *Modern Insurgencies and Counter-Insurgencies*, 32–4.
12. Beckett, *Modern Insurgencies and Counter-Insurgencies*, 42–3.
13. Alex P. Schmid, ed., *The Routledge Handbook of Terrorism Research* (New York: Routledge, 2011), 86–7.
14. The classic study is now Christopher R. Browning, *Ordinary Men: Reserve Police Battalion 101 and the Final Solution in Poland* (New York: Harper Collins, 1992).

15 In this context, see Gordon H. Chang's fascinating account of Japanese internees in the United States during World War II, who were subjected to an all-encompassing program of "social engineering" intended to instill in them an "American" civic identity. This project was supported not only by military internment officials but by a wide array of educators, researchers, and political leaders on the left as well as right. Gordon H. Chang, "Social Darwinism versus Social Engineering: The 'Education' of Japanese Americans during World War II," in *Landscaping the Human Garden: Twentieth-Century Population Politics in a Comparative Framework*, 189–204.

16 For a definitive catalog of Soviet-era repressions, and despite the often contentious tone of the rest of the volume, see Nicolas Werth, "A State against Its People: Violence, Repression, and Terror in the Soviet Union," in *The Black Book of Communism: Crimes Terror, Repression*, ed. Stéphane Courtois et al., 33–268 (Cambridge, MA: Harvard University Press, 1999); here 71–80.

17 On repressions of intellectuals after 1917, see Stuart Finkel, *On the Ideological Front: The Russian Intelligentsia and the Making of the Soviet Public Sphere* (New Haven, CT: Yale University Press, 2007). On the repression of the Don Cossacks, see Peter Holquist, *Making War, Forging Revolution: Russia's Continuum of Crisis, 1914–1921* (Cambridge, MA: Harvard University Press, 2002).

18 Jörg Baberowski and Anselm Doering-Manteuffel, "The Quest for Order and the Pursuit of Terror," in *Beyond Totalitarianism: Stalinism and Nazism Compared*, ed. Michael Geyer and Sheila Fitzpatrick (New York: Cambridge University Press, 2009), 202–3.

19 Eric Lohr, *Nationalizing the Russian Empire: The Campaign against Enemy Aliens during World War I* (Cambridge, MA: Harvard University Press, 2003).

20 The standard account of the early years of the Red Army remains Mark von Hagen, *Soldiers in the Proletarian Dictatorship: The Red Army and the Soviet Socialist State, 1917–1930* (Ithaca, NY: Cornell University Press, 1993).

21 The literature on the Russian Civil War is vast, but readers interested in the complex mechanisms of state violence in this period should begin with two exceptional works not of history but fiction: Mikhail Bulgakov, *White Guard*, trans. Marian Schwartz (New Haven. CT: Yale University Press, 2008); and Isaac Babel, *Red Cavalry*, trans. Peter Constantine (New York: W. W. Norton, 2002).

22 For more on state terrorism in the Russian Empire, as well as the more familiar story of Russian revolutionary terrorism, see Chapter 7 by Martin A. Miller in this volume.

23 Terry Martin, *The Affirmative Action Empire: Nations and Nationalism in the USSR, 1923–1939* (Ithaca, NY: Cornell University Press, 2001); and David L. Hoffmann, *Cultivating the Masses: Modern State Practices and Soviet Socialism, 1914–1939* (Ithaca, NY: Cornell University Press, 2011).

24 For a wide-ranging exploration of the effects of war on the emerging Soviet system that, despite its publication in the 1980s, continues to reflect the basic contours of the field, see Diane P. Koenker, William G. Rosenberg, and Ronald Grigor Suny, eds., *Party, State, and Society in the Russian Civil War: Explorations in Social History* (Bloomington: Indiana University Press, 1989).

25 See, for example, Wendy Z. Goldman, *Terror and Democracy in the Age of Stalin: The Social Dynamics of Repression* (Cambridge: Cambridge University Press, 2007); and *Inventing the Enemy: Denunciation and Terror in Stalin's Russia* (Cambridge: Cambridge University Press, 2011).

26 Lynne Viola, *The Unknown Gulag: The Lost World of Stalin's Special Settlement* (Oxford: Oxford University Press, 2009).

27 Werth, *The Black Book of Communism*, 146–58; mortality estimate on 155.

28 David R. Shearer, *Policing Stalin's Socialism: Repression and Social Order in the Soviet Union, 1924–1953* (New Haven, CT: Yale University Press, 2009).

29 For a guide to the most recent work on Stalinist repression, see James Harris, ed., *The Anatomy of Terror: Political Violence under Stalin* (Oxford: Oxford University Press, 2013).

30 Few accounts have done more to shape the popular understanding of the "Great Terror" than Arthur Koestler's semi-fictional account of Nikolai Bukharin's downfall in *Darkness at Noon* (London: J. Cape, 1940). The metaphor of the "whirlwind" comes from the equally influential memoir by Eugenia Ginzburg, *Journey into the Whirlwind* (New York: Harcourt Brace & World, 1967).

31 Baberowski and Doering-Manteuffel, "The Quest for Order," 223.

32 Aristotles A. Kallis, "Fascism, Violence and Terror," in *Terror: From Tyrannicide to Terrorism*, 192–4.

33 Chief among these accounts are the many works of Renzo De Felice, including his four-volume, eight-book biography of Mussolini, unfinished at his time of death: *Mussolini il fascista* (Turin: Einaudi, 1966–8); *Mussolini il duce* (Turin: Einaudi, 1974–81); and *Mussolini l'alleato*,

1940–45 (Turin: Einaudi, 1990–7). For a comprehensive guide in English to these controversies, see R. J. B. Bosworth, *The Italian Dictatorship: Problems and Perspectives in the Interpretation of Mussolini and Fascism* (New York: Hodder, 1998).
34 For a guide to recent literature on the Fascist Italian state, see Patrick Bernhard, "Renarrating Italian Fascism: New Directions in the Historiography of a European Dictatorship," *Contemporary European History* 23, no. 1 (2014): 151–63.
35 Michael Ebner, *Ordinary Violence in Mussolini's Italy* (Cambridge: Cambridge University Press, 2011), esp. 5–11.
36 Bernhard, "Renarrating Italian Fascism," 153–60.
37 Kallis, "Fascism, Violence and Terror," 199.
38 Kallis, "Fascism, Violence and Terror," 199–200.
39 Ruth Ben-Ghiat, "Response to Matteo Millan: Mapping Squadrist Violence," *Contemporary European History* 22, no. 4 (2013): 582, citing Aram Mattioli, *Experimentierfeld der Gewalt: Der Abessinienkrieg und seine internationale Bedeutung 1935–1941* (Zurich: Orell Füssli, 2005).
40 Ben-Ghiat, "Response to Matteo Millan," 583.
41 Joanna Bourke, "Barbarisation vs. Civilisation in Time of War," in *The Barbarization of Warfare*, ed. George Kassimeris (New York: New York University Press, 2006), 35.

Further reading

Ebner, Michael. *Ordinary Violence in Mussolini's Italy*. Cambridge, UK: Cambridge University Press, 2011.

Gellately, Robert. *Backing Hitler: Consent and Coercion in Nazi Germany*. Oxford: Oxford University Press, 2001.

Geyer, Michael, and Sheila Fitzpatrick, eds. *Beyond Totalitarianism: Stalinism and Nazism Compared*. New York: Cambridge University Press, 2009.

Harris, James, ed. *The Anatomy of Terror: Political Violence Under Stalin*. Oxford, UK: Oxford University Press, 2013.

Holquist, Peter. *Making War, Forging Revolution: Russia's Continuum of Crisis, 1914–1921*. Cambridge, MA: Harvard University Press, 2002.

Scott, James. *Seeing Like a State: How Certain Schemes to Improve the Human Condition Have Failed*. New Haven: Yale University Press, 1999.

Viola, Lynne. *The Unknown Gulag: The Lost World of Stalin's Special Settlement*. Oxford: Oxford University Press, 2009.

Weiner, Amir, ed. *Landscaping the Human Garden: Twentieth-Century Population Politics in a Comparative Framework*. Stanford: Stanford University Press, 2003.

Werth, Nicolas. "A State against Its People: Violence, Repression, and Terror in the Soviet Union." In *The Black Book of Communism: Crimes, Terror, Repression*, edited by Stéphane Courtois, 33–268. Cambridge, MA: Harvard University Press, 1999.

12

BRITAIN'S SMALL WARS

The challenge to Empire, 1881–1951

Benjamin Grob-Fitzgibbon

In 1921, the British Empire began to lick its wounds after a decade of violence that had threatened to bring the whole edifice tumbling down. The Great War had caused the most severe disruption: almost 900,000 British subjects had lost their lives, with 200,000 more from the empire also falling.[1] The impact of the war was profound. In the Dominions of Canada, Australia, New Zealand, and South Africa, there was widespread dismay at the costs of this European adventure and a sense that the imperial masters in London were perhaps not as wise as they had once believed them to be. Throughout the 1920s, they began to redefine the relationship between the United Kingdom and the Dominions as one of "autonomous communities within the British Empire, equal in status, in no way subordinate one to another," a concept that was enshrined into British law by the 1931 Statute of Westminster. No longer would the Dominions be subject to British control.[2]

If the Dominions sought greater independence through conferences, treaties, and acts of Parliament, others were less inclined to adopt such pacific means. It is the purpose of the next two chapters to explore this "other path" taken on the road to self-governance, the path of insurgency and terrorism rather than moderate constitutional evolution.

Ireland

In no place was this secondary path more apparent than in Ireland, which had in one way or another been a thorn in England's side ever since its incorporation into the United Kingdom in 1801. It was from Irish hands that the British state first experienced the phenomenon of terrorism and while it could be argued that "insurgent" movements of one form or another had always existed in Anglo-Irish relations, it was not until the middle of the nineteenth century that anything resembling modern nationalism could be identified in Ireland and not until the latter part of that century that these Irish nationalists first turned to terrorism.

The Fenian Movement and Irish Republican Brotherhood (IRB) – as the ancestral fathers of the contemporary Irish Republican Army (IRA) – have often been cited as the first Irish "terrorists" following their founding in the United States, Canada, and Britain in 1858. In their initial incarnation, however, the Fenians can best be understood as the last of a series of Irish discontents who sought to use overt methods of insurgency and uprising rather than terrorism to achieve their ends. The IRB's rising in Ireland in 1867 followed the more conventional approach of an open display of opposition than a surprise act of political violence, a tactic that was assured no more success than its attempted invasion of Canada later that year. Historians have sometimes cited the Clerkenwell Prison bombing of

December 1867 as the first act of Irish terrorism, when 548 pounds of gunpowder were used to create an explosion outside Clerkenwell Prison in Dublin where the leaders of the failed Fenian uprising were being held. However, as the intent was not to cause civilian casualties (although twelve did die) or make a political statement, but rather to blow a hole in the prison wall to free those within, it cannot truly be regarded as terrorism. Indeed, had it not been for the continuity of the organizational name into the twentieth century, the Fenians of the mid-nineteenth century might have gone down as one of the less illustrious movements in Irish history.[3]

Nevertheless, if the IRB of the 1850s and 1860s cannot truly be understood as terrorist, the same cannot be said of the organization as it evolved into the 1880s. In 1881, it launched a bombing campaign against targets throughout Great Britain, planting devices at military barracks in Manchester, the Mansion House in London, and police stations and the Town Hall in Liverpool. To carry out these attacks, the IRB evolved into a more secretive organization, with circles commanded by a center, the circles in turn divided into cells, and lower-level members knowing only their own cell comrades. Cell leaders knew their circle leaders but not the leadership or membership of other circles and cells. Thus each member of the IRB could identify only a handful of others if captured.[4] In 1883 and 1884, the IRB expanded its campaign from state targets to civilians, planting bombs at a canal viaduct and gasworks in Glasgow, the offices of *The Times* in Fleet Street, various stations of the London Underground, the London train stations at Victoria, Ludgate Hill, and Paddington, and, in January 1885, the House of Commons. While most of these bombs were diffused by London's Metropolitan Police, there were several dozen injuries and three IRB members lost their lives when a bomb exploded prematurely on London Bridge.[5] This dynamite campaign was accompanied in May 1882 by the stabbing assassination of the Irish chief secretary and his undersecretary as they walked through Phoenix Park in Dublin.[6] With an intent to cause widespread civilian casualties beyond what could be argued to be military or political targets, the IRB actions of the 1880s were the first time the British government encountered what is today understood as terrorism, and they represented one of the first attempts by an insurgent group to rock the status quo of the British Empire, at that time reaching its jingoistic heights.

Yet the empire did not fall under the weight of Irish bombs, and, following first William Gladstone's (unsuccessful) Home Rule Bills of 1886 and 1893 and then A. J. Balfour's (more successful) policy of "killing Ireland with kindness" in the 1890s and early 1900s, Ireland became more happy and content within the United Kingdom than at any time before.[7] Irish crowds lined the streets in Dublin for Queen Victoria's Diamond Jubilee in 1897 as elsewhere in the empire, and when Great Britain declared war on Germany in 1914 Irishmen flocked to the cause, 75,314 volunteering for armed service in the first twelve months of the conflict alone.[8] Not all was well, however, and in December 1911, militant Protestants, openly opposed to the government's policy of introducing a Home Rule Bill, formed the Ulster Volunteer Force (UVF), an overt paramilitary army committed to using force to shut down any Home Rule Parliament that might be established. In response, Catholic nationalists formed the Irish Volunteers, a second paramilitary army just as committed to using force to protect Home Rule as the UVF was to preventing it. By the summer of 1914, these two armies had between them over 200,000 well-armed men; in July of that year, the British Army Council warned that civil war in Ireland was imminent.[9] But then came the shot heard around the world, shattering not just the peace of Europe but, in time, the very foundations upon which the British Empire stood. The UVF (in a show of loyalty to the United Kingdom to which the volunteers were proud to belong) and the Irish Volunteers (in a demonstration that despite their calls for Home Rule they were still loyal Britons) volunteered their ranks en masse; they were destined to die side by side at the Somme two years later.[10]

As tens of thousands of Irishmen – Protestant and Catholic – flocked to France, a small minority remained at home, arguing that Irish Home Rule was needed *before* they could support the British war effort. By doing so, they split the Irish Volunteers into the majority (newly named the Irish National Volunteers) and a much smaller anti-war minority (retaining the old name of the Irish Volunteers), numbering just 3,000 individuals. Within the Irish Volunteers, a still smaller group argued that Ireland needed not a Home Rule Parliament within the British Empire but a republic outside it. It was these men and women who on Easter 1916 launched the most serious rebellion the British government had faced since the Indian Mutiny of 1857–8, seizing various buildings within Dublin and elsewhere in Ireland and declaring the establishment of the Irish Republic. The British government dealt with the rising swiftly, sailing a gunboat up the River Liffey to shell Dublin from its center, rounding up more than 3,500 Irishmen and women to intern without trial, and sentencing ninety of the ringleaders to death by firing squad. By the time fourteen had been shot, public opinion had so soured against the government that all further capital sentences were commuted to life in prison.[11] Yet W. B. Yeats's "terrible beauty" had been born, and not only Ireland but the Empire as a whole was "changed, changed utterly."[12]

Following the 1916 Easter Rising, the IRB renamed itself the Irish Republican Army (IRA) and joined with the political party Sinn Féin to pursue complete independence. In 1917, Sinn Féin candidates stood in Westminster by-elections against established Irish nationalist candidates; upon winning, however, they refused to take their seats, claiming they did not recognize Westminster's authority to govern Ireland, a policy known as abstentionism. By the end of the year, Sinn Féin candidates had won all four by-elections and the party had increased its membership to more than 66,000. In the November general election of the following year, Sinn Féin won seventy-three of the 105 Irish seats. When the new session of the Westminster Parliament began in January 1919, these members instead met at the Mansion House in Dublin, where they established the Dáil Éireann (the Irish Parliament), announced that the Irish Republic had come to pass, and declared that the IRA was the only legitimate security force in Ireland. Given the British "occupation" continuing beyond that date, the newly proclaimed Irish Republic and the British state were at war.[13]

When all was said and done and the Anglo-Irish Treaty of 1921 was signed, the southern twenty-six counties of Ireland had left the Union. Proclaimed the fifth dominion and named the Irish Free State, they were given their own parliament, the Dáil Éireann, although they remained with the British Commonwealth. The northern six counties were named Northern Ireland, remained within the Union, and were also given their own Home Rule parliament at Stormont, ironically the very thing the Ulster Volunteer Force had formed to prevent a decade earlier. The treaty did not bring peace to Ireland, as the southern states descended into civil war and a Catholic minority in the north grew increasingly discontented under a state designed to be a Protestant polity for a Protestant people. The story of this discontent will be told later by Cillian McGrattan in Chapter 14 in this volume, but its consequences for the wider empire were very real. The Irish experience from 1916 to 1921 pointed the way forward for other unsatisfied subjects within the empire, demonstrating that where constitutionalism failed, force and violence could succeed. The fires of war in France had convinced the first four dominions that greater autonomy from Westminster was needed and that the British Empire as it had existed throughout the nineteenth century could no longer continue. The fires of terrorism and insurgency in Ireland taught a similar lesson to other areas of the empire, although with very different implications.

India, Egypt, and Iraq

In India, there was likewise a reaction against the sacrifices demanded by the war and the seemingly little that had been gained in return. Already on the subcontinent, a militant party called the Jungantar had formed in Bengal, committed to using violence to protest British rule and the 1905 partition of Bengal.[14] Fearful of an Irish-like rebellion on the subcontinent, in 1919 the government decided to continue the emergency powers of detention and trial that had been introduced during the war, turning them now not against potential wartime subversives but on the followers of a new revolutionary leader named Mohandas K. Gandhi, who was introducing novel concepts of non-violent non-cooperation to the Indian people. Edwin Montagu, the British secretary of state for India, warned the cabinet in October 1920 that an outbreak in India would dwarf what had happened in Ireland: "a campaign comparable to the Sinn Féin campaign in Ireland would be almost impossible to deal with except by punishment and revenge, certainly not by prevention."[15] Throughout the 1920s and 1930s, the Indian people increased the intensity of their resistance to the British government, although they did so by following the model of Gandhi rather than the IRA, at turns infuriating and flummoxing the British government, which found it increasingly difficult to bring a mailed fist against pacifist resisters.[16] While there was some violence in India in the 1920s and 1930s,[17] it never reached the levels of Ireland, and the subcontinent followed a path to self-government more similar to the one taken by the Dominions – that is, at least, until the very last months, when things went quite awry.[18]

Egypt, too, experienced violent upheaval in 1919, and in Iraq an Arab uprising in 1920 erupted that was 130,000 strong, eventually requiring fifty-one British battalions to contain it on the ground and the development of strategic bombing from the air to persuade those who might be minded otherwise to rethink before launching a similar rebellion.[19]

Mandatory Palestine

However, it was from the new mandate of Palestine that the British government received its greatest shock in the interwar years and Palestine also that would present the government with its first sustained terrorist campaign since the flames were extinguished in Ireland. At the end of World War I, the territory of Palestine – previously part of the Ottoman Empire – was being pulled three ways: promised in 1915 by Sir Henry McMahon (the British high commissioner in Egypt) to Husain ibn Ali (the grand sharif of Mecca) as a reward for helping the British overthrow the German-allied Ottoman Empire; promised to be shared with the French government in the colonial horse-trading of the secret Sykes–Picot Agreement in 1916; and in 1917 promised by the British foreign secretary A. J. Balfour as a national home for the Jewish people. Such contradictory promises were inevitably going to breed postwar conflict. When in 1922 the newly formed League of Nations granted Palestine to the British as a "mandate," neither Arab nor Jew were happy, leading to widespread and deadly rioting in 1928, 1929, and 1933. This rioting eventually evolved into a full-scale Arab Revolt against British rule and Jewish ambitions in 1936.[20]

The Arab Revolt began as an urban-based general strike intended to highlight purported British favoritism toward the Jewish minority, particularly regarding increased Jewish immigration into Palestine. The strike soon evolved into a rural peasant revolt, becoming increasingly violent and culminating in the assassination of Lewis Andrews, the district commissioner of the Galilee district in September 1937.[21] In response, the British government appointed Sir Charles Tegart as "chief advisor on terrorism and policing in Palestine,"[22] the first time since the Irish War of Independence that the government had employed an official directly tasked with counter-terrorism. Tegart, like so many of the police and intelligence officials in Palestine, was intimately connected with the past troubles in both India and Ireland. Born in Ireland in 1881, he joined the Indian Police in 1901, quickly becoming head of the Calcutta Detectives Department. In 1919, as a brief respite from his work in India, he traveled to Ireland to serve as intelligence advisor for the government's counter-insurgency campaign there, remaining in Ireland until 1921. He then returned to India, becoming commissioner of Calcutta Police from 1923 to 1931. Having survived at least six assassination attempts, in December 1931 he was appointed a member of the secretary of state's India Council, where he recommended the creation of the Indian Special Branch and continued to serve as the top Indian police official responsible for intelligence.[23]

While Tegart had returned to India after the Irish War of Independence, many of his colleagues traveled instead to seek work in Palestine, including Major General Henry Hugh Tudor, the head of police intelligence in Ireland and Tegart's direct supervisor, who in 1922 was tasked with establishing a Palestine gendarmerie along the lines of the by-then demobilized Royal Irish Constabulary (RIC). Nearly all the gendarmerie's initial cohort came from Ireland; by 1943, the inspector general, his deputy, and more than half of the district commanders of the Palestine Police Force had served in Ireland during the War of Independence.[24] When Tegart arrived in Palestine to advise the government on counter-terrorism, he was far from the first man in the mandate to have experience of terrorism and insurgency within the British Empire.

Yet Tegart's security recommendations went beyond anything attempted before in Ireland, India, or elsewhere in the empire: the British built seventy concrete fortresses throughout the Palestinian countryside, erected an eighty-kilometer fence along the border with Lebanon and Syria, imported Doberman dogs from South Africa to work as "terrorist trackers," and declared each village in Palestine either "good" or "bad," with the good ones receiving rewards for their cooperation and the bad ones suffering collective punishment.[25] The use of fortresses, officially part of a "village control scheme," together with the placing of Palestine under the command of the mandate's military commander, achieved what the British had hoped, and by the eve of World War II, the Arab Revolt had been broken. Employing what one historian has called the "banality of brutality,"[26] the British had thwarted a threat to their empire. As in the Irish War of Independence, the British faced a mixture of terrorism and insurgency during the Arab Revolt, with guerrilla attacks the preferred method in rural areas and assassinations and bombings more common in urban areas.[27]

There were great consequences stemming from the Arab Revolt. Mindful of the manpower and expense that had been required to suppress the revolt and sensing trouble on the European continent, in May 1939 the British government published a White Paper intended to remove the main Arab grievance; its chief recommendation was that further Jewish immigration to Palestine be restricted and that the government move toward an independent Palestinian state with an Arab majority within ten years.[28] While this temporarily salved the

Arabs, it enraged the Jewish population, who saw it as a reneging of the promises given in the Balfour Declaration of 1917. Consequently, in 1939 Avraham Stern formed Lohamel Herut Israel (LEHI – Fighters for the Freedom of Israel), a violent breakaway group from Irgun Zvai Leumi (the National Military Organization), itself formed in 1931 as a Jewish defense organization at the height of the rioting in Palestine. After only the briefest of respite, terrorism was once again to plague the British Empire.[29]

In its initial stages, Irgun condemned the actions of LEHI, which were characterized by the assassination of British officials, bank robberies, and the use of small explosive devices against police stations and government buildings. On September 5, 1939, the leadership of Irgun declared full support for the British war effort, theorizing that it was better to support the British war effort and defeat the Nazi menace before launching a campaign for independence.[30] This support hardened after Stern turned to Germany's Nazi government for assistance in his fight against the British, a strange move given the intent of Germany during the war to eliminate Jewish citizenry worldwide.[31] In any case, Hitler spurned Stern's advances, and LEHI was left to terrorize the British alone. The generally pro-British attitude of Irgun began to change in 1943, however, with the arrival of Menachem Begin into Palestine. Begin, born in Brest-Litovsk, had remained in Poland until the beginning of the war, when he was imprisoned in a Soviet labor camp before being released in 1942 to join the Polish Free Army in its fight against Germany. Traveling with this army in campaigns through Iraq and Iran, he first set foot in Palestine in 1943. Begin soon deserted the Polish Free Army to become leader of Irgun.[32] He immediately rejected the standing policy of support for the British war effort, arguing – as those in Ireland had before him – that England's difficulty was Palestine's opportunity; the time to strike for independence was while the United Kingdom was at its lowest.

On February 1, 1944, Irgun issued a declaration of revolt against the British government.[33] Reorganized by Begin along the lines of an underground guerrilla army, Irgun launched its terrorist campaign on February 12 with simultaneous bombing attacks on immigration offices in Jerusalem, Tel Aviv, and Haifa.[34] There followed attacks on police targets and intelligence institutions; on March 23 alone, four police constables, one police superintendent, and one chief clerk were murdered during attacks on three separate police stations. That same day, LEHI re-launched its campaign of violence. Before the year was out, the two organizations had expanded their targets from immigration offices and police stations to the Land Registry Office, an assassination attempt on the British high commissioner, and a successful assassination of the British minister resident in the Middle East.[35] With the end of the war in Europe in May 1945, violence accelerated in Palestine.[36] In November, Irgun launched attacks on police naval vessels, railway lines, train stations, and the trains themselves, and stole two truckloads of arms from a Royal Air Force (RAF) camp. By the end of December, they had launched attacks against the Jerusalem and Jaffa CID (Criminal Investigations Department) headquarters and the Tel Aviv workshop of the British Army's Royal Electrical and Mechanical Engineers.[37]

The year 1946 began no less quietly. On January 12, the Jewish insurgency destroyed the railway line near Benyamina, before stealing £35,000 worth of payroll from the grounded train and injuring the three police constables who attempted to prevent the robbery; five days later, Irgun attempted to destroy the headquarters of the Palestine Broadcasting Service, the Coast Guard station at Givat Olga, and the RAF radar station on Mount Carmel; and on January 29, members of Irgun, dressed in RAF uniforms, entered the RAF base at Aqir, bound and gagged the four RAF personnel at the arms hut, and escaped with numerous arms.[38] Throughout the spring, the intensity of the violence increased. On April 25, LEHI launched a machine gun attack against the Sixth Airborne Division, killing six soldiers instantly. As the other soldiers scattered to escape the fire, they encountered pre-laid mines; a seventh soldier was killed as he stepped on a mine and three more were wounded. LEHI bombings continued into May and June, and on the night of June 16/17, Irgun kidnapped six British army officers.[39]

In late June 1946, the British government launched Operation Agatha, a search-and-arrest operation against Irgun and LEHI centered on Jerusalem, Tel Aviv, and Haifa. Ten thousand British soldiers and 7,000 members of the Palestine Police had by July 1 taken 2,718 persons into custody and seized over 500 arms from thirty-three separate weapons caches.[40] The revenge of Irgun was swift. On July 22, 1946, it planted several bombs hidden in milk churns beneath the King David Hotel, half of which served as the administrative headquarters of British rule while the remaining half continued to function as a hotel and the center of social life for the British community in Palestine at large. The bombs exploded at 12:37 p.m., when the hotel's restaurants and bars were crowded; the toll was deadly. When the final count was taken, the bombs had killed ninety-one and wounded a further forty-five, many of whom were civilians.[41] Following Operation Agatha in June and the bombing of the King David Hotel in July, there could be no compromise for either the Jewish insurgents or the British government. As the summer turned into autumn, the belligerents continued to fight in a bloody war of attrition.

It was into this abyss that Henry Gurney arrived as chief secretary in October 1946, from that date forward responsible for all British administration in Palestine. Gurney quickly determined that the best way to tackle the violence was with a policy of restraint by the British security forces and renewed engagement by the British government with moderate elements of the Jewish community.[42] With the support of the colonial secretary, Arthur Creech Jones, Gurney suspended all army sweeps and searches of residential properties and on November 5 released from internment the leaders of the Jewish Agency's executive committee, who had been held without trial since Operation Agatha.[43] Despite Gurney's olive branch, terrorist violence continued throughout the remaining weeks of 1946, and on January 1, 1947, the cabinet instructed him to implement a policy of military action over political settlement, leading to a declaration of statutory martial law on March 2.[44] In the meantime, on February 14, the cabinet voted to formally abandon future British aspirations in Palestine and to instead turn over the mandate to the newly formed United Nations (UN); four days later, on February 18, it likewise voted to relinquish British control of India.[45] From February 1947 onwards, the British response to terror and insurgency in Palestine was simply to restrain the level of violence to the greatest extent possible using military force, while allowing an outside, transnational organization to develop a political settlement.

After several months of deliberations, on November 29 the UN General Assembly voted by thirty-three votes to thirteen to partition Palestine into separate Arab and Jewish states, a decision which, while pleasing Irgun and LEHI, dragged the territory into ever deeper levels of violence as the Arab population responded with outrage. From the UN vote in late November until December 12 of that same year, 125 Arabs, ninety-five Jews, and nine British soldiers lost their lives in the violence. The tit-for-tat killing between Jew and Arab and between the British and Palestinians (both Arab and Jew) continued throughout the winter of 1947 and into the spring of 1948. Finally, without resolution of the conflict, British forces withdrew on May 15, having suffered the loss of 338 British citizens since the revolt began in 1944. That same day, the Jewish leadership proclaimed the State of Israel, incorporating all Palestinian territory. Before the sun had set, troops from Egypt, Syria, Jordan, Lebanon, and Iraq mobilized to begin what has since become known as the First Arab–Israeli War.[46] In Palestine, terrorism had succeeded in forcing the world's largest empire to withdraw from a strategically important territory. There were others throughout the British Empire who were watching this development with interest.

The Malayan Emergency

If the government had expected a period of quiet following the independence of India in August 1947 and the withdrawal from Palestine in May 1948, they were sorely mistaken. Half a world away on the Malayan peninsula, the British high commissioner declared a state of emergency in June 1948 – almost a month to the day after the British withdrawal from Palestine – and in October, Sir Henry Gurney (newly knighted for his services in Palestine) was appointed the new high commissioner.[47] The situation Gurney encountered in Malaya was in many ways more grave than that which he had faced in the Middle East. Malaya had been controlled by the British in one sense or another since the 1700s, with a formal crown colony established in 1867. Throughout the latter half of the nineteenth century, British authorities steadily replaced the traditional feudal structure of Malay society with Western notions of law and property, cleared the swamps to prevent the spread of malaria, and from 1884 opened and operated a Malayan railway system. More importantly, the colonial administration replaced coffee with rubber as the staple crop of the Malayan economy, encouraging the immigration of Chinese and Indian migrant workers to man the labor-intensive plantations. By 1945, Malaya's population of 5.3 million people included 49 percent Malays, 38 percent Chinese, 11 percent Indians, and 12,000 Europeans.[48]

The Chinese, separated from the Malays by culture, language, and ethnic quarrel, drifted to the Chinese Communist Party following World War I, eventually establishing an independent Malayan Communist Party (the MCP) in 1930. Following the December 1941 Japanese invasion of Malaya, the MCP played a leading role in organizing a guerrilla campaign against the occupation, liaising with British Special Forces and forming the Malayan People's Anti-Japanese Army (MPAJA). By December 1943, the British Special Operations Executive was supplying the MPAJA with £3,000 a month to finance its insurgency; by August 1945, there were eighty-eight British officers present in Malaya working with the MPAJA.[49] On September 28, 1945, the MPAJA finally defeated the Japanese in Malaya. After four years of guerrilla warfare against the Japanese occupiers, the MCP and MPAJA expected to reap the benefits of victory and establish a communist republic. Instead, in October, the British government announced the establishment of the Malayan Union and, in December, staged a disbandment ceremony for the MPAJA. In March 1946, they appointed the Union's first governor, Sir Edward Gent.[50]

Initially, the British government welcomed the MCP into the Union as an important participant. By the middle of 1946, however, both the MCP and the rulers of the traditional Malay States were growing anxious about a return to the prewar days of British colonialism. To assuage their fears, the government worked throughout 1947 to develop a new constitutional settlement that included greater levels of power-sharing. The result was the Federation of Malaya, announced on February 1, 1948, with Gent appointed its first high commissioner. The Malay States rulers were appeased, but the MCP remained antagonistic to British rule. In May, the MPAJA reconstituted itself as the Malayan People's Anti-British Army (MPABA) and on June 15, the MCP – with the MPABA acting as its armed wing

– declared war against the British colonial administration. The following day, they murdered three British rubber planters and their Chinese assistants. Gent immediately declared a state of emergency, thus creating the name by which the ensuing conflict came to be known: the Malayan Emergency.[51]

When Gurney arrived in the Federation in October 1948 as the new high commissioner (Gent having been killed in a plane accident earlier that summer), the British community in Malaya was in a state of panic. The MPABA had staged guerrilla raids throughout the territory and had murdered more than fifty plantation owners and workers in ambushes and direct assassinations. The British authorities at first preferenced a military solution over a political one. For the remainder of 1948 and throughout 1949, police and civil authorities were sidelined while generals dictated the pace of the campaign, using conventional search and destroy operations to combat the MPABA. The British security forces initially referred to the insurgents as "bandits," but by May 1952 had instead officially termed them "Communist Terrorists," or CTs for short.[52] For their own part, the insurgents renamed themselves the Malayan Races Liberation Army (MRLA) in February 1949.[53]

Gurney was troubled by the military focus of the campaign. Drawing on his experience from Palestine, in April 1949 he wrote to Creech Jones – still colonial secretary in London – that "the lesson has not apparently yet been generally learnt that the answer to Communist terrorism equipped with modern arms is not the soldier but the policeman." He continued: "It is of immense political advantage in restoring confidence if the inhabitants of this country can be organised and led to put their own security house in order, rather than have the impression that it is being done for them by troops on whose inevitable departure there will be no guarantee of peace."[54] He wrote again to the colonial secretary six weeks later, warning that terrorism was impossible to defeat completely, since "the terrorist tends always to have the initiative. It is impracticable to defend against assassination all the individuals who may be attacked, or to defend against sabotage all the railway tracks, telephone and electric power lines, factories, Government offices and other installations that are vulnerable." He argued that British failure in Palestine had become inevitable once martial law was introduced, as "the withdrawal of the civil power and the substitution of military control represent the first victory for the terrorists."[55] To succeed in Malaya, the British would have to try something different.

For the remainder of 1949, Gurney's pleas fell on deaf ears, and by January 1, 1950, the MRLA had killed 850 Malay and British civilians, 325 Malay policemen, and 150 British soldiers.[56] During that same time period, the security forces had killed or captured 1,752 insurgents, but still the terrorist campaign showed no signs of abating, with the rate of ambushes and assassinations increasing following each army sweep rather than declining.[57] For that reason, on February 23, 1950, Gurney suggested to Creech Jones that a radical departure in British anti-terrorism/counter-insurgency strategy was needed. He recommended that a single officer – either a civilian or retired military – be appointed as director of operations to command and coordinate all elements of the campaign in an integrated fashion. Under his direction all officers – civil, military, and police – would serve together in shared committees to jointly plan Emergency operations.[58]

Gurney's telegram was one of the last Creech Jones would receive as colonial secretary, as he lost his seat in parliament and had to resign from the cabinet that same day. However, his successor, James Griffiths, continued to support Gurney's approach, and, in March 1950, the government announced that retired general Sir Harold Briggs would serve as the first Malayan director of operations, to arrive in the Federation on April 3.[59] In consultation with

Gurney, Briggs immediately issued the Briggs Plan, which created a Federal War Council. Under the council sat a series of State War Executive Committees (SWECs) and District War Executive Committees (DWECs). In each, soldiers served side by side with policemen and civil servants. Within the committees, Briggs forbade the ranking of army, police, and civil personnel with one claiming superiority over the other. All would work in absolute coordination.[60] With an inter-agency hierarchy established, Briggs implemented his plan: he would resettle the Malayan squatters who illegally occupied plantation lands during the Japanese occupation into "New Villages," where they would receive education, social welfare, and instruction in the practices of good governance. Once these Malays were separated and protected by British forces, the army would destroy the Communist Terrorists without fear of adversely affecting the most vulnerable elements of the civilian population.[61]

This resettlement process began in July 1950, and within a year 240,000 squatters had been resettled into New Villages. Furthermore, the larger aims of the strategy seemed to be working. Briggs and Gurney reported that in the first six months of 1951, terrorist surrenders had increased by 180 percent and terrorist casualties by 42 percent, while security force casualties had increased by just 11 percent and civilian deaths had actually gone down by 3.5 percent.[62] It had been three years since the Emergency began – and seven since the start of the revolt in Palestine – but the British government finally appeared to have settled on a strategy that was having success against terrorism and insurgency. For Gurney, however, such success came too late. On October 6, 1951, his car was ambushed by the MPLA as he traveled with his wife and private secretary for a weekend's retreat at Fraser's Hill. In an effort to protect his wife and secretary, Gurney left his vehicle to draw away the assassins' bullets. His ploy worked, but he was shot multiple times, falling dead to the ground.[63]

In many ways, Gurney's promising plan followed by his untimely death epitomized the British experience with terrorism in the British Empire in the years 1921–52. Threats arose again and again, only to be knocked down, to arise again. In Ireland, Palestine, and Malaya, the government initially responded to terrorism and insurgency with military force, combining large-scale sweep operations with punitive measures. In doing so, they created more terrorists than they were able to kill, only further exacerbating the situation. Not until the arrival of Gurney in Malaya did the government begin to adopt a more nuanced approach, encapsulated in the Briggs Plan and supported by successive colonial secretaries. Nevertheless, when Gurney died, the situation in Malaya was by no means under control. Furthermore, within a year of his death, a new emergency had erupted in Kenya, followed shortly thereafter by terrorist violence in Cyprus and Aden. As dawn broke on the year 1952, the British Empire was in flames, from Southeast Asia through the Middle East and Mediterranean to Africa. How the British government grappled with and eventually defeated that threat is the subject of the next chapter of this volume.

Notes

1 Commonwealth War Graves Commission, *Annual Report 2011–2012* (London, 2012), 46, available in print or online at: www.cwgc.org (accessed June 23, 2014).
2 For more, see Nicholas Mansergh, *The Commonwealth Experience*, vol. 2, *From British to Multiracial Commonwealth*, rev. ed. (Toronto: University of Toronto Press, 1982), ch. 1, 3–42.
3 Thomas E. Hachey, Joseph M. Hernon, Jr., and Lawrence J. McCaffrey, *The Irish Experience: A Concise History*, rev. ed. (London: M. E. Sharpe, 1996), 102–5; and T. W. Moody and F. X. Martin, *The Course of Irish History*, rev. and enl. ed. (Cork, Ireland: Mercier Press, 1995), 278–80.

4 Many of the practices of organizing a centrally run revolutionary terrorist group, including the use of a secretive, insulated cell structure, originated in Russia in the 1870s. There is some evidence that the IRB learned of this through the writings of Sergei Kravchinsky-Stepniak, a Russian revolutionary terrorist who relocated to London in 1880. For more on these practices, see Chapter 7 by Martin A. Miller in this volume. For more on what came to be known – outside of Russia – as "the Russian Method," see Chapter 8 by Richard Bach Jensen.
5 Bernard Porter, *The Origins of the Vigilante State: The London Metropolitan Police Special Branch before the First World War* (Rochester, NY: Boydell and Brewer, 1987), 27–8.
6 Hachey et al., *The Irish Experience*, 122.
7 For more on this, see James Loughlin, *Gladstone, Home Rule and the Ulster Question, 1882–93* (Atlantic Highlands, NJ: Humanities Press, 1987); and Eunan O'Halpin, *The Decline of the Union: British Government in Ireland, 1892–1920* (Dublin: Gill and Macmillan, 1987).
8 Keith Jeffrey, *Ireland and the Great War* (Cambridge: Cambridge University Press, 2000), 7.
9 The National Archives (TNA), Cabinet Office (CAB) 37/120/1914:81, "A Memorandum by the Military Members of the Army Council on the Military Situation in Ireland," July 4, 1914.
10 For more, see Benjamin Grob-Fitzgibbon, *Turning Points of the Irish Revolution: The British Government, Intelligence, and the Cost of Indifference, 1912–1921* (New York: Palgrave Macmillan, 2007).
11 For more on this, see Charles Townshend, *Easter 1916: The Irish Rebellion* (London: Allen Lane, 2005).
12 These references are taken from W. B. Yeats's poem, "Easter, 1916," which is well worth reading to understand how violence can lead to a profound change in political sensibilities. It highlights better than many academic treatises the potential effects of terrorism and government attempts to quell such.
13 See Grob-Fitzgibbon, *Turning Points of the Irish Revolution*, 115–49.
14 See Peter Heehs, *The Bomb in Bengal: The Rise of Revolutionary Terrorism in India, 1900–1910* (New York: Oxford University Press, 2004).
15 Quoted in Deirdre McMahon, "Ireland and the Empire-Commonwealth, 1900–1948," in *The Oxford History of the British Empire*, vol. 4, *The Twentieth Century*, ed. Judith M. Brown and Wm. Roger Louis (Oxford: Oxford University Press, 1999), 146.
16 Barbara D. Metcalf and Thomas R. Metcalf, *A Concise History of India* (Cambridge: Cambridge University Press, 2002), 165–99.
17 See Kate O'Malley, *Ireland, India and Empire: Indo-Irish Radical Connections, 1919–64* (Manchester: Manchester University Press, 2008); and Michael Silvestri, "'The Sinn Féin of India': Irish Nationalism and the Policing of Revolutionary Terrorism in Bengal," *Journal of British Studies* 39, no. 4 (October 2000): 454–86.
18 See Stanley A. Wolport, *Shameful Flight: The Last Years of the British Empire in India* (Oxford: Oxford University Press, 2006).
19 See Anthony Clayton, "Imperial Defence and Security, 1900–1968," in *The Oxford History of the British Empire*, 4:287; and Priya Satia, *Spies in Arabia: The Great War and the Cultural Foundations of Britain's Covert Empire in the Middle East* (Oxford: Oxford University Press, 2009).
20 Benjamin Grob-Fitzgibbon, *Imperial Endgame: Britain's Dirty Wars and the End of Empire* (New York: Palgrave Macmillan, 2011), 7–10. See also: David Fromkin, *A Peace to End All Peace: The Fall of the Ottoman Empire and the Creation of the Modern Middle East* (New York: Owl Books, 1989); Martin Kolinsky, *Law, Order and Riots in Mandatory Palestine, 1928–35* (London: St. Martin's Press, in association with King's College, London, 1993); and Y. Porath, *The Palestinian Arab National Movement: From Riots to Rebellion*, vol. 2, *1929–1939* (London: Frank Cass, 1977).
21 Jacob Norris, "Repression and Rebellion: Britain's Response to the Arab Revolt in Palestine of 1936–1939," *Journal of Imperial and Commonwealth History* 36, no. 1 (2008): 28.
22 Ibid.
23 Jason Tomes, "Tegart, Sir Charles Augustus (1881–1946)," *Oxford Dictionary of National Biography*, Online Edition, www.oxforddnd.com/view/article/36447 (accessed June 23, 2014); and Michael Silvestri, "'An Irishman is specially suited to be a policeman': Sir Charles Tegart and Revolutionary Terrorism in Bengal," *History Ireland* 8, no. 4 (Winter 2000), Online Edition, www.historyireland.com/volume8/issue4/features/id=242 (accessed June 23, 2014).
24 Benjamin Grob-Fitzgibbon, "Intelligence and Counter-Insurgency: Case Studies from Ireland, Malaya and the Empire," *RUSI Journal* 146, no. 1 (February/March 2011): 74–5. See also

Richard Andrew Cahill, "Going Berserk: 'Black and Tans' in Palestine," *Jerusalem Quarterly* 10, no. 1 (Summer 2009): 59–68.
25 Norris, "Repression and Rebellion," 28.
26 Matthew Hughes, "The Banality of Brutality: British Armed Forces and the Repression of the Arab Revolt in Palestine, 1936–39," *English Historical Review* 124, issue 507 (2009): 313–54.
27 See ibid.; and Norris, "Repression and Rebellion."
28 Grob-Fitzgibbon, *Imperial Endgame*, 10.
29 Ibid., 10–11.
30 J. Bowyer Bell, *Terror out of Zion: Irgun Zvai Leumi, LEHI, and the Palestine Underground, 1929–1949* (New York: St. Martin's Press, 1977), 51.
31 Ibid., 64–5.
32 For more on Begin's early life, see: Eitan Haber, *Menahem Begin: The Legend and the Man*, trans. Louis Williams (New York: Delacorte Press, 1978); Amos Perlmutter, *The Life and Times of Menachem Begin* (New York: Doubleday & Company, 1987); and Eric Silver, *Begin: The Haunted Prophet* (New York: Random House, 1984).
33 John Newsinger, *British Counter-Insurgency: From Palestine to Northern Ireland* (New York: Palgrave Macmillan, 2002), 7.
34 Grob-Fitzgibbon, *Imperial Endgame*, 12–13.
35 Ibid., 15.
36 Ibid., 22.
37 Bell, *Terror Out of Zion*, 145–52.
38 Grob-Fitzgibbon, *Imperial Endgame*, 43.
39 Ibid., 45.
40 Charters, David A., *The British Army and Jewish Insurgency in Palestine, 1945–47* (New York: St. Martin's Press, 1989), 117–18; and TNA, War Office (WO) 275/27, "Report on Operation Agatha."
41 Bell, *Terror Out of Zion*, 169–73.
42 TNA, Colonial Office (CO) 967/102, Letter from Henry Gurney, Chief Secretary, Palestine, to John Martin, Assistant Undersecretary, Cabinet Office, November 5, 1946.
43 Bell, *Terror Out of Zion*, 183.
44 Ibid., 190.
45 John Darwin, *Britain and Decolonisation: The Retreat from Empire in the Post-War World* (New York: St. Martin's Press, 1988), 94–5.
46 Benjamin Grob-Fitzgibbon, "Securing the Colonies for the Commonwealth: Counterinsurgency, Decolonization, and the Development of British Imperial Strategy in the Postwar Empire," *British Scholar* 2, no. 1 (September 2009), 23. See also Grob-Fitzgibbon, *Imperial Endgame*, 80–100.
47 Grob-Fitzgibbon, *Imperial Endgame*, 102–103.
48 Robert Jackson, *The Malayan Emergency: The Commonwealth Wars, 1948–1966* (London: Routledge, 1991), 4–6; and John A. Nagl, *Learning to Eat Soup with a Knife: Counterinsurgency Lessons from Malaya and Vietnam* (Chicago: University of Chicago Press, 2002), 60.
49 Richard Clutterbuck, *Conflict and Violence in Singapore and Malaysia, 1945–1983* (Boulder, CO: Westview Press, 1985), 37–41.
50 Grob-Fitzgibbon, *Imperial Endgame*, 106.
51 Ibid., 106–12. For more on the broader questions concerning the relationship between terrorism and insurgency, see Chapter 25 by Geraint Hughes on that topic in this volume.
52 For the evolution of this terminology, see Phillip Deery, "The Terminology of Terrorism: Malaya, 1948–52," *Journal of Southeast Asian Studies* 34, no. 2 (June 2003): 231–47.
53 Grob-Fitzgibbon, *Imperial Endgame*, 124.
54 TNA, CO 537/4751, no. 80, [security situation]: Dispatch (reply) no. 4 from Sir Henry Gurney, British High Commissioner in Malaya, to Arthur Creech Jones, Colonial Secretary, April 11, 1949, in *British Documents on the End of Empire*, series B, vol. 3, *Malaya: Part II: The Communist Insurrection, 1948–1953*, ed. A. J. Stockwell (London: Her Majesty's Stationary Office, 1995), 73–5.
55 TNA, CO 537/4773, no. 3 [insurgency and counter-insurgency]: Despatch no. 5 from Sir Henry Gurney, British High Commissioner in Malaya, to Arthur Creech Jones, Colonial Secretary, May 30, 1949, in ibid., 133–43.

56 Benjamin Grob-Fitzgibbon, "Counterinsurgency, the Interagency Process, and Malaya: The British Experience," in *The US Army and the Interagency Process: Historical Perspectives*, ed. Kendall D. Gott and Michael G. Brooks (Fort Leavenworth, KS: Combat Studies Institute Press, 2008), 95.
57 Rhodes House Library, Oxford University, Creech Jones Papers, Box 57, File 2, Dispatch from Sir Henry Gurney, British High Commissioner in Malaya, to Arthur Creech Jones, Colonial Secretary, January 12, 1950.
58 TNA, Foreign Office (FO) 371/84477, Telegram from Sir Henry Gurney, British High Commissioner in Malaya, to Arthur Creech Jones, Colonial Secretary, February 23, 1950.
59 Anthony Short, *The Communist Insurrection in Malaya, 1948–1960* (New York: Crane, Russak, 1975), 235.
60 Grob-Fitzgibbon, "Securing the Colonies for the Commonwealth," 27.
61 Ibid., 27–8.
62 TNA, Cabinet Office (CAB) 21/2884, Sir Harold Briggs, Director of Operations, and Sir Henry Gurney, High Commissioner in Malaya, "Combined Appreciation of the Emergency Situation," circulated to the Malaya Committee of the Cabinet, June 4, 1951.
63 Grob-Fitzgibbon, *Imperial Endgame*, 166.

Further reading

Bell, J. Bowyer. *Terror out of Zion: Irgun Zvai Leumi, LEHI, and the Palestine Underground, 1929–1949*. New York: St. Martin's Press, 1977.

Charters, David A. *The British Army and Jewish Insurgency in Palestine, 1945–47*. New York: St. Martin's Press, 1989.

French, David. *The British Way in Counter-Insurgency, 1945–1967*. Oxford: Oxford University Press, 2011.

Grob-Fitzgibbon, Benjamin. *Imperial Endgame: Britain's Dirty Wars and the End of Empire*. New York: Palgrave Macmillan, 2011.

Heller, Joseph. *The Stern Gang: Ideology, Politics and Terror, 1940–1949*. London: Frank Cass, 1995.

Jackson, Robert. *The Malayan Emergency: The Commonwealth's Wars, 1948–1966*. London: Routledge, 1991.

Stubbs, Richard. *Hearts and Minds in Guerrilla Warfare: The Malayan Emergency, 1948–1960*. Oxford: Oxford University Press, 1989.

Townshend, Charles. *Easter 1916: The Irish Rebellion*. London: Allen Lane, 2005.

13

BRITAIN'S SMALL WARS
The Empire strikes back, 1952–68

Benjamin Grob-Fitzgibbon

As dawn broke on the year 1952, the British government was perhaps better manned to oversee security operations in the Empire than at many other times in the twentieth century. On October 26, 1951 – just three weeks after Sir Henry Gurney, the British high commissioner in Malaya, was assassinated by Communist Terrorists – Sir Winston Churchill replaced Clement Attlee as British prime minister, bringing to power a Conservative cabinet more robust in its commitment to empire and more willing to use military force to defend it than its Labour predecessors. Between them, the cabinet and its junior ministers had much wartime service: the Colonial Secretary Oliver Lyttelton and future prime ministers Harold Macmillan and Anthony Eden fought together in World War I, and War Secretary Anthony Head, future prime minister Edward Heath, future defence secretary Lord Carrington, and future colonial secretary Iain Macleod all served in World War II.[1] Yet it was not just military service but the political management of conflict that the cabinet had in droves. During World War II, Eden served first as dominions secretary, then as war secretary, and finally foreign secretary; Lyttelton served as president of the Board of Trade, then as minister of state in the Middle East, and finally as minister of production; and Macmillan served successively as parliamentary secretary to the Ministry of Supply, undersecretary in the Colonial Office, minister resident in the Mediterranean, and air secretary.[2] In their recent history, members of Churchill's cabinet had killed and had led others to kill on their behalf, and they brought this experience with them into the government in October 1951.[3]

The conclusion of the Malayan Emergency

This change of leadership had an immediate effect on the way the government viewed the insurgency in the Malayan Federation, now dragging into its fourth year, and it shaped how they approached the problem. As the newly appointed colonial secretary with ultimate responsibility for Malaya, Lyttelton despised his predecessor's "emotional approach to public affairs" and believed that "to imagine that universal suffrage, elections and self-government with a few trades unions and co-operative wholesale societies thrown in spell immediate peace, prosperity and happiness" was an "outrage" to historical good sense and an "affront" to reason.[4] Democracy was important, yes, but democracy had to be protected with a mailed fist; put another way, the fruit of democracy could only be expected to grow if the field of civil society had first been tilled with heavy machinery, eradicating any weeds that might grow there. In Malaya as elsewhere in the empire, any opposition to British interests had to be eliminated before Westminster could successfully grant self-government to the colonial peoples. Yet in Malaya, Lyttelton was faced not only with the death of Gurney but also with the retirement of Sir Harold Briggs, the Malayan Director of Operations.[5] With Briggs and Gurney gone, the guiding lights behind the Briggs Plan (see the previous chapter) were dimmed. Consequently, Lyttelton embarked on a tour of the Federation to assess for himself the situation, arriving in the country in late November 1951. Within a week, he determined that more rigorous leadership was needed. In early December, he therefore recommended to Churchill that the recently vacated positions of high commissioner (Gurney) and director of operations (Briggs) be merged into a single position that would have complete control over all aspects of the Emergency, from policing operations to military campaigns to civil administration.[6]

Lyttelton expanded his vision further in a memorandum to the cabinet in late December, suggesting that Briggs' system of integrating military, police, and civil operations through State War Executives (SWECs) and District War Executives (DWECs) be retained but that the system be controlled by a war cabinet operating from within a single Executive Council rather than under joint control by a Federal War Council (military) and a Federal Executive Council (civil), as was the practice under Briggs. Any separation of civil and military power should be removed with all power invested in a single individual at the top of a rigid hierarchy. Finally, Lyttelton argued that the administration should not rush to introduce self-governance to Malaya but should first establish the solid foundations of civil society, eliminating all existing security threats. The government, he wrote, must adopt the philosophy of *festina lente* – make haste slowly.[7] The cabinet agreed. In early January 1952, Churchill contacted General Sir Gerald Templer, at that time serving as general officer commanding Eastern Command, to offer him the position of high commissioner and director of operations. In a little over a month, Templer arrived in Malaya.[8]

Templer immediately took a more aggressive approach than his predecessors. Within two days of arriving in the colony, he gathered together all leading civil officers to demand personal responsibility for their actions and to insist that they implement a more rigorous approach to their counter-insurgency operations.[9] Yet individual accountability was only the beginning. As suggested by Lyttelton, Templer reformed the system of operational control that Briggs had put into place, creating a single Executive Council. Within this council, he established a Director of Operation's Committee (with himself in the chair) that would run the SWECs and DWECs, "advise" the Executive Council on what policies to follow, and in general streamline the management of the Emergency, bringing together all aspects of it under the control of a single committee led by the director of operations – a man who also happened to be the high commissioner chairing the Executive Council to whom the director of operations and his committee reported![10]

Within the Director's Committee, Templer accepted only individuals who were as dedicated to a successful outcome in the Emergency as he was. He began by replacing the police commissioner with the forty-four-year-old Arthur Young, at that time commissioner of the City of London Police.[11] Young and Templer developed a close working relationship, Young accompanying Templer on many of the forty-five tours of Malaya – each two to three days long – that he carried out in his first twelve months in the Federation alone.[12] Young would subsequently become commissioner of police in Kenya in 1954 (at the height of the Mau Mau Emergency – see below) and eventually chief constable of the Royal Ulster Constabulary in 1969, just as the Troubles in Northern Ireland were beginning (see the next chapter, by Cillian McGrattan). However, policing in a counter-insurgency environment was only as good as the intelligence that fed it, and Templer recognized the importance of sound information to his overall strategy. For that reason, less than a week after arriving in Malaya he contacted Lyttelton to ask that a high-ranking official from MI5 (Britain's security service) be seconded to Malaya to serve as director of intelligence.[13] Within days, MI5's Jack Morton, at that time heading up the joint MI5/MI6 Security Intelligence Far East Office in Singapore, was approached, arriving in the Federation in April 1952.[14] Morton took up residence in what Templer called the "inner keep" of the police headquarters, a room established by Templer in February 1952 where high-ranking representatives from the police special branch, the armed forces, the civil service, the Malayan Ministry of Defense, and the intelligence services were physically grouped together in what today would be called an intelligence fusion center.[15]

Despite his robust approach, Templer shared Gurney's skepticism of large-scale army sweep operations. Nevertheless, he maintained that the army still had a role to play in the conflict. In addition to conventional operations, Templer believed that special forces would be necessary, and he turned to 22 SAS Regiment to assist him in this.[16] Twenty-two SAS, initially called the Malayan Scouts (SAS), was born in July 1950, when General John Harding, the commander-in-chief, Far East, summoned former wartime SAS commander Mike Calvert to assess the best way out of the Malayan quagmire. Calvert spent close to five months traveling throughout the Federation, speaking to police commanders and men, officers and soldiers, and civil authorities, undertaking police and army patrols, and witnessing the implementation of counter-insurgency policy. He reported to Harding that current operations were "making a lot of noise and achieving very little" and recommended the formation of a special forces unit modeled on the wartime SAS.[17] This Harding authorized him to do, and in July the Malayan Scouts (SAS) received its first volunteers.[18] By January 1951, men from the UK-based 21 SAS (Artists Rifles) regiment were dispatched to form B Squadron, Malayan Scouts (SAS), and by the summer of 1951, the Malayan Scouts had increased its numbers to four squadrons.[19]

By February 1952, SAS squadrons had been operating largely autonomously for half a year, broken down into smaller troops that would each carry out operations.[20] Templer expanded their use. In February, they launched Operation Helsby, a large three-squadron offensive designed to break the communist base area. The operation was a disaster, with C and D squadrons unable to cross swollen rivers and B squadron missing its drop zone from the air. Nevertheless, Helsby signaled a new approach. By the summer of 1954, when Templer's successor, General Geoffrey Bourne, arrived in the country, the "specialized work" undertaken by the SAS squadrons had become an essential part of military operations.[21]

It was not only in his use of police, intelligence, and military resources that Templer brought innovation to Malaya. Shortly after he arrived in the Federation, Templer uttered his famous words, "The answer lies not in pouring more troops into the jungle, but in the hearts and minds of the people," popularizing the notion of "hearts and minds" in unconventional warfare.[22] However, this did not mean that he was opposed to military action nor that he intended to take a "soft" approach. Under Templer's tenure, "kills" and "surrenders" of insurgents increased as British violence became more targeted and the security forces as a whole became more aggressive.[23] Within the New Villages, conditions became for a time *more* draconian rather than less. For Templer, winning the hearts and minds of the population did not mean distributing milk and cookies but rather triumphing in an ideological struggle between communism and the West; if the Malayan people did not voluntarily adopt Western norms, then punitive action would encourage them to do so. As early as March 1952, Templer began to use collective punishments such as curfews, the reduction of rice rations, and fines imposed on villages suspected of aiding the enemy. In at least one case, he sent all sixty-two village residents to detention camps and destroyed their property as punishment for not providing intelligence information.[24] Templer's strategy was one of the carrot and the stick, with the carrot given for cooperation but the stick swiftly wielded if cooperation turned out to be less than forthcoming.

With his approach firmly entrenched by the summer of 1952, Templer worked to secure the loyalties of those within the New Villages while isolating and destroying the insurgency at ever growing distances from the civilian population. In September 1953, Templer devised a system of rewarding villages that had been compliant over a prolonged period of time by designating them "White Areas," where all emergency restrictions were lifted and freedom of movement and action were returned to the people.[25] By June 1954, 1.3 million people were living within White Areas.[26] When Templer returned to visit Malaya as chief of the Imperial General Staff in October 1955, he was informed that the security situation had improved to such an extent that the security forces were now more interested in the Federation Football Final than best counter-insurgency practices.[27]

By then, the positions of director of operations and high commissioner had once again been separated, with Sir Donald MacGillivray taking the latter and General Sir Geoffrey Bourne the former. In October 1954, MacGillivray invited five local political leaders onto the Director of Operation's Committee (chaired by Bourne, but now reporting to MacGillivray) and from January 1955 he instructed the chairs of the SWECs and DWECs to likewise introduce indigenous representation. In March 1956, the British transferred all operational responsibility for the Emergency from the director of operations to Tunku Abdul Rahman, the Malay chief minister; from that point forward, British officials began to intentionally devolve more and more power to local authorities. On August 31, 1957, the British government relinquished all sovereignty over the territory, and Malaya took its place as an independent state within the Commonwealth of Nations.[28] Although British troops remained in the country until 1960, to all intents and purposes the back of the insurgency had been broken.

In all, between 1948 and 1957, the communist insurgency took the lives of 1,851 members of the security forces and 2,461 civilians, making it one of the deadliest terrorist campaigns of the postwar empire. Yet the insurgents suffered still more, with 6,398 killed, 2,760 wounded, and 1,938 captured after surrender.[29] The Malayan Emergency was a long and drawn-out struggle, a close-run affair, but it also proved a testing ground for British counter-insurgency/anti-terrorist tactics, tactics that would be used by the government for many years to come throughout the British Empire and beyond.[30]

The Mau Mau Insurgency in Kenya

If the conflict in Malaya was a protracted but straightforward struggle against communist insurgents whose aims were clear and whose strategy was understood, the violence that erupted in Kenya in 1952 was far less comprehensible. The first Briton arrived in what became known as Kenya in 1883; before the close of the century, the British government declared a protectorate and by 1901 had laid 582 miles of railway track, assisted the immigration of 30,000 Indians for labor purposes, and encouraged adventurous British settlers with promises of large tracks of farmland. Following World War I, the government launched a settlement scheme for newly demobilized officers, and in 1920 the protectorate was declared an official crown colony.[31] The British met tribes that opposed their expansion with force and between 1895 and 1920 launched nineteen punitive expeditions against ten separate tribes. Kenya's largest tribe, the Kikuyu, was pacified earlier than most and as such retained a greater level of cohesiveness into the post-World War I period. Consequently, it was Kikuyu lands that felt the greatest impact of the British settlement.[32]

Within the Kikuyu areas, British settlers were joined by missionaries who by 1920 had established Christian missions and church schools, aiming to create an African Christian elite within the tribe. Those who accepted Christianity were rewarded with increased involvement in the political sphere, primarily through the Kikuyu Association (established in 1921). Those who refused were ostracized and formed their own organization, the East African Association, which was explicitly opposed to European settlement in Kenya. The Kikuyu Association was supported by the Local Native Councils, local government institutions established by the British, while the East African Association was allied with the Kikuyu Central Association, which opposed the settler-friendly practices of the Kikuyu Association and Local Native Councils. This political separation was amplified by the migration of Kikuyu squatters to settler lands; by 1931, 1,850,000 acres of a total 6,847,000 acres of settler lands was occupied by squatters. In response to this perceived "crisis," in 1940 the colonial government proscribed the Kikuyu Central Association and between 1946 and 1952 embarked upon a policy of repatriation of Kikuyu squatters onto specially created reservations. By 1952, over 100,000 Kikuyu had been removed in this way. Those repatriated created new pressures on those already living on the reservations, leading in 1947 to a land crisis and peasant revolt that continued to simmer for many years afterwards.[33]

In this climate, some Kikuyu who were not loyal to British rule restored the old Kikuyu tradition of oathing when faced with war or crisis, beginning in Olenguruone in 1943, spreading beyond that village by 1945, and becoming a movement known to the British and loyalist Kikuyu as Mau Mau by 1948. While there was no rigid hierarchical structure in Mau Mau such as could be found in other organizations such as the Irish Republican Army, nor any distinct event such as the 1916 Easter Rising that gave it its birth, what in 1943 had been a spontaneous and localized response to perceived crisis had by 1948 evolved into a recognizable and widespread movement among the Kikuyu tribe.

Oath-takers pledged their opposition to the colonial government and took part in rituals involving animal sacrifice, sexual intercourse, and the smearing of animal blood on one's genitalia – all repulsive to British and settler sensibilities. It was the nature of these oaths, rather than the level of violence, that shocked the British government, as demonstrated by an army report written in 1953:

> The only possible deduction to be drawn from the details of the bestiality and perversion connected with the ceremonies is the horrible one that we are now faced in Kenya with a terrorist organisation composed not of ordinary humans fighting for a cause but of primitive beasts who have forsaken all moral codes in order to achieve the subjugation of the Kikuyu tribe and the ultimate massacre of the European population of the Colony.[34]

Oliver Lyttelton, colonial secretary until 1954, shared the army's assessment that the Mau Mau threat was of a special nature, writing in his memoirs: "I can recall no instance when I have felt the forces of evil to be so near and so strong. As I wrote memoranda or instructions, I would suddenly see a shadow fall across the page – the horned shadow of the Devil himself."[35]

Mau Mau moved beyond oathing to violently intimidate Kikuyu workers on settler farms and estates in 1949, attacks that escalated into the destruction of Kikuyu property on these farms by 1951. Consequently, the colonial government banned Mau Mau, but to no avail. In January 1952 alone, there were eleven cases of arson against the property of Kikuyu loyalists; in February, there were fifty-eight unexplained grass fires on European estates. Police investigations of these crimes went nowhere, as the Kikuyu population refused to cooperate, so in April 1952 the colonial government enacted the Collective Punishments Ordinance, allowing fines against communities that would not cooperate with the police. The ordinance failed to have the desired effect; by September 1952, the police had documented forty cases of confirmed arson against African loyalists and the murder of twenty-three Kikuyu by Mau Mau.[36]

It was into this rapidly deteriorating situation that Sir Evelyn Baring arrived as the new governor to Kenya. Baring's first action was to take a seven-day tour of the colony, during which Mau Mau murdered Chief Waruhiu wa Kungu, the most senior African in the colonial administration. Upon his return to Nairobi, Baring laid bare for Lyttelton the gravity of the situation: "There is the attempt to gain control over the whole Kikuyu tribe by attacks on those who refuse to take the Mau Mau oath. There is the determination to destroy all sources of authority other than Mau Mau, hence the attacks first on headmen and now on chiefs." He closed, warning that if Mau Mau could not be quelled quickly, "first there will be an administration breakdown and next a great deal of bloodshed amounting, possibly, even to something approaching civil war."[37] Consequently, after less than two weeks in the colony, he recommended that a state of emergency be declared in Kenya. This he was granted, and on October 20, 1952, Baring issued an emergency proclamation and initiated Operation Jock Scott, a security operation intended to arrest the principal ring leaders of Mau Mau and break the movement before it could escalate further.[38]

Before daybreak on October 21, the British security forces had arrested 106 of the 150 identified leaders. The following day, Mau Mau hacked to death a prominent Kikuyu tribal leader as he attempted to break up an oathing ceremony. When the police and army arrived, they could find nobody in the crowd willing to give evidence against the killers. Five days later, Mau Mau murdered its first European victim, a British veteran of both world wars who was slashed in his bathtub alongside his two Kikuyu house servants.[39] Following his murder, Lyttelton decided that he ought to see for himself the situation in Kenya and on October 29 flew to Nairobi.[40] The colonial secretary recognized immediately that there was an unsustainable settler–African dynamic in the colony and warned the European representatives of the Legislative Council that "sixty thousand Europeans cannot expect to hold all the political power and to exclude Africans from the legislature and from the Government. The end of that will be to build up pressures which will burst into rebellion and bloodshed." He also cautioned that Kenya's future security could not rest on the British security forces but only on the "building of a multiracial society."[41]

Nevertheless, if Lyttelton's long-term vision was for a multiracial society, in the short term Mau Mau had to be dealt with. Because it came from within the Kikuyu tribe – and because intimidation of Kikuyu loyalists made accurate information on who was or was not Mau Mau difficult – Lyttelton gave Baring permission to institution a wide-scale "screening" of the Kikuyu population to separate the wheat from the chaff. By November 15, 31,450 members of the Kikuyu tribe had been screened, of whom 8,500 were arrested for association with Mau Mau.[42] In addition to the screenings, Baring instituted a system of collective punishments that was entirely punitive, rather than linked to the collection of intelligence as was the case in Malaya. By November 10, the security forces had seized nearly 10,000 cattle, sheep, and goats in areas with a high proportion of Mau Mau adherents.[43]

Such screenings, arrests, and collective punishments did little to quell Mau Mau. On November 22, a retired British naval officer and his wife were attacked in their sitting room following dinner. She survived (albeit with mutilated wrists, breasts, and torso), but he died of his injuries. Four days later, a Kikuyu member of the Nairobi city council and a prominent critic of Mau Mau was hacked to death in a marketplace, his body left on the road for several hours until found by a settler. On December 24, Mau Mau simultaneously attacked five separate Kikuyu homesteads, killing six, and on January 1, 1953, murdered two more British settlers as they shared an evening meal. The most shocking crime to date, however, occurred on January 24, 1953. Mau Mau murdered a settler mother and father outside their home by the porch but slayed their six-year-old son as he slept in his bed, teddy bear in his arms. The press reported widely that one of those who had assisted in the murder was a domestic servant who just days earlier had carried the child when he fell from his pony.[44]

Baring did not stand idly by as these attacks occurred. Soon after the emergency began, he requested assistance from MI5, and a delegation arrived in Nairobi in late November, led by Sir Percey Sillitoe, the director-general. Sillitoe brought with him MI5 officers A. M. MacDonald and Alex Kellar, the latter of whom had worked as head of Security Intelligence first in Palestine from 1946 to 1948 and then in Malaya since 1948. Sillitoe recommended that an intelligence center be established to coordinate all police and military intelligence, and he left MacDonald in Kenya to run it, while Kellar returned to Malaya.[45] Furthermore, in late November Baring changed the emergency regulations to allow any district officer in Kenya to direct Kikuyu males over the age of eighteen into manual service on behalf of the police or military, and he instituted a large-scale sweep of the Thompson's Falls area where many settlers lived, interning without trial 750 Kikuyu men and 2,200 women and children, and confiscating 5,000 cattle.[46] Beyond these measures, Baring imposed a special tax of twenty shillings on each member of the Kikuyu tribe for a period of two years to force them to contribute to the cost of the Emergency. In January 1953, he approved a measure passed by the Legislative Assembly that imposed the death penalty on any Kikuyu taking the Mau Mau oath. By the end of the Emergency seven years later, 1,090 members of the Kikuyu tribe had been hanged for this crime.[47]

Nevertheless, Mau Mau violence continued, climaxing in March 1953 at the Kikuyu village of Lari, where Mau Mau burned to the ground fifteen homesteads and murdered 120 people, primarily women and children, as their men were lured away from the village. That same night, Mau Mau attacked the police station at Naivasha, killing six African constables and stealing forty-seven weapons and 4,000 rounds of ammunition.[48] In response to the Lari Massacre and the attack at Naivasha, Baring increased the mass-screening of the Kikuyu population; by the end of April, 82,840 members of the Kikuyu tribe had been screened, 28,912 of whom were tried and sentenced for association with Mau Mau, 38,947 of whom were released without charge, with the remainder charged but still awaiting trial.[49] For those interned by the colonial government, conditions were bleak, with a primitive detention system that eventually housed tens of thousands of Kikuyu throughout the duration of the Emergency.[50]

With the Kikuyu population separated, screened, and interned in large numbers, Baring turned next to tackle the Mau Mau fighters who had withdrawn to the forests. To assist him in this task, he appointed General George Erskine as director of operations.[51] Erskine adopted the committee structure pioneered by Gurney and Briggs in Malaya, working on the one hand to deal ruthlessly with Mau Mau while on the other encouraging the European settlers to give a greater role in governance to the African population. Nevertheless, while the general principle of separating the insurgents from the civilian population was implemented in both Kenya and Malaya, Erskine's task was made considerably more difficult in Kenya by the fact that the separation of the civilian population was into camps under deplorable conditions rather than into New Villages where increasing levels of personal freedom were granted. Consequently, Erskine was never able to integrate the Kikuyu people into his emergency planning and execution in the same way that Templer did in Malaya. Through the brutal application of force, the Mau Mau threat in the forests was largely destroyed by 1956, and by 1959 the government had released close to 77,000 of the more than 80,000 it had held in camps. In 1960, the government declared the Emergency over and in 1963 granted Kenya full independence. Nevertheless, while the insurgency in Kenya had taken considerably fewer lives than in Malaya, the government had viewed Mau Mau as deserving of greater levels of force than the Communist Terrorists in Malaya. This was a dirty war and the civilian population of the Kikuyu people felt the brunt, with ramifications that continue to this day.[52]

The Cyprian Emergency

If the violence in both Malaya and Kenya could best be characterized as insurgencies – one communist, the other anti-colonial – the violence that erupted in Cyprus in 1955 bore closer resemblance to the terrorism that Britain had faced in Palestine a decade earlier. Cyprus had been in the empire since 1878 when the British seized it from the Ottoman Turks, declaring it a British Protectorate and conferring crown colony status in 1923. Following the collapse of their own empire, the Turks were happy with this arrangement, content to see the island controlled by the British rather than the Greeks, who since the 1880s had been calling for *enosis*, the incorporation of Cyprus into Greece based on its historical Greek culture and civilization. This call for *enosis* provoked riots in 1931, causing the colonial government to react with draconian measures. During World War II, the strategic position of Cyprus became clear, a position made all the more important following the loss of Palestine in 1948, after which all the air bases and military garrisons previously housed in Palestine were transferred to Cyprus. In the face of the increased British presence, the movement for *enosis* picked up pace and in an illegal referendum held in January 1950, 96.6 percent of the Greek Cypriot population voted in favor of *enosis* (the Turkish Cypriots refused to take part, still preferring British governance to Greek).[53]

In 1951, Lieutenant George Grivas, a retired Cypriot officer who had served in the Greek Army during World War II, returned to Cyprus to advocate a more active campaign for *enosis*. Beginning the following year, he began to clandestinely organize men and weapons for an armed struggle against British rule, preparation that was largely complete by November 1954 when he persuaded Archbishop Makarios of Cyprus of the need for an armed campaign. With the support of Makarios, Grivas organized his men into a terrorist organization called the Ethniki Organosis Kyprion Agoniston (the National Organization of Cypriot Fighters), or EOKA for short. On April 1, 1955, EOKA launched its terrorist campaign against the colonial government, detonating a series of bombs in or around government buildings in the capital Nicosia, Limassol, and Larnaca and distributing leaflets claiming credit for the bombings.[54]

Using its recent experiences in Palestine, Malaya, and Kenya, the government responded proactively, forming a new committee called the Cyprus Internal Security Committee, chaired by the governor, Sir Robert Armitage, and including in its membership the army, air, and naval commanders in Cyprus, the commissioner of police, and a newly created director of intelligence, first held by MI5 officer Donald Stephens. The latter position was suggested by Templer, who at the prime minister's request traveled to Cyprus to advise the government immediately after the outbreak of violence.[55] In contrast to Kenya and Malaya, however, no declaration of emergency was issued, the government in London concerned about overstretch given the ongoing conflicts in Malaya and Kenya.[56] Nevertheless, violence in Cyprus continued, as EOKA detonated bombs at police stations in Nicosia and Kyrenia on June 19, destroyed the front of a police headquarters in Ataturk Square on June 21, attacked with machine guns the police station in Amiandos, and assassinated a police sergeant who had been attached to the newly created Special Branch on June 22.[57]

In the face of this violence, the British government followed a two-pronged strategy, on the one hand refusing Armitage's request for a declaration of emergency, instead requesting that he deal with EOKA through existing police powers, while on the other attempting to establish tripartite political talks between Greece, Turkey, and the United Kingdom to find a lasting resolution to the Cyprus problem. However, the proposed tripartite conference was overshadowed when on the morning it began – August 29, 1955 – EOKA assassinated a police constable in Nicosia. Harold Macmillan, at that time serving as foreign secretary in the new cabinet of Prime Minister Anthony Eden, predicted the conference would fail and an emergency would become inevitable; he therefore arranged for the transfer of seven senior police officers from Kenya and Malaya who had experience countering insurgencies and terrorism, two concepts that were indistinguishable in the British mind at the time.[58] Macmillan turned out to be right; on September 7, the conference collapsed.

Following its collapse, Eden agreed with Macmillan that tougher action was needed in Cyprus but felt that Armitage was the wrong man to lead such action. Consequently, on October 3 he removed Armitage from the governorship and replaced him with Field Marshal Sir John Harding, who had from 1949 to 1951 been responsible for all British Army troops in Malaya as the commander-in-chief, Far East, and since 1952 had been serving as chief of the Imperial General Staff, holding ultimate responsibility for all military action throughout the empire. Harding attempted political settlement with the Greek Cypriots for a little over a month but was met with more EOKA violence. Therefore, with the cabinet's backing, he declared an emergency in Cyprus on November 26, 1955, making it the third colony in the empire to simultaneously experience a state of emergency.[59]

As in Malaya and Kenya, the emergency in Cyprus was a protracted affair, lasting until February 1959. Throughout its four years, EOKA violence steadily rose, averaging ten kills per month by the summer of 1956 and peaking at twenty-six per month in early 1957. While many of these deaths were the result of simple assassinations or bombings, on some occasions EOKA attempted more audacious attacks, such as in October 1956 when it rigged explosive devices to the water tap used at the rugby practice fields of the Highland Light Brigade, leading to the disembowelment of two soldiers and other serious injuries to four more.[60] The British security forces in Cyprus did not establish mass internment camps as in Kenya or create New Villages as in Malaya, but their widespread use of curfews, fines, and collective punishment mirrored those earlier conflicts, as did the destruction of property in a punitive manner. Furthermore, in 1956 allegations of torture of EOKA prisoners by British soldiers began to emerge, with the Nicosia Bar Council establishing a Human Rights Commission to investigate the claims. Although it had no legal authority for action, its findings nevertheless made uncomfortable reading for the British government and drew international attention to Britain's robust approach to terrorism and insurgency.[61]

In October 1957, Harold Macmillan – prime minister since January 1957 – replaced Harding with the civilian Sir Hugh Foot, a man who had already served as colonial secretary in Cyprus from 1943 to 1945 and, as brother of the prominent Labour politician Michael Foot, could help with parliamentary opposition to some of the more ruthless aspects of the government's counter-insurgency/anti-terrorism policies. Foot's task was to find a constitutional settlement and end the emergency as quickly as possible. His job was not an easy one, as EOKA murdered the wives of two British servicemen in Cyprus just prior to his arrival, escalating tensions precipitously. Foot would not be deterred, however. When his first plan – announced in January 1958 – failed due to lack of Turkish and then Greek cooperation, he involved the prime minister directly. In June 1958, Macmillan announced in parliament a provisional constitutional plan that he hoped would lead to a permanent settlement. Eight months of tense negotiations between the British, Turks, and Greeks followed, but in February 1959, the three governments issued a joint communiqué announcing a power-sharing plan for the island. EOKA immediately declared a cease-fire, and Foot lifted all emergency regulations. The British government then established a joint constitutional committee to manage the transfer of power. On August 16, 1960, the government granted Cyprus independence. As with Malaya and Kenya, upon independence the new state chose to remain within the Commonwealth; on May 1, 2004, it entered the European Union as a democratic, presidential republic, still within the Commonwealth.[62]

The Aden Emergency

The Malayan, Kenyan, and Cyprus emergencies were resolved in a manner acceptable to the British government, each remaining within the Commonwealth upon independence and broadly speaking within the British sphere of influence. The same could not be said of the troubles facing the government in Aden. The British occupied Aden in 1839, making it the first colony acquired under the reign of Queen Victoria and the first European possession in the Middle East. Controlled initially by the East India Company, Aden was administered by the colonial government in India until 1937 when it finally received crown colony status, coming under the control of the Colonial Office rather than the India Office. As with Palestine and Cyprus, World War II highlighted the strategic significance of Aden. Furthermore, following the Iranian oil crisis of 1951, the British opened an oil refinery in Aden, relying on the labor of Yemini migrant workers who by 1959 outnumbered the Adenis. These Yeminis, developing a strong sense of Arab nationalism, sought to undermine British rule at every instance, launching eighty-nine industrial strikes in 1959 alone.[63] This opposition evolved into two militant organizations, the National Liberation Front (NLF) and the Front for the Liberation of Occupied South Yemen (FLOSY). On December 10, 1963, the NLF launched a grenade attack against the British high commissioner, Sir Kennedy Trevaskis, killing two and injuring 24. In response, Trevaskis declared an emergency in Aden.[64]

The NLF and FLOSY adopted a dual approach to oppose British rule, waging an Egyptian-supported overt insurgency in the countryside, while in the cities organizing in a clandestine cell structure to practice terrorism.[65] As in previous campaigns, the British formed a centralized intelligence system to combat this terrorism but opted not to form a committee structure to manage it, as there were no civilian political officials to help facilitate it.[66]

Furthermore, in Aden the British made no effort to separate and protect the broader civilian population; as such, they neglected the "hearts and minds" component of a counter-insurgency campaign that Templer had argued was so important.[67] After just four years of emergency regulations – compared to eight in Kenya and twelve in Malaya – and facing a financial crisis at home, the British decided to cut their losses in Aden and abandon the campaign. In contrast to the orderly final transfer of power in Malaya, Kenya, and Cyprus, the British withdrawal in Aden resembled that of Palestine, with a departure surrounded by violence and those who had waged the terrorist campaign seizing power. On November 30, 1967, the NLF proclaimed the People's Republic of South Yemen, the only former British colony to fall under communist influence during de-colonization and one of the few not to remain within the Commonwealth upon independence.[68] If some success could be claimed in Britain's other postwar campaigns against insurgency and terrorism, the same could not be said of Aden.[69]

Conclusions

When British forces withdrew from Aden in 1967, the British government had been fighting insurgency and terrorism on a continuous basis since Irgun re-launched its revolt in Palestine in 1944, twenty-three years earlier (and arguably since the beginning of the Irish War of Independence in 1919). And it would not end there. Less than two years after the last soldier left Aden, British troops were once again deployed, this time to Northern Ireland in the face of a new outbreak of terrorism. They would remain there as part of Operation Banner until July 31, 2007, the longest continuous military operation in British history. In the closing years of Northern Ireland's Troubles, violence declined precipitously, particularly after the Good Friday Peace Agreement of April 1998, but for the British government the struggle with insurgency and terrorism would continue, as the wars in Afghanistan and Iraq have created new problems since 2001. As the past two chapters of this volume have demonstrated, the terrorism and insurgency that plagued the British Empire in the postwar period cannot be separated from its larger historical context – from the legacies of World Wars I and II, from the grievances and causes of the insurgent groups themselves, and from Britain's struggles to manage its own imperial decline and de-colonization. It is a story that continues to this day, and will endure for as long as Britain's new post-imperial role remains unwritten.

Notes

1 Roy Jenkins describes Churchill's 1951 cabinet as being "like the organization of a vast commemorative pageant for the great days of the war", *Churchill: A Biography* (New York: Farrar, Straus and Giroux, 2001), 842). For more on the individual biographies, see Simon Ball, *The Guardsmen: Harold Macmillan, Three Friends, and the World They Made* (London: Harper Perennial, 2004); Alistair Horne, *Macmillan: The Official Biography* (London: Macmillan, 2008); D. R. Thorpe, *Eden: The Life and Times of Anthony Eden, First Earl of Avon, 1897–1977* (London: Chatto & Windus, 2003); and individual entries in the *Oxford Dictionary of National Biography* (Oxford: Oxford University Press, 2004).
2 Ibid.
3 Oliver Lyttelton perhaps best sums up this attitude, writing in his memoirs of his disappointment at initially being offered the position of minister of Materials and Rearmament and then his subsequent elation at instead being appointed colonial secretary. His sentiments on entering political service well represented other members of the cabinet: "[H]igh political office is only attractive to me in war or times of crisis." Oliver Lyttelton, *The Memoirs of Lord Chandos: An Unexpected View from the Summit* (New York: New American Library, 1963), 328.

4 Ibid., 332.
5 Benjamin Grob-Fitzgibbon, *Imperial Endgame: Britain's Dirty Wars and the End of Empire* (New York: Palgrave Macmillan, 2011), 176.
6 The National Archives [TNA], Prime Minister's Office [PREM] 11/639, f. 51, Telegram from Oliver Lyttelton, Secretary of State for the Colonies, to Winston Churchill, Prime Minister, December 8, 1951, in *British Documents on the End of Empire*, series B, vol. 3, *Malaya: Part II: The Communist Insurrection*, ed. A. J. Stockwell (London: Her Majesty's Stationary Office, 1995), 317–18.
7 TNA, Cabinet Office [CAB] 129/48, C (51) 59, "Malaya," Cabinet Memorandum by Oliver Lyttelton, Secretary of State of the Colonies, December 21, 1951, in ibid., 318–31.
8 Grob-Fitzgibbon, *Imperial Endgame*, 185–7.
9 Richard Stubbs, *Hearts and Minds in Guerilla Warfare: The Malayan Emergency, 1948–1960* (Oxford: Oxford University Press, 1989), 145; and Rhodes House Library, Oxford University, Mss. Brit. Emp. S. 527, "End of Empire" Transcripts, 527/9/1, Interview with Leslie Davis, Malayan Civil Service, interviewed by Desmond Smith, August 1981.
10 Grob-Fitzgibbon, *Imperial Endgame*, 194–5.
11 Noel Barber, *The War of the Running Dogs: The Malayan Emergency, 1948–1969* (New York: Weybright and Talley, 1971), 147; and Stubbs, *Hearts and Minds in Guerilla Warfare*, 143.
12 Stubbs, *Hearts and Minds in Guerilla Warfare*, 146.
13 Benjamin Grob-Fitzgibbon, "Intelligence and Counter-Insurgency: Case Studies from Ireland, Malaya and the Empire," *RUSI Journal* 156, no. 1 (February/March 2011): 76–7.
14 Leon Comber, *Malaya's Secret Police, 1945–60: The Role of the Special Branch in the Malayan Emergency* (Victoria, Australia: Monash University Press, 2008), 179.
15 Grob-Fitzgibbon, "Intelligence and Counter-Insurgency," 77.
16 Grob-Fitzgibbon, *Imperial Endgame*, 193.
17 Michael Asher, *The Regiment: The Real Story of the SAS* (London: Penguin Books, 2008), 302.
18 Ibid., 302–3.
19 David Rooney, *Mad Mike: A Life of Michael Calvert* (London: Leo Cooper, 1997), 148–50; and Michael Calvert, *Fighting Mad: One Man's Guerrilla War* (Barnsley, UK: Pen & Sword, 1964), 208.
20 Grob-Fitzgibbon, *Imperial Endgame*, 193.
21 TNA, War Office [WO] 216/874, Letter and Appreciation of the Situation in Malaya from Lieutenant General G.K. Bourne, Director of Operations in Malaya, to Field Marshal Sir John Harding, Chief of the Imperial General Staff, July 17, 1954.
22 Grob-Fitzgibbon, *Imperial Endgame*, 192. These words have long been attributed to Templer. That he said them is beyond dispute. However, there is some controversy about whether the phrase actually originated with him. Tim Jones, for example, has attributed the phrase to Sir Henry Gurney as early as late 1948. Tim Jones, *Postwar Counterinsurgency and the SAS, 1945–1952: A Special Type of Warfare* (New York: Routledge, 2001), 100.
23 Grob-Fitzgibbon, *Imperial Endgame*, 232–3.
24 See Stubbs, *Hearts and Minds in Guerilla Warfare*, 165–70.
25 TNA, Colonial Office [CO] 1022/58, Telegram from General Sir Gerald Templer, High Commissioner and Director of Operations in Malaya, to Oliver Lyttelton, Secretary of State for the Colonies, August 28, 1953.
26 John Cloake, *Templer: Tiger of Malaya: The Life of Field Marshal Sir Gerald Templer* (London: Harrap, 1985), 260; and Stubbs, *Hearts and Minds in Guerilla Warfare*, 180.
27 TNA, WO 216/875, Letter from Lieutenant-General Sir Geoffrey Bourne, Director of Operations in Malaya, to General Sir Gerald Templer, Chief of the Imperial General Staff, October 3, 1955.
28 TNA, WO 106/5990, "Review of the Emergency in Malaya from June 1948 to August 1957, by the Director of Operations, Malaya," September 12, 1957. For more on the constitutional developments that accompanied this counter-insurgency operation, see Short, *The Communist Insurrection in Malaya*; and Stubbs, *Hearts and Minds in Guerilla Warfare*. Malaya adopted its current name, Malaysia, in 1963 when it united with territories on the island of Borneo to create a new federative state.
29 TNA, WO 106/5990, "Review of the Emergency in Malaya from June 1948 to August 1957, by the Director of Operations, Malaya," September 12, 1957.

30 For example, the most current (at time of writing) British Army counter-insurgency manual still references Malaya, as does the American version. See *Army Field Manual: Countering Insurgency: Volume 1: Part 10* (Warminster, UK, 2010); and *U.S. Army/Marines Field Manual No. 3–24* (December 2006).
31 For more on the establishment of Kenya, see Elspeth Huxley, *White Man's Country: Lord Delamere and the Making of Kenya: Volume One, 1870–1914* (London: Chatto and Windus, 1953); John S. Galbraith, *Mackinnon and East Africa, 1878–1895: A Study in the "New Imperialism"* (Cambridge: Cambridge University Press, 1972); and G. H. Mungeam, *British Rule in Kenya, 1895–1912: The Establishment of Administration in the East Africa Protectorate* (Oxford: Clarendon Press, 1966).
32 Grob-Fitzgibbon, *Imperial Endgame*, 209–10.
33 David Anderson, *Histories of the Hanged: The Dirty War in Kenya and the End of Empire* (New York: W. W. Norton, 2005), 15–18; and David Throup, *Economic and Social Origins of Mau Mau, 1945–53* (Athens: Ohio University Press, 1988), 91–100.
34 Imperial War Museum [IWM], Department of Documents [DoD], "Mau Mau Oath Ceremonies," 1953, in the Papers of Lt. Col. J.K. Windeatt (305 90/20/1).
35 Lyttelton, *The Memoirs of Lord Chandos*, 380.
36 Anderson, *Histories of the Hanged*, 44–53; and TNA, CO 822/438, "Memorandum on Mau Mau Intimidation," Criminal Investigation Department, Kenya, September 12, 1952.
37 TNA, CO 822/444, Letter from Sir Evelyn Baring, Governor of Kenya, to Oliver Lyttelton, Secretary of State for the Colonies, October 9, 1952.
38 Anderson, *Histories of the Hanged*, 63.
39 Ibid., 88–9.
40 Lyttelton, *The Memoirs of Lord Chandos*, 382.
41 Ibid., 383.
42 TNA, CO 822/438, Telegram from Sir Evelyn Baring, Governor of Kenya, to Oliver Lyttelton, Secretary of State for the Colonies, November 15, 1952.
43 Ibid.
44 Grob-Fitzgibbon, *Imperial Endgame*, 237–48.
45 Christopher Andrew, *The Defence of the Realm: The Authorized History of MI5* (London: Allen Lane, 2009), 456.
46 TNA, CO 822/462, Telegram from Sir Evelyn Baring, Governor of Kenya, to Oliver Lyttelton, Secretary of State for the Colonial Affairs, November 24, 1952; and Anderson, *Histories of the Hanged*, 90.
47 For a detailed account of these trials, see Anderson, *Histories of the Hanged*.
48 Grob-Fitzgibbon, *Imperial Endgame*, 251–4.
49 TNA, CO 822/440, Telegram from Sir Evelyn Baring, Governor of Kenya, to Oliver Lyttelton, Secretary of State for Colonial Affairs, April 24, 1953.
50 For the fullest account of these internment camps, see Caroline Elkins, *Imperial Reckoning: The Untold Story of Britain's Gulag in Kenya* (New York: Henry Holt, 2005).
51 Grob-Fitzgibbon, *Imperial Endgame*, 255–6.
52 In June 2013, the British government agreed to pay reparations to Mau Mau fighters who had been tortured in British camps.
53 R. F. Holland, *Britain and the Revolt in Cyprus, 1954–1959* (Oxford: Oxford University Press, 1998), 5–37.
54 Ibid., 52–5.
55 TNA, CO 926/517, Letter from the Colonial Secretary, Cyprus, to Sir John Martin, Colonial Office, April 27, 1955.
56 TNA, Foreign Office [FO] 371/117640, Telegram from Alan Lennox-Boyd, Secretary of State for the Colonies, June 20, 1955.
57 Grob-Fitzgibbon, *Imperial Endgame*, 302.
58 Bodleian Library, Oxford, Harold Macmillan Papers, Dep. c. 301, Memorandum from Harold Macmillan, Secretary of State for Foreign Affairs, to Anthony Eden, Prime Minister, August 29, 1955. For more on the relationship between terrorism and insurgency, see Chapter 25 by Geraint Hughes on that subject in this volume.
59 Grob-Fitzgibbon, *Imperial Endgame*, 317–24.
60 Holland, *Britain and the Revolt in Cyprus*, 154.

61 Ibid., 171–2.
62 For a more detailed account of these negotiations, see Grob-Fitzgibbon, *Imperial Endgame*, 368–74.
63 Ronald Hyam, *Britain's Declining Empire: The Road to Decolonisation, 1918–1968* (Cambridge: Cambridge University Press, 2006), 288–9; and Harvey Sicherman, *Aden and British Strategy, 1839–1968* (Philadelphia, PA: Foreign Policy Research Institute, 1972), 1–17.
64 David French, *The British Way in Counter-Insurgency, 1945–1967* (Oxford: Oxford University Press), 51.
65 Ibid., 52.
66 Ibid., 100.
67 Ibid., 242.
68 Grob-Fitzgibbon, *Imperial Endgame*, 376.
69 For more on Aden, see Jonathan Walker, *Aden Insurgency: The Savage War in South Arabia, 1962–67* (Staplehurst, UK: Spellmount Publishers, 2003).

Further reading

Anderson, David. *Histories of the Hanged: The Dirty War in Kenya and the End of Empire*. New York: W. W. Norton, 2005.

Bennet, Huw. *Fighting the Mau Mau: The British Army and Counter-Insurgency in the Kenya Emergency*. Cambridge: Cambridge University Press, 2012.

Elkins, Caroline. *Imperial Reckoning: The Untold Story of Britain's Gulag in Kenya*. New York: Henry Holt, 2005.

French, David. *The British Way in Counter-Insurgency, 1945–1967*. Oxford: Oxford University Press, 2011.

Grob-Fitzgibbon, Benjamin. *Imperial Endgame: Britain's Dirty Wars and the End of Empire*. New York: Palgrave Macmillan, 2011.

Holland, R. F. *Britain and the Revolt in Cyprus, 1954–1959*. Oxford: Oxford University Press, 1998.

Jackson, Robert, *The Malayan Emergency: The Commonwealth's Wars, 1948–1966*. London: Routledge, 1991.

Stubbs, Richard, *Hearts and Minds in Guerilla Warfare: The Malayan Emergency, 1948–1960*. Oxford: Oxford University Press, 1989.

Walker, Jonathan, *Aden Insurgency: The Savage War in South Arabia, 1962–67*. Staplehurst, UK: Spellmount Publishers, 2003.

14

THE NORTHERN IRISH TROUBLES

Cillian McGrattan

As the first of Benjamin Grob-Fitzgibbon's chapters outlined, Ireland has endured a long relationship with terror. The Northern Irish "Troubles" – the colloquial term given to the conflict that took place between 1966 (or sometimes dated from the arrival of British troops in 1969) and 2005 – claimed almost 4,000 lives and left upwards of 50,000 people injured. In a population of around 1.5 million, this equates to one in three families having been directly affected by the violence, which itself took the form of rioting, shootings, and bombings (particularly car bombs and mortars). The violence peaked in the early 1970s (1972 witnessed 496 deaths) but continued sporadically and relentlessly into the 1990s and early 2000s.[1] Although these figures may seem small when placed in absolute terms against other conflicts, in proportional terms the killing toll would translate as around 100,000 deaths in the United Kingdom or 500,000 in the United States. Less overt forms of violence included threats and intimidation, collusion between state forces and paramilitary organizations, (intra)community "policing" in the form of "punishment beatings" and "kneecappings," and a climate of sectarianism and segregation the residual effects of which continue to be felt at many levels in contemporary Northern Irish society. These include continued sectarian attacks on homes and places of symbolic and cultural importance, rioting and protest, perceptions of alienation and marginalization by groups and individuals (including the victims and survivors of terror and violence) along with a renewed armed campaign by a range of anti-peace process "spoiler" organizations.

Northern Ireland's experience of terror therefore in some ways represents a further development in the Irish history of violence: it may be seen as a re-run of ancient Catholic–Protestant, Irish–British enmities. Certainly, its psychological, social, and physical effects are still being reckoned with and are, arguably, exacerbated by the efforts of political elites to justify, defend, minimize, whitewash, and commemorate the violence. In this way, history itself becomes an oppressive weight: a Joycean nightmare from which Ireland continues to try to awaken. On the other hand, the historical record of the tactics and strategies deployed in the terror campaigns in Northern Ireland suggests distinctions with other historical outbreaks of violence in Ireland: these include the prolonged nature of the conflict, its pronounced ethnic characteristics, and the fact that the violence involved the two sovereign states of the Republic of Ireland and the United Kingdom. Despite its seeming ubiquity, terror in Northern Ireland was (and remains) a backdrop to everyday life. The history of the Northern Ireland conflict, in this view, is not only concerned with the destructive, bloodied nature of terror but also the ways in which it can be lived with, endured, and perhaps even surmounted.

Background to the conflict

The Northern Irish conflict is often seen as a problem of "double minorities": the Ulster unionist community, which is mainly Protestant and British in religious and cultural outlook and which wishes to maintain the constitutional link with the rest of Great Britain, is in the majority in Northern Ireland but is a minority on the island of Ireland; the Irish nationalist community, which is mainly Catholic and Irish in religious and cultural outlook and wishes to end the partition of Ireland, is part of a broad Catholic–Irish majority on the whole island but a minority within Ulster.[2] A zero-sum contest thus haunts much of what passes for political debate in Northern Ireland – for example, disputes over cultural or religious symbols inevitably seem to become concerned with one "side" losing and another winning. The flipside of this contest is a "what-we-have-we-hold" approach to politics in which territory, votes, and rights are divided up between the two main ethno-national blocs; pressure points where control is ambiguous or the two communities (particularly in urban areas) live side by side symbolize the broader contest. Policing and security is one such "interface issue" that has resulted in a kind of détente where the building of "peace lines" or "peace walls" around communities is seen as a (temporary) solution to the problem of guaranteeing safety in urban districts.

The fact that the two ethno-nationalist blocs have different perspectives on the origins of the conflict underpins and helps to sustain debates about terror in Northern Ireland. At the level of bare figures, the story is easily told: Irish Republican terror groups – the main one being the Provisional Irish Republican Army (PIRA), an offshoot and reinvention of the IRA described in Chapter 12 – were responsible for almost sixty percent of violent deaths.[3] Republicans share basic ideological aspirations with Irish nationalists but differ on strategies: nationalists, who tend to be more middle class, prefer constitutional, peaceful, and democratic methods to reunify Ireland. Republicans, on the other hand, tend to be from more working-class backgrounds and believe that partition is linked to a British imperialist presence in Ireland, the end of which will require tactics involving physical force. During much of the conflict, the moderate strain of Irish nationalism was represented politically by the Social Democratic and Labour Party (SDLP), while the physical force tradition was represented by the PIRA's political wing, Sinn Féin (since around 2003, the latter has become the dominant electoral force in nationalist politics in Northern Ireland). Ulster loyalist paramilitary groupings – such as the Ulster Volunteer Force (UVF) and the Ulster Defence Association (UDA) – were responsible for thirty percent of the killings. Loyalists form part of the Ulster unionist community; they tend to be from working-class backgrounds and see violence as a fundamental means of defending their districts and their culture against encroachment and attack by republicans.[4] Loyalist paramilitaries have not been able to develop anything like the kind of party political machine that Sinn Féin provides for republicans. Instead, loyalist voters have mainly looked to the Democratic Unionist Party (DUP) to serve their interests. Part of the reason why loyalists have been unable to develop political representation is that unionist politicians have sought to marginalize rather than accommodate or tolerate terror and violence, thereby successfully shutting down any space within that broad constituency for voices linked to paramilitary organizations. The remaining ten percent of deaths are attributable to British state security forces – the British Army and the local police, the Royal Ulster Constabulary (RUC).

Divided histories

Republicans and nationalists argue that Northern Ireland was founded in 1920–2 by a gerrymandered peace settlement that was specifically designed to give unionists a permanent majority. Nationalists point to a subsequent history of discrimination and violence on the part of the unionist-dominated government towards its Catholic citizens as evidence of its illegitimacy and irreformability. Although discrimination in official employment, voting procedures, and housing did exist and was widespread, it cannot be linked, despite nationalist perceptions, to a dedicated governmental policy.[5] The emergence of a civil rights movement in the 1960s represented the first non-violent and cross-community attempt to tackle these issues. The idea of "equal rights for British citizens" caught both the IRA and the Northern Irish authorities – who had been used to political issues being framed in nationalistic or constitutional rather than civic language – off guard. For it was concerns with socio-economic injustices rather than simply questions about the border or reunification that were uppermost in the minds of those Catholics and Protestants who mobilized in the tens of thousands in a series of marches and rallies from late 1968 onwards. The response by loyalists, the Northern Irish government, and the British government to what was a genuinely mass peace movement represents a core facet in the nationalist narrative of the Troubles. Nationalists, for example, point to the fact that the first killings took place in 1966 when two Catholics were shot by a loyalist terror organization, the UVF. Several factors – the heavy-handed response by the police in attacking marchers, the behavior of counter-demonstrations by loyalist protesters led by the then youthful, firebrand preacher, the Rev. Ian Paisley, and the seeming lack of interest on the part of Whitehall – suggests, for nationalists, a certain inevitability: peaceful protest against injustice did not work, runs the logic, so the subsequent emergence of violence was understandable and perhaps even predictable.

Unionists, on the other hand, point to the instability caused by successive republican terror campaigns. The new and vocal civil rights movement, for example, had followed from – though was not connected in any real way with – the IRA's "border campaign," code-named Operation Harvest, which ran from 1956 until 1962.[6] Republican terror had remained a feature of the history of Northern Ireland long after the vast majorities of warring factions in the civil war had formed themselves into political parties and begun to take seats in the Dáil – the Irish parliament in Dublin. During World War II, for example, the IRA worked closely with the Nazi regime to mount attacks in several British cities. Although the bombing campaign was largely suppressed through internment, the IRA regrouped in the 1950s under the direction of a new military chief, Sean Garland. Although the 1956 campaign was launched with a fanfare of millenarian bluster ("Irishmen have again risen in armed revolt against British aggression in Ireland"), the limiting of operations to the border region was itself a sign of weakness. The immediate strategy was to attack police stations and retreat to the Irish Republic, but implicit in this was the acknowledgment that the organization did not have the capacity to work in towns or cities further inland, such as Belfast. Indeed, as the petering out of the campaign demonstrated, radical, violent republicanism no longer seemed convincing to the vast majority of Catholics in the context of the welfare state, which, from the late 1940s, guaranteed rights of access to social security, health care, education, and housing. Nonetheless, Operation Harvest precipitated disquiet among the Ulster unionist population of Northern Ireland, and Protestant groups intimated that unless the government responded forcefully they would organize resistance themselves. Internment was introduced on both sides of the Irish border, and the unionist government went on to impose curfews and prohibit publication of subversive material. In the end, Operation Harvest achieved nothing in military terms, while it heightened sectarian tensions and fears and pushed republican leaders in the direction of civil rights and leftist ideological ideas. In turn, unionists saw the appearance of republican leaders within the civil rights movement as evidence that it was no more than an umbrella movement or a conspiracy to achieve goals that had been unachievable through terror.

Although loyalists hold to the same chronology as do unionists, the former's understanding of the conflict emphasizes different factors; in particular, loyalist terror can be explained by recourse to ideas about defense. Thus, the UVF was formed in 1965 as a "preemptive measure to defend Northern Ireland against an anticipated IRA threat."[7] Adopting the name of the organization that had been set up to resist the devolving of governance to Ireland in the 1910s, the UVF used history to claim legitimacy for their aims and promoted a chilling contemporary agenda:

> From this day we declare war against the IRA and its splinter groups. Known IRA men will be executed mercilessly and without hesitation. Less extreme measures will be taken against anyone sheltering or helping them, but, if they persist in giving them aid, then more extreme measures will be adopted. . . . We are heavily armed Protestants dedicated to this cause.[8]

By making new demands and using new mass mobilization tactics, the civil rights movement inspired "street" politics and contributed to an increasingly fissiparous political environment. The re-emergence of terror within this context should be seen as an example of terrorists always being "something else" – that is, something inspired by a different form of politics and political expression than those contained in the civil rights movement.[9] While terror, therefore, was not linked directly to the peaceful civil rights movement, it nevertheless grew and took sustenance from the uncertainties, confrontations, and fears that the civil rights era precipitated. The loyalist and republican terror campaigns, therefore, may have been reprisals, but they were not insurgencies nor were they simply responses to repression: they were opportunistic and deliberately planned strategies of violence. While the goals and the tactics of terror and civil rights protest were at opposite ends of the political spectrum, it was not surprising to find radical republicans sharing civil rights platforms with trade unionists, communists, and moderate nationalists, owing to their shared contexts and cultural backgrounds.

In this instance, terrorists could be identified as part of a community but were also undeniably something other. There is no doubt that the actions and strategic visions of loyalist and republican terrorists in Northern Ireland were profoundly amoral and often straightforwardly anti-democratic. Political representatives, even in this early period, were attacked in their homes, and both sets of terror organizations consistently opposed dialogue between elected politicians until the 1990s (see the last section below). Yet it would be inaccurate to dismiss the terror campaigns simply (or infamously, as Margaret Thatcher did in 1981) as criminal.[10] While they cannot be seen as anything other than retrograde in terms of deepening or furthering democracy in Northern Ireland, the two sets of terrorists arguably represented a democratic surfeit. Although some overt support was offered within both the Catholic and Protestant communities to the terror campaigns, more typical was the phenomenon of "sneaking regard," a complex system of vicarious support or, more accurately, disgusted admiration for people who were willing to commit acts (and atrocities) ostensibly in the name of a common ideology that "ordinary" people could not countenance doing themselves. In this regard, the relationship of everyday life and democracy to violence and terror in Northern Ireland is comparable to that of any liberal democratic state in which individuals and groups are tacitly empowered to protect communities; where Northern Ireland's relationship to terror differs – and, arguably, where the *political* appropriateness of the use of the term is justified – resides in the fact that the means to afford democratic legitimacy to the violence were not present and were in fact contested. The key indicator of this is that while the PIRA's campaign continued, Sinn Féin could count on no more than one in every three Catholic votes, but when the PIRA began to move towards acceptance of peaceful elections in the 1990s, Sinn Féin began to make real electoral progress.

The origins of the conflict

Following the failed terror campaign that was Operation Harvest, the febrile atmosphere of civil rights marches, counter-demonstrations, riots, and police repression at the end of the 1960s provided republican militants with opportunities to both recruit and push forward this teleological agenda by radicalizing Catholic youths. The key mechanism for doing so was the coordination of riots, which became more intense during the summer of 1969, culminating in an almost total breakdown of the police in August, which necessitated the introduction of troops to maintain law and order. At this point, the army's brief was to bolster the police and maintain the coherence of Northern Ireland. Yet, in effect, two security regimes came into existence – while the police was answerable to the devolved Stormont government, the army was answerable to London. Both regimes sought to restore peace. Differences in approach quickly became apparent, however: the police's role was to restore order and arrest lawbreakers, but in an escalating climate of violence and killing, the army's role of tackling gunmen and bombers soon took precedence.

The army's focus also moved towards the terrorism of the anti-state republican movement. (Although the army was also charged with stopping loyalist violence, it was not their direct target. For their part, loyalists were mainly concerned with, first, killing republican terrorists and second, by way of deterrence, Catholics. For loyalists, the army and the police were occasional nuisances.) The PIRA's terror campaign began at the end of 1969 through the beginning of 1970 following a split between the Marxian "Officials" and the more nationalistic "Provisionals" over the question of ending a policy of abstentionism and contesting parliamentary seats in the Irish Republic. Although the immediate question concerned the idea of affording recognition (and legitimacy) to partition, at a deeper level the debate was concerned with and was influenced by the IRA's role within Northern Ireland. The Provisional movement responded to these issues by offering an alternative to the leftist ideas that had dominated republican thinking after the 1956–62 campaign. In their place, the PIRA concentrated on northern Catholic working-class alienation, fear, and anger against loyalists, the RUC, and the army.[11]

The summer of 1969 is crucial in the republican mythos, which emphasizes how loyalist mobs conspired to perpetrate pogroms on Catholic areas of Belfast. This sense of threat was crystalized in the burning of Bombay Street, which lies at an intersection of Catholic and Protestant areas of west Belfast. Father Des Wilson (a priest who self-consciously harnessed the language of liberation theology and embraced various aspects of community life in west Belfast) recalled:

> I remember the lead up [to August 1969] alright.... There was tremendous tension and it was quite obvious that the Loyalists were ready to spring. I believe it was supposed to be the final solution. You know, that this was the wipe out, when Catholics would be finally driven into ghettos and intimidated for the next 30 years.[12]

The absence of the IRA in this rendering is crucial because what the events of August 1969 seemed to demonstrate was that the organization had run down and left working-class Catholics at the mercy of loyalist and state forces. While loyalists emphasize preemption to justify terror, republicans, on the other hand, emphasize self-defense – in each case, the underlying logic is defense. In other words, terror is justified when it is a response to something far worse: namely, the annihilation of working-class communities by their ethnic neighbors. Following heavy-handed tactics and unlawful killings by the army and the police, the state began to feature as strongly (if not more so) in the republican imagination as did loyalist terrorists. One of the foundational events for this collective memory occurred the following summer when the British Army cordoned off the Catholic sections of lower Falls Road for three days during which houses were searched and ransacked and five people killed. The template of justification through defense and victimhood was thus established early in the conflict: perpetrators were easily identified, and rather than simply "refereeing the fight," as British politicians liked to see themselves,[13] state forces quickly became implicated as another belligerent.

Although Father Wilson's recollections undoubtedly capture something of the palpable paranoia and fear of the time, they jar with the recent work of historians such as Brian Hanley, who has observed that despite there being over 200 journalists in Belfast at the time, there is not one extant photograph of the infamous graffito "IRA = I Ran Away."[14] They also obscure the fact that IRA recruitment had been rising steadily during the 1960s (from 657 volunteers in 1962 to 1,039 by 1966)[15] and other memories such as those of the journalist Malachi O'Doherty, who grew up in the area and recalled how in the late 1960s republicans engineered riots to provoke the authorities.[16] The arrival of the British Army in August 1969 also opened the way for what one historian, Thomas Hennessey, has called "the single most disastrous decision" that would produce the next thirty-plus years of violence: namely, "the decision of the Provisional IRA's army council in January [1970] to begin a war – their war – against the British state."[17] Thus, while claims to self-defense and victimhood and the attribution of perpetrator status help to establish a narrative of self-exculpation on the part of terror groups and allow the communities from which they arose to develop a sense of blamelessness and even bystander status, historical consensus has begun to form around less abstract or even structuralist explanations. In these explanations, the terror campaigns, while occurring in the context of societal upheaval, were the result of conscious, strategic choices. Rather than being somehow inevitable, the decision to "go to war" was avoidable; after all, politics, in the form of dialogue and contact between the communities and their elected representatives, continued. The origins and persistence of conflict lay in the fact that that type of political behavior was, first, seen as irrelevant by the terrorist leaders of the PIRA, who wished to complete their 1916 Revolution under the guise of defense; second, seen as irrelevant by loyalists who saw killing as the best means of defending their beliefs; and third, seen as irrelevant by the state forces that were driven by the military imperatives of quashing insurrection.

Development and persistence of conflict

The escalation of PIRA activities during 1970–71 persuaded the prime minister of Northern Ireland, Brian Faulkner (of the largest party, the Ulster Unionist Party [UUP]), to introduce internment without trial in August 1971. The move was disastrous from a public relations point of view: although state forces arrested over 300 republicans, the intelligence lists they had been operating from were woefully out of date and included mostly middle-aged men who had been active in the pre-1969 period. Stories about mistreatment of the prisoners ("in-depth interrogation" techniques including food, sleep, and drink deprivation and being hooded and forced to listen to white noise) quickly began to filter out. These, together with the fact no loyalists were arrested, only added to the growing sense of Catholic alienation from the state.[18] British state papers reveal that for the United Kingdom's prime minister, Edward Heath, internment was Faulkner and the UUP's last chance: although the British government had no appetite to end devolution, the subsequent inability of Faulkner to alleviate Catholic disquiet forced Heath's hand, and London assumed direct control of the administration of Northern Ireland in March 1972.

The killing of thirteen unarmed protesters on an anti-internment march in Derry (a fourteenth died in hospital later) on January 30, 1972, is often seen as a pivotal event in the history of the Troubles.[19] The traumatic brutality of the events of that day has given rise to a totalizing narrative that ignores historical distinction. This narrative tends to form the basis of nationalist collective memory.[20] P. J. McLoughlin, for example, contends that "Bloody Sunday also dealt a devastating blow to constitutional nationalism. . . . The [P]IRA reaped a bitter harvest from the British army's actions, as scores of young nationalists, convinced of the need to defend their community, swelled the Republican ranks."[21] This assessment may, arguably, be overstating the case since it remains unlikely that an underground terrorist organization would recruit any and all aggrieved individuals. Instead, the atrocity was likely used in a post-hoc way to justify stepping up the PIRA's campaign. As such, what is true is that Bloody Sunday represented a further step in the polarization of Northern Ireland's two communities and remained an open sore within the Catholic collective memory. Its impact allowed the PIRA to press ahead, regardless of it having (notionally) achieved one of its central aims – namely, the fall of the unionist-dominated government at Stormont. Thus, the PIRA's leader in Derry (today the deputy first minister of Northern Ireland, Martin McGuinness) dismissed political developments with the message that "people are going around seeking for peace. They are wasting their time. We are fighting on. We are not stopping until we get a united Ireland."[22]

In response to republican violence, loyalist terrorists also increased their activities, particularly under the direction of what was to become the main loyalist organization, the Ulster Defence Association (UDA). Superficially a community-defense grouping, the UDA carried out a campaign of sectarian assassination, including, for example, the brutal and bloody killing of the moderate nationalist SDLP politician Paddy Wilson in 1973 under what was effectively a nom de guerre, the Ulster Freedom Fighters (UFF). Both the UFF and the UVF quickly refined their methodologies of terror that led seamlessly to drink-fueled sadistic orgies of torture. Thus, innocent Catholics and members of their own organizations (suspected of being informants but often just unfortunate to say the wrong thing at the wrong time) met pitiless, horrible deaths in the so-called "romper rooms" within drinking dens in loyalist-dominated estates. The most notorious "refinement" of these practices took place at the end of the 1970s among a group of UVF loyalists under the direction of Lenny Murphy. Between 1975 and 1979, the so-called Shankill Butchers were suspected of killing thirty Catholics. Michael Burleigh describes their modus operandi:

> The gang would always claim that the idea (and the victim) just popped into their heads whenever they went out for bags of chips. In fact, each killing was hatched as they talked themselves into it during all-day drinking sessions in loyalist bars. They would drag some unfortunate fellow into a black taxi after hitting him on the head with a wheel brace. Inside the victim would be brutally assaulted, while the taxi stopped off to collect butcher's knives or a hatchet for the wet work. Then there would be a long torture session at some dingy loyalist drinking den, which ended when Murphy sawed through the victim's throat and spinal column. Then the corpse would be driven away and dumped – near a republican area if the victim was a fellow Protestant.[23]

The shape of terror

The Troubles witnessed few gun battles between terror organizations and state forces; instead, the main tactics consisted of car bombings or the shooting of people identified as "justifiable targets." Both "sides" were responsible for horrific tragedies such as the bomb that republicans planted in the village of Claudy in 1972 that killed nine people; the Dublin–Monaghan bombings of 1974 by loyalists that killed thirty-four; or the human proxy bombs of the late 1980s in which the PIRA held families hostage until the fathers would detonate a car bomb inside an army or police barracks.

The longest period of non-violence was the PIRA's decision to call a cease-fire at the end of 1974. British officials sought to use the cease-fire to keep the PIRA locked in interminable talks in an attempt to wind the organization down; for their part, republicans called the cease-fire because they believed British suggestions that they were going to withdraw.[24] The cease-fire broke down in an orgy of killings in August 1975. Demoralized and deeply infiltrated, the PIRA moved to a cellular structure to limit the number of other volunteers any single person would know (though in practice in tight-knit communities like west and north Belfast, Derry, or south County Armagh, everyone knew everyone else anyway).[25] It also dropped the "year of victory" rhetoric from its Easter messages and began to plan for a "long war" that would sap the will of the British population to keep troops in Northern Ireland – a policy McGuinness succinctly, if euphemistically, defined as "blattering on until the Brits leave."[26] In response to these developments, the British embarked on a dual strategy, the first part of which was "normalization," that is, treating paramilitary actions as criminal rather than political. The second was "Ulsterization": reducing the numbers of troops from the United Kingdom and, instead, bolstering the numbers of the RUC and the Northern Irish army regiment, the Ulster Defence Regiment. The latter strategy had the deleterious consequence of exacerbating the sectarian dimensions of the situation since it increased the chances that PIRA victims would be Northern Irish Protestants known to many people in the areas where they were killed.

As applied to the prisons, normalization in effect entailed a criminalization of terror: prisoners lost any special dispensations they had gained as "political" groupings and instead were subjected to "normal" prison regulations. Republican prisoners began a series of ineffectual protests that culminated in the decision to launch hunger strikes in 1980. A journalist and cultural commentator, Fintan O'Toole, argues that the hunger strikes, in which ten men starved to death before families intervened to authorize medical care, were ready-made histories that literally incorporated tropes of victimhood and self-sacrifice. In the process of inscribing those tropes on their own transforming bodies, the prisoners transformed themselves from criminals and terrorists into martyrs. The "whole point of the hunger strikes," O'Toole writes, "was that aesthetics trumps politics. The fusion of a visual imagery that deliberately tapped into images of Christ and the potent drama of slow death worked to simplify and transform a complex political reality. It obliterated the reality that the prisoners were killers."[27] The reality for the victims of the ten men was somewhat different, as one police officer recalled of Francis Hughes, the second hunger striker to die: "He was an extremely good terrorist. He killed a lot of people. A terrible and ruthless opponent – and in some way brave. But I saw a lot of people he murdered, including a child, which gives a different perspective." The ethnicization of terror in places like Northern Ireland gives a new gloss to the terrorist–freedom fighter cliché: whereas one community saw the hunger strikers as martyrs, the other saw them as callous killers and child-murderers.[28]

The strikes revealed a residual Catholic support and respect for the Provisional movement. On the back of the victory of the strike leader, Bobby Sands, who stood as an Independent in a Westminster by-election in Fermanagh–South Tyrone (on the border with the Irish Republic), the PIRA's political wing, Sinn Féin, re-entered electoral politics. The British and Irish governments responded to the renewed political mobilization of republicans by reinitiating talks aimed at a significant political intervention. For its part, the British government under Margaret Thatcher hoped to tie Dublin into a more cooperative security strategy, while the Irish hoped to create institutions to tackle nationalist disaffection. In her autobiography, Thatcher expressed disappointment that the Irish government emphasized the latter aspects of the resultant Anglo-Irish Agreement (AIA) at the expense of the former. The unionist community was outraged that its future had been negotiated without its consent or the input of its political representatives; and it was particularly upset that the AIA offered nationalists a consultative role for the Dublin government in Northern Ireland. Although some scholars have dated the peace process from this event, it is also possible to argue that the agreement delayed the cause of peace as it provided no incentive for nationalists to enter into dialogue with unionists. Nationalists had achieved a key objective (Dublin's involvement) under the AIA; that objective would be watered down through actually taking on political responsibility within Northern Ireland by working with unionists. Seemingly recognizing the logic of this position, the SDLP's leader, John Hume, agreed instead to an invitation by the president of Sinn Féin, Gerry Adams, to explore avenues for "identifying a common strategy for bringing about unity."[29] Soon after, the pair entered into a series of secret talks that lasted from 1988 to 1993. The strategy of violence-with-politics would be slowly phased out and replaced by a politics-first strategy based on targeting the "soft underbelly" of the SDLP (that is, by attempting to "outbid" the more moderate party by developing a more robust defense of nationalist rights and grievances) and building links with Irish America.

As part of an incipient and implicit recognition of the futility of the "long war," both republicans and loyalists began developing position papers during the 1980s. Predating Ulster unionist thinking in this regard (and prefiguring most of what would later appear in the 1998 Belfast/Good Friday Agreement), in 1985 loyalist political strategists called for a return to devolution on a power-sharing basis and noted the acceptability (on the basis of transparency) of cross-border cooperation. Republicans also began to try to develop a more coherent political position. The year 1987 saw a series of important changes within republicanism. First, the PIRA's hopes of escalating its campaign suffered setbacks when French authorities intercepted a vessel containing a major quantity of armaments bound for Ireland, and, as Geraint Hughes points out in Chapter 25, "Terrorism and Insurgency," when a particularly brutal and effective cell was eliminated by the SAS in Loughgall (the eight killings representing PIRA's greatest loss of life in a single incident). Second, the Remembrance Day bombing at Enniskillen, which killed eleven people, provoked a massive public backlash against the armed campaign. Third, Sinn Féin produced a discussion paper, *A Scenario for Peace*, that made two advancements on its previous position: namely, that dialogue rather than violence might further republican objectives and that unionists existed in their own right (rather than as deluded Irish people). Although republicans created an opening for abandoning terror in favor of negotiation, they refused to forgo the utility of violence in achieving their ends. This cul-de-sac arose simply because those ends remained solidly unrealistic: republicans, in short, still held fast to the doctrine of a united Ireland or nothing. Within this vision, unionists would remain unionists but would do so within a reunified country. Thus, as the party made clear the following year: "Sinn Féin is totally opposed to a power sharing Stormont assembly and states that there cannot be a partitionist solution. Stormont is not a stepping-stone to Irish unity."[30]

Ending the terror campaigns

The peace process saw an evolution of thinking in which republicans moved from the position of anti-power-sharing to the view that it "could become a transitional stage towards reunification."[31] If we take the peace process to be a narrative of the British state winding down the PIRA, then Sinn Féin's position can only be explained through willful amnesia or outright betrayal. The latter, of course, is the preferred explanation of anti-peace-process, "dissident" republicans. As one spokesperson put it: "If we were wrong now, then they were wrong for all them [sic] years: and if we are right now then they are wrong."[32] Sinn Féin explains the evolution as being congruent with the PIRA's campaign: violence and terror were once necessary, but the "current phase" in the struggle necessitates dialogue and politics. In other words, the political ends that fueled the terror campaign remain; it is the tactical utility of violence that is no longer appropriate.

The key events of the peace process themselves are easily told: the Hume–Adams talks produced a document in May 1993 that called on the British government to declare that it had no "selfish, strategic, political, or economic interest" and that it would use its "influence and energy to win the consent of a majority in Northern Ireland" to agree to self-determination. Westminster agreed with the former suggestion – albeit with the crucial exception of "political" – and stated that it would not persuade anyone in Northern Ireland but would remain open to the democratically expressed wishes of a majority. Placing its faith in the development of a pan-nationalist alliance (incorporating Ireland and the diaspora in the UK and North America), the PIRA called a cease-fire in September 1994. Loyalists followed shortly afterwards. In a leaked document, republicans explained this strategy as "TUAS." Although it was never defined, it is suspected that TUAS stands for either Totally Unarmed Strategy or, for the less sanguine, Tactical Use of the Armed Struggle. Although the PIRA's cease-fire broke down in 1996 over the question of decommissioning as a precondition to negotiations, it was restored following the landslide victory of New Labour in 1997, since Labour has traditionally been seen as more sympathetic to Irish nationalism than have Conservatives. Loyalism, meanwhile, began to fissure during these years, with hard-line elements indulging in power battles and stoking the flames of ethnic violence during the summer marching "seasons" to further their interests – which largely involved drugs, prostitution, and racketeering.[33]

Conclusion

Loyalist politics collapsed in the years after devolved power-sharing. Sinn Féin, on the other hand, grew to become the largest nationalist party in Northern Ireland and, by 2010, a major player in the Dáil. At the time of writing, it aims to be a party of government on both sides of the Irish border by 2016. The Ulster Unionist Party also experienced a backlash following the release of paramilitary prisoners, the continued refusal of the PIRA to disarm, and the reformation of the police. Republicans resisted decommissioning until led to do so by the combination of several factors: a changed geopolitical climate against terror post-9/11, the revelation that republicans were involved in training the Colombian FARC in 2003, the massive bank robbery of the Northern Bank in Belfast in 2004, and the sordid murder and cover-up by members of the PIRA of a Catholic in a bar in Belfast after the Bloody Sunday commemorative march in 2005. In 2007, Martin McGuinness, a former PIRA leader, and Ian Paisley, of the Democratic Unionist Party (DUP), headed up the Northern Ireland Executive. The Sinn Féin–DUP partnership has subsequently given Northern Ireland its most enduring period of devolved governance in a power-sharing framework in its entire history.

The DUP has seemingly squared the circle of sitting in government with those it previously (and still does) consider "terrorists" – those whose armed campaign it considers arbitrary, unjust, and often inhumane – by invoking "African proverbs," which equate to a pragmatic understanding of peace: "Peace is costly but worth the expense."[34] For anti-peace-process "dissident" republicans opposed to the Good Friday Agreement (GFA), the circle cannot be squared. Holding that "GFA = Got Fuck All,"[35] they persist in an ETA-style campaign: not having the resources or support to rival the PIRA's violence, they have seemingly opted to keep the pot boiling through a series of assassinations (mainly targeting Catholic police officers in an effort to drive a wedge between that community and the police). As the killing of over thirty people in the 1998 Omagh bomb showed, this threat should not be taken lightly.[36]

Many victims also feel short-changed by the new political dispensation. Within the police service, a Historical Enquiries Team has been established to deal with unsolved murders. However, it is underfunded and understaffed and faces the additional challenge that former terrorists collude to provide alibis for comrades under suspicion. Since ex-prisoners have been released under the GFA, the question facing any process of truth recovery remains: why would they re-implicate themselves and risk going back to jail by divulging secrets about the past? In this way, the Joycean nightmare continues: unable to bring into the light the atrocities of the past, Northern Ireland lives in a kind of traumatic suspension, lacking resolution and, in some ways, fearful of what a thorough revisiting of the past might entail. The victims of terror, then, remain cut off from the wider society. "It was something at the end of all these years," said one eighty-one-year-old mother following an apology from the Ministry of Defence for the unlawful shooting of her daughter. "But nothing brings her back," she continued. "I feel lonely and sad."[37]

Therefore, republicans – and loyalists, to a lesser extent, given their tendency to fissure – have seemingly little to fear from "truth recovery": the repainting of the past is almost secure, and its tenor is condescension. As a Sinn Féin Assembly member explained to Ann Travers, whose sister had been killed by a PIRA gunman who had been driven away by a woman later appointed as a special advisor to the Minster for Culture, Arts, and Leisure: "[Yours] is a heart-rending story, but you will acknowledge . . . that we are not dealing with your case on its own. We are dealing with many, many other cases and people who are screaming for help and support." Travers' response said something about where victims and history find themselves in Northern Ireland:

> [A]s I pointed out, two gunmen murdered Mary [her sister] . . . and I do not know who they are. . . . Like the other people you talked about, I do not know who these people are. Mary McArdle [the gunwoman convicted of the killing] knows who they are, but she will not give their names. Waiting for the truth and for an international truth body is not doing the victims much good. It does not really wash with me at the moment.[38]

Joyce's metaphor of the nightmare of history captures something about trauma that resonates with Travers' sentiments: there is a consciousness but also a state of powerlessness within the Joycean predicament (of "trying to awake"). Working through the past then becomes a matter of trying to articulate that disorientation; the nightmarish quality occurs when the process is somehow interrupted. The inability of Northern Ireland to work through its terror-filled past should not be taken as a sign of the victory of violence. Indeed, the key historical lesson of the Northern Irish Troubles is that terrorists were only admitted to talks gradually as they disavowed their tactics, although they retained their aims (at least at a rhetorical level). The continued marginalization of victims of terror points to this lack of assimilation. Former terrorists can partake in democracy if they follow the rules of the game, so to speak, but reconciliation and justice require more fundamental reappraisals of the ideologically inspired explanations that excused violence in the first place.

Notes

1 These figures are taken from what remains (and is unlikely to be surpassed) the most accurate and comprehensive account of the impact of the Northern Irish conflict, David McKittrick, Seamus Kelters, Brian Feeney, and Chris Thornton's *Lost Lives: The Stories of the Men, Women and Children Who Died as a Result of the Northern Ireland Troubles* (Edinburgh: Mainstream, 1999).

2 See Christopher Farrington, *Ulster Unionism and the Peace Process* (Basingstoke: Palgrave Macmillan, 2006) and Henry Patterson and Eric Kaufmann, *Unionism and Orangeism since 1945: The Decline of the Loyal Family* (Manchester: Manchester University Press, 2007) for two recent analyses of Ulster Unionism. See Gerard Murray's *John Hume and the SDLP: Impact and Survival in Northern Ireland* (Dublin: Irish Academic Press, 1998) and Enda Staunton's *The Nationalists of Northern Ireland, 1918–1973* (Dublin: Columba Press, 2001) for historical overviews of Northern Irish nationalism.

3 The most recent and most thorough general history of nationalism and republicanism in Ireland is Richard English, *Irish Freedom: The History of Nationalism in Ireland* (London: Macmillan, 2006). A large number of political science works and political histories exist on republicanism. Henry Patterson's *The Politics of Illusion: A Political History of the IRA* (London: Serif, 1997) remains a key text; Ed Moloney's *A Secret History of the IRA* (London: Penguin Books, 2002) contains a wealth of hitherto unpublished interview material, as does Rogelio Alonso's *The IRA and Armed Struggle*

(London: Routledge, 2006), which is a perceptive analysis of the IRA's campaign and a subtle but devastating deconstruction of its war aims and strategies.
4 See Graham Spencer, *The State of Loyalism in Northern Ireland* (Basingstoke: Palgrave Macmillan, 2008), for a recent appraisal of Loyalism.
5 Moreover, despite the importation of a repertoire of protest methods and language from the American Civil Rights Movement, the position of Catholics in Northern Ireland could not realistically be compared to that of African Americans. See Thomas Hennessey, *Northern Ireland: The Origins of the Troubles* (Dublin: Gill & Macmillan, 2005).
6 See Aaron Edwards and Cillian McGrattan, *The Northern Ireland Conflict: A Beginner's Guide* (Oxford: Oneworld, 2010), 12–15.
7 Aaron Edwards, "Abandoning Armed Resistance? The Ulster Volunteer Force as a Case Study of Strategic Terrorism in Northern Ireland," *Studies in Conflict & Terrorism* 32, no. 2 (2009): 150.
8 UVF Statement, May 1966, cited in ibid., 151.
9 Randall D. Law, *Terrorism: A History* (Cambridge: Polity, 2009), 3.
10 Paul Bew and Gordon Gillespie, *Northern Ireland: Chronology of the Troubles: 1968–1999* (Dublin: Gill & Macmillan, 1999), 148.
11 Henry Patterson, *Ireland since 1939: The Persistence of Conflict* (Dublin: Penguin, 2006), 216.
12 Des Wilson interview, 26 June 2000, Dúchas Living History Project, Falls Community Council.
13 Edwards and McGrattan, *Northern Ireland*, 57–80.
14 Brian Hanley, "'I Ran Away?' The IRA and 1969," *History/Ireland* 17, no. 4 (2009): 24–7.
15 Timothy Shanahan, *The Provisional IRA and the Morality of Terrorism* (Edinburgh: Edinburgh University Press, 2009), 22.
16 Malachi O'Doherty, *The Trouble with Guns: Republican Strategy and the Provisional IRA* (Belfast: Blackstaff Press, 1998).
17 Hennessey, *Northern Ireland*, 394.
18 Patterson, *Ireland*, 220–1.
19 Cillian McGrattan, *Northern Ireland, 1968–2008: The Politics of Entrenchment* (Basingstoke: Palgrave Macmillan, 2010), 58–61.
20 Cillian McGrattan, *Memory, Politics and Identity: Haunted by History* (Basingstoke: Palgrave Macmillan, 2013), 65.
21 P. J. McLoughlin, *John Hume and the Revision of Irish Nationalism* (Manchester: Manchester University Press, 2010), 217.
22 Cited in McGrattan, *Northern Ireland*, 62.
23 Michael Burleigh, *Blood and Rage: A Cultural History of Terrorism* (London: Harper Press, 2008), 306–7.
24 Edwards and McGrattan, *Northern Ireland*, 71.
25 Cell structures of this sort were first pioneered by the People's Will in Russia and the Irish Republican Brotherhood (for more on this, see Chapter 12 in this volume by Benjamin Grob-Fitzgibbon) and later used by the National Liberation Front in Algeria in the 1950s.
26 Charles M. Drake "The Provisional IRA: A Case Study," *Terrorism and Political Violence* 3, no. 1 (1991): 44.
27 Cited in McGrattan, *Memory*, 89.
28 Paul Bew, *Ireland: The Politics of Enmity, 1789–2006* (Oxford: Oxford University Press, 2007), 529.
29 Edwards and McGrattan, *Northern Ireland*, 86.
30 Edwards and McGrattan, *Northern Ireland*, 88–9.
31 McGrattan, *Northern Ireland*, 161.
32 Ruth Dudley Edwards, "Being an Irish Republican Means Never Having to Say You're Sorry," *The Telegraph*, November 2, 2012. Available at: http://blogs.telegraph.co.uk/news/ruthdudleyedwards/100187539/being-an-irish-republican-means-never-having-to-say-youre-sorry/ (accessed November 28, 2012).
33 See Ian Wood, "Loyalist Paramilitaries and the Peace Process," in *The Northern Ireland Question: The Peace Process and the Belfast Agreement*, ed. Brian Barton and Patrick J. Roche, 181–204 (Basingstoke: Palgrave Macmillan, 2009).
34 Ian Paisley [Jr.], "Peace Must Not Be the Victim of International Justice," *New York Times*, March 16, 2012. Available at: www.nytimes.com/2012/03/17/opinion/peace-must-not-be-the-victim-of-international-justice.html?_r=2& (accessed November 28, 2012).

35 Richard English, *Armed Struggle: The History of the IRA* (Basingstoke: Macmillan, 2003), 318.
36 MI5, the British internal security agency, reportedly continues to dedicate between around a quarter and a fifth of their budget to tackling dissidents. The secretary of state for Northern Ireland recently issued the government's latest assessment of terror threats from Northern Ireland, which, she said, remain "severe." Her report stated that there were twenty-four "national security attacks" during 2012 compared with twenty-six in 2011 and ten this year so far. However, these attacks, she said, seem to be targeted at killing prison and police officers. Punishment beatings, she said, "continued with involvement by both republican and loyalist groups." House of Commons, Official Report, June 17, 2013. Available at: www.publications.parliament.uk/pa/cm201314/cmhansrd/cm130717/wmstext/130717m0001.htm#13071774000260 (accessed August 1, 2013).
37 Cillian McGrattan, "'Moving On': The Politics of Shared Society in Northern Ireland," *Studies in Ethnicity and Nationalism* 21, no. 1 (2012): 183.
38 Northern Ireland Assembly, Committee for Finance and Personnel, Official Report (Hansard), "Civil Service (Special Advisers) Bill: Ann Travers/Catherine McCartney Briefing," November 21, 2012, 6. Available at: www.niassembly.gov.uk/Documents/Official-Reports/Finance_Personnel/2012-2013/121121_CivilServiceSpecialAdvisersBillAnnTraversCatherineMcCartneyBriefing.pdf (accessed November 28, 2012).

Further reading

Aughey, Arthur. *The Politics of Northern Ireland: Beyond the Belfast Agreement*. Abingdon: Routledge, 2005.

Barton, Brian, and Patrick J. Roche, eds. *The Northern Ireland Question: The Peace Process and the Belfast Agreement*. Basingstoke: Palgrave Macmillan, 2009.

Bew, Paul, Peter Gibbon, and Henry Patterson. *Northern Ireland, 1921–2001: Political Forces and Social Classes*. London: Serif, 2002.

Breen-Smyth, Marie. *Truth Recovery and Justice after Conflict: Managing Violent Pasts*. Abingdon: Routledge, 2007.

Dixon, Paul, and Eamonn O'Kane. *Northern Ireland since 1969*. London: Longman, 2011.

Edwards, Aaron, and Cillian McGrattan. *The Northern Ireland Conflict: A Beginner's Guide*. Oxford: Oneworld, 2012.

Hennessey, Thomas. *A History of Northern Ireland, 1921–1996*. Dublin: Gill & Macmillan, 1997.

McGarry, John, and Brendan O'Leary. *Explaining Northern Ireland: Broken Images*. Oxford: Blackwell, 1995.

McGrattan, Cillian, and Elizabeth Meehan, eds. *Everyday Life after the Irish Conflict: The Impact of Devolution and Cross-Border Cooperation*. Manchester: Manchester University Press, 2012.

Ruane, Joseph, and Jennifer Todd. *The Dynamics of Conflict in Northern Ireland: Power, Conflict and Emancipation*. Cambridge: Cambridge University Press, 1996.

Tonge, Jonathan. *The New Northern Irish Politics?* Basingstoke: Palgrave Macmillan, 2005.

15

VIOLENCE IN THE ALGERIAN WAR OF INDEPENDENCE

Terror, counter-terror, and compliance

Martin C. Thomas

The French colony of Algeria was agonizingly put together; it was even more agonizingly dissolved. Slow to take shape, slower still to disintegrate, it was always subject to bitter conflict within and between its communities of European settlers and indigenous North Africans. Early decades of military rule shaded into a protracted colonization process that hardened the territory's inter-communal antagonisms and ensured that colonial Algeria was also steeped in violence. Estimates vary, but some calculate that 825,000 Algerians fell victim to violence during the first forty-five years of colonial conquest after 1830, a figure broadly comparable to the number who succumbed to famine and epidemic disease over the same period.[1] Figures for the number of Algerians who perished during the country's War of Independence between 1954 and 1962 range from 300,000 to one million within a population then approaching nine million.[2]

Is this enough to warrant a discrete chapter on forms of terroristic conflict at the end of Algeria's anti-colonial struggle? It is not difficult, after all, to find evidence of bitter contestation, systemic discrimination, even mass killing elsewhere in the history of modern European colonialism. What set French Algeria apart are matters of scale and form. On the one hand, as suggested by the estimates above, levels of Algerian political violence and criminality during the 130 years or so of French rule were persistently high, especially in those areas worst affected by European expropriation of Muslim landholders.[3] On the other hand, rural dispossession, forcible relocation of populations, insurgency, and repression defy characterization as mere by-products of colonial domination. Each registered major societal effects, changing Algeria's socio-economic structure, refashioning its demography, and promoting new forms of cultural resistance. Registering its impact cumulatively (by quantity) and longitudinally (over time), violence became integral to the political culture of an intensely conflicted society.[4]

Viewed from a more theoretical perspective, these societal divisions promoted what sociologists, following the insights of Roberta Senechal de la Roche and Donald Black, have described as the preconditions for a particular "social geometry" of collective violence. Terroristic violence, defined here in Black's terms as "self-help by organized civilians who covertly inflict mass violence on other civilians," took root in colonial Algeria because the socio-economic gulf between Europeans and Algerians, their profound cultural division (in sociological terms, their relational distance), and the resultant inequality between them fostered the social polarization necessary to make political violence more likely. Despite falling infant mortality rates and net rises in overall living standards in the ten years between the end of World War II and the beginning of Algeria's War of Independence, the inequality gap between settlers and Algerians, starkest of all in the rural interior, remained yawningly wide. Educational provision, particularly for Muslim girls and Algerians of high school age, was scanty; industrial concentration minimal. Each severely limited Algerians' capacity for wealth creation and social advancement.[5] Meanwhile, the physical interactions between Algerians and settlers in the colony's cities, market towns, farms, government offices, police stations, and other workplaces created multiple opportunities – and offered multiple sites – for terroristic acts.[6]

Before plunging into the details of Algeria's independence struggle, we should pause briefly to consider what is being analyzed. If we are to follow Omar Carlier's suggestion that an understanding of Algerian colonial violence must include not only physical assaults against the person but resource denial and the psychological violence done to individuals and groups by means of discrimination and threat, then it becomes harder to confine a review of terror and terrorism in French Algeria to the colony's final years of outright war.[7] Certainly, it was during that conflict that a non-state group committed to the achievement of national independence employed varying forms of lethal violence – assassinations of alleged "collaborators," bombings of symbolically meaningful sites, guerrilla warfare and, above all, the elimination of political opponents – to force an end to colonial rule. (See Chapter 25 by Geraint Hughes in this volume for broader consideration of these forms of insurgent violence.) But anti-colonial, if not anti-state, violence was already endemic in Algerian society, its emergence the product of the particular socio-economic conditions and cultural discriminations created by French colonialism. Thus, while focusing primarily on the fight for independence between 1954 and 1962, this chapter will also consider the roots of terror and terrorist methods – French and Algerian – over the preceding decades of colonialism in Algeria.

A single item of legislation makes the case for such an approach. On April 23, 1955, six months after the nationalist rebellion began in earnest, specially constituted army courts in Algeria were authorized to punish terrorist attacks under the terms of a law passed 110 years earlier, in 1845, at the height of the army's suppression of last-ditch resistance to French colonization. The first tranche of martial law restrictions imposed after the start of the Algerian War of Independence was thus emblematic of colonial Algeria's continuity of terror, re-designating a broad range of criminal acts as inherently subversive.[8] Within a year, these restrictions were extended colony-wide. Recourse to martial law, in effect a return to military governance in response to colonial civil war, signified that the French state would tackle Algerian insurgency, not by means of criminal law and judicial punishment but by waging war against it. More than anything else, it was this French counter-terror that set the violence of the Algerian War apart.[9]

Pre-histories of the Algerian War

Harmonious inter-ethnic cooperation was hardly the norm in early colonial Algeria. The first wave of colonization in the 1830s and early 1840s was only made possible by the suppression of indigenous resistance through a campaign combining scorched-earth violence with population displacement. Both were directed by the French military administration, first under Marshal Bertrand Clauzel and then his successor, Thomas-Robert Bugeaud.[10]

Tensions over land rights and native policy between Algeria's army governors and the growing numbers of European colonists arriving and organizing in Algeria, in turn, shaped official attitudes toward those members of the indigenous elite recruited as junior administrators and Muslim judges (*qadis*) in the first decades of conquest.

The incidence of rural uprisings and the terms on which indigenous auxiliaries were co-opted to the military administration were subject to constant change and mirrored local variations in landholding and levels of agricultural self-sufficiency among the Muslim peasantry.[11] But only after the vicious repression of Muhammad al-Muqrani's 1871 revolt in Kabylia, Algeria's Berber heartland, did the balance of power in the colony's politics shift decisively away from the military and toward the settlers. Their representatives challenged the army's preference for the conciliation of a Muslim administrative elite.[12] By the 1880s, the army's *bureaux arabes* were therefore at odds with the expanding cadre of European mayors installed across Algeria's rural interior.[13] For every Muslim official or cleric willing to acknowledge French authority in Algeria as in other Muslim territories, the silent Muslim majority remained overwhelmingly hostile to French infringement of sacred spaces, Muslim religious observance, and Islamic juridical authority.[14]

Regional disorders and urban protests there certainly were, notably as a result of wartime demands imposed on Algerian families and conscripts in World Wars I and II, but it would be many years before Algeria erupted into sustained anti-colonial revolt. The May 1945 rebellion centered in and around the towns of Sétif and Guelma in eastern Algeria began with political violence against a particular type of state, one that relied on its security forces and information-gathering networks to maintain hierarchies of colonial privilege to the exclusion of the indigenous majority. This violence was pre-planned – and it was meant to instill terror. The action was coordinated by nationalist activists from two main groups – the integral nationalist Algerian People's Party (rendered in French as the PPA) and its more moderate cousin, the Democratic Union for the Algerian Manifesto (the UDMA in French). It was also backed by local supporters of Algeria's leading Muslim cultural association. They, in turn, endorsed a number of Muslim scouting organizations, teenagers and young men from which took part in street protests and mob violence. Between May 8 and 11, 1945, 102 Europeans were killed, several of them in acts of collective violence against specific targets, such as settler farms, isolated gendarmerie posts, and public transport.[15]

The rapid escalation in violence against settlers was facilitated by an extraneous factor: once the social constraints implicit in the threat of state sanction collapsed, the punitive costs of violent disorder – briefly – disappeared. Muslim attacks on settlers were instrumental. They served a distinct ideological purpose, demonstrating the PPA's capacity to harness popular anger over long-standing economic hardship and cultural marginalization to nationalist political ends. Yet the violence was also functional insofar as attacks on infrastructure, police buildings, and farmsteads destroyed the fabric of French hegemonic control, thereby fulfilling the political objectives of PPA-directed insurrection. The specific forms that this Algerian violence took were rooted in a colonial culture that imposed sharp divisions between Europeans and indigenous Algerians, meaning that demonstrative violence against French settlers signified much more than an act of physical violation. Inexcusable though the initial May 1945 killings were, they were politically legible: targeting particular sites and persons was attacking the colonial state.

This was not how the French authorities locally, in Algiers, and in Paris interpreted events. The original violence of what would come to be known as the Sétif uprising was instead categorized as not merely unjustified but intrinsically emotive, even irrational.[16] The reality was quite different. The dismissal of grassroots nationalism as unrepresentative and unjustifiable pointed to the cognitive inability of French colonial officials to make sense of popular fury. Contrary to the administration's assertion that the pre-rebellion status quo signified some sort of normative standard to which Algeria could and should revert, the explosion of political violence in 1945 augured a future in which inter-communal peace would be harder to sustain. The Algiers government's intelligence sources actually confirmed this. Indeed, an overhauled Algerian colonial security establishment operated from an assumption of communal irreconcilability in the months ahead. Collated into a discrete account of violence foretold, police statements, trial reports, and political intelligence suggested that erstwhile practices of internal colonial policing were insufficient. Relying on local informants to explain rumors circulating in mosques, cafés, and other meeting points; searching for signs of dissent in the local-language press and other forms of Algerians' cultural expression from work-songs to itinerant theaters; even occasional police raids against known nationalist organizers: these methods were once the basis for a more economical recourse to security force repression.[17]

No longer: after Sétif, colonial and police officials gathered covert intelligence more systematically, exploiting it as the pretext for Draconian judicial powers that marked a de facto reversion to martial law. Thereafter, the army worked more closely with police and gendarmerie commanders in refining techniques of social control that included collective punishments against rural settlements, mass detention (predominantly of young adult males), and the use of torture in suspect interrogations.[18] Days after the Sétif outbreaks, the provisional coalition government in Paris, with Charles de Gaulle at its head, reversed course over Algeria. Anticipating the end of World War II and a transition to more "normal" peacetime conditions, instructions had been prepared to end the internment of nationalist activists and ease wartime restrictions on freedom of movement. Instead, both were shelved.[19] In their stead, locations were agreed for improvised detention centers required to hold the thousands of political prisoners, principally agricultural workers caught up in the violence of May 1945.[20] Even when most of these detainees were freed under a political amnesty in March 1946, the Algiers colonial government could authorize mass arrests and preventive detentions on suspicion of seditious activity.[21]

Meanwhile, consistent with the official characterization of the 1945 rebellion as egregious and unwarranted, the retributive violence of army, police, and settler vigilantes was sanitized in official reportage, depicted not as an instrument of terror but as a curative procedure to restore orderliness to colonial society. These medical metaphors could, of course, be interpreted in contrary fashion. As the Martinican psychiatrist Frantz Fanon, a literary protagonist of Algerian revolution, insisted, violence and psychiatric disorder were inherent to the lived experience of colonialism: the individual and communal antagonisms in colonial society were inseparable from the racial iniquities underlying it.[22] An uncomfortable truth here is that these diametrically opposing viewpoints – one official and pro-settler, the other revolutionary and anti-colonial – each concluded that recourse to extreme violence was the logical path to follow, whether for French security forces or for the impoverished Algerian majority.

Beginnings: the War and the FLN

Taking the long view of social conflict in colonial Algeria, Sétif could be read as the bridge spanning the grinding poverty and political crackdowns of the Depression and wartime years and the eventual resumption of nationalist rebellion in November 1954. Certainly, for those who directed the latter, the repression of 1945 and after was a formative experience.

The National Liberation Front (rendered as the FLN in French) was a small, secretive organization at its inception in late 1954. Its core membership, including the "historic nine" leaders who comprised the movement's executive, were young men from both Arab and Berber families, predominantly in eastern Algeria. Most became politically active during World War II or, more often, immediately after it, typically as young militants within the integral nationalist group, the Movement for the Triumph of Democratic Freedom (in French: MTLD). For some, the lived experience of participating in the first anti-colonial rebellion of the post-World War II era – the Sétif uprising of May 1945 – was pivotal. Others were radicalized by the ensuing French crackdown. Its severity was such that the Algerian death toll probably exceeded 7,000 civilian victims, possibly many more. Arguably, Sétif's aftermath did more to radicalize the emerging generation of nationalist activists than the preceding wartime years.[23] Yet both were of a piece insofar as World War II had also brought martial law, political crackdowns, mass arrests, and chronic foodstuff shortages rendered more iniquitous by a highly racialized system of colonial rationing. Not surprisingly, then, young Algerian adults flocked to join the MTLD's nascent paramilitary wing, the Special Organization (in French: the OS). Secretive and broadly modeled on French-style resistance groups, the OS also marked out several future FLN leaders. So, too, did years of imprisonment, whether in the lockdown following Sétif or as a result of French infiltration and dismantlement of the OS in the early months of 1950.[24] Years spent in imperial prisons, as in the case of other insurgent movements from the Viet Minh to the Provisional IRA, recast the emergent FLN leadership's sense of its distinctiveness, of its mission, and of its methods.

Initially describing itself as an Algerian Revolutionary Committee, by the time the FLN mounted its first wave of insurgent attacks on All Saints Day, November 1, 1954, several broad outlines of future Algerian nationalist strategy were falling into place. A vertical structure connecting the FLN executive to its local party cells and regional guerrilla army (the Army of National Liberation – the ALN) commands promoted an authoritarian style but also chronic, often violent factional rivalry.[25] Belief that eventual independence could only be secured by and through the people impelled the movement towards popular mobilization and – often coercive – community activism.[26] Acts of demonstrative, public violence were central to these objectives. Bombings of government buildings, police outposts, and electricity sub-stations illustrated the FLN's capability to strike at the heart of colonial administration and infrastructure. Killings of government servants pointed to the prohibitions to come. Yet, to characterize this as just terrorism misses the political point.

Rather, targeted violence was integral to FLN strategies of social control within the Muslim community. Some of these were consensual: charitable redistribution of money and food as well as rudimentary local welfare, for instance. But others were proscriptive: bans on certain employments, on social contact with Europeans, and on the purchase of French and other Islamically proscribed (*haram*) goods. FLN fund-raising was pivotal. Regular cash-flow made possible these apparently contradictory traits of voluntarism and coercion. Small-scale weekly donations built up the movement's growing war chest and, equally significant, lent tangible force to the FLN's political claims. Boycotts, bans, and fund-raising were more than just materially useful. Rather, they were developed at first to counter French official claims that the FLN was marginal and unrepresentative and, subsequently, to underline the singularity of the movement's nationalist vision and the illegitimacy of its local rivals.[27]

Central to everything was compliance. Party members, male and, even more so, female, were subject to rigorous, sometimes arbitrary, discipline.[28]

Lauded in FLN–ALN pronouncements for their heroism and purity, Algerian women were also expected to conform to FLN dictates and the patriarchal norms of Muslim society.[29] Penalties for transgression and, most especially, for perceived fraternization or disloyalty were as arbitrary as they were severe.[30] Their Algerian confrères were required, at minimum, to remain silent and, at maximum, to sacrifice home, family, and career to the national cause. After a decisive shift in their insurgent strategy – and in the balance of influence between the FLN's increasingly foreign-based political leadership and its domestic guerrilla bands – in November 1956 new recruits were instructed to abide by the ALN's "ten commandments." Alongside appeals to bravery, sacrifice, and unwavering commitment to total independence were instructions to deepen FLN influence in society, to gather intelligence from – and about – the local population, and to adhere to a strict discipline in conformity with Islamic ethics.[31]

At much the same time, ALN commanders of *wilaya 4* in the Algiers hinterland codified the penalties for "basic misdemeanors" (*fautes simples*), such as slovenliness or poor hygiene, and those for *fautes graves* for which demotion, public denunciation (and resultant ostracism), and a death sentence could be applied without right of appeal.[32] Other regional commanders issued similar edicts, whose scope progressively widened. By September 1957, for example, the fighters in neighboring *wilaya 3* (north-central Algeria) faced capital punishment not just for desertion or insubordination but for "conduct deleterious to ALN and Islamic principles" and for "all anti-patriotic activity damaging to unity or general discipline."[33] At a more mundane level, the nationwide proliferation of local fund collectors, the widening boycotts on French goods and services, as well as the indictments against inter-communal mixing offered day-by-day proof of the FLN's growing reach into Muslim society. Little by little, the movement changed the rhythms of workaday life for Algerians and, by extension, their settler neighbors.

Politically, a commitment to highly centralized but collective decision-making enabled the party executive to define early priorities, operational practices, and targets. Admittedly, rivalries and disagreements within and between the movement's political and military wings had ramifications for the direction and intensity of the revolutionary violence to come. Challenged by the hard-pressed ALN front-liners, from 1956 onward the party executive would, in addition, splinter into competing factions based inside and outside Algeria. Ideologically, the FLN oscillated between a color-blind vision of socialist modernity and a reanimation of Algeria's Muslim, Arabo-Berber culture. The FLN did not espouse holy war, nor was it wholly secular or un-Islamic.[34] This basic ambiguity affected the way that violence unfolded insofar as it determined the nature and scope of the revolutionary transformation sought.

On certain fundamentals, though, executive members and ALN commanders did agree. Less critical than the fine detail of their visions for a post-independence future was the message, unvaryingly repeated, that there could be no compromise short of total national independence.

This demand was also disseminated internationally. The FLN's first proclamation pleaded for United Nations support. Identifying with other North African national movements, it also represented Algeria's claim for freedom as universalist in its core aspiration that all people be accorded equal rights under law.[35] By 1955, the movement was working closely with the Arab League and consolidating its relationship with India, Indonesia, and Gamal

Abdul Nasser's Egypt, the trio of states that set the early agenda for the Non-Aligned Movement at its defining conference at Bandung in May of that year.[36] FLN Algeria, then, although not yet constituted as a government-in-waiting, still less a state, was there at the inception of the new global radicalism that, after the Bandung moment, would be defined as Third Worldism.[37] A slow-burn whose intensity would become clearer over time, this internationalization of the conflict was something that successive French governments and military commanders proved powerless to reverse. Between 1955 and 1962, the FLN cause went global, part of a transnational interest in de-colonization as a central preoccupation of governments and peoples throughout the developing world.[38]

Meanwhile, the FLN continued to make its mark domestically. Determined to sever connections between Algeria's nine-tenths Muslim majority and the colonial administrative apparatus, alleged "collaborators" with the French authorities would remain acutely vulnerable to intimidation, violence, or assassination. Local government officials, public sector workers, village headmen, and, of course, Muslim police and paramilitary auxiliaries were all judged culpable if they chose to remain in post. These were the individuals most liable to face what Jeff Goodwin has dubbed "categorical terrorism," the exemplary violence of a revolutionary movement determined to use the killing of its domestic political opponents to sway the opinion of the surrounding community.[39] White settlers, while undoubtedly subject to FLN violence throughout the war, were never the movement's principal targets. Most Europeans in Algeria lived in the colony's coastal cities – Oran, Algiers, and Bône (Annaba) – where, in the war's first years, FLN violence was sporadic. Even settler landowners and farmers, although more exposed to attack, were of secondary concern to FLN strategists, if only because their opposition to Algerian nationalism could be taken for granted. More imperative was to secure the allegiance or, perhaps more accurate, the obedience of their Algerian farmhands and of their village neighbors. Only then could the developing strategy of rural insurgency be effectively pursued.

It is well here to recall the conflict's military asymmetries. These were typified by the presence of an experienced French colonial army, the availability of large-scale troop reinforcements from the mainland as well as from other French African territories, and huge technological advantages of firepower, aerial surveillance, and helicopter transport. None of these could ALN units hope to match. Guerrilla units relied instead on concealment, something that required the provision of food and shelter within "safe zones" in Algeria's highland interior. Networks of local support were thus fundamental to ALN capacity to make rural insurgency self-sustaining. Breaking these hand-to-mouth connections between fighters and villagers by extension became a critical aspect of French military patrolling. Victory for either side, in other words, rested on the efficacy of their population control. On this depended the ALN's ability to evade capture and the FLN's capacity to build alternative structures of state power – fiscal, juridical, and military – with which Algerians would eventually align, whether from conviction or fear. Conversely, destroying what their opponents in the French army's psychological warfare bureau labeled the FLN's Political and Administrative Organization underpinned a widening counter-terror as security forces tried to dismantle the FLN's local networks of material sustenance and political support.[40] It was in these local contests for civilian allegiance, most of them fought out in agricultural market centers, farming villages, and remote upland hamlets far from media scrutiny, that the greater part of the war's violence – and its abuses – occurred. If this could be defined as terrorism, it is because its primary targets were the people themselves.

Some of the FLN's practices drew on perceived lessons of recent Chinese and, more especially, Vietnamese communist victories through adaptive practices of Maoist revolutionary war. Some built on precedents closer to home. Of these, three stood out. One was the developing rural insurgencies and urban protest movements in neighboring French-ruled Morocco and Tunisia. In Tunisia, especially, a rural insurgency impelled the French authorities towards a fundamental revaluation of the costs of clinging on after 1954.[41] Second was the propagandist styling of Egypt's Free Officers' Movement, increasingly identifiable with the charismatic figure of Nasser and his calls to pan-Arabist unity, socialist modernization, and militant rejection of Western imperialism. Third were the diverse appeals to Algerian wage workers, to rural laborers, and to devout Muslims made by home-grown communist, nationalist, and Islamist groups of much older vintage than the FLN. Each conveyed powerful lessons to FLN organizers despite the fact that all were considered their bitter rivals. With organizational roots traceable to the interwar period, the first-wave Algerian nationalists loyal to Messali Hadj offered a model for the implantation of party networks at the local levels of workplace, café, and mosque. The Algerian Communist Party, although tainted in FLN eyes by association with its larger French Communist cousin, illustrated the utility of cellular organization, clandestine action, and targeted propaganda.[42] Islamist groups, among which the Association of Reformist Ulama and various Muslim scouting bodies stood out, confirmed that appeals to devotion, ascetic virtue, and cultural pride resonated strongest for many Algerian Muslims of all ages.[43]

Massacres and terror

Massacres and, more particularly, the retributions they provoked, changed the cultural codes, the military rules, and the permissible limits to mass violence within Algeria's population and between French security forces and local insurgents.[44] Why this should be the case demands closer examination. The demonstrative horror of mass killing intentionally shrinks the middle ground. It destroys the prospects for compromise, denying political and personal space to the otherwise non-committal.[45] Meant to polarize, its violence signifies the ultimate rhetoric of shock. Little wonder that historians of Algeria's war concur that massacres served as decisive conflict escalators, whether strategically, symbolically, or both.

This escalatory dynamic is something with which analysts of asymmetric warfare, civil conflict, and revolutionary insurgencies – not to mention the witnesses to such dreadful events – have long been familiar.[46] Less well understood is why the perpetrators of such actions should resort to such extreme terror in furtherance of their cause. Did the mass killing of civilians during the Algerian War represent an extreme iteration of what Charles Tilly identified as the "repertoire of protest"? Were such actions rendered logical to some because opportunities to influence the actions of the state were otherwise so limited? In the Algerian Revolution as in the French, violence remained a last resort for the marginalized, not the first.[47] To follow Tilly's logic, the repressive action of colonial authorities rather than the FLN's ruthlessness must be held accountable for precipitating such killings.[48] This was certainly the FLN's assertion but it was hotly contested by French authorities at the time.

The intended audience of such actions must be central to resolving this argument. Equally, the focus on massacres, while discomfiting, makes sense insofar as widespread killing, usually of unarmed victims, generated rumor, contestation, even conspiracy theories about FLN power and, by extension, the colonial state's incapacity. This was something that, in turn, drove French military commanders to harsher collective punishments in their efforts to destroy the FLN's Political and Administrative Organization at village and city district level.[49] A parallel war of information and disinformation accelerated this discursive restructuring of the relative strengths of the war's antagonists. It signified what Paul Silverstein, in the context of Algeria's civil war of the 1990s, has characterized as "vernacular knowledge production," a means of communication with discrete rules and styles of diffusion. The rhetorical depiction of massacres and the rumors they generated, in other words, gave rise to a new "regime of truth." Regardless of its objective veracity, this was one that the French authorities struggled to control.[50] Driven by growing popular unease about FLN ruthlessness and security force retribution, rumors became harder to refute. Spreading such rumors – or constructing this form of vernacular knowledge – was not just part of the rhetorical battle between French and Algerian version of events, it was integral to the FLN's psychological warfare.[51]

Alongside the analysis of massacres as calculated practices of demonstrative violence – and, as such, phenomena without any uniquely "colonial" dimension – it is useful, if also troubling, to recall that such mass killings in de-colonization conflicts spoke to at least three discrete audiences. The first of these was the surrounding civilian population to whom demonstrations of collective punishment functioned for all warring parties as a means to deny agency, either by silencing dissent or by narrowing the spaces, public and private, in which the non-committal could avoid taking sides.[52] The resultant slippage between civilian neutral and compromised inhabitant was itself part of the terror process. For the greater probability was not that you and yours would be caught in a cross-fire between rebels and security forces. It was, rather, that one might be identified by informants, ostracized by one's community, or targeted by combatants for actions that, in less tense societies, would seem unremarkable: a conversation overheard, a commercial transaction involving French-made goods, a readiness to provide shelter to a relative known to have taken sides. The grinding fear that resulted did more, perhaps, than anything else to erode everything from social cohesion to mental health amongst populations that conventional accounts of the Algerian War might simply label "civilian."[53] One index of such collective anxiety is provided by the outpouring of retributive violence at the war's conclusion. In the summer months after the Algerian cease-fire, tens of thousands of Algerian auxiliary troops, the *harkis* – at the time still denied access to France whether as citizens, ex-servicemen, or refugees – faced retribution, incarceration, or worse.[54] Massacres of these alleged collaborators were commonplace.[55] Many killings, it appears, were carried out by Algerian civilians anxious to demonstrate their support for the victorious FLN.[56]

The second target audience were the political elites and domestic publics of the imperial power. All strata of the metropolitan population, regardless of status, gender, or age, might be counted here. For all of them, the increasing incidence of Algerian massacre, the press commentaries it elicited, and the lingering unease it created, changed the terms by which the colonial presence was evaluated and understood. On the one hand, insurgent groups employed massacres, whether of civilians (and settlers especially) or of captured military personnel, to cultivate revulsion, war fatigue, and consequent public pressure for withdrawal. What for some remained incomprehensibly extreme violence still conveyed its own logic, fostering the sense that compromise was impossible and lasting colonial attachment unachievable.[57] The uncompromising rhetoric of extreme violence thereby generated what political scientist Gil Merom describes as a "normative gap" between the French state's official justifications for the war and the wider French public's growing sense that the conflict's costs were intolerable.[58] On the other hand, imperial security forces undertook retributive violence to affirm the colonial state's greater capability to impose, or re-impose, security on its own terms. Retributive certainly, state violence of this type was also inherently reactive. It was less a means to sustain social control in the affected colony than a bid to convince home audiences that the advances made by insurgents in attaining such local control could yet be reversed.[59]

To audiences "back home" increasingly exasperated by the war, such violence thus became integral to a rhetoric that combined appeals to European supremacy and technological superiority with an invocation of triumph over adversity, of redoubtable and immovable colonial power.[60] In the first case, massacre conjured an image of anti-colonial violence as the expression of unstoppable popular will. In the second, retributive violence was invoked as the restoration of security, of certainty, of the triumph of military modernity over colonial primitivism. For officers of the highly influential army psychological warfare bureau, physical violence was useful as a means of psychological coercion. Tightly regulated and carefully measured, both were integral to the social control over Algerian minds and bodies that they sought to achieve.[61]

Increasingly, however, it was the third audience of massacres that acquired singular importance, not least in the Algerian case. For it was in its appeals to a transnational and global audience of "world opinion" that the FLN most comprehensively defeated the French security forces.[62] The FLN persuaded much of the foreign press, the majority of UN General Assembly members, and countless observers the world over that it would win. Its strategies for doing so made violence the decisive rhetorical tool, albeit in different ways. Ruthless elimination of local opponents confirmed the movement's unalterable resolve. Shining a light on human rights abuses and the increasing disproportionality of French military reprisal against Algerian civilians mocked French insistence that right was on their side. The FLN's rhetorical story here was less one of justice denied to colonial subjects than of the compelling force of nationalist mobilization. In this reading, the FLN alone represented the "tide of history" inexorably rising towards sovereign independence. Reduced to its essence, the message was clear: the FLN was the future, French colonial authority the past. Framed in the light thrown upon it by Fanon's laudatory writings, FLN violence was in every sense liberating, both for the nation and the individual actors involved. Indeed, the movement's public defense of their actions became what Robert Malley calls "hallmarks of an assertive Third Worldism." Violence was, at once, culturally deterministic and politically inescapable. It remade Algerian society by purging it of its colonial remnants. And it affirmed the irreversible course of national liberation.[63] French military violence was, by extension, repressive and backward. Whether perpetrating massacre or provoking French military counter-killings, the FLN retained a singularity of purpose that the French civil and military authorities, their ethical restraint cast aside, had lost. These theoretical perspectives may go some way to explaining the first decisive escalation in the terrorism of the Algerian War: the Constantine massacres of August 1955.

August 20, 1955, was a memorable date in the calendar of anti-colonial nationalism in the French Maghreb. It marked the second anniversary of the French deposition of Morocco's pro-independence Sultan Mohammed V, an event that had come to symbolize the arrogance and arbitrariness of imperial rule in the region. With Morocco's nationalists planning simultaneous attacks, the FLN was gifted the opportunity to demonstrate its transnational connections and increase the depth of its public support – and all of this barely a month before the UN General Assembly was due to go into session with France's colonial misrule high on its agenda.[64] There were other, more negative reasons to target civilians by their ethnicity and political affiliation. Within Algeria, the revolution's first phase of targeted ambushes and assassinations seemed to be running out of steam. Tougher legal restrictions in notorious rebel "zones" and an influx of army and police reinforcements were taking effect. Some FLN leaders were hesitant. But, determined to strike a blow for their uncompromisingly militant version of total insurgency, FLN supporters in north-eastern Algeria struck. Mass killing of civilians, largely avoided hitherto, marked a vile but decisive statement of intent. The reprisals sure to follow would restore the revolution's impetus by driving Algeria's differing ethnic communities apart. With violence so embedded, no one within the affected communities could avoid taking a position. Governor-General Jacques Soustelle's integrationism would be dead; its underlying goal of lessening inter-communal difference exploded.[65]

In a south-easterly arc from the coastal city of Philippeville to the town of Guelma, coordinated attacks were launched against European settlers, workers, and their families. Also targeted were colonial government installations, alleged Muslim "collaborators," and supporters of the Mouvement National Algérien (MNA), still the FLN's main local rival. In the larger urban centers of Constantine and Philippeville, ALN fighters placed bombs, threw grenades, and, in some cases, held out, urban-guerrilla style, against the army reinforcements sent in to restore order.[66] In most cases, though, the violence was more demonstratively terroristic. Settlers, young and old, were hacked down in full gaze of the local population. And in the worst single instance of anti-European violence, at El Halia, an isolated pyrite mining settlement, the thirty-six victims were butchered and left to be discovered by security forces, administrators, and press.

Planned by the FLN's northern Constantine (*wilaya* 2) leaders, Youssef Zighoud and Lakhdar Ben Tobbal, these killings performed four functions. The first was political: an unequivocal show of mass support for the FLN intended to silence more moderate voices and marginalize the MNA. The people, it would be claimed, were solidly behind the FLN's first "general offensive," something that the United Nations would do well to note.[67] The second was strategic: an act of provocation sure to trigger retribution, thus driving settlers and Algerians apart. This would, in turn, discredit France in Algeria, making it harder still for the undecided to avoid taking sides. Intrinsic to this logic was the expectation that martial law, hitherto confined to Kabylia and the Aurès mountains, the highland centers of the first-stage rebellion, would be applied nationwide. The third function was cultural: affirmation that bonds of lineage, clan, and community amongst Algerian town dwellers and villagers could be harnessed to the cause of anti-colonial revolution. And the fourth was rhetorical: a replication of the abortive uprising in eastern Algeria a decade earlier, the repression of which had catalyzed the original foundation of the FLN. The Constantine massacres of 1955, in other words, served symbolically to reaffirm the FLN's regional roots, the implacability of the surrounding population, and the irreversibility of the war's outcome. If, for some, the August 1955 killings marked the true beginning of the Algerian War, for others they proved that it could have only one end.[68]

The war expands

As predicted by the FLN's eastern regional leadership, the upturn in security force violence after the Constantine massacres demonstrated that the escalatory dynamics of terror and counter-terror began to accelerate from late 1955 onward. Still rigidly hierarchical in its internal organization, the FLN's political militancy was matched by the willingness of

ALN commanders to enforce popular compliance, employing violence to do so. The movement's uncompromising politics and the widening scope of its attacks meanwhile impelled the government in France to concede greater powers to the in situ army command at the direct expense of civil administration in Algiers. Martial law, still confined in spring 1955 to the rebellion's epicenters in eastern Algeria and the highlands of Kabylia, was, as we shall see, extended throughout the colony twelve months later. With extended military powers, the scope for searches and arbitrary arrests, mass detentions, and other juridical abuses increased. While military rule might not be inherently abusive, its logic was to make speedy punitive action the measure of success. Its tragic irony was thus that heightened violence was rendered justifiable as the quickest route to peace; it was order before reform.

Martial law represented the suspension of basic protections to the individual – even those at the bottom of colonial society. An abnegation of established criminal and civil law, a marginalization of civil authority, and a nullification of due process, the creeping extension of military powers inevitably fostered a more permissive environment for human rights violations, whether committed against civilian victims of army round-ups or against ALN detainees denied the status of recognized combatants. Once reinforcement made possible the adoption of search-and-destroy tactics by the colonial army's professional units, the indiscriminate targeting of populations accused of concealing ALN supporters set in train a pattern of army violence that would spiral ever upwards between 1955 and 1959. But strategic choices were also the product of the military culture peculiar to any military organization. In this respect, too, the French security forces in Algeria were institutionally inclined towards a counter-terror solution.

After the events of August 1955 in Constantine, there was no question that the French colonial military would cleave towards a "minimum force" solution to the Algerian rebellion. Collectively, the professional regiments that policed France's overseas empire constituted an institution whose identity, ethos, and practices were fundamentally different from those of the metropolitan French army. Most of the former had served extensively in the recent conflict in Indochina. Long-service troops, noncommissioned officers (NCOs), and officers nursed the scars of defeat by the Viet Minh. Many had been on active colonial service for eight years by the time the Algerian conflict erupted. Ruminations on how and why the Indochina War was lost generated dangerous conclusions that were quickly transposed from Vietnam to North Africa. Certain that throughout their time in Southeast Asia the colonial security forces had been inadequately supported and poorly understood by government and people "back home" in France, the troops reassigned to restore order in Algeria were never likely to be restrained in their application of force.

Grudging respect for the Viet Minh's adaptation of Maoist ideas of revolutionary war inclined numerous colonial army officers to write approvingly about manipulative techniques of population control. Several of these army strategists had been incarcerated in Vietnamese prison camps during the Indochina War. Their own experiences of deprivation and torture as instruments of brainwashing and forcible indoctrination were not forgotten; far from it. Members of the army's psychological warfare bureau were intellectually drawn to the Viet Minh's techniques of manipulation, which were adapted for use both against the army's FLN opponents and against Algerian society more widely. Among the officer corps deployed to Algeria in late 1954 and 1955, the conviction was that the civilian population not only spawned but gave succor to guerrilla forces. This, in turn, informed a reductive logic that conflated civilian and combatant, rendering the pursuit of counter-terror among Algerian Muslim communities permissible. The boundaries between the legal protection of civilian populations and unlimited pursuit of armed insurgents collapsed within weeks of the war's outbreak.[69] The army's first major sweep of the war, Operation Orange Amère (bitter orange) launched in late December 1954, was indicative. Hundreds of nationalist sympathizers in the regional capitals of Algiers, Constantine, and Oran were herded onto army transports, turned over to police custody, and tortured. Wanted individuals in the rebellion hot spots of Kabylia and the Aurès Mountains were more likely to be shot on sight.[70]

Identification of the civilian as the critical object of army action was reflected in the legislative apparatus erected by French governments, colonial authorities, and the army command in Algiers in their quest to root out the FLN. Martial law, as we have seen, was introduced relatively early, in April 1955 within the interior regions where rebel attacks were most intense. Military law – exemplified by the suspension of habeas corpus, the introduction of fast-acting military courts, detention without trial, and the criminalization of meetings, actions, and statements deemed a threat to social order – corroded the limited rights of association and expression that Algerians had previously enjoyed.[71] On March 16, 1956, Guy Mollet's Socialist-led government secured overwhelming support in the French National Assembly for a raft of emergency legislation that heralded the introduction of conscripts to the Algerian War, further eroded the rights of detainees, and prefigured the delegation of police powers to army commanders in the field. Collectively, the so-called Special Powers signified the government's acquiescence to the demands of military rule in Algeria. Through these dubious legal means, the door was opened to a counter-terror strategy built on the twin foundations of intelligence-led operations and harsher methods of population control. Over subsequent months and years, torture became a key weapon of the former strategy; forcible relocation of rural populations to internment camps the principal instrument of the latter.[72]

The Battle of Algiers, 1957

Algeria's further descent into terror and counter-terror was symbolized by the infamous "Battle of Algiers." Although the Algerian capital witnessed its share of killings in the war's first years, it was only in 1956 that the city's FLN commanders turned to urban guerrilla warfare. Street shootings of administrators and police personnel, strict enforcement of the party's boycotts, tighter political control over the capital's Muslim districts, and bombings of chosen sites frequented by Europeans brought the conflict to the colony's administrative core.[73] But it was the FLN's call for a January 1957 general strike, an action designed to show a global audience that Algeria's people stood behind the FLN, that triggered the opening of the decisive ten-month "Battle." As we will see, that decisiveness derived less from the FLN's more systematic resort to urban bombings as an instrument of insurgency than from the French army's casual disregard of human rights in its efforts to bring that insurgency to an end. In a war the outcome of which would be governed by shifting patterns of allegiance – of Algerians to their nationalist leadership; of French society to its republican institutions; of wider global opinion to a continued European colonial presence in the global South – it was the army's violence against civilian detainees, rather than the more limited FLN terrorism, that wrought the more fundamental change.

The process began in January 1957 when elite units of General Jacques Massu's 10th Parachute Division transferred into the capital. Massu's forces were among those compelled to pull out from operations in Egypt during the abortive Suez operation against Colonel Nasser's Cairo regime two months earlier. This was an action that Guy Mollet's government chose to justify as a war against the FLN's major Arab backer. Massu's commanders, assigned sweeping police powers by Robert Lacoste, head of the Algiers civil administration, on January 7, were adamant that they should not be thwarted again. Initially ordered to break the strike by forcing shops and businesses to resume work after stoppages began on January 28, their broader task was to destroy Saadi Yacef's urban guerrilla network. Dismantling the cellular structure of party activists, fund-raisers, and bombing teams within the FLN's "Autonomous Algiers Zone" (ZAA in French) looked difficult because it depended on securing actionable information from ZAA members who typically only knew their immediate contacts.[74] Massu's senior officers thought otherwise. They exploited their devolved powers to their fullest extent. And they drew on funds of bitter experience garnered from World War II and the more recent conflict in Indochina. Their unscrupulousness in extracting intelligence from detainees turned the conflict in Algiers from a battle against individual terrorist acts into a larger terror program with a momentum of its own – so much so that surviving members of the FLN's executive Coordination Committee went into exile after their colleague Larbi ben M'Hidi was killed by his army captors in February.

M'Hidi's murder epitomized the moral bankruptcy of a repressive colonial strategy whose extreme violence eclipsed the horror of the urban terrorism it was supposed to eradicate. The army's decision to use torture to extract the desired information from detainees before their comrades could evade capture turned what was advertised as the restoration of order to a terrorized city into systematic violations of human rights that utterly delegitimized the French presence in Algeria.[75] Far from stemming these abuses, the French judicial system became complicit in the process. Some 1,500 death sentences were pronounced. Of these, nearly 200 were carried out, often on the basis of evidence extracted by professional torturers well versed in dehumanizing physical and sexual violence.[76] Thousands of Algiers residents, only a minority directly linked to FLN actions, were swept up in mass arrests. Many were tortured. Countless more were "disappeared" by Massu's loyal lieutenants. Revelations about the scale of the "dirty war" in Algiers helped bring other abuses to light. Especially powerful was a shocking compilation of soldiers' testimonies, the vividness of which made plain that what was being practiced in Algiers had been going on in the Algerian countryside for years. Edited by an anti-war committee of French university professors, *Reservists Testify* (*Des Rappelés témoignent*) cataloged the army's violations of basic human rights with graphic details of on-the-spot execution of Algerian suspects and shootings of unarmed civilians during village searches.[77]

Viewers of Gillo Pontecorvo's 1966 film dramatizing the Battle of Algiers will recall that women couriers – Djamila Bouazza, Djamila Bouhired, and Zohra Drif among others – brought terrorist bombing to the capital's European districts. Defying the gendered norms of a conflict that objectified Algerian women as subordinate to the will of the warring parties, they placed bombs in station foyers, bars, and sports stadiums. Terroristic to be sure, this bombing campaign was devastatingly effective as an indicator to the world of the FLN's singularity of purpose.[78] Although most of these bombers were soon captured (and tortured), inhabitants of the city's Muslim quarters were made to pay. The hillside *casbah*, home to Yacef's clandestine terror network until his capture in late September, came under siege. Thanks to relentless FLN publicity and, later, Pontecorvo's film (made with the assistance of the post-independence Algerian regime), this battle within a battle transformed global attitudes toward the war. Defiance of curfews and other restrictions by the *casbah*'s embattled population came to symbolize a people's resolve to resist colonial oppression.

Perhaps fittingly, it was in the *casbah* that the Battle of Algiers reached its bloody climax. It was there on October 8, 1957, that Massu's troops surrounded the hideout of the only surviving team of FLN bombers. Neither the group's leader, Ali Ammar (better known by his nom de guerre, Ali La Pointe); his bomb maker, Mahmoud Bouhamidi; their female assistant, the teenaged Hassiba Ben Bouali; nor Yacef Omar, a boy of only twelve years old, heeded calls to surrender. All four perished when army engineers blew up their apartment in an explosion so large that it destroyed the entire block, killing an additional seventeen residents. This last bombing of the Battle of Algiers spoke volumes about the disproportionate violence of a colonial system whose military enforcers had been freed to act without political checks or ethical balances.[79] For the time being, the guerrillas' state-within-a-state in the *casbah*'s narrow confines was disrupted. But the FLN's global standing was transformed. In the eyes of much of the world, the sacrifices of the Battle of Algiers were those of a representative resistance movement, not a terrorist organization. France's political counter-claims and, more specifically, French military actions were thereby undermined.[80] The presumptive connection between restoring colonial authority and promoting constructive social reform was made to appear ridiculous.

The role of violence in victory and defeat

As the Battle of Algiers indicated with sickening clarity, the military authorities presumed that the effectiveness of counter-terror rested, in part, on demonstrating a capacity to outdo FLN displays of retributive violence. Responding to nationalist tactics of street killings, throat cutting, and the dumping of alleged traitors in sight of their local community, army units, too, began putting executed "terrorists" on display. In a practice refined against Madagascan rebels in 1947–8, torture victims in the Algerian capital were dropped from army helicopters into the sea. But the site chosen was anything but remote. Dropping the bodies into Algiers harbor in the knowledge that they would be washed ashore, the city's army command reversed the logic of "disappearing" victims. Secrecy was abandoned, even mocked, making such actions demonstrative and thus terroristic. Similar practices were adopted elsewhere. In February 1959, inhabitants of the city of Tiaret in western Algeria were made to file past a recently executed FLN supporter, Maarouf Addi, his corpse bearing a sign in French and Arabic describing his crime. A month later, two more prominent FLN leaders, Amirouche and Si Haouès, were killed in a firefight with French troops at Djebel Tsaneur. The army then ordered their bodies embalmed. Each was then put on public display as symbolic evidence that the era of FLN control was over.[81]

Grotesquely macabre, these activities seemed at variance with the rising transnational chorus of disapproval for European colonialism, a hostility that increased markedly after seventeen newly independent – and predominantly Francophone – states joined the UN in 1960. Less persuasive is the suggestion that the French army's unrestrained war against the FLN was somehow out of kilter with President Charles de Gaulle's gradual shift toward negotiation, settlement, and withdrawal from Algeria. Quite the reverse: during 1959 and beyond, Gaullist eagerness to bring France's draining commitments in North Africa to an end required commanders on the ground to widen their offensive against the ALN in order to coax the nationalists' political leaders into talks. Only when the full extent of de Gaulle's readiness to sever France's Algerian connections became apparent during 1960 and, still more so, 1961 did army and settler hard-liners irredeemably turn against the Paris authorities, adopting the strategy of counter-terror and political murders identifiable with the Secret Army Organization (the OAS, from its French name). With a negotiated settlement crystallizing over the winter of 1961–2, the OAS became the foremost perpetrator of assassinations, urban bombings, and terror threats.[82]

This is not somehow to let the FLN off the terrorism hook. Consensual nationalist politics were inhibited by a number of factors: the fragmentation within the FLN's political leadership after French capture of four of its senior figures in October 1956, the flight overseas of remaining executive members during 1957, and the emergence of splinter groups within various ALN *wilaya* commands as the ground war intensified.[83] Murderous rivalry with Messali Hadj's MNA meanwhile continued unabated, ultimately leading to the deaths of thousands in Algeria and within Algerian immigrant communities in France as well.[84] The killing of political opponents, vicious purges within the ALN, and, above all, the emergence of Abdelhafid Boussouf's ruthless security apparatus at the movement's heart pointed to the uncompromising repression characteristic of certain phases of FLN rule after independence.[85] Even so, it bears repeating that in the last days of Algeria's colonial history, as at its beginning, the principal source of terrorist violence was French in origin, as exemplified by the OAS campaign to derail negotiations in the war's final months.

Conclusions

The development of terroristic violence, actual and psychological, during Algeria's War of Independence is inherently unsettling, not least in the conclusions that it suggests. What emerge clearly are the parallels and reciprocity between FLN and French security force terror practices. Originating in ideas of psychological warfare and population control, the two were mutually reinforcing. Their impact was registered in systematic human rights abuses and forcible relocation of populations. Marnia Lazreg, an astute commentator on the sociology of terror in the Algerian War, captures another dangerous symbiosis, this one between government in Paris and military authority in Algiers. It, too, generated heightened violence as the army accrued greater repressive powers:

> The militarization process also created a relationship of dependency between the military and civil authorities.... The state thus had its dirty job done by the military, which it, when need arose, strategically and formally sought to restrain in the name of civil rights. Conversely, the military did its best to administer, control, and manage a civilian population in the name of the state, which it then blamed for its incompetence, and in a quid pro quo demanded silence regarding its methods of "pacification". In this sense, militarization enabled the state to violate its own legal safeguards by proxy, through the army, and the army to unleash repressive methods, which it justified as necessary correctives to the state's incompetence.[86]

The escalatory dynamic underlying the French terroristic practices that Lazreg describes raises an obvious question: how did things come to this? At the level of abstraction, political scientist Christian Davenport offers answers. So it is perhaps worth concluding our survey by considering them. Davenport identifies two distinct categories of threats in the literature on state repression: those that are "behavioral" and others that are "systemic." The first of these relates to sustained actions taken by groups of people, usually against political leaders or economic overseers. Examples include street protests, boycotts, strike actions, and guerrilla warfare. Clearly the organized Algerian violence of proto-nationalist groups as well as that of their FLN successor fits this model. The second refers to large-scale changes taking place within a particular polity, perhaps as part of broader social or international change. These dangers are less tangible. They do not involve individuals opposing authority but, rather, refer to structural change liable to render the state more insecure.

Governments often respond to such threats with political repression for which analysts have applied one or more of three main categories. These are, first, "negative sanctions." A broad term, it includes the curtailment of political freedoms and civil liberties and may include arrests for specific public order or seditionist offences, the imposition of martial law, and aggressive state propaganda. Here, too, pre-rebellion Algeria, with its prolonged periods of political lockdown and martial law, witnessed precisely such negative sanctions imposed by colonial government. But negative sanctions usually stop short of major acts of violence. This, then, brings us to the second category: "state terror," by which is meant the use of force, violence, or the threat that these methods will be applied. Third are human rights abuses, which may range from killings and disappearances to torture and arbitrary imprisonment. Both the second and third categories of systemic threat were increasingly in evidence during the eight years of the Algerian War after 1954. Davenport argues that all three responses to systemic threat amount to the same thing: government operations designed to enforce popular compliance and political quiescence. His insight is that the distinction between the non-violent repression of negative sanctions and systemic state terror may collapse in practice.[87] Again, transposing these models to late colonial Algeria, we find a massive French security apparatus confronted with FLN insurgency unable and unwilling to resist such a collapse from taking place. The result was a vicious cycle of terror and counter-terror from which only France's final 1962 withdrawal offered some way out.

Notes

1 Kamel Kateb, *Européens, "indigènes," et juifs en Algérie, 1830–1962* (Paris: EINED, 2001), 47, 66–7; also cited in Benjamin Claude Brower, *A Desert Named Peace: The Violence of France's Empire in the Algerian Sahara, 1844–1902* (New York: Columbia University Press, 2009), 4.
2 Guy Pervillé, "La guerre d'Algérie: Combien de morts?" in *La guerre d'Algérie, 1954–2004: la fin de l'amnésie*, ed. Mohammed Harbi and Benjamin Stora, 476–93 (Paris: Robert Laffont, 2004).
3 Brower, *A Desert Named Peace*, 6–26; Olivier Le Court Grandmaison, *Coloniser, Exterminer: Sur la guerre et l'Etat colonial* (Paris: Fayard, 2005), 146–56, 219–23; and Jean-Pierre Peyroulou, *Guelma, 1945: une subversion française dans l'Algérie coloniale* (Paris: Editions la découverte, 2009), 61–73.
4 For reflections on violent social conflict in post-colonial Algeria, see: James D. Le Sueur, *Algeria since 1989: Between Terror and Democracy* (London: Zed Books, 2010), especially chapters 4–8.
5 Daniel Lefeuvre, *Chère Algérie: comptes et mécomptes de la tutelle coloniale, 1930–1962* (Paris: SFHOM, 1997), 52, 196–9, 215–19, 240–2.
6 Roberta Senechal de la Roche, "Collective Violence as Social Control," *Sociological Forum* 11, no. 9 (1996): 118–22; and Donald Black, "The Geometry of Terrorism," *Sociological Theory* 22, no. 1 (2004): 18–22.
7 Omar Carlier, "Violence(s)," in Harbi and Stora, *La guerre d'Algérie*, 347–67.
8 Marnia Lazreg, *Torture and the Twilight of Empire: From Algiers to Baghdad* (Princeton, NJ: Princeton University Press, 2007), 36–7; for the 1840s repression, see Jennifer E. Sessions, *By Sword and Plow: France and the Conquest of Algeria* (Ithaca, NY: Cornell University Press, 2011), chapter 2; and William Gallois, *A History of Violence in the Early Algerian Colony* (Basingstoke: Macmillan, 2013), 100–21 passim.
9 M. L. R. Smith and Sophie Roberts, "War in the Gray: Exploring the Concept of Dirty War," *Studies in Conflict & Terrorism* 31, no. 5 (2008): 377–98; see also Chapter 25 by Geraint Hughes in this volume.
10 John Ruedy, *Modern Algeria: The Origins and Development of a Nation* (Bloomington: Indiana University Press, 1992), 55–76; Brower, *A Desert Named Peace*, 21–41 passim.

11 Peter von Sivers, "Rural Uprisings as Political Movements in Colonial Algeria, 1851–1914," in *Islam, Politics, and Social Movements*, ed. Edmund Burke III and Ira M. Lapidus, 41–57 (Berkeley: University of California Press, 1988).
12 Peter von Sivers, "Insurrection and Accommodation: Indigenous Leadership in Eastern Algeria, 1840–1900," *International Journal of Middle East Studies* 6, no. 3 (1975): 259–75; and Ruedy, *Modern Algeria*, 76–9.
13 Ibid., 262. Von Sivers notes that by 1884 there were 289 mayors in Algeria, a larger administrative group than the army's Arabist specialists.
14 Allen Christelow, "The Mosque at the Edge of the Plaza: Islam in the Algerian Colonial City," *Maghreb Review* 25, no. 3–4 (2000): 296–8.
15 Jean-Louis Planche, *Sétif 1945: Histoire d'un massacre annoncé* (Paris: Perrin, 2006), 114–43.
16 Archives Nationales (AN), Paris, F60/871, no. 1319/CIE renseignements, "A/S état d'esprit dans la région de Sétif," May 28, 1945.
17 AN, F60/871, Constantine prefecture, CIE, "Rapport mensuel d'information sur l'activité indigène, Département de Constantine, période du 22 avril au 21 mai 1945."
18 Archives Nationales d'Outre-Mer (ANOM), Aix-en-Provence, Gouvernement Général d'Algérie (GGA), 40G/32, "Règlement relatif au fonctionnement et à l'emploi des Groupes Mobiles de Police Rurale," Algiers GGA, May 12, 1955.
19 ANOM, GGA, Centre d'Informations et d'Etudes (CIE)/Services des Liaisons nord-africains (SLNA), Carton 40G/32: Police activité 1945–50, no. 675, Adrien Tixier circular, August 30, 1945: "Mesures préparatoires en vue de la suppression de l'internement administratif."
20 ANOM, GGA, 40G/32, no. 16,570/POL/A, Ministre plenipotentiaire, GGA, to Commandant, 19e Corps d'Armée, May 20, 1945, "A/S/ de la création d'un Centre de Séjour Surveillé destiné à recevoir des internés politiques musulmans."
21 ANOM, GGA, 40G/32, no. 1899, Police des Renseignements Généraux, district de Constantine, to Prefect, March 18, 1946: "Libération des détenus de la Maison centrale de Lambèse"; GGA SIDM, "Note pour M. Paye," Alger, May 23, 1946.
22 Keller, *Colonial Madness*, 161–5; see also Hussein Bulhan, "Revolutionary Psychiatry of Fanon," in *Rethinking Fanon: The Continuing Dialogue*, ed. Nigel Gibson, 141–75 (Amherst, NY: Humanity Books, 1999).
23 Gilbert Meynier, *Histoire intérieure du FLN, 1954–1962* (Paris: Fayard, 2002), 59–84.
24 Ministère des Affaires Etrangères, sous-série: Algérie 1944–1952, vol. 6, Algiers prefecture, "Note sur l'activité subversive du PPA-MTLD dans le Département d'Alger," n. d. 1950.
25 Meynier, *Histoire intérieure*, 137–41.
26 Meynier, *Histoire intérieure*, 153–6, 213–17.
27 "Directives politiques de l'état-major général aux wilayas, 1er semester 1961," in *Le FLN: Documents et histoire, 1954–1962*, ed. Mohammed Harbi and Gilbert Meynier (Paris: Fayard, 2004), 305–6 (hereafter, *FLN:Documents*).
28 Neil MacMaster, *Burning the Veil: The Algerian War and the 'Emancipation' of Muslim Women, 1954–1962* (Manchester: Manchester University Press, 2009), 322–41.
29 ALN "Directives sur la propagande et la contre-propagande au sujet de la femme," 2e semestre, 1958, in *FLN:Documents*, 609–12.
30 "Directives de la wilaya 2 mintaqa 2 sur les 'questions féminine' et le mariage," in *FLN:Documents*, 614–15.
31 "Les dix commandements de l'A.L.N.," November 30, 1956, in *FLN:Documents*, 52.
32 "Règlement intérieur de la *wilaya* 4," 2e semestre 1956, in *FLN:Documents*, 53.
33 *Wilaya 3*, "Règlement intérieur de l'A.L.N.," n.d. September 1957, in *FLN:Documents*, 64–6.
34 "Procès-verbal du congrès de la Soummam," August 20, 1956, and "Directives au responsables des biens *habûs* en *wilaya 3*," n.d 1956 or 1957, in *FLN:Documents*, 241–5, 586–7.
35 Martin Evans, *Algeria*, 114–16.
36 Christopher J. Lee, "Between a Moment and an Era: The Origins and Afterlives of Bandung," in *Making a World after Empire: The Bandung Moment and its Political Afterlives*, ed. Christopher J. Lee (Athens: Ohio University Press, 2010), 9–15.
37 Odd Arne Westad, *The Global Cold War: Third World Interventions and the Making of Our Times* (Cambridge: Cambridge University Press, 2005), 100–5.

38 Support from revolutionary Cuba provides one such instance among many: see Piero Gleijeses, "Cuba's First Venture in Africa: Algeria, 1961–1965," *Journal of Latin American Studies* 28, no. 1 (1996): 159–63.
39 Jeff Goodwin, "A Theory of Categorical Terrorism," *Social Forces* 84, no. 4 (2006): 2027–31.
40 Lazreg, *Torture*, 16, 29–30.
41 Martin Thomas, *The French North African Crisis: Colonial Breakdown and Anglo-French Relations, 1945–1962* (Basingstoke: Palgrave-Macmillan, 2000), 47–51, 58–68.
42 Allison Drew, *We Are No Longer in France: Communists in Colonial Algeria* (Manchester: Manchester University Press, 2014).
43 James McDougall, *History and the Culture of Nationalism in Algeria* (Cambridge: Cambridge University Press, 2006), especially chapters 2–4.
44 Joshua Cole, "Massacres and their Historians: Recent Histories of State Violence in France and Algeria in the Twentieth Century," *French Politics, Culture, and Society* 28, no. 1 (2010): 107–22.
45 My thanks to Talbot Imlay for his insights on this point.
46 Outstanding examples include: Elisabeth Wood, *Insurgent Collective Action and Civil War in El Salvador* (Cambridge: Cambridge University Press, 2003); Greg Grandin, *The Last Colonial Massacre: Latin America in the Cold War* (Chicago: University of Chicago Press, 2004); Stathis Kalyvas, *The Logic of Violence in Civil War* (Cambridge: Cambridge University Press, 2006); and Daniel Branch, *Defeating Mau Mau, Creating Kenya: Counterinsurgency, Civil War, and Decolonization* (Cambridge: Cambridge University Press, 2009).
47 Micah Alpaugh, "The Politics of Escalation in French Revolutionary Protest: Political Demonstrations, Non-Violence and Violence in the *grandes journées* of 1789," *French History* 23, no. 3 (2009), 336–8.
48 Charles Tilly, "Collective Violence and Collective Loyalties in France: Why the French Revolution Made a Difference," *Politics & Society* 18, no. 4 (1990): 527–52.
49 Lazreg, *Torture*, 29–30.
50 Paul A. Silverstein, "An Excess of Truth: Violence, Conspiracy Theorizing and the Algerian Civil War," *Anthropological Quarterly* 75, no. 4 (2002): 643–6.
51 Charles-Robert Ageron, "La 'guerre psychologique' de l'Armée de libération nationale algérienne," in *La guerre d'Algérie et les Algériens, 1954–1962*, ed. Ageron (Paris: Armand Colin, 1997), 227–9.
52 Neil MacMaster, "The 'Silent Native': *Attentisme*, Being Compromised, and Banal Terror during the Algerian War of Independence, 1954–1962," in *The French Colonial Mind*, vol. 1, *Mental Maps of Empire and Colonial Encounters*, ed. Martin Thomas, 283–303 (Lincoln: University of Nebraska Press, 2011.
53 Ibid., 289–90, 293–6.
54 Evans, *Algeria*, 325–8.
55 Sylvie Thénault, "Massacre des *harkis* ou massacres de *harkis*? Qu'en sait-on?" in *Les Harkis dans la colonisation et ses suites*, ed. Fatima Besnaci-Lancou and Gilles Manceron, 81–91 (Paris: Éditions de l'Atelier, 2008).
56 Matthew Connelly, *A Diplomatic Revolution: Algeria's Fight for Independence and the Origins of the Post-Cold War Era* (New York: Oxford University Press, 2002).
57 For a meticulous reassessment of the socio-cultural conditions that generated Algerian colonial violence, see: James McDougall, "Savage Wars? Codes of Violence in Algeria, 1830s–1990s," *Third World Quarterly* 26, no. 1 (2005): 117–31.
58 Gil Merom, *How Democracies Lose Small Wars: State, Society, and the Failure of France in Algeria, Israel in Lebanon, and the United States in Vietnam* (Cambridge: Cambridge University Press, 2004), 78–80, 121–35.
59 Martin Thomas, "Colonial Violence in Algeria and the Distorted Logic of State Retribution: The Sétif Uprising of 1945," *Journal of Military History* 75, no. 1 (2011): 523–56; and Lazreg, *Torture*, 61–72.
60 As Jean-Pierre Rioux has stressed, opinion poll evidence confirms that, by 1956, most French voters favored peace and withdrawal from Algeria. The essential dilemma for political historians of the war is to reconcile the existence of this "pacifist majority" with the conflict's escalating violence between 1956 and 1962: see Rioux, "Les Français et la guerre des deux Républiques," in Harbi and Stora, *La Guerre d'Algérie, 1954–2004*, 17–26.

61 Richard C. Keller, *Colonial Madness: Psychiatry in French North Africa* (Chicago: University of Chicago Press, 2007), 152–60.
62 This is the core argument of Connelly, *A Diplomatic Revolution*.
63 Robert Malley, *The Call from Algeria: Third Worldism, Revolution, and the Turn to Islam* (Berkeley: University of California Press, 1996), 104.
64 Martin Thomas, "France Accused: French North Africa before the United Nations, 1952–1962," *Contemporary European History* 10, no. 1 (2001): 95, 103–4. More broadly, see Matthew Connelly, "Rethinking the Cold War and Decolonization: The Grand Strategy of the Algerian War for Independence," *International Journal of Middle East Studies* 33, no. 2 (2001): 223–37.
65 Le Sueur, *Uncivil War*, 31, 98.
66 Merom, *How Democracies Lose Small Wars*, 100. On August 22, Edgar Faure's government announced both an additional 100,000 troops for Algeria and the retention on active service of a further 120,000.
67 Mahfoud Kaddache, "Les tournants de la Guerre de libérationau niveau des masses populaires," in Ageron, *La guerre d'Algérie et les Algériens*, 52–4.
68 Benjamin Stora, "Le massacre du 20 août 1955: Récit historique, bilan historiographique," *Historical Reflections* 36, no. 2 (2010): 97–107.
69 Troubling implications of the combatant/non-combatant divide are explored in Maja Zehfuss, "Killing Civilians: Thinking the Practice of War," *British Journal of Politics and International Relations* 14, no. 3 (2012): 424–38.
70 Lazreg, *Torture*, 36.
71 Lazreg, *Torture*, 35–8.
72 Lazreg, *Torture*, 44–50.
73 Guy Pervillé, "Une capital convoitée," in *Algier, 1940–1962: Une ville en guerres*, ed. Jean-Jacques Jordi and Guy Pervillé (Paris: Autrement, 1999), 138–44.
74 Christopher Cradock and M. L. R. Smith, "'No Fixed Values': a Reinterpretation of the Influence of the Theory of *Guerre révolutionnaire* and the Battle of Algiers, 1956–1957," *Journal of Cold War Studies* 9, no. 4 (2007): 68–105.
75 The most thoughtful account of this process remains Raphaëlle Branche, *La torture et l'armée pendant la Guerre d'Algérie: 1954–1962* (Paris: Gallimard, 2002).
76 Sylvie Thénault, *Une drôle de justice: Les magistrats dans la guerre d'Algérie* (Paris: La Découverte, 2001), part II.
77 Le Sueur, *Uncivil War*, 150–62.
78 Djamila Amrane, *Des femmes dans la guerre d'Algérie: Entretiens* (Paris: Karthala, 1994); and Judith Surkis, "Ethics and Violence: Simone de Beauvoir, Djamila Boupacha, and the Algerian War," *French Politics, Culture, and Society* 28, no. 2 (2010): 38–55.
79 Evans, *Algeria*, 201–21.
80 Mahfoud Kaddache, "Le tournants de la Guerre de liberation au niveau des masses populaires," in Ageron, *La guerre d'Algérie et les Algériens*, 55–6, 61, 67.
81 Lazreg, *Torture*, 54–5.
82 Olivier Dard, *Voyage au coeur de l'OAS* (Paris: Perrin, 2005), deuxième partie.
83 For instance, "Rapport du Colonel Amirouche sur le 'complot bleu' en *wilaya* 3," August 3, 1958, in *FLN:Documents*, 546–50.
84 Linda Amiri, "La guerre dans la guerre: la lutte entre le FLN et le MNA en métropole, 1954–1962," *Cahiers d'Histoire sociale* 23 (2004): 81–109.
85 "Le système de terreur de Boussouf vu par Fathi Al Dib," in *FLN:Documents*, 310–14.
86 Lazreg, *Torture*, 60.
87 Introduction to Christian Davenport, ed., *Paths to State Repression: Human Rights Violations and Contentious Politics*, 5–17 (Oxford: Rowman and Littlefield, 2000).

Further reading

Brower, Benjamin Claude. *A Desert Named Peace: The Violence of France's Empire in the Algerian Sahara, 1844–1902*. New York: Columbia University Press, 2009.

Connelly, Matthew. *A Diplomatic Revolution: Algeria's Fight for Independence and the Origins of the Post-Cold War Era*. New York: Oxford University Press, 2002.
Evans, Martin. *Algeria: France's Undeclared War*. Oxford: Oxford University Press, 2013.
Kalyvas, Stathis. *The Logic of Violence in Civil War*. Cambridge: Cambridge University Press, 2006.
Lazreg, Marnia. *Torture and the Twilight of Empire: From Algiers to Baghdad*. Princeton, NJ: Princeton University Press, 2007.
MacMaster, Neil. *Burning the Veil: The Algerian War and the 'Emancipation' of Muslim Women, 1954–1962*. Manchester: Manchester University Press, 2009.
Merom, Gil. *How Democracies Lose Small Wars: State, Society, and the Failure of France in Algeria, Israel in Lebanon, and the United States in Vietnam*. Cambridge: Cambridge University Press, 2004.
Meynier, Gilbert. *Histoire intérieure du FLN, 1954–1962*. Paris : Fayard, 2002.
Peyroulou, Jean-Pierre. *Guelma, 1945: une subversion française dans l'Algérie coloniale*. Paris: Editions la découverte, 2009.

16

ISRAEL AND THE PALESTINE LIBERATION ORGANIZATION

Boaz Ganor

The state of Israel has dealt with political violence and Palestinian terrorism since its inception and even prior to its establishment. As one of the countries most affected by terrorism, Israel has become something of a test case and model for democratic countries dealing with terrorism. Israel was among the first countries challenged by a wide variety of terrorist attacks, including hijackings, explosions in crowded areas, hostage barricade situations, suicide attacks, and more. The scale of these terrorist attacks and the numbers of casualties have varied over the years, depending on the operational capacity of the Palestinian terrorist organizations and their level of motivation at a given time and the result of the regional processes and the interests of their patron states.

The challenge of terrorism in Israel after the establishment of the state (1948–67)

The violent conflict between the Jewish and Arab inhabitants of Israel–Palestine started way before the founding of Israel in 1948. As a protest against the waves of Jewish immigration in the 1930s and following internal processes within the Palestinian population, a general Arab strike was declared in 1936. The end of the strike after six months marked the beginning of three years of violent rebellion against British rule and the Jewish population. The suppression of the rebellion by the British and World War II brought relative peace, which was preserved until November 1947. (For more on Mandatory Palestine before the creation of the state of Israel, see Chapter 12 by Benjamin Grob-Fitzgibbon, "Britain's Small Wars: The Challenge to Empire, 1881–1951," in this volume.)

Immediately after the declaration of independence of the state of Israel in 1948, the neighboring Arab countries together with the local Palestinian community provoked an overall war against the newborn state. After the cessation of the hostilities, Israel had to deal with a new type of military challenge – the intrusion of *fedayeen* into Israeli territory. These were Palestinian refugees, terrorists, and criminals who infiltrated Israel for the purposes of agricultural cultivation, theft, robbery, looting, killing, assassination, and sabotage. From 1951 to 1955, more than 800 Israeli civilians and soldiers were injured by *fedayeen* penetrating the border (mostly from Jordan), with the casualty count rising every year.[1] These penetrations into Israel over the years challenged Israel's sovereignty within its territory and tarnished the status quo Israel was attempting to achieve through stabilizing its borders.

Against this backdrop, the idea began to develop that there was a need to conduct offensive retributions against various targets in Arab countries, in order to alleviate, at least partially, the anxiety and low morale of Israeli citizens affected by the infiltrations. Thus, efforts were directed towards deterrence and retaliation against Arab and Palestinian targets outside Israeli territory, consistent with the notion of "an eye for an eye and a tooth for a tooth." Initially, these operations were carried out by one local commander or another and were usually directed against Arab or Palestinian targets that had a direct or symbolic connection with the preceding attacks, or against the bases from which the attacks were launched.

In an attempt to formalize the sporadic Israeli military activity, in 1953 the Israeli Defense Forces (IDF) established a military unit trained for special missions under the command of Major Ariel Sharon. This unit came to be called Unit 101. Its successes and Israel's retaliatory actions strengthened morale amongst the Israeli public and IDF soldiers, who began to volunteer for the unit. Nevertheless, the activities of the *fedayeen* continued to expand every year. After several months of activity and dozens of reprisals, Unit 101 consolidated with the paratroopers' battalion in early 1954. The Israeli retaliatory operations at that time were not necessarily designed to deter the *fedayeen* but to punish them and their supporters as an end unto itself.[2]

One retaliatory operation that drew widespread criticism and protest took place against the village of Kibiya on October 14, 1953. It followed a month of attacks on Israel that had killed twelve people, culminating two days earlier when infiltrators from Jordan threw a hand grenade into a house in the Jewish town of Yehud, killing a mother and her two young children. The response was immediate. Unit 101, reinforced by paratroopers, raided three Jordanian villages, including Kibiya, the main target of the operation since it was an established *fedayeen* base. The paratroopers blew up several houses and dozens of villagers were killed, despite claims by the force commanders that the residents had been warned before the attack.

The Kibiya operation was a turning point, spurring the Jordanian Legion into intensive efforts to curb infiltration: Jordanian forces in the West Bank were increased, more ambushes and patrols were carried out to prevent *fedayeen* infiltrations, orders were given restricting the activities of citizens along the border, and penalties were imposed for those who violated these orders.[3] In the years that followed, the number of thefts, robberies, and casualties along this border decreased.

The shock caused by the mass strike on Palestinian civilians brought on a gradual shift in the focus of Israeli's retaliatory efforts, from civilian targets to military ones. Indeed, from the end of 1954, retaliation efforts focused on the bases and training facilities of the Palestinian organizations themselves and even more so on military and police installations of the Arab countries, principally Jordan and Egypt, which sponsored the *fedayeen* or allowed them to operate from their territory. It was at this time that Israel openly adopted the principle of placing the responsibility for the *fedayeen*'s activity on the shoulders of the Arab governments.

The Sinai Campaign marked the end of the first period of terrorism against Israel – that of the infiltration of the *fedayeen*. The war that took place between Egypt and Israel in fall 1956, during which Israel occupied the Sinai Peninsula, was coordinated both politically and militarily with Britain and France. The operation was designed to root out *fedayeen* bases in the Gaza Strip and prevent further acts of terrorism and sabotage in Israel's south.[4] Indeed, in the short period of occupation of the Gaza Strip in the months after the war, Israel located the terrorist bases in Gaza and neutralized them. In this respect, the Sinai Campaign was crowned with success, bringing a cessation to *fedayeen* operations against Israel from Egypt for nine years, until 1965.

On the other hand, the Sinai Campaign was one of the motives for the establishment of Fatah three years later by a number of Palestinian students in Egypt, headed by Yasser

Arafat. With Fatah's creation, terrorist activities against Israel took on another face: national terrorism carried out by Palestinian groups led by this new Palestinian national movement. Fatah proclaimed the operational strategy of "armed struggle" and refrained from adopting a defined social philosophy. The organization saw the question of the nature of the future state as an issue to be discussed only after the "liberation of Palestine." In the eyes of Fatah's founders, the goal of armed violence was the extermination of the military, political, economic, financial, and cultural institutions of the state of Israel, as well as the prevention of any possibility of a resurgence of a new Zionist society. Military defeat of Israel, in their view, was not the only goal of the Palestinian liberation war. The real purpose was "the abolition of the Zionist character of the occupied land (i.e., the whole territory of Israel); the eradication of the society."[5]

Fatah's strategy was based on two basic principles: the independence of the Palestinian national movement from any Arab rule, and the supremacy of the armed struggle as the only means of the liberation of Palestine. According to the founders of Fatah, the military failure of the Arab states in 1948 was due mainly to the prevention of the Palestinians from engaging in armed struggle to free their homeland.[6] The armed struggle, in their opinion, was intended to simultaneously serve three main goals of the liberation movement: to actively bring about Israel's destruction, to unify the Palestinian people and involve them in the liberation of Palestine, and to make the existence of the Palestinian people known and to demand a solution to their problems.

Fatah was aware that the destruction of Israel required massive force which could only be found amongst the regular Arab armies. Therefore, its leaders did not object to a conventional war but proposed that it be conducted in stages and be propelled by the action of the Palestinian masses as a "war of liberation."[7] Guerrillas would pave the way for the actions of regular units, but unlike the theory outlined by Mao Zedong, it would not be the guerrilla units themselves that would become more powerful, but rather the regular Arab armies.[8] Palestinian armed struggle would thus be used primarily as a catalyst for the war that would destroy Israel.

On May 28, 1964, the first Palestinian national conference convened in east Jerusalem (under Jordanian rule) and decided to establish the Palestine Liberation Organization (PLO). The conference, attended by 422 people, defined itself as the Palestinian National Council (PNC) and chose Ahmad Shukeiri as the chair of the PLO.[9] This body was intended to work with the Arab countries and to coordinate the political and military activities of the Palestinians.

At the first meeting of the PNC, the Palestinian National Charter was formulated, defining the Palestinian national identity and the borders of Palestine. The second paragraph of the charter stated that the borders of Palestine were the same as those under the British Mandate.

Alongside its political activity, the PLO also turned to the military arena and initiated the establishment of a "Palestinian Liberation Army" (PLA). Units of this army were established within the framework of various Arab militaries. Recruits came from among the Palestinian population, while training and operations were the responsibility of the "host" Arab army. PLA units were closely monitored by the Arab governments sharing a border with Israel and could not take any military action against Israel without their approval. In September 1964, the second Arab League summit officially recognized the PLO and approved the establishment of the Palestinian Liberation Army.[10]

The establishment of the PLO was an anathema to members of Fatah, as it represented everything Fatah had sought to avoid – the patronage of the Arab countries and the attempt to use the Palestinian issue to further the interests of the Arab states (especially Egypt) – and did not adhere to the principle of the independence of Palestinian decision-making or the Fatah banner of "Palestinian revolution."

Fatah and the radicals argued that since Palestinian organizations had no value without the actions of the *fedayeen*, a small core of Palestinian fighters should begin to fight immediately in small arenas: "The armed struggle is what will allow for the establishment of a Palestinian organization; it is not the organization that will allow for armed struggle. From the flames of combat real leadership will arise."[11]

Terrorism against Israel was renewed in the mid-1960s. Fatah became operational and made its first attempt at an attack on January 1, 1965, on Israel's National Water Carrier, under the name "al-Asifa" ("The Storm"). Despite disapproval from Arab countries (with the exception of Syria), Fatah continued its terrorist activities until the Six Day War (1967). The Arab countries, particularly Jordan and Egypt, tried to damage Fatah via propaganda but were unsuccessful. Gamal Nasser feared that Fatah attacks at this stage would lead to a loss of control over the course of events, so he issued an order to the Arab armies to view themselves as in a state of war with "al-Asifa."[12]

After Fatah began carrying out attacks, Israel renewed its retaliatory actions in the Arab countries with the purpose of achieving an effective warning and deterrence policy, but again, as in the past, these messages did not appear to achieve their goal. Fatah's terrorist activity was not stopped and in fact even increased. In 1965, connections were formed between Fatah and Syria, which, among other things, led to Fatah receiving modest amounts of weapons and explosives from Syrian military intelligence. In mid-1965, Arafat, Khalil al-Wazir, and other senior Fatah members moved to Damascus,[13] and from the beginning of 1966 Syria allowed Fatah terrorists to infiltrate into Israel via the slopes of the Golan Heights. The Fatah–Syria honeymoon was short-lived; already in mid-1966 tensions arose between the parties, manifested in arrests, defections, and murders which stemmed from the claim that the organization was not coordinating the attacks it carried out through the Syrian border with the Syrian leadership. However, the cause of the rift was actually the attempts by the new Ba'ath Party leadership to impose its authority on Fatah and make it a Syrian satellite.[14]

On the eve of the Six Day War, during the first half of 1967, there was a significant increase in the number of attacks carried out by Palestinian organizations (thirty-seven, compared to thirty-five in 1965 and forty-one in 1966). Thirteen infiltrations were carried out from Syria, thirteen from Jordan, and eleven from Lebanon. Only the Gaza Strip border crossing remained sealed.[15] Despite the rise in the number of attacks, Israel suffered no significant damage; the attacks were more of a nuisance than anything else.

The Six Day War, the Yom Kippur War, and their aftermaths (1967–80)

The Arab defeat in the Six Day War and Israel's occupation of the West Bank and Gaza Strip reinforced the notion that the Palestinians were the only Arab actors that could preserve the violent conflict with Israel.[16] In December 1967, George Habash, a Christian Palestinian, founded the Popular Front for the Liberation of Palestine (PFLP). The new organization adopted a rigid ideological approach combining Marxist–Leninist social and economic values and principles of popular resistance and armed struggle for "the liberation of Palestine and the destruction of Arab imperialism and Arab reactionism." Since its establishment, the

PFLP has been careful to avoid total dependence on any country and has sought independence in decision-making on political, military, and organizational issues. Throughout the years, the PFLP advocated the overthrow of the Jordanian Hashemite regime and its replacement by a popular government sympathetic to the Palestinian cause. The establishment of the PFLP symbolized the beginning of a split amongst the Palestinians, which continued in the years that followed with the establishment of other organizations.

In October 1968, Ahmed Jibril left the PFLP due to personal rivalries with the organization's leaders. In an attempt to demonstrate his connection to the mother organization, Jibril called his new organization the Popular Front for the Liberation of Palestine-General Command (PFLP-GC). Jibril, who had served as an officer in the Syrian army, had close ties with Syria, and the organization soon secured complete Syrian sponsorship. The PFLP-GC did not adopt coherent ideological positions on social and political issues, only the commitment to liberate Palestine through armed struggle.

In 1968, the Syrian Ba'ath regime established another organization, al-Saika. In this way, Syria sought to strengthen its influence on the Palestinian movement without it being considered an external intervention. In 1969, the Iraqi Ba'ath regime established the Arab Liberation Front as a counterweight to al-Saika and the Syrian penetration into the Palestinian arena. These organizations did not reflect the authentic interests of the Palestinians but were designed primarily to promote the sponsoring states' interests in the Palestinian arena.

In 1969, a faction led by Nayef Hawatmeh left the PFLP and established the Democratic Front for the Liberation of Palestine. Over the years, the Democratic Front formed closer ties with Syria and Iraq and developed a close relationship with communist countries, in particular the Soviet Union.

The founding of numerous Palestinian terrorist organizations was not the only consequence of the 1967 Six Day War. A no less important development was Fatah's attempt to move the center of gravity of the armed struggle to the occupied West Bank and Gaza Strip themselves. The presence of a million Palestinians under Israeli occupation allowed, in its opinion, for guerrilla activities along the lines of those formulated by Mao, with the troops coming from within the local population, as "fish in water." Paradoxically, the occupation allowed the Palestinians to take their fate into their own hands without being dependent on the auspices of the Arab countries.[17]

Immediately after the occupation of the territories, Defense Minister Moshe Dayan formulated the three basic principles that guided Israeli policy in the years that followed: minimal military presence in Palestinian towns and villages, minimal involvement of the military government in everyday life, and, above all, the "Open Bridges" policy that allowed residents of the West Bank to pass freely into Jordan and maintain family ties and commerce with neighboring Arab countries. In addition to these principles, Israel allowed residents of the territories to join the Israeli labor market. This policy almost completely eradicated unemployment in the territories and raised the average wage significantly. As a supplementary measure intended to demonstrate goodwill, the Israeli government decided to let Palestinian residents of the territories approach the Israeli Supreme Court of Justice asking to remedy problems with Israeli activities in the territories.

This policy led to the failure of Fatah's attempts to organize civil disobedience in the territories and mobilize the population for terrorist activities against Israel. In less than a year, Fatah forces in the West Bank suffered a serious blow, with most of their members arrested and imprisoned, killed in clashes with IDF commanders, or having fled to Jordan or other Arab countries. The Palestinian public, moreover, refrained from cooperating with them. By the end of 1968, approximately 1,700 terrorists and collaborators were imprisoned in Israeli jails, and a year later this number increased to 2,800. By the end of 1969, 1,354 terrorists were killed in Israeli operations in the territories, and this number increased to 1,828 by the end of 1970.[18] As a result, Fatah dropped its idea of "self-liberation" in favor of the old familiar strategy of embroiling Israel in a war with the Arab armies.[19]

Meanwhile, the relationship between Egypt and Fatah was strengthened at the end of 1967. Nasser had come to the conclusion that there was a need to reshuffle the PLO and replace Shukeiri. Therefore Arafat was appointed PLO spokesperson in April 1968. Fatah members were elected to senior positions in PLO institutions, thereby effectively allowing for the takeover of the PLO by Palestinian organizations, led by Fatah. The Palestinian Liberation Organization went from being a symbolic, futile framework to becoming an umbrella organization coordinating the military and political activities of all of the various organizations.

At the same meeting of the PNC, it was decided that changes should be made to the Palestinian National Charter in order to reflect the transformation in the character of the PLO. These changes included the addition of several sections emphasizing the exclusivity of the armed struggle as the way to achieve the national aspirations of the Palestinians. Article 9 of the Charter stated that "armed struggle is the only way to liberate Palestine," and Article 10 added that "Fedayeen (Commando) actions constitute the nucleus of the Palestinian popular liberation war." Article 21 stated that the Palestinian Arab people "reject all solutions which are substitutes for the total liberation of Palestine."[20] At the PNC's next meeting, Fatah's takeover of the PLO was completed when Yasser Arafat was appointed PLO chairman.

Contrary to the Israeli policy in the West Bank of minimum military presence, it was decided that the opposite approach would be taken in the Gaza Strip with maximum IDF presence through the physical reinforcement of troops, multiple patrols in population centers, and, depending on the period, both a fixed and a temporary presence in the refugee camps. Nonetheless, one of the most prominent achievements of its Gaza policy was the continued enablement of Palestinians to work in Israel, despite repeated attempts by terrorist organizations to harm Palestinian citizens who did so. Defense Minister Moshe Dayan saw this as an important achievement and as proof that the PLO could not disrupt what was in the common interest of Israel and the Palestinian residents of the territories.[21]

Israel's actions undermined the confidence of the terrorists, as they turned their natural environment into a potential threat. The most significant step taken was the decision to demolish dozens of homes in Gaza refugee camps. These measures were effective; the number of attacks in the Gaza Strip gradually decreased, and by mid-1972 terrorist activity in the Gaza Strip had subsided.

Following its failure in the West Bank and Gaza Strip, the PLO set more symbolic goals for the armed struggle. Fatah spokespeople repeatedly stated that their actions would be sufficient even if they were sporadic, as a symbol and a reminder of the Palestinian cause.[22] They explained to the Palestinian public that the terrorist attacks were intended to harm the Israeli economy by deterring tourists and disrupting trade in Israel but were above all designed to prevent Jewish immigration to Israel and encourage the emigration of Israelis back to their countries of origin; in other words, the goal was to make Israelis feel that life in Israel was intolerable.[23]

Toward this end, the PLO struck new targets in new locations. Therefore, in addition to their activities in Israel and along its borders, in the late 1960s the Palestinians began to hit Israeli and foreign targets abroad, in part to disrupt the relationship between Israel and other countries, as well as to cause harm to the Israeli economy.[24] In July 1968, an El Al plane en route from Rome to Lod was hijacked by a PFLP terrorist cell. The airplane and crew were held hostage in Algeria. Bruce Hoffman claims that this attack represented the beginning of the phenomenon of modern international terrorism as the objective of the hijacking was to make a clear political statement. Unlike earlier hijackings, this plane was selected because it belonged to the national Israeli airline and the terrorists realized that by putting civilians' lives at stake, they could attract the attention of the media.[25] The negotiations between Israel and the hijackers lasted two months, and the incident only ended when the International Federation of Airline Pilots' Associations threatened to boycott Algeria.[26]

The hijacking in Algeria was the first in a long series of operations against Israeli and Jewish targets outside of Israel, which at first were carried out mainly by the PFLP. The most notorious of these in the late 1960s and early 1970s were attacks against aircraft traveling to Israel. In February 1970, Ahmed Jibril announced his intention to stop the movement of aircraft into Israel, and on the 21st his accomplices planted explosives on foreign airlines making their way to Israel. One Swissair plane crashed, and forty-seven passengers, including fifteen Jews, were killed.[27] In September 1970, four planes belonging to foreign airlines were hijacked by the PFLP. Three were landed at Zarqa Airport in Jordan and the fourth in Cairo. After a short time, the planes were blown up in Jordan by the terrorists, although no passengers were killed. In response to the wave of attacks on the Israeli airline industry, Israel decided to take dramatic action in Lebanon. On December 12, 1968, IDF forces stormed the Beirut airport and blew up thirteen passenger planes belonging to Arab airlines. The retaliation was designed to cause heavy damage to Lebanon's aircraft industry while avoiding any loss of human life.

The PFLP soon acquired an international reputation for its "expertise" in aircraft hijacking. The terrorist organization claimed that the attacks on air and sea transport to Israel should not be considered attacks on civilians due to the militarization of Israeli society. Moreover, they argued, airports and harbors were used for military purposes, and El Al pilots were actually plainclothes military personnel, making them legitimate targets.[28] The wave of Palestinian terrorism outside of Israel naturally led to the capture and arrest of Palestinian terrorists in different countries. The hijacking tactic soon proved effective as a method to secure their release.[29]

The end of the terrorist attacks in the air in the early 1970s did not lead to the abandoning of Palestinian terrorist activities against Israeli targets internationally. Various organizations – such as Black September (a pseudonym for Fatah's overseas operations, which possibly worked in cooperation with the PFLP), Wadie Haddad's various PFLP splinter groups, and later Abu Nidal fractions – focused on carrying out attacks on Israel-related targets abroad, such as embassies, official Israeli representatives, and Jewish institutions.

One of the most nefarious attacks took place on September 5, 1972, with the murder of Israeli athletes at the Munich Olympics. Despite the criticism voiced from all over the world following the brutal attack in Munich, it was an unprecedented media achievement for the Palestinians. An estimated 900 million people from at least 100 countries watched the events unfold on their TV screens. The brutal nature of the attack convinced many in the world that the Palestinians could not be ignored, and Yasser Arafat posited that perhaps it was not just a coincidence that eighteen months after the Munich massacre, as PLO chairman he was invited to address the United Nations General Assembly. Soon after, the PLO was accepted as a UN Special Observer.[30]

Israel's policy in responding to attacks outside of its borders consisted of three main strata: offensive operations, defensive operations, and the development of skills to solve hostage crises.

Offensive operations The basis for this activity was the desire for revenge as much as deterring others from attacking Israel. These goals led to the use of Israeli targeted killings designed to cause panic among the heads of organizations and those involved in terrorist attacks, disrupt their operations and preparations, and deter them from carrying out further attacks.

Defensive operations Shortly after the wave of hijackings began, Israel invested large sums of money to secure El Al aircraft and protect its embassies around the world. Passengers now had to undergo extensive security checks, including luggage inspections, metal detectors, and questioning before boarding the plane. Security guards were positioned on the plane itself, in order to take on terrorists who had managed to sneak through the security mechanisms. Israeli security guards protected Israeli embassies around the world, and alarm systems were put into place. Israeli officials visiting foreign countries were escorted closely by bodyguards.

Skill in solving crises Terrorist attacks against Israel on foreign soil, particularly those involving bargaining, such as the hijackings, required Israel to train experts for solving such crises. Special units were established and trained to deal with such situations on short notice by using military action. At the same time, Israel formulated a tough policy (at least on a declarative level) that made clear its refusal to negotiate with terrorists and its unwillingness to make concessions in hijacking and bargaining situations.

In 1970, tensions in Jordan rose and peaked in September after the Democratic Front attempted to assassinate King Hussein. On September 6, the PFLP blew up three hijacked planes in Zarkqa, as described above, and at the same time the PLO declared the city of Irbid a "liberated area." On September 17, the Jordanian army attacked PLO outposts, first in Amman and then in northern Jordan. Hussein had to agree to a cease-fire and to the presence of the PLO in Jordan, as was dictated by the Arab leaders in the framework of the Cairo Agreement of September 27. But peace was not restored. Repeated fire between Palestinians and the Jordanian army in November 1970 were sufficient grounds for Jordan to embark on an extensive operation to re-establish law and order and to expel the PLO from, first, the major cities and then from all of Jordan. This military campaign against the Palestinian organizations in Jordan, colloquially known as "Black September," lasted until July 1971 and brought about the virtual elimination of their bases in the country.[31] Many militants were killed in battle, others were imprisoned, and the rest were expelled or fled from Jordan. These events led to the creation a few months later of Fatah's special force under the alias Black September, headed by Salah Khalaf. Black September concentrated on attacking Israeli, Jordanian, and Arab civilian targets around the world. The first attack that Black September claimed responsibility for was the assassination of Jordanian Prime Minister Wasfi al-Tal on November 28, 1971, when he was in Cairo for the Arab League summit. With the loss of the Palestinian terrorist organizations' stronghold in Jordan, their military forces moved to southern Lebanon to launch a new front against Israel's northern border.

The Yom Kippur War (1973) and its outcomes marked another change in the strategy of the armed struggle. Whereas the Palestinians had already recognized the fact that the armed struggle alone could not lead to the liberation of Palestine, after the war it was clear that they should also reconsider the strategy of armed struggle as a catalyst for an Arab war against Israel. The war proved that even when the Arab countries succeeded in catching Israel off-guard in a surprise attack, they still lost at the end of the day. Thus, pressure mounted from the residents of the territories to formulate a new strategy following the failure of the war. This, in turn, forced Palestinian leaders to consider the possibility of achieving their goal – the complete liberation of Palestine – in stages, step by step. Another factor was the PLO leaders' fear that if they did not take part in the political process that began with the postwar interim arrangements, Jordan would take their place as the representative of the Palestinian people.[32]

In order to ensure that the PLO would be integrated into any future negotiation, in June 1974 the Palestinian National Council adopted what was referred to as the "strategy of stages." This strategy encountered strong opposition both from Arafat's rivals in the PLO, and within the ranks of Fatah itself. Critics argued that even if it was not the intention at the outset, this strategy would eventually lead to a compromise that would be less than the liberation of all of Palestine, making it unacceptable. In their opinion, the strategy also contradicted the pillar of the Charter that held that the armed struggle was the only way to liberate Palestine. Those groups that opposed the PLO initiative formed a new Syrian-sponsored coalition dubbed the Rejectionist Front.

The PLO's primary task was now to secure its status as the body authorized to negotiate on behalf of the Palestinians and as the sole legitimate representative of the Palestinian people. At the Arab League summit in Rabat, Morocco, in October 1974, this notion won the support of Jordan. One of the direct results of the Rabat summit was the invitation extended to Yasser Arafat on November 13, 1974, to address the United Nations General Assembly. Arafat, who was wearing a gun and holding an olive branch, was received with applause and a standing ovation by members of the UN. This represented a high point in the international standing of the PLO.

On November 22, the General Assembly adopted UN Resolution 3236, recognizing the right of self-determination of the Palestinian people and granting the PLO observer status at the United Nations as the representative of the Palestinians. Six days after Arafat's speech at the UN, four Israeli civilians were killed in an apartment building in Beit She'an. The Democratic Front for the Liberation of Palestine, a member of the Rejectionist Front, claimed responsibility for the attacks, stating that despite Arafat's waving of the olive branch, the Palestinians had not abandoned their weapons.[33] Indeed, at the 13th Palestinian National Council it was announced that "the PLO is determined to continue the armed struggle along with the other forms of political and popular struggle."[34]

At this point, it was clear to Fatah leaders that terrorist attacks abroad impeded their stated goals, as they damaged the PLO's image in the eyes of the international public. Thus, in July 1974, the PLO took the decision to cease terrorist attacks abroad, a decision that applied to all PLO member organizations, including the PFLP. To substantiate this decision, the PLO announced in January 1975 that hijackers would be executed if their attacks caused any loss of human life and would receive a prison sentence of up to 15 years if there were no casualties.[35] At the same time, however, it was important for the PLO to clarify that this decision did not imply the cessation of the armed struggle and that it intended to escalate terrorist activities in Israel. Indeed, the list of terrorist attacks during this period is long and the number of victims high, but Israel was successful in thwarting many attacks, often before they were carried out. Israel was also often successful in taking action for the release of hostages. The most well-known operation in this context was the release of the airplane passengers held hostage in Entebbe on July 3, 1976. The attack was on an Air France flight from Paris to Tel Aviv with many Israelis on board. In order to avoid an Israeli military takeover, the hijackers flew the plane to Uganda, a country hostile towards and far away from Israel. However, despite the distance and the objective difficulties, Israel conducted an extremely successful rescue operation and released almost all of the hostages.

After Fatah and the other Palestinian organizations moved to Lebanon following the events of Black September in Jordan, resources were allocated towards consolidating and buttressing their forces there. They established new, expanded military frameworks and recruited many Palestinians from the refugee camps in Lebanon. Palestinian organizations succeeded in penetrating the population by operating welfare institutions and paying salaries to Palestinians who served in the organizations' bureaucracies. Joining the ranks of the Palestinian organizations in Lebanon was therefore not only an expression of national aspirations but also a means of employment and livelihood. As far as the organizations were concerned, the paying of salaries ensured loyalty to the organization and its leader.

The strengthening of these Palestinian organizations created friction with other forces in Lebanon, most notably the Maronite Christians. In April 1975, these power struggles led to the outbreak of battles between the PLO and Maronite Christian militias around Beirut. These battles marked the beginning of the Lebanese Civil War.

While the battle was waged in Lebanon, in early 1976 a rift developed between the PLO and Syria. Syria urged the Palestinian factions under their authority, chief among these al-Saika, to work alongside the Christians against Fatah. The entrance of the Syrian army into Lebanon at the invitation of the Christian leadership caused another rift among the Palestinian organizations. The alignment of Jibril's PFLP-GC with the Syrians in their conflict with the PLO in Lebanon during the civil war caused a split in the organization in April 1977. A number of its members, led by Mahmoud Zeidan and Talaat Yaqub, withdrew from the organization and set up a rival faction called the Palestinian Liberation Front (PLF). The new faction did not adopt a defined ideological strategy, aside from adherence to the liberation of Palestine through armed struggle. Early on the PLF received the backing of Iraq, which supported the organization financially and helped it organize militarily.

The fighting in Lebanon ended following heavy pressure from the Arab states, which at the end of October at the Arab League summit in Riyadh and then in Cairo agreed on a timetable for the withdrawal of combat forces.

Egyptian President Anwar Sadat's visit to Jerusalem in November 1977 and the peace process that led to the signing of the peace treaty between Israel and Egypt once again reshuffled the cards in the Middle East and led to the escalation of the Palestinian armed struggle. The Camp David Accords stated that within five years the residents of the territories would be self-governed and that afterwards a final settlement would be signed by all parties.

The peace process between Israel and Egypt was perceived by the Palestinian organizations as a betrayal of the Palestinian cause by the Arab countries and a serious threat to the future of the struggle. Opposition to the Israeli–Egyptian peace process, was, at least on the surface, shared among all of the Palestinian organizations and in fact led to the healing of the rift within the PLO and the return of the Rejectionist Front groups to it. The local leadership in the territories also disapproved of the agreement, and demonstrations were held in most of the universities there.[36]

The Palestinian struggle against the peace process focused on two areas: increased political pressure on the Arab countries, and the escalation of terrorist attacks against Israel on all fronts. In March 1978, a Fatah terrorist cell from Lebanon sailed to Israel and landed on the beach of Kibbutz Maagan Michael (next to the coastal highway). This deadly attack in the heart of the country, during which the terrorists seized a civilian bus and killed 36 people, shook the Israeli public. Israel's response to the so-called Coastal Road attack was not long in coming. Two days later, the IDF launched a large-scale operation in Lebanon ending with the occupation of areas south of the Litani River. After a stay of several months, the IDF withdrew from the conquered territory as part of an agreement that included the deployment of the United Nations Interim Force in Lebanon (UNIFIL) south of the Litani River.

Despite the presence of UNIFIL and the South Lebanese Army after Operation Litani, the PLO continued to launch terrorist attacks against Israel from Lebanese territory. After Israel built a security fence and reinforced security measures along the northern border, Palestinian terrorists sought other ways to penetrate Israel. One of these was from the sea, and another, in the late 1970s, was via makeshift aircraft (hot-air balloons and motorized hang gliders).

The disintegration of the Lebanese central government and along with it the military and police forces following the civil war in Lebanon led to the division of Lebanon between various power players. The areas under Palestinian control included West Beirut and most of South Lebanon. In these territories, Palestinian organizations built infrastructure including regular military units, training bases, support units, militia forces, and civilian administrative offices that provided social, education, and healthcare services to their constituencies. Relatively soon, extraterritorial areas were created in which the Palestinians controlled traffic routes and Palestinian population centers, carried weapons openly, set up checkpoints on the roads, and in essence enforced their rule (similar to what they had done ten years earlier in Jordan). These autonomous regions formed a "state within a state" ruled by the organizations from their headquarters in Beirut. The accelerated building up of Palestinian military forces marked a new stage in the strategic development of the armed struggle – that of military institutionalization.

From the Lebanon War to the Palestinian "Intifada" (1982–91)

The Israeli occupation of southern Lebanon during Operation Litani allowed Israel and its Christian allies to create a new reality, such that after Israel's withdrawal, the area was controlled by the Christians, preventing the return of the PLO. This is how the "security zone" came into being. With the bolstering of defense and deterrence mechanisms along the northern border, Israel was able to thwart many terrorist attacks by cells attempting to infiltrate into Israel. Even so, terrorist organizations quickly discovered that with artillery fire, they could strike northern Israeli settlements without physically entering the country and without risk of the attack being thwarted ahead of time. This recognition led to Palestinians arming themselves with mobile artillery weapons and preparing ammunition depots and supplies that would enable a drawn-out conflict with Israel.

In July 1981, hostilities between Israel and the Palestinians escalated when the Israeli Air Force attacked targets in Beirut and elsewhere deep inside Lebanon, and terrorists shelled all of the northern Israeli towns with artillery and Katyusha rockets. After ten days of fighting and following international intervention, mainly American (including direct pressure on Israel by suspending its supply of US F-16 aircraft), a cease-fire was reached.

The PLO used the year following the artillery battles to rehabilitate and strengthen their military forces in Lebanon, with particular emphasis on enlarging and optimizing its artillery systems based on lessons learned in battle. Thus, on the eve of the Lebanon War (1982), Palestinian military forces in Lebanon included approximately 15,000 people belonging to semi-regular battalions and brigades, as well as several thousand militiamen.[37]

Following the attempted assassination of Shlomo Argov, the Israeli ambassador in London (which was carried out by Abu Nidal's terrorist group, which was hostile to Arafat), Israel decided to end the cease-fire and ordered its air force to operate against Palestinian terrorist bases and forces in Lebanon. After a brief period of exchanging artillery fire with terrorists and semi-regular forces in Lebanon, the Israeli government decided to implement its plan to embark on an unprecedented ground operation against the Palestinians in Lebanon. On June 6, 1982, the IDF launched Operation Peace for the Galilee. The alliance of IDF forces with Christian units in the area of the Beirut–Damascus road led to the imposition of a blockade on West Beirut, which entrapped some of the leaders of the PLO and many terrorists. During this period, Christian militants penetrated to the Sabra and Shatila Palestinian refugee camps in Beirut and killed hundreds of Palestinians. Israeli leaders were blamed for not anticipating and preventing this massacre, and an Israeli investigation committee brought the resignation of Ariel Sharon, the Israeli minister of defense. After two and a half months of the blockade, 8,000 Palestinians were evacuated from Beirut and taken to eight Arab countries: Syria, Iraq, South Yemen, North Yemen, Tunisia, Algeria, Jordan, and Sudan.

The IDF's occupation of southern Lebanon and the evacuation of Palestinian militants from Beirut dealt a fatal blow to the military forces of most of the organizations. Units were disbanded, their members were scattered in different countries, most of their weapons were lost, and morale was very low. After the war, attacks on Israel's border communities became almost impossible due to the retreat of the Palestinians from the northern border and the refusal of the Arab states bordering Israel to allow the terrorist groups to operate from their borders.[38]

Syria, which sought to exploit the results of the Lebanon War to take over the PLO, began to confine the movements of the Fatah operatives remaining in Lebanon and Syria, and for this purpose once again recruited pro-Syrian terrorist organizations. In addition, in May 1983, a faction in Fatah opposed to Arafat was established, led by several commanders of the forces in Lebanon who were close to Syria.[39]

Despite Israel's achievements in destroying the Palestinian military forces in Lebanon, the IDF was still entrenched in Lebanon, and hundreds of its soldiers had been killed and wounded. Shi'ite terrorist organizations, which had developed at this time, began to target the bases of the IDF and the multinational forces in Lebanon. (For more on Hizbullah and other radical Islamist groups during this period, see Chapter 18 by David Cook in this volume.) On January 1985, Israel began a staged withdrawal from Lebanon that was completed by June 1985 (except the "security zone" bordering Israel). The IDF withdrawal propelled the Palestinian terrorist organizations to bring their people back into Lebanese territory and rebuild their military infrastructure. This enabled them to resume their attacks and infiltrate into Israel through the security fence.

The PLO's military defeat in Lebanon spurred Arafat into vigorous political and diplomatic activity with the assistance and patronage of King Hussein of Jordan. In an attempt to arbitrate between the United States and the PLO, Egyptian President Hosni Mubarak demanded that Arafat publicly denounce terrorism. Arafat agreed, and on

November 10, 1985, he declared in Cairo his condemnation "of all types of terrorism" but clarified that one must differentiate between terrorism and "legitimate armed struggle which every nation living under occupation is entitled to use."[40]

One of the most significant Israeli offensives against terrorist organizations took place on October 1, 1985, when the Israeli Air Force bombed PLO offices and the Force 17 commando unit in Tunisia (approximately 2,500 kilometers from Israel). Ninety percent of the Hammam al-Shatt base on the Tunisian coast was destroyed, and sixty terrorists were killed and sixty injured.[41] This attack came a few days after Fatah's Force 17 hijacked a yacht carrying Israeli tourists in the port of Larnaca in Cyprus and killed them, and a few months after Israel foiled an attempted terrorist attack by Fatah using the vessel Ataviros that was intended to land terrorists on the Tel Aviv coast to raid the IDF General Staff headquarters on Independence Day. The Tunisia operation reinforced three of Israel's stated positions that reflected its policy with regards to the war on terrorism over the years. One was its reliance on the long arm of its air force, which allowed for effective and accurate strikes on specific terrorist targets. The second was the pursuit of terrorists wherever they were, and the third was the assignment of direct responsibility for terrorist attacks on the countries that offered terrorist organizations sponsorship and the use of their territory for the planning and carrying out of terrorist attacks.

Until the mid-1980s, the majority of the Palestinian population in the territories was not actively involved in terrorist activities against IDF forces and Israeli civilians. Terror in Israel and the territories was generally carried out by Palestinians recruited by organizations and who acted according to their instructions. These recruits were only a small minority of the residents of the West Bank and Gaza.

In late 1987, riots began in the West Bank and Gaza Strip as an outcome of growing frustration from PLO failures and weaknesses. The violent street protests and occurrences of civil disobedience deteriorated rapidly into a wave of violence that was named the "Intifada" or the Palestinian Uprising. The violent demonstrations became more and more frequent and well attended and were accompanied by the throwing of stones and Molotov cocktails. Despite the PLO's attempt to present itself, in retrospect, as having initiated and directed the uprising in the territories, the Intifada actually broke out gradually as a result of local initiatives.

The uprising surprised the Israeli security forces, which were not prepared for it. IDF forces operated in the territories in small formations, equipped with firearms and a sense that their lives were in jeopardy. Consequently, in the first month of the uprising (December 9 to January 8), twenty-six Palestinians were killed, which caused the situation to escalate even more. A month or so after the riots began, the IDF changed its strategy, augmenting its forces in the territories and enforcing punishments such as curfews and administrative detention. The army was equipped with cold weapons appropriate for self-defense and close contact with the rioters, including steel helmets, tear gas, rubber bullets, and batons. Israel also started to operate special units that acted undercover amongst the crowds by adopting the appearance of Palestinians. However, none of these tactics were successful. The Intifada expanded, with violent protests spreading to all parts of the West Bank and Gaza Strip.

The issue of the popular struggle versus the armed struggle constantly hovered over Palestinian militants in the territories. Some Palestinian leaders saw the Intifada as a direct result of the armed struggle over the years, a complementary method designed to involve the masses in the armed struggle. Others saw the Intifada as an alternative to the armed struggle and stressed the need to maintain the popular struggle without terrorist attacks. The Intifada activists ignored the PLO's instructions to use firearms and explosives.[42]

Meanwhile, on the eve of the Intifada, the Palestinian Islamist movements Hamas and Palestinian Islamic Jihad started to gain support among the territory's population. This was due in part to events unfolding in the Arab world, most notably the rise of Khomeini to power in Iran and the search for alternatives to the national–secular movement of the PLO.

During the six years of the Intifada, approximately 1,100 Palestinians and over 120 Israelis were killed.[43] Another 1,000 Palestinians were assassinated by other Palestinians as a result of internal rivalries or out of suspicion of collaboration with Israel. On April 16, 1988, against the backdrop of the Intifada in the territories, Khalil al-Wazir – "Abu Jihad" – Yasser Arafat's deputy and the head of the Fatah's military arm, was killed in Tunis. This killing was a milestone in the Israeli government's policy of targeted killings as part of its war on terror.

The Israeli–Palestinian peace process and its implications (1992–2013)

The Intifada left its mark on the political scene as well. In July 1988, King Hussein made a strategic decision, the essence of which was Jordanian disengagement from the West Bank. In a speech to the Jordanian people, the king announced that he would "dismantle the legal and administrative links between the two banks," in response to "the wishes of the PLO."[44]After the 1991 Gulf War in Iraq, the United States was initiating a new political initiative to resolve the Israeli–Palestinian conflict. The American initiative led to an international conference in Madrid in which Palestinian and Israeli representative held direct talks within the framework of a larger Israeli–Arab negotiation to achieve peace in the Middle East. The Madrid talks died out, but simultaneously a second track of peace talks that were held between Israeli scholars and PLO representatives in Oslo accelerated in 1992 after a government change in Israel in which Yitzhak Rabin replaced Yitzhak Shamir as the Israeli prime minister.

Over the next few years, several interim agreements were signed between the PLO and Israel, in which Israel gave the Palestinians control over more territory in Judea and Samaria as well as increased self-government. In exchange for this transfer of territories and autonomy, Israel repeatedly demanded that the Palestinians commit to stopping terrorist attacks on Israel, but the Islamist terrorist organizations continued to carry out attacks, while Arafat turned a blind eye or sometimes even encouraged them.

The signing of the Oslo Accords and then of the Gaza and Jericho agreements, the establishment of Palestinian autonomy in Gaza and the West Bank, and the entry of Arafat and his loyalists into the autonomous areas constituted an important landmark in Palestinian history. For the first time, the Palestinians had their own territory, with the understanding and the hope that after a few years of self-government, this autonomy would turn into sovereignty over an independent state. The PLO, which only three and a half decades earlier had been no more than a handful of people trying to convince the world that it represented a landless nation of refugees, had become the sole legitimate representative of the Palestinian people and the legal sovereign over their territory.

Trying to scuttle peace and reconciliation between Israel and the Palestinians, the Islamist terrorist organizations Hamas and Palestinian Islamic Jihad recommenced their terror attacks and began employing a new modus operandi – suicide attacks – which caused multiple casualties in Israel and spread fear and anxiety.

Arafat consciously gave ample support to the social, economic, and religious development of the Islamist terrorist organizations in the Palestinian autonomous regions. From time to time, he even made pacts with them regarding the use of or abstention from terrorism. These agreements allowed the Islamist organizations to continue to carry weapons and to operate within the autonomous regions, as long as they did not execute attacks that would "embarrass" the PLO leadership or allow Israel to place responsibility on the Palestinian Authority (PA). In other words, terrorist attacks were allowed if their perpetrators did not carry them out from those cities controlled exclusively by the Palestinian Authority, but rather from the territories controlled by the IDF, even if these attacks were organized, prepared, and controlled by officials of Hamas and Islamic Jihad residing in these cities.[45] When it was estimated that terrorist attacks would harm immediate Palestinian interests, Arafat communicated to the Islamist organizations that the damage caused by the attacks could outweigh their benefits and ordered them to refrain from attacks for a certain period of time. Arafat refrained from taking action to eliminate the military capabilities of these organizations. He never destroyed the operational infrastructures of terrorist organizations or their laboratories nor did he ban their illegal weapons; above all, he did not stop the incitement against Israel. Instead, Arafat chose to ignore the military buildup of the Islamist terrorist groups and even helped prepare them for the possibility of a conflict with Israel.

Israel's withdrawal from the autonomous Palestinian areas severely limited the intelligence capability of the Israeli security services in the territories and made Israel largely dependent on the intelligence and security services of the Palestinian Authority. Palestinian intelligence officials generally refrained from giving Israel early information about plans for terrorist attacks, or any other intelligence information. Also, the Palestinians often did not use information that they received from Israel to thwart specific terrorist attacks.

In light of the Palestinian Authority's conduct, the assassination of Israeli Prime Minister Yitzhak Rabin by a Jewish fundamentalist, and the establishment of the first Benjamin Netanyahu government in the late 1990s, the Oslo process dwindled as both sides exchanged accusations concerning responsibility for its failure. In Israeli elections in 1999, Ehud Barak won due in part to his promise to withdraw the remaining Israeli forces from Lebanon, a commitment he fulfilled in 2000. In an attempt to save the Oslo Accords and reach a permanent agreement that would end the Israeli–Palestinian conflict, Prime Minister Barak met with Chairman Yasser Arafat under the auspices of US President Bill Clinton at Camp David in July 2000. These talks failed, and soon after, riots – dubbed the Second or "al-Aqsa" Intifada – broke out all over Judea, Samaria, and Gaza. The supposed trigger for these violent events was the visit of opposition leader Ariel Sharon and his entourage to the Temple Mount. But according to Israeli officials, the Second Intifada was planned in advance by the Palestinian Authority with the purpose of dragging in the international community, particularly the United States, which, it was hoped, would force Israel to make concessions beyond those it had been prepared to undertake in the Camp David talks.[46] The al-Aqsa Intifada, which lasted five years, was significantly different from the First Intifada. Whether or not its outbreak was an initiative of the Palestinian Authority, the violence erupted after long-term and focused incitement by the PA aimed at stirring up the masses. Unlike the mass demonstrations that characterized the events of the late 1980s, most of the violence of the Second Intifada took the form of various types of terrorist attacks, most notably a record number of suicide bombings. For the first time in a decade, Fatah activists rather than the Islamist organizations led the Palestinian violence. During the conflict (September

2000–December 2005), 1,080 Israelis were killed in 25,375 terrorist attacks; 146 suicide bombings were carried out, killing 518 Israelis and injuring 3,350. The number of Palestinians killed during this period was 3,405.[47] One of the events that most shocked the Israeli nation at the beginning of the Intifada was a public lynching, filmed by television cameras, of two Israeli reserve soldiers who accidentally drove into Ramallah in December 2000.

After several meetings between Barak and Arafat failed to bring about a cease-fire, and following the early Israeli elections that brought Ariel Sharon to power, the debate in Israel over whether Arafat was responsible for the Intifada ended. Thus, in December 2001, after Israel killed the secretary general of the PFLP, Abu Ali Mustafa, and the Palestinians killed the Israeli tourism minister, Rechavam Zeevi, and following a series of suicide bombings in Jerusalem and Haifa, Israel decided to cease all negotiations with Arafat and cut off contact with him; he had become, in the words of the Israelis, "irrelevant."[48] This Israeli decision – combined with US pressure on Arafat and the September 11 attacks in the US which resulted in even lower tolerance of those involved in terror – led Arafat to declare a cease-fire. During this brief break from terrorist attacks, the Palestinian terrorist groups continued to arm themselves, and in January 2002, Israel intercepted the ship Karine A making its way from Iran to the Gaza Strip and carrying on board large quantities of advanced weapons for Fatah.

The cease-fire ended when, in mid-January 2002, Israel killed Fatah's Raed Karmi, head of the military wing in Tul Karm. The violence and terrorist attacks resumed and reached a new peak in March 2002, when in that month alone, 133 Israelis were killed in terror attacks. Among the attacks that month was a suicide bombing on Passover Eve at the Park Hotel in Netanya, which caused the deaths of thirty Israelis who were celebrating the festive Passover Seder. This attack triggered a large-scale ground operation named Defensive Shield, in which the IDF reoccupied Palestinian cities in the West Bank. After a month and a half of fighting, the terrorist groups as well as the PA were disarmed, and many terrorists were caught and arrested. The Palestinian Authority lost its sovereignty over the cities and Arafat was placed under siege and isolation in Ramallah. The results of Defensive Shield led to a drastic decline in the number of terrorist attacks in general and that of suicide bombings in particular, until they essentially ceased a few years later. However, this decline in terrorism is also attributed to the physical security barrier that was built around the same time between the West Bank and Israel. The barrier includes a security fence stretching hundreds of kilometers, equipped with electronic sensors and a high concrete wall along part of it. The difficulties that Hamas and other terrorist organizations had in penetrating into Israel led these organizations to equip themselves with high trajectory weapons.

In light of the collapse of the Oslo Accords, the Saudis launched a peace initiative that was later adopted by the Arab League and that paved the way for the "Road Map" for resolving the Israeli–Palestinian conflict put forward by President George W. Bush in late 2002. Attempts to resume negotiations after Arafat's death in late 2004 with his successor, Mahmoud Abbas (also known as Abu Mazen), were unsuccessful. Abbas, unlike his predecessor, wanted to reach an agreement to end the conflict with Israel, but, unlike Arafat, he lacked the leadership qualities, public support, control, and charisma necessary to enforce such an agreement on his rivals, the Islamists. Against this backdrop, the Israeli government headed by Ariel Sharon undertook a unilateral disengagement from Gaza in the summer of 2005, which included the withdrawal of IDF forces and the evacuation of all Israeli settlements from the Gaza Strip. Hamas, which claimed that Israel's disengagement was a capitulation that stemmed from Hamas's terrorist attacks against it, translated these claims of victory into an electoral win, defeating Fatah in the Palestinian Authority's parliamentary elections in January 2006. The Hamas takeover of Gaza was completed after the elections with a violent military revolution during which Hamas militants slaughtered Fatah members and expelled them from the Strip. Mahmoud Abbas, with aid from Israel and generous international backing, consolidated his power in the West Bank and renewed security cooperation with Israel, bringing relative stability, improving the economic situation, and preventing terrorist attacks from the West Bank. The center of gravity of the struggle against Israel moved back to the Islamist organizations. This time, salafi Palestinian organizations inspired by the global jihad movement began operating in the Gaza Strip along with Hamas and Palestinian Islamic Jihad. These organizations began firing rockets at civilian communities in southern Israel and sometimes even carried out terrorist attacks within Israel, either by infiltrating the border fence between Gaza and Israel, or by going from Gaza to Sinai and entering Israel from Egypt. This rocket fire has intensified over the years, both in terms of the number of rockets fired into Israel and the increase of their range. This prompted a number of large-scale IDF ground operations in Gaza, including Operation Hot Winter in February 2008, Operation Cast Lead in January 2009, and Operation Pillar of Defense in 2012.

Conclusions

The scope, characteristics, methods, and theaters of terrorist activity against Israel were the result of processes that occurred within the Palestinian arena, such as internal and inter-organizational tensions and pressure from Palestinian society. At the same time, Palestinian terrorist activity reflected external influences such as pressure from sponsoring countries that utilized Palestinian terrorism to promote their interests, and, of course, Israeli counter-terrorism. Israeli action took the form of offensives against terrorist organizations, their facilities, members, and leaders, as well as diverse defensive operations and pressure against the terrorists and their supporters. These actions were designed mainly to reduce the terrorists' capabilities and maneuverability and in many cases achieved their goals. However, all attempts to deal with the motivations driving the terrorists through political processes aimed at resolving the conflict, especially in the case of the Oslo process, were unsuccessful and in some cases led to an escalation in terrorism against Israel. This failure to remedy the motivations for terrorism can be explained in several ways, but it would appear that one of the main reasons is the fact that the Israeli–Palestinian conflict, in contrast to its name, has never been just a two-sided conflict between the Palestinians and Israelis. There have always been many players involved in this conflict – the Arab states, the superpowers, and other players whose conflicting interests influenced the positions of the two major players and often led to an escalation of the conflict.

Notes

1 Herb Keinon, "Foreign Ministry Arms Israelis Traveling Abroad with Terror Statistics," *Jerusalem Post*, March 27, 2002.
2 Shlomo Aronson and Dan Horowitz, "The Strategy of Controlled Retaliation: The Israeli Example," *Political Science and International Relations* (1976): 78.

3. Benny Morris, *Israel's Border Wars, 1949–1956* (Tel Aviv: Am Oved, 1996), 98, 211.
4. Gal-Or, Noemi, "Tolerating Terrorism in Israel," in *Tolerating Terrorism in the West*, ed. Noemi Gal-Or (London: Routledge, 1991), 69.
5. Yehoshafat Harkaby, *Fatah bastrategia Ha'aravit – Yionim Be'etmol vs Be'machar* [Fatah in Arab Strategy: Looking at Yesterday and Tomorrow] (Tel Aviv: Maarachot, 1969), 34–5.
6. Yezid Sayigh, *Armed Struggle and the Search for State: The Palestinian National Movement 1949–1993* (Oxford: Clarendon Press, 1997), 89.
7. Sayigh, *Armed Struggle*, 120.
8. Yehoshofat Harkaby, *On Guerrilla Warfare* (Hebrew) (Tel Aviv: Maarachot, 1983), 306.
9. Sayigh, *Armed Struggle*, 98.
10. Eliezer Ben-Rafael, *Israel–Palestine: A Guerrilla Conflict in International Politics* (Westport, CT: Greenwood Press: 1987), 36.
11. Yehoshafat Harkaby, *Ha'Palestinim Mitrodama Le'atraorerot* [The Palestinians: From Quiescence to Awakening] (Jerusalem: Magnus, 1979), 106.
12. Alan Hart, *Arafat: The Definitive Biography* (London: Sidgwick Jackson, 1994), 159.
13. Ehud Yaari, *Fatah* (New York: Sabra Books, 1971), 47, 57.
14. Yaari, *Fatah*, 59.
15. Yaari, *Fatah*, 75.
16. Yuval Arnon-Ohana and Aryeh Yodfat, *Ashaf–Dyokno shel Irgun* [The PLO: Portrait of an Organization] (Tel Aviv: Ma'ariv Library, 1985), 118.
17. Hart, *Arafat*, 204.
18. Sayigh, *Armed Struggle*, 203.
19. Yaari, *Fatah*, 129.
20. www.mfa.gov.il/MFA/Peace%20Process/Guide%20to%20the%20Peace%20Process/The%20Palestinian%20National%20Charter (accessed May 15, 2014).
21. Moshe Dayan, *al-tahalich ha-shalom ve-atida shel Y Israel* [On the Peace Process and the Future of Israel], ed. Natan Yanai (Tel Aviv: Ministry of Defense Publishing House, 1988), 14.
22. Harkaby, *The Palestinians*, 183–4.
23. Sayigh, *Armed Struggle*, 211.
24. Ariel Merari and Shlomo Elad, *The International Dimension of Palestinian Terrorism 1968–1986* (Hebrew) (Tel Aviv: Hakibbutz Hameuchad, Kav Adom, 1986), 31.
25. Bruce Hoffman, *Inside Terrorism* (New York: Columbia University Press, 2006), 68. For more on international terrorism and the Palestinians' contribution to its emergence, see Chapter 25 by Geraint Hughes in this volume.
26. Peter St. John, "Counterterrorism Policy-Making: The Case of Aircraft Hijacking, 1968–1988," in *Democratic Responses to International Terrorism*, ed. David A. Charters (New York: Transnational Publishers, 1991), 75.
27. St. John, "Counterterrorism," 75.
28. Sayigh, *Armed Struggle*, 214.
29. Merari and Elad, *International Dimension*, 26, 28, 31.
30. Hoffman, *Terrorism*, 75. For more on the Munich massacre, see Chapters 25 by Hughes on international terrorism and 28 by Robert A. Saunders on terrorism and the media, both in this volume.
31. Asher Susser, *The PLO after the War in Lebanon* (Tel Aviv: Hakibbutz Hameuchad, 1985), 123–38.
32. Matti Steinberg. "Trends and Changes in the PLO," *The Lebanon War* (Hebrew) (Tel Aviv: Hakibbutz Hameuchad, Kav Adom, 1983), 62.
33. Hart, *Arafat*, 371.
34. Yuval Arnon, "The PLO's Stance towards Israel: Ideology Put to the Test" (Hebrew), *Skira Chodshit* 27, no. 10 (1980): 24.
35. Merari and Elad, *International Dimension*, 46.
36. Ben-Rafael, *Israel–Palestine*, 84.
37. Rashid Khalidi, *Under Siege: PLO Decision Making During the 1982 War* (New York: Columbia University Press, 1986), 31.
38. Merari and Elad, *International Dimension*, 9–10.
39. Joseph Olmert, "The Rebellion within Fatah: Background, Process, Results, and the Role of Syria," (Hebrew), *Skira Chodshit* 30, no. 9 (Sept 1983): 4.

40 Hart, *Arafat*, 448–9, 456–7.
41 Mike Eldar, *Shayetet 13: The Story of the Naval Commando* (Hebrew) (Tel Aviv: Maariv Book Guild, 1993), 645.
42 Ze'ev Schiff and Ehud Ya'ari, *Intifada* (Jerusalem: Schocken Publishing House, 1990), 116.
43 www.btselem.org/hebrew/statistics/first_intifada_tables (accessed May 17, 2014).
44 Aryeh Shalev, *The Intifada: Causes and Effects* (Tel Aviv: Papyrus Press, 1990), 147, 151.
45 *Ha'aretz*, April 29, 1994; *Ma'ariv*, April 24, 1994; *Ha'aretz*, April 18, 1995; and *Ma'ariv*, April 24, 1995.
46 Eran Halpering and Daniel Bar-Tal, "The Fall of the Peace Camp in Israel: The Influence of Prime Minister Ehude Barak on Israel Public Opinion," *Conflict and Communication online* 6, no.2 (2007): 5.
47 These numbers are based on several sources, including the Shin Bet, the IDF (Military Intelligence/Spokesperson's Unit), the Center for Special Studies, and Amos Harel and Avi Issacharoff, *The Seventh War* (Yediot Aharonot, 2004).
48 Safire William, "The Irrelevant Man," *New York Times*, December 17, 2001, www.nytimes.com/2001/12/17/opinion/the-irrelevant-man.html (accessed May 16, 2014).

Further reading

Arnon-Ohana, Yuval, and Aryeh Yodfat. *Ashaf–Dyokno shel Irgun* [The PLO: Portrait of an Organization]. Tel Aviv: Ma'ariv Library, 1985.
Ben-Rafael, Eliezer. *Israel–Palestine: A Guerrilla Conflict in International Politics*. Westport, CT: Greenwood Press, 1987.
Dayan, Moshe. *al-tahalich ha-shalom ve-atida shel Y Israel* [On the Peace Process and the Future of Israel]. Edited by Natan Yanai. Tel Aviv: Ministry of Defense Publishing House, 1988.
Harkaby, Yehoshafat. *Fatah bastrategia Ha'aravit – Yionim Be'etmol vs Be'machar* [Fatah in Arab Strategy: Looking at Yesterday and Tomorrow]. Tel Aviv: Maarachot, 1969.
—. *Ha'Palestinim Mitrodama Le'atraorerot* [The Palestinians: From Quiescence to Awakening]. Jerusalem: Magnus, 1979.
Hart, Alan. *Arafat: The Definitive Biography*. London: Sidgwick Jackson, 1994.
Hoffman, Bruce. *Inside Terrorism*. New York: Columbia University Press, 2006.
Khalidi, Rashid. *Under Siege: PLO Decision Making During the 1982 War*. New York: Columbia University Press, 1986.
Merari, Ariel, and Shlomo Elad. *The International Dimension of Palestinian Terrorism, 1968–1986*. Tel Aviv: Hakibbutz Hameuchad, Kav Adom, 1986.
Morris, Benny. *Israel's Border Wars, 1949–1956*. Tel Aviv: Am Oved, 1996.
Sayigh, Yezid. *Armed Struggle and the Search for State: The Palestinian National Movement, 1949–1993*. Oxford: Clarendon Press, 1997.
Schiff, Ze'ev, and Ehud Ya'ari. *Intifada*. Jerusalem: Schocken Publishing House, 1990.
Shalev, Aryeh. *The Intifada: Causes and Effects*. Tel Aviv: Papyrus Press, 1990.
Yaari, Ehud. *Fatah*. New York: Sabra Books, 1971.

17

THE ROOTS OF ISLAMISM AND ISLAMIST VIOLENCE

John Calvert

The past 75 years have witnessed the appearance in the Middle East, Africa, Southeast Asia, and elsewhere of political parties and other formal organizations with Islamic agendas. The last 30 years have been especially active in this regard. Events from the Revolution of 1978–9 in Iran to the attacks on New York and Washington of September 11, 2001, have led some to conclude that the United States and European nations are on a collision course with Islam, the religion of one-fifth of the world's population. Although the view of a monolithic Islamic threat ranged against the West is problematic, not least because it ignores the diversity within global Muslim communities and many fruitful relationships that exist between Muslims and non-Muslims, it is true that Muslim populations around the world are exhibiting heightened religiosity, oftentimes within the context of doctrinally and socially conservative organizations and mass movements.

Observers outside of the phenomenon have adopted a number of terms to refer to these manifestations of Islamic resurgence. One of the most widely used is Islamic fundamentalism. Other terms include political Islam, Islamic revivalism, Islamic extremism, and, more controversially, Islamo-fascism. Although these terms denote aspects of the phenomenon – Islamic fundamentalism, for example, connotes its emphasis on the revival of original principles – none covers its entire meaning. A better term, increasingly employed by scholars and journalists, and the one adopted here, is Islamism. In common with other ideological systems of the modern era, including communism and fascism, Islamism subscribes to a comprehensive view that seeks to stimulate and guide major social and political change. However, those whom we call "Islamist" rarely apply that term to themselves. Islamists may oppose the term because it suggests that their philosophy is a political extrapolation from Islam rather than a straightforward expression of Islam as a way of life. In fact, most Islamists identify themselves simply as concerned Muslims working for the restoration of authentic Islam.

Following Graham E. Fuller, I define an Islamist as "one who believes that Islam as a body of faith has something to say about how politics and society should be ordered in the contemporary Muslim world and who seeks to implement this idea in some fashion."[1] Inclining toward activism, Islamism differs from the faith of "ordinary" Muslims who may not emphasize the need for Islamic-oriented socio-political change. Feeling their Islamic identity at risk, Islamists focus on the "pure" Islam of the earliest generations of Muslims in order to fortify contemporary Muslim communities against states, regimes, social groups, and belief systems that they regard as damaging to their faith. The restoration of authentic Islam, Islamists say, will guarantee social justice, fair economic practice, and probity in public affairs. Empowered by Islamic principles, Muslims will find their potential as shining examples of modernity imbued with spiritual value. Inherent to Islamism is the sense of Islam's manifest destiny to liberate benighted humanity from the dross and distortions incumbent upon disbelief.[2]

In some ways, modern Islamist organizations are similar to earlier Islamic movements. Like the tribally organized jihad movements in the pre-modern era – including those of Usman dan Fodio who founded the Fulani Empire in what is now northern Nigeria in 1804–8, Muhammad Ibn Ali al-Sanusi (d. 1859) in Cyrenaica, and Muhammad Ahmad (d. 1885), the self-styled Mahdi who fought to rid the Sudan of the disruptive features of Anglo-Egyptian colonialism – Islamists see themselves as participants in a continuum of Islamic reassertion that dates from the earliest decades of Islam. In common with the nineteenth-century jihad movements, Islamists seek to restore Islam to its original purity. But, unlike these earlier movements, Islamists implicitly or explicitly address challenges to Islam that stem from social antipathies and oppositional stances intrinsic to global modernity.

Islamism is a diverse phenomenon. Yet a number of common features can be identified. One is obvious: the tendency to ground activism in the teachings of the Qur'an and the example of the Prophet Muhammad as documented in the *hadith* – reports of what Muhammad said and did during his career as a prophet. Islamists regard Islam not as a private affair but as a *nizam*, by which they mean an "integrated system" or "closed order" that includes all aspects of life, including public matters. There is legitimacy in this claim. Since the earliest days of Islam, Muslims have recognized that the vocation to implement God's will is a communal as well as an individual responsibility, a mandate reflected in the division of the *shari'a* between issues relating to social and economic transactions *(mu'amalat)* and those dealing with ritual, faith, and worship *(ibadat)*. In putting forward the idea of Islam's comprehensive nature, Islamists draw upon a concept of social order that has deep roots in Islamic tradition.

Islamists may also differ from other Muslims in their attitude toward extraneous influences on Islam. Whereas the Islam of many Muslims is a hybrid of beliefs and practices, some of them derived from non-Muslim cultures, Islamists are careful to pattern their lives on scriptural and canonical principals. In the Islamist view, practices such as visiting tombs of Muslim "saints" *(awliya)* or the free mixing of the sexes are "innovations" that should be purged from the lives of Muslims. True Islam, Islamists stress, is based not on culture but on Qur'anic norms that are enduring and universal. In referring to an unblemished identity, Islamists attempt to undercut the legitimacy of existing socio-political orders, which they deem to be insufficiently Islamic.

Islamists also tend to be critical of Islamic scholars (*'ulama*) whom they regard as peddlers of dry and irrelevant scholasticism and the co-opted mouthpieces of corrupt, secular political leaders; it is a fact that in modern history, many Sunni *'ulama* have been absorbed into the state as salaried employees (their Shi'a counterparts have maintained a greater degree of autonomy), a dependency that has compromised their standing as champions of the people's interests. Many Islamist thinkers and activists are laymen who have by-passed the specialized juridical and theological training of the scholars; this was the case with Hasan al-Banna, founder of Egypt's Muslim Brotherhood. Others are renegade scholars operating on the fringes of the Islamic establishment. Shaykh Umar 'Abd al-Rahman, the former spiritual guide of Egypt's al-Jama'a al-Islamiyya (The Islamic Group), is an example of a trained scholar (he is a graduate of the Azhar, Cairo's hallowed mosque-university) who abandoned the religious institution for a career of Islamist militancy.[3]

Islamist beginnings

Islamism must be seen within a framework of Muslim responses to Western imperialism. Islamism's remote origins can be traced back to the long and slow decline in Muslim fortunes that began in the 1700s. It was then, at the height of the early modern age, that Europe's powerful new nation-states began to impose, oftentimes forcefully, degrees of economic and political control over the swath of Muslim lands stretching from Morocco to the South China Sea. Muslim sultanates and princedoms were incorporated as subordinates into a growing European order of culture and economic exchange.

The reversal of Muslim power and influence encouraged the quest for solutions. One response was to emulate the success of the West by adopting secularism – the explicit removal of Islam from some or all areas of public life; this was the approach famously taken during the early decades of the twentieth century by Mustafa Kemal Ataturk in the Turkish Republic and in Pahlavi Iran by Reza Shah.

Another solution lay in strengthening Islam by accommodating pure Qur'anic principles to the requirements of Western modernity. Throughout the Islamic world, but especially in Cairo, Istanbul, and the cities of the Indus-Gangetic plain, modernist reformers attempted to justify in Islamic terms the adoption by Muslims of Western political, economic, and civic institutions necessary, in their view, for the empowerment, independence, and eventual political unity of Muslim lands. Thus, for example, several reformers, including the Ottoman Turkish Namik Kemal (d. 1888) and the Egyptian Muhammad 'Abduh (d. 1905), redefined the old Islamic principle of *shura* ("consultation") to legitimize the writing of political constitutions.[4] In India, the reformer Sayyid Ahmad Khan, who received a knighthood from the British government in 1888, attempted to demonstrate the Qur'an's compatibility with reason and "nature."[5] Thus Islamic modernism came to be a wedge that allowed the Muslim political class to adopt, under the cover of Islam, secular attitudes and institutions.

Despite promising starts, the secularist and modernist approaches did not gain traction with most Muslims. In many colonized or semi-colonized countries, Muslims associated Westernization, in all of its forms, with the European imperial order and with the indigenous political elite that was prepared to accept the tutelage of European overlords as a prelude to full self-determination.

By the mid-1930s, many Muslims, especially those belonging to modernizing middle classes, were gravitating to the more vigorous and confrontational Islamist posture. In contrast to the secularists and Islamic modernists, both of whom admired much of what the West had to offer, the Islamists distanced Islamic civilization from the West. Islamists claimed that the failure of modern-era Muslims to construct strong and viable states and societies had a moral and ethical source, namely, the promotion of individualism, materialism, and relativism. In the Islamist view, modernization should be accomplished in an Islamic spirit and not as a cover for Europeanization. Only by returning to authentic Islam, they said, would Muslim populations be able to restore their inner strength and thus resist prevailing forms of tyranny, exclusion, and debilitating vice.

Islamism's popularity accelerated during the middle decades of the twentieth century, when Muslim peoples struggled for independence from formal or informal modes of Western authority. In the end, it was the secular, technocratic wings of the anti-colonial movements rather than the Islamist organisations that gained freedom for their countries. Secular nationalism reached the peak of its influence in the Muslim world in the 1960s, as leaders such as Pakistan's Ayub Khan, Tunisia's Habib Bourguiba, and Indonesia's Sukarno forcibly limited the presence of Islam in the public sphere. The anti-colonial pedigrees and state-directed modernization programs of these regimes initially gained them considerable legitimacy. But already in the late 1960s, cracks were beginning to appear in their systems. All over the Muslim world, populations felt crushed by failing economies, rising unemployment, and by the closed political orders imposed by dictatorships and monarchies. Many saw Israel's decisive defeat of the Arab armies during the June 1967 Arab–Israeli War as symptomatic of the problem. The failure of the nationalist regimes to address the needs of the people reinvigorated Islamism and made it the primary expression of popular protest. Whereas in the 1940s and 1950s, Islamists primarily targeted Western imperialism, now they challenged nominally Muslim governments. The ensuing contest abetted the confrontational mode inherent in Islamism, resulting in episodes of radicalism and violence that stretched into the 1980s and 1990s and laid the foundations of the al-Qaeda phenomenon. (For more on the radical Islamist groups that have used violence, see Chapter 18 by David Cook in this volume. See Chapter 22 by Daveed Gartenstein-Ross for the contemporary history of al-Qaeda.)

Islamist variants

Islamism is a phenomenon that springs from, and responds to, tensions in social, economic, and political environments. It takes the form of diverse kinds of social movements and smaller organizations. Most Islamists focus on preaching and political activity to bring about their moral revolution. Here the goal is to build a modern Islamic society from the ground up by means of missions of reconversion and pragmatic involvement in politics. These moderate, political Islamists may work toward limited reforms in the existing regime or push for the restructuring of the social, political, and economic realms in ways that reflect Islamic values. Although political Islamists propagate the ideal of political unity in the Muslim world, they tend to recognize the validity of the nation-states in which they operate for pragmatic reasons.

Examples of Islamist organizations that have worked within political systems include the Muslim Brotherhood (al-Ikhwan al-Muslimun) in Egypt, the Justice and Development Party (Adalet ve Kalkinma Partisi) in Turkey, the Prosperous Justice Party (Partai Keadilan Sejahtera) in Indonesia, and the Party for Justice and Development (Parti pour la justice et le développement) in Morocco. In recent years, all of these organizations have attempted to prove Islam's compatibility with pluralist democracy, or at least with some of its basic elements. In the modernist vein, they uphold *shura* – the idealized Islamic concept of political consultation. Since the 1980s, moderate Islamists have sought, oftentimes successfully, to participate in parliamentary elections.

Yet, despite their doctrinal flexibility, political Islamists are in the end bounded by a premise basic to Islamism as a whole: the idea that political sovereignty resides with God, not with people. God holds dominion over His creation and through the agency of prophecy has provided humankind with laws, regulations, and advice for righteous living. Such strictures have the potential to block legislation with a secular bent. They can also encourage intolerance and aggression. Although moderate Islamists by definition eschew the tactical use of violence, beneath most political Islamist organizations lurks an original militant spirit, which in contexts of social or political struggle may manifest in the form of political violence.

Other Islamists, often labeled "radicals" or "jihadis," abjure the gradualist strategy and instead demand a complete end to the power structure of the prevailing political order. The radicals' goals, in other words, tend toward unqualified change rather than incremental reform through political channels. Throughout the world, radical Islamists combat what they regard as insufficiently Islamic Muslim regimes, foreign occupiers of Muslim lands – as in Afghanistan, Chechnya, Bosnia, and Kashmir – and domineering Western states that they hold responsible for the enervating political, economic, and social conditions under which many Muslims live. In contrast to political Islamists, who advance a political agenda and engage with society to meet the challenges facing Muslims, radicals disavow the legitimacy of political processes and set themselves up as self-appointed vanguards apart from the general population and in judgment of it.[6]

Not only that, many radicals, especially those like al-Qaeda dedicated to internationalist and anti-Western global jihad, disavow the legitimacy of the nation-state altogether, regarding it as serving the interests of man rather than God. In place of the nation-state, the radicals speak of reviving the caliphate, an institution of pre-modern provenance that represents the unity of Muslims, which Mustafa Kemal Ataturk officially abolished in 1924. As of this writing, the Islamic State in Iraq and Syria (ISIS), a radical organization with roots in a former al-Qaeda affiliate, had made moves to establish the foundations of a caliphate in the areas it controls in Syria and Iraq. However, radicals are generally vague as to what form a new caliphate should take. For now, their imperative of a revived caliphate stands merely as a potent unifying symbol.

Islamists may adopt political gradualism or they may attempt the revolutionary overthrow of a government. They may harness the discourse of Islam to liberate a Muslim territory under the control of putative *kuffar* ("disbelievers"), as did Muslim volunteers from around the world in Soviet-occupied Afghanistan in the 1980s, or else establish a base for permanent jihad to fight the West, the so-called "Far Enemy" identified by al-Qaeda. Whether one strategy prevails over another is contingent on context. In this sense, Islamist solidarities are conditional, accidental, and secondary to the local and practical struggles waged by Muslims.

Especially important is the attitude of state authorities toward Islamist movements. The historical record suggests a pattern: where states allowed Islamist movements to access the political field or provided them with a modicum of organizational autonomy, Islamists adapted their purposes to the state regime, sometimes at the cost of modifying their demands and tactics. This was the case as regards Egypt's Muslim Brotherhood during the former presidency of Hosni Mubarak (1981–2011): in return for compliance, the Mubarak regime allowed the Brothers to propagate their message and even participate in elections, although the regime was quick to curtail the Brotherhood whenever it became too prominent or overstepped explicit political boundaries.

However, even dedicated moderates have turned to violence when excluded entirely from the political system. Then violence is the consequence of triggering factors, which can include the state's outlawing of an Islamist movement and the savage persecution of its members and supporters. Under the impact of state oppression, it has not been unusual for a cohesive radical wing to break away from the moderate parent movement. The violence perpetrated by these groups on state officials or even on the general population has often had the effect of further polarizing the conflict.[7]

One clear example of anti-regime radicalization relates to Sayyid Qutb (1906–66), an Egyptian man of letters who joined the Muslim Brotherhood in 1953. Qutb was originally a supporter of the nationalist government of Gamal Abdel Nasser but turned against the regime when it retained the prevailing secular character of the Egyptian state. Imprisoned and subjected to brutal torture, Qutb transferred the odium he had previously directed at the politicians of Egypt's Old Regime to Nasser's government. In Qutb's new view, although Nasser's government claimed to represent the interests of Muslims, its refusal to fully implement *shari'a* qualified it as a usurper of God's sovereign authority over the Earth. Qutb wrote of the need for a circle of adroit Muslims, a vanguard, to awaken the masses from the deception and mobilize them in the direction of comprehensive change. (For more on Sayyid Qutb and his influence on subsequent generations of Islamists, see Chapter 18 by Cook in this volume.)

In coming to this tactic, Qutb had in mind the model of the Prophet Muhammad and the first Muslims, who from an initial position of weakness gradually built up their power so that they could confront head-on the oppressors of their period. But Qutb was also inspired by modern currents of rebellion and political change, at least unconsciously. That is to say, he repackaged in Islamic form the Jacobin characteristics of the European revolutionary tradition, which in his time were common currency throughout much of Africa and Asia. Like his global counterparts, Qutb enumerated grievances and laid claim to truth in an effort to realize the utopian dream, in his case, of an Islamic state. The Egyptian regime released Qutb from prison in 1964 but soon rearrested him on the charge that he and dozens of other Muslim Brothers belonged to an underground cell intent on overthrowing the government. On August 29, 1966, he and two of his colleagues were executed.[8]

The radicalism inherent in this and other cases of Islamist contestation is circumstantial, shaped by events on the ground, including institutional political environments and international trends. The exclusionary and repressive practices of post-colonial authoritarian regimes have been especially important in encouraging components within established Islamist organizations to pick up the gun. It is not going too far to say that in instances, Islamist violence reflects the violence perpetrated on Muslim populations by the authoritarian state. Once engaged in a conflict, it is easy for radicals to further sharpen the lines of division between insiders and outsiders, thus producing an environment conducive to total war.[9]

Ideological framing

Islamism is tangled in the dynamics of the modern world. Yet we must not neglect the role of ideas in the formation of Islamist-oriented dissent. Steeped in a received history that extends to the time of the Prophet Muhammad, both mainstream and radical Islamists interpret the Islamic heritage through a lens of discontent, focusing on understandings that justify, but also shape, their responses to situations of stress, conflict, and contestation. The Islamic symbols and doctrines that Islamists resuscitate resonate with authenticity and emotional energy. From them Islamists create counter-discourses that challenge perceived enemies from positions of ostensible religious legitimacy.

Islamists draw inspiration and doctrine from the *al-salaf al-salih* – the "pious forefathers of the faith" who comprised the first three generations of Muslims, including the Prophet, his loyal companions, and the scholars who followed in their footsteps (*al-tabi'un*). It is important to emphasize that *salafism* – the term applied to those who follow the *salaf* – predated the rise of Islamism and, to a large extent, remains independent of it. In the contemporary period, most self-described salafis have little or nothing to do with the Islamist phenomenon. Yet salafism, as a mood if not a precise doctrine, inhabits a great deal of Islamist ideology.

Salafi Muslims uphold the teachings of the *al-salaf al-salih* as representative of original, unblemished Islam. They therefore consider these teachings as exemplary. Distrustful of reason as a basis in discerning God's will, salafis take the Qur'an and the example of the

Prophet Muhammad (*Sunna*) as their sole sources of guidance. In the salafi view, God is the sole legislator and He alone has the power to define right and wrong, good and evil. To this extent, salafis decry slavish adherence to the four Sunni schools of law, which make use of imperfect human judgment in the construction of legal rulings. Against the tradition of religious tolerance and accommodation within Islam, salafis rigorously distinguish between themselves and "infidel" Christians and Jews, in addition to other Muslims who do not live up to their strict standards. Rooted in this attitude of exclusion is the potential for assertiveness and even violence against persons or governments considered by salafis as wayward or insufficiently Islamic. Historically, however, most salafis have adopted the established Sunni view that rulers – including imperfect rulers – should be obeyed in order to avoid the chaos that is the inevitable consequence of rebellion.[10]

Salafism emerged as a coherent religious orientation in the fourteenth century. Its great champion was the Damascene scholar Ibn Taymiyya (d. 1328), who objected to the innovations and accretions he believed had crept into Islam over the centuries, including the intercessory beliefs and practices of Sufis (Islamic mystics) and the Shi'as. In Ibn Taymiyya's view, both the Sufi cult of saints and the Shi'a's veneration of their imams (lineal descendants of the Prophet Muhammad's family) compromised the unity of God's lordship over the universe (*tawhid*) – an accusation that became standard among salafi Muslims.

In the 1910s and 1920s, a tribal chieftain from Nejd, 'Abd al-'Aziz Ibn Sa'ud, conquered most of the Arabian Peninsula in the name of a puritanical creed closely identified with salafism. The movement took its immediate inspiration from Muhammad 'Abd al-Wahhab (d. 1792), a religious reformer educated at Mecca and Medina who harshly criticized the lax religious practices of the Peninsular Arabs. Consequently, outsiders often refer to this Arabian movement as "Wahhabism," although the early Saudis preferred the name "People of Unity" (*al-Muwahhidun*); today many refer to themselves simply as salafis. As the Saudi state consolidated, its ruling house abandoned its penchant for territorial conquest in favor of mostly peaceful methods of propagation. In the 1960s and 1970s, 'Abd al-'Aziz ibn Sa'ud's successors began to channel Saudi assertiveness into a strong missionary impulse that targeted Muslim populations in the Middle East, South Asia, and elsewhere to counter the Arab socialism spilling out of Nasser's Egypt and, after 1979, to stem the spread of the Shi'a Iranian Revolution.

From the outset, Islamists identified with the salafi quest for authentic origins. Hasan al-Banna claimed that in its effort to revive Islamic first principles, the Muslim Brotherhood was in part a salafi organization, although many Wahhabis in Saudi Arabia came eventually to disagree, citing the Brotherhood's political activism, eventual acceptance of democracy, and emphasis on narrow national concerns. More pronounced was the appropriation of the tenets and doctrines of traditional salafi theology and jurisprudence by radical Islamists. This overlapping was an outcome of the insurgencies and protest movements that rocked the Middle East and South Asia between the 1970s and 1990s, especially the Islamist rebellions in Egypt and Algeria and the Muslim resistance to the invading Soviet Red Army in Afghanistan. The international networks of activists formed as a result of these struggles provided opportunities for Saudi Arabian puritanism – by that time widespread in the world – to mingle with the revolutionary trend associated with the Muslim Brother Sayyid Qutb. The merging of the two was evident in the writings of the Palestinian advocate of jihad, 'Abdullah 'Azzam (d. 1989) who took his inspiration from Qutb and was also a beneficiary of Saudi Arabian patronage.[11] In the 1990s, many radicals acknowledged this hybrid form by referring to themselves as "jihadi salafis," a self-descriptor meant to signify vociferous activism propelled by religious correctness. However, the radicals' understanding of the Islamic tradition is often at odds with the consensus of salafi scholars, both state-supported, as in Saudi Arabia, and independent, as in Egypt. Whereas mainstream salafis appeal to canonical Islamic texts in efforts to address issues of religious purity and transgression, Islamist radicals use these sources to change political systems and to justify their assault on those whom they identify as enemies.

Nowhere is the radical Islamist appropriation of salafism more explicit than in its attention to group exclusivity. Dividing the world into spheres of good and evil, Islamists fortify salafism's inherent intolerance toward other beliefs, thus strengthening boundaries that align with struggles over the public sphere in which they are engaged. They find justification for the practice of strong group loyalty in the writings of Ibn Taymiyya, who warned Muslims against associating with Christians and Jews. More influential, especially among Islamist radicals, is the salafi injunction of "Loyalty and disavowal" (*al-wala' wa al-barra'*) enunciated by eighteenth- and nineteenth-century Wahhabi clerics like Sulayman Ibn 'Abdullah Al al-Shaykh (d. 1818), which similarly encourages Muslims to sever relations between believers and non-Muslims. According to the doctrine, Islam is constructed according to the opposites of love and hatred: love for true Islam and hatred for its antithesis. The doctrine has a natural appeal to radical Islamists who modify it in order to assert their spiritual superiority over opponents. In their view, true believers are few and are chosen by God above all others. Contemporary ideologues, like the al-Qaeda-affiliated Abu Muhammad al-Maqdisi (b. 1958), use the doctrine to judge the legitimacy of Muslim political leaders who dispense man-made law, or to delegitimize competing Muslim communities such as the Shi'a. In so doing, they transform what was originally a command to enhance religious purity into an ideological tool to provoke and sustain conflict.[12] We have a conceptual dynamic of in-group radicalization familiar to students of revolution, but which is here expressed in terms of religion.

Qutb formulated a similar, though not identical, exclusionary principle that likewise draws upon ideas associated with Islam's formative period. During his tryst with Egypt's Nasser regime, Qutb claimed that the world was enveloped in *jahiliyya* – "ignorance" of the divine mandate – a Qur'anic term well placed in classical Islamic thought. Muslim thinkers, including Arabian Wahhabis, had applied *jahiliyya* to the condition of "ignorance" that prevailed in west-central Arabia prior to the advent of Islam's "civilizing mission." *Jahiliyya*, in this sense, was a temporal designation that distinguished Islam from pre-Islamic heathendom. Following the lead of the South Asian Islamists Abu l-A'la Mawdudi (d. 1979) and his disciple Abu Hasan Nadwi (d. 1999), Qutb defined the concept as an existential condition caused by people's willful dismissal of God's sovereignty, which prevails almost everywhere in the modern world, including Muslim countries like Egypt that were infected with secularism. As a result, the strong oppressed the weak and wickedness triumphed over goodness.[13] Qutb's adoption of ideological totality anticipated, and in part inspired, the "friend–enemy" distinctions made by subsequent radicals, including those of a salafi bent such as Egypt's Islamic Group (al-Jama'a al-Islamiyya) in their violent confrontations with the powers-that-be.

Many radicals have taken the next step of explicitly excising putatively wayward Muslim rulers and populations from the realm of Islam. The practice is called *takfir* – literally, the branding of a person previously considered Muslim a *kafir* or "infidel" – and is based on the Qur'anic prooftext (5:44): "and whoever did not judge by what Allah revealed, those are they that are unbelievers." The charge is serious – the traditional punishment for apostasy is death. The first practitioners of *takfir* were the Kharijites, literally, "those who secede" or "go out," an Islamic sect that during Islam's formative period assassinated its erstwhile leader, the fourth caliph 'Ali Ibn Abi Talib, on account of his alleged apostasy. Islamic jurists eventually restricted *takfir* in order to prevent civil unrest and to keep the Muslim community intact. According to the developing consensus of the scholars, only God knows what is in the heart of a person; as a result, Muslims must postpone their judgment on the fidelity (or lack thereof) of co-religionists. By separating faith and works, the jurists justified the authority of strong rulers capable of maintaining political order.[14]

Yet the practice of *takfir* persisted within the context of emergent salafism. In 1300, Ibn Taymiyya issued a *fatwa* (Juridical opinion) that permitted Muslims to fight the recently converted Mongols then invading Syria and Palestine. According to Ibn Taymiyya, despite the Mongols' conversion to Islam, their Islam was compromised by their continuing adherence to the *Yasa* code of laws of Genghis Khan. As a result, the Mongols were apostates, and their challenge to the Islamic authority of the Cairo-based Mamluk Sultanate could be lawfully met with force.[15]

In Arabia, Wahhabi clerics attached to the House of Sa'ud went a step further in ascribing unbelief to all except their own adepts, thus justifying violence against competing tribes. Yet, as noted above, the Saudi state eventually exchanged peaceful propagation for territorial conquest; Ibn Saud did not want to provoke the intervention into Saudi affairs of Great Britain, which had interests in the nearby Arab states of Iraq, Jordan, and Palestine. Consequently, Saudi Arabia's Wahhabi clerics fell into line with earlier Sunni scholars in placing limits on *takfir*. They were careful to make the point that there are levels of impiety that require judgmental caution.

Radicals, however, were under no such constraint. As they did in the case of the doctrine of "loyalty and disavowal," they renewed the practice of *takfir* as an ideological weapon within the context of the Islamist insurgencies of the late twentieth century. In Egypt, in 1981, the Jihad Group (Jama'at al-Jihad) interpreted Ibn Taymiyya's *fatwa* in a way that justified its assassination of Egypt's President Anwar Sadat; Sadat, they said, had left the faith on account of his refusal to fully implement Islamic law and look after the interests of Muslims. Egypt's state-sponsored clerical establishment labeled the assassins "Neo-Kharijites" – a term of reproach. In the 1990s, Algeria's Armed Islamic Group excommunicated a wide range of the country's Muslim population, including many ordinary citizens whom they accused of being in league with the government. One of the most notorious practitioners of *takfir* was Abu Mu'sab al-Zarqawi (d. 2006), the former leader of al-Qaeda in Iraq and one-time disciple of Abu Muhammad al-Maqdisi. Following the fall of Iraq's Baathist regime at the hands of the US-led coalition in 2003, Zarqawi pronounced anathema on the whole Shi'a community. His goal was to encourage civil strife, which his organization could then exploit to enhance its influence in the country.

Jihad

Islamists of all varieties hold that Muslims have a responsibility to reactivate the principle of *jihad*, literally, "striving" or "exertion" in pursuit of God's way. The injunction to jihad comes from divergent texts in the Qur'an. While some verses caution Muslims against confronting enemies and others allow fighting disbelievers only in self-defense, a select few verses appear to sanction jihad in all circumstances. The medieval exegetes regarded these divergent texts as corresponding to the changing circumstances of the Prophet Muhammad's career. According to this method, the divine revelations encouraged Muslims to avoid physical conflict during the Meccan period when they were weak but expanded the conditions under which they could wage war once the Muslims attained a position of strength at Medina. The medieval jurists held that the earlier verses dealing with jihad related to a specific situation, while the latter verses were enduring and universal. It was this aggressive understanding of jihad that legitimized the Muslim conquest movements of the early Middle Ages. According to the classical Islamic doctrine, offensive jihad of this kind is an obligation of the Muslim community as a whole (*fard kifaya*), although it can be carried out by some on behalf of the others. However, when Muslims are on the defensive, it becomes a personal duty of every adult male Muslim (*fard 'ayn*). In both cases, jihad is contingent on the approval of a legitimate community leader.[16]

Islamists honor the classical jurisprudence on jihad as a template for sustaining the struggle against Islam's enemies in the modern period, although in ways that suit their specific purposes. They downplay definitions that define jihad primarily as a spiritual struggle meant to tame base desires – the designation popularized by the Islamic modernists Sir Sayyid Ahmad Khan and Muhammad 'Abduh in the late nineteenth century. For Islamists, jihad is primarily a duty to resist the political and social manifestations of infidelity in the world.

According to political Islamists, like the Muslim Brotherhood, jihad connotes forms of activism, short of violence, which aim to create a state governed by Islamic values. Radical Islamists, while they accept the validity of "jihad of the tongue" and of "the pen," emphasize jihad's militant dimension, both as a goad against foreign occupation and as an essential component of a revolutionary discourse directed at Muslim regimes they consider apostate. Because Muslim-majority lands are occupied or threatened by purported infidels, radicals tend to delimit jihad as an individual obligation on par with prayer and fasting. And because, in their view, no legitimate political authority exists, they believe that they have the right to interpret the sacred texts directly, thus circumventing the normative deliberations and possible prohibitions of the religious establishment. Bereft of institutional constraints, radical jihadis interpret God's will in ways that authorize their oftentimes violent methods. Depending on local or regional conditions, cultures, and histories, these methods may include the vociferous moral policing of communities, targeted assassinations of enemies, or mass-casualty terrorism of the kind perpetrated by al-Qaeda and its affiliates on populations around the world, including the attacks on New York and Washington (2001), Bali (2002), Madrid (2004), London (2005), and various places in Iraq (2006 to the present, as of this writing).

Conclusion

Islamism is a phenomenon of the twentieth and twenty-first centuries. It is a product of tensions and dilemmas that have beset many Muslim-majority societies in the late-colonial and post-colonial eras, including Westernization, the perseverance of authoritarian regimes, and a general sense of Muslim powerlessness vis-à-vis the United States and Europe. What sets Islamism apart from other types of protest or insurrection is the inclination of Islamist thinkers and activists to interpret the world in terms of Islam's foundational texts and religious inheritance. The Islamists' revival of the heritage is necessarily selective, and the purposes and methods of its deployment contingent on particular situations and contexts.

What all varieties of Islamism share in common is an attitude of confrontation – a desire to change the status quo – which in environments of political oppression, institutional blockage, or revolutionary fervor can devolve into violence.

Notes

1. Graham E. Fuller, *The Future of Political Islam* (New York: Palgrave Macmillan, 2003), xi.
2. Islamism's engagement with the politics of authenticity is treated in Aziz al-Azmeh, *Islams and Modernities* (London: Verso, 1993). A good overview of Islamism is Gilles Kepel, *Jihad: On the Trail of Political Islam* (Cambridge, MA: Belknap Harvard, 2002).
3. See Malika Zeghal, *Gardiens de L'islam: Les oulemas d'al Azhar dans l'Egypte contemporaine* (Paris: Presses de la Fondation nationale des sciences politiques, 1996).
4. Albert Hourani, *Arabic Thought in the Liberal Age*, rev. ed. (London: Cambridge University Press, 1983).
5. Aziz Ahmad, *Islamic Modernism in India and Pakistan, 1857–1964* (Oxford: Oxford University Press, 1967).
6. The categorization of Islamism is well treated in Jillian Schwedler, "Can Islamists Become Moderates? Rethinking the Inclusion–Moderation Hypothesis," *World Politics* 63, no. 2 (April 2011): 347–76.
7. See Mohammed M. Hafez, *Why Muslims Rebel: Repression and Resistance in the Islamic World* (Boulder, CO: Lynne Rienner, 2003); and Quintan Wiktorowicz, ed., *Islamic Activism: A Social Movement Theory Approach* (Bloomington: Indiana University Press, 2004).
8. On Sayyid Qutb, see John Calvert, *Sayyid Qutb and the Origins of Radical Islamism* (London: Hurst and Columbia University Press, 2010); and Roxanne Euben, *Enemy in the Mirror: Islamic Fundamentalism and the Limits of Modern Rationalism* (Princeton, NJ: Princeton University Press, 1999).
9. See Luis Martinez, *The Algerian Civil War 1990–1998* (New York: Columbia University Press, 2000); and Michael Willis, *The Islamist Challenge in Algeria: A Political History* (New York: New York University Press, 1996) for case studies of state-driven Islamist radicalization.
10. On salafism, see the essays in Roel Meijer, ed., *Global Salafism: Islam's New Religious Movement* (London: Hurst, 2009).
11. See Thomas Hegghammer, "Abdullah Azzam, the Imam of Jihad," in *Al Qaeda in its Own Words*, ed. Gilles Kepel and Jean-Pierre Milelli, 81–101 (Cambridge, MA: Harvard University Press, 2008).
12. Joas Wagemakers, "The Transformation of a Radical Concept: al-wala' wa-l-barra'," in *Global Salafism*, 81–106.
13. William Shepard, "Sayyid Qutb's Doctrine of Jahilyya," *International Journal of Middle East Studies* 35, no. 4 (2003): 521–45.
14. On the Kharijites and their relation to *takfir*, see Nelly Lahoud, *The Jihadis' Path to Self-Destruction* (New York: Columbia University Press, 2010).
15. Mona Hassan, "Modern Interpretations and Misinterpretations of a Medieval Scholar: Apprehending the Political Thought of Ibn Taymiyya," in *Ibn Taymiyya and His Times*, ed. Yossef Rapoport and Shahab Ahmed, 338–66 (Oxford: Oxford University Press, 2010).
16. On the classical doctrine and practice of jihad, see Michael Bonner, *Jihad in Islamic History* (Princeton, NJ: Princeton University Press, 2006).

Further reading

al-Azmeh, Aziz. *Islams and Modernities*. London: Verso, 1993.
Calvert, John. *Sayyid Qutb and the Origins of Radical Islamism*. London: Hurst and Columbia University Press, 2010.
Commins, David. *The Wahhabi Mission and Saudi Arabia*. London: I. B. Tauris, 2009.
Cook, Michael. *Forbidding Wrong in Islam*. Cambridge: Cambridge University Press, 2003.
Hafez, Mohammed M. *Why Muslims Rebel: Repression and Resistance in the Islamic World*. Boulder, CO: Lynne Rienner, 2003.

Hourani, Albert. *Arabic Thought in the Liberal Age*. Rev. ed. London: Cambridge University Press, 1983.

Lia, Brynjar. *The Society of the Muslim Brothers in Egypt: The Rise of an Islamic Mass Movement, 1928–1942*. Reading, UK: Ithaca Press, 1998.

Meijer, Roel, ed. *Global Salafism: Islam's New Religious Movement*. London: Hurst, 2009.

Shepard, William. "Sayyid Qutb's Doctrine of Jahilyya." *International Journal of Middle East Studies* 35, no. 4 (2003): 521–45.

Wiktorowicz, Quintan, ed. *Islamic Activism: A Social Movement Theory Approach*. Bloomington: Indiana University Press, 2004.

18

ISLAMIST TERRORISM FROM THE MUSLIM BROTHERHOOD TO HAMAS

David Cook

This chapter will discuss Islamist terrorism in its more mainstream variety associated with the Sunni Muslim Brotherhood (*al-Ikhwan al-Muslimin*) and its offshoots as well as the various Lebanese Shi'ite radical groups associated with Hizbullah by tracing the principal political Islamist organizations and their use of political violence and terror from the 1930s until the first decade of the 2000s in the region of Egypt and the Levant. Although these various groups are disparate in their origins and span the doctrinal divide that exists between Sunnism and Shi'ism, they share a common commitment to the mainstream political process that is not shared by salafi-jihadis. All of the groups descended from the Muslim Brotherhood, not to speak of Hizbullah, have been accepted in some way by the broader Muslim society – either into government or as legitimate resistance movements – and in some cases eventually as part of the religious establishment. Although some of the radicalized groups (in Egypt primarily) that descended from the Muslim Brotherhood during the 1970s and 1980s fought their government (an action which did not command broad support), the ideologues of these offshoots, such as Sayyid Qutb, were frequently accepted by the mainstream and even venerated. Similarly, the position of Hizbullah, as a radical Shi'ite organization in a mostly Sunni Arab world, has been ambiguous but always bolstered by the perception that it was primarily a resistance movement against Israel, as well as by the judicious moderation (towards other Muslims) of its leader Hassan Nasrullah.

However, in contradistinction to purely quietist (non-violent) political Islamic parties and groups throughout the Muslim world, Islamist terrorist groups also share the willingness to apply violence in order to force the political–religious pace of change, that is, create a *shari'a* state. Whereas on the one side quietists reject violence entirely and on the other side jihadis reject the political process entirely, Islamist terrorist groups have at different times embraced both processes.

Mainstream Muslim radicalism has its roots in the political organization of Islam during the early part of the twentieth century, which until that period had relied upon the institution of the caliphate (abolished in 1924) in order to provide the political basis of the faith and the religious authority of the *'ulama* (religious hierarchy) to provide the boundaries of the faith, the limits of what constitutes a Muslim. Lacking the symbolic leadership of the caliph during the 1920s at the same time when most governments in the Arabic-speaking world (together with their subordinate religious establishments) were directly or indirectly controlled by non-Muslim Europeans, there was a strong and broad need for some type of political activism that would renew political Islam.[1] This need was eventually fulfilled by the Muslim Brotherhood and its offshoots. (For more on the origins of Islamism, as well as a discussion of its variants and their relationship to salafism and jihadism, see Chapter 17 by John Calvert in this volume.)

However, it is important to note that the Muslim Brotherhood was not an acceptable organization to all strands of Islam and most especially not to governments. The latter saw the Brotherhood as a representative of the pre-modern attitudes they were trying to excise and overcome during the period of its rise (1930–50), and they feared its fanaticism. The Muslim Brotherhood's Muslim opponents included conservative *'ulama*, which rejected the political activism of the Brothers, as well as Sufi orders, which were usually quietist and rejected violence from a political and religious point of view. Liberal Muslim intellectuals were often the victims of Brotherhood attacks, whether physical or verbal, and Christian minorities throughout the Middle East feared the rise of political Islam and tended to support secular or at least non-confessional political parties.

Given the power and prestige of these numerous opponents, it is not surprising that the Muslim Brotherhood and its offshoots have often seen the world arrayed against them (especially when one considers that the colonial powers and then later the United States and the Soviet Union all sided with the semi-secular elites of the Arabic-speaking Middle East) and found recourse to violence in order to even the field. This Muslim Brotherhood violence then, in its turn, justified repression and demonization of even mainstream Islamists who by the late 1980s and 1990s had acquired the aura of being both the primary danger to the established order as well as the primary justification for its existence.[2]

The Muslim Brotherhood in Egypt

The Muslim Brotherhood was founded by Hasan al-Banna in 1931 as a specifically political movement to re-establish the dominance of Islam within the Arabic-speaking Muslim world (first, prior to the projected unification of all Muslims) and to implement the *shari'a* (divine law), understood by the Brotherhood to be a unified code (for more on this, see Chapter 17 by Calvert).[3] Its opponents were numerous and included the British masters of Egypt (until 1952), then the secularizing elites surrounding first the monarchy and later the military dictatorship that replaced it (in 1952), and finally the Muslim religious elites, which the Brotherhood held to be medieval in their religious and political attitudes.

Al-Banna wrote extensively on the issue of jihad (divinely mandated warfare) and considered, in the words of Brynjar Lia, that it

> was not only a duty to wage war against the occupying colonial power ... but was also a pledge to eradicate the deeply ingrained resignation of the souls and minds of their co-religionists and remove their inferiority complexes. Jihad became a keyword denoting all self-initiated productive work or activities aimed at bettering the conditions of the Islamic community. Furthermore, jihad also implied a solemn avowal to fearlessly reproach and correct unjust rulers by demanding justice and reform, thereby abandoning the traditional political quietism which characterized other contemporary Islamic groups.[4]

In such a statement we see all of the hallmarks of the success of the Brotherhood: the use of violence as a force to overcome inferiority (heralding a similar move by Frantz Fanon during the Algerian War of Independence, 1954–62) as well as the social basis of a mass movement through which the militants can gain access to the wider society (key to the success of Hamas and other Brotherhood-related groups). During this early period of the Muslim Brotherhood, political violence was usually of a personal nature (assassinations, local intimidation) or involved mass demonstrations.

These limitations are reflected in what al-Banna writes concerning jihad:

> God ordained jihad upon the Muslims not as a means of aggression, nor as a method for personal aggrandizement, but in order to protect the call (*da'wa*), and as a guarantee for peace – and as a means for the greater message to be undertaken by the Muslims, which is the message of guiding the people to the right and to justice, and to Islam.[5]

One should remember that during al-Banna's time, the presence of political Islam at the higher reaches of political power was almost non-existent, and that nationalist leaders, while frequently applying violence against the colonial powers, did not utilize the term jihad. It was not until al-Banna's emphasis upon jihad that the term began to be utilized again, and it did not become truly popular until after the Six Day War in 1967 (both under the influence of the radical ideologue Qutb and under Egyptian governmental influence through the mainstream *'ulama*). Further, al-Banna laid down the elevated nature of the jihad, as he perceived it: during jihad Muslims would not loot, rape, dismember bodies, or hurt innocent people.[6] It is, however, difficult to reconcile these descriptions with the actual facts of the Brotherhood during the period 1931–49.

For the most part, there were two aspects to the Brotherhood's violence at this time. The first was through the service of volunteers in the Egyptian army as volunteers, mainly fighting against Israel in 1948–9 (Brothers from Syria also aided the Syrian army in the same way); the second was assassinations of prominent Egyptian personalities said to have betrayed the Muslim cause. Probably the best known of the latter group was the killing of Nokrashy Pasha, who was prime minister during much of the war with Israel in 1948 and to whose incompetence the defeat in battle was attributed. Almost immediately after Pasha's death, Hasan al-Banna was himself assassinated (by unknowns, but presumably government-inspired), and the Muslim Brotherhood lost its most potent ideologue.[7]

Radicalism in the Muslim Brotherhood

After the assassination of al-Banna, the Brotherhood effectively went through a gradual split. Its political prominence rose tremendously during and immediately following the Revolution of 1952; however, Gamal Abdel Nasser (who ultimately became the ruler of Egypt) violently suppressed the group starting in 1954.[8] Nasser pursued a socialist, secularizing agenda for Egypt and believed that the Brothers constituted a dangerous opposition. As elation turned to disappointment, the leadership of the Brotherhood assumed a quietist role that they would play for the next forty-some years. This trend is important mainly for the fact that the mainstream Brotherhood gradually assumed the social and community-based responsibilities that the Egyptian government was either unwilling or unable to take upon itself, thereby laying the basis for the strong showing it made as a political party starting in the 1990s when it was once again legalized.

The more activist wing of the Brotherhood was led and influenced by Sayyid Qutb (executed 1966), a former literary critic who had then been employed by the Ministry of Education, which sent him to the United States for a time to study American methods of education. Qutb's writings became highly influential in moving elements of the Brotherhood away from quietism into activism; they bore fruit not during his lifetime but during the 1970s and 1980s, after which they were gradually superseded by salafi-jihadis radicalized by the Afghan War (1979–89). Salafis were those who took Qutb's ideas and, using the basic idea of *takfir* (the willingness to label apparent Muslims non-Muslims), attempted to create doctrinal boundaries around Islam. Not all salafis are violent; some are quietist. But those who are salafi-jihadis accept that in order to create the Islamic state one needs to apply violence.

Essentially Qutb was a protestant (in the sense of rejecting the interpretative writings around the sacred text of the Qur'an) and sought to focus the entirety of Islamic (Sunni) teaching upon the Qur'an, to the detriment of the tradition (*hadith*) literature. In practice, this meant unifying Islamic teaching as opposed to allowing for internal variations that previously had characterized Sunnism. This revolutionary conception of Islam moved the radical away from the centuries of jurisprudential discussion that characterize mainstream conservative Islam (and also the quietist Muslim Brotherhood) and focused him or her upon the life example of Muhammad and the text of the Qur'an. In turn, this had the effect of presenting history in a cyclical manner; indeed, during the course of conceptualizing this idea, Qutb decided that contemporary Islam is reliving the period of ignorance (*Jahiliyya*) against which Muhammad struggled and fought.

Although all Sunni Muslims try to follow the life-example of Muhammad (which is the meaning of Sunnism), Qutb's conception of *jahiliyya* more clearly emphasized the fact that the Prophet led and participated in numerous battles (up to approximately eighty-three) against the *jahiliyya*. In Qutb's conception, *jahiliyya* is the code word for the contemporary secular Arab state, in which the *shari'a* is not implemented and in which the ruler not only does not promote Islamic norms but is often subservient to non-Muslim powers (either the United States or the USSR). Qutb states in his definitive work, *Ma'alim fi al-tariq* (*Signposts along the Way*):

> Since this movement comes into conflict with the *jahiliyyah* which prevails over ideas and beliefs . . . the Islamic movement had to produce parallel resources to confront this *jahiliyyah*. This movement uses the methods of preaching and persuasion for reforming ideas and beliefs; and it uses physical power and *jihad* for abolishing the organizations and authorities of the *jahili* system which prevents people from reforming their ideas and beliefs but forces them to obey their erroneous ways and make them serve human lords instead of the Almighty Lord.[9]

This statement and Qutb's ideology as a whole led to the major conceptual foundation of salafi-jihadism as it developed after his death in 1966. For Qutb, the main starting point was the re-establishment of the general principle of *takfir*, which in turn would enable Muslim radicals to unleash violence against, first, their governments in order to establish the Islamic state and then ultimately against the society as a whole. This process was a gradual one and stands at the heart of the differences between the mainstream Brotherhood and the salafi-jihadis: while the Brotherhood believed in the necessity of jihad, for them the focus was outward, usually towards Israel or other non-Muslim entities. For salafi-jihadi radicals, these enemies were important as well, but only secondarily. They believed that the primary necessity was to establish the Muslim state, and that the true enemies of Islam were those – including nominal Muslims – who prevented that end from coming about.

Qutb wrote further concerning the goals of the jihad:

> The reasons for jihad which have been described in the above verses are these: to establish God's authority in the earth, to arrange human affairs according to the true guidance provided by God, to abolish all the Satanic forces and Satanic systems of life, to end the lordship of one man over others, since all men are creatures of God, and no one has the authority to make them his servants or to make arbitrary laws for them. These reasons are sufficient for proclaiming jihad.[10]

These goals are grand in nature and do not cease with the creation of the Islamic state but, in fact, as Qutb repeatedly points out, involve forcible removal of all systems that preclude humanity from freely choosing Islam. Although Qutb himself never participated in any violence, it should be clear that his conceptual framework – of non-Muslim governments and systems constituting *jahiliyyah* – was the basis for much of the radical violence during the period since his death.

At first, Egyptian radical Muslims were marginalized. Through the 1970s, they built counter-societies, such as the group known popularly as Takfir wa-l-Hijra group (actual name: Gama'at al-Muslimin), which was discovered in 1977 but had roots going back to 1971. The group was led by Shukri Mustafa and is best known for assassinating the Muslim religious leader al-Dhahabi in 1977 (after which it was suppressed by the government),[11] as well as for attacking Coptic Christians. Takfir wa-l-Hijra received its name from its methodology, which was to declare the Egyptian society to be an infidel (*kafir*) one, to emigrate from it (*hijra*) following the example of the Prophet Muhammad, and then to declare war against it. Nasser's successor, Anwar Sadat, alternately propitiated and suppressed Takfir wa-l-Hijra and other radical groups, but in the end their hatred for him, as a result of the peace agreement he signed with Israel in 1979, led to his assassination by a cell of radicals.

This cell, whose ideological leader was Muhammad 'Abd al-Salam Farag (executed in 1982), wrote the most important conceptual work on jihad to come out of the world of radicalism since the time of Qutb. Entitled *al-Farida al-gha'iba* (*The Neglected Duty*), referring to jihad, this comparatively short document is a polemic against the quietistic policies of the Brotherhood and specifically rejects peaceable alternatives to jihad. These alternatives are listed, among others, as mission work, education, withdrawal from society, and charitable work. All of these are specifically rejected because they allow the state to carry out its campaign of secularism and do not fulfill the obligation for Muslims to establish an Islamic state. When dealing with the question of who is the enemy, Farag states:

> First: to fight an enemy who is near is more important than to fight an enemy who is far [Israel]. Second: Muslim blood will be shed in order to realize this victory. Now it must be asked whether this victory will benefit the interests of an Islamic State?. . . It will mean the strengthening of a State which rebels against the Laws of God. . . . Fighting has to be done (only) under the Banner of Islam and under Islamic leadership. Third: The basis of the existence of Imperialism in the lands of

Islam are (precisely) these rulers.... We must concentrate on our own Islamic situation: we have to establish the rule of God's religion in our own country first.[12]

Unlike Qutb, Farag delineates and justifies a wide range of specifically violent actions, making sure to root them in Islamic law (according to a salafi interpretation) or at least to excuse those who carry out such actions from any repercussions. Probably the most problematic among these violent actions are the inadvertent deaths of bystanders who will inevitably be killed by the militants in their efforts to overthrow the tyrannical rulers. These, according to Farag, fall into two groups: the first includes the supporters of the government who are paid, such as soldiers, policemen, government officials, and the like, while the second is composed of entirely innocent bystanders who could be killed or injured in such operations. Farag does not flinch from declaring the first group to be essentially guilty by its association with the rulers and states that killing them is permitted. He is more hesitant about the second group, but later salafi-jihadi religious literature would sanction such deaths as well, under the rubric of the general *takfir* of the society.

Usually salafi-jihadi literature during the later 1990s and early 2000s would use the example of the *majaniq* (mangonels) that the Prophet Muhammad was said to have used against the city of al-Ta'if (in 630) as a precedent. If those mangonels could lob rocks over the city walls, presumably killing any innocents on the other side without discrimination between combatants and non-combatants, then it should be possible to justify killing innocents in the pursuit of the greater good of the Islamic state. In other words, those seeking to establish an Islamic state could ultimately attack and kill whomever they wished because their goal was right.

These points are still problematic for many jihadis, and almost every operation during the low-level war they carried out against Sadat's successor, Husni Mubarak, during the 1990s was characterized by inadvertent deaths of innocents. Probably the best-known of those was the death of the young girl Shayma' during the botched assassination attempt against Egyptian prime minister 'Atef Sedki ('Atif Sedqi) in 1993. Even in 2007, the then deputy leader of al-Qaeda, Ayman al-Zawahiri (who during the mid-1990s had commanded the Egyptian Islamic Jihad group that carried out the action) had to defend himself against the accusation that her inadvertent death was murder.[13] Although the justifications Islamist terrorists wrote during the 1990s usually only sought to explain the inadvertent deaths of Muslim innocents, mass attacks on non-Muslims also became impossible for them to justify successfully to the Egyptian public. The Egyptian public first began to turn against the Islamists in the 1990s, and many of the radical leaders began issuing re-evaluations of their tactics and/or denunciations of them in the later 1990s and early 2000s.

But in the short term during the 1990s, there were two major spin-offs of the Brotherhood that fought the Mubarak regime: the larger al-Jama'a al-Islamiyya (Islamic Group) and the much smaller al-Jihad al-Islami al-Masri (Egyptian Islamic Jihad, usually referred to as EIJ). Both took part in multiple assassination attempts (some successful, most not) against Egyptian officials but engaged more often in attacks on the economic basis for the regime by focusing upon its most vulnerable component, tourism. Attacks upon Western tourists served the dual purpose of highlighting the group's message to the outside world as well as depriving the Egyptian state of the revenues generated from the industry. This approach culminated in the barbarous attack of six Gama'at operatives upon (mostly) Swiss tourists at the Temple of Queen Hatshepsut at Luxor on November 17, 1997, killing sixty-two people. Egyptians reacted extremely negatively towards the attack, and within several days the Islamists were forced to first issue denials and then apologies and finally to initiate a cease-fire. There can be no doubt that the public reaction turned this event into a watershed in the attempt to violently overthrow the government.

For the most part, the activist salafi-jihadi movement in Egypt was split after 1997, with most in Egypt either in jail or beginning to retract their previous stance of global *takfir*, while the leadership in exile (al-Zawahiri and his small group) encouraged operations but ultimately in frustration were forced to amalgamate themselves with Osama bin Laden's al-Qaeda group. This remained the situation until the fall of Mubarak in 2011 when the salafis effectively rejoined the Brotherhood as a political force. While they continue to participate in violence against Coptic Christians and secularists, salafis today do not substantially differ from the Brotherhood in their ideological stances.

Radicalism among Sunnis and Shi'ites in Syria and Lebanon

The Brotherhood spread early to Syria and Lebanon and was already prominent in both countries at the time of independence in the 1940s. In Syria especially, the Brotherhood achieved political prominence that it was not to attain in Egypt until the fall of Mubarak. However, with the rise of the regime of Hafiz al-Asad (1970–present, now under his son, Bashshar al-Asad), the government began to target the Brotherhood as its primary enemy. In general, the Brotherhood has been strong in the central and northern regions of Syria, farther from the secularized capital Damascus and the Alawite stronghold along the coast. However, like in Egypt, the difficulty with this central region, from a revolutionary point of view, is its flatness, making it easy for the regime to level massed forces against the Brotherhood's strongholds in Hama, Homs, and Aleppo.

During the 1970s, the Brotherhood leader in Syria was Marwan al-Hadid, who principally opposed the regime because of its secularization efforts. He was ultimately taken prisoner while fighting in an early attempt against the government (he later died in prison).[14] Subsequently, the Muslim Brotherhood attempted a rising in the city of Hama (central Syria) in 1982, to which the regime responded with extraordinary brutality, surrounding the city with tanks and bombarding it until the entire city was leveled and approximately 45,000 people were killed.[15] It is highly doubtful whether the Brotherhood ever carried out terrorist operations in Syria during this period. But there is no doubt that the destruction of Hama and the subsequent repression of political Islam in Syria were successful in retarding the development of radicalism in the country.

Sunni radicals were also active in Lebanon, with a Takfir wa-l-Hijra group under Bassam Kanj taking over the region of Diniyye (northern Lebanon) in 2000. This group was also closely connected with Jordanian radicals discussed below and was violently suppressed by the Lebanese army. It is unclear whether Kanj really believed that he could found an Islamic ministate in such a region, hemmed in as it was at the time between the Christian Maronites to the south and the Syrian army to the north. Nonetheless, in 2007 and later, salafi-jihadi groups, such as Fatah al-Islam, managed to take over the Nahr al-Bared Palestinian refugee camp.

As in both Syria and Lebanon, the Jordanian Muslim Brotherhood has fairly deep roots and has also gone through the usual split between mainstream radicals and salafis. Quintan Wiktorowicz cites a salafi informant thusly:

> [T]here are two descriptions [of the government]: it is either a Muslim leadership or non-Muslim. There is a sect of Salafis that believe that [even if] a Muslim leader

is doing injustice, we have to tolerate this and try to resurrect the people, including the leader, by praying for a change. . . . [Another] say[s] that the leader is a *kafir* (a person who becomes a Muslim and then is non-Muslim) [*sic*] to begin with because he adopted an ideology that is not in accordance with Islam, such as communism or liberalism. The first way is by peaceful means. The second is more violent and is called jihad. Because the leader is a *kafir*, he deserves to die; he deserves elimination.[16]

This is a classic summary of the duality of quietism and activism which we have seen in the Egyptian paradigm. However, the difference in Jordan was the nature of the government, for its leader was a monarch descended of the Prophet Muhammad. Like in Morocco (the other case where a monarchy is ruled by a Prophetic descendant), this fact has hampered the growth of overt radical Muslim opposition to the regime. Salafis may resent the pro-Western attitude of the Hashemite dynasty, but they have not succeeded in convincing large numbers of Jordanians to rise up against it, nor have they been able to carry out successful operations inside the country. In general, Jordanian salafis have either focused their violence upon Israel or joined other arenas of fighting (Iraq mainly).

With the general revolt against the Asad regime in Syria starting in the spring–summer of 2011, Syrian radicals have once again come into view. With the foundation of Jabhat al-Nusra (which in 2013 proclaimed its identity with and allegiance to al-Qaeda) on January 23, 2012, once again Syrian radicals have a practical expression for fighting. Almost immediately after its foundation, al-Nusra began to take credit for suicide attacks throughout the country, of which there have been several hundred thus far. Far and away the most successful of these was that of July 18, 2012, in which the minister of defense, the minister of the interior, and the national security adviser (Bashshar al-Asad's brother-in-law) were killed, among others. This was one of the most successful assassination suicide attacks on record anywhere. Although these suicide attacks are only part of the larger pattern of guerrilla fighting, kidnapping, rocket-launching, and other tactics that have torn the country apart, they do imprint the signature of radical Islam upon the struggle. With the influx of foreign fighters into the Syrian arena, it is clear that al-Nusra would be a powerful contender for government if the Asad regime were to fall.

Hamas

Palestinian Muslim radicalism has its roots in the figure of 'Izz al-Din al-Qassam, who was a Muslim Brotherhood fighter against the British mandate in Palestine, killed by them in 1935. There are, however, no other prominent examples of Muslim figures in the Palestinian quest to establish a state until the mid-1980s. Starting with its spiritual leader, Shaykh Ahmad Yassin, the Muslim Brotherhood began activities under various different names in the West Bank and in Gaza (and even in Israel itself), but it was eight months into the First Intifada (1987–93) before Hamas was established. (For more on the First Intifada and the broader Israeli–Palestinian conflict, see Chapter 16 by Boaz Ganor in this volume.) During the 1980s (and earlier), Palestinian Muslim radicals often had to face the question of why exactly they had not participated in the various violent confrontations waged by the Palestine Liberation Organization (PLO) against Israel. The most likely answer given by scholars today – outside of the Palestinian movement – is that Islamists during this period were more influenced by the Brotherhood's quietist attitudes (in Egypt). Hamas, especially in Gaza, has generally looked to the Egyptian Muslim Brotherhood for guidance, a pattern that is still reflected to some extent at present.

It should be noted that there were smaller radical Muslim organizations during the early 1980s before the rise of Hamas. Most notable among them was the Islamic Jihad (no relation to the EIJ), which ideologically was a by-product of the Islamic Revolution in Iran. Its leader, Fathi Shiqaqi (assassinated in 1995), never converted to Shi'ism (in spite of the accusations of his opponents) but fostered a revolutionary movement that was designed to be a vanguard rather than a popular movement. Its activities during the months of October–November 1987 are generally understood to have precipitated the outbreak of the First Intifada on December 3, 1987.

Unlike the Islamic Jihad, Hamas was from its inception designed to be a mass movement and took upon itself not only militant actions against Israel (and also against the PLO) but also quietist activities such as providing social, medical, and educational services for the Palestinians.[17] Due to these services, Hamas gradually became a counter-state and by 2006 was able to win elections against the PLO, supplanting it in the Gaza Strip region. Its charter, written at the time of its founding in August 1988, states that in contradistinction to salafi-jihadis, Hamas is a "Palestinian movement" (Article 6, also 12).[18] This led to salafi-jihadi critiques of Hamas as merely a nationalist organization, which grew ever more vociferous during the early 2000s and have led to the establishment of salafi-jihadi splinter groups in Gaza.

From a methodological point of view, the principal difference between Hamas and the PLO has been the fact that Hamas viewed (and still does view) the entirety of historical Palestine (today the countries of Israel and the territories of the West Bank and the Gaza Strip) as being a divine and inalienable endowment (*waqf*) from God to the Muslims. Thus – quite aside from the fact that others besides Muslims, including Jews and many Palestinian Christians, have lived there – Hamas believes that it cannot negotiate with Israel at all (Article 11). The division between Hamas and the PLO, therefore, is the same sort of division that one finds in many other Islamic/nationalist conflicts (such as those in the Philippines, Bosnia-Herzegovina, and Chechnya), where the Islamic side of the movement has proven to be inflexible while the nationalist side has shown itself willing to negotiate.

This stance is stated clearly in Article 15 of Hamas' charter: "We must instill in the minds of the Muslim generations that the Palestinian cause is a religious cause. It must be solved on this basis because Palestine contains the Islamic holy sanctuaries of al-Aqsa Mosque and the Haram Mosque [the Dome of the Rock] which are inexorably linked . . . to the night journey of the Prophet of God."

During the period of the First Intifada, the tactics of Hamas did not differ substantially from those of the other secular Palestinian organizations. Only in the leaflets it produced can one see the Islamic content: Muslim themes and history are emphasized, heroes from the early Islamic conquests and the period of the Crusades are highlighted, and the terminology is suffused with citations from the Qur'an and the traditions that call for jihad. By the period of the Oslo peace negotiations in1993–2000, however, the tactics of Hamas had changed. During this time, it was willing to part with the PLO and use the 'Izz al-Din al-Qassam Brigades to continue attacks on Israel, starting during 1994 with the use of suicide attacks (also pioneered by the Islamic Jihad). These attacks were at first usually synchronized to some type of specific perceived provocation by Israel and were comparatively few (although quite devastating to the peace negotiations, most probably resulting in the election of Benjamin Netanyahu in 1996).

With the collapse of the Camp David talks in 2000, however, the Second Intifada began, and Hamas began to use suicide attacks en masse. (Again, one should note that the Islamic

Jihad, Fatah's al-Aqsa Martyrs Brigade, and the smaller – and Marxist – Popular Front for the Liberation of Palestine also used suicide attacks during this period. Hamas, however, was able to carry out about forty percent of the total.) These suicide attacks were perceived by Hamas as a way to close the disparity between the Israelis and Palestinians in weaponry and resources. However, the fact is that the extensive use of suicide attacks and violence that characterized the Second Intifada did not result in obvious political gains for the Palestinians, nor did it garner them the political support they needed from the outside world. This was the result of the sense that while the First Intifada had been based upon demonstrations and classic civil disobedience methods that resonated with the outside world, the Second Intifada was militarized. Just as with the splinter radical Muslim groups in Egypt described above, Hamas and the other Palestinian groups that used suicide attacks tended to view such attacks as being justified because of the occupation, but they were unable to translate that belief to the mass media (except in Muslim countries) effectively.

With the building of Israel's security wall in 2004, there was a sharp decline in Hamas' use of suicide attacks, which in retrospect were a function of the easy access that Palestinians had to Israeli society. Israel, in the end, could actually wall itself off from its Palestinian neighbor, and thus the "weapon of the weak" was nullified. In response, Hamas turned to the use of rockets, appropriately called Qassam, which it began firing over the security barriers that Israel had constructed. Although these largely primitive rockets were ineffective in hitting targets for the most part and until recently have not had sufficient range to reach major Israeli population centers, they have made certain that Israel is unable to forget about the Hamas-ruled entity in Gaza and periodically have caused mini-wars to erupt.

At present, the tactics of Hamas are at a standstill. The organization has become a popular one rather than a strictly terroristic one, but it retains the ability and willingness to wage war against Israel. After the loss of suicide attacks as a primary weapon, however, its tactics are nowhere near as glamorous (as the firing of rockets do not allow for the direct engagement in battle so lionized by Muslim radicals) or successful as they once were. Thus the impasse remains.

The victory of Hizbullah

Like Hamas, Hizbullah is an organization that has deep roots within its community, which is Shi'ite rather than Sunni, and was born out of resistance to Israel's occupation of southern Lebanon (1982–2000) (for more on this, see Chapter 16 by Ganor in this volume). Throughout the 1950s and 1960s, the Lebanese Shi'ite population was largely quietist, having been activated to some extent by the charismatic Musa al-Sadr (d. 1977), who founded the mainstream organization Amal. During the early 1980s, the Shi'ite population in southern Lebanon was heavily dominated by the local Palestinians who used the region to initiate attacks on Israel, to which Israel responded in 1982, invading and occupying the region. Although the Shi'ites went through a brief period of pro-Israeli feeling, that quickly turned to hostility as the Israelis sought to re-impose the Maronite Christian hegemony in the area. This feeling of hostility was redoubled as the United States, France, and Italy sent troops into West and South Beirut (the latter a Shi'ite stronghold) to enforce a peace.

Hizbullah (Arabic for "the Party of God") was born of this (for the Shi'ites) desperate moment and was nurtured by the support of the Islamic Republic of Iran. It began operations with nearly simultaneous suicide attacks against US Marines and French paratroopers on October 23, 1983; these attacks killed 241 marines and others, while fifty-eight French were killed. Similar powerful suicide attacks struck sensitive Israeli targets as well during the period 1982–5, although Hizbullah gradually came to realize that such attacks were subject to the laws of diminishing returns in terms of those killed.[19] These tactics were supplemented by the kidnappings of Westerners during the mid-1980s, especially those still living in West Beirut (some of whom were not released until the early 1990s). Throughout the 1990s, therefore, Hizbullah adopted a classic guerrilla tactics approach: ambushes, rocket fire into northern Israel, and occasionally other sensational tactics. In spite of the cessation of suicide attacks against Israel, it is strongly suspected that Hizbullah carried out the suicide attack against the Jewish Center in Buenos Aires in 1994, although definitive proof is lacking.

Like Shi'ites overall but unlike Sunni radicals, Hizbullah has always been closely tied to religious authority. Its first major spiritual leader, Muhammad Fadlallah (d. 2010) laid down the methodology by which Hizbullah sought to frame its conflict with Israel. Placing the Shi'ites within the Qur'anic context of the "down-trodden" who rise up against their oppressors – a common Qur'anic narrative – he states:

> God allows them to fight, pointing to the aspects of this permission and its causes, which are represented in the defense of their legitimate right to protect their homes and be free to practice their creed and work. God has promised them victory over their enemies if, in their means and goals, they follow the path God has assigned them so as to be sure that the process of resistance of the weak against their oppressors matches the natural law of life.[20]

In 1992, the charismatic Hassan Nasrullah assumed the leadership of Hizbullah and immediately began to further integrate the organization into the Shi'ite Lebanese community but also made considerable headway into the southern Christian Lebanese communities, which hitherto had been the backbone of support for the Israeli occupation. After the Israeli withdrawal in 2000, Nasrullah described the organization's approach thusly: "Hizbullah utilized the methodology of guerrilla groups in its military activities against Israel, together with suicide attacks. Mostly these were used together with IEDs, explosive charges and rockets (Katyushas) against Israeli settlements."[21]

After 2000, Hizbullah marketed itself as a major political force in Lebanon and came to be seen as such, although it has struggled to justify its continued deployment of armed forces against Israel in southern Lebanon. During 2006, Nasrallah launched a full-scale war against Israel in an effort to free Hizbullah captives still in Israeli prisons (an operation known as *al-Wa'd al-sadiq*, "the true promise"). This operation backfired to a large extent, as a wide range of Lebanese perceived Hizbullah to be endangering the entire country for its own private sectarian interests. Similarly, the Hizbullah domination of West Beirut in 2007–9 triggered a panic among the rest of the Lebanese sectarian communities that had grown alarmed at the concentration of power in the hands of the Shi'ites. During this period, Hizbullah is widely suspected of having carried out targeted assassinations of key Sunni figures (such as former prime minister Rafiq al-Hariri in February 2005) and a number of prominent Christian and Druze politicians.

Although one can say that Hizbullah's position is strong, in the sense that it is both a political and a military force and dominates Lebanon as a whole, it is also fairly isolated with its primary political support coming from Syria and Iran. In the Syrian Civil War, Hizbullah has supplied thousands of fighters for the al-Asad regime, a fact that could rebound against it if and when the next government of Syria is Sunni (and most probably from the Muslim

Brotherhood). But in the short term, there is no more successful mainstream radical Muslim group in the Middle East than Hizbullah. That is most likely due to the support of its allies but also to the strong links between the religious and political wings of the movement as well as the discipline that Shi'ites bring to bear (as a result of the religious hierarchy). Today, over a decade after its victory in southern Lebanon, Hizbullah still commands prestige as the only radical group that has defeated Israel.

Conclusion

The dominant feature in the discussion of these Islamist groups and their recourse to terrorism and violence is that the Sunni groups have splintered off towards the radical wing on a continual basis and that most of them have been more consumed with fighting their secular (Arab) opponents than an outside enemy (Israel, Western tourists). This does not mean that these radical Muslim groups did not utilize violence against outsiders – merely that when one compares the extensive use of violence they manifested against their internal opponents to the more occasional attacks against outsiders, it is clear which one is predominant. With the exception of Hizbullah, all Islamist groups became enamored with the idea of *takfir* during the 1990s, and all of them lived to regret that choice by the early 2000s. By 2013, all of these groups (with the exception of the Syrians still fighting the Asad regime) have made the transition into political parties, and all, in at least a symbolic manner (with the exception of Hamas), have turned their backs on overt violence. Thus, the paradigm for these groups has been: foundation in the 1960s as a result of dissatisfaction with Muslim political quietism; a period of extreme activism in the 1980s, 1990s, and early 2000s; which by 2006 (again with the exception of the Syrians) had resulted in their reintegration with the quietists into political power (or at least the political process).

From a summary of the violent terroristic methods utilized by these groups one can say the following: no group on its own has been able to take and hold territory that its opponent has valued (with the possible future exception of the Syrians). This is true with regard to Hizbullah, which although it was able to defeat Israel in 2000, has never successfully managed to attack Israel proper. Hizbullah was victorious in southern Lebanon because Israel did not value it; the same is true of the Gaza Strip and Israel's withdrawal from it in 2005. Hizbullah has been unable to impose itself upon the Lebanese political structure – in fact, its attempts to do so have caused the opposition to unite against it. Nor were the radical Muslims successful in toppling Mubarak in the 1990s; when he finally fell in 2011, it was the result of a broad-based movement in which the radicals had little part.

Thus, one can say that although Islamist terrorists have viewed their violence as being different and more dangerous to their enemies than violence associated with non-Islamists and more likely to lead to substantial victories for the Muslim world, there is no real evidence to substantiate this idea. Suicide attacks were supposed to be a field-leveler, but instead every group (including Hizbullah) has allowed them to run wild and have utilized them against their political enemies, thereby destroying their own popularity and legitimacy.

Notes

1 Articulated by 'Ali al-Nadwi, *Madha khasara al-'alam bi-inkhitat al-Muslimin*, 416ff.
2 See Daniel Lav, *Radical Islam and the Revival of Medieval Theology* (Cambridge: Cambridge University Press, 2012), chapter 6.

3 As opposed to its classical understanding of being the sum total of jurisprudential discussions and debates, without any particular unity.
4 Brynjar Lia, *The Society of the Muslim Brothers in Egypt* (Reading: Ithaca Press, 1998), 83. For more on jihad, see Chapter 17 by Calvert in this volume.
5 Hasan al-Banna, *Majmu'at rasa'il al-Imam al-Shahid Hasan al-Banna* (Beirut: al-Mu'assasa al-Islamiyya li-l-Tiba'a wa-l-Sahafa wa-l-Nashr, n.d.), 297.
6 Ibid, 299.
7 See al-Wa'i, *Mawsu'at al-shuhada' al-haraka al-Islamiyya* (Cairo: Dar al-Tawzi', 2006), 1:25–51.
8 For an account, see Rawa'if, *Saradib al-shaytan: safahat min ta'rikh al-ikhwan al-Muslimin* (Cairo: al-Zahra' li-I'lam al-'Arabi, 1990), 605ff.
9 *Ma'alim*, 8–9, quoted in Albert Bergesen, *The Sayyid Qutb Reader* (New York: Routledge, 2008), 36.
10 Ibid, 39.
11 Giles Kepel, *Muslim Extremism in Egypt: The Prophet and Pharaoh* (Berkeley: University of California Press, 1984), 96–101.
12 Johannes Jansen, ed. and trans., *The Neglected Duty: The Creed of Sadat's Assassins and Islamic Resurgence in the Middle East* (New York: Macmillan, 1986), 192–3.
13 In his *al-Tabri'a*, 212ff., www.e-prism.org/images/kitab_al-Tabrieah_-_2-3-08.pdf (accessed September 16, 2014).
14 For a hagiography, see: http://iskandrani.wordpress.com/2008/02/09/the-soul-shall-rise-tomorrow-the-story-of-marwan-hadid/ (accessed February 3, 2013).
15 For a description, see Nina Wiedl, *The Hama Massacre – Reasons, Supporters of the Rebellion, Consequences* (München: GRIN Verlag für Akademische Texte, 2006).
16 Quintan Wiktorowicz, *The Management of Islamic Activism: Salafis, the Muslim Brotherhood and State Power in Jordan* (Albany: State University of New York Press, 2001), 122.
17 See Matthew Levitt, "Hamas from Cradle to Grave," in *Political Islam*, ed. Barry Rubin (London: Routledge, 2007), 2:408–21.
18 This and all other excerpted translations of Hamas' charter are taken from Khaled Hroub, *Hamas: Political Thought and Practice* (Washington, DC: Institute for Palestine Studies, 2000), appendix.
19 See the table in Robert Pape, *Dying to Win* (Chicago: University of Chicago Press, 2004), appendix 1 (pp. 253–4).
20 Muhammad Hussain Fadlallah, "Islam and the Logic of Power," in *The Contemporary Arab Reader of Political Islam*, ed. Ibrahim M. Abu-Rabi (London: Pluto, 2010), 60.
21 Hassan Nasrullah, *Mawsu'at Nasrullah* (Beirut: Manshurat al-Fajr, 2006), 1:173.

Further reading

Abu-Rabi', Ibrahim, ed. *The Contemporary Arab Reader on Political Islam*. London: Pluto, 2010.
—. *Intellectual Origins of Islamic Resurgence in the Modern Arab World*. Albany: State University of New York Press, 1996.
al-Banna, al-Hasan. *Majmu'at rasa'il al-Imam al-Shahid Hasan al-Banna*. Beirut: al-Mu'assasa al-Islamiyya li-l-Tiba'a wa-l-Sahafa wa-l-Nashr, n.d.
Bergesen, Albert, ed., *The Sayyid Qutb Reader: Selected Writings on Politics, Religion and Society*. New York: Routledge, 2007.
Carré, Olivier. *Les Frères musulmans: Egypte et Syrie (1928–1982)*. Paris: Gallimard, 1983.
Hroub, Khaled, ed. *Political Islam: Context versus Ideology*. London: Saqi, 2010.
—. *Hamas: Political Thought and Practice*. Washington, DC: Institute for Palestine Studies, 2000.
Jansen, Johannes, ed. and trans. *The Neglected Duty: The Creed of Sadat's Assassins and Islamic Resurgence in the Middle East*. New York: Macmillan, 1986.
Kepel, Gilles. *Muslim Extremism in Egypt: The Prophet and Pharaoh*. Berkeley: University of California Press, 1984.
Lav, Daniel. *Radical Islam and the Revival of Medieval Theology*. Cambridge: Cambridge University Press, 2012.
Lia, Brynjar. *The Society of Muslim Brothers in Egypt 1920–42*. Reading: Ithaca Press, 1998.
Mitchell, Richard P. *The Society of the Muslim Brothers*. Oxford: Oxford University Press, 1993.

al-Nadwi, 'Ali. *Madha khasara al-'alam bi-inkhitat al-Muslimin*. Reprint ed. Cairo: Maktabat al-Sunna, 1990.

Nasrullah, Hassan. *Mawsu'at Nasrullah*. 3 vols. Beirut: Manshurat al-Fajr, 2006.

Pape, Robert. *Dying to Win*. Chicago: University of Chicago Press, 2004.

Qutb, Sayyid. *Ma'alim fi al-tariq*. Riyad: al-Ittihad al-Islami al-'Alami li-Munazzamat al-Tullabiyya, n.d.

Rawa'if, Ahmad. *Saradib al-shaytan: safahat min ta'rikh al-ikhwan al-Muslimin*. Cairo: al-Zahra' li-I'lam al-'Arabi, 1990.

Rubin, Barry, ed. *Political Islam*. Vol. 2. Oxford: Routledge, 2007.

Sa'd al-Din, 'Adnan. *al-Ikhwan al-Muslimin fi Suriya*. 5 vols. Amman: Dar 'Ammar, 2010.

Shammakh, 'Amir. *al-Ikhwan wa-l-'unf: qira'a fi fikr wa-waqi' jama'at al-Ikhwan al-Muslimin*. Cairo: Maktabat Wahba, 2011.

al-Wa'i, Tawfiq Yusuf, ed. *Mawsu'at shuhada' al-harakat al-Islamiyya fi al-'asr al-hadith*. 5 vols. Cairo: Dar al-Tawzi', 2006.

—. *Qadat al-jihad al-Filistini fi al-'asr al-hadith*. Kuwayt: Dar al-Buhuth al-'Ilmiyya, 2004.

Wiedl, Kathrin Nina. *The Hama Massacre – Reasons, Supporters of the Rebellion, Consequences*. München: GRIN Verlag für Akademische Texte, 2006.

Wiktorowicz, Quintan. *The Management of Islamic Activism: Salafis, the Muslim Brotherhood and State Power in Jordan*. Albany: State University of New York Press, 2001.

19

THE URBAN GUERRILLA, TERRORISM, AND STATE TERROR IN LATIN AMERICA

Jennifer S. Holmes

Since the mid-twentieth century, Latin America has suffered from some of the highest incidents of terror, both state and non-state. From Mexico to the southern cone, Latin America has had more terrorist incidents than all other regions of the world, making up more than a quarter of the world's attacks (according to the Global Terrorism Database, and including the Caribbean). As a region, the groups that have carried out these attacks have been both homegrown and inspired from abroad. Latin America has also suffered from some of the most brutal examples of state terror, including the notorious cases of Argentina and Guatemala. Typically, violence from small groups was met with indiscriminate repression, which then spawned more violent groups, creating a cycle of escalation and human rights violations.

The decision to call these groups terrorists, guerrillas, revolutionaries, or insurgents has been controversial given the academic and political uses of the term terrorism. Some of the groups discussed in this chapter may not be universally labeled as terrorist or, at least, not at all times. For example, in Colombia, FARC (Fuerzas Armadas Revolucionarias de Colombia/Revolutionary Armed Forces of Colombia) violence can be labeled as terrorist, guerrilla, or revolutionary, given that the group targets both civilians and the government forces in the same campaign. Moreover, after the September 11 attacks on the United States, it became more common to label non-state violence as terrorism. Nonetheless, in each case discussed, typically groups engaged in activities that could either be called terrorist, revolutionary, or insurgent.

What kind of terror

Latin America is recognized as having suffered from many different types of violence, including rural insurgencies, urban terror, and state violence. Martha Crenshaw, one of the first academics to study terrorism, counsels scholars to situate terrorism in its context and to identify the "causal relationship between terrorism and its political, social and economic environment" and the "impact of terrorism on this setting."[1] Following this advice, it is prudent to examine the emergence of non-state terror and state terror in their historical contexts, instead of extracting similar types of attacks and treating them as causally equivalent acts. One of the best typologies of terrorism was created by David Rapoport. Rapoport situates most Latin American terrorism in the third wave, which is anchored by groups inspired by the success of the Vietcong against US forces in Vietnam. Rapoport specifically includes the Nicaraguan Sandinistas and the Colombian M-19 revolutionary groups in the third wave.[2] In fact, Ernesto "Che" Guevara, an Argentine who became one of the heroes of the Cuban Revolution and the author of *Guerrilla Warfare*, once stated a desire to make multiple Vietnams in the region.[3] The success of the 1959 Cuban Revolution inspired many to try to unseat their own governments. Che advocated a *"focista"* approach, in which a "small cadre of revolutionary fighters in the countryside, or *foco*, would create this subjective condition by igniting the spark of rural based revolution."[4] In response, many governments attempted to implement land reform to pre-empt possible peasant unrest in the countryside. Some groups were inspired by the urban Uruguayan Tupamaros. Certainly, groups learned from each other and earlier experiences. However, other groups, like the Colombian FARC, had historical antecedents decades older than the 1959 Cuban Revolution. This entry will examine four main types of Latin American terror: violence in the Cold War context, groups responding to regimes with low legitimacy, urban terrorism, and state terror.

Cold War and Latin American terror

Latin America was a strategic battlefield for much of the Cold War. Che Guevara did try to foment revolution in countries such as Bolivia, while Fidel Castro's Cuba attempted to incite uprisings and revolutions throughout the region. Dozens of guerrilla movements influenced by the Cuban example emerged, such as the ELN in Colombia, but the process did not stop there. According to the historian Hal Brands, "By the early 1960s the Cuban revolution had stimulated the Left, terrified the Right, and intensified existing internal conflict throughout the region."[5] The leftist groups generally failed in their desired impact, and the Cuban attempt to instigate revolution was abandoned by the early 1970s. In general, the government response was harsh and there were few converts to a foreign-led insurgency.

Despite the lack of desired direct impact, there was a large unwanted influence through the external meddling of competing foreign powers like the United States and the Soviet Union (or its proxy, Cuba). External actors also began to fight Cold War battles on Latin American terrain. Both Cuba and the Soviet Union provided a range of assistance to friendly governments, including arms, training, and diplomatic support. The United States supported the other side, often anti-communist authoritarian regimes (including interventions in Guatemala in1954, Dominican Republic in 1965, Chile under Pinochet in 1973, Nicaragua in the 1980s, etc.).

Nonetheless, it would be incorrect to assume that the unrest emerging in Latin America was due primarily to foreign intervention. Inadvertently and indirectly, interventions had long-lasting effects when US or Latin American governments assumed that all credible terrorist activity was sponsored by other governments. The Cold War context encouraged the assumption that "insurgencies had a strong element of the ideological conflict between the East and West, and involved, directly or indirectly, the support for the insurgents of the prime Communist states . . . on the one hand, and Western governments . . . on the other. Almost inevitably, they equated insurgencies with revolutionary, Communist movements."[6] This faulty assumption often resulted in mischaracterizing fundamental causes of unrest in the region. The Cold War lens through which the US viewed internal turmoil in the region understated how domestic pressures, such as long-standing exclusion and inequality, could result in formidable violent movements. Although the majority of Latin American countries gained their independence around 1820, independence was not accompanied by significant social or economic change. Additionally, most Latin American countries maintained a hierarchical society, inherited from colonial rule, based on race and class that perpetuated an unequal distribution of land and wealth.[7] Political and social openings were often met with backlash. In other words, many countries were ripe for rebellion without any foreign instigation.

However, the Cold War perspective did influence how groups were perceived by governments. For example, in Peru when Sendero Luminoso (the Shining Path) emerged, government "officials thought Senderistas were common criminals or a product of an international subversive movement.... The left thought they were part of a CIA plot to discredit them. The right believed that Sendero was merely a covert arm of the left."[8] In fact, despite the end of the Cold War, not all Latin American countries experienced a decline of terrorism or guerrilla conflict as many expected. Other internal factors were present to encourage conflict.

Rural unrest, grievance, and weak states with legitimacy problems

Many countries, such as Colombia and Uruguay, experienced upheavals due to stagnation in the agricultural sector or rural unrest. Long-standing land conflict was the spark for much conflict. One of the longest-lived groups, the Colombian FARC, emerged out of periods of rural discontent in the 1920s and a mid-century civil war. After its official founding in 1964, it increased its foothold during periods of crisis in certain commodities such as coffee. Other groups emerged out of frustration with closed political systems, regimes with weak legitimacy, or festering unresolved conflicts. Andreas Feldmann and Maiju Perälä state that "nongovernmental terrorism in Latin America has been more likely to occur in weakly institutionalized regimes, characterized by some measure of political and civil liberties but concomitantly by a deficient rule of law and widespread human rights violations."[9] Some of the most active terrorist groups emerged in countries with historical challenges of exclusion, inequality, and weak legitimacy. Moreover, many rebels, guerrillas, and revolutionaries justify their violence by attacking the legitimacy of the targeted regime, further undermining them. Two of the most fearsome terrorist groups in the region, Shining Path and the FARC, shared a frustration with relatively closed political systems (until 1980 in Peru and 1991 in Colombia), a weak state, and accusations of clientelism in government. However, even efforts to democratize did not always stifle the growth of existing groups (like the FARC) or the emergence of new ones (like Shining Path in Peru).[10]

Peru

In the twentieth century, the Peruvian state was still weak, unstable, offered few services, and excluded the participation of the indigenous through restricting the suffrage of illiterates (until 1980). Moreover, the state was widely viewed as corrupt. The main populist political party, APRA, was banned or prevented from winning major elections for much of the time from its founding in 1924 until the return to democracy in 1980. In the twentieth century, no regime lasted longer than twelve years. In the 1960s, there were short-lived Cuban-inspired rural guerrilla movements that were quickly defeated by the police or the military. In 1963, Hugo Blanco led an uprising in Cuzco. In 1965, both the MIR (Movimiento de la Izquierda Revolucionaria/Leftist Revolutionary Movement) and the ELN (not to be confused with the

Colombian group of the same name) were active for a few months before being dismantled by government forces. Peru had a military regime from 1968 to 1980 that attempted major land reform but still failed to quell dissent.

However, the major Peruvian terrorist group was not related to these earlier Cuban-inspired groups, nor was it related to Cold War interventions. PCP–Sendero Luminoso (Partido Comunista del Peru–Sendero Luminoso/the Communist Party of Peru in the Shining Path of José Carlos Mariátegui), became one of the most brutal groups in the hemisphere. Sendero had two main influences. First, they were inspired by the Peruvian intellectual José Carlos Mariátegui (1894–1930), who believed in a nationalist, democratic revolution as a step towards socialism. Mariátegui founded the Peruvian Communist Party and was author of *Seven Interpretive Essays on Peruvian Reality* (1928), which painted rural Peru as a neo-feudal hacienda system. Second, its founder, the charismatic philosophy professor Abimael Guzmán, was influenced by Mao and made numerous trips to China in the 1960s and 1970s.[11] Despite this influence, the group received no international support. According to William Ratliff, "Sendero seems to have no international ties; even its friendship with China was directed toward Mao Zedong rather than the present Chinese leadership."[12] The group, founded in 1970 by Guzmán, became the PCP–SL after splitting off from the Communist Party of Peru, which had rejected arguments for clandestine organization and armed struggle advocated by Guzmán. The early base of the new Sendero organization was universities in highland provinces, such as the rural Universidad de Huamanga in Ayacucho, but not among the indigenous. The Cold War, however, influenced how the group was perceived. Despite the initial assessments, as noted above, by the government and the left, Sendero was an entirely Peruvian movement that would kill tens of thousands in the next twenty years.

Shining Path was estimated to have approximately 10,000 active members with a peak network of 50,000 to 100,000 supporters. Sendero grew out of a movement mobilized on the historical exclusion and neglect of the rural areas, gained some support from coca growers frustrated with eradication efforts, and took advantage of the government's early reliance on arbitrary repression and brutal force. Sendero's plan was to develop the movement in the rural areas, cut off supply lines, and then take over the cities, with support from workers and peasants. The initial state response under President Fernando Belaúnde was indiscriminate repression against the indigenous and rural populations, who were assumed to be friendly to Shining Path because the group was in the area. In reality, the indigenous were attacked by both the government and the Shining Path. Instead of reducing Shining Path violence, the government counter-insurgency (COIN) campaign reduced government support and reinforced old distrust. The group increased its activities in the 1980s and pushed the country to the point of a civil war. After the election of President Alberto Fujimori in 1990, the government began to have more success with a more targeted counter-insurgency strategy. However, Fujimori quickly turned to authoritarian means. Under the guise of responding to a corrupt state, Fujimori closed Congress and dissolved the judiciary in 1992. The new regime benefited greatly when Guzmán was captured in September 1992 with many important files. This intelligence jackpot facilitated more government victories using police tactics (as opposed to COIN) and the eventual surrender of thousands of Sendero members. According to the Peruvian Comisión de la Verdad y Reconciliación (Truth and Reconciliation Committee – CVR), 69,280 Peruvians were killed from 1980 to 2000, most by Shining Path. The most human rights violations inflicted by the state paradoxically occurred during the democratic period of President Belaúnde (1980–85) and President Alan Garcia (1985–1990). Under

Belaúnde, rural peasants were attacked by Sendero members and then suffered from indiscriminate counter-insurgency operations by the Peruvian military. Under Garcia, mutinous prisons were shelled by the air force. There were egregious violations as well under Fujimori (1990–2000), including those carried out by the Colina Group which targeted suspected insurgents, but the repression was not as widespread or indiscriminate as during the previous ten years. Nonetheless, serious violations occurred and Fujimori was later convicted and imprisoned for ordering killings and kidnappings.

Since 2003, two remnants of Sendero Luminoso have been active, one in the Upper Huallaga Valley region that is loyal to the traditional leadership and another in the valleys of the Apurímac, Ene, and Mantaro rivers (known as the VRAEM) that is not. The second group tries to link Guzmán and Sendero with the atrocities committed against the peasants and the indigenous. It should be noted that Sendero is unusual in that the group killed more civilians than the government counter-insurgency forces – an uncomfortable fact that the VRAEM faction tries to distance itself from. This group is led by Victor Quispe Palomino, aka "Camarada José." The VRAEM group, which calls itself the Communist Party of Peru, rejects calls for peace and believes that the revolution can continue without the founder. It is increasing its activities and is regarded as a smart, well-equipped, and formidable foe. The other group is active in the Upper Huallaga Valley and was led by "Artemio" until his capture in 2012. This group should be considered coordinated with the traditional Shining Path-oriented, contemporary amnesty group, MOVADEF (Movimiento por Amnistía y Derechos Fundamentales/Movement for Amnesty and Basic Rights), which was founded by Guzmán's lawyers in 2010 and which advocates for the amnesty of imprisoned Sendero members. This group has been denied permission to run candidates by the Peruvian government, which views it as a terrorist front.

In addition to the Maoist Shining Path, there was another group, MRTA (Movimiento Revolucionario Túpac Amaro/Túpac Amaru Revolutionary Movement), active in the country. MRTA is more of a *focista* movement that aims for a socialist revolution. MRTA first attacked a police station in Villa El Salvador, in the outskirts of Lima in January 1984. The group extended its activities to other departments, including San Martín and Cusco. In contrast to Sendero, MRTA's members portrayed themselves as the "good guerrillas." For example, when they invaded villages, they would often announce that they did not come to engage in summary executions, as Shining Path was known to do, but instead wanted to begin a conversation with the citizens. MRTA even suspended attacks at the beginning of the first Garcia presidency (1985–1990) in the hopes that he would comply with his campaign promises. MRTA's leaders, Luis Varesse and Víctor Polay Campos, issued demands that the Peruvian government stop debt payments, not cooperate with the International Monetary Fund, raise the minimum wage, declare an amnesty for all political prisoners, and end the "dirty war." MRTA's most notorious attack was the December 1996 takeover of the Japanese embassy and the capture of more than 400 hostages. Many of the hostages were released, but seventy-two were held for 126 days until Peruvian government forces stormed the embassy. All of the MRTA fighters, including leader Nestor Cerpa, were killed. In recent years, the group has been capable of only sporadic activity.

Colombia

Colombia has experienced political violence from the left and right, drug violence, out of control common crime, and state violence. The consequences of the violence were not limited to its direct targets but also affected state institutions and the state's ability to respond effectively to violence or crime. Current fault lines should be understood in a post-civil war context. The civil war, known as La Violencia (1948–57), was fought between the Liberal and Conservative parties and their supporters. Part of the agreement to end the conflict included a power-sharing pact called the National Front (1958–74). Guerrilla groups mobilized partially in response to the National Front period when the traditionally dominant Liberal and Conservative parties had a power-sharing agreement that excluded other political parties and popular movements. The pact's rigidity and exclusion encouraged the emergence of radical movements geared toward revolution.

Two groups still active today formed in this period. The ELN (Ejército Liberación Nacional/Army of National Liberation) formed after sixteen Colombian youth visited Cuba in 1962. An early member was the revolutionary priest Camilo Torres. The group raised substantial sums from extorting the oil companies in the area and was known for frequently bombing the oil pipelines. Infamous attacks include two from 1999: the kidnapping of 186 people in a church in Cali, and the hijacking of an Avianca plane, the passengers of which were held for a year. The FARC (Fuerzas Armadas Revolucionarias de Colombia/the Revolutionary Armed Forces of Colombia) officially formed after an uprising and its violent but unsuccessful repression in 1964 in Marquetalia. The FARC is the one of the oldest and most active guerrilla groups in the hemisphere. The group is Marxist but does not identify as a *focista*, Cuban-inspired group. Both claim earlier precursor groups in the Liberal Party guerrilla movements of the 1940s and 1950s during the Colombian civil war. The FARC's long-time leader, Manuel Marulanda ("Tirofijo"), was active in campaigns waged by Liberal militias against the Conservatives. Eventually, in a context of continuing government repression and the absence of a political solution or significant reform, these militias evolved from unorganized peasant resistance into guerrilla groups. Despite the proclaimed commitment of the Colombian Communist Party (PCC) to peaceful change instead of supporting revolution, the party remained illegal and faced repression. In response, a group that initially called itself the Bloque Sur de Guerrilla separated from the PCC and eventually became the FARC. By the 1980s, the FARC had evolved from its rural origins, with both urban aspects and increasing involvement in the drug trade. Despite attempts to label the contemporary FARC as nothing more than a drug cartel, the extent to which the original ideological motivation has been subsumed by the lucrative drug business is a hotly debated topic. The reality is likely mixed, with some members and fronts participating more for illicit business opportunities and others out of their original demands for reform.

There were failed peace talks in 1982, 1984, and 1991–2. In 1984, some FARC members demobilized and formed a political party called the UP (Unión Patriótica/Patriotic Union), but the group was brutally targeted for assassination by paramilitary groups that will be discussed next. In the late 1990s, the FARC was granted control over a Switzerland-sized area of the country as a precondition of peace talks. Many in the country doubted that the FARC was sincere throughout President Andrés Pastrana's peace efforts. Instead, it was widely believed by many citizens and some within the security forces that the FARC used the opportunity of peace talks to plan attacks and dig in. In 2002, days after the FARC hijacked an airplane and kidnapped a prominent senator, Pastrana ended peace talks and ordered the military to retake the peace zone. His successor, President Álvaro Uribe instead focused on a military response to the FARC and no negotiations. The next president, Juan Manuel Santos, began a new round of peace talks in late 2012. The original motivation of land reform has remained strong. The FARC demanded that more than twenty percent of the country's land (62 million acres) be redistributed to the poor. Although peace talks have so far been successful in coming to agreements on land and rural development, talks on illicit drugs have been difficult, although the FARC has promised to end the drug trade if a final peace accord is reached.

Other groups emerged in Colombia as well. The EPL or (Ejército Popular de Liberación/Popular Liberation Army) was founded in Antioquía in 1967 but never grew into a large group. It attempted to demobilize in the 1980s, but its demobilized soldiers were targeted by paramilitaries. Most of the group disbanded in 1991. Finally, an urban guerrilla group, the M-19 (Movimiento 19 de Abril/Nineteenth of April Movement) emerged out of the ANAPO movement after it "lost" presidential elections in 1970, widely considered to be fraudulent. This group, drawn from students and urban residents, should be considered more nationalist. In fact, one of its first high-profile acts was the theft of the sword of the independence hero, Simón Bolívar. In 1985, thirty-five members of the group seized the Palace of Justice, demanding that President Belisario Betancur be put on trial. Instead, the government stormed the palace, resulting in more than 100 deaths, including the head of the Supreme Court, almost half the justices, and all the M-19 members. The M-19 later demobilized in an agreement that also included the government's commitment to a new constitution. Since 1990, M-19's members have participated in elections and held more than a quarter of the seats in the National Constitutional Assembly. They are now a legal political party (Alianza Democrática M19/the Democratic Alliance M19).

Partially in response to the government's inability to respond to guerrilla groups, privately funded paramilitary groups formed. The government encouraged this initially and considered them legal under decree 3398 of 1965 and Law 48 of 1968. Their purpose was to bolster Colombian counter-insurgency efforts. Many landowners created paramilitary groups, since they were on the front lines of the land conflict that fueled many guerrilla groups. However, as their violence increased, they were declared illegal in 1989. At the same time, drug-related violence increased in the 1980s and 1990s because of retaliatory cycles of violence and government crackdowns and a fight for dominance between the Cali and Medellín cartels. Additionally, many *narcos* bought land and inherited traditional land conflicts with groups like the FARC, while some paramilitaries entered the drug business to fund operations. Beginning in late 2002, the main umbrella paramilitary group, the AUC (Autodefensas Unidas de Colombia/United Self-Defense Forces of Colombia) declared a cease-fire with the government (despite not targeting government forces in the past) in preparation for peace talks and a demobilization effort under President Uribe (2002–10). Despite their illegality, there have been persistent concerns over government complicity in paramilitary violence. Francisco Leal Buitrago and Andrés Dávila Ladrón de Guevara have criticized the state as being captured by clientelism,[13] while others warn of state capture by violent groups.[14] Some human rights groups have accused the government of using paramilitary violence as an unofficial government strategy to contract out *mano dura* ("firm hand") COIN efforts and avoid responsibility for human rights abuses.[15] There has been success in professionalizing the government security forces since the 1990s, although questions remain about factions and individuals within the different agencies.[16]

Urban terror

Whereas Guevara thought that rural areas would be the key to the struggle and any "suburban" guerrilla movements would never emerge independently because they should be considered in "exceptionally unfavorable ground,"[17] Latin America is also home to the most well-known urban terrorist groups. The success of groups like the urban Tupamaros quickly challenged Che's assumption, especially as most rural movements failed in countries including Venezuela, Argentina, and Bolivia. Paul Wilkinson notes the growing abandonment of rural guerrilla conflict and a growing adoption of terrorism as Cuban-inspired groups failed: "Furthermore, the revolutionaries came to realize that in heavily urbanized states like Brazil and Argentina where well over half the population was in cities, they had to win power in the cities as a condition for seizing state power."[18] Instead of Che's guide to rural guerrilla conflict, Carlos Marighella and his *Minimanual of the Urban Guerrilla* became the inspiration and guide for another model of revolutionary activity pioneered by the Tupamaros of Uruguay. Soon, other groups began to imitate the Tupamaros and their urban rebellion. Even the Cubans took notice and began to distribute Marighella's *Minimanual*.[19] Marighella was a Brazilian guerrilla leader (Action for National Liberation – ALN) who was killed by the Brazilian police in 1969. Before his death, he wrote the short *Minimanual* to outline the role and strategy of urban guerrilla conflict, which he saw as the adaptation of Guevara's model to urban areas. According to Marighella, the urban guerrilla attacks the "government, the big businesses, and the foreign imperialists, particularly North Americans." Specific goals include targeting leaders from the security forces (military and police) and expropriation of the resources of the regime and its supporters. Marighella envisioned rural conflict as different from traditional peasant struggles. He did not believe that these conflicts would evolve into a rural guerrilla force. However, he did view the peasants as an ally when they saw the attacks against the landlord that would not go against their own interests: "The armed alliance of the proletariat, peasantry, and the middle class is the key to victory."[20]

Internationally, Uruguay had a reputation of being the Switzerland of the South because of its relative democratic stability and long-consolidated party system. However, the country had experienced a long period of economic stagnation since the 1950s. Strikes were responded to with states of siege, which were then used to respond to general unrest, including actions by the new urban terrorist group. The Uruguayan Tupamaros (MLN-T) (Movimiento de Liberación Nacional – Tupamaros) were founded by Raúl Sendic, Julio Marenales, and Jorge Maner Lluveras in 1962. Five years later, they started releasing communiqués to the public decrying the Uruguayan state as illegitimate and for the benefit of an oligarchy. The Tupamaros' actions were designed not to militarily defeat the government, but to increase their own support and delegitimize the government. Although delegitimizing the government is a classic goal of terrorist and guerrilla groups, in doing this, the Tupamaros more explicitly followed the advice of Marighella's *Minimanual*, according to which "the primary task of the urban guerrilla is to distract, to wear down, to demoralize the military regime and its repressive forces, and also to attack and destroy the wealth and property of the foreign managers." Among the tactics that Marighella advised for urban guerrillas were bank robberies; raids; the occupation of radio stations, schools, factories or other public places; prison breaks; kidnapping as propaganda; and the spread of propaganda in general. Throughout, the quest for popular support was paramount. "Where government actions become inept and corrupt, the urban guerrilla should not hesitate to step in and show that he opposes the government, and thus gain popular sympathy."[21] The principal strategy was to create a permanent political crisis and provoke the government into a repressive response. Before censorship was routine, the Tupamaros regularly released communiqués to the media, distributed leaflets and posters, and even took control of businesses and radio stations to deliver speeches to their captive audiences.

The Tupamaros were an authentic and self-sufficient Uruguayan group. Arturo Porzencanski wrote that "no evidence has been found that the Tupamaros ever received either money or arms from other countries or from social movements abroad."[22] The Tupamaros explained:

> We do not go outside the country to seek financing for our revolution, but seize from our enemies the money to mount the necessary revolutionary campaign.... We must make a clear distinction between what the bourgeoisie's property and the worker's property really is. The former is, beyond a doubt, the outcome of workers' exploitation; the latter is a result of work and individual effort. Therefore, the bourgeoisie's property is our natural fountain of resources and we have the right to expropriate it without compensation.[23]

Some of their thefts were spectacular, including $6 million in jewelry and $400,000 in gold from a branch of the Banco de la República. They also raided army garrisons for weapons and ammunition and industry for chemicals and explosives.

The Tupamaros also kidnapped prominent and symbolically important officials, diplomats, businesspeople, and landowners. Some were held for ransom while others were put on trial and held in a Tupamaro "people's jail." In 1969, about ten were kidnapped, and this tactic increased each year through 1971, with more than thirty kidnapped that year. There were few murders, although one was of Dan Mitrione, a CIA agent who was alleged to have taught the police torture techniques. In 1972, the Tupamaros killed four officials who were alleged to be members of an anti-Tupamaro group, Caza Tupamaros.

The Tupamaros provided a vision of an alternate state. For example, after the kidnapping and trial of prosecutor general Dr. Guidi Berro Oribe, the Tupamaros released recordings to the press. The group also succeeded in outsmarting the police by avoiding capture and escaping when imprisoned. They had four successful mass prison breaks, some involving prison disguises, others using tunnels, and some with bribes or threats to prison workers.

Despite not having broad support for their illegal tactics, the Tupamaros did have wide support for their reform goals. According to a 1969 Gallup poll, about half of the respondents viewed them as a dangerous group. In April 1971, a presidential contender, Alberto Heber, from one of the main political parties (Blanco) suggested that the government should negotiate with the Tupamaros on policy issues. Some senators and representatives agreed with some of the Tupamaro policy proposals, although they disagreed with their means of achieving them. However, as their activity became more violent, the Tupamaros lost support. Their activity was also met with increasing brutality by the government forces, suspension of civil liberties, and the extensive use of torture by police in interrogations. Although the Tupamaros had basically already been crushed and defeated by a brutal counter-insurgency campaign, unrest was one of the main justifications given for a military coup in 1973. In short, both Tupamaro violence and the government's repression undermined democracy in this era.

Despite their defeat, the Tupamaros also inspired others in the region. The Colombian M-19 emphasized political tactics learned from the Uruguayan Tupamaros.[24] The Tupamaros themselves went on to have a significant second act. After the return to democracy in 1985, traditional (Colorado and Blanco) presidential candidates were elected until 2004, when Tabaré Vázquez of the Encuentro Progresista – Frente Amplio (Progressive Encounter – Broad Front) was elected. Prominent former Tupamaros became politically active within the Broad Front, including Nora Castro, who became the leader of the Chamber of Deputies, and José Mujica, who became leader of the Senate. Mujica, who was imprisoned for fourteen years (most of it in solitary confinement) during the military regime, was elected president in 2009.[25]

State terror, civil–military relations, and the national security doctrine

From the 1950s on, a pattern emerged in the region. Unrest was responded to with government crackdown, followed by a proliferation of violent groups across the ideological spectrum. Mitchell Seligson highlights the combustive nature of repression: "It may well be that massive repression launched by the state to root out what are initially small groups of guerrillas ... initiates a cycle of violence that eventually brings others into the fray."[26] This cycle escalated in a region with tense civil–military relations, frequent military coups, and weak democratic accountability for security forces. Historically, a major issue in Latin American politics has been the phenomenon of politicians repeatedly "knocking on the barrack doors" and the belief of militaries that they are the ultimate protectors of the constitution, as they interpret it. J. Samuel Fitch described the main challenge of balancing security and democracy in Latin America:

> At a minimum, democratic governments must clearly delineate the lines between police and military roles in internal security. Insofar as possible, the armed forces should be removed from primary responsibility for internal security, without denying the need for trained counterinsurgency forces to intervene when antidemocratic forces attempt to establish a territorial base.[27]

However, when governments have put the military in charge of internal security without clear limits and guidelines on the use of force, bloody counter-insurgency often gave the guerrillas at least the moral victory of portraying their governments as illegitimate and brutal. This persistent tradition continued into the twentieth century as the military turned against internal enemies, subversives, terrorists, or revolutionaries.[28]

Argentina in the 1960s and 1970s typifies this pattern of a proliferation of terrorist groups in response to state repression after failed attempts at political reform and opening. In 1955, populist president Juan Perón was ousted in a military coup and forced into exile. General Pedro Aramburu led an attempt by the military to purge the country of Peronism before allowing elections with restrictions in 1958 – elections that were annulled in 1962 because the Peronist party received more votes than other parties. New elections were held in 1963, in which President Arturo Illia of the centrist Radical Party won. In June 1966, General Juan Onganía seized power and banned political parties. However, instead of promoting calm, this repression resulted in the emergence of numerous terrorist groups and uprisings, beginning with the 1969 Cordobazo. This spontaneous eruption of riots was followed by the emergence of more dissent and a government crackdown. The crackdown was met with the violence of new Peronist groups such as the Montoneros, the Fuerzas Armadas Peronistas/ Peronist Armed Forces, and the Fuerzas Armadas Revolucionarias/Revolutionary Armed Forces. Other leftist (but non-Peronist) groups included the Ejercito Revolucionario del

Pueblo/People's Revolutionary Army, and the Ejercito Revolucionario de los Trabajadores. By 1970, rightist vigilante groups, such as Mano (Hand) – composed of off-duty police – had emerged in response. These groups were not truly independent of the government but represented an effort by the state to distance itself from the worst of the violence. General Onganía was replaced by General Roberto Levingston in July 1970, who was ousted and replaced by General Alejandro Lanusse in March 1971. Under Lanusse, the military became directly involved in the counter-insurgency campaign. Disappearances were rampant by 1971. Incidents of monthly violence increased from fewer than ten a month in 1965 to more than 100 by December 1972. In an effort to remove incentives to violence, the military allowed elections in March 1973. Perón, who had been in exile in Spain, returned to the country in time for new elections in September. After a brief decline in violence, the cycle continued. Perón died in office in July 1974 and was succeeded by his wife Isabel. By the beginning of 1976, the average rate of violence was 300 incidents per month.[29] It continued to increase and a cycle of increasing violence quickly emerged. The far right responded with their own violent groups, including the AAA (Alianza Anticomunista Argentina/Argentine Anticommunist Alliance). As violence from multiple sources proliferated, Isabel Perón lost support. She was removed in a March 1976 coup that installed a *mano dura* authoritarian regime. State terror was extreme, and the military launched what is commonly described as the "dirty war" (1976–83) against anyone it suspected of being a subversive. It is estimated that up to 30,000 Argentines were killed or tortured by the government. At the same time, the governments of Argentina, Bolivia, Brazil, Chile, Paraguay, and Uruguay worked together to track and eliminate each other's internal opponents. Cooperation included intelligence and joint operations that crossed boarders. Prominent assassinations of dissidents in exile included former Chilean foreign minister Orlando Letelier in Washington, DC, by Chilean intelligence, and Uruguayan former congressmen Hector Gutiérrez Ruiz and Zelmar Michelini in Buenos Aires by Argentine forces.

Other countries experienced state terror, including Guatemala (1960–96), Chile under Augusto Pinochet (1973–90) and even Uruguay (1973–85), which became infamous for the extensive use of torture, with estimates of up to twenty percent of the population interrogated and tortured by state forces. Many of these authoritarian regimes shared a "national security" ideology, which, according to George Lopez, "served to support, if not predict, the use of terror as a preferred ruling style in a number of Latin American political systems."[30] The legacy of the "national security" doctrine was entrenched in the region and contributed to state terror. Chilling accounts of government human rights violations can be found in the *Nunca Más (Never Again)* report (1984) submitted by Argentina's National Commission on the Disappearance of Persons (Comisión Nacional sobre la Desaparición de Personas). The report documented the disappearances of 8,960 people, with the total feared to be at least double that, in addition to tens of thousands imprisoned. In the aftermath of other authoritarian regimes, similar truth commissions were formed, including Uruguay's *Uruguay: Nunca Más* (1989), Chile's *Nunca Más en Chile* (1991), and Guatemala's *Guatemala: Nunca Más* (1998).

Conclusion

This chapter has provided an overview of exemplars of different types of Latin American terrorism and violence. Instead of extracting out of the historical context particular tactics, this piece has tried to illustrate how violent movements emerged out of long-standing inequalities and political exclusion and in response to state repression. Violent challengers to the state tended to result in intensification of cycles of violence and repression, sometimes even resulting in state terror.

Notes

1. Martha Crenshaw, "Relating Terrorism to Historical Contexts," in *Terrorism in Context*, ed. Martha Crenshaw (University Park: Pennsylvania State University Press, 1995), 4.
2. David C. Rapoport, "The Fourth Wave: September 11 in the History of Terrorism," *Current History*, no. 650 (2001).
3. Che Guevara, "Message to the Tricontinentals," in Che Guevara, *Guerrilla Warfare* (Lincoln: University of Nebraska Press, 1985).
4. Brian Loveman and Thomas M. Davies, Jr., introduction to *Guerrilla Warfare*, by Che Guevara (Lincoln: University of Nebraska Press, 1985), 12.
5. Hal Brands, *Latin America's Cold War* (Cambridge, MA: Harvard University Press, 2010), 27–8.
6. Beatrice Heuser, "The Cultural Revolution in Counter-Insurgency," *Journal of Strategic Studies* 30, no. 1 (2007): 155.
7. Howard Handelman, *Mexican Politics: The Dynamics of Change* (New York: St. Martin's Press, 1997), 26.
8. Jennifer S. Holmes, *Terrorism and Democratic Stability Revisited* (Manchester: Manchester University Press, 2008), 90.
9. Andreas E. Feldmann and Maiju Perälä, "Reassessing the Causes of Nongovernmental Terrorism in Latin America," *Latin American Politics & Society* 46, no. 2 (2004): 102.
10. Gustavo Gorriti Ellenbogen, *The Shining Path: A History of the Millenarian War in Peru* (Chapel Hill: University of North Carolina Press, 1999); and Jennifer S. Holmes, Sheila Amin Gutiérrez de Piñeres, and Kevin Curtin, *Guns, Drugs and Development* (Austin: University of Texas Press, 2008).
11. See David Scott Palmer, ed., *The Shining Path of Peru* (New York: St. Martin's Press, 1992).
12. William Ratliff, "Revolutionary Warfare," in *Violence and the Latin American Revolutionaries*, ed. Michael Radu (New Brunswick, NJ: Transaction Books, 1988), 27.
13. Francisco Leal Buitrago and Andrés Dávila Ladrón de Guevara, *Clientelismo: El sistema politico y su expression regional* (Bogotá, Colombia: Tercer Mundo Editores, 1990).
14. See Aldo Civico "'We are Illegal, but not Illegitimate': Modes of Policing in Medellin, Colombia," *PoLAR* 35, no. 1 (2012): 89. Civico states: "One afternoon in a villa of an upper-class neighborhood in Medellin, Job, one of the main leaders of the Cacique Nutibara, explained to me that the paramilitary 'do not side with the government but are not against the state' [field notes, July 2006]. This was a further illuminating statement. It hinted at the way in which the paramilitaries in Colombia are a criminal organization of the mafia kind. In fact, they are not just a parallel organization, but also one that is working hand-in-hand with the state. Like the Sicilian Mafia, the paramilitaries in Colombia have been at the same time against the state and within the state; both a parallel system and a strategic ally; and a vital part of the *intreccio* to reterritorialize, which is the ultimate goal of policing."
15. Human Rights Watch, "The 'Sixth Division': Military–paramilitary Ties and U.S. Policy in Colombia," October 4, 2001.
16. See Jennifer S. Holmes and Sheila Amin Gutiérrez de Piñeres, "Violence and the State: Lessons from Colombia," *Small Wars and Insurgencies* 25, no. 2 (2014): 372–403.
17. Guevara, *Guerrilla Warfare*, 76–8.
18. Paul Wilkinson, *Terrorism versus Democracy: The Liberal State Response*, 3rd ed. (New York: Routledge, 2011), 27.
19. Ratliff, "Revolutionary Warfare," 28.
20. Carlos Marighella, *Minimanual of the Urban Guerrilla* (Montreal: Abraham Guillen Press, 1969). Quoted material is on 4, 39, 41. See Chapter 20 by Hanno Balz in this volume for a discussion of the influence of Marighella, the Tupamaros, and the urban guerrilla movement on Western European armed groups in the 1970s and 1980s.
21. Ibid., 4, 36.
22. Arturo Porzencanski, *Uruguay's Tupamaros* (New York: Praeger, 1973), 41.
23. Ibid., 40.

24 Arturo Alape, *La Paz, la violencia: Testigos de excepción* (Bogotá: Editorial Planeta, 1985), 324.
25 Simon Romero, "After Years in Solitary, an Austere Life as Uruguay's President," *New York Times*, January 3, 2014.
26 Mitchell Seligson, "Agrarian Inequality and the Theory of Peasant Rebellion," *Latin American Research Review* 31, no. 2 (1996): 154.
27 J. Samuel Fitch, *The Armed Forces and Democracy in Latin America* (Baltimore: Johns Hopkins University Press, 1998), 132–2.
28 For more on state terror and its relationship with various forms of sub-state violence, see Chapters 7, 11, and 24 by Martin A. Miller, Paul M. Hagenloh, and Roger Griffin, respectively, in this volume.
29 Jennifer S. Holmes, "Political Violence and Regime Change in Argentina: 1965–1976," *Terrorism and Political Violence* 13, no. 1 (2001): 134–54.
30 George Lopez, "The National Security Ideology as an Impetus to State Terror," in *Government Violence and Repression: An Agenda for Research*, ed. Michael Stohl and George A. Lopez (New York: Greenwood Press, 1986), 75.

Further reading

Bergquist, Charles, Ricardo Peñaranda, and Gonzalo Sánchez, eds. *Violence in Colombia: The Contemporary Crisis in Historical Perspective.* Wilmington, DE: SR Books, 1992.

Brands, Hal. *Latin America's Cold War.* Cambridge, MA: Harvard University Press, 2010.

Corradi, Juan E., Patricia Weiss Fagen, and Manuel Antonio Garretón. *Fear at the Edge: State Terror and Resistance in Latin America.* Berkeley: University of California Press, 1992.

Crenshaw, Martha, ed. *Terrorism in Context.* University Park: Pennsylvania State University Press, 1995.

Feldmann, Andreas E., and Maiju Perälä. "Reassessing the Causes of Nongovernmental Terrorism in Latin America." *Latin American Politics & Society* 46, no. 2 (2004): 101–32.

Fitch, J. Samuel. *The Armed Forces and Democracy in Latin America.* Baltimore, MD: Johns Hopkins University Press, 1998.

Generals and Tupamaros: The Struggle for Power in Uruguay 1969–1973. London: Latin American Review of Books, 1974.

Guevara, Che. *Guerrilla Warfare.* Lincoln: University of Nebraska Press, 1985.

Holmes, Jennifer S. "Political Violence and Regime Change in Argentina: 1965–1976," *Terrorism and Political Violence* 13, no. 1 (2001): 134–54.

Koonings, Kees, and Dirk Kruijt, eds. *Societies of Fear: The Legacy of Civil War, Violence and Terror in Latin America.* London: Zed Books, 1999.

McClintock, Cynthia. *Revolutionary Movements in Latin America.* Washington, DC: US Institute of Peace Press, 1998.

Porzencanski, Arturo. *Uruguay's Tupamaros.* New York: Praeger, 1973.

Radu, Michael, ed. *Violence and the Latin American Revolutionaries.* New Brunswick, NJ: Transaction Books, 1988.

Seligson, Mitchell. "Agrarian Inequality and the Theory of Peasant Rebellion," *Latin American Research Review* 31, no. 2 (1996): 154.

Wilkinson, Paul. *Terrorism versus Democracy. The Liberal State Response.* 3rd ed. New York: Routledge, 2011.

20

MILITANT ORGANIZATIONS IN WESTERN EUROPE IN THE 1970s AND 1980s

Hanno Balz

When looking at the postwar societies of Western Europe, we can observe a tantalizing contrast between, on the one hand, a tendency towards liberalization and, on the other, a series of domestic crises and the antagonisms and tensions of the Cold War condition. While it appears to be common sense that the student revolt of the late 1960s had a lasting liberalizing effect on most societies, its offshoots, the armed groups of the 1970s and 1980s, are regarded as their perverted epigones – the black sheep of the radical family. The threat of "terrorism" caused a considerable perception of crisis, mainly in West Germany and Italy, where in the late 1970s the threatened state became a "state of emergency," and the mass media repeatedly created moral panics.[1]

In this chapter I will first examine the origins of this outbreak of left-wing political violence in West Germany and Italy and the connections between the armed groups of the 1970s and the protest movement of the 1960s, which eventually became a serious threat to internal security. Furthermore, I will explore how armed groups like the Red Army Faction (Rote Armee Fraktion or RAF) in West Germany and the Red Brigades (Brigate Rosse or BR) in Italy operated transnationally and what caused their decline in the 1980s.

In the second part of this chapter I will focus on right-wing (neo-Nazi and neo-fascist) armed groups in Italy and West Germany. Surprisingly, this facet of political violence in the 1970s and 1980s has been repeatedly neglected and plays a minor role in public memory compared to the attacks from the Left, although the bombings of right-wing groups caused a higher death toll. However, in the last twenty years there have been many investigations into the involvement of the security and military apparatus concerning right-wing bombings, which have shed new light on this form of domestic terrorism in Western Europe.

Talking about revolution: the revolt of the 1960s

At the 1967 convention of the West German Socialist German Student League (Sozialistischer Deutscher Studentenbund or SDS), one of the topics was the discussion of Che Guevara's "*foco* theory" of guerrilla intervention and direct action. Members of SDS were not the only ones who hoped that the guerrilla concept would win support for the New Left, as may be seen if we take a closer look at the post-1968 movements in Western Europe.[2] After revolutions failed to break out following the tumultuous events of 1968 in most Western

European countries, activists longed to take the revolt to a "higher level," as was the dictum of the times. From here on, the movements, predominantly supported by students, underwent major splits and ventured in different directions. A major fraction saw political salvation in a neo-orthodox turn to Maoist or Leninist party organization. In London, the well-known intellectual and student-activist Tariq Ali called for a "Revolutionary Socialist Party," while in France the Proletarian Left (Gauche prolétarienne) was founded in late 1968. The next year saw the emergence of Unceasing Struggle (Lotta Continua) and Worker's Power (Potere Operaio) during Italy's "hot autumn." While these neo-orthodox militant groups were focusing on workers' struggles in the factories and beyond, the offspring of the anti-authoritarian Left proved to be rather short-lived in most Western European countries besides West Germany and Italy. Groups such as the Angry Brigade in Great Britain and the Red Youth in the Netherlands acted on a considerably smaller scale than the aforementioned groups, choosing symbolic actions without causing any casualties.

In West Germany, the split between proletarian and anti-authoritarian groups was more profound than elsewhere. While the emerging "Communist Groups" (K-Gruppen) focused on party organizations and discipline, the anti-authoritarian movement and its later offspring, the so-called Sponti Groups (believers in the "spontaneity of the masses"), pursued organization by militant action.[3]

Although the omnipresent Che Guevara was executed in 1967, the late 1960s saw a sudden emergence of militant revolutionary struggles all over the world. In Northern Ireland, the all-but-civil-war known as "The Troubles" gave rise to the Provisional IRA; the People's Front for the Liberation of Palestine hijacked their first airplane; and Basque's ETA militants engaged in their first shootout. Large parts of the world seemed to be going up in flames – the success of anti-colonial liberation movements changed global power relations and it seemed that even the US could be defeated, as was about to happen in Vietnam. For self-declared Western revolutionaries, the Cuban Revolution, as well as the Maoist takeover in China, appeared to serve as blueprints for a revolution beyond the orthodoxies of the Leninist model. Were not Fidel Castro and his 82 comrades who entered Cuba in 1956 to overthrow the Batista dictatorship historic proof that you did not need a proletarian mass organization for starting an armed rebellion? The anti-authoritarian New Left rejected the Leninist idea of building up a proletarian party that would eventually form the avant-garde for a future revolution. In opposition to the new Maoist splinter parties of the 1970s, which would turn back to the orthodox model of mass organization, the anti-authoritarian political current served as the background for the manifold groups that waged an armed struggle from the late 1960s on.

Germany: from the West German student movement to "building up the Red Army"

In Berlin, the first militant attacks started in 1969 after the members of the counter-culture militant group Tupamaros West-Berlin were the first to visit a Fatah camp in Jordan to get military training. The following year, the group carried out arson attacks against police and US facilities in Berlin. It gained notoriety when it took responsibility for an attempted bombing of the Jewish Community Center in West Berlin on November 9, 1969, to protest Israeli policies against the Palestinians. Although the bomb didn't go off, it set off a debate on anti-Semitism in the German radical Left. In 1972 the group merged with the newly founded June 2nd Movement.[4]

Yet the organization with the most militant approach and the biggest impact on West German society emerged in May 1970 and shortly after began calling itself the Red Army Faction. In the early years (1970–5) of this tightly organized urban guerrilla group, it was mainly called the Baader-Meinhof Group or Gang. The choice of label followed the speaker's political attitudes. On the one hand were those who sought to delegitimize the RAF by emphasizing its merely criminal character. On the other hand, the name Red Army Faction was meant to conjure up emotional images of Germany's archenemy during World War II. Herein lies the legacy of the West German student movement's confrontation with the German past.

Featuring no more than two dozen members in the early 1970s, the RAF's members were mostly young Germans with academic backgrounds. A distinguishing characteristic of the first RAF generation, compared to their successors after 1972, was the fact that the individuals who went underground in 1970 were already prominent figures. Ulrike Meinhof was editor of the left-wing magazine *konkret* and a radio personality. Similarly famous was Horst Mahler, who as a lawyer defended SDS spokesman Rudi Dutschke in court. Finally, Andreas Baader and Gudrun Ensslin gained substantial media attention in 1968 when they were sentenced for arson in the bombing of a Frankfurt shopping center. Thus a paradoxical situation emerged: the people in the early urban guerrilla movement were prominent personalities, yet their political program was hardly known at all. Being a VIP "terrorist" influenced to some extent public perception and caused a stronger focus on the personal stories of the RAF members in the media.[5]

The strategy of the RAF, as well as that of the Red Brigades, was to unveil the "open fascism" of contemporary politics by provoking the state monopoly on the use of force through specific guerrilla attacks. The RAF's "propaganda of the deed," a concept that goes back to nineteenth-century anarchist Paul Brousse and was later manifested by the Tupamaros of Uruguay, was to serve as a call to arms for the radical Left after the revolt of '68 had diversified and radicalized itself.[6] RAF's propaganda was that of an avant-garde that sought to escalate a growing conflict by what they thought were military means. The RAF believed that the only answer to the provocation would be massive repression by the state which would cause it to drop its "democratic mask." A revolutionary situation would then follow. By conjuring up the repression – which the Left already experienced and would have to suffer much more of – this strategy embodied a constitutive, cynical "ends justify the means" rationality that was common within RAF and BR ideology. Assuming that the revolutionary process was not emancipation from present living conditions but passage through a "new fascism," the RAF detached itself from the New Left. This could also be called "armed propaganda" by the RAF to raise public awareness about issues that were neglected before (like the fact that US bombings in Vietnam were coordinated at the US Army headquarters in Heidelberg).

During the first two years of its existence, the group predominantly tried to organize a clandestine infrastructure and to raise money and arms by robbing banks and weapon stores. This was also the formative propaganda phase. The RAF issued four lengthy theoretical communiqués in 1971 and 1972 that were mostly written by Meinhof.[7] Her ideology could be called Marxist–Leninist with a Maoist, even anarchist, influence, reflecting the radical eclectic political belief system of the New Left since the late 1960s. Meinhof's "revolutionary subject" (which, ironically had to be led by an armed avant-garde) was not the prototypical proletariat, but rather the radical students and the fringe groups of West German society.[8]

Eventually, the RAF would orient itself more towards the anti-imperialist struggle in the "third world."

In the year after the RAF's emergence, it seems there was considerable backing for the urban guerrilla movement in West German society, at least with the rebellious youth: polls revealed in 1971 that twenty-five percent of West Germans under the age of thirty held "certain sympathies" for the RAF and one out of twenty said they would even help to shelter its members.[9] This stirred up serious concern among the political elite and especially within the Federal Criminal Police Office, which from then on focused not only on increased prosecution but on its own propaganda, which one federal attorney called the "aggressive informing of the public."[10]

While three police officers had been killed in shootouts with RAF members in 1971 and 1972, sympathies for the RAF didn't dwindle until its lethal May Offensive in 1972 when, seeing itself at war with the US Army, the RAF bombed the US Army Headquarters in Frankfurt and Heidelberg, killing four GIs and injuring eighteen. People were also injured after bombings of the Augsburg police headquarters and the Hamburg branch of the Springer Publishing Company – the latter expressing the RAF's preoccupation with the media, especially with Springer's tabloid *Bild*.

Shortly after, the first generation cadres – among them Meinhof, Baader, Ensslin, Meins, and Raspe – were arrested, and the RAF appeared to be history for the next three years. Nevertheless, the imprisoned members gained considerable media attention when they conducted several hunger strikes until 1977; in fact, Meins died in November 1974. Meanwhile, a second generation of the RAF was emerging, organized by one of the former attorneys of RAF members, Siegfried Haag, who was eventually captured in 1976.

It wasn't until April 1975 that the next generation would spring into action, when RAF members seized the German embassy in Stockholm and demanded the release of twenty-six German militants. Two diplomats were shot during the takeover, and accidental explosions killed two RAF members before the police could storm the building. After this incident, Chancellor Helmut Schmidt decided that in the future the federal government would never give in to "terrorist blackmail."[11]

Between 1975 and 1978, the RAF solely focused on freeing their imprisoned mentors and therefore set aside their armed propaganda. Nonetheless, the prison conditions of the RAF members – especially Meinhof's incarceration in an isolation cell during her first year in prison – became a highly contentious issue in West German discourse. The highly controversial trial did not start until 1975 and was held on the grounds of the Stammheim prison in a newly erected courtroom, often called the "bunker" in the media. "Stammheim" became a synonym for courtroom confrontation, the dubious ad hoc tightening of laws, hunger strikes, the secret service's eavesdropping on advocates, and prison cell suicides, like that of Meinhof on May 8, 1976, which a majority of the radical Left believed was a state murder for the years to follow.

Shortly before the end of the "trial of the century," as it was dubbed by the press, RAF "commandos" – called thusly by both the RAF and the media – killed the federal attorney general Siegfried Buback and his escort in plain view. This was the first assassination of a leading "representative of the system," as the RAF denounced him in West Germany. During the following '77 Offensive, as it was called by the RAF's second generation, the federal government was pressured to release RAF prisoners once again. The first attempt to kidnap a representative of the German economic elite failed when, in July 1977, the chairman of Dresdner Bank, Jürgen Ponto, was killed when he resisted his kidnapping.

Just a few weeks later on September 4, the RAF succeeded when members kidnapped Hanns-Martin Schleyer and killed his escort of three bodyguards and a driver. Schleyer was the most influential, yet controversial, economic leader in West Germany at that time. He was a former manager for Mercedes-Benz and in 1977 was head of the two most important German employers' associations, which made him the "boss of the bosses."[12] For the Left, he was a prominent enemy, for Schleyer used to be a middle-rank SS officer and was known for his tough stance against striking workers.[13]

The six weeks that followed are still considered the Federal Republic's moment of greatest existential danger. The federal government and especially Chancellor Helmut Schmidt were adamant in not giving in to the kidnappers' demands to release the Stammheim prisoners. During these weeks, an extra-legislative administration led by the former Wehrmacht officer Schmidt handled all affairs. This crisis squad immediately established a news ban and even discussed the reintroduction of the death penalty.[14] Palestinian commandos further escalated the crisis when they hijacked a Lufthansa plane with German tourists on October 13 in support of the RAF's demands. When four days later all hostages were freed by West Germany's new counter-terrorism unit GSG-9, it became clear that the RAF's '77 Offensive was a train wreck. The next morning, October 17, Baader, Ensslin, and Raspe were found dead in their high-security cells.[15] Schleyer's dead body was discovered a day later.

While what came to be known as the German Autumn is the most referenced phase of the RAF's attack on the state, it must be seen as a culmination of what happened in the years before. In the 1970s, the conflict between the RAF and the West German state proved to be a paradigm for the growing political polarization of communications in German society.

Italy: "Carry the attack to the heart of the state!"

Like those that emerged in West Germany, the clandestine groups that sprung up in 1969–70 in Italy were also ideologically and personally connected to the revolt of 1968. But radical activism in Italy followed the neo-Marxist trend of Workerism (Operaismo). After the events of Italy's "hot autumn" and with the addition of more and more public support after 1969, groups like Worker's Power and Unceasing Struggle saw the political struggle taking place in the factories in Milan and Turin rather than at the universities. Eventually an increasing militancy accompanied "operaist" and later "autonomous" activism. The year 1969 saw a wave of strikes and unrest in northern Italian factories. This industrial militancy was fed by the precarious conditions that millions of marginalized migrant workers from the impoverished Italian South encountered in the production plants in Milan and Turin. To the radical "operaistii," the Communist Party of Italy and the opportunistic trade unions were turning their backs on unorganized workers. Added to this, a growing number of university graduates who found it increasingly difficult to find employment saw themselves as a new "proletarian intelligentsia."[16]

Historic legacies also played an equally important role in the self-conception of militant Italian groups. Like the RAF, they shared the assumption that the state would become openly fascist again and even believed in the possibility of a right-wing coup d'état, but they also linked themselves to the history of anti-fascist partisans during World War II.[17]

Among all European states, Italy had the largest number of revolutionary armed factions, which also enjoyed more mass support than, for example, in Germany. Nearly 500 left-wing groups – most of them rather obscure – claimed responsibility for militant attacks involving nearly 3,000 participants between 1969 and 1980.[18] With 426 members overall, the Red

Brigades was the largest armed group in Italy by far, and it developed a strictly hierarchical organization from 1974 on, when most of its members began to live clandestinely. Thereafter, a Strategic Command and an Executive Committee were the organization's highest political authorities, while five regional "columns" operated in Milan, Turin, Genoa, Rome, and the Veneto. The "columns" were supported by "irregulars" who managed logistics and who had not gone underground.[19] While the different cells might not know of each other, they were given orders by a central command at the top level.

When the Red Brigades were founded in October 1970, they were still taking part in militant movements in factories, especially those of Fiat, Sit-Siemens, and Pirelli in Milan and Turin. Thus, the formation of the Red Brigades was announced as "the first moments of the Proletariat's self-organization in order to fight the bosses and their henchmen."[20] Founding members Renato Curcio, Margherita Cagol, and Alberto Franceschini had been active in the short-lived Metropolitan Political Collective (Collettivo Politico Metropolitano) and now discussed strategies of armed struggle with other militants.[21]

The radicalization of the movements that existed in Italy in the early 1970s was, to a certain extent, the result of attacks by fascist groups from the late 1960s onwards – groups that, in turn, saw themselves as a reaction to the student unrest and strike waves of 1968/69. When sixteen people were killed and eighty-seven injured in the Piazza Fontana bombing in Milan in December 1969 (which is described below), it was the radical Left that was blamed first. But to the activists on the Left, it was clear that this was carried out by neo-fascists from the Italian Social Movement (Moviemento Sociale Italiana or MSI). Even more, these atrocities were observed to be part of a greater "strategy of tension" aimed at preparing the ground for an authoritarian coup d'état in Italy with support from the Italian police force, secret service, and army.[22] For that reason, the BR repeatedly targeted members of the MSI and shot two of them in 1974.

At first, the Red Brigades were active in the factories and saw their actions as strategic interventions on behalf of militant workers. BR militants burned managers' cars and sabotaged factory equipment.[23] Still, the *brigatisti* tried to keep their links with the radical workers in the factories, which in the ensuing years proved to be more difficult. In 1972, BR shifted its tactics: the attacks grew more and more personal and began to include temporary kidnappings of managers and later their notorious kneecappings of managers and state-officials, thus furthering the goal of "armed propaganda" as well as a crude notion of political revenge.

Caselli and della Porta have identified four distinct periods in the history of the Red Brigades. As with the RAF, we can speak of the group's succeeding generations: "(1) the period of 'armed propaganda' (1970–4); (2) the 'attack on the heart of the state' (1974–6); (3) the 'strategy of destruction' (1977–8); and (4) the military confrontation with the state for survival of the organization (1979–82)."[24] In 1974 and 1975, BR's leading members were captured: Curcio and Franceschini were arrested, while Cagol was shot by police in a gunfight. By then, the Red Brigades engaged in high-profile kidnappings (e.g., Assistant State Attorney Mario Sossi) and demanded the release of militant prisoners. In 1974, BR's tactics radicalized when most moderate and some radical leftist social movements underwent a partial institutionalization and underwent the *riflusso*, or withdrawal from the radical Left.[25] Since Italy experienced economic crises after 1973, a 1975 manifesto from BR stated that its new goal was to "carry the attack to the heart of the state! Transform the crisis of the regime into the armed struggle for communism."[26] Given this, the "SIM" (the "Imperialist State of the Multinationals," as the BR called the combined Italian system of governmental, business, and military institutions) became a primary target of the group that by now was being led by the hardliner Mario Moretti.[27]

After the trial against the captured *brigatisti* started in May 1976 in Turin, a BR "commando" team committed the group's first assassination of a high-ranking member of the judiciary when they shot Genoese Attorney General Francesco Coco and his bodyguards a month later. By this point, it proved to be more and more difficult to find judges and prosecutors for terrorism trials since militant groups issued threats against anyone who would participate in them.[28]

After 1977, when Italy experienced widespread street violence during the inner city protests carried out by the autonomous Movement of '77, which was made up of counter-culture youths who had turned away from the factories to broader societal issues, the Red Brigades benefited from an inflow of radicalized youth who wanted to leave street battles behind and take up arms.[29] Also at this time, Front Line (Prima Linea), the second largest armed organization of the Italian Left, emerged from Unceasing Struggle (Lotta Continua), which had dissolved earlier. This group was responsible for more than twenty assassinations – mainly of those who were associated with the executive authority and the penal system.[30]

The year 1978 proved to be the peak of the "anni di piombo" (the Years of Lead), the term later applied to the escalation of the violent confrontation between the Italian state and militant groups on both the left and the right. By that year, the second generation of BR deployed their "strategy of destruction" primarily against the ruling Christian Democratic Party (DC) – twelve of their politicians were injured in attacks. This strategy of intimidating political personnel was exemplified in the slogan "strike one to educate a hundred," which was written on the sign that the Red Brigades' first kidnapping victim had to wear around his neck. The phrase comes from Mao Zedong's guerrilla strategy, according to which the aim is not to defeat the enemy directly but to win over public opinion – but it also bluntly encapsulates the general communicative nature of the "terrorist" act.[31] BR hoped to follow such strikes by quickly escalating toward an even greater "direct confrontation" based on a plan to physically eliminate those politicians at the state's nerve center.[32]

This is why the Red Brigades came to blame one man for the groundbreaking rapprochement – known as the "historic compromise" – between the conservative Christian Democrats and the Italian Communist Party (PCI), which had recently turned towards euro-communism. That man was the former prime minister Aldo Moro, the leader of the Christian Democrats. Large segments of the radical Left saw the Communist Party as corrupted by the Christian Democrats when the PCI agreed to tolerate Giulio Andreotti's minority cabinet in 1978. Devoted from the start to bringing the PCI "back into revolutionary line," the Red Brigades decided to maximize the confrontation by kidnapping Moro on March 16, 1978, during which five of his bodyguards were killed. After his kidnapping, Moro was held for fifty-five days in what the BR in their communiqués called a "people's prison." The Red Brigades became an important political factor, and the ensuing crisis can be compared to the events of the German Autumn half a year earlier with a de facto state of emergency and widespread public expressions of insecurity. BR demanded the release of thirteen political prisoners and gained considerable media attention, issuing nine communiqués during the kidnapping, while public and political life in Italy seemed to be paralyzed.[33] However, Prime Minister Andreotti, like Helmut Schmidt before him, adamantly refused to give in to the kidnappers' demands. Decades later, after the Italian judiciary investigated the Moro affair, it became clear that the US Central Intelligence Agency (CIA) had obviously influenced the Italian government's decision-making. For the CIA, Moro's efforts to include the PCI in the political process posed a threat at a time when the United States feared the growing influence of euro-communism.[34] In the end, Moro was submitted to a "political process" and then "executed," with his body abandoned in the trunk of a car in Rome, where it was found on May 9, 1978.

Like the Red Army Faction, the Red Brigades experienced a lasting defeat after the killing of Moro, which produced strong controversy among the Italian Left and within the organization itself, although BR cells engaged in more deadly attacks than ever before between 1978 and 1981. Nevertheless, many observers have understood this expansion as a sign of desperation and with it a first step of the Red Brigades' decline.[35] Furthermore, Italian law enforcement reacted strongly after the Moro kidnapping, and the so-called government of national unity issued several anti-terrorist emergency laws. Still, BR continued its lethal attacks. In fact, the highest concentration of militant attacks occurred in Italy during the period between 1977 and 1980.[36] But, at the same time, the armed groups lost their support within the radical Left and especially with workers, who, for example, were alienated by the BR's killing of a trade unionist who reported a BR activist.[37] The ebbing support in the factories and from the Left led to major internal divisions from 1979 onwards. One of the main accusations was that after the Moro kidnapping, the Red Brigades featured a form of "militarismo" that was detached from political struggle outside of the armed groups.[38] New factions emerged, like the Communist Combatant Party (BR-PCC). In the meantime, the state went on the offensive: the new laws of December 1979 and especially the "legge Cossiga" (the laws introduced by Prime Minister Francesco Cossiga) of February 1980 were a general blow to civil liberties and broadened the powers of the police, but they also granted benefits to repentant BR members who would collaborate (the *pentiti*). More than 130 *pentiti* collaborated with the police in the early 1980s, and their information, such as that provided by Petrizio Peci, weakened BR even more than did the internal rifts.[39] The Red Brigades' attacks grew more personal, as when they shot Peci's brother as retaliation for his collaboration. Yet, the decline continued. By the end of 1983, there were some 3,000 militants in Italian jails, some of whom were organized by the old BR avant-garde.[40] The Red Brigades ceased to exist as a unified organization around 1981, but its core successor, the BR-PCC, continued to stage high-profile attacks throughout the decade, until its leaders formally declared the armed struggle finished in 1988. From 1970 to 1988, the Red Brigades were responsible for some seventy-five assassinations, 115 attempted assassinations, and seventeen political kidnappings – unlike other armed organizations in Western Europe, bombings were not part of its tactics.[41]

The "European front" in the 1980s

In the late 1970s, militant groups emerged that weren't directly linked to the movement of 1968. Two groups founded in 1975, Spain's GRAPO (First of October Anti-Fascist Resistance Groups) and the Greek 17N (Revolutionary Organization 17 November), understood their attacks as anti-fascist interventions during the transitional periods following the collapse of authoritarian governments in each country. In West Germany, the RZ (Revolutionary Cells) emerged from the autonomous wing of the German radical Left in the mid-1970s. While these cells did not go underground and refrained from using lethal violence (although they did carry out kneecappings), an international arm of the RZ gained notoriety when its members joined the international terrorist group led by Carlos the Jackal and participated in the 1975 raid on the Vienna OPEC conference. In 1976, they took part in the hijacking of an Air France plane with Israeli passengers that was then redirected to Entebbe. This action provoked angry reactions from the German Left and led to some efforts to tone down expressions of anti-Zionism even as armed groups and others continued to denounce Zionism as an ideology.

The French group Action Directe (AD) emerged in 1979, followed somewhat later by the Belgian Communist Fighting Cells (CCC), both of which cooperated to a certain extent with the re-emerging RAF in the early 1980s. In the late 1970s and early 1980s, Western European armed groups generally developed a more transnational strategy with the focus shifting to attacking NATO infrastructure in Western Europe. The RAF, after its major defeat in 1977, regrouped in the Middle East and was joined by the remaining members of the June 2nd Movement. Ten RAF members of the second generation quit the armed struggle and found refuge in East Germany, where they lived a normal life under new identities provided by that country's government.[42] The remaining RAF members nevertheless started a new campaign in 1979 by attempting to assassinate NATO's commander-in-chief, General Alexander Haig, in Belgium. Shortly after, they released a communiqué containing the first hint of a significant change in perception, one that would subsequently turn into a strategic shift, based on what the RAF believed to be a fundamental change in the international balance of power in the post-Vietnam era. "With the victories of the liberation struggles in Southeast Asia and Africa," the communiqué stated, "the front line has moved closer to the centre, it has fallen back to the metropole itself and is making the tactical and strategic retreat of U.S. imperialism – the so-called shift of the strategic core to Western Europe – inevitable."[43]

As we can see with the call to arms beyond national borders, RAF's second (and then third) generation sought combined efforts to attack NATO structures. In fact, the RAF and the Red Brigades probably began to cooperate as early as 1977.[44] Although BR leadership disapproved of the RAF's lack of building a "proletarian fighting party," cooperation intensified in the early 1980s.

During the 1970s the Red Brigades, unlike the RAF, only attacked Italian targets. Even in their "war against imperialism," they hadn't attacked NATO or American targets. This changed when BR kidnapped NATO Deputy Chief of Staff James Dozier in Verona in December 1981. Dozier, one of the highest ranking US officers in Italy, was rescued some weeks later.[45]

Meanwhile, the RAF had to regroup after most of the second generation was arrested by 1982. Even today there is a considerable lack of established knowledge about RAF's third generation and its hard core of an estimated fifteen members. However, after the RAF carried out another assassination attempt against a high-ranking NATO officer – the commander of NATO's Central Army Group, General Frederick Kroesen – in September 1981, its new anti-NATO agenda became more obvious. The RAF published its new political platform, the so-called May Paper, in May 1982. In this, its first theoretical paper in ten years, the RAF called for a single "front" uniting the "urban guerrilla" and the growing militant Left (the "resistance"), which came from the influential West German "Autonomen" movement. More than that, this new "front," as the RAF declared, should demonstrate the combined effort of different anti-imperialist armed groups in Western Europe. By 1982, these groups oriented themselves towards the non-working-class New Social Movements which had gained momentum since the late 1970s. In fact, the massive anti-nuclear and anti-war movements in Western Europe seemed to offer new possibilities for armed intervention. Since all of the armed groups lost significance and lost the support of left-wing activists from the late 1970s onwards, critical observers saw the RAF, BR-PCC, and others' new orientation as an attempt to ingratiate themselves.

Although it is doubtful that there were established links between most of the armed groups in Western Europe in the 1980s, we can observe certain cross-references in different groups' communiqués and actions. For example, Action Directe and the RAF claimed joint responsibility for the 1985 bombing of the US Rhein-Main Airbase in Frankfurt. Furthermore, Action Directe and the RAF targeted representatives of the "military-industrial complex," such as, for example, the French general René Audran, and Ernst Zimmermann, chairman of the German armaments firm MTU, both in 1985.[46]

As it turned out, transnational cooperation between the armed groups proved to be rather problematic. Although Action Directe seemed to look up to the RAF (or perhaps just the RAF's legacy), the more or less open claim of RAF to a leadership position stirred major objections from others, including the BR-PCC.[47]

The latter half of the 1980s saw the dissolution of the Western European "front": Action Directe was broken by arrests in 1987, and the BR-PCC in 1988. The RAF held on to its notion of anti-imperialism but, in its final years in the late 1980s and early 1990s, it turned towards domestic issues. This became manifest when RAF militants assassinated Deutsche Bank chairman Alfred Herrhausen in 1989 and in 1991 shot Detlev Carsten Rohwedder, who was responsible for the privatization of the former German Democratic Republic's (GDR) state economy. The latter proved to be the last deadly assault by the RAF; eventually its members dissolved the organization in 1998.

The major global cataclysm of the collapsing communist world affected the final days of armed struggle in Western Europe. While that ended with a whimper, the anti-terrorist apparatus remained in existence, with its massive limitations on civil liberties, expanded police and intelligence administrations, and a history of dubious counter-terrorism.

"Strategy of tension": attacks from the Right

Regarding counter-terrorism, there is still an ongoing debate about the involvement of various Western European states in right-wing terrorist attacks. In Italy at least, several parliamentary commissions of inquiry have found proof of the high-level governmental involvement in nearly 200 lethal attacks between 1969 and the early 1980s.[48] The blueprint for this came from Greece's authoritarian coup in 1967, which was supported by the CIA and influenced the radical Right in Western Europe. And in the late 1960s and early 1970s, radical right-wing parties enjoyed some electoral success in Italy and Germany.[49] The neo-fascist MSI became Italy's fourth largest party in the 1960s. Its offshoot, New Order (Ordine Nuovo or ON) – later the Black Order (Ordine Nero) – engaged in militant bombings and assassinations starting in the late 1960s.[50]

In Italy, right-wing terrorists were responsible for the highest death toll of all militant attacks during the Years of Lead, although in most instances these acts cannot be attributed to a specific organization. The major difference between attacks from the militant Left and the Right, besides the fundamental political antipode, was the latter's strategy of causing massive insecurity through indiscriminate attacks on the population as well as the total lack of a political agenda published in communiqués. While left-wing organizations always claimed responsibility for their attacks and tried to elaborately explain their motives, there was nothing but unsettling silence after the radical Right attacked. Another, even more striking difference was the neo-fascists' ability to mysteriously escape after each bombing.

Unlike the members of the Red Brigades, neo-fascists were never caught red-handed and it was not until the mid-1980s that trials against the militant Right began to shed some light on these incidents. Slowly, it became obvious that the Italian security apparatus, especially the military secret service, had spread its wings of protection over New Order and others. In 1984, Vincenzo Vinciguerra, a member of the neo-fascist National Vanguard, testified in court that the Italian state heavily supported right-wing terrorism. In 1990, he told the British *Guardian* newspaper: "Avanguardia Nazionale, like Ordine Nuovo, were being mobilised into the battle as part of an anti-communist strategy originating not with organisations deviant from the institutions of power, but from within the state itself, and specifically from within the ambit of the state's relations within the Atlantic Alliance."[51]

The first bomb to shatter Italian society and to set an example for the Italian militant Right was set off in a bank in Piazza Fontana in Milan in December of 1969. Sixteen people, mostly customers, were left dead, and eighty-seven were injured. For some time, the extreme Left was blamed for the bombing, as was presumably the goal of the bombers. Investigations were frustrated by segments of the police and the military secret service. This major "false flag" attack was part of a "strategy of tension" (as the British *Observer* newspaper first labeled it in 1970) that garnered considerable support from influential right-wing elements in Italian politics, the secret service, judiciary, and the military.[52] Since the growth of the communist Left after 1968 and the fragmenting of the Christian Democratic Party, there were two elements to this strategy. First, attacks were to be carried out which would lead the Left to be blamed for a new wave of violence that affected everyone. This would mean the marginalization of the Left in general and calls for a "strong state." Second, it was hoped these attacks would eventually prepare the ground for a possible coup d'état (as happened earlier in Greece) via the declaration of a "state of emergency." In fact, elements of the military nearly seized power in Italy in December 1970 in what was known as the Borghese Putsch, which was named after the influential leader of the neo-fascist movement, Junio Valero Borghese. This right-wing takeover was called off at the last moment, and the already mobilized neo-fascists from the National Vanguard and military units returned home.[53] In any case, the Right soon turned away from its goal of carrying out a coup. This helps explain the emergence in the 1970s of a new generation of militant neo-fascists, like those in the Armed Revolutionary Nuclei (Nuclei Armati Rivoluzionari or NAR) and Third Position. Presenting themselves as a "spontaneous movement" without a central command or a program, they were not linked to traditional Italian fascism and lacked a coherent strategy.[54]

The early 1970s saw a rise in right-wing attacks, including the bombing of trains (the Rome–Messina train in 1970 and the "Italicus" train in 1974) which left eighteen people dead. Additionally, there were numerous attacks on the Left, most notably a hand grenade attack on an anti-fascist rally in Brescia that killed eight in May 1974.[55] Attacks by neo-fascist organizations against members of the police and the judicial system were often blamed by officials on the Red Brigades and other organizations from the Left. Extensive manipulation of the investigations by police and secret service helped to uphold these accusations and were part of the "strategy of tension."[56]

The attacks from the Right seemed to ebb by the mid-1970s, but in the early 1980s, there was a return of even deadlier attacks, predominantly committed by NAR, which was founded in 1980 and had close ties to the Italian mafia. On August 2, 1980, the group carried out the most devastating act of domestic terrorism in postwar Western Europe when it detonated a bomb in the railway station of Bologna during the peak of the holiday season, killing eighty-five people and injuring about 200. Unlike the 1969 Piazza Fontana bombing, this time everyone accused the neo-fascists of being responsible. What followed was a crackdown on right-wing organizations, so that after the mid-1980s right-wing attacks ceased.

In the following years, numerous official investigations revealed that the "strategy of tension" was supported by the Italian SISMI intelligence service, members of the Italian judiciary, the CIA, and NATO.[57] In the early 1990s, Italian Prime Minister Giulio Andreotti publicly recognized the existence of Operation Gladio, NATO's top secret, paramilitary "stay behind" organization, the purpose of which was to wage guerrilla warfare in the event of a Warsaw Pact invasion of Western Europe. Investigations after the end of the Cold War revealed the existence of such organizations in most NATO member states and that some of them did not "stay behind" but lived a life of their own. Soon, more facts, as well as more conspiracy theories, about Gladio's involvement with the attacks from the radical Right came to light. Later, Colonel Oswald LeWinter, a CIA liaison officer for Europe, revealed that there existed a secret NATO policy which consisted of tolerating anti-communist extreme-Right activities.[58] Still, the precise role played by Gladio has not yet been uncovered, even though the controversial publications of Daniele Ganser shed light on the dimension of state-sponsored terrorism.[59] There is evidence that the Italian mafia was heavily involved in the "strategy of tension." It has even been argued that the Red Brigades were infiltrated by secret service informants and that the Italian state was somehow involved in the Aldo Moro kidnapping.[60] Since much of the debate on these issues belongs to the realm of conspiracy theories, further speculation is not warranted. But many questions regarding the state's involvement in Italian armed groups remain, and there certainly is more to discover in the future. There is, however, broad agreement on the fact that the Italian state apparatus, the CIA, and NATO played a considerable role in the "strategy of tension." Beyond that, newer publications even take a closer look at the Soviet KGB's involvement.[61] Anna Bull summarized the "strategy of tension" by defining it as "destabilizing in order to stabilize the political system."[62]

In the case of West Germany, there is no such evidence of a "strategy of tension." Nevertheless, West Germany experienced its own attacks by the militant Right in the late 1970s and early 1980s. These were carried out by militant neo-Nazi groups such as the German Action Groups (Deutsche Aktionsgruppen), the Hoffmann Militia Group (Wehrsportgruppe Hoffmann), and the People's Socialist Movement of Germany/Labor Party (VSBD/PdA). As with neo-fascists in Italy, German neo-Nazis were increasingly active in the public sphere. Many Germans dismissed them as obsessed with paramilitary training and Nazi uniforms and firearms, referring to them as "kooks" and "nutcases" and stuck in the past.[63] But by the late 1970s, they emerged as a growing threat, with the number of neo-Nazi incidents tripling to 1,533 from 1977 to 1980.[64] The first neo-Nazi assassination attempt to attract major attention occurred in April 1968 when the unskilled worker Josef Bachmann, who had contacts in the neo-Nazi world, shot and severely injured the speaker of the West German student movement, Rudi Dutschke.[65] In the early 1970s, there were attacks on communist party structures and Jewish facilities, although these did not cause any casualties. Some small neo-Nazi militant cells planned bombings and assassination in the 1970s, but in all cases the police were able to break them up before they were launched. This was because the Office for the Protection of the Constitution (Verfassungsschutz) and other West German intelligence offices had recruited informers who were quite involved in neo-Nazi groups. In the wake of the deadly attacks in 1980, some Germans grew concerned that the authorities were better informed about what was going on with the militant Right than they dared to admit. This is still a highly controversial issue today.[66]

During the second half of the 1970s, some fringe groups also engaged in militant attacks from the Right. The Ludwig Group, which consisted of only two members, committed arson attacks and assassinations that left fifteen dead between 1977 and 1984. They were mostly active in northern Italy, where they targeted homosexuals, minorities, and sex clubs. Quite unusually for the militant Right, they left behind leaflets with Nazi symbols and crude slogans.[67] During these years, police investigators discovered more and more militant neo-Nazi cells that apparently modeled themselves after organizations from the Left like the RAF or the Revolutionary Cells.

The most notorious neo-Nazi group was the Hoffmann Militia Group (WSH, from its German name), founded in 1973 by the neo-Nazi Karl-Heinz Hoffmann as a paramilitary organization. It had some 400 members over the seven years of its existence. In a manifesto explaining his neo-Nazi agenda, Hoffmann called for the establishment of an authoritarian state, "a dictatorship with the right man at the helm."[68]

After engaging in paramilitary training, members of the group later stockpiled weapons and attacked members of the radical Left. In the second half of the 1970s, WSH members carried out several attacks, although it is unclear whether these actions were part of the group's overall strategy or the deeds of "lone wolves," an explanation that was given for nearly all neo-Nazi attacks. Although the WSH was outlawed by the Federal Minister of the Interior in January 1980, that year saw the climax of deadly attacks by the group's former members.

There is still much debate over whether the most deadly militant attack in the history of the Federal Republic of Germany, the Oktoberfest bombing of September 26, 1980, in Munich, was the work of a "lone wolf." This attack killed thirteen people and injured 211. As in many Italian cases, militants from the Left were initially blamed. Finally evidence was uncovered that the bomber was twenty-one-year-old Gundolf Köhler, who died in the explosion and who had links to WSH.[69] The bombing happened just a few days before West German general elections, and it has been argued that it created an atmosphere of instability that was meant to help the right-leaning Christian Democrat candidate Franz-Josef Strauß win the election – which he did not.[70]

It is still unclear whether Köhler was the lone perpetrator. For instance, another WSH member claimed to be involved in the attack shortly before he committed suicide after a shootout in 1982.[71] Daniele Ganser even links the Oktoberfest bomb to remnants of the German branch of Operation Gladio, suggesting that the explosives were drawn from one of its many secret arms caches found a year later.[72] The West German authorities were reluctant to follow up these leads and preferred to close the file soon after. Recently, researchers have also found links between the German and the Italian militant Right. Since Italy's NAR carried out a very similar attack on the Bologna rail station just weeks earlier, some have speculated that there was a coordinated strategy between the two groups.[73] German neo-Nazis also received assistance from their neo-fascist counterparts in France and Belgium.[74] Astonishingly, WSH even received support from East Germany's secret police, the Stasi, as part of the GDR's propaganda efforts to discredit West Germany's government.[75]

The Oktoberfest attack was not the last by WSH members. In December 1980, a former WSH member shot dead the Jewish publisher Schlomo Lewin and his partner, Frida Poeschke. Hoffmann was himself accused of the assassination and fled to Lebanon with fourteen of his followers to train with the PLO's Fatah faction. He was arrested after his 1981 return to Germany and in 1986 was sentenced to nine years imprisonment for illegal possession of firearms and explosives as well as aggravated assault, although the judge found him not guilty in the case of the Lewin murder. WSH's responsibility for the attack has also still not been verified.[76]

The early 1980s were the most deadly period of neo-Nazi attacks in West Germany. In addition to attacks carried out by the WSH, other groups attacked foreigners (two Vietnamese refugees died in an arson attack by members of the German Action Groups in 1980) and US Army personnel (carried out by the Hepp-Kexel Group) and were engaged in bank robberies and deadly shootouts with police (VSBD/PdA).[77]

Conclusions

The militant neo-Nazi attacks of the 1970s and 1980s did not leave a big footprint in the nation's public memory (this is somewhat less the case in Italy). How can this be explained? First, right-wing bombings were carried out like covert secret service operations – no one was meant to know who was behind the assaults. In most cases there was no coherent program or strategy – except for the spreading of fear and uncertainty – visible behind the attacks. It is worth noting that the public was less fearful of being a potential victim of right-wing bombs despite the fact that right-wing extremists chose arbitrary targets more often than did their left-wing counterparts. For example, more than fifty percent of West Germans interviewed in a 1977 survey stated that attacks like those by the RAF (this was even before the hijacking of the Lufthansa plane) could "hit any of us. I'm personally afraid of that."[78]

This suggests that it was predominantly the media and the political elite who were responsible for these very different perceptions. Left-wing militants indeed struck at the "heart of the state," challenging those in power, while right-wing groups targeted those, at least in the German case, who were already the subject of discrimination in society (refugees, Jews, homosexuals). Most of all, the period examined here is subject to the dichotomies of the Cold War. It was the Left that was blamed as a "fifth column" of Moscow, while, on the contrary, the radical Right was not understood to have a greater power behind it pulling the strings.[79] It was implicit from the start – and later became obvious – that everyone who was drawn into the terrorist spectacle in the 1970s and 1980s – the militants, the state apparatus, the media – were actors on a greater stage. It became self-evident that militant organizations were a threat to the Cold War balance of power in Europe, even as they were being used to maintain that very balance. The dictum that "the enemy of my enemy is my friend" never appeared to be more applicable as with the covert support of terrorism by intelligence and security agencies on both sides of the Iron Curtain.

When the Cold War eventually ended in 1991, social-revolutionary terrorism ultimately ebbed. A communist utopia seemed further away than ever, and the global Left found itself in disintegration. Furthermore, the Cold War condition in which militant organizations worldwide found sponsors or safe havens from the "other side" was over, and the remaining armed groups struggled with this lack of support and soon ceased to exist. One obstacle that makes it difficult to write a complete history of the conflicts between armed groups and the state in Europe – one that could, in particular, shed more light on the most dubious forms of state involvement in the terrorism spectacle – is the fact that while states like the GDR are no longer around, most of the state apparatuses that left a legacy of counter-terrorism are still in existence. Therefore, the task remains for future historians to ask the necessary discomforting questions.

Notes

1. H. Balz, "Throwing Bombs in the Consciousness of the Masses: The Red Army Faction and Ist Mediality," in *Media and Revolt: Strategies and Performances from the 1960s to the Present*, ed. K. Fahlenbrach et al. (New York: Berghahn, 2014), 270.
2. B. Davis, *Changing the World, Changing Oneself: Political Protest and Collective Identities in West Germany and the U.S. in the 1960s and 1970s* (New York: Berghahn, 2012), 161.
3. M. Klimke, "West Germany," in *1968 in Europe: A History of Protest and Activism, 1956–1977*, ed. M. Klimke and J. Scharloth (New York: Palgrave Macmillan, 2008), 101.
4. See A. Reimann, *Dieter Kunzelmann: Avantgardist, Protestler, Radikaler* (Göttingen: Vandenhoeck & Ruprecht, 2009), 237–54. The group named itself after the date the student Benno Ohnesorg was shot by a police officer at a demonstration against the Shah of Iran in Berlin in 1967.
5. See H. Balz, *Von Terroristen, Sympathisanten und dem starken Staat* (Frankfurt am Main: Campus, 2008), 52.
6. For more on the origins of the term "propaganda of the deed," see Chapter 8 by Richard Bach Jensen on European and world anarcho-terrorism in this volume. For more on the Tupamaros of Uruguay and the origins of the "urban guerrilla" movement, see Chapter 19 by Jennifer S. Holmes in this volume on terrorism in Latin America.
7. "The Urban Guerilla Concept" (1971), "On the Armed Struggle in Western Europe" (1971), "Serve the People: Urban Guerilla and Class Struggle" (1972), and "The Action of 'Black September' in Munich" (1972). See J. Smith and A. Moncourt, *The Red Army Faction: A Documentary History*, vol. 1, *Projectiles for the People* (Oakland, CA: PM Press, 2009).
8. Meinhof – as well as Ensslin, Baader, and Raspe – had been involved in working with fringe groups, especially asylum runaways. See S. Aust, *Baader-Meinhof: The Inside Story of the R.A.F.* (London: Bodley Head, 2008), 46.
9. "Politische Überzeugung," *Der Spiegel*, July 26, 1971, 16.
10. Balz, *Von Terroristen*, 125.
11. Smith and Moncourt, *Red Army Faction*, 331–2.
12. "Der Boss der Bosse," *Stern*, 1974, no. 51, 76–86.
13. J. Varon, *Bringing the War Home: The Weather Underground, the Red Army Faction, and Revolutionary Violence in the Sixties and Seventies* (Berkeley: University of California Press, 2004), 197.
14. "Exotische Lösung," *Der Spiegel*, February 11, 1980, 27.
15. This remained a controversial issue for at least two decades and was the subject of many conspiracy theories, concerning whether these were suicides or murders carried out by the state. For details – for which room does not exist here – see K. Hanshew, *Terror and Democracy in West Germany* (Cambridge: Cambridge University Press, 2012), 231. Also see H. Lehmann, *Die Todesnacht in Stammheim. Eine Untersuchung: Indizienprozess gegen die staatsoffizielle Darstellung und das Todesermittlungsverfahren* (Köln: Pahl-Rugenstein, 2012).
16. R. C. Meades, Jr., *Red Brigades: The Story of Italian Terrorism* (London: Palgrave Macmillan, 1990), 20.
17. P. Cooke, *The Legacy of the Italian Resistance* (New York: Palgrave Macmillan, 2011), 119.
18. D. Hauser, "Terrorism," in Klimke and Scharloth, *1968 in Europe*, 272–3.
19. A. Orsini, *Anatomy of the Red Brigades: The Religious Mind-set of Modern Terrorists* (Ithaca, NY: Cornell University Press, 2011), 56.
20. M. Burleigh, *Blood & Rage: A Cultural History of Terrorism* (New York: Harper Perennial, 2009), 198.
21. G. C. Caselli and D. della Porta, "The History of the Red Brigades," in *The Red Brigades & Left-wing Terrorism in Italy*, ed. R. Catanzaro (London: Pinter, 1991), 72.
22. J. E. Engene, *Terrorism in Western Europe: Explaining the Trends since 1950* (Cheltenham: Edgar Elgar, 2004), 136–7; and D. Ganser, *NATO's Secret Armies: Operation Gladio and Terrorism in Western Europe* (Milton Park, UK: Frank Cass, 2005), 76–83. See also: A. C. Bull, *Italian Neo-Fascism: The Strategy of Tension and the Politics of Non-Reconciliation* (New York: Berghahn, 2007); and F. Ferraresi, *Threats to Democracy: The Radical Right in Italy after the War* (Princeton, NJ: Princeton University Press, 1996).
23. Burleigh, *Blood & Rage*, 199.

24 Caselli and della Porta, "History of the Red Brigades," 71.
25 D. della Porta, *Social Movements, Political Violence, and the State: A Comparative Analysis of Italy and Germany* (Cambridge: Cambridge University Press, 1995), 30.
26 Meades, *Red Brigades*, 52.
27 Caselli and della Porta, "History of the Red Brigades," 79–89.
28 Burleigh, *Blood & Rage*, 203.
29 One example of the widespread support for the Red Brigades among the radical Left was the demonstration of 5,000 youths in favor of the assassination of the neo-fascist party member Enrico Pedenovi in 1976. See Richard Drake, *The Aldo Moro Murder Case* (Cambridge, MA: Harvard University Press, 1995), 172. A newspaper reported that BR could rely on more than 10,000 supporters in Italy. See "Italien: Terror nach deutscher Art," *Der Spiegel*, March 27, 1978, 120.
30 See C. Novaro, "Social Networks and Terrorism: The Case of Prima Linea," in Catanzaro, *The Red Brigades*, 144–73.
31 A. P. Schmid and J. de Graaf, *Violence as Communication: Insurgent Terrorism and Western News Media* (London: Sage, 1982), 20.
32 Caselli and della Porta, "History of the Red Brigades," 91.
33 Burleigh, *Blood & Rage*, 209–12.
34 M. Moore, "US Envoy Admits Role in Aldo Moro Killing," *The Telegraph* (London), March 11, 2008 (accessed March 5, 2014); and R. Igel, "Linksterrorismus ferngesteuert? Die Kooperation von RAF, Roten Brigaden, CIA und KGB," *Blätter für deutsche und internationale Politik* 52, no. 10 (2007): 1222.
35 M. Wieviorka, *The Making of Terrorism* (Chicago: University of Chicago Press, [1993] 2004), 90.
36 Engene, *Terrorism*, 135.
37 Burleigh, *Blood & Rage*, 212.
38 Caselli and della Porta, "History of the Red Brigades," 97.
39 Meades, *Red Brigades*, 216.
40 A. Jamieson, "Identity and Morality in the Italian Red Brigades," *Terrorism and Political Violence* 2, no. 4 (1990): 510.
41 Y. Alexander and D. A. Pluchinsky, *Europe's Red Terrorists: The Fighting Communist Organizations* (London: Frank Cass, 1992), 194.
42 The GDR also presumably provided support to active RAF cadres. To what extent they offered military training to RAF members is still debated today. See J. Smith and A. Moncourt, *The Red Army Faction: A Documentary History* (Oakland, CA: PM Press, 2013), 2:183–4.
43 Smith and Moncourt, *Red Army Faction*, 2:116–18.
44 E. Karmon, *The Red Brigades: Cooperation with the Palestinian Terrorist Organization (1970–1990)*, (Israel: International Institute for Counter-Terrorism (ICT), 2001).
45 Meades, *Red Brigades*, 206.
46 Alexander and Pluchinsky, *Europe's Red Terrorists*, 57, 136.
47 A. Straßner, "Perzipierter Weltbürgerkrieg: Rote Armee Fraktion in Deutschland," in *Sozialrevolutionärer Terrorismus: Theorie, Ideologie, Fallbeispiele, Zukunftsszenarien*, ed. A. Straßner (Wiesbaden: VS Verlag, 2008), 232. When the RAF issued a communiqué under the name of "Commando Patrick O'Hara," the Irish National Liberation Army denounced this as a misappropriation.
48 See for example: Ganser, *NATO's Secret Armies*; Bull, *Italian Neofascism*; and Ferraresi, *Threats to Democracy*.
49 H.-G. Jaschke, "Right-wing Extremism and Populism in Contemporary Germany and Western Europe," in *Right-Wing Radicalism Today: Perspectives from Europe and the US*, ed. S. von Mering and T. W. McCarty (Milton Park, UK: Routledge, 2013), 24.
50 See R. Chiarini, "The 'Movimento Sociale Italiano': A Historical Profile," in *Neofascism in Europe*, ed. L. Cheles, R. Ferguson, and M. Vaughan, 19–42 (London: Longman, 1991).
51 E. Vulliamy, "Secret Agents, Freemasons, Fascists . . . and a Top-level Campaign of Political 'Destabilisation,'" *The Guardian*, December 5, 1990, 12.
52 Bull, *Italian Neofascism*, 30–5; and Ferraresi, *Threats to Democracy*, 90–115. There is a wide range of literature on the Piazza Fontana bombing that links this attack to the Italian Secret Service and the Army. For example, see L. Lanza, *Bombe e Segreti. Piazza Fontana: Una Strage Senza Colpevoli* (Milano: Eleuthera, 2005).

53 Ganser, *NATO's Secret Armies*, 76–7.
54 Chiarini, "Movimento," 37; and D. della Porta, *Clandestine Political Violence* (Cambridge: Cambridge University Press, 2013), 160.
55 Engene, *Terrorism*, 137.
56 Ganser, *NATO's Secret Armies*, 4.
57 P. Willan, "Terrorists 'Helped by CIA' to Stop Rise of Left in Italy," *The Guardian*, March 25, 2001 (accessed March 5, 2014); and, in particular, R. Igel, *Terrorjahre: Die dunkle Seite der CIA in Italien* (München: Herbig, 1997).
58 Bull, *Italian Neofascism*, 59. Bull uses an incorrect spelling of LeWinter's name in her text.
59 Ganser, *NATO's Secret Armies*.
60 G. Fasanella, C. Sestieri, and G. Pellegrino, *Segreto di stato: La Verità da Gladio al Caso Moro* (Turin: Einaudi, 2000); Igel, *Terrorjahre*, 162–202; and Ganser, *NATO's Secret Armies*, 80.
61 R. Igel, "Linksterrorismus ferngesteuert?"
62 Bull, *Italian Neofascism*, 76. For a more critical stance on the existence and significance of the Gladio network and its "false-flag" operations, see Chapter 25 by Geraint Hughes on international terrorism in this volume.
63 B. Hoffman, "Right-wing Terrorism in Europe," in *European Terrorism*, ed. E. Moxon-Browne (New York: Macmillan, 1994), 96.
64 Ibid.
65 A. Röpke and A. Speit, *Blut und Ehre: Geschichte und Gegenwart rechter Gewalt in Deutschland* (Berlin: C.H. Links, 2013), 46.
66 It proved, for instance, to be a major political scandal when the German Federal Constitutional Court decided that the planned governmental ban of the National Democratic Party (NPD) was to be called off due to the fact that Verfassungsschutz informants were active even in the highest ranks of the party.
67 Röpke and Speit, *Blut und Ehre*, 54.
68 L. McGowan, *The Radical Right in Germany: 1870 to Present* (Harlow, UK: Pearson Education, 2002), 182–3.
69 Ibid., 183.
70 Röpke and Speit, *Blut und Ehre*, 68.
71 Ibid., 69.
72 Ganser, *NATO's Secret Armies*, 206–9. See also T. von Heymann, *Die Oktoberfest-Bombe: München, 26. September 1980* (Berlin: Nora, 2008); and U. Chaussy, *Oktoberfest: Das Attentat. Wie die Verdrängung des Rechtsterrors begann* (Berlin: Ch. Links, 2014).
73 P. Fahrenholz, "Zweifel an der Einzeltäterthese," *Süddeutsche Zeitung*, January 16, 2014. Doubts about the German investigative agencies were aggravated when it recently became public that all court exhibits from the attack were thrown away in 1997.
74 Hoffman, "Right-wing Terrorism," 101.
75 M. A. Lee, "Strange Ties: The Stasi and the Neo-Fascists," *Los Angeles Times*, September 10, 2000.
76 McGowan, *The Radical Right*, 183.
77 Ibid., 182–4.
78 Balz, *Von Terroristen*, 11.
79 P. Lehr, "Still Blind in the Right Eye? A Comparison of German Responses to Political Violence from the Extreme Left and the Extreme Right," in *Extreme Right-Wing Political Violence and Terrorism*, ed. M. Taylor, P. M. Currie, and D. Holbrook (London: Bloomsbury, 2013), 207.

Further reading

Alexander, Yonah, and Dennis A. Pluchinsky. *Europe's Red Terrorists: The Fighting Communist Organizations*. London: Frank Cass, 1992.
Bull, Anna Cento. *Italian Neofascism: The Strategy of Tension and the Politics of Nonreconciliation*. New York: Berghahn, 2007.
Engene, Jan Oskar. *Terrorism in Western Europe: Explaining the Trends since 1950*. Cheltenham: Edgar Elgar, 2004.

Ganser, Daniele. *NATO's Secret Armies: Operation Gladio and Terrorism in Western Europe.* Milton Park, UK: Frank Cass, 2005.

McGowan, Lee. *The Radical Right in Germany: 1870 to Present.* Harlow, UK: Pearson Education, 2002.

Meades, Robert C., Jr. *Red Brigades: The Story of Italian Terrorism.* London: Palgrave Macmillan, 1990.

della Porta, Donatella. *Social Movements, Political Violence, and the State: A Comparative Analysis of Italy and Germany.* Cambridge: Cambridge University Press, 1995.

Smith, J., and André Moncourt. *The Red Army Faction: A Documentary History.* 2 vols. Oakland: PM Press, 2009 and 2013.

Part IV

RECENT DECADES

21

CONTEMPORARY DOMESTIC TERRORISM IN THE UNITED STATES

Carolyn Gallaher

We can learn a good deal about how Americans understand terrorism by the adjectives we place in front of it. When scholars, pundits, and everyday citizens modify terrorism with adjectives like "homegrown" or "domestic," they signal that terrorism, in its most essential form, is something that happens "over there," "outside" American borders. Likewise, when journalists and pundits describe terrorism occurring in the US as "attacks on American soil," they suggest the terrorism in question is an aberration by virtue of its location. After the attacks of September 11, 2001, commentators started modifying terrorism more frequently with adjectives such as "Islamic" or "Middle Eastern." The adjective assured us that even if the terrorists lived here, they were not from here or like "us" (citizens of a presumably Christian nation).

Despite the assumption that terrorism happens over there, and that when it does happen here, it is wrought by foreigners, American history provides countless examples to the contrary (in this volume see Chapters 6, 9, and 10 by Matthew Jennings, Thai Jones, and R. Blakeslee Gilpin, respectively). Violence meant to terrorize, or otherwise cow an opponent with different political aims, is as much a part of the American political landscape as primaries, debates, and conventions.[1]

In this chapter, I explore so-called domestic terrorism. Before proceeding, however, a few definitions are in order. Although terrorism is a deceptively simple concept – presumably a "you know it when you see it" phenomenon – there are a multitude of debates[2] about how to define it (see Randall D. Law's introduction to this volume). Here I use a simple definition. Terrorism is the use of violence or the threat of violence to meet a political objective, albeit with one important caveat. Unlike other forms of political violence, terrorist violence is focused (whether by purpose or necessity) on people not intimately or often even tangentially involved in the political issue at hand. Indeed, the terrorizing of innocents is the crucial thing that distinguishes terrorism from other forms of violence – spilling innocent blood is seen as necessary, or inevitable, to secure political victory. The term domestic terrorism refers to terrorist violence that occurs within a country rather than across its borders and in cases where the perpetrator and the victim live in the same country. The intended audience of domestic terrorism is usually a domestic audience as well (e.g., the US government or a group the perpetrator wants to intimidate). However, the audience can also be international inasmuch as domestic terrorists often want their attack to embarrass a domestic target on the international stage.

The goal of this chapter is to provide a panoramic view of domestic terrorism in the US since 1970, with a particular focus on definitional debates and key patterns across the period. Other chapters in this volume cover domestic terrorism in earlier periods of US history. The remainder of this chapter is organized in the following manner. I begin with a brief appraisal of the terrorism literature. I then discuss three key debates that drive the literature on domestic terrorism. In the third section I overview key patterns in domestic terrorism and discuss changes in them over time, using a wide array of examples in illustration.

A vast literature and a very brief summary

Thousands of articles and books have been devoted to the subject of terrorism. Not surprisingly, the ground covered is immense. The literature can be categorized in various ways. Some scholarship is regional in nature – i.e., works that look at terrorism in the Middle East,[3] Asia,[4] Central Asia,[5] or Latin America.[6] There are even entire bodies of literature devoted to particular terrorist groups. The literature on Peru's Sendero Luminoso is so immense it constitutes its own field of study – Senderology.[7] Other scholarship is focused on ideological variants of terrorism, such as right-wing terrorism.[8] Some terrorism scholarship is associated with particular theoretical stances, such as rational choice, liberal interventionism, and constructivism.[9] There are even debates about whether terrorism has changed so much in the last few decades that it amounts to something new.[10]

Although the definition of terrorism does not include geographic limits, most American scholarship is, as I suggest in the introduction, focused outside of the US. The literature on domestic terrorism is, therefore, much smaller and less readily categorized than the wider literature. In the discipline of history, for example, Beverly Gage observes that domestic terrorism has only been covered in a scattershot fashion (usually tracking current event trends), and what is covered is often of limited depth. As she notes:

> But even into the 1990s, there was little effort to assess these events [terrorist attacks in the US] in the context of domestic political trends or even U.S. foreign policy; nor was there much attempt to integrate them into historical debates about the nature of American national identity, social conflicts, and political traditions.[11]

There are a number of reasons for the disparity. When compared to many other countries in the world, for example, the US has had relatively little terrorist violence. The US has not experienced any guerrilla wars or insurgencies within its borders since the Civil War. Although guerrillas and insurgents are not necessarily terrorist organizations, they often adopt terrorist tactics over time. The Shining Path in Peru and the Basque separatists in Spain both began as classic guerrilla groups but soon employed tactics that killed innocent civilians and threatened others not willing/able to submit to their demands.

After Timothy McVeigh bombed the Murrah Federal Building in Oklahoma in 1995, US law enforcement officials began paying closer attention to domestic terrorist groups. However, that focus was diverted after nineteen men, fifteen of them Saudi nationals, hijacked four planes on September 11, 2001, hitting the World Trade Center towers in New York, the Pentagon in Virginia, and a field in Pennsylvania.[12] Given the anxiety about the "other" engendered by the attack – as well as the government's response to it – most law enforcement and scholarly attention shifted quickly to focus on terrorism committed by foreigners in the US or against US targets abroad. When domestic terrorists (i.e., people from the US) are examined, they tend to be terrorists embracing foreign ideologies. Much less attention is given to terrorists who are from the US and who are motivated by domestic ideologies rooted in American history and given form through its culture or regional cultures within it.

The limited and disparate work on domestic terrorism has important implications for how we understand domestic terrorism. Most importantly, there is a general fuzziness that surrounds the concept. In the next section, I highlight this fuzziness by examining three debates within the field of scholars and practitioners dealing with domestic terrorism. The nature of these debates suggests that there is not even a basic agreement on what constitutes a domestic terrorist.

Debates within the field of domestic terrorism

Where does ideology end and terrorism begin?

The first debate centers on the criteria used to define a person or group as a terrorist or terrorist group respectively. In the domestic context, this debate has focused on the question of whether espousing a hate-filled ideology is sufficient basis for using the terrorist label. Some argue that the terrorist label should be reserved for those who have actually committed a terrorist act. Others argue for a broader definition, noting that hateful ideologies – i.e., ones that subject an entire group of people to suspicion and hate because of biological traits, such as skin color, and/or cultural traditions, like religion or dress – create a discursive space for justifying and encouraging terrorist violence. As such, the groups built up around these ideologies can rightly be labeled as terrorists. In the US, this debate has tended to play out in policy conversations about right-wing ideology.

Although this debate has simmered for decades, it became a headline issue in the spring of 2009 when an internal Department of Homeland Security (DHS) intelligence assessment was leaked in the media.[13] Although the title of the report did not describe right-wing extremist groups as terrorists, the executive summary did:

> The DHS/Office of Intelligence and Analysis (I&A) has no specific information that domestic rightwing terrorists are currently planning acts of violence, but rightwing extremists may be gaining new recruits by playing on their fears about several emergent issues. The economic downturn and the election of the first African American president present unique drivers for rightwing radicalization and recruitment.[14]

The report engendered a quick and angry response by self-described right-wing commentators and bloggers. On her self-named blog, Michelle Malkin wrote a post on April 14, 2009, describing the report as "one of the most embarrassingly shoddy pieces of propaganda I'd ever read out of DHS." In a blog posting on The Liberty Papers two days earlier, Stephen Gordon argued that the assessment "targets most conservatives and libertarians in the country," observing that "all it takes to fit the terrorist profile is to have general anti-government feelings or prefer local/state government to federal control over everything." Critics also took issue with the report's warning that right-wing extremist groups might actively recruit veterans that were "disgruntled, disillusioned, or suffering from the psychological effects of war."[15] And, they were especially angry that the report cited Timothy McVeigh as an example. As the American Legion explained in a blog post on April 16, 2009, about the initial report and secretary Janet Napolitano's subsequent apology, "To continue to use McVeigh as an example of the stereotypical 'disgruntled military veteran' is as unfair as using Osama bin Laden as the sole example of Islam."

The furor led the Department of Homeland Security to officially recall the report, even though the secretary had been briefed on the report before its release, and it had already been sent to fusion centers[16] and selected law enforcement agencies across the country. The report's main author, Daryl Johnson, left the department in 2010. In 2011, he gave an interview to the Southern Poverty Law Center (SPLC) defending the report's findings and condemning its critics for politicizing the issue.

> I'd also like people to know that we were not directing LEOs [law enforcement officials] to do anything. We were prohibited from doing so. All we could do was say there is a trend emerging, and if you have these folks in your jurisdiction, perhaps you should think about how you are using your resources.[17]

He also rebuffed the charges that the report was aimed at conservatives. As he told Heidi Beirich at SPLC, "they [my critics] would have been shocked to know that I personify conservatism. I'm an Eagle Scout. I'm a registered Republican. I'm Mormon."[18]

While the furor over the report, as well as Johnson's public discussions of it, focused on whether the report was partisan in nature, Johnson did address the wider question of interest here: was it appropriate to label anti-government groups on the right as terrorists when they had not been involved in any acts of violence? Indeed, though the report he helped author never included a working definition of the term "right-wing extremism," Johnson acknowledged in the interview that his group intentionally used a broad working definition of the term, which allowed them to discuss a variety of right-wing groups and movements, not all of which had been involved in recent criminal or terrorist activity. Explaining the internal review process for the report, for example, he noted:

> One office [inside DHS] raised issues – the Office of Civil Rights and Civil Liberties [CRCL]. At the time, we weren't required to give them the report, but my boss thought we should run it past them. They had edits, but the main issue related to the definition of right-wing extremism. That office wanted a narrow definition limited to violent groups and individuals. Our subject-matter experts and management felt the definition needed to be broader. Under CRCL's definition, if you were in the Klan, burned crosses, had a terrorist in your house and donated money to groups advocating violence, you still would not qualify as a right-wing extremist.[19]

While the furor has largely subsided over the recalled report, many groups still use the terrorist label to describe groups that have not committed any crime. In its most recent (2013) annual publication *The Year in Hate and Extremism*, for example, the Southern Poverty Law Center used the words "terror," "conspiracy," and "political violence" interchangeably to label the right-wing extremist groups it tracks.[20]

Healthy debates about terminology can be good. Efforts to sharpen or change the meaning of a category can, for example, be useful when the previous definition no longer captures the behavior it is meant to describe. For law enforcement purposes, there is also some benefit to having broad categories because more potential cases can be tried under them.[21] However, the flexibility of the categories we use to capture certain kinds of violence make counting and tracking domestic terrorism difficult. If there is not clarity or agreement on who is being counted, then it is hard for a researcher to combine existing datasets or to use a dataset whose definition does not match his/her own.

What counts as domestic?

Another line of debate concerns how to define the parameters of the domestic. In particular, while scholars and experts tend to agree that a terrorist act is domestic if it is committed in the US by someone from or living in the US, there is no consensus on whether that person's ideology must also be "homegrown."

In many ways this is a new debate. It is a product of the conceptual confusion that ensued in the wake of 9/11. Before it, ideology was not a factor in distinguishing the domestic from the international. Rather, the question hinged on geography – where the attack occurred (at home or abroad) and where the person or group that directed it came from (home or abroad). For example, the FBI's 1999 definition of terrorism, excerpted below, makes no mention of the terrorist's ideology or origin:

> Domestic terrorism is the unlawful use, or threatened use, of force or violence by a group or individual based and operating entirely within the United States or its territories without foreign direction committed against persons or property to intimidate or coerce a government, the civilian population, or any segment thereof, in furtherance of political or social objectives.[22]

The 1994 definition of international terrorism is equally silent on the geographic origins of ideology. As above, the geography of the attack and the attackers are central.

> International terrorist acts occur outside the United States or transcend national boundaries in terms of the means by which they are accomplished, the persons they appear intended to coerce or intimidate, or the locale in which the perpetrators operate or seek asylum.[23]

In response to the 9/11 attacks, the US launched its "global war on terror." This war upended the unspoken geography that underpinned American notions of domestic (and international) terrorism. Americans were suddenly confronted with the fact that a terrorist act with mass casualties could not only occur at home but be launched by foreigners who were living/working/studying in our country. Suddenly, the lines between "us" and "them" and "here" and "there" were blurred. They grew even blurrier when American citizens were implicated in terrorist activity inside the US that explicitly invoked the ideology of al-Qaeda, the organization behind the 9/11 attacks. A year after the 9/11 attacks, for example, an American-born citizen named José Padilla was arrested for plotting a dirty bomb attack in the US. Other attacks followed. In 2009, an Army psychiatrist named Nidal Hasan went on a shooting rampage at Fort Hood to avenge American violence in Afghanistan and Iraq.

In a discursive sense, people like Padilla and Hasan are categorically troubling. Although both were American citizens, they justified their attacks using foreign ideology. Indeed, it was not their anger at the US government that made them stand out – plenty of US domestic terrorists have targeted the US government – but rather the "foreignness" of the ideologies they used to defend their actions.

In response to this discursive unease, there were calls to refine definitions of domestic terrorism to account for terrorists influenced by foreign ideology. The impetus behind these calls did not, however, emerge from scholarly quarters. Rather, it came from the US government and, within it, the newly created Department of Homeland Security. Although

DHS's mandate was to track all threats to the domestic sphere, it was clear that the new agency would focus on individuals and groups inspired by al-Qaeda. And that focus would require disaggregation of the data on domestic threats to account for differences between those influenced by domestic ideology and those driven by foreign ideology. The result was a new category of domestic terrorism – homegrown violent extremism. DHS and the FBI made the category official in 2011:

> DHS and FBI define an HVE as a person of any citizenship who has lived and/or operated primarily in the United States or its territories who advocates, is engaged in, or is preparing to engage in ideologically-motivated terrorist activities (including providing support to terrorism) in furtherance of political or social objectives promoted by a foreign terrorist organization, but is acting independently of direction by a foreign terrorist organization.[24]

Supporters of the new categorization argue that Americans have categorized terrorism incorrectly for far too long. Erroll Southers, for example, points to two common mistakes. First, Americans tend to look at terrorism as something that happens "over there" or that it is otherwise an anomaly inside the US. Unfortunately, this view blinds us to the fact that "dogmatic zealotry has embedded itself into the fabric of communities throughout the United States."[25] As an example, he points to the initial search for the perpetrators of the Boston Marathon bombing in April 2013. Officials originally thought a Saudi national with shrapnel wounds was a likely suspect. It soon became apparent, however, that the true perpetrators – Dzhokhar and Tamerlan Tsarnaev – were "homegrown." Although they were born in Chechnya, both grew up in the US. In this regard, the category of homegrown violent extremism is important because it forces us to look at home for the source of threats. As Southers argues, "the origin of the ideology is irrelevant . . . what matters is where it was embraced."[26]

The second mistake is to treat terrorism as a uniform phenomenon. There is no single terrorist threat, so there can be no unitary approach to combating it. Southers argues, for example, that developing threat profiles within the category of homegrown violent extremists is crucial so that law enforcement officers know the complexity of the phenomena they are meant to track and ultimately counter.[27] For those interested in stopping the HVE threat, the most important thing to understand is the multitude of ways that people are radicalized, rather than the ideology that frames their radicalization.

The concept of radicalization is fairly new in terrorism studies.[28] The literature used to explain individual participation in terrorism as the result of macro-level factors such as poverty, limited avenues for political expression, or cultural values. Radicalization was embraced in the immediate post-9/11 atmosphere when attempts to explain terrorist motivations using these variables were often equated with support for such groups. As Peter Neumann, one of the founders of contemporary radicalization studies explains:

> In the highly charged atmosphere following the September 11 attacks, it was through the notion of radicalization that a discussion about the political, economic, social and psychological forces that underpin terrorism and political violence became possible again.[29]

Despite the growing acceptance of the HVE category (and the attendant focus on radicalization) across US government agencies, the shift is not without criticism. As a person who has studied the US patriot movement,[30] for example, I disagree that ideology is what distinguishes terrorists like Hasan and the Tsarnaev brothers from terrorists like Timothy McVeigh. In fact, on the face of it, these three attacks have a number of things in common. All three perpetrators acted as "lone wolves," and all three appeared to have been motivated to some extent by a desire to enact revenge against the US government. The primary difference between these attacks is the scale of violence. McVeigh killed many more people (168) than either Hasan (thirteen) or the Tsarnaev brothers (three) did, suggesting that tactical sophistication was the primary dividing line between them. In this light, categorizing Hasan and the Tsarnaev brothers differently from McVeigh seems less about empirics than politics. That is, the HVE designation reifies the foreign heritage of Hasan and the Tsarnaev brothers even though it is not a trait that empirically distinguishes their attacks from those of other domestic terrorists. It also encourages Americans to continue seeing terrorism as something that happens "over there" or that is imported from abroad. In so doing, it diverts our attention away from the long-standing use of terrorism by American citizens drawing on American ideologies.

A related critique concerns the growth of counter-radicalization programs to thwart HVEs. While critics agree that the concept of radicalization *was* useful in creating a space to talk about the "why" behind terrorist attacks, a veritable industry of experts has emerged to deal with HVEs, and their practices are often quite problematic.[31] In particular, counter-radicalization singles out a subset of domestic terrorists for special scrutiny that other equally dangerous groups do not receive. In his study of Britain's Prevent Violent Extremism program, Paul Thomas notes that the program was monocultural because it focused almost exclusively on Muslim youth.[32] Moreover, the monocultural nature of the program tended to work at cross-purposes with the program's stated goal. Specifically, instead of mitigating the alienation that many Muslim youth in Britain feel, it ended up reinforcing their differences from the British mainstream. Likewise, Arun Kundnani argues that the Muslim-centric focus of counter-radicalization programs have opened Muslim communities up to surveillance by government officials, scholars, and other experts. This scrutiny has, in turn, contributed to an erosion of trust between Muslims and the wider communities in which they live. Many Muslims feel like they are considered "suspect" simply because they are Muslim.[33]

Can we categorize violence fueled by bigotry as terrorism?

In October 2012, Wade Michael Page entered a Sikh temple in Oak Creek, Wisconsin, and started shooting. He killed six people before turning the gun on himself. Although the investigations into Wade's motives were complicated by his suicide, Wade's history with white supremacist groups and the white power music scene suggested that he was motivated by hatred of non-white racial groups. Although US Attorney General Eric Holder initially labeled the shooting a hate crime,[34] the police investigating the scene described it as "a domestic terrorist-type incident."[35]

The different labels suggest another unanswered question within the scholarly and policy circles focused on domestic terrorism. Indeed, though most definitions of domestic terrorism cite terrorists as having "political" motivations, there is no agreement on what constitutes "politics." Classic notions of politics revolve around matters of governance – how an economy should be organized, what rights citizens will have, and how crimes will be adjudicated. In the context of terrorism, this view of politics would see the terrorist desire to replace a sitting government or get it to do (or stop doing) something as political.

However, "identity politics," which can be broadly defined as the politics of defending or advocating for groups defined by a shared identity (e.g., religious, ethnic/racial, etc.), casts a broader definitional net. In this conception, politics also involves questions over cultural and social dominance. In the context of terrorism, groups defending a given ethnic group – or, more precisely attacking all other ethnic groups – would be viewed as political, even if the attackers made no claim on formal government power. Claudia Card observes that scholars using the first definition of politics to define terrorism (she calls this the coercion model) do not typically view hate as part of the equation. Indeed, when innocents are killed, they are more often than not viewed as "throwaways," as pawns whose death will coerce the group's primary target.[36] Moreover, terrorist political rationality – evidenced by the clear articulation of a goal to take over government – means they can be negotiated with. By contrast, scholars who adopt the second view (Card refers to this approach as the group target model) think hate – and the related racial, cultural, and social dimensions – is often a vital part of the terrorist logic because it is about establishing dominance over a particular group. As such, hating and attacking another group can be political.

This debate is more than scholarly. Formal definitions of "hate crime" and domestic terrorism do not offer much clarification. Although hate can be the motivating factor in a hate crime or domestic terrorism event, the distinction used by the FBI – individual malice for a hate crime and ideological malice for terrorists – can be difficult to delineate on the ground.[37] In the Oak Creek case, for example, sorting through a dead perpetrator's motives is as much an art as a science. Nor is there a clear agreement on what the balance between individual malice and malice driven by ideology would need to be to select the "proper" category for a given perpetrator.

Recent patterns in domestic terrorism

Given the debates outlined above, it is difficult to discuss patterns in domestic terrorism using quantitative data without making definitional sacrifices. And because there are no consensus standards for defining domestic terrorism, most databases will include or leave out instances that a particular author or analyst would otherwise include. However, the databases that do exist can serve as a broad guide for looking at patterns of contemporary terrorism. In this section, I rely on two databases for quantitative data, the Global Terrorism Database[38] and the Homegrown Threat Database.[39] The first database (1970 to present) includes terror acts committed by so-called traditional[40] terrorists and HVEs. The second database, which also includes traditional terrorists and HVEs, is smaller in temporal scope. It only includes terrorist acts between 2000 and 2013. I also rely on individual, often ethnographic, work to lend texture to some of the statistical patterns.

A politics with limited appeal

In a relative sense, the US has been lucky. Although terrorism has been a part of the political landscape since the country's inception, citizens have not routinely resorted to terrorism to meet their political goals. This is not to suggest that the violence that has occurred is excusable or can be dismissed as a marginal phenomenon. Even one act of terrorism is too much. However, a quick survey of the Global Terrorism Database[41] demonstrates that the North American region has, since 1970, been spared the scale of terrorism found in other regions.[42] Between 1970 and 2012, for example, North America has had fewer incidents (2,896) of terrorism than Western Europe (15,115), Sub-Saharan Africa (8,175), Central America and the Caribbean (10,567), South America (17,997), and the Middle East and North Africa (23,118). And, though the US has more incidents (2,242) than many of its fellow NATO members – Germany (542), France (1,101), Italy (1,413) – it ranks below both Great Britain[43] (3,267) and Spain (2,752). The number of US incidents also pales in comparison to developing countries that have had civil wars or other lengthy insurgencies, such as Peru (5,408) and El Salvador (3,699).[44]

Terrorist incidents in the United States have also involved relatively few deaths. Between 1970 and 2012, just over ninety percent of attacks involved no fatalities (1,986).[45] Of the attacks that did involve fatalities (197), ninety-six percent involved ten or fewer people. Only four attacks involved more than 100 fatalities – the 1995 bombing of the Murrah Federal Building in Oklahoma City and the attacks on the Pentagon and two World Trade Towers on 9/11.[46] When non-fatal injuries are examined, a similar pattern emerges. Casualties per attack tended to be only slightly higher than fatalities. Just over eighty-eight percent of incidents (1,923) involved no injuries, and ninety-three percent of attacks that did involve injuries (248) involved ten or fewer people.[47] When compared to patterns in global terror attacks, these numbers suggest that attacks in the US are less intense, as measured by human toll. Indeed, only fifty-seven percent of total global terror attacks involved no fatalities (the percentage for attacks with no injuries is 69.5 percent), and in attacks that did, 90.7 percent involved ten or fewer fatalities (the corresponding percentage for injuries is 78.7 percent).[48] These data suggest that most domestic terrorists focused their attacks on property[49] (e.g., police patrol cars, buildings) or were unable/unwilling to successfully carry off attacks involving large numbers of people.

Incidents of terrorism in the United States are also on the decline. In 1970, for example, there were more than 450 recorded cases of terrorist attacks. After the early 1970s, the number of incidences decreases sharply; after 1977, the number of recorded cases never exceeds 100. In 2012, there were thirteen recorded cases.

The numbers are also low if we narrow our focus to incidents of domestic terrorism in the Homegrown Threat Database (recall that this dataset includes traditional terrorists and HVEs). This database indicates that between September 11, 2001, and June 17, 2013, there were 309 individual indictments against domestic terrorism suspects. Just under half of these (178 indictments or forty-six percent of the total) involve citizens influenced by domestic ideologies. This translates to an average of fifteen so-called traditional domestic terrorist attacks a year. And the total number of people killed by domestic terrorists between 2000 and the present was twenty-nine. These are low numbers. Consider, for example, that an average of fifty-three people are killed a year by lightning strikes in the US.[50]

Shifting patterns

During the forty plus years covered by the Global Terrorism Database, there have been a number of shifting patterns. To demonstrate these, I will take a snapshot of patterns from the decade of the 1970s and compare them to more recent decades. In the 1970s, domestic terrorism exhibited several key characteristics. First, most terrorist attacks (where a perpetrator is known) were associated with a group. Second, it was a busy decade for domestic terrorism. Fifty-eight percent of all terrorist attacks occurring in the US in the Global Terrorism Database occurred during the 1970s. It was, in a sense, domestic terrorism's heyday, even if the death toll was fairly low (156). Indeed, the total number of terrorist-related fatalities in the 1970s is less than the total number of people killed in either the 1995 Oklahoma City bombing or the attacks on 9/11.

During the 1970s, a slightly greater share of terrorists can also be classified as left-wing than right-wing. Although the political categories of "left" and "right" are themselves fungible, they are a useful, if imperfect way to capture political variation within the universe of domestic terrorism. Typically, right-wing politics refers to groups who support limited government involvement in the economy and traditional social hierarchies of race, tribe, sect, gender, etc. Left-wing politics refers to groups who believe government intervention in the economy is necessary to ensure a more level playing field between social and cultural groups. Left-wing groups also support expanding/improving the participation of minority or stigmatized groups in social, economic, and political life.

In the 1970s, left-wing terrorist groups were strongly focused on oppression and the US's role in perpetrating it at home and abroad. The Fuerzas Armadas de Liberacion Nacional, a terrorist group devoted to securing independence for the island of Puerto Rico, was involved in eighty-one terrorist incidents between 1970 and 1979. Likewise, the New World Liberation Front (NWLF), which was devoted to "liberating" African Americans from conditions of oppression, engaged in eighty-five terrorist incidents during the same time period. NWLF, which was largely active in the San Francisco Bay area, focused on bombing property associated with individuals or companies seen as oppressing minorities. They also firebombed police cars. The Weather Underground also organized against what it saw as US oppression at home and abroad. The Weather Underground's stated goal was to overthrow the US government, and most of their forty-one attacks were lodged against government buildings. In 1972, for example, the group placed a bomb in a women's restroom at the Pentagon to protest the US government's bombing of Hanoi. However, the group was also involved in one of the era's more peculiar crimes, when it helped break Timothy Leary, a psychologist and advocate of LSD therapy, out of a California prison in 1970.

There were, of course, right-wing groups active during the 1970s as well. The Jewish Defense League[51] was involved in forty-four acts of terrorism in that decade. The group's primary targets were neo-Nazis and Arab Americans. It also attacked the property of Arab governments inside the country. The right-wing group Omega-7, formed by Cuban exiles, was engaged in twenty-three terror attacks during the 1970s. The group attacked people and property associated with Cuba as well as American citizens seen as supporting the Castro regime.[52] During the 1970s, the group killed one person and injured four. The nascent anti-abortion movement also began to engage in terrorism during this decade. Nine attacks against abortion providers or property where abortions were provided occurred during the 1970s.

Today, the character of domestic terrorism is quite different. A primary difference is that acts of terror have declined significantly from their 1970s heyday. Attacks between 2000 and 2011, for example, only account for nine percent of total terror attacks since 1970. However, the largest death toll is found in the contemporary period. There are a number of potential explanations for the larger death toll, including a growing technological sophistication (e.g., larger bombs) and recognition that a twenty-four-hour news cycle requires more carnage to get attention.

A second difference is that attacks are increasingly launched by individuals who are not directly connected to any group. Between 2000 and 2010, thirty-two percent of attacks in the Global Terrorism Database were by people "with no apparent affiliation to a known extremist group."[53] Two terrorists personify this move away from group-sanctioned terrorism.

Timothy McVeigh, the perpetrator of the Oklahoma City bombing, worked with one accomplice and was not a formal member of any militia groups, though he is believed to have attended militia meetings in Michigan and read militia/patriot literature. Likewise, Nidal Hasan, the Army psychiatrist who shot and killed thirteen people at Fort Hood in 2009, is known to have developed sympathy for radical interpretations of Islam but is not believed to have been directly affiliated with any group.

Perhaps not surprisingly, given the 9/11 attacks, which were perpetrated by a group of mostly Saudi nationals working for al-Qaeda, radical Islamism and salafi jihadism are behind a growing number of domestic terror threats. (For more details on Islamism/jihadism see Chapters 18, 17, and 22 by Cook, Calvert, and Gartenstein-Ross, respectively, in this volume.) According to the Homegrown Threat Database, for example, fifty-four percent of domestic terror attacks between September 11, 2001, and June 17, 2013, were conducted by "jihadist" terrorists.[54] While these data are suggestive, a note of caution is warranted. In particular, the Homegrown Threat Database includes attacks that were not seen to fruition. Moreover, when the database compares "deadly" attacks across groups, the number of attacks by "jihadists" (twenty) is actually one-third smaller than the number attributed to "right wing" groups (twenty-nine).

Some scholars also argue that the concentration of domestic terrorist activity not perpetrated by radical Islamists and jihadists has shifted from the left to the right on the political spectrum.[55] The Homegrown Threat Database indicates that between 2000 and 2013, seventy-six percent of all domestic terrorists (i.e., "traditional" and HVEs) may be classified as right-wing. Many of these terrorists are associated with either white supremacist or militia/patriot groups. Although outsiders often see these groups as synonymous, there are important differences between them. White supremacist groups place the racial dominance of whites at the top of their agenda. Most militia/patriot groups, by contrast, do not openly advocate for the dominance of one racial group over another. Although most patriot groups have an all-white membership, minorities are not usually prevented from joining militias. Militia/patriot groups are primarily concerned with fighting the "new world order," which they define as an international conspiracy, aided and abetted by US government officials, to erode the sovereignty of the United States. Other right-wing attacks are associated with the anti-abortion movement, though these attacks are linked to individual activists rather than specific anti-abortion groups. Of the nineteen attacks against abortion-related targets between 2000 and 2011 in the Global Terrorism Database, for example, none was associated with an anti-abortion group.

Terrorism from the left remains, however, an important part of the domestic terrorist scene. The Homegrown Threat Database notes, for example, that seventeen percent of domestic terrorist cases involve animal rights and environment-focused groups. Two of the biggest groups in action today are the Animal Liberation Front (ALF) and the Earth Liberation Front (ELF). The ALF, which was founded in 1976, advocates the ideas of Peter Singer, whose touchstone book, *Animal Liberation*, first published in 1975, argues that animals should have the same rights as humans.[56] ALF's mission is to destroy the capacity of organizations that abuse animals. Activists typically target animal-holding facilities; after freeing animals, the group inflicts damage to the property.[57] The Earth Liberation Front, founded in 1992, deploys a similar approach to ALF. The group targets businesses that it thinks are contributing to the destruction of the environment. They often target building sites in environmentally sensitive areas.[58] ALF and ELF have also worked together. In 1997, the two groups set fire to Bureau of Land Management property in Oregon reserved for wild horse corrals. In the Global Terrorism Database, the ALF and the ELF are responsible for eighty-seven terrorist acts (thirty-seven by ALF and fifty for ELF) between 2000 and 2010.

Discursive shifts

To some degree, all terrorists cite oppression to justify their actions. However, if we look at domestic terrorism in the US and confine it to groups that are not connected to radical Islamism/jihadism, discourses around who is doing the oppression and how they are doing it have changed. These changes broadly reflect the emergence of globalization and the new anxieties it has produced. We can see this trend by examining who terrorists target, and how conceptualizations of the "who" have changed over time.

Although the government is a consistent rhetorical and physical target throughout the period covered here, how terrorist groups view the government has varied over time. In the 1970s, the US government was depicted by terrorists across the political spectrum as a menacing, unchecked force. In the domestic sphere, it could oppress minorities and women (a concern of left-wing groups) as well as fetuses (the fear of right-wing groups). In the foreign realm, it could start wars and abuse peasants and other poor people with little regard for domestic or international laws. Today, terrorists on the left and right still see the government as a powerful entity, but they no longer see its power as unchecked. Indeed, a central point of the militia/patriot movement during the 1990s was that the US was slowly divesting its sovereignty to global institutions. As such, while militia and patriot groups described government agents as jack-booted thugs, they believed their thuggish behavior could be traced to the fact that the US government was no longer controlled by Americans, but rather by supranational organizations like the UN.[59]

Likewise, when animal rights groups attack slaughterhouses or government labs, they situate their attack in a wider corporate context. Indeed, in this manner, US laws meant to protect animals or accord them humane treatment are poorly enforced because the US government is seen as beholden to wider corporate interests. Carl Boggs, who studies and advocates animal rights from a self-described "critical left" perspective, refers to this center of power as "the corporate-imperial order," signifying that something greater than the state is holding the oppressive reins of power.[60]

Domestic terrorism going forward

Although the patterns suggested here are provocative and certainly useful for those interested in stopping terrorist attacks, our ability to fully understand domestic terrorism is limited by our inability to define what we are talking about. Of course, definitional muddiness is not confined to domestic terrorism. Debates about what does and does not constitute an act of terror are just as strong in circles looking at international terrorism. However, in the domestic sphere, these debates matter because the denominator (or total cases) is quite small. If we take a broader definition of what constitutes domestic terrorism, for example, our denominator can more than double. Adding attacks against property, for example, increases the numbers. So, too, does adding HVEs.

The fact that the terrorism denominator is not fixed also suggests that in many respects "terrorism" is a discursive strategy. That is, the ability and power to name someone (or his/her group) as a terrorist is a powerful thing. We can ruin or protect people simply by how we label them. The fact that corporate crackdowns on American labor unrest – some of the bloodiest episodes in American history outside of the Civil War – are never discussed in the context of terrorism also suggests the terrorist label is value laden. Indeed, though I have not discussed state terrorism in this chapter, Chapters 7, 11, and 24 by Miller, Hagenloh, and Griffin, respectively, make it clear in this volume that the state (ours and others) can conduct terrorism or support entities that do. The data presented here, then, are more than an objective presentation of facts and patterns. They are also mirrors that show us what the powerful hold dear and who they believe threaten it. In this regard, the old saw that one man's terrorist is another's freedom fighter captures the fact that political, social, and economic interests govern even our most sacred categories.

Notes

1 Catherine McNicol Stock, *Rural Radicals: Righteous Rage in the American Grain* (Ithaca, NY: Cornell University Press, 1996); and Beverly Gage, "Terrorism and the American Experience: A State of the Field," *Journal of American History* 98, no. 1 (2011): 73–94.
2 Richard Jackson and Samuel Sinclair, eds., *Contemporary Debates on Terrorism* (New York: Routledge, 2012).
3 Mahmood Mamdani, "Good Muslim, Bad Muslim: A Political Perspective on Culture and Terrorism," *American Anthropologist New Series* 104, no. 3 (2002): 766–75; and Konstantinos Drakos and Ali M. Kutan, "Regional Effects of Terrorism on Tourism in Three Mediterranean Countries," *Journal of Conflict Resolution* 47, no. 5 (2003): 621–41.
4 Zachary Abuza, "Funding Terrorism in Southeast Asia: The Financial Network of Al-Qaeda and Jemaah Islamiya," *Contemporary Southeast Asia* 25, no. 2 (2003): 169–99.
5 Cerwyn Moore, "Suicide Bombing: Chechnya, the North Caucasus and Martyrdom," *Europe–Asia Studies* 64, no. 9 (2012): 1780–807; and Valery Tishkov, *Chechnya: Life in a War-torn Society* (Berkeley: University of California Press, 2004).
6 Andreas Feldmann and Maiju Perälä, "Reassessing the Causes of Nongovernmental Terrorism in Latin America," *Latin American Politics and Society* 46, no. 2 (2004): 101–32.
7 Cynthia McClintock, "Why Peasants Rebel: The Case of Peru's Sendero Luminoso," *World Politics* 37, no. 1 (1984): 617–36; David Scott Palmer, "Rebellion in Rural Peru: The Origins and Evolution of Sendero Luminoso," *Comparative Politics* 18, no. 2 (1986): 127–46; Carlos Ivan Degregori, *Las Rondas Campesinas y la Derrota de Sendero Luminoso* (Lima: IEP Ediciones, 1996); and Orin Starn, *Nightwatch: The Politics of Protest in the Andes* (Durham, NC: Duke University Press, 1999). See Chapter 19 by Jennifer S. Holmes on Latin American terrorism in this volume.
8 Daniel Levitas, *The Terrorist Next Door: The Militia Movement and the Radical Right* (New York: Thomas Dunne Books, 2002); and Daryl Johnson, *Right-wing Resurgence: How a Domestic Terrorist Threat is Being Ignored* (Lanham, MD: Rowman and Littlefield, 2012).
9 For a rational choice perspective, see Martha Crenshaw, "The Logic of Terrorism: Terrorist Behavior as a Product of Strategic Choice," in *Origins of Terrorism: Psychologies, Ideologies, Theologies, States of Mind*, ed. Walter Reich, 7–24 (Washington, DC: Woodrow Wilson Center Press, 1998). For a liberal interventionist perspective, see Paul Berman, *Terror and Liberalism* (New York: Norton, 2003). For constructivist accounts, see James Horley and Ian McPhail, "What's in a Name? Interpreting Terrorism from the Perspective of Personal Construct Theory," in *Engaging Terror: A Critical and Interdisciplinary Approach*, ed. J. Haig et al., 119–28 (Boca Raton, FL: Brown Walker, 2008); and Rainer Hülsse and Alexander Spencer, "The Metaphor of Terror: Terrorism Studies and the Constructivist Turn," *Security Dialogue* 39, no. 6 (2008): 571–92.
10 For an argument that contemporary terrorism is different from earlier epochs, see Ian O. Lesser, Bruce Hoffman, John Arquilla, David Ronfeldt, Michele Zanini, and Brian Michael Jenkins, *Countering the New Terrorism* (Santa Monica, CA: Rand Corporation, 1999); and Alejandra Bolanos, "The 'New Terrorism,' or the 'Newness' of Context and Change," in *Contemporary Debates on Terrorism*, ed. Richard Jackson and Samuel Sinclair, 29–34 (London: Routledge, 2012). For an opposing view, see Isabelle Duyvesteyn, "How New is the New Terrorism?" *Studies in Conflict and Terrorism* 27, no. 5 (2004): 439–54; and Isabelle Duyvesteyn and Leena Malkki, "No: The Fallacy of the New Terrorism Thesis," in *Contemporary Debates on Terrorism*, 35–42.

11 Gage, *Terrorism and the American Experience*, 79. For an important exception to this trend see Michael Fellman, *In the Name of God and Country: Reconsidering Terrorism in American History* (New Haven, CT: Yale University Press, 2010).
12 Jerome Bejlopera, *American Jihadist Terrorism: Combating a Complex Threat* (Washington, DC: Congressional Research Service, 2013).
13 Office of Intelligence and Analysis Assessment, *Rightwing Extremism: Current Economic and Political Climate Fueling Resurgence in Radicalization and Recruitment* (Washington, DC: Department of Homeland Security, 2009). This report was produced for law enforcement personnel and not designated for widespread, public release. The report is no longer available on the DHS website, but a full copy is archived on the Federation of American Scientists' website at: www.fac.org/irp/eprint/rightwing.pdf (accessed July 18, 2014).
14 Office of Intelligence and Analysis Assessment, *Right Wing Extremism*, 2.
15 Office of Intelligence and Analysis Assessment, *Right Wing Extremism*, 7.
16 Fusion centers are designed to bring together law enforcement officers from different agencies (e.g., Customs and Border Patrol and the Drug Enforcement Administration [DEA]) and scales (e.g., federal, state, and local) to combat sophisticated criminal activity such as terrorism or drug trafficking. Fusion centers are primarily organized to share intelligence, but some also encourage joint operations. Although fusion centers were in existence before 9/11, their numbers increased substantially after it. By 2008, the Department of Homeland Security was funding 58 new or retooled fusion centers. For more detail, see Torin Monahan and Neal A. Palmer, "The Emerging Politics of DHS Fusion Centers," *Security Dialogue* 40, no. 6 (2009): 617–36.
17 As quoted in Heidi Beirich, "Inside the DHS: Former Top Analyst Says Agency Bowed to Political Pressure," *Intelligence Report*, no. 142 (Summer 2011), www.splcenter.org/get-informed/intelligence-report/browse-all-issues/2011/summer/inside-the-dhs-former-top-analyst-says-agency-bowed (accessed July 18, 2014).
18 As quoted in Beirich, "Inside the DHS."
19 As quoted in Beirich, "Inside the DHS."
20 Mark Potok, "The Year in Hate and Extremism," *Intelligence Report*, no. 149 (Spring 2013).
21 Bejelopera, *American Jihadist Terrorism*, 41–2.
22 Federal Bureau of Investigations, *Terrorism in the United States 1999: Thirty Years of Terrorism, a Special Retrospective Edition* (Washington, DC: US Department of Justice), ii.
23 Federal Bureau of Investigations, *Terrorism in the United States* 1999, ii.
24 Department of Homeland Security and the Federal Bureau of Investigations, *Use of Small Arms: Examining Lone Shooters and Small-unit Tactics: Joint Intelligence Bulletin*, August 16, 2009, 3.
25 Southers made this comment in an April 17, 2013, blog post on ElsevierConnect.
26 Erroll Southers, *Homegrown Violent Extremism* (Amsterdam: Anderson Publishing, 2009), xi.
27 Southers, *Homegrown Violent Extremism*, 115–17.
28 Peter Neumann, "Introduction," in *Papers from the First International Conference on Radicalisation and Political Violence*, ed. Henry Sweetbaum, 1780–807 (London: International Centre for the Study of Radicalisation and Political Violence, 2008).
29 Neumann, "Introduction," 4.
30 Carolyn Gallaher, *On the Fault Line: Race, Class, and the American Patriot Movement* (Lanham, MD: Rowman and Littlefield, 2003).
31 Arun Kundnani, "Radicalisation: The Journey of a Concept," *Race and Class* 54, no. 2 (2012): 3–25.
32 Paul Thomas, "Failed and Friendless: The UK's 'Preventing Violent Extremism' Programme," *British Journal of Politics and International Relations* 12, no. 3 (2010): 442–58.
33 Kundnani, "Radicalisation," 19.
34 Eric Holder, Speech Given at Oak Creek Memorial Service, August 10, 2009, www.justice.gov/iso/opa/ag/speeches/2012/ag-speech-1208101.html (accessed July 18, 2013).
35 Michael Yaccino, Michael Schwirtz, and Marc Santora, "Gunman Kills 6 at a Sikh Temple Near Milwaukee," *New York Times*, August 5, 2012.
36 Claudia Card, "Recognizing Terrorism," *Journal of Ethics* 11, no. 1 (2007): 4.
37 Bejelopera, *American Jihadist Terrorism*, 71, 125.
38 The National Consortium for the Study of Terrorism and Responses to Terrorism, Global Terrorism Database [Data File], 2012. Available online at: www.start.umd.edu/gtd (accessed July 12, 2013).

39 New America Foundation and Syracuse University. The Homegrown Threat Database: Homegrown Terrorism Cases, 2001–2013, 2013. Available online at: http://web.archive.org/web/20131218083954/http://homegrown.newamerica.net/ (accessed July 18, 2013).
40 My use of the word traditional here refers to people/groups inspired by ideologies that are domestic in origin or were brought to the US decades if not centuries ago and retooled for American grievances.
41 The National Consortium for the Study of Terrorism and Responses to Terrorism, "Global Terrorism Database."
42 It is worth noting that between 1850 and 1930s, there was more terrorist violence in the US than in most other countries in the world. White supremacist violence related to the Civil War and its aftermath (such as Klan-related violence and systematic lynching) explains why the US was at the top of the list for much of the period. See Chapter 10 by R. Blakeslee Gilpin on white supremacist terrorism in this volume.
43 The data for Great Britain includes Northern Ireland.
44 These numbers were calculated using the START database's online search (available at: www.start.umd.edu/gtd/search/). The database defines terrorist acts using three criterion: (1) "the act must be aimed at attaining a political, economic, religious, or social goal"; (2) "there must be evidence of an intention to coerce, intimidate, or convey some other message to a larger audience (or audiences) than the immediate victims"; and (3) "the action must be outside the context of legitimate warfare activities, i.e. the act must be outside the parameters permitted by international humanitarian law (particularly the admonition against deliberately targeting civilians or non-combatants)."
45 This percentage figure was not calculated using the total number of attacks (2,242) in the denominator because the START database lists fifty-nine attacks with an unknown death toll. My denominator (2,183) does not include these fifty-nine attacks.
46 Although we tend to think of the 9/11 attacks as one attack occurring in multiple places, the START database includes a separate entry for each place/building effected (e.g., each of the twin towers is given its own entry).
47 This percentage figure was not calculated using the total number of attacks (2,242) in the denominator because the START database lists seventy-one attacks with unknown injuries. My denominator (2,171) does not include these seventy-one attacks.
48 Like the percentage calculations for the US, I do not include the total number of worldwide attacks in the denominators for global fatalities and injuries – that is, I removed attacks where fatalities and injuries respectively are unknown.
49 Some people do not believe that attacks against property should be described as terrorism. However, most databases in the US include these attacks; without them there would be very few data points to consider. Moreover, a number of groups attack both property and humans through the course of their existence, so including both sorts of attacks allows for a fuller picture of a group's activities.
50 National Oceanic and Atmospheric Administration, "Lightning Safety," www.lightningsafety.noaa.gov/fatalities.htm (accessed July 18, 2013).
51 Although the Jewish Defense League could be described as a left-wing group, I designate it as a right-wing group because the FBI categorizes the group as right-wing (FBI 2001).
52 Harvey, Kushner, *The Encyclopedia of Terrorism* (Thousand Oaks, CA: Sage Publications, 2003), 272.
53 The National Consortium for the Study of Terrorism and Responses to Terrorism, "Global Terrorism Database."
54 New America Foundation, "The Homegrown Threat Database." This database defines a jihadist terrorist as someone who was "indicted on terrorism-related charges or killed before an indictment could be handed down" and "subscribe[d] broadly to the ideology of Osama bin Laden's al-Qaeda." This definition is essentially synonymous with "radical Islamism."
55 New America Foundation, "Homegrown Threat Database." See also Daryl Johnson, *Right-wing Resurgence*, x.
56 Peter Singer, *Animal Liberation* (New York: Harper Perennial Modern Classics, 2009).
57 Kushner, *The Encyclopedia of Terrorism*, 33–4.
58 Kushner, *The Encyclopedia of Terrorism*, 112.

59 Gallaher, *On the Fault Line*, 16–18.
60 Carl Boggs, "Corporate Power, Ecological Crisis, and Animal Rights," in *Critical Theory and Animal Liberation*, ed. John Sanbonmatsu, 71–90 (Lanham, MD: Rowman and Littlefield, 2011).

Further reading

Card, Claudia. "Recognizing Terrorism." *Journal of Ethics* 11, no. 1 (2007): 1–29.

Gage, Beverly. "Terrorism and the American Experience: A State of the Field." *Journal of American History* 98, no. 1 (2011): 73–94.

Gallaher, Carolyn. *On the Fault Line: Race, Class, and the American Patriot Movement*. Lanham, MD: Rowman and Littlefield, 2003.

Johnson, Daryl. *Right-Wing Resurgence: How a Domestic Terrorist Threat is Being Ignored*. Lanham, MD: Rowman and Littlefield, 2012.

Kundnani, Arun. "Radicalisation: The Journey of a Concept." *Race and Class* 54, no. 2 (2012): 3–25.

Levitas, Daniel. *The Terrorist Next Door: The Militia Movement and the Radical Right*. New York: Thomas Dunne Books, 2002.

Mamdani, Mahmood. "Good Muslim, Bad Muslim: A Political Perspective on Culture and Terrorism." *American Anthropologist New Series* 104, no. 3 (2002): 766–75.

Southers, Errol. *Homegrown Violent Extremism*. Amsterdam: Anderson Publishing, 2009.

Stock, Catherine. *Rural Radicals: Righteous Rage in the American Grain*. Ithaca, NY: Cornell University Press, 1996.

Thomas, Paul. "Failed and Friendless: The UK's 'Preventing Violent Extremism' Programme." *British Journal of Politics and International Relations* 12, no. 3 (2010): 442–58.

22

THE GENESIS, RISE, AND UNCERTAIN FUTURE OF AL-QAEDA

Daveed Gartenstein-Ross

Al-Qaeda has already upended traditional understandings of terrorism in several important ways. Until the 9/11 attacks, most observers accepted Brian Michael Jenkins's observation that "terrorists want a lot of people watching and a lot of people listening and not a lot of people dead."[1] But on September 11, 2001, the world was given conclusive and grisly proof that some groups did in fact want a lot of people to die in their terrorist attacks and possessed the deadly competence to make it happen.

While Jenkins's famous statement was certainly accurate at the time he wrote it, by 2001, al-Qaeda was distinct from previous groups that employed terrorism in three important ways. Unlike the nationalist terrorist groups prominent in the 1970s that required international recognition to achieve their statehood goals, al-Qaeda rejected the very legitimacy of the international system and thus was largely uninterested in persuading neutral and objective non-Muslim observers. Unlike the communist terrorist groups of that era, al-Qaeda was for the most part not dependent on state support and didn't need to fear alienating state patrons. And finally, al-Qaeda – as will be discussed subsequently – wasn't primarily a terrorist group in its outlook but rather possessed the goals of an insurgent organization "that seeks to impose revolutionary change worldwide."[2] Though the line between terrorist and insurgent groups can be unclear, al-Qaeda possessed several important characteristics of an insurgency that would become more pronounced over time. Insurgents had been ratcheting up the levels of violence that they inflicted – something that can be discerned in jihadist groups' actions in the Algerian Civil War – and though al-Qaeda's decision to carry out history's most notorious terrorist attack may have been out of step with the modus operandi of terrorist groups, it fit more comfortably with the violence carried out by insurgents.

Al-Qaeda also differed from previous terrorist groups because it was global in reach and able to challenge the world's most powerful states at a strategic level. Despite the attention devoted to al-Qaeda in the thirteen years following the September 11 attacks, the group remains poorly understood in many ways, with analysts having widely divergent views about such matters as the relevance of al-Qaeda's senior leadership, the organization's strategy, and its future prospects. This chapter traces the history of al-Qaeda, beginning with its origins in the Afghan–Soviet War, then examines the group's rise and execution of the world's most notorious terrorist attack. The chapter goes on to explain how al-Qaeda survived, adapted, and rebounded after a vigorous counter-attack by the United States and its allies. Finally, the chapter explores al-Qaeda's prospects after longtime leader Osama bin Laden's death, the onset of the Arab Spring, and a challenge for supremacy of the global jihadist movement in the form of its offshoot known as the Islamic State.

A careful reading of al-Qaeda's history and evolution reveals three overarching themes. The first is the question of whether al-Qaeda should primarily be understood as a terrorist group. Although the US's first encounters with the organization were through spectacular terrorist attacks against American targets, its strategy has always been broader than just terrorism. Viewing al-Qaeda primarily as a terrorist group impeded the US's understanding in the years following the 9/11 attacks. The second theme is that al-Qaeda possesses impressive, albeit imperfect, strategic thought. The group has many weaknesses, some of which stem from its propensity to overplay its hand and descend into brutality, but al-Qaeda has been able to adapt to opportunities and to some extent mitigate its worst habits. Third, in interpreting al-Qaeda, analysts need to be modest and be cognizant of areas where their understanding suffers from a dearth of information. The analytic community has a record that is mixed at best in its efforts to understand, interpret, and predict this group, and there is a need to do better.

Al-Qaeda's founding and outlook

Al-Qaeda was born during the Afghan–Soviet War, a conflict that began with the Soviet Union's ill-fated invasion of Afghanistan in December 1979. The precise rationale for the invasion remains hazy – the meeting that authorized this action was memorialized by only a single handwritten note, and all participants are now dead. However, the most persuasive explanations involve the Soviet Union's extreme dissatisfaction with Afghan leader Hafizullah Amin. Politburo members believed Amin was mishandling anti-government uprisings, was untrustworthy, and might even reorient the country toward the West; and they were also angry over the undignified end that Amin had inflicted upon his predecessor (who was smothered to death with a pillow while incarcerated despite Soviet pleas not to harm him).[3]

Soviet special forces attacked the Taj-Bek palace on the outskirts of Kabul, where Amin was holed up – after being told by the Soviets that they could better protect him in that location. The invasion began well, as the Soviets quickly killed Amin, but the backlash in the Muslim world was immense and immediate. In January 1980, Egypt's prime minister declared the Soviet invasion "a flagrant aggression against an Islamic state" and condemned the Soviet Union as "but an extension of the colonialist Tsarist regime."[4] By the end of the month, foreign ministers of thirty-five Muslim countries, as well as the Palestine Liberation Organization, passed a resolution through the Organization of the Islamic Conference declaring the invasion of Afghanistan a "flagrant violation of all international covenants and norms" and "a serious threat to peace and security" both regionally and globally.[5]

These thundering condemnations were representative of the anger felt on the Arab street. Thus, even as the anti-Soviet Afghan mujahideen received state support (primarily from the United States, Pakistan, and Saudi Arabia), thousands of Arabs also flocked to South Asia to aid the Afghan cause. American aid to the mujahideen was channeled to Afghan factions; it did not reach such anti-Soviet Arab groups as that led by a young bin Laden.[6]

Many Arabs who traveled to South Asia during the war provided humanitarian aid, but there was also a contingent of Arab foreign fighters. Bin Laden transitioned from being part of the former group – a humanitarian worker and mujahideen financier – to proving himself on the battlefield. Born in the late 1950s to Mohammad bin Laden, who from humble beginnings in Yemen rose to become a multibillionaire construction magnate and confidant of Saudi Arabia's royal family, Osama was pious and religiously conservative when growing up in Jeddah, Saudi Arabia. The Soviet invasion of Afghanistan was a galvanizing event for bin Laden, as it was for many young Arab men of his generation. In 1984, bin Laden and his mentor, the influential Palestinian cleric 'Abdullah 'Azzam, founded the Services Office, a Peshawar-based organization designed to place Arab volunteers in the region with either humanitarian organizations or else "with the Afghan factions fighting the communists on the front lines."[7]

After his first trip to the front lines the same year that he founded the Services Office, bin Laden developed a thirst for more action and established a base for Arab fighters near Khost in eastern Afghanistan. The exploits of the fighters bin Laden led were irrelevant to the broader war, a fact substantiated by even a cursory glance at the number of men who fought on the rebels' side. Journalist Peter Bergen, a well-regarded chronicler of the "war on terror," notes that around 175,000 Afghan mujahideen battled the Soviets but that "the largest number of Arabs fighting the Soviets inside Afghanistan at any given moment amounted to no more than several hundred."[8] Despite this, bin Laden's involvement launched him to prominence in the Arab media as a war hero.[9]

Al-Qaeda was founded in 1988, in the waning days of the Afghan–Soviet War. At the time, bin Laden and 'Azzam agreed that the organization they had built during the conflict shouldn't simply dissolve when the war ended. Rather, they wanted the structure they had created to serve as "the base" (*al-qaeda*) for future efforts. Al-Qaeda's mission was initially broad, with its founding minutes describing the organization as "basically an organized Islamic faction" whose goal was lifting "the word of God, to make His religion victorious."[10]

Although bin Laden disdained the United States even while they both supported the same side in the Afghan–Soviet War, initially al-Qaeda wasn't focused on the United States as its pre-eminent enemy. The group's original mission focused on the threat that communism posed to the *umma* (worldwide community of Muslims), especially the communist regime that then ruled South Yemen.[11] In part, bin Laden's initial focus on South Yemen may be explained by his familial roots in the country; but surely another factor was the apparent similarity between that country and Afghanistan. In both cases, a godless communist regime had taken root in the heart of the Islamic world. But Iraq's August 2, 1990, invasion of Kuwait transformed bin Laden's priorities.

Saddam Hussein's invasion of the tiny monarchy to his south posed a clear threat to Saudi Arabia. With 100,000 Iraqi troops massed in Kuwait, which shares a border with Saudi Arabia, the Saudis feared that they could be next. President George H. W. Bush offered to furnish 250,000 US soldiers to defend the Saudi monarchy. Though American troops were on Saudi soil for defensive reasons, bin Laden perceived the US presence as a violation of his faith, a view informed by a famous *hadith* (part of the collection of the customs and sayings of Prophet Muhammad) in which the prophet, on his death bed, ordered that "two *deens* [faiths] shall not co-exist in the land of the Arabs."[12]

In the spring of 1991, bin Laden left Saudi Arabia for Sudan, where he decided to sponsor attacks on the United States. It is not clear whether his initial attacks were merely retaliatory for America's growing global presence, including in the Arabian Peninsula, or if al-Qaeda's mastermind had a broader strategy even then – but, as will be discussed shortly, bin Laden's anti-US attacks soon came to serve several purposes at once.

However, bin Laden's initial attacks against America were not an auspicious debut. Al-Qaeda's first known attack against an American target was the December 1992 bombing of two hotels in Yemen, which housed US soldiers en route to the Horn of Africa for Operation Restore Hope, a UN-sanctioned humanitarian mission to Somalia. The bombings "killed a tourist but no Americans."[13] Neither that attack nor the indeterminate role that al-Qaeda played in the October 1993 downing of a US helicopter in Mogadishu launched bin Laden into the Western public's consciousness.[14] Nonetheless, his involvement in terrorism caught the attention of the American and Saudi intelligence services. Resulting political pressure on Sudan caused the Sudanese regime to appropriate the construction equipment that formed the backbone of bin Laden's business in that country, repaying only a fraction of its value.[15]

Afghan mujahideen leader Yunus Khalis invited bin Laden back to Afghanistan, an offer that he accepted.[16] Just as bin Laden was able to first make his reputation there in the 1980s, he carved out an even bigger name for himself the second time around.

Within a few months of arriving in Afghanistan – on August 23, 1996 – bin Laden issued a manifesto proclaiming himself at war with the world's only remaining superpower. Bin Laden's overarching grievance in this declaration was the US military presence in Saudi Arabia, which he described as "one of the worst catastrophes to befall the Muslims since the death of the Prophet."[17] Bin Laden also named America's support for Israel and US-led sanctions against Saddam's regime in Iraq as additional justifications for his fight. (No fan of Saddam, bin Laden's criticism of the sanctions focused on their humanitarian impact.)

Bin Laden's articulated grievances were political in nature, but al-Qaeda cannot be understood without reference to its theological outlook, which is properly classified as salafi-jihadist. Salafism – a term referring to the "pious predecessors" – can be defined broadly as a movement striving for a practice of Islam that its adherents believe to be consonant with that of Prophet Muhammad and the first three generations of Muslims. Salafism is not a monolith, possessing both non-violent and violent variants, but salafi-jihadism falls within the latter category. As the scholar Quintan Wiktorowicz notes, salafi-jihadists "take a more militant position" than other salafi strains, believing "that the current context calls for violence and revolution."[18]

Strains of salafism that deem it appropriate to work within the political system to make religion a more powerful force in society may be understood as Islamist but not jihadist. While some observers place Islamism and jihadism in entirely separate categories, in practice it is problematic to do so. For one thing, jihadism is best understood as a subset of Islamism, in the manner that John Calvert characterizes it in Chapter 17 in this volume, rather than as a completely different category. A second problem is that Islamist organizations that once worked through the political system may come to embrace jihadist violence, while it is conversely possible that jihadist groups will adopt a more pragmatic outlook and eventually embrace reformist tactics, thus moving toward more mainstream Islamism. Moreover, sometimes Western analysts classify groups as Islamist and not jihadist when these groups do believe in violent revolution but think that developing a larger grassroots following is necessary before this turn to violence. When a group's non-violence primarily represents a strategic pause allowing it to gain adherents without meeting a state crackdown, it's not clear that this classification is sensible.

That being said, while it is problematic to argue that Islamism and jihadism are entirely separate, the distinction between what David Cook dubs "mainstream Muslim radicalism" (in Chapter 18 in this volume) and jihadism is real, even if some observers draw too sharp a line between them. The primary distinction can be found in the relationship to violence that the two strands have. Mainstream Islamist groups should not be understood as non-violent, but as Cook's contribution explains, groups like the Muslim Brotherhood tend to focus their violence "outward, usually towards Israel or other non-Muslim entities," while jihadists believe it is necessary "to establish the Muslim state, and that the true enemies of Islam were those who prevented that end from coming about."[19] Thus, mainstream Islamists may be understood as gradualists or reformists within the Islamic societies they inhabit, while jihadists function as violent revolutionaries within those same societies. The distinction between mainstream jihadism and Islamism mirrors the distinction within salafism between salafi-jihadism and strands that eschew revolutionary violence.

Al-Qaeda's religious outlook shaped both the group's immediate grievances, such as those articulated in bin Laden's declaration of war, and also its more expansive goals. As Michael Scheuer, the former head of the CIA's Bin Laden Unit, has written, the political grievances in bin Laden's declaration of war were intended to place al-Qaeda's fight within the realm of "a defensive jihad sanctioned by the revealed word of God."[20] That is, in contrast to an "offensive jihad," expansionist warfare designed to enlarge the abode of Islam, bin Laden framed this as a case where the faith itself was under attack. In such circumstances, each Muslim has an individual obligation to join the battle.

But in al-Qaeda's vision, the group is, in fact, not constrained to defensive jihad. Though the group's grievances are somewhat narrow, its ultimate goals are broad. One goal is to forcibly impose *shari'a* (Islamic law). For example, jihadist strategist Abu al-Harith al-Ansari wrote in an essay posted to Ansar al-Mujahideen Network in February 2011 that the implementation of *shari'a* was a critical religious obligation, as "the duty of Muslims is to rule Muslims by Islam."[21] A militant's notebook that Reuters journalists unearthed from the site of an al-Qaeda leadership camp near the Yemeni town of al-Mahfad memorializes similar goals: "Establishing an Islamic state that rules by Islamic *shari'a* law."[22] These statements are typical of the jihadist genre, as bin Laden, new al-Qaeda emir Ayman al-Zawahiri, and other jihadist leaders have repeatedly emphasized the importance of establishing *shari'a*.[23] Al-Qaeda's goal of imposing religious law is rooted in its salafi-jihadist outlook: in addition to the fact that the first generations of Muslims lived under *shari'a*, salafists hold that the religious concept of *tawhid* (unity of God) means that if only Allah can be worshiped and obeyed, then only Allah's laws have legitimacy.[24]

The desire to replace regimes in Muslim countries with theocratic governments also contributed to al-Qaeda's decision to make war against the United States. Peter Bergen explains that this was an instrumental decision on bin Laden's part, because fighting the US was seen as the road to toppling regional governments:

> The al-Qaeda leader lectured to his followers [in Sudan] about the necessity of attacking the United States, without which the "near enemy" regimes could not survive. Noman Benotman, the Libyan militant who knew both of al-Qaeda's leaders, recalled that, "Osama influenced Zawahiri with his idea: Forget about the 'near enemy'; the main enemy is the Americans." The intense Syrian jihadist intellectual Abu Musab al-Suri explains that bin Laden came to this strategic analysis because "Sheikh Osama had studied the collapse of the Soviet Union and of the dictator governments in Warsaw Pact countries and, as had happened in East Germany, Romania, Poland and other countries; he was convinced that with the fall of the United States, all the components of the existing Arab and Islamic regimes would fall as well."[25]

A 2009 study by a jihadist "think tank" that supported al-Qaeda's decision to concentrate its efforts on the United States, rather than focusing primarily on the "near enemy," reached a similar conclusion. The study explained that in waging war against the Saudi regime, al-Qaeda was faced with the decision of fighting Saudi Arabia directly or striking at the American presence in that country. If it fought Saudi Arabia, the attacks would have been condemned by the Saudi *ulema* (religious scholars). Al-Qaeda's war against the Saudis would then have been a losing effort, "given the size and weight of the religious institution, and the legitimacy and prestige it instilled in the people's minds across more than 70 years." On the other hand, the study viewed striking the Americans as a wise choice, because the kingdom would be forced to defend their presence, "which will cost them their legitimacy in the eyes of Muslims."[26] Thus, fighting the United States is seen by many jihadists as a way to simultaneously strike at "apostate" regimes of the region.

An even more ambitious goal of al-Qaeda's is re-establishment of the caliphate, a theocratic government that would rule a united Muslim world. Current al-Qaeda emir Ayman al-Zawahiri has written that the group's "intended goal in this age is the establishment of a caliphate in the manner of the Prophet."[27] The desire to re-establish the caliphate is an important overarching goal for the jihadist group that tells a great deal about its strategy and prioritization, and hence this goal has a concrete impact on al-Qaeda's actions.

Al-Qaeda's rise and involvement in violence

Yunus Khalis, who was instrumental to bringing bin Laden back to Afghanistan from Sudan, was not a member of the Taliban, the fundamentalist group that came to control about ninety percent of the country at its apex. Indeed, bin Laden initially chose to base himself in Nangarhar in part because it was still not ruled by the Taliban, who hadn't yet earned his trust. But when the Taliban entered Nangarhar, they "immediately sought to reassure bin Laden that they would protect him."[28]

Taking advantage of this safe haven, al-Qaeda grew significantly during its time in Afghanistan. The jihadist group established a powerful network of militant training camps, and perhaps as many as 20,000 people received training in them.[29] It also developed connections to other militant organizations and grew its insurgent and terrorist capabilities.

Al-Qaeda possessed an extremely hierarchical and bureaucratized organizational structure during this period. The group was led by an advisory (*shura*) council in which bin Laden held the dominant position. The group had an intricate command structure under this council, including military, financial, and political committees, an intelligence wing, and a media/propaganda wing. In addition to this hierarchical structure, the group had specific bureaucratic requirements for both leadership positions and even membership. The commander, for example, was required to have been a member of al-Qaeda for at least seven years, have a sufficient understanding of Islamic law and jihad, and "have operational experience from jihad." Below the commander were a deputy, who was required to share the same qualifications; a secretary, whom the commander appointed; and a command council.[30] Other documents from this period also detailed members' duties, salaries, and even vacation allowances.[31] Under this system, bachelors qualified for a round-trip plane ticket home after a year but also had the option of using the ticket for the *hajj* instead. The application to train for jihad in one of al-Qaeda's camps inquired about the applicant's education level, professional experience, medical history, and how much of the Qur'an he had memorized.[32]

Al-Qaeda carried out two skilled and deadly terrorist attacks against the United States prior to 9/11. On August 7, 1998, near-simultaneous truck bombs destroyed the US embassies in Nairobi, Kenya, and Dar es Salaam, Tanzania, killing 212 (twelve of whom were Americans) and injuring over 5,000 people. On October 12, 2000, a suicide bombing struck the destroyer USS Cole in the Yemeni port of Aden, killing seventeen American sailors and wounding thirty-nine.

Because the US's initial encounters with al-Qaeda involved terrorist attacks executed by the jihadist group, it is natural that American analysts understood it as primarily a terrorist organization and also perceived it as predominantly focused on the United States. However, even in this early stage, al-Qaeda was at least as devoted to insurgent warfare as to terrorism. As James Khalil has noted, analysts and scholars contrasting terrorism with insurgency generally believe that terrorists "(a) are less reliant on the use of nonviolent methods, (b) apply uniquely uncompromising forms of violence, (c) operate with limited community support, (d) are numerically smaller, and (e) do not maintain territorial control."[33] Looking at these factors:

(a) Al-Qaeda has long incorporated non-violent methods, such as *da'wa* (evangelism), and these techniques would become significantly more refined in the new environment brought by the Arab Spring.[34]
(b) Al-Qaeda can accurately be regarded as applying uniquely uncompromising forms of violence, as it far exceeded previous terrorist groups in this regard, but it has also attempted to constrain its violence for strategic reasons, particularly when compared to other jihadist groups. One example is Ayman al-Zawahiri issuing new guidelines for jihad in 2013 that were designed to mitigate the group's previous excesses.[35]
(c) Al-Qaeda is a vanguard movement, but it would be inaccurate to say that the group lacks community support. It has a transnational vision and seeks to appeal to Muslims across many countries: although the overwhelming majority of Muslims have a negative view of al-Qaeda,[36] when the militant group's support is aggregated across all the theaters in which it operates, al-Qaeda in fact has a large base of support, perhaps one of the larger of any militant organization. This was true even before the 9/11 attacks.
(d) Al-Qaeda was neither numerically small at the time of 9/11, nor is it today, especially if one includes affiliated organizations in this count.
(e) Al-Qaeda has always sought to maintain control of territory. Its branches have become increasingly successful at doing so over time. Since 2006, al-Qaeda branches have controlled and governed territory in Iraq, Mali, Somalia, and Yemen.

So, looking at these traditional factors for distinguishing terrorism from insurgency, some seem to push in favor of the group being classified as terrorist, while others are in favor of it being classified as insurgent. James Khalil warns against imposing "binary distinctions on continuous variables" and concludes that many or most militant groups "obtain intermediate scores" for the variables he outlines, thus "falling into the in-between 'grey areas.'"[37] Pre-9/11 al-Qaeda may fall into these gray areas, though as time has passed, the group has come to increasingly resemble an insurgency rather than a terrorist group. The US was thus wrong to see al-Qaeda largely through the lens of terrorism, and this focus on terrorism to the exclusion of other modes that al-Qaeda would employ was strategically costly.[38]

Prior to 9/11, al-Qaeda devoted fighters and resources to several insurgencies. Its members fought in the country where they found safe haven, as an estimated 2,000 to 3,000 al-Qaeda fighters supported the Taliban in its struggle to push the rival Northern Alliance from the small portion of Afghanistan that it still managed to control.[39] Al-Qaeda also devoted resources to insurgencies in Algeria, Bosnia, and Chechnya.

But the group's crowning achievement was the notorious 9/11 attack. That attack was both tactically brilliant and devastating, killing almost 3,000 on US soil while shattering previous assumptions about terrorism – the idea that terrorists wanted a lot of people watching but not a lot of people dead – and making the world suddenly seem overwhelmingly unsafe for Americans.

Bin Laden spoke of the strategic logic of the attack shortly after al-Qaeda carried it out. On October 21, 2001, he spoke at length to Al Jazeera's Taysir Allouni, even as American bombs were falling on Afghanistan, and his observations provided great insight into al-Qaeda's approach to fighting its superpower opponent. When Allouni asked the jihadist leader to speak of the impact of the 9/11 attacks, bin Laden first turned to the economic damage they caused. "According to their own admissions," he said, "the share of the losses on the Wall Street market reached 16%. They said that this number is a record, which has never happened since the opening of the market more than 230 years ago."[40]

Bin Laden then provided an extended exposition of the economic numbers, as well as associated costs, that showed he had given much thought to the economic implications of 9/11. "The gross amount that is traded in that market reaches $4 trillion," he said. "So if we multiply 16% [by] $4 trillion to find out the loss that affected the stocks, it reaches $640 billion of losses from stocks, with Allah's grace. So this amount, for example, is the budget of Sudan for 640 years." He also referenced lost productivity, claiming (inaccurately) that the United States did not work for an entire week after the attacks because of the psychological impact; and referred to building and construction losses (which he estimated at $30 billion), as well as lost American jobs (claiming that 170,000 employees were fired from the airline industry and that the InterContinental Hotel chain had been forced to cut 20,000 jobs).[41]

Essentially, bin Laden saw the American economy as its center of gravity. He believed that if al-Qaeda could significantly damage the US economy, it could force America to the sidelines while al-Qaeda toppled the regimes of the region and installed its theocratic rule. Although the 9/11 attack struck at the US economy through terrorism, al-Qaeda would use increasingly varied means after America's counter-attack deprived the group of its Afghanistan safe haven.

The post-9/11 period: al-Qaeda scatters and regroups

The United States began a bombing campaign against the Taliban, which refused to hand bin Laden over for trial, on October 7, 2001. When it inserted troops into the country later in the month, America employed a decidedly light footprint. About 300 Special Forces soldiers and 110 CIA officers liaised with tens of thousands of fighters from the Northern Alliance, the Taliban's only real opposition in the country.[42]

Essentially, the Northern Alliance became the bulk of the US's ground forces in the country, with the United States supporting their efforts with its airpower. American airstrikes were devastating to the Taliban's ranks, possessing such deadly accuracy that some Northern Alliance commanders thought US soldiers had death rays – an idea that American soldiers made little effort to debunk. The combination of US airpower and the light counter-attack toppled the Taliban from power within weeks. Although the US's initial counter-attack was a stunning success, bin Laden managed to escape across the border into Pakistan. He left Afghanistan demoralized and injured but didn't stay that way for long.

Al-Qaeda's comeback began in some of Pakistan's remote regions, as his wife Amal has said that she and her husband were reunited "in 2003 in a remote part of Pakistan's Swat district."[43] The group benefited from the fact that its ideology and worldview became popularized during this period for a variety of reasons, including a backlash against US military operations in Afghanistan. By 2005, bin Laden was ready to relocate his family to a compound in Abbottabad, Pakistan.[44]

As al-Qaeda had been rather quiet, observers began to publicly state that it had been defeated. A couple of representative pieces from the period described it as having become "more of an ideology than an organization" and "a fragmented terrorist group living on the run in the caves of Afghanistan."[45] Despite these confident pronouncements, al-Qaeda's senior leadership began to again play a significant role in terrorist attacks as it recovered from the damage inflicted upon it.

On July 7, 2005, four British-born suicide bombers blew themselves up on London's public transit system during rush hour, killing fifty-two. The authorities were hesitant to acknowledge that al-Qaeda had played a role, as two official British reports released the following year described the cell as autonomous and self-actuating rather than tied to al-Qaeda.[46] But shortly after these reports came out, the idea that the London bombings were completely unrelated to al-Qaeda was definitively refuted by a commemorative video that the jihadist group released in July 2006 featuring a martyrdom tape recorded by Mohammad Sidique Khan. Al-Qaeda's leadership simply could not have obtained this footage had the plot proceeded completely independent of them. Another plot that was disrupted on August 10, 2006 – which was designed to blow up with liquid explosives seven planes bound for the United States from Britain – further underscored the fact that al-Qaeda was back as an operational force.

As it recovered in Pakistan, al-Qaeda underwent several adaptations. During the organization's time in Afghanistan, it was highly bureaucratized, and though it had significant connections to militant organizations and operations throughout the world, it didn't recognize other groups as official branches. After the relocation to Pakistan, al-Qaeda's senior leadership took on official branches in Iraq (al-Qaeda in Iraq), Yemen (al-Qaeda in the Arabian Peninsula), North Africa (al-Qaeda in the Islamic Maghreb), and Somalia (al-Shabaab).

In an article published in *Foreign Affairs* in early 2011, Leah Farrall, a senior counter-terrorism intelligence analyst for the Australian federal police, provided a balanced conceptual analysis of al-Qaeda.[47] Farrall argued that by 2011, al-Qaeda's strength could no longer be evaluated in isolation from that of its branches. She noted that al-Qaeda's organizational structure was dispersed and that the group "operates as a devolved network hierarchy, in which levels of command authority are not always clear; personal ties between militants carry weight and, at times, transcend the command structure between core, branch, and franchises." Farrall portrayed al-Qaeda's senior leadership as focusing on "strategic command and control" rather than micromanaging its affiliates' affairs. For example, al-Qaeda's senior leadership pre-approved some types of attacks by branches on "preapproved classes of targets" but required the branches to consult with the group's leadership prior to undertaking "large-scale plots, plots directed against a new location or a new class of targets, and plots utilizing a tactic that has not been previously sanctioned, such as the use of chemical, biological, or radiological devices."[48]

With these organizational adaptations, al-Qaeda also adapted its means of targeting the US economy. In addition to terrorist attacks that could damage the US economy, al-Qaeda involved its operatives in insurgent warfare designed to bleed the American economy in both Afghanistan and Iraq – and the group's involvement in insurgent warfare easily eclipsed its use of terrorism. Bin Laden underscored this strategic shift with a dramatic October 2004 video address to the American people that came out just before the US presidential election. He compared the wars in Afghanistan and Iraq to his first encounter with a superpower adversary, saying that just as the Afghan mujahideen and Arab fighters had destroyed the Soviet Union economically, al-Qaeda was now doing the same to the United States, undertaking a policy of "bleeding America to the point of bankruptcy."[49]

Another adaptation was related to the purpose of terrorist attacks during this period. The dramatic collapse of the US economy in September 2008 was significant for the jihadist movement. Some representatives claimed credit: al-Zawahiri, for example, said that "the battles and raids against America" resulted in the Federal Reserve significantly decreasing interest rates, which in turn "increased fluidity and competition to lend, which pushed the public to borrow more than they can pay back. That caused incapability by the public to pay back, so the financial institution fell, and that was followed by a disastrous economic crisis."[50] Hyperbole of this view aside, al-Qaeda and its affiliates were able to see that the subprime mortgage crisis and its aftermath allowed them to undertake a strategic adaptation: attacks could more explicitly target the US's and other countries' economies, and even unsuccessful plots could serve their purpose.

Exemplifying this adaptation, the November 2010 issue of *Inspire*, the English-language online magazine produced by al-Qaeda in the Arabian Peninsula (AQAP), was dedicated to an apparently unsuccessful plot. The publication's cover featured a somewhat blurry photograph of a United Parcel Service plane on a runway, along with the crisp headline "$4,200." This was a reference to a terrorist plot AQAP had launched the previous month involving bombs hidden in printer cartridges. The group's operatives successfully placed bombs aboard a FedEx and UPS plane, each of which flew through several stops, but authorities managed to locate and disable the explosive devices before they were timed to explode.

The magazine made clear that AQAP's reason for celebrating an attack that killed nobody was the tremendous disparity between what the ink-cartridge plot cost the terrorists and what it was expected to cost their enemies: a $4,200 price tag for AQAP versus, according to the magazine, "billions of dollars in new security measures" for the United States and other Western countries. AQAP's late head of external operations, Anwar al-Awlaki, explained that the jihadists' foes were faced with a dilemma once AQAP was able to successfully place the ink-cartridge bombs on cargo planes. "You either spend billions of dollars to inspect each and every package in the world," he wrote, "or you do nothing and we keep trying again."[51] Awlaki explained that this would be a difficult decision for Western countries because "the air freight is a multi-billion dollar industry," with FedEx alone flying "a fleet of 600 aircraft and ship[ping] an average of four million packages per day." *Inspire* lucidly explained that large strikes, such as those of 9/11, were no longer required to defeat the United States. "To bring down America we do not need to strike big," it claimed. "In such an environment of security phobia that is sweeping America, it is more feasible to stage smaller attacks that involve less players and less time to launch and thus we may circumvent the security barriers America worked so hard to erect."[52] The clearly expressed plan was to launch smaller yet more frequent attacks to drive up the security costs of the jihadists' foes – "a death by a thousand cuts," as several commentators have noted. These adaptations demonstrate that al-Qaeda is a strategic organization that is capable of learning.

But its efforts weren't always successful, and often al-Qaeda and its branches ended up being the organization's own worst enemy. Abu Mu'sab al-Zarqawi, who led al-Qaeda in Iraq (AQI) until his death in June 2006, was extraordinarily brutal, even by jihadist standards.

Images of beheadings and sectarian killings became associated with AQI, prompting al-Zawahiri, who was then al-Qaeda's deputy leader, to send al-Zarqawi a letter reprimanding him. Al-Zawahiri warned al-Zarqawi not to "be deceived by the praise of some of the zealous young men and their description of you as the shaykh of the slaughterers." Al-Zawahiri warned that these fanatics "do not express the general view of the admirer and the supporter of the resistance in Iraq."[53]

In addition, the totalitarian rule that the group forcibly implemented engendered a backlash. The Sahwa (Awakening) movement, which was announced by Sunni sheikhs in Iraq's Anbar province on September 9, 2006, was a manifestation of the growing anger at AQI. The Sahwa would prove instrumental in driving AQI from Anbar, and the model was later expanded to other Iraqi provinces through a program known as the "Sons of Iraq." At its height, more than 100,000 predominantly Sunni Iraqis took part in the program. In addition to suffering through this backlash that pushed AQI from its once-dominant position in Iraq, the group's brutality damaged al-Qaeda's worldwide reputation.

Al-Qaeda in the Arab Spring

When 2011 began with the long-standing dictators of Tunisia and Egypt being toppled from power in rapid succession, it was clear that an important new dynamic was sweeping the region. A newly empowered Arab public was capable of sweeping away regimes that had been in power for decades, hopefully bringing democratic change after they fell. Commentators referred to this dynamic as the "Arab Spring," a term that reached widespread acceptance even though it is in many ways problematic.[54] After revolutionary events struck, US analysts overwhelmingly believed that the changes were devastating for al-Qaeda and other jihadist groups because they undermined the group's narrative and could remove the underlying grievances that drew people to jihadism.[55]

The notion that al-Qaeda had finally been neutralized was given even more credence when a US raid in Abbottabad, Pakistan, killed bin Laden on May 1, 2011. Bin Laden was replaced by his longtime deputy, Ayman al-Zawahiri. In contrast to Western analysts, the jihadist movement's strategists did not view the Arab Spring as a devastating set of events. Rather, they perceived more opportunity for the movement, and less peril, than Western analysts believed. As previously discussed, the United States was seen by jihadists as a major barrier to overthrowing Arab regimes, and so jihadist observers believed the uprisings demonstrated the limits of US and Western power. Some jihadists believed, for example, that "global infidelity" would have intervened to prop up Tunisia's Ben Ali regime had Western countries not realized that the government was doomed regardless of what actions they took.[56] Al-Zawahiri said that the "tyrants" the US supported were seeing their thrones crumble at the same time "their master," the United States, was being defeated. He pointed to the 9/11 attacks, the US "defeats" in Iraq and Afghanistan, and still more defeats during the Arab Spring: "It was then defeated in Tunisia, losing its agent there. Then it was defeated in Egypt, losing its greatest agents there." Even in Libya, where NATO intervened to topple Muammar Qaddafi's regime, al-Zawahiri framed the West as losing an "agent."[57] (One may argue that al-Zawahiri's framing of Qaddafi as a Western agent betrays a fundamental misunderstanding of geopolitics. However, there is also a converse argument that the growth of jihadism in Libya subsequent to NATO's intervention shows that al-Zawahiri was in fact prescient.) In other words, jihadists thought the US now lacked the will or means to intervene to protect its client states. This perception in turn altered the movement's strategies.

Al-Qaeda's adaptations were tied to two specific advantages that its leading thinkers discerned. The first was prisoner releases. A lengthy hagiographical account of how "the mujahideen" had escaped from the Abu Zaʿbal prison appeared on the Ansar al-Mujahideen Network, a jihadist web forum, soon after the Egyptian uprising began. Thereafter, jihadist thinker Hani al-Sibaʿi published multiple lists of violent Islamists who had been released from Egyptian prisons.[58] The second perceived operational advantage was that the fall of established regimes would usher in an era of greater openness that would create unprecedented opportunities to undertake *daʿwa*.[59] Salafi-jihadists' *daʿwa* efforts would focus not on leading non-Muslims to Islam but on persuading other Muslims to accept their particular version of the faith.

Earlier, this chapter mentioned the need for analytic humility when interpreting al-Qaeda. Many US-based analysts thought it inconceivable that al-Qaeda and jihadism might benefit from the revolutionary changes that convulsed the region – but they proved to be wrong, and the predictions of al-Qaeda's strategists were right. In fact, jihadism benefited from the revolutions.

Prisoner releases were, of course, not uniformly bad. In many cases, it was good that prisoners went free, as the Arab dictatorships were notorious for unjustly incarcerating and abusing political prisoners. But jihadists were part of this wave of releases. One example is Muhammad Jamal, an Egyptian whose network the Senate Select Committee on Intelligence has fingered as a part of the notorious September 2012 attack on the US consulate in Benghazi, Libya.[60] Other prominent figures from Egypt's jihadist movement were also freed. The most well known is Muhammad al-Zawahiri, the brother of al-Qaeda's emir and a former member of Egyptian Islamic Jihad. Al-Zawahiri played a prominent role in encouraging jihadists to join a September 2012 attack on the US embassy in Cairo. Other released Egyptian inmates returned to operational and media roles, including Murjan Salim. Figures like Jalal al-Din Abu al-Fatuh and Ahmad ʿAshush helped loosely reorganize networks through media outlets al-Bayyan and al-Faruq. Prisoner releases helped regenerate jihadist networks in the Sinai that have caused a great deal of bloodshed since Egypt's July 2013 coup.

The growth of the jihadist group Ansar al-Sharia in Tunisia (AST) in the Arab Spring environment was also assisted by prisoner releases. AST leader Abu Iyadh al-Tunisi had been imprisoned since 2003 for involvement in terrorism abroad but was released in the general amnesty of March 2011, as were other leading members of the group. In Libya, some released prisoners have returned to jihadist violence. Ansar al-Sharia in Libya's Mohammed al-Zahawi and Shaykh Nasir al-Tarshani both spent years in Qaddafi's notorious Abu Salim prison.[61] Abu Sufyan bin Qumu, another Ansar al-Sharia leader based in Derna, was formerly imprisoned in both Guantánamo Bay and Abu Salim.

This renewed manpower was bolstered by the growth in *daʿwa* opportunities anticipated by movement strategists. In Egypt, salafi-jihadists such as Muhammad al-Zawahiri and Ahmad ʿAshush were able to personally advocate for the movement on television for the first time. In Tunisia, AST developed a sophisticated *daʿwa* strategy. Some of AST's *daʿwa* efforts were traditional, such as holding *daʿwa* events at markets or universities, holding public protests, and dominating physical spaces, such as cafés near places of worship. But AST also used innovative approaches to *daʿwa*, including provision of social services (something other militant Islamic groups like Hizbullah and Hamas have also done) and sophisticated use of social media. Almost immediately after it undertook humanitarian efforts, AST would post information about its latest venture, including photographs, to Facebook and Twitter. Social media served as a force multiplier: even if AST didn't provide consistent services to an area (as was often or always the case), its social media activity portrayed a rapid pace of humanitarian assistance and thus helped the group achieve its goal of visibility.

But the most significant post-Arab Spring development that will influence the future of jihadism is the Syrian Civil War. The impact it will have on this generation of jihadists will be every bit the equal of what the Afghan–Soviet War meant for militants coming of age in the 1980s. Both conflicts were first-order humanitarian disasters that inflamed passions throughout the Muslim world and beyond. Both conflicts thus attracted a large number of Sunni foreign fighters from abroad, most of whom were drawn to the battlefield by grisly representations of what was happening and the desire to battle repressive forces who willingly shed innocent blood. (The Syrian Civil War, in contrast to the Afghan–Soviet War, has also seen a significant influx of Shi'a foreign fighters.)[62] Despite the often noble intentions for being drawn to the battlefield, many foreign fighters joined jihadist factions. But while communists were the enemy in the Afghan–Soviet War, the Syrian war has taken on a sectarian hue. The foreign fighters attracted to the battlefield as well as the growth in sectarianism will have far-reaching implications.[63]

Though the environment is conducive to the growth of jihadist movements, questions remain about some of the new groups' connections to al-Qaeda. Many of the new jihadist organizations that emerged are either unconnected or have only minimal connections to al-Qaeda, while others have, at the very least, a deeper relationship and may perhaps have been functioning as unacknowledged al-Qaeda affiliates.[64]

At this point, though new jihadist groups were able to experience growth in the Arab Spring environment, the openness they once enjoyed in Egypt and Tunisia has largely been lost. The post-coup government in Egypt has reined in both Islamist and jihadist groups, while Tunisia banned AST following an escalation in violent incidents attributed to it. Since its August 2013 ban, AST youth leader Youssef Mazouz said the group now carries out "less than half the work it used to before August when it could plan events openly and post details on Facebook."[65]

But while al-Qaeda may have gained some new affiliates from the Arab Spring environment, it recently lost the most powerful organization in its network. On February 2, 2014, al-Qaeda's senior leadership announced it was no longer affiliated with its Iraq franchise, the Islamic State of Iraq and the Levant, which would subsequently rename itself the Islamic State (IS). IS had been fighting with other Syrian rebel factions – including al-Qaeda's official Syrian affiliate, the al-Nusra Front – and al-Qaeda's senior leadership had ordered it to submit to mediation to resolve these tensions. IS paid lip service to these demands but in practice flouted the mediation orders. In addition to IS's insubordination, there were strategic differences between al-Qaeda and IS. Al-Zawahiri's al-Qaeda had absorbed the lessons of al-Zarqawi's failures and was set on not repeating his brutal errors, while IS's strategy embraced brutality.

Following its expulsion from al-Qaeda, IS began actively lobbying for al-Qaeda's affiliates to defect and join its cause. Following a major offensive IS was able to execute in Iraq, capturing a number of cities at lightning speed and then promptly declaring that it had re-established the caliphate, many analysts began to openly state that IS had eclipsed al-Qaeda as the world's pre-eminent jihadist organization.[66] Author Kurt Eichenwald went so far as to claim that al-Qaeda "faces a growing risk of irrelevance" because of IS's gains.[67]

With its control of a significant amount of territory that spans Syria and Iraq, IS can definitively be called an insurgent group rather than simply a terrorist organization. However, the fact that IS is in a position where it can govern territory is not unique among jihadist organizations: al-Qaeda affiliates have also governed territory in North Mali, Somalia, and Yemen. But which jihadist group has the brighter future, IS or al-Qaeda? It is worth questioning the conventional wisdom that IS has become the dominant global force. Al-Qaeda's network has remained intact, as IS's bid to win over its affiliate organizations has yet to gain a single defection. Al-Qaeda's senior leadership is also primed to recover some of its operational abilities as US forces draw down from Afghanistan. Moreover, IS possesses a more problematic strategy than does al-Qaeda, not only emulating the brutality of al-Zarqawi but surpassing it. Members of IS have flooded social media with pictures in which they pose with severed heads, as well as videos of the humiliation and execution of captured members of the Iraqi security forces. The many claims that IS has permanently pushed al-Qaeda to the side assume that the kind of tactics that led al-Qaeda to near ruin after 2006 – as al-Qaeda's global brand was significantly diminished by al-Zarqawi's brutality – are today primed to succeed.

Conclusion

As of this writing, al-Qaeda faces significant challenges, including the possibility that another jihadist group could eclipse it. However, this is a group that has confronted numerous challenges previously, including its near destruction after the US invasion of Afghanistan destroyed its safe haven, the tarnishing of its brand through al-Zarqawi's brutality, and the new political environment produced by the Arab Spring. It has also survived a heavy pace of drone strikes that rocked al-Qaeda's senior leadership in Pakistan. The respected terrorism scholar Bruce Hoffman summarizes the reasons that it has thus far been premature to pen al-Qaeda's obituary:

> Although one cannot deny the vast inroads made against Core Al Qaeda in recent years ... the long-established nucleus of the Al Qaeda organization has proven itself to be as resilient as it is formidable. For more than a decade, it has withstood arguably the greatest international onslaught directed against a terrorist organization in history. Further, it has consistently shown itself capable of adapting and adjusting to even the most consequential countermeasures directed against it, having, despite all odds, survived for nearly a quarter century.[68]

Overall, the current environment is favorable to the growth of jihadism. If al-Qaeda proves unable to capitalize, as some commentators now believe, then another group surely will. But al-Qaeda has also made clear over the past fifteen years that one should be hesitant before declaring its future to be bleak.

Notes

1 Brian Michael Jenkins, "International Terrorism: A New Mode of Conflict," in *International Terrorism and World Security*, ed. David Carlton and Carlo Schaerf (London: Croom Helm, 1975), 15.
2 *The U.S. Army/Marine Corps Counterinsurgency Field Manual* (FM 3-24), Kindle ed. (Chicago: University of Chicago Press, 2007), loc. 931 of 8639.
3 See Gregory Feifer, *The Great Gamble: The Soviet War in Afghanistan* (New York: Harper, 2009), 11–14, 48.
4 "Egyptian Prime Minister on Middle East and Afghanistan," BBC Summary of World Broadcasts, January 5, 1980.

5 James Dorsey, "Islamic Nations Fire Broadsides at Soviet Military Interventions," *Christian Science Monitor*, January 30, 1980.
6 Richard Miniter, *Disinformation: 22 Media Myths that Undermine the War on Terror* (Washington, DC: Regnery, 2005), 11–21.
7 Peter L. Bergen, *The Longest War: The Enduring Conflict between America and al-Qaeda*, Kindle ed. (New York: Free Press, 2011), 14.
8 Ibid., 16.
9 Steve Coll, *Ghost Wars: The Secret History of the CIA, Afghanistan, and bin Laden, from the Soviet Invasion to September 10, 2011* (New York: Penguin Books, 2004), 163.
10 Tareekh Osama memorandum, 1988, introduced by prosecution at Benevolence International Foundation trial, Northern District of Illinois, 2002–3.
11 Vahid Brown, "Al-Qaeda Central and Local Affiliates," in *Self-Inflicted Wounds: Debates and Divisions within al-Qaeda and Its Periphery*, ed. Assaf Moghadam and Brian Fishman (West Point, NY: Combating Terrorism Center, 2010), 80; and Lawrence Wright, *The Looming Tower: Al-Qaeda and the Road to 9/11* (New York: Vintage Books, 2007), 173–5.
12 Malik's Muttawa, Book 45, *hadith* number 45.5.17.
13 Bergen, *The Longest War*, 20.
14 It is known that al-Qaeda dispatched trainers to Somalia prior to the famous incident in which a Black Hawk helicopter was shot down in Mogadishu and eighteen Americans died in the ensuing melee. However, observers disagree on whether these trainers were likely to have played any role in the helicopter being shot down. For more on al-Qaeda's possible role, see Evan F. Kohlmann, *Shabaab al-Mujahideen: Migration and Jihad in the Horn of Africa* (New York: NEFA Foundation, 2009), 4; and Bergen, *The Longest War*, 20 (noting that Somalis trained by al-Qaeda operatives "had been taught that the most effective way to shoot down a helicopter with a rocket-propelled grenade was to hit the vulnerable tail rotor," but that due to "fog of war, it remains unclear who exactly brought down the American helicopter in Mogadishu").
15 Bruce Riedel, *The Search for al-Qaeda: Its Leadership, Ideology, and Future* (Washington, DC: Brookings Institution Press, 2008), 56.
16 Kevin Bell, *Usama bin Ladin's "Father Sheikh": Yunus Khalis and the Return of al-Qa`ida's Leadership to Afghanistan* (West Point, NY: Combating Terrorism Center, 2013).
17 Osama bin Laden, "Declaration of Jihad against the Americans Occupying the Land of the Two Holy Mosques," trans. Open Source Center, August 23, 1996.
18 Quintan Wiktorowicz, "Anatomy of the Salafi Movement," *Studies in Conflict & Terrorism* 29, no. 3 (2006): 208.
19 The Muslim Brotherhood hasn't always focused its violence on external foes. As scholar Lorenzo Vidino notes, Brotherhood founder Hasan al-Banna developed a clandestine paramilitary wing called the Special Section, which initially focused its attacks on British interests in Egypt and the nascent state of Israel, but soon moved on to internal targets: "But soon the Special Section extended its violent actions against domestic targets, bombing sites owned by or linked to Egyptian Jews and killing prominent politicians, judges, and government officials. Tensions reached their peak when members of the Brotherhood were accused of killing Prime Minister Mahmud Fahmi al-Nuqrashi, and Egyptian authorities banned the organization in December 1948." (Lorenzo Vidino, *The New Muslim Brotherhood in the West*, Kindle ed. (New York: Columbia University Press, 2010), 22. See also Richard P. Mitchell, *The Society of Muslim Brothers* (New York: Oxford University Press, 1969), 30–64.)
20 Michael Scheuer, *Imperial Hubris: Why the West is Losing the War on Terror* (Washington, DC: Potomac Books, 2004), xviii.
21 Abu al-Harith al-Ansari, "Statement on the Events in Egypt," published on Ansar al-Mujahideen Network, February 10, 2011.
22 Yara Bayoumy and Mohammed Ghobari, "In al-Qaeda Camp, Notes on an Islamic Caliphate," Reuters, July 8, 2014.
23 See, for example, "Bin Laden: Expel Jews, Christians from Holy Places," *Jang* (Rawalpindi), trans. Open Source Center, November 18, 1998; Ayman al-Zawahiri, "The Fourth Episode: Message of Hope and Glad Tidings to Our People in Egypt," trans. Open Source Center, March 4, 2011, posted on Ansar Dawlat al-Iraq al Islamiyah; and "Al-Qaeda Commander Calls for Overthrow of Qaddafi and Introduction of *Sharia* Law," Kavkaz Center (Jihadist news agency), March 14, 2011.

See also the following Open Source Center translations: "Sirajuddin Haqqani Interview on Jihad in Afghanistan, Palestinian Cause," April 27, 2010; "Islamic Army in Iraq Calls upon Mujahedin to Unite, Abide by *Sharia* Rules," April 9, 2010; and "Jihadist Leader al Qar'awi Interviewed on Jihad in Arabian Peninsula, Levant," April 4, 2010.

24 Mary Habeck, *Knowing the Enemy: Jihadist Ideology and the War on Terror* (New Haven, CT: Yale University Press, 2006), 60–5. For an extended salafi treatise on this point, see Abu Ameenah Bilal Philips, *The Fundamentals of Tawheed (Islamic Monotheism)* (Riyadh, Saudi Arabia: Tawheed, 1990).

25 Bergen, *The Longest War*, 23.

26 Historical Studies and Strategic Recommendations Division, "Strategic Study on Global Conflict and the Status of the Jihadist Trend," trans. Open Source Center, July 4, 2009. For discussion of the debate within jihadism over whether to fight the near or far enemy, see Fawaz A. Gerges, *The Far Enemy: Why Jihad Went Global* (Cambridge: Cambridge University Press, 2009).

27 Ayman al-Zawahiri letter to Abu Mu'sab al-Zarqawi, July 2005, full text reprinted in "English Translation of Ayman al-Zawahiri's Letter to Abu Musab al-Zarqawi," *Weekly Standard*, October 12, 2005.

28 Bell, *Usama bin Ladin's "Father Sheikh"*, 60.

29 National Commission on Terrorist Attacks Upon the United States, *Staff Statement No. 15*, June 16, 2004, 10.

30 "Interior Organization," Combating Terrorism Center at West Point, Harmony Database, released February 16, 2006.

31 "Employment Contract," Combating Terrorism Center at West Point, Harmony Database, released February 16, 2006.

32 "Camp Acceptance Requirements," Combating Terrorism Center at West Point, Harmony Database, released March 17, 2006.

33 James Khalil, "Know Your Enemy: On the Futility of Distinguishing between Terrorists and Insurgents," *Studies in Conflict & Terrorism* 36, no. 5 (2013): 426–7. For more on the relationship between terrorism and insurgency, see Chapter 25 by Geraint Hughes on that topic in this volume.

34 See Daveed Gartenstein-Ross and Tara Vassefi, "Perceptions of the 'Arab Spring' within the Salafi-Jihadi Movement," *Studies in Conflict & Terrorism* 35, no. 12 (2012): 831–48.

35 Ayman al-Zawahiri, "General Guidelines for Jihad" (2013), available at: https://azelin.files.wordpress.com/2013/09/dr-ayman-al-e1ba93awc481hirc4ab-22general-guidelines-for-the-work-of-a-jihc481dc4ab22-en.pdf (accessed August 5, 2014).

36 "Concerns about Islamic Extremism on the Rise in Middle East," Pew Research Global Attitudes Project, July 1, 2014.

37 Khalil, "Know Your Enemy," 427.

38 I have written extensively about the US's strategic errors in the war on terror in Daveed Gartenstein-Ross, *Bin Laden's Legacy: Why We're Still Losing the War on Terror* (New York: Wiley, 2011). As Brian Michael Jenkins told me during the course of my research for the book, "At the governmental level, we need to have a better understanding of our foe's approach to warfare and strategy. One of the reasons we haven't done so is that we're trapped by the word *terrorism* itself" (ibid., 42).

39 Ahmed Rashid, "Afghan Resistance Leader Feared Dead in Blast," *Telegraph* (UK), September 11, 2001.

40 Quoted in Taysir Allouni, "A Discussion on the New Crusader Wars," trans. Open Source Center, October 21, 2001.

41 Ibid.

42 Bergen, *The Longest War*, 59.

43 Abdel Bari Atwan, *After bin Laden: Al-Qaeda, The Next Generation*, Kindle ed. (New York: New Press, 2012), 22.

44 Ibid.

45 Douglas Frantz et al., "The New Face of al-Qaeda," *Los Angeles Times*, September 26, 2004; and Derek Reveron, "Tuned to Fear," *National Review Online*, January 13, 2005.

46 Stationery Office, Intelligence and Security Committee, "Report into the London Terrorist Attacks on 7 July 2005," May 11, 2006; and British House of Commons, "Report of the Official Account of the Bombings in London on 7th July 2005," May 11, 2006.

47 Leah Farrall, "How al-Qaeda Works," *Foreign Affairs* 90 (March/April 2011): 128–38.
48 Ibid., 135.
49 "Bin Laden Addresses American People on Causes, Outcome of 11 Sep Attacks," Al Jazeera, trans. Open Source Center, October 29, 2004.
50 Ayman al-Zawahiri, "The Facts of Jihad and the Lies of the Hypocrites," trans. Al Sahab, Nine Eleven Finding Answers (NEFA) Foundation, August 5, 2009. For another jihadist claim of responsibility for the subprime mortgage crisis, see "The West and the Dark Tunnel," trans. Al Sahab, Open Source Center, September 22, 2009.
51 Head of Foreign Operations [Anwar al-Awlaki], "The Objectives of Operation Hemorrhage," *Inspire*, November 2010, 7.
52 Editorial, *Inspire*, November 2010, 4.
53 Al-Zawahiri letter to al-Zarqawi.
54 Marc Lynch, who seems to have coined the term "Arab Spring," later commented that it "does not do justice to the nature of the change." Lynch explained that "the uprisings are an exceptionally rapid, intense, and nearly simultaneous explosion of popular protest" and that the uprisings "are playing out very differently across the region and are likely to produce new, very mixed regional politics – some new democracies, some retrenched dictatorships, some reformed monarchies, some collapsed states, and some civil wars." Marc Lynch, *The Arab Uprising: The Unfinished Revolutions of the New Middle East*, Kindle ed. (New York: PublicAffairs, 2012), 9.
55 One media report illustrating the widespread analytic view that the revolutions were harmful to al-Qaeda is Scott Shane, "As Regimes Fall in Arab World, al-Qaeda Sees History Fly By," *New York Times*, February 27, 2011. In the article, several analysts describe the revolutions as extremely harmful to al-Qaeda. Paul Pillar of Georgetown University commented, "So far – and I emphasize so far – the score card looks pretty terrible for al-Qaeda. Democracy is bad news for terrorists. The more peaceful channels people have to express grievances and pursue their goals, the less likely they are to turn to violence" (ibid.). Brian Fishman of the New America Foundation said, "Knocking off [Hosni] Mubarak has been Zawahiri's goal for more than 20 years, and he was unable to achieve it. Now a nonviolent, nonreligious, pro-democracy movement got rid of him in a matter of weeks. It's a major problem for al-Qaeda" (ibid.). Steven Simon of the Council on Foreign Relations described the uprisings as a strategic defeat for jihadism, explaining that "these uprisings have shown that the new generation is not terribly interested in al-Qaeda's ideology" (ibid.).

For other writings arguing that the Arab Spring would undermine al-Qaeda, see Fawaz Gerges, "The Rise and Fall of al-Qaeda: Debunking the Terrorism Narrative," *Huffington Post*, January 3, 2012; Dan Murphy, "The Future of al-Qaeda and Its Likely Leader," *Christian Science Monitor*, May 9, 2011; "Bergen Correctly Predicted bin Laden's Location," NPR, May 3, 2011; Fareed Zakaria, "Al-Qaeda is Over," CNN, May 2, 2011; Jason Burke, "Amid All the Turmoil in the Middle East, al-Qaeda Remains Invisible," *Guardian* (UK), February 25, 2011; Paul Cruickshank, "Why Arab Spring Could be al-Qaeda's Fall," CNN, February 21, 2011; and Paul Cruickshank, "Why Egypt Revolt Threatens al-Qaeda," CNN, February 6, 2011.
56 See forum member Imarat al-Jihad, "Tunisian Incidents: Did Infidelity Shed Its Skin and Have a Conscience Awakening?" Ansar al-Mujahideen Network, January 17, 2011.
57 Ayman al-Zawahiri, "And the Americans' Defeats Continue," posted on Global Jihad Network, October 12, 2011.
58 See Hani al-Siba'i, "The Release of Prisoners after Nearly Twenty Years of Injustice," Ansar Dawlat al-Iraq al-Islamiyah, February 23, 2011; Hani al-Siba'i, "The Release of a New Batch after Long Years Behind Bars," Al-Jahafal, February 27, 2011; Hani al-Siba'i, "Urgent: The Release of a New Batch of Those Charged with Military Verdicts," Ansar Dawlat al-Iraq al-Islamiyah, March 4, 2011; and Al-Maqrizi Center for Historical Studies, "Names of the Released Detainees from the al-Aqrab, al-Istiqbal, al-Wadi, and Burj al-Arab Prisons," Shumukh al-Islam Network, March 18, 2011.
59 See Ayman al-Zawahiri, "And be Neither Weakened nor Saddened," Al-Sahab Media, August 15, 2011; Hamzah bin Muhammad al-Bassam, "Heeding the Advantages and Lessons of the Two Uprisings in Egypt and Tunisia," Ansar Dawlat al-Iraq al-Islamiyah, February 25, 2011; Hamid bin Abdallah al-Ali, "The Joy Lies in the Harvest of the Two Revolutions," posted on al-Ali's

official website, February 15, 2011; and Atiyatallah Abd al-Rahman, "The People's Revolt … The Fall of Corrupt Arab Regimes … The Demolition of the Idol of Stability … and the New Beginning," distributed by the Global Islamic Media Front, February 16, 2011.
60 US Senate Select Committee on Intelligence, "Review of the Terrorist Attacks on US Facilities in Benghazi, Libya, September 11–12, 2012," January 15, 2014.
61 Mary Fitzgerald, "It Wasn't Us," *Foreign Policy*, September 18, 2012.
62 The most comprehensive resource on Shi'a foreign fighters in Syria is "Hizballah Cavalcade," which is maintained by analyst Phillip Smyth at: http://jihadology.net/hizballah-cavalcade/ (accessed August 5, 2014).
63 On the growth of sectarian strife engendered by the Syria conflict, see Aaron Y. Zelin and Phillip Smyth, "The Vocabulary of Sectarianism," *Foreign Policy*, January 29, 2014.
64 One example of a group that was likely an unacknowledged al-Qaeda affiliate is Ansar al-Sharia in Tunisia. See discussion in Daveed Gartenstein-Ross, Bridget Moreng, and Kathleen Soucy, *Raising the Stakes: Ansar al-Sharia in Tunisia's Shift to Jihad* (The Hague: ICCT, 2014), 13–15.
65 "The Salafist Struggle," *The Economist*, January 1, 2014.
66 See Barak Mendelsohn, "Collateral Damage in Iraq: The Rise of ISIS and the Fall of al-Qaeda," *Foreign Affairs*, June 15, 2014; Olivier Guitta and Jacob Zenn, "ISIS is Alive and Kicking while al-Qaeda is Passé," *Times* (UK), July 1, 2014; and "Al-Qaeda's Next Move: Battling 'the Islamic State' & Irrelevancy," The Soufan Group, July 3, 2014.
67 Kurt Eichenwald, "Iraq's ISIS is Eclipsing al-Qaeda, Especially with Young Jihadists," *Newsweek*, July 7, 2014.
68 Bruce Hoffman, "Al-Qaeda's Uncertain Future," *Studies in Conflict & Terrorism* 36, no. 8 (2013): 636.

Further reading

Atwan, Abdel Bari. *After bin Laden: Al Qaeda, The Next Generation*, Kindle ed. New York: New Press, 2012.

Bergen, Peter L. *The Longest War: The Enduring Conflict between America and al-Qaeda*. New York: Free Press, 2011.

Coll, Steve. *Ghost Wars: The Secret History of the CIA, Afghanistan, and bin Laden, from the Soviet Invasion to September 10, 2011*. New York: Penguin Books, 2004.

Gartenstein-Ross, Daveed. *Bin Laden's Legacy: Why We're Still Losing the War on Terror*. New York: Wiley, 2011.

Gerges, Fawaz A. *The Far Enemy: Why Jihad Went Global*. Cambridge: Cambridge University Press, 2009.

Habeck, Mary. *Knowing the Enemy: Jihadist Ideology and the War on Terror*. New Haven, CT: Yale University Press, 2006.

bin Laden, Osama. "Declaration of Jihad against the Americans Occupying the Land of the Two Holy Mosques." Translated by Open Source Center. August 23, 1996.

National Commission on Terrorist Attacks Upon the United States. *Staff Statement No. 15*. June 16, 2004.

Riedel, Bruce. *The Search for al-Qaeda: Its Leadership, Ideology, and Future*. Washington, DC: Brookings Institution Press, 2008.

Wright, Lawrence. *The Looming Tower: Al-Qaeda and the Road to 9/11*. New York: Vintage Books, 2007.

23

POLITICS, RELIGION, AND THE MAKING OF TERRORISM IN PAKISTAN AND INDIA

Eamon Murphy

In recent times, especially since the terrorist attacks on September 11, 2001, scholars and media commentators have paid close attention to violent acts committed in the name of religion, especially Islam. Pakistan, in particular, has been identified as a major center of extremism, the epicenter of global terrorism, and allegedly a failing state facing the threat of nuclear weapons falling into the hands of extremists. In contrast, its neighbor and main rival, India, is very often held up as a model of a tolerant, secular democratic Asian state whose numerically dominant religion, Hinduism, is viewed as a pacifist, non-violent religion. Innocent citizens of both states, however, have been the victims of acts of violence committed in the name of religion since the 1980s.

While extremist groups based in Pakistan have been responsible for acts of terrorism abroad, particularly in India, by far the most deadly of the attacks have occurred within Pakistan itself, perpetuated by extremist followers of the Sunni Muslim tradition against the minority Shi'a or against state security forces. In direct contrast, in India, followers of the minority religious community of Muslims have been the victims of terrorist acts perpetuated by groups claiming to be devotees of the Hindu religion. In many instances, the terrorist attacks have been encouraged and supported by agents of the state or, indeed, have been committed by the state itself. Analysis of the two histories demonstrates the complexities of the origins, causes, and nature of terrorism in the Indian subcontinent in modern times. It also challenges the use of the term "religious terrorism" which implies that religious beliefs are the primary driving force motivating terrorists.

The central focus of this chapter then is to explore the growth of violence committed in the name of Islam and Hinduism in Pakistan and India, particularly from the 1980s when terrorism emerged as a major security concern in both countries. The chapter will first explore the nature of Islam in Pakistan and delineate the specific historical developments that help explain the growth of terrorism in that country. Second, the chapter will analyze the complex nature of what is labeled Hinduism and how it came to provide the ideological basis for the perpetuation of terrorist violence against the Muslim minority in India. The concluding section will make some general observations, particularly regarding the role of religion in the making of terrorism in the Indian subcontinent in modern times.

The two major religions of the subcontinent, Islam and Hinduism, are, on the surface, diametrically opposed. Islam was originally foreign to the region, having originated in Saudi Arabia in the seventh century and been introduced into the subcontinent over a long period of time by merchants, warriors, Sufi mystics, and other migrants. The main impact of Islam came from the northwest, which is closest to the Muslim-dominated regions of Afghanistan, Central Asia, Persia, and the Middle East, or through the ports on the west coast which have had long-established trading links with the Middle East.[1] Most Muslims in the subcontinent live in the Islamic state of Pakistan and its neighbor, the Republic of India. In Pakistan, which is located in the northwest of the subcontinent, they comprise a population of over 180,000,000, about ninety-five to ninety-seven percent of the total population. In India, around 170,000,000, approximately fourteen to twenty percent of the total population, are Muslim. The majority of Indian Muslims live mainly in the north of the country.[2] Contrary to popular belief, force was seldom used by Muslim rulers to convert Hindus to Islam. Hindus and Muslims, for most of the time, have lived peacefully side by side for well over a thousand years.

While there are major sectarian and doctrinal differences among Muslims in Pakistan and India as in the rest of the Islamic world, all Muslims believe in the one God Allah and the prophetic mission of Muhammad and adhere to a single religious text, the Qur'an. This common belief system is what separates Muslims, with their manifold distinctive class, linguistic, ethnic, and other differences, from Hindus and other religious groups in the subcontinent.

The dominant religion numerically in India is Hinduism, although many scholars argue that the use of the label Hinduism to embrace the many divergent religious traditions in India is highly contestable. Romila Thapar, one of India's most eminent historians, argues that it is analytically far more useful to use the term Hindu religions rather than the singular Hindu religion.[3] Unlike Islam, Hinduism has no single text, no common belief in any one God, and no founder. Indeed, the term Hindu originally had no religious connotations and simply referred to the peoples who lived east and south of the Indus River, which bifurcates Pakistan today.[4] The term Hinduism can be considered a convenient label for describing the numerous religious beliefs, philosophies, and religious practices of the majority of the people who live in India. These range from the highly sophisticated philosophical speculations of the educated elite belonging to the Great Tradition based on Sanskrit and Brahmanical teachings with its emphasis upon vegetarianism to the simple animal sacrifices comprising part of the folk religion practiced by the largely undereducated poor. The majority of the population – who are made up of Dalits (the oppressed, who also are known as Harijans or by the more pejorative label untouchables), tribal peoples known as Adivasis, and lower castes – have their own priests, rituals, and their worship of local gods and spirits which have little in common with the Great Tradition of the elite.[5]

Sectarian divisions among Pakistani Muslims

Like Hinduism, Islam in the Indian subcontinent, as in other parts of the world, is characterized by its extraordinary sectarian and doctrinal diversity. In Pakistan, the main sectarian division is between the Sunni majority, who make up between seventy-five and eighty percent of Muslims, and the followers of minority Shi'a sects, who make up about twenty percent.[6] The main doctrinal difference between Shi'a and Sunni is that the former believe that the legitimate leader of the Muslim community should be a direct descendent of the prophet Muhammad, while Sunnis accept that leadership can come from any individual from among the Muslim community. Despite their relatively low numbers, Shi'as have been particularly important in Pakistan as they comprise a relatively high proportion of the elite as landlords, professionals, merchants, and politicians. For example, the highly revered founder of Pakistan, Muhammad Ali Jinnah, came from a minor Shi'a sect.[7]

Both Sunnis and Shi'as are divided into a large number of sub-sects. The two major groups within Pakistani Sunni Islam are the Barelvi, so-called traditionalists, representing the popular face of Islam in Pakistan, particularly in the countryside, and the Deobandi, who see themselves as reformers promoting what they claim is a purer form of Islam similar to what is practiced in the Middle East. Like many Shi'a, the Barelvis are strongly influenced by mystical Sufism and follow many Sufi practices, such as the use of music and dance, and worship at the shrines of Sufi saints. These practices are regarded as sacrilegious by those of the Deobandi tradition, who espouse a more literal and austere interpretation of Islam. Further complicating this diversity has been the recent growth in influence, particularly among some followers of the Deobandi tradition, of Saudi Arabian Wahhabism, an extremely narrow and legalistic sect which regards virtually all other Muslim sects, both Sunni and, even more so Shi'a, as infidels. Wahhabis are particularly hostile to what they regard as the worship of Sufi saints.[8]

The origins of sectarian violence and terrorism in Pakistan

When Pakistan was established as an independent state in 1947, there was little to suggest that internal sectarian violence and terrorism were to emerge as serious problems facing the state and its people towards the end of the twentieth century. Until the 1980s, the relationship between the Shi'as and the majority Sunnis was generally peaceful. Mixed marriages between Sunnis and Shi'as were acceptable, and followers of both sects often participated in each other's rituals.[9] Of all the newly independent Islamic states that emerged in the postwar period, Pakistan was regarded as the most liberal in its acceptance of a wide variety of Muslim sects and of other religious traditions. In recent times, however, much of this tolerance and acceptance of religious diversity has, unfortunately, disappeared.

The tension between the sects first developed in the 1980s and greatly escalated from the 1990s.[10] Between 1990 and 1997 alone, Sunni extremists killed over 581 Shi'as and left over 1,600 injured through assassinations, attacks on mosques and shrines, and other public places.[11] The year 2012 was the worst on record for sectarian violence, with over 400 Shi'as being killed, mainly in drive-by shootings.[12] On February 18, 2013, a suicide bomb in a busy market in the provincial capital of Baluchistan, Quetta, targeted Shi'a Hazaras, an ethnic group originally from Afghanistan, killing eighty-four people and wounding over 200. Among the dead were women and schoolchildren whose burnt books and school bags were found among the debris. A spokesperson for the violent Sunni sectarian organization Lashkar-e-Jhangvi claimed responsibility for the bombing.[13]

The major political and religious goal of Sunni-sectarian-based terrorism is to establish a Sunni state and impose Sunni-based *shari'a* law by intimidating Shi'as and secularists through acts of terrorism. Attacks on Shi'a religious processions and mosques are designed not just to kill or intimidate Shi'as but to warn off Sunnis, particularly those of the Barelvi tradition, who traditionally had participated in some Shi'a rituals. Sunni terrorists not only agitate to have the Shi'as declared to be *kafirs* (unbelievers) but also to prevent Sunnis from eating with Shi'as, worshiping with them, or marrying them.[14]

The single most important factor in the growth of sectarian violence in Pakistan was the attempts by the dour religious conservative and military dictator General Muhammad Zia ul-Haq during the 1980s to turn Pakistan into a state ruled according to Islamic principles.[15]

Zia began a process that was intended to Islamize Pakistani society according to his own narrow interpretation of puritanical Sunni Deobandi Islam. Zia saw Islamization as a way of strengthening Pakistan's identity as a Muslim state threatened by its much more powerful Hindu neighbor, India.[16] He believed that Islamization would set the country apart from, and by implication be superior to, its archrival.[17] Zia's motivations were also strongly motivated by self-interest. By depicting himself as a champion of Islam, Zia hoped to legitimatize his rule which was unpopular at home and abroad.[18]

One of the major unintended consequences, however, of Zia's state-sponsored Islamization was the intensification of sectarian divisions. The problems and inherent dangers of Zia's attempts to Islamize Pakistani society became obvious when his government attempted to impose a legal system based on one particular school of Islam – the Hanafi, as interpreted by the Deobandis – and thus create a strong unified Islamic state. Ironically, it had the opposite effect, accentuating and widening the differences between Sunnis and Shi'as. One of the first rabidly anti-Shi'a Sunni terrorist organizations that emerged during the rule of Zia was Sipah-e-Sahaba (Army of the Prophet's Companions), which was founded in 1985 in the district of Jhang in the center of the Punjab province. The organization has targeted Shi'a processions, places of worship, and individuals ever since. In 1995, a faction broke away from the Sipah-e-Sahaba to form the even more violent Lashkar-e-Jhangvi.[19] Since then, numerous even more violent extremist groups have broken away from Sipah-e-Sahaba and the other major sectarian groups partly because of disputes over leadership and factional rivalries as well as tactics, goals, and the control of finances.[20]

Zia's unpopular rule and his attempts to impose a Sunni form of Islam on Pakistan may well have come to nothing except that it coincided with the decision in 1979 by the Soviet Union to invade Afghanistan, the communist government of which was being threatened by insurgents. The spontaneous uprising of the Afghans against the Soviets assumed the form of a holy war – jihad – waged by the mujahideen (holy warriors) from among various tribal groups, particularly the Pashtun tribes of Afghanistan and Pakistan who inhabit the region straddling the Pakistan–Afghanistan border and who have a long history of resisting the invasion of foreigners. This jihad was eagerly supported by Pakistan, fearful of the Soviet threat and anxious to increase its influence in Afghanistan to counter Indian influence there. As part of the jihad, the mujahideen resorted to terrorist actions directed against the Soviet military and their Afghan allies and later were to use the same tactics against the United States and its allies when they invaded Afghanistan in 2001.[21]

The military, particularly the Inter-Services Intelligence (ISI), Pakistan's major intelligence service, supported the more extreme jihadi groups among the Pashtun tribes in southern Afghanistan whose leaders were influenced by Wahhabi ideas. In turn, Pakistan was supported by the US in order to weaken its archrival, the Soviet Union. The US channeled funds and weapons through the ISI which greatly strengthened the power and influence of the organization.[22] US support for the Afghanistan jihad also greatly boosted Zia as the champion of Islam against the godless Soviets.

The Afghan jihad also provided a golden opportunity for Saudi Arabia to promote its extremist form of Wahhabi Islam throughout Afghanistan and Pakistan, particularly among the tribal areas along the Pakistan–Afghanistan border. Saudi Arabia and other Gulf States have financed Wahhabi-influenced *madrassas* (educational institutions) in the Pashtun tribal belt and in other parts of Pakistan, particularly in the Punjab. Saudi Arabia's actions were motivated in part by its desire to curb the influence of its archrival the Shi'a state of Iran. Pakistan and Afghanistan consequently became a battleground for a proxy war between

Shi'a Iran and Wahhabi Saudi Arabia. Wahhabi-influenced *madrassas* have continued to preach jihad against the US and its allies and other Muslim sects.[23] The baneful influence of Saudi Arabian Wahabbism in promoting sectarian hatred in Pakistan and hostility to the US and its allies in Pakistan and Afghanistan has, surprisingly, been largely understated in the literature on terrorism.

After the Soviets decided to leave Afghanistan in 1989, the US turned its back on the region because it was no longer important for US geopolitical goals. This shortsighted policy, just one of a number of blunders the US has made over Pakistan, has strengthened the anger felt towards the US in Pakistan and left Afghanistan to be fought over by rival well-armed mujahideen groups.[24] The result was the seizing of power in Afghanistan by the Taliban, graduates of Wahhabi-influenced *madrassas* imbued with a harsh version of Islam opposed to secularism, women's rights, and Shi'a sects.

The withdrawal of Soviet troops from Afghanistan in 1989 provided a golden opportunity for Pakistan to renew its agitation against Indian occupation of the Kashmir Valley. The valley has been a source of perpetual conflict between India and Pakistan ever since it was partitioned between the two states in 1947. Pakistan has consistently and stridently asserted that as the valley is dominated by Muslims, who comprise about ninety-seven percent of the population, the entire area should be incorporated into Pakistan, a claim vigorously rejected by India. In 1989, a spontaneous revolt broke out among Muslims in the Kashmir Valley against the abuses of Indian power. With the withdrawal of the Soviets from Afghanistan, Pakistan saw the opportunity through the ISI to channel the unemployed battle-hardened mujahideen groups, armed with the numerous weapons left over from the Afghan jihad, into supporting the revolt. Attacks on military and civilian targets in Kashmir and in other parts of India by Pakistan jihadi groups have threatened to break out into full-scale war with the possibility of the use of nuclear weapons.

In addition to funding, training, and arming terrorist groups in Kashmir as part of Pakistan's war of attrition against India, the Pakistan military, particularly the ISI, has been accused by India and Western intelligence sources of supporting state-sponsored terrorist attacks in India itself. In 2001, terrorist attacks on the Jammu and Kashmir Legislative Assembly killed thirty-eight people and the five terrorists involved. One of the most serious events was the 2001 suicide attack on the Indian Parliament by five gunmen who killed five policemen before they were killed themselves. In 2006, the holy city of Varanasi was rocked by bomb blasts which killed about twenty and injured 101.

The most serious attack on Indian soil took place on November 26, 2008, when a group of heavily armed militants, who had arrived by boats from Pakistan, terrorized downtown Mumbai, India's most heavily populated city and its commercial heart. They targeted two five-star hotels, the major train terminus where two gunmen killed fifty-eight and wounded 104 civilians, a Jewish center, a movie theater, and a hospital. The Mumbai attacks highly embarrassed Pakistan's government, particularly when Western intelligence sources claimed that the ISI was actively involved in training the terrorists. While the Pakistan government vehemently denied any knowledge of this, the evidence clearly suggests that former officers of the Pakistan military and the ISI were involved in training the terrorists in camps in Pakistan, probably without the knowledge of senior government officials.[25] In a confession to police, the sole survivor of the attack on the train terminus, Mohammad Qasab, described how he had received rigorous military training in a camp in Pakistan-controlled Kashmir. It is not clear whether this assault squad belonged to one of Pakistan's largest terrorist groups, Lashkar-e-Taiba, or to a more extremist splinter group.[26]

The policy of the Pakistani state supporting jihadis backfired dramatically when Pakistan attempted under pressure from the US, particularly after 9/11, to curb the activities of terrorist organizations. These groups turned viciously on the state itself that had, ironically, once nurtured them. General Pervez Musharraf, for example, survived numerous assassination plots against his life. The resistance to the state and security forces increased dramatically when the US forced Pakistan to support the highly unpopular invasion of Afghanistan by the US and its allies on October 7, 2001. Currently, members of the security forces, politicians, and other opponents of the jihadis are still the targets of assassination attempts and other acts of terrorism.[27]

The political, social and economic roots of sectarian terrorism

The third factor in the rise of terrorist sectarian organizations in Pakistan during the 1980s and 1990s can be traced to the political, economic, and social changes that took place from the 1970s in Pakistan, particularly in the most important province, Punjab. The impact of these developments was initially most closely felt in that province's Jhang District. The major urban center Jhang City became the birthplace of sectarian violence which then spread to other parts of Punjab and elsewhere.[28]

Jhang District has a population of around three million, of which about twenty-five percent are Shi'a. Among the Sunnis, many of their poor had gone to work in the Middle East, particularly Saudi Arabia. This led to upward social mobility by the workers and their families during the 1970s and 1980s because many who had remitted comparatively large sums of money home returned themselves after a few years relatively wealthy and settled in urban centers. The quest for social recognition attracted these newly affluent to the ideology of Sunni sectarian groups, particularly the many who had been influenced by Wahhabism while working in the Gulf States. In fact, many Sunni sectarians who became activists had spent time working in the Middle East.[29] One of the most rabidly anti-Shi'a Sunni terrorist organizations to emerge in Jhang was Sipah-e-Sahaba, founded in 1985 by a Deobandi Sunni cleric, Maulana Haq Nawaz Jhangvi, who wanted Pakistan to be officially declared a Sunni Muslim state and Shi'as to be classified as *kafirs* or non-Muslims.[30] Politics in Jhang, particularly in the countryside, had been dominated by large Shi'a landlords who controlled about sixty-five percent of land in the district.[31] Shi'a political and social dominance was challenged by Sunni politicians in the urban centers and supported by Sunni traders, shopkeepers, and businesspeople as well as the new rich who had worked in the Middle East.[32] Merchant organizations supported strikes and demonstrations and financially contributed to the printing of sectarian books, journals, magazines, and pamphlets that were distributed free in mosques and other public places.[33] According to the propaganda of the Sunni sectarians, Shi'a landlords not only had exploited their Sunni tenants economically but also had led them astray in respect to religious affairs.

Initially, the sectarian terrorism involved the assassination of prominent Shi'as but by the 1990s had escalated into bombings of religious processions, mosques, and public places with accompanying civilian casualties. Sectarian violence spread from Jhang to other parts of Punjab, particularly in the less developed center and south. In one incident alone, a bomb attack resulted in the deaths of twenty-five Shi'a mourners at a Lahore cemetery in January 1998.[34] One consequence of the violence was the formation in 1991 of a Shi'a self-defense group, the Sipah-e-Muhammad, which itself began to engage in terrorist acts and tit-for-tat revenge killings.

Much of the leadership for sectarian organizations came from poorly educated *ulema* (scholars) seeking power, status, and wealth.[35] For many Sunni extremists, becoming involved in sectarian politics was good for business, money, and power. Moreover, by appealing to sectarian interests, politicians developed successful careers both locally and nationally. Sipah-e-Sahaba had contested national elections since 1988, and successful candidates were incorporated into government coalitions at both the national and provincial levels.[36] In 1990, for example, the deputy leader of Sipah-e-Sahaba defeated a powerful Shi'a landlord in the contest for a seat in the National Assembly.[37] Thus, sectarianism in Jhang can in large part be attributed to the frustration of the Sunni middle classes striving to break the hold that the Shi'a landed elites had on local politics.[38] Sectarian violence, therefore, was largely an urban phenomenon and a consequence of modernization with religion providing the ideology but not the motivation.

Hindu nationalism and anti-Muslim terrorism in India

Political and social change associated with modernization is also evident in the origins of anti-Muslim terrorist activities in India.[39] One of the major problems facing Indian democracy is that since independence in 1947 the Muslim minority has suffered from economic, social, and political marginalization. Today, the vast majority of Indian Muslims are impoverished descendants of low castes, Adivadis (tribals), and Dalits (formerly known as untouchables), who converted to Islam in part at least to try to overcome the social stigma of being at the bottom of the caste hierarchy. In 2005, the government appointed the Sachar Commission to examine the problem. Among its findings was that there was great concern about the poor educational standard among Muslims at all levels, including graduates.[40] The majority eke out a precarious existence as casual laborers and are very poorly represented in prestigious government and large public sector jobs.[41] Although some Indian Muslims have played a key role in Indian politics and have been highly successful as businesspeople, professionals, and industrialists, they are a small minority. Many of the more affluent and better educated fled to Pakistan when the Indian subcontinent was partitioned in 1947. A large proportion of Muslims live in slums and ghettos in the urban centers, such as Mumbai, India's largest city, where they are often the victims of violence. Moreover, they are overrepresented in prisons and have experienced discrimination by the police and the judiciary. For example, between 2006 and 2008, a series of bomb blasts orchestrated by Hindu extremists targeted Muslim neighborhoods and mosques. Instead of conducting a rigorous impartial investigation, the police rounded up young Muslim men and then tortured and extracted false confessions from them claiming that they had set off the bomb blasts in order to foment violence between Hindus and Muslims.[42]

Although there were occasional outbreaks of communal violence between Hindus and Muslims over many centuries, these were largely localized and spontaneous, erupting, for instance, in the wake of reports of Muslims slaughtering sacred cattle or Hindus playing loud music outside mosques during prayer services. One of the reasons why relations between Hindus and Muslims were generally peaceful during the early years of Indian independence was that politics was dominated since 1947 by the Congress Party which, in the early years at least, had been committed to a policy of secularism and Hindu–Muslim unity. However, the Congress Party's domination of Indian politics was challenged by a new political phenomenon that emerged during the 1980s: the rise of Hindu nationalism known as the Hindutva movement.[43] One important consequence of this new political development was the growth of anti-Muslim terrorism, particularly in northern India.

The Hindutva movement is made up of a number of organizations under the umbrella term the Sangh Parivar, or "family" of Hindu right-wing organizations.[44] The largest and most important of these many organizations is the highly organized and disciplined RSS (the Rashtriya Swayamsevak Sangh or National Volunteer Organization). Founded in 1925, RSS members are involved in a number of charitable activities and other forms of social work. However, some individuals and cells among the RSS have been involved in spreading strident anti-Muslim propaganda and in some instances have encouraged terrorist actions against Muslims. The youth wing of the Sangh Parivar, the Bajrang Dal, has been labeled a Hindu extremist organization whose violence against Muslims and Christians has embarrassed more moderate followers of the Sangh Parivar.[45]

The ideological goal of Hindu nationalism is to build a strong, united, and proud Indian nation around the concept of Hindutva or Hindu-ness, the political ideology that aims to create the Hindu Rashtra or Hindu nation. According to this ideology, to be a patriotic Indian is to be a Hindu or at least to adhere to Hindu values and to the Hindu way of life.[46] The more extreme followers of the Hindutva movement claim that Muslims and Christians are all potential traitors because of their alleged loyalty to foreign religions. Muslims in particular are regarded as dangerous and subversive because they are the largest single minority in India and because of the suspicion that they are all potential fifth columnists for India's greatest enemy, the Islamic state of Pakistan. For the very extreme proponents of Hindutva ideology, the choices for Muslims living in India are very clear: either go to Pakistan or be killed. The insistence that Muslims do not belong in India ignores the fact that the majority of Muslims in India are descended from indigenous ancestors who have generally lived peacefully alongside Hindus for many centuries.

Hindu nationalism is one of the oldest ideological streams in modern Indian history. As an ideology and a movement, it paralleled the development of the Indian National Congress led by Gandhi. It rejected the Gandhian plea for non-violence, drawing upon the Hindu tradition of violent action advocated by anti-British figures such as Bal Gangadhar Tilak (1856–1920), who drew upon Hindu scripture to justify violent action against an unjust government. In contrast to Gandhi's universalist view of India incorporating all religions, including Islam and Christianity, the Hindu nationalists defined their national identity as one that grew out of indigenous culture and religions, primarily Hinduism.[47]

Although the Hindutva movement has ideological and organizational roots in the 1920s and 1930s, it has had little influence until recently. Over time, however, the Hindutva political wing, the Bharatiya Janata Party (BJP; the Indian People's Party), which was founded in 1980, was able to achieve rapid widespread support and electoral successes in some parts of north India. In 1984, the party performed dismally in the national elections, but by the 1990s, the extensive organizational activities and propaganda of the Hindu nationalists had begun to pay off with the BJP winning strong support among upper and middle castes, including government bureaucrats and the police.[48]

Strong support for the Hindutva movement came largely from the new vibrant middle class that has emerged with the economic growth and prosperity that globalization and economic liberalism has brought to many parts of India, particularly since the 1990s. For many among the newly middle class, the history of India had been a history of shame as for over 1,000 years Hindu India had been a conquered state under initially foreign Muslim and later British rule. According to Hindutva ideology, for far too long Hindus had been humiliated by foreigners, especially Muslims, who in the past had destroyed Hindu culture. Hindutva propaganda emphasizes that the weakness of the Hindu nation has been largely due to the oppressive rule of various Muslim dynasties that ruled much of India before the advent of British rule. Muslim rule in India is portrayed as a disaster for the Hindu motherland. Hindutva literature portrays former Muslim rulers as violent religious bigots who destroyed numerous Hindu temples and persecuted the Hindus whom they had conquered.[49] According to the Hindutva view of history, the Muslim invasions ended a golden age of peace and prosperity.[50]

Indian Muslims have been portrayed in Hindutva literature as the Other: fanatical, backward, violent, and dirty, a people whose existence would unite all Hindus through fear and hatred of the common enemy. As lower-caste university lecturer and journalist Kancha Ilaiah succinctly put it, the Hindu nationalists successfully created a "deliberately constructed enemy – Muslims."[51]

The BJP and its allies were therefore skillfully able to exploit this sense of insecurity, low self-esteem, and irrational fear of Muslims. The Hindutva fear campaign culminated in two major events that have had far-reaching consequences for politics in India and for terrorism against Muslims: the Babri Masjid controversy and state terrorism in the state of Gujarat. An analysis of both events provides an understanding of the outbreaks of communal violence against Muslims, mainly in urban centers in northern India, in recent times.

Communal violence and politics: the Babri Masjid controversy

In order to win popular support among the middle class, particularly traders and professionals, organizers of the Hindutva movement identified a single issue that appealed to the national pride of many Hindus and which could be translated into organizational and electoral successes in many north Indian state elections and at the national level. That issue was the campaign to build a temple dedicated to the Hindu King Ram, an avatar or incarnation of the great god Vishnu, at his alleged birthplace in the small north Indian town of Ayodhya.

Hindu nationalists claimed that Ram's birthplace lay under a mosque, the Babri Masjid, built by a general of the Mughal Empire in the sixteenth century on the site of a Hindu temple he destroyed. Through the use of propaganda, Hindu nationalists were able to turn what had been a very minor local dispute into a national issue for political advantage. Hindutva propagandists skillfully began to portray Ram as not just the god of one of India's numerous sects but rather the god of all Hindus in order to create a fictitious Hindu and national identity.

Hindutva leaders demanded at emotional public meetings that the Babri Masjid should be pulled down and a brand new Hindu temple be erected in its place. From 1990 to 1992, Hindu nationalist politicians embarked on a number of campaigns to publicize the Ayodhya issue, including religious processions from various parts of north India to Ayodhya carrying statues of Ram and his wife Sita. The processions were greeted by large, highly emotional crowds in major north Indian cities. At huge public meetings, leading Hindu nationalist politicians and *sadhus*, Hindu holy men, attacked Islam and Muslims in highly emotional and inflammatory speeches, which provoked attacks on Muslim quarters of the cities.

The political agitations culminated in the destruction of the Babri Masjid by Hindu mobs on December 6, 1992. The campaign and destruction of the Masjid inflamed communal hatreds, leading to riots throughout north India and the death of over 2,000 people, mostly Muslims. It also translated into political support for the BJP; the party became the country's largest after the 1996 general elections, and its leader became prime minister. The complicated nexus between religion, politics, and terrorism in India was soon to be demonstrated even more clearly in one of the most terrible outbreaks of communal violence in Indian history.

State terrorism, politics, and communal violence in Gujarat, 2002

One of the most violent and destructive instances of anti-Muslim terrorism took place in the northwest state of Gujarat in 2002, ironically one of the most prosperous and modernizing states in India. The key to understanding state terrorism and communal violence in Gujarat and elsewhere in India lies in an analysis of caste and religion and their complex role in electoral politics in the state.[52]

About ninety percent of the population of Gujarat can be grouped into four broad caste groups.[53] First, there is a numerically small group of higher and middle castes – about twenty-five percent of the population – who traditionally have controlled land, the professions, education, dominated the bureaucracy and business, and who until recently had traditionally held political power in Gujarat. Second, there is a numerically much larger group – about forty-three percent – of lower castes who are mainly small landowners, sharecroppers, artisans, and laborers. The third group, the Dalits, comprise about seven percent. Finally, the tribal Adivasis are about fourteen percent. Previously, most Adivasis had lived in remote areas away from settlements, but now they mainly live in poverty either in their own settlements or in slums in urban centers.

The largest religious minority in Gujarat are Muslims, comprising about nine percent of the population. Most of the Muslims in Gujarat are descendants from lower caste groups, Dalits, and Adivasis who had converted to Islam, but, in most respects, their economic and social position had not changed despite their conversion.[54] Gujarat had experienced occasional communal rioting in some urban centers, but until the 2002 riots, Muslims generally had lived peacefully with their Hindu neighbors, especially in rural areas.

Higher caste dominance of society and politics in Gujarat, as elsewhere in India, was challenged by the introduction of democratic politics along with independence in 1947. Voting rights to all adult Indians had given the numerically larger lower castes, Dalits, Adivasis, and Muslims great electoral power. From around 1969, Gujarati politics began to be dominated by the Congress Party, which built a mass-based party in Gujarat committed at least in principle to social justice and abolishing poverty. Congress Party success was based on a coalition made up predominantly of the lower castes, Dalits, Adivasis, and Muslims. Comprising between seventy and seventy-five percent of Gujarat's population,[55] this voting bloc enabled Congress to dominate electoral politics and thus threaten the political, economic, and social dominance of Gujarat's upper castes, the main supporters of Hindutva.

This environment does much to explain the emergence of state terrorism. Moreover, a close analysis of Gujarati state terrorism provides a very useful insight into the origins and nature of anti-Muslim terrorism in other parts of India as well. In particular, it demonstrates how the Hindu nationalists were able, at least temporarily, to unite followers of all castes from very high to the lowest by a common ideal of the Hindu state and opposition to the Muslim enemy.

The trigger for the state terrorism and the subsequent outbreak of communal violence that followed between February 28 and mid-June was a train fire on February 27, 2002, which broke out in the Sabarmati express that had halted in the town of Godhra in Gujarat. The train was packed with Hindu pilgrims known as *karsevaks* who were returning from a pilgrimage to Ayodhya. A dispute broke out between the *karsevaks* and Muslim vendors at the station, which led to name calling and stone throwing. The cause of the fire, in which fifty-eight men, women, and children were burnt alive, is still hotly debated, although the cause was probably accidental. Nonetheless, the state's BJP politicians immediately identified Muslims as the culprits. A great deal of the blame for the communal violence, then, can be attributed to the state's ruling Hindu nationalist party, the BJP, and its chief minister, Narendra Modi, who initiated, encouraged, and condoned the violence.[56]

The next day saw the beginning of systematic violence when Hindus embarked on a campaign of revenge throughout the state against Muslims, who were innocent of any wrongdoing. In the massacres that followed, around 2,000 men, women, and children were murdered across Gujarat, many in hideously cruel ways. Both the living and the dead were mutilated. Women and young girls were raped in their homes, farms, factories, and by the side of the road.

According to numerous media, civil rights activist, and eyewitness accounts, the mob attacks on the Muslims were carefully planned and coordinated by government ministers and officials. Two cabinet ministers had on February 27, 2002, met with senior members of Hindu nationalist organizations to coordinate the unleashing of violence against Muslims.[57] The Gujarati riots, therefore, can be regarded as a form of state terrorism in that it was used to terrorize the state's political opponents. On the day after the fire, attackers arrived in trucks dressed in saffron robes and khaki shorts, the uniform of Hindu nationalist groups. The mobs were armed with swords, explosives, gas cylinders, and other weapons, which they used to set houses and businesses alight. They also had computer printouts obtained from government officials listing the addresses of the homes of Muslims and their businesses. The attacks were carefully coordinated through the use of mobile phones. In numerous cases, Muslim businesses were looted and burnt while neighboring Hindu businesses were left untouched.[58] Many attacks were made close to police stations and in view of the police, but no attempts were made to stop the violence. Frantic calls by terrified men, women, and children were answered by the police, "We have no orders to save you."[59] In some instances the police fired on Muslims who attempted to defend themselves.

The main motivation for the state-supported terrorist actions against Muslims in Gujarat was political. The BJP had become the major party in the political coalition that ruled Gujarat state in 1995. The electoral successes in Gujarat were in large part built upon the fact that the Hindu nationalists were very well organized at a grassroots level. Hindu nationalists working through the media, local organizations, propaganda, and education were able to proselytize widely the Hindutva message of Hindu pride and unity, particularly amongst the low castes, Dalits, and Adivasis. The Hindu nationalists thus embarked on a novel policy of constructing a new Hindu identity that would include the lower castes, Dalits, and Adivasis, all of whom previously had been excluded from higher caste worship.

For the first time in history, Dalits were invited to attend upper-caste religious rituals, such as chariot processions of Hindu gods. Hindu nationalist activists distributed idols of the two very popular Indian gods, Ganesh and Ram, throughout tribal areas.[60] Members of the youth wing of the Hindutva movement, the Bajrang Dal, were asked to dedicate themselves to the abolition of untouchability and to work for the social, economic, and educational uplift of their new Hindu brothers. Hindutva forces were particularly successful in winning support in the Adivasi areas of central and east Gujarat by offering the Adivasis incorporation into what they regarded as a superior religion and culture.[61] Dalits and Adivasis were given leadership positions at the lower levels in Hindutva organizations, thus enhancing their self-respect and sense of their acceptance by the upper castes.[62]

Crucial for the construction of a new Hindu identity was the projection of Muslims as a common enemy of all. All Muslims were tarnished with the label of being fundamentalist, anti-national, and pro-Pakistan.[63] However, this unity was fragile, as many still resented higher-caste dominance of the top leadership positions in Hindutva organizations as well as what they perceived as the arrogance of the higher castes who, despite the rhetoric of equality, still deep down were contemptuous of those below them in the caste hierarchy. The BJP desire to strongly coalesce the various castes and tribal groups became more urgent with the forthcoming state elections in 2002 in which the BJP was predicted to lose support.

The Hindutva strategy of winning the electoral support of the lower castes, Dalits, and Adivasis by marginalizing and demonizing Muslims worked brilliantly. In December 2002, the BJP won a landslide victory in the Gujarat state assembly elections, the best result for any BJP state party.[64] During the 2002 electoral campaign, anti-Muslim propaganda by the chief minister and his supporters proved to be a highly successful political strategy. Muslims were portrayed as traitorous supporters of global Islamic terrorism, a task made easier by the worldwide anti-terrorist hysteria following the events of September 11, 2001.[65] A vote for the BJP, therefore, would demonstrate to Pakistan and the traitorous Muslims living in Gujarat that terrorism would be resisted at all costs.[66]

Conclusion

The case studies of terrorism in Pakistan and India are, in many ways, very dissimilar. In summary, the most noteworthy difference between the acts of political violence that emerged in the name of religion in Pakistan and India was that in Pakistan Muslims belonging to the Sunni tradition perpetuated terrorist acts against the minority Shi'as, whereas in India the main victims of terrorist acts were members of the minority Muslim religion. But an analysis of both cases of terrorism also reveals many similarities. Previously, violence in the name of religion in both states had been largely spontaneous and localized. The terrorism that emerged towards the end of the twentieth century, however, differed in respect to its widespread nature, the far greater number of casualties, and the motivations of the protagonists who initiated the violence. Both cases of terrorism were largely a consequence of the development of modern politics in both India and Pakistan. Shi'as in Pakistan and Muslims in India became the innocent scapegoats of ambitious politicians' quest for personal power. In Pakistan, the political ambitions of Zia saw the beginnings of sectarian violence during the 1980s, which ever since has become a feature of modern Pakistani politics; in India, the BJP's attempt to win electoral support by demonizing Muslims during the 1990s was a brilliant political strategy but has had disastrous consequences for communal harmony. In neither India nor Pakistan can the origins of terrorism in modern times be linked to the actual teachings of the religions but rather were the result of the exploitation of religious feeling for political ends.

Notes

1 Although now somewhat dated, two very useful introductory volumes to the history of Islam in the Indian subcontinent are P. Hardy, *The Muslims of British India* (Cambridge: Cambridge University Press, 1972); and S. M. Ikram, *Muslim Civilization in India* (New York: Columbia University Press, 1964).

2. www.mapsofworld.com/world-top-ten/world-top-ten-countries-with-largestmuslim-populations-map.html http://features.pewforum.org/muslim-population/ (accessed January 21, 2013). In addition, Bangladesh, located in the northeast of the subcontinent and which was once part of the Pakistani state, has a population of nearly 150,000,000 Muslims.
3. One of the best discussions of the "making of Hinduism" is Romila Thapar, "Syndicated Hinduism," in *Hinduism Reconsidered*, ed. Gunther-Dietz Sontheimer and Hermann Kulke, 54–81 (New Delhi, Manohar, 1997).
4. Ibid., 295.
5. Ibid., 87.
6. Hassan Abbas, "Shiism and Sectarian Conflict in Pakistan Identity Politics, Iranian Influence, and Tit-for-Tat Violence," in *Combating Terrorism Center at West Point Occasional Paper Series* (2010), 7, www.ctc.usma.edu/wp-content/uploads/2011/05/CTC-OP-Abbas-21-September.pdf (accessed January 21, 2012).
7. For the key role of Jinnah in the formation of Pakistan, see chapter 2, "The Colonial Legacy and the Making of Pakistan," in Eamon Murphy, *The Making of Terrorism in Pakistan: Historical and Social Roots of Extremism* (Abingdon, Oxon: Routledge, 2013), 30–47.
8. For an overview of Islam in Pakistan, see chapter 1, "Islam in Pakistan: An Overview," in ibid., 14–29.
9. Abbas, "Shiism and Sectarian Conflict in Pakistan Identity."
10. For details, see Murphy, *The Making of Terrorism in Pakistan*, 128–31.
11. Vali R. Nasr, "International Politics, Domestic Imperatives, and Identity Mobilization: Sectarianism in Pakistan, 1979–1998," *Comparative Politics* 32, no. 2 (2000): 171.
12. Syed Ali Shah, "Quetta Blast Death Reaches 84," Dawn.com, February 17, 2013 (accessed December 12, 2013).
13. Ibid.
14. Murphy, *The Making of Terrorism in Pakistan*, 31. For more on radical Islamism and salafi-jihadism, see Chapter 17 by John Calvert and Chapter 18 by David Cook in this volume.
15. For an overview of Islamization, see Murphy, *The Making of Terrorism in Pakistan*, 84–201.
16. Husain Haqqani, *Pakistan: Between Mosque and Military* (Washington, DC: Carnegie Endowment for International Peace, 2005),136.
17. Ibid.
18. Kunal Mukherjee, "Islamic Revivalism and Politics in Contemporary Pakistan," *Journal of Developing Societies* 26, no. 3 (2010): 342.
19. S. V. R. Nasr, "Islam, the State and the Rise of Sectarian Militancy in Pakistan," in *Pakistan: Nationalism without a Nation?*, ed. Christophe Jaffrelot (New Delhi: Manohar, 2002), 99.
20. Ibid., 98.
21. For an excellent analysis that is sympathetic to the Russian perspective and that dispels many of the myths about the Soviet invasion and occupation of Afghanistan, see the account by the former British ambassador to Moscow, Rodric Braithwaite, *Afgantsy: The Russians in Afghanistan, 1979–89* (London: Oxford University Press, 2011).
22. Steve Coll, *Ghost Wars: The Secret History of the CIA, Afghanistan, and Bin Laden, from the Soviet Invasion to September 10, 2001* (New York: Penguin Press, 2004).
23. Imtiaz Gul, *The Most Dangerous Place: Pakistan's Lawless Frontier* (London: Penguin, 2010), 200.
24. Coll, *Ghost Wars*, 239.
25. Murphy, *The Making of Terrorism in Pakistan*, 153.
26. Ibid.
27. Ibid., 137–59.
28. There are a number of excellent analyses of the growth of sectarianism in the Punjab and other parts of Pakistan. One of best is Muhammad Qasim Zaman, "Sectarianism in Pakistan: The Radicalization of Shi'i and Sunni Identities," *Modern Asian Studies* 32, no. 3 (July 1998): 689–716.
29. Ibid., 708–10.
30. Murphy, *The Making of Terrorism in Pakistan*, 98–9.
31. S. V. R. Nasr, "The Rise of Sunni Militancy in Pakistan: The Changing Role of Islamism and the Ulema in Society and Politics," *Modern Asian studies* 34, no. 1 (2000): 166.
32. Zaman, "Sectarianism in Pakistan," 700.
33. Nasr, "Islam, the State and the Rise of Sectarian Militancy in Pakistan," 91.

34 Ibid., 86.
35 Nasr, "The Rise of Sunni Militancy in Pakistan," 150.
36 Ibid., 165.
37 Zaman, "Sectarianism in Pakistan," 712.
38 Nasr, "The Rise of Sunni Militancy in Pakistan," 167.
39 For a brief description of terrorism in India before independence, see Chapter 12 by Benjamin Grob-Fitzgibbon in this volume.
40 Government of India, Report, "Social, Economic and Educational Status of the Muslim Community in India," New Delhi, 2006, http://minorityaffairs.gov.in/sites/upload_files/moma/files/pdfs/sachar_comm.pdf (accessed June 11, 2013).
41 Ibid., 91.
42 Alastair Scrutton, "The Dark Side of Hindu Nationalism," *India Insight*, November 3, 2008, http://blogs.reuters.com/india/2008/11/03/the-dark-side-of-hindu-nationalism/ (accessed March 3, 2013).
43 There is an extensive literature on the Hindutva movement. For example, see Basu et al., eds., *Khaki Shorts, Saffron Flags: A Critique of the Hindu Right* (Delhi: Orient Longman, 1993); and Christophe Jaffrelot, *The Hindu Nationalist Movement and Indian Politics: 1925 to the 1990s* (London: Hurst, 1996).
44 The Sangh Parivar or "family" of Hindu right-wing organizations includes the militant Rashtriya Swayamsevak Sangh (the National Volunteer Organization); the Vishva Hindu Parishad (World Hindu Council); the youth wing of the Vishva Hindu Parishad, the Bajrang Dal; and the Sangh Parivar's electoral arm, the Bharatiya Janata Party (BJP; the Indian People's Party).
45 Jaffrelot, *The Hindu Nationalist Movement*, 478.
46 For Hindutva ideology, see Christophe Jaffrelot, ed., *The Sangh Parivar: A Reader* (New Delhi: Oxford University Press, 2005).
47 For an excellent summary of the origins of Hindu nationalism, see "Introduction: The Invention of an Ethnic Nationalism," in *Hindu Nationalism: A Reader*, ed. Christophe Jaffrelot (Princeton, NJ: Princeton University Press, 2007).
48 Ibid., 63–410.
49 Ibid., 19–25.
50 Martha C. Nussbaum, *The Clash Within: Democracy, Religious Violence, and India's Future* (Cambridge, MA: Harvard University Press, 2007), 212.
51 Kancha Ilaiah, "The rise of Modi," *The Hindu*, December 26, 2002, www.hindu.com/2002/12/26/stories/2002122600461000.htm (accessed April 15, 2013).
52 For a more detailed discussion of the communal violence in Gujarat, see Eamon Murphy, "'We Have No Orders to Save You': State Terrorism, Politics and Communal Violence in the Indian State of Gujarat, 2002," in *Contemporary State Terrorism: Theory and Practice*, ed. Richard Jackson, Eamon Murphy, and Scott Poynting, 86–106 (Abingdon, Oxon: Routledge, 2010).
53 The caste and religious statistics are based on the 1971 census. See Atul Kohli, *Democracy and Discontent: India's Growing Crisis of Governability* (Cambridge: Cambridge University Press, 1991), 241.
54 "Marginalization of Muslim Minority in India," *The Islamic Workplace*, December 29, 2006, http://makkah.wordpress.com/ (accessed April 21, 2013).
55 Nikita Sud "Secularism and the Gujarat State: 1960–2005," *Modern Asian Studies* 42, no. 6 (2008): 262.
56 Murphy, "'We Have No Orders to Save You,'" 87.
57 Nikita Sud, "Secularism and the Gujarat State," 1272.
58 Human Rights Watch, "'We Have No Orders to Save You': State Participation and Complicity in Communal Violence," April 30, 2002, www.hrw.org/reports/2002/india/ (accessed November 26, 2112).
59 Ibid.
60 Vidya Subrahmania, "The Muslim Question in Gujarat," *The Hindu*, October 9, 2007, www.hindu.com/2007/10/09/stories/2007100956230800.htm (accessed November 11, 2012).
61 Ibid.

62 Ghanshygam Shah, "The BJP's Riddle in Gujarat: Caste, Factionalism and Hindutva," in *The BJP and the Compulsions of Politics in India*, ed. Thomas Blom Hansen and Christophe Jaffrelot (Delhi: Oxford University Press, 1998), 257.
63 Davindar Kumark, "Poisoned Edge: The Sangh Exploits Dalit and Tribal Frustration to Recruit Soldiers for Hindutva's 'War,'" *Outlook Magazine*, June 24, 2002, http://cac.ektaonline.org/updates/2002_06_23_archive.htm (accessed April 23, 2013).
64 Dibyesh Anand, "The Violence of Security: Hindu Nationalism and the Politics of Representing 'the Muslim' as a Danger," *The Round Table: The Commonwealth Journal of International Affairs* 94 (April 2005): 203–15.
65 Paula Chakravartty and Srinivas Lankala, "Media, Terror, and Islam: The Shifting Media Landscape and Culture Talk in India," in *Violence and Democracy in India*, ed. Amitra Basu and Srirupa Roy (Calcutta: Seagull Books, 2007).
66 Ibid., 189.

Further reading

Abbas, Hassan. *Pakistan's Drift into Extremism: Allah, the Army, and America's War on Terror*. New York: M. E. Sharpe, 2005.
Basu, Amitra, and Srirupa Roy, eds. *Violence and Democracy in India*. Calcutta: Seagull Books, 2007.
Bennett Jones, Owen. *Pakistan: Eye of the Storm*. 3rd ed. New Haven, CT: Yale University Press, 2009.
Hansen, Thomas Blom, and Jaffrelot Christophe, eds. *The BJP and the Compulsions of Politics in India*. Delhi: Oxford University Press, 1998.
Jackson, Richard, Eamon Murphy, and Scott Poynting, eds. *Contemporary State Terrorism: Theory and Practice*. Abingdon, Oxon: Routledge, 2010.
Jaffrelot, Christophe, ed. *Pakistan: Nationalism without a Nation?* New Delhi: Manohar, 2002.
—. *The Hindu Nationalist Movement and Indian Politics: 1925 to the 1990s*. London: Hurst, 1996.
Kaur, Ravinder. *Religion, Violence and Political Mobilisation in South Asia*. New Delhi: Sage Publishers, 2005.
Murphy, Eamon. *The Making of Terrorism in Pakistan: Historical and Social Roots of Extremism*. Abingdon, Oxon: Routledge, 2013.
Nussbaum, Martha C. *The Clash Within: Democracy, Religious Violence, and India's Future*. Cambridge, MA: Harvard University Press, 2007.

Part V

CRITICAL THEMES IN THE HISTORY OF TERRORISM

24

MODERNITY AND TERRORISM

Roger Griffin

"Finally, he was quartered.... This last operation was very long, because the horses used were not accustomed to drawing; consequently, instead of four, six were needed; and when that did not suffice, they were forced, in order to cut off the wretch's thighs, to sever the sinews and hack at the joints."[1] This brief extract from the protracted description of Robert-François Damiens' execution in 1757 in Paris by the French absolutist regime for the attempted regicide of Louis XV forms the famous opening to Michel Foucault's classic study of the birth of the modern prison, *Discipline and Punish*. The elaborate public execution of Guy Fawkes and his accomplices in 1605 in the Old Palace Yard in Westminster under James I was only marginally less refined.

The descriptions of such gruesome state murders are not isolated episodes. The ritual infliction of extreme pain calculated to spread terror among potentially "subversive" elements in the population who threaten its moral norms or institutional power has been a recurrent feature of the pre-modern state. At least within Christian culture, the crucifixion of Jesus Christ is the most famous historical example of how states in antiquity routinely deployed terror to counter the threat of popular sedition. Attempts by the Roman Empire to halt the spread of Christianity led to the even more exotic forms of public execution documented in the first chapter of *Fox's Book of Martyrs*, "History of Christian Martyrs to the First General Persecutions Under Nero."

So there is nothing particularly modern about a state deploying terror as a means of social control, reinforcing its hegemony, and asserting its absolute, unimpeachable power over its enemies, no matter how much the means deployed may have been transformed through technology and the nature of the state since the eighteenth century. Perhaps more surprisingly, anti-state terrorism[2] is of comparable antiquity. One of the earliest examples of it documented in any detail is the resistance movement that arose in the first century AD opposed to the Roman occupation of Judea and to the extensive collaboration with it promoted by the Herodian faction. In his *The Jewish War*, Josephus – a first-century Romano-Jewish historian who embodied the "Herodization" of Judaic culture in his fusion of Judaic Orthodoxy with Graeco-Roman thought and culture – described the particular tactics adopted by the Sicarii, a group fanatically opposed to Roman rule on the basis of a religious fundamentalism akin to that of the Zealots and to those who supported it like Josephus himself. Precluded from fighting the type of guerrilla war against the Romans that the Maccabees had waged successfully to resist the absorption of Judea into the Seleucid Empire, they turned to the last resort of fanatics engaged in an "asymmetrical conflict" with overwhelming state power: terrorism. They carried out acts of sporadic violence against individuals representing the oppressors or their Herodian collaborators with a view to forcing them into ending Rome's annexation of Judea.

In the defense of their unique culture and religion, these men, who would now be called "religious terrorists," carried out a number of assassinations literally using cloak and dagger tactics (*sicarius* means "dagger-man") to obtain maximum proximity to the victim in a crowd, to enable them to escape undetected, and, most significantly, to disseminate fear and anxiety in civic society among the occupiers and their "collaborators," their target audience. (For more on the Sicarii, see Chapter 3 by Donathan Taylor and Yannick Gautron in this volume.) To corroborate the credentials of the Sicarii as forerunners of modern terrorism, it is significant that in 1931, some nineteen centuries after their defeat, a new generation of Zionist militants fighting for a Jewish homeland in Palestine formed the League of Sicarii in a conscious act of "recovering roots."[3] It was set up by the Achimeir circle of radicalized Zionist youth, a group dedicated to "direct" (i.e., terrorist) action in the pursuit of their cause. This terrorist strain in Zionism played a key role in the creation of the modern state of Israel,[4] but it is clear that some of its protagonists saw themselves as the modern heirs of the Sicarii and Zealots who had fought a paramilitary war against Roman occupation nearly two millennia before.

If both the state's use of terror as a tool of governance and acts of terror carried out against the state or foreign occupation are ancient – if, as Randall D. Law indicates in the introduction to this book, terrorism is as old as human civilization – then the central question for this chapter to address is whether there is anything special about them under the conditions of modernity. This highly contested term is taken here to refer to a nexus of anti-traditional forces, notably the secularization of society, politics, and cosmology; intensified social mobility; the rise of science, materialism, individualism, globalized consumerism and media, mass migration (much of it coerced through famine, poverty, and war), and the resulting multiculturalism and relativism; the waning of dynastic absolutism; technological advances in surveillance and weapons; and the breakdown of relatively homogeneous cultures based on religion and tradition that is the concomitant of this nexus.[5] The chapter argues that globalizing Western modernity has indeed generated new forms of terrorism in both its state and anti-state forms, as well as proliferating its deployment to the point where acts of terrorism to defend or attack the status quo can be considered no less integral and endemic to the modern world than ethnic or sectarian violence or financial scandals. We will start by considering state terrorism and its complex relationship to modernity.

The semiotic dimension of terrorism

Before we focus on the modernity of terrorism in the context of the assertion of state power and anti-state protest, it is as well to clarify what is being understood here by the term. Among the several perceptive components of Alex Schmid's twelve-point "revised academic consensus definition," one important distinction that he draws is between the direct victims of the violence and its ultimate targets, the victims serving primarily as "message generators."[6] My own attempt to contrive an ideal type of terrorism chimes with these insights when it opens with the statement that:

> Terrorism is a generic term for extremely heterogeneous acts of violence originating from an asymmetrical relationship of force with the perceived source of oppression, injustice, or decadence, and carried out within civic space (or at least outside

the traditional contexts/spaces of military conflict), generally targeting non-combatants. The violence has a direct object, the human or material targets of the attack which are typically destroyed, and an indirect object, the third parties for whom the violence is a "message", a performative, semiotic act conceived to force them to change their behavior, policies, actions, or way of thinking by undermining their sense of security and disseminating fear, both rational and irrational, of further outrages.[7]

Terrorism is thus distinguished from other forms of violence by the triadic relationship between perpetrators, victims, and targets, and by the importance and intended receivers of the symbolic message. This is carried by the calculated cultural and mythic significance of the object of the violence beyond the immediate reality of the physical pain, murder, and material destruction itself to become an act of "propaganda by the deed,"[8] one aimed in the first instance not at the military and political defenders of state power (a point of contrast with guerrilla warfare) but at chosen segments of society at large. It stands out from most other political "isms" by defining not a particular ideology but a particular tactic used to achieve ends which may be overtly political – at practically any point in the left–right spectrum – or appear utterly nihilistic, but generally prove to have a more profound cosmological and psychological component associated with such terms as fanaticism, Jacobinism, extremism, and fundamentalism.

The performative dimension of state terrorism

The triadic, semiotic component of terrorism means that it is misleading to portray the Gunpowder Plot of 1605 as an example of anti-state terror because the intended victims, the "Protestant" King James I and all the ministers and politicians gathered for the state opening of parliament, were also the targets of the destruction. This was conceived to be the first act in an attempted coup designed to culminate in the installation of the king's daughter, Elizabeth, the "Winter Queen," as a Catholic monarch. It was no more an act of terrorism than the attempted assassination of Hitler was in the context of the Stauffenberg Plot of 1944 – unless, that is, the "conspiracy" version of events is believed, which claims the Gunpowder Plot was engineered by the king's ministers in order to legitimize a draconian campaign of repression against English Catholics. In this case, the gruesome public execution of Guy Fawkes and the annual burning of the "Guy" are fine examples of the Machiavellian use of state terrorism, rather than the crushing of anti-state terrorism.

Following such distinctions, it becomes clear that in the context of state power, "terrorism" excludes torture primarily to extract suffering when it serves a sadistic purpose, as was the case in many of the atrocities ordered – and sometimes participated in – by Ivan the Terrible. But it does include Ivan's calculating use of public torture and executions, as well as arbitrary "disappearances" of powerful men, intended to spread fear among the nobles and destroy their capacity to mount a concerted assault on his absolute rule. Similarly, it excludes the extensive use of torture behind closed dungeon doors by the Spanish Inquisition to extract confessions. Yet it certainly includes the elaborate ritual of penance known by the extraordinary euphemism *auto-da-fé* (act of faith) and the subsequent burning of effigies or living human beings as punishment for the sins once confessed. Such public displays of horrific penitential suffering served the dual purpose of punishing "sinners" for their sins and defending the Catholic Church from the threats of apostasy and the invasion of the allegedly Satanic forces represented by Protestantism, the Renaissance, freedom of thought and intellectual enquiry, and the alleged decay of morality under the sway of the Devil – the latter to be done by terrifying society into compliance.

The elaborately stage-managed rituals of penitence and execution enacted by the Inquisition in Catholic Europe and overseas colonies highlight the central importance of the spectacular dimension of state terrorism. It is a central theme of Foucault's *Discipline and Punish* that for the rulers of pre-modern societies every serious crime against the state was experienced like a rent in the "Code," the semiotic thread that seamlessly held together the fabric of society and protected it from the forces of anarchy, evil, and darkness. Expiation of the crime through a public spectacle of punishment visibly exacting excruciating suffering from the condemned was the only way to mend the tear and re-establish the cosmological equilibrium, laying bare the etymological link between pain and punishment contained in the Latin *poena* (which still reverberates in the expression "under pain of death"). Before the "birth of the prison," punishment was thus the "reactivation of the Code": "Rather than seeing the presence of the Sovereign, one will read the laws themselves."[9] Terror is intrinsic to this process: "In physical torture the example was based on terror: physical fear, collective horror, images which must be engraved on the memories of the spectators, like the brand on the cheek or the shoulder of the condemned man."[10] Thus in the pre-parliamentary age, terror ritually reaffirmed absolutism and, in fact, continued to be used in Britain to reinforce the law even in the early phase of constitutional monarchy.

> Broadly speaking, one might say that, in monarchical law, punishment is a ceremonial of sovereignty; it uses the ritual marks of the vengeance that it applies to the body of the condemned man; and it deploys before the eyes of the spectators an effect of terror which is as intense as it is discontinuous, irregular, and always above its own laws, the physical presence of the sovereign and of his power.[11]

Foucault demonstrates in disturbingly graphic detail the profound link between punishment and state terrorism before the Enlightenment transformed the theory and practice of justice. To be understood by the victim and the spectators, the transgression against instituted authority and the sentence it had incurred were to be inscribed through the pain experienced in the nerves and limbs of the offender's body in the way so graphically explored by Franz Kafka in his short story "The Penal Colony," in which the victim has his alleged crime literally engraved or tattooed into his skin by a grotesque machine to the point where he understands it on his flesh and it is expiated.

Foucault's analysis is supplemented by Patrick Lenta's distinction, sometimes difficult to draw in practice, between "spectacular torture" and another form, "terroristic torture," in which punishment is not involved, torture being used solely for its deterrent, coercive power, the "message" being enacted solely for the benefit of the "spectators," the public at large.[12] Another important insight is added by Mikkel Thorup, who establishes that throughout history the degree of humaneness with which both subversive citizens and foreign enemies have been treated by states has been conditioned, consciously or subliminally, by the degree of *humanness* accorded them.[13] It is an argument powerfully reinforced by Michael Fellman's account of the central role played by state terrorism in the making of America, *In the Name of God and Country*, a story of the official deployment of torture uninterrupted by the advent of modernity.[14] It is clear from all these accounts that the roots of modern state terrorism are plunged deep into a pre-modern past.

The modern practice of state terrorism

On the basis of such considerations it can be seen that when terror is deployed by a modern state, considerable care needs to be taken before its genesis is attributed to the impact of modernity. There are strong continuities in the way the Romans practiced barbarity as a weapon of war in the conquest of Gaul and the suppression of the Spartacus revolt, the way the conquistadors used it to commit genocide and "culturecide" in Latin America on behalf of Spain, the Nazis' use of it in Operation Barbarossa to advance the cause of the Third Reich, and the Japanese armies' deployment of it to establish the "Greater East Asia Co-Prosperity Sphere." In each case, the state, launching a campaign of aggression against allegedly "primitive," "degenerate," "racially inferior" people, fought with no moral restraints. It would be reassuring to think that states fighting "tyrannies" in the name of liberal humanistic values were immunized against dehumanizing the enemy and the propensity to commit the ensuing atrocities. However, the behavior of "liberal democratic" states when seeking to overwhelm enemies who have been dehumanized and demonized has sometimes been disturbingly similar, as a study of the Entente's conduct of World War I, the Allied terror bombing of Nazi Germany, the US war in the Pacific and Vietnam, and the campaign of "Shock and Awe" in Iraq all testify too vividly.[15] State terrorism in one form or the other is probably as old as the state itself.

But state terrorism can be associated with two species of government unknown to pre-modern society: the authoritarian state and the totalitarian state. The first arose because under the impact of modernity, the evaporation of "traditional" power associated with feudal and absolutist regimes all over the world created political spaces that, when liberal democratic forces were not powerful enough to fill them, have allowed the establishment of regimes based on personal or military dictatorship with no genuine revolutionary aspirations and no genuine democratic consensus to build on. Instead, they have disguised extensive coercion behind a façade of democratic, charismatic, or revolutionary fascist or Marxist legitimacy. Dictatorships of this sort were established in the twentieth century not just in Europe (e.g., Franco's Spain and Ceaușescu's Romania) but in Latin America, former African colonies, the Middle East, and Indonesia. A number of modern authoritarian regimes had recourse to extreme violence to crush democratic, left-wing, secessionist, or anti-colonial movements. Emblematic of this "modern" state terrorism are Pinochet's Chile,[16] Saddam Hussein's Iraq,[17] Mugabe's Zimbabwe,[18] Suharto's Indonesia,[19] Kim Il-sung's North Korea,[20] and apartheid South Africa.[21] Egypt, Libya, Tunisia, and Syria before and after the "Arab Spring" of 2011 all had recourse to different degrees of "terror" in enforcing their rule, a policy often actively supported by Western powers in order to defend their perceived interests. More recently, the modern world has seen the installation of Islamic theocratic states in Afghanistan (1996–2001) and Iran (1979–present) that deployed and continue to deploy terror as a means of social control, and a number of Middle Eastern dynastic states combining the extremes of material modernization with state oppression, including the use of torture.

Max Weber's famous triadic scheme of "traditional," "rational," and "charismatic" power does not seem to have allowed for the emergence of modern militaristic and authoritarian regimes with a pseudo-populist base of largely coerced enthusiasm for the ruler, or for a ruling elite's development of debased forms of bureaucratic and instrumental rationality to terrorize segments of their population. However, this has been the reality in which many millions of "modern" lives have been lived out since the turn of the twentieth century.

Nor did Weber envisage situations in which genuine charismatic forces would give rise to a special form of dictatorship which, though far outnumbered by coercive authoritarian states, has in its several permutations led to the loss of far more military casualties and civilian deaths than the state terrorism of all modern authoritarian regimes, whether of the extreme left[22] or extreme right,[23] put together. What have come to be known as "totalitarian societies" set out to do more than repress anarchy, liberal freedoms, religious sectarianism, or fascism – or whatever is a threat to their control of society – and create a modern travesty of traditional authority. Like Revolutionary France, they set out to institute a new society with a new type of human being in a new historical era and thus pursue goals that would simultaneously bring about a socio-economic, political, anthropological, and temporal revolution. Their goal is not authoritarian stability but revolutionary rebirth: total palingenesis. Even if the ultimate aim of such regimes is the creation of an egalitarian, post-absolutist society, the very radicalness of their palingenetic project demands a sustained process of "creative destruction," conjuring up regenerative myths of purging through war and violence against enemies that are turned into lethal state policies. The French Revolution anticipated the dark logic of twentieth-century totalitarian regimes when one of the most vociferous ("liberal fundamentalist"?) Jacobins, Jean-Baptiste Carrier, could exclaim, "We will make France a graveyard, rather than not regenerating it our own way!" And Marc-Antoine Baudot, true to the "instrumental reason" of all totalitarian terror, declared to a Jacobin club on the subject of the enemies of the Revolution, "Were they a million, would not one sacrifice the twenty-fourth part of one's self to get rid of a gangrene which might infect the rest of the body?"[24]

The deeper significance of the use of this metaphor drawn from eugenic thinking *avant la lettre* for understanding the peculiar nature of modern totalitarian terroristic regimes[25] has been illuminated in masterly fashion by Zygmunt Bauman, particularly in his two major works, *Modernity and the Holocaust* and *Modernity and Ambivalence*. Taken together, these show first that it was the overwhelming power of instrumental and bureaucratic reason (Weber's "rationalization"), combined with the full arsenal of the technological processes and logistical instruments available to the modern bureaucratic state, that made the Holocaust possible. It was realization of the Nazis' extensively scientized myth that the destruction of the Jews formed the precondition for Aryan rebirth. Its multi-process, multi-stage technocratic execution by hierarchically obedient and uniformed men and women doing their duty broke down any residual guilt for the inhumanity caused into minute hosts of collective responsibility that the party faithful could swallow without sullying their consciences. The attempted extermination not just of the Jews but of the many other categories of the Reich's enemies was thus facilitated by the fullest embrace of modernity's unique temporality of secular progress brought about through human action, and was neither a rebellion against it nor a throwback to primitive, barbaric times.

Bauman's second contribution is to show that the Reich's comprehensive extermination policies directed at racial, social, and ideological enemies were the expression of a new type of regime peculiarly founded on the right it arrogated to exercise terrorism on its subjects in the name of a greater good: the "gardening state." Such a state is dedicated to defeating the specters of anarchy and ambivalence that haunt the inhabitants of the modern world in times of crisis by creating a *new* order. This means the use of social engineering not just to create new institutions and power structures but a new type of human being. This in turn demands not just mass organizations to mold the "new man" but instruments of terror, repression, and elimination to crush opposition and "weed out" those who embody the decadence of the old system or stand in the way of the transformation project. This revolutionary logic creates a Manichaean worldview dividing human beings into those who are healthy or capable of regeneration, on the one hand, and the "unhealthy," the "parasitic," the "degenerate," the "subhuman," on the other. It is a logic that informed the Russian and Chinese communist revolutions in their most radical anti-capitalist phases of total revolution as well as, more recently, Khmer Rouge rule in Cambodia.

The Pol Pot regime, though conceived as a violent war against Western modernity and against all Cambodians accused of colluding with it, was actually the supreme expression of radical modernity in its vision of social transformation. The New Cambodia, a synthesis of organic nationalism centered on the ancient Khmer kingdom and a radical version of agrarian communism, was to be brought about through human agency and state-inflicted violence to build a secular utopia, no matter how many "gangrenous" lives of those contaminated by the influence of the West had to be removed as a precondition of national palingenesis. Estimates put the total number of people killed as a direct result of these four experiments (in the Soviet Union, Germany, China, and Cambodia) in utopian social engineering in the twentieth century at over 100 million. Each regime ran its own unique terror apparatus and precise forms of terror, some of which continue to be used to this day in the People's Republic of China, though in much muted form in comparison with the heights of the Cultural Revolution.

It is clear from these considerations that, although state terrorism is as ancient as the state itself, it has acquired powerful new tools and techniques thanks to bureaucratic and technological advances in the modern age which have led to refinements in both surveillance and the techniques of torture unimaginable at the time of the Terror presided over by the Jacobins. Under the secularizing, rationalizing, and disenchanting conditions of a globalizing modernity, new types of autocratic or authoritarian states have arisen that use terror to keep at bay the forces of sedition and subversion as they see them, dismissing any struggle for freedom or rights (ironically) as "terrorism." North Korea, with its grotesque blend of atrophied state socialism and personal dictatorship, perhaps provides the most potent contemporary case study in this type of modern terrorist state. Or else, in the case of genuine totalitarian states – at least in their idealistic, utopian phases – terror apparatuses of varying sophistication and savagery are used for purposes of repression, coercion, and mass-extermination so as to be able to pursue unimpeded a revolutionary program of social engineering – inevitably with catastrophic consequences.[26] In short, modernity has done more than modernize the apparatus of state terrorism. It has brought into being a new type of state dedicated to the realization of a totalizing vision of a new society prepared to deploy systemic terror long after the pursuit of its utopian dream has turned into a daily hell for millions.

Modernity and anti-state terrorism: defending or creating the nomos

The "evil twin" of state terrorism is anti-state terrorism. Though its victims since the nineteenth century run into tens of thousands rather than tens of millions, since 9/11 it is the threat of anti-state violence – not the continuation of government repression in regimes in many parts of the world – that springs immediately to mind at the mention of "terrorism" and that lurks in the back of people's minds in crowded public spaces and transport systems in ostensibly peaceful, politically stable societies all over the world.

Certainly in terms of perception, there has been a dramatic escalation in the frequency and violence of such terrorism globally since the early 2000s on a scale that far eclipses anything produced by the pre-modern era, or for that matter the two other modern periods of intense terroristic activity in the West, namely the period of anarchist violence (1890–1910) and of "red" and neo-fascist attacks (1968–1982). To understand the multiple drivers at work in the extraordinary proliferation of anti-state terrorism under modernity since the late nineteenth century we have to begin at the beginning. This means starting with a premise that belongs more to anthropological speculation than political science.

Living out brief lives on a small planet in an inconceivably vast and (according to the assumptions of secular science) absurd universe devoid of higher purpose and consciousness, human beings have an innate need for a sense of supra-personal belonging, identity, and purpose. It is a need that evolutionists would probably argue is crucial to the human species' ability to survive in a hostile environment while endowed with the blessing and the curse of reflexive self-consciousness. Throughout pre-modern history, this purpose was hardwired by myriad cultures, each of which passed down a cosmology – usually linked to religious beliefs and rituals, language, customs, social laws, eating traditions – and a physical territory, that together formed a sacred canopy and homeland. A shorthand for this blend of homeland and culture used by some specialists is the *nomos* (the cosmic "law" in Greek).[27]

It was this nomos, in this case their sacred homeland, that the Sicarii and later the Assassins defended against destruction, and that has been fought for, often against overwhelming odds, by all those warriors, known and unknown, from recorded history, who bravely resisted invasion, occupation, culturecide, and even genocide by enemies down through the centuries on behalf of their people. In the modern age, the Aztec warriors and Amazonian tribespeople who resisted the Spanish and Portuguese invaders would have doubtlessly been portrayed in the media and history books of the invading forces as terrorists, which is how the Nazis described French resistance fighters. The battle of an indigenous people against alien occupiers is the archetypal one dramatized in such films as Kevin Costner's *Dances with Wolves* and James Cameron's *Avatar*. It is consistent with this analysis that a recurrent form of terrorism that continues to arise under the impact of a globalizing modernity based on centralized nation-states is one in which a regime based on an ethnic majority threatens the very existence of a minority ethnic group that responds by resorting to violence to defend itself from extinction as a cultural entity. Such terrorism is driven by the fanatical commitment to defending the nomos from destruction or to re-establishing it once the sacred homeland has been lost, and examples can be found in the modern history of the Irish, the Basques, the Kurds, the Tamils, the Sikhs, the Zionists, the Palestinians, and the Chechens. All their struggles to defend or restore their nomos are akin to the attempts by Zealots and Sicarii to achieve liberation from Roman control and can be usefully termed "Zealotic" terrorism.

While separatist struggles in the modern age perpetuate an ancient phenomenon, modernity's constant erosion of the homogeneity and metaphysical basis of religious cultures has brought about a new type of terrorism altogether, one dedicated not to defending a nomos but creating a new one. The history of human culture is one of permanent evolution in religious beliefs and values, and has seen the rise of entirely new major religions through a complex process of synthesis and syncretism carried out by what are known to anthropologists as "revitalization movements." The rise of secularism in the West, a process accelerated by the rise of science and the Enlightenment, was accompanied by what has been described as "the temporalization of utopia."[28] This process, which drove the French

Revolution as well as the creation of totalitarian regimes seeking to establish utopian societies, also manifests itself in revitalization movements, sometimes carried out by lone actors, that attempt to impose not a new religion but a new type of society, one brought about not through state power from above but "from below."[29]

The first examples of the new, essentially *modern* type of terrorism that resulted were produced in the fin-de-siècle by the Russian "nihilists" and their anarchist counterparts in Europe and the US. The nihilists set about liberating Russia from feudalism and a "foreign" model of progress by blowing up Tsar Alexander II of Russia, which they naively took to be the first step in creating a modernity distinct from the one emerging so rapidly in Western Europe and the US. Their acts of "creative destruction" carried into devastating political practice what Nietzsche was to call "positive nihilism," crystallized in a dual myth: first, that the destruction of what Sergei Nechaev, the main ideologue of political nihilism, called in his "Revolutionary Catechism" of 1869 the "whole filthy system"[30] could be brought about by extreme acts of symbolic violence (in this case assassinating the tsar); and second, that a nebulously conceived new age (in this case of a truly Russian form of freedom and equality) would automatically dawn after the equally nebulous "revolution." Their counterparts in the West entertained similar delusions. The newly invented nitroglycerine-based dynamite became their weapon of choice, no doubt partly for its symbolic value as a means to blow to smithereens a human target who embodied the hated "system" in a spectacular fashion. (For more on Russian revolutionary terrorism, see Chapter 7 by Martin A. Miller in this volume.)

Clearly, anarchist violence in Europe and the United States aimed not to defend any existing nomos but to create a new one altogether, one so radical in its utopian aspect that it was indescribable except in the most nebulous terms in the works of Proudhon, Bakunin, and Kropotkin. In the 1970s too, while Lebanon and Palestine were being torn apart by movements attempting to impose hegemony for their nomos through violence, forms of communist and neo-fascist terrorism arose that, as for the anarchists before them, were rationalized by the belief that attacks carefully targeted against civil or political society to bring about its disintegration would eventually lead to the installation of a new secular nomos inconceivable from the vantage point of the present.

It is worth considering the dynamics of this new, nomos-*creating* terrorism in more detail. The relentless "nomocidal" impact of modernity has been steadily creating a worldwide social habitat in which, using the metaphor of the sociologist Zygmunt Bauman, previously "solid" realities of faith, identity, culture, fact, and moral or metaphysical truth have become "liquid."[31] Modernity is a paradoxical blend of the "materialization" of reality and its "dematerialization," producing an age that Karl Marx already described in 1848 as one where "all that is solid melts into air." For millions, the liquefying character of modernity is accentuated objectively by displacement, diaspora, multiple cultural realities, loss of identity or excess of identities, spiritual crisis, nameless angst, cultural rootlessness, and spiritual homelessness – all of which are summed up in the word "anomy."[32] Particularly when combined with serious socio-economic and political issues apparently unresolvable within the status quo, modernity can generate for some not depression but the permanent feeling that reality can be experienced differently, that values can be changed, that an alternative future is possible, that some sort of rebirth is possible. Expressed aesthetically, the resulting art is associated with artistic "modernism." However, it is also legitimate to identify this term with utopian attempts to bring about radical social and political change in the modern age, banish anomy, and restore collective social meaning and purpose. When expressed in the form of fanatical violence against the "system" in order to establish a new order, rather than defend or restore an old one in a Zealotic spirit, then a futural terrorism can result which we have termed "modernist."[33]

Modernist terrorism of the left has become a staple component of the modern world, whether carried out by post-1945 communists, such as the Red Brigades in Italy, the Red Army Faction in Germany, the Shining Path in Peru, the Golden Path of Nepal, or the Revolutionary Armed Forces of Colombia. The latter has employed the full gamut of modern terrorist techniques, such as vehicle bombings, gas cylinder bombs, killings, landmines, kidnapping, extortion, hijacking, as well as guerrilla and conventional military techniques. But the far right has also been a source of modernist terrorism, in the form of neo-Nazi attacks on Jews, asylum seekers, immigrants (all three favorite targets in Western Europe and the US), and Turks (Germany).[34]

But in terms of media impact and scale of destructiveness, the most potent forms of terrorism since the 1990s have been hybrids of Zealotic and modernist terrorism. Ted Kaczynski, the Unabomber, who for a time became the US's enemy number one, planted bombs targeting those working in science labs to alert the world to the dangers posed to the environment by the technocracy, thereby both protecting the ultimate nomos, the Earth itself, and promoting the emergence of a new, post-industrial society. Timothy McVeigh, who blew up the Alfred P. Murrah building in Oklahoma City, wanted to trigger a war against the federal state that he believed was dominated by ZOG (the Zionist Occupation Government), while David Copeland, the "London nail-bomber," thought his explosions in the heart of London would trigger a race war. Both convinced themselves that they were defending the white race from (self-)destruction while laying the foundation for a new society based on Aryan supremacy. Anders Breivik also developed his own hybrid ideology by wanting to save Norway and Europe from Islamization (Zealotic) while also creating a new Europe based on a reborn sense of European identity and roots (modernist).

By far the most potent source of terrorism in the modern world, and the one that has become synonymous with modern terrorism in many minds, is Islamism – sometimes known as salafist jihadism and also misleadingly reduced to the shorthand "al-Qaeda," as if it were a single organization or homogeneous ideology. To identify the link between modernization as a nomocidal force and the rise of Islamist terrorism, it is worth citing in full Slavoj Žižek's analysis of the relationship between the impact of a globalizing modernity on Islamic societies and the rise of fundamentalist violence:

> In Europe, where modernisation took place over several centuries, there was time to adjust to this break, to soften its shattering impact, through *Kulturarbeit*, the work of culture. New social narratives and myths slowly came into being. Some other societies – notably the Muslim ones – were exposed to this impact directly, without a protective screen or temporal delay, so their symbolic universe was perturbed much more brutally. They lost their (symbolic) ground with no time left to establish a new (symbolic) balance. No wonder then, that the only way for some of these societies to avoid total breakdown was to erect in panic the shield of "fundamentalism," that psychotic-delirious-incestuous reassertion of religion as direct insight into the divine Real, with all the terrifying consequences that such a reassertion entails, and including the return with a vengeance of the obscene superego divinity demanding sacrifices.[35]

This observation, which it should be stressed concerns only *some* societies and, I would add, only some small groups and individuals within the vast Islamic world, corroborates the theory that Islamism arises at least in part as a fundamentalist, Zealotic reaction to the existential need to preserve the sacred canopy afforded by Islam against modernity and its encroaching secularization and anomy. But it is important to stress that at the same time Islamism is a deeply futural movement analogous to other global secular creeds such as Enlightenment rationalism, anarchism, communism, and capitalism,[36] one that seeks to impose Islam as the sole world religion in order to save it from spiritual decay and moral decadence.[37]

Islamism can assume a number of different tactics in its bid to overcome worldwide *jahiliyyah* (decadence and apostasy). However, the terrorist permutation of global jihadism put into such apocalyptic effect on 9/11 in New York and Washington in the full glare of the global media – followed by devastating attacks against civilians in London, Madrid, Bali, Amsterdam, Russia, and Boston, and against a soldier in broad daylight in Woolwich, a series of narrowly averted plane explosions over the Atlantic, and countless plots foiled before they did any harm – at least partially succeeded in its aim. It forced the US and some of its allies to react "true to type" (in Islamist eyes) by precipitating the invasion by Western powers of Afghanistan and Iraq (where Islamist and sectarian terrorism has only become part of daily life since the Anglo-American occupation), causing many thousands of deaths, and leading to numerous abuses of human rights committed in the name of the "war on terror." Even more insidiously, the radical Islamist campaign has significantly undermined the sense of security previously enjoyed by liberal democracies, disseminating an unspoken fear of an attack wherever civilians are amassed for an event or take to public transport. (For more on al-Qaeda, 9/11, and the Global War on Terror, see Chapter 22 by Daveed Gartenstein-Ross in this volume.)

Conclusion: the link between modernity and terrorism

This necessarily brief chapter on a highly complex topic has suggested that, however ancient both state terrorism and anti-state terrorism may be, the nexus of forces known as "modernity" has created a political ecology and social habitat particularly conducive to the proliferation of both in particularly unfortunate conjunctures of forces and events. The breakdown of society in Syria has seen a bloodcurdling escalation in the incidence of both state terrorism and anti-state terrorism during the writing of this chapter, and other maelstroms of terroristic energies may well have emerged like sunspots by the time it is published or read.[38] State terrorism will be a fact of modern life as long as authoritarian states feel threatened by religious, secular, capitalist, populist, or democratic forces they identify with anarchy and cannot afford. Meanwhile, anti-state terrorism will continue to be driven by the primordial human capacity for such fanatical devotion to a cause – whether a sacralized secular or secularized sacral cause – that it becomes morally acceptable to kill and even be killed, a belief given a modernist twist by the fact that most terroristic violence is committed under the delusion that it will somehow change the course of history within human not divine time. The ultimate roots of fanaticism, whether of the henchmen of a totalitarian state or of anti-state terrorism, lie not just in material exigencies but overwhelmingly in the species-defining capacity to create a set of mythic beliefs that furnish a sense of identity and purpose – a nomos – and then to defend or assert that nomos to the death for reasons that extend far beyond the realm of practical considerations.

Since modernity seems set to remain a permanent source of anomy, there is every prospect that it will continue to be a generator of anti-state terrorism taken up not just by "religious fundamentalists," separatists, and (neo-)Marxists, or racial supremacists, but by representatives of a wide range of utopian, unrealizable "causes" espoused by international networks, local groupuscules, and "lone wolves" alike, to right the wrongs of modern states, neo-colonial powers, multicultural society, or finance capitalism as they see them. As I write, the Mexican government is, for example, engaged in combating the terrorist group ITS (Individualidades Tendiendo a lo Salvaje) which has declared war on the nanotechnology they believe is destroying the planet. In pursuit of their ideal society, such idealists become "cosmic warriors"[39] in their own privately constructed Manichaean universe, impervious to reason, discussion, empirical refutation, or doubt, and immune to compassion for the countless innocent citizens they may kill in the process. Indeed, they may even experience bliss in the completion of their murderous task.[40] Under modernity, the metaphysical and the terrestrial become inextricably entwined in the terrorist's motivation. The 9/11 hijackers pursuing the goal of a global caliphate to put an end to planetary decadence were promised earthly pleasures in paradise as long as it was their heroic avatar who prevailed over their merely mortal selves. They also used holy scripture as a manual for murder:

> When the confrontation begins, strike like champions who do not want to go back to this world. Shout, "Allahu Akbar," because this strikes fear in the hearts of the non-believers. God said: "Strike above the neck, and strike at all of their extremities."[41]

The same letter combines instrumental reason with sacral consciousness when it uses the Arabic verb for the ritual killing of animals to refer to the passengers who will have their throats slit with a box-cutter: "Check your weapon before you leave and long before you leave. (You must make your knife sharp and must not discomfort your animal during the slaughter)."[42]

Meanwhile, the authoritarian regimes that still remain in the world will continue to deploy state terrorism in the name of crushing "terrorists," in at least one case prepared to deliberately torture children and release their martyred bodies as a deterrent against further uprisings,[43] thereby fulfilling Friedrich Nietzsche's declaration in the section "The New Idol" of *Thus Spoke Zarathustra*: "State is the name of the coldest of all cold monsters. Coldly it lies; and this lie slips from its mouth: 'I, the state, am the people.'"[44]

Notes

1 *Gazette d'Amsterdam*, April 1, 1757, cited in Michel Foucault, *Discipline and Punish: The Birth of the Prison* (New York: Vintage, 1977), 3–4.
2 There is little scholarly consensus about the connotations of the terms "state terrorism" and "state terror," but it seems appropriate in this volume to use "terrorism" rather than just "terror" to refer to acts of violence and atrocities carried out in the pursuit of an ideologically conceived cause, either in the interests of the state or against the state. On the grounds of familiarity and euphony, however, "state terror apparatus" will be preferred to "state terrorism apparatus." For more on the definition of terrorism, see the "Introduction" by Randall D. Law in this volume. For more on the relationship between terrorism and state terrorism, see Chapters 7, 11, and 32 in this volume by Martin A. Miller, Paul M. Hagenloh, and Richard Jackson, respectively.
3 Yael Zerubavel, *Recovered Roots: Collective Memory and the Making of Israeli National Tradition* (Chicago: University of Chicago Press, 1995).
4 Ami Pedhazur and Arie Perliger, *Jewish Terrorism in Israel* (New York: Columbia University Press, 2009).

5 See Roger Griffin, *Modernism and Fascism: The Sense of a Beginning under Mussolini and Hitler* (Basingstoke: Palgrave, 2007), chapter 2. On modernity understood in this way, the key works are Antony Giddens, *The Consequences of Modernity* (Cambridge: Polity Press, 1990); and Zygmunt Bauman, *Liquid Modernity* (Cambridge: Polity, 2000).
6 Alex P. Schmid, ed., *The Routledge Handbook of Terrorism Research* (London: Routledge, 2011), 86–7.
7 Roger Griffin, *Terrorist's Creed: Fanatical Violence and the Human Need for Meaning* (London: Palgrave, 2012), 11.
8 On the origins of the term "propaganda of the deed," see Chapter 8 by Richard Bach Jensen in this volume.
9 Foucault, *Discipline and Punish*, 110.
10 Ibid. In the *auto-da-fé*, the offending part of the body associated with the "crime" was marked in fabric of a different color.
11 Ibid., 130.
12 Patrick Lenta, "Symposium: Torture and the Stoic Warrior: The Purposes of Torture," *South African Journal of Philosophy* 25, no. 1 (2006): 54.
13 See Mikkel Thorup, *An Intellectual History of Terror: War, Violence and the State* (Abingdon: Routledge, 2010), 137–69.
14 Michael Fellman, *In the Name of God and Country: Reconsidering Terrorism in American History* (New Haven, CT: Yale University Press, 2010).
15 In this context, see particularly Noam Chomsky, *Power and Terror: Post-9/11 Talks and Interviews* (New York: Seven Stories, 2003).
16 John Dinges, *The Condor Years: How Pinochet and His Allies Brought Terrorism to Three Continents* (New York: New Press 2004/2005).
17 Samir al-Khalil, *Republic of Fear: The Politics of Modern Iraq* (Berkeley: University of California Press, 1989).
18 Documentary Storm, *The Terror of Zimbabwe: Mugabe*, http://documentarystorm.com/the-terror-of-zimbabwe-mugabe/ (accessed January 8, 2012).
19 Richard Tanter, Desmond Ball, and Gerry Van Klinken, eds., *Masters of Terror: Indonesia's Military and Violence in East Timor* (Lanham, MD: Rowman & Littlefield, 2006).
20 Bruce E. Bechtol, "North Korea and Support to Terrorism: An Evolving History," *Journal of Strategic Security* 3, no. 2 (2010): 45–54.
21 See, "State Terrorism in South Africa," special issue, *Crime and Social Justice*, no. 24 (1985).
22 E.g., communist Romania under Ceaușescu, and the German Democratic Republic.
23 E.g., the various military dictatorships of Argentina and contemporary Myanmar.
24 B. Buchez et P. Roux, *Collection of Authentic Documents for the History of the Revolution at Strasbourg*, 34:204 (testimony of François Lameyrie), 2:210 (speech by Baudot, Frimaire 19, year II, in the Jacobin club at Strasbourg), cited in Hippolyte Taine, *The Origins of Contemporary France* (1880), 3:40.
25 It is worth noting that fascist Italy was also a totalitarian regime but not a terror state as far as domestic social control was concerned.
26 See note 25.
27 The classic exposition of this approach to human culture is Peter Berger, *The Sacred Canopy Elements of a Sociological Theory of Religion* (New York: Doubleday, 1967).
28 A term coined by Reinhardt Koselleck in *The Practice of Conceptual History: Timing History, Spacing Concepts* (Stanford, CA: Stanford University Press, 2002).
29 A key book for understanding the metaphysical dimension of both modern state terrorism and modernist anti-state terrorism is Luciano Pellicani, *Revolutionary Apocalypse: The Ideological Roots of Terrorism* (Westport, CT: Praeger, 2003).
30 See Sergei Nechaev, *The Revolutionary Catechism*, www.marxists.org/subject/anarchism/nechayev/catechism.htm (accessed June 19, 2014).
31 See Bauman, *Liquid Modernity*.
32 Peter Berger chooses this spelling to dissociate himself from Émile Durkheim's closely related concept of *anomie*.
33 For an extensive exploration of this distinction, see Griffin, *Terrorist's Creed: Fanatical Violence and the Human Need for Meaning*.

34 For more on left- and right-wing terrorism in Europe in the 1970s and 1980s, see Chapter 20 by Hanno Balz in this volume. For more on terrorism in Latin America, see Chapter 19 by Jennifer S. Holmes in this volume.
35 Slavoj Žižek, *Violence* (London: Profile Books, 2008), 70.
36 On this neglected aspect of Islamism, see in particular John Gray, *Al Qaeda and What It Means to Be Modern* (London: Faber & Faber, 2003).
37 The global, futural scope of the Islamist project is clearly laid out in Sayyid Qutb, *Milestones* (New Dehli: Islamic Book Services, 2002). For more on Qutb, as well as radical Islamism and terrorism, see Chapters 17 and 18 by John Calvert and David Cook, respectively, in this volume.
38 Since this chapter was written, Jihadism has succeeded in demonstrating the ability of a counter-state terrorist movement to mutate into a terrorist state. The new "caliphate" or Islamic State straddling Syria and Iraq fuses elements of both, and of Zealotic and modernist terrorism, in the most spectacular fashion.
39 I have adapted Reza Aslan's use of this term in his book on jihadism (*How to Win a Cosmic War: God, Globalization, and the End of the War on Terror* (New York: Random House, 2009)) to refer to all contemporary anti-state, "modernist" terrorists.
40 Bliss is recognized as a key experience of terrorists in Jessica Stern, *Terror in the Name of God: Why Terrorists Kill* (New York: Ecco, 2002).
41 Kanan Makija and Hassan Mneimneh, "Manual for a Raid", *New York Review of Books*, 17 January 2002, www.nybooks.com/articles/archives/2002/jan/17/manual-for-a-raid/ (accessed June 19, 2014).
42 Ibid.
43 An allusion to the repressive actions of the Syrian state under Bashar al-Assad in the civil war of 2012–13.
44 Friedrich Nietzsche, *Thus Spoke Zarathustra: A Book for Everyone and No One* (Harmondsworth, UK: Penguin, 1999), 30.

Further reading

Aslan, Reza. *How to Win a Cosmic War: God, Globalization, and the End of the War on Terror*. New York: Random House, 2009.
Bauman, Zygmunt. *Liquid Modernity*. Cambridge: Polity, 2000.
Berger, Peter. *The Sacred Canopy: Elements of a Sociological Theory of Religion*. New York: Doubleday, 1967.
Giddens, Antony. *The Consequences of Modernity*. Cambridge: Polity Press, 1990.
Gray, John. *Al Qaeda and What It Means to Be Modern*. London: Faber & Faber, 2003.
Griffin, Roger. *Terrorist's Creed: Fanatical Violence and the Human Need for Meaning*. London: Palgrave, 2012.
Pellicani, Luciano. *Revolutionary Apocalypse: The Ideological Roots of Terror*. Westport, CT: Praeger, 2003.
Qutb, Sayidd. *Milestones*. New Dehli: Islamic Book Services, 2000.
Thorup, Mikkel. *An Intellectual History of Terror: War, Violence and the State*. Abingdon: Routledge, 2010.

25

TERRORISM AND INSURGENCY

Geraint Hughes

As noted previously in this volume, there is no common, internationally agreed-upon definition of "terrorism," and in texts written both by scholars and practitioners the terms "terrorism" and "insurgency" are commonly conflated with each other.[1] For armed forces in particular, "counter-terrorism" and "counter-insurgency" are often treated as the same activity. This was evident not only with the Russians in Chechnya (1994–6 and 1999–2009) and Serbia's military and security forces during the Kosovo conflict (1998–9), but also with the British Army's traditional approach to "small wars" (described in more detail in Chapters 12 and 13 by Benjamin Grob-Fitzgibbon in this volume).[2] According to the United States' official terminology, the "Global War on Terror"/"Long War" that followed the al-Qaeda attacks on New York and Washington, DC, on September 11, 2001, incorporates not only a global effort (quoting former US Secretary of State Hillary Clinton) to "dismantle, eradicate, and defeat" al-Qaeda and affiliated groups,[3] but also the conflicts pitting the US and other Western powers either directly against Islamist insurgents – in Afghanistan and Iraq (2003–11) – or in support of friendly governments fighting internal revolts – notably in Pakistan, the Philippines, Yemen, and Somalia. Critics argue that in the process, the US and its allies are conflating a number of disparate conflicts, committing troops and funds to a perpetual conflict against a multiplicity of adversaries, without defining any discernible "end-state" (a clear strategic objective that can be accomplished by both non-military and military means).[4]

There are clear risks involved in the militarization of counter-terrorism, and from an official perspective the key danger is that the states involved can expend vast amounts of money and resources for little effect. This attitude has influenced US Vice President Joseph Biden's efforts to change the mission in Afghanistan from one of nation-building to a narrow counter-terrorist focus, in which US and allied forces focus purely on operations to kill and capture members of al-Qaeda.[5] The problem here is that there is little understanding within Western governments and militaries as to what the conceptual differences between terrorism and insurgency are.[6] Recent history shows that the terms one uses to define a problem shape the manner in which it is to be resolved, and this is particularly evident with the language of counter-insurgency (COIN) and counter-terrorism (CT).

It is also important to note that since 1945, wars within states have been more commonly waged than wars between states, and in certain conflicts (for example, the Vietnam War [1961–75], the Israeli intervention in Lebanon of 1982, or the US-led invasion and occupation of Iraq) campaigns between regular armed forces (armies, navies, and air forces) have been fought concurrently with conflicts involving irregular belligerents, with the latter being described as "insurgents," "guerrillas," "terrorists," "militias," "rebels," "militants," "proxies," and other myriad terms.[7] For the purposes of this chapter, terrorism is defined as the use of violence by an armed non-state group to coerce a government and to intimidate its population into acceding to its political demands. (For analyses of terrorism that explore its similarity to state terror, see Chapters 7, 11, and 24 in this volume by Martin A. Miller, Paul M. Hagenloh, and Roger Griffin, respectively.) Terrorism is a tactic that can be employed as part of a wider insurgency, which involves a paramilitary and subversive campaign waged by an irregular paramilitary faction to overthrow a state's government, secede from a state, or (as is the case currently with Hamas and Israel) destroy a state. Insurgencies can use terrorist methods (kidnappings, hijackings, and bomb and gun attacks against officials, security force personnel, and civilians) along with guerrilla warfare and the promotion of civil unrest; as was the case with the Algerian War of Independence, Vietnam, Angola, the Afghan insurgencies (both against the Soviets and in the aftermath of the Taliban's fall), Colombia, Sri Lanka, and Iraq. Terrorism can also be a by-product of civil war and state failure, such as with Lebanon (1975–91) and Somalia now.[8] In contrast, some insurgent groups may renounce terrorist tactics on moral and practical grounds, concluding that attacks that kill civilians will discredit their cause as far as international opinion is concerned. To take one example, the PULO – a Muslim minority insurgent movement in southern Thailand – confines its operations to the Patani region, eschewing attacks against Bangkok or cities and resorts where foreign tourists congregate.[9]

The problem for scholars is that it has proved impossible to provide a clear and objective definition that distinguishes between "terrorism" and "insurgency" as a whole. This is not just because of the conceptual complexity of intra-state wars (described by a variety of terms, such as "insurrections," "civil wars," "rebellions," and "revolutionary wars"), but also because it is implicitly in the interests of governments, armed forces, and non-state combatants involved in such conflicts to obscure any distinctions between "insurgent" and "terrorist" violence that can be used either to discredit them or (in the case of state actors) to provide their enemy with a propaganda advantage that comes from employing language that legitimizes their cause; hence the cliché that "one man's terrorist is another man's freedom fighter." As George Orwell observed with his 1946 essay "Politics and the English Language," words do not come with value-free definitions, and as John Shy and Thomas W. Collier point out, in the types of conflicts discussed in this book "there can be no neutral, apolitical vocabulary; words themselves are weapons."[10] As this chapter demonstrates, even if one tries to depoliticize terminology by basing definitions on characteristics such as the size, capability, and tactics employed by irregular armed groups, it is still difficult to apply labels such as "terrorist" and "insurgent" with any impartial analytical rigor. (See Chapter 32 by Richard Jackson in this volume for more discussion of the linguistic and cultural construction of terrorism.)

Conceptual challenges

Amongst others, Gerd Nonneman reminds us that terrorism is "not an ideology, but a tactic," and one that can be applied by states, individuals, or groups. A common trait is that it involves "the act or threat of violent targeting of non-combatant populations and/or institutions, often but not always in arbitrary fashion, in order to create fear and/or to damage the institutions being challenged." In this respect, political activism or dissent does not necessarily lead to radicalism, which in turn does not always take a violent form. Terrorism (which involves the deliberate infliction of lethal violence) can also be distinguished from other forms of violence that occur as a consequence of radicalization – a good example includes clashes between demonstrators and police or counter-demonstrators at a protest march.[11] Stathis Kalyvas also reminds us that in a variety of internal conflicts, government forces and its adversaries have used violence with varying degrees of discrimination in order to intimidate the civilian population and to force them to offer allegiance to them.[12]

Audrey Kurth Cronin notes that terrorism itself picks "at the vulnerable seam between domestic law and foreign war. . . . [Arguing] over which paradigm best fits the threat – war or crime – says more about the rigid intellectual and bureaucratic structures of the state than it does about the nature of terrorism."[13] Defining terrorism becomes harder when it occurs as part of a wider phenomenon of civil strife, coexisting with a significant challenge to the authority of the state (such as in Northern Ireland from 1969 to 1998, or in Indian-ruled Jammu and Kashmir since 1989), or where terrorism is a transnational phenomenon that transcends boundaries. In the context of the "long war," Thomas Rid and Thomas Keaney note that "succeeding against an insurgency and succeeding against specific terrorists that are part of a wider global ideological movement may be two different things," and this point has indeed been demonstrated by the fact that the killing of Osama bin Laden by US Navy special forces on May 1–2, 2011, has had little apparent effect on the insurgency in Afghanistan.[14]

Analysts now reject the term "low intensity warfare" as a catch-all term to describe those conflicts that fall short of inter-state war. All conflict is "intense," and American, British, and other NATO soldiers and marines who have served in southern Afghanistan would probably offer a blunt response to the idea that their experiences of combat lacked the ferocity of a "conventional" war. As M. L. R. Smith observes, the term "guerrilla war" itself lacks utility, as it refers to a series of tactics (hit-and-run raids, partisan operations, sabotage attacks) which can be practiced by the special forces units of regular armed forces in inter-state conflicts.[15]

Our conceptual challenges become far harder when we consider the fact that in internal conflicts, belligerents – both military/security forces and their opponents – can receive substantial external support in the form of arms, safe havens, training, equipment, funds, and volunteers, and that non-state armed groups can indeed exert as much influence on international politics as the governments of internationally recognized states.[16] From the early 1970s, the Palestine Liberation Organization (PLO) sought diplomatic recognition as part of its own claim to statehood,[17] mirroring the example of the Algerian National Liberation Front's (FLN) successful campaign to rally non-aligned opinion within the United Nations.[18] Some "insurgent" or "terrorist" groups established "states-within-a-state" in countries with weak or non-existent central governments, notably the PLO's "Fatahland" in Lebanon (from the late 1960s to 1982), Hizbullah in southern Lebanon, and al-Qaeda in Taliban-ruled Afghanistan.[19] In all these cases, the movements concerned were able to arrogate the powers of governance for themselves.

Armed forces themselves devise doctrine – defined by NATO members as "[the] fundamental principles by which military forces guide their actions in support of [their] objectives" – to prepare for the types of operations they may be expected to conduct, and both the US and British Army's manuals on COIN describe insurgency as an act of war. Military professionals seek conceptual clarity as a precondition for the application of armed force, while their critics point out that this could lead to the adoption of terminology which oversimplifies the complexities of armed conflict. If terrorism is interpreted as being part of a wider phenomenon called "insurgency," then implicitly a state's military will become the lead agency – or at least an important one – when its authority is challenged by armed internal opposition.[20]

The problem of terminology

As Magnus Ranstorp and Paul Wilkinson observed, the term "terrorism" has become a "'boo'-word," which when applied to armed non-state groups (or their adversaries) is automatically intended to demonize them.[21] The last organization to accept the "terrorist" label was the Stern Gang, a Zionist group active in Palestine during the 1930s and 1940s, and since then no organization has claimed this appellation.[22] Lawrence Freedman states that "[the] presentation of terrorism as inherently illicit or immoral conduct ensures that it is put in a separate category to other forms of action and so is subject to different considerations to those that normally govern political affairs or even most types of military operations."[23] As a consequence, it is therefore extremely difficult to analyze this phenomenon dispassionately.

Governments have certainly used the "t-word" to de-legitimize their foes. With Britain's COIN campaigns in Malaya (1947–60), Kenya (1952–7), and Cyprus (1955–9), British politicians, military commanders, and colonial administrators labeled the MRLA, Mau-Mau, and EOKA as "terrorists," or chose other pejorative terms such as "bandits."[24] The Syrian regime uses similar phraseology to describe armed opponents to the Ba'ath regime, whilst the Chinese government goes as far as to accuse Tibetan exiles who immolate themselves as an act of protest of committing an act of "terrorism" – even though the individuals concerned do harm to no one but themselves.[25] One of the most chilling abuses of the term the author has found was that employed by General Jorge Videla, Argentina's military dictator from 1976 to 1981, who stated that "a terrorist is not just someone with a gun and a bomb but also someone who spreads ideas that are contrary to Western and Christian civilization."[26] Even with democracies, officials may prefer the label of "terrorism" because it implies that the non-state armed group(s) concerned has no legitimate cause for which to fight. Governments are not often intellectually honest enough to accept that paramilitary violence can be caused by specific grievances, such as nationalist anger at the presence of foreign troops. To cite one example, the Bush administration preferred to deny the existence of a growing insurgency in Iraq in 2003–4, claiming that violence against coalition occupation forces was merely committed by Ba'athist "dead enders." Any acknowledgment that the US was facing an insurgent campaign would involve accepting that there was considerable resistance in Iraq, would expose flaws in the administration's own policies, and also embarrass it at a time when the president was preparing for re-election.[27]

For their part, non-state armed groups, their sympathizers and other parties – notably the media – prefer terms such as "guerrillas" or "freedom fighters." The choice of alternative words is often in part due to an effort by uninvolved diplomats, academics, or journalists to find less emotive phrases (such as "militant" or "gunman"), but it also reflects an effort by the groups concerned to shift opprobrium from themselves to their adversaries, as like the state governments they fight, they have their own interest in blurring any distinction between terrorism and insurgency.[28] Irregular combatants can in turn adopt the language of a military formation, a prime example being the "Provisional Irish Republican Army" (PIRA), with its "Army Council," "chief of staff," "quartermasters," "brigades," and "companies." For other organizations, the terms "liberation" and "self-defense" are common.[29] Irregular fighters may also use the trappings of a regular military force, which can include the incorporation of uniforms (berets and similar headdress, combat jackets and trousers, insignia, boots, etc.) to distinguish themselves from mere criminals. Ali Ahmeti, the former leader of the ethnic Albanian National Liberation Army during the Macedonian civil war of 2001, stated that "[a] person cannot be a terrorist who wears an army badge, who has an objective for which he is fighting . . . who acts in public with name and surname, and answers for everything he does."[30] However, this is a functional definition that breaks down in practice. The Tamil Tigers conducted terrorist atrocities during the Sri Lankan Civil War (1976–2009), but it also had a sophisticated military apparatus that was able to confront the government's armed forces in open combat.[31] The Algerian FLN had a uniformed guerrilla formation (the ALN) that fought the French, and they hid terrorist cells amongst the civilian population, such as the ones that conducted "the Battle of Algiers" during 1957.[32] (For more on the role of terrorism in the Algerian War of Independence, see Chapter 15 by Martin C. Thomas in this volume.)

Thomas Mockaitis defines insurgents and terrorists according to their objectives, stating that the former have realistic ones which are based on goals that are attainable and practical, whilst the latter are either completely utopian or utterly nihilistic.[33] This distinction is, however, difficult to apply to specific groups. In Northern Ireland, PIRA arguably had a feasible and limited objective (the end to British rule and the creation of a united Ireland), but the "armed struggle" was strategically flawed because, as Cillian McGrattan notes in Chapter 14 in this volume, it overlooked the fact that the Protestant majority wanted to remain part of the UK. In Spain, the campaign by Euskadi Ta Askatasuna (ETA) for Basque independence continued for over two decades after Francisco Franco's death (in November 1975), even though the political autonomy conceded by successive democratic governments satisfied the national aspirations of the majority of Basques.[34]

The context in which a non-state armed group emerges is important for analysts to consider. Is it involved primarily in a domestic conflict? Has it been established in response to colonial rule or foreign occupation, or is the government it opposes indigenous? Is its violence directed against the state and its security forces or against a different ethnic, confessional, or sectarian group within the community (as was the case with the loyalist paramilitaries in Northern Ireland)? Is the state concerned a democracy where dissent and non-violent political opposition is feasible, or is it an authoritarian or totalitarian state? Has governmental authority been weakened or has it even collapsed? It is also important to recognize that insurrections can change in character. The Kashmir insurgency began in 1989–90 in response to Muslim anger against Indian repression, and the Jammu and Kashmir Liberation Front fought for national independence. However, Pakistani aid to the insurgency led to its takeover by religiously inspired groups such as Laskhar-e-Taiba and Harkat ul-Mujahideen, which aimed to establish an Islamist state in South Asia.[35] The First Chechen War of 1994–6 pitted nationalist fighters against Russian Federation forces and was largely confined to Chechnya itself. The Second Chechen War (1999–2009) involved an Islamist insurgency waging war against a pro-Moscow regime in Grozny and also incorporated terrorist atrocities against Russian civilians, such as the Moscow theater siege (March 2002) and the Beslan school massacre (September 2004) in Ossetia.[36]

The motivations of the individuals and factions involved also deserve consideration. Nasir Abbas, an Indonesian defector from Jemaah Islamiyah (al-Qaeda's Southeast Asian network), joined the jihad in Afghanistan against the Soviets during the 1980s, but he became a police informant because he felt personal revulsion after the Bali bombings of October 2002.

Abbas justified his betrayal of Jemaah Islamiyah by saying that he took up arms to protect fellow Muslims from infidel invaders, not to kill nightclub revelers. The Libyan Islamic Fighting Group (LIFG) was affiliated with al-Qaeda before 9/11, but broke ranks with Osama bin Laden's movement in protest against its attacks on civilians, both in the West and in the Muslim world. Ironically enough, LIFG joined the revolution which overthrew Muammar Qaddafi's regime with NATO support (March–August 2011), even though its leader, Abdelhakim Belhadj, was "rendered" to Libya seven years beforehand by the Central Intelligence Agency and its British counterpart, the Secret Intelligence Service (MI6).[37]

What both terrorism and insurgency have in common conceptually is that both seek to challenge state-based adversaries by using tactics that those institutions are ill-suited to counter.[38] Terrorist groups within liberal democracies will exploit the normative characteristics of the state (freedom of assembly, constraints on the legal system and police powers, an abundance of potential targets, and freedom of association) to launch their attacks, whilst insurgents in a variety of conflicts employ guerrilla tactics because they risk destruction if they confront the government's military and security forces in direct combat.[39] In general, irregular groups aspire to wage a wider insurgency but may lack either the means (in terms of volunteers, professional expertise, and weaponry) to wage guerrilla warfare, or the state's military and security forces are in such a position of strength that terrorist attacks are the only feasible option (as was the case with Fatah against Israel from the early 1960s, and for ETA, EOKA, and PIRA after the early 1970s). The practitioners of terrorism can even be "lone wolves" (such as the "Unabomber" Theodore Kaczynski, David Copeland in London in 1999, Anders Breivik in Oslo in 2011, and Mohamed Merah in Toulouse in 2012), whose atrocities are individual acts, even if they may be inspired by a wider extremist ideology (radical environmentalism for Kaczynski, neo-Nazism for Copeland and Breivik, extreme Islamism for Merah) and may hope that they can incite a wider community to emulate their acts. Some non-state armed groups may develop a sophisticated organization and also acquire the weaponry needed to pose a major challenge to conventional forces – as demonstrated by Hizbullah, the Revolutionary Armed Forces of Colombia (FARC), and the Tamil Tigers. Since the Communist victory in the Chinese Civil War (1926–49) and the Viet Minh victory over the French at Dien Bien Phu (1954), the aspiration for many insurgencies has been to conquer territory and defeat the government's forces prior to the seizure of power.[40]

As noted in the introduction, analysts may seek to distinguish between terrorists and insurgents by observing their capabilities and the tactics they employ. Bruce Hoffman asserts that unlike insurgent groups, "[terrorists] do not function in the open as armed units, generally do not attempt to seize or hold territory, deliberately avoid engaging enemy forces in combat, are constrained both numerically and logistically from undertaking concerted mass political mobilization efforts, and exercise no direct control or governance over a populace at either the local or national level." The ability of the group to mobilize mass support or exert political control can be viewed as a distinguishing factor. Assessments can focus on the size of a non-state armed group, how lethal it is, how much of a challenge it poses to a state's control over its territory, how effective it is in combat against security forces (the question here being whether its members can do more than pick off individual soldiers and police in sniping and bombing attacks), and how much of a support base it possesses. Martha Crenshaw states that terrorists are "[cut off] from society; they inhabit a closed community that is forsaken only at great cost. . . . Isolation and internal consensus explain how the beliefs and values of a terrorist group can be so drastically at odds with that of a society at large," and this indeed can be seen with the rise and fall of groups such as the German Red Army Faction.[41]

Nonetheless, a degree of caution should be exercised with these distinctions. In Northern Ireland after the early 1970s, neither the republicans nor the loyalists could recruit active members beyond triple figures. By the 1980s, PIRA had only 300–400 "volunteers" pitted against around 25,000 military and police personnel, and it could not confront the British in open battle as the Taliban have repeatedly done against NATO forces in Afghanistan. While the Taliban's heavy combat losses have not impeded its insurgency, with PIRA the impact of security force successes such as the Loughgall ambush (May 8, 1987) had a disproportionate effect on its strength. Yet there is also no doubt that both PIRA and its loyalist adversaries exercised considerable influence over the Catholic and Protestant communities respectively, whether in the form of votes for their political wings in elections, informant and support networks for their operations, or the coercive effect of extortion and "punishment beatings."[42] In South Africa from 1961 to 1994, Umkhonto we Sizwe, the paramilitary wing of the African National Congress (ANC), failed to launch a successful insurgency due to the pervasiveness of the apartheid regime's security forces and also South Africa's use of coercive military raids to force "front-line" states such as Mozambique to cease support for the ANC. Yet in political terms, the ANC unquestionably commanded the allegiance of the majority of black South Africans, and this support was not only evident with the mass protest movement of the 1980s, but the ANC's victory in South Africa's first democratic elections in April 1994.[43]

The state's response: counter-terrorism and counter-insurgency

No government – democratic or otherwise – can accept the existence of an armed challenge to its authority, and terrorism/insurgency explicitly challenges what Max Weber (in a lecture to students at Munich University in January 1919) called the state's "monopoly of violence."[44] The terminology of COIN and CT needs to be treated with care because some authors draw a distinction between anti-terrorism (the defensive measures the state takes to protect itself and its citizens) and more offensive counter-terrorist measures. The latter may incorporate measures that are of contested legitimacy (such as the shooting of armed terrorists during hostage rescue missions or arrests) and those which Charles Townshend describes as "counter-terror," which are often flagrantly illegal (including death squad violence and the use of torture against suspects).[45] In this respect, a common feature of CT in contemporary democracies is the concern by human rights activists that the state's response to acts of violence committed by a handful of its citizens can lead to the erosion of civil liberties and the eventual imposition of authoritarianism. In Britain during the 1970s, there were widespread fears that military intervention in Northern Ireland would destabilize the UK as a whole and that the armed forces would even seize power in a coup.[46]

Scholars describe two competing models of CT. The criminal justice model treats terrorists as felons and emphasizes the use of policing and judicial methods to defeat them. In contrast, the war model treats terrorism as an existential threat requiring a military response.[47] Western theories of COIN also draw a contrast between an enemy-centric approach, which concentrates on the physical eradication of insurgents, and a population-centric approach which focuses on both the security of the civil populace and the application of political reforms to address the socio-economic grievances that have provoked insurgent violence. In practice, the theoretical distinctions between these models are easily blurred. Even with criminal justice approaches, the adoption of legislation designed to aid CT (the banning of political groups, looser regulations on police powers such as surveillance, or "control orders" allowing for conditions of house arrest) can arouse concerns over civil liberties. For democratic states waging COIN campaigns, a balance often has to be struck between "civil affairs" work amongst the population and military operations to stop insurgents from disrupting the former. Nonetheless, the conceptual definitions offered here provide a useful template for interpreting the state's response to the challenge to its "monopoly of violence." Does the government seek the obliteration of its internal adversaries, or does it counter the challenge to its own legitimacy? Is its main focus the attrition of the enemy through the death or capture of its cadres, or the undermining of its ideology and strategy?[48]

The war/enemy-centric models tend to be applied by authoritarian/totalitarian regimes, in addition to states with weak democratic foundations (for example, post-Soviet Russia).[49] One democratic state, Israel, has adopted a counter-terrorist strategy similar to the war model because of the existential threat posed by the PLO (historically) and Hamas and Hizbullah (currently).[50] In other cases, state law and established norms shape a country's response to internal security threats. Prior to 9/11, the Posse Comitatus Act imposed significant constraints on the use of the US armed forces in domestic operations. Institutional memories of Nazism, fascism, and the military junta of 1967–74 led the democratic governments of Germany, Italy, and Greece, respectively, to adopt counter-terrorist measures reflecting the criminal justice model.[51] Even in liberal democracies, however, state authorities can become embroiled in "counter-terror" practices that mirror terrorist tactics and violate the law. In Northern Ireland, the British Army and Royal Ulster Constabulary (RUC) have been accused of collusion with loyalist paramilitaries,[52] whilst in Spain's case, officials within the Socialist government ran a death squad (the GAL) against ETA during the 1980s.[53]

The British example offers an interesting case study, with its contrast between domestic and colonial traditions of countering internal violence. Aside from the RUC, British police forces were unarmed, and the armed forces can offer "military assistance to the civil authorities" in a variety of scenarios, from disaster relief to intervention in conditions bordering on insurrection (most notably with Northern Ireland in 1969). However, the British also have a tradition of imperial policing within their former empire that involves the overt use of coercion to intimidate the civilian population into acquiescence.[54] Both these traditions collided in Northern Ireland during the early 1970s, where the Army's heavy-handedness contributed to Catholic anger, increased support for PIRA, and the catastrophe of "Bloody Sunday" (January 30, 1972). Henceforth, the British authorities sought to demilitarize their confrontation with terrorism, symbolized by the policy of "police primacy" in 1977, which emphasized that the Army supported the civil authorities' efforts to restore order and that republican and loyalist terrorism was a criminal rather than a military problem.[55] The experience of Northern Ireland has particularly shaped the British government's current **Coun**ter-**Te**rrorism **St**rategy (CONTEST), which emphasizes the need to restrict radicalization and to address grievances within communities (notably the UK's Muslims), thereby avoiding the counter-productive tactics that antagonized Northern Ireland's Catholic population forty years ago.[56]

For some scholars, CT should be exclusively a problem for the police and judiciary,[57] although such an argument overlooks certain issues. For example, in Northern Ireland in

1969, the RUC was seen by Catholics as a sectarian force. British military intervention was originally intended both to restore authority and reform a governing system biased towards the Protestant community, although as one former British Army colonel noted, the early phases of its involvement demonstrated that "no army, however well it conducts itself, is suitable for police work."[58] In cases where states face terrorist violence combined with significant internal disorder, the established legal and policing apparatus may be stretched to breaking point, although it is worth noting that several countries have gendarmerie forces specifically trained to deal with internal disorder, some of which (such as Russia's Interior Ministry troops) are configured almost like regular armies and which take a direct role in fighting insurgents/terrorists.[59]

In certain cases, mass casualty attacks can impel governments to retaliate by military means, and such a response can have a cathartic effect on public opinion. In the aftermath of 9/11, it would have been politically impossible for any US president to suggest a "business as usual" approach to al-Qaeda, whilst a series of apartment bombings in Russia in September 1999 led Prime Minister Vladimir Putin to order the invasion of the separatist republic of Chechnya.[60] Yet while democracies may be obliged to use military means to protect their constitutions and citizens against non-state armed groups, it is important to consider the exact roles the armed forces should perform and their legal and political parameters. John Mackinlay's "global insurgency" thesis has been criticized for its proposals to militarize domestic British counter-terrorism, which could lead to a dangerous estrangement between the civil authorities and the UK's Muslims.[61] Scholars would also do well to contemplate the absurdity of South Africa's "total national strategy" in 1977, which treated every challenge to the apartheid system as a manifestation of a global Soviet-inspired conspiracy, and which led the white regime in Pretoria to order a series of actions (death squad killings against political opponents at home, terrorist attacks against ANC activists overseas, "false-flag" attacks to incite internecine violence in black townships, and military raids against neighboring countries) which combined ethical nihilism with an absence of a strategic rationale.[62]

When states are involved in CT or COIN overseas, the challenges of fighting insurgents/terrorists can be combined (as in Afghanistan) with the task of supporting a weak indigenous government. Afghanistan itself represents a unique case, as prior to October–November 2001 it represents the only case in which a transnational terrorist organization was able to effectively "hijack" an entire country, subverting the authority of the Taliban and co-opting it to its own ends.[63] Since the Taliban's overthrow, US-led coalition operations have involved both special forces raids and drone strikes to eliminate terrorist/insurgent leaders (CT), and a more complicated process of countering Taliban guerrilla activity, building up Afghan government forces, whilst conducting "civil affairs" work to rally the populace behind Hamid Karzai's regime (COIN). The problem in Afghanistan is that while militarily the Taliban are no match for NATO, in political terms the Kabul regime's fragility and corruption mean that it is losing the battle for governance against its internal foes, making it likely that Karzai's government will collapse after Western forces withdraw from the country.[64] Cronin notes that when facing non-state armed groups, "a government's top priority should not be to win people's hearts and minds, but rather to amplify the natural tendency of violent groups to *lose* them." Yet this becomes a far harder task if the state's authorities lose both their monopoly of violence and their ability to exercise political control, as is evident not only in Afghanistan but also in Somalia and North-West Pakistan[65]

Concluding points

In essence, terrorism is a tactic that – if employed by a non-state armed group – can indicate both weakness in numbers and support. Purely terrorist campaigns have not overthrown governments, unless the groups that have initiated them have successfully made a transition to a full insurgency. States can themselves erode the foundations of their constitutions by their own reactions to internal violence. Two prime examples include Uruguay during the early 1970s, where a military-led campaign against left-wing terrorists led to the overthrow of democracy and the establishment of a right-wing junta, and more recently Sri Lanka where the military suppression of the Tamil Tigers in the spring of 2009 has contributed to the rise of a more authoritarian system of governance.[66]

In the aftermath of 9/11, US, British, and other Western officials assert that "failed states" could – like Taliban-ruled Afghanistan – become havens for terrorist groups, although an observation of Lebanon since the early 1970s and Somalia after 1991 suggests that this is not entirely a new phenomenon. Yet al-Qaeda and its affiliates have demonstrated that they have no capability to exercise political authority, and while they can have a parasitical relationship with insurgencies they cannot actually initiate them, let alone use them to seize political power.[67] Other movements that have waged armed campaigns that have destabilized states also lack either the ideology or capacity to govern, and rather than follow the Maoist model of building a support base, the insurgent groups involved have resorted to indiscriminate violence against civilians. A prime example of this phenomenon is the Revolutionary United Front during the civil war in Sierra Leone (1991–2000).[68] A further conceptual issue involves the tendency of insurgent/terrorist movements to become criminalized (as demonstrated by PIRA and loyalist groups in Northern Ireland, and both the FARC and right-wing paramilitaries in Colombia) and the fact that organized criminal syndicates can employ terrorism in order to thwart a crackdown by the authorities; prime examples include the Sicilian Cosa Nostra during the 1980s and 1990s, the Medellín cartel in Colombia during the same period, or Mexican drug gangs at the time of writing.[69]

The Prussian military theorist Carl von Clausewitz (1780–1832) offers us a framework of analysis for examining the phenomena discussed here. Clausewitz's *On War* is often dismissed as a work relevant only for inter-state conflicts, but he reminds us that wars are fought for political objectives and that the belligerents involved seek to use violence in order to fulfill strategic ends. He emphasizes that "wars will always vary with the nature of their motives and the situations which gave rise to them" and stresses the importance of understanding the characteristics of a given conflict, "neither mistaking it for, nor trying to turn it into something alien to its nature." Whenever a non-state group launches an armed campaign to fight for a political outcome – whether the Red Army Faction in Germany during the 1970s or the Taliban in Afghanistan and Pakistan today – it is important to analyze each case on its own terms, assessing the characteristics of the conflicts concerned. What this chapter ultimately discusses is the ability and the will of non-state groups to employ lethal violence in support of their objectives, and the reality that any state's response in the ensuing conflict depends on its own analysis of its enemy's goals, capabilities, the extent of its support, and own weaknesses. These can indeed prove crucial in determining whether the state's efforts at COIN or CT, on the one hand, contain or defeat non-state armed groups or, on the other, instead incite more violence by and more popular support for the latter. Terrorism/insurgency involves a convergence among war, crime, and politics, and it is important for both academic specialists and officials to recognize and accept its conceptual complexity.[70]

Notes

The analysis, opinions, and conclusions expressed or implied here are those of the author and do not necessarily represent the views of the JSCSC, the Defence Academy, the MOD, or any other UK government agency.

1. See, for example, Bard O'Neill, *Insurgency and Terrorism: Inside Modern Revolutionary Warfare* (Dulles, VA: Brassey's, 1990). The British theorist and practitioner General Frank Kitson uses the term "wars of subversion" to discuss both phenomena, and "counter-subversive warfare" to describe the state's response. See Frank Kitson, *Low Intensity Operations: Subversion, Insurgency and Peacekeeping*, 2nd ed. (London: Faber & Faber, 1991), 28, 38.
2. Tim Judah, *Kosovo: War and Revenge* (New Haven, CT: Yale University Press, 2000); Tracey German, *Russia's Chechen War* (Abingdon, UK: Routledge, 2003); and AC71876, AFM1/10, *Countering Insurgency* (London: MOD, 2010), CS1-3.
3. "Mme Clinton; le but est 'd'éradiquer' Al-Qaida," *Le Monde*, November 17, 2009.
4. Warren Chin, "The United Kingdom and the War on Terror: The Breakdown of National and Military Strategy," *Contemporary Security Policy* 30, no. 1 (2009): 125–46; and Patrick Porter, "Long Wars and Long Telegrams: Containing Al-Qaeda," *International Affairs* 85, no. 2 (2009): 285–305. For more on the Global War on Terror, see Chapter 22 by Daveed Gartenstein-Ross in this volume.
5. Austin Long, "Small is Beautiful: The Counterterrorism Option in Afghanistan," *Orbis* 54, no. 2 (2010): 199–214; and Michael J. Boyle, "Do Counterterrorism and Counterinsurgency Go Together?' *International Affairs* 86, no. 2 (2010): 333–53.
6. David Martin Jones and M. L. R. Smith, "Whose Hearts and Whose Minds? The Curious Case of Global Counter-Insurgency," *Journal of Strategic Studies* 33, no. 1 (2010): 81–121.
7. Geraint Hughes, *My Enemy's Enemy: Proxy Warfare in International Politics* (Brighton: Sussex Academic Press, 2012), 7, 160; and Isabelle Duyvesteyn and Mario Fumerton, "Insurgency and Terrorism: Is There a Difference?' in *The Character of War in the 21st Century*, ed. Caroline Holmqvist-Jonsater and Christopher Coker (Abingdon, UK: Routledge, 2010), 27–8.
8. Bruce Hoffman, *Inside Terrorism*, 2nd ed. (New York: Columbia University Press, 2006), 1–41; Magnus Ranstorp and Paul Wilkinson, "Introduction: International Conference on Terrorism and Human Rights," *Terrorism & Political Violence* 17, no. 1 (2005): 3–4; Paul Wilkinson, *Terrorism Versus Democracy: The Liberal State Response* (London: Frank Cass, 2001), 1; FM3/24, *Counterinsurgency* (Washington, DC: Department of the Army, 2006), 1-1/1-29; and AFM1/10, 1-5/1-6.
9. David Kilcullen, *The Accidental Guerrilla: Fighting Small Wars in the Midst of a Big One* (London: C. Hurst, 2009), 59, 223.
10. George Orwell, "Politics and the English Language" (1946), http://iis.berkeley.edu/sites/default/files/Politics_%26_English_language.pdf (accessed July 19, 2013); and John Shy and Thomas W. Collier, "Revolutionary War," in *Makers of Modern Strategy: From Machiavelli to the Nuclear Age*, ed. Peter Paret (Princeton, NJ: Princeton University Press, 1986), 821.
11. Gerd Nonneman, "'Terrorism' and Political Violence in the Middle East and North Africa," in *International Terrorism Post-9/11*, ed. Asaf Siniver (Abingdon, UK: Routledge, 2010), 12–13, 17.
12. Stathis N. Kalyvas, *The Logic of Violence in Civil War* (Cambridge: Cambridge University Press, 2006).
13. Audrey Kurth Cronin, *How Terrorism Ends: Understanding the Decline and Demise of Terrorist Campaigns* (Princeton, NJ: Princeton University Press, 2009), 116.
14. Thomas Rid and Thomas Keaney, "Counterinsurgency in Context," in *Understanding Counterinsurgency: Doctrine, Operations and Challenges*, ed. Thomas Rid and Thomas Keaney (Abingdon, UK: Routledge, 2007), 256–7.
15. Kitson, *Low Intensity Operations*, passim; Christopher Bellamy, *The Evolution of Modern Land Warfare* (Abingdon, UK: Routledge 1990), 10; and M. L. R. Smith, "Guerrillas in the Mist: Reassessing Strategy and Low Intensity Warfare," *Review of International Studies* 29, no. 1 (2003): 19–37.
16. Daniel Byman et al., *Trends in Outside Support for Insurgent Movements* (Santa Monica, CA: RAND, 2001); Ideán Saleyhan, *Rebels without Borders: Transnational Insurgencies in World Politics*

(Ithaca, NY: Cornell University Press, 2009); and Anthony Vinci, *Armed Groups and the Balance of Power: The International Relations of Terrorists, Warlords and Insurgents* (Abingdon, UK: Routledge, 2008).

17 Yezid Sayigh, *Armed Struggle and the Search for State: The Palestinian National Movement, 1949–1993* (Oxford: Oxford University Press, 1997), 343–5.
18 Alistair Horne, *A Savage War of Peace: Algeria 1954–1962*, 2nd ed. (Basingstoke: Macmillan, 2002), 464–5.
19 Hughes, *My Enemy's Enemy*, 60–1, 99–102, 107, 109–11.
20 Smith, "Guerrillas in the Mist," 24; AFM1/10, 1-1. FM3/24, 1-1; and Steven Metz, "Rethinking Insurgency," in *The Routledge Handbook of Insurgency and Counterinsurgency*, ed. Paul B. Rich and Isabelle Duyvesteyn (Abingdon, UK: Routledge, 2012), 36; and Jones and Smith, "Whose Hearts and Whose Minds?" passim.
21 Ranstorp and Wilkinson, "Introduction," 4; and Freedman, "Terrorism as a Strategy," 317.
22 Lawrence Freedman, "Terrorism as a Strategy," *Government & Opposition*, 42, no. 3 (2007): 315.
23 Hoffman, *Inside Terrorism*, 1; and Christopher Andrew, *The Defence of the Realm: The Authorized History of MI5* (London: Penguin, 2010), 350.
24 David French, *The British Way in Counterinsurgency, 1945–1967* (Oxford: Oxford University Press, 2011), 42–73.
25 International Crisis Group, Middle Eastern Report No. 143, *Syria's Metastasising Conflicts*, Brussels, June 27, 2013, 3, 19–21; and "Tibetan Activism: No Impact," *The Economist*, March 31, 2012.
26 Richard Gillespie, "Political Violence in Argentina: Guerrillas, Terrorists, and *Carapintadas*," in *Terrorism in Context*, ed. Martha Crenshaw (University Park: Pennsylvania State University Press, 1995), 243.
27 Linda Robinson, *Tell Me How This Ends: General David Petraeus and the Search for a Way out of Iraq* (New York: Public Affairs, 2008), 5.
28 Hoffman, *Inside Terrorism*, 29–30; and Freedman, "Terrorism as a Strategy," 315.
29 Hoffman, *Inside Terrorism*, 21.
30 Timothy Garton Ash, "Is there a Good Terrorist?" *New York Review of Books*, November 29, 2001.
31 David Lewis, "Counterinsurgency in Sri Lanka: A Successful Model?' in *Insurgency and Counterinsurgency*, ed. Rich and Duyvesteyn, 312–23.
32 Martha Crenshaw, "The Effectiveness of Terrorism in the Algerian War," in *Terrorism in Context*, ed. Crenshaw, 473–513.
33 Thomas Mockaitis, *The "New" Terrorism: Myths and Reality* (London: Praeger, 2007), 5, 7.
34 Goldie Shabad and Francisco Jose Llera Ramo, "Political Violence in a Democratic State: Basque Terrorism in Spain," in *Terrorism in Context*, ed. Crenshaw, 410–69.
35 Victoria Schofield, *Kashmir in Conflict: India, Pakistan and the Unending War* (London: I. B. Tauris, 2003).
36 James Hughes, *Chechnya: From Nationalism to Jihad* (University Park, PA: Pennsylvania State University Press, 2007).
37 "The Jihadi Who Turned 'Supergrass,'" BBC News, September 13, 2006, news.bbc.co.uk/1/hi/programmes/5334594.stm (accessed June 18, 2014); and Lindsay Hilsum, *Sandstorm: Libya from Gaddafi to Revolution* (London: Faber & Faber, 2013), 129–30.
38 Audrey Kurth Cronin, *Ending Terrorism: Lessons for Defeating al-Qaeda*, Adelphi Paper No. 394 (Abingdon, UK: Routledge for International Institute of Strategic Studies, 2008), 16.
39 Metz, "Rethinking Insurgency," 38; and Alex P. Schmid, "Terrorism and Democracy," in *Western Responses to Terrorism*, ed. Alex P. Schmid and Roland Crelinstein (Abingdon, UK: Frank Cass, 2003), 14–19.
40 Freedman, "Terrorism as a Strategy," 325–6.
41 Hoffman, *Inside Terrorism*, 35; and Duyvesteyn and Fumerton, "Insurgency and Terrorism," 31. Crenshaw is quoted on 38.
42 Peter Bergen, "Mowing the Lawn," *Prospect*, no. 152 (November 2008); and Ed Moloney, *A Secret History of the IRA* (London: Penguin, 2002), 318–19.
43 Kevin O'Brien, "A Blunted Spear: The Failure of the African National Congress/South African Communist Party Revolutionary War Strategy 1961–1990," *Small Wars & Insurgencies* 14, no. 2 (2003): 27–70; and Stephen Ellis, *External Mission: The ANC in Exile 1960–1990* (London: C. Hurst, 2012).

44 Max Weber, *Politics as a Vocation* (Philadelphia, PA: Fortress Press, 1965); and Freedman, "Terrorism as a Strategy," 324.
45 Randall D. Law, *Terrorism: A History* (Cambridge: Polity Press, 2009), 7; Metz, "Rethinking Insurgency," 35; and Charles Townshend, *Terrorism: A Very Short Introduction* (Oxford: Oxford University Press, 2002), 114–15.
46 Roger Faligot, *Britain's Military Strategy in Ireland: The Kitson Experiment* (London: Zed Press, 1983); and Hew Strachan, *The Politics of the British Army* (Oxford: Clarendon Press, 1997), 184–90.
47 M. L. R. Smith and Sophie Roberts, "War in the Gray: Exploring the Concept of Dirty War," *Studies in Conflict & Terrorism* 31, no. 5 (2008): 385–8.
48 Geraint Hughes, "The Cold War and Counter-Insurgency," *Diplomacy & Statecraft* 22, no. 1 (2011): 145; and Cronin, *Ending Terrorism*, 32. The tensions between coercion and conciliation can, to take one example, be seen in Annex A to CGS/1180, *Directive for General Officer Commanding Northern Ireland*, December 15, 1972, DEFE25/282, National Archives of the United Kingdom, Kew, London.
49 Cerwyn Moore and David Barnard-Wills, "Russia and Counter-terrorism. A Critical Appraisal," in *International Terrorism*, ed. Siniver, 144–67.
50 Daniel Byman, *A High Price: The Triumphs and Failures of Israeli Counterterrorism* (Oxford: Oxford University Press, 2011); and Aaron J. Klein, *Striking Back: The 1972 Munich Olympics Massacre and Israel's Deadly Response* (New York: Random House, 2005). For more on the histories of these organizations, as well as Israel's counter-terrorist practices, see Chapters 16 and 18 by Boaz Ganor and David Cook, respectively, in this volume.
51 Geraint Hughes, *The Military's Role in Counterterrorism: Examples and Implications for Liberal Democracies* (US Army War College, Carlisle PA: Strategic Studies Institute, 2011), 25–7.
52 Peter Taylor, *Brits* (London: Bloomsbury Press, 2002), 288–94.
53 Paddy Woodworth, *Dirty War, Clean Hands: ETA, the GAL and Spanish Democracy* (Cork: Cork University Press, 2001).
54 James Salt and M. L. R. Smith, "Reassessing Military Assistance to the Civil Powers: Are Traditional British Anti-Terrorist Responses Still Effective?" *Low Intensity Conflict & Law Enforcement* 13, no. 3 (2005): 227–49; and French, *British Way in COIN*, passim.
55 Huw Bennett, "From Direct Rule to Motorman: Adjusting British Military Strategy for Northern Ireland in 1972," *Studies in Conflict & Terrorism* 33, no. 6 (2010): 511–32; Peter Neumann, *Britain's Long War: British Government Strategy in Northern Ireland, 1969–98* (Basingstoke: Palgrave, 2003); and *Joint Directive by General Officer Commanding Northern Ireland and Chief Constable Royal Ulster Constabulary*, January 12, 1977, DEFE11/917 (NAUK).
56 Cm.8123, *The United Kingdom's Strategy for Countering International Terrorism* (2011), 11–12, 58–71.
57 George Kassimeris, "Introduction," in *Playing Politics with Terrorism: A Users Guide*, ed. George Kassimeris (London: C. Hurst, 2007), 11–12.
58 Michael Dewar, *The British Army in Northern Ireland* (London: Arms and Armour Press, 1997), 38; Adam Roberts, "Ethics, Terrorism and Counter-Terrorism," *Terrorism & Political Violence* 1, no. 1 (1989): 60; and Thomas Hennessey, *The Evolution of the Troubles, 1970–72* (Dublin: Irish Academic Press, 2007).
59 Alice Hills, "Insurgency, Counterinsurgency and Policing," in *Insurgency and Counterinsurgency*, ed. Rich and Duyvesteyn, 103, 106.
60 Cronin, *Ending Terrorism*, 21; and Robert Saunders, "A Conjurer's Game: Vladimir Putin and the Politics of Presidential Prestidigitation," in *Playing Politics*, ed. Kassimeris, 220–49.
61 Hughes, *Counterterrorism*, 24–37, 139–43; John Mackinlay, *The Insurgent Archipelago* (London: C. Hurst, 2009), 213–14; and Paul Rich, "Counterinsurgency or a War on Terror? The War in Afghanistan and the Debate on Western Strategy," *Small Wars & Insurgencies* 21, no. 2 (2010): 415–20.
62 Annette Seegers, *The Military in the Making of Modern South Africa* (London: I. B. Tauris, 1996), 164; and James Sanders, *Apartheid's Friends: The Rise and Fall of South Africa's Secret Service* (London: John Murray, 2006), 198–219, 255–79.
63 Roy Gutman, *How We Missed the Story: Osama bin Laden, the Taliban, and the Hijacking of Afghanistan* (Washington, DC: United States Institute of Peace, 2008).
64 Boyle, "Counterterrorism and Counterinsurgency," 343–4, 352–3; Chin, "United Kingdom," 136–7; and "Afghan Surprise in Ghazni Province," *The Independent*, April 10, 2012.

65 Chin, "United Kingdom," 127–8; and Cronin, *Ending Terrorism*, 29. Emphasis as in original.
66 Cronin, *How Terrorism Ends*, 125–7, 129–31; Freedman, "Terrorism as a Strategy," 319; and Boyle, "Counterterrorism and Counterinsurgency," 340–1.
67 Boyle, "Counterterrorism and Counterinsurgency," 335; Chin, "United Kingdom," 133–5; and Porter, "Long Wars," 288, 303–4.
68 Ibrahim Abdullah, "Bush Path to Destruction: The Origin and Character of the Revolutionary United Front/Sierra Leone," *Journal of Modern African Studies* 36, no. 2 (1998): 203–35.
69 John Dickie, *Cosa Nostra: A History of the Sicilian Mafia* (London: Hodder & Stoughton, 2007), 379–90; Mark Bowden, *Killing Pablo* (New York: Atlantic Books, 2002); and "Drug Policy in Latin America: Burn-out and Battle Fatigue," *The Economist*, March 16, 2012.
70 Salt and Smith, "Military Assistance," 236; Carl von Clausewitz, *On War*, trans. and ed. Michael Howard and Peter Paret (Princeton, NJ: Princeton University Press, 1984), 87–9; and Smith, "Guerrillas in the Mist," passim.

Further reading

Boyle, Michael J. "Do Counterterrorism and Counterinsurgency Go Together?" *International Affairs* 86, no. 2 (2010): 333–53.
Cronin, Audrey Kurth. *How Terrorism Ends: Understanding the Decline and Demise of Terrorist Campaigns*. Princeton, NJ: Princeton University Press, 2009.
Duyvesteyn, Isabelle, and Mario Fumerton. "Insurgency and Terrorism: Is There a Difference?" in *The Character of War in the 21st Century*, edited by Caroline Holmqvist-Jonsater and Christopher Coker, 27–41. Abingdon, UK: Routledge, 2010.
Jones, David Martin, and M. L. R. Smith. "Whose Hearts and Whose Minds? The Curious Case of Global Counter-Insurgency." *Journal of Strategic Studies* 33, no. 1 (2010): 81–121.
Kalyvas, Stathis N. *The Logic of Violence in Civil War*. Cambridge: Cambridge University Press, 2006.
Kitson, Frank. *Low Intensity Operations: Subversion, Insurgency and Peacekeeping*. 2nd ed. London: Faber & Faber, 1991.
O'Neill, Bard. *Insurgency and Terrorism: Inside Modern Revolutionary Warfare*. Dulles, VA: Brassey's, 1990.
Saleyhan, Idean. *Rebels without Borders: Transnational Insurgencies in World Politics*. Ithaca, NY: Cornell University Press, 2009.
Smith, M. L. R. "Guerrillas in the Mist: Reassessing Strategy and Low Intensity Warfare." *Review of International Studies* 29, no. 1 (2003): 19–37.
Vinci, Anthony. *Armed Groups and the Balance of Power: The International Relations of Terrorists, Warlords and Insurgents*. Abingdon, UK: Routledge, 2008.

26

SUICIDE TERRORISM

Susanne Martin

If airline hijackings were the "emblematic" deed of terrorists of the 1970s and 1980s, suicide attacks would seem to be the equivalent today.[1] Like skyjackings, suicide attacks are dramatic events that are disturbing for their unpredictable nature and high death tolls. Suicide attacks perpetuate fear and insecurity, emotions the groups employing these tactics use for political effect. For terrorist groups, adopting suicide tactics is a sign of adaptation or innovation, a response to changing circumstances, such as improvements in airport security and permissive ideologies.[2] Using suicide attacks also allows actors to signal the highest devotion to a cause and the likely limits of counter-strategies aimed at deterring those who are already willing to die.[3]

Although there have been variations in the intensity and frequency of suicide attacks across time and space, evidence suggests a growing threat from this type of attack, with increases in the number of groups using suicide tactics, the lethality of these attacks, and the number of countries affected by them.[4] Suicide attacks are horrific, with at least one terrible death or dismemberment at the site of each attack. In most places, however, suicide terrorism is not part of everyday life; it has typically been considered something that happens elsewhere or rarely, something that affects others. Such perceptions of suicide terrorism as a faraway threat changed with the surprising scale of the attacks in the United States on September 11, 2001. A large volume of research devoted to explaining the changing nature of terrorist threats and the modern advent of suicide tactics dates from this time.

The pages that follow offer an overview of the evolution of suicide tactics as a form of terrorism. As is customary, and necessary, this chapter begins with a discussion of definitions. More than being concerned with the definition of terrorism, which is addressed elsewhere in this volume,[5] the focus here is on defining suicide terrorism. The chapter continues with a survey of the predecessors of modern suicide terrorists, giving attention to historical examples of suicide tactics in terrorism and warfare and changes in the uses and users of these tactics over time. It would be impossible in these few pages to include a complete overview of research on suicide terrorism. Instead, the chapter concludes with an assessment of what is known and not yet known about modern-day suicide terrorism, including suggestions as to why individuals and groups choose to carry out these types of attacks.

Defining suicide terrorism

It is impossible to arrive at a consensus definition of suicide terrorism so long as debates continue regarding the definition of terrorism.[6] The lack of consensus is not surprising given disagreements over definitional elements, problems associated with identifying whether or not definitional elements are present in a given case, and inconsistencies in applications of the terrorism label. At the same time, even though "one man's terrorist" may play the part of "another man's freedom fighter," this is no reason to assume that a "freedom fighter" will not use terrorist tactics while fighting for "freedom."[7] After all, freedom is an objective; terrorism is a tactic.[8] Moreover, a group that uses terrorism is a terrorist group, but a terrorist group may use any number of other tactics.

One "consensus" definition of terrorism includes three elements: terrorists use or threaten to use violence; they seek publicity so as to influence a larger audience; and, they do so in order to achieve political goals.[9] The definition may or may not include two additional elements. First, if terrorism is defined by the terror its agents create or desire to create, then a reference to this presumed psychological impact seems relevant. Second, if a distinction is to be made between terrorism and other types of violence, such as guerrilla warfare, comments regarding the targets of attacks would be appropriate.

In fact, questions regarding the targets of attacks and deaths of attackers are crucial in the study of suicide terrorism. Suicide attacks garner public attention when the immediate targets are viewed as innocent civilians as well as when the targets may be identified as "combatants." While terrorists have used suicide tactics in modern times, a large number of suicide attacks have been perpetrated against "combatant" targets or in the context of war. Attacks such as these may create terror; yet they might not be labeled as terrorist attacks.

Many questions follow from the coincidence of tactics often associated with terrorism being used against targets not typically associated with terrorism. One of the most relevant disagreements is the designation of "combatant." We know that terrorist groups have targeted civilians in some attacks and the military or police in others. If military and police are considered to be combatants, attacks on these targets might not be labeled as terrorism. A similar question may be raised regarding attacks directed at a state (e.g., infrastructure, personnel). Must combatants wear uniforms or carry weapons; does the label apply to peacekeeping forces; what about diplomats; would an attack on an embassy be an attack on a state? Are attacks against such targets, when perpetrated by non-state actors, more appropriately labeled as guerrilla warfare? Moreover, does the context – the time, location, prevalence of peace or war – within which an attack takes place matter? Suicide attacks on the US marine barracks in Beirut in 1983, American embassies in Kenya and Tanzania in 1998, and the *USS Cole* in a Yemeni harbor in 2000 have been called terrorist attacks, while the same label was at least initially withheld in the case of the September 11, 2012, attack on the American embassy in Libya.[10] One may wonder whether the "terrorism" designation would have been forthcoming – or easier – had the 2012 attack been a suicide attack. One also may ponder the meaning implicit in the choosing of words that included general references to "acts of terror" while withholding the "terrorism" label from this particular act. Because suicide terrorism is, first, a form of terrorism, the above considerations should precede discussions of what is, and perhaps is not, suicide terrorism.

Once the meaning of terrorism has been established, suicide terrorism can be differentiated from non-suicide terrorism by the death of the attacker at his or her own hand in the process of carrying out an attack.[11] The designation of an attack as a suicide attack requires more than an attacker's death. There is a presumption that the attacker must die in order for a mission to be successful and that the attacker will kill others or attempt to do so in the process of carrying out an attack. Moreover, perpetrators of suicide attacks must be willing to die, expect to die, or must die in order to complete their missions. These are premeditated, life-taking acts perpetrated with murderous intent. They are not life-saving acts, as might best describe the acts of soldiers who make split-second decisions that may result in their own deaths but will likely save others.

Some attacks are relatively easy to identify as suicide attacks, especially when attackers use the types of weapons (e.g., suicide vests) that are most likely to result in their deaths. The designation is less clear for attackers using other types of weapons (such as knives or guns), even though they may expect to die in the process of carrying out an attack. There are also problems associated with an unknown number of cases in which missions do not go as planned (for instance, explosives detonate accidentally), an individual embarks upon a suicide mission unwillingly (i.e., by force) or unknowingly (perhaps by driving an explosive-laden vehicle that is detonated remotely), or an attacker survives an attempted suicide mission. There may also be questions regarding consent. It is unlikely that an eight-year-old girl who is asked to carry a satchel full of explosives would be considered a suicide terrorist – or even a suicide attacker. Would the same be true for a fourteen-year-old boy who participates in such acts but may not be sufficiently mature to understand the implications of these acts or his alternatives?[12] The problem is more than one of conceptual confusion.

Scholars focusing on suicide terrorism have dealt with questions regarding targets, intent, and consent by using alternative labels. It is not uncommon to find studies broadened to include suicide attacks, missions, or operations; or narrowed to focus on a type of suicide attack, such as suicide bombings.[13] A focus on suicide bombings, strictly interpreted, would likely exclude some suicide attacks, including those on September 11, 2001, while including other attacks, such as suicide bombings carried out in the context of war. Although the preference for alternative concepts is partly a response to problems associated with defining terrorism, it is also a consequence of the expectation that terrorists perpetrate similar types of attacks against military, state, and civilian targets and may do so for similar reasons or in pursuit of the same objectives.[14] It is also likely that terrorists do not distinguish between combatant and non-combatant targets in the same ways or for the same reasons that other audiences do.

Ancient and pre-modern "suicide terrorists"

Attacks involving the death of the attacker are not unique to modern times. There are numerous historical examples of terrorists expecting death as part of carrying out a mission. One of the best known were the so-called Assassins, followers of an extremist branch of Shi'a Islam in medieval Syria and Persia who used assassinations as a form of terrorism.[15] The Assassins wanted to create a single Islamic community that would abide by their sect's religious views. This was not a popular position, as most Muslims considered the Assassins heretical. The Assassins, viewing other Muslims similarly, began a campaign of assassinations of opposing leaders. In a time before mass media, the Assassins attacked in places where there would be many witnesses. Their method of attack was stabbing, requiring attacks to take place at close range. Rather than hiding within the crowd of witnesses, individual Assassins are said to have accepted capture and subsequent execution. Assassins expected death, which made embarking upon an attack a type of suicide mission.

Suicide attacks would be used again by members of Sunni Muslim communities in Malabar, India; Atjeh in Sumatra, Indonesia; and Mindanao and Sulu in the Philippines as early as the 1500s and into the twentieth century. Traders from the Middle East began visiting and settling these coastal regions at least as early as the first century CE. Islam spread along these same trade routes centuries later, after being established in the Middle East.

These earlier colonizers were followed by a wave of European expansion. From the fifteenth century, European traders and settlers brought economic and political competition as well as a cultural challenge. By attempting to spread Christianity, the newcomers threatened Islamic culture in the region. Adding to the threat, local Muslims tended to be militarily weak in comparison to the Europeans. Their weakness was demonstrated by the many failed attempts of established Muslim communities to rout the waves of Spanish, Portuguese, Dutch, and British colonizers.

One response to the European-Christian threat involved the religious framing of the threat posed to local Muslim societies by these foreign cultures. Zayn al-Din, a Sunni in southern India, framed the Muslims' resistance to the newcomers as a jihad and those who died in the process of carrying out jihad as *shahuda*, or martyrs. His ideas, put in writing in the sixteenth century, presumably inspired militants in Malabar to begin using suicide attacks against the Europeans, with the expectation that the attackers would become martyrs. Suicide attacks became part of anti-colonial warfare, which later evolved into anti-colonial terrorism as the militants weakened.[16]

As with the Assassins, there are similarities and differences between these anti-colonial terrorists and other terrorists, past and present. For these Muslim communities in India, Indonesia, and the Philippines, suicide terrorism was the weapon of the weakest, most vulnerable actors, likely used when the militants could no longer challenge the Europeans militarily. Unlike the first modern suicide terrorists, the Muslims of these communities were Sunnis. As such, their acceptance of jihad and martyrdom challenges any view that the "culture of martyrdom" is unique to Shi'a Islam.

Although far less may be known about the ancient Shi'a Assassins and their pre-modern Sunni counterparts, it is possible to draw many parallels between them and their modern-day counterparts.[17] Much like the latter, the Assassins' strategy and acceptance of death drew on precedents established centuries earlier within what would become the Shi'a branch of Islam. Also, like some of their successors, the Assassins used their acceptance of death to send a message. In this way, it is possible to view the Assassins' deaths as necessary for the success of their operations, even though the Assassins' did not kill themselves while killing their victims. Also like their successors, the Assassins sought large audiences for their attacks; unlike some of their successors, they did not seek large numbers of victims.[18]

Perhaps because more is known about the pre-modern suicide attackers of India, Indonesia, and the Philippines, it is easier to identify apparent parallels between them and their modern counterparts. Much as modern groups have done, there is evidence that the pre-modern terrorists reinforced beliefs regarding self-sacrifice as an altruistic act for the benefit of larger communities through songs, poems, and literature. Pre-modern terrorists also used rituals associated with preparing for a suicide attack and threats of public shaming, making it difficult for would-be martyrs to retreat from a commitment, once made. Typical pre-modern suicide attackers tended to be younger, be poorer, and have fewer ties to their community, a pattern apparent in some modern-day examples. Moreover, although religious precedents and interpretations gave support to ideas associated with jihad and martyrdom, there is a suggestion that, over time, these attacks became "culturally sanctioned forms of suicide rather than true jihads."[19] Perhaps these developments were a result of a weakening of the guiding ideologies and the failures of suicide attacks to achieve desired goals. It is also interesting to note that, much like in other time periods, not all of the Muslim groups facing European colonization used suicide tactics, even in the pre-modern era. Among South Asian Muslims, for instance, it was only those in Malabar (on the southwest coast of India) who used suicide tactics. As true today as in the past, the attacks were not as important militarily as they were psychologically.[20]

Modern-day suicide attacks

Based on what is known about ancient and pre-modern groups, many of the earliest suicide attacks do not meet the definition of suicide terrorism discussed earlier. Their targets could be designated as combatant, and some of the suicide attacks took place in the context of warfare. In many cases, it could be argued that the attackers' deaths were of qualified necessity for the success of their missions. The same is true of some early terrorist attacks in the modern period.

The first "modern" terrorists of the late 1800s and early 1900s were not like the suicide attackers who would later embark upon their missions with the expectation of dying in the process.[21] Although they may have expected to be captured, with the possible exception of some of those carrying out attacks with volatile weapons, such as dynamite,[22] most attackers expected to survive their missions. In this way, the anarchist "martyrs" were much like the Assassins when they took credit for their attacks and accepted the consequences, both as a means of differentiating themselves from criminals and communicating and legitimizing their "terrorism" to a broader audience.[23]

Suicide tactics were also part of twentieth-century warfare. One of the best-known examples occurred during the final stages of World War II. Japan's loss was almost certain when the Japanese military began sending soldiers on suicide missions. Japan's arsenal for one-way missions included planes (*tokkotai* or *kamikazes*), gliders (*oka*), underwater torpedoes (*kaiten*), and motorboats (*shinyo*). Although they could not change the outcome of the war, the Japanese were able to raise the costs of war. They also created what might be best described as terror among the Allied forces in the Pacific.[24] In fact, the Japanese military was not alone in its use of suicide missions during World War II. Soviet and German soldiers used suicide planes. The Italians attempted a suicide attack with torpedoes and boats. Like the Japanese attacks, these were planned and premeditated.[25]

The Viet Cong created terror a generation later with their targeting of local Vietnamese populations. In November 1967, a Viet Cong directive called for the creation of "suicide cells," the presumed purpose of which was to incite mass uprisings, similar to what the "first wave" anarchists before them had sought.[26] This was part of a strategy, which included intimidating local Vietnamese while simultaneously engaging opposing military forces. The members of suicide cells were reportedly young, mostly teenagers.[27]

In 1981, another group of young people began a campaign that would make some of them "martyrs" for their cause.[28] Like the anarchists, Provisional Irish Republican Army prisoners in Northern Ireland wanted to be recognized as political prisoners rather than as criminals. To this end, the inmates began a hunger strike, the results of which were public attention and, eventually, their desired status. Ten died during the strike, including the strike's leader, Bobby Sands, who nevertheless survived long enough to defeat a high-profile unionist candidate and become an elected member of the UK Parliament in a by-election that was deliberately uncontested by other republican or nationalist parties. The hunger strikers who died are memorialized in murals, including several in West Belfast.[29]

It was also around this time that voluntary death became a tactic of warfare in Iran. Most Iranians are Shi'a. As with the ancient Assassins, Shi'ite readings of history and veneration for martyrdom provided favorable conditions for encouraging voluntary death among Iran's soldiers in their war against the secular, Sunni-led Iraq. In Iran, a young Iranian soldier is celebrated as the first suicide bomber of his time; he would also be the youngest. At thirteen years of age, Hossein Fahmideh reportedly detonated the explosives he was carrying in an attempt to halt an approaching Iraqi tank. Fahmideh became famous, a national hero and an example for other Iranian soldiers.[30]

Although Fahmideh is known, especially in Iran, as the first suicide bomber, he was not a suicide terrorist. His attack took place in war, and his target was the opponent's military. In carrying out his attack he presumably thought of saving some lives while taking others. Fahmideh reportedly decided to carry out the attack only moments before acting, allowing for limited premeditation. In these ways, Fahmideh's act may not differ much from those of soldiers who have made similar decisions on battlefields that would result in their deaths and opponents' deaths but could save others' lives. Fahmideh's attack is, however, different from other split-second decisions, such as a decision to throw oneself upon a grenade within a confined space. In such a scenario, deaths would be likely regardless of one soldier's intervention; however, without this intervention, the death count would likely be higher. More importantly, an intervention of this sort is not an attack. Neither scenario makes a soldier a terrorist, much less a suicide terrorist.

Fahmideh's act also differs from those of many of Iran's young soldiers who presumably followed his example. Iran's developing "culture of martyrdom" provided inspiration for the young soldiers, who seemed to accept, even seek, death.[31] Those who were tasked with clearing minefields were more effective than the animals that had been used previously; they were described as "machine-like in their mass sacrifice" and as "dehumanized weapons for the larger jihad."[32] Iran's young soldiers may have behaved in a way that appears suicidal; however, this understanding would be debatable on the basis of their beliefs and motivations. Regardless, their acts are not examples of suicide terrorism.

There are numerous other examples, among them the case of Dalal al-Mughrabi, a Palestinian teenager and a leader within the secular Fatah movement when she led a mission into Israel that would become the country's deadliest terrorist attack.[33] Thirty-eight Israeli civilians and one American were killed, the majority when their hijacked bus exploded.[34] This attack took place in March 1978, prior to the Islamic Revolution and the Iran–Iraq War, before Hossein Fahmideh reached his teenage years. Even though al-Mughrabi was viewed by some Palestinians "as a heroine and a martyr," it was some time later that her attack was retrospectively labeled a suicide attack.[35] The attack on civilians was terrorism; the presumed absence of a plan of escape gives the appearance of a suicide mission. As such, the attack may be labeled suicide terrorism.

Contemporary suicide terrorism

The story of contemporary suicide terrorism typically begins in 1979 with Iran's Islamic Revolution and with events that, as described above, were not terrorism. Iran's revolution brought the first modern Islamist government to power, in spite of (perhaps also in response to) America's support for the shah's pro-Western regime. The Islamists' success in overthrowing the regime demonstrated that a weaker party could challenge a greater power's influence, at least on their home turf. Communist and secular Vietnamese insurgents also learned that weaker actors could withstand superior foreign armies on their soil; in contrast, the Islamists understood their own victory in religious terms. Theirs was not simply a victory of the weak over the strong; it was also seen as a victory of good over evil. Such a lesson was reinforced a decade later by the "Afghan Arabs" when their comparatively weak forces confronted another great power, the Soviet Union. The Soviets eventually withdrew from Afghanistan and, not long afterwards, the USSR collapsed. This was not a victory over capitalists or communists; it was the expulsion of "infidels".

The spread of Iran's martyrdom culture outside that country was not an accident. Iran provided support for the militant Shi'a Islamists in Lebanon who introduced suicide attacks in the early 1980s in the midst of that country's fifteen-year sectarian war.[36] The first suicide attack in Lebanon occurred on December 15, 1981, with the bombing of Iraq's embassy in Beirut. Within two years, four suicide attacks targeted foreign government and military installations, including the November 11, 1982, attack on the Israeli military in Tyre, Lebanon; an April 18, 1983, attack on the American Embassy in Beirut; and near-simultaneous attacks on the barracks of American and French peacekeepers in Beirut on October 23, 1983. The American embassy in Beirut was attacked again on September 2, 1984. It was not long before references to "suicide terrorism" became "virtually synonymous with the Hezbollah organization," which was at this time the party responsible for most of these attacks.[37] Despite references to terrorism, however, the majority of suicide attacks in Lebanon were aimed at government and military targets.

This began to change in 1987 as suicide tactics were adopted by groups operating outside of Lebanon.[38] The leader of Sri Lanka's Tamil Tigers, Velupillai Prabhakaran, is said to have been "impressed" by Hizbullah's use of suicide car bombings. As a result, he formed a "special unit" called the Black Tigers to carry out similar attacks and sought training in these tactics in Lebanon.[39] On July 5, 1987, the Tigers carried out their first suicide attack, a truck bombing at a Sri Lankan military base in Jaffna. The Tigers would quickly become the most prolific users of suicide tactics, carrying out more suicide attacks than "all other Islamic groups combined" between 1983 and 2000.[40] This was, of course, prior to the advent of suicide attacks in Iraq.

Despite their affinity for the Islamists' tactics, the Tigers were a secular group with nationalist–separatist aspirations: they were Tamils while the majority of the Sri Lankan population is Sinhalese. Their motivation for adopting suicide tactics seems to be their presumed effectiveness against greater powers.[41] After all, the Americans left Lebanon after the attacks on the American embassy and military.

While most of the suicide attacks in the 1980s were directed at military or government targets, civilian targets became more common during the 1990s. This is the time when Palestinian groups Hamas and Islamic Jihad (PIJ) began carrying out suicide attacks. Both groups were Islamist with ties to Egypt's Muslim Brotherhood. The fact that most Palestinians were Sunni did not prevent them from seeking assistance from their Shi'a neighbors in Lebanon; nor did this difference prevent Hizbullah from wanting to assist the Palestinians.[42] After all, the Palestinian groups and Hizbullah recognized a common adversary in Israel.[43]

The timing of the first Palestinian suicide attacks coincided with the implementation of the Oslo Accords and dissatisfaction with the slow pace of Israel's exit from Palestinian territories.[44] Hamas's first suicide attack was on April 16, 1993, a car bombing targeting civilian and military buses at the Mechola Junction, near the Mechola settlement in the West Bank. Two people died in the attack; both were Palestinian. PIJ followed with suicide attacks targeting buses in the West Bank and Gaza Strip in September and October 1993.

Thus, within a few years of the contemporary advent of suicide terrorism, the main perpetrators were religious and secular groups with Hindu and Shi'ite and Sunni Muslim members. Some had religious objectives; others were nationalist–separatists; some were both. Suicide attacks were carried out in states with Muslim, Buddhist, Christian, and Jewish majorities.[45]

By the mid-1990s, suicide tactics were being used by groups operating in Algeria, Egypt, India, Pakistan, Saudi Arabia, and Turkey. Some of the attacks were carried out on foreign soils. Still active, Hizbullah carried out a 1992 suicide attack in Buenos Aires, Argentina, against the Israeli embassy. Two years later, a suicide bomber targeted a Jewish center, also in Buenos Aires, killing at least eighty-five and injuring hundreds. The Armed Islamic Group (GIA) of Algeria began its suicide campaign with attacks on a power plant and market in 1995.[46] The same year, in the context of the Bosnian War, affiliates of Egypt's al-Jama'a al-Islamiyya attempted to destroy a police station in Rijeka, Croatia, with a suicide car bombing. Suicide attacks continued in Lebanon with an attack on a naval target on May 19, 1997, the first for Amal, Hizbullah's secular competitor for the support of Lebanon's Shi'a population.

The Kurdistan Workers' Party (PKK), a secular nationalist and leftist group, began carrying out suicide attacks against police and military targets in Turkey in 1996 and against civilians in 1998. The 1998 attack was followed by at least nine attacks within a year, seven of which were aimed at civilian targets. For the PKK, suicide missions were undertaken from a position of weakness in terms of popular support among the Kurdish population and from a position of "strategic inferiority" in relation to the Turkish government.[47]

Sikh terrorists seeking to create an autonomous state in the Punjab region of India were similarly disconnected from their presumed constituency. Among their activities, the group claimed a single suicide attack in 1995; three other attacks were either unclaimed (1993) or thwarted (1999 and 2000).[48]

Whereas the Sikh terrorists may have been motivated primarily by nationalist–separatist objectives, Kashmiri and Chechen terrorists combined nationalist–separatist and religious objectives. Although Kashmiri separatists first used suicide tactics in 1996 in an attack on a bus in Lahore, Pakistan, which claimed fifty-two lives, a concerted "suicide terrorist campaign" did not begin until 2000.[49] Kashmiri groups Lashkar-e-Taiba and Jaesh-e-Mohammed began their campaigns with attacks on the military and police in India.[50] Chechen separatists began their campaign around the same time in June–July 2000 with a cluster of suicide attacks aimed primarily at Russian military and police. Among their suicide attacks, which numbered 28 by 2006, were attacks on civilians in a Moscow theater in October 2002, an attack on a school in Beslan, North Ossetia, in September 2004, and bombings on two passenger planes in August 2004.[51]

Around this time, particularly between 2000 and 2003, there was a significant increase in the use of suicide terrorism by the militant wings of Hamas and Islamic Jihad. This timing corresponded with the Second Intifada and with the adoption of suicide tactics by secular groups, including Fatah's al-Aqsa Martyrs Brigade and the Popular Front for the Liberation of Palestine (PFLP). Although the Palestinian groups attacked military, police, and government targets, the main targets of their suicide attacks were civilians. Palestinian suicide terrorists targeted Israel's buses, shopping centers, and restaurants.[52]

Suicide terrorism in the twenty-first century

The terrorist groups discussed thus far used suicide tactics to achieve local objectives, such as national autonomy, regime change, political power, or the imposition of Islamic law within the borders of a state. While some of these groups continued their operations into the twenty-first century, there are important differences between the suicide terrorism that dominates the twenty-first century and the suicide terrorism of earlier periods.

The first difference concerns religion. Although religious "narratives"[53] are not new to suicide terrorism, the decline of secular actors and the growing relevance of Islamist and salafi-jihadist ideologies are. The Taliban is an Islamist group that maintains primarily local ambitions. Jemaah Islamiyah is a salafi-jihadist group seeking to establish an Islamic state in the vicinity of Indonesia. Both groups are fundamentalist and violent, though the two labels do not necessarily go together. Islamist groups tend to be fundamentalist but not necessarily violent. Salafism is also fundamentalist but not violent. In contrast, salafi-jihad is the most extreme version of salafism, and it is violent. Some salafi-jihadist groups, such as Jemaah al-Islamiyah, maintain local objectives; others, such as al-Qaeda and its network of affiliates and "franchises,"[54] have global objectives. Al-Qaeda formed in the context of the Soviet withdrawal from Afghanistan in the late 1980s, and its far-reaching objectives are framed as a global jihad. The group seeks to place separate Muslim states within a single political and religious entity and favors a single interpretation of Islam and Islamic rule over an otherwise diverse religious community. National identities and local rule would presumably disappear.[55]

The second difference involves the sectarian allegiances of the main actors. The new suicide terrorists tend to be Sunnis, including salafi-jihadists, rather than Shi'a. The former were not the first modern users of suicide tactics but, like the secular Tamil Tigers, they may have adopted suicide tactics on the basis of a belief that these types of attacks would work. They also adopted these tactics from positions of relative weakness. When al-Qaeda began perpetrating suicide attacks against American targets in Saudi Arabia, Kenya, Tanzania, Yemen, and, later, within the United States itself, it did so from a position of weakness. This position has been exacerbated by the continuing – if not increasing – lack of popularity of al-Qaeda's guiding ideology and its objectives. Even though there have been pockets of support for the challenge al-Qaeda has posed to the West, the group's objectives are not well received by the more moderate Muslim majority. The group's objectives are also not well received by nationalist–separatist Islamists, such as Hamas.[56]

The main actors are also more deadly than their predecessors. Suicide attacks perpetrated by salafi-jihadists have been "far more lethal" than those perpetrated by others; and salafi-jihadists have become "the predominant employers of this tactic."[57] Al-Qaeda's attack on September 11 remains the single most lethal suicide attack. Jemaah Islamiya was tied to the October 12, 2002, suicide bombing of a Bali nightclub and other attacks, which have killed hundreds. British terrorists detonated multiple suicide bombs in an attack on London's mass transit system on July 7, 2005. Between 2001 and 2007, salafi-jihadist groups perpetrated nearly four times as many suicide attacks as "mainstream Islamist/nationalist–separatist" groups and more than 100 times the number of suicide attacks perpetrated by Shi'a.[58]

The third difference is a matter of the location of suicide terrorist attacks today. By 2007, suicide attacks had been carried out in at least thirty-five countries, yet the majority of suicide attacks occur in only a few.[59] Much of the suicide terrorism today is in Iraq. Pakistan and Afghanistan also figure prominently in reports of suicide terrorism.[60] More recently, Lebanon has seen a return of suicide attacks, though perpetrated by outsiders. Explanations for these trends lie in local and regional political competitions.

Sunni militants in Iraq have become the most prolific users of suicide tactics in recent years.[61] There is more to this increase than the adoption of a "culture of martyrdom." The introduction of suicide attacks follows a change in the distribution of political power within Iraq. Once Iraq's privileged minority under Saddam Hussein's secular regime, Sunnis are now among the weakest actors in domestic politics. They are also divided. Although competing groups, including the salafi-jihadists, Ba'athists, and Islamic nationalists, may have the same targets – Shi'a, Sufis, and Kurds – they have competing objectives ranging from inciting sectarian war to state failure.[62]

In contrast, the regime change that followed the 2003 invasion of Iraq empowered the country's Shi'a majority. After their common religion is taken into account, the Shi'a in Iraq differ in an important way from the Shi'a in Iran and Lebanon. Although the Shi'a were a majority in Iran, they were the weaker party in the Iran–Iraq War. Lebanon's Shi'a were a minority within a multi-confessional state and in a position of relative weakness during and after the country's sectarian civil war. The Shi'a in Iraq, on the other hand, are now a majority and the main beneficiaries of the regime change that followed the 2003 invasion. As such, the empowered Iraqi Shi'a need not rely on the "weapon of the weak" used by their counterparts in Lebanon and Iran. More importantly, Iran's "culture of martyrdom" did not find a place among Iraq's Shi'a. It was and is still being used against Iraqis. In Iraq and elsewhere, suicide tactics have become a tactic of Sunni rather than Shi'a militants.

The fourth difference reflects a change in the targets of attacks. Whereas the first suicide "terrorists" targeted militaries and states, suicide terrorists now increasingly target civilians. Al-Qaeda did not adopt suicide tactics until the mid-1990s, after the Saudi regime accepted American assistance instead of that offered by Osama bin Laden. Before 9/11, al-Qaeda attacked American diplomatic and military targets overseas. September 11 differed from these earlier attacks in scale, location, and means of attack; it also differed in terms of the targets of the attacks, which included civilians and the state.

Suicide terrorist targets are also increasingly local in that Muslims are mostly attacking Muslims. Religious differences have been redefined as existing within religions rather than between religions.[63] Iraq's Sunnis, and perhaps a cadre of non-Iraqi jihadists,[64] are attacking Iraq's Shi'a. Syrian rebels reportedly perpetrate suicide attacks against Lebanese militants, presumably in response to Hizbullah's active support of Syria's Assad regime. Ironically, the original suicide terrorists have become the newest targets.[65] Pakistani militants, including some identifying as Taliban, use suicide attacks against local Pakistanis, creating terror and instability within the country. The reasons seem to have a lot to do with local politics and power. The result is a serious challenge to the Muslim world. It is, at the very least, an indication of the heterogeneity of identities and interests within the larger community.

Remaining questions

In the post-9/11 era, much of the attention has been directed toward understanding why individuals and groups have chosen to carry out suicide attacks. Such questions are particularly problematic from the perspectives of individual suicide terrorists, who presumably expect to die in the process of carrying out their attacks. Regardless of presumed psychological or social vulnerabilities of individual attackers, the fact remains that very few people become suicide terrorists and, among these few, there is "no single profile."[66] From the perspectives of groups, however, explanations tend to draw on the presumed strategic benefits associated with suicide terrorism. Whether or not suicide terrorism "works" is beside the point; leaders of terrorist groups must simply think that it might work.[67]

Neither of the answers focusing on individual susceptibility or group strategy adequately explains why suicide tactics were adopted after 1979 or why these tactics have been used in some places and not others, and by some groups and not others. Even though suicide tactics are not reserved for religious groups, much less Islamist groups, with few exceptions they have been used mostly by groups employing Muslim attackers and operating in Muslim-majority countries. Perhaps the communities where suicide attacks take place or from where the attackers originate have populations that are more sympathetic or susceptible to the "martyrdom mythology."[68] Perhaps these are communities with internal divisions and unpopular or weak regimes offering the most fertile grounds for suicide terrorism. Perhaps these communities are the only places where violent groups and the populations supporting them have not yet learned that suicide terrorism does not work.

While there are many "maybes," at least one answer is known. Modern terrorists have access to the tools their predecessors lacked, and it is these tools that increase the destructiveness of suicide attacks. Unlike their earlier counterparts, modern terrorists have explosives, which are deadlier and more destructive than knives or guns. Moreover, explosives packed on the bodies or in the vehicles of terrorists may be the smartest weapons available to the weakest actors. Suicide attacks are, by some estimates, twelve times deadlier than non-suicide attacks.[69] As such, it is not surprising that bombings have become one of the most feared and frequently used tools of suicide terrorists.

Notes

1 Leonard Weinberg, "Observations on the Future of Terrorism," in *Terrorism: What's Coming, The Mutating Threat*, ed. James O. Ellis III (Oklahoma City, OK: Memorial Institute for the Prevention of Terrorism, 2007), 41, mipt.publishpath.com/terrorism-whats-coming (accessed September 9, 2014).
2 For instance, see Martha Crenshaw, "Explaining Suicide Terrorism: A Review Essay," *Security Studies* 16, no. 1 (2007): 152; and Assaf Moghadam, "Motives for Martyrdom: Al-Qaida, Salafi Jihad, and the Spread of Suicide Attacks," *International Security* 33, no. 3 (2007): 46–78.
3 See, for instance, Mohammed M. Hafez, *Suicide Bombers in Iraq: The Strategy and Ideology of Martyrdom* (Washington, DC: United States Institute of Peace Press, 2007), 11–14.
4 For instance, see Moghadam, "Motives for Martyrdom." See also Moghadam, *The Globalization of Martyrdom: Al Qaeda, Salafi Jihad, and the Diffusion of Suicide Attacks* (Baltimore, MD: Johns Hopkins University Press, 2008).
5 See Randall D. Law's introduction to this volume.
6 Assaf Moghadam, "Defining Suicide Terrorism," in *Root Causes of Suicide Terrorism: The Globalization of Martyrdom*, ed. Ami Pedahzur (New York: Routledge, 2006), 14.
7 David C. Rapoport, "Before the Bombs There Were Mobs: American Experiences with Terror," *Terrorism and Political Violence* 20, no. 2 (2008): 168–9.
8 See, for instance, Leonard Weinberg, *Global Terrorism* (Oxford: OneWorld, 2008), 2.
9 This discussion of the elements of a "consensus" definition draws on Leonard Weinberg, Ami Pedahzur, and Sivan Hirsch-Hoefler, "The Challenges of Conceptualizing Terrorism," *Terrorism and Political Violence* 16, no. 4 (2004): 777–94.
10 For instance, see White House, Office of the Press Secretary, "Statement by the President on the Anniversary of the Attack on the US Marine Barracks in Beirut, Lebanon," October 23, 2009; "Statement by the President on the 10th Anniversary of the al-Qa'ida Terrorist Attack Against the USS Cole," October 12, 2010; "Statement by the President on the 13th Anniversary of the Embassy bombings in Kenya and Tanzania," August 7, 2011; and "Remarks by the President on the Deaths of the U.S. Embassy Staff in Libya," September 12, 2012; all can be found at: www.whitehouse.gov/briefing-room/statements-and-releases (all accessed September 5, 2014). It should be noted that references to "act of terror" and "terrorism" were debated in the aftermath of the statement about the Benghazi attack. See, for instance, the commentary by Glenn Kessler,

"Obama's Claim He Called Benghazi an 'Act of Terrorism,'" *Washington Post*, May 14, 2014, www.washingtonpost.com/blogs/fact-checker/post/obamas-claim-he-called-benghazi-an-act-of-terrorism/2013/05/13/7b65b83e-bc14-11e2-97d4-a479289a31f9_blog.html (accessed September 6, 2014).

11 For further discussion, see Moghadam, "Defining Suicide Terrorism"; and Crenshaw, "Explaining Suicide Terrorism," 134–40.

12 Stories such as these have been reported in various news outlets. See, for instance, *BBC News South Asia*, "Afghanistan: Eight-year-old Girl 'Used in Attack,'" June 25, 2011, www.bbc.co.uk/news/world-south-asia-13919946, and "Pakistan: Teenager Tells of Failed Suicide Bomb Mission," April 18, 2011, www.bbc.co.uk/news/world-south-asia-13111948 (both accessed September 5, 2014).

13 See, for instance, Crenshaw, "Explaining Suicide Terrorism," 135–40; and Moghadam, "Defining Suicide Terrorism."

14 For further discussion, see Susanne Martin and Leonard Weinberg, "Terrorism in an Era of Unconventional Warfare," *Terrorism and Political Violence* (forthcoming in print, available online at: www.tandfonline.com/doi/abs/10.1080/09546553.2014.895330#.VGYcg4dOWM9 [accessed November 14, 2014]).

15 For further discussion of the Assassins, refer to Chapter 3, "Pre-modern Terrorism: The Cases of the Sicarii and the Assassins," by Donathan Taylor and Yannick Gautron in this volume. For a comparison of the Assassins and other ancient terrorists, see David C. Rapoport, "Fear and Trembling: Terrorism in Three Religious Traditions," *American Political Science Review* 78, no. 3 (1984): 658–77.

16 Stephen Frederic Dale describes these pre-modern cases of anti-colonial suicide terrorism and discusses several of the parallels between pre-modern and modern suicide terrorism mentioned below. See Dale, "Religious Suicide in Islamic Asia: Anticolonial Terrorism in India, Indonesia, and the Philippines," *Journal of Conflict Resolution* 32, no. 1 (1988): 37–59; and Dale, "The Islamic Frontier in Southwest India: The Shahid as a Cultural Ideal among the Mappillas of Malabar," *Modern Asian Studies* 11, no. 1 (1977): 41–55.

17 See, for instance, Dale, "Religious Suicide in Islamic Asia," 51–4.

18 See, for instance, Brian Michael Jenkins, *Unconquerable Nation: Knowing Our Enemy, Strengthening Ourselves* (Santa Monica, CA: RAND Corporation, 2006), 9.

19 Dale, "Religious Suicide in Islamic Asia," 54.

20 Dale, "The Islamic Frontier in Southwest India," 41.

21 David C. Rapoport, "The Four Waves of Modern Terrorism," in *Terrorism Studies: A Reader*, ed. John Horgan and Kurt Braddock, 41–60 (New York: Routledge, 2011).

22 Ibid., 44.

23 See, for instance, Rapoport, "Fear and Trembling"; Rapoport, "Before the Bombs There Were Mobs," 185; and Rapoport, "The Four Waves of Modern Terrorism." See also Chapter 8 by Richard Bach Jensen, "Anarchist Terrorism and Counter-terrorism in Europe and the World, 1878–1934," and Chapter 9 by Thai Jones, "Anarchist Terrorism in the United States," both in this volume.

24 See, for instance, Peter Hill, "Kamikaze, 1943–5," in *Making Sense of Suicide Missions*, ed. Diego Gambetta, 1–42 (New York: Oxford University Press, 2005).

25 Ibid., 42.

26 Rapoport, "The Four Waves of Modern Terrorism."

27 These discussions of Viet Cong suicide terrorism draw on two sources: Stephen T. Hosmer, *Viet Cong Repression and Its Implications for the Future* (Lexington, MA: Heath Lexington Books, 1970), 53–6; and Leonard Weinberg, "Suicide Terrorism for Secular Causes," in *Root Causes of Suicide Terrorism: The Globalization of Martyrdom*, ed. Ami Pedahzur, 108–21 (New York: Routledge, 2006).

28 Andrew Silke, "The Role of Suicide in Politics, Conflict, and Terrorism," *Terrorism and Political Violence* 18, no. 1 (2006): 39.

29 For more on the PIRA's hunger strikes, see Chapter 14 by Cillian McGrattan in this volume.

30 For an overview of Fahmideh and the young *basij* soldiers discussed in these paragraphs, see Denis MacEoin, "Suicide Bombing as Worship: Dimensions of Jihad," *Middle East Quarterly* 16, no. 4 (2009): 15–24, www.meforum.org/2478/suicide-bombing-as-worship (accessed September 6, 2014).

SUICIDE TERRORISM

31 For detailed discussions of the "culture of martyrdom," see Hafez, *Suicide Bombers in Iraq*; and Moghadam, "Motives for Martyrdom."
32 See Adam Lankford, *Human Killing Machines: Systematic Indoctrination in Iran, Nazi Germany, al Qaeda, and Abu Ghraib* (Lanham, MD: Lexington Books, 2009), 105. See also Weinberg, "Suicide Terrorism for Secular Causes."
33 Mia Bloom, *Bombshell: Women and Terrorism* (Philadelphia: University of Pennsylvania Press, 2011), 23.
34 Ibid. See also Isabel Kershner, "Palestinians Honor a Figure Reviled in Israel as a Terrorist," *The New York Times*, March 11, 2010, www.nytimes.com/2010/03/12/world/middleeast/12westbank.html?_r=0 (accessed September 7, 2014).
35 Ibid. See also Reuters, "Palestinians Honor Fatah Terrorist, Despite Israel's Protests," *Haaretz*, March 13, 2011, www.haaretz.com/news/diplomacy-defense/palestinians-honor-fatah-terrorist-despite-israel-s-protests-1.348939 (accessed September 7, 2014).
36 See, for instance, Moghadam, "Motives for Martyrdom."
37 Ami Pedahzur, *Suicide Terrorism* (Malden, MA: Polity Press, 2005), 45. See also Chapter 18 by David Cook on Islamist terrorism in this volume.
38 Much of the information regarding specific suicide terrorist events, including groups, dates, targets, casualties, and locations, detailed in the paragraphs here and below comes from data provided separately by Pedahzur and Pape. See Pedahzur, *Suicide Terrorism*, "Appendix: Suicide Bombings (December 1981–June 2005)," 241–53; and Robert A. Pape, *Dying to Win: The Strategic Logic of Suicide Terrorism* (New York: Random House, 2005). In Pape, see, for instance, Table 1, "Suicide Terrorist Campaigns, 1980–2003," 15.
39 Pape, *Dying to Win*, 142.
40 Rapoport, "The Four Waves of Modern Terrorism," 52.
41 See, for instance, Crenshaw, "Explaining Suicide Terrorism." There are indeed religious differences at work as well – most Tamils are Hindu, while most Sinhalese are Buddhist – but this has always played a secondary role in the Tamil Tigers' self-conception and their stated goals. Strong evidence for this point is that Tamil Tiger suicide and terror attacks have been carried out by Christians as well as Hindus.
42 See, for instance, Pedahzur, *Suicide Terrorism*, 52–3.
43 Ibid., 51–8.
44 Ibid., 55–8.
45 For instance, during the 1990s, suicide attacks were carried out in Argentina and Croatia, two Christian-majority countries.
46 See, for instance, Shaul Shay, *The Shahids: Islam and Suicide Attacks* (Piscataway, NJ: Interdisciplinary Center for Herzliya/Transaction Publishers, Rutgers), 95–6.
47 Pedahzur, *Suicide Terrorism*, 91; and Crenshaw, "Explaining Suicide Terrorism," 149.
48 Pape, *Dying to Win*, 15, 157.
49 Ibid. Pape's focus is on "suicide terrorist campaigns" rather than individual attacks.
50 See, for instance, Jamal Afridi, "Kashmir Militant Extremists," Council for Foreign Relations (CFR) Backgrounder, July 9, 2009, www.cfr.org/kashmir/kashmir-militant-extremists/p9135 (accessed September 7, 2014).
51 Regarding Chechen attacks, see Anne Speckhard and Khapta Ahkmedova, "The Making of a Martyr: Chechen Suicide Terrorism," *Studies in Conflict and Terrorism* 29, no. 5 (2006): 429–92.
52 For more on Palestinian groups and the Second Intifada, see Chapter 16 by Boaz Ganor in this volume.
53 Mohammed M. Hafez, "Martyrdom Mythology in Iraq: How Jihadists Frame Suicide Terrorism in Videos and Biographies," *Terrorism and Political Violence* 19, no. 1 (2007): 95–115.
54 See, for instance, Moghadam, *Motives for Martyrdom*.
55 For more on Islamism and salafi-jihadism, see Chapters 17 and 18 by John Calvert and David Cook, respectively, in this volume. On al-Qaeda, 9/11, and the "War on Terror," see Chapter 22 by Daveed Gartenstein-Ross.
56 For more on this discussion, see Charles Kurzman, *The Missing Martyrs: Why There Are So Few Muslim Terrorists* (New York: Oxford University Press, 2011).
57 Moghadam, *The Globalization of Martyrdom*, 253.
58 Moghadam, "Motives for Martyrdom," 50, 70.

59 Ibid., 46, 49–50. With data covering 1981 and 2007, Moghadam reports that more than half of all "suicide missions" were carried out in Iraq; another forty percent were carried out in six countries (Afghanistan, Israel, Sri Lanka, Pakistan, Lebanon, and Russia, in descending order with between 12.7 percent and two percent of the total number), several of which are no longer experiencing high rates of such attacks; twenty-nine countries shared the remaining 7.5 percent.
60 See, for instance, Kurzman, *The Missing Martyrs*, 14.
61 For further discussion of the use of suicide tactics in Iraq, see Hafez, *Suicide Bombers in Iraq*. See also Moghadam, "Motives for Martyrdom."
62 Hafez, *Suicide Bombers in Iraq*, 109–10.
63 In *Dying to Win*, Pape highlights religious differences as among the reasons groups have used suicide tactics. The suggestion here is that relevant differences also exist within religions.
64 See, for instance, Kurzman, *The Missing Martyrs*.
65 See, for instance, Hafez, *Suicide Bombers in Iraq*. For additional information on attacks, refer to "Recent Highlights in Political Violence" (column), *CTC Sentinel*, Countering Terrorism Center at West Point, www.ctc.usma.edu/publications/sentinel (accessed September 7, 2014); and "Al-Nusra Front," Mapping Militant Organizations, Stanford University, web.stanford.edu/group/mappingmilitants/cgi-bin/groups/view/493 (accessed September 7, 2014).
66 Crenshaw, "Explaining Suicide Terrorism," 141.
67 See, for instance, Max Abrahms, "Are Terrorists Really Rational? The Palestinian Example," *Orbis* 48, no. 3 (2004): 533–49.
68 Hafez, *Suicide Bombers in Iraq*.
69 Ibid., 9.

Further reading

Crenshaw, Martha. "Explaining Suicide Terrorism: A Review Essay." *Security Studies* 16, no. 1 (2007): 133–62.

Dale, Stephen Frederic. "Religious Suicide in Islamic Asia: Anticolonial Terrorism in India, Indonesia, and the Philippines." *Journal of Conflict Resolution* 32, no. 1 (1988): 37–59.

Hafez, Mohammed M. *Suicide Bombers in Iraq: The Strategy and Ideology of Martyrdom*. Washington, DC: United States Institute of Peace Press, 2007.

Kurzman, Charles. *The Missing Martyrs: Why There Are So Few Muslim Terrorists*. New York: Oxford University Press, 2011.

Moghadam, Assaf. "Motives for Martyrdom: Al-Qaida, Salafi Jihad, and the Spread of Suicide Attacks." *International Security* 33, no. 3 (2007): 46–78.

Pape, Robert A. *Dying to Win: The Strategic Logic of Suicide Terrorism*. New York: Random House, 2005.

Pedahzur, Ami. *Suicide Terrorism*. Malden, MA: Polity Press, 2005.

Rapoport, David C. "Fear and Trembling: Terrorism in Three Religious Traditions." *American Political Science Review* 78, no. 3 (1984): 658–77.

Weinberg, Leonard. "Suicide Terrorism for Secular Causes." In *Root Causes of Suicide Terrorism: The Globalization of Martyrdom*, edited by Ami Pedahzur, 108–21. New York: Routledge, 2006.

27

COUNTER-TERRORISM AND CONSPIRACY

Historicizing the struggle against terrorism

Beatrice de Graaf

To write a history of *counter*-terrorism pushes the limits of possibility even beyond the plausibility of producing a comprehensive history of terrorism. Terrorism is an "essentially contested concept."[1] The term is almost always used as an attributed pejorative within a specific political and historical context and seldom provides a neutral description of the phenomenon as it lives and moves "out there." Counter-terrorism, all the more so, reflects an explicit political strategy: that of defining and identifying (in that order) a type of violence in order to invoke special legal and administrative measures to neutralize and combat it.[2] Hence, counter-terrorism is not an easy category to work with. Even in scholarly work it is easy to unwittingly reinforce the existing political paradigm or lend a hand to oppressive counter-terrorist strategies intended to quell democratic opposition.[3]

To study terrorism from a perspective of non-state actors alone (and not including the possibility of state terrorism) runs the risk of affirming the status quo and of academically buttressing the defense of the existing order against potential revolutionaries. The linguistic turn in history combined with a myriad of studies from the social constructivist corner, most notably works from the "Copenhagen school" of securitization and *Critical Studies in Terrorism*, have taught us important lessons about the danger of running into positivist pitfalls and adhering to an overly governmental interpretation of history.[4]

Given these observations, this chapter adopts a historicizing approach, i.e., we will try to stick to definitions and interpretations that were in use by the contemporaries themselves. This means that we have to admit that our perspective is inevitably tainted by a Western bias and directed towards non-state terrorism; and that all modern discourse on terrorism originates within this Western, transatlantic world and has been developed by states and communities of states (e.g., the League of Nations, the United Nations, the European Union, etc.) to deal with their contenders. As a result, when turning to the development of this concept over time, we explicitly leave out forms of pre-modern political violence, projections of terrorist activity in Asia in pre-colonial times, or other post hoc interpretations of thug violence and the like. The only justification for this immense academic caveat is the fact that a *Begriffsgeschichte* (conceptual history, or history of semantics, as founded by Reinhart Koselleck)[5] and genealogies necessarily follow the line of history.[6] By historicizing counter-terrorism we can at least be sure that we are not imposing our normative biases and post hoc amendments onto the past.

As is the case with so many novel political concepts, a history of (counter-)terrorism will always be written from the author's historical point of view and more often than not clearly evidence the signs of one's times. No one in the nineteenth or early twentieth centuries, or even in the 1960s, had an inkling about writing a book on terrorism. Doing so is, with a few exceptions, a distinctively post-1960s sport. David Rapoport's four-waves theory is a case in point.[7] This illustrative and helpful tool for teaching and understanding terrorism is a socially constructed and highly teleological approach. It is presentist in perspective, because the prequels to current contractions of violence can only be viewed in time and space from the vantage point of surfing on the fourth wave. However, from a *begriffsgeschichtliche* perspective it falls short. An ideal, value-free, theoretical framework for the interpretation of terrorism does not derive from top-down political or power structures, or as post hoc interpretations by researchers, but should also include how contemporary actors perceived the issue: the terrorists themselves (some explicitly called themselves "terrorists" and directly challenged authorities to counter them), the society surrounding them, the media, foreign nations, international institutions, private companies, or the petty despots or bureaucrats that executed their power at the local level.

This chapter, therefore, modestly aims to combine an overview of existing secondary literature with some primary research about a few Western countries in order to develop an initial, grounded, conceptual history of counter-terrorism. To limit our survey, we take as our cues any mention of *international* terrorism[8] (as an indicator for a widely perceived problem), parallel developments in *national* counter-terrorism efforts, and the manifest political transfer of these efforts across countries and continents. Of course, many individual national counter-terrorism campaigns were quite different from international efforts, such as the approach taken by the French in Algeria. However, the decision to restrict this overview to international terrorism enables us here to concentrate on a very essential, specific, and recurrent feature of the struggle against terrorism: namely, the attempt to legitimate and stylize counter-terrorism efforts by framing the purported terrorist enemy as part of a wider conspiracy, preferably by pointing to a transnational menace behind the single incident, and by soliciting international solidarity in combating this purported plot.

In each chronologically defined section, we will describe how a wave of terrorism was defined and mediated by contemporaries and how terrorism "stories" spread through media and society. Subsequently, we will map the parallel national or joint transnational efforts in combating this wave, and we will assess whether this led to a formalized, international framework of legal and administrative initiatives, e.g., to an institutionalized and widely accepted form of counter-terrorism.

Entering the conspiracy

The pivotal point on which this very brief overview of counter-terrorism history hinges is thus the concept of *conspiracy* as it was restyled in the nineteenth century.[9] By introducing the concept of conspiracy we can secure the conceptual side of terrorism, both empirically and conceptually. The assumption is that eras with a high circulation of conspiracy theories are often also eras with a higher frequency of actual assassination attempts, plots, and attacks, although it remains difficult to discern which tends to precipitate the other. Authorities and societies use and even concoct these conspiracy theories in order to make sense of shocking incidents and disparate attacks – as Randall D. Law already explicitly mentioned in his introduction to this volume. For security institutions, conspiracy theories are an essential rhetorical, practical, and philosophical means to justify their regime and expansion. Naming alleged conspiracy threats offers a framework within which to identify enemies that have not yet manifested themselves. Though spread over countries and continents, disconnected in time and place, they are jolted together by the lens of the alleged conspiracy. By expanding the geographical and temporal scope of the projected threat, security operations receive a boost as well.[10] The alleged risk of the global terrorist threat posed – e.g., recently by the purported global al-Qaeda network – dictated a new security logic: not just a reactive one, but a proactive, preventative, and even pre-emptive one. This was demonstrated in the years after 9/11 when the US government's pre-emptive attacks against Iraq were justified by the stated risk that Iraq's dictator Saddam Hussein might give weapons of mass destruction to terrorist groups.[11]

On the other hand, conspiracy theories are also used as political mechanisms for oppressed or disadvantaged groups seeking redress for their conditions, or they can be used as a political weapon by political entrepreneurs claiming to speak for a threatened majority. Conspiracy thinking is an integral part of almost every extremist ideology in which the legitimacy of the existing political and societal order is condemned.[12] In jihadist texts – e.g., from Sayyid Qutb, Osama bin Laden, or Anwar al-Awlaki – a recurrent theme is the purported "War against Islam" that is being waged by the Western world, that is, by *kuffars* (infidels), against the *ummah* (the world Islamic community).[13] That said, social conflicts can be simplified by both sides, by the government and the opponents thereof, by attributing all kinds of malicious intent to demonized populations.[14]

Pairing the concept "conspiracy" with the study of (counter-)terrorism is crucial because the challenge to defining something as a threat or even as a legal offense before it has empirically manifested itself is not dissimilar to the challenges of definition faced by scholars in the field of terrorism and counter-terrorism. Moreover, counter-terrorism efforts are almost without exception legitimated and executed by projecting an overarching threat and connecting incidents into one large-scale conspiracy that is intended to mobilize a population, constituency, parliament, or other factions to rally behind the flag – as Adam Curtis claims, for example, was the case with the War on Terror after 9/11.[15]

However, rather than attempting to discern between "real" conspiracies and purported ones, or trying to assess the historical truth behind the conspiracists' grievances, the focus here is on the functional character of conspiracy thinking at a given moment in time. On an epistemological plane, distinguishing between imagination and reality is impossible because a conspiracy theory is preconceived to rationalize and integrate all cognitive dissonances into its master narrative, leaving no room for alternative explanations. Therefore, in what follows we will focus on the empirical occurrence and frequency of conspiracy thinking as a function bearer and sanctioning tool for counter-terrorism politics.

The first global counter-terrorism debate: the Black conspiracy, 1880–1930

The anarchist wave

In Europe between 1880 and 1914, more than 500 people were wounded by anarchists and around 160 persons, mostly prominent officials and state representatives, fell victim to anarchist attacks. Some of the most significant were King Umberto of Italy (1900), US President William McKinley (1901), three prime ministers, as well as a host of cabinet ministers, police officials, and politicians. The popular empress Elisabeth of Austria ("Sissi") was stabbed to death by the Italian anarchist Luigi Lucheni in 1898.[16] In Chapters 8 and 9 in this volume, Richard Bach Jensen and Thai Jones, respectively, elaborate extensively on this first wave of modern terrorism, and Jensen convincingly describes how "anarchism," "terrorism," "assassins," and "revolutionaries" became synonymous.

"Worldwide conspiracy" was first of all the specter invoked by the anarchists themselves to describe their millenarian and apocalyptical utopia (or dystopia), on the one hand, and to boost their small number, on the other. Anarchists operated new, very visible, and fearsome technologies of destruction, using, for example, the automobile as both a means of transport and, when augmented with dynamite (another new technology), as vehicle-borne improvised explosive device *avant la lettre*. Anarchist associations gratefully exploited new technologies to communicate and to travel around the world much more quickly than before. A Polish anarchist took his cue to attack the tsar from a newspaper report on the impending state visit of the Russian head of state to France. Russian nihilist Sergei Nechaev turned to cheaper printing techniques to help disseminate his *Catechism of a Revolutionist* abroad in translation. His anarchist colleague Mikhail Bakunin issued his handful of disciples four-digit membership cards to suggest a constituency of thousands of adherents to his World Revolutionary Alliance. And the French League of Nihilists disseminated a leaflet in 1881, which bragged that it would poison hundreds of bourgeois families by adding toxins to the potable water supply of Paris.[17] Anarchists published their threats in newspapers, traveled by steamships, and contacted each other by telegraph.[18]

The anarchists' self-stylization as a global conspiracy was adopted and aggravated by the newspapers. Newspapers connected strikes, worker riots, and communist meetings to attacks by Russian nihilists and French anarchists. Incidents in Europe, Australia, and the United States were linked to attacks in Egypt, China, and Japan. Fear soared high in 1898 when the German emperor Wilhelm II cancelled a state visit to Egypt because of rumors about Italian anarchists conspiring to attack him there.[19] Thus, the global threat of the so-called "Black International" (the global anarchist conspiracy) played into the vignette of the "new political era, experimental, positive, scientific."[20]

Emerging counter-terrorism practices

From the 1880s onwards, the struggle against the Black International rose on the political agenda of most nations of Europe and beyond. "Technologies of imagination" transformed the faraway, imagined threat of anarchist violence into a vivid and material danger. Around 1890, police commissioners in Europe assembled and disseminated "wanted" posters and pictures of fugitive anarchists within the country and abroad and assisted their foreign police colleagues when possible. Newspapers, telegraph, telephone, and café rumors contributed to this process of public dissemination and securitization of these global anarchist threats.

In all these efforts, the specter of the anarchist threat served to frame these disparate incidents and attacks as a real international and homogeneous threat. Conspiracy was a fruit of modernism: it combined reactionary fear for chaos and socialism with a new reliance on and faith in modern technological innovations and in managerial progress and engineering. In the Hamidian era (1878–1908), even the Ottoman Empire used the global anarchist threat as a pretext to impose and implement all kinds of new technologies of surveillance and population control (such as registration techniques and new extradition and administrative procedures). Sultan Abdülhamid II justified the harsh repression of the

Armenian rebellion, the prosecution of vagrants, and the deportation of Italian immigrants by pointing to the "trouble of anarchism" – which was only partially causing his troubles.[21] The specter of the Black International provided operational clues to the nascent police and security centers throughout Europe. Even seemingly harmless meetings, such as completely legal gatherings of social–democratic parties and associations, could be framed as a decoy to conceal deceitful activities and illegal conspiracies to overthrow the government, as police officials in Germany and the Netherlands pointed out to their ministers, partly in order to convince their ministers to invest more in new anti-terrorist techniques.

For example, police forces in Europe and the Ottoman Empire joined forces and implemented the system of Bertillonage, developed around 1882 by the French police prefect Alphonse Bertillon. So-called *portraits parlés* registered a series of bioanthropological facial and bodily traits and measures based on a system of numbers and codes. This "scientific" method was informed by the notion that a deviational, criminal nature manifested itself in facial features and other anthropometric characteristics. These data could be transmitted on short notice to fellow police forces abroad in order to identify and arrest fugitive criminals or suspects, which was something of a revolution, since most suspects up to that time often managed to keep their identity hidden or were able to escape with forged identity cards. So, too, new shipping lines and railroad connections helped expedite the dispatch of photographs.[22]

These novel anti-terrorist techniques served to identify suspects and to improve prosecution, but they also symbolized the state of modernity to which security forces aspired. Within the context of increasing bilateral and transnational cooperation, these modern methods were thought to offer a fast track to the elite circle of the – supposedly – most advanced and professionalized forces. Hence, police forces in the Netherlands also pressed their minister to tune in to these new scientific insights and international developments. The Bertillonage system had already been adopted in France, and Germany and the United Kingdom were quick to follow suit.[23] Due to the ambitious police commissioner of Rotterdam, Willem Voormolen, the system also got a foothold in the Netherlands as well. In February 1896, Bertillon was invited to the Netherlands and received a royal decoration, together with Voormolen, from the Dutch queen regent Emma.[24] Per royal decree, the Bertillon system was now available to the Dutch police and judicial forces.[25] Although nary a single anarchist attack took place in the Netherlands, the global conspiracy discourse, the securitization of terrorism, and the desire to modernize the forces helped Voormolen and his officers to implement new techniques and professionalize their capacities.[26]

In this way the departments of justice in almost every European country, seeking to professionalize and centralize their respective police systems, embraced "modern" scientific insights from the young discipline of criminology. Even the Dutch police were elevated to the status of an international player. Dutch police and their newly constituted criminal investigators joined in collecting material on suspected anarchists, exchanging details and photographs with colleagues over the world, including colleagues from authoritarian police forces, such as Russia's Okhrana.[27] These international counter-terrorism practices and standards emerged quite clearly in response to an alleged global threat.

International transfer and cooperation of police organizations

International collaboration between European police forces, including the Dutch, profited from these trends in bureaucratization and professionalization. This supports Mathieu

Deflem's hypothesis on the close connection between more autonomy in terms of bureaucratization and professionalization and more international contacts.[28] This internationalization was cemented when the first international anti-anarchist conference was organized in 1898, three weeks after the murder of Empress Elisabeth.[29] Participating states agreed on a definition of anarchist crimes. The signatories also adopted a central system of registration and, in the years that followed, created central investigative forces and trained new detectives. The system of Bertillonage was accepted as the international standard. The signatories likewise promised to assist each other with rendition and information requests and resolved to implement the death penalty. In the end, not all of the countries ratified the treaty. No further international conventions were held, but the meeting did herald the beginning of organized international police cooperation and can be seen as the forerunner of Interpol.[30]

In short, the nexus between terrorism and counter-terrorism through the mutual use of the conspiracy debate could not be better illustrated than G. K. Chesterton did in his 1908 novel *The Man Who Was Thursday*. In this brilliant story, the menacing and secretive high council of international anarchists turns out to be set up and staffed without exception by police officials. In the end, the protagonist (a police inspector who writes poetry) laments that good and evil overlapped: "[E]ach man fighting for order may be as brave and good a man as the dynamiter. . . . We have descended into hell."[31] Indeed, as Jensen describes in Chapter 8 in this volume, this "cultural construction" tied all kinds of actions together, from mere socialist gatherings to nihilist propaganda, but also inspired numerous agents provocateurs to play a shadowy role in instigating real acts of terrorism.

A second wave of anarchism: national confinement of conspiracy theories in the 1930s

Although anarchist attacks took place from the 1880s on, and a first international language on countering terrorism emerged from the international conferences in 1898 and again in 1904, (international) counter-terrorism efforts were mainly executed at the sub-state police level. It was not until the 1930s that actual inter-state cooperation in the struggle against terrorism took shape, enabled and mediated by the League of Nations, which was founded in 1919.

It was the assassination of King Alexander I of Yugoslavia while on a state visit to Marseille on October 9, 1934, by a Bulgarian marksman of the Internal Macedonian Revolutionary Organization, that precipitated the first international political debate on terrorism.[32] This regicide proved that the anarchist wave of assassinations prior to World War I was experiencing an upsurge again.

A Commission on the Responsibility of the Authors of the War had tried earlier to define the "systematic terrorism" that occurred during World War I.[33] But public indignation and shock after "Marseille," and the collective fear that "Sarajevo" (i.e., the assassination of Archduke Franz Ferdinand, which triggered World War I) might happen all over again, convinced the League of Nations to put "terrorism" on the international agenda. A Committee of Experts was set up to study the question and to draw "a preliminary draft of an international convention to assure the repression of conspiracies or crimes committed with a political or terrorist purpose."[34] The final Convention for the Prevention and Punishment of Terrorism, consisting of twenty-nine articles, defined acts of terrorism "as criminal acts which are directed against a State and which are intended or calculated to create a state of terror among individuals, groups of persons, or the general public" and committed states to cooperate "for the prevention and punishment of such acts when they are of an international character." States were further encouraged to refrain from supporting or enabling terrorist activity directed against other states.[35]

The novelty of this convention was not the attempt to come to a definition; the 1898 conference had already tried that much. The intention was to create binding international law that would compel states to adhere to the principle of *aut dedere aut judicare* (extradite or prosecute). Terrorists should no longer be able to flee to another country; the principle of "no impunity" should be upheld. This was the first attempt at an internationally binding judicial definition of terrorism as a crime – a milestone in the history of counter-terrorism.[36]

However, establishing this global conspiracy plot of worldwide anarchist violence was thwarted by national political sentiments. Many countries, priding themselves on having exceptions for political crime in their constitution, were not immediately willing to accept another country's definition of a terrorist as theirs. Conceptual and semantic difficulties arose. For example, to the Belgians, a terrorist was someone who committed crimes against a head of state. For the Bulgarians, any Bolshevik was considered a terrorist. For the Soviets, "revisionism" was already considered an act of terrorism; but for the British, political crimes were excluded. As the British Home Office deputy legal adviser L. S. Brass wrote:

> If all states were at all times decently governed, presumably anyone who attempted by force to overthrow an existing government should be a *hostis humanae generis* [enemy of the human race]; but when the government is itself a terrorist government, I think the person who endeavours to overthrow it by the only means available is not necessarily to be so regarded.[37]

In July 1938, twenty-three of the thirty-five plenipotentiaries signed the terrorism convention (including the Soviet Union, but not the UK) and twelve countries ratified the convention establishing the International Criminal Court. However, at that time, both the Convention and the League of Nations were heading towards a dead end.

Contrary to the international threat discourse on anarchism, which was more or less consistent throughout Russia, Europe, North America, and Latin America and did inspire at least some solidarity among the regimes of the late nineteenth century, conspiracy theories did not transcend borders easily in the 1920s and 1930s. With the rise of regimes in the Soviet Union and Germany that embraced tactics of terror as core elements to their rule, the generally accepted threat of global anarchism and revolution seemed to give way to national caveats and even sincere doubts about politicizing terrorism.

The global wave of "revolutionary violence": 1940s–80s

Anti-colonial uprisings in the 1940s–60s

Counter-terrorism, both in its conceptual and tactical sense, further developed during the years of de-colonization after World War II. European powers fought in Malaya, Kenya, Palestine, Indochina, and Algeria to defend their colonial empires. Successes and failures in those conflicts have been studied ad infinitum for clues as to how to counter terrorism today.[38] In this case, the idea of fighting a conspiracy of rebels or "savages" was inspired by notions of a racial struggle and justified at home by relating stories of purported indigenous savagery in Kenya and Algeria that should be put to an end. At the same time, counter-terrorist tactics – including the use of concentration camps, torture, and other extrajudicial counter-terrorist and counter-insurgency strategies – were honed to perfection. The incipient Cold War served to disseminate the fabrication of conspiratorial communist plots. The rebellion of Mau Mau insurgents in Kenya was depicted as a communist conspiracy,[39] although even the British Colonial Office could find no evidence for that allegation. The Mau Mau were moreover portrayed as coming straight out of the heart of darkness, as savages "who indulged in cannibalism, witchcraft, devil worship and sexual orgies and who terrorised white settlers and mutilated women and children."[40] The Battle of Algiers, the Dutch campaigns in Indonesia, and the British counter-insurgency campaigns also developed along such lines.[41] In this volume, Chapters 25, 15, and 12 and 13 by Geraint Hughes, Martin C. Thomas, and Benjamin Grob-Fitzgibbon, respectively, describe counter-insurgency campaigns and instances of counter-terrorism approaches that were justified and defended by appealing to purported plots.

A radical decade

A new "global conspiracy plot" emerged in the 1970s, a decade that stands out for Western Europe and the US as another moment of global (counter-)terrorism activity. Student protesters, trade unions, and extra-parliamentary demonstrators clashed with police forces. Actually or seemingly spontaneous acts of sabotage, arson, and explosions were common in almost every Western European or American country, as Chapters 19, 20, and 21 by Jennifer S. Holmes, Hanno Balz, and Carolyn Gallaher, respectively, in this volume aptly illustrate. Domestic, imported, and international terrorism were recurring threats. The various terrorist statements and manifestos suggested an immediate revolutionary takeover, starting with the revolutionary hotbeds in the Third World, spreading from the student and factory workers' movement into the "imperialist" headquarters of the world. "New Left" or "revolutionary terrorism" accounts for the sharp uptick in terrorist incidents in Europe, the Americas, and even in Iran in the period from 1978 onwards.[42]

A "terror network" engineered by Moscow?

New Left terrorism spread internationally, but the groups, cells, and organizations as such were much less connected and interwoven than was often presumed. Nevertheless, already early in the 1970s a "terror network" theory developed, assuming an "all roads lead to Moscow" framework. This theory of "Cold War by proxy" still runs deep and has credentials dating back to the shock of the 1968 revolts in capitals all over the world.[43] With the May revolt of 1968 in Paris, which even saw French president Charles de Gaulle temporarily fleeing the country, the perceived threat of a "global" revolution was born. Left-wing activists exploited the public's fear of a revolution, quoting and distributing Chinese Maoist, Cuban, and South American strategies for stirring up a revolution as we saw above.

In April 1969, US president Richard Nixon gained international notoriety when interpreting demonstrations, occupations, and arson attacks on university campuses as traits of one global communist terror plot. In his "Campus Unrest Speech," for example, he branded simple student demonstrations as the "next to last step along the road to terrorism."[44] A year later, on June 5, 1970, he took his verdict a step further: "We have moved from the 'student activism' which characterized the civil rights movements in the early '60s through the 'protest movements' which rallied behind the anti-war banner beginning with the March on the Pentagon in 1967 to the 'revolutionary terrorism' being perpetrated today by determined professionals." He likewise told US intelligence chiefs, "We are now confronted with a new and grave crisis in our country – one which we know too little about. Certainly hundreds, perhaps thousands, of Americans – mostly under 30 – are determined to destroy our society."[45]

Nixon repeatedly voiced his perception that student and anti-war protests were being funded and initiated by Moscow or Havana, a perception that kept returning to the political and public scene, culminating in the 1981 study by publicist Claire Sterling in the guise of a solid academic monograph on the communist "terror network."[46] In the book of the same name, Sterling introduces the idea of a communist-backed network of terrorists in order to make sense of a wave of seemingly interconnected terrorist attacks, starting with the Munich hostage-taking in September 1972 and climaxing in the German Autumn and the Italian Moro kidnapping in 1977/78 that swept through Western countries. Although the Central Intelligence Agency's Soviet analysts dismissed the gist of the book in 1981,[47] the dispositive of an international terror network directed by the communist world was a common feature in Western media throughout the 1970s. This schema was taken over by many more security agencies in the Western world.

To be sure, communist world capitals did try to meddle with the disparate groups of revolutionary students. The East German secret service and other East Bloc agencies offered Red Army Faction terrorists, Palestinian freedom fighters, and conspirators like Carlos the Jackal safe haven and weapons. However, these "contacts" were often motivated more by a defensive wish to keep an eye on these loose cannons for security reasons than by proactive ambitions of sabotage.[48] Archival research has refuted the idea that Moscow, East Berlin, or Havana were puppeteers manipulating revolutionary violence. On the contrary, communist agencies for their part suspected the CIA of aiding and abetting left wing terrorism in order to discredit the communist world.[49] Daniel Cohn-Bendit, Rudi Dutschke, and Bernardine Dohrn were certainly not activists that could be kept on a leash by some murky communist agency, although Western agencies were prone to identify them as Moscow's cronies. Moscow's arm simply wasn't that long or powerful – as many intelligence officials knew all too well at that time. Intelligence services and politicians alike nevertheless did find merit in keeping the menace of a global communist terrorist conspiracy alive – for budgetary, electoral, or political reasons. The United States' Federal Bureau of Investigation did so in the 1960s with the creation of their counter-intelligence programs and the Nixon administration revived the menace in the 1970s, as have the Italian security services since the 1980s.[50] A number of Latin America regimes in the 1980s stirred the pot as well to justify their gruesome campaigns of state terror.

International cooperation: intelligence and UN efforts

Given these claims, it is no wonder that premonitions of a "terror network" menace grew within governmental agencies and political centers. In 1971, the "Club de Berne" and NATO's Special Committee were established to enable heads of intelligence and security services, police forces, and high ranking civil servants to exchange information, assist each other with specific counter-terrorist operations, and join hands in countering international terrorism.[51]

The trigger for moving the series of disparate attacks taking place all over the world higher on the international *political* agenda was the attack by the Palestinian group Black September on the dormitories of the Israeli Team at the Olympic Games in Munich, Germany, on September 5, 1972. At the UN General Assembly, the terrorist acts sparked heated debates. Its Resolution 3034 defined three committees that had to deal with (1) finding a common definition of terrorism, (2) examining the causes of terrorism, and (3) proposing measures to prevent terrorism. Again, interpretations of the terrorist threat went in opposite directions, dictating competing and conflicting approaches. Whereas the so-called First World (the Western world) saw the terrorist attacks as a more or less global wave inspired by leftist revolutionary sentiments or even steered by Moscow, East Berlin, Beijing, or Havana to overthrow the existing (capitalist) order, the Second World (the communist states) did not know quite what to make of them and tried to influence the course of terrorist action, but perceived them equally as a problem and threat to the political status quo.[52] The countries of the so-called Third World, which had joined the UN after the wave of independence in the former colonies during the 1950s and 1960s, had a totally different view. To them, attempts by organizations such as the South West Africa People's Organization (SWAPO), the People's Liberation Army of Namibia, and other liberation movements within the Organization of African Unity to liberate oppressed minorities or to fight back against oppressive "state terrorism" was a legitimate goal.[53] Yasser Arafat's speech before the UN Assembly in 1974 is a case in point. "International terrorism," however defined, may not be used to criminalize national liberation movements; for the "desperate, colonized, persecuted and underprivileged," political violence comes as their last resort and such terrorism is legitimate, as the country of Guinea acknowledged in its statements.[54]

Consequently, as before, police cooperation and intelligence sharing increased, but a political definition was stalemated. A binding definition of the nature of terrorist crime, its intentions, or consequences was not to be had. In the course of the 1970s and 1980s, only certain well-described concrete *acts* of terrorism came to be described and penalized by binding law. This was facilitated by a number of developments. The Palestine Liberation Organization (PLO) officially renounced terrorism in 1974; the struggles for national liberation petered out; and Third World countries were faced with acts of terrorism themselves, such as the raid on a meeting of oil ministers of the Organization of Petroleum Exporting Countries (OPEC) in Vienna in 1975.[55] As a result, their collective resistance to the international codification of terrorist violence eroded. The Convention for the Suppression of Unlawful Seizure of Aircraft was concluded in 1970 and expanded upon in 1971. Other conventions dealt with nuclear material (1979), airports (1988), maritime navigation (1988), and fixed platforms on the continental shelf (1988). In 1977, a European Convention on the Suppression of Terrorism was ratified; a similar Organization of American States convention had already been drafted in 1971. On a practical level, airport security, gates, and tighter controls were introduced by aviation and transport companies.

In sum, competing definitions were launched and defended by larger country "blocs" within the UN, each of which advocated its own interpretive framework or conspiracy theory regarding the origins, causes, nature, and intention of the global terrorist wave. A shared discourse, let alone a generic solution, regarding the terrorist problem never materialized. Progress was made, however, in a convergence of national and international *practices* for countering terrorism.

Epilogue: al-Qaeda and the War against Terror, 2001–present

The 9/11 al-Qaeda attacks on the World Trade Center returned terrorism to the top of the political agenda. The nature of the event and its death toll marked a spectacle that in its impact and consequences could perhaps only be compared to the assassination of Archduke Franz Ferdinand in Sarajevo on June 22, 1914, an incident that helped trigger World War I. But owing to the new media, the impact of 9/11 was distinctly larger.[56] The intensity of video footage had the veritable "power of nightmares,"[57] which immediately after 9/11 translated into an equally dazzling cascade of academic and expert interpretations, on the one hand, and corresponding counter-terrorism measures, practices, legislation, and even military operations, on the other.

To be sure, Middle Eastern terrorism had never dropped off the threat lists of security agencies in the United States and Europe.[58] In the Arab and North African world, combating jihadist movements had been an ongoing struggle over the course of the 1980s and 1990s, as David Cook and Daveed Gartenstein-Ross describe in Chapters 18 and 22, respectively, in this volume. Even Dutch intelligence (BVD-AIVD) commented already in 1992 about the mounting threat of radicalized youths among second-generation immigrants with a Muslim–Moroccan background.[59] In 1994, the UN passed a resolution defining terrorism as "criminal acts intended or calculated to provoke a state of terror in the general public, a group of persons or particular persons for political purposes."[60] And in 1996, a new UN ad hoc committee was created to negotiate sectoral conventions on the elimination of terrorist acts. Other resolutions in 1998–2000 by the UN Security Council prescribed sanctions against the Taliban and al-Qaeda.[61]

However, al-Qaeda assumed its leading role within the specter of global terrorism only after the attacks on New York and Washington. In his statements, Osama bin Laden repeatedly argued the legitimacy of waging "global jihad" against the "infidel regimes," "apostate rulers," and the "Crusaders alliance."[62] Similarly, the interpretation of 9/11 and the compelling and ongoing supply of media "evidence" regarding a global terror plot heralded a new security age. Directly after the attacks, US President George W. Bush condemned the 9/11 attacks as an assault on the whole of the civilized world. He immediately received congressional approval for the use of military force and ordered the invasion of Afghanistan to overthrow the Taliban as the sponsors of Osama bin Laden and al-Qaeda. In the state of the union address of January 2002, Bush drew a menacing picture of an "axis of evil," comprising North Korea, Iran, and Iraq that was "arming to threaten the peace of the world" and "posed a grave and growing danger."[63] The Bush doctrine of pre-emptive war and a "Global War on Terror" (GWOT) was born.[64] Underpinning this counter-terrorism dispositive was the threat description of a global terrorist plot of jihadists – a "leader-led jihad" in the words of Bruce Hoffman – that connected pockets of resistance all over the globe to the mastermind of Tora Bora.[65]

Domestically, organizational changes fundamentally altered the security infrastructure of the US. On both the national and international level, the intelligence community – which endured widespread criticism reminiscent of the Pearl Harbor debacle – underwent a total overhaul.[66] The Patriot Act of 2002 enabled the US government to engage in military activities and covert operations around the world in order to capture, detain, and interrogate terrorism suspects using a new range of extra-legal practices.[67] By locating the terrorist enemy outside the international community of states and citizens, the Bush presidency and its allies blurred the lines between war and peace and even designed a new category of "unlawful combatants."

Globally, the American call to arms was followed by NATO and the UN, first through the United States' Operation Enduring Freedom in Afghanistan, then through the NATO-led International Security Assistance Force (ISAF) mission that was established by the UN Security Council in December 2001. More UN Resolutions were adopted, legitimized by the "dialectic of unprecedented threat and the need for dramatic action."[68] The terrorist threat was addressed militarily but also through criminal law and administrative and financial procedures. Banking secrecy acts, money laundering control acts, a European arrest warrant, new immigration procedures, and shared "black lists" and no-fly lists made sure that every legal and administrative loophole for international terrorists was closed.[69]

Only after US Special Forces killed Osama bin Laden in his compound in Pakistan in 2011 did the leader-led jihad specter start to fade. However, newly perceived threats, such as "foreign fighters" and "homegrown terrorists," are still being caught in the frame of a worldwide terror plot, albeit a plot without clearly identifiable "puppeteers." At the same time, the waning power of the alarmist global terrorist conspiracy did not go hand in glove with a decrease of counter-terrorism measures. On the contrary, vast intelligence competencies crept into other policy areas (e.g., cybersecurity) and were appropriated for classical espionage or commercial gain. It took the Manning and Snowden revelations from 2011 to 2013 to (temporarily?) stem the tide.

In short, counter-terrorism measures may well have enhanced the "Theater of Terror" caused by the terrorists. Governments cannot dictate what attacks take place and how footage and images of these attacks are spread, but they do have some impact on the public's imagination. They can affect the social impact of terrorist attacks with their response.[70] Governments still have a monopoly on the use of violence, and they are the ones citizens turn to in times of national crises. Moreover, they often fuel these crises and use them to further their own political and military agendas.[71] With vast conspiracy theories or highly unsubstantiated interpretive frameworks in the air, they can easily amplify the "moral panic" in society with military metaphors ("we are at war"). That said, they might also be equally able to exert a moderating influence by providing more realistic threat descriptions and by appealing to the social resilience in a society.[72]

The need for historicizing counter-terrorism

Conspiracy is a tool that is employed by both the defenders and the opponents of the existing order in their battle. They wield it to mobilize resources, to make sense of the tactics of brute violence, and to justify a limitless approach in fighting the enemy. Counter-terrorism is always occasioned by a political crisis of some sort; the crisis is the question and most often conspiracy theories are crafted to provide an answer.

Counter-terrorism is not the simple consequence of physical or political circumstances and incidents. People and organizations have to attribute meaning to circumstances and incidents. When these incidents are seen as elements of a conspiracy, the perceived threat of terror increases. These perceptions are then incorporated into political, administrative, and bureaucratic decision-making processes and procedures. This may seem obvious, but the history of (counter-)terrorism is usually not described in these terms.

This chapter suggests a new approach to the history of counter-terrorism, one that takes into account (a) a shift from a fixed, ahistorical take on (counter-)terrorism to a more dynamic understanding of the constructivist nature and volatility of security considerations, and (b) a historicizing of the dominant presentist-oriented theoretical underpinnings to terrorism research as provided by the social sciences. This very brief overview has first of all made the case that the contested character of terrorism becomes manifest in the framing of terrorist practices and discourses as conflicting *conspiracy* theories; second, that these conflicting conspiracy theories are interpretive frameworks that dictate equally competing "solutions" to the perceived crisis; and third, that inflating these frameworks and conspiracies through the use of the media and the invasive techniques of counter-terrorism (and upheld by the "invisible college of terrorism researchers themselves"[73]) increasingly erodes the remaining checks and balances when it comes to the use of counter-terrorism measures. Legal safeguards wither when the threat of a perceived limitless terrorist plot looms. By deconstructing terrorist conspiracies as cultural scripts and by historicizing the threat of terrorism and the corresponding counter-terrorism measures, we will be in a position to track down and unpack the different interlocking and interwoven notions of terrorism and counter-terrorism as they emerged in discourse, rule, and praxis. Doing so will allow us to avoid absolutist applications of the notion of security and afford us insight into the ways we perceive and sometimes inflate security threats and, one may hope, into possible alternative courses of counter-terrorist action.

Notes

The research leading to these results has received funding from the European Research Council under the European Union's Seventh Framework Programme (FP/2007–2013)/ERC Grant Agreement n.615313. The author furthermore thanks John Kok for his assistance in editing the text.

1. William E. Connolly, *The Terms of Political Discourse* (Princeton, NJ: Princeton University Press, 1993), 10. See also Alex Schmid, "Terrorism: The Definitional Problem," *Journal of International Law* 36 (2004): 375–420.
2. See Beatrice de Graaf, *Evaluating Counterterrorism Performance: A Comparative Study* (London: Routledge, 2011), chapter 1.
3. See Richard Jackson, "Knowledge, Power and Politics in the Study of Terrorism," in *Critical Terrorism Studies: A New Research Agenda*, ed. Richard Jackson et al., 66–83 (London: Routledge, 2009).
4. Barry Buzan, Ole Waever, and Jaap de Wilde, *Security: A New Framework for Analysis* (Boulder, CO: Lynne Rienner, 1998); Michael C. Williams, *Culture and Security: Symbolic Power and the Politics of International Security* (London: Routledge, 2007); and Thierry Balzacq, *Securitization Theory: How Security Problems Emerge and Dissolve* (London: Routledge, 2011).
5. See Reinhart Koselleck, *Begriffsgeschichten* (Frankfurt am Main: Suhrkamp, 2006).
6. The best example of such a conceptual genealogy of security is still Werner Conze, "Sicherheit, Schutz," in *Geschichtliche Grundbegriffe: Historisches Lexikon zur politisch-sozialen Sprache in Deutschland*, ed. O. Brunner, W. Conze, and R. Koselleck, 5:831–62 (Stuttgart: Kohlhammer, 1984).
7. David Rapoport, "The Four Waves of Modern Terrorism," in *Attacking Terrorism: Elements of a Grand Strategy*, ed. Audrey Kurth Cronin and James Ludes, 46–73 (Washington, DC: Georgetown University Press, 2004).
8. See Thomas J. Badey, "Defining International Terrorism: A Pragmatic Approach," *Terrorism and Political Violence* 10, no. 1 (1998): 90–107.
9. Beatrice de Graaf and Cornel Zwierlein, "Security and Conspiracy in Modern History," *Historical Social Research* 38, no. 1 (2013): 7–45.
10. Beatrice de Graaf and Cornel Zwierlein, "Historicizing Security: Entering the Conspiracy Dispositive," *Historical Social Research* 38, no. 1 (2013): 46–64.
11. Michael Gordon, "Papers from Iraqi Archive Reveal Conspiratorial Mind-Set of Hussein," *New York Times*, October 25, 2011; Abraham D. Sofar, "On the Necessity of Pre-emption," *European Journal for International Law* 14, no. 2 (2003): 209–26; and Liesbeth van der Heide, "Cherry-picked Intelligence: The Weapons of Mass Destruction Dispositive as a Legitimation for National Security in the Post 9/11 Age," *Historical Social Research* 38, no. 1 (2013): 286–307.

12 Bartlett and Miller, *The Power of Unreason*, 21; Jonathon R. White, "Political Eschatology: A Theology of Antigovernment Extremism," *American Behavioral Scientist* 44, no. 6 (2001): 940.
13 A few examples of such remarks by the late American–Yemeni Islamist militant Anwar al-Awlaki can be found here: "The Evolution of a Radical Cleric: Quotes from Anwar al-Awlaki," *New York Times*, May 8, 2010.
14 Bartlett and Miller, *The Power of Unreason*, 54.
15 Adam Curtis, *The Power of Nightmares: The Rise of the Politics of Fear*. Documentary, 2005. www.archive.org/details/ThePowerOfNightmares (accessed on November 11, 2012).
16 Alex Butterworth, *The World That Never Was: A True Story of Dreamers, Schemers, Anarchists, and Secret Agents* (London: Random House, 2010).
17 Ibid., 181–2.
18 For more on the relationship between technology and terrorism, see Chapter 29 by Ann Larabee in this volume.
19 See Carola Dietze, "Terrorismus im 19. Jahrhundert: Politische Attentate, rechtliche Reaktionen, Polizeistrategien und öffentlicher Diskurs in Europa und den Vereinigten Staaten 1878–1901," in *Vom Majestätsverbrechen zum Terrorismus*, ed. Karl Härter and Beatrice de Graaf, 179–96 (Frankfurt am Main: Klostermann, 2012).
20 Butterworth, *The World That Never Was*, 46.
21 See Noémi Levy-Aksu, *Ordre et désordres dans l'Istanbul ottomane (1879–1909)* (Paris: Karthala, 2013).
22 Cyrille Fijnaut, *De geschiedenis van de Nederlandse Politie. Een staatsinstelling in de maalstroom van de geschiedenis* (Amsterdam: Boom Uitgevers, 2007), 283; and J. Jäger, *Verfolgung durch Verwaltung. Internationales Verbrechen und internationale Polizeikooperation 1880–1933* (Konstanz: UVK, 2006), 196–221.
23 F. Lignian, "De anthropometrische signalementen volgens Alphonse Bertillon," *Nederlands Tijdschrift voor Geneeskunde* 38 (1894): 987–96.
24 "Het Bertillonage-stelsel," *De Nederlandsche Politiegids* 10, no. 113 (May 1895) and National Archive, The Hague/Netherlands, pl.no. 2.09.05, inv.no. 6488, exchange between the minister of justice, the minister of foreign affairs, and the Cabinet of the Queen-Regentess, January 22, 1896, no. 12; February 12, no. 5; February 15, no. 7; and February 19, no. 11.
25 Koninklijk Besluit (Royal Decree), *Staatsblad*, February 22, 1896. See also "Antropometrisch stelsel," *Nieuws van de Dag*, January 3, 1896.
26 Beatrice de Graaf, "Van 'helsche machines' en Russische provocateurs. De strijd tegen het anarchisme in Nederland," *Tijdschrift voor Geschiedenis* 125, no. 3 (2012): 313–31.
27 Beatrice de Graaf, "The Black International as Security Dispositive in the Netherlands, 1880–1900," *Historical Social Research* 38, no. 1 (2013): 142–65.
28 Mathieu Deflem, "International Police Cooperation – History of," in *The Encyclopedia of Criminology*, ed. Richard A. Wright and J. Mitchell Miller, 795–8 (New York: Routledge, 2005).
29 Ministère des Affaires Étrangères, *Conférence Internationale de Rome pour la défence sociale contre les anarchistes. 24 novembre–21 décembre 1898* (Rome 1898). National Archive, The Hague/Netherlands, Justitie Geheim, inv.nr. 6496.
30 See Richard Bach Jensen, "The International Anti-Anarchist Conference of 1898 and the Origins of Interpol," *Journal of Contemporary History* 16, no. 2 (1981): 323–47. Also see Chapter 8 by Jensen in this volume.
31 G. K. Chesterton, *The Man Who Was Thursday: A Nightmare* (London: [1908] 2008), 172–3. For more on Chesterton's novel as well as the broader pattern of literary reactions to terrorism, see Chapter 31 by Lynn Patyk in this volume.
32 *New York Times*, October 10, 1934. See also Ondrej Ditrych, "From Discourse to Dispositif: States and Terrorism between Marseille and 9/11," *Security Dialogue* 44, no. 3 (June 2013): 223–40.
33 Ditrych, "From Discourse to Dispositive," 225.
34 League of Nations Council resolution, December 10, 1934. Proceedings of the International Conference on the Repression of Terrorism (C.94.M.47.1938.V), League of Nations, Geneva, June 1, 1938. Annex 1, p. 183. Quoted in Charles Townshend, "'Methods Which All Civilized Opinion Must Condemn': The League of Nations and International Action against Terrorism," in *An International History of Terrorism: Western and Non-Western Experiences*, ed. J. M. Hanhimäki and B. Blumenau (London: Routledge, 2013), 35.

35 Ibid., 36–7.
36 See Karl Härter, "Die Formierung transnationaler Strafrechtsregime: Auslieferung, Asyl und grenzübergreifende Kriminalität im Übergang von gemeinem Recht zum nationalstaatlichen Strafrecht," *Rechtsgeschichte* 18 (2011): 36–65.
37 Townshend, "Methods Which All Civilized Opinion Must Condemn," 40–1.
38 See Michael E. Brown et al., eds., *Contending with Terrorism: Roots, Strategies, and Responses: An International Security Reader* (Cambridge, MA: MIT Press, 2010), 32–5.
39 See for example the 1955 novel by Robert Ruark, *Something of Value*. For a discussion of these presentations see Susan Carruthers, "Two Faces of 1950s Terrorism: The Film Presentation of Mau Mau and the Malayan Emergency", in *Terrorism, Media, Liberation*, ed. J. David Slocum, 70–93 (Piscataway, NJ: Rutgers University Press, 2005).
40 Mark Curtis, "The Mau Mau War in Kenya, 1952–60," February 12, 2007, http://markcurtis.wordpress.com/2007/02/12/the-mau-mau-war-in-kenya-1952-60/ (accessed on July 16, 2014). See also Mark Curtis, *Secret Affairs: Britain's Collusion with Radical Islam* (London: Serpent's Tail, 2010).
41 See David French, *The British Way in Counter-Insurgency, 1945–1967* (Oxford: Oxford University Press, 2011); Roger Trinquier, *Modern Warfare: A French View of Counterinsurgency* (Fort Leavenworth, KS: US Combat Studies Institute, [1961] 1985); and J. J. P. de Jong, *Diplomatie of strijd: Het Nederlands beleid tegenover de Indonesische Revolutie 1945–1947* (Amsterdam: Boom, 1988).
42 See Jerrold D. Green, "Terrorism and Politics in Iran," in *Terrorism in Context*, ed. Martha Crenshaw, 553–94 (University Park: Pennsylvania State University Press, 1995). See also Jan Oskar Engene, *Terrorism in Western Europe: Explaining the Trends since 1950* (Cheltenham, UK: Edward Elgar, 2004). For charts and statistics, and an introduction into these statistics, see Jan Oskar Engene, "Five Decades of Terrorism in Europe: The TWEED Dataset," *Journal of Peace Research* 44, no. 1 (January 2007): 109–21.
43 Even Steven Pinker recently characterized the terrorism bulge in the 1970s and 1980s as a "Cold War by proxy," suggesting a causal connection with the life cycle of communist regimes in the East. *The Better Angels of Our Nature: Why Violence Has Declined* (New York: Viking, 2011), 352.
44 William Safire (Nixon's speech writer), "2nd Draft: Campus Unrest Speech," April 30, 1969, 2. White House Special Files (WHSF), Staff Member and Office Files (SMOF), Krogh, Box 66, "Campus Disorder." National Archives and Records Administration (NARA), Washington, DC.
45 "Internal Security and Domestic Intelligence Presidential Talking Paper," June 5, 1970. White House Central Files (WHCF), ND 6, Box 41, "Intelligence." NARA, Washington, DC.
46 Claire Sterling, *The Terror Network: The Secret War of International Terrorism* (New York: Berkley Books, 1981).
47 Central Intelligence Agency. Special National Intelligence Estimate. *Soviet Support for International Terrorism and Revolutionary Violence*. SNIE 11/2–81 (May 27, 1981).
48 See Jens Bauszus, "Die RAF–Stasi-Connection," *Focus Magazine*, May 8, 2007; and Tobias Wunschik, "Die 'Bewegung 2. Juni' und ihre Protektion durch den Staatssicherheitsdienst der DDR," *Deutschland-Archiv* 6 (2007): 1014–25.
49 See Hermann Mierecker, "So schuf die CIA die 'Roten Brigaden.' Über die Steuerung linksextremistischer Terrorbanden in Italien durch imperialistische Geheimdienste," *Informationen* (Abteilung Agitation, SED) 4 (1984): 9–18. The article appeared in the East German magazine *Militärwesen*, no. 7–8, as early as 1980. Archives of the *Bundesbeauftragten für die Unterlagen des Staatssicherheitsdienstes der ehemaligen Deutschen Demokratischen Republik* (BStU), Ministerium für Staatssicherheit (MfS), SED-KL, 3503, p. 9–18; MfS/Abt. XII, "Hinweise zu einigen Aspekten des links-bzw. rechtsextremistischen Terrors in Italien," Berlin April 26, 1979. BStU MfS HA VI no. 1406: 21.
50 See Philip Willan, *Puppetmasters: The Political Use of Terrorism in Italy* (San Jose, CA: iUniverse, 2002); and de Graaf, *Evaluating Counterterrorism Performance*, 116–18.
51 Ursula C. Schroeder, *The Organization of European Security Governance: Internal and External Security in Transition* (London: Routledge, 2013), 118.
52 Based on my research in the MfS/KGB Archives, this chapter does disagree with Thomas Riegler's interpretation of the findings of connections between the secret services of the Soviet satellite states and revolutionary terrorist groups. These links did exist, but they have to be carefully

assessed and embedded within the communist states' own security strategies, rather than projecting new conspiracies upon them. Riegler, "Quid Pro Quo: State Sponsorship of Terrorism in the Cold War," in *An International History of Terrorism*, ed. Hanhimäki and Blumenau, 115–32.
53 See Shaloma Gauthier, "SWAPO, the United Nations, and the Struggle for National Liberation," in *An International History of Terrorism*, ed. Hanhimäki and Blumenau, 169–88.
54 Doc. A/C.6/SR.1362 (1972), Minutes of the Sixth Committee, statement by Guinea.
55 Bernhard Blumenau, "The UN and West Germany's Efforts against International Terrorism in the '70s," in *An International History of Terrorism*, ed. Hanhimäki and Blumenau, 79.
56 David Altheide, *Creating Fear: News and the Construction of Crisis* (New York: Aldine de Gruyter, 2002), ix–x; and Brigitte L. Nacos and Oscar Torres-Reyna, *Fueling Our Fears: Stereotyping, Media Coverage, and Public Opinion of Muslim Americans* (Lanham, MD: Rowman and Littlefield, 2007), 101.
57 Curtis, *The Power of Nightmares*.
58 Mattia Toaldo, "Reagan and Libya: A History of Pre-emptive Strikes and (Failed) Regime Change," in *An International History of Terrorism*, ed. Hanhimäki and Blumenau, 210–27.
59 Binnenlandse Veiligheidsdienst (BVD), *Ontwikkelingen op het gebied van de binnenlandse veiligheid. Taakstelling en werkwijze van de BVD* (The Hague: MinBZK, 1992), 25; P. H. A. M. Abels and R. Willemse, "Veiligheidsdienst in verandering. De BVD-AIVD sinds het einde van de Koude Oorlog," *Justitiële Verkenningen* 30, no. 3 (2004): 91.
60 UN General Assembly Resolution 49/60 para. 3 (1994).
61 UN Security Council Resolutions 1189 (1998), 1193 (1998), 1214 (1998), 1267 (1999), 1333 (2000). See also Ditrych, "From Discourse to Dispositive," 18.
62 See Osama bin Laden, *Messages to the World: The Statements of Osama bin Laden*, ed. Bruce Lawrence, trans. David Howarth (London: Verso, 2005). See also bin Laden, "Declaration of Jihad," www.terrorismfiles.org/individuals/declaration_of_jihad1.html (accessed February 24, 2014).
63 Liesbeth van der Heide, "Cherry-picked Intelligence."
64 See Bob Woodward, *Bush at War* (New York: Simon & Schuster, 2002); and Bob Woodward, *Plan of Attack* (New York: Simon & Schuster, 2004).
65 See Bruce Hoffman, "The Leaderless Jihad's Leader: Why Osama bin Laden Mattered," *Foreign Affairs*, May 13, 2011.
66 See James Risen, *State of War: The Secret History of the CIA and the Bush Administration* (New York: Simon & Schuster, 2006); National Commission on Terror Attacks, *The 9/11 Commission Report: Final Report of the National Commission on Terrorist Attacks upon the United States* (New York: Norton, 2004); and Gerald Posner, *Why America Slept: The Failure to Prevent 9/11* (New York: Random House, 2004).
67 Karen J. Greenberg and Joshua L. Dratel, eds., *The Torture Papers: The Road to Abu Ghraib* (New York: Cambridge University Press, 2005); and Abraham R. Wagner, "The US Response to Contemporary Terrorism," in *An International History of Terrorism*, ed. Hanhimäki and Blumenau, 244–62.
68 Ditrych, "From Discourse to Dispositive," 230.
69 See Marieke de Goede, "Blacklisting and the Ban: Contesting Targeted Sanctions in Europe," *Security Dialogue* 42, no. 6 (December 2011): 499–515; and Marieke de Goede, *Speculative Security: The Politics of Pursuing Terrorist Monies* (Minneapolis: University of Minnesota Press, 2012).
70 See de Graaf, *Evaluating Counterterrorism Performance*; and Frank Furedi, *Invitation to Terror: The Expanding Empire of the Unknown* (New York: Continuum, 2007).
71 See David Altheide, *Terror Post 9/11 and the Media* (New York: Peter Lang, 2009), especially chapter 7, "Terrorism Programming."
72 Recall how immediately after the London bombings of July 7, 2005, British Prime Minister Tony Blair did exactly this: "Terror will not win, we will not be intimidated." "Blair Says 'Terror Will Not Win,'" *BBC News*, July 7, 2005.
73 Magnus Ranstorp, "Mapping Terrorism Studies after 9/11: An Academic Field of Old Problems," in *Critical Terrorism Studies*, ed. Jackson et al., 14.

Further reading

Alexander, Yonah, ed. *Combating Terrorism: Strategies of Ten Countries*. Ann Arbor: University of Michigan Press, 2002.

Art, Robert J., and Louise Richardson, eds. *Democracy and Counterterrorism: Lessons from the Past.* Washington, DC: United States Institute of Peace Press, 2007.

Bartlett, Jamie, and Carl Miller. *The Power of Unreason: Conspiracy Theories, Extremism and Counter-terrorism.* London: Demos, 2010.

De Graaf, Beatrice. *Evaluating Counterterrorism Performance: A Comparative Study,* London: Routledge, 2011.

Deflem, Mathieu, ed. *Terrorism and Counterterrorism: Criminological Perspectives.* Amsterdam: Elsevier/JAI Press, 2004.

Forest, James J. F., ed. *Influence Warfare: How Terrorists and Governments Fight to Shape Perceptions in a War of Ideas.* Westport, CT: Praeger Security International, 2009.

Härter, Karl, and Beatrice de Graaf, eds. *Vom Majestätsverbrechen zum Terrorismus. Politische Kriminalität. Recht, Justiz und Polizei zwischen Früher Neuzeit und 20. Jahrhundert.* Frankfurt am Main: Klostermann, 2012.

Jensen, Richard Bach. *The Battle against Anarchist Terrorism, 1878–1934: An International History.* Cambridge: Cambridge University Press, 2014.

Masferrer, Aniceto, and Clive Walker. *Counter-Terrorism, Human Rights and the Rule of Law: Crossing Legal Boundaries in Defence of the State.* Cheltenham, UK: Edward Elgar, 2013.

Schmid, Alex, and Ronald Crelinsten, eds. *Western Responses to Terrorism.* London: Frank Cass, 1993.

White, Nigel D. "Preventive Counter-terrorism and International Law." *Journal of Conflict Security and Law* 18, no. 2 (Summer 2013): 181–92.

28

MEDIA AND TERRORISM

Robert A. Saunders

At its core, terrorism is political theater intended to convey a series of messages via symbolic acts of death and destruction. Prior to the advent of mass media (books, newspapers, radio, television, Internet, etc.), the effective reach of terrorists, whether state or non-state actors, remained comparatively weak, typically dependent on word of mouth, rumor, and intrigue. However, beginning with the introduction of the steam-powered rotary printing press in the mid-nineteenth century, the ability of political actors to inspire terror expanded exponentially. In our current era of globally linked networks of information and communications technologies (ICTs), terrorist organizations now enjoy the ability to broadcast their propaganda around the world at little to no cost, while also simultaneously benefiting from the deterritorialized nature of the Internet, which provides diverse mechanisms for recruitment, fund-raising, and surreptitious communication. Recognizing the historical import of such a transformation, this chapter presents a tripartite analysis of the relationship between media and terrorism, focusing on the "mediatization" of terrorism, or how the media coverage of terrorism facilitates and conditions human understanding and behavior.[1] Put more simply, this chapter investigates how the media make terrorism "real." The initial section explores the role of mass media as a tool of terrorists for the purposes of publicity, intimidation, propaganda, recruitment, fund-raising, communication, and, most importantly, legitimacy. In the second section, the focus is on governmental responses to mediatized terror, including censorship, counter-messaging, and public diplomacy, as well as media-based manipulation of the terrorist threat for political purposes. The final section interrogates political violence (both historical and fictional acts of terror) as a source of entertainment and popular culture, examining the role of cultural producers in shaping attitudes towards terrorism and counter-terrorism; the role of popular media in predicting and even shaping terrorist plots is also discussed. This exploration of the actual and symbolic relationships between various forms of mass media and terrorism, and particularly how terrorism has been facilitated by the media as well as transformed by it over time, aims to provide both an explanation of and a rejoinder to former British prime minister Margaret Thatcher's oft-echoed assertion that "publicity is the oxygen of terrorism."

A brief history of media as a tool of terror and terrorism as a media obsession

In a 1976 article in *Harper's* magazine, the noted historian of political violence Walter Laqueur stated that "The media are the terrorist's best friend. The terrorists' act by itself is nothing. Publicity is all."[2] Laqueur effectively applied the principle of the "the tree falling in the forest" to the practice of terrorism, suggesting that without "the media" any act of political violence was worthless as no one would "hear" it, i.e., be influenced by it. Whether one dates the origins of terrorism to the Sicarii attacks on Roman officials, the Assassins' reign of fear, or political violence during the French Revolution, publicity has been key to achieving the political aims of the perpetrators of such violence, whether through word of mouth, a hastily painted mural, or the most sophisticated form of digital media. In fact, many – if not most – definitions of terrorism implicitly or explicitly reflect the centrality of "messaging," that is, the transmission of actionable information associated with the act of terror.[3] According to terrorism expert Alex P. Schmid, terrorism is symbolic violence "aimed at behavior modification by coercion. Propaganda aims at the same by persuasion. Terrorism can be seen as a combination of the two."[4] Carlo Pisacane, who coined the phrase "propaganda by the deed," was perhaps the first to make this link explicit (though the anarchist aristocrat Peter Kropotkin popularized the notion), stating: "Ideas spring from deeds and not the other way around."[5] Pisacane, a supporter of social revolution as well as a unified Italy, influenced the generation of leftist revolutionaries who took acute advantage of burgeoning literacy, the ubiquity of newspapers, international telegraphy, and the power of the image to advance their causes. During the twentieth century, emergent media platforms from radio and television to the Internet would expand and amplify the ability of terrorist groups to "speak" to their various audiences, including but not limited to current and potential supporters, adversaries (the state), pro-state constituencies (society), "neutral" (often foreign) publics, other terrorist organizations, and the media.

In the pre-mass media era, terrorist "messaging" proved quite difficult, though not impossible. With abysmal levels of literacy and the high price of books, the printed word did not serve the terrorist well; instead, terror needed to be conveyed via speech acts. The Sicarii of Judea and Nizari Ismailis killed their foes in broad daylight, often in crowded places, to guarantee the reports of their acts traveled far and wide, whereas the Jacobins turned the public square into a murderous grotesquerie for all to witness the deadly fruits of counter-revolution. Whispers in the bazaar, bardic ditties about assassinations, and hanging corpses all served as pre-modern "technologies" of communication for non-state actors, spreading the discourse of fear ever outwards from the site of the attack. Conversely, as the state apparatus expanded, governments enjoyed an ever-increasing capacity to strike fear in the hearts of the citizenry through public executions, propaganda, and a visible police presence combined with the use of informers and undercover agents. The systemic and ideologically justified terror of the French Revolution exemplified this new shift; however, it was not until a half-century later that new technologies began to emerge that would literally "electrify" the message of terror.

The first generation of terrorists to yoke the power of new information and communications platforms included the Russian populists, Irish revolutionaries, and transnational anarchists of the latter half of the 1800s. From Chicago, Illinois, to St. Petersburg, Russia, radicals of every stripe quickly came to understand the powerful connection between bombs, blood, and newspaper headlines. While these terrorist groups tended to be quite small and had little recourse to the traditional channels of mass communication (political rallies, schools, churches, etc.), their actions commanded outsize attention in the burgeoning "free" press. From the mid-1800s to the end of the century, the number of newspapers worldwide increased ten-fold to well over 30,000, with over 2,000 daily newspapers with a total circulation of 15 million in the US alone; meanwhile, male literacy started to approach 100 percent in developed economies like England, France, and Germany (female literacy lagged well into the twentieth century) and showed dramatic increases in developing countries like India and the Philippines.

The widespread availability of the daily newspaper combined with an increasingly literate middle and working class ushered in the first era of mediatized terror, and, with new processes that allowed for reprinting of illustrations (and later photographs), the imagery of certain terror attacks such as Auguste Vaillant's 1893 bombing of the French Chamber of Deputies or the 1894 explosion at the Royal Observatory in Greenwich Park were etched in the collective memory. Likewise, high-profile assassinations, including Narodnaia Volia's murder of Tsar Alexander II and Leon Czolgosz's shooting of US President William McKinley in 1901, became mainstays of international media reporting, encouraging even more acts of individuated terror across Europe and North America. Even in states like tsarist Russia, where the government maintained strict controls on journalism, news of terrorist attacks – both at home and abroad – garnered valuable publicity for these groups, allowing them to challenge the state on a symbolic level. As non-state actors, such groups lacked control over the messaging of their acts and were thus consigned to the structural limitations of Pisacane's dictum, i.e., the deed must speak for itself, although public trials afforded certain radicals a further opportunity to propagandize. However, the emergence of underground printing presses did allow for the widespread distribution of incendiary manifestos like Sergei Nechaev's *Catechism of a Revolutionary* (1869) and periodicals such as the *United Irishman* (1885–1910) and *Cronaca Sovversiva* (1903–18), which served as mechanisms for fund-raising and recruitment, as well as propaganda. Following the 1914 assassination of the heir apparent to the Habsburg throne, Archduke Franz Ferdinand, by a Serbian nationalist influenced by the terrorist propaganda of the day, Europe was engulfed by war and the forces of history pushed the threat of anti-state terrorism to the backburner.

In the last century of the millennium, emergent media platforms began to transform the relationship between terrorism and journalism. Unlike newspapers, nascent broadcast media tended to be either run by the state or dependent on it (directly in authoritarian countries or indirectly in more liberal states), thus putting in place new safeguards against the manipulation of the press by terrorist organizations which did not exist in print media. Reflecting the new regime of informational power, authoritarian and totalitarian regimes in Soviet Russia, fascist Italy, and Nazi Germany employed mass media technologies in their own campaigns of political terror, resituating the notion of terrorism within its Jacobin roots.[6] The loudspeaker, motion pictures, and radio endowed the modern state with untold capacities to demonize one's enemies, put fear in the hearts of the opposition, and indoctrinate the masses (a process that would be repeated throughout the twentieth century, with the tragic coda of the 1994 broadcasts of Radio Television Libres des Mille Collines which encouraged Rwandans to slaughter their compatriots by the thousands). However, the "statist" domination of mass media proved ephemeral. Shortwave radio – a relatively inexpensive and slippery medium of mass communication – soon punctured the state's monopoly. A particularly telling example occurred in 1940s Palestine, as British power was targeted by the Voice of the Haganah, an underground Tel Aviv radio station supporting attacks on the imperial power in advance of the establishment of Israel. As de-colonization moved apace, national liberation struggles invaded the airwaves with clandestine radio stations popping up in Malaya, Vietnam, the Dominican Republic, and elsewhere. Moreover, transnational broadcasting – particularly via the Voice of the Arabs, a pan-Arab radio channel based in Cairo, Egypt – allowed groups like the National Liberation Front (FLN) to broadcast anti-colonial propaganda and reach receptive audiences in Algeria during the long struggle against French colonial rule. However, the genuine transformation of broadcast media into a tool of "international terrorism" came later with the rise of satellite television.

Once an experimental and geographically bound medium, by the 1970s television had emerged as the ultimate propaganda tool for terrorists, combining the power of visuality, immediacy, and – through satellite distribution – deterritorialization. Not coincidentally, the scale and scope of this "new breed of media-aware terrorists" who operated on "image and illusion" allowed for sub-state terrorism to become increasingly unmoored from individual states, effectively allowing it to "go global."[7] In 1972, several highly publicized terrorist attacks demonstrated the dark side of Marshal McLuhan's long-prophesied "global village,"[8] with the Black September attack on the Olympic village in Munich being the most (in)famous as an estimated audience of some 500 million people around the globe watched the tragedy unfold.[9] The world's media outlets, which had covered the incident at the Olympic Games in excruciating detail, had no shortage of terrorist acts to publicize during the decade following Munich, which ultimately became a byword for mediatized terror. Recognizing the media allure of hijacking airliners, terrorist organizations made the practice an almost commonplace occurrence between 1968 and the early 1980s. Combining suspense, danger, and a guaranteed international component, the spate of "skyjacking" acts during this period relied on media coverage for purposes of political extortion, recognition, and legitimacy, while also demonstrating the increasing connections between entities as disparate as the Japanese Red Army, Carlos the Jackal, and the Popular Front for the Liberation of Palestine.[10] Both the Munich massacre and the rise in airline and airport attacks during the 1970s demonstrated the centrality of global media coverage for certain types of terror organizations, specifically those seeking international attention.[11]

On the domestic level, groups like the Red Army Faction, the Red Brigades, and even Quebec separatists publicized their platforms and political demands through kidnapping and killing prominent state officials, typically in a prolonged and theatrical manner designed to reach large audiences and keep their organizations "in the news." To a certain extent, these strategies reflected the intellectual direction of the Brazilian Marxist Carlos Marighella whose *Minimanual of the Urban Guerrilla* became required reading for a generation of revolutionaries, insurgents, and terrorists. In his text, Marighella instructs the reader to make "direct or indirect use of mass means of communication and news transmitted orally in order to demoralize the government"[12]; while this echoes the maxims of earlier theorists, the specificity reflects a novel understanding about the reach of "new media." This period saw a purposefully exaggerated linkage between mass media and terrorism when the Symbionese Liberation Army kidnapped Patricia Hearst, scion of the media magnate William Randolph Hearst, and employed her as a mouthpiece for armed revolution, knowing the photogenic heiress would dramatically increase their public profile. Overall, this period represented a sea change in terrorist manipulation of the media wherein journalists could be relied on to cover political violence and the viewing public could be trusted to watch such coverage, thus guaranteeing an information channel for non-state actors who would otherwise be denied mass communication platforms. Scope also influenced this new dynamic as the ubiquity of satellite TV allowed any event anywhere to be beamed into the living room. In the words of Paul Wilkinson, the press and terrorist organizations became "locked in a relationship of considerable mutual benefit," whereby the terrorists attempt to use the media to convey propaganda, mobilize support, and frustrate their enemies, while the media are bound to report acts of terror to attract viewers, satisfy the demands of the market, and provide better coverage than their rivals.[13] The ramifications of this symbiosis were not lost on Iranian radicals who stormed the US embassy in Tehran in 1979 and held more than sixty Americans hostage for 444 days, an act which riveted American media outlets and even precipitated the (still-running) news program *Nightline*, which, during its days as "America Held Hostage," reached approximately 12 million viewers per night.[14]

In the midst of the Iran hostage crisis, the American media mogul Ted Turner launched the Cable News Network (CNN), heralding the rise of global twenty-four-hour news networks, which today include the international English-language news channels BBC World (UK), Al Jazeera (Qatar), Euronews (France), DW-TV (Germany), and RT (Russia). As a result, terrorist attacks could now be covered around the clock rather simply accounting for a portion of the evening news broadcast. The demands of filling hourly segments with content also served the interests of terrorist organizations hungry for publicity. Consequently, the 1980s saw a steady shift towards calculated terrorist "media events," prompting conservative commentator Charles Krauthammer to describe the actions of certain organizations as "pure media terrorism."[15]

> In this curious incarnation, terrorism became a form of political advertising. Barred from buying television time, the enterprising revolutionary decided to barter for it. Like the early commercial sponsors who produced their own television dramas in order to be able to show their ads, the media terrorists provided irresistible action – kidnapping and murder, live – in return for a chance to air their message.[16]

The 1985 hijacking of TWA Flight 847 and subsequent hostage-taking exemplified this trend. According to terrorism analyst Gabriel Weimann, "News organizations, and especially the US networks, gave the story impressive coverage, turning it into a dramatic, emotionally charged crisis that was rich in incident and interest."[17] Media framing soon came to characterize the journalistic approach to terrorist events, including personalization of the victims and victimizers, spectacularization of events, use of symbolism, and articulation of values.[18] During the 1980s, coverage of other high-profile incidents, sometimes referred to as "spectaculars," saw this approach honed. The hijacking of the Achille Lauro cruise ship in 1985 (which personalized the murder of the wheelchair-bound passenger Leon Klinghoffer) and the 1988 midair bombing of Pan Am Flight 103 over Lockerbie, Scotland (which was transformed into international geopolitical theater wherein democratic values and "justice" competed against tyranny and "evil"), were particularly emblematic of this trend. Terrorists soon took note of the efficacy of media-centric attacks, frequently contouring their operations for the television camera.

The end of the Cold War transformed the global terrorism milieu, as ideological as well as material support for left-wing terrorist organizations evaporated almost overnight. While nationalist groups such as the Provisional Irish Republican Army (PIRA), the Basque separatists Euskadi Ta Askatasuna (ETA), the Liberation Tigers of Tamil Eelam, and the various affiliates of the Palestine Liberation Organization continued their campaigns of terror, a palpable shift towards religiously affiliated terrorism came to define media coverage in the 1990s. Certainly, radical Islamist terrorist organizations – the most prominent of these religiously motivated organizations – were, in fact, not new to the scene, having assassinated Anwar Sadat in 1981 and bombed the US embassy in Beirut in 1983; however, with the changing state of international geopolitics, their relative position dramatically rose in terms of news coverage after 1989. As a number of scholars have pointed out, injecting religiosity into the mix triggered multiple shifts in terrorist practices.[19] Two of the most important were the introduction of suicide bombings, typically attributed to the Lebanese Shi'ite group Hizbullah,[20] and the tendency among religiously inspired groups to seek as many deaths as possible. The latter reflects an important shift in the mediated power of such attacks, given that the emphasis is now on sheer violence rather than an act's symbolic value. During the 1990s, Hamas and Islamic Jihad attacks on Jewish Israelis in shopping malls, restaurants, and public transportation certainly fit this mold, producing high numbers of casualties and graphic scenes of blood, body parts, and physical carnage that were transmitted to Israelis and the world via media outlets.[21] In the United States, the 1993 bombing of the World Trade Center by followers of the blind sheik Umar 'Abd al-Rahman targeted a near-universally recognizable icon (and potent symbol of the power of the "West"), generating what some have called the age of "spectacular terrorism" in which a so-called "image-event" – inherently visual and infinitely replicable in nature – is created for the purpose of constant remembering and reinterpretation.[22] Although not an example of religiously motivated terror, Timothy McVeigh's bombing of the Alfred P. Murrah Federal Building in Oklahoma City proved to be just as "spectacular" three years later. By targeting the federal facility at 9:00 a.m., McVeigh hoped to spill "as much blood as possible," while his timing ensured that television cameras would be able to cover the story throughout the day.[23] As Bruce Hoffman points out, international media coverage and the undeniable globality of terrorist attacks were factors as well, as McVeigh wanted to guarantee that his actions were not overshadowed by the (religiously inspired) Aum Shinrikyo's "dramatic and more exotic nerve gas attack on the Tokyo subway" a month earlier.[24]

During the 1990s, transnational terrorist organizations developed highly sophisticated media strategies. Perhaps most illustrative of this phenomenon was the establishment of Al-Manar ("The Beacon"), a Hizbullah-owned and operated satellite television station in 1991 (today, the network has approximately 15 million daily viewers, as well as reaching a larger audience via its webcasts). However, less costly innovations also characterized the decade, including the employment of video recordings of "martyrs" (suicide bombers) for propaganda purposes, as well as the widespread use of computer diskettes, satellite telephones, fax machines, email, websites, and electronic bulletin boards for communication and intelligence exchange.[25] Hizbullah, in particular, proved to be a pioneer in the adoption of emerging media technologies, being one of the first groups on the Internet; however, other organizations were quick to follow, and the Web soon became a factor in terrorist activities from Ireland to Chechnya to Indonesia. According to Marc Sageman, Osama bin Laden's sojourn in Sudan and subsequent return to Afghanistan in 1996 coincided with a massive transformation of media, which bin Laden incorporated into his day-to-day practices, ultimately transforming the salafi-jihadi movement into a global force with al-Qaeda serving as its "base."[26] Using such tools, bin Laden and the Egyptian Ayman al-Zawahiri directed their affiliates to undertake the highly publicized bombings of two US embassies in East Africa (1998) and the naval warship USS Cole (2000), before undertaking the ultimate "spectacle": the September 11, 2001 attacks on the World Trade Center and the Pentagon. According to one scholar: "The 9/11 terror spectacle was obviously constructed as a media event to circulate terror and to demonstrate to the world the vulnerability of the epicenter of global capitalism and American power."[27] The seminal event of the new millennium, 9/11 transformed geopolitics, international relations, and the global economy, while linking media coverage and acts of terror more closely together than at any time in the history of political violence,[28] a fact underscored by subsequent acts of terrorism including the coordinated attacks on high-profile sites in Mumbai, India, in 2008, and the 2010 bombings of the Moscow Metro. (For more on al-Qaeda, 9/11, and the Global War on Terror, see Chapter 22 by Daveed Gartenstein-Ross in this volume.)

Following the October 2001 US invasion of Afghanistan, al-Qaeda's ability to operate was severely compromised; however, the physical limitations placed on the organization led to a greater reliance on new media, with al-Qaeda effectively becoming a virtual entity sustained by the Internet and satellite television. Bin Laden's organization, coordinating with "start-up" branches of like-minded jihadis in North Africa, Iraq, and elsewhere, developed a heavy presence in cyberspace during the decade following 9/11. Al-Qaeda deployed an online public relations campaign that advanced a coherent narrative through its As-Sahab ("The Cloud") propaganda arm, its *al-Hussam* ("The Sword") online magazine, and affiliations with the loosely connected network of friendly programmers known as al-Fajr Media Center.[29] As new platforms such as YouTube emerged, al-Qaeda and other jihadist groups were quick to take advantage of the Internet's ability to function as a single-source platform for all forms of broadcast media, allowing for the transmission of items as mundane as policy statements on climate change to videos showing the beheading of American Nicholas Berg in 2004. Freed from the shackles of the "old media" relationship, terrorists could now represent themselves without relying on journalistic intermediaries.[30] Security analyst and journalist Peter Bergen once noted that al-Qaeda's leadership argues that "90% of [the] battle is conducted in the media,"[31] thus requiring real-world attacks to take a back seat to "e-jihad."[32] For audiences without access to the Internet, the Arabic-language satellite network Al Jazeera served as a fairly reliable venue for distributing video and audio recordings (often in raw form) made by bin Laden and al-Zawahiri, particularly during the early years of the "War on Terror," thus earning the broadcaster a host of epithets including "jihad TV," "killers with cameras," and "the most powerful ally of terror in the world."[33] Following in al-Qaeda's wake, other violent organizations from the Earth Liberation Front to neo-Nazis have adapted to the Internet era, folding new media into their overall strategies for winning hearts and minds, as well as vilifying their enemies.

Looking beyond the realm of propaganda, the evolution of new media technologies and the expansion of cyberspace since the late 1990s have proved a boon to terrorist organizations. The decentralization, anonymity, and speed of the Internet allow terrorists to use cyberspace as a "safe haven" for the distribution of training manuals, as well as a realm for various forms of communication, logistical support, and coordination (even the deployment of videogames meant to "prime the pump" for future terrorists or suicide bombers); the Internet also functions as the primary tool for collecting intelligence on enemy activity, potential targets, etc.[34] The murkier corners of the Web allow for fund-raising and recruitment, as do mainstream social networking sites like Facebook and Twitter.[35] In an exceptional case, Palestinian militants even used an Internet chat room to lure an Israeli teenager to the West Bank where he was killed. More recently, the Taliban has used fake profiles of attractive women to obtain geo-tagged information from coalition soldiers in Afghanistan in order to help plan attacks.[36] Most disturbingly, cyberspace has become such a repository of propaganda and terrorist "know-how" that minuscule cells and "lone wolf" individuals are able to "self-radicalize" via the Web and learn what they need to know to commit major acts of terrorism, including the 7/7 attacks in London (2005) and Anders Breivik's terror spree in Norway (2011). The benefits of the Internet do come with a price, however, as counter-terrorism operatives enjoy significant intelligence gathering capabilities over the Internet, allowing the US's National Security Agency, Britain's Security Service (MI5), and France's

General Directorate for External Security to ferret out terrorist cells in cyberspace. Given the increasingly networked nature of critical infrastructure (transportation, water supplies, etc.), there is the possibility that information and communications technologies may eventually be used to carry out terrorist attacks; however, such dangers remain the preserve of science fiction for the immediate time being.

Mediatization and state responses to terrorism

As discussed in the previous section, terrorist organizations are ineluctably linked to media coverage and the use of ICTs to achieve their political goals; however, states – often the primary targets of terrorist activity – are also key players in the mediatization of terror. By choosing to engage in censorship, (dis)information campaigns, or to ignore the relationship between the press and terrorists, governmental actors shape the milieu in which political violence effects political outcomes; similarly, manipulation of the terror threat has also been a common ploy for governments to achieve discrete political gains (often ones with only minimal links to national security).

Historically, the political system of a given state tended to inform its response to the media coverage of terrorism. Censorship has often been the redoubt of autocratic regimes, with tsarist Russia and Ottoman Turkey representing examples of such an orientation. During the reign of Nicholas I (1825–55), which coincided with the dawn of mass media, Russia instituted a reign of "censorship terror" to provide "intellectual dams against destructive European ideas" against which future tsarist policies would be measured.[37] While future leaders would not be as restrictive, the Russian state possessed all the tools necessary to censor mass media (including plays, literature, the visual arts, and even popular ballads) with the aim of squashing revolutionary ideals. Heavy fines, arrests, destruction of presses, and a host of other mechanisms were at the disposal of the secret police whose job it was to ensure the state against "inimical interests." In certain cases, even articles of "nihilist fashion" (seen as a form of visual media) were prohibited in an effort to forestall further terrorist acts.[38] Despite such measures, anti-state propaganda still managed to find its way to the public eye, particularly via publications that were smuggled in from abroad. Under Alexander II (1855–81), significant reforms were undertaken to lessen censorship, resulting in increasingly "lurid descriptions" of assassinations and acts of terrorism, which in turn led to increasingly effective propaganda of the deed on the part of Russian nihilists and leftists,[39] including multiple assassination attempts on the reforming tsar (one was ultimately successful). In the Ottoman Empire, the Sultan willfully ignored the dramatic political transformations occurring across the continent, expecting his subjects to do likewise. In fact, newspapers were forbidden to even mention the word assassination; accordingly, "Empress Elizabeth of Austria died of pneumonia, President Carnot of France of apoplexy, US President McKinley of anthrax, and the King and Queen of Serbia simultaneously of indigestion."[40]

Liberal, democratic states were certainly not above employing censorship to undermine the propaganda value of terrorist acts; however, the laissez-faire structure of the press in countries like the United States and Britain often made for a difficult balancing act. Generally speaking, both Washington and London proved to be rather lax in policing terrorist propaganda as long as it targeted regimes overseas, thus providing safe havens for Fenian propagandists in America and a host of European radicals in England. As the US did not suffer from a sustained terrorist threat until the current century (other than the spate of violent radicalism in the 1880s–1910s), censorship related to the reporting of acts of terror has not generally been an issue. Britain, however, responded to violence in Northern Ireland by instituting the 1988 Broadcasting Ban, which by most accounts represented an instance of direct censorship.[41] The measure prohibited televising or broadcasting the voices of representatives of organizations seen to be supporting terrorism. While a number of organizations were included under the ban, Sinn Féin – the political arm of the PIRA – was its main target. Interestingly, Russia used a similar ban to bar ABC News from the country in 2005 following its airing of a *Nightline* interview with the now-deceased Islamist terrorist Shamil Basayev on grounds the US network was "abetting the propaganda of terrorism."[42] During its long war in Algeria (1954–62), France instituted pre- and post-publication censorship, shuttering presses and seizing newspapers and even books deemed to be supportive of FLN terrorism.[43] As the birthplace of the *Declaration of the Rights of Man*, intellectuals and eventually the masses rallied against such measures, ultimately forcing the government to abandon overt efforts at silencing discourse related to terrorism. As mentioned above, post-Soviet Russia has taken a hard stance on media reporting of terrorism, both by domestic and international media organizations. New laws enacted under Vladimir Putin allowed the government to shut down television and radio stations who contravened the edict on real-time reporting during the Nord-Ost hostage crisis in 2002 on grounds these media were "promoting terrorism"; subsequent attacks, like Beslan in 2004, received almost no live coverage as journalists feared government reprisals for doing their jobs.[44]

In lieu of outright censorship, many governments have engaged in systemic policies of disinformation (purposefully spreading false reports to influence public opinion) and misinformation (non-factual reporting) to counter terrorist propaganda. In cases where the press is government-controlled, such policies have been rather ineffective; however, in countries where the media are perceived to be free from state control, such policies have produced tangible results. When conducted in concert with strategic public diplomacy campaigns to mobilize popular opinion, state actors have been able to manipulate the "signal-to-noise" ratio so effectively that terrorist organizations' ability to use the media is almost totally negated, as in the case of the PIRA and ETA which came to see media coverage as counter-productive.[45] In such cases, these organizations began to shun press coverage and eschewed standard post-attack propagandizing. Historically, advocates of the state have used a cooperative press to buttress their own positions and weaken those of their terrorist adversaries often through loaded language, e.g., the labeling of the Red Army Faction as the "Baader-Meinhof Gang" or Ilich Ramírez Sánchez as "The Jackal."

Perhaps nothing better exemplifies this trend than the introduction of the catchphrase "War on Terror" by the Bush administration following the 9/11 attacks. By framing the government's response to the attacks as the equivalent of a "world war" (and playing on deeply embedded strands of racism and xenophobia), the state was generally able to rely on the media to treat its actions accordingly, as well as portray criticisms of national policy as seditious, if not outright treasonous.[46] Consequently, mainstream mass media outlets tended to engage in significant levels of self-censorship and pro-government bandwagoning on issues related to terrorism. While many in America were genuinely "terrorized" by the original attack, daily media coverage of the Department of Homeland Security's color-coded threat-level system and constant "terrorist threat" stories (often without any specific information) led to intense criticism of the press as a complicit partner in the US government's manipulation of an exaggerated perception of danger to achieve its domestic and foreign policy goals, most notably the decision to go to war with Iraq.[47] Around the globe, other states have massaged media coverage of anti-state activists in similar fashion. In the wake of 9/11, China's press, reflecting a shift in government policy, began branding Uighur separatists as "Islamic fundamentalists" and "violent jihadis," descriptors that went unchallenged in much of the international press.[48] Similar discursive manipulation occurred in Russia, Sri Lanka, and Syria. However, such media "management" has not always been successful. In 2004, Spanish Prime Minister José María Aznar's government fell following an ill-conceived attempt to blame ETA terrorists for an Islamist bombing of the Madrid metro system. His personal assurances to the press of Basque responsibility for the attacks were eventually exposed as incontrovertible lies and the opposition won the election that followed.[49]

Of mirrors and oracles: terror as entertainment

The "wild-eyed terrorist" is a perennial subject of fascination for authors and film makers, and through constant mass mediation forms a powerful myth in modern global culture.[50] During the nineteenth and early twentieth centuries, scores of popular novels and even works of high literature dramatized the anarchist or nihilist terrorist, thus reflecting the public interest in the bloody paroxysms of the time, and providing what Lynn Patyk characterizes as "a symbolic intermediary between terrorism and its audiences."[51] Fyodor Dostoevsky's *Demons* (1872), the "best known 'terrorist' novel in world history,"[52] critiqued the "devilish" fundaments of contemporary Russian radicals bent on the violent overthrow of the tsarist regime. In a case of art imitating life and vice versa, Joseph Conrad took inspiration from the failed Greenwich Park bomber Martial Bourdin for his novel *The Secret Agent: A Simple Tale* (1907); the character of "The Professor," an anarchist bomber, would later serve as inspiration for Unabomber and former mathematics professor Theodore Kaczynski.[53] Frank Harris's *Bomb* (1908) similarly ripped its topic from the headlines, providing a fictional account of an escaped Haymarket Riot bomber who exacts a horrible revenge. Other fictional works of the period that both drew inspiration from terror attacks and contributed to the stereotype of the unstable and malevolent terrorist include Robert Louis Stevenson's *The Dynamiter* (1885), Henry James's *The Princess Casamassima* (1886), and Edward Douglas Fawcett's *Hartmann the Anarchist* (1892). Popular novels such as Frederick Forsyth's *The Day of the Jackal* (1971) and John le Carré's *The Little Drummer Girl* (1983) continued to play on fears of terrorism in the ensuing decades, but by the second half of the twentieth century the written word had taken a backseat to visual media.

The advent of the motion picture introduced a new medium that would eventually link the power of image and sound to the storyteller's vision. Laqueur dates the first "terrorist" film to 1917 with the premiere of Russian director Yakov Protazanov's *Andrey Kozhukov*.[54] The interwar period saw a number of important pictures on the topic of terrorism, including John Ford's 1935 adaptation of Liam O'Flaherty's novel *The Informer* (1925). In the wake of World War II, national liberation terrorism was prominently showcased in *Exodus* (1960) and *The Battle of Algiers* (1966). Based on the novel by Leon Uris, *Exodus* presents a fictional and highly positive vision of the Jewish underground fighting against the British in Palestine, personified by the handsome Ari Ben Canaan (Paul Newman). Positing Israeli identity as a correlate for "Americanness," director Otto Preminger scripted violent extremism as the "good fight" for North American audiences.[55] As relevant today as when it was filmed, Gillo Pontecorvo's *The Battle of Algiers* represents the most important film on the topic of terrorism. A stunning example of *cinéma vérité*, Pontecorvo reproduced actual FLN terror attacks in

Algiers on celluloid and even cast a local cell commander, Saadi Yacef, as himself in the film; according to film historian Peter Matthews, "The details are so explicit that *The Battle of Algiers* was adapted into a training manual by the Black Panthers and the IRA – even screened (for a more cautionary purpose, one assumes) at the Pentagon."[56]

In the wake of the Munich massacre, popular culture began to reflect the growing obsession with international terrorism, and especially Arab terrorists. Based on Thomas Harris's novel, the motion picture *Black Sunday* (1977) centered on a Palestinian terrorist plot to attack the Super Bowl with a blimp, eerily reminding viewers of the attack on a premier sporting event five years prior (nearly three decades later Steven Spielberg directed *Munich*, which dealt with the Olympic terrorist attack and the centrality of media coverage to the event). During the following decades, films such as *Back to the Future* (1985), *The Delta Force* (1986), *Navy SEALs* (1990), *True Lies* (1994), *Executive Decision* (1996), and *The Siege* (1998) presented a terrorist threat emanating from the Arab–Muslim world, retooling old prejudices and capitalizing on contemporary fears.[57] Arab terrorists were not the only organizations to be dramatized on the big screen, as films like *Year of the Gun* (1991) and *Patriot Games* (1992) explored themes in Italian and Irish terrorism, respectively. In an instance in which popular media actually triggered an act of terror, the liberal, Jewish radio host Alan Berg was gunned down by the right-wing terrorist group The Order in 1984; the events of this political murder were later fictionalized in *Talk Radio* (1988) and *Betrayed* (1988).

In the wake of the 9/11 attacks, the "War on Terror" naturally came to influence cultural production, with nearly every popular medium reflecting some aspect of the US and allied campaign to eradicate Islamist terror. Captain America took on terrorists on the pages of comic books, while Jack Bauer tortured them on the television show *24*; meanwhile, country music singers railed against Arab bombers and ventriloquist Jeff Dunham rode to fame on the back of his dummy Achmed the Dead Terrorist as the notoriously liberal director Oliver Stone sculpted a cinematic paean to the victims of 9/11 in his 2006 film *World Trade Center*.[58] Cultural producers who had once been criticized for "giving ideas" to terrorists (e.g., flying airplanes into buildings) were called upon by Washington to support the "global response" against jihadist "evil."[59] While a few films such as *Syriana* (2005) and *Rendition* (2007) would question the role of US foreign policy in shaping the current terrorist threat, as well as post-9/11 policies intended to thwart political violence, most mainstream mass media throatily supported the governmental response to international terrorism.

Paul Wilkinson contends that "When one says 'terrorism' in a democratic society, one also says 'media'" as the two concepts are inextricably bound together.[60] However, as we have seen above, even the most autocratic societies must also confront the undeniable realities of the terror–media nexus. Since the advent of genuinely "mass" media in the mid-nineteenth century, terrorists have increasingly modeled their propaganda, attacks, and targets with the media in mind. Not surprisingly, states have attempted to negate any benefits provided by the emerging media forms and new ICTs, while concurrently making use of their own power to influence the mediatization of terror and terrorist groups (for good or ill). Reflecting the intense interest of the public in issues related to political violence, cultural producers have incorporated contemporary and long past acts of terrorism into their own work, from novels to films to comedy skits. While the twenty-first century has witnessed a widening and deepening of the interconnectedness of terrorism and media (particularly through the continued rise of the Internet and other forms of new media), such trends serve only to remind us of how established the historical relationship between these two entities actually is.

Notes

1. Knut Lundby, *Mediatization: Concept, Changes, Consequences* (Bern: Peter Lang, 2009).
2. Walter Laqueur, "The Futility of Terrorism," *Harper's* 252 (1976): 104.
3. See, respectively, Randall D. Law, *Terrorism: A History* (Cambridge: Polity, 2009); Michael Burleigh, *Blood and Rage: A Cultural History of Terrorism* (New York: HarperCollins, 2009); and Barry Cooper, *New Political Religions, Or an Analysis of Modern Terrorism* (Columbia: University of Missouri Press, 2005).
4. Alex P. Schmid, "Frameworks for Conceptualising Terrorism," *Terrorism and Political Violence* 16, no. 2 (Summer 2004): 206.
5. Carlo Pisacane, "Political Testament," in *Anarchism: A Documentary History of Libertarian Ideas, Volume One*, ed. Robert Graham (Montreal: Black Rose Books, [1857] 2004), 68. For more on "propaganda of the deed" and anarchist terrorism in Europe in the late nineteenth century, see Chapter 8 by Richard Bach Jensen in this volume.
6. See Chapter 7 by Martin A. Miller in this volume for more on the roots of state terror in Imperial Russia, as well as Chapter 11 by Paul M. Hagenloh on state terror in the Soviet Union and Nazi Germany.
7. Desmond Smith, "A New Brand of Terrorism," *Nation* 218, no. 13 (1974): 393.
8. Marshall McLuhan, *The Gutenberg Galaxy: The Making of Typographic Man* (Toronto: University of Toronto Press, 1962).
9. Paul Wilkinson, "The Media and Terrorism: A Reassessment," *Terrorism and Political Violence* 9, no. 2 (1997): 52.
10. Adam Dolnik, *Understanding Terrorist Innovation* (London: Psychology Press, 2007), 32.
11. For more on the Munich attack, the development of international terrorism, and the manipulation of public opinion around the globe, see Chapter 25 by Geraint Hughes in this volume.
12. Carlos Marighella, *Minimanual of the Urban Guerrilla* (Washington, DC: Citizens Committee for a Free Cuba), n.p. For more on Marighella and the emergence of the urban guerrilla movement in Latin America, see Chapter 19 by Jennifer S. Holmes in this volume.
13. Paul Wilkinson, "The Media and Terrorism," 52.
14. Melani McAlister, *Epic Encounters: Culture, Media, and U.S. Interest in the Middle East since 1945* (Berkeley: University of California Press, 2005), 205.
15. Charles Krauthammer, "The New Terrorism," *New Republic* 191, nos. 7–8 (1984): 11.
16. Ibid., 12.
17. Gabriel Weimann, "Media Events: The Case of International Terrorism," *Journal of Broadcasting & Electronic Media* 31, no. 1 (1987): 24.
18. Pippa Norris, Montague Kern, and Marion Just, *Framing Terrorism: The News Media, the Government and the Public* (New York: Routledge, 2003).
19. See, for instance, Burleigh, *Blood and Rage*; Mia Bloom, *Dying To Kill: The Allure of Suicide Terror* (New York: Columbia University Press, 2005); and Bruce Hoffman, *Inside Terrorism*, 2nd ed. (New York: Columbia University Press, 2006).
20. Mahmood Mamdani, *Good Muslim, Bad Muslim: America, the Cold War, and the Roots of Terror* (New York: Random House, 2005). However, as Susanne Martin discusses in Chapter 26 in this volume, the Tamil Tigers were the most prolific employers of suicide terrorism until the early part of the twenty-first century.
21. For more on radical Islamist terrorism, see Chapters 17 and 18 by John Calvert and David Cook, respectively, in this volume.
22. Luke Howie, *Terror on the Screen: Witnesses and the Reanimation of 9/11 as Image-Event, Popular Culture and Pornography* (New York: New Academia Publishing, 2011).
23. Robert L. Snow, *Terrorists among Us: The Militia Threat* (Cambridge, MA: Da Capo Press, 2002), 97.
24. Hoffman, *Inside Terrorism*, 248.
25. See John Arquilla and David F. Ronfeldt, *Networks and Netwars: The Future of Terror, Crime, and Militancy* (Washington, DC: RAND Corporation, 2001).
26. Marc Sageman, *Understanding Terror Networks* (Philadelphia: University of Pennsylvania Press, 2011).
27. Douglas Kellner, *From 9/11 to Terror War: The Dangers of the Bush Legacy* (Lanham, MD: Rowman & Littlefield, 2003), 41.

28 Walter Enders and Todd Sandler, *The Political Economy of Terrorism*, 2nd ed. (Cambridge: Cambridge University Press, 2011).
29 See Jarret Brachman, Afshon Ostovar, and Lianne Kennedy Boudali, *The Islamic Imagery Project: Visual Motifs in Jihadi Internet Propaganda* (West Point, NY: Combating Terrorism Center at the United States Military Academy, 2006); and Craig Whitlock, "Al-Qaeda's Growing Online Offensive," *Washington Post*, June 24, 2008, http://articles.washingtonpost.com/2008-06-24/world/36885241_1_zawahiri-qaeda-al-qaeda (accessed January 12, 2013).
30 Bruce Klopfenstein, "Terrorism and the Exploitation of the New Media," in *Media, Terrorism, and Theory: A Reader*, ed. Anandam P. Kavoori and Todd Fraley, 107–20 (Lanham, MD: Rowman & Littlefied, 2006).
31 Peter Bergen, "Reassessing the Threat: The Future of al Qa'ida and Its Implications for Homeland Security," in *House Committee on Homeland Security's Subcommittee on Intelligence, Information Sharing and Terrorism Risk Assessment* (Washington, DC: US Congress, 2008).
32 Brigitte L. Nacos, *Mass-Mediated Terrorism: The Central Role of the Media in Terrorism and Counterterrorism* (Lanham, MD: Rowman & Littlefield, 2007).
33 Marc Lynch, "Watching al-Jazeera," *Wilson Quarterly* 29, no. 3 (2005): 36.
34 See David H. Gray, and Albon Head, "The Importance of the Internet to the Post-Modern Terrorist and Its Role as a Form of Safe Haven," *European Journal of Scientific Research* 25, no. 3 (2009): 396–404.
35 Gabriel Weimann, "Terror on Facebook, Twitter, and Youtube," *Brown Journal of World Affairs* 16, no. 2 (2010): 45–54.
36 Ben Farmer, "Taliban Pose as Women to Friend Soldiers on Facebook," *Telegraph*, September 11, 2012, www.telegraph.co.uk/news/worldnews/asia/afghanistan/9535862/Taliban-pose-as-women-to-friend-soldiers-on-Facebook.html (accessed December 12, 2012).
37 Daniel Balmuth, "The Origins of the Tsarist Epoch of Censorship Terror," *American Slavic and East European Review* 19, no. 4 (1960): 498.
38 Claudia Verhoeven, *The Odd Man Karakozov: Imperial Russia, Modernity and the Birth of Terrorism* (Ithaca, NY: Cornell University Press, 2009).
39 Law, *Terrorism*, 75.
40 Jason Goodwin, *Lords of the Horizons: A History of the Ottoman Empire* (New York: Macmillan, 2003), 313.
41 See Kent Roach, *The 9/11 Effect: Comparative Counter-Terrorism* (Cambridge: Cambridge University Press, 2011).
42 "Russia Bars ABC over Interview," *BBC News*, August 2, 2005, http://news.bbc.co.uk/2/hi/europe/4739619.stm (accessed June 28, 2006).
43 Raymond Kuhn, *The Media in France* (London: Routledge, 1994).
44 Robert A. Saunders, "A Conjurer's Game: Vladimir Putin and the Politics of Presidential Prestidigitation," in *Playing Politics with Terrorism: A User's Guide*, ed. George Kassimeris, 220–49 (London: Hurst, 2007).
45 Boaz Ganor, *The Counter-Terrorism Puzzle: A Guide for Decision Makers* (Piscataway, NJ: Transaction Publishers, 2007).
46 Richard Jackson, *Writing the War on Terrorism: Language, Politics and Counter-terrorism* (Manchester: Manchester University Press, 2005).
47 John Mueller, *Overblown: How Politicians and the Terrorism Industry Inflate National Security Threats, and Why We Believe Them* (New York: Simon and Schuster, 2006).
48 Diane Winston, *The Oxford Handbook of Religion and the American News Media* (Oxford: Oxford University Press, 2012), 488.
49 George Kassimeris, "Introduction," in *Playing Politics with Terrorism*, ed. George Kassimeris, 1–14.
50 Jamal Raji Nassar, *Globalization and Terrorism: The Migration of Dreams and Nightmares* (Lanham, MD: Rowman & Littlefield, 2010).
51 See Lynn Patyk, "The Age of Terrorism in the Age of Literature," Chapter 31 in this volume.
52 Walter Laqueur, *A History of Terrorism* (Piscataway, NJ: Transaction Publishers, 1977), 156.
53 Ramón Spaaij, *Understanding Lone Wolf Terrorism* (New York: Springer, 2012).
54 Laqueur, *A History*, 149.
55 McAlister, *Epic Encounters*, 161.

56 Peter Matthews, "The Battle of Algiers: Bombs and Boomerangs," *Current* (2004), www.criterion.com/current/posts/342-the-battle-of-algiers-bombs-and-boomerangs (accessed August 26, 2004). For more on the FLN's use of terrorism during the Algerian War of Independence, see Chapter 15 by Martin C. Thomas in this volume.
57 Jack Shaheen, *Reel Bad Arabs: How Hollywood Vilifies a People* (New York: Olive Branch Press, 2001).
58 See, respectively, the following: Jason Dittmer, "Captain America's Empire: Reflections on Identity, Popular Culture, and Post-9/11 Geopolitics," *Annals of the Association of American Geographers* 95, no. 3 (2005): 626–43; Adam Green, "Normalizing Torture on '24,'" *New York Times*, May 22, 2005, www.nytimes.com/2005/05/22/arts/television/22gree.html?pagewanted=all&_r=0 (accessed March 28, 2012); Andrew Boulton, "The Popular Geopolitical Wor(l)ds of Post-9/11 Country Music," *Popular Music and Society* 31, no. 3 (2008): 373–87; Darren Purcell, Melissa Scott Brown, and Mahmut Gokmen, "Achmed the Dead Terrorist and Humor in Popular Geopolitics," *Geoforum* 75 (2010): 373–85; and Klaus Dodds, "Hollywood and the Popular Geopolitics of the War on Terror," *Third World Quarterly* 29, no. 8 (2008): 1621–37.
59 Matthew Alford, *Reel Power: Hollywood Cinema and American Supremacy* (New York: Pluto Press, 2010), 14.
60 Wilkinson, "The Media," 54.

Further reading

Altheide, David L. *Terror Post-9/11 and the Media*. New York: Peter Lang, 2009.

Howie, Luke. *Terror on the Screen: Witnesses and the Reanimation of 9/11 as Image-Event, Popular Culture and Pornography*. New York: New Academia Publishing, 2011.

Kavoori, Anandam P., and Todd Fraley. *Media, Terrorism, and Theory: A Reader*. Lanham, MD: Rowman & Littlefield, 2006.

Martin, Andrew, and Patrice Petro. *Rethinking Global Security: Media, Popular Culture, and the "War on Terror."* New Brunswick, NJ: Rutgers University Press, 2006.

Nacos, Brigitte L. *Mass-Mediated Terrorism: The Central Role of the Media in Terrorism and Counterterrorism*. Lanham, MD: Rowman & Littlefield, 2007.

Tuman, Joseph S. *Communicating Terror: The Rhetorical Dimensions of Terrorism*. 2nd ed. Thousand Oaks, CA: Sage, 2010.

Wilkinson, Paul. "The Media and Terrorism: A Reassessment." *Terrorism and Political Violence* 9, no. 2 (1997): 51–64.

29

TERRORISM AND TECHNOLOGY

Ann Larabee

The role of technology is fundamental to our understanding of modern terrorism, and yet historians have largely viewed technology – especially the bomb – as merely incidental or instrumental objects, vehicles for violently carrying out pre-existing political aims. To borrow philosopher Carl Mitcham's definition, technologies are not only objects but also activities, ways of knowing, and volitions.[1] When we look at the ways groups embed technologies in their repertoire of political action, we find that technologies are important agents that have reshaped activities, networks, identities, and goals.[2] Technologies are also important as the contexts in which terrorist acts unfold, including, for example, urban geographies that concentrate populations in small areas, communications media that carry news of these acts, and targets like transportation systems. Most importantly for this chapter, the flow of technological projects from one group to the next reveals much about the disturbingly porous borders between state and non-state actors, and among those defined as terrorists, insurgents, soldiers, and military engineers. It troubles the tendency to characterize groups as defined by their political beliefs, as diabolical inventors removed from any sources of invention, and as anomalies in societies that wage war through arms development and trade. There is no such thing as a terrorist technology, but only technologies that have been disseminated through circuitous pathways to those who have been deemed the wrong hands. This chapter proposes that it is well worth adding the question of technology to the subfield of the history of terrorism, which has been mostly focused on definitions, typologies, psychological and political motivations, and ideological conflicts.[3]

Terrorism and the development of modern technological systems

The late nineteenth century witnessed a confluence of scientific and technical development energized by patent systems, a more pervasive science education and formal technical training for ordinary citizens, the rise of a robust global print media that carried news through the telegraph, new fast and efficient printing technologies, the development of an effective postal system, urbanization, the railroad and faster ocean travel, and an arms race among the Western empires. As Robert A. Saunders points out in the previous chapter, new communications technologies allowed revolutionary groups to get their messages out and were a mode of propaganda, but they also allowed the migrations from places like Germany, Austria, Spain, India, and Ireland to keep revolutionary fervors alive and for revolutionary groups worldwide, whatever their local conflicts, to position themselves within global social movement frameworks like anarchism, communism, and nihilism. For example, in the early twentieth century, the Chinese radical Liu Shifu was inspired by Russian nihilism while he was a student in Japan where a robust alternative press operated, and then returned home to participate in the Chinese Assassination Corps, a group that attempted bombing assassinations of military officials. Like many violent radicals from this period, Shifu turned to peace after realizing the disastrous consequences of bombings, including his own injuries in a failed attempt on a naval officer.[4]

A robust print media presented opportunity in a flow of technical ideas from mainstream sources like university chemists, explosives manufacturers, and military developers into the hands of small, potentially violent groups. These groups then adapted and disseminated these ideas through their own small, easily hidden printing presses. However, an extremely important difference exists between abstract threats of political violence and murderous acts of terrorism. The first is protected in the most robust democracies, although that protection has recently eroded in the pursuit of alleged al-Qaeda sympathizers through laws like Britain's Terrorism Act and US laws against an ill-defined "material support" for designated terrorist groups. These laws punish persons on the basis of speech alone, including the weapons-making texts they collect on their computers and are used against them in court. Speech – even seemingly instrumental technical speech – is never a sole cause of terrorism. Many groups have bellicose rhetoric and an interest in weapons but never become violent; some may talk their way towards peace. The historical definition of terrorism must be kept sufficiently narrow to avoid bolstering current political and legal arguments that erode free speech. If one claims that *terrorist* groups use the media to propagandize, it raises the question of whether the speakers are indeed terroristic (and why) and what the relationship is between speech and act. Terrorism is a violent act directed at a specific object, is brought about by direct conspiratorial speech if enacted by a group, and includes technical and tactical preparations for an imminent action. Propagandizing in newsletters and books does not fall under conspiracy, and even claims of responsibility by radical speakers must be viewed with caution.

Many historians and terror experts have seen the Irish Fenians, Russian People's Will (Narodnaya Volya), and anarchist groups like the Galleanisti as the progenitors of modern terrorism.[5] These groups have been seen as modern, in large part, because they turned to complicated technological projects like bomb making, exploited the news media, and targeted technological systems, like transportation, in urban areas.[6] In her biography of the failed assassin Dmitry Karakozov, Claudia Verhoeven places the emergence of terrorism in the late nineteenth century with a new subjective sense of historical belonging and change made possible by communications technologies: "Violence is promptly communicated to everyone everywhere, and ... this message guarantees meaning: the action will have happened, and the world will not be the same."[7] Revolutionary groups shaped their identities and purposes around being modern and mastering the advanced technologies of their time to birth the new post-revolutionary society. Indeed, a central argument went that if governments could command violent technologies, so could they. At the 1881 International Social Revolutionary Congress, for example, speakers called for scientific and technical education and the formation of a military school to carry out socialist revolutionary goals.[8]

Violent radical groups like the Irish Clan na Gael and People's Will were slanted mirrors of warring empires, which provided them with technical aspirations, education, and means to become occasionally effective at disturbing imperial power. Some American Fenians who were trained on the battlefields of the Civil War coveted its weapons for their revolutionary aspirations against England; they had the hubris to attempt armed invasions of Canada and built a submarine that sank in New Jersey's Passaic River.[9] *Irish World* editor Patrick Ford, who financially supported skirmishing missions against the British, imagined sending chemistry teachers to Ireland to teach the science of explosives, which would also lend itself to social uplift of the people through science education.[10] After a successful bombing against government offices in London, the *Irish World* declared that it was now "blow for blow": the "modern Babylon" was "getting a taste of the resources of civilization."[11] That latter, oft-repeated phrase was a reference to Prime Minister William Gladstone's famous threat in 1881 to use the "resources of civilization" against Irish radicals.[12] The *Irish World* interpreted the phrase to mean Gatling guns and rockets using high explosives, the cutting-edge military weapons of the day, used to suppress anti-colonial movements.[13] To be a viable contender for state power meant to possess these resources of civilization and the scientific and technical training that went with them.

The development of high explosives in the mid-nineteenth century was key to the formation of modern terrorism; at least by one count, bombings account for half of terrorist incidents identified by the Rand Corporation from 1972 to 2009.[14] Producing shock and fear, with great destructive force, bombs are still the primary means of creating a terrorist spectacle. The history of bomb making outside official military research and development or organizations is less about progress than it is dissemination and repetition. Before the Italian chemist Antonio Sobrero synthesized the first nitroglycerin in 1847 and Alfred Nobel stabilized it in dynamite, bombs were filled with gunpowder or highly volatile substances like silver fulminate that put bombers at great risk. To get a really large effect, bombers had to use barrels of gunpowder – like Guy Fawkes in his attempted attack on the British House of Lords in 1605 – or use small gunpowder devices as primary detonators to blow up military gunpowder stores or steam boilers. Early on, the American inventor David Bushnell created floating bombs using barrels of gunpowder and clockwork mechanisms to blow up British ships harbored in Philadelphia during the Revolutionary War, but, as in many such schemes, he failed. Bushnell went on to become the commander of the US Army Corp of Engineers at West Point, the site of much dissemination of information about the chemistry of explosives and pyrotechnics throughout the nineteenth century. A chemistry professor at West Point, James Cutbush, wrote the early nineteenth century's standard work on pyrotechnics that included instructions on how to make fuses, mortars, grenades, and rockets.[15] The inventor of the landmine, Confederate General Gabriel Rains, was educated at West Point, and this device widely introduced the idea that one could anonymously blow up one's enemies from a safe distance using simple booby traps.[16] Indeed, mostly from the Confederate side, the American Civil War produced a plethora of "infernal machines" and "torpedoes" justified in their use by whatever seeming noble cause.[17] These provided the blueprints for mechanisms that the new nitro and chlorate explosives made more portable and exponentially more powerful. Stable explosives like guncotton and dynamite miniaturized the explosive device, leading to deployment of sea and landmines in imperial wars and to concealed handheld bombs and booby traps.

The engineering aspirations of People's Will

While it may seem, from reading histories of terrorism, that nineteenth-century terrorists were diabolically inventive, with technologies of time bombs and percussion grenades sprung full blown from evil genius, their ideas came from a dissemination of technical knowledge through military service and science education. The nineteenth century saw the professionalization of the sciences and engineering along with the spread of formal education to produce experts who could contribute to industrial and military expansion. Even for those who could not afford to attend science and engineering schools, textbooks, encyclopedias of practical knowledge, compendiums of pyrotechnics, and scientific books and journals appeared in the popular market, describing ways to make and use the new explosives. These works traveled along the communication roads of the colonial powers, with their ambitious and often violent engineering projects and military conquests, reaching an increasingly literate audience, especially in the cities. Despite an institutional faith that literacy produced less criminality and greater social stability,[18] it also provided encouragement and information for violent technical pursuits, including the unintended consequence of training terrorists who were mirrors of the military engineers. These conditions created the ecology in which a terrorist act could be formulated.

As a young man, the bomb maker for the People's Will, Nikolai Kibalchich, was trained at the Institute of Transportation Engineers in St. Petersburg.[19] He was part of a cadre of smart young men who were expected to contribute to the monumental project of extending Russia's railroad system, and thus its dominion, across Siberia. Railroad engineering education included the physics and chemistry of explosives and instruction in blasting. Kibalchich was also trained in chemistry at the Medico-Surgical Academy. By that time, nitroglycerine was being used to treat heart ailments, so even in medical study the science of explosives was introduced. Kibalchich emerged from these academies with a practical knowledge of explosives chemistry and blasting along with a radicalized political point of view. At first, Kibalchich wanted to offer his medical training to the cause of revolution, a peaceful aim that was hardened into violence through harsh treatment and encounters with more aggressive revolutionaries. Imprisoned for possessing subversive literature, Kibalchich wrote to a fellow prisoner: "I possess a certain amount of knowledge which will enable me and my comrades to exploit my capabilities in the cause of revolution. Very possibly it will require years of study before my knowledge is sufficiently complete to be of real help."[20] After his release, he perfected his knowledge by obsessively reading books on explosives from a St. Petersburg library and experimenting in a household laboratory.

Kibalchich's involvement with the group of radicals who became People's Will allowed them to imagine grand schemes for assassinating the tsar. (For more on the People's Will and the Russian revolutionary movement in general, see Chapter 7 by Martin A. Miller in this volume.) Others of the group had dabbled in explosives or had served in the Russian military. Andrei Zhelyabov had taken a course on explosives to kill fish.[21] Killing fish was an industrial use of dynamite enthusiastically promoted by the explosives industry, which offered training to potential consumers. Alexander Filippov directed fireworks displays for the government's Okhtenskii gunpowder factory.[22] Associated with military display, pyrotechnics was an important pathway for explosives information, providing access to explosives, designs for explosive devices, and cultural enthusiasm for explosive spectacles. F. I. Zavalishin was a student at the Krondstadt naval base who worked at radicalizing other sailors and military officers.[23] Beginning in the 1840s, the Russian Navy carried out experimentation with land and sea mines that used pressure detonators. This concentration of technological enthusiasm and expertise, honed in the contexts of Russia's military and industrial expansion, gave shape to People's Will, a secretive organization devoted to assassinating Tsar Alexander II and other officials using much more spectacular means than the gun.

Making a bomb was a very different enterprise than using a gun. While the gun required some training to fire effectively, it could be used immediately and impulsively and was an intimate encounter with the enemy who stood within range. The bomb was a long-term enterprise that required study, planning, and testing, a coldly distant project during which over days or months the technician channeled violent impulse into an assemblage. Kibalchich experimented with the kind of electrical detonators found in blasting projects to attempt to bomb trains traveling on predictable schedules. The Fenians developed timed detonators using clocks or layers of paper that filtered acid at a deliberate rate. In this way, they absorbed military science's view of armies as clockwork mechanisms, with synchronized movements, and battles as predictable action sequences.[24] Whoever wielded them, bombs were, as Joseph Conrad's anarchist professor put it, "a combination of time and shock" that created a hole in the flow of everyday life.[25] That revelation is a definition of "terror." Conrad understood that bombs were aesthetic craft objects that reflected the preoccupations of their makers.

Like most groups of its kind, People's Will had many more failures at its bomb attacks than successes. The efforts to control time were not as easy as anticipated. Poor organization, lack of foresight, encounters with unforeseen obstacles like delayed trains, and personnel with less expertise than Kibalchich led to several failures. Then one of the members managed to let off a successful explosion during an otherwise ineffective grenade attack on Tsar Alexander II's carriage in 1881. These grenades used a chemical detonator provided by Zavalishin and were filled with guncotton, which was widely used in state military operations and not especially difficult to make.[26] Of great interest to imperial powers, the sensational news of the tsar's assassination traveled around the world, carried not only by mainstream newspapers but also by a robust alternative press through which political radicals networked across the seas. People's Will inspired many other radicals to believe that they could make high explosives, even under the watchful eyes of secret police, and successfully deploy them. Kibalchich and several of his co-conspirators were executed for the crime, though not before he had tried to return to the fold of the empire, offering a design for a manned, jet-propelled rocket to the minister of the interior. Later, the Soviet Union named one of the craters on the dark side of the moon after him, showing how well he fit into the long tail of technological development.

The activities of People's Will are indicative of many other groups of this period who organized around violent technological projects. They had a fascination with science and engineering that was in harmony with the public promotion of these fields as driving the progress of civilization. They were not at all anomalies but in some ways ideal modern citizens, interested in technical education, technological progress, and military dominance. People's Will did not see "terror" as directed towards the mass of people, who might end as collateral damage, but at a small population of rulers and capitalists. The terror was to come from a demonstration that the revolutionist could be as technologically adept and as scientifically advanced as these masters, who were blasting holes through mountains and blowing up bridges, firing rockets into civilian populations, and pacifying populations with high explosives wielded by corps of sappers and military engineers.[27] What has seemed like the terrorists' slide into the unethical tactic of endangering civilians was already widely practiced by regular armies to coerce populations and gain territory in protracted colonial wars.[28] The development of controversial, automated weapons that killed from a distance, like the landmine, was underway. In their technical works, regular military engineers displayed little interest in the human consequences of their developments, except to occasionally laud the progress of the field and its importance to civilization.[29]

Indeed, with their political sensitivities and need to persuade populations to their cause, the nineteenth century's terrorist bombers were more aware than engineers of the ethical problems in turning from guns to more indiscriminate weapons like bombs and rockets. Kibalchich deliberately designed his explosions to have a small radius so as to not kill anyone outside the immediate circle of his target, the tsar.[30] With a much more expansive view of possible targets to include monuments, public offices, and public transport, the Fenians were more willing to cause mass casualties, but they thought about the efficacy and consequences, as did the larger community of supporters of Irish independence.[31] One of the Fenian bomb makers, Richard Rogers, aka Professor Gaspodin Mezzeroff, presented his thinking on the subject in a pamphlet in which he justified the use of dynamite. The Civil War had legitimated the use of "diabolical, hellish, unchristian, and fiendish infernal machines," he said, which killed more quickly, and thus more humanely.[32]

Stealing the tools of empire

In the late nineteenth century, experimentation with the advanced weapons technology of the time was still within reach of the amateur with some training from educational institutions or workplaces like the mine and the railroad. As Kilbachich demonstrated, high explosives could be manufactured in a household lab and bombs could be cobbled together using readily available equipment and supplies. Still, making a foolproof electrical or percussion detonator was complicated, and most ingredients for explosives were commercially available only in an unrefined, unpredictable form. Homemade detonators failed much more often than they worked, and in the history of terrorist attacks one can tally up many more technical failures than successes. The landscape of history is littered with unexploded bombs picked up by the police as evidence. In 1884, for example, a portmanteau containing dynamite and a pistol mechanism was found in London's Charing Cross Station after other explosions in the train system. The bomb had failed because of a flaw in the mechanical arrangement, leaving the bag with important clues that the plot had a US origin.[33] Clockworks jammed, triggers missed their aim, wires didn't connect, fuses got wet, or the explosive was incorrectly mixed. In numerous instances, inexperienced bombers have been maimed and killed in accidents in household laboratories and while transporting bombs to targets. For example, in 1914, three Galleanisti were killed in a New York tenement constructing bombs in a plot to attack John D. Rockefeller.[34] In 1970, three members of the Weather Underground were killed in Greenwich Village devising explosives to attack soldiers at an army base dance. Amateurs experiment with high explosives at their great peril. The most successful bomb makers, like Kilbachich, were trained by civil or military engineers. War and industry made basic training in blasting widely available, but this training did not often translate into an effective household science.

With their concentrations of expertise, nineteenth-century military research labs and explosives manufacturers developed ways to refine, mix, package, and detonate chemical substances with complex, sophisticated equipment. These processes could never be emulated in a household laboratory. The dream of making explosives in the back of a paint or cheese shop (to cover the smell) evaporated quickly, as violent radicals turned to stealing dynamite. Other explosives introduced in the nineteenth century were more manageable and safer to mix. It was known that ammonium nitrate (later used in the 1995 Oklahoma City federal building bombing) and urea nitrate (used in the 1993 World Trade Center bombing) could cause explosions, but these would not become terrorist weapons until their military use in

World War II and their commercial availability as fertilizer.[35] The zeal for organic chemistry in the late nineteenth and early twentieth centuries created a plenitude of explosive compounds. A vast technical literature, much of it coming out of military laboratories and explosives manufacturers (especially the E. I. Dupont Nemours Company), disseminated information that was then popularized in general science magazines, encyclopedias, and almanacs. Fragments of this literature were circulated in popular weapons handbooks published by radicals – like Johann Most's *Science of Revolutionary Warfare*, *l'Indicateur Anarchiste*, and *La Salute é en Voi!* Much later, Kurt Saxon compiled his infamous *Fireworks & Explosives Like Granddad Used to Make* from nineteenth-century works like *Dick's Encyclopedia of Formulas and Processes*. Circulated among anarchists from Italy to the United States, the Galleanisti bomb-making manual, *La Salute é en Voi!*, was written by a respected professional chemist, Ettore Molinari, who also wrote regular textbooks for science and engineering students.[36] Yet, despite the infusions of expertise, the individual experimenter was left behind as the chemical and explosives industries, entwined with military development, created large-scale systems that organized scientific innovation and technical production of weapons like torpedoes and rockets.[37]

In their attempts to resist the technically equipped nation-state, non-state actors understood the difficulties and either recruited scientists and engineers to join them or sent their members for training through military service or matriculation at institutions of higher education. In India, angry at the British partition of Bengal in 1905, a group of assassins aspired to bomb making and began setting up a laboratory in a residential house. Their experiments with chemicals were extensive and sophisticated, though their deployment was flawed. They came to police attention when they tried to assassinate a local judge, killing two Englishwomen instead. They were also accused of four other bombings, including two failed attempts to blow up trains carrying British officials. When police raided the lab, they collected not only bomb-making materials like picric acid and ammonium nitrate but also technical literature on explosives, including a standard for civil and military engineers, *Nitro Explosives: A Practical Treatise* by Percy Gerald Sanford, a fellow of the British Chemical Society and Institute of Chemistry.[38] At the trial, known as the Alipore bomb trial, one of the members, who had turned informant, reported that the group had sent revolutionaries abroad for science training in Japan, France, England, and the United States.[39] Hem Chandra Das had gone to France for technical and explosives training and brought back an explosives manual that was widely circulated among young male students.[40] Like many twentieth-century young people with scientific interest, some of the bomb makers were self-taught, using books and shared expertise, refining their technique through contact with professionally trained scientists.

As imperial powers, like Britain, carried out their transformations of the colonies with what Daniel Headrick has called "the tools of empire," they brought with them knowledge, skill, and aspiration.[41] European experts were in charge of these technologies – the railroads, the mines, the gunboats, the telegraph – and were reluctant to share any power, such as extending technical education beyond semi-skilled training to workers in the colonies.[42] The Alipore bomb factory demonstrated that a group of Indian resistors could acquire scientific and technical expertise for a chemical laboratory and carry out experiments sophisticated enough to impress an investigating chemist. The formation of the shadow lab was a symbol of independence in itself. Despite their ambitions, the group failed in their deployment of weapons, incorrectly mixing chemicals or creating powerful blasts but missing their targets. A larger organization, like a military research and development laboratory, could absorb failures with investments in repetition and redundancy, but small groups had only limited means and few opportunities that depended on unpredictable circumstances. Failure was much more significant, not only because the action could not be easily repeated but also because it left evidence and exposed the group to watchful eyes.

The emphasis on science, the formation of a testing laboratory, and the formalization of experimentation through process and record keeping created non-state terrorist organizations that mirrored their official counterparts in military research and development. Further, information and personnel traveled between these two seemingly opposing camps. Through the twentieth century, every war created new experts – disgruntled veterans, agents provocateurs, counter-insurgency operatives, radicalized scientists and engineers – who joined militant groups to provide know-how and encouragement. The bureaucratic organization, training procedures, and covert operations of regular armies produced a flow of weapons information that traveled around the world. By the 1960s, private publishing operations were set up in the United States to reprint army manuals on booby traps, landmines, and improvised explosive devices used in covert operations. For example, the 1965 *Special Forces Handbook* (ST131-80) was created by the Special Warfare team at Fort Bragg, North Carolina, to train "indigenous forces" in guerrilla operations "in support of US Cold War objectives."[43] It gave instructions for making ANFO, the ammonium nitrate fertilizer–fuel oil mix that has often been used for powerful bombs carried in cars and trucks. As it said, ammonium nitrate fertilizer is "readily available in many parts of the world," and "motor oil may be drained from a crankcase."[44] Because it is bulky, sensitive to moisture, and requires two stages to detonate, ANFO is not a widely used military explosive, but it has been used to make improvised bombs because the ingredients are easily available. Busy inventing and testing destructive devices, US Army technicians produced many other similar handbooks on explosives, mines, and booby traps that leaked from the bases or were kept by veterans. Although in the early 1970s the US government attempted to recall these military handbooks and reclassify them as "confidential," private publishing houses like Paladin Press, located in Boulder, Colorado, had already reprinted and sold them, providing circulation to a worldwide audience.[45]

The determined and organized Provisional Irish Republican Army (PIRA), formed in 1969, relied, in part, on military and paramilitary manuals imported from the United States for making its early explosives and switches. The recipe for an ammonium nitrate and sugar explosive, which PIRA used in car bombs, can be found in the *Improvised Munitions Handbook*, which at the time was Paladin Press's new reprint of an army manual.[46] For the most part, these manuals turned out to be ineffective, producing dangerous and unreliable devices. PIRA's efforts began with a series of failures that were lethal to dozens of bomb makers and carriers. Yet, PIRA's members had embraced the idea of innovation, experimenting with explosives made from substances extracted from bacon fat, dyes, and cleaning fluids and devices from domestic appliances and door handles.[47] They kept copious notes. To create a more proficient bomb-making enterprise, PIRA organized its own "Engineering Department," setting up a formal military research-and-development unit that introduced radio-detonated mines using model airplanes. Writing in *New Scientist*, a Belfast correspondent, Robert Rodwell, explained that these devices were unsophisticated, and that because the Irish Republic lacked weapons manufacturers and advanced technology industries, PIRA was unable to draw expertise "above the level of the average quarryman."[48] Yet PIRA aspired to be an army engaging in legitimate struggle, despite Rodwell's withering appraisals of an illiterate, technologically backward people. They organized enough expertise to engage in a "mini arms race," evolving their wireless operations to match counter-terrorism technologies, earning the admiration of terror experts.

The infamous 7,000 page *Encyclopedia of Afghan Jihad*, a set of training documents compiled by members of al-Qaeda, had origins in US army manuals. A condensed version found in northern Iraq in 2003 contained diagrams from US army manuals, including the *Improvised Munitions Manual*.[49] A shady al-Qaeda operative, military trainer, and double agent, Ali A. Mohamed, served in the US Army at Fort Bragg, North Carolina – the source of many such publications – and smuggled military manuals from the base, delivering them to El Sayyid Nosair who was convicted of conspiracy in the 1993 World Trade Center bombing. One of the recipients of these manuals told reporter Peter Bergen, "I was capable of making explosives from a pile of aspirin."[50] Despite their aura of ease, the military guides – like all technical manuals – outlined processes that were much more complex in their implementation, requiring materials acquisition, skill, experience, hands-on practice, and effective planning and foresight. Few individuals and groups can successfully aspire to this level of complexity.

The construction and deployment of even conventional weapons requires some training, expertise, and a special knowledge of the environment. This has made the role of the agent provocateur – who typically offers a seductive résumé of specialized technical expertise and access to materials – an important but largely overlooked one in the history of violent radicalism. For example, a contemporary of Kibalchich, Arkadiy Harting, also trained to be an engineer but veered in another direction as an operative for the tsarist police. Under the alias Landezen, Harting organized Russian exiles in Paris in a plot to assassinate the tsar, concocted by the police to discredit anti-tsarist sentiments in France. Harting provided information on bomb instruction and alleged that he had a rich uncle who would fund the project.[51] The conspirators were subsequently exposed and arrested. Such measures have often been used in police operations against domestic radicals, providing another conduit of technical information and material support from the state. Nevertheless, the modern industrial and post-industrial state has far greater means for organizing violence, and it protects the technical means through classification systems and the sheer complexity of the enterprises.

Rough knowledge and failed innovation

Over the twentieth century, most amateur bomb makers – despite their aspirations – were left in the nineteenth century with pipe bombs and battery- and chemical-initiated bombs using whatever explosive could be obtained, while governments created complex, powerful weapons of mass destruction. Even the Unabomber, Ted Kaczynski, who was popularly regarded as a scientific genius, made primitive (though murderous) booby trap bombs using gunpowder, batteries, and lamp wire. Yet as many violent radical groups found, even a fuse-lit pipe bomb – a design known since the nineteenth century – could be powerful enough to cave in walls and kill those in its path. An undercurrent of rough, dangerous knowledge has circulated through word of mouth and publications that explain how to blow things up, while emulating the advanced technical power of the state has become increasingly difficult.

The Internet now provides a vast library of older information, much of it chaotic, unsourced, and unreliable, more threat than danger, despite alarms from the army of terror experts who serve as government consultants and advise on regulations and legal cases.[52]

Historical analysis can provide a much-needed perspective on the extent to which the Internet is providing an unprecedented flow of new information and means for terrorist conspiracy (as distinct from mere political association). In his study of terrorist networks, Michael Kenney has refuted the hyperbole that the Internet is an online terrorist training camp delivering weapons of mass destruction: "Some Internet-directed amateurs may succeed in building crude devices with the power to maim and kill, but the quality – and lethality – of these munitions will be limited by the perpetrators' lack of technical knowledge and practical experience."[53] Formal training in engineering, chemistry, and military sciences, along with field experience, is a much more important requirement for organized, large-scale terrorist violence.

Adam Dolnik writes that weapons innovation – as in the cases of al-Qaeda's 9/11 transformation of planes into missiles and Aum Shinrikyo's release of sarin gas on the Tokyo subway – is dependent on a group's fascination with innovation as a goal, need to outwit government countermeasures, robust financial resources, and acquisition of technically adept members.[54] The Aum Shinrikyo attack revealed how sophisticated such a project could be. With a compelling vision of a new society, its leader, Shoko Asahara, attracted smart, socially alienated people with advanced science training to work in a large, well-funded, secret chemical laboratory. Aum Shinrikyo's technological obsessions drew Robert Jay Lifton to place the group alongside nuclear weapons developers and Nazi researchers: "In the hands of more 'stable' leaders and groups, weapons-centered projects take on the illusion of sanity."[55] Despite the inevitable failure of its apocalyptic plans, Aum Shinrikyo built a slanted mirror to the high-tech projects of chemical and pharmaceutical industries and to prior official military production of biological and chemical weapons. The group worked to acquire technologies – botulism, anthrax, sarin – from these domains and reinvent them as agents of creative destruction in the birthing of a new social order. Aum Shinrikyo's production of biological and chemical weapons fit with its leader's hubristic desire to penetrate and manipulate bodies and minds and to fulfill his own visions and prophecies derived from popular culture. The result was "an erratic course, rather than . . . a methodical research and development program."[56]

Because of the complex factors involved, radical innovation is rare and deployment of new and unusual weapons difficult, as is born out in the history of terrorist crimes. Violent groups have most often turned to familiar techniques and devices with the most symbolic value in articulating the history and meaning of the act. For example, despite the availability of many bomb designs, the late nineteenth-century anarchists often talked about, and occasionally used, modifications of the Orsini bomb – an iron globe studded with nipples containing a primary explosive used to detonate a main secondary charge. The Orsini bomb was named after Felice Orsini, who attacked Napoleon III in 1858 with three of the devices. The Orsini bomb became a symbol of anarchist resistance against imperial and capitalist hegemony, publicly reviled in the caricature of the shaggy anarchist wielding a globe bomb (erroneously given a lit fuse).[57] Likewise, the long history of the car bomb shows it to be an ideal weapon for revealing the vulnerability of capitalism's urban centers and the state's architectural symbols.[58] Weapons of choice – from the Kalishnikov rifle to the package bomb – are chosen for their accessibility and ease of use and construction but also for their symbolic resonance, since terrorists attempt to use weapons as conduits for political messages. The weapon itself declares group identity and purpose, often without the need for a stated declaration of responsibility. A small innovation – such as a particular detonating system or way of addressing a package bomb – serves as a signature. Terrorists may covet the state's technical proficiency and efficacy but not its large-scale innovation which requires substantial resources.

In his intellectual history of terrorism, Mikkel Thorup explains that the idea of terrorism has mutually evolved with the state:

> The terrorist . . . is to be understood in relation to the state, both as his or her object of rage and as the one whose organizational and legitimating order one has to challenge. A violent challenger will always try to mimic his or her opponent, whether the object is to usurp or destroy the power of the adversary. And the state is also to be understood in relation to the terrorist, both because the state "creates" the terrorist . . . but also because the state came into being and continues to be shaped by its response to violent challenges.[59]

The mutually constituting relationship between the terrorist and the state is not only conceptual but unfolds in the material practices of weapons making. Terrorists not only get weapons from the state, they get training, information, and inspiration for technological projects, even if they lack innovation and complexity. In the name of security, governments are unlikely to acknowledge or reveal the extent of this relationship and terrorist bomb makers operate secretly and anonymously, making this a very difficult avenue of historical research. Nevertheless, it is an important one, revealing how the most violent technologies come to permeate societies so that militarization is not an abstraction but a shared set of violent practices.

Notes

1 Carl Mitcham, *Thinking Through Technology* (Chicago: University of Chicago Press, 1994), 1–18.
2 Some political scientists have touched on this question. See David C. Rapoport, "Before the Bombs Were the Mobs: American Experiences with Terror," in *Terrorism, Identity and Legitimacy: The Four Waves Theory and Political Violence*, ed. Jean Elizabeth Rosenfeld, 137–67 (New York: Oxford University Press, 2011).
3 Major works include Gerard Chailan and Arnaud Blin, eds., *The History of Terrorism from Antiquity to Al Qaeda*, trans. Edward Schneider (Berkeley: University of California Press, 2007); Walter Laqueur, *History of Terrorism* (New Brunswick, NJ: Transaction, 2001); Randall D. Law, *Terrorism: A History* (Malden, MA: Polity, 2009); Michael Burleigh, *Blood and Rage: A Cultural History of Terrorism* (New York: HarperCollins, 2009); and Matthew Carr, *The Infernal Machine: An Alternative History of Terrorism* (New York: New Press, 2007).
4 Edward S. Krebs, *Shifu: Soul of Chinese Anarchism* (Oxford: Rowman & Littlefield, 2007), 6–11.
5 People's Will called themselves "terrorists." The Fenian group the United Brotherhood referred to themselves as "skirmishers," but greatly admired and in some ways emulated the tactics of People's Will.
6 Bruce Hoffman, *Inside Terrorism*, 2nd ed. (New York: Columbia University Press, 2006), 10–11; Lindsay Clutterbuck, "The Progenitors of Terrorism: Russian Revolutionaries or Extreme Irish Republicans?" *Terrorism and Political Violence* 16, no. 1 (2004): 154–81; David Rapoport, "The Four Waves of Modern Terrorism," in *Attacking Terrorism: Elements of a Grand Strategy*, ed. Audrey Kurth Cronin and James Ludes (Washington, DC: Georgetown University Press, 2004): 48–9; Martin A. Miller, "The Intellectual Origins of Modern Terrorism in Europe," in *Terrorism in Context*, ed. Martha Crenshaw (University Park: Pennsylvania State University Press, 1995), 30–1; and Burleigh, *Blood and Rage*, 1–66. For a somewhat different understanding of the relationship between terrorism and modernity, see Chapter 24 by Roger Griffin in this volume.
7 Claudia Verhoeven, *The Odd Man Karakozov: Imperial Russia, Modernity and the Birth of Terrorism* (Ithaca, NY: Cornell University Press, 2009), 7.

8 Paul Avrich, *The Haymarket Tragedy* (Princeton, NJ: Princeton University Press, 1984), 58.
9 Hereward Senior, *The Last Invasion of Canada: The Fenian Raids, 1866–1870* (Quebec: Canadian War Museum, 1991), 40; and James Delgado, *Silent Killers: Submarines and Underwater Warfare* (Oxford: Osprey, 2011), 75–7.
10 "A Sacred Trust," *Irish World*, December 30, 1876. For discussions of the Fenian dynamite campaign, see K. R. M. Short, *The Dynamite War: Irish–American Bombers in Victorian Britain* (New York: Gill and Macmillan, 1979); and Niall Whelehan, *The Dynamiters: Irish Nationalism and Political Violence in the Wider World, 1867–1900* (New York: Cambridge University Press, 2012).
11 "Blow for Blow," *Irish World*, March 31, 1883.
12 Richard Shannon, *Gladstone* (London: Penguin, 1999), 2:282.
13 "England's Resources of Civilization," *Irish World*, August 26, 1882.
14 Adam Dolnik, *Understanding Terrorist Innovation: Technology, Tactics and Global Trends* (New York: Routledge, 2007), 36–41.
15 James Cutbush, *System of Pyrotechny: Comprehending the Theory and Practice, With the Application of Chemistry* (Philadelphia, PA: Clara F. Cutbush, 1825).
16 Norman Youngblood, *The Development of Mine Warfare: A Most Murderous and Barbarous Conduct* (Westport, CT: Praeger Security International, 2006), 25–7.
17 For overviews of the Confederate guerrilla war, see Jane Singer, *The Confederate Dirty War: Arson, Bombings, Assassination and Plots for Chemical and Germ Attacks on the Union* (Jefferson, NC: McFarland, 2005); William A. Tidwell, *April '65: Confederate Covert Action in the American Civil War* (Kent, OH: Kent State University Press, 1995); and Ann Larabee, *The Dynamite Fiend: The Chilling Tale of a Confederate Spy, Con Artist, and Mass Murderer* (New York: Palgrave Macmillan, 2005).
18 Harvey J. Graff, *The Literacy Myth: Cultural Integration and Social Structure in the Nineteenth Century*, 2nd ed. (New Brunswick, NJ: Transaction, 1991), 235–51.
19 Lee B. Croft, *Nikolai Ivanovich Kibalchich: Terrorist Rocket Pioneer* (Tempe, AZ: Institute for Issues in the History of Science: 2006), 25.
20 Croft, *Kibalchich*, 49.
21 David Footman, *The Alexander Conspiracy: A Life of A. I. Zhelyabov* (LaSalle, IL: Open Court, 1974), 69.
22 Croft, *Kibalchich*, 81.
23 Lynn Hartnett, "The Making of a Revolutionary Icon: Vera Nikolaevna Figner and the People's Will in the Wake of the Assassination of Tsar Aleksandr II," *Canadian Slavonic Papers* 43, no. 2–3 (2001): 260.
24 Antoine Bousquet, *The Scientific Way of Warfare: Order and Chaos on the Battlefields of Modernity* (New York: Columbia University Press, 2009), 53–62.
25 Joseph Conrad, *The Secret Agent* (1907; New York: Vintage, 2007), 69.
26 Richard Bach Jensen, *The Battle against Anarchist Terrorism: An International History, 1878–1934* (New York: Cambridge University Press, 2014), 24–5; and Burleigh, *Blood and Rage*, 27–66. For overviews, see Deborah Hardy, *Land and Freedom: The Origins of Russian Terrorism, 1876–1879* (Westport, CT: Greenwood, 1987); Franco Venturi, *Roots of Revolution: A History of the Populist and Socialist Movements in Nineteenth-Century Russia* (New York: Knopf, 1960); and Astrid von Borcke, "Violence and Terror in Russian Revolutionary Populism," in *Social Protest, Violence and Terror in Nineteenth- and Twentieth-Century Europe*, eds. Wolfang J. Mommsen and Gerhard Hirschfeld, 48–62 (New York: St. Martin's Press, 1982).
27 In 1879, as the Fenian terrorist skirmishing began in earnest, the *Irish World*, a newspaper devoted to Irish independence, discussed the British firing naval rockets into Alexandria, Egypt, and placing guncotton in caves in Zululand where the Pedi had fled. "England's Resources of Civilization."
28 Most historical discussions of the targeting of civilians have focused on the twentieth century, but some scholars have written of the extensive use of the practice in earlier periods. Most agree that civilians are targeted for instrumental reasons, rather than a lack of moral judgment. See Mark Grimsley and Clifford J. Rogers, eds., *Civilians in the Path of War* (Lincoln: University of Nebraska Press, 2002); and Alexander Downes, *Targeting Civilians in War*, Cornell Studies in Security Affairs (Ithaca, NY: Cornell University Press, 2008).
29 See, for example, Charles Munroe's regular column surveying US and European developments in military uses of explosives, "Notes on the Literature of Explosives," in the *Proceedings of the United States Naval Institute*, Vols. 5–23 (1875–1898), Hathitrust Digital Library.

30. Croft, *Kibalchich*, 85.
31. Whelehan, 145–57.
32. "An Advocate of Dynamite: Outlines of a Pamphlet Issued by Prof. Mezzeroff," *New York Times*, April 27, 1883. For more on the Fenians, including their dynamite campaign of the 1880s, see Chapter 12 by Benjamin Grob-Fitzgibbon in this volume.
33. Joseph McKenna, *The Irish–American Dynamite Campaign: A History, 1881–1896* (Jefferson, NC: McFarland, 2012), 69.
34. Nunzio Pernicone, *Carlo Tresca: Portrait of a Rebel* (New York: Palgrave-Macmillan, 2005), 80–2. For more on the Galleanisti, see Chapter 9 by Thai Jones in this volume.
35. Ian D. Rae and James H. Whitehead, "Rackarock: On the Path from Black Powder to ANFO," in *Gunpowder, Explosives and the State*, ed. Brenda J. Buchanan, 367–85 (Burlington, VT: Ashgate, 2006); and G. S. Scott and R. L. Grant, *Ammonium Nitrate: Its Properties and Fire and Explosion Hazards*, Information Circular, Bureau of Mines, United States Department of the Interior, June 1948, Hathitrust Digital Library.
36. Paul Avrich, *Sacco and Vanzetti: The Anarchist Background* (Princeton, NJ: Princeton University Press, 1991), 98.
37. Thomas P. Hughes, *American Genesis: A Century of Invention and Technological Enthusiasm, 1870–1970* (1989; Chicago: University of Chicago Press, 2004).
38. Bejoy Krishna Bose, *The Alipore Bomb Trial* (London: Butterworth, 1922), 60–6.
39. "Indian Telegrams. Bengal Sedition. King's Evidence," *Times of India*, June 24, 1908. See also Sailendra Nath Sen, *Chandernagore: From Bondage to Freedom* (Delhi: Primus, 2012), 9–16; and Peter Heehs, *The Bomb in Bengal: The Rise of Revolutionary Terrorism, 1900–1910* (New York: Oxford University Press, 2004).
40. Peter Heehs, "Revolutionary Terror in British Bengal," in *Terror and the Postcolonial*, ed. Elleke Boehmer and Stephen Morton (Chichester: Wiley-Blackwell, 2010), 168.
41. Daniel R. Headrick, *The Tentacles of Progress: Technology Transfer in the Age of Imperialism, 1850–1940* (New York: Oxford University Press, 1988).
42. Headrick, 382
43. *Special Forces Handbook* (Fort Bragg, NC: US Army Special Warfare School, 1965), n.p. A facsimile was published in 1992 by Paladin Press.
44. *Special Forces Handbook*.
45. Ann Larabee, *The Wrong Hands: Popular Weapons Manuals and Their Challenges to Democracy* (New York: Oxford University Press, 2015).
46. John Allison, "Terrorist Weapons and Technology," in *Combating Terrorism in Northern Ireland*, ed. James Dingley (New York: Routledge, 2009), 104.
47. Robert Rodwell, "Army Uncovers a Mrs. Beeton for Bombers," *New Scientist*, May 3, 1973, 276–7.
48. Rodwell, "Technology in the Streets of Ulster," *New Scientist*, April 6, 1972, 16.
49. C. J. Chivers, "Instruction and Methods from Al Qaeda Took Root in North Iraq with Islamic Fighters," *New York Times*, April 27, 2003, accessed via Proquest (August 18, 2014).
50. Quoted in Peter L. Bergen, *An Oral History of Al Qaeda's Leader: The Osama bin Laden I Know* (New York: Free Press, 2006), 115.
51. Rita T. Kronenbitter, "The Illustrious Career of Arkadiy Harting," in *Okhrana: The Paris Operations of the Russian Imperial Police*, ed. Ben B. Fischer (n.p.: Central Intelligence Agency, 1997), 77.
52. See, for example, Gabriel Weimann, *Terrorism on the Internet: The New Arena, the New Challenges* (Washington, DC: United States Institute, 2006).
53. Michael Kenney, "Beyond the Internet: Mētis, Techne, and the Limitations of Online Artifacts for Islamist Terrorists," *Terrorism and Political Violence* 22, no. 2 (2010): 192.
54. Dolnik, 147–72.
55. Robert Jay Lifton, *Destroying the World in Order to Save It: Aum Shinrikyo, Apocalyptic Violence, and the New Global Terrorism* (New York: Macmillan, 2000).
56. Richard Danzig, et al., *Aum Shinrikyo: Insight into How Terrorists Develop Biological and Chemical Weapons*, Report, Center for a New American Security (July 2011), 20. Available online at: www.cnas.org/files/documents/publications/CNAS_AumShinrikyo_Danzig_0.pdf (accessed August 19, 2014).
57. For more on turn-of-the-century European anarchist terrorism, see Chapter 8 by Richard Bach Jensen in this volume. For more on the literary construction of the same, see Chapter 31 by Lynn Patyk.

58 Mike Davis, *Buda's Wagon: A Brief History of the Car Bomb* (New York: Verso, 2007).
59 Mikkel Thorup, *An Intellectual History of Terror: War, Violence and the State* (New York: Routledge, 2010), 53.

Further reading

Bousquet, Antoine. *The Scientific Way of Warfare: Order and Chaos on the Battlefields of Modernity*. New York: Columbia University Press, 2009.

Davis, Mike. *Buda's Wagon: A Brief History of the Car Bomb*. New York: Verso, 2007.

Dolnik, Adam. *Understanding Terrorist Innovation: Technology, Tactics and Global Trends*. New York: Routledge, 2007.

Headrick, Daniel R. *The Tentacles of Progress: Technology Transfer in the Age of Imperialism, 1850–1940*. New York: Oxford University Press, 1988.

Larabee, Ann. *The Wrong Hands: Popular Weapons Manuals and Their Challenges to Democracy*. New York: Oxford University Press, 2015.

———. *The Dynamite Fiend: The Chilling Tale of a Confederate Spy, Con Artist, and Mass Murderer*. New York: Palgrave Macmillan, 2005.

Singer, Jane. *The Confederate Dirty War: Arson, Bombings, Assassination and Plots for Chemical and Germ Attacks on the Union*. Jefferson, NC: McFarland, 2005.

Thorup, Mikkel. *An Intellectual History of Terror: War, Violence and the State*. New York: Routledge, 2010.

Verhoeven, Claudia. *The Odd Man Karakozov: Imperial Russia, Modernity and the Birth of Terrorism*. Ithaca, NY: Cornell University Press, 2009.

Whelehan, Niall. *The Dynamiters: Irish Nationalism and Political Violence in the Wider World, 1867–1900*. New York: Cambridge University Press, 2012.

30

INTERNATIONAL TERRORISM

Geraint Hughes

On Sunday, September 6, 1970, the Popular Front for the Liberation of Palestine (PFLP) hijacked three airliners (one each from TWA, Pan Am, and Swissair), taking 300 hostages and flying them to a commandeered airfield in Jordan. They were joined three days later by the passengers and crew of a British airliner taken by the PFLP en route from Bombay to London. The hostage-takers issued demands to the United States, British, West German, and Swiss governments to release Palestinian terrorists in their custody, and on September 12, they blew up their captured planes in front of assembled journalists. "Skyjack Sunday" and its aftermath was a stunning *coup de théâtre* for the PLFP comparable in its effect to 9/11. Furthermore, the hijackings not only forced Britain, Switzerland, and the Federal Republic of Germany to free convicted terrorists, but it brought global political and media attention to the Palestinian cause. It was truly an act of "international" terrorism.[1]

For the US and British governments, "international" or "global" terrorism is synonymous with al-Qaeda and affiliated groups,[2] and even in academic literature there is no agreed-upon definition as to the characteristics of international terrorism, as opposed to more parochial forms of terrorist violence.[3] The debate concerning "old" and "new" terrorism also has its methodological limitations, as some "new terrorist" groups operate only domestically (prime examples here include Aum Shinrikyo and far-right militias in the US).[4] The aim of this chapter is to offer a terminological definition for this phenomenon and also to describe what constituted the three waves of international terrorism in history: anarchist violence in late nineteenth-/early twentieth-century Europe and North America, the coalescence of "rejectionist" Palestinian groups (those that opposed any peace settlement with Israel) with far-left movements (notably the Japanese Red Army [JRA] and German leftist terrorists) in the 1970s, and the rise of Islamist terror from the late 1980s onwards.[5]

Terminology

Terrorists may use (or threaten to use) lethal violence for political objectives against specific states and their citizens, but they do not necessarily confine their operations to their home countries. The Provisional Irish Republican Army (PIRA) targeted British military personnel in mainland Europe during the 1980s,[6] whilst the Armenian group ASALA assassinated Turkish diplomats overseas.[7] Embassies, state agencies (such as the offices of national airlines), and expatriate businesses offer tempting targets for terrorist groups, particularly for diaspora-based organizations (like ASALA) or ones which are restricted in their domestic operations due to the effectiveness of their adversary's military and security forces. An external "spectacular" represents an opportunity for any organization to gain international media attention. This explains why, for instance, Ahvaz (ethnic Arab) gunmen took over the Iranian embassy in London between April 30 and May 5, 1980.[8] For the purposes of this chapter, international terrorism is defined as the use of lethal violence by an array of groups against several states and societies, with the specific objective of overthrowing the basis of an international order, rather than provoking political change within a specific country. Yet four complicating actors need to be considered with reference to terrorism's international dimensions:

- *State sponsorship* – the involvement of Serbian military officers in the plot to assassinate Archduke Franz Ferdinand (on July 28, 1914) and Fascist Italy's role in sheltering and training the Croatian Ustaše demonstrates that state support for terrorism is not a new phenomenon.[9] Arab regimes have backed subversive groups in order to weaken adversarial powers,[10] and from the late 1960s, Libya, Syria, Iraq, and South Yemen backed various factions within the Palestine Liberation Organization (PLO) not only to wage proxy war against Israel, but also to exploit the Palestinians whilst pursuing their own intra-Arab feuds. From 1989, Pakistan fostered jihadi groups such as Lashkar-e-Taiba (LET) and Harkat ul-Mujahideen (HUM), treating them as strategic assets against its economically and militarily stronger neighbor and enemy, India.[11]
- *Diasporas* – ethno-nationalist terrorists in particular can exploit links with expatriate communities to generate money, arms, and recruits. From the emergence of the Fenian Brotherhood in the mid-nineteenth century to PIRA in the 1970s and 1980s, Irish terrorists had some residual support amongst émigrés in the US, and the Tamil Tigers (LTTE) have been able to raise – or extort – funds from Tamil communities in Europe, North America, and Australasia.[12]
- *Cross-training* – terrorist groups can collaborate by sharing technical knowledge, dispersing weapons, providing sanctuary and training facilities, or by conducting attacks on each other's behalf. On October 9, 1934, a member of the Macedonian group IMRO shot dead King Alexander of Yugoslavia during a state visit to France, although the gunman involved was working for the Ustaše.[13] The PLO's camps in Jordan (until 1970) and Lebanon (until 1982) accommodated fighters from an array of "national liberation" movements, and in August 2001, the Colombian authorities arrested three PIRA members in Bogota, charging them with training the FARC in urban bombing tactics.[14] Such cooperation is often purely tactical in nature and does not necessarily symbolize any ideological solidarity between the groups concerned (as demonstrated, for example, by the training that future members of the Iranian Revolutionary Guards Corps (committed to an Islamist revolution) received from Fatah (a secular–nationalist movement) in Lebanon during the 1970s).[15]
- *Nomenclature and aggregation* – as Jason Burke notes, "al-Qaeda" does not exist as an organization but as a mobilizing idea, and in the aftermath of 9/11, governments across the globe opportunistically sought to associate domestic insurgents and dissidents with Osama bin Laden's cause.[16] Adam Curtis goes as far as to claim that al-Qaeda itself is largely the conceptual creation of US officials and neo-conservative ideologues who sought to rally the American public behind an illusory threat.[17] The phenomenon of international terrorism is a complicated one, and there is a clear risk that oversimplified narratives can be used to lump disparate groups together and to impose an artificial framework of unity and strategic cohesion.

Audrey Kurth Cronin comments on the fact that al-Qaeda's "most potent threat [is] its ability to transcend borders and governments and mobilize people in a violent jihad,"[18] and in this respect international terrorist movements are able to recruit and mobilize support worldwide to serve objectives which involve a global revolution – against the concept of government and hierarchical authority in the case of the anarchists; capitalism, imperialism, and colonialism (which included "Zionism") on the part of "rejectionist" Palestinians and far-left allies from Europe and Japan; and the West and "apostate" regimes in the Muslim world as far as the radical Islamist movements are concerned.

Above all, international terrorists are far less discriminatory in conducting their attacks. George Habash, the leader of the PFLP, justified the hijacking and bombing of airliners by stating that "[in] today's world, no one is innocent, no one a neutral. A man is either with the oppressed or he is with the oppressors. He who takes no interest in politics gives his blessing to the prevailing order, that of the ruling classes and exploiting forces."[19] The vast majority of the hostages taken by the PFLP in September 1970 had no connection with the plight of the Palestinians. Most of the dead and wounded in the East African embassy bombings (August 7, 1998) were Kenyan and Tanzanian civilians, who could not by any criteria be accused of responsibility for the grievances which motivated al-Qaeda. If traditional terrorists confine their attacks against citizens of a particular nationality – or specifically against government officials, police, and military personnel – then a common facet between the international movements discussed below is that their perpetrators do not believe that there are innocent bystanders or non-combatants.

Caveats

The linkages between terrorism and the development of communications technology is an established one (for more on the relationship between terrorism and the media, see Chapter 28 by Robert A. Saunders). The anarchists of the late nineteenth/early twentieth century could exploit the mass production of newspapers and books – not to mention the growth of literacy in the West – to publicize their actions. Terrorists of the 1970s and 1980s had television, whilst radical Islamist groups have the Internet and 24-hour rolling news. A generation of protesters from 1968 were outraged by US military intervention in Vietnam, whilst from the 1990s European Islamists were motivated by anger over the persecution of co-religionists in Kashmir (1989 onwards), Bosnia (1992–5), Chechnya (1994 onwards), Palestine, Afghanistan (after October 2001), and Iraq (during the imposition of sanctions on Saddam Hussein's regime in the 1990s, and the Anglo-American invasion and occupation from 2003 to 2011). For the second and third waves of international terrorism, air travel itself provided both targets and examples of the "propaganda of the deed." Once commercial flight became affordable and common (notably in the West), the hijacking of an airliner or a bomb attack at an airport provided terrorist groups involved with a global audience for publicity and intimidation.[20]

It is nonetheless important to emphasize that the processes of political radicalization discussed in this chapter did not inevitably lead to violence. Dissatisfaction in Europe and America a century ago over endemic poverty, social stratification, political autocracy (in much of Europe), and predatory big business (in the US) influenced trade unionism and the rise of democratic socialism.[21] Joschka Fischer, Daniel Cohn-Bendit, Jack Straw, and Tariq Ali were more typical of the 1968 generation than Andreas Baader or Ulrike Meinhof, insofar as the former either abandoned revolutionary politics or found non-violent means of pursuing them.[22] Likewise, Muslim anger over Israel's occupation of the West Bank or the presence of Western troops in Afghanistan is far more widespread than support for al-Qaeda and affiliated groups,[23] and as is evident with the Justice and Development Party (Adalet re Kalkina Partisi, or AKP in Turkey) – not to mention the evolution of both the Muslim Brotherhood in Egypt and Enhada in Tunisia after the 2011 revolutions – Islamism can have a non-violent (and even a democratic) dimension.[24]

Finally, readers should be wary of conspiratorial explanations of international terror, or indeed the self-serving notion that Western societies constitute its primary victims.[25] Claire Sterling's claim (expressed in her 1981 book, *The Terror Network*) that terrorism was part of a coordinated strategy of proxy warfare waged by the USSR against the West aroused controversy amongst US intelligence analysts, but the Reagan administration supported Sterling's thesis because it confirmed its collective view of the Soviet threat.[26] The Soviet bloc and its intelligence/secret police services (notably the KGB, the East German MfS (better known as the Stasi), and the Czechoslovak StB) did provide arms, training, and shelter to European far-left groups and the Palestinians, although this derived from political opportunism rather than any grand strategic concept.[27] The Soviets backed the PLO (and its principal faction, Fatah) mainly in order to bolster their ties with Arab allies and to gain a propaganda advantage against the US and other Western states, which could be portrayed as being pro-Israeli. However, the USSR's relations with the Palestinians were problematic, first, because Moscow recognized Israel's claim to statehood,[28] and, second, because the PLO often clashed with the USSR's other Arab clients, most notably Syria. When Fatah fought Syrian forces in Lebanon in 1976 and 1983, Yasser Arafat discovered on both occasions that the Soviets valued their relationship with Hafez al-Asad more than the one they had with the PLO.[29]

On the opposite side of the political spectrum from Sterling, Daniele Ganser links both far-left and far-right terrorism in Europe from the 1970s to the existence of "stay-behind" groups, paramilitary formations established by West European states from the late 1940s to act as embryonic resistance movements in the event of a Soviet invasion. While there are grounds for believing that some "stay-behind" units (notably the Italian Gladio network) became involved with extreme-right paramilitary violence, Ganser went as far as to allege that these groups were coordinated by the US and Britain to conduct "false-flag" attacks intended to discredit left-wing movements, thereby keeping Western Europe within the NATO alliance. Ganser's thesis was weakened by his reliance on a forged US military manual, and on closer examination his sources are either of questionable reliance or they do not support his thesis.[30] In a similar manner, both 9/11 and the London bombings of July 7, 2005, have attracted the attention of conspiracy theorists who seek to prove that the attacks were committed not by Islamist terrorists but by the US and British authorities. Proponents of such claims are if anything less careful than Ganser about critically examining the "evidence" they cite.[31]

From anarchism to revolutionary terrorism

In 2001, the RAND analysts John Arquilla and David Ronfeld discussed the evolution of "netwar," in which "dispersed organizations, small groups and individuals . . . communicate, coordinate and conduct their campaign in an internetted manner, without a precise central command."[32] This pattern of violence echoes that of European and American anarchist groups operating from the 1880s to the 1920s (which are discussed in more detail in Chapters

8 and 9 by Richard Bach Jensen and Thai Jones, respectively, in this volume). Anarchists assassinated three heads of state – the French President Sadi Carnot (June 24, 1894), King Umberto I of Italy (July 29, 1900), and US President William McKinley (September 14, 1901). They also caused a public sensation through clashes with the authorities (notably the gun-battle between Latvian émigrés and police and soldiers in London on January 2, 1911, that became known as the "Siege of Sidney Street"), and major attacks such as the Wall Street car bombing of September 16, 1920.[33]

Following the Russian Revolution (1917), anarchism was conflated by Western governments and public opinion with Bolshevism, in particular during the politically inspired "red scare" in the US in 1919–20. In fact, Karl Marx and his adherents had an ambivalent attitude towards the effectiveness of "propaganda of the deed"; Lenin and Trotsky treated terrorism by itself (as opposed to the application of state terror by a revolutionary regime in power) as futile, and after the Revolution of 1917 the Bolshevik regime subjected Russian anarchists to a far more ruthless process of repression than their counterparts experienced elsewhere.[34] Anarchism survives as a political force, although with a few exceptions (such as the somewhat ludicrous Angry Brigade in London in the early 1970s), "black bloc" terrorism faded into insignificance in the 1920s.[35]

The late 1960s–early 1970s saw a confluence of two radicalized ideologies. In the industrialized world, the New Left rejected the iniquities of capitalism as well as traditionalist communism as represented by the USSR and its affiliated parties (in particular the Italian PCI, which outraged the "extra-parliamentary" Left in Italy by participating in coalition politics). Concurrently, certain Palestinian groups, such as the PFLP, opted to wage an international campaign to further their objectives. Bold pledges by states such as Egypt, Syria, and Iraq to "liberate Palestine" had been exposed by their crushing defeat in the Six Day War (June 5–11, 1967), whilst Fatah guerrilla raids against Israel were generally ineffectual. As a consequence, Habash and his deputy, Wadie Haddad, concluded that aircraft hijackings would focus international attention to their cause, and the first of these took place with the capture and diversion of an El Al jet to Algeria on July 23, 1968. The PFLP also used hijackings as a means of competing with its main rival within the PLO, Fatah, and Habash also had a declared objective of overthrowing conservative Arab regimes, in particular that of Jordan.[36] This provided the basis for an "anti-imperialist" alliance between the Palestinian *fedayeen* and far-left groups such as the JRA and the German Red Army Faction (RAF; known also by its nickname as the Baader-Meinhof Group), not to mention individuals such as the Venezuelan gun-for-hire Ilich Ramírez Sánchez (nicknamed Carlos the Jackal).

European and Japanese terrorists trained at *fedayeen* camps in Jordan until the civil war between King Hussein's forces and the Palestinians in September 1970.[37] The JRA conducted a bloody attack on Lod Airport on May 31, 1972, killing twenty-four people. Carlos led a mixed German–Palestinian team which held delegates at the OPEC summit in Vienna hostage for twenty-four hours on December 21–22, 1975, and on June 27, 1976, the PFLP and the German "Revolutionary Cells" hijacked an Air France jet from Tel Aviv to Paris, diverting it to Uganda and holding its crew and Jewish passengers hostage. On October 13, 1977, the PFLP took over a Lufthansa plane in an attempt to force the West German authorities to release Andreas Baader, Gudrun Ensslin, and other Red Army Faction prisoners from jail. Fatah became involved in overseas attacks following the PLO's expulsion from Jordan (January 1971), establishing the Black September Organization as a front for its operations. Black September's most notorious atrocity was its assault on Israel's team at the Munich Olympics (September 5–6, 1972). The ruthlessness of its operatives, combined with the incompetence of the German authorities, led to the killing of eleven Israeli athletes, nine of whom perished during a botched attempt by the Bavarian police to rescue them.[38] (For much more on the PLO, the PFLP, and the Munich massacre, see Chapter 16 by Boaz Ganor in this volume.)

The Munich massacre not only caused international outrage, but it forced Western governments to prepare for similar attacks either in their own countries or against citizens overseas. As one senior official from the UK's domestic counter-intelligence and security agency, MI5, warned the British home secretary three days after Munich, the fact that Palestinian and affiliated terrorist groups had sanctuaries in Arab states (and the support of their secret police and intelligence agencies) meant that governments were unlikely to receive any prior intelligence warning for future attacks.[39] Negotiations and concessions to terrorist demands could incite future attacks, whilst the bungling the authorities displayed at Munich illustrated the need for governments to prepare for analogous emergencies.[40] Following 1972, Western states also established military or police units specifically trained to rescue hostages in future scenarios; these included the Pagoda troop of the UK's 22nd Special Air Service Regiment (22SAS), the French GIGN, Germany's GSG-9, and the US Army's Delta Force. Whilst the specter of international terrorism inspired the foundation of these anti-terrorist units, they could also be employed against internal groups as well. Hostage-rescue missions tended to work if the special forces units involved operated in their own country (as was the case with 22SAS's storming of the Iranian embassy on May 5, 1980, and the Italian Carabinieri's rescue of Brigadier James Dozier, a US Army officer held by the Red Brigades in May 1982) or if assisted by sympathetic authorities overseas (as demonstrated by GSG-9's assault on the Lufthansa jet held by the PFLP at Mogadishu on October 18, 1977). Aside from the Israeli operation at Entebbe on July 4, 1976 – which rescued the Air France crew and passengers held by German and PFLP terrorists (with the connivance of the Ugandan dictator, Idi Amin) – governments could not employ military or paramilitary means to end a similar crisis if it occurred abroad and if the local authorities aided the hostage-takers.[41]

Yet governments not only had the challenge of coordinating their political, legal, intelligence, and military responses to international terrorism, but also had the problem of international cooperation to address. The fact was that different states followed diverging approaches to the problem concerned. Whilst certain West European governments (notably the French) were inclined to negotiate and compromise when dealing with hostage crises, the Israeli response to terrorist attacks against its own citizens has invariably involved retaliation (as Ganor notes in Chapter 16 in this volume). Following the Munich massacre, Prime Minister Golda Meir ordered Israel's foreign intelligence and counter-terrorism agency, Mossad, to assassinate members of Black September responsible for orchestrating the attack, and even before the Israeli invasions of Lebanon in 1978 and 1982, the governments of Yitzhak Rabin and Menachem Begin ordered air and artillery strikes against PLO camps in response to Palestinian attacks. US policy alternated between public declarations of resolution and private acts of compromise; the Central Intelligence Agency actually established covert contacts with the Black September leader, Ali Hasan Salameh, until Mossad killed him in January 1979. Ronald Reagan ordered the bombing of Libya on April 15, 1986 (Operation El Dorado Canyon) because of Muammar Qaddafi's sponsorship of the Abu Nidal Organisation (ANO), but he also authorized clandestine talks with Iran in an effort to secure the release of American hostages held by Hizbullah in Beirut.[42] Neither military pressure nor negotiations had any discernible long-term effect, and Qaddafi's response to El Dorado Canyon included the bomb attacks that destroyed Pan Am Flight 103 over Lockerbie, Scotland, on December 21, 1988, and that blew up a French Airliner over Niger nine months later.[43]

Ultimately, terrorism proved to be a futile tactic for its far-left practitioners. The JRA imploded as a result of an internal purge in the winter of 1971–2.[44] During the 1980s, the Red Army Faction and its French counterpart, Action Directe, attempted to establish a pan-European alliance of far-left groups directed against NATO and US military establishments in the continent, but both groups crumbled as a result of German and French police pressure (as described in Chapter 20 by Hanno Balz). The fall of the Berlin Wall, the end of the Cold War, and German reunification robbed the RAF and its peers of their political rationale and also deprived them of the refuges they had had in the former Eastern Bloc.[45] The failure of the "red" groups reflected the ideological bankruptcy of the likes of Carlos, whose revolutionary pretensions were those of a dilettante playboy, and Andreas Baader, whose infantile rationalization of terrorism was best expressed by his assertion that "[fucking] and shooting are the same." The tenuous nature of the far-left/Palestinian alignment was also illustrated by the Red Army Faction's short-lived experience training in Jordan in 1970. The more puritanical *fedayeen* were scandalized by the Germans' insistence on cohabiting and the tendency of female terrorists to sunbathe naked, and it is hardly surprising that Baader and his comrades were eventually invited to leave.[46]

The degree to which terrorism suited the Palestinian cause is more open to debate. Skyjack Sunday and Munich may have brought the plight of the Palestinians to the forefront of international attention, but it was the Intifada in the West Bank and Gaza (1986–9) that did more to mobilize global opinion for Palestinian emancipation and statehood than the paramilitary operations of the PLO.[47] Fatah actually ceased operations against US and European targets (although not Israeli ones) after Arafat's speech to the UN General Assembly in November 1974, although this did not stop groups such as the PFLP and the Abu Nidal Organization from conducting repeated overseas attacks. Abu Nidal's atrocities – which included bomb and gun attacks at airports in Rome and Vienna on December 27, 1985, and a similar massacre on a Greek passenger ship on July 11, 1988 – highlighted not only the bloodlust of its leader but also the destructive internecine rivalry between the Palestinian groups, which was often deliberately incited by their sponsors, notably Libya, Syria, Iraq, and Iran. In an interview in April 1986, the PLO's intelligence chief, Abu Iyad, stated that the Israelis were responsible for only a quarter of the Palestinians killed in their struggle for statehood.[48] The PLO's problems were compounded by its bureaucratization and corruption as it settled into its sanctuary in Lebanon, and in Tunisia after 1983. The contrast between the destitution in refugee camps and the opulent lifestyle of Palestinian leaders reflected the ideological decline of pan-Arab nationalism as a whole, which in turn fostered the rise of radical Islamism.[49]

The rise (and fall?) of Islamist terrorism

The rise of al-Qaeda and affiliated groups from the Maghreb to Pakistan derived to considerable degree from an ideological reaction against the failure of pan-Arab nationalism – as associated with Gamal Abdel Nasser in Egypt and the Ba'ath regimes of Syria and Iraq; and resentment over the misrule, corruption, and socio-economic stagnation within Arab states coexisted with bitter hostility towards the West and the US in particular.[50] The Iranian revolution of 1978–9 provided inspiration for Sunni radicals such as the salafis. Even though the latter despised the Ayatollah Khomeini's regime because it was Shi'ite, the fact that it had overthrown a pro-Western monarch and defied America made it a source of emulation. Hizbullah's suicide attacks against Israeli troops and the ill-fated Multi-National Force in Lebanon in 1983–4 also inspired Sunni groups from Hamas to al-Qaeda to adopt similar tactics.[51] Certain governments also contributed to the rise of radical Islamism as an ideology by fostering clerics and parties associated with fundamentalist variants of Islam, such as Wahhabism in Saudi Arabia and Deobandism in Pakistan.[52]

Al-Qaeda's evolution can be traced from the siege of the Grand Mosque in Mecca in November–December 1979;[53] the Soviet intervention in Afghanistan (1979–89), which encouraged thousands of Muslims worldwide (including Osama bin Laden) to fight alongside the Afghan mujahideen;[54] bin Laden's estrangement from the Saudi monarchy after it invited US troops to help defend their country in August 1990 (following the Iraqi invasion of Kuwait); and (after April 1996) his coordination of an array of Islamist terrorist groups from the Arab world, Central, South, and Southeast Asia from his sanctuary in Taliban-ruled Afghanistan.[55] Al-Qaeda's ideological objectives involved the eviction of Western power and influence from the Islamic world, the destruction of Israel, the overthrow of "hypocritical" (*munafiq*) and "apostate" governments in Muslim countries, and the establishment of a global caliphate covering the entire extent of the Islamic world (*ummah*). As efforts by Islamist militants to overthrow the "near enemies" faltered during the 1990s – notably with the Algerian Civil War and the failure of Egyptian Islamists to overthrow Hosni Mubarak's regime – bin Laden's attention focused on the "far enemy," that is, the US and other Western powers. The suicide bomb attacks on the US embassies in Nairobi and Dar-es-Salaam (August 7, 1998) demonstrated al-Qaeda's determination to cause maximum damage to American interests, regardless of the civilian casualties involved. Consciously or not, bin Laden took to extremes Habash's statement that "no one is an innocent, no one a neutral." The aircraft hijackings and suicide attacks against New York and Washington, DC, on September 11, 2001, can be compared to Skyjack Sunday in terms of the global political, diplomatic, and media reaction. The crucial difference with the PFLP's operation in September 1970 was that while the former avoided civilian casualties, Mohammed Atta and the other eighteen hijackers sought to massacre the largest number of people possible.[56] (For more on al-Qaeda, 9/11, and the Global War on Terror, see Chapter 22 by Daveed Gartenstein-Ross in this volume.)

The consequences of 9/11 are no doubt familiar to the reader. In October–November 2001, a US-led coalition orchestrated the overthrow of the Taliban in Afghanistan and the destruction of al-Qaeda's infrastructure, although bin Laden and several hundred of his fighters were able to escape across the border into Pakistan. Al-Qaeda's survival after the winter of 2001–2 depended on its evolution into a decentralized network, with the Internet providing a means of recruitment and organization, as well as a tool for disseminating tactical expertise (notably with the construction of bombs). Volunteers across the globe could conduct their operations with the leadership's sanction but not their explicit direction. The Bush administration's conduct of the Global War on Terror actually helped al-Qaeda recruit terrorists across the globe through its militarized reaction to the 9/11 attacks. In this respect, the most counter-productive response involved the US-led invasion and occupation of Iraq (2003–11), which provided some of the motivation for the al-Qaeda cells responsible for the bombings of Madrid (March 2004) and London (July 2005). One of the key concerns for critics such as Richard Clarke was that US policies and actions actually helped confirm bin Laden's claims that the

West was waging war against Islam itself and that al-Qaeda would grow inevitably stronger as a result.[57]

However, al-Qaeda was hampered by two key flaws. First, the very fact that it was a decentralized network made it impossible for its leadership to impose any overall direction over its disparate membership. Al-Qaeda did have a strategy, best expressed in the writings of the Syrian jihadist Abu Mu'sab al-Suri, but it had few means of implementing it. Its problem was illustrated by the letter which bin Laden's deputy, Ayman al-Zawahiri, wrote to the leader of al-Qaeda in Iraq (AQI), Abu Mu'sab al-Zarqawi, on July 9, 2005. Al-Zawahiri tried in vain to persuade al-Zarqawi that the objective of rallying Iraqis against the US-led coalition was being fatally undermined by its terrorist attacks against Iraqi civilians, most notably the sectarian killings directed against the country's Shi'a majority.[58] A second weakness lay in the mismatch between its propaganda and the fact that most of its victims were Muslims. As a consequence, the bloodshed inflicted by al-Qaeda and its affiliates proved to be strategically damaging, as it undermined bin Laden's dream of mobilizing Muslim support internationally against the Western "Crusaders," Israel, and the "hypocritical"/"apostate" regimes of Saudi Arabia, Egypt, Pakistan, and other Islamic states.[59]

Algerian and Egyptian militants had estranged themselves from their domestic countries through their atrocities against civilians during the civil wars of the 1990s, and al-Qaeda also experienced the desertion of both its Libyan branch (the Libyan Islamic Fighting Group) and Zawahiri's former mentor, Sayyed Imam al-Sharif ("Dr. Fadl"), whose condemnation of al-Qaeda echoed popular anger within the Islamic world over the senselessness of its attacks, including 9/11.[60] Al-Zarqawi and like-minded individuals hid behind the concept of *takfir*, which declared that "faithful" Muslims could kill their co-religionists if they were apostates to the true faith. For Muslim critics, al-Qaeda's leaders were claiming for themselves the right to decide religious law, despite their lack of recognized scholarly credentials. The Iraqi tribal revolt against al-Qaeda – in which former insurgents fought alongside American soldiers and marines against a common adversary – illustrated the collective failure of the "global jihad," as did both al-Qaeda's irrelevance during the Arab Spring revolutions of 2011 and the sense of anti-climax surrounding bin Laden's death at the hands of US commandos during a raid on his compound at Abbotabad, Pakistan (May 1–2, 2011).[61]

Conclusions

Al-Qaeda may have suffered serious blows inflicted by the US-led global counter-terrorist campaign, but it is far too soon to predict its demise. Its regional "franchises" (notably al-Shabaab in Somalia, al-Qaeda in the Arabian Peninsula in Yemen, and al-Qaeda in the Islamic Maghreb in the Sahara region) continue to wage insurgencies in weak states, while like European and American anarchist bombers a century ago, "lone wolves" like Mohamed Merah, Umar Farouk Abdulmutallab, Michael Adebolajo, and Michael Adebowale are still inspired to enlist in a global jihad.[62] Moreover, one cannot rule out the possibility that affiliated groups could provoke a major crisis through future atrocities, similar in scale and character to the Lashkar-e-Taiba assault on Mumbai in November 2008. In this respect, any Mumbai-style attack committed against Indian civilians by a Pakistani-backed jihadi group could exacerbate the tensions between India and Pakistan, inciting a military confrontation between the two nuclear-armed states. The possibility of Iraq being destabilized following the US withdrawal by a renewed sectarian terrorist campaign by AQI against Shi'ites cannot be discounted, and there are indicators to suggest that al-Qaeda-inspired militants are fighting alongside the Baath regime's foes in the current civil war in Syria.[63]

Nonetheless, in strategic terms, al-Qaeda and its affiliated groups have been as unsuccessful as the far-left movements of the 1970s and the anarchists of the late nineteenth/early twentieth centuries. This failure is not just a product of military intervention in Afghanistan, drone strikes in Pakistan, or the global collaboration of police and intelligence services to roll up militant cells from Manchester to Jakarta. Al-Qaeda's propaganda of both word and deed may have radicalized thousands of Muslims, but it has also appalled and repelled millions of co-religionists. In much the same way that the Red Army Faction, JRA, and other leftist groups were completely unable to act as the vanguard of a revolutionary "proletariat," the gulf between bin Laden and the majority of the Muslim *ummah* he claimed to defend was widened by atrocities committed against civilians by his followers across the globe. The strategic failure of al-Qaeda's actions is illustrated starkly by the fact that bin Laden's eventual objective was to expel Western influence from the Muslim world, but that the 9/11 attacks in particular served only to entrench the US's military presence in the Middle East and contributed also to the overthrow of its patron, the Afghan Taliban.[64]

Essentially, al-Qaeda's problem was similar to that of the late nineteenth-/early twentieth-century anarchists and the likes of Habash, Baader, and Abu Nidal. The ideologies behind both "red" and "green" (radical Islamist) terrorism could not provide the basis for a popular mobilization in any country, far less a "global insurgency,"[65] and this is illustrated by the fact that its adherents inspired widespread scorn as well as repulsion. The gulf between the RAF's proletarian pretensions and its dilettantism was reflected by its tendency throughout the 1970s to buy or steal luxury cars as getaway vehicles, hence the contemporary German quip that BMW stood for "Baader-Meinhof Wagen."[66] The senselessness of international terrorism was epitomized even before 9/11 by atrocities such as the Lod Airport massacre. Most of the victims of this particular attack were pilgrims from Puerto Rico, whose bewilderment was expressed thus by one survivor: "[how] does it happen that Japanese kill Puerto Ricans because Arabs hate Israelis?" More recently, atrocities by al-Qaeda inspired a combination of popular disgust and ridicule, demonstrated, for example, by the British satirical film *Four Lions* (2010).[67]

It is nonetheless conceivable that for a minority across the globe, utopian or apocalyptic ideologies may well inspire future outbreaks of international terrorism. In the same way that Francis Fukuyama's prediction that the end of the Cold War and the triumph of political and economic liberalism meant "the end of history" – using the Hegelian concept that "history" involved the confrontation between rival ideologies – was invalidated by the rise of radical Islamism, contemporary scholars of terrorism may likewise ignore other trends which may inspire international terror. The global financial crisis of 2007–8, fiscal austerity in the US and Europe, and the emergence of the "Occupy" protest movement may re-energize the far-left and provide a handful of individuals with the justification to follow the examples of the Red Army Faction, Red Brigades, and Action Directe.[68] "Brown" (neo-Nazi) terrorists have as yet been unable to achieve the levels of transnational cooperation achieved by "black," "red," or "green" counterparts, mainly due to the intense feuding and internecine strife which characterizes far-right politics. Yet extremist politics tend to thrive in periods of economic crisis, so analysts cannot necessarily discount the emergence of a common front of European or American neo-Nazis mobilizing against Muslims, immigrant communities, or white "race traitors."[69] Environmentalism may also provide the ideological justification for a terrorist fringe, particularly given the apocalyptic predictions of the consequences of climate change.[70] Predictions about the precise course of international terrorism are unwise, but while we may not anticipate its future ideological foundations, we can safely conclude that it will never disappear as a phenomenon.

Notes

The analysis, opinions, and conclusions expressed or implied here are those of the author and do not necessarily represent the views of the JSCSC, the Defence Academy, the MOD, or any other UK government agency.

1 Mark Ensalaco, *Middle Eastern Terrorism: From Black September to September 11* (Philadelphia: University of Pennsylvania Press, 2008), 19–27. The PFLP failed in its efforts to hijack an El Al jet on September 6, and the surviving terrorist, Leila Khaled, was arrested by British police after the Israeli airliner made a forced landing at Heathrow. Khaled's release was therefore added to the list of the PFLP's demands.
2 Cm.8123, *The United Kingdom's Strategy for Countering International Terrorism* (2011), 21–37. See also MI5's depiction (www.mi5.gov.uk/home/the-threats/terrorism/international-terrorism.html [accessed June 18, 2014]); and *National Strategy for Counterterrorism* (Washington, DC: The White House, 2011).
3 See, for example, Asaf Siniver, ed., *International Terrorism Post-9/11* (Abingdon, UK: Routledge, 2010).
4 For a more detailed description of this debate, see Bruce Hoffman, *Inside Terrorism*, 2nd ed. (New York: Columbia University Press, 2006).
5 David C. Rapoport, "The Four Waves of Modern Terrorism," in *Attacking Terrorism: Elements of a Grand Strategy*, ed. Audrey Kurth Cronin and James M. Ludes, 46–73 (Washington, DC: Georgetown University Press, 2004). Rapoport describes a fourth wave of anti-colonial terrorism from the 1940s to the 1960s as an "international" phenomenon. The author argues that because Kenyans, Algerians, and Cypriots fought for nationalistic objectives – using violence for the specific objective of independence – means that they cannot be considered to be involved in "international" terrorism as described in this chapter.
6 Ed Moloney, *A Secret History of the IRA* (London: Penguin, 2003), 336–7.
7 Michael M. Gunter, "Armenian Terrorism: A Reappraisal," *Journal of Conflict Studies* 27, no. 2 (2007), online at: http://journals.hil.unb.ca/index.php/jcs/article/view/10546/11761 (accessed June 18, 2014).
8 *SAS: Embassy Siege*, broadcast on BBC2 (UK television), 21:00 on July 25, 2002.
9 Hoffman, *Inside Terrorism*, 12–14; and Zara Steiner, *The Lights that Failed: European International History 1919–1933* (Oxford: Oxford University Press, 2007), 502.
10 Andrew Rathmell, *Secret War in the Middle East: The Covert Struggle for Syria, 1949–1961* (London: I. B. Tauris, 1995), 1–5, 166–7.
11 Daniel Byman, *Deadly Connections: States that Sponsor Terrorism* (Cambridge: Cambridge University Press, 2005).
12 Isabelle Duyvesteyn, "How New is the New Terrorism?" *Studies in Conflict & Terrorism* 27, no. 5 (2005): 444; and Thomas Mockaitis, *The "New" Terrorism: Myths and Reality* (London: Praeger, 2007), 43.
13 R. J. Crampton, *Eastern Europe in the Twentieth Century* (London: Routledge, 1994), 139.
14 Ensalaco, *Middle Eastern Terrorism*, 35; and Moloney, *IRA*, 486–91.
15 Ronen Bergman, *The Secret War with Iran: The 30-Year Covert Struggle for Control of a "Rogue" State* (Oxford: Oneworld, 2008), 53–4.
16 Jason Burke, *Al-Qaeda* (London: Penguin, 2007), xvi–xvii.
17 *The Power of Nightmares: The Rise of the Politics of Fear*, broadcast on BBC2, 23:20 on January, 18, 19, and 20, 2005.
18 Audrey Kurth Cronin, *Ending Terrorism: Lessons for Defeating al-Qaeda*, Adelphi Paper No. 394 (Abingdon, UK: Routledge for International Institute of Strategic Studies [IISS], 2008), 51.

19 Quoted in Jillian Becker, *The PLO: The Rise and Fall of the Palestine Liberation Organization* (London: Weidenfeld & Nicholson, 1984), 106.
20 Hoffman, *Inside Terrorism*, 173–228; and Ed Husain, *The Islamist: Why I Joined Radical Islam in Britain, What I Saw Inside and Why I Left* (London: Penguin, 2007).
21 See, for example, Henry Pelling, *A Short History of the Labour Party*, 8th ed. (Basingstoke: Macmillan 1985), 1–17.
22 Jeremi Suri, *The Global Revolutions of 1968* (New York: W. W. Norton, 2007). Fischer was Germany's foreign minister from 1998 to 2005. Cohn-Bendit (a Parisian student leader during the *événements* of May 1968) is now co-president of the Green Bloc in the European Parliament. Straw was a senior minister in the British Labour governments of 1997–2010, holding amongst other portfolios the posts of home secretary and foreign secretary. Ali, a Pakistani-born British radical, remains active in fringe far-left politics.
23 Marc Lynch, "Islam Divided between *Salafi-jihad* and the *Ikhwan*," *Studies in Conflict & Terrorism*, 33, no. 6 (2010): 467–87.
24 "Turkey: A Special Report," *The Economist*, October 21, 2010. Ashraf el-Sherif, "Islamism after the Arab Spring," *Current History* 110 (December 2011): 358–63.
25 Christopher Dobson, et al., *The Weapon of Terror: International Terrorism at Work* (Basingstoke, UK: Macmillan, 1979); and Benjamin Netanyahu, ed., *Terrorism: How the West Can Win* (New York: Farrar Straus Giroux, 1986).
26 Claire Sterling, *The Terror Network: The Secret War of International Terrorism* (London: Weidenfeld & Nicholson, 1981); SNIE11/2-81, *The Soviet Bloc Role in International Terrorism and Revolutionary Violence*, May 15, 1981, www.foia.cia.gov (accessed July 9, 2013); and Timothy Naftali, *Blind Spot: The Secret History of American Counterterrorism* (New York: Basic Books, 2006), 117–18, 123–4.
27 Christopher Andrew and Vasili Mitrokhin, *The Mitrokhin Archive I: The KGB in Europe and the West* (London: Allen Lane, 1999), 389, 501–3; Andrew and Mitrokhin, *The Mitrokhin Archive II: The KGB and the World* (London: Penguin, 2006), 246–59; and Markus Wolf (with Anne McElvoy), *Memoirs of a Spymaster* (London: Pimlico, 1998), 249–81.
28 Rami Ginat and Uri Bar-Noi, "Tacit Support for Terrorism: The Rapprochement between the USSR and Palestinian Guerrilla Organizations following the 1967 War," *Journal of Strategic Studies* 30, no. 2 (2007): 255–84.
29 Galia Golan, *Soviet Policies in the Middle East: From World War II to Gorbachev* (Cambridge: Cambridge University Press, 1990), 110–56.
30 Daniele Ganser, *NATO's Secret Armies* (London: Frank Cass, 2005). See also Peer Henrik Hansen's review article, "Falling Flat on the Stay-Behinds," in *International Journal of Intelligence and Counterintelligence* 19, no. 1 (2005): 182–6. For more authoritative analyses of the "stay-behind" formations, see the special edition of the *Journal of Strategic Studies* 30, no. 6 (2006), edited by Leopoldo Nuti and Olav Riste. For more analysis of the cultural and political contexts of the Gladio network and left- and right-wing violence in Europe in the 1970s and 1980s, see Chapter 20 by Hanno Balz in this volume.
31 David Aaronovitch, *Voodoo Histories: The Role of the Conspiracy Theory in Shaping Modern History* (London: Jonathan Cape, 2009), 219–58.
32 John Arquilla and David Ronfield, "The Advent of Netwar (Revisited)," in *Networks and Netwars: The Future of Terror, Crime and Militancy*, ed. John Arquilla and David Ronfeld, 1–25 (Santa Monica, CA: RAND Corporation, 2001).
33 Michael Burleigh, *Blood and Rage: A Cultural History of Terrorism* (London: Harper Perennial, 2009), 78–87; and Mike Davis, *Buda's Wagon: A Brief History of the Car Bomb* (London: Verso, 2008), 1–3.
34 Randall D. Law, *Terrorism: A History* (Cambridge: Polity Press, 2009), 91–2, 98–125; and Walter Laquer, *A History of Terrorism* (New Brunswick, NJ: Transaction Publishers, 2001), 54–69.
35 "Generation Terror: The Angry Brigade," broadcast on BBC4 at 21:00, November 20, 2002.
36 Hoffman, *Inside Terrorism*, 63–78; Ensalaco, *Middle Eastern Terrorism*, 8–19; and Yezid Sayigh, *Armed Struggle and the Search for State: The Palestinian National Movement, 1949–1993* (Oxford: Oxford University Press, 1999).
37 William R. Farrell, *Blood and Rage: The Story of the Japanese Red Army* (Lexington, MA: Lexington Books, 1990).

38 Ensalaco, *Middle Eastern Terrorism*, 32–117; and Simon Reeve, *One Day in September* (London: Faber & Faber, 1999). "Black September" was the name the PLO gave to the Jordanian civil war of 1970.
39 Christopher Andrew, *The Defence of the Realm: The Authorized History of MI5* (London: Penguin, 2010), 613.
40 The British response, to take one example, can be seen with the papers of the Cabinet Working Group on Terrorist Activities meeting in October 1972 (GEN129(72), CAB130/616), at the National Archives, Kew, London.
41 Geraint Hughes, *The Military's Role in Counterterrorism: Examples and Implications for Liberal Democracies* (Carlisle, PA: Strategic Studies Institute, US Army War College, 2011), 37–9, 44–7, 63–6.
42 Joseph T. Stanik, *El Dorado Canyon: Reagan's Undeclared War with Qaddafi* (Annapolis, MD: Naval Institute Press, 2003); and Naftali, *Blind Spot*, 184–90.
43 Ronald Bruce St. John, *Libya: From Colony to Revolution* (Oxford: Oneworld, 2011), 196–7.
44 Farrell, *Blood and Rage*.
45 Hoffman, *Inside Terrorism*, 77–8; and Peter H. Merkl, "West German Left-Wing Terrorism," in *Terrorism in Context*, ed. Martha Crenshaw (University Park: Pennsylvania State University Press, 1995), 166–73.
46 Burleigh, *Blood and Rage*, 179–82; and Hoffman, *Inside Terrorism*, 246–7.
47 Lawrence Freedman, "Terrorism as a Strategy," *Government & Opposition*, 42, no. 3 (2007): 334–5.
48 Barry Rubin, *Revolution until Victory? The History and the Politics of the PLO* (Cambridge: Cambridge University Press, 1994), 61–3, 138–9, 155; and St. John, *Libya*, 179.
49 Hoffman, *Inside Terrorism*, 77–8; and Thomas Friedman, *From Beirut to Jerusalem: One Man's Middle Eastern Odyssey* (London: HarperCollins, 1998), 117–20.
50 Gilles Kepel, *Jihad: Expansion et déclin de l'islamisme* (Paris: Editions Gallimard, 2003); and Lawrence Wright, *The Looming Tower: Al-Qaeda's Road to 9/11* (London: Penguin, 2007). For more on radical Islamism and terrorism, see Chapters 17 and 18 by John Calvert and David Cook, respectively, in this volume.
51 Hoffman, *Inside Terrorism*, 145–65; and Freedman, "Terrorism as a Strategy," 331–3.
52 Kepel, *Jihad*, 105–35; and Ahmed Rashid, *Descent into Chaos: The World's Most Unstable Region and the Threat to Global Security* (London: Penguin, 2009), 37–8.
53 Yaroslav Trofimov, *The Siege of Mecca: The Forgotten Rising in Islam's Holiest Shrine and the Birth of Al Qaeda* (New York: Doubleday, 2007).
54 Steve Coll, *Ghost Wars: The Secret History of the CIA, Afghanistan and Bin Laden, from the Soviet Invasion to September 10, 2001* (London: Penguin, 2005); and Geraint Hughes, *My Enemy's Enemy: Proxy Warfare in International Politics* (Brighton, UK: Sussex Academic Press, 2012), 122–3.
55 Rohan Gunaratna, *Inside Al Qaeda* (New York: Berkley Books, 2003), 24–52; Burke, *Al-Qaeda*, 136–78; and "Bin Laden 'Leads Global Islamic Militants'," *The Independent*, November 6, 1998.
56 Daniel Benjamin and Steven Simon, *The Age of Sacred Terror* (New York: Random House, 2002).
57 Patrick Porter, "Long Wars and Long Telegrams: Containing Al-Qaeda," *International Affairs* 85, no. 2 (2009): 288–96; and Richard Clarke, *Against All Enemies: Inside America's War on Terror* (London: Free Press, 2004), 262–87.
58 Brynjar Lia, *Architect of Global Jihad: The Life of al-Qaida Strategist Abu Musab al-Suri* (London: C. Hurst, 2007); Porter, "Long Wars," 296–300; and Lawrence Freedman, *The Transformation of Strategic Affairs*, Adelphi Paper No. 379 (Abingdon, UK: Routledge for IISS, 2006), 90–1.
59 Christopher C. Harmon, *How al-Qaeda May End*, Heritage Foundation Backgrounder No. 1760, May 19, 2004, 7.
60 Lawrence Wright, "The Rebellion Within," *New Yorker*, June 2, 2008; and Peter Bergen, "The Unravelling," *New Republic*, June 11, 2008.
61 "They Took Osama's Image along with His Life," *The Times*, May 1, 2012; and "The Arab Spring: A Long March," *The Economist*, February 18, 2012.
62 "Osama bin Laden: The Evolution of al-Qaeda," *The Economist*, May, 2 2011. Merah was responsible for the Toulouse killings of March 2012, whilst Abdulmutallab was the failed "underwear bomber" involved in an abortive suicide attack on a flight from Amsterdam to Detroit on December 25, 2009. Adebolajo and Adebowale murdered an off-duty British soldier in a street attack in Woolwich, South London, on May 22, 2013. "Al-Qaeda vs Christmas," *The Economist*,

December 21, 2010; "Mohamed Merah, un membre actif de la mouvance djihadiste internationale," *Le Monde*, March 22, 2012; and "Return to Old-style Terror," *The Economist*, May 25, 2013.
63 "One Year after Death of Osama bin Laden, What Next for al-Qa'ida?" *The Independent*, May 1, 2012; and "Iraqi al-Qa'ida Declares Takeover of Leading Syrian Rebel Group," *The Independent*, April 9, 2013.
64 Freedman, "Terrorism as a Strategy," 332.
65 To use the phrase coined by John Mackinlay. See his *Globalisation and Insurgency*, Adelphi Paper No. 352 (Abingdon, UK: Routledge for IISS, 2002), 80–92.
66 Burleigh, *Blood and Rage*, 239–40. The West German media dubbed the RAF the "Baader-Meinhof Gang" under the presumption that the two named individuals were the movement's leaders.
67 Christopher Dobson, *Black September: Its Short, Violent History* (London: Robert Hale, 1975), 79; and *Four Lions* (2010), www.imdb.com/title/tt1341167/ (accessed June 18, 2014).
68 Francis Fukuyama, *The End of History and the Last Man* (New York: Free Press, 1992); and Alan Johnson, "The New Communism: Resurrecting the Utopian Delusion," *World Affairs Journal* May/June 2012, www.worldaffairsjournal.org/article/new-communism-resurrecting-utopian-delusion (accessed June 18, 2014).
69 Christopher C. Harmon, "The Myth of the Invincible Terrorist," *Policy Review* 142 (April–May 2007): 71–3; and Roger Griffin and Matthew Feldman, eds., *Fascism*, vol. 5, *Post-war Fascisms* (Abingdon, UK: Routledge, 2003).
70 Eco-terrorism is at present a minor threat, and most environmental activism involves non-violent protest by groups such as Greenpeace. "As Eco-terrorism Wanes, Governments Still Target Activist Groups Seen as Threat," *Washington Post*, February 28, 2012; and Pascal Bruckner, "Apocalyptic Daze," *City Journal*, 22, no. 2 (2012), www.city-journal.org/2012/22_2_apocalyptic-daze.html (accessed June 18, 2014).

Further reading

Burleigh, Michael. *Blood and Rage: A Cultural History of Terrorism*. London: Harper Perennial, 2009.

Byman, Daniel. *Deadly Connections: States that Sponsor Terrorism*. Cambridge: Cambridge University Press, 2005.

Cronin, Audrey Kurth. *Ending Terrorism: Lessons for Defeating al-Qaeda*. Adelphi Paper No. 394. Abingdon, UK: Routledge for International Institute of Strategic Studies, 2008.

Ensalaco, Mark. *Middle Eastern Terrorism: From Black September to September 11*. Philadelphia: University of Pennsylvania Press, 2008.

Freedman, Lawrence. "Terrorism as a Strategy." *Government & Opposition* 42, no. 3 (2007): 314–39.

Gunaratna, Rohan. *Inside Al Qaeda*. New York: Berkley Books, 2003.

Hoffman, Bruce. *Inside Terrorism*. 2nd ed. New York: Columbia University Press, 2006.

Kepel, Gilles. *Jihad: Expansion et déclin de l'islamisme*. Paris: Editions Gallimard, 2003.

Lia, Brynjar. *Architect of Global Jihad: The Life of al-Qaida Strategist Abu Musab al-Suri*. London: C. Hurst, 2007.

Porter, Patrick. "Long Wars and Long Telegrams: Containing Al-Qaeda." *International Affairs* 85, no. 2 (2009): 285–305.

31

THE AGE OF TERRORISM IN THE AGE OF LITERATURE

Lynn Patyk

The "Age of Terrorism," as Walter Laqueur has called it, was not coincidentally "the Age of Literature": the age when imaginative literature was the art form unrivaled both for its social relevance and its capacity to render the depth and variety of human experience. At the historical moment when literary art attained what some might see as its apogee in the great realist novel's extraordinarily verisimilar recreation of the social world, modern terrorism declared its abhorrence for that world and the passion for its destruction a "creative passion."[1] If terrorism is understood in part as an art form and, inseparably from that, as a communicative act, then it stands at a pole opposite the novel.[2] While the novel is characterized by its openness to other literary forms and democratic inclusiveness of contesting voices, terrorism enacts a linguistic totalitarianism that seeks to supersede words with an unambiguously monologic Deed capable of transforming social and political realities with one blow.[3]

It would be a mistake, however, to suppose that the relationship between terrorism and literature has been an unremittingly hostile one. Even though terrorism styled itself as a rejection of the Word, it is difficult to imagine the emergence of a strategy of violence so entirely predicated upon symbolization and instantaneous legibility without literature's long tutelage in the narrative and interpretive arts.[4] Much as terrorists declared their contempt for the word as opposed to the deed, they in fact resorted to a variety of genres (proclamations, "catechisms," memoirs, etc.) in order to control the interpretation of their own acts.[5] Coming at the same point from the opposite direction, literary and popular fiction have participated in the mediatization that is said to be the hallmark of modern terrorism.[6] In other words, literary fiction may be considered one form of media that has served as a symbolic intermediary between terrorism and its audiences, recasting its messages and reframing the phenomenon itself. The earliest studies of terrorism and literature, such as Barbara Melchiori's indispensible *Terrorism and the Victorian Novel*, noted the alacrity with which Victorian writers of high- and low-brow fiction latched onto the terrorism plot, and their reliance on the mass circulation press for their inspiration and forensic details. The recent, post-9/11 effusion of literary studies of terrorism has in turn built upon Melchiori's work to emphasize the symbiosis of terrorism and literature as a form of media, arguing that literary fiction eagerly capitalized upon terrorism by adopting it as a ready-made plot with all the devices (both literary and explosive) to attract a suspense- and sensation-craving mass public, while literary depictions shaped the way in which terrorism and the terrorist were perceived by the public.[7]

This chapter endeavors to go beyond these generalizations to a historicist, transnational, and comparative discussion of literature and terrorism. Neither of these terms refers to monoliths. "Literature," in fact, encompasses distinctive national literary traditions evolving through transnational period styles, and modern terrorism refers to widely differing practices of violence by state or sub-state actors that grew out of unique national political contexts in an increasingly globalizing world. That is to say, modern terrorism matured concurrently in two distinctive political and cultural contexts – Russia and the West – that were increasingly opened to, and therefore shaped by, international forces in the key years of the 1870s–90s.

This chapter, therefore, offers a historicized interpretation of the relationship between literature and terrorism in Russia and Western Europe (with a focus on Great Britain and France) in the years of modern terrorism's ascendance to its eclipse just prior to the outbreak of World War I. The fact that in autocratic Russia power was still personally embodied by the tsar conditioned the emergence of what the historian Manfred Hildermeier has called populist political terrorism, in which revolutionary terrorists targeted the tsar or other officials held responsible for the regime's malfeasance.[8] This became the paradigmatic form of terrorism practiced by the members of the People's Will in 1878–82 and revived by the Combat Organization of the Party of Socialist Revolutionaries in 1902–7. By contrast, in Western European states where power was diffused throughout institutions and discourses, terrorism took a wide variety of forms, from the murder and sabotage of Land Leaguers in Ireland, to the anarchist bombings of popular cafés frequented by the local bourgeoisie.[9] Whereas in Western Europe, literary and popular fiction immediately recognized terrorism's potential as entertainment, in tsarist Russia terrorism was at the heart of society's most pressing questions and confronted each individual with a harrowing political and moral choice. In Russia, moreover, censorship made the explicit representation of terrorism or anything remotely resembling a violent challenge to the state impossible, except by means of the famous Aesopian language (through allegory and allusion), until after 1905. Finally, recent studies accept it as a given that in Western Europe representations of terrorism follow on the heels of a historically pre-existing terrorism, whereas this is not the case in Russia.[10] The specter of terrorism haunted Russia as surely as communism's specter haunted Europe, and literature was the first medium for its ghostly communications. The second would be blood.

Word and deed: the Russian invention of terrorism

While there is no consensus definition of terrorism, scholars have reached a degree of consensus in locating modern terrorism's birthplace in mid-nineteenth-century Russia. If these claims are parsed, Russia is awarded priority less on the basis of chronology (the Irish were technically first) than on the basis of their "spectacular successes," or more often on the basis that Russians *wrote*. Terrorism in Russia was the invention of a relentlessly literate and literary oppositional intelligentsia that had itself been succored by enlightened absolutists (first Peter I, then Catherine II) only as recently as the eighteenth century. The institutionalized censorship and state repression that perennially menaced the literary enterprise went far in enhancing the writer's charismatic aura of prophet and martyr, and Russia's first major secular writer/publicists, Nikolai Novikov (1744–1818) and Alexander Radishchev (1749–1802), were also political martyrs who were sentenced by their erstwhile patroness, Catherine II, for their subversive writings, thereby foreshadowing the vicious circle of state terror and sub-state terrorism that was to emerge.[11]

In Russia, the writer, therefore, came to define himself in opposition to the state that sired him and to identify instead with challenges to the state system and social order. In contrast to Western Europe, where the figure of the terrorist would always be a shadowy "other" hell-bent on civilization's destruction, in the Russian literary tradition the terrorist was hatched virtually simultaneously with the modern personality (in Russia, itself the product of European literature) with its aspiration to human dignity, personal wellbeing, and agency in a system inimical to it. In fact, these anticipatory stories spotlight an unlikely challenger in an asymmetrical contest and portray terrorism as the product of the state's real overreaction to a threat that is purely symbolic or even imaginary.

In this regard, Alexander Pushkin's famously ambivalent paean to Peter the Great, the narrative poem *The Bronze Horseman* (1833), is seminal. While Pushkin had found himself on the outskirts of the aristocratic conspiracy to prevent Nicholas I's ascension to the throne (known as the Decembrist Rebellion in December 1825), even as a young poet he had fallen in with republican sentiments and declared his approval of heroic tyrannicides such as Brutus and Charlotte Corday ("The Dagger," 1819).[12] By the early 1830s, Russian society had been brought to heel by Nicholas I's repressive policies, and the autocrat demonstrated his appreciation of Pushkin's talents in particular and the power of the literary word in general by appointing himself Pushkin's personal censor. It is, therefore, no surprise that only a fragment of *The Bronze Horseman* could be published in Pushkin's lifetime. The poem begins with an ambivalent panegyric to Peter I and the capital he founded with willful disregard of topography, climate, and human life; it abruptly shifts focus from the grandeur of Peter and his city to the tragic ordeal of Pushkin's hero, Evgenii, whose humble dreams of future happiness are destroyed when flood waters submerge the city and sweep away his sweetheart, Parasha.

Pushkin makes it a point that Evgenii is a new type of hero: an ordinary hero with ordinary hopes for a good life. But the trauma of natural disaster unhinges Evgenii and leaves him a homeless outcast, a being of indeterminate ontological status that can be expressed only in terms of what it is *not*. "Not a beast, not human being – Not this or that – not an inhabitant of the earth, Not ghost of the dead."[13] Evgenii is "tortured" by "strange thoughts" that crystallize only when he finds himself standing opposite Falconet's imposing equestrian statue of Peter I. These "strange thoughts" amount to a narrative of blame (Peter I's responsibility for the tragedy that has befallen his subjects) and consequent revenge. "Well builder of miracles," he whispered, shaking with fury, "Just you wait!"[14] Evgenii's vague threat provokes a disproportionate response: it galvanizes the bronze autocrat "with a wrath suddenly embraced" to descend from his pedestal and pursue the terrified civil servant through the city streets. In the aftermath of the encounter, Evgenii is terminally afflicted with terror and perishes as a hunted man. Nevertheless his threat, predicated upon its future realization ("Just you wait!"), remains vital.

Ten years later at the height of Nicholas I's stifling reign, the even more insignificant hero of Nikolai Gogol's *The Overcoat* (1842) suffers a fate similar to Evgenii's, albeit in a purely satirical key, when he is "roasted" by a "certain important person," an unnamed bureaucrat of unspecified rank who delights in terrorizing subordinates and petitioners alike. When Akaky's new overcoat, acquired with much scrimping and sacrifice, is stolen, the "important person" reacts to Akaky's direct appeal for help in recovering the overcoat as nothing short of sedition and bombastically underscores his unchallengable authority: "Do you know to whom you are saying this? Do you realize who is standing before you?"[15] "Akaky Akakievich was simply stricken, he swayed, shook all over and was unable to stand . . . He was carried out almost motionless." Like Evgenii, Akaky dies a victim, not of irrecoverable personal loss but of *terror*.

The story does not end there, however, because Gogol proceeds to shed the most prescient and piercing satirical light on the birth of revolutionary terrorism from state terror's corpses. Rumors begin to circulate about the nocturnal depredations of a dead clerk, who, on the pretext of his stolen overcoat, terrorizes St. Petersburg officialdom by stripping the overcoats willy-nilly from all shoulders, regardless of rank. Ultimately, the "important person" gets his come-uppance when he is accosted by Akaky Akakievich's ghost, who predictably demands the "important person's" overcoat. Not only does the VIP "nearly die" of fear and hasten to give the spectral avenger his overcoat, but thereafter he substantially modifies his despotic behavior.

The narrative of "terrorism," therefore, lay in wait, even while no actual terrorists or strategy of political violence had yet appeared on the historical scene. No sooner did Alexander II's ascension to the throne betoken a period of liberalization and reform than a troika of extraordinarily talented and politically radical literary critics – Nikolai Chernyshevsky, Nikolai Dobroliubov, and Dmitry Pisarev – used their journal, *The Contemporary*, as a forum to envision new forms of struggle and a "new person" to wage it. The liberal author Ivan Turgenev responded to these rabid exhortations by immortalizing his radical adversaries in the figure of Evgenii Bazarov (*Fathers and Sons*, 1862) and coining the word "nihilist" to convey their defining characteristic: violent opposition to traditional institutions and the received truths upon which they stood. Bazarov's declaration of his intentions – "we want to fight.... We want to smash other people"[16] – intentionally echoed Pisarev's battle cry: "In a word, here is the ultimatum of our camp: what can be broken should be broken; what resists the blow is worth keeping, what flies to pieces is rubbish; in any case, strike right and left, no harm can come of it and no harm will come."[17]

Bazarov, however, was not up to the task because he conspicuously failed to live up to his utilitarian doctrine and subdue his unruly passions (he was undone by a love affair). It was left to Pisarev's senior colleague, Chernyshevsky, to create a genuinely extraordinary man in his wildly influential novel, *What Is to Be Done?* (1863). Rakhmetov is extraordinary principally because of the rigor with which he is able to embody his ideological principles and put them into action. He mortifies his flesh – and more importantly, his heart – by sleeping on a bed of nails so that he can accomplish any mission, no matter how emotionally repugnant. Contemporary readers and posterity have taken Rakhmetov as the prototypical revolutionary, although none of his revolutionary activity seems to involve terrorist conspiracy. But when Dmitry Karakozov stepped out of the shadows and made the first attempt to assassinate Alexander II on April 4, 1866, certain of Karakozov's acquaintances and, more importantly, the Supreme Criminal Court, concluded that "the novel of that criminal [Chernyshevsky] had the most destructive influence on many of the defendants" and that Karakozov had modeled himself on the "extraordinary man," Rakhmetov.[18]

No matter that Karakozov bore a more striking resemblance to "the insignificant man" – Pushkin's Evgenii driven mad (Karakozov, in fact, used the recently introduced insanity plea as his defense) – than an extraordinary one. So does Rodion Raskolnikov, whose murder of an old pawnbroker and her younger sister unfolded on the pages of Fyodor Dostoevsky's latest novel, *Crime and Punishment*, just prior to Karakozov's attempt. Three of Dostoevsky's greatest novels, *Crime and Punishment* (1866), *Demons* (1870–3), and *The Brothers Karamazov* (1878–80), directly reflect events that marked important phases in the evolution of revolutionary terrorism in Russia.

In *Crime and Punishment*, Dostoevsky's Raskolnikov commits the common crime of murdering a repulsive pawnbroker, but for uncommon, humanitarian reasons – and to prove Pisarev's thesis regarding the right of extraordinary people (naturally, he considers himself one of them) to transgress moral law, "to struggle and err" (where "to err" is understood as to commit a crime). Thus, as Claudia Verhoeven has pointed out, while committing what for all intents and purposes resembles a common crime, Raskolnikov is not a common criminal, and his desire to be a Napoleon is a challenge to the established order and a metaphorical tsaricide.[19]

While *Crime and Punishment* was uncannily in sync with Karakozov's attempted tsaricide, Dostoevsky's novel *Demons* was based on the revolutionary agitator Sergei Nechaev's murder of one of his own followers, the student Ivan Ivanov, in November 1869. Initially obscure, the murder made headlines once the outline of a broader political conspiracy became visible. The historical Nechaev's most notable achievement was not an act of revolutionary terrorism but the infamous terrorist playbook and manual for revolutionary self-fashioning, *Catechism of a Revolutionary*. Dostoevsky, however, allowed his Peter Verkhovensky to surpass Nechaev's accomplishments. With the enigmatic and "satanically proud" Nikolai Stavrogin as his front man, Peter, using violence, mischief, and manipulation, realizes his goal of "shaking the foundations" of an obscure, provincial backwater. As the town is wracked by violence and destruction, Dostoevsky tests the limits of any definition of terrorism by illustrating the way in which the public reception and interpretation of the violence is key to making it "terrorism" or not.

For all his remarkable insight into the emerging phenomenon, Dostoevsky was taken somewhat by surprise in 1878, when a young woman named Vera Zasulich attempted to assassinate the governor of St. Petersburg for ordering the illegal flogging of a political prisoner. Dostoevsky's magnum opus, *The Brothers Karamazov* (1880), should be considered his extended response to the Zasulich affair and his most profound reckoning with the phenomenon of revolutionary terrorism as it coalesced in the years 1878–80.[20] Dostoevsky's novel about four brothers who share culpability for their despicable father's murder is a transparent allegory for the "emperor hunt" then underway by the first terrorist organization, the People's Will, and the Russian public's general indifference to it. His extraordinary conclusion in *The Brothers Karamazov* is that even – and especially – the most compassionate among us can be driven to acts of terrorism in the name of retributive justice. The only way to overcome this proclivity, counsels the novel's spiritual authority, the Elder Zosima, is to acknowledge one's own responsibility for evil in the world, rather than multiply that evil through retaliation.

The avowed hero of *The Brothers Karamazov*, the youngest brother Alyosha, was by many accounts to become a revolutionary and "kill the tsar" in Dostoevsky's planned sequel to the novel.[21] The fact that Dostoevsky's contemporaries considered this a credible trajectory indicates that the image of the revolutionary terrorist was evolving in an unexpected way: it was in the process of acquiring the halo of purity and self-sacrifice. This image had gained traction thanks to the impressive performances of the young political defendants in the great trials of 1877–8, and especially since Vera Zasulich's acquittal on March 31, 1878. "For 48 hours" Zasulich captivated a world (i.e., Western European) public united by the telegraph and mass circulation newspapers.[22] The only internationally famous Russian writer at the time, Ivan Turgenev, was called upon as the resident (he was living in France) expert on Russia and the Zasulich affair, but he wisely declined to comment directly. Instead, a month after Zasulich's trial, he wrote a prose poem entitled "The Threshold." It takes the form of a dialogue overheard between a "Russian girl" and the guardian of the threshold, who tests the girl's commitment and resolve through a series of initiatory questions, the climactic one being:

> "Are you prepared to commit a crime?"
> The girl lowered her head . . .
> "And I'm prepared to commit a crime."[23]

Turgenev's poem, as laconic and balanced as it was, ends with a voice declaring the Russian girl a "saint" and therefore could not be published in Russia until 1905. It was, however, printed and circulated at Turgenev's funeral in 1882 by members of the People's Will who claimed this isolated Russian liberal known as "The American" for their own.

A new sensation

In *Fathers and Sons*, Ivan Turgenev had coined the term "nihilist" to refer to the iconoclastic generation of the 1860s, and it wasn't long before the Russian "nihilists" colonized the Western imagination through every available media, including the wax museum.[24] Turgenev's nihilists of the 1860s were conflated with the revolutionary populists of the 1870s who adopted terrorism as a strategy of political protest only after other means had been exhausted, and the anachronistic term "nihilist" would be used interchangeably with the still relatively rare neologism "terrorist" until the end of the nineteenth century. Most Western European writers of popular and even serious literary fiction were completely slipshod when it came to specifying the national or ideological stripe of their fictional terrorists. Instead, like Robert Louis Stevenson in *The Dynamiter* (1885), they were primarily interested in terrorism as a potentially best-selling plot device. In this sense, the terrorism plot was deeply bound with capitalist modernity that traded in up-to-the-minute topicality and strong sensation. Even writers of serious literary works, such as Henry James, Émile Zola, and Joseph Conrad, overcame any squeamishness about writing for the market and tapped the terrorism plot to boost sales. Their deeper anxieties, however, were cultural–historical and existential, and the terrorism plot served as the perfect vehicle for their dramatization.

The twenty-two-year-old Oscar Wilde was one of the first to capitalize upon the historical emergence of terrorism. The young playwright's first dramatic attempt, *Vera, or the Nihilists* (1879), was intended as a serious statement about liberty and tyranny, but also to cash in at the box office.[25] Wilde's *Vera* takes nothing from Zasulich but her given name (the character's family name is Souboroff) and, in fact, is anachronistically set in the early nineteenth century. Unlike the real Zasulich, who was deliberately plain and unkempt in the style of the female nihilist (*nigilistka*), Wilde's Vera is so beautiful that she repeatedly attracts the notice of government officials whom she must elude and so reputedly dangerous that she is the most prized quarry of the police (wo)manhunt. Vera's immediate impetus for joining the nihilists is her brother's conviction and exile to Siberia for nihilist propaganda, and the nihilist plot dramatically – and again, improbably – thickens when Vera's co-conspirator and beloved, Alexis, is unmasked as the tsarevich. When Alexis ascends the throne after the nihilists' successful assassination of his father, Vera is tasked with assassinating him, but instead she decides to save the new, potentially reforming tsar (whose fate she equates with Russia's) by killing herself and throwing the bloody dagger down to her waiting comrades as evidence of her deed.

Such a representation of Russia and its nihilists (to whom Britain offered political asylum, much to Russia's ire) held great appeal for the English, with their unshakable self-image as a bastion of humane and enlightened liberalism. It also allowed them to dismiss, criminalize, and demonize the terrorists in their own backyard, the Land Leaguers and the Fenians. The Russians, after all, were engaged in a struggle with an arbitrary and crushingly absolute (read: "oriental") power, and such desperate measures as tsaricide could be excused and even glamorized. Substantial media coverage of the nihilist attacks and trials in metropolitan and local British newspapers, as well as a spate of non-fictional books, catered to this interest and provided an abundance of material for novelists. *Underground Russia: Profiles and Sketches from Life* (1882) by the Russian terrorist Sergei Kravchinsky, who wrote under the pseudonym Stepniak, was a particularly captivating introduction to the terrorist as a figure who combined "the two sublimities of human grandeur: the hero and the martyr."[26]

By contrast, the Fenians were not exotic denizens of a rapacious enemy empire but insubordinate colonial subalterns, rebels (coddled by that ultimate rebel, the United States), and murderers. Although there were Fenian-linked attempts on the life of the British sovereign, their signature tactic beginning in the early 1880s was the dynamite outrage targeting a strategic or symbolic location, such as Scotland Yard or, in the great dynamite campaign of 1885, Nelson's Column, the Tower of London, and the House of Commons.[27] At the same time, the Land League wreaked terror in the Irish countryside, committing acts of murder (landlords or their agents), arson, and cattle mutilation that hearkened back to early modern forms of social protest. For reasons of class, ethnicity, religion, geopolitics, and finally gender (no Fenians were women), but above all, because the dynamite outrages directly menaced the English public, Fenians did not lend themselves to romanticization by English authors. In Joseph Hatton's *By Order of the Czar, Anna Queen of the Ghetto* (1890), this difference in perception/reception is made explicit, when the artist Philip Forsyth rejects that quintessential scene of injustice, the eviction of Irish peasants from their cottage, as insufficiently noble for his planned painting "Tragedy." He elects instead the more exotic – and needless to say noble – subject matter of Russian political prisoners on their way to exile in Siberia.[28]

Most striking in English-authored works about terrorism in the 1880s is the complete absence of the Fenians or, as in the case of Anthony Trollope's 1883 little-known novel *The Landleaguers*, the complete absence of sympathy or understanding for their grievances.[29] Just as Dostoevsky's *Demons* indicts Western European ideas as transmitted by Francophilic Russians and then "dragged around in the street" by unscrupulous radical demagogues, *The Landleaguers* lays the blame for Irish troubles upon insidious American influence ("The tuition had come from America! That no doubt was true; but it had come by Irish hearts and Irish voices, by Irish longings and Irish ambition") and smuggled arms.[30]

By contrast, the Irish novelist George Moore allows the reader to perceive the economic and social injustice that gave rise to Land League violence in his more nuanced and artistically accomplished *Drama in Muslin* (1886). Moore's proto-symbolist novel funnels the political turmoil and volatility of early 1880s Ireland through the perspectives and experiences of five young debutantes in Dublin. As the young women marry and mature in an atmosphere of relative privilege, decadence, violence, and fear (at the debutante ball, a clap of thunder is mistaken for a dynamite explosion), they experience their own personal travails as connected to the seemingly insoluble problems that afflict their homeland. In important respects, these hot-house blossoms of Irish society are no less exploited subalterns than the poor family that is evicted from its home before the heroine's horrified eyes: "Is it not terrible that human beings should endure such misery," exclaims the novel's heroine, Alice Barton. While her husband agrees that it is "horrible" and "shocking," the young couple can only alleviate the suffering of the family in front of them and acknowledge their impotence before the seemingly inexorable tide of human misery.

Only Tom Greer's adventure/science fiction novel for boys, *A Modern Daedalus*, openly embraces terrorism as a weapon of the weak, in the process envisioning new weapons of mass destruction and tactics of warfare. Greer's 1885 novel presents the moral dilemma of terrorism from the perspective of a young Irish man, John O'Halloran (the name James Joyce took as his first pseudonym), who is deeply attuned to Irish grievances but loyal to England. The novel was set in the very near future (1887) when John invents a primitive flying machine consisting of wings strapped to his back. While he is enamored by the humanitarian potential of his invention, his father and brother, both rebel leaders against the British, immediately perceive the potential terrorist/military use of the flying machine. Though clearly sympathetic to the Irish cause, John refuses to participate in the family business of revolt, but his naive public debut of his flying machine in the skies above London gets him mistaken as a Fenian terrorist nonetheless. With bitter sarcasm, John observes the media's role in "making terrorism": "the inventive genius of writers had no difficulty in discovering the motive that had prompted me. Undoubtedly it was part of a dynamite conspiracy, and the police were at that moment on the roof of St. Paul's, searching for the infernal machine I had been seen to carry there."[31]

Ultimately, John is forced by the British government's presupposition that he is a rebel and a terrorist to become one, and he lends his "humanitarian" invention to the complete defeat and destruction of British forces in Ireland. Greer was a writer by inclination and a doctor by profession, and his novel is significantly complicated by pacifist sentiments openly expressed and implicit in his naturalistic depictions of the horrors of war. His novel "for boys" deals more profoundly with the question of violence and morality than most and arrives at the surprising advocacy of war without restraint for moral reasons. "But when men do make war, they ought to in earnest. Their weapons should be the deadliest they can use; their blows the heaviest they can deal. To say that they may make war, indeed, but that they must not make it too effectively . . . is a species of cant born of the idea that war is a magnificent game for kings and nobles, and must be carried on under rules that disguise its essentially revolting nature."[32]

While Greer seems intent on exploding hypocritical distinctions between legitimate and illegitimate violence, more often Victorians were simply captivated by big guns and more spectacular explosions. Terrorism provided all the elements necessary for truly popular fiction at precisely the moment when visual media (early cinema) was gaining ground. Published the same year as Greer's *Daedalus*, *The Dynamiter*, by the Scotsman Robert Louis Stevenson and his wife Fanny Van Der Grift Stevenson, comprises a volume of his aptly entitled *New Arabian Nights*. A burlesque of the dynamite genre that nonetheless capitalizes upon it, no work better demonstrates the windfall that terrorism constituted for imaginative literature than these tales spun from a few sensational newspaper headlines and thin air. Fittingly, Stevenson's detectives are not real detectives, but down-on-their-luck loafers in pursuit of adventure and a story. Stevenson's tales, despite their complete unconcern with realism and historical fidelity, provide a certain insight into terrorism's modus operandi. In keeping with his name, the terrorist mastermind and "Irish patriot" Zero fails at all his endeavors, including his ultimate aspiration, which is to blow up the monument to Shakespeare. Zero ultimately suffers the fate of so many literary terrorists, when, attracted by newspaper headlines, he bangs his bomb-toting bag against the news-stand, blowing it and himself sky-high.

Class, culture, and the bomb

Ultimately, the pleasurable frisson of fear and catastrophe is experienced only at a safe distance. By 1886, Fenianism had fizzled and its sponsored dynamite outrages had ceased, so that terrorism in Great Britain receded safely into literary and popular fiction. Those British authors who sought to evoke melodramatic pathos and capitalize on the exoticism of the "other" followed Oscar Wilde's lead in portraying Russian nihilist terrorists, as did Ouida in her 1884 novel *Princess Napraxine*, and the accomplished journalist and novelist Joseph Hatton, in his three-volume potboiler *By Order of the Tsar* (1890). By contrast, those authors who used terrorism in order to express class, cultural, or more broadly existential anxieties characterized their terrorists as "anarchist" in the vaguest sense, less in terms of a clearly defined political and ideological programs than by means of class, gender, racial, and other physical markers that would support a diagnosis of degeneracy. Henry James's novel *The Princess Casamassima* involves its protagonist Hyacinth Robinson in a strictly hierarchical secret society with all the sinisterly ritualistic trappings – including a compelling but absent leader, Hoffendahl – but of indeterminate political stripe.[33] While James is sympathetic to a protagonist whose sensitivity and refinement reflects his own, he nevertheless underscores Hyacinth's otherness by a variety of means. In terms of national origins, Hyacinth is half-French, half-British; in terms of class origins, he is half-criminal (his mother murdered his father), half-aristocrat; and in terms of gender and sexual orientation, as his name indicates, he is somewhat effeminate.

The eponymous Princess Casamassima (the American Christina Light of James's 1875 novel, *Roderick Hudson*) is Hyacinth's double, although she follows a trajectory opposite to that of Hyacinth and the novel's other male characters. Both the Princess and Hyacinth are parvenus straining against the limitations of class, gender, and sexuality. As an antidote to an abusive marriage to an Italian prince, the Princess plunges lustily into the revolutionary underworld, which welcomes her money and her sex but bars her from any significant role.[34] James's Hyacinth ultimately undergoes a conversion from a revolutionist to a cultural preservationist and at the critical moment recoils from his role of assassin, choosing to kill himself instead. The Princess, by contrast, becomes increasingly radicalized, disposing of her wealth and assuming an ascetic lifestyle that verges on self-mortification in the style of Chernyshevsky's Rakhmetov. By novel's end, she embodies political, sexual, and economic rebellion against the status quo and has transformed herself into a weapon of revolution.

In the mid-1880s, the hub of the Russian nihilist movement had relocated from St. Petersburg to Parisian exile, and the Paris prefecture entered into official cooperation with the Russian secret police.[35] At the same time, veterans of the Paris Commune were returning from prison or exile and enjoyed the cultural cachet of the revolutionary martyr, while homegrown anarchists unleashed a wave of terrorism from 1892 to1894. The rising modernists were keen to associate themselves with anarchist "propaganda by the deed," more as a fashion statement and for its individualist ethos than for its ideology.[36] The handful of genuinely anarchist writers and publishers tended to have more conservative literary tastes. These included the editor of *La Révolte*, Jean Grave, as well as Charles Chatel, Felix Fénéon, and Zo d'Axa, all of whom were charged with the journalistic encouragement of terrorism under the infamous *lois scélérates* (the three Exceptional Laws) in the Procès de Trente (1894). Even prior to this onslaught of anarchist terrorism, Émile Zola had imagined infernal attacks as the logical extreme of social unrest and the burgeoning workers' movement. In both *Germinal* (1883) and *Paris* (1895), Zola's working-class heroes are the ones who sensibly resist the lure of hatred, *ressentiment*, and dynamite, and instead choose a more conciliatory path and, needless to say, a more fecund future for France (hence "Germinal"). While in *Paris* the notorious plan to bomb the Sacre Coeur is foiled, in *Germinal* it is notably a Russian anarchist, Souveraine, who detonates a bomb in the coal pits where the workers (on whose behalf he ostensibly acts) are trapped and incinerated. Zola uses "speaking names" for his revolutionary characters, and Souveraine ("Sovereign") is one of the most aloof and unfathomable characters in terrorist fiction.

Male degeneracy, agency panic, and provocation

By the time that Joseph Conrad embarked on the writing of his devastatingly ironic novel *The Secret Agent*, the anarchist as a degenerate was both a medical and literary cliché. While Conrad endows his anarchist characters with the most unattractive "degenerate" qualities, he goes quite beyond caricature and defamation. *The Secret Agent* is a vertiginously ironic tragedy: unlike Zola's *Germinal* or *Paris*, it does not pretend to offer a positive alternative or vision. Terrorism as a form of social protest is manifest only in words of the simple-minded Stevie ("Bad world for poor people"), who is duped by his brother-in-law into participating in an attempt to blow up the Greenwich Observatory (based on Martial Bourdin's failed attempt in 1894). Instead, Stevie trips over a tree root en route and blows himself up. Rather than political conviction, commitment, and self-sacrifice, *The Secret Agent* is a tale of self-seeking opportunism, deception, masquerade, and accident. In David's Weir's perceptive reading, Conrad's novel itself displays anarchist tendencies. Not only does its chronological deformation produce a type of formal anarchy ("as if time itself had been exploded"), but Conrad's ironic distance from his characters and subject matter is so extreme as to suggest a "man who has cut himself off," like Nechaev's Revolutionist.[37]

The almost contemporaneous (1908) novel by G. K. Chesterton, *The Man Who Was Thursday*, has similar themes but in the key of good-natured satire and merry absurdity. Chesterton's deliciously clever novel satirizes everything to do with anarchist conspiracy, from the artist/anarchist as a pretentious poseur, to society's knee-jerk and manipulated fear of anarchists, to the necessary interdependence of political conspirators and the police. But the deeply religious, inveterately mischievous lover of paradox Chesterton's ultimate target is man's desire for order and control – in other words, to be God. The "God" of *The Man Who Was Thursday*, in which the members of the Supreme Anarchist Council code-named for days of the week are in fact undercover policemen charged with spying on each other, is Sunday, and his principle role is to expose them as "a set of highly well-intentioned young jackasses" and confound their desires for order and security.

While Western Europe wallowed in its cultural anxieties, Russia in 1905 was finally in the throes of its first official revolution. Sensational acts of populist political terrorism (under the aegis of the newly founded Party of Socialist Revolutionaries) had contributed to revolutionary ferment and revitalized the image of the terrorist as heroic martyr. "How can I condemn terrorism," wrote the most celebrated poet of his generation, Alexander Blok, "when I clearly see, as if by the light of an enormous tropical sun, that the revolutionaries who are worth speaking about (and there are dozens of them) kill like true heroes, with the halo of the truth of martyrdom about their faces, without the slightest self-interest, and without the slightest hope of salvation from torture, penal servitude and execution."[38] Although the revolution was ultimately quashed, a relaxation in censorship allowed the international best-selling author Leonid Andreev to explore every aspect of revolutionary terrorism in his short stories "The Governor" (1905, the psychology of the terrorist's victim), "Darkness" (1907, the terrorist's self-doubt), and "The Story of the Seven Who Were Hanged" (1909, the terrorist's apotheosis). Andreev had dedicated the latter to Count Leo Tolstoy as a sign of his solidarity in the campaign against the death penalty; unfortunately, the international bestseller also inflamed the imaginations of future terrorists, most consequentially Archduke Francis Ferdinand's future assassin, Gavrilo Princip.

Andreev's attempt to retrofit the heroic image of the terrorist was both timely and doomed. The publication of Conrad's and Chesterton's novels eerily anticipated the December 1908 unmasking of Evno Azef, who as liaison between the Party of Socialist Revolutionaries and its terrorist unit, the Combat Organization, had presided over two high-profile assassinations – even while serving as an agent for the political police. Azef's unmasking and the shocking revelations of police provocation collapsed the bipolar field of revolution and identities firmly grounded in those oppositions. The former head of the Combat Organization, the dashing and dandyesque Boris Savinkov, simultaneously realized his literary aspirations and funneled his disappointment in terrorism into two novels, *The Pale Horse* (1909) and *That Which Never Happened* (1911). At the same time, the brilliant Symbolist poet and novelist Andrei Bely claimed to take Savinkov (whom he had met) as the prototype for his effeminate terrorist with mystical proclivities, Alexander Dudkin, in his epochal novel *Petersburg* (1916/1922). Bely grafts the terrorist plot onto a family plot with oedipal themes, when a ne'er-do-well son, Nikolai Apollonovich Ableukhov, rashly promises the revolutionary party to assassinate his father, a powerful government minister. As in Conrad's *The Secret Agent*, the plot, in fact, originates not with the revolutionaries but with the political police as represented by the grotesque figure of the agent provocateur Lippanchenko (modeled on Azef). Using Pushkin's *The Bronze Horseman* to ingenious symbolic effect and taking it to its logical conclusion, Bely portrays the chimerical city of Petersburg as a synecdoche for modern Russia, itself a "provocation" on a world-historical scale: for what could be more provocative to the modern state than the invention of terrorism? And vice versa, more provocative *of terrorism* than the invention of the modern state?

As this brief and admittedly incomplete survey of the age of terrorism in the age of literature suggests, literature played a seminal role in the emergence and maturation of modern terrorism. While it certainly participated in what is referred to as terrorism's mediatization, literature enjoys a privileged status among media because its panoply of devices – and above all, its special status as *fiction* – allows it to suggest and uncover more meanings and hence to produce more precocious and penetrating analyses. Of these, the most precocious was perhaps literature's consciousness of its own and the media's role in generating and regenerating the narrative of terrorism – by lending it its symbolic constructs, among other things. The literary age, it seems, was a necessary but insufficient condition for the emergence of modern political terrorism, if for no other reason than shared basic premises: the still intact belief in meaning and its safe conduct through narrative and symbolization. It is no coincidence that modernist literary works portray personal agency and meaning in grave jeopardy while effectively annulling terrorism, rendering it instead as a "provocation" beyond/without meaning and human agency. Post-modern literary works, as Margaret Scanlan has recently argued, display a pessimism verging on despair vis-à-vis both the literary work's and the terrorist act's ability to signify in an environment dominated by instantaneous communication and ceaseless stream of images and information that guarantees equally instantaneous oblivion.[39] In the wake of September 11, however, contemporary writers' need to address terrorism and the War on Terror was accompanied by an acute awareness of their role in its mediatization and a desire to avoid the complicity of literal re-representation and the reproduction of dominant discourse(s).[40] Literary fiction, therefore, remains the most conscientious, nuanced, and inventive form of mediation between terrorism and us, if only we would read it.

Notes

1 Mikhail Bakunin, "The Reaction in Germany," in *Notebooks of a Frenchman* (October 1842, signed "Jules Elysard"), www.marxists.org/reference/archive/bakunin/works/1842/reaction-germany.html (accessed July 23, 2014).
2 Even prior to the spectacular attacks of 9/11, numerous scholars suggested that terrorism be understood as performance art or, alternatively, some type of hybrid of art and life, or as ritual. These include Anthony Kubiak, *Stages of Terror: Terrorism, Ideology and Coercion as Theatre History* (Bloomington: Indiana University Press, 1991); and Joseba Zulaika and William A. Douglass, *Terror and Taboo: The Follies, Fables and Faces of Terrorism* (New York: Routledge, 1996). Alex Schmid's model of terrorism as a communicative act originated in Schmid and Janny de Graf's *Violence as Communication: Insurgent Terrorism and the Western News Media* (London: Sage, 1982).
3 This brief discussion of terrorism and the novel is indebted to the Russian literary theorist Mikhail Bakhtin's understanding (and valorization) of the novel, most expansively in his essay "Epic and Novel" in *The Dialogic Imagination: Four Essays*, trans. Caryl Emerson and Michael Holquist (Austin: University of Texas Press, 1981).
4 For a discussion of the way in which terrorists, in their rhetoric at least, revile words, see Richard Leeman, *The Rhetoric of Terrorism and Counterterrorism* (New York: Greenwood Press, 1991).
5 Following Leeman, Zulaika and Douglass's work was one of the first to remark terrorists' fundamental dependence on words, and specifically on particular genres.
6 In this volume, see Chapter 28 by Robert A. Saunders, "Media and Terrorism."
7 Nicholas Daly, *Literature, Technology, and Modernity* (Cambridge: Cambridge University Press, 2004), 13.
8 Manfred Hildermeier, *The Russian Socialist Revolutionary Party before the First World War* (New York: St. Martin's Press, 2000).
9 For more on anarchist terrorism in Europe, see Chapter 8 by Richard Bach Jensen in this volume.
10 What some scholars consider a precursor of modern terrorism, the Gunpowder Plot of 1605, was reflected in literary works by Thomas Dekker, Ben Jonson, and William Shakespeare, among others. See Dimiter Daphinoff, "Catastrophe Observed from an Unsafe Distance: Terrorism and the Literary Imagination," in *Terrorism and Narrative Practice*, ed. Thomas Austenfeld, Dimiter Daphinoff, and Jens Herlth, 81–98 (Berlin: LitVerlag, 2011).
11 See also Chapter 7 by Martin A. Miller in this volume – as well as his *The Foundations of Modern Terrorism* (Cambridge: Cambridge University Press, 2013) – for the vicious circle of state sub-state terrorism in Russian history in particular, but also as the key dynamic of modern terrorism.
12 The Decembrist conspirators were among the most educated and worldly members of the Russian aristocracy and counted several accomplished writers, including the poets Kondraty Ryleev and Wilhelm Kiukhel'beker, among them. Their rebellion and fate on the scaffold or in Siberian exile formed the basis for the Russian revolutionary mythology. Several references in Pushkin's diaries, including doodles of the Decembrist leaders' hanging bodies, indicate that the revolt and the execution "shook the foundations of [Pushkin's] world." See Liudmilla A. Trigos, *The Decembrist Myth in Russian Culture* (London: Palgrave Macmillan, 2009), 8.
13 Alexander Pushkin, "Mednyi vsadnik" [The Bronze Horseman] in *Sobranie sochinenii A.A. Pushkina* [The Collected Works of Alexander Pushkin] (Moscow: Khudozhestvennaia literatura, 1960), 296.

14 Ibid., 298.
15 Nikolai Gogol, *The Complete Tales of Nikolai Gogol*, ed. Leonard J. Kent (Chicago: University of Chicago Press, 1985), 2:327.
16 Ivan Turgenev, *Fathers and Sons* (Oxford: Oxford University Press, 2008), 181.
17 D. I. Pisarev, *Sochineniia* [Essays] (Moscow, 1955), 1:135.
18 Claudia Verhoeven, *The Odd Man Karakozov: Imperial Russia, Modernity, and the Birth of Terrorism* (Ithaca, NY: Cornell University Press, 2009), 40.
19 Ibid. Verhoeven's larger argument, though, involves the assertion of the complete originality of Karakozov's deed of tsaricide and does not admit any cultural influences or sources.
20 Lynn Ellen Patyk, "'The Double-edged Sword of Word and Deed': Revolutionary Terrorism and Russian Literary Culture" (PhD diss., Stanford University, 2005), 29–31.
21 See James Rice, "Dostoevsky's Endgame: The Projected Sequel to The Brothers Karamazov," *Russian History/Histoire Russe* 33, no. 1 (Winter 2006): 45–62.
22 See Ana Siljak, *Angel of Vengeance: "The Girl Assassin," the Governor of St. Petersburg and Russia's Revolutionary World* (New York: St. Martin's Press, 2008), 9–10, for Vera's instant celebrity. See also Richard Pipes, "The Trial of Vera Z," *Russian History* 37, no. 1 (2010).
23 Ivan Turgenev, *Polnoe sobranie sochinenii* [Complete Collected Works] (Moscow: Izdatel'stvo "Nauka," 1982), 10:147–8.
24 The diorama entitled "The Arrest of the Russian Nihilists" won critical acclaim for its authenticity upon the Musée Grevin's opening in Paris in June 1882. See Vanessa Schwartz, *Spectacular Realities: Early Mass Culture in Fin-de-Siècle Paris* (Berkeley: University of California Press, 1999), 113, 139.
25 Elizabeth Carolyn Miller, *Framed: The New Woman Criminal in British Culture at the Fin de Siècle* (Ann Arbor: University of Michigan Press, 2008), 194.
26 Sergei Kravchinskii, *Underground Russia: Revolutionary Profiles and Sketches from Life; By Stepniak; with a preface by Peter Lavroff; translated from the Italian* (New York: Charles Scribner's Sons, 1883).
27 For more on the Fenians' dynamite campaign, see Chapter 12 by Benjamin Grob-Fitzgibbon in this volume.
28 Joseph Hatton, *By Order of the Czar, Anna Queen of the Ghetto* (London, 1890), 1:241.
29 Melchiori expresses her astonishment that Trollope could dismiss Irish grievances so completely when he knew them from long personal observation and "was actually living and working in Ireland, where the estimated deaths from famine in the decade [1840s] were 800,000." Barbara Melchiori, *Terrorism in the Victorian Novel* (London: Croom Helm, 1985), 88.
30 Melchiori, *Terrorism*, 84.
31 Thomas Greer, *A Modern Daedalus* (London: Griffith, Farran, Okeden and Welsh), 82.
32 Greer, *Daedalus*, 247.
33 Although James's novel was taken by early critics such as Lionel Trilling to be a faithful portrait of anarchism, more recent critics have insisted that James's representation of terrorist conspiracy lacks all historical fidelity and is completely the product of authorial fantasy. See David Weir, *Anarchy and Culture: The Aesthetic Politics of Modernism* (Amherst: University of Massachusetts Press, 1997), 71.
34 Miller, *The New Woman Criminal*, 166.
35 Frederic Zuckerman, "Policing the Russian Emigration in Paris, 1880–1914. The Twentieth Century as the Century of the Political Police," www.h-france.net/rude/rude%20volume%20ii/Zuckerman%20Final%20Version.pdf (accessed July 30, 2014).
36 Weir, *Anarchy and Culture*, 123.
37 Weir, *Anarchy and Culture*, 84.
38 Alexander Blok, excerpt from a letter to V. V. Rozanov, *Sobranie sochinenii* [Collected Works] (Moscow: Gosudarstvennoe izdatel'stvo khudozhestvennoi literatury, 1960–3), 8:267–7.
39 Margaret Scanlan, *Plotting Terror: Novelists and Terrorists in Contemporary Fiction* (Richmond: University of Virginia Press, 2001, 44.)
40 Birgit Däwes, "We don't know what the next sentence will be: Post 9-11 Narrative and the Labyrinths of Representing Terror," in *Terrorism and Narrative Practice*, ed. Thomas Austenfeld, Dimiter Daphinoff, and Jens Herlth, 177–88 (Berlin: LitVerlag, 2011).

Further reading

Bakhtin, Mikhail. *The Dialogic Imagination: Four Essays*. Translated by Caryl Emerson and Michael Holquist. Austin: University of Texas Press, 1981.

Febles, Eduardo A. *Explosive Narratives: Terrorism and Anarchy in the Works of Emile Zola*. Amsterdam: Rodopi, 2010.

Houen, Alex. *Terrorism and Modern Literature*. Oxford: Oxford University Press, 2002.

Laqueur, Walter. *The Age of Terrorism*. Boston, MA: Little, Brown, 1987.

Melchiori, Barbara. *Terrorism in the Late Victorian Novel*. London: Croom Helm, 1985.

Miller, Elizabeth. *Framed: The New Woman Criminal in British Culture at the Fin de Siècle*. Ann Arbor: University of Michigan Press, 2008.

Miller, Martin A. *The Foundations of Modern Terrorism: State, Society, and the Dynamics of Political Violence*. Cambridge: Cambridge University Press, 2013.

O'Donghaile, Deagla'n. *Blasted Literature, Victorian Political Fiction and the Shock of Modernism*. Edinburgh: Edinburgh University Press, 2011.

Phillips, Wm. M. *Nightmares of Anarchy: Language and Cultural Change, 1870–1914*. Lewisburg, PA: Bucknell University Press, 2003.

Scanlan, Margaret. *Plotting Terror: Novelists and Terrorists in Contemporary Fiction*. Richmond: University of Virginia, 2001.

—. "Terrorism and the Realistic Novel: Henry James and the Princess Casamassima." *Texas Studies in Literature and Language* 34, no. 3 (1992): 380–402.

Singer, Ben. "Modernity, Hyperstimulus, and the Rise of Popular Sensationalism." In *Cinema and the Invention of Modern Life*, edited by Leo Charney and Vanessa R. Schwartz, 72–99. Berkeley: University of California Press, 1995.

Sonn, Richard. *Anarchism and Cultural Politics in Fin de Siècle France*. Lincoln: University of Nebraska Press, 1989.

Verhoeven, Claudia. *The Odd Man Karakozov: Imperial Russia, Modernity, and the Birth of Terrorism*. Ithaca, NY: Cornell University Press, 2009.

Weir, David. *Anarchy and Culture: The Aesthetic Politics of Modernism*. Amherst, MA: University of Massachusetts Press, 1997.

Part VI

THE HISTORIOGRAPHY OF TERRORISM

# 32

THE LITERARY TURN IN TERRORISM STUDIES

Richard Jackson

It is fair to argue that, notwithstanding the Reagan administration's first "war on terrorism" in the 1980s and the rise of so-called "new terrorism" in the 1990s, without the events of September 11, 2001, terrorism studies would likely have remained a fairly small though not necessarily unimportant field of study within the academy. The terrorist attacks were the impetus to a period of unprecedented growth in terrorism-related research, leading to what one observer has called "a golden age" of terrorism studies.[1] A study in 2006 noted that 14,006 articles about terrorism had been published between 1971 and 2002, with fifty-four percent of the articles published in 2001 and 2002.[2] Another study found that 2,281 non-fiction books with the term terrorism in the title had been published between September 2001 and June 2008; in comparison, only 1,310 such books had been published in the entire period prior to 2001.[3]

This rapid expansion in the literature, which continues apace today, has resulted in a welcome diversification in the field in both disciplinary and epistemological terms.[4] Once arguably dominated by social science, in particular political science and international relations, the terrorism field is now far more genuinely multidisciplinary, with important research also being contributed by, among many others, historians,[5] anthropologists,[6] psychologists,[7] economists,[8] lawyers,[9] and philosophers.[10] Perhaps more importantly, and partly as a result of increasing multidisciplinarity, the field has also witnessed a growing epistemological pluralization, with increasing numbers of studies that take reflectivist, post-positivist,[11] as well as historical–materialist[12] approaches.

It is within this broader context of rapid growth and diversification that this chapter examines the so-called "literary turn" within terrorism studies. Not to be confused with the analysis of terrorism in literature,[13] the literary turn in terrorism studies falls within the broader "post-modern" or "post-structuralist turn" within social science. Focusing on the role of language and discourse in constructing both reality and our attempts to study aspects of it, it refers to those studies that treat terrorism (and by extension, counter-terrorism) not as a distinct, ontologically stable, trans-historical phenomenon, but rather as a social and cultural construct, defined within a particular historical–cultural context and shaped by the assumptions embedded within it. Typically, such studies employ various forms of discourse analysis or critical constructivist analysis as their primary methodological orientation.

The aim of this chapter is to survey the rise, development, and impact of the literary turn on the broader terrorism studies field, and to explore some of the ways in which it has made its presence felt in historical studies of terrorism. I also discuss a few of the key challenges to historical accounts of terrorism posed by the literary turn, and some of the ways in which historians can contribute to a better understanding of the current terrorism *episteme* – the broader social body of ideas, narratives, and unwritten assumptions that have arisen to give shape and legitimacy to the widely accepted knowledge about terrorism at the present historical juncture.[14] The terrorism episteme, and its accompanying *dispositif* [15] – a related term that refers to the underlying logic or orientation which ties together all the discourses, laws, institutions, regulatory decisions, security practices, scientific statements, and philosophical propositions relating to terrorism in a kind of strategic apparatus – point to the role that academic research has played, and continues to play, in establishing how "terrorism" is understood, spoken about, studied, and acted upon in contemporary society. In other words, the academic study of terrorism occurs within a broader epistemological–historical context and simultaneously co-constructs that same context.

The literary turn

The literary turn in terrorism research refers to the body of research that implicitly or explicitly adopts a social constructivist or post-structuralist ontology in relation to its primary subject, "terrorism." Scholars in this tradition assume that "terrorism" derives its ontological status primarily from its existence as a commonly used rhetorical term and cultural construct; that is, "terrorism" is fundamentally a social fact rather than a brute fact.[16] Thus, while political violence is obviously experienced as a brute fact by its direct victims, its wider cultural–political meaning and its analytical–descriptive status – as "war," "crime," "insurgency," or "terrorism," for example – is decided by socially negotiated agreement and inter-subjective practices involving political authorities, investigators, judges, the media, academic experts, opinion leaders, and others.[17] In this sense, just as "races" do not have an independent ontological existence but classifications of humankind do, so too "terrorism" does not exist as an objective, externally recognizable phenomenon, but classifications of different forms of political violence do.[18] To put it another way, "The nature of terrorism is not inherent in the violent act itself. One and the same act ... can be terrorist or not, depending on intention and circumstance"[19] – and, we might add, historical juncture. Who is a terrorist – Menachem Begin, Nelson Mandela, Yasser Arafat – and which acts of political violence are considered acts of terrorism – the assassination of Archduke Franz Ferdinand or President John F. Kennedy, the atomic attack on Hiroshima, the Lockerbie bombing – are not independently verifiable facts but interpretations liable to change over time, place, and observer. Begin, Mandela, and Arafat were all transformed within their lifetimes from "terrorists" to Nobel Peace Prize winners, for example.

From the perspective of the literary turn, "terrorism" is an empty signifier; we cannot know the thing itself with any certainty, only the way in which it is discursively constructed through language usage and social practices.[20] Partly as a result, and parallel to this, within academia "terrorism" is also a quintessential example of a "contested concept," as it lacks "one clearly definable general use ... which can be set up as the correct or standard use."[21] This is reflected in the well-worn observation that there are now over 200 definitions of terrorism currently in use by scholars, governments, and international organizations.[22] In the end, because "terrorism" exists solely as a socially constructed (and highly pejorative) label, scholars from within this perspective argue that it is the language games, narratives, and representational practices of the term that should be the primary focus of academic research, not necessarily the phenomenon itself.[23]

The origins of the literary turn in terrorism studies

The origins of the literary turn can first be found in some important research within political science on the academic and political construction of terrorism as a specific form of political violence, primarily during Reagan's first "war on terrorism."[24] Analyzing the rhetoric of scholarly experts, politicians, and the media, this work demonstrated some of the ways in which terrorism, as an essentially contested concept, was produced as an object of knowledge through certain kinds of rhetorical strategies and practices, and how a coherent community of experts and practitioners came together to shape public and political understandings of the phenomenon. As this and later research[25] demonstrated, it was during this period that terrorism was rhetorically reconstructed from being a rational insurgent (and counter-insurgent) strategy to a form of irrational, decontextualized, and essentially purposeless political violence.

For example, at the first American conference on terrorism held at the State Department in 1972, participants agreed that terrorism was a tool that both opposition forces and established regimes could employ and that it was driven by unresolved political grievances. More broadly, the violent tactics later defined as "acts of terrorism," such as bombings, assassinations, and hijackings, were at this time framed within a discourse of "insurgency."[26] Over the next few years, however, the discourse among scholars and policy makers changed dramatically and, by the late 1970s, terrorism had been rhetorically separated from insurgency by virtue of its inherent moral degeneracy, its irrationality, its lack of justification, and, importantly, its exclusive use by non-state actors. By the early 1980s, "terrorism" had been established as a separate, morally defined category of political violence in the media, in policy circles, and in the scholarly network of the new "terrorism experts."

Importantly, these early studies on the rise of terrorism discourse also adopted an openly critical and normative perspective in which the political effects of certain kinds of rhetoric about terrorism were traced. For example, they highlighted some of the inherent contradictions in the dominant political discourse at the time, such as the way in which the Reagan administration lauded and materially supported the Contras in Nicaragua, UNITA in Angola, and the mujahideen in Afghanistan, among others, despite the clear involvement of these groups in a great many acts of terrorism, while at the same time condemning acts of terrorism by certain other groups and so-called state sponsors of terrorism, and declaring a broader American-led "war on terrorism."[27] In other words, these studies demonstrated some of the ways in which the construction of terrorism fulfilled the political propagandistic function of condemning groups and states that opposed Western interests, while supporting groups and states that were friendly to Western interests. They also demonstrated the way in which the meaning and definition of the term terrorism evolved to explicitly exclude the actions of states, especially Western states. While certain anti-Western states were frequently described as "state sponsors of terrorism," the notion of "state terrorism" – that is, acts of terrorism committed directly by state as opposed to non-state agents – had largely disappeared from view in policy, media, and expert circles. In addition, these studies criticized the often violent and counter-productive counter-terrorism policies this reconstruction of the problem of terrorism engendered.

A second important early strand of the literary turn came from a series of anthropological studies on the role of terrorism, violence, and resistance within different societies, as well as studies of societies which were deemed to be "terrorist" in some way – such as Catholic Irish, Basque, Sikh, and the like.[28] In particular, Zulaika and Douglass's seminal work, *Terror and*

Taboo, provided a powerful deconstruction of terrorism as a cultural construct and modern taboo within contemporary Western society. It demonstrated, among other things, the changing meanings of terrorism over historical periods, the "reality gap" between the perception and actual risk of terrorism at the time, the role of so-called experts in constructing political and public knowledge of terrorism, the way in which terrorism functions culturally as a form of taboo, and the violent and repressive counter-terrorism policies the dominant discourse engendered.

This approach – using deconstructive theoretical tools drawn from anthropology as well as post-structuralism to analyze terrorism as a discursive cultural object – was to prove highly influential in later years, even if it did not penetrate the epistemological boundaries of the terrorist studies field at the time.[29] Such studies were largely ignored in the main forums of the established terrorism field, such as its major conferences, journals, and core texts, in part because the field was at the time very small and dominated by political science approaches, particularly security studies and international relations. More significantly, it was oriented towards the counter-insurgency and security agendas of the United States and its allies. As an influential review of the field concluded, much of the terrorism field's output in the 1970s and 1980s appeared to be "counterinsurgency masquerading as political science."[30] However, in combination with studies of terrorism rhetoric from political science, anthropological studies such as that by Zulaika and Douglass were to form the intellectual foundation for a proliferation of discourse-oriented studies after September 11, 2001.

The critical turn in terrorism studies after 2001

It is perhaps not surprising that within the widely documented[31] broader growth in terrorism studies that took place after the 2001 terrorist attacks, as discussed below, there was an important strand of research that built on earlier deconstructive studies, questioning the discursive construction of terrorism under the George W. Bush administration and the subsequent policies and practices of the global war on terrorism. This increasingly large literature emerged initially out of the sudden academic cachet generated by the spectacular attacks and their aftermath. Political, security, media, and public interests combined to make terrorism-related research, including research on its rhetorical and cultural construction, something of a glamour subject in academia, with enhanced funding, media, and professional opportunities. In addition to the enhanced status of existing "terrorism experts"[32] who were now in great demand, virtually overnight there were also a great many new "instant experts" on all subjects related to terrorism.[33] Many of the new experts brought with them the traditional security studies paradigm.

Perhaps more importantly, a widespread sense of unease and disquiet engendered by the apparent abuses and overreaction of the war on terrorism, particularly after the Abu Ghraib scandal in 2004, directly contributed to what might be termed the "critical turn" in terrorism studies.[34] Inspired by and drawing directly upon the earlier deconstructive literature, a group of scholars in the United Kingdom purposefully tried to spark a new debate in the field about the ontology, epistemology, and ethics of terrorism and counter-terrorism – as a way of challenging the dominant discourse of the so-called "terrorism experts" and opening up new areas of investigation. At this time, the dominant orthodox terrorism discourse largely reflected political and media discourses in which terrorism was viewed as a serious existential threat, driven by religious extremism, and requiring extraordinary measures to effectively defeat.[35] In contrast, terming their approach "critical terrorism studies" (CTS), this group of scholars sought to institutionalize their activities in a scholarly network, a peer-reviewed journal (*Critical Studies on Terrorism*), regular conferences, an academic book series, an undergraduate textbook,[36] research, and teaching. Moreover, these activities provoked a series of scholarly debates about the nature and study of terrorism within the wider field.[37]

Today, and partly as a consequence of this critical turn in terrorism studies, there is a large and ever-growing body of literature that approaches terrorism as a socially constructed category or discourse, and that seeks to examine its construction; its discursive conditions; its dominance as a truth regime, *episteme*, and *dispositif*; and its broader ideological consequences in society. This literature comes out of international relations, political science, media studies, anthropology, literary studies, communication, sociology, law, and many others. It can be broadly divided into five main strands.

First, there is a fairly large literature which examines the discursive construction of terrorism within political rhetoric, particularly the war on terror.[38] These studies look at the way political leaders, primarily in the United States but also in other countries like the United Kingdom and Australia, deployed particular words, collective narratives, and cultural resources to construct terrorism as a specific kind of "evil," for example, and as an existential threat to the values of society, part of the ongoing struggle between civilization and barbarism, one of the new security risks of the globalized era, and so on. More importantly, these studies examine some of the key ideological and political consequences of constructing the terrorism subject in this way, such as how it normalizes and legitimizes a "war" against terrorism,[39] constructs a particular sense of national identity,[40] contributes to the creation of a torture culture,[41] and normalizes a culture of fear.[42]

For example, there are a growing number of studies which examine the rhetorical construction of the threat of terrorism, noting how political leaders, the media, and terrorism experts have articulated public narratives that highlight the potentially catastrophic and existential threat posed by terrorism, and how the "new" brand of fanatical terrorists are eager and willing to employ weapons of mass destruction (WMD).[43] Moreover, these narratives are then deployed by political elites to legitimize expanding national security powers, engaging in mass surveillance, restricting civil liberties, clamping down on dissent, and pursuing foreign-policy objectives. These studies then set about deconstructing the narratives of terrorist threat by demonstrating the empirical gap between the perception and reality of the terrorist threat, countering the WMD terrorism argument, and revealing the political interests involved in maintaining public fear of terrorism.

Related to this, a number of studies have attempted to trace the continuities in political rhetoric about terrorism, noting that the Bush administration's "war on terrorism" discourse did not suddenly emerge from a vacuum but was rooted in earlier eras.[44] These studies clearly demonstrate that the current "war on terrorism" or "war against extremism"[45] is rooted in the earlier "war on terrorism" declared by the Reagan administration, and that there was already a kind of commonsense knowledge about terrorism in American society that political leaders could appeal to and draw upon. The commonsense view of terrorism was that it was a growing scourge upon the civilized world, a major threat to the lives of Americans, and linked to both Soviet expansionism and Islamic fundamentalism following the revolution in Iran.[46] More importantly, they show that the terrorism discourse has been normalized and embedded in security, political, and cultural systems since 9/11, which makes it highly resistant to change. In other words, they suggest that President Barack Obama would find it extremely difficult to change the dominant language and paradigm of terrorism, even if he was inclined to, because the terrorism discourse has become sedimented in society and institutionalized in politics and security.[47]

Second, there is a large and growing body of research on the cultural construction of the terrorism subject in the media.[48] This literature examines the way terrorism and its threat is represented in news media, film, television, novels, and other cultural forms. Importantly, it finds that with few exceptions, there is a high degree of convergence between the way terrorism is discursively constructed as a modern form of "evil" and existential threat by political leaders, and the way it is portrayed in both news and entertainment media. In part, this is because the primary media frame for stories of terrorism is as decontextualized, ahistorical, and inexplicable violence, which obviously lends itself to the exaggeration of threat and notions of "evil." Moreover, this framing goes back to the beginnings of mass media when newspapers first covered anarchist bombings in the late nineteenth century.[49] Consequently, this reinforces political discourse and simultaneously provides a set of cultural resources that politicians can draw upon to construct their rhetoric and justify their counter-terrorism policies. More broadly, this research demonstrates how the terrorism discourse has been embedded into Western culture since 9/11 in particular and become part of a broader cultural–political complex that takes in security practices, political rhetoric, law, media, entertainment, and other forms of social regulation.

A third strand of research within the current literary turn focuses on academia, the terrorism studies field, and the sociology of terrorism knowledge.[50] Building on a number of earlier studies on the production of terrorism knowledge,[51] this research has focused on the role that academics and so-called "terrorism experts" have played in the construction of "terrorism" as an object of knowledge, policy, and public discourse. These studies demonstrate how terrorism studies initially emerged from counter-insurgency studies during the Cold War, an origin that has continued to shape its problem-solving, statist orientation. They also demonstrate the degree of convergence between political and academic narratives of terrorism and reveal some of the network and revolving-door linkages between political and academic elites in the "terrorism expert" network. In other words, this research demonstrates how the broader terrorism discourse is shaped and supported by academic as well as political and cultural knowledge production processes.

Fourth, there is a growing literature that examines the discourse of terrorist leaders, groups, and associated movements in an attempt to understand their motivations, worldviews, and strategic action frames.[52] In other words, this literature adopts a similar theoretical and methodological approach but then switches the focus to the way in which militant groups construct their own subjectivity and political action. These studies are important for the way they deconstruct and challenge dominant narratives and beliefs about terrorists and terrorism. They demonstrate that terrorist groups are not driven by bloodlust or "evil" but by, for example, a sense of duty, sacrifice, and often quite understandable political grievances. They are also important for revealing the rhetorical and normative resources common to both terrorists and counter-terrorists: both sets of actors construct and try to legitimize their violence by appealing to notions of existential threat, the right to self-defense, cosmic struggle, the demonization of "the other," and the like. Bruce Lincoln, for example, analyzes speeches by George W. Bush and Osama bin Laden and finds that they deploy almost identical rhetorical appeals and normative arguments for why the Other is evil and why counter-violence is necessary.[53]

Finally, emerging from and parallel to these strands, there are a variety of discourse-focused critical studies on terrorism and counter-terrorism-related issues, including studies on the social construction of risk and risk-management in the war on terror,[54] urban planning and counter-terrorism practices,[55] counter-radicalization programs,[56] profiling and border security regimes,[57] urban counter-insurgency practice,[58] and the like. This body of work reveals how counter-terrorism discourse and practice has infiltrated ever more areas of modern society, and how it is having transformative effects across a range of groups, identities, and practices. Brad Evans, for example, has explored how security management practices have expanded from attempting to control terrorism to a broader security rationality that takes in an expanding range of threats – natural disasters, disease, immigration, crime, digital security, and so on.[59] He argues that, paradoxically, within this logic, attempts to secure life have normalized terror whilst also creating a passive liberal subjectivity. In effect, this literature explores the ways in which counter-terrorism has morphed into an important contemporary *dispositif* or apparatus of state control and biopolitical population management.

Historical research and the literary turn

For a number of understandable reasons related to ontological, epistemological, and methodological issues (see below), and perhaps also because historians of terrorism remain a small and marginalized section within the academy,[60] it is only fairly recently that the literary turn has started to have a noticeable impact on the historical study of terrorism. For the most part, previous research within history has tended to approach terrorism as an objective, trans-historical, and generalizable phenomenon, although there is currently a small but growing body of work which examines the discourse and social construction of terrorism in historical context,[61] as well as other studies that examine state terrorism, the gap between the "real" and perceived threat of terrorism, and the meaning of the term in specific cultural contexts[62] – even if these studies do not always explicitly employ discourse analytic tools or deconstructive approaches. However, there is no reason why the literary turn should remain a minority approach within the field, as there are a number of important real and potential intersections between the history of terrorism and the literary turn approach.

In the first instance, there is a fairly long-standing debate within the philosophy of history about the importance of narrative in the production of historical knowledge. Hayden White[63] has argued that narrative is the paradigmatic historical style and, in the words of David Campbell, that "through the operation of 'emplotment,' facts are structured in such a way that they become components in a particular story."[64] This means that the narration of events is inescapably bound up in the politics of representation, and "events in a chronology do not by themselves legitimate one particular narrative over and above another."[65] In other words, the historical record itself is a site of narrative contestation and discursive construction. Such an approach to historical analysis sits comfortably with the literary turn and provides the impetus and theoretical tools for historians to re-examine existing narratives (histories) of terrorism, with attentiveness to the conditions and politics of their production and with a view to assembling alternative and competing narratives.

Second, the history of ideas is an important subfield within history, and the ideas of terrorism and anti-terrorism are perfect subjects for such an analysis. It is striking that in a relatively short space of time, in historical terms, "terrorism" has come to dominate so much of Western society and global culture. Before the early 1970s, terrorism was rarely described in such terms in the media, there was no academic field to speak of, and the term was not yet part of the diplomatic lexicon.[66] However, from 1972, events that were previously described as assassination, bombing, massacre, hijacking, and the like, started to be classified as "terrorism" in major news outlets[67] and later in academic conferences and publications. Tracing the evolution of terrorism and anti-terrorism, their conceptual development and their incorporation into legal, political, academic, and cultural discourse and understandings would appear to be an important lacuna in need of more sustained and systematic historical research. Importantly, Mikkel Thorup's *An Intellectual History of Terror*[68] constructs a narrative – in the Hayden White sense – of how ideas and concepts of state, terrorism, order, disorder, territory, violence, and others have evolved over the past centuries, and how they consequently continue to influence the struggle between the modern state and its challengers.

Third, and related to the history of ideas, Michel Foucault's broader notion of – and theoretical tools for the analysis of – "the history of the present"[69] provides an important impetus for a more systematic analysis of how "we" as both a global and national society reached the present historical moment in which terrorism defines social and political reality so powerfully, and constructs human subjects in particular ways. Employing Foucault's deconstructive historical tools, including genealogy and archeology, a small but important number of studies have started to examine the origins of this present moment – in the archives of international organizations such as the League of Nations and the United Nations, for example.[70]

Finally, a potentially productive intersection between the literary turn and the history of terrorism lies in the so-called "new terrorism" debate,[71] which posits that since the 1990s, the aims, actors, and modes of terrorism have changed so substantively that there is a "new" type of terrorism in existence. Historical studies on terrorism in previous eras,[72] particularly comparative studies with contemporary cases,[73] speak directly to, and are crucial for, challenging and deconstructing the "new terrorism" narrative, particularly given the way the narrative is employed politically to legitimize "new" forms of counter-terrorism, including methods previously considered illegitimate such as torture, rendition, targeted assassination, and the like.

In short, there are a number of potentially productive intersections between the literary turn and the history of terrorism. At the very least, the approaches and tools of the literary turn can be usefully turned towards the critical examination of current and past historical narratives of terrorism and the way in which different emplotments can generate alternative readings of the historical record. Such a task is important for greater understanding of how terrorism came to assume such a dominant place in our current historical juncture, as well as for understanding the politics and ethics of contemporary counter-terrorism.

Conclusion

In this brief chapter I have attempted to provide an overview of the origins and current state of the literary turn within the terrorism studies field. I have suggested that while there is by now a large and diverse body of work from many disciplines that treats terrorism as a social construction or discursive object, the literary turn has only just started to make a significant impact on the history of terrorism. In part, this is due to a number of inherent tensions generated by the literary turn due to its particular ontological, epistemological, and normative commitments. For example, treating terrorism as an unstable discursive category bound up in historically and spatially contingent truth regimes, employing discourse analytic and deconstructive techniques, and adopting an openly normative commitment to human rather than state security and critical praxis[74] does not always sit easily with approaches that would seek to chronicle terrorism as an objectively observable, trans-historical, and generalizable phenomenon. Such tensions come to the fore particularly when researchers read back the contemporary discourse of terrorism to historical eras when the language and concept of terrorism did not exist, or when they treat terrorism as a self-evident, discrete category and phenomenon of political violence without paying attention to its status as an empty signifier and the politics of representation.

At this point, the question of state terrorism arises as an additional important tension generated by the emergence of the literary turn. It is a long-running criticism of the terrorism studies field and broader "terrorism industry" that it has largely followed official government practice of applying the terrorism label only to non-state actors, when an objective approach would have to include states among the primary actors who employ terror as a political tactic.[75] As a consequence, and notwithstanding the potential ontological contradictions involved, some within the literary turn have advocated that the systematic study of state terrorism, including the construction of major datasets, ought to be undertaken as a means of bringing greater balance and narrative contestation to the broader study of terrorism.[76] Such an undertaking would have obvious normative value in de-legitimizing state oppression and violence, and might also contribute to broader discursive change in the meaning of the term, ironically, back towards an earlier historical era when it was understood primarily as a form of state violence. The inclusion of several chapters which engage directly with the subject of state terrorism in this volume[77] is a promising step forward in this regard.

It is something of a truism that state terrorism has been far more widespread and far more serious than non-state terrorism, despite its notable absence from the broader field of study[78] – the aforementioned chapters on state terrorism in this volume notwithstanding. Interestingly, there are a number of important historical studies on state terror,[79] including some in this volume, although these studies have not necessarily framed the research in terms of the terrorism phenomenon and are not usually considered as studies on terrorism per se within the terrorism studies field. It is important that historians of terrorism more systematically chronicle and analyze state use of terrorism historically as a tool of repression, conquest, and state-building (as Chapters 24, 11, and 7 in this volume by Roger Griffin, Paul M. Hagenloh, and Martin A. Miller, respectively, do), examine the means by which states have controlled the public discourse of terrorism such that their own use of exemplary forms of violence has been excluded from the "terrorism" label (as Chapter 24 by Roger Griffin in this volume does to some degree), and dissect the dynamic ways in which state and non-state terrorism have evolved in tandem with, and fed on, each other.[80]

In short, there is a great deal that historians can contribute to the contemporary study of terrorism. One way is through more methodical and meticulous research on some of the more neglected non-state terrorist campaigns that do not directly involve Western states or their geopolitical interests, such as various right-wing terrorist campaigns in Latin America and anti-colonial and pro-colonial terrorism during independence struggles in sub-Saharan Africa and elsewhere. Clearly, a more methodical, richer chronicling of state terrorism up to the contemporary era, including imperial and colonial terror, post-colonial regime terror in Africa and Asia, and the state terror of the ongoing "war on terrorism" would also be beneficial. More importantly in terms of this chapter's focus, adopting the tools of the literary turn, or simply taking seriously Hayden White's narrative paradigm, historians can play an important role in uncovering the genealogy of the current terrorism discourse and tracing its emergence as one of the constitutive ideas and *dispositifs* of our current era, as well as deconstructing the ways in which academic research itself, including the history of terrorism, is an important part of this genealogy.

Notes

1. Magnus Ranstorp, "Mapping Terrorism Studies after 9/11: An Academic Field of Old Problems and New Prospects," in *Critical Terrorism Studies: A New Research Agenda*, ed. Richard Jackson, Jeroen Gunning, and Marie Breen Smyth (Abingdon, UK: Routledge, 2009), 17.
2. Cynthia Lum, Lesley Kennedy, and Alison Sherley, "Are Counter-terrorism Strategies Effective? The Results of the Campbell Systematic Review on Counter-terrorism Evaluation Research," *Journal of Experimental Criminology* 2 (2006): 491–2.
3. Andrew Silke, "Contemporary Terrorism Studies: Issues in Research," in *Critical Terrorism Studies: A New Research Agenda*, ed. Richard Jackson, Jeroen Gunning, and Marie Breen Smyth (Abingdon, UK: Routledge, 2009), 17.
4. Richard Jackson, "The Study of Terrorism 10 Years after 9/11: Successes, Issues, Challenges," *Uluslararası İlişkiler: Journal of International Relations* 8, no. 32 (Winter 2012): 1–16.
5. Richard English, *Armed Struggle: The History of the IRA* (London: Pan Macmillan, 2003); and Randall D. Law, *Terrorism: A History* (Cambridge: Polity Press, 2009).
6. Scott Atran, *Talking to the Enemy: Faith, Brotherhood, and the (Un)Making of Terrorists* (New York: HarperCollins, 2010).
7. John Horgan, *The Psychology of Terrorism* (London: Frank Cass, 2005).
8. Alan Krueger, *What Makes a Terrorist: Economics and the Roots of Terrorism* (Princeton, NJ: Princeton University Press, 2007).
9. Tal Becker, *Terrorism and the State: Rethinking the Rules of State Responsibility* (Oxford: Hart Publishing, 2006).
10. Robert Goodin, *What's Wrong with Terrorism?* (Cambridge: Polity Press, 2006).
11. Joseba Zulaika, *Terrorism: The Self-fulfilling Prophesy* (Chicago: University of Chicago Press, 2009).
12. Ruth Blakeley, *State Terrorism and Neoliberalism: The North in the South* (Abingdon, UK: Routledge, 2009).
13. For that, see Chapter 31 in this volume by Lynn Patyk.
14. Michel Foucault, *The Order of Things: An Archaeology of the Human Sciences* (London: Tavistock Publications, 1970).
15. Ondrej Ditrych, "'International Terrorism' in the League of Nations and the Contemporary Terrorism *Dispositif*," *Critical Studies on Terrorism* 6, no. 2 (2013): 225–40.
16. Richard Jackson, Lee Jarvis, Jeroen Gunning, and Marie Breen Smyth, *Terrorism: A Critical Introduction* (Basingstoke: Palgrave-Macmillan, 2011).
17. Philip Jenkins, *Images of Terror: What We Can and Can't Know about Terrorism* (New York: Aldine de Gruyter, 2003).
18. Jeffrey Sluka, "Comment: What Anthropologists Should Know about the Concept of 'Terrorism,'" *Anthropology Today* 18, no. 2 (2002): 23.
19. Alex P. Schmid and Albert J. Jongman, *Political Terrorism: A New Guide to Actors, Authors, Concepts, Databases, Theories and Literature* (Oxford: North Holland, 1988), 101.
20. Joseba Zulaika and William Douglass, *Terror and Taboo: The Follies, Fables, and Faces of Terrorism* (London: Routledge, 1996).
21. W. B. Gallie, "Essentially Contested Concepts," *Proceedings of the Aristotelian Society* 56 (1955–6): 168.
22. Richard Jackson, "In Defence of 'Terrorism': Finding a Way through a Forest of Misconceptions," *Behavioral Sciences of Terrorism and Political Aggression* 3, no. 2 (2011): 116–30.
23. Rainer Hulsse and Alexander Spencer, "The Metaphor of Terror: Terrorism Studies and the Constructivist Turn," *Security Dialogue* 39, no. 6 (2008): 571–92; Joseba Zulaika and William Douglass, "The Terrorist Subject: Terrorism Studies and the Absent Subjectivity," *Critical Studies on Terrorism* 1, no. 1 (2008): 27–36; and Zulaika and Douglass, *Terror and Taboo*.
24. See Noam Chomsky, *The Washington Connection and Third World Fascism* (Boston, MA: South End Press, 1979); Noam Chomsky, "International Terrorism: Image and Reality," in *Western State Terrorism*, ed. Alexander George (Cambridge: Polity Press, 1991); Edward Herman,

The Real Terror Network: Terrorism in Fact and Propaganda (Boston, MA: South End Press, 1982); Edward Herman and G. O'Sullivan, *The "Terrorism" Industry: The Experts and Institutions that Shape our View of Terror* (New York: Pantheon Books, 1989); Edward Herman and G. O'Sullivan, "'Terrorism' as Ideology and Cultural Industry," in *Western State Terrorism*, ed. Alexander George (Cambridge: Polity Press, 1991); Michael Gold-Biss, *The Discourse on Terrorism: Political Violence and Subcommittee on Security and Terrorism 1981–1986* (New York: Peter Lang, 1994); and Steven Livingston, *The Terrorism Spectacle* (Boulder, CO: Westview Press, 1994).

25 See Lisa Stampnitzky, *Disciplining Terror: How Experts and Others Invented Terrorism* (Cambridge: Cambridge University Press, 2013); and Carol Winkler, *In the Name of Terrorism: Presidents on Political Violence in the Post-World War II Era* (Albany: State University of New York Press, 2006).
26 See Stampnitzky, *Disciplining Terror*; and Zulaika and Douglass, *Terror and Taboo*.
27 See Livingston, *The Terrorism Spectacle*; and David Wills, *The First War on Terrorism: Counter-terrorism Policy during the Reagan Administration* (Lanham, MD: Rowman & Littlefield, 2003).
28 See among others, Allen Feldman, *Formations of Violence: Narratives of the Body and Political Terror in Northern Ireland* (Chicago: University of Chicago Press, 1991); Cynthia Mahmood, *Fighting for Faith and Nation: Dialogues with Sikh Militants* (Philadephia: University of Pennsylvania Press, 1996); Jeffrey Sluka, *Hearts and Minds, Water and Fish: Popular Support for the IRA and INLA in a Northern Irish Ghetto* (Greenwich, CT: JAI Press, 1998); E. V. Walter, *Terror and Resistance* (New York: Oxford University Press, 1969); and Joseba Zulaika, *Basque Violence: Metaphor and Sacrament* (Reno: University of Nevada Press, 1984).
29 Stampnitzky, *Disciplining Terror*.
30 Schmid and Jongman, *Political Terrorism*, 182.
31 The following sources detail the rapid expansion of the terrorism field after 9/11 in terms of the increase in numbers of published books and articles, and the new journals, university teaching programs, scholarly associations, think tanks and research centers, and new sources of funding for terrorism research: Magnus Ranstorp, *Mapping Terrorist Research: State of the Art, Gaps and Future Direction* (Abingdon, UK: Routledge, 2007); Andrew Silke, ed., *Research on Terrorism: Trends, Achievements and Failures* (London: Frank Cass, 2004); and Jackson, "The Study of Terrorism 10 Years after 9/11."
32 David Miller and Tom Mills, "The Terror Experts and the Mainstream Media: The Expert Nexus and its Dominance in the News Media," *Critical Studies on Terrorism* 2, no. 3 (2009): 414–37.
33 Silke, "Contemporary Terrorism Studies."
34 See Richard Jackson, Marie Breen Smyth, and Jeroen Gunning, eds., *Critical Terrorism Studies: A New Research Agenda* (Abingdon, UK: Routledge, 2009); and Richard Jackson, "On How to Be a Collective Intellectual – Critical Terrorism Studies (CTS) and the Countering of Hegemonic Discourse," in *Security Expertise: Practices, Power and Responsibility*, ed. Trine Villumsen Berling and Christian Bueger (Abingdon, UK: Routledge, forthcoming).
35 The main narratives of the dominant terrorism studies discourse are detailed in Richard Jackson, "Constructing Enemies: 'Islamic Terrorism' in Political and Academic Discourse," *Government & Opposition* 42, no. 3 (2007): 394–426; and Richard Jackson, "Knowledge, Power and Politics in the Study of Political Terrorism," in *Critical Terrorism Studies*, ed. Jackson, Breen Smyth, and Gunning, 66–83.
36 Jackson et al., *Terrorism: A Critical Introduction*.
37 See Charlotte Heath-Kelly, "Critical Terrorism Studies, Critical Theory and the 'Naturalistic Fallacy,'" *Security Dialogue* 41, no. 3 (2010): 235–54; Eric Herring and Doug Stokes, "Critical Realism and Historical Materialism as Resources for Critical Terrorism Studies," *Critical Studies on Terrorism* 4, no. 1 (2011): 5–21; John Horgan and Michael Boyle, "A Case Against 'Critical Terrorism Studies,'" *Critical Studies on Terrorism* 1, no. 1 (2008): 51–64; Hulsse and Spencer, "The Metaphor of Terror"; Jonathan Joseph, "Critical of What? Terrorism and its Study," *International Relations* 23, no. 1 (2009): 93–8; Torsten Michel and Anthony Richards, "False Dawns or New Horizons? Further Issues and Challenges for Critical Terrorism Studies," *Critical Studies on Terrorism* 2, no. 3 (2009): 399–413; Douglas Porpora, "Critical Terrorism Studies: A Political Economic Approach Grounded in Critical Realism," *Critical Studies on Terrorism* 4, no. 1 (2011): 39–55; Doug Stokes, "Ideas and Avocados: Ontologising Critical Terrorism Studies," *International Relations* 23, no. 1 (2009): 85–92; Jacob Stump, "The Artful Side of the Terrorism Discourse: A Response to Hulsse and Spencer," *Security Dialogue* 40, no. 6 (2009): 661–5; Leonard Weinberg and William

Eubank, "Problems with the Critical Studies Approach to the Study of Terrorism," *Critical Studies on Terrorism* 1, no. 2 (2008): 185–95; and Thomas Wright, *State Terrorism in Latin America: Chile, Argentina, and International Human Rights* (Lanham, MD: Rowman & Littlefield, 2006).

38 See, among others, John Collins and Ross Glover, eds., *Collateral Language: A User's Guide to America's New War* (New York: New York University Press, 2002); Krista De Castella, Craig McGarty, and Luke Musgrove, "Fear Appeals in Political Rhetoric about Terrorism: An Analysis of Speeches by Australian Prime Minister Howard," *Political Psychology* 30, no. 1 (2009): 1–26; Jack Holland, *Selling the War on Terror: Foreign Policy Discourses after 9/11* (Abingdon, UK: Routledge, 2012); Richard Jackson, *Writing the War on Terrorism: Language, Politics and Counterterrorism* (Manchester: Manchester University Press, 2005); Lee Jarvis, *Times of Terror: Discourse, Temporality and the War on Terror* (Basingstoke: Palgrave-Macmillan, 2009); Trevor McCrisken, "Ten Years On: Obama's War on Terrorism in Rhetoric and Practice," *International Affairs* 87, no. 4 (2011): 781–801; Trevor McCrisken, "Justifying Sacrifice: Barak Obama and the Selling and Ending of the War in Afghanistan," *International Affairs* 88, no. 5 (2012): 993–1007; John Murphy, "'Our Mission and Our Moment': George W. Bush and September 11," *Rhetoric and Public Affairs* 6, no. 4 (2003): 607–32; Joseph Tuman, *Communicating Terror: The Rhetorical Dimensions of Terrorism* (London: Sage, 2003); Sandra Silberstein, *War of Words: Language, Politics and 9/11* (London: Routledge, 2002); and Winkler, *In the Name of Terrorism*.

39 Jackson, *Writing the War on Terrorism*.

40 Holland, *Selling the War on Terror*; and Winkler, *In the Name of Terrorism*.

41 Richard Jackson, "Language, Policy and the Construction of a Torture Culture in the War on Terrorism," *Review of International Studies* 33, no. 3 (2007): 353–71.

42 Richard Jackson, "The Politics of Terrorism Fear," in *The Political Psychology of Terrorism Fears*, ed. Justin Sinclair (Cambridge: Cambridge University Press, 2013).

43 Jackson, "The Politics of Terrorism Fear"; Richard Jackson, "Playing the Politics of Fear: Writing the Terrorist Threat in the War on Terrorism," in *Playing Politics with Terrorism: A User's Guide*, ed. George Kassimeris, 176–202 (New York: Columbia University Press, 2007); John Mueller, *Overblown: How Politicians and the Terrorism Industry Inflate National Security Threats and Why We Believe Them* (New York: Free Press, 2006); John Mueller, *Atomic Obsession: Nuclear Alarmism from Hiroshima to Al-Qaeda* (Oxford: Oxford University Press, 2009); and John Mueller and Mark G. Stewart, *Terror, Security and Money: Balancing the Risks, Benefits, and Costs of Homeland Security* (Oxford: Oxford University Press, 2011).

44 Richard Jackson, "Genealogy, Ideology, and Counter-Terrorism: Writing Wars on Terrorism from Ronald Reagan to George W. Bush Jr," *Studies in Language & Capitalism* 1, no. 1 (2006): 163–93; Richard Jackson, "Culture, Identity and Hegemony: Continuity and (the Lack of) Change in US Counter-terrorism Policy from Bush to Obama," *International Politics* 48, no. 2/3 (2011): 390–411; Erik Ringmar, "'How to Fight Savage Tribes': The Global War on Terror in Historical Perspective," *Terrorism and Political Violence* 25, no. 2 (2013): 264–83; and Winkler, *In the Name of Terrorism*.

45 Richard Jackson, "Bush, Obama, Bush, Obama, Bush, Obama . . .: The War on Terror as a Durable Social Structure," in *Obama's Foreign Policy: Ending the War on Terror*, ed. Michelle Bentley and Jack Holland (Abingdon, UK: Routledge, 2013).

46 Zulaika and Douglass, *Terror and Taboo*.

47 See Jackson, "Bush, Obama, Bush, Obama, Bush, Obama"; McCrisken, "Ten Years On"; and McCrisken, "Justifying Sacrifice."

48 See, among many others, David Altheide, *Terrorism and the Politics of Fear* (Lanham, MD: Alta Mira Press, 2006); Robert Appelbaum and Alexis Paknadel, "Terrorism and the Novel, 1970–2001," *Poetics Today* 29, no. 3 (2008): 387–436; Stuart Croft, *Culture, Crisis and America's War on Terror* (Cambridge: Cambridge University Press, 2006); Pippa Norris, Montague Kern, and Marion Just, eds., *Framing Terrorism: The News Media, the Government, and the Public* (New York: Routledge, 2003); Margaret Scanlan, *Plotting Terror: Novelists and Terrorists in Contemporary Fiction* (Charlottesville: University of Virginia Press, 2001); and Silberstein, *War of Words*.

49 Matthew Carr, *The Infernal Machine: An Alternative History of Terrorism* (London: Hurst, 2011).

50 See among others, Jonny Burnett and David Whyte, "Embedded Expertise and the New Terrorism," *Journal for Crime, Conflict and the Media* 1, no. 4 (2005): 1–18; Jeroen Gunning and Richard Jackson, "What's so 'Religious' about 'Religious Terrorism'?" *Critical Studies on Terrorism* 4,

no. 3 (2011): 369–88; Christina Hellmich, *Al-Qaeda: From Global Network to Local Franchise* (London: Zed, 2011); Christina Hellmich and Andreas Behnke, eds., *Knowing al-Qaeda: The Epistemology of Terrorism* (Farnham: Ashgate, 2012); Richard Jackson, "Terrorism Studies and Academia," in *Weapon of the Strong: Conversations on US State Terrorism*, ed. Jon Bailes and Cian Aksan, 118–31 (London: Pluto Press, 2012); and Richard Jackson, "Bin Laden's Ghost and the Epistemological Crisis of Counter-Terrorism," in *Covering bin Laden: Global Media and the World's Most Wanted Man*, ed. Susan Jeffords and F. al-Sumait (Champaign: University of Illinois Press, forthcoming).
51 See, for example, Edna Reid, "Terrorism Research and the Diffusion of Ideas," *Knowledge and Policy* 6, no. 1 (1993): 17–37; and Edna Reid, "Evolution of a Body of Knowledge: An Analysis of Terrorism Research," *Information Processing and Management* 33, no. 1 (1997): 91–106.
52 See, among many others, Faisel Devji, *Landscapes of the Jihad: Militancy, Morality, Modernity* (Ithaca, NY: Cornell University Press, 2005); Roxanne Euban, "Killing (for) Politics: Jihad, Martyrdom, and Political Action," *Political Theory* 30, no. 1 (2002): 4–35; Melissa Finn, *Al-Qaeda and Sacrifice: Martyrdom, War and Politics* (London: Pluto, 2012); Guy Fricano, "Horizontal and Vertical Honour in the Statements of Osama bin Laden," *Critical Studies on Terrorism* 5, no. 2 (2012): 197–217; Diego Gambetta, ed., *Making Sense of Suicide Missions* (Oxford: Oxford University Press, 2005); and Quintan Wiktorowicz and John Kaltner, "Killing in the Name of Islam: Al-Qaeda's Justification for September 11," *Middle East Policy* 10, no. 2 (2003): 76–92.
53 Bruce Lincoln, *Holy Terrors: Thinking about Religion after September 11* (Chicago: University of Chicago Press, 2003).
54 See Louise Amoore and Marieke de Goede, *Risk and the War on Terror* (London: Routledge, 2008).
55 Jon Coaffee, Paul O'Hare, and Marion Hawkesworth, "The Visibility of (In)security: The Aesthetics of Planning Urban Defences against Terrorism," *Security Dialogue* 40, no. 4–5 (2009): 489–511.
56 Jonathan Githens-Mazer and Robert Lambert, "Why Conventional Wisdom on Radicalization Fails: The Persistence of a Failed Discourse," *International Affairs* 86, no. 4 (2010): 889–901.
57 Nicholas Vaughan-Williams, "The Shooting of Jean Charles de Menezes: New Border Politics?," *Alternatives: Global, Local, Political* 32, no. 2 (2007): 177–95.
58 Matthew Hidek, "Military Doctrine and Intelligence Fusion in the American Homeland," *Critical Studies on Terrorism* 4, no. 2 (2011): 239–61.
59 Brad Evans, *Liberal Terror* (Cambridge: Polity, 2013).
60 I am grateful to Randall D. Law for this point.
61 See, for example, Jeffory Clymer, *America's Culture of Terrorism: Violence, Capitalism, and the Written Word* (Chapel Hill: University of North Carolina Press, 2002); and Eva Hershinger, "A Battlefield of Meanings: The Struggle for Identity in the UN Debates on a Definition of International Terrorism," *Terrorism and Political Violence* 25, no. 2 (2013): 183–201.
62 See John Merriman, *The Dynamite Club: How a Bombing in Fin-de-Siècle Paris Ignited the Age of Modern Terror* (New York: Houghton Mifflin Harcourt, 2009); Claudia Verhoeven, *The Odd Man Karakozov: Imperial Russia, Modernity, and the Birth of Terrorism* (Ithaca, NY: Cornell University Press, 2008); Michael Fellman, *In the Name of God and Country: Reconsidering Terrorism in American History* (New Haven, CT: Yale University Press, 2010); and James Green, *Death in the Haymarket: A Story of Chicago, the First Labor Movement and the Bombing that Divided Gilded Age America* (New York: Pantheon Books, 2006). I am grateful to Randall D. Law for pointing this out.
63 Hayden White, *Metahistory: The Historical Imagination in Nineteenth-century Europe* (Baltimore, MD: John Hopkins University Press, 1973); and Hayden White, *The Content of the Form: Narrative Discourse and Historical Representation* (Baltimore, MD: John Hopkins University Press, 1987).
64 David Campbell, "MetaBosnia: Narratives of the Bosnian War," *Review of International Studies* 24, no. 2 (1998): 262.
65 Ibid., 279.
66 Remi Brulin, "Defining 'Terrorism': The 1972 General Assembly Debates on 'International Terrorism' and their Coverage by the New York Times," in *Societies Under Siege: Media, Government, Politics and Citizens' Freedoms in an Age of Terrorism*, ed. Banu Hawks (Cambridge: Cambridge Scholar Press, 2012).
67 Zulaika and Douglass, *Terror and Taboo*, 46.
68 Mikkel Thorup, *An Intellectual History of Terror: War, Violence and the State* (Abingdon, UK: Routledge, 2010).

69 See Ditrych, "'International Terrorism' in the League of Nations."
70 See Remi Brulin, "A History of the American Discourse on 'Terrorism' and of the New York Times Coverage of the 'Terrorism' Question" (PhD dissertation, La Sorbonne Novelle, France, 2011); Brulin, "Defining 'Terrorism'"; and Ditrych, "'International Terrorism' in the League of Nations."
71 See Thomas Copeland, "Is the New Terrorism Really New? An Analysis of the New Paradigm for Terrorism," *Journal of Conflict Studies* 21, no. 2 (2001): 91–105; Martha Crenshaw, "'New' vs 'Old' Terrorism: A Critical Appraisal," in *Jihadi Terrorism and the Radicalisation Challenge in Europe*, ed. Rik Coolsaet (Aldershot: Ashgate, 2008); Isabelle Duyvesteyn, "How New is the New Terrorism?" *Studies in Conflict & Terrorism* 27, no. 5 (2004): 439–54; and Alexander Spencer, "Questioning the Concept of 'New Terrorism,'" *Peace, Conflict & Development*, no. 8 (February 2006): 1–33.
72 See Carr, *The Infernal Machine*.
73 Mark Sedgwick, "Al-Qaeda and the Nature of Religious Terrorism," *Terrorism and Political Violence* 16, no. 4 (2004): 795–814.
74 See Jackson, Breen Smyth, and Gunning, *Critical Terrorism Studies*.
75 See Richard Jackson, "The Ghosts of State Terror: Knowledge, Politics and Terrorism Studies," *Critical Studies on Terrorism* 1, no. 3 (2008): 377–92; Richard Jackson, "Conclusion: Contemporary State Terrorism: Towards a New Research Agenda," in *Contemporary State Terrorism: Theory and Cases*, ed. Richard Jackson, Scott Poynting, and Eamon Murphy (Abingdon, UK: Routledge, 2010).
76 Jackson, "Conclusion: Contemporary State Terrorism."
77 See Chapters 24, 11, and 7 by Roger Griffin, Paul M. Hagenloh, and Martin A. Miller, respectively, in this volume.
78 Jackson, "The Ghosts of State Terror."
79 David Chandler, *Voices from S-21: Terror and History in Pol Pot's Secret Prison* (Berkeley: University of California Press, 2000); Eric Johnson, *Nazi Terror: Gestapo, Jews and Ordinary Germans* (New York: Basic Books, 2000); and Colin Wight, "Theorising Terrorism: The State, Structure and History," *International Relations* 23, no. 1 (2009): 99–106.
80 Martin A. Miller, *The Foundations of Modern Terrorism: State, Society and the Dynamics of Political Violence* (Cambridge: Cambridge University Press, 2013); see also, Goodin, *What's Wrong with Terrorism?*

Further reading

Croft, Stuart. *Culture, Crisis and America's War on Terror*. Cambridge: Cambridge University Press, 2006.
Goodin, Robert. *What's Wrong with Terrorism?* Cambridge: Polity Press, 2006.
Jackson, Richard. *Writing the War on Terrorism: Language, Politics and Counterterrorism*. Manchester: Manchester University Press, 2005.
Jackson, Richard, Marie Breen Smyth, and Jeroen Gunning, eds. *Critical Terrorism Studies: A New Research Agenda*. Abingdon, UK: Routledge, 2009.
Jenkins, Philip. *Images of Terror: What We Can and Can't Know about Terrorism*. New York: Aldine de Gruyter, 2003.
Stampnitzky, Lisa. *Disciplining Terror: How Experts and Others Invented Terrorism*. Cambridge: Cambridge University Press, 2013.
Thorup, Mikkel. *An Intellectual History of Terror: War, Violence and the State*. Abingdon, UK: Routledge, 2010.
Tuman, Joseph. *Communicating Terror: The Rhetorical Dimensions of Terrorism*. London: Sage, 2003.
Winkler, Carol. *In the Name of Terrorism: Presidents on Political Violence in the Post-World War II Era*. Albany: State University of New York Press, 2006.
Zulaika, Joseba, and William Douglass. *Terror and Taboo: The Follies, Fables, and Faces of Terrorism*. London: Routledge, 1996.

INDEX

Abane, Ramdane 3
Abarno, Frank 136
Abbas, Mahmoud 254–5
Abbas, Nasir 387–8
Abbasid Caliphate 34–5, 38
Abbottabad 341, 343
ABC News 436
'Abd al-Rahman, Umar 259, 433
'Abduh, Muhammad 260, 267
Abdülhamid II, Sultan of Ottoman Empire 414–15
Abdulmutallab, Umar Farouk 464, 468n62
abolitionism 88, 143–4
abschreckung 164
abstentionism 179, 208
Abu Ghraib 490
Abu Iyad (PLO) 462
Abu Iyadh al-Tunisi (AST) 344
Abu Nidal 245, 250, 461–2
Abu Salim prison 344
Abu Sufyan bin Qumu 344
Abu Za'bal prison 344
academic consensus definition of terrorism, revised 7, 370
Académie française 63
Achille Lauro 432, 462
Achimeir 370
Achmed the Dead Terrorist 438
Action Directe (France) 305–6
Action for National Liberation (ALN) (Brazil) 291
Action Française 123
Adam of Fleury 51
Adam, Guillaume 41–2
Adams, Gerry 212–13
Addi, Maarouf 232
Adebolajo, Michael 464, 468n62
Adebowale, Michael 464, 468n62
Aden 199–200, 339
Aden Emergency 199–200
Adivasis 352, 360–2
al-Afdal 39, 44n41

Afghan War (2001–) 340, 379, 383, 389, 391, 421; and Pakistan 356; and al-Qaeda 340–2, 346, 385, 434, 463
Afghanistan 336, 339, 373
Afghan–Soviet War 262, 273, 334–5, 354–5, 363n21, 403, 463
African Americans 82–3, 85–8, 145–51, 216n5, 326
African National Congress 389, 391
Agatha, Operation 183
agents provocateurs 111–12, 114, 117, 120, 136–7, 140–1, 416; in Russia 93, 96, 102, 104, 450, 480
Ahala 17
Ahmeti, Ali 387
Air France 248
airport security 246, 420
Al Jazeera 340, 434
al- *see* word or proper noun that follows the article
Alabama 1, 151–2
Alamut 35, 38, 41
Albanian National Liberation Army 387
Albigensian Crusade 54, 63
Albinus, Lucceius 29–30
Albrecht, Bernard 306
Aleksei, Tsar of Russia 94
Alexander I, King of Yugoslavia 125, 416, 457
Alexander I, Tsar of Russia 94
Alexander II, Tsar of Russia 97, 100–1, 377, 430, 435, 473; death celebrated abroad 112, 119, 133, 446
Alexander III, Tsar of Russia 101, 103
Alexandria 33
Alfonso XIII, King of Spain 120–1
Alfred P. Murrah Federal building 318, 378, 433
Algeria 3, 245, 266; as French colony 218–34, 235n13, 236n60; jihadism in 339
Algerian Civil War 333, 464
Algerian National Movement (MNA) 228, 233
Algerian People's Party 220

501

INDEX

Algerian War of Independence 3, 218–19, 222–34, 237n66, 271, 436; casualties of 218; massacres in 225–8
Algiers 230–2
Ali La Pointe 232
Ali, Tariq 298, 458, 467n22
Alimamu 78–9
Alipore bomb trial 448
Allouni, Taysir 340
ALN *see* National Liberation Army (Algeria)
Amal 279, 404
Ambrose of Milan 47
American Civil War 144–6, 153n12, 443–4, 447
American Indians *see* Native Americans
American Legion 319
American Revolutionary War 84–6, 444
Ames, Adelbert 148
Amherst, Jeffrey 84
Amin, Hafizullah 334
Amin, Idi 461
Amirouche 232
ammonium nitrate 447–8
ammonium nitrate fuel oil bomb (ANFO) 449
Ananias, High Priest 30–1
anarchism 2–3, 103, 111–12; in Europe and Russia 103, 106, 119, 166; ideology of 111, 117–18, 131–2, 139–40; as international movement 114, 131; as pejorative 130, 414, 478–9; and socialism 111–12, 114, 122, 125n6, 132–3; and uprisings 112, 115, 121; in US 130–3, 138–40; and violence 111, 125n6, 130–1, 140; *see also* anarchist terrorism
Anarchist Exclusion Act 135–6
Anarchist Fighters 137
Anarchist Squad 136–7
anarchist terrorism 377, 401, 413–14; in Argentina 113, 118, 121, 124; in Austria-Hungary 114, 122, 127n36; in Belgium 115; in Brazil 124; in China 122; decline of 124–5; four phases 114; in France 114–15, 118, 123; by Germans abroad 124; in Germany 112, 114–15; and international counter-terrorism 413–17; by Italians abroad 114–15, 117, 124, 137; in Italy 116, 123; in Japan 122; and leaderless organization 459–60; in Russia/USSR 119, 122–3; by Russians abroad 120–1, 127n40, 134; in Spain 112–13, 115–16, 120–1, 123–4, 127n36; by Spaniards abroad 121, 124; understood as global conspiracy 111, 413–16; in Uruguay 124; in US 120, 122, 130–41, 153n12, 154n33; in US, seen as foreign 133, 135, 141; and women 123–4; *see also* anarchism
Anastasius, Emperor of Rome 47
Anbar 343
Andreev, Leonid 480

Andreotti, Giulio 303, 308
Andress, David 68
Andrews, Lewis 181
Andrey Kozhukov (Protazanov) 437
Anglo-Irish Agreement 212
Anglo-Irish Treaty 179
Angry Brigade 298, 460
Animal Liberation (Singer) 327
Animal Liberation Front 140, 327
animal rights 327–8
anomy 377
Ansar al-Mujahideen Network 337, 344
Ansar al-Sharia in Libya 344
Ansar al-Sharia in Tunisia 344–5, 350n64
al-Ansari, Abu al-Harith 337
anti-abortion movement 326–7
anti-lynching activism 150, 155n40, 155n42
anti-Semitism 101, 105, 162–3
anti-terrorism 389
anti-Zionism 305
APRA (Peru) 286
al-Aqsa Intifada *see* Intifada, Second
al-Aqsa Martyrs Brigade 279, 404
Aquinas, Thomas 19, 55
Arab Americans 326
Arab League 223, 241, 246–8, 254
Arab Liberation Front 243
Arab Revolt (1936) 180–1, 239
Arab Spring 339, 343–6, 349n54, 349n55, 373, 464
Arab–Israeli War, First 184, 241
Arabs, in Palestine 180–1, 183–4
Arafat, Yasser 240–2, 244–5, 247, 251–4, 488; and Soviet Union 459; and UN 420, 462
Aramburu, Pedro 293
Arenal 79
Arendt, Hannah 108n4, 162, 168–9
Argentina 280, 293–4, 386, 404; anarchist terrorism in 113, 118, 121, 124; counter-terrorism in 121
Argentine Anticommunist Alliance (AAA) 294
Argov, Shlomo 250
Aristogeiton 15–16
Aristotle 16–17
Armed Islamic Group (Algeria) 266, 404
Armed Revolutionary Nuclei (NAR) (Italy) 307, 309
armed struggle (Fatah/PLO) 241, 244, 247, 249, 251
Armitage, Robert 198
Arnold of Lübeck 39
Arquilla, John 459
Artemio (Shining Path leader) 288
al-Asad, Hafiz 276
Asahara, Shoko 451
ASALA (Armenian group) 456

502

INDEX

'Ashush, Ahmad 344
al-Asifa 242
al-Askari Shrine 2
Aslan, Reza 382n39
As-Sahab 434
assassination 15–16, 35, 37–8, 41, 65, 72–3
Assassins 28, 33–42, 44, 54, 400; and messaging 429; Muslim perceptions of 36–7; source of term 37; as suicide terrorists 399–400; Western perceptions of 39–42
Association of Reformist Ulama (Algeria) 225
Ataturk, Mustafa Kemal 260, 262
Ataviros 251
Athens 15–16, 21
attentats 2, 3; defined 134
Attlee, Clement 190
Audran, René 306
Augustine of Hippo 18, 21, 47–8
Aum Shinrikyo 433, 451, 456
Austria 174n9
Austria–Hungary 119, 161; anarchist terrorism in 114, 122, 127n36
authoritarianism 373, 390; and state terror/ism 373–5, 379–80
auto-da-fé 371, 381n10
Autonomous Algiers Zone 231
Avatar (Cameron) 376
Awakening movement (Iraq) *see* Sahwa
al-Awlaki, Anwar 342, 424n13
axis of evil 421
Ayodhya, India 359
Azef, Evno 92–3, 105–6, 110n46, 480
Aznar, José María 437
'Azzam, 'Abdullah 264, 335

Ba'ath Party (Iraq) 243
Ba'ath Party (Syria) 242
Baader, Andreas 299–301, 458, 460, 462
Baader-Meinhof Group/Gang *see* Red Army Faction
Babeuf, Gracchus 71
Babri Masjid mosque 359
Bachmann, Josef 308
Bajrang Dal 358, 361
Bakhtin, Mikhail 481n3
Bakunin, Mikhail 98–9, 111–12, 131–2, 414
Balfour Declaration 180, 182
Balfour, A. J. 178, 180
Bali nightclub bombings 387–8, 405
Balmashov, Stepan 104
Baltics 169
Banco de la República (Uruguay) 292
Bandung Conference 224
Bangladesh 363n2
al-Banna, Hasan 259, 264, 271–2, 347n19
Banner, Operation 200

Barak, Ehud 253–4
Barcelona 115–16, 120–3
Barelvi *see* Islam, Barelvi
Barère, Bertrand 63, 67
Baring, Evelyn 195–6
Basayev, Shamil 436
Basques 387
batin 34, 36–7
Battle of Algiers 230–2
Battle of Algiers, The (Pontecorvo) 231, 437–8
Baudot, Marc-Antoine 374
Bauer, Jack 438
Bauman, Zygmunt 168, 174n6, 374, 377
Beauharnois, Charles de la Boische de 82
Begin, Menachem 182, 461, 488
Beirut 249–50, 279–80
Belaúnde, Fernando 287
Belfast 208–9, 214
Belgian Clause 118
Belgium, anarchist terrorism in 115
Belhadj, Abdelhakim 388
Bell, The 97, 99
Bely, Andrei 480
Ben Ali, Zine El Abidine 343
Ben Bouali, Hassiba 232
Ben Tobbal, Lakhdar 228
Benckendorff, Alexander 94–6
Bengal 180
Benghazi, Libya 344, 407n10
Benotman, Noman 337
Bentham, Jeremy 132
Berg, Alan 438
Berg, Nicholas 434
Bergen, Peter 335, 337, 381n32, 434, 450
Berkman, Alexander 134, 137
Berro Oribe, Guidi 292
Berry, Duc de 73
Bertillon, Alphonse 415
Bertillonage 415–16
Berton, Germaine 123
Beslan school massacre 387, 404, 436
Betancur, Belisario 290
Betrayed 438
Bharatiya Janata Party 358–62
Bible 18, 21, 79, 87, 143–4
Biden, Joseph 383
Bin Laden Unit (of CIA) 337
bin Laden, Mohammad 334
bin Laden, Osama 276, 334–8, 340, 342–3, 421–2, 463, 492; death of 385, 422, 464
biological weapons 341, 451
Birjandi, Hasan Ibn Salah 38
Birth of a Nation, The (Griffith) 149, 151, 154n30
Bismarck, Otto von 114, 161
Black Band (France) 114
Black Hand (Spain) 114

503

INDEX

Black Hundreds 104–5, 109n43
Black International 112, 414–15
Black Legend 80, 82
Black Order (Italy) 306
Black Panthers 139
Black Power 138
Black Reconstruction (Du Bois) 150
Black Repartition 100
Black September (operation) 246, 460
Black September (organization) 245–6, 420, 431, 460–1
Black Sunday 438
Black Tigers (Sri Lanka) 403
Black, Donald 218
Blair, Tony 426n72
Blanco Party (Uruguay) 292
Blanqui, Louis-Auguste 71–2
Bloch, Marc 52
Blok, Alexander 479
blood eagle 49–50
Bloody Sunday (Northern Ireland) 210
Bloody Sunday (Russia) 106
Bloque Sur de Guerrilla (Colombia) 289
Bodin, Jean 22
Boer War 161
Boggs, Carl 328
Bogolepov, Nikolai 104
Bogrov, Dmitry 106
Bologna railway station bombing 307–9
Bolsheviks 107 *see also* Communist Party of the Soviet Union; Russian Social Democratic Labor Party
Bomb (Harris) 437
Bombay Street (Belfast) 208
Bookchin, Murray 139–40
Booth, John Wilkes 144–5, 153n8, 12
border campaign (Ireland) 206
Borghese Putsch 307
Bosnia and Herzegovina, jihadism in 339
Bosnian War 404
Boston 138
Boston Marathon bombing 322
Boston Tea Party 85
Bouazza, Djamila 231
Bouhamidi, Mahmoud 232
Bouhired, Djamila 231
Bourdin, Martial 437, 479
Bourne, Geoffrey 192–3
Bourse (Paris) 115
Boussouf, Abdelhafid 233
Bradford, William 81
Brands, Hal 285
Brass, L. S. 417
Brazil 124, 291
Breivik, Anders 378, 434

Bridge and Structural Iron Workers, International Association of 136
Brigate Rosse *see* Red Brigades
Briggs Plan 186, 191
Briggs, Harold 185–6, 191, 197
Britain 82–5, 113, 117, 161, 178–9, 190, 240, 298, 323, 325, 341; and Aden 199–200; censorship in 435; and counter-insurgency 181, 185–6, 191–200, 202n30, 386; and counter-terrorism 391; and Cyprus 197–9; and Dominions 177; and Egypt 180, 271, 347n19; and imperial policing 390; and India 180, 183, 358; and international counter-terrorism 119; and Ireland 177–80, 204; and Irish Fenians 444; and July 7, 2005, attacks 341, 405, 426n72, 434, 463; and Kenya 191, 193–8, 202n52; and Malaya 184–6, 190–3, 198; and Middle East 266; Ministry of Defence, 215; and Native Americans 82–4; negotiating with terrorists 456; and Northern Ireland 204–5, 209–13, 217n36, 389; and Palestine 180–4, 197; suicide terrorism in 405; *see also* British Army; British Commonwealth; British Empire; England; United Kingdom
British Army 183, 202n30; and counter-insurgency 385; in Northern Ireland 205, 208–11, 390–1; and "small wars" 383
British Army Council 178
British Commonwealth 179, 193, 199–200
British East India Company 85
British Empire 177, 180, 186, 190, 200 *see also* Britain
British Special Operations Executive 184
Broadcasting Ban (UK) 436
Bronx County Court House 136
Bronze Horseman, The (Pushkin) 472
Brothers Karamozov, The (Dostoevsky) 474
Brousse, Paul 112, 299
Brown, John 88–9, 143–4, 153n7–8, 153n12
Brownshirts 4, 162–3
Brutus, Marcus Junius 18, 472
Buback, Siegfried 300
Buenos Aires 121, 404
Bugeaud, Thomas-Robert 219
Buitrago, Francisco Leal 290
Bulgaria 119
Burchard of Strasbourg 39
Bureau of Investigation (US) 120, 137–8; *see also* Federal Bureau of Investigation
Bureau of Land Management (US) 327
Burke, Edmund 1–2
Bursuqi 38–9
Burtsev, Vladimir 106, 109n46
Bush, George H. W. 335

INDEX

Bush, George W. 254, 386, 421, 436, 490, 492
Bushnell, David 444
Bu-Tahir 35–6
By Order of the Czar, Anna Queen of the Ghetto (Hatton) 476, 478

Cable News Network 432
Čabrinović, Nedeljko 122
Cacique Nutibara 295n14
Caesar, Julius 17–18, 65
Cafiero, Carlo 112
Cagol, Margherita 302
Cahokia 78
Cairo Agreement 246
Cali cartel 290
caliphate 262, 270, 338, 345
Callwell, Charles 164
Calvert, Mike 192
Calvin, John 22
Cambodia 375
Camp David Accords 248
Campbell, David 493
Canada 177
Canalejas, José 121, 127n36, 128n61
Cánovas del Castillo, Antonio 116
Captain America 438
car bomb 211, 451
Carbonari 72
Carbone, Carmine 136
Carlier, Omar 219
Carlos the Jackal 304, 436, 460, 462
Carnegie Steel 134
Carnot, Sadi 115, 459
Carolingians 48–50
Carové, Friedrich 73
Carr, Caleb 11n17
Carrier, Jean Baptiste 374
Carrington, Peter 190
casbah 231–2
Caselli, Gian Carlo 302
Caserio, Sante 115
Cast Lead, Operation 255
Castro, Fidel 298
Castro, Nora 293
Catechism of a Revolutionary (Nechaev) 98–9, 111, 377, 430, 474, 414
categorical terrorism 224
Cathars 54
Catherine II, Tsarina of Russia 471
Catholic Church 47–8, 55–7, 66, 69, 171, 371–2; and Peace and Truce of God 50–3; and religious violence 53–55; and tyrannicide 20–4; violence against members of 87, 116; *see also* Catholics
Catholics: in Ireland 178–9; in Northern Ireland 205–6, 208–212, 216n5, 389–91

Caucasus 167, 170
Caza Tupamaros 292
cells, organization of 178, 216n25, 231, 302
censorship 291, 428, 435–6; in Russia 95, 97, 430, 435–6, 471–2, 480
Central Intelligence Agency (US) 292, 303, 306, 308, 337, 340, 388, 419, 461
Cerpa, Nestor 288
Chaadaev, Peter 96
Chaco Canyon Native Americans 78
Chamber of Deputies (France) 115, 430
Charbonnerie 72
Charlemagne 48–9, 52, 57
Charles the Good 57
Charles Town 84
Chechens 167, 170
Chechnya 383, 387, 391, 404; jihadism in 339
Cheka 166
chemical weapons 172, 341, 433, 451
Chernyshevsky, Nikolai 97, 99, 473
Cherokee 84–6
Chesterton, G. K. 92, 416, 479
Chicago 114, 133–6, 139
Chile 294, 373
China 122, 287, 298, 375, 386, 437
Chinese Assassination Corps 443
Chinese, in Malaya 184
chivalry 55–6
Christian Democratic Party (Italy) 303, 307
Christian Democratic Party (West Germany) 309
Christianity 46–57, 79, 194; Christianity, relations with Islam 49, 53–4, 400; and tyrannicide 18–19, 21 *see also* Catholic Church; Christians; Crusades; Reformation
Christians: Coptic 274, 276; and Islamism 264–5, 271; in India 358; in Lebanon 248–50; Maronite 248, 276, 279
Church *see* Catholic Church
Churchill, Winston 190–1, 200n1
Cicero, Marcus Tullius 17–18, 47, 64–5
cinematic depictions of terrorism 231, 437
civil rights movement (Northern Ireland) 206, 216n5
Civil Rights Movement (US) 151–2, 216n5
Civil War *see* American Civil War
Clan na Gael 443
Clansman, The (Dixon) 149
Clark, George Rogers 85
Clarke, Richard 463–4
Claudy bombing 211
Clausewitz, Carl von 392
Clauzel, Bertrand 219
Clemenceau, Georges 123
Clément, Jacques 23
Clerkenwell Prison 177–8
Clinton, Hillary 383

505

INDEX

Clinton, William Jefferson 253
Clovis I, King of the Franks 48
Club de Berne 419
Coastal Road attack 249
Coco, Francesco 303
Cofitachequi 79
Cohn-Bendit, Daniel 419, 458, 467n22
COIN *see* counter-insurgency
Colby, Abram 147
Cold War 5–6, 139, 297, 310, 418; impact of end of 139, 286, 310, 462, 465; and Latin America 285–7; and terrorism studies 492
Colina Group 288
Collective Punishment Ordinance (Kenya) 195
collective punishment: in Algeria 226; in Cyprus 198; by Israel against Palestinians 239–40; in Kenya 195–6; in Malaya 192–3; in Mandatory Palestine 181
collectivization (USSR) 168
Collier, Thomas W. 384
Colombia 284, 286, 288–90, 295n14, 392
colonialism: in Africa by Germany 164; in Africa by Italy 172; in Algeria by France 218–21, 222, 224, 226–7, 232, 235n13; in Asia by Europeans 399–400; in Caucasus and Central Asia by Russia 167; in Kenya by Britain 193–4; in Malaya by Britain 184; in North America by Europeans 77, 79, 80, 82, 84, 155n44; and state terror/ism 159–61, 167, 170, 172, 220–1; and technology 448; *see also* de-colonization; imperialism
Colorado Fuel and Iron Company 136
Colorado Party (Uruguay) 292
color-coded threat level system (US) 436
Combat Organization 92, 104–6, 471, 480; *see also* Socialist Revolutionary Party (Russia)
combatants, and definition of terrorism 398
Committee of General Security 67–8
Committee of Public Safety 64, 67, 70, 94
committees of surveillance (in French Revolution) 67–9
communism 138, 192, 200, 298–9, 301; and Islam 335
Communist Combatant Party (BR-PCC) (Italy) 304, 306
Communist Fighting Cells (Belgium) 305
Communist Groups (West Germany) 298
Communist Party of Algeria 225
Communist Party of China 184
Communist Party of Colombia 289
Communist Party of Germany 162
Communist Party of Italy 301, 303, 460
Communist Party of Malaya 184
Communist Party of Peru 287–8
Communist Party of Peru in the Shining Path of José Carlos Mariátegui *see* Shining Path

Communist Party of Soviet Union 123, 168, 170; *see also* Bolsheviks; and Russian Social Democratic Labor Party
Communist Party USA 138
communist terrorism, understood as global Soviet plot 418–19
Communist Terrorists (in Malaya) 185–6, 190, 197
concentration camps 4, 196–7, 230
Conestoga Native Americans 84
Confederación National del Trabajo 123
Confederate States of America 146
Congress (US) 147
Congress Party (India) *see* Indian National Congress
Conquest, Robert 108n4
conquistadors 373
Conrad of Montferrat 40
Conrad, Joseph 437, 446, 475, 479
Conservative Party (Colombia) 289
conspiracy: and counter-terrorism 412–13, 422–3; and terrorism 413, 422–3
conspiratorial methods 72
Constantine 230
Constantine massacres 227–8
Contemporary, The 473
Continental Army (US) 82, 85
Contras 489
Convention (in French Revolution) 66–70
Convention for the Prevention and Punishment of Terrorism 125, 416–17
Convention for the Suppression of Unlawful Seizure of Aircraft 420
Copeland, David 378, 388
Corday, Charlotte 65, 472
Cordobazo 293
Coronado, Francisco Vázquez de 79
Corps of the Imperial Guards (Russia) 94
Cossacks 166–7
Cossiga, Francesco 304
Council of Charroux 50–1
Council of Constance 20–2
Council of Narbonne 53
counter-insurgency 493; in Argentina 294; and Britain 202n30; by Britain in Aden 199–200; by Britain in Cyprus 198–9; by Britain in Kenya 194–7; by Britain in Malaya 185–6, 191–3; by Britain in Palestine 181; in Colombia 289–90; by France in Algeria 221, 224, 229; and colonialism 161, 164; and counter-terrorism 383, 389–92, 393n1; and democracy 390; enemy-centric approach to 389–90; in Latin America 293; in Peru 287–8; population-centric approach to 389–90; and terrorism studies 490, 492; and US 202n30; in World War II 164

INDEX

counter-radicalization 323, 492
counter-terror 389; by France in Algeria 219, 224–32; by Israel 246; *see also* state terror
counter-terrorism 411–12, 422, 489, 493; against anarchists 117; vs. anti-terrorism 389; in Argentina 121; in Britain 391; by Britain in Northern Ireland 208, 210–11, 213, 217n36; by Britain in Palestine 181; and counter-insurgency 383, 389–92, 393n1; criminal justice model of 389–90; as cultural/linguistic construct 411, 422–3; in democracies 391; by France in Algeria 224, 231; international 3, 125; international, against anarchism 117–19, 124, 413–17; international, against global jihadism 421–2, 465; international, against revolutionary terrorism 419–20, 461; in Israel 390; by Israel in Palestine 243–4, 246, 253, 255; in Italy 118, 304; militarization of 383; in Russia 92–3, 101–7, 119–20; and terrorism studies 3, 320, 323, 490; in Uruguay 292; in US 118–19, 133–4, 136–8, 322, 330n16, 390; war model of 389–90; in West Germany 301, 308; in Western Europe 306; *see also* counter-terror; War on Terror
Counter-Terrorism Strategy (CONTEST) (Britain) 390
Coushatta Massacre 148
Crain, Caleb 153n12
Creech Jones, Arthur 183, 185
Crenshaw, Martha 284, 388
Crime and Punishment (Dostoevsky) 473–4
crime, and terrorism 4, 6, 32, 99, 104, 113–14, 120, 211–12, 299, 392
criminology 3, 415
Critical Studies in Terrorism 411
critical terrorism studies 490–1
Croatia 404
Cronaca Sovversiva 430
Cronin, Audrey Kurth 385, 391, 458
Crow Creek Native Americans 78
Crusades 37, 39–40, 53–4, 56
Cuba 236n38, 285, 289, 291, 326
Cuban Americans 326
Cuban Revolution 298
Curcio, Renato 302
Curry, John Steuart 155n40
Curtis, Adam 413, 457
Cutbush, James 444
Cyprian Emergency 198–9
Cyprus 197–9, 251
Czolgosz, Leon 134–5, 430

da'i see da'wa
da'wa 34, 272, 339, 344–5
Dáil Éireann 179, 206, 214
Dale, Stephen Frederic 408n16

Dalits 352, 360–2
Damiens, Robert-François 64, 369
Dances with Wolves (Costner) 376
Danton, Georges 68–9
Darrow, Clarence 135
Dato, Eduardo 123, 127n36
Davenport, Christian 233
Dayan, Moshe 243–4
Daylam 35
Days of Rage 139
de Gaulle, Charles 221, 232, 418
de Soto, Hernando 78–9
Dearborn, Henry 87
Debs, Eugene V. 137
Decembrists 71–3, 94–5, 99, 472, 481n12
Declaration of Independence (US) 85, 133
de-colonization 4, 200, 224, 226, 232, 298, 305, 417; and Islam 260–1; and media 430; *see also* colonialism
Defensive Shield, Operation 254
Deflem, Mathieu 415–16
Degaev, Sergei 102
della Porta, Donatella 302
Delta Force 461
democracies: and counter-terror 390; and counter-terrorism 391; and state terror/ism 373; terrorism in 239, 388
democracy 293; and counter-insurgency 390; and de-colonization 190; and Islam 261; in Northern Ireland 207–8; and terror 63, 68; and terrorism 386; and tyrannicide 16
Democratic Alliance M19 (Colombia) 290
Democratic Front for the Liberation of Palestine 243, 246–7
Democratic Party (US) 146–7
Democratic Union for the Algerian Manifesto 220
Democratic Unionist Party (Northern Ireland) 205, 214
Demons (Dostoevsky) 437, 474
Demophantos 16
Denmark 119
Deobandi *see* Islam, Deobandi
Derry 210
Desmoulins, Camille 69
al-Dhahabi 274
Diana Theater (Italy) 123
al-Din Abu al-Fatuh, Jalal 344
dirty bomb 321
dirty war: in Algeria 231; in Argentina 294; in Kenya 197; in Peru 288
disappearing: in Algeria 231–2; in Argentina 294
Discipline and Punish (Foucault) 369, 372
Dixon, Thomas 149
Dobroliubov, Nikolai 97
Dobrovin, A. I. 105

INDEX

Doherty, Chris 374–5
Dolgorukov, Vasily 97–8
Dolnik, Adam 451
domestic terrorism, definition of 317, 321, 323
Donatists 47–8
Dostoevsky, Fyodor 96, 437, 473–4, Fyodor 96
double minorities, in Northern Ireland 205
Douglass, William A. 5, 489–90, 481n5
Dozier, James 305, 461
Drama in Muslin (Moore) 476–7
Dray, Philip 151
Drenteln, Alexander 100–1
Drif, Zohra 231
drones 346, 391, 465
drugs: and terrorism 289
Du Bois, W. E. B. 150
Dublin 178–9
Dublin-Monaghan bombings 211
Duby, Georges 50
Duma 105–6
Dunham, Jeff 438
Dunmore, Lord 85
Durnovo, Peter 110n47
Dutschke, Rudi 299, 308, 419
Dylan, Bob 152–3
dynamite 113, 132, 137, 377, 444, 447; *see also* explosives
Dynamiter, The (Stevenson) 475, 477

E. I. Dupont Nemours Company 448
Eager, Scipio 147, 150
Earth Liberation Front 140, 327, 434
East African Association 194
East Germany 305, 309, 312n42
East India Company 199
"Easter, 1916" (Yeats) 187n12
Easter Rising 179
Eastern Europe, in World War II 163, 169–70
eco-terrorism 327, 465–6, 469n70
Eden, Anthony 190, 198
Egypt 180, 184, 199, 264, 271, 334, 345; and Algeria 223–4, 230–1; ancient, 33; and Arab Spring 343–4; Islamism in 259, 262–6, 271–6, 347n19; and Israel 240, 248, 272, 274; and Palestinians 240, 242, 244; and PLO 241–2, 250
Egyptian Islamic Jihad 275, 344, 464
Eichenwald, Kurt 345
Einsatzgruppen 164
El Al 245–6, 460
El Dorado Canyon, Operation 461–2
El Halia 228
El Salvador 325
Eleazar ben Ananias 30
Elisabeth, Empress of Austria-Hungary 117
ELN (Colombia) 285

Emancipation Proclamation (Russia) 97, 108n21
Encyclopedia of Afghan Jihad 450
Encyclopedia of the Social Sciences 3
Enduring Freedom, Operation 422; *see also* Afghan War (2001–)
Engedi 31–2
England 23, 50, 53; and Native Americans 79–82; *see also* Britain; and United Kingdom
Enlightenment 94, 376
Enniskillen 213
enosis 197
Enragés 69
Ensslin, Gudrun 299–301, 460
Entebbe raid 248, 305, 460–1
environmentalism 139–40
EOKA 197–9
Erskine, George 196–7
Espionage Act 137
Ethiopia 172
ethnic cleansing 86, 167, 169
Ethniki Organosis Kyprion Agoniston *see* EOKA
European Convention on the Suppression of Terrorism 420
Euskadi Ta Askatasuna (ETA) 318, 387, 390
Evans, Brad 493
Evers, Medgar 152
Exceptional Laws (France) 478–9
execution 64, 369
executive protection 116–17, 127n36
Exodus (Uris) 437
explosives 112–13, 443–501; and aesthetics 446, 451; key nineteenth century inventions 444; laws against criminal use of 117; and suicide terrorism 399, 401, 407; *see also* ammonium nitrate; dynamite; nitroglycerine
expropriations 105, 292

Facebook 344–5, 434
Fadlallah, Muhammad 280
Fahmideh, Hossein 402
al-Fajr Media Center 434
Falcon, Ramon 121
Falkenberg, Johannes 20
Falls Road (Belfast) 209
false flag operations 307, 391, 459
Fanon, Frantz 221, 227, 271
Farag, Muhammad 'Abd al-Salam 274–5
FARC *see* Revolutionary Armed Forces of Colombia
Farrall, Leah 341
Fascist Italy *see* Italy, Fascist
Fascist Party (Italy) 171; *see also* neo-fascism
Fatah 241–4, 247–255, 460, 462; camps attended by foreign terrorists 298, 310; founding of 240–1; and Intifadas 251, 253; and Iranian Revolutionary Guards 457; and

INDEX

Popular Front for the Liberation of Palestine 460; and Soviet Union 459; strategy of 241; *see also* Palestine Liberation Organization
Fatah al-Islam 276
Fatahland 385
Fathers and Sons (Turgenev) 473, 475
Fatimid Caliphate 34, 36, 38–9, 44n41
fatwa 266
Faulkner, Brian 210
Faure, Edgar 237n66
Favier, Jean 49
Fawkes, Guy 369, 371, 444
fedayeen (Palestinian) 239–40, 242, 244
Federal Bureau of Investigation (US) 140, 321–2, 324, 419; *see also* Bureau of Investigation
Federal Criminal Police Office (West Germany) 300
Federal Republic of Germany *see* West Germany
FedEx 342
Feldmann, Andreas 286
Fellman, Michael 145, 372
Felton, Rebecca 151
feminism 139
Fenians 177–8, 446–7, 453n27, 476; in Britain 476; support in North America 443–4, 457, 476
Ferguson, Patrick 85
Ferrer y Guardia, Francisco 121
fida'i 35, 38
Fields, Factories, and Workshops (Kropotkin) 139
Fieschi, Joseph 73
Figner, Vera 102
Filippov, Alexander 445
firearms, vs. bombs 445–7
Fireworks & Explosives Like Granddad Used to Make (Saxon) 448
First of October Anti-Fascist Resistance Groups 304
Fischer, Joschka 458, 467n22
Fishman, Brian 349n55
Fitch, J. Samuel 293
Five-Year Plans 168
FLN *see* National Liberation Front (Algeria)
focista 285, 288–9, 297
Foot, Hugh 199
Force 17 251
Ford, John 437
Ford, Patrick 444
Fort Caroline 81
Fort Hood shooting 321, 327
Fort Mims 86
Fort Pitt 84
Fort William Henry 84
Foucault, Michel 64, 369, 372, 494

Four Lions (Morris) 465
Fox Native Americans *see* Mesquakie
Fox's Book of Martyrs 369
France 64, 71–3, 81–4, 213, 240, 298, 325; and Algeria 3, 218–34; anarchist terrorism in 114–15, 118, 123; censorship in 436; cooperation with Russian counter-terrorism 102–3, 450, 478; early modern 22–4; May 1968 revolt in 418; medieval 19–20; and Native Americans 82–3; newspapers in 113; peacekeepers bombed in Lebanon 279; police in 415; Second Republic 71; Wars of Religion 22, 64; *see also* French Army; French Revolution; Reign of Terror, French
Franceschini, Alberto 302
Franco, Francisco 124, 170
Franco-Prussian War 161
Franz Ferdinand 122, 416, 457
Franz Joseph 122
Frederick Barbarossa 19, 39
Free Officers' Movement 225
Freedman, Lawrence 386
Freiheit, Die (*Freedom*) 112
Freikorps 162
French and Indian War *see* Seven Years' War
French Army, in Algeria 219–21, 224, 227, 229–30, 235n13
French League of Nihilists 414
French Revolution 1–2, 63–6, 68, 73–4, 113, 160–1, 374, 376; influence of 67, 71–4, 94, 161; and messaging 429; French Revolution, relationship with the Reign of Terror 67; *see also* Reign of Terror, French
Frick, Henry Clay 134
Fromkin, David 5
Front for the Liberation of Occupied South Yemen 199
Front Line (Italy) 303
Fuerzas Armadas de Liberacion Nacional 326
Fujimori, Alberto 287–8
Fukuyama, Francis 465
Fuller, Graham E. 258
fusion centers 330n16

Gabinius, Aulus 28–9
Gage, Beverly 318
Gage, Thomas 85
Galleani, Luigi 126n11, 137–88; followers of 137–8, 140, 447–8
Gallo, Charles 115
Gallup 292
Gama'at al Muslimin *see* Takfir wa-l-Hijra
Gandhi, Mohandas 180, 358
Ganser, Daniele 308–9, 459
Garcia, Alan 287–8
gardening state 164, 168, 374–5

INDEX

Garland, Sean 206
Garrison, William Lloyd 143
Gaza Strip 242–4, 251–2, 254–5, 278–9
Geiking, G. E. 100
Gelasius I, Pope 47
gendarmerie 391
General Directorate for External Security (France) 435
genocide 159, 165, 167, 430; compared to state terror/ism 165
Gent, Edward 184–5
George I, King of Greece 121
Georgia 147
Gerasimov, A. V. 105
German Action Groups (DA) 308, 310
German Autumn 301
German Democratic Republic *see* East Germany
Germania monument plot 114–15
Germany *see* East Germany; Imperial Germany; Nazi Germany; Weimar Germany; West Germany
Germinal (Zola) 479
Gershuni, Grigory 104–5
Gerson, Jean 20
Gerwarth, Robert 174n9
Ghodelive 53
GIGN (France) 461
Giovanni, Severino di 124
Girondins 65–6
Gladio, Operation 308–9, 459
Gladstone, William 178, 444
Global Terrorism Database 284, 324–7
Global War on Terror *see* War on Terror
globalization 114, 139–40, 328, 431, 471
Gogol, Nikolai 472–3
going to the people movement (Russia) 99–100
Golan Heights 242
Goldenberg, Grigory 100–1
Goldman, Emma 134, 137, 139
Gone with the Wind (Fleming) 154n30
Good Friday Agreement 212, 214
Goodwin, Jeff 224
Gordon, Stephen 319
Gotz, Mikhail 127n40
Grand Mosque in Mecca, seizure 463
Grant, Ulysses S. 147
Grave, Jean 478
Great Depression (1880s–90s) 113
Great Depression (1920s–30s) 162
Great Recession 342, 465
Great Terror (French) 70
Great Terror (Soviet) 166, 169
Greece 121–2, 171–2, 197–9, 306; ancient 15–17, 21
Green, James 146
Greenwich Observatory bombing 430, 437, 479

Greer, Tom 477
Gregory of Tours 48
Griffith, D. W. 149
Griffiths, James 185
Grivas, George 197
GSG-9 (Germany) 301, 461
Guardian 307
Guelma 220, 228
guerrilla war 385, 398
Guerrilla Warfare (Guevara) 285
Guevara, Ernesto "Che" 285, 290–1, 297–8
Guibert of Nogent 53
Gujarat 360–2
Gulag 166, 168
Gulf War 252
Gunpowder Plot 23, 369, 371, 444, 481n10
Gurney, Henry 183–6, 190–191, 197, 201n22; on counter-terrorism 185
Gutiérrez Ruiz, Hector 294
Guzmán, Abimael 287–8

Haag, Siegfried 300
Habash, George 242, 458, 460
Haddad, Wadie 245, 460
al-Hadid, Marwan 276
hadith 259, 335
Hadj, Messali 225, 233
Haig, Alexander 305
Hakluyt, Richard 79–80
Hale, Grace 146
Hama 276
Hamas 252–5, 277–9; and Hizbullah 403; and al-Qaeda 405; and suicide terrorism 403–4
Hampton, Fred 139
Hand (Argentina) 294
Hanley, Brian 209
Haq Nawaz Jhangvi, Maulana 356
Harding, John 192, 198–9
al-Hariri, Rafiq 280
Harkat ul-Mujahideen 387, Mujahideen 457
harkis 226
Harmodios 15–17
Harpers Ferry, Virginia 86–8, 143
Harris, Frank 437
Harris, Thomas 438
Hart, Brooke 155n40
Hartmann, Lev 102
Harvest, Operation 206–7
Hasan, Nidal 321, 323, 327
Hasan-i Sabbah 34–7
Hashemite dynasty 277
hate crime 324
hate: and terrorism 319, 324
Hatton, Joseph 476, 478
Hawatmeh, Nayef 243
Hawkins, Samuel 145

510

INDEX

Hay, John 118–19
Haymarket Square bombing 114, 133–4, 146, 153n12, 437
Haywood, "Big Bill" 135
Hazaras 353
Head, Anthony 190
Headrick, Daniel 448
Hearst, Patricia 431
hearts and minds 192–3, 391
Heath, Edward 190, 210
Heber, Alberto 292
Hébert, Jacques-René 69
Hekkelman, Abram *see* Landezen
Helsby, Operation 192
Hem Chandra Das 448
Hennessey, Thomas 209
Henri of Champagne 40
Henry I, King of England 52
Henry III, King of France 22–4
Henry IV, King of France 23–4, 64
Henry, Émile 115
Hepp-Kexel Group 310
Herero revolt 164
Herodotus 15
Herrhausen, Alfred 306
Herzen, Alexander 96–7, 99, 108n20
hijackings, airplane 245–8, 456, 458, 460; and media 431
Hildermeier, Manfred 471
Hillenbrand, Carole 54
Hindu nationalism *see* Hindutva
Hinduism 351–2, 357
Hindutva 357–62
Hipparchus 15–16
historians, and terrorism studies 6–7, 493–6
Historical Enquiries Team (Northern Ireland) 214
Hitler, Adolf 182, 371
Hizbullah 270, 279–81, 463; and Hamas 403; and Internet 433; and Islamic Jihad (Palestine) 403; and suicide terrorism 403–4; and Syria 345, 350n62, 406; and television 433
Hoedel, Max 112
Hoffman Militia Group (WSH) 308–10
Hoffman, Bruce 245, 346, 388, 421, 433
Hoffmann, Karl-Heinz 309–10
Hofstadter, Richard 132
Holder, Eric 323
Holiday, Billie 152
Holocaust 164, 374
Holy Brotherhood 101–2
Home Rule (Ireland) 178–9
Homegrown Threat Database 324–5, 327, 331n54
homegrown violent extremism (US) 322–3, 327

Homeland Security, Department of (US) 319–21, 322, 330n13, 330n16, 436
Homestead, Pennsylvania 134
Hoover, J. Edgar 137–8
Horne, John 174n9
Horsey, Jerome 108n8
Hospitallers, Order of 41
hostages 52–3, 79, 164, 166, 174n1, 246; government agencies created to rescue 461
hot autumn (Italy) 297, 301
Hot Winter, Operation 255
House of Commons (Britain) 178–9
Huamanga, Universidad de 287
Hughes, Francis 212
Human Rights Commission (for Cyprus) 198–9
Hume, John 212–13
hunger strikes: by PIRA 212, 401; by RAF 300
Husain ibn Ali 180
al-Hussam 434
Hussein, King of Jordan 246, 250, 252
Hussein, Saddam 373, 413

Ibn 'Abdullah Al al-Shaykh, Sulayman 265
Ibn Sa'ud, 'Abd al-'Aziz 264, 266
Ibn Taymiyya 264–6
identity politics 323–4
Ilaiah, Kancha 359
Ilich Ramírez Sánchez *see* Carlos the Jackal
illegalism 114; *see also* expropriations
Illia, Arturo 293
Imperial Germany 112, 114–15, 119, 164
imperialism, by West in Muslim regions 260, 270; *see also* colonialism
Improvised Munitions Handbook (Paladin Press) 449
India 223–4, 351–2, 355, 357–62; and Britain 120, 180–1, 183, 260, 448; and Pakistan 387, 464; suicide terrorism in 404
Indian National Congress 357–8, 360
Indian Parliament, attack on 355
Indian People's Party *see* Bharatiya Janata Party
Indian Police 181
Individualidades Tendiendo a lo Salvaje 380
Indochina War 229, 231
Indonesia 223–4, 387–8, 405
Industrial Workers of the World 135, 137
Informer, The (Ford) 437
Innocent III, Pope 54
Innocent IV, Pope 40, 55
innovation, in terrorism 397, 433, 451–2
Inquisition 55, 57, 63; *see also* Spanish Inquisition
Inspire (al-Awlaki) 342
insurgency, and terrorism 198, 333, 339, 345, 383–9, 392, 393n1, 489
Intellectual History of Terror, An (Thorup) 494
Internal Macedonian Revolutionary Organization 125, 416, 457

INDEX

Internal Troops for Defense of the Republic (USSR) 166, 169
International Convention for the Suppression of the Financing of Terrorism 10n13
International Criminal Court 417
International Security Assistance Force 422
International Social Revolutionary Congress 443
international terrorism 4–6, 245, 385, 412, 456–66; definition of, 321, 456–7; in films, 438; and mass media 431; and no innocent bystanders 458; understood as global Soviet conspiracy 5–6, 419–20, 459
International, First or Socialist 112
Internet 139, 428–9, 433–4, 438, 450–1, 458, 463
Inter-Services Intelligence (Pakistan) 354–5
Intifada, First 251–2, 277–8, 462
Intifada, Second 278–9, 253–4, 404
Iran 260, 278–9, 354, 373, 402, 431–2; and culture of martyrdom 401–3; embassy in London seized 457, 461; and Hizbullah 280; and Shi'a Muslims in Lebanon 403; see also Iranian Revolution
Iran hostage crisis 431–2
Iran-Contra 461
Iranian Revolution 258, 264, 402; as inspiration for Islamists 402–3, 462–3
Iran-Iraq War, suicide tactics in 401–2
Iraq 180, 184, 335–6, 373, 464–5; embassy bombed in Lebanon 403; jihadism in 345–6; and Palestinians 243, 248; and al-Qaeda 341; see also Iraq War
Iraq War 2, 266, 341–3, 379, 383, 386, 437, 463–4; suicide terrorism in 405–6, 410n59
Ireland 205, 177–81, 482n29
Ireland, Republic of 204, 206, 208
Irgun Zvai Leumi 182–3
Irish Free State 179
Irish National Liberation Army 312n47
Irish National Volunteers 179
Irish Republican Army 179, 205–7, 209
Irish Republican Army, Official 208
Irish Republican Brotherhood 177–9
Irish Volunteers 178–9
Irish War of Independence 179, 181
Irish World 444, 453n27
Irish: in North America 87, 212–13, 443–4
Iroquois 85
IS *see* Islamic State of Iraq and Syria
Isfahan 35
Islam 2, 6, 8, 34, 36–7, 48–9, 53–4, 258–9, 267, 270–1, 273; Barelvi 353; and Christianity, in Asia 400; and democracy 261; Deobandi 353, 463; in India 351–2; Isma'ili 34–37 (*see also* Assassins); and modernity 260–1; and National Liberation Front (Algeria) 223;

Nizari 36–39 (*see also* Assassins); in Pakistan 351–4; Sufi 264, 271, 353; and West 258, 260, 262; *see also* Islamism; Muslims; Shi'a Islam; Sunni Islam
Islamic Conference, Organization of the 334
Islamic Group (Egypt) 259, 265, 275, 404, 464
Islamic Jihad (Palestine) 278, 403–4
Islamic State of Iraq and Syria 33, 262, 345–6, 382n38
Islamism 258, 260, 267–8, 281, 336–7, 378–9; in Algeria 225; and Christians 264–5, 271; defined 258; in Egypt 345; in Europe 458; and Islam 258–9; and Jews 264–5; and jihad 267; and modernity 258–61; in Palestine 252–5, 277–9; political vs. radical 261–3, 267; political/quietist 261, 270–2, 276, 336; radical 261–6, 273–4, 281, 327, 331n54, 432, 462, 465 (*see also* jihadism); and salafism 263–4; and Shi'a 264–6; terminology 258, 336; and terrorism 270, 275, 378; and violence 261–3, 267–8, 270
Isma'ilis *see* Assassins; Islam, Isma'ili
Israel 183–4, 239–55, 278–9, 336; and counter-terror 246; and counter-terrorism 243–4, 246, 253, 255, 390; and Egypt 248, 272, 274; embassy in Argentina, bombing of 404; and Entebbe Raid 248, 305, 460–1; and Hamas 252–5, 278–9; and Lebanon 249–50, 253, 279–81, 383, 403; and mediatized terrorism 433; response to international terrorism 246; and suicide terrorism 402, 404
Israeli Air Force 249, 251
Israeli Defense Forces 240, 244–5, 249–51, 254
Italian Social Movement (MSI) 302, 306
Italian Socialist Party 116
Italy 71–2, 113, 161, 297–8, 301, 307, 325; anarchist terrorism in 116, 123; counter-terrorism in 116–18; Fascist 381n25; Fascist, sponsorship of Ustaše 457; Fascist, state terror/ism in 170–3; labor movement in 118; left-wing terrorism in 301–4; right-wing terrorism in 302, 306–10
Ivan IV the Terrible, Tsar of Russia 93, 371
'Izz al-din al-Qassam Brigades 278

Jacobins 1–2, 65–71, 74, 160; and messaging 429
Jaesh-e-Mohammed, and suicide terrorism 404
jahiliyyah 265, 273–4, 379
al-Jama'a al-Islamiyya (Egypt) *see* Islamic Group (Egypt)
al-Jama'a al-Islamiyya (Indonesia) *see* Jemaah Islamiyah (Indonesia)
Jama'at al-Jihad *see* Jihad Group (Egypt)
Jamal, Muhammad 344
James I, King of England 23, 371

512

INDEX

James, Henry 475, 478, 482n33
Jamestown 80
Jammu and Kashmir 385
Jammu and Kashmir Legislative Assembly, attack on 355
Jammu and Kashmir Liberation front 387
Japan 122, 169, 288, 373, 401, 433, 443
Japanese internees in US in World War II 175n15
Japanese Red Army 460–1, 465
Jemaah Islamiyah (Indonesia) 387–8, 405
Jenkins, Brian Michael 333, 348n38
Jerez, Spain 115
Jerusalem 28, 30–31, 54, 182–3
Jesuit debate 22–3
Jesus Christ 47, 369
Jewish Agency 183
Jewish center, in Argentina, bombing of 404
Jewish Defense League (US) 326, 331n51
Jewish War, The (Josephus) 29, 32, 369
Jews 28–33, 54, 167, 171–2, 374; and Islamism 264–5; and Nazi Germany 163–5; in Palestine 180–4, 239; in Russia 104–5; *see also* Judaism; Judea/Judaea
Jhang District, Pakistan 356–7
Jibril, Ahmed 243, 245
jihad 54, 262, 264, 273–4, 277, 337; defined 266–7; and Muslim Brotherhood 271–2; *see also* jihadism
al-Jihad al-Islami al-Masri *see* Egyptian Islamic Jihad
Jihad Group (Egypt) 266
jihadism 259, 261, 267, 275, 331n54, 336–7, 379, 382n38; and conspiratorial thinking 413; in Libya 343; *see also* salafi jihadism
Jinnah, Muhammad Ali 352
Jock Scott, Operation 195
John of Salisbury 18–19
John the Fearless 19–20
Johnson, Daryl 320
Jonathan R. White 11n17
Jonathan, High Priest 30
Jones, Jame 468n62
Jordan 184, 277; and Palestinians 240, 242–3, 245–7, 252
Jordanian Legion 240
Josephus, Flavius 29–32, 43, 369
Joyce, James 215, 477
Juan de Mariana 22–4
Judaea *see* Judea
Judaism 32–3, 43n23; *see also* Jews
Judea/Judaea 28–33, 42n2, 369–70
Julian the Apostate 18
July 7, 2005, attacks in London 341, 405, 426n72, 434, 463; conspiracy theories about 459

Jumonville, Joseph Coulon de Villiers de 83
June 2nd Movement (West Germany) 298, 305, 311n4
Jungantar 180
just war 46–7
Justice and Development Party (Turkey) 261, 458
Juwayni 35–6

Kaczynski, Theodore 378, 388, 437, 450
kafir 277, 353; *see also takfir*
Kafka, Franz 372
Kalyaev, Ivan 105
Kalyvas, Stathis 385
Kamal al-Din 38
kamikazes 401
Kanj, Bassam 276
Kansas 88
Karakozov, Dmitry 92, 97–8, 443, 473, 482n19
Karine A 254
Karmi, Raed 254
Karpovich, Peter 104
Kashmir 355, 387, 404
Keaney, Thomas 385
Kellar, Alex 196
Kemal, Namik 260
Kennedy, John F. 152
Kenney, Michael 451
Kensington, Pennsylvania, Bible Riots 87
Kentucky 145
Kenya 191, 193–7
Kenya Emergency 195–7
Khalaf, Salah 246
Khaled, Leila 466n1
Khalil, James 339
Khalis, Yunus 336, 338
Khalturin, Stepan 101
Khan, Sayyid Ahmad 260, 267
Khan, Sidique Mohammad 341
Kharijites 266
Khmer Rouge 375
Kibalchich, Nikolai 445–7
Kibiya 240
kidnapping 30, 291–2, 280, 302, 431
Kiev 101, 106, 167
Kikuyu 194–6
Kikuyu Association 194
Kikuyu Central Association 194
King David Hotel 183
King Philip's War *see* Metacom's War
King's Mountain, Battle of 85
Kitson, Frank 393n1
Kletochnikov, Nikolai 100–1
Klinghoffer, Leon 432
Köhler, Gundolf 309
konkret 299
Koran *see* Qu'ran

Kosovo 383
Kosto, Adam 53
Kotzebue, August von 73
Krauthammer, Charles 432
Kravchinsky-Stepniak, Sergei 1, 99, 109n29, 187n4, 476
Kristallnacht 163, 165
Kritsky circle 96
Kroesen, Frederick 305
Kropotkin, Dmitry 100–1
Kropotkin, Peter 2, 10n6, 102, 112–13, 122, 131–2, 139, 429
Ku Klux Klan 1, 145–9, 151
Ku Klux Klan Act 147
kulaks 168
Kurdistan Workers' Party 404
Kuwait 335

La Salute é en Voi! 448
labor movement: in Britain 117; international 112–13, 132; in Italy 118, 301–2, 304; in Russia 104, 106; in Spain 121, 123; in US 114, 118, 130, 132–5, 137–8, 328; in Western Europe 298
Labour Party (UK) 214
Lacoste, Robert 231
Laden, Osama bin *see* bin Laden, Osama
Ladrón de Guevara, Andrés Dávila 290
Lahore cemetery bombing 356
Land and Freedom 99–100
Land League (Ireland) 476
Landezen (A. M. Harting) 103, 450
Landleaguers, The (Trollope) 476
landmines 444
Lane, Ralph 80
Lanusse, Alejandro 294
Laqueur, Walter 428–9, 437, 470
Lari Massacre 196
Las Casas, Bartolomé de 80
Lashkar-e-Jhangvi 353–4
Lashkar-e-Taiba 355, 387, 404, 457, 464
Latin America 284, 286, 293–5
Latvians 120, 459
Lavrov, Peter 99, 102
Law, Randall D. 55, 65
Lazreg, Marnia 233
Le Jau, Francis 83
leaderless organization 139–40, 459
League of Nations 125, 180, 416–7, 494
Leary, Timothy 326
Lebanese Civil War 248–9
Lebanon 184, 249, 276, 279–81, 377; and Israel 249–50, 253; and Palestinians 242, 245, 248; suicide terrorism in 403
Leftist Revolutionary Movement (MIR) (Peru) 286

LEHI 182–3, 386
Lemann, Nicholas 148
Lenin, Vladimir 106, 460
Lenta, Patrick 372
Letelier, Orlando 294
Levingston, Roberto 294
Lewin, Schlomo 309
LeWinter, Oswald 308
Lewis, Daniel Levering 150
Lexington Avenue bombing 136
Lia, Brynjar 271
Liberal Party (Colombia) 289
liberalism 72, 117
Liberation Tigers of Tamil Eelam *see* Tamil Tigers
Libya 172, 343–4, 461–2
Libyan Islamic Fighting Group 388, 464
Lifton, Robert Jay 451
Lincoln Center 139
Lincoln, Abraham 144–5, 153n7, 153n12
Lincoln, Bruce 492
linguistic turn in terrorism studies 411
Litani, Operation 249
literacy 429–30, 445, 458
literary depictions of terrorism 3, 92, 149, 437–8, 470, 474–80, 492
literary turn, in terrorism studies 487–96
literature, and terrorism 470–1, 480–1; in Britain and Ireland 475–9, 482n33; in France 478–9; in Russia 471–5, 479–80
Livius, Titus 17
Lockerbie, Scotland 432, 461
Lod Airport attack 460, 465
Lohamei Herut Israel *see* LEHI
Lombroso, Cesare 3
London 112, 114, 178, 341, 405, 426n72, 460
London nail-bomber 378
London transportation bombings (July 7) 341, 405, 426n72, 434, 463
lone wolves 388, 434, 464
long war (Northern Ireland) 211–12
Lopez, George 294
Lopukhin, A. A. 100, 106
Loris-Melikov, Mikhail 101
Los Angeles Times 135–6
Loughgall ambush 389
Louis IX, King of France 41
Louis XV, King of France 64, 369
Louis XVI, King of France 64–6
Louis, Duke of Orléans 19–21
Louisiana 148
Louis-Philippe, King of France 73
Louvel, Louis-Pierre 73
Lovejoy, Elijah 88
low intensity warfare 385

INDEX

loyalists, in Northern Ireland 205–15, 389–90, 392
Ludwig Group 309
Lufthansa hijacking (1977) 248, 301, 305, 460–1
Luther, Martin 21–2
Luxor, Egypt 275
Lynch, Marc 349n54
lynching 145, 150–2, 155n40, 155n42
Lyttelton, Oliver 190–2, 194–5, 200n3

M'Hidi, Larbi ben 231
M-19 (Colombia) 285, 290, 292
Maccabees 369
MacDonald, A. M. 196
Macedonia 387
MacGillivray, Donald 193
Machiavelli, Niccolò 64
Mackinlay, John 391
Macleod, Iain 190
Macmillan, Harold 190, 198–9
Madagascar 232
Madrid train bombings (M-11) 437, 463
mafia, Italian 307–8
Mahler, Horst 299
mail bombs 137
Makarios, Archbishop 197
Malabar, India 399–400
Malatesta, Errico 112, 123
Malaya 184–6, 190–3, 201n28
Malayan Emergency 184–6, 190–3, 197
Malayan People's Anti-British Army 184–5
Malayan People's Anti-Japanese Army 184
Malayan Races Liberation Army 185
Malayan Scouts (SAS) 192
Mali 346
Malik Shah 35–6, 38
Malkin, Michelle 319
Malley, Robert 227
Mamluks 266
Mamluks 41
Man Who Was Thursday, The (Chesterton) 92, 416, 479
Al-Manar 433
Mandatory Palestine *see* Palestine
Mandela, Nelson 488
Manning, Chelsea 422
Mao Zedong 241, 243, 287, 303
Maoism 225
al-Maqdisi, Abu Muhammad 265–6
Marat, Jean-Paul 65
Mariátegui, José Carlos 287
Marighella, Carlos 291, 431
Marston, B. W. 148
martial law: in Algeria 219, 221–2, 228–30, 234; in Argentina 121; in Mandatory Palestine 183, 185; martial law, in Russia 106; in Spain 116

martyrdom 34, 37, 74, 144, 212, 400–3, 407; and Shi'a Islam 400–2
Marulanda, Manuel 289
Marx, Karl 132
Marxism: and denunciation of terrorism 99; and terrorism 460
Masada 31–2
Mason, John 81
mass media 428–31, 438, 442–3, 446, 458, 492; and international terrorism 431; *see also* Internet; media; newspapers; television
Massu, Jacques 230–2
material support for terrorism, laws against 443
Matthews, Peter 438
Mau Mau 194–7, 202n52, 418
Mau Mau Emergency 191
Maura, Antonio 120
Mawdudi, Abu l-A'la 265
Maximum, Law of the 68, 71
May 1968 revolt, in France 418
Mayer, Arno 65–6
Mazouz, Youssef 345
Mazzini, Giuseppe 71–2
McArdle, Mary 215
McGuinness, Martin 210–11, 214
McKinley, William 111, 118, 134, 430, 459
McLoughlin, P. J. 210
McLuhan, Marshal 431
McMahon, Henry 180
McVeigh, Timothy 318–19, 323, 326–7, 378, 433
Mechola Junction suicide bombing 403
Medellín cartel 290
media 3, 7, 103, 111, 152, 326, 490, 492; and anarchist terrorism 414; and (counter)terrorist conspiracies 423; and radical Islamism 432; technology 428–30, 433; *see also* mass media; newspapers
mediatization 428, 470, 480–1, 492; and state responses to terrorism 435–7; and sub-state terrorism 428–35, 438, 477
Meeropol, Abel 152
Meinhof, Ulrike 299–300, 311n8, 458
Meins, Holger 300
Meir, Golda 461
Melchiori, Barbara 470, 482n29
Meloy, Colin 94
Menachem (Sicarii leader) 31
Menéndez de Avilés, Pedro 81–2
Mensheviks 166
Merah, Mohamed 388, 464, 468n62
Merom, Gil 226
Merovingians 48
Mesquakie 82
Metacom's War 81
Metropolitan Police (London) 178

INDEX

Metropolitan Political Collective (Italy) 302
Mexico 87, 380, 392
Mezentsev, Nikolai 1, 99
MI5 (Britain) 192, 196, 198, 217n36, 434, 461
MI6 (Britain) 388
Michelini, Zelmar 294
Middle Ages in Europe: terror/terrorism in 46–57; tyrannicide in 18–21, 24
Mikhailov, Alexander 100–1
Milan 123, 302
militia movement (US) 327–8, 456
Minimanual of the Urban Guerrilla (Marighella) 291, 431
Mississippi 148
Mississippian-era Native Americans 78–9
Mitcham, Carl 442
Mitrione, Dan 292
MNA *see* Algerian National Movement
mob violence 87, 151, 155n40
Mockaitis, Thomas 387
Modern Daedalus, A (Greer) 477
modernity 174n6, 370, 377; and Islam 260–1; and Islamism 261; and state terror/ism 372–5, 379; and terrorism 376–80, 382n38, 443, 471–2, 475
Modernity and Ambivalence (Bauman) 374
Modernity and the Holocaust (Bauman) 374
Modi, Narendra 361
Mogadishu 336, 347n14, 461
Moghadam, Assaf 410n59
Mohamed, Ali A. 450
Mohammed V, Sultan of Morocco 227
Molinari, Ettore 126n11, 448
Mollet, Guy 230
Moltke, Helmuth von 161
monarchomachs 22
Mongols 41, 266
Montagu, Edwin 180
Montjuich 116
Montoneros 293
Moore, George 476–7
Moretti, Mario 303
Mormons 87
Moro, Aldo 303, 308
Morocco 225, 227
Morral, Mateo 121
Morton, Jack 192
Moscow 105
Moscow Metro bombings 434
Moscow theater siege 387, 404, 436
Moscow University 96, 98
Mossad 461
Most, Johann 112–13, 119, 133–4, 448
Motherfuckers (US) 139
Movement for Amnesty and Basic Rights (MOVADEF) (Peru) 288

Movement for the Triumph of Democratic Freedom (Algeria) 222
Movement of '77 (Italy) 303
Mubarak, Hosni 250, 262, 275–6, 281, 349n55
al-Mughrabi, Dalal 402
Muhammad 34, 259, 263, 267, 273; descendants of 264, 277; and jihad 267; and violence 275
mujahideen, in Afghanistan 334, 354–5, 489
Mujica, José 293
Mumbai attacks 355, 434, 464
Munich (Spielberg) 438
Munich Olympics attack 245, 431, 460–1; Israeli reaction to 461; Western reaction to 4, 245, 420, 438, 461–2
al-Muqrani, Muhammad 220
Murphy, Lenny 211
Musée Grevin 482n24
Musharraf, Pervez 356
Muslim Brotherhood 270–1, 336, 347n19; and democracy 458; in Egypt 259, 261–4, 267, 271–4, 276, 282n3; in Jordan 276–7; in Lebanon 276; in Palestine 277; in Syria 276
Muslims: in Algeria 220, 224–5, 231; in India 352, 357–62; in Pakistan 352; in UK 391; *see also* Islam; Shi'a Islam; Sunni Islam
Mussolini, Benito 123, 125, 127n36, 170–2
Mustafa, Abu Ali 254
Mustafa, Shukri 274

Nadezhdin, Nikolai 96
Nadwi, Abu Hasan 265
Nahr al-Bared 276
Napoleon Bonaparte 65, 161
Napolitano, Janet 319
Nasrullah, Hassan 270, 280
Nasser, Gamal Abdel 223–5, 242, 244, 262–4, 272
Nat Turner 88
National Association for the Advancement of Colored People 149, 152, 155n40
National Commission on the Disappearance of Persons (Argentina) 294
National Constitutional Assembly (Colombia) 290
National Democratic Party (West Germany) 313n66
National Front (Colombia) 289
National Liberation Army (Algeria) 222–4, 228–9, 233
National Liberation Army (ELN) (Colombia) 289
National Liberation Army (ELN) (Peru) 286
National Liberation Front (Aden) 199–200
National Liberation Front (Algeria) 3, 222, 224–8, 230–4, 387; and Islam 223; and mass media 430; and United Nations 385

INDEX

National Security Agency 434
national security ideology 294
National Socialism *see* Nazi Germany; Nazi Party
National Vanguard (Italy) 307
nationalists, in Northern Ireland 205–6, 210, 212, 214
Native Americans 77–8, 82, 85–6; and England 79–82; and Spain 78–80, 82; and US 82–4; US attitudes toward 77–8, 85–6; *see also* specific tribes and groups
NATO *see* North Atlantic Treaty Organization
Nazi Germany 3–4, 162–5, 169, 171, 182, 206, 374–5, 417; and state terror/ism 162–5
Nazi Party 3–4, 162; *see also* Nazi Germany; neo-Nazism
Nechaev, Sergei 98–100, 111, 377, 414, 430, 474
Neglected Duty, The (Farag) 274
negotiating with terrorists 213–14, 245–7, 292, 300, 456, 461
neo-fascism 306–7, 312n29
neo-Nazism 308–10, 313n66, 326, 434, 465
Netanyahu, Benjamin 253, 278
Netherlands 298, 415, 421
netwar 459
Neumann, Peter 322
Never Again (Argentina) 294
New England 80–1
New Journalism 113
New Left 297–9, 418, 460
new media 433–4, 438; *see also* mass media
New Order (Italy) 306–7
new terrorism 318, 456, 487, 491, 494; and new counter-terrorism 494
New Villages (Malaya) 186, 192–3, 197
New World Liberation Front (US) 326
new world order 327
New York City 133, 136–7, 139
New York Times 139, 145
newspapers 113, 134, 429–30, 474; *see also* mass media, media
Nicaragua 489
Nicholas I, Tsar of Russia 94–6, 435, 472
Nicholas II, Tsar of Russia 106, 110n47
Nicosia 197–8
Nietzsche, Friedrich 380
Nightline 432, 436
nihilism *see* Russia, nihilism 475–6, 478
1905 Revolution (Russia) 103, 105–6, 119, 479–80
Nineteenth of April Movement *see* M-19 (Colombia)
nitroglycerin 377, 444–5; *see also* explosives
Nixon, Richard 418–19
Nizam al-Mulk 35–7
Nizar 36

Nizaris *see* Assassins; and Islam, Nizari
NKVD (USSR) 166, 168–70
Nobel Peace Prize 488
Nobel, Alfred 113
nomos 376–9
Non-Aligned Movement 224
Nonneman, Gerd 384
non-violence 180
North Atlantic Treaty Organization 305, 307–8, 343, 419, 422
North Korea 375
Northern Alliance (Afghanistan) 339–40
Northern Bank (Belfast) 214
Northern Ireland 179, 191, 200, 204–15, 216n25, 217n36, 385, 388–91; casualties during Troubles 204
Northern Ireland Executive 214
Northern Society (Russia) 94
Norway 119
Nosair, El Sayyid 450
Novikov, Nikolai 471
Núñez Florencio, Rafael 120
al-Nuqrashi, Mahmud Fahmi 347n19
Nuremberg Trials 3–4
al-Nusra Front 277, 345

O'Doherty, Malachi 209
O'Flaherty, Liam 437
O'Toole, Fintan 212
Oak Creek, Wisconsin 323–4
Obama, Barack 491–2
Occupy Wall Street 140, 465
October Manifesto 106
Odo of Déols 51
Office for the Protection of the Constitution (West Germany) 308, 313n66
Official Nationality (Russia) 95
Ohnesorg, Benno 311n4
Okhrana 92, 101–6
Oklahoma City bombing 318, 378, 433, 447; *see also* McVeigh, Timothy
Oktoberfest bombing 309, 313n73
Old Man of the Mountains 39–41
Oliva y Moncasi, Juan 112
Omagh bombing 214
Omar, Yacef 232
Omega-7 326
On War 392
Onganía, Juan 293–4
"Only a Pawn in Their Game" (Dylan) 152–3
Opechancanough 80
Open Bridges policy (Israel) 243
Oprichnina 93, 108n8
Orange Amère, Operation 230
Orchard, Harry 135
Order, The 438

517

Organization of Petroleum Exporting Countries, summit in Vienna 420, 460
Orsini bomb 451
Orsini, Felice 451
Orthodox Church (Russia) 96, 166
Orwell, George 384
Oslo Accords 252–4
Ottoman Empire 161, 180, 197, 414–15, 435
Ouida 478
Overcoat, The (Gogol) 472–3

Padilla, José 321
Page, Wade Michael 323
Pahlen, Konstantine 99
Paisley, Ian 206, 214
Pakistan 340–1, 351, 353–6, 358, 362; and Afghan-Soviet War 334, 354; and India 387, 464; al-Qaeda in 340–1, 343, 346; state-sponsored terrorism against India 355, 457; suicide terrorism in 404, 406
Paladin Press 449
Pale of Settlement 105
Palestine 180–4, 370, 377; Zionist insurgency aided by radio 430
Palestine Liberation Organization 462; and armed struggle 244; competing Arab-sponsored factions of 243, 255, 457, 462; and Egypt 241–2, 250; founding 241; in Jordan 244–6; in Lebanon 246, 248–51; in Palestinian Authority 253, 278; renounces terrorism 420; and strategy of stages 247; training for other militants 298, 309–10, 457, 460, 462; in Tunisia 251–2; and UN 385; *see also* Fatah and other individual groups
Palestine Police Force 181–3
Palestinian Authority 252–5
Palestinian Islamic Jihad 252–3, 255
Palestinian Liberation Army 241
Palestinian Liberation Front 248
Palestinian National Charter 241, 244, 247
Palestinian National Council 241, 244, 247
Palestinians 239, 251; and Arab states 240–3; in Lebanon 276; most deaths not caused by Israel 462
palingenesis 374–5
Pallás, Paulino 115
Palmer Raids 137–8
Palmer, A. Mitchell 137–8
Pan Am Flight #103 432, 461
pan-Arabism 225
paramilitaries 174n9; in Colombia 290, 295n14; in Italy 171; in Weimar Germany 162–3
Paris (Zola) 479
Paris 49, 66, 68–70, 73, 103, 115, 120–1, 478
Paris Commune 101, 132, 140, 161, 478
Park Hotel bombing (Israel) 254

Parsons, Albert 133
Pasha, Nokrashy 272
Paspahegh 80
Pastrana, Andrés 289
Patriot Act (US) 421
patriot movement (US) 327–8, 323
Patriotic Union (UP) (Colombia) 289
Paxton Boys 84
Peace for Galilee, Operation 250
Peace League 51
Peace of God 50–3, 56
peace walls, in Northern Ireland 205
Peci, Petrizio 304
Pedenovi, Enrico 312n29
Peletier de Saint-Fargeau, Louis Michel le 65
Pemisipan *see* Wingina
"Penal Colony, The" (Kafka) 372
Pentagon (US) 139, 326, 438
People's Republic of China *see* China
People's Socialist Movement of Germany/Labor Party (VSBD/PdA) 308, 310
People's Vengeance 98
People's Will 100–2, 112, 443, 452n5, 471, 474–5; bomb-making 445–7
Pepin the Short, King of the Franks 48
Pequots 81
Perälä, Maiju 286
Percy, George 80
Perón, Isabel 294
Perón, Juan 293–4
Persia 34–6, 41
Peru 286–8, 325
Pestel, Pavel 71, 94, 108n13
Peter the Great, Tsar of Russia 93, 472
Petersburg (Bely) 480
Petit, Jean 20, 26n22–3
Petrashevsky, Mikhail 96
Philippe VI, King of France 41
Philippeville 228
Phoenix Park 178
Piazza Fontana bombing 302, 307, 312n52
Picqueray, May 123
Pillar of Defense, Operation 255
Pillar, Paul 349n55
Pinochet, Augusto 294, 373
Pisacane, Carlo 125n7, 429
Pisarev, Dmitry 98, 473–4
pistoleros 123
Pittsburgh 134
Pittsburgh Manifesto 133
Plant, Robert 355
Plato 16
Plehve, Vyacheslav von 92, 104–5
Plymouth 80–1
Pobedonostsev, Konstantine 101
Pocahontas 80

INDEX

Poeschke, Frida 309
pogroms 101, 104–5, 167
Pol Pot 375
Poland 72, 96, 169
Polay Campos, Víctor 288
Poles 164
Polevoi, Nikolai 96
police: in Algeria 221; in Argentina 294; in Britain 117; in Fascist Italy 171; in France 415; in India 357, 361; in Italy 117; in Latin America 293; in literature 92, 416, 479; in Northern Ireland 208, 214, 390 (*see also* Royal Ulster Constabulary); posing as anarchists 112–13; in Russia 92–106, 119–20; in Spain 117; in Netherlands 415; in US 119, 133–4, 136, 140; in West Germany 300
Political and Administrative Organization (Algeria) 224, 226
Polo, Marco 41
Pompey 28
Pontecorvo, Gillo 231, 437
Pontiac 84
Ponto, Jürgen 300
Popular Front for the Liberation of Palestine 242–3, 245–7, 254, 279, 456, 458, 460, 466n1; Fatah 460; and RAF 460; and Revolutionary Cells 460; and suicide terrorism 404
Popular Front for the Liberation of Palestine-General Command 243, 248
Popular Liberation Army (EPL) (Colombia) 290
popular sovereignty 24, 64, 67, 71–2, 94
portrait parlé 118, 415
Portugal 72, 119
Porzencanski, Arturo 292
Posse Comitatus Act 390
Potawattomie Creek, 88
Powhatan 80, 89n13
Prabhakaran, Velupillai 403
Preminger, Otto 437
Preobrazhensky Prikaz 93
Preparedness Day bombing 141
Prevent Violent Extremism program (Britain) 323
Prince, The (Machiavelli) 64
Princess Casamassima, The (James) 478
Princess Napraxine (Ouida) 478
Princip, Gavrilo 480
Procès de Trente 478–9
Progressive Encounter-Broad Front (Uruguay) 293
Proletarian Left (France) 298
propaganda by the deed 2–3; aircraft hijackings 458; and anarchism 113, 115, 132–41; confused with Russian Method 119; and John Brown 143; laws against 117, 479; and leftist revolutionary terrorism 299; and modernist writers 478; origins of 111–12, 125n7, 429; and symbolism 371
property, terrorism against 331n49
Protazanov, Yakov 437
Protestant Reformation 21–4, 63–4, 371–2
Protestants: in Ireland 179; in Northern Ireland 205–7, 211, 389, 391
Proudhon, Pierre-Joseph 111, 132
Provisional Government (Russia) 106
Provisional Irish Republican Army 205, 208–211, 213–15, 387, 389, 392; bomb-making 449–50; in Britain and Europe 456; and FARC 457; and hunger strikes 212, 401; support for in US 457; use of military terminology 386
psychological warfare bureau of French Army 227, 229
public diplomacy 428, 436
Puerto Rico 326
PULO (Thailand) 384
Punjab 354, 356, 404
Purishkevich, Vladimir 105
Pushkin, Alexander 96, 472, 481n12
Putin, Vladimir 391, 436
pyrotechnics 444–5

Qaddafi, Muammar 343, 388, 461–2
al-Qaeda 262, 275–6, 331n54, 333–5, 341, 343, 346, 392, 421; and affiliates 277, 339, 341–2, 345–6, 350n64, 387–8, 463–4; and affiliates' targeting of Muslims 265–6, 275–6, 464; in Afghanistan 336, 338; and Arab Spring 339, 344, 349n55; and bomb-making 450; and domestic terrorism in the US 321–2; and global jihad 458; and Hamas 405; as idea not group 457; as insurgent group 333, 339, 341; as invented US bogeyman 413, 421–2, 457; lack of success of 465; and media 433–4; organization of 338, 341; overview 463; in Pakistan 340–1, 343, 346; religious views of 336–7; in Somalia 336, 347n14; strategy of 334, 337–8, 340–1, 343, 464; in Sudan 335–7; and suicide terrorism 405–6; and US 336–40, 342–3, 348n38
al-Qaeda in Iraq 2, 266, 341–3, 464
al-Qaeda in the Arabian Peninsula 341–2
al-Qaeda in the Islamic Maghreb 341
al-Qassam, 'Izz al-Din 277
Qasab, Mohammad 355
Quebec 84
Queen Hatshepsut Temple 275
Quispe Palomino, Victor 288
Qur'an 34, 259–60, 263, 265–6, 273, 280
Qutb, Sayyid 262–5, 270, 272–4, 382n37

INDEX

Rabin, Yitzhak 252–3, 461
race riots 150
Rachkovsky, Peter 103
racial terrorism *see* white supremacist terrorism
radicalization 322–3, 385, 390, 434, 458
radio 430
Radio Television Libres des Mille Collines 430
Radishchev, Alexander 471
Radowisky, Simon 121
Rains, Gabriel 444
Ram (Hindu god) 359, 361
Ramallah 254
RAND Corporation 444, 459
Ranstorp, Magnus 386
Rapoport, David 284–5, 412
Rashid al-Din (Persian chronicler) 37
Rashid al-Din Sinan (Assassin leader) 39–40
Rashtriya Swayamsevak Sangh 358
Raspe, Jan-Carl 300–1
Ratliff, William 287
Ravachol, François Claudius 115, 118
Ravaillac, François 24, 64
Raymond of Tripoli 39
Reagan, Ronald 6, 459, 461, 487, 489, 491
Reconstruction (US) 145–8, 150–1;
  historiography and memory of 145, 149–50
Red Army 166–7, 169–70
Red Army Faction (RAF) 297, 299–301, 305–6, 310, 311n15, 312n42, 312n47, 436; and Action Directe 305–6, 461; dilettantism of 465; in Jordan 462; and PFLP 460
Red Brigades (BR) 297, 299, 301–5, 307–8, 312n29, 461
Red Front-Fighters Alliance 162
Red Scare of 1880s 134
Red Scare of 1910s–20s 138, 460
Red Terror (Soviet) 166
Red Youth (Netherlands) 298
Redemption *see* Reconstruction (US)
Reformation *see* Protestant Reformation
Reign of Terror, French 63–5, 67–71, 73–4, 101; influence of 71–2
Rejectionist Front (Palestinian) 247–8, 458
religion: and terrorism 2, 8–9, 351
Remembrance Day bombing 213
Rendition (Hood) 438
representatives on mission (France) 67, 69
Republic of Virtue 70
Republic, The (Plato) 16
Republican Party (US) 147–8
republicans; in Northern Ireland 205–15, 389–90; dissident, in Northern Ireland 213–14, 217n36
Requirimiento (Spain) 79, 89n9
Reservists Testify 231
Restore Hope, Operation 335

Reuters 337
Révolte, La 478
revolution 67, 374
revolutionary (left-wing) terrorism; in Americas 418–19; in Europe 418–19; in France 67; in Italy 301–4; in Russia 1, 92–3, 97–107, 124, 377, 473–5, 479–80; in Third World 418–20; in US 326–7; in West Germany 298–301, 310;
Revolutionary Armed Forces of Colombia (FARC) 214, 284–6, 289, 290, 378, 457
revolutionary armies (in French Revolution) 68–9
Revolutionary Cells (RZ) (West Germany) 304–5, 460
Revolutionary Organization 17 November 304
Revolutionary Tribunal (France) 67–8, 70
Revolutionary United Front (Sierra Leone) 392
Revolutionary War *see* American Revolutionary War
Revolutions of 1848 71, 96
Reza Shah 260
Rhein-Main Airbase 306
Richard the Lionheart 40
Rid, Thomas 385
Riegler, Thomas 425n52
Rioux, Jean-Pierre 236n60
Risorgimento 113
Roanoke 80
Robert of Bellême 52, 57
Robespierre, Maximilien 63–5, 67, 69–71, 74, 94
Rockefeller, John D. 136, 447
Rodwell, Robert 449
Rogers, Richard 447
Rohwedder, Detlev Carsten 306
Roland 49
Romania 119, 171
Roman-Jewish War, First 29, 31–3
Rome Accord 117–18, 416–17
Rome, ancient 17–18, 21, 46–7; and Christianity 369; and Germany 32; influence on French Revolution 64, 71; and Judea/Judaea 28–33, 369–70; and North Africa 32; and state terror 373
romper rooms (Northern Ireland) 211
Ronfeld, David 459
Roosevelt, Theodore 118, 120, 136
Roscigna, Arcangel 124
Rote Armee Fraktion *see* Red Army Faction
Royal Air Force 182
Royal Frankish Annals 48–9
Royal Irish Constabulary 181
Royal Ulster Constabulary 191, 205, 211, 390–1
Rull, Joan/Juan 120
Rushdy, Ashraf 155n44

520

INDEX

Russia; agents provocateurs in 93, 96, 102, 104, 450, 480; anarchist terrorism in 119; apartment bombings in 1999, 391; and Chechnya 383, 387, 391; birthplace of terrorism 1, 471; imperial budgetary allocation for internal security 109n36; censorship in 95, 97, 430, 435–6, 471–2, 480; counter-terrorism in 119–20; entangled terrorism of state and opponents 92–3, 100–4, 106–7, 471–3, 480; explosives in 445–7; Imperial 92–107; Imperial, and state terror/ism 167; and international counter-terrorism 119; Ministry of Police 94; Muscovite 93; nihilism 117, 377, 414, 435, 437, 473, 475–6, 478; revolutionary terrorism in 1, 71, 92–3, 97–107, 124, 377, 473–5, 479–80; right-wing terrorism in 104–5; *see also* Soviet Union
Russian Civil War 167
Russian Justice (Pestel) 71
Russian Method 119–22, 187n4, 452n5
Russian Navy 445
Russian Revolution 106, 122; influence of 122–3, 137; western fear of 122–3, 137, 460
Russian Social Democratic Labor Party 104
Russo-Japanese War 106
Rwanda 430
Rysakov, Nikolai 101

Sabra and Shatila refugee camps 250
Sacco, Nicola 124, 138
Sachar Commission 357
al-Sadah, Amal 340
Sadat, Anwar 248, 266, 274
al-Sadr, Musa 279
Sageman, Marc 433
Sahwa (Awakening) 343
al-Saika 243
Saint-Just, Louis-Antoine 65, 67, 70–1
salafi jihadism 264–5, 270, 273–4, 327, 336–7, 378; and Arab Spring 344; defined 264–5, 274; in Egypt 274–6, 344–5; in Iraq 262; and lone wolves 464; near enemy or far enemy 337–8, 463; in Pakistan 353, 355–6; and satellite television 434; and suicide terrorism 405; in Syria 262
salafism 263–6, 273, 336–7; defined 263–4; and Islamism 263–4; in Jordan 276–7; in Palestine 255
Salah al-Din 54
Salameh, Ali Hasan 461
Salim, Murjan 344
Samara 2
Sand, Karl 73
Sandinistas 285
Sands, Bobby 212, 401
Sanford, Percy Gerald 448

Sangh Parivar 357–8, 364n44
sans-culottes 66, 68–9, 71, 160
Santos, Juan Manuel 289
Sanusi 172
Saragossa, Cardinal Archbishop of 123
Saudi Arabia 334–8, 354–5; and Afghan-Soviet War 334; and Israeli-Palestinian conflict 254; and Wahhabism 264–6, 354–5
Savinkov, Boris 106, 480
Saxon, Kurt 448
Saxons 48–9, 52, 57
Sazonov, Igor 105
Scanlan, Margaret 480–1
Scenario for Peace, A (Sinn Féin) 213
Scheuer, Michael 337
Schinas, Aleko 121
Schleyer, Hanns-Martin 301
Schmid, Alex P. 5–7, 65, 165, 170, 370, 429
Schmidt, Helmut 300–1
schrecklichkeit 164
Schutzstaffel (SS) 163
Science of Revolutionary Warfare, The (Most) 112–13, 448
scientific policing 117
scientism 415, 444, 446, 449
Scotland Yard 118
Scottsboro case 151–2
Seattle 139
Secret Agent: A Simple Tale, The (Conrad) 437, 446, 479
Secret Army Organization (OAS) 233
Secret Chancellery (Russia) 93–4
Secret Intelligence Service (Britain) *see* MI6
security barrier between Israel: and Gaza Strip 279; and West Bank 254
Security Service (Britain) *see* MI5
Sedition Act 137
Sedki, 'Atef 275
Seligson, Mitchell 293
Seljuk Turkish Empire 34–5, 37
Sendero Luminoso *see* Shining Path
Sendic, Raúl 291
September 11, 2001 attacks 6, 340, 379–80, 391, 397, 421, 463; conspiracy theories about 459; economic impact of 340; impact on perception/definition of terrorism in US 317–18, 321–2, 487; and media 433
September Massacres (France) 66, 68
Serbia 119, 383, 457
serfdom 71, 96–7
Sergei Aleksandrovich, Grand Duke 104–5
Services Office 335; *see also* al-Qaeda
Sétif 220–2
Seven Interpretive Essays on Peruvian Reality (Mariátegui) 287
Seven Years' War 82–3

sexual violence 1, 49, 53, 85, 87, 151
al-Shabaab 341
shahuda 400
Shami, Yitzhak 252
Shankill Butchers 211
shari'a 259, 270–1, 282n3, 337
al-Sharif, Sayyed Imam 464
Sharon, Ariel 240, 250, 253–4
Shawnee 85
Shayma' (Egyptian girl) 275
Shi'a Islam 2, 34, 36–7, 259, 264, 270, 280, 352; in Iran 406; in Iraq 406; in Lebanon 279–81, 401–2, 406; in Pakistan 352–4, 356, 362; and suicide terrorism 403, 406; *see also* Islam; Muslims
Shi'ites, in Lebanon 250
Shifu, Liu 442–3
Shining Path 286, 288, 318; VRAEM faction 288
Shiqaqi, Fathi 278
Shukeiri, Ahmad 241, 244
Shuvalov, Peter 98
Shy, John 384
Si Haouès 232
al-Siba'i, Hani 344
Siberia 109n44
Sicarii 28–33, 42–3n8, 369–70, 376; and messaging 429; term defined 30, 43n14
Sidney Street Siege 120, 460
Sierra Leone 392
Sigismund, Holy Roman Emperor 20
Sikhs 404
Sillitoe, Percey 196
Silva, L. Flavius 31–2
Silverstein, Paul 226
Simon, Steven 349n55
Sinai/Suez Campaign 230, 240
Singer, Peter 327
Sinn Féin 179–80, 205, 208, 212–15, 436
Sipah-e-Muhammad 356
Sipah-e-Sahaba 354, 356–7
Sipiagin, Dmitry 104
SISMI (Italian intelligence service) 308
Six Day War 242, 261, 460
Siyar al-Muluk 36
Skyjack Sunday 245, 456, 462, 466n1
slavery 77, 82–3, 85, 87–8, 144–5, 151, 155n44; as terrorism 82–3, 88
Small Wars: Their Principles and Practice (Callwell) 164
Smith, John 80
Smith, Joseph 87
Smith, M. L. R. 385
Snowden, Edward 422
Sobrero, Antonio 444

Social Democratic and Labour Party (Northern Ireland) 205, 210, 212
Social Democratic Party, German 112
social engineering 70, 374–5
social media: and Arab Spring 344
Social Question 113
Social Revolutionary Club (US) 133
Socialist Party of America 137
Socialist Revolutionary Party (Russia) 92, 104–5, 109n46–7, 118–19, 122–3, 166, 471, 479–80; *see also* Combat Organization
Société des Droits de l'Homme et du Citoyen 73
Socrates 17
Soloviev, Alexander 100
Somalia 335–7, 341, 346, 347n14
Sons of Iraq 343
Sons of Liberty (American colonies) 84
Sossi, Mario 302
Soustelle, Jacques 228
South (US) 145–53
South Africa 389, 391
South Carolina 145, 147
South Lebanese Army 249
South West Africa 164
South Yemen, People's Republic of 200, 335; *see also* Yemen
Southern Poverty Law Center 320
Southern Society (Russia) 94
Southers, Erroll 322
Soviet Union 107n4, 139, 162, 375, 417; anarchist terrorism in 122–3, 460; and Fatah 459; and Latin America 285; and Middle East 271; and Palestinians; state terror/ism in 165–70; and strategy of tension 308; support for international revolutionary terrorism 419, 425–6n52, 459; *see also* Bolsheviks; Red Army; Russia; Russian Revolution; Russian Social Democratic Labor Party
soviets 106
Spain 72, 81–2, 114, 121, 123, 161, 171, 325; anarchist terrorism in 112–13, 115–16, 120–1, 123–4, 127n36; counter-terrorism against anarchists in 116–17; and ETA 390; and international counter-terrorism 119; labor movement in 121, 123; and media manipulation 437; and Native Americans 78–80, 82 (*see also* Black Legend); and state terror/ism of conquistadors 373
Spanish Civil War 170
Spanish Inquisition 371–2; *see also* Inquisition
Special Air Service (UK) 192, 213
Special Forces Handbook (US) 449
Special Organization (Algeria) 222
Special Powers (Algeria) 230
Special Section (Muslim Brotherhood) 347n19
spectacle 2–4, 444–5

INDEX

Spielberg, Steven 438
Spies, August 133
Sponti Groups 298
Springer Publishing Company 300
squadristi 171–2
Sri Lanka 387, 392, 403, 409n41
St. Alphonsus' Church 136
St. Patrick's Cathedral 136–7
St. Petersburg 97–9, 104–6, 472, 480
St. Petersburg Protocol 119
St. Petersburg University 104
Stalin, Joseph 70, 107–8n4, 166, 168–9
Stammheim prison 300–1
Stasi (East Germany) 309, 419
state as terrorist 1, 4–5, 8, 92–3, 109n29, 417; *see also* state terror/ism
state terror/ism 1–2, 4, 8, 233–4, 328–9, 369; in Algeria by France 233–4; and decline of anarchism 417; in ancient Rome 373; in Argentina 294; and authoritarianism 373–5, 379–80; and colonial wars 446; and colonialism 159–61, 167, 170, 172; definition of 159, 165, 380n2; and democracies 373; in Fascist Italy 170–3; by French in North America 82; in French Revolution 65–70, 160; in Imperial Russia 92–3, 96, 98, 101–2, 106 (*see also* Russia, entangled terrorisms); in India 360–1; in Latin America 284, 293–4; and messaging 429; and modernity 372–5, 379; in Nazi Germany 162–5; pre-modern 63–4, 373; and punishment 371–2; and slavery 82–3; in Soviet Union 165–70; and terrorism 382n38; and critical terrorism studies 489, 495; and totalitarianism 172–3, 374–5; in Uruguay 294; in US 77; and war 159–61, 163, 167, 169–70, 172; and World War II 373; state terror *see also* counter-terror; state as terrorist
state-sponsored terrorism 86, 105, 240, 243, 251, 280, 308, 417, 457, 489
Statkovsky, P. S. 102
Statute of Westminster 177
Stauffenberg Plot 371
stay-behind forces 308, 459
Stedman, E. C. 144
Stephens, Donald 198
Stepniak *see* Kravchinsky, Sergei
Sterling, Claire 5–6, 419, 459
Stern, Avraham 182
Steunenberg, Frank 135–6
Stevenson, Fanny Van Der Grift 477
Stevenson, Robert Louis 475, 477
Stolypin, Peter 105–6, 119
Stone, Oliver 438
Stono Rebellion 83
"Strange Fruit" (Holiday) 152
strategy of tension, in Italy 302, 307–8

Strauß, Franz-Josef 309
Straw, Jack 458, 467n22
Students for a Democratic Society 139
Stürgkh, Karl von 127n36
Sturmabteilung (SA) *see* Brownshirts
Suárez, Francisco 23–4
Sudan 335
Sudeikin, G. P. 102
suicide tactics, in warfare 401
suicide terrorism 17, 38, 281, 397, 400–1, 410n59, 433; changes in recent years 406; contemporary 402–7; definition of 397–9; and explosives 399, 401, 407; in Israel 252–3, 278–9; pre-modern 399–401, 408n16; in Syria 277; tactical/strategic reasons for 397, 403–6; used by Christians 404, 409n45; used by secular groups 403–4, 409n41
Sulla, Lucius Cornelius 43n14
Sullivan, John 85
Summers, Andy 117
Sunni Awakening 464
Sunni Islam 2, 34, 36–7, 259, 264, 270, 273, 352; in Iraq 405–6; in Pakistan 352–4, 356, 362; and suicide terrorism 403, 405–6; *see also* Islam; Muslims
Supreme Court (US) 149
Supreme Court of Justice (Israel) 243
al-Suri, Abu Mu'sab 337, 464
Suspects, Law of (France) 68
Sweden 119
Switzerland 119, 456
Sykes-Picot Agreement 180
Symbionese Liberation Army 431
Syria 39–41, 184, 272, 277, 386; and Hizbullah 280, 406; jihadism in 345; Muslim Brotherhood in 276; and Palestinians 242–3, 247–8, 250; political Islamism in 276
Syrian Civil War 277, 280–1, 345, 379, 382n43, 406, 465
Syriana (Gaghan) 438
systemic violence 168, 172

ta'lim 34, 36–7
takfir 265–6, 273, 281, 464
Takfir wa-l-Hijra: in Egypt 274, in Lebanon 276
al-Tal, Wasfi 246
Talib, 'Ali Ibn Abi 266
Taliban 338–40, 355, 389, 391, 421; and new media 434; and suicide terrorism 405
Talk Radio (Stone) 438
Tallien, Jean-Lambert 2, 71
Tamil Tigers 387, 392, 403, 409n41, 457
Tanaghrisson 83
Tarleton, Banastre 85
al-Tarshani, Nasir 344
tawhid 337

INDEX

technical education 443–52
technology: and terrorism 103, 374, 442; see also explosives; media
Tegart, Charles 181
Tel Aviv 182
television 431, 434, 458
Temple, Order of 41
Templer, Gerald 191–3, 197–8, 201n22
Terror and Taboo (Zulaika and Douglass) 489–90
Terror Network, The (Sterling) 5, 419, 459
Terrorism Act (Britain) 443
terrorism studies 3–6, 423, 487–96, 497n31; and counter-insurgency 490, 492; and counter-terrorism 3, 320, 323, 490; critical 490–1; during Cold War 492; and historians 6–7, 493–6; literary turn in 487–96
terrorism, anarchist *see* anarchist terrorism
terrorism, international *see* international terrorism
terrorism, revolutionary *see* revolutionary terrorism
terrorism, state *see* state terror/ism
terrorism, state-sponsored *see* state-sponsored terrorism
terrorism, suicide *see* suicide terrorism
terrorism, white supremacist *see* white supremacist terrorism
terrorism: as art form 470, 481n2; and audiences 4–5, 7, 55, 165, 225–7, 317, 429; birth of modern 1, 471; brute vs. social fact 8, 488; as communicative act 2–3, 5, 7, 55, 57, 152, 165, 225–8, 303, 370–1, 428, 470, 481n2 (*see also* mediatization); competing national definitions of 417; as contested concept 8, 370, 411, 488–9; and crime 4, 6, 32, 99, 104, 113–14, 120, 211–12, 299, 392; cultural/linguistic construct 5, 8, 111, 328, 384, 422–3, 487–8, 490–2, 494; defined by League of Nations 416–17; defined by UN 420; definition of 2–9, 11n17, 15, 18, 63, 93, 174n1, 218, 317, 331n44, 370–1, 383–5, 397–8, 474, 488; definition of, and media messaging 429; definition of, and speech 443; and democracy 215, 386; and hate 319, 324; as ideology 3, 5–6; and insurgency 198, 333, 339, 345, 383–9, 392, 393n1, 489; means vs. ends 6, 63, 73; and modernity 376–80, 382n38, 471–2, 475; as pejorative 386, 411, 488–9, 491–2; and popular support 73; pre-modern 9, 24, 28, 42, 46, 77, 84; as provocation 291, 299, 379, 480; and religion 2, 8–9, 351; and social sciences vs. humanities 6–7; as spectacle 2–4, 444–5; and state terror/ism 165, 382n38; as symbolism 3, 5, 7, 31, 143, 371, 428–30, 451, 470; as tactic/strategy 2–4, 5–6, 9–10, 31, 33,
371, 384, 392; as term 63; and war 4, 127n36, 159
Thailand 384
Thapar, Romila 352
Thatcher, Margaret 207, 212, 428
Theodosius, Emperor of Rome 47
Third Position (Italy) 307
Third Section of his Majesty's Imperial Chancellery (Russia) 95–101
Third World, and attitudes toward terrorism 420
Third Worldism 224, 227
Thirteenth Amendment to US Constitution 145
Thoreau, Henry David 139
Thorup, Mikkel 372, 452, 494
"Threshold, The" (Turgenev) 474–5
Thucydides 15–16
Thus Spoke Zarathustra (Nietzsche) 380
Tibet 386
Tikhomirov, Lev 102
Tilak, Bal Gangadhar 358
Tilly, Charles 225
Tokyo subway nerve gas attack 433, 451
Tolstoy, Dmitry 101–2
Torres, Camilo 289
torture 55, 64, 116, 198–9, 229, 371–2; in Algerian War of Independence 230–1; in Uruguay 294
totalitarianism 92, 162, 168, 170–3, 374, 376, 390; and state terror/ism 374–5
Toulouse attacks 388, 468n62
Townshend, Charles 389
Travers, Ann 215
Treasury Department (US) 138
Trelease, Allen 147
Trepov, Dmitry 104
Trepov, Fyodor 98–9
Trevaskis, Kennedy 199
Trial of the 193 (Russia) 99, 474
Trial of the 50 (Russia) 99, 474
Trilling, Lionel 482n33
Trollope, Anthony 476, 482n29
Trotha, Lothar von 164
Trotsky, Lev 106, 107n4, 460
Troubles 191, 200, 204; casualties of 204; *see also* Northern Ireland
Truce of God 50–1, 53, 56
Truth and Reconciliation Committee (Peru) 287
Tsarnaev, Dzhokhar and Tamerlan 322–3
Tudor, Henry Hugh 181
Tunisia 225, 251, 343–5, 458
Tunku Abdul Rahman 193
Túpac Amaru Revolutionary Movement (MRTA) 288
Tupamaros 285, 291–2, 299
Tupamaros West-Berlin 298
Turchetti, Mario 26n22

524

INDEX

Turgenev, Ivan 473–5
Turkey 119, 197–9, 260–1, 404, 458
Turkish Muslims 167
Turner, Ted 432
TWA Flight #847 432
24 (television show) 438
22 SAS Regiment 192, 461
Twitter 344, 434
Two Powers (or Two Swords) 47
tyrannicide 15, 21, 24, 25n3, 37, 57, 65, 113, 122; in ancient Greece 15–17, 21; in ancient Rome 17–18, 21; in early modern Europe 21–3; in medieval Europe 18–21; Pushkin's approval of 472

Uganda 248, 460–1
Uighur separatists 437
Ukraine 167, 170
Ulster 205; *see also* Northern Ireland
Ulster Defence Association 205, 210
Ulster Defence Regiment 211
Ulster Freedom Fighters 210
Ulster Unionist Party 210, 214
Ulster Volunteer Force (1910s) 178–9
Ulster Volunteer Force (1960s–2010s) 205–7, 210–11
Umberto I, King of Italy 116, 118, 134, 459
Umkhonto we Sizwe 389
Unabomber 378, 388, 437, 450
Unceasing Struggle (Italy) 298, 301, 303
Underground Russia: Profiles and Sketches from Life (Kravchinsky-Stepniak) 476
underwear bomber 468n62
Union of the Russian People 105
Union Square (New York City) 136
unionists, in Northern Ireland 205–7, 212–13
unions *see* labor movement
Unit 101 (Israel) 240
United Brotherhood (Fenians) 452n5
United Irishman 430
United Kingdom *see* Britain; England
United Nations 183, 232, 494; and Afghan War 422; and Algeria 223, 227; definition of terrorism 4, 420–1; and FLN 385; Interim Force in Lebanon 249; and Palestinians 247; and PLO 246, 385; and al-Qaeda 421; and Taliban 421
United Parcel Service 342
United Self-Defense Forces of Colombia (AUC) 290
United States Army 299–300, 310; Corps of Engineers 444; and counter-insurgency 385; Headquarters in West Germany 300; manuals, as sources for terrorists 449–50
United States of America 77, 86–7, 113, 118, 155n44, 273, 331n42; and Afghan War (2001–) 340–1, 346, 356; and Afghan-Soviet War 334–5, 354–5; anarchist terrorism in 120, 122, 130–41, 153n12, 154n33; censorship in 435; counter-terrorism in 118–19, 133–4, 136–8, 390; Department of State 489; diplomats in Libya, attacked 344, 407n10; domestic terrorism inspired by foreign ideologies 321–3, 327; during Civil War 146; embassies in Kenya and Tanzania, bombings of 338–9, 433, 458, 463; embassy in Egypt 344; embassy in Iran 431–2, seized; embassy in Lebanon, bombing of 403; and euro-communism 304; immigration to 114, 118, 132–5; and Iraq War 2, 341; Irish in 443–4; and Israeli-Palestinian conflict 250, 253–4; labor movement in 114, 118, 130, 132–5, 137–8, 328; and Latin America 285; and Lebanon 279, 403; left-wing terrorism in 326–7; and left-wing terrorism in Europe 303–5; and Libya 461–2; and media manipulation after 9/11 436–7; and Middle East 271; militia movement in 327–8, 456; and Native Americans 85–6, 161; and negotiations with terrorists 461; patriot movement in 327–8, 323; and al-Qaeda 335–40, 342–3, 348n38; recent domestic terrorism in 317–29; Revolutionary War 84–6, 444; right-wing terrorism in 326–7; and security infrastructure after 9/11 421; slavery in 87–9; and Vietnam War 285, 298–9, 383, 458; and War on Terror 6, 321, 346, 379, 383, 413, 421–2, 463, 481, 490–1, 495 (*see also* counter-terrorism, international, against global jihadism); and War on Terror, and popular entertainment 438; and War on Terror, impact of term 436–7; war on terrorism (1980s) 6, 487, 489, 491; *see also* United States Army
United States of America, white supremacist terrorism in *see* white supremacist terrorism, in US
unlawful combatants 421
urban guerrilla terrorism 290–2, 299–300, 305
Urban II, Pope 53–4
Uribe, Álvaro 289–90
Uriburu, José Félix 124
Uris, Leon 437
Uruguay 124, 291–2, 294, 392
US Marine barracks bombing 279, 403
USS Cole bombing 339, 433
USSR *see* Soviet Union
Ustaše 457

Vaillant, Auguste 115, 118, 430
Vanzetti, Bartolomeo 124, 138

INDEX

Varanasi, India 355
Varela, Hector 124
Varesse, Luis 288
Vázquez, Tabaré 293
Vendeé 66, 69
Vera, or the Nihilists (Wilde) 475
Verhoeven, Claudia 443, 474, 482n19
Videla, Jorge 386
videogames 434
Vidino, Lorenzo 347n19
Viet Cong 401
Viet Minh 229
Vietnam 225, 229
Vietnam War 285, 298–9, 383, 401, 458; *see also* Indochina War
Vikings 49–51, 57
Vincent, Howard 118
Vinciguerra, Vincenzo 307
violence, and destruction of middle ground 225–6, 228; public vs. private 47, 50–1, 56, 77
Violencia, La (Colombia) 289
Virginia 80, 88, 143–4
Vitalis, Orderic 52
Vock, M. Ia. von 95
Voice of the Arabs 430
Voice of the Haganah 430
Voormolen, Willem 415

al-Wahhab, Muhammad 'Abd 264
Wahhabism 264, 266, 463
Wahhabism, in Pakistan 353–6
Wall Street bombing 138, 460
Walter, Eugene 4
Wampanoags 81
war crimes 87
War on Terror 6, 321, 346, 379, 383, 413, 421–2, 463, 481, 490–1, 495; impact of term 436–7; and popular entertainment 438; *see also* counter-terrorism, international, against global jihadism
war on terrorism (1980s) 6, 487, 489, 491
war: rules of 56, 82 (*see also* Peace of God; Truce of God); and terrorism 159
Waruhiu wa Kungu 195
Washington, DC 87, 137
Washington, George 83, 85
Waxhaws massacre 85
al-Wazir, Khalil 242, 252
weapons of mass destruction 413, 450–1, 477, 491
Weather Underground 139, 326, 447
Weatherman 139
Weber, Max 373–4, 389

Wehrmacht 163–4
Weimann, Gabriel 432
Weimar Germany 162, 174n9
Weir, David 479
Wells-Barnett Ida B. 150
West Bank 240, 242–3, 251–5
West German Socialist German Student League 297, 299
West Germany 297–8, 325; embassy in Sweden, attacked 300; left-wing terrorism in 298–301, 310; negotiating with terrorists 456; right-wing terrorism in 308–10, 313n66
West Point 444
Western Federation of Miners 135
What Is to Be Done? 473
White Areas (Malaya) 193
White League (US South) 148
White Line (US South) 148
White Paper (on Palestine) 181
white supremacist terrorism: in Europe 378; in US 1, 84, 132, 143–53, 154n33, 155n44, 331n42; *see also* white supremacy
white supremacy, in US 143, 145–9, 151, 153, 155n44, 323, 327; *see also* white supremacist terrorism
White Terror (France) 65
White Terror (Russia) 98, 101
White, Edward 149–50
White, Hayden 493–5
Wiktorowicz, Quintan 276, 336
Wilde, Oscar 475
Wilhelm I, Kaiser of Germany 112
Wilkinson, Paul 291, 386, 431, 438
William the Conqueror, King of England 53
Wilson, Des 208–9
Wilson, Paddy 210
Wilson, Woodrow 149
Wingina 80
Winter Palace 100–1, 105–6
Witte, Sergei 104
Wobblies *see* Industrial Workers of the World
Wolfe, James 84
women 53, 98, 123–4; in Algerian War of Independence 223, 231
Wood, Amy Louise 152, 155n42
Worker's Power (Italy) 298, 301
Workerism 301
World Trade Center (Stone) 438
World Trade Center attacks (2001) *see* September 11, 2001, attacks
World Trade Center bombing (1993) 433, 447, 450
World Trade Organization 139

INDEX

World War I: and British Empire 177–8, 180; decline of anarchism during 122; impact of in US 137, 150; and state terror/ism by European countries 161, 164, 167, 416

World War II 301; and British Empire 182, 184, 190, 197, 206; and French Empire 221–2; and state terror/ism 163–4, 169, 172, 373; suicide tactics in 401

Yacef, Saadi 231, 438
Yair, Eleazar ben 31–2
Yaqub, Talaat 248
Yassin, Ahmad 277
Year in Hate and Extremism, The (SPLC) 320
Years of Lead (Italy) 303, 306
Yeats, W. B. 179, 187n12
Yehud 240
Yemen 335, 337, 339, 341, 346
Yom Kippur War 247
York, Canada 87
Young Bosnia 122
Young Italy 72
Young, Arthur 191
YouTube 434
Yreka Herald 86

Yrigoyen, Hipólito 124
Yugoslavia 172

Zachary, Pope 48
al-Zahawi, Mohammed 344
al-Zarqawi, Abu Mu'sab 266, 342–3, 346, 464
Zasulich, Vera 99, 112, 474
Zavalishin, F. I. 445–6
al-Zawahiri, Ayman 275–6, 337–9, 342–3, 349n55, 433, 464
al-Zawahiri, Muhammad 344
Zayn al-Din 400
Zealotic terrorism 376, 378–9, 382n38
Zealots 29, 43n8, 369–70, 376
Zeevi, Rechavam 254
Zeidan, Mahmoud 248
Zhelyabov, Andrei 101, 445
Zia ul-Haq, Muhammad 353–4, 362
Zighoud, Youssef 228
Zimmermann, Ernst 306
Zionism 241, 370
Zionist Occupation Government 378
Žižek, Slavoj 378
Zola, Émile 475, 479
Zubatov, Sergei 104–5
Zulaika, Joseba 5, 481n5, 489–90

Printed in Great Britain
by Amazon

44414194R00310